ON THIS DAY

The history of the world in 366 days

April 6, 1814 French emperor Napoleon
Bonaparte abdicates and is exiled to Elba.

December 25, 440 AD Christ's birth date becomes official.

March 17, 1766 Britain repeals the controversial Stamp Act in America.

January 6, 1540 Henry VIII marries his fourth wife Anne of Cleves.

September 2, 1945 Ho Chi Minh proclaims Vietnam independent.

July 25, 1917 Femme fatale Mata Hari is found guilty of spying.

May 25, 1935 Athlete Jesse Owens sets five new world records.

August 6, 1945 The *Enola Gay* drops an atom bomb on Hiroshima.

ON THIS DAY

The history of the world in 366 days

November 12, 1919 Start of the first flight from England to Australia.

June 2, 1953 Queen Elizabeth II is crowned in Westminster Abbey.

October 18, 1989 A powerful earthquake rocks San Francisco.

February 27, 1991 The Gulf War ends as Kuwait City is liberated.

BB Bounty Books

Contributors: Keith Addison; Marilyn Inglis; Mike Petty; Carolyn Pyrah; Tessa Rose; Diana Vowles; Joanna Smith

Editor: Sian Facer
Art Editor: Leigh Jones
Designer: Stephen Cary
Picture Research: Liz Fowler
Production: Nick Thompson

First published in 1992 by Octopus Publishing Group Ltd.

This edition published 2004 by Bounty Books,
a division of Octopus Publishing Group Ltd,
2-4 Heron Quays. London E14 4JP

Reprinted 2005,2006

Copyright © 2004 Octopus Publishing Group Ltd

A catalogue record for this book is available from the British Library

ISBN-13: 978-0-753710-11-1
ISBN-10: 0-753710-11-0

Printed in Dubai by Oriental Press

What is *On This Day*? An encyclopedia, a history book, a trivia book, a book of days, a source of quirky anecdotes or a serious reference work? It can be used as all these. With a whole page for each of the 366 days of the calendar it describes all the major events (and a lot of the minor ones) that happened throughout history on each day of the year in a lively and accessible way.

However, *On This Day* doesn't just tell you when an event happened but sets it in context. The announcement of the death of Charlie Chaplin (Christmas day, 1977) for example provides the opportunity for a biography, and the article on the Japanese attack on Pearl Harbor

December 25, 1977 Actor and comedian Charlie Chaplin dies.

explains why it took the Americans so much by surprise. It can also be used as a source of background information on areas such as the history of space travel, recent developments in Eastern Europe, the American Civil War, or the women's liberation movement. And, if you want to follow a sequence of events, for example the battles of World War II, then you can do so using the index which will point you to all the articles on one particular

August 30, 30BC Roman ruler Mark Antony commits suicide at the court of Cleopatra.

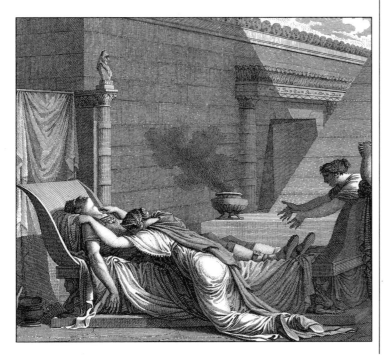

May 19, 1980 At least 15 people were killed when long-dormant volcano Mt. St. Helens, Washington State. explodes.

subject. There are no page numbers in the book, so everything is indexed by day of the year.

On This Day is wide ranging both in terms of time span and subject matter. From Julius Caesar to the present day, it covers over 2000 years of history and a multitude of subjects including sporting records, exploration, film and entertainment, music and literature, fashion, scientific achievements, politics, inventions, quotations, birthdays, wars, and royalty.

Did you know that Siamese twins Chang and Eng married and fathered several children although joined at the chest? Did you know that Batman's sidekick Robin was dynamited by the Joker following a readers' poll which voted that he had to go ? Did you know that in Germany in 1923 a loaf of bread cost 200 million marks? As well as providing factual information on history's great events *On This Day* can be dipped into as a fun source of weird and wonderful anecdotes and trivia.

September 1, 1939 Nazi troops march into Poland.

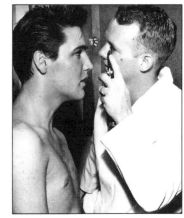

January 4, 1957 Elvis Presley has his army medical check-up.

JANUARY

"I must point out that my rule of life prescribed as an absolutely sacred rite smoking cigars and also the drinking of alchohol before, after, and if need be, during all meals and in the intervals between them."

Sir Winston Churchill
British statesman, died January 24, 1965.

Flight to freedom by banned journalist

1978 Banned South African newspaper editor Donald Woods of the *Daily Dispatch* has fled to Lesotho after escaping from house arrest in East London. Woods gained notoriety for his support of black leader Steve Biko, who was killed while in police custody last September. Woods' daughter was later injured when white extremists sent her a T-shirt soaked in acid through the post. Woods used a number of disguises to elude South African police and reach neutral Lesotho, where he was joined by his wife and family. They will fly to London on United Nations passports. Woods is planning to write a book on Biko's fate.

World's richest man in Brunei takeover

1984 The Sultan of Brunei, said to be the world's richest man, today appointed himself prime minister, finance minister and home affairs minister as the tiny British protectorate gained its independence. Sandwiched between parts of Malaysia in what used to be called Borneo (now Kalimantan), Brunei's fortune lies in the necklace of oil wells strung along its coast – hence its ruler's wealth, and his subjects' per capita income of US$13,663. There is no tax on citizens, and no unemployment. The Sultan has bestowed upon his Muslim people a large mosque commissioned from the world's best Islamic architects. His Royal Highness has also bought a Boeing 747 jet, equipped to carry himself and his polo team, horses and all, to compete at international venues. The oil is expected to last another 20-30 years.

AMERICAN SLAVES "MUST BE UNCHAINED"

1863 As civil war rages in America, President Abraham Lincoln today declared freedom for all slaves in the southern states that have rebelled against his government. In Washington huge crowds of emancipated slaves celebrated the announcement, which honours a pledge made by the President before the war began. "The old South must be destroyed and replaced by new propositions and new ideas," said Lincoln in a speech. But his order does not apply to slaves in border states fighting on the Union side against the South, nor does it affect slaves in southern areas already under Union control – and, of course, the rebel Confederates will not act on Lincoln's order. What the proclamation does show is that the Civil War is really being fought to end slavery. The issue has dominated the election campaign, with Democrats claiming that the Northern states will be overrun with "semi-savages". Meanwhile, all-black army units are being formed to fight the South.

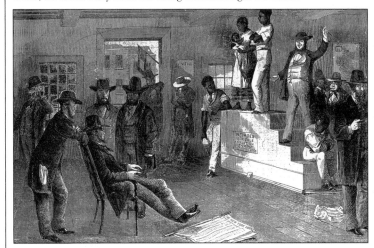

Queen spices up world trade

1600 Queen Elizabeth I today granted a charter establishing the British East India Company. The company will trade in the Eastern Hemisphere, and the charter gives George Clifford, Earl of Cumberland, and 215 other knights a 15-year franchise. Its purpose is to break into the Indonesian spice trade, which is dominated by the Dutch. The company will also operate on the Indian subcontinent and is to establish a base at Surat to exploit this region's wealth. Members of the company have invested £72,000 to equip five ships for the first voyage. It will be led by James Lancaster and John Davis, experienced mariners in both the South Seas and the Arctic.

> *Men their rights and nothing more; women their rights and nothing less.*
> **Susan B. Anthony,** American feminist – motto of the first issue of the suffragette journal *The Revolution*, 1868.

Castro topples Cuban dictator

1959 Cuban dictator Fulgencio Batista has fled from his war-torn island after failing to secure the support of the US in his struggle against the revolutionary forces of Fidel Castro. Castro, 32, is expected to declare Santiago de Cuba, from where he commands his rebel army, Cuba's provisional capital. Dr Manuel Urrutia is to be the new president and will fly to Havana, bringing to a formal end Castro's 25-month struggle against the hated Batista regime. Castro's ragged army grew from a core of 81 guerrillas who returned from exile in Mexico in 1956 to harry Batista's army from hide-outs in the Sierra Maestra mountains. Castro has been welcomed to power by adoring crowds and by liberal politicians alike. Mobs have burned down casinos, the government newspaper building and other symbols of Batista's rule.

44 BC Julius Caesar, founder of the Roman Empire, introduces the Julian calendar.

1538 German and Swiss states introduce the Gregorian calendar.

1804 After an 11-year slave rebellion against France, Haiti declares its independence, becoming the first Latin-American state to gain its freedom.

1901 The Commonwealth of Australia is established with Edmund Barton as the country's first prime minister.

1958 The European Economic Community, an alliance between France, Italy, West Germany, Belgium, Holland and Luxembourg, comes into being.

1961 The British farthing ceases to be legal tender.

1965 British footballer Stanley Matthews is the first professional footballer to be knighted.

1990 A week after the death of the Ceaucescus, Romania abolishes the death penalty.

1991 Albanian president Ramiz Alia promises that democratic elections will be held to bring an end to 43 years of communist dictatorship.

1999 The Euro becomes the official currency of 11 european countries.

BIRTHDAYS

Paul Revere 1735, American silversmith and patriot who carried the news of the British approach to Lexington and Concord.

Baron Pierre de Coubertin 1863, French founder of the modern Olympic Games.

E. M. Forster 1879, British novelist, whose books included *A Passage to India*.

J. Edgar Hoover 1895, American founder and head of the FBI.

Harold 'Kim' Philby 1912, British traitor who spied for Russian intelligence.

J. D. Salinger 1920, American author whose novels include *Catcher in the Rye*.

17 AD The poet Ovid and the historian Livy die in Rome.

1635 Cardinal Richelieu establishes the Académie Française to safeguard the purity of the French language.

1769 The British Royal Academy opens with painter Sir Joshua Reynolds as its first president.

1788 Georgia becomes the fourth state of the Union.

1900 The first electric omnibus runs in New York City.

1900 Queen Victoria writes her famous line, "We are not amused".

1900 Britain's first municipal crematorium is opened by the Lord Mayor of Hull.

1903 President Roosevelt closes a Missouri post office which refused to employ a black postmistress.

1952 Pope Pius XII declares that television is a threat to family life.

1959 The Soviets launch *Luna I*, the first unmanned space rocket to pass close to the moon.

1965 Under President Sukarno, Indonesia quits the UN.

1974 Death of Tex Ritter, singing cowboy of the silver screen.

1976 Britain grants limited self-government to the Solomon Islands.

1980 US president Jimmy Carter tells the Senate it should not ratify the SALT nuclear arms treaty with the USSR until the Soviets withdraw from Afghanistan.

1991 Soviet interior ministry troops seize the Communist Party headquarters in Vilnius, capital of Lithuania, and Lithuanians demonstrate in protest.

BIRTHDAYS

James Wolfe 1727, British general who played a major part in fighting the French in Canada.

Sir Michael Tippett 1905, British composer whose works include the oratorio *A Child of our Time*.

Isaac Asimov 1920, Russian-born American scientist and author of science-fiction novels.

David Bailey 1938, British photographer whose subjects include many icons of the 1960s.

BLACK HOLE OF CALCUTTA AVENGED

1757 Robert Clive's forces have recaptured Calcutta and avenged the infamous "Black Hole" incident when, last year, the Nawab of Bengal captured the city and imprisoned the British defenders in a tiny airless room, where 123 died. Calcutta was founded by the British East India Company, which bought the villages of Sutanati, Kalikata, and Govindapur in 1698. Its recapture now was seen as essential to British prestige in India.

Clive went to India as a clerk in 1743 and joined the company's army four years later. He was appointed lieutenant governor of Fort St David, near Madras, in 1755. Now Clive is expected to challenge the Nawab in an attempt to bring Bengal under British rule. If he succeeds, Clive can expect to become governor of Bengal, known for its vast wealth.

1987 Macdonald's, publishers of Enid Blyton's Noddy books for children, announced today that future editions will lack the traditional black gollywogs. The publisher has bowed to pressure groups and agreed to excise all "racism" from the series.

Muslims lose grip on Spain

1492 Seven hundred years of Arab rule in Spain ended today when Granada, the last Spanish Muslim stronghold, fell to the army of the Christian Queen Isabella I of Castile. Muslims are regarding this as Islam's worst-ever catastrophe, while Christians hail it as "the most blessed day in Spain's history". With today's Reconquest, Muslim invasions from North Africa are no longer a threat. At a time when Europe was rural and impoverished, Moorish Spain was a flourishing economic and cultural centre where science, medicine, and philosophy thrived. The final ousting of the Moors is the work of a gifted royal pair, Isabella I of Castile and Ferdinand II of Aragon, who married in 1479. Their kingdoms have been fighting the Moors for centuries, in what finally became a crusade.

Army fiasco triggers Boer War

1896 The three-day raid by Starr Jameson and 500 British soldiers into the Boer republic of the Transvaal, purportedly in support of British settlers, has ended in defeat, capture and humiliation with 17 men killed and 55 missing. The Parliaments in both Cape Town and London are in an uproar over what is being termed "a colossal folly". Jameson, a close associate of British imperialist and Prime Minister of the Cape Colony Cecil Rhodes, had planned to overthrow the Boer government of President Paul Kruger. Instead, he and the bedraggled remainder of his men are today languishing in a Pretoria jail. Jameson's folly could now tip Britain into war with the Boer republics. Rhodes' political career can hardly survive this disaster – questions are already being asked about whether the raid was his idea and just how much Colonial Secretary Joe Chamberlain knew about it.

Cartel takes control of US oil

1882 John D. Rockefeller has become the most powerful American outside the White House by gaining a stranglehold on the fast-growing oil industry. A "Trust" agreement signed today in New York will give the Rockefeller brothers and seven others the power to create or dissolve corporations in any state and allocate funds of more than $70 million. In effect, nine men now control the oil industry in an atmosphere of secrecy and intrigue. In 1863 Rockefeller and his partners formed an oil business that absorbed many Cleveland refineries and expanded into the Pennsylvania oil fields, becoming the world's largest refining concern. In 1870 Rockefeller founded the Standard Oil Company of Ohio. Today's Standard Oil Trust, formed to avoid

state controls, can expect opposition from Ohio's legal authorities who regard it as restraint of trade. In Washington, politicians are warning of the dangers of such Trusts and proposing legislation to break them.

Ibrox disaster – soccer fans crushed

1971 Sixty-six people died today at the Ibrox Park stadium in Glasgow in Britain's worst-ever soccer disaster. Two hundred fans were crushed when metal barriers gave way and a mass of fans swept on to the terraces. By the time rescuers were able to reach the trampled and injured, many could not be revived.

1942 Manila has fallen to Japanese forces and US General Douglas MacArthur has started evacuating the Philippines. The Japanese landed on the island of Luzon on December 22. Successive waves of Japanese aircraft struck at Manila for two days, and today the Japanese took the city and naval base of Cavite.

LUTHER PROVOKES PAPAL WRATH

1521 A Papal bull from Pope Leo X has ordered the excommunication of Martin Luther after a deadline for him to recant his heretical views expired. In 1520, Luther completed three celebrated works in which he stated his views: in his *Address to the Christian Nobility of the German Nation*, he invited the German princes to take the reform of the church into their own hands; in *A Prelude Concerning the Babylonian Captivity of the Church*, he attacked the papacy and the current theology of sacraments; and in *On the Freedom of a Christian Man*, he stated his position on justification and good works. Luther's dispute with Rome began when he challenged the doctrine of Indulgences (the remission of punishments for sins confessed) and their sale to raise funds for the church. The rift widened in 1517 when Luther posted his famous "95 Theses" on the door of the castle church at Wittenberg.

Hated Nazi Haw-Haw hangs

1946 Nazi propagandist William Joyce – known to British wartime radio listeners as Lord Haw-Haw – was hanged today for treason. Speaking in a high nasal voice and using outdated jingoistic slang, he parodied the tones of BBC announcers as he broadcast reports from Germany, often false, of Hitler's military advances. At the war's end, he was captured by the British. Though born in the United States, he had a British passport and was sent for trial at a British military court.

Human law is law only by virtue of its accordance with right reason, and by this means it is clear that it flows from eternal law. In so far as it deviates from right reason it is called an unjust law; and in such a case, it is no law at all, but rather an assertion of violence.

Thomas Aquinas, who died today in Rome, 1274.

1940 British aristocrat Unity Mitford, who has been on intimate terms with Adolf Hitler since 1935 and has thus gained the nickname "The Storm Troop Maiden", came home from Germany on a stretcher today. She shot herself when Britain declared war on her hero, Hitler.

1777 George Washington defeats the British at the Battle of Princeton.

1795 Josiah Wedgwood, original creator of the famous blue and white china, dies in Staffordshire.

1870 Work begins on the Brooklyn–New York bridge.

1911 Three anarchists are burnt to death after a gun battle with troops and police in Sidney Street, East London.

1918 New Zealand-born scientist Ernest Rutherford announces he has split the atom.

1947 The US House of Representatives is televised for the first time.

1958 British explorer Sir Edmund Hillary reaches the South Pole.

1959 Alaska becomes the 49th and largest state of the USA.

1961 The USA severs diplomatic links with Cuba.

1961 The millionth Morris Minor car rolls off the assembly line in Britain.

1962 Pope John XXIII excommunicates Cuban premier Fidel Castro.

1967 Jack Ruby, killer of Lee Harvey Oswald who was alleged to be the assassinator of John F. Kennedy, dies in hospital, thus avoiding execution.

1979 Death of Conrad Hilton, founder of the Hilton Hotel Group and one-time husband of Zsa Zsa Gabor.

1980 British naturalist Joy Adamson, author of the book *Born Free*, is murdered in a Kenyan game park.

BIRTHDAYS

Marcus Tullius Cicero 106 BC, Roman statesman and orator.

Clement Attlee 1883, British politician and Labour Prime Minister 1945-51.

J. R. R. Tolkien 1892, South African-born novelist and author of *The Lord of the Rings* and *The Hobbit*.

Victor Borge 1909, Danish pianist and entertainer.

Victoria Principal 1945, American actress most famous for her role in *Dallas*.

Boy emperor to head Japan

1868 The 16-year-old Japanese emperor Meiji today seized power from the Tokugawa Shogun, ending 700 years of military rule. The beginning of the end for the Tokugawas, rulers for two centuries, came with a national humiliation in 1854 when, in a classic example of gunboat diplomacy, US Commodore Matthew Perry's warships forced Japan's proud lords to scrap their traditional policy of isolation. Japanese leaders have now backed the young emperor in the first move of their plan to transform the country into a world power within one generation. A new government is to be formed in Tokyo to implement a policy of rapid industrialization, and a conscript army will be established.

Pharaoh's treasures may unleash curse

1924 British archaeologist Howard Carter has made a dazzling discovery in Egypt's Valley of Kings – a pharaoh's tomb filled with treasure, including a solid gold coffin, a gold mask, jewellery and other artifacts. The tomb is that of Tutankhamen, a

pharaoh of the 18th dynasty who died 3276 years ago. Egyptologists say this is by far the richest of the few royal burial chambers that survived comparatively intact. The Valley of Kings contains royal burial sites dating from the 18th and 19th dynasties of the New Kingdom, from about 1570-1200 BC. More than 60 royal tombs are known, including that of Ramses VI. It was below his tomb that Carter unearthed the new find. Carter joined the Egypt Exploration Fund in 1891 as a draughtsman and was trained by Sir Flinders Petrie. He became Egypt's Inspector-General of Antiquities in 1899. Since 1907 he has worked with Lord Carnarvon in the hunt for this tomb, locating its entrance two years ago.

1884 The Fabian Society is formed in London to promote socialist ideals.

1885 The first successful appendix operation is performed in Iowa by Dr Williams West Grant.

1896 Utah becomes the 45th state of the Union.

1936 *Billboard* publishes the first-ever pop chart in New York.

1948 Burma leaves the British Commonwealth to become fully independent.

1958 Death of Ralph Vaughan Williams, British composer.

1961 Apprentice barbers in Copenhagen finally end a strike which began in 1938, the longest-running industrial dispute in history.

1972 Rose Heilbron becomes the first British female judge at the Old Bailey.

1981 The show *Frankenstein* opens and closes on Broadway, losing $2 million.

1986 Phil Lynott of the rock group Thin Lizzy dies of a drug overdose.

1988 Karni Bheel, who boasted the longest moustache in India at 2.3 m (7 ft 10 in) from tip to tip, is found decapitated.

1990 President Gorbachev tells Lithuania's communists they can leave the Soviet Communist party.

BIRTHDAYS

Sir Isaac Newton 1643, British physicist and mathematician who discovered the law of gravitation.

Jakob Grimm 1785, eldest of the two Grimm brothers who wrote *Grimm's Fairy Tales*.

Louis Braille 1809, French inventor of an alphabet system for the blind.

Augustus John 1878, British painter with a fondness for gypsy subjects.

Floyd Patterson 1935, US heavyweight boxing champion and youngest holder of the world title.

Grace Bumbry 1937, American opera singer who was the first black singer to take the stage at Bayreuth.

REBEL ELVIS GETS GI SHOW ROLLING

1957 Two days before what is being billed as his final appearance on the *Ed Sullivan Show*, rock star Elvis Presley today underwent his pre-induction army medical checkup at the Kennedy Veterans' Hospital in Memphis. Though his formal drafting is some months off – he could remain a civilian until early next year – Presley's willingness to serve his country has already done much to tame the image of a rock'n'roll rebel that has entranced youngsters and maddened parents. Since his debut in July 1954 he has proved a brilliant investment for promoter Colonel Tom Parker; last year his "Hound Dog" became the fastest-selling single ever. His appearances on the *Ed Sullivan Show* have helped generate an adoring fan club that sends him 3000 letters a week.

Rail tycoon's $100 million

1877 Cornelius Vanderbilt has died in New York at 83, leaving a fortune estimated at $100 million. Vanderbilt's life was a classic American enterprise story. When he was 16, he started a ferry service to Staten Island. By the time he was 30 he virtually controlled the Hudson River shipping business, expanding by undercutting his competitors. During the gold rush he opened a fast and cheap steamship service linking New York and California, crossing the isthmus in Nicaragua. In the 1860s Vanderbilt starting buying small railroad holdings, and his New York Central Railroad eventually controlled the vital New York-Chicago route.

1967 A 300-mph (482 kph) somersault has ended the career of British speed king Donald Campbell, whose jet-powered speedboat *Bluebird* went out of control today on Coniston Water in northern England as he tried to beat his own record of 276 mph (444 kph). He made a good first run and then turned for a second attempt without stopping to refuel. The end came when the boat ran into its own wake at full speed and lifted out of the water. Divers searching for Campbell's body found only his helmet and teddy bear mascot.

DESPERATE HITLER DRAFTS CHILDREN

1944 The increasingly desperate plight of Hitler's military commanders became clear today when Berlin issued an order mobilizing all children over the age of 10 to be ready to fight in the war. Boy-soldiers as young as 15 have already been captured in the front lines by Allied troops. The Third Reich is suffering spectacular reverses on several fronts. Allied troops are known to be massing for an invasion somewhere in southern Europe. In Berlin it is reported that the RAF, which began its raids last November, has dropped over 17,000 tons of bombs on the city in two months, and further mass raids are expected. On the Eastern Front Hitler's forces besieging Leningrad are reported to fear defeat as Stalin's armoured columns race toward the city from the south and, for the first time, Russian troops have recrossed the old Polish border moving westward.

His refusal to take solace in a concept of divine or cosmic meaning for human life did not conflict with Camus' humanistic attitude that man is capable of a certain degree of dignity in honestly facing his solitary condition.

William Benét, on French Nobel Prize-winning novelist Albert Camus, who was killed today in a car crash, aged 46 – 1960.

THE SWAN SONG OF T.S. ELIOT

1965 Thomas Stearns Eliot, the Anglo-American poet and Nobel Prize-winner who took poetry into the modern era by renouncing the Romantic values of the Victorian age, has died in London. Eliot's career spanned daring iconoclasm to High Church Anglicanism, and ranged across poetry, drama, criticism and journalism. His most revolutionary poem was *The Waste Land*, but critics found deepest meaning in his *Four Quartets*. The descendant of a distinguished New England family, Eliot studied at Harvard, the Sorbonne and Oxford. In 1914 he took up permanent residence in England, becoming a British subject in 1927. After eking a living as a teacher and bank clerk during his most creative period, Eliot finally found stability at the publishers Faber & Faber.

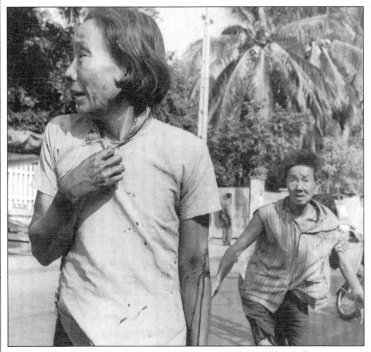

Khmer Rouge blitz Cambodian capital

1975 The Cambodian capital Phnom Penh today came under direct siege by Khmer Rouge communist rebels using heavy rocket and artillery attacks. The Khmer Rouge advance has been relentless, in spite of massive economic and military aid from the United States to Lon Nol's government. Military experts predict the capital can hold out for no more than four months. North Vietnam and the Viet Cong have helped the Khmer Rouge in their war against the government of Prince Norodom Sihanouk and Lon Nol. Their sanctuaries in the mountains of southern Cambodia have been the subject of massive bomb attacks by US planes, but by 1970 the Khmer Rouge already controlled about two-thirds of Cambodia. Their leader is Pol Pot, a shadowy figure who joined Ho Chi Minh's Indochinese Communist party in the 1940s.

Unknown Austrian forms Nazi party

1919 The political turmoil of the Weimar Republic has given rise to yet another tiny faction based in Munich: the National Socialist German Workers' party. Little is known about the new grouping, led by an Austrian-born former soldier in the defeated German Army who received the Iron Cross for bravery. His name is Adolf Hitler and he is known to be radically opposed to the rise of communism and to the humiliating terms being imposed on Germany at the Peace of Versailles. Herr Hitler says he will direct the organization with an iron hand and use its meetings to deliver forceful rhetorical assaults on Germany's "enemies", of which he says there are many. Hitler was a poor student in Austria's classical secondary schools and became an artist. He went to Vienna in 1907 but failed to enter the Academy of Fine Arts. Acquaintances describe him as beset by melancholy, aimlessness and racial hatred, and obsessed by the idea that world Jewry threatens his own Aryan race.

How could they tell?
Dorothy Parker, US writer, on being told John Calvin Coolidge, 30th US president, had died today, 1933.

US FIGHTERS CLASH WITH GADDAFI JETS

1989 Two Libyan fighters were shot down over the Mediterranean today after approaching a US aircraft carrier with "hostile intent", according to the US navy pilots. Libya's leader, Col. Muammar Gaddafi, described the incident as "premeditated aggression" and demanded a meeting of the UN Security Council to discuss it. The clash comes just days after the US government claimed that Libya is building a chemical weapons plant and three years after the US attack on Benghazi that flattened Gaddafi's house and killed relatives. The Pentagon is insisting its Tomcat F14 pilots fired in self-defence as the USS *John F. Kennedy* was cruising off Benghazi.

1896 A German physicist, Wilhelm Roentgen, today demonstrated what he calls the X-ray. This is a form of high-energy radiation which allows him to see through solid objects. It is thought the technique may prove useful in medicine. Roentgen discovered the new ray last year, quite by accident.

1922 The British polar explorer, Sir Ernest Shackleton, has died at sea while on his way to lead a fourth expedition to the Antarctic. His 1914 expedition to cross the Pole collapsed when his ship, *Endurance*, became trapped in ice. Shackleton led his men to the edge of the ice and then sailed hundreds of miles in an open boat – an extraordinary feat during which no lives were lost.

1066 Death of Edward the Confessor, the English king renowned for his piety.

1589 Death of Catherine de' Medici, Italian wife of Henry II of France.

1818 The first regular trans-Atlantic service begins between New York and Liverpool.

1925 Mrs Nellie Taylor Ross of Wyoming becomes the first woman governor in the US.

1930 Joseph Stalin collectivizes Soviet farms, forcing wealthy peasants off their land.

1941 Amy Johnson, the British aviator who flew solo from Britain to Australia, crashes and dies on a flight across the Thames estuary.

1964 Pope Paul VI meets the Ecumenical Patriarch of Constantinople in Jerusalem, the first meeting between the heads of the Roman Catholic and Orthodox churches in 500 years.

1968 Alexander Dubcek becomes Secretary of the Czechoslovakian Communist Party.

1971 Former world heavyweight boxing champion Sonny Liston is found dead at his home in the US.

1971 England play Australia in the first-ever one-day cricket match in Melbourne.

2003 Death of Roy Jenkins, the former Labour chancellor and leader of the SDP.

BIRTHDAYS

John Burke 1781, British genealogist and founder of *Burke's Peerage*, first published in 1826.

Stella Gibbons 1902, British novelist and journalist, author of *Cold Comfort Farm*.

Alfred Brendel 1931, Austrian concert pianist.

Robert Duvall 1931, US film actor who appeared in *To Kill a Mockingbird* and *Apocalypse Now*.

King Juan Carlos of Spain 1938.

Diane Keaton 1946, US film actress and photographer, star of several Woody Allen films including *Sleeper* and *Annie Hall*.

JANUARY 6

Twelfth Night

1066 Harold II of England is crowned.

1840 Death of Fanny Burney, British novelist and diarist and close friend of Dr Johnson.

1884 Gregor Mendel, the Austrian botanist who discovered the principles governing the inheritance of characteristics in living things, dies aged 62.

1916 The British government institutes conscription to replace the many thousands of fighting men killed in the trenches in France.

1928 The River Thames bursts its banks, drowning four people.

1930 Australian cricketer Don Bradman scores 452 not out against Queensland in his first innings as he bats for New South Wales.

1931 The New Sadler's Wells Theatre opens in London.

1988 La Coupole, the famous Parisian brasserie, is sold to be turned into an office block.

1995 Death of South African communist leader Joe Slovo.

BIRTHDAYS

King Richard II of England 1367, son of Edward the Black Prince.

Joan of Arc 1412, French heroine who fought to drive the British from France.

Gustave Doré 1832, French artist and illustrator.

Max Bruch 1838, German Romantic composer whose works included the much-loved first violin concerto.

Carl Sandburg 1878, American author and folk singer who wrote a biography of Abraham Lincoln.

Tom Mix 1881, American film actor and most popular cowboy of the silent screen.

Loretta Young 1913, American film actress who won an Oscar for *The Farmer's Daughter*.

Nancy Lopez-Melton 1957, American professional golfer voted Sportswoman of the Year in 1978.

SEX PISTOLS FIRED BY EMI

1977 Unable to handle further controversy, the record company EMI has kicked out the British punk rock group the Sex Pistols – with a £40,000 payoff. A statement issued today said the company can no longer promote the group's records in view of recent adverse publicity. All publicity is good in the pop business, and it is no coincidence that the group's latest album, *Anarchy in the UK*, has sold 50,000 copies. EMI is withdrawing the record. Taunted by interviewer Bill Grundy on ITV's evening magazine programme, *Today*, last month, the Sex Pistols responded with language considered unsuitable for family viewing time. "They're foul-mouthed yobs," Grundy commented. It got them on to every front page in the country and it got Grundy suspended.

1838 Samuel Morse today demonstrated a revolutionary electromagnetic telegraph that promises to open up a new world in long-distance communications. The device sends a pulse of current down a line, energizing an electromagnet at the receiving end which pulls an iron armature attached to a pencil. The pulses are short or long, producing "dots" or "dashes" which can be used as a code to represent the letters of the alphabet.

Last-ditch Nazi assault fails

1945 Germany's desperate attempt to break the advancing Allied line by thrusting through the Ardennes forest has been turned back, Field Marshal Montgomery said today. The Battle of the Bulge has resulted in 10 German armoured divisions being "written off", according to the Allied commander. The attack, which began on December 16, was a last-ditch attempt by Germany to turn back the Allies. Forces under generals Gerd von Rundstedt and Hasso von Manteuffel drove their wedge of tanks (the Bulge) into Allied lines, but were finally halted mainly by the US 1st and 3rd armies (the latter under General George Patton) and forced to retreat.

> *What progress we are making. In the Middle Ages they would have burned me. Now they are content with burning my books.*
> **Sigmund Freud** today after fleeing the Nazi persecution of Jews in Vienna, 1938.

Theodore Roosevelt dies

1919 Theodore Roosevelt, the American president who occupied the White House for two terms died today at Oyster Bay after a life dedicated to politics, literature and adventure. He once said, "I wish to preach . . . the doctrine of the strenuous life." He will be remembered as the president who restrained big business, pushing through anti-Trust legislation which discouraged market control and price rigging. In international affairs he won a Nobel Prize for mediating peace between Russia and Japan, and was responsible for widening America's international influence; in the Roosevelt Corollary to the Monroe Doctrine, he also enshrined America's right to interfere in Latin America. He began his career running the New York police, then became state governor. First taking power after the assassination of William McKinley in 1901, he was elected in his own right in 1904, serving until 1909.

Henry VIII – fourth time lucky?

1540 King Henry VIII of England married his fourth wife, Anne of Cleves, today in an alliance that could secure the King both an heir and powerful friends – though it has deepened his rift with Rome. Anne's brother, the Duke of Cleves, is a powerful German Protestant prince with whom Henry shares political interests. Henry's chief minister, Thomas Cromwell, negotiated the marriage, gaining Lutheran support to counter a Catholic alliance against England. The king's marital affairs have so far been a catalogue of disaster: he divorced Catherine of Aragon and had Anne Boleyn executed, while Jane Seymour died. When Henry first saw his fourth wife at the wedding today, he bellowed: "You have sent me a Flanders mare!"

HERO WASHINGTON IS FIRST US PRESIDENT

1789 George Washington, hero of America's revolutionary wars, has been unanimously elected as the first president of the United States. Members of the electoral college in New York gave an overwhelming vote to the hero of Yorktown, who is expected to take office on April 30. Washington was closely involved in drafting the constitution two years ago. Despite his audacity in the war against England, Washington is expected to move cautiously. He is acutely aware of the need to build an executive structure that can accommodate future presidents.

Calais calamity

1558 France today fulfilled Joan of Arc's ancient dream of ousting the English from her shores by seizing Calais, the first and last foothold of British invaders. Calais, which had fallen in 1346, was finally reclaimed by the Duke of Guise in an operation that began on New Year's Day. The English reverse should bring over 60 years of intermittent warfare between France, England and Spain to an end. In 1346, after almost a year of siege by the English armies, six Calais burghers surrendered themselves to avoid a massacre. Today's loss is a major setback for the English Queen, Mary Tudor, whose unpopular marriage to a Spanish prince provoked the war with France that led to the defeat at Calais.

Sex is one of the nine reasons for reincarnation. The other eight are unimportant.
Henry Miller, whose explicit novels were banned in the US until 1961, died today, 1980.

1536 Death of Catherine of Aragon, King Henry VIII of England's first wife whom he divorced to marry Anne Boleyn.

1610 Galilei Galileo, Italian mathematician, scientist and astronomer, announces his discovery of the four moons circling Jupiter.

1618 Francis Bacon, lawyer, philosopher and writer, becomes Lord Chancellor of England.

1785 Dr John Jeffries and Jean-Pierre Blanchard cross the English Channel in a hot-air balloon, an American-French adventure.

1905 The US Senate approves the first government appointment of a black man, as head of South Carolina customs services.

1927 The Harlem Globetrotters basketball team is founded.

1927 A transatlantic telephone link between London and New York is opened.

1943 Death of Nikola Tesla, the Croatian-American electrical engineer who developed the alternating current.

1945 Allied forces complete the construction of the new Burma Road, a vital supply line into China since the old Burma Road was closed by Japanese troops.

1975 The Organization of Petroleum Exporting Countries (OPEC) raises the price of crude oil by 10 per cent.

1990 The Leaning Tower of Pisa is closed to the public as its rate of movement accelerates.

BIRTHDAYS

Joseph Bonaparte 1768, Corsican, eldest brother of Napoleon Bonaparte and King of Naples and Spain.

Marie-Bernard Soubirous 1844, French visionary who became St Bernadette of Lourdes.

François Poulenc 1899, French composer best-known for his ballet *Les Biches*.

Gerald Durrell 1925, British author and naturalist who wrote *My Family and Other Animals*.

Wall Street tycoon loses final gamble

1872 American financier and stock speculator James Fisk has died aged 38 after being shot by a business associate. Fisk, known as the "Barnum of Wall Street", left school early and worked at first as an odd-job man, subsequently becoming an agent for financier Daniel Drew, who helped him set up as a broker. Fisk later fought and lost the "Erie War" to keep Cornelius Vanderbilt from gaining control of the Erie Railroad. In 1869, Fisk's efforts to corner the gold market ended in the Black Friday market panic. Fisk lived as he liked, unconcerned by his reputation. He was killed in an argument over his favourite mistress.

1970 Woodstock Festival – the biggest-ever rock event, held over three days last August with an attendance of half a million – caused $35,000 damage, neighbours claimed today in a civil action against Max Yasgur, the farmer who owned the land on which the festival was held.

Last rites for Emperor who was last of the gods

1989 Hirohito, the Japanese emperor who disavowed his ancient claim to divinity in an act of contrition for World War II, died today after a 62-year reign. He is succeeded by Crown Prince Akihito. After the 1946 constitution stripped him of all but ceremonial powers, he devoted himself to ceremonial duties and to marine biology, a subject on which he wrote several books. Hirohito opposed war with the United States in the 1930s, including Japan's invasion of Manchuria and her alliance with Nazi Germany, but was later powerless to restrain the generals. In 1941 he favoured peace with Washington, but his war minister convinced him that a pre-emptive strike at Pearl Harbor was necessary. Hirohito's broadcast confirming Japan's surrender after the destruction of Hiroshima and Nagasaki tested the post-feudal fabric of Japanese society: many believed surrender impossible for a Japanese emperor.

794 Danish Vikings attack Lindisfarne Island off the north-east coast of England and destroy its famous church.

1800 London sees the opening of its first soup kitchens for the poor.

1895 French poet Paul Verlaine dies in poverty.

1889 New Yorker Dr Herman Hoperith patents the first computer.

1921 Lloyd George becomes the first British Prime Minister to take up residence at Chequers, a Buckinghamshire mansion presented to the nation by Lord Lee of Fareham.

1941 Robert Baden-Powell, founder of the Boy Scouts, dies.

1942 German troops begin the retreat from Leningrad, defeated by the Russian winter.

1948 Death of Kurt Schwitters, German painter and writer who spent a major part of his life in the British Lake District.

1948 Richard Tauber, the much-loved Austrian tenor, dies in Australia.

1963 Fire damages seven floors of the Empire State Building in New York.

1976 Zhou En-Lai dies, Chinese Communist premier 1949–76.

1979 Vietnamese troops crush the Khmer Rouge and occupy Phnom Penh, capital of Cambodia.

1996 Death of French socialist president François Mitterrand who lost the fight against cancer at 80.

BIRTHDAYS

Wilkie Collins 1824, British master of the suspense novel who wrote *The Woman in White*.

Solomon Bandaraike 1899, Prime Minister of Sri Lanka 1956-59.

Georgi Malenkov 1902, President of the Soviet Union 1953-5.

Elvis Presley 1935, first American rock 'n' roll icon.

Shirley Bassey 1937, Welsh singer whose international hits include "Goldfinger" and "Hey Big Spender".

David Bowie 1947, British rock musician and actor.

DEATH OF GALILEO

1642 Galileo Galilei, the mathematician and astronomer, has died at Arcetri. Galileo rose to prominence as professor of mathematics at the University of Padua, where he challenged key assumptions in Aristotelian physics. He was the first to exploit the telescope to gaze on lunar mountains, the Milky Way, and the moons of Jupiter. Galileo became convinced that Copernicus had been right: the earth rotates around the sun, not vice-versa as the Bible teaches. The Holy Office at Rome issued an edict against Copernicanism and in 1632 Galileo was called to Rome by the Inquisition. He was condemned to life imprisonment for heresy and forced to recant. Even so, he said under his breath, "But it still goes round the sun."

How can you govern a country which produces 265 different kinds of cheese?
General Charles de Gaulle, on his appointment as French premier, 1958.

Boeing jet kills 44 in motorway crash

1989 A Boeing 737 crashed today on the M1 motorway in central England. At least 44 people died. The plane was carrying 117 passengers and eight crew on a flight to Ireland when the pilot reported engine trouble. Witnesses said they saw flames from the port wing, but in a radio message the pilot said he was shutting off the starboard engine – leaving the plane without any power.

Our man in Uruguay kidnapped

1971 Britain's ambassador in Uruguay, Geoffrey Jackson, has been kidnapped by left-wing Tupamaros guerrillas in the capital, Montevideo, it was reported today. The hijackers used five cars to seize 53-year-old Mr Jackson on his way to work, while local police were distracted by a diversionary movement. This is the first time a British envoy has been kidnapped in the volatile Latin continent, and Britain is pressing hard for Uruguayan troops to be deployed in the search for Mr Jackson, who suffers from heart disease. There are rumours that the Tupamaros would exchange Mr Jackson for political prisoners held in Montevideo jail, and would like the authorities to arrange for them to "escape".

1982 Armed barriers between Algeciras and the British colony of Gibraltar came down today as Spain ended its 12-year siege of "The Rock" in return for British agreement to Spanish membership of NATO and the EC.

1973 Rock idol Elvis Presley, on his 38th birthday, today sued Priscilla, his wife of six years, for divorce – and recorded a new single, "Separate Ways". The lyrics are obviously based on "the King's" marriage breakup.

1815 US forces led by Major General Andrew Jackson have crushed an invading British army at New Orleans in an engagement that could be the last of this war. Now English diplomats have begun to negotiate a peace settlement. It was British insistence on the right to commandeer US vessels and their men that originally sparked off the conflict in 1812.

Lean times for wartime Britain

1940 Britain went back to food rationing today for the first time since 1918 as the U-boat war in the Atlantic starts to affect ordinary housewives. Consumption of most meat has not yet been limited but ration books have been issued for butter, sugar, bacon and ham. Tough new laws oblige every household to register with its local shop, while hotel guests will have to hand in ration books to get a meal. The British are facing the new wartime limitations stoically. A government campaign is encouraging the nation to "Dig for victory" to boost home-grown food production.

Saudis execute invaders of Mecca

1980 Saudi Arabia announced today that 63 of the Shi'ite extremists who seized the Great Mosque in Mecca last November have been executed. This has inflamed already tense relations with nearby Iran and could complicate the three-month-old US hostage crisis in Tehran. Saudi troops captured the ringleaders of the Shi'ite invasion of Islam's holiest place when they stormed the Great Mosque on November 23. Some 500 heavily-armed extremists were holding thousands of pilgrims hostage and blood was spilled close to the Kaaba, which houses the holy Black Stone. Their leader belonged to the same religious sect as Iran's Ayatollah Khomeini and Saudis fear Tehran is trying to subvert the right-wing kingdom's Sunni Muslim rule.

Wave of immigration hits Britain's shores

1955 A ship with 400 Jamaican immigrants aboard docked in Britain today – the latest in a growing influx of West Indians arriving to help in the reconstruction of Britain's war-ravaged cities. Conservative politicians are pressing for legislation to control the numbers of immigrants.

Mystery fire sinks grand lady of luxury travel

1972 The *Queen Elizabeth* – once the greatest of the trans-Atlantic liners – was destroyed today by a mysterious fire in Hong Kong harbour, where she has been berthed for some time as a floating university. There are no reports of deaths in the fire that scuttled the former pride of the Cunard fleet, but police are investigating allegations that the fire was started deliberately to recoup insurance cash from the flagging university project. The *Queen Elizabeth* was launched in 1938 and, with her sister ship the *Queen Mary*, operated as a troop ship during World War II.

She returned to commercial service in 1946. Jet travel killed the trans-Atlantic sea voyage, and in 1969 the ship was sold to American investors who planned to use her as a tourist attraction – the same fate as that of the *Queen Mary*. Then Hong Kong shipping magnate C.Y. Tung bought her and she became the Seawise (C.Y.'s) University.

This vice brings in one hundred million francs in taxes every year. I will certainly forbid it at once – as soon as you can name a virtue that brings in as much revenue.
Napoleon III, upon being asked to ban smoking. The emperor died today in exile in Kent at the age of 65 – 1873.

Eden resigns: Suez cited as real reason

1957 Sir Anthony Eden's rash decision to go to war over the Suez Canal cost him his job as Britain's prime minister today. He was said to be resigning for reasons of health, but few doubt that American rage over the Anglo-French occupation of Suez, in connivance with Israel, is really the cause. Before the troops were pulled out a month ago in response to a United Nations mandate, Britain had to plead with the US Treasury for funds to stop a run on the pound, which is at an all-time low. The price of US support was Britain's withdrawal from Suez.

1806 Lord Nelson, naval commander and hero of the Battle of Trafalgar, is buried at St Paul's Cathedral in London.

1811 The first women's golf tournament takes place in Scotland.

1878 Death of Victor Emmanuel. first King of Italy.

1909 Ernest Shackleton's polar expedition is forced to turn back just 11 miles from the South Pole.

1920 Alexander Fleming pioneers the use of penicillin at St Mary's Hospital in London.

1923 Katherine Mansfield, New Zealand-born author renowned for her short stories, dies in France of tuberculosis.

1951 *Life After Tomorrow*, the first film to receive an 'X' rating in Britain, opens in London.

1972 British miners strike for the first time since 1926.

1995 Death of Peter Cook, comedian, broadcaster and writer.

1996 Rebels seize 3,000 hostages in Chechnya.

BIRTHDAYS

Lady Randolph Churchill 1854, American-born mother of Sir Winston Churchill.

Sir Rudolf Bing 1902, Austrian-born conductor and founder of the Edinburgh festival.

George Balanchine 1904, Russian-born choreographer who moved to the USA and was co-founder of the New York City Ballet.

Simone de Beauvoir 1908, French novelist, critic, early feminist and long-time companion of Jean-Paul Sartre.

Richard Nixon 1913, 37th President of the USA who resigned in disgrace after the Watergate scandal.

Gypsy Rose Lee 1914, American strip-tease artist, actress and author whose biography *Gypsy* was the basis of the Broadway musical of the same name.

Joan Baez 1941, American singer who came to prominence in the 1960s with her protest songs.

Unwelcome cost of war with France

1799 William Pitt the Younger introduced income tax in Britain today, at two shillings in the pound (10 per cent). This unpopular move is to pay for the even more unpopular war against Napoleon's France. Pitt, Prime Minister since he was 24, is a liberal reformer who revived Britain's economy following the American Revolution, but the French Revolution has brought different pressures; radical groups inspired by France have found the ear of disgruntled workers and troops have been called out as mass meetings demanding change have turned into riot. War has turned Pitt the reformer into an oppressor: he has enforced summary trial for trade unionists, banning and arrest of radical workers, and total press censorship. The new income tax is being seen as part of the same unwelcome parcel.

BIRTHDAYS

GOVERNMENT SAYS BRITONS CAN'T JOIN ANTI-FRANCO FORCES

1937 Britain has announced a ban on its nationals joining the International Brigades now gathering in Spain to defend the Constitutionalist Republican forces against General Franco's Nationalists in the civil war that has erupted there. The US is to impose a ban on Americans joining the fighting. 59,000 idealists from all countries have flocked to Spain to join the "fight

for liberty". The eight-month-old conflict has gained international overtones with Nazi and fascist troops fighting for Franco, while the USSR has sent weapons and military advisers to the Republicans. The Comintern, the international communist brotherhood, has organized thousands of liberals and leftists from 53 countries into volunteer International Brigades to fight fascism.

Crisis? What crisis? for Sunny Jim

1979 Britain's "Winter of Discontent" finally caught up with Labour premier Jim Callaghan today when he returned to London from a comfortable four-day "sunshine summit" in the West Indies to face charges that he had let the country slip into chaos. Hundreds of thousands of workers have been laid off as a rash of strikes sweeps the country. The Cabinet has refused to seek emergency powers to deal with industrial unrest because it fears a union backlash – but with disruptions in the distribution of food and fuel, few believe that Mr Callaghan's government can have many months of life left to it.

British flag flying over strategic Cape

1806 The Cape of Good Hope is now a British colony. A British fleet today defeated the Dutch colonists at the Battle of Blaauwberg, and the British flag is flying at the Fort. Control of the strategic Cape is a key factor in the European war, as it commands the route between the European powers and their rich Eastern dominions. This is the second time the Dutch colonists who founded the Cape Colony 150 years ago have had to surrender to British forces – the first was in 1795, after the Battle of Muizenberg. The British ruled the Cape for the next seven years. In 1803 the colony reverted to Napoleonic Holland under the treaty of Amiens, but again came under threat when the treaty broke down and the European war resumed.

1863 London's first underground railway, the Metropolitan, opened today, inaugurating a new era in city travel that could do much to help clear the congested roads of carriages and pedestrians. Passengers are delighted with the new service, but some foresee problems because of the smoke the trains spew from their chimneys.

1918 Women's rights on both sides of the Atlantic took a huge stride forward today when legislatures in London and Washington gave women the right to vote. In Britain, the House of Lords gave its approval to the Representation of the People Bill, which gives women over 30 the vote. Royal Assent is expected next month. In Washington the House of Representatives also voted in favour of suffrage for women.

Buffalo Bill goes West

1917 William "Buffalo Bill" Cody, the man who brought the world the romantic image of the Wild West, died today, aged 71. He began his career as a Pony Express rider in the days before the Civil War, served as a soldier in the war, and then became a contractor supplying meat to the workers of the Kansas Pacific Railroad in the 1860s, hence his name. As chief of scouts for the Fifth US Cavalry he fought in several battles against the Indians. A novel about his exploits brought him fame; he went on to organize a travelling Wild West show that toured in Europe before the Great War.

You're lucky I don't shove your beard down your gullet! . . . Get out, viper! . . . Sheer off, filibuster! Out of my sight, you gallows bird! . . . Baboon! . . . Carpet-seller! . . . Pockmark! . . . Cannibal! . . . Duck-billed platypus! . . . Jellied-eel! . . . Er. .
Captain Haddock, irate, sees off a slave-trader in *The Red Sea Sharks* – Herge's Tintin first appeared today, 1929.

HARDY'S HEART STAYS IN BELOVED WESSEX

1928 Thomas Hardy, the chronicler of a rural England whose pulse is changing as the modern world bears down on the vanishing world of the yeoman, has died today, aged 87. His body will be buried in Westminster, beside Dickens, in the presence of his wife Florence. His heart, however, is to be buried in his native Wessex, at the country churchyard at Stinsfield – in the grave of his first wife, Emma, to whom he wrote a long series of impassioned love poems after her death. Hardy lived in Wessex for 40 years. "There was quite enough human nature in Wessex for one man's literary purpose," he once said. Hardy's own domestic arrangements are perhaps a case in point. Certainly his dual burial,

showing as it does the loyalties his heart held in life, must go down in legend. Hardy's novels described a vanished way of life which he knew intimately, in which the fate of his characters was often circumscribed by the looming nature of the landscape they lived in.

13-year-old bride for painter Gauguin

1892 French Impressionist painter Paul Gauguin, now 44, has married a 13-year-old Tahitian girl. Gauguin, who abandoned his Danish wife and four children in Copenhagen eight years ago, arrived in Tahiti last year, and has started a series of paintings of the islanders and their religious myths. The painter was riding in the hills when he was invited to eat with a group of villagers – and was offered a wife. Finding the girl in question charming, Gauguin asked: "Would you like to live always in my hut?" "Yes," she answered. The couple then rode off together, and by the time they reached his home Gauguin had fallen in love with her. In accordance with local traditions, if the girl is not happy after eight days, she will leave the French painter.

> *My great fear is that by the time the whites have turned to loving, the blacks will have turned to hating.*
>
> **Alan Paton**,
> South African author,
> in *Cry the Beloved Country*
> (1948) – born today, 1903.

Hong Kong talks overshadowed by Tianenmen memories

1990 China today lifted martial law, seven months after the horrific military massacre of 2600 pro-democracy demonstrators in Peking's Tianenmen Square. The troops withdrew from Tianenmen Square in honour of Hong Kong's governor, Sir David Wilson, who arrived for talks with the Peking regime on the colony's future. In 1997 the colony reverts to Chinese control as Britain's 99-year lease runs out. Sir David is to meet Chinese premier Li Peng, who praised the withdrawing troops for their role in "crushing the emerging anarchy", as he put it. "For this, the people will never forget them," he added. There were huge turnouts in Hong Kong in support of the pro-democracy demonstrators. Confidence died, the economy stumbled, and an exodus began – led by the skilled professionals the colony will desperately need if Hong Kong is to survive into the future.

1569 The first state lottery is held in England, with tickets on sale at the West Door of St Paul's Cathedral in London.

1753 Sir Hans Sloane, British physician, naturalist and botanist, dies aged 93.

1864 Charing Cross railway station is opened in London.

1867 Mexican president Benito Juarez returns to Mexico City following the defeat of French forces.

1891 Baron Georges-Eugène Haussman, architect who replanned Paris as a city of long boulevards, dies in poverty.

1898 Major Esterhazy is wrongly acquitted in Paris of forging documents which had been used to establish the charge of treason against French army officer Captain Alfred Dreyfus.

1922 Insulin is first used with success in the treatment of diabetes.

1954 All Comet aircraft are grounded following a mysterious crash off the island of Elba.

1959 In Karachi, Pakistani cricketer Hanif Mohammad hits a record-breaking 499 runs in an innings lasting more than 10 hours.

1963 The club Whisky-Au-Go-Go opens in Los Angeles.

1966 Death of Alberto Giacometti, Italian painter and sculptor.

1970 Rebel Biafran leader General Ojukwe flees the country as the Nigerian civil war reaches a bitter end.

1974 The first surviving sextuplets are born to Mrs Sue Rosenkowitz of Cape Town, South Africa.

1989 President Ronald Reagan bids goodbye to the American people after two terms in office.

BIRTHDAYS

Ezra Cornell 1807, American founder of Cornell University, New York.

Sir John Alexander 1815, Canada's first Prime Minister.

It's a Zog's life

1946 King Zog, the colourful monarch who started life as Ahmed Zogu, a conservative northern tribal chief in Albania, has been dethroned and the country declared a republic again. Zog elevated himself to the monarchy after seizing power in 1925 in the turbulent period following the collapse of Ottoman Turkish rule. Allying himself with Italy, Zog carried out some modernizations, but his entanglement with Italy's fascist dictator, Benito Mussolini, backfired; in 1939 Italian fascist forces invaded Albania and Zog was forced into exile. During the war he was unable to exploit a power struggle between the communist and non-communist liberation forces to his advantage and when the communists won, Zog lost.

> *'Tis the star-spangled banner;*
> *O long may it wave*
> *O'er the land of the free,*
> *and the home of the brave!*
> **Francis Scott Key**,
> lyricist, who died today, 1814.

1519 Death of Maximilian I, King of Germany and Holy Roman Emperor from 1493.

1879 The British-Zulu War begins in South Africa.

1948 The London Co-op opens the first British supermarket at Manor Park.

1954 Queen Elizabeth II opens the New Zealand parliament.

1957 President Eisenhower urges the Soviet Union to agree a ban on space warfare.

1959 British boxer Henry Cooper becomes British and European heavyweight boxing champion after defeating Jack London on points.

1959 A $400 million contract for the Mercury space programme is awarded to the McDonnell Aircraft Corporation of St Louis.

1964 The Sultan of Zanzibar is banished and the country becomes a republic.

1970 A Boeing 747 (Jumbo) jet touches down at Heathrow Airport after its maiden transatlantic flight from New York.

1977 France releases PLO terrorist Abu Davoud, leader of the Black September group who claimed responsibility for the killing of 11 Israeli athletes at the Munich Olympics.

1989 Former Ugandan leader Idi Amin is expelled from Zaire and takes refuge in Senegal.

BIRTHDAYS

Charles Perrault 1628, French writer and collector of fairy tales.

Johann Pestalozzi 1856, Swiss educationist who founded a new principle of teaching.

John Singer Sargent 1856, American painter best-known for his portraits of society figures.

Jack London 1876, American author whose books include *White Fang* and *Call of the Wild*.

Hermann Goering 1893, commander of the German Air Force during World War II.

Joe Frazier 1947, American holder of the world heavyweight boxing title from 1970 to 1975.

PEACE IN BIAFRA BUT FAMINE LOOMS

1970 The secessionist Nigerian state of Biafra today surrendered to Nigerian federal troops after a disastrous three-year war likely to be even more catastrophic in its aftermath as starvation grips the population. As the last Biafran airstrip was taken by federal troops, reports began to emerge of rape and pillage by the victors on a horrifying scale. During its brief existence, the oil-rich state of Biafra covered 44,000 sq miles. It was created by the Ibo, the dominant ethnic group in Nigeria, and led by Lt Col. Chukwuemeka Odumegwu Ojukwu. He is said to be demanding political asylum in nearby Ivory Coast.

> *In a hierarchy, every employee tends to rise to his level of incompetence. Work is accomplished by those employees who have not yet reached their level of incompetence.*
> **Peter Lawrence**, Canadian author of *The Peter Principle*, who died today, 1990.

Mark Thatcher "lost" in desert

1982 There was concern last night in Downing Street as Britain's premier Margaret Thatcher fretted over an affair close to her heart – her son Mark is reported missing in the Sahara Desert, where he is taking part in the gruelling Paris-Dakar Motor Rally. Search planes have been sent out to look for young Thatcher and his team-mate, and the Prime Minister has been advised that there is little cause for alarm. This is not the first anxiety Mark has caused his mother: his misadventures on the racetrack and in the world of business have already raised eyebrows.

Music to Ludwig's ears

1809 Ludwig van Beethoven, Vienna's musical genius, has been given a guaranteed yearly income by three Viennese noblemen – on the single condition that he stays in Vienna. Beethoven first came to Vienna from Bonn in 1892 to study under Josef Haydn, and has never left. He is now half-deaf, able still to hear his music, but not human speech. Over the years his music has reflected his struggle against loss of hearing. In 1802 he resolved to "seize fate by the throat" and emerged with a series of triumphant works, such as the Eroica Symphony (1803), that quite transcended his earlier work. In more recent compositions, however, such as the Violin Concerto of 1806 or last year's Sixth Symphony, this heroic quality alternates with a new serenity. Beethoven has conquered his fate: although trapped in a muffled world, he has produced some of the finest music ever written. He is now working on his fifth piano concerto. The Viennese princes have bought a bargain.

Ford speeds to new record on frozen lake

1904 The American automobile engineer and racing driver Henry Ford has achieved a new land speed record of 91.37 mph in his "999" car on frozen Lake St Clair outside Detroit. Ford, who has built several racing cars and fruitlessly tried to put them into production, has been experimenting with motor transport for some years – he built his first car, the quadricycle, in 1896. Ford is said to be raising $100,000 in capital for a new business venture in which he plans to produce automobiles in series for the American people. "Make them all alike" is the principle he aims to work to in the interests of keeping costs down.

Queen of Crime dies with mystery unsolved

1976 The queen of crime fiction breathed her last today at the age of 85, carrying her most enigmatic mystery to the grave unsolved. Dame Agatha Christie's books have been translated into every major language since the first one appeared in 1920. She was the creator of the Belgian dandy martinet Hercule Poirot and the parochial, English Miss Jane Marple. Of nearly 100 novels, many were made into films, while the stage play *The Mousetrap* has now run for 24 years in London's West End. Agatha Christie never revealed the truth of her missing weekend in 1926, after which she reappeared in a Harrogate Hotel with no recollection of where she had been.

LABOUR PARTY BORN: SOCIALISM GETS SERIOUS

1893 James Keir Hardie, the new member of parliament for West Ham who last year arrived to take his seat at Westminster dressed in yellow trousers and to the tune of the Marseillaise, has fathered an organization that could in time shock Britain's frock-coated Tories even more deeply than his dress sense. It is called the Labour Party and results from an alliance of British trade union and socialist movements. The Fabian Society, the newly-formed Independent Labour Party, and Keir Hardie's own Scottish Labour Party will all be united under the Labour Representation Committee. Hardie, who started work as a miner at the age of 10 and educated himself at night school, secured election as an independent socialist, but now he has a party to back him.

1897 Mr and Mrs Bradley Martin, high-flyers in the "400", New York's gilt-edged society set, were making a bid for the party of the year. The ballroom of the Waldorf Astoria was converted into a Palace of Versailles replica. No expense was spared. The next day's newspapers said that in the face of the nation's worst ever depression, the party was a disgrace. The Martins fled public outrage and have just arrived in England, leaving only 398 top people in New York.

FAB FOUR HIT US CHARTS

1964 The Beatles, the subject of massed teenage hysteria in Britain and irate debate in London's House of Commons, have entered the US pop charts at No 45, climbing fast. The group's new single, *I Wanna Hold Your Hand*, brings America its first taste of the new Mersey Beat from Liverpool. *Billboard* magazine described the new single as "a driving rocker with surf on the Thames sound", predicting it would be a chart-topper.

> When the Lord sent me forth into the world, He forbade me to put off my hat to any high or low.
> **George Fox**, oft-imprisoned founder of the Quakers, who died today, 1691.

Soviet rebuke to Lithuanian challenge

1991 At least 13 demonstrators were killed as Soviet troops cracked down on the Lithuanian pro-independence movement in Vilnius today. Soviet paratroopers tried to seize television broadcasting installations in the capital. Lithuania lost independence in 1939 because of a deal between Stalin and Hitler. The Lithuanian Communist party has separated itself from the Soviet Communist party, and in March 1990 Lithuania proclaimed its independence. Moscow responded with an economic blockade, and in June the Lithuanians agreed to suspend their independence declaration during negotiations. These have broken down, leading to today's tragedy – in spite of a visit to Vilnius by Mikhail Gorbachev two days ago.

DREYFUS VICTIM OF RACISM SAYS NOVELIST ZOLA

1898 The distinguished novelist Emile Zola today stunned the Parisian literary and political world with an open letter on the front page of *L'Aurore* entitled "J'accuse", which makes a blistering attack on the French army over the affair of Captain Alfred Dreyfus. His letter forces simmering conflicts between the republicans and right-wing pro-monarchists into the open, showing just how deeply rooted anti-semitism is in French society. Officials are now examining the letter for a possible

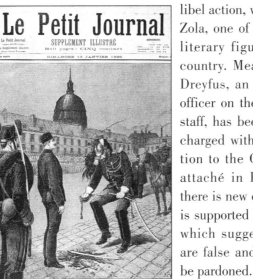

libel action, which could force Zola, one of France's leading literary figures, to flee the country. Meanwhile Captain Dreyfus, an Alsatian Jewish officer on the French general staff, has been sent to prison charged with giving information to the German military attaché in Paris. However, there is new evidence – which is supported by Zola's letter – which suggests the charges are false and Dreyfus should be pardoned.

1599 Death of Edmund Spenser, English poet who wrote *The Faerie Queene*.

1864 Death of Stephen Foster, American composer whose songs include "Swanee River" and "Beautiful Dreamer".

1910 Caruso is broadcast by radio singing at the New York Metropolitan Opera House.

1915 South African troops occupy Swakopmund in German South West Africa.

1926 Wyatt Earp, American lawman and hero of the gunfight at OK Corral, dies peacefully at the age of 81.

1941 Irish author James Joyce, whose book *Ulysses* caused outrage because of its sexual frankness, dies after surgery in Zurich.

1957 Elvis Presley records the hit "All Shook Up" in a Hollywood studio.

1974 The world's largest airport is opened at Dallas, Texas.

1978 Death of Hubert Humphrey, Vice-President to Lyndon Johnson.

1979 Concorde begins regular flights from Washington D.C. to Dallas.

1982 An Air Florida jet plunges into the frozen Potomac River near the White House, killing 78 people.

1988 Death of Chiang Ching-kuo, President of the Republic of China of Taiwan since 1978.

1990 Twenty-four people die in riots in Baku, Soviet Azerbaijan.

BIRTHDAYS

Sophie Tucker 1884, Russian-born singer and vaudeville star in America.

Lord Ted Willis 1918, British screenwriter and playwright who created the TV series *Dixon of Dock Green*.

Robert Stack 1919, American actor whose films included *Nice Girl* and *Written on the Wind*.

Michael Bond 1926, creator of the much-loved children's character Paddington Bear.

1742 Death of Sir Edmund Halley, British Astronomer Royal who gave his name to a comet.

1814 Denmark cedes Norway to Sweden.

1867 Death of Jean-Auguste-Dominique Ingres, French Romantic painter.

1878 Queen Victoria is given a demonstration of Alexander Graham Bell's new invention, the telephone.

1900 Puccini's opera *Tosca* is staged for the first time, in Rome.

1907 An earthquake in Kingston, Jamaica, destroys most of the capital and kills over 1000 people.

1938 *Snow White and the Seven Dwarfs*, Walt Disney's first full-length Technicolor cartoon, goes on general release in the USA.

1947 The newly renovated Covent Garden Opera House opens with a staging of Bizet's *Carmen*.

1953 Marshal Tito, Yugoslavia's communist leader since the end of World War II, is elected president of his country.

1957 Humphrey Bogart, Hollywood star, dies of cancer.

1977 Death of Sir Anthony Eden, former Prime Minister of Britain.

1982 Mark Thatcher, son of the British Prime Minister, is found after being lost in the Sahara Desert while competing in the Paris-Dakar car rally.

1990 Forty-three people die as fire sweeps through a disco in Saragossa, Spain.

BIRTHDAYS

Henri Fantin-Latour 1836, French painter who excelled in still-lifes and portraits.

Albert Schweitzer 1875, French theologian, organist and missionary surgeon, winner of the Nobel Peace Prize in 1952.

Cecil Beaton 1904, British stage designer and photographer.

Jack Jones 1938, American popular singer.

Faye Dunaway 1941, American actress, star of *Bonnie and Clyde* and *The Thomas Crown Affair*.

Marilyn Monroe becomes Mrs DiMaggio

1954 Marilyn Monroe, the screen star of *How to Marry a Millionaire*, has followed her own advice and found herself a wealthy new husband. This time it's 1940s baseball hero Joe DiMaggio. After a checkered start to her career, actress Norma Jean Baker (her real name) has nowhere to go but up, as Hollywood vies for the talents of this new international sex goddess. DiMaggio, now 40, led the New York Yankees to 10 pennants and 9 World Series titles. In 1941 he hit safely in 56 consecutive games, an all-time record. Soft-spoken and courteous, DiMaggio has endeared himself to the American public – and now wed one of America's most desirable women.

De Gaulle says emphatic *non* to Britain in EEC

1963 France today delivered a stunning rebuke to Britain for its years of hesitation over closer ties with Europe. Britain has now finally applied for membership of the European Economic Community, but President Charles de Gaulle virtually dismissed the plea with a single "non". At a Paris news conference he said Britain would only be ready for membership when it started thinking like a Continental country and severed its ties with the Commonwealth. He also criticized Britain for its subservience to the US. De Gaulle had haughty words for the Americans: he rejected US offers to station Polaris missiles on French soil and said France would rather look after its own nuclear defence than be "swallowed" by Washington. In London the Prime Minister said de Gaulle is trying to dominate Europe. A forthcoming royal visit to Paris may be cancelled.

Bradford book burnings as Rushdie takes cover

1989 Angry British Muslims today burned copies of Salman Rushdie's book *The Satanic Verses* in public. Rushdie has been catapulted to the centre of an international furore over the book, which has caused fury throughout the Islamic world for its alleged blasphemies against the Prophet Mohammed. Many of the Muslim community in Bradford publicly support Iranian leader Ayatollah Khomeini's call for the author's assassination. Rushdie has prudently gone into hiding and is under British police protection. The issue has caused Muslim indignation that western blasphemy laws only apply in a Christian context.

Thames freezes: crowds celebrate

1814 London crowds braved biting cold today and flocked to what could be the city's last Frost Fair on the frozen River Thames. The fair offered the traditional Punch and Judy shows and spit-roasts and the city's vendors were out in force, selling pies, oysters – and a very great deal of mulled ale to warm the bones of the revellers.

"If everyone minded their own business," the Duchess said in a hoarse growl, *"the world would go round a deal faster than it does."*

Lewis Carroll (Charles Dodgson), author of *Alice's Adventures in Wonderland* (1865), died today aged 66 – 1898.

Italian assassin misses Napoleon III

1858 An Italian assassin threw a bomb at French Emperor Napoleon III and Empress Eugenie tonight as they drove to the Paris Opera. But the bomb, thrown at their carriage by a Republican extremist police have named as Felice Orsini, caused eight other deaths, and up to 100 bystanders were reported injured. It has been revealed that Orsini planned the attack and made his bomb in London at a gathering of Italian emigré republicans. Anti-British sentiment is running strongly in Paris. Under interrogation the detained man told police that he regarded the Emperor as a traitor to the Italian cause because of his support for the Carbonari movement, an Italian secret society.

Visitor for far-flung Uranus

1986 Voyager 2, the only spacecraft to reach the planet Uranus, today passed within 50,625 miles of the planet's cloud tops. Voyager 2 has been collecting data on Uranus and its rings and satellites for four months. The planet's rings were only discovered in 1977, one of the most unexpected events in modern astronomy. Uranus, the seventh planet from the sun, is about four times the size of the Earth. Voyager 2 has detected an ocean perhaps 6000 miles deep.

NIXON HALTS US BOMBING OF VIETNAM

1973 US President Nixon today ordered a halt to all bombing of Vietnam by American warplanes, less than a month after the massive US "Christmas bombing" raids hit North Vietnam's capital, Hanoi. This initiative comes as the Paris peace conference opens, with a cease-fire to end the conflict believed to be imminent. The Christmas bombing was planned by White House strategists as a means of forcing Viet Cong leaders to moderate their demands at the Paris negotiating table. Women and children were evacuated as Hanoi hospital was hit by bombs, and 1600 civilians killed when more than 36,000 tons of bombs fell on the city over 12 days, leaving Hanoi a wasteland. In Washington a hostile congress had signalled its intention to limit Nixon's power to wage war if bombing continued.

Television brought the brutality of war into the comfort of the living room. Vietnam was lost in the living rooms of America - not on the battlefields of Vietnam.
Marshall McLuhan.

Stasi secrets plundered

1990 Thousands of furious East Germans today tore apart the machinery of post-war communist repression when they invaded the Berlin headquarters of the Stasi, the old regime's secret police. Offices were wrecked and police summoned as demonstrators from a rally in support of the New Forum opposition ran amok. No one was hurt.

Opening day at British Museum

1759 From today Londoners will be able to visit a "general repository for all arts and sciences" in Montague House, to be known as the British Museum. The museum, the first great public assembly of antiquities, is based on the famous collection of books, manuscripts, and objects of natural history amassed by the physician and naturalist Sir Hans Sloane, together with similar collections made by Edward and Robert Harley and Sir Robert Bruce Cotton. The museum was conceived when £300,000 was raised in a lottery. It will be administered by trustees, drawn from both church and state.

QUEEN BESS CROWNED

1559 Elizabeth I was today formally crowned Queen of England at the age of 26. The brilliant young queen took the throne from her Catholic half-sister, Mary Tudor, last year. Elizabeth is rapidly consolidating her control in a volatile political situation. She is trying to outflank both Rome and the equally radical Puritans by introducing a more moderate Protestant faith similar to that initiated by her father, King Henry VIII. Elizabeth wants to repudiate the Catholic church without provoking a continental Catholic alliance to unseat her. Though there is nervousness about a Queen who shows no inclination for marriage, the English are impressed with their new highly intelligent and well-educated monarch. Elizabeth is the daughter of Henry's second wife, Anne Boleyn, whom he later executed.

Irish glimpse independence

1922 The Provisional Irish Parliament, Dail Eireann, is tonight passionately debating a new treaty proposal that could finally make Ireland an independent nation. The Irish Free State proposal has split Ireland's nationalist politicians, as perhaps has been Britain's intention: Foremost nationalist Eamon de Valera has refused to sit in the proposed new chamber because an oath to the British Crown is required. But the IRA's Michael Collins – reported to have been holding secret talks with British Home Secretary Winston Churchill – insists Ireland must accept the flawed treaty.

1790 Fletcher Christian and other mutineers from the *Bounty* land on Pitcairn Island in the South Pacific.

1797 James Hetherington is fined £50 for wearing the first bowler hat.

1815 Emma, Lady Hamilton, former mistress of Lord Nelson, dies in poverty at Calais.

1867 Forty people drown in frozen Regent's Park when ice gives way.

1877 Torrential rain causes the railway tunnel between Dover and Folkestone to collapse, but no lives are lost.

1878 Women receive degrees for the first time at London University.

1880 The first telephone directory is published in London.

1890 The first performance of Tchaikovsky's ballet *The Sleeping Beauty* is given in St Petersburg.

1964 Death of Jack Teagarten, American jazz trombonist.

1971 President Sadat of Egypt officially opens the Aswan High Dam on the River Nile.

1971 The currency of Britain changes from pounds, shillings and pence to the decimal pound.

BIRTHDAYS

Jean-Baptiste Poquelin Molière 1622, French dramatist who wrote *Le Malade Imaginaire*, *Tartuffe* and many other satirical plays.

Mazo de la Roche 1885, Canadian novelist who wrote the "Whiteoaks of Jalna" series.

Aristotle Onassis 1906, Greek shipowner, lover of opera diva Maria Callas and second husband of Jackie Kennedy.

Lloyd Bridges 1913, American actor.

General Gamal Nasser 1918, first president of the republic of Egypt.

Martin Luther King 1929, American clergyman, leader of the civil rights movement in the 1960s and winner of the Nobel Peace Prize in 1964.

Margaret O'Brien 1937, American child actress who won a special Academy Award in 1944, at just seven years old.

1547 Ivan the Terrible is crowned the first Tsar of Russia.

1780 British forces under Admiral Rodney defeat the Spanish at Cape St Vincent and relieve Gibraltar.

1794 Death of Edward Gibbon, British historian and author.

1891 Death of French composer Leo Delibes, best-known for his ballet *Coppélia*.

1924 The BBC broadcasts the first play written specifically for radio – *Danger*, by Richard Hughes.

1932 Duke Ellington records "It Don't Mean a Thing" in New York.

1942 American actress Carole Lombard, wife of Clark Gable, dies in a plane crash.

1944 General Eisenhower is appointed Supreme Commander of the Allied Forces in Europe.

1957 The Sadler's Wells Ballet is granted a royal charter and becomes the Royal Ballet.

1957 The Cavern Club opens in Liverpool as a venue for rock groups.

1957 Italian conductor Arturo Toscanini dies at the age of 90.

1970 Colonel Gaddafi becomes Chairman of the Revolutionary Command Council in Libya.

1975 Angola gains its independence from Portugal.

1979 The Shah of Iran dies in exile in Egypt.

1979 American singer and actress Cher files for divorce just nine days after her wedding to musician Greg Allman.

BIRTHDAYS

André Michelin 1853, French manufacturer of rubber tyres.

Alexander Knox 1907, Canadian actor whose films include *Reach for the Sky* and *The Sea Wolf*.

Ethel Merman 1909, American singer and actress who starred in the musicals *Call Me Madam*, *Annie Get Your Gun* and *There's No Business Like Show Business*.

Lord Thomson of Fleet 1921, Canadian newspaper magnate.

USA bans booze

1920 With heavy hearts, party-going Americans raised their glasses for the last time today in the final hours before the 18th Amendment to the Constitution came into force, banning the consumption of alcohol in the United States. Many foresee trouble and lawlessness as the price of restraining individual liberty with the "Noble Experiment". New York's police chief says 250,000 extra officers will be needed to enforce the ban, though the provisions planned in the new Volstead Act should do much to stop contraband liquor entering the country. America is not going dry overnight: liquor has been banned in some states since before the Civil War and the Prohibition Party fielded a presidential candidate 50 years ago. Today's legislation is the culmination of a long temperance battle.

RED ROSA MURDERED

1919 "Red Rosa" Luxembourg and Karl Liebknicht, the two revolutionary leaders of last week's abortive communist uprising in Berlin, have been murdered by army officers, it was reported today. Soldiers escorting the two captives to prison yesterday killed them instead, and threw their bodies into a canal. Two soldiers have been arrested. "Red Rosa", who spent years in prison for her attempts to mobilize German workers against the Great War, founded the Spartacist movement. Last week the movement tried to establish a Bolshevik republic in Berlin. Revolutionaries took over streets and seized public buildings, hoping that the workers would rally to their cause; the workers more or less ignored them. Loyal troops were called in and the revolt degenerated into confused street battles before the Spartacists were dislodged. Reports speak of hundreds of bodies littering the capital's streets.

> *An ally has to be watched just like an enemy.*
>
> **Leon Trotsky**, who was today removed from the leadership of the Communist Party by Joseph Stalin and placed under house arrest – 1925.

Test-tube fibre: great on legs

1937 The Du Pont Company has patented a revolutionary "miracle" yarn made entirely from chemicals. The new fibre is called Nylon, and members of the research team, headed by Wallace H. Carothers, say it is strong even when knitted into the sheerest of fabrics and can be washed and dried quickly. It can be made into filaments, sheets or a variety of finished products. One possible fashion use is to replace natural silk stockings. Du Pont says the new material's strength, durability, and resistance to moisture and mildew could interest the US Army. It is not the first artificial fabric: rayon, made from pulped wood, was first produced in 1884.

Protest lands Baez behind bars

1966 Protest singer Joan Baez is in jail. The left-wing 25-year-old American singer was amongst 124 anti-Vietnam War demonstrators arrested for blocking the entrance to a US Army induction centre at Oakland, California, and has been sent to prison for 10 days. Baez is no stranger to trouble. She refused to pay 60 per cent of her income tax in protest at US government armaments spending. Six months ago she opened the Institute for the Study of Non-Violence in Carmel, California, and withheld a further 10 per cent of her tax. Last year she and British folk singer Donovan led a massed Vietnam protest march in London.

DESERT STORM BREAKS WITH BOMBS ON BAGHDAD

1991 Allied jets bombed Baghdad as war broke out early today. In spite of desperate last-minute peace efforts, the UN deadline for Iraq's Saddam Hussein to withdraw his troops from Kuwait expired at midnight without an Iraqi response. The action started when US warships in the Gulf launched Cruise missiles at Iraqi targets. In the next four hours allied aircraft flew 400 missions against 60 targets in Iraq. UN Secretary General Perez de Cuellar, President Mubarak of Egypt and King Fahd of Saudi Arabia all sent urgent appeals to Iraqi strongman Saddam Hussein yesterday. Perez de Cuellar promised that if the present crisis was averted concrete progress could immediately be made on the Arab-Israeli conflict and the Palestinian question, which Saddam has consistently linked to his invasion of Kuwait. The appeals were fruitless.

Bodyline bowling just not cricket

1933 A row over cricket is threatening friendly relations between England and Australia. Lord's Cricket Ground in London, home of England's MCC (Marylebone Cricket Club), has received an angry telegram from the Australian Cricket Board demanding that the English bowlers change their bowling tactics in the third Test match now being played at Adelaide. The English fast bowling, led by Harold Larwood, has injured several players and dispatched the wicket-keeper with head injuries. These tough tactics are intended to counter Australian Donald Bradman's incomparable batting. "Bodyline" bowling forces batsmen to play leg strokes into the waiting hands of slip fielders. However, when the popular Bert Oldfield was carried off unconscious it was feared the Australian crowds would riot. The MCC may have to recall its aggressive touring team, captained by Douglas Jardine.

1773 Captain Cook's *Resolution* crosses the Antarctic Circle, the first ship ever to do so.

1781 American revolutionary troops rout a British force in South Carolina.

1827 The Duke of Wellington is appointed Commander-in-Chief of the British Army.

1852 The British recognize the independence of the Transvaal Boers.

1934 A "poor white" called Pohl finds a 500-carat diamond near Pretoria in South Africa.

1961 Patrice Lumumba, first president of the Democratic Republic of the Congo, is assassinated.

1966 A B-52 carrying four hydrogen bombs collides with a refuelling tanker, killing eight and releasing the weapons.

1983 The BBC pioneers breakfast television in Britain.

1988 The Nicaraguan Sandinista leader Daniel Ortego offers a ceasefire to the Contras.

1995 5,000 people die in an earthquake which strikes Kobe, Japan, at dawn. It is the biggest Japan has seen for 47 years.

SCOTT REACHES SOUTH POLE BUT NORWEGIANS WERE FIRST

1912 Britain's polar explorers completed a terrible overland journey to reach the South Pole today – only to find they were not the first. A Norwegian tent showed Roald Amundsen had beaten Captain Robert Falcon Scott's party by a month. "Great God, this is an awful place," wrote Scott in his diary as his party swallowed their disappointment. Poor logistics and unreliable equipment hampered the expedition, resulting in the ill-equipped party travelling far more slowly than Amundsen, whose men raced along behind dog-sleds.

Shah of Iran out, Khomeini in

1979 In one of contemporary history's most extraordinary reverses, the once-mighty Shah of Iran fled from his Peacock Throne at the command of an aged and still exiled priest. Jubilant Iranians danced for joy when Tehran Radio announced today that the Shah and his family had fled to Cairo, unable to resist the mounting opposition masterminded by Ayatollah Ruholla Khomeini, whose portrait is now omnipresent in the capital. In contrast, the crowds lost no time in toppling surviving statues of the Pahlavi dynasty begun by the Shah's father, a former mule-driver. The deposed ruler's powerful armed forces, his grandiose plans to restore Persia's former greatness, his modernizations using oil revenues and US support all counted for nothing in the face of discontent at his regime's corruption and brutality. Now the way is open for a triumphal return of the exiled Ayatollah, still living on the outskirts of Paris.

1874 Chang and Eng, the famous Siamese twins, have died within three hours of each other aged 62. They were joined at the hip, chest, abdomen and head, and even shared some organs. Chang and Eng mean "left" and "right" in Thailand, where they were born. They married sisters and fathered 10 and 12 children respectively.

Gilmore gets death wish

1977 For the first time in a decade an American prisoner was today taken from Death Row to face execution, ending a lengthy campaign to abolish the death penalty. "Let's do it," said murderer Gary Gilmore as prison officials led him out to face a firing squad at the State Prison in Provo, Utah. Seconds later, four bullets thudded into his heart. Gilmore had been found guilty of killing two students at Brigham Young University last year. Despite his wish for the death penalty to be carried out protesters made an appeal on his behalf. Norman Mailer is already planning a book about the case.

Benjamin Franklin 1706, American statesman and scientist who helped draft the Declaration of Independence.

David Lloyd George 1863, British prime minister 1916-1922.

Neville Shute 1899, British novelist who settled in Australia where he set his most famous book, *A Town Like Alice*.

Al Capone 1899, American gangster known as "Scarface".

Moira Shearer 1926, British ballerina and star of the film *The Red Shoes*.

Clyde Walcott 1926, Barbadian cricketer who, with Frank Worrell, hit an unbroken 544 against Trinidad.

Muhammad Ali 1942, American world heavyweight boxing champion three times over.

1485 The Houses of Lancaster and York are united by the marriage of Henry VII to Elizabeth, the eldest daughter of Edward IV.

1871 Wilhelm of Prussia is proclaimed the first German emperor.

1911 Eugene Ely is the first pilot to land his aircraft on a ship when his Curtis pusher bi-plane lands on the US cruiser *Pennsylvania* in San Francisco Bay.

1919 Twenty-seven nations convene the Paris Peace Conference following World War I – Germany is not allowed to attend.

1934 The first arrest is made in Britain by policemen using pocket radios.

1954 Death of Sydney Greenstreet, British actor who appeared in *Casablanca*, *The Maltese Falcon* and *The Woman in White* among many other films.

1972 Former prime minister Garfield Todd and his daughter are placed under house arrest by Ian Smith's government in Rhodesia.

1977 Eighty-two die in Australia when a Sydney-bound train is derailed.

BIRTHDAYS

Peter Mark Roget 1779, British doctor and lexicographer whose *Thesaurus* remains an indispensable tool for writers.

Emmanuel Chabrier 1841, French composer whose most famous work is the orchestral rhapsody *España*.

A. A. Milne 1882, British author who created Winnie the Pooh.

Thomas Sopwith 1888, British aircraft designer best-known for the World War I biplane the Sopwith Camel.

Oliver Hardy 1892, American half of the comedy team Laurel and Hardy.

Cary Grant 1904, British-born actor who became a Hollywood star.

Danny Kaye 1913, American actor and comedian whose films include *The Secret Life of Walter Mitty* and *Hans Christian Andersen*.

Russian forces break siege of Leningrad

1943 The Red Army has broken the 890-day siege of Leningrad and re-established land communications with the city, which since September 1941 has been subject to terrible air and artillery bombardment from German forces. During the siege the city received only irregular supplies over the frozen Lake Ladoga and its inhabitants consumed everything near-edible they could lay their hands on. The city's relief is the high point of the current massive Soviet counter-offensive which moved into top gear as the roads and waterways froze. The Red Army is now moving toward Voroshilovsk and its divisions are threatening the main German invading force at Stalingrad, where a battle is expected.

Verdi scores second success

1843 *I Lombardi*, Guiseppe Verdi's new opera set in the Crusades, opened in Milan tonight to instant success. This follows the extraordinary popularity of Verdi's third opera, *Nabucco*, which inspired near-riots when it was first performed here last year – the "Va pensiero" chorus is now the anthem of the Italian resistance movement against Austrian domination. With *I Lombardi*, Verdi, son of an innkeeper, is now the foremost composer of Italian romantic opera, although it once seemed as if his career had ended after his wife and two children died in the space of 22 months. It was only last year his producer persuaded him to write *Nabucco*.

Gulf War protests – and support

1991 Anti-Gulf War demonstrators across the US clashed violently with police today, and 1400 demonstrators were arrested – more than in any of the Vietnam War marches of the 1960s and 70s. After three days of war between the allied forces and Iraq, there were also massed anti-war demonstrations in most European capitals, with 300,000 gathering in Bonn and 50,000 in Paris. In Berlin, 10,000 children carried candles through the streets in protest. In spite of the riots, majority public opinion in the US is strongly behind military action. Current polls show 75 per cent of people favour the attack on Iraq – an increase from 50 per cent just before the war started. British polls show 80 per cent of respondents are in favour of Britain's involvement. The Arab world is in a furore over the allied attack, with pro-Iraqi demonstrations in many Muslim countries. There have also been angry protests in many Third World countries.

> *Though I've belted you an' flayed you,*
> *By the livin' Gawd that made you,*
> *You're a better man than I am, Gunga Din!*
>
> **Rudyard Kipling**, novelist, poet and chronicler of imperial Britain, who died today aged 70 – 1936.

1879 First edition of *Boy's Own Paper* published 1879–1967, created by the Religious Tract Society.

COOK DISCOVERS HAWAII

1778 The English navigator James Cook has discovered a new group of islands in the Pacific Ocean on his third voyage of discovery aboard his ship *Resolution*. The islands, inhabited by a powerful race of Polynesians, are called Hawaii in the local tongue, but Captain Cook today claimed the territory for the Crown and named them the Sandwich Islands. In his attempt to discover a northwest passage from Europe to the Orient from the Pacific side, Captain Cook sailed from the Cape of Good Hope in 1776 to meet the survey vessel *Discovery*, and then onward to the North American coast via the Pacific. His plan is to force a passage through the Bering Straits into the Arctic Ocean, and return to Europe this way. If no such passage exists, then the *Resolution* can return the way it came. Cook aims to use the newly-discovered islands as ports of call. However, the island's inhabitants have shown some animosity toward their first European visitors.

1990 Englishman Terry Marsh, former world welterweight boxing champion, was charged today with trying to kill his ex-manager, Frank Warren, last November. Warren was shot in the face.

Free love guru dies

1990 Bhagwan Shree Rajneesh, the Indian guru who owned nearly 100 Rolls-Royces, has died of a heart attack at his commune in Poona, barred from nearly 20 countries. He was 58. Rajneesh was the guru of free love: according to his teaching, celibacy was a crime, and a great obstacle on the path towards enlightenment. One of his books was entitled *Meditation: The Art of Ecstasy*. During the 1970s he had hundreds of thousands of ardent followers in the West, keenly practising the guru's principles. Known as the Orange People because, for no known reason, his disciples wore only orange clothing, those converted to his teaching lost their names, adopting Indian names Rajneesh gave them. Rajneesh was recently expelled from the US and his commune in Oregon was closed.

Washington mayor stung in crack bust

1990 FBI agents using an attractive black actress as bait have caught Washington's mayor Marion Barry red-handed as he smoked a cocaine-laced cigarette in a hotel room. The "sting" operation came as Barry – long suspected of illegal drug consumption – accepted a "crack" cigarette from the police informer while hidden FBI video cameras recorded the event. Seconds later one of America's best-known black leaders was under arrest.

1547 Henry Howard, Earl of Surrey, is beheaded in the Tower of London for treason.

1729 English Restoration playwright William Congreve is killed in a carriage accident.

1793 King Louis XVI of France is sentenced to the guillotine.

1853 Verdi's opera *Il Trovatore* is premiered in Rome.

1884 Massenet's opera *Manon* receives its first performance in Paris.

1942 The Japanese invade Burma.

1966 Sir Robert Menzies resigns as Prime Minister of Australia.

1969 Twenty-one-year-old student Jan Palach sets fire to himself in Wenceslaus Square in Prague as a protest against the Soviet invasion of Czechoslovakia.

1988 Severely disabled Irish writer Christopher Nolan wins the Whitbread Book of the Year Award at the age of only 22 for his autobiography *Under the Eye of the Clock*.

1995 Russian troops seize the presidential palace in Grozny, Chechnya.

Zeppelin bombs British towns

1915 A new and sinister form of destruction has been added to the already terrifying catalogue of modern warfare: aerial bombardment. For the first time since the war began last year German Zeppelin airships tonight crossed the eastern English coast to bombard towns in East Anglia. Great Yarmouth and King's Lynn, brilliantly lit and unsuspecting, were hit, with more than 20 people killed. The attacks follow last month's shelling of Whitby and Hartlepool, further to the north, by German warships, when more than 100 people lost their lives. Germany's airship mastery could be ominous for Britain: the Zeppelins can patrol the North Sea at altitudes no British plane is able to reach. Steps are being taken with all possible speed to protect London from bombardment.

> *My act has fulfilled its purpose, but let nobody else do it.*
> **Jan Palach**, 1969.

Palach remembered

1989 Police today used tear gas, water cannon and baton charges to break up a huge demonstration taking place in the centre of Prague. The demonstrators were commemorating the 20th anniversary of the death of Jan Palach, the Czechoslovak student who burned himself to death in Jan Palach Square in violent protest against the Soviet invasion of 1968. The demonstration today was led by dissident writer Vaclav Havel of the Charter 77 human rights movement.

James Watt 1736, Scottish inventor of the steam engine.
Robert E. Lee 1807, American general and Commander-in-Chief of the Confederates in the Civil War.
Edgar Allan Poe 1809, American writer of macabre and detective stories.
Paul Cézanne 1839, French Post-Impressionist painter.
Javier Pérez de Cuéllar 1920, Peruvian Secretary General of the United Nations since 1982.
Nina Bawden 1925, British author of novels for both adults and children.
Phil Everly 1939, American singer and half of the duo the Everly Brothers.
Janis Joplin 1943, American rock singer.
Dolly Parton 1946, American country singer.
Simon Rattle 1955, British conductor.

Indira Gandhi is India's first woman PM

1966 Indira Gandhi today became India's first woman leader, following in the footsteps of her father, Jawaharlal Nehru, India's first prime minister. Mrs Gandhi, a widow, is no relation of Mahatma Gandhi. She was sworn into power today following the sudden death last week of Prime Minister Lal Bahadur Shastri as he was signing a peace pact with Pakistan. She has been president of the ruling National Congress Party since 1959. She follows Sri Lanka's Mrs Sirimavo Bandaranaike, who took office as the world's first woman prime minister in 1960.

Tour de France will test cyclists to limit

1903 Sports promoter and journalist Henri Desgrange today announced plans to hold a gruelling bicycle race across France this summer. It will be called the Tour de France, and will cover around 2500–3000 miles (4000–4800 km) of roads and mountain passes throughout the country and into parts of its five neighbours. About 60 top cyclists will follow a route from Paris to Marseilles and back again in six stages over three weeks. The new race reflects the recent increase in competitive cycling which has brought world cycling championships and an International Union of Cyclists.

1779 Death of David Garrick, British actor.

1779 Death of David Garrick, British actor.

1841 Hong Kong is ceded to Britain from China.

1878 The 3500-year-old obelisk known as Cleopatra's Needle arrives in London from Alexandria in Egypt.

1882 A draper's shop in Newcastle-upon-Tyne becomes the first shop in the world to be lit by electric light.

1892 The first baseball game is played in Springfield, Massachusetts.

1900 Death of John Ruskin, British art critic and social reformer.

1944 The RAF drop 2300 tons of bombs on Berlin.

1958 Edmund Hillary reaches the South Pole, the first explorer to do so since Captain Scott.

1964 The Great Train Robbers go on trial in Britain.

1965 American disc jockey Alan Freed, creator of the phrase "rock 'n' roll" dies in California.

1971 The RAF Red Arrows aerial display team collide in mid-air, killing four.

1981 Ronald Reagan is inaugurated as President of the USA, the oldest candidate to take office.

1981 Fifty-two American hostages are released from Iran.

1988 Palestinians begin the intifada (uprising) to protest against Israeli occupation of the West Bank.

BIRTHDAYS

Mischa Elman 1891, Russian-born violinist who became a US citizen in 1923.

George Burns 1896, American comedian and film actor.

Federico Fellini 1920, Italian film director whose works include *La Dolce Vita* and *La Strada*.

Slim Whitman 1924, American country singer.

Edwin "Buzz" Aldrin 1930, American astronaut and second man on the moon.

England's first Parliament to meet at Westminster

PARLIAMENT of EDWARD I.

1265 A new era in relations between the English king and his people opened today with the summoning of a parliament in London that includes both gentry from the shires and burgesses from the towns. For the first time, the whole country is represented in a single chamber at Westminster Hall. The parliament was convened by the Earl of Leicester, Simon de Montfort, the king's troublesome brother-in-law. Since his return to this country in 1262, de Montfort has built a hegemony of power. His military victory over King Henry III at Lewes last year in the Barons' War gives the tired king (Henry has been on the throne since he was nine) no option but to acquiesce to the new parliament. But Henry's son Edward has promised to seek revenge against the French-born Earl on the battlefield for these affronts to royal prerogative.

Vive l'existentialisme!

1943 Jean Paul Sartre has published a monumental work, *Being and Nothingness*, a treatise on his existentialism. The French thinker has explored the nature of existence, and comes up with – basically, nothing. He rejects the supernatural and ideas of humanity and morality, concluding that existence is absurd – life is merely "contingent". A thing simply is; objects crowd upon humans by sheer virtue of their abundance. What distinguishes humanity is consciousness – "being-for-itself" – and the ultimate freedom to build an identity. The use of this freedom is the basis of existential living. *Being and Nothingness* also probes responsibility, and the limits of freedom. "Man is a useless passion," Sartre proclaims – though that doesn't mean that all is futile, to judge from his own very active life.

DOWNED ALLIED PILOTS ON IRAQI TV

1991 Iraq today paraded a group of captured allied jet pilots in front of the television cameras. The men – Americans, Britons, an Italian and a Kuwaiti – have made confused statements saying they do not agree with the war. Meanwhile, new US Patriot anti-missile missiles are arriving in Tel Aviv to counteract Iraqi Scud missile attacks on Israel, which could carry biological warheads. Israel has already been hit by Scuds since the war started two days ago, but has not so far responded. Allied leaders say it is essential that Israel be kept from the conflict – to maintain US support by Saudi Arabian, Syrian and Egyptian forces.

Britain mourns George V

1936 Britain is today mourning the death of King George V after his 26-year reign. The grandson of Queen Victoria, he was responsible for changing the name of the Royal Family from Saxe-Coburg-Gotha to Windsor during the Great War in order to emphasize the distance from his German cousins. He also initiated the tradition of the monarch's Christmas radio broadcasts. George V had never expected to be king and was forced to give up a career in the Royal Navy to take the throne when his elder brother died. He steered Britain through the Great War, through the Irish Home Rule crisis, and through the reform of the House of Lords. A countryman at heart, King George V died at his beloved Sandringham estate in Gloucestershire. He always loathed foreign travel and once said, "I don't like abroad, I've been there." His last words were "How is the Empire?" King George V is succeeded by Edward VIII, his eldest son.

> *We stand on the edge of a new frontier.*
> **John F. Kennedy**, on his inauguration as US president, 1961.

Roosevelt does it again

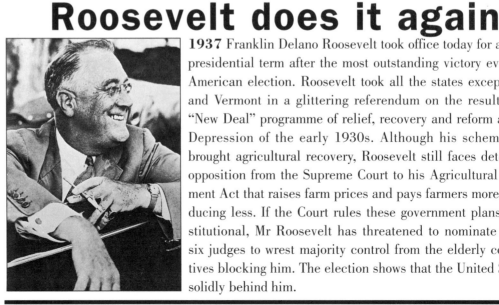

1937 Franklin Delano Roosevelt took office today for a second presidential term after the most outstanding victory ever in an American election. Roosevelt took all the states except Maine and Vermont in a glittering referendum on the results of his "New Deal" programme of relief, recovery and reform after the Depression of the early 1930s. Although his schemes have brought agricultural recovery, Roosevelt still faces determined opposition from the Supreme Court to his Agricultural Adjustment Act that raises farm prices and pays farmers more for producing less. If the Court rules these government plans unconstitutional, Mr Roosevelt has threatened to nominate another six judges to wrest majority control from the elderly conservatives blocking him. The election shows that the United States is solidly behind him.

1648 The first woman lawyer in the American colonies has been denied the right to vote. Margaret Brent, a wealthy landowner, has challenged the ruling on the grounds that the proceedings were unlawfully conducted in her absence. All landowners vote in Maryland, and she is the first woman to hold land in her own right in the colony.

Ruskin loses a farthing – and his reputation

1878 The American artist James Whistler has won damages of one farthing in a London libel action against critic John Ruskin. On seeing the 200-guinea price tag on Whistler's painting *Nocturne in Black and Gold – The Falling Rocket*, Ruskin accused the American of "flinging a pot of paint in the public's face". Ruskin's reaction is unexpected, for he has always championed the imagination against "mere realism". He defended J.M.W. Turner at a time when the painter's vivid colours and vague forms were bringing charges of madness. Ruskin can certainly afford the one farthing damages, but perhaps not the damage to his credibility.

America's Tehran hostages go free

1981 America's 444-day agony over the hostages held in Iran ended today as the 52 diplomats landed safely in Algiers. Looking exhausted but still smiling, the senior US diplomat Bruce Laingen stepped to freedom from the aircraft, flanked by the two women hostages, Kathryn Koob and Elizabeth Ann Swift. Iran's ruler, Ayatollah Khomeini, at first insisted that the students who took over the US embassy in Tehran were beyond his control. He has now doubly humiliated US President Jimmy Carter by releasing the captives just hours after Carter handed over the presidency to Ronald Reagan. No one knows what concessions Reagan, who triumphantly announced the resolution of the crisis, has had to make. The crisis was sparked by the decision to allow the ailing and exiled Shah of Iran into the US for medical treatment.

All animals are equal but some animals are more equal than others.

George Orwell, who died today, 1950.

LENIN DIES

1924 Vladimir Ilyich Lenin, the Father of the Russian Revolution, who started out as a country lawyer but went on to topple an emperor and shake the world with a new creed, has died at the age of 53. In the Communist pantheon he was second only to Karl Marx, and a special mausoleum is being built in Moscow's Red Square where his embalmed body will be on display in a glass coffin. A triumvirate is expected to succeed him. Lenin's political conversion came in 1887 when his brother was hanged after plotting against the Tsar. In 1917, after years of exile, he jumped at a German offer to return him to Russia aboard a sealed train. He quickly toppled the liberal provisional government and consolidated the Bolshevik hold on power by ruthless use of the Party, the secret police and the Red Army. Lenin's agricultural policies caused a famine that claimed more than five million lives. According to Lenin's theory, the nature of capitalism makes socialist revolution possible, and leaders of the working class from the proletariat and peasantry are able to overthrow the capitalist class that dominates the world.

CLINTON DENIES AFFAIR WITH INTERN

1998 President Clinton has denied all allegations that he had a relationship with a 24-year-old former White House intern, Monica Lewinsky. He also rejected claims that he asked her to lie under oath about the affair. The president made his statement after increasing media pressure amid rumours of the 18-month relationship in 1995. Miss Lewinsky has made no public statement although it is understood she has admitted to the affair on tape. She is currently in hiding. President Clinton made his denial at a news conference at the White House today, saying: "I did not have sexual relations with that woman, Miss Lewinsky. I never told anybody to lie, not a single time, never. These allegations are false and I need to get back to work for the American people." Clinton then left the room without answering any questions.

1793 France is today without a monarch and the Revolution has blood on its hands. At 10.30 this morning the head of Louis Capet – as Louis XVI is now known – rolled into a waiting basket as the guillotine claimed its most illustrious victim yet. He had been found guilty of treason. Crowds cheered as he died.

1790 In Paris, Dr Joseph Guillotin demonstrates a new device for performing executions whereby a heavy blade drops from a frame on to the neck of the victim.

1846 The first edition of the *Daily News*, edited by Charles Dickens, is published in London.

1879 Zulus massacre British troops at Isandlwana in Natal.

1907 Taxi cabs are officially recognized in Britain.

1911 The first Monte Carlo car rally takes place.

1932 Death of Lytton Strachey, author of *Eminent Victorians* and founder-member of the Bloomsbury Group.

1935 Snowdonia, Wales, is designated a national park.

1941 The *Daily Worker*, Britain's communist newspaper, is banned as a result of wartime restrictions.

1951 Atomic bombs are tested in Nevada for the first time.

1954 The USA launches *Nautilus*, its first nuclear submarine.

1959 Death of Cecil B. de Mille, American film director, producer and screenwriter renowned for his biblical epics.

1976 British and French Concordes make their inaugural commercial flights, from London to Bahrain and Paris to Rio de Janeiro.

1988 Briton Brian Milton lands his microlight aircraft in Darwin after a 51-day flight from London.

BIRTHDAYS

Thomas "Stonewall" Jackson 1824, American general who commanded Confederate forces in the Civil War.

Christian Dior 1905, French fashion designer.

Paul Schofield 1922, British stage and film actor.

Telly Savalas 1925, American film actor best-known for his role of Kojak.

Jack Niklaus 1940, American champion golfer.

Placido Domingo 1941, Spanish operatic tenor.

JANUARY 22

1824 The Asante army crushes British troops in the Gold Coast.

1879 Zulus massacre British forces at Isandlwana.

1901 Queen Victoria dies at Osborne House on the Isle of Wight at the age of 81, ending a 64-year reign.

1924 Ramsay MacDonald becomes Britain's first Labour Prime Minister.

1941 The British capture Tobruk from German forces.

1959 Mike Hawthorn, British and world motor racing champion, is killed on the Guildford bypass.

1964 Kenneth Kaunda is sworn in as the first Prime Minister of Northern Rhodesia.

1972 The United Kingdom, Denmark and the Irish Republic join the EEC.

1972 As he prepares to sign the Treaty of Brussels securing British entry into the Common Market, British prime minister Edward Heath has ink thrown over him by protesters against the redevelopment of Covent Garden, London.

1973 Death of Lyndon Baines Johnson, President of the United States after John F. Kennedy.

1988 Schipol Airport in Amsterdam opens a departure lounge for cattle.

BIRTHDAYS

Francis Bacon 1561, English statesman, essayist, lawyer, philosopher and Lord Chancellor of England.

André Ampère 1775, French physicist who gave his name to "amp" as a unit of electricity.

Lord Byron 1788, English poet with a scandalous private life.

August Strindberg 1849, Swedish playwright and novelist.

Beatrice Webb 1858, British founder member of the Fabian Society.

D. W. Griffith 1875, American film director whose pioneering works include *Birth of a Nation*.

John Hurt 1940, British actor who starred in *The Elephant Man*.

BLOOD OF MASSACRE STAINS TSAR'S HANDS

1905 A mass march to the Winter Palace in St Petersburg today turned into a horrifying slaughter as Cossack troops fired salvo after salvo into the crowd at close range, leaving the snow red with the blood of at least 500 people. This "Red Sunday" massacre of strikers could ignite the long-simmering discontent with the rule of Tsar Nicholas II. His regime is weakened by the turmoil of military defeat at the hands of Japan, and today's massacre could lead feuding liberal and radical groups to unite against the government. The outrage is all the greater because the peaceful march of 1000 demonstrators was led by a St Petersburg priest – Father Gapon – while other marchers carried crosses, icons, and even the Tsar's portrait.

Borg's game, set and match

1983 Tennis star Bjorn Borg retired today at 26, a wealthy man with an unequalled record. Borg made his professional debut at 14. Two years later he earned £40,000 in prize money. By 1981, Borg had won six French Open titles and five consecutive Wimbledon championships – an all-time record. Borg is a powerful player with unbeatable speed and great concentration. Last year Borg was barred from the major championships because he had not entered the minimum number of tournaments. A request to reduce his commitments was turned down.

Hiss case starts McCarthy's Communist witch-hunt

1950 Alger Hiss, a former adviser to US President Franklin Roosevelt, has been convicted of perjury for denying contacts with a Soviet agent. Whittaker Chambers, an editor of *Time* magazine and a former agent for the USSR, had accused Hiss of having been a secret member of the Communist Party and of giving him State Department documents for the Soviets. Chambers took Republican congressman Richard M. Nixon to his farm, where he produced microfilms of the documents, allegedly typed on Hiss's typewriter. The microfilms were hidden in a hollowed-out pumpkin. Hiss denied ever knowing Chambers and said the documents were forged. A first trial ended with a hung jury, but today he was jailed for five years. Senator Joseph R. McCarthy has now charged that the State Department is riddled with Communists.

> *Today 23 years ago dear Grandmama died. I wonder what she would have thought of a Labour Government.*
> **George V of England**, as Britain's first Labour Government is formed, 1924.

Mao's peasant army marches into Peking

1949 Chinese leader Mao Tse-Tung marched into Peking today at the head of a battle-hardened guerrilla army to make the Communists virtual masters of China. The vanquished Nationalist leader Generalissimo Chiang Kai-shek appealed for immediate peace talks, but Mao contemptuously dismissed the appeal. The guerrillas crossed the Yangtze to defeat a huge Nationalist army at Huai Hai north of the capital, taking over 300,000 prisoners. Mao now plans to march on to Shanghai to mop up Chiang's fleeing forces, completing the task he began by leading a ragged peasant army to freedom back in 1935.

Death of a Mogul Emperor

1666 Shah Jahan, the mighty Mogul emperor of India who built the Taj Mahal as a mausoleum for his beloved wife Mumtaz-i-Mahal, died today in the fort where his son, Aurangzeb, imprisoned him eight years ago. He was 74. He is to be entombed in the Taj Mahal beside his wife. Aurangzeb had fought and killed his brothers to seize the throne, as Shah Jahan had done before him in 1628. Aurangzeb confined his father to his harem in the fort at Agra, from where the old man could gaze at the magnificent white marble mausoleum in which his empress lay. He was a direct descendant of both Genghis Khan and Timur.

Third Man Philby disappears

1963 Kim Philby is today considered missing after failing to meet his wife at a dinner party in Beirut. Now a foreign correspondent, Philby was formerly a high-ranking intelligence officer and in 1955 was accused in the British Parliament of being a Soviet spy. It took Britain's security services four years to admit that former intelligence officers Guy Burgess and Donald Maclean, who fled to Moscow in 1951, were indeed spies. Philby received a clean bill of health from Prime Minister Harold Macmillan, who said there was no "Third Man" inside MI5 (Britain's military intelligence agency). Now doubts are resurfacing about the missing journalist.

Treaty of Utrecht redraws Europe

1713 The map of Europe has been redrawn in a treaty to end the long and bloody War of Spanish Succession. The Peace of Utrecht, signed today in the Lowlands, preserves Europe's fragile power balance by preventing either Bourbon France or Habsburg Austria from dominating the old territories of the Spanish Succession. It is a masterpiece of diplomacy: Philip V gets the Spanish throne and its overseas colonies but must renounce all claims to the French crown. Britain gets Minorca and Gibraltar as well as territory in the Americas and West Indies. Prussia gets Upper Gelderland, Neuchatel, and Valengin, while the Duke of Savoy wins Sicily. The truth is that everyone was thoroughly worn out by a senseless war which had dragged on for 12 years.

Verne's fantasy now a reality

1960 Two men have ventured down 35,800 ft into the world's deepest ocean trench inside a bathyscope, challenging Jules Verne's famous fiction with fact. French scientist Jacques Piccard and US Navy lieutenant Donald Walsh made their world-record dive for the purpose of deep-sea exploration into the Challenger Deep of the Marianas Trench near the Philippines. Their bathyscope, the Trieste, was built in 1953 by Jacques Piccard's father, Auguste Piccard.

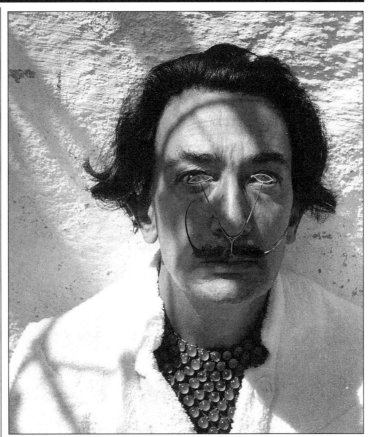

Salvador Dali fails to live forever

1989 "Geniuses don't die, I'm going to live forever," the Spanish surrealist painter Salvador Dali is on record as saying. Nevertheless, he died today, at his Spanish castle in Figueras. He was 78. Famed for his varnished moustache, flowing capes and outrageous behaviour, Dali had been a recluse since the death in 1982 of his wife Gala. Dali was a technical virtuoso and his dreamlike scenes – melting watches and painstakingly detailed beauties supported by fantastical crutches – commanded huge prices. He once said his paintings were motivated by his megalomania. The art world was angered by recent confirmation that he had been signing blank canvases for others to paint.

THE WAR IN VIETNAM IS OVER, SAYS NIXON

1973 US President Richard Nixon tonight told American TV viewers his government has achieved an agreement that will bring "peace with honour" and an end to the war in Vietnam. Negotiators in Paris are hammering out the final text of a peace treaty to be signed in the next few days. Its central provision is a ceasefire that must hold long enough for the Americans to withdraw. Though Nixon, buoyed up by his massive election victory, claims the peace agreement will preserve the principle so many Americans and Vietnamese have died for – the right of the South Vietnamese to settle their own political future – the draft text does not actually say what will happen to South Vietnam's President Thieu. He is refusing to sign it because Viet Cong troops will remain inside his country, but US troops will get out and prisoners of war will be exchanged. Ominously, Hanoi's chief negotiator Le Duc Tho concluded, "Right has triumphed over wrong."

1556 An earthquake in Shanxi Province, China, kills 830,000 people.

1571 Queen Elizabeth I opens the Royal Exchange in London.

1793 Poland is partitioned by Russia, Austria and Prussia.

1806 William Pitt the Younger, twice British prime minister, dies aged 47, having first taken office at the age of only 24.

1823 The USA recognizes Argentina and Chile.

1849 British-born Elizabeth Blackwell qualifies in the USA as the first woman doctor.

1908 A 7000-mile telegraph from London to India is introduced.

1931 Anna Pavlova, Russian prima ballerina, dies in Holland at the age of 45.

1943 The British capture Tripoli from the Germans.

1955 Spanish dictator General Franco decides to reinstate the monarchy and Prince Juan Carlos is allowed to claim the crown.

1968 North Korean patrol boats attack and capture a US Navy intelligence ship in the Sea of Japan, killing several of its crew.

1976 Paul Robeson, black American singer, actor and campaigner for civil rights, dies in Harlem aged 77.

BIRTHDAYS

Edouard Manet 1832, French Impressionist painter who scandalized the public with his *Déjeuner sur l'herbe*, which depicted the nude for the first time in a naturalistic setting.

Sergei Eisenstein 1898, Russian film director who made *The Battleship Potemkin*, *Ivan the Terrible* and *Alexander Nevsky*.

Bob Paisley 1919, British football player, trainer and manager of Liverpool.

Jeanne Moreau 1928, French actress whose films include *Jules et Jim* and *Viva Maria*.

Bill Gibb 1943, British fashion designer who had great influence in the 1960s and '70s.

41 AD Roman emperor Caligula, renowned for his excesses, is murdered by a tribune of the guard.

1236 King Henry III of England marries Eleanor of Provence.

1895 Death of Lord Randolph Churchill, leader of the British Conservative party.

1915 The British fleet defeats the Germans at the Battle of Dogger Bank.

1916 Conscription is introduced in Britain.

1920 Italian painter Amadeo Modigliani dies from alcohol and drug abuse.

1935 Canned beer is sold for the first time in Richmond, Virginia.

1961 A US B-52 bomber breaks up in mid-air, killing three crew and releasing two 24-megaton nuclear bombs.

1976 The *Olympic Bravery*, a 270,000 ton oil tanker, runs aground off France.

1976 A Russian satellite crashes near Yellowknife in north-west Canada.

1983 Death of George Cukor, American film director.

2001 Five million Hindus attend the Maha Kumbh Mela at Allahabad, India, in the largest ever gathering of humans. The crowds flock to bathe in the river Ganga at dawn.

BIRTHDAYS

Hadrian 76 AD, Roman emperor who built Hadrian's Wall across northern England to keep out the Scots.

Ernest Borgnine 1917, American actor whose many films include *The Poseidon Adventure* and *The Wild Bunch*.

Desmond Morris 1928, British zoologist and writer, author of *The Naked Ape*.

Neil Diamond 1941, American singer and songwriter.

Nastassja Kinski 1961, German-born actress who starred in the film *Tess of the D'Urbervilles* at the age of 18.

Gold strike in California

1848 What could turn out to be the greatest gold rush in the history of the United States began today when James Marshall made a rich strike at Sutter's sawmill on the American River in northern California. It is several years since farmer Francisco Lopez found traces of gold on a freshly-dug onion nearby, but the stampede is now just beginning. The government of the Mexican-owned territory is spreading the news of the find in the hope of increasing the population of California, which now has just 14,000 inhabitants. A gold strike of this magnitude will bring fortune-hunters from all over the world.

I could not understand from them why they made war upon each other, considering that they held no private property or sovereignty of empire and kingdoms. They said that this curse came upon them in ancient times and they sought to avenge the deaths of their forefathers.

Amerigo Vespucci, Italian explorer, reporting on a month with the natives of Brazil, 1502.

New World settlers break with Britain

1639 American settlers meeting in Hartford have voted to adopt a new constitution called the Fundamental Orders of Connecticut. This written body of laws is believed to be the first such constitution in the colonies: it is notable for the fact that it makes no mention at all of allegiance to the British Crown, and it allows colonists both to administer their own taxes and to summon their own legislature without the prior permission of the King's appointed governor.

The lion lies down

1965 Sir Winston Churchill, dubbed the "last lion of British politics" and perhaps Britain's greatest statesman since his ancestor the Duke of Marlborough, died today aged 90, exactly 70 years after his father. He never recovered after suffering a stroke last week. His body is to lie in state in Westminster Hall. His career stretched back to the Victorian era and he left his stamp on many of the great theatres of modern history: India, Africa, Ireland, the Middle East and above all the Europe of two World Wars. The son of an American society beauty, Churchill pursued a second career as one of the world's most successful journalists.

1616 The Dutch navigator Willem Schouten today rounded the perilous cape at the southern tip of the Americas. He has named it Cape Hoorn after his birthplace in Holland. The Cape was first sighted by Sir Walter Raleigh, while in 1520 Ferdinand Magellan passed through the straits to the north.

Waite mission ends in kidnap

1987 Terry Waite, the special representative of the Archbishop of Canterbury, has been kidnapped in Beirut. Waite had hoped to negotiate the release of foreign hostages held by Islamic extremists. He left five days ago for a meeting with Shi'ite Muslims, followers of the Iranian leader Ayatollah Khomeini, who are believed to be holding hostages. Waite's Druze bodyguards say he dismissed them and then vanished. Waite may have opted for silence because he is near to a breakthrough in releasing the captives. However, there are fears that the recent linking of his name with the Iran-Contra scandal in the US means he can expect little mercy from the Shi'ite "Hezbollah" militants.

1962 Jeanne Moreau stars in the latest film by "nouvelle vague" director François Truffaut, premiered in Paris today. *Jules et Jim* is the romantic tale of two close friends with a shared mistress who end up fighting on separate sides in World War One.

First Winter Olympics under starter's orders

1924 The first Winter Olympics are being held in the shadow of Mont Blanc at Chamonix in France, despite the reluctance of the International Olympics Committee to give them their full title. Competitors from 18 countries are taking part, and the Scandinavians are seizing the lion's share of the medals. Ski-jumping, cross-country skiing and speed skating are among the new sporting categories being inaugurated this week, although it is still felt in some quarters that the traditional Nordic Games would be a more suitable recipient of the Olympic title.

Secret wedding for Henry VIII and Anne Boleyn

1533 England's King Henry VIII has married his lover, Anne Boleyn, in secret – and in some haste, since she is pregnant. The birth is expected in September. Last month Anne and the King visited King Francis of France at Calais, where they stayed in adjoining suites. Anne is Henry's second wife, though he is not yet free of the first: His determination to divorce Catherine of Aragon, who has failed to bear him a son and heir, has brought him into collision with the Roman church, which refuses to allow the divorce.

Big Apple's subway vigilante gets lesser charge

1985 New York's white "subway vigilante" Bernard Goetz will not stand trial for shooting four black youths at close range, a grand jury ruled today. But it accepted the prosecution's demand that Goetz stand trial for illegal possession of the handguns he used on his self-appointed mission to "clean up" the city's crime-infested subway system. The case has divided New Yorkers: some see Goetz as a hero, others as a dangerous racist. The prosecution says it will still press for murder charges.

Few mourn penniless Capone

1947 "Scarface" Al Capone, America's most feared mobster, is dead. An Italian-born New Yorker who made Prohibition-era Chicago his power-base, Capone's bloody battles for control of the bootleg liquor smuggling business are legendary – more than 200 of his rivals met a violent end. "I've been accused of every death except the casualty list of the World War," he once said. It was estimated he made $105 million in 1927 alone. It was not murder or smuggling but income-tax evasion that finally tripped him up, and in 1931 he was fined $80,000 (£44,000) and sentenced to 11 years in jail. He was released from Alcatraz in 1939, old before his time and terminally ill with syphilis. He died today at his home in Florida of a massive brain haemorrhage, unmourned and virtually penniless. He was 48.

Mao widow sentenced to death

1981 Madame Chiang Ch'ing, Mao Tse-tung's 67-year-old widow and former actress and a leader of China's Cultural Revolution, has been given a suspended death sentence for "counter-revolutionary crimes" committed with the "Gang of Four" in the mid-1970s. She was dragged from the courtroom screaming abuse. The defendants insisted their actions had been at Mao's behest.

There's no starvation in Uganda. If you get hungry you can go into the forest and pick a banana.
Idi Amin Dada, who seized power in Uganda today, 1971.

Manson guilty of Sharon Tate murders

1971 Macabre cult leader Charles Manson was found guilty today of murdering actress Sharon Tate and four others in a ritual slaughter in August 1969 that stunned America. Satanist Manson, who led a drug-ridden Californian commune or "family" of disturbed women, warned the judge, "You won't outlive this, old man," as the court took the next legal steps to have him and his accomplices sent to the gas chamber. The trial was punctuated by Manson's outpourings about race war and Satan. As the death penalty has in fact been suspended in California, Manson and his co-convicts face life terms instead.

1327 Edward III accedes to the English throne.

1832 The state of Virginia rejects the abolition of slavery.

1878 A Russian boat fires the first torpedo used in war and sinks a Turkish steamer.

1882 The London Chamber of Commerce meets for the first time.

1895 Wales loses 3-0 to the Irish in the first-ever hockey international, held at Rhyl in Wales.

1917 The USA buys the Virgin Islands from Holland for a sum of $25 million.

1934 Bank robber John Dillinger is captured in Tucson, Arizona.

1938 The aurora borealis (northern lights) are seen as far south as western Europe.

1944 In Macao, the Reverend Florence Tim-Oi Lee becomes the first woman Anglican priest.

1952 Vincent Massey is appointed first Canadian-born Governor-General of Canada.

1957 The UN orders Israel to quit Aqaba and Gaza.

1980 Japan orders the deportation of ex-Beatle Paul McCartney after keeping him in prison for nine days following the discovery of marijuana in his luggage.

1981 Roy Jenkins, Dr David Owen, Shirley Williams and Bill Rodgers break away from the British Labour Party to form the Social Democrats.

1990 American actress Ava Gardner dies in London, aged 68.

BIRTHDAYS

Robert Burns 1759, Scottish poet who wrote many poems in dialect.

William Somerset Maugham 1874, British novelist and dramatist.

Virginia Woolf 1882, British novelist, critic and leading member of the Bloomsbury Group.

Edvard Schevardnadze 1928, Russian politician and former foreign minister under Gorbachev.

1500 Explorer Vicente Yáñez Pinsón discovers Brazil and claims it for Portugal.

1827 Peru ends its union with Chile and declares independence.

1828 The Duke of Wellington becomes prime minister of Britain.

1871 The Rugby Football Union is formed in London.

1886 Karl Benz patents a three-wheel drive motor car and the internal combustion engine.

1926 The British Surgeon-General links cigarette-smoking with cancer.

1931 Mahatma Gandhi is released from prison to have talks with the British colonial government in India.

1939 In Spain, General Franco's rebel troops capture Barcelona from the Republicans.

1947 Prince Gustav of Sweden is killed in an air crash near Copenhagen.

1950 India becomes a democratic republic within the Commonwealth.

1960 Rioters greet British prime minister Harold Macmillan in Rhodesia.

1973 Death of Edward G. Robinson, American actor who was best-known for his gangster roles.

2001 Thousands die in a powerful earthquake which strikes Western Indian and parts of Pakistan. Nearly all the victims are from the Indian town of Bhuj in Gujarat.

BIRTHDAYS

Douglas MacArthur 1880, American general and Supreme Commander of the Allied Forces in the Pacific during World War II.

Stephane Grappelli 1908, French jazz violinist who played in the quintet known as the Hot Club of France.

Paul Newman 1925, American actor, director and producer.

Eartha Kitt 1928, American singer and actress.

GORDON KILLED AS KHARTOUM FALLS TO DERVISHES

1885 In a stunning reverse for the British, the Mahdi Muhammad Ahmad is today master of Khartoum. The British commander General Charles Gordon is dead, killed by a dervish spear and decapitated, his forces overrun even as a British force speeds to relieve the beleaguered city. Disobeying Prime Minister Gladstone's orders to evacuate, Gordon held the city for almost a year against the Mahdi's army, showing himself to be almost as fanatical as his charismatic Muslim foe. Gordon fought in the Opium War in China, and helped to put down the Taiping anti-foreigner rebellion there, earning him the name "Chinese" Gordon. His pointless heroism at Khartoum will surely become a legend.

"Playboy" in scandal

1907 A new play by Irish playwright J.M. Synge is causing riots at the Abbey Theatre in Dublin because of its "foul language", while the opera *Salome* by the German composer Richard Strauss was today banned by the Metropolitan Opera House in New York as obscene. Synge's *Playboy of the Western World* caused such outrage that the audience stopped the play on its opening night. While the play's coarse language reflects the character of the peasants it portrays, its rich, lyric beauty seems to have gone unnoticed. Synge is not the critics' favourite – his work is often censured as "un-Irish". *Salome*, Strauss's third opera, was premiered in Munich in 1905 to critical acclaim, not a moralistic fuss – after all, the Biblical princess's seductive aspect can hardly be ignored.

Huge diamond found in South Africa

1905 A magnificent diamond has been discovered in South Africa, the largest rough stone ever found. Weighing nearly 1 1/2 lb or 3106 carats (621.2g), the Cullinan diamond is also of high-quality. It is literally priceless – and far outweighs the previous record-holder, the 995.2-carat Excelsior, found in South Africa 12 years ago. The Cullinan is to be cut into a number of stones, some of which are destined for the British Crown Jewels.

Convict ships arrive in Sydney

1788 Captain Arthur Phillip of the HMS *Endeavour* and his fleet of six transport ships today dropped anchor in what Captain Phillip describes as "the finest harbour in the world" to begin the dismal task of establishing a penal settlement in the new Australian colony. His first landfall was Botany Bay, but he preferred to forge on to Port Jackson or Sydney. Aboard the ships were 570 men and 160 women, the survivors of a 36-week voyage from England during which the pox carried off 48 of the prisoners. A stern critic of the slave trade, Captain Phillip preferred to take convicts to provide the manpower for his settlement, which is intended to deter French ambitions in the region. The new settlers have already encountered the indigenous dwellers of Australia, first seen by Captain Cook in 1770 when he claimed the territory for Britain. Captain Phillip is to administer the colony.

> *Yes, I'd like to be President. Hell, yes.*
>
> **Nelson Rockefeller**, Vice-President to Gerald Ford, when asked his political intentions. He died today, 1979.

Over here again: US troops back in Europe

1942 For the first time since American "doughboys" left France soon after the 1918 Armistice, US ground troops arrived in Europe today to join the struggle against Adolf Hitler's Nazis. Sir Archibald Sinclair, Britain's Minister for Air, was in Northern Ireland to welcome the shipload of American soldiers as they stepped ashore to the tune of "The Star-Spangled Banner" – played by a British military band who hadn't known to rehearse it because the arrival of the American troops was kept secret. But not everyone welcomed them: the Dublin government said the troop landings violated Eire's neutrality.

Wildlife artist dies

1851 John Audubon, the French-born naturalist who painted the birds and animals of America, has died. He originally made his living painting portraits and teaching art in New Orleans, but came to devote his life to his bird studies. Audubon concentrated on the character of his subjects, setting them in their natural context. A Scottish publisher printed his *Birds of America* between 1827 and 1838, by which time he had painted hundreds of birds. Five volumes of descriptive text followed. Audubon also experimented with bird-banding to study migration patterns.

1822 Greece declares independence following her war against Turkey.

1868 The missing explorer Dr Livingstone is found in Africa by Sir Henry Morton Stanley.

1901 Death of Giuseppe Verdi, Italian composer whose operas include *Rigoletto*, *La Traviata*, *Aida* and *Otello*.

1901 King Edward VII makes his cousin Kaiser William II of Germany a field-marshal in the British army.

1923 Former German army corporal Adolf Hitler holds the first congress of the National Socialist Party in Munich.

1943 The US Air Force bombs Germany for the first time.

1952 The Shepheard Hotel in Cairo is burnt down during an anti-British riot, killing 17 people.

1967 Round-the-world yachtsman Francis Chichester is knighted on the quay at Greenwich by Queen Elizabeth II.

1969 Flooding in California leaves thousands homeless.

1972 Death of Mahalia Jackson, American gospel singer.

1973 US military action in Vietnam comes to an end as the ceasefire is signed.

1989 death ofSir Thomas Octave Sopwith, British aircraft designer best known for the World War I biplane the *Sopwith Camel*.

Launch pad fire kills astronauts

1967 US astronauts Virgil "Gus" Grissom, Edward White and Roger Chafee died on the ground today of asphyxiation when fire broke out in their Apollo 1 Command Module during a flight simulation on the launch pad. The fire was caused by a short circuit in the cabin. Plastics which are normally fire-resistant ignited in the pure oxygen used by astronauts. The tragedy is a serious setback for the Apollo programme, which is geared to put a man on the moon by 1970, fulfilling John F. Kennedy's dream.

It could never be a correct justification that, because the whites oppressed us yesterday when they had power, the blacks must oppress them today when they have power.

Robert Mugabe, guerrilla chief, on return from exile, 1980.

1913 The US athlete Jim Thorpe has lost his Olympic titles. Thorpe won gold medals in the pentathlon and decathlon events, but he was disqualified today after it was discovered he had received $50 a week to play baseball, making him a professional. The Olympics are strictly an amateur contest.

Ace woman pilot arrives in a bomber

1942 Jacqueline Cochran, the American aviator, has brought a US bomber to Britain. She is the first woman to fly one of the big American planes here for action against Germany. She started her working life in a cotton mill, and gained her pilot's licence after only three weeks' training. The world's leading aviatrix, in 1938 she won the Bendix transcontinental air race, and now holds more speed, altitude and distance records than any other pilot.

Murdoch takes over *Times*

1981 Australian press baron Rupert Murdoch has bought 'The Thunderer' – the *Times* of London, Britain's most venerated newspaper – and the *Sunday Times*. Murdoch first bought into the British press in 1969 when he acquired the *News of the World* – more in keeping with his sensationalist style than the august *Times*. He has overcome considerable British opposition to the takeover with the clearance of the purchase today by the Monopolies Commision.

1980 Robert Mugabe, the leader of Rhodesia's guerilla army, has returned to Salisbury after five years of exile to take part in forthcoming elections that will transfer the country to majority rule. Mugabe is tipped to win the election, which is the result of last month's Lancaster House settlement. The country will be renamed Zimbabwe.

Flickering threat to silver screen

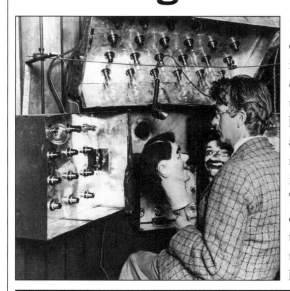

1926 Members of the Royal Institution in London today peered at crude and flickering images of a ventriloquist's doll as electrical engineer and inventor John Logie Baird unveiled his new "television" machine. Baird's home-made equipment successfully transmitted a radio signal from a camera that is partly mechanical and partly electrical. The resulting image was sent electrically to a small screen. Two years ago Baird was able to transmit the outline of shapes, and he has progressed from there. The Scottish inventor's far-fetched idea is that his device could one day provide every home with a substitute for the cinema.

BIRTHDAYS

Wolfgang Amadeus Mozart 1756, Austrian composer and child prodigy.

Charles Dodgson 1832, British mathematician who, under the name of Lewis Carroll, wrote *Alice in Wonderland* and *Alice Through the Looking Glass*.

Kaiser William II 1859, third German emperor and grandson of Queen Victoria.

Jerome Kern 1885, American composer of much-loved musicals.

John Ogdon 1937, British pianist whose brilliant career was sadly interrupted by schizophrenia.

JANUARY 28

BIRTHDAYS

MILLIONS SEE SPACE SHUTTLE EXPLODE

1986 America's space shuttle Challenger exploded in a ball of fire today soon after blasting off for its tenth flight, killing all seven aboard instantly. Millions of viewers saw the televised launch turn to tragedy as the space shuttle's fuel tanks, containing liquid hydrogen and oxygen, exploded 10 miles from the ground. This is NASA's second space tragedy and is a major blow to the shuttle programme. The crew included Christa McAuliffe, a high school teacher who had won her place on the flight in a nationwide competition. It is unlikely that the "citizen in space" programme involving congressmen, teachers and journalists will continue. Challenger itself seemed reluctant to undertake its final mission: the launch was postponed five times and only went ahead after unseasonal ice was chipped from the skin of the shuttle.

Japan occupies Shanghai in China invasion

1932 Japanese troops have occupied Shanghai. This follows Japan's seizure last year of Manchuria, the former Chinese province, as the first step in its drive to create a new Asian empire. Fighting continues on the northern front in Manchuria, as well as close to Nanking, in a full-scale invasion of China. Attempts to bring peace have been fruitless: Tokyo has paid no attention either to the League of Nations or to the overtures of US Secretary of State Henry Stimson. In Japan it is known that army officers acted without government authorization last year in precipitating the Mukden incident

that has sparked off the current troubles, but the power of the militarist faction and public hunger for new territories now seems to have overwhelmed the more liberal instincts of Japan's emperor himself.

Prussians crush Paris resistance

1871 After a five-month siege Paris has fallen and the Franco-Prussian War is virtually ended. The armistice signed today with Prussian Prime Minister Bismarck gives the French three weeks to elect a national assembly to negotiate peace after the 44-day war. The end came after three weeks of intensive artillery bombardment that reduced the population to starvation – all the animals in the Paris zoo were eaten and balloons were the only means of communication – carrying mail, passengers and homing pigeons to the rest of France. The fall of Paris was only a matter of time after Emperor Louis Napoleon's humiliating defeat at the Battle of Sedan last year. Bismarck has made the Prussian king Europe's most powerful monarch.

> *I don't know anything about music.*
> *In my line you don't have to.*
> **Elvis Presley**, who made his first TV appearance today. 1956.

German physicist discovers how to split the atom

1939 The German chemist and Nobel Prizewinner Otto Hahn is reported to have discovered a means of unleashing the immense power stored inside the atom. In Stockholm, his scientific colleague of many years' standing, Lise Meitner, has just announced that in Germany Hahn recently succeeded in transforming uranium-92 by means of nuclear fission. Bombarding the uranium with neutrons produced barium – contrary to all theoretical expectations. Nuclear fission could unlock a massive amount of energy and has enormous military potential.

All-American axeman carves name in flesh

1978 Rock guitarist Ted Nugent has caused a storm of criticism by carving his autograph on a fan's arm with the point of a Bowie knife. Nugent, who has hit the mega-grossing league amongst heavy rock stars, is a clean-living family man with an aversion to drugs. An important part of his image is that of the all-American huntin' and shootin' frontiersman – hence the Bowie knife.

Sailor hero Francis Drake buried at sea

1596 A national hero to the English and a bloodthirsty pirate to the Spanish, Sir Francis Drake has been buried at sea off the coast of Panama after suffering weeks of dysentery. The most famous English seaman of the Elizabethan Age, Drake first put to sea in 1566. Eleven years later, when the Queen gave him command of five ships, he became the second commander after Magellan to sail around the world, returning laden with treasure and spice. From his native Plymouth Drake went to defeat the Spanish Armada in 1588 and was acclaimed as England's hero. His final voyages to the West Indies, however, were unsuccessful.

KARL BENZ PATENTS FIRST PETROL-DRIVEN CARRIAGE

1886 Three German engineers are vying to perfect a horseless carriage driven by petroleum spirit. Nikolaus August Otto has just patented his "Silent Otto" gas engine, with four cycles: intake, compression, stroke, and exhaust. His design is a considerable improvement on Jean Joseph Etienne Lenoir's noisy two-cycle engine introduced in 1862. But the new motor needs something to drive, and Karl Benz today patented his design for an automobile to be powered by Otto's engine. Gottlieb Daimler, a younger engineer, is meanwhile working on a high-speed internal-combustion engine.

1820 King George III of England dies at 81, having reigned for over 59 years.

1853 Napoleon III marries Eugénie de Montijo in Paris.

1856 Britain's highest military decoration, the Victoria Cross, is instituted by Queen Victoria.

1861 Kansas becomes the 34th US state.

1899 Alfred Sisley, Impressionist painter born in Paris to English parents, dies in poverty.

1916 Britain begins military tank trials at Hatfield.

1916 German Zeppelins bomb Paris for the first time.

1947 Buckingham Palace is lit by candles as lowest-ever temperatures cause nationwide power cuts.

1960 President de Gaulle of France makes a TV address attacking Algerian rebels planning civil war.

1964 American actor Alan Ladd, who specialized in cowboys and tough guy roles, dies.

1978 Sweden bans the use of ozone-depleting aerosol sprays.

1980 American comedian Jimmy Durante dies at the age of 87.

1988 Unsuccessful opera singer Bantcho Bantchevsky commits suicide by hurling himself from the balcony of the Metropolitan Opera House in New York during a performance of Verdi's *Macbeth*.

PATTY HEARST GOES FREE

1979 US President Jimmy Carter today commuted Patricia Hearst's prison sentence. The millionaire kidnap victim had joined her Symbionese Liberation Army captors in armed bank robberies and half-baked plots to overthrow American capitalism. A year after the granddaughter of the newspaper magnate William Randolph Hearst was kidnapped, the FBI tracked her down and she was sentenced to seven years for criminal activities with the Los Angeles-based terror group. Miss Hearst is to be released, having served just three years of her term. She will be watched closely by a guard.

Marcos supporters thwarted by Aquino

1987 President Corazon Aquino of the Philippines put down another attempted coup against her two-year-old administration today, forcing rebels to abandon the Manila television station they seized two days ago. Loyal troops stopped the rebels broadcasting to the nation by cutting off power to the transmitters, but another rebel force attacked the Villamor air base near the capital. Once again, supporters of exiled and ailing ex-dictator Ferdinand Marcos and his wife Imelda are behind the troubles.

If with me you'd fondly stray,
Over the hills and far away.
John Gay,
from The Beggar's Opera,
first performed today – 1728.

Gorbachev calls for democracy

1987 Soviet leader Mikhail Gorbachev has taken his policy of Glasnost – "openness" – right to the heart of the Communist Party. He told the party's Central Committee today that the time had come for greater "control from below", which means free elections for local councils. He also said the Party bears a heavy responsibility for the USSR's crippling economic and social problems. In line with the new openness in the media and tolerance of criticism, Gorbachev is expected to announce the freeing of imprisoned dissidents. Glasnost is the first political step in Gorbachev's wider plan of perestroika – restructuring and economic reforms. Western analysts say he may face greater difficulties here because of entrenched and corrupt Party interests.

BIRTHDAYS

Thomas Paine 1737, English philosopher and writer famed for his "Give me liberty or give me death" speech, given in pre-Revolutionary America.

W. C. Fields 1879, American actor and comedian who exploited his genuine eccentricity and intolerance of sentimentality.

Germaine Greer 1939, Australian feminist writer best known for *The Female Eunuch*.

Katherine Ross 1943, American actress who won an Academy Award for her performance in *The Graduate*.

1606 Four conspirators involved in Guy Fawkes' Gunpowder Plot are hanged, drawn and quartered in London.

1858 The Hallé Orchestra is founded in Manchester by Charles Hallé.

1945 The Duke of Gloucester becomes the first member of the British royal family to be appointed Governor General of Australia.

1948 Orville Wright, one of the Wright brothers who made the first powered flight, dies.

1961 The contraceptive pill goes on sale in the UK, although it is not available on the National Health Service.

1963 The French composer and pianist Francis Poulenc dies.

1965 Winston Churchill is buried.

1969 The Beatles make their last live performance on the roof of the Apple building in London - singing "Get Back".

1973 Watergate conspirators Gordon Liddy and James McCord are convicted of spying on Democratic headquarters.

1983 A massive African exodus begins as Nigeria expels Ghanaians living within Nigerian borders.

1989 Five black Pharaonic figures dating from 1470 BC are found in Luxor in Egypt.

BIRTHDAYS

Anton Chekhov 1860, Russian playwright and short story writer whose plays include *The Cherry Orchard* and *The Seagull*.

John Profumo 1915, British cabinet minister caught up in the "Profumo Affair" involving Christine Keeler and a Russian naval attaché.

Harold Prince 1928, American stage producer and director of *West Side Story, Cabaret, Evita* and *The Phantom of the Opera*.

Gene Hackman 1931, American actor who won an Oscar for *The French Connection*.

Vanessa Redgrave 1937, English actress well-known for her brilliance on stage and screen.

Mahatma Gandhi gunned down

1948 Mahatma Gandhi, India's "Great Soul" and prophet of non-violence, has been assassinated. Still weakened from a lengthy fast to urge peace between Muslims and Hindus, Gandhi was walking through a New Delhi garden on his way to prayer when a Hindu fanatic stepped from the crowd and fired three shots into his emaciated body. Gandhi's last words were "Ram, Ram", meaning "Oh God, Oh God". His killer, Nathuram Godse, made no attempt to flee and was saved from a lynching at the hands of the furious crowd by air force officers. It was Gandhi's fervent opposition to the painful partition of India on independence in 1947 that brought about his death: his Hindu killer thought Gandhi's anti-partition sentiment was pro-Muslim and pro-Pakistan. Tomorrow his body will be cremated and its ashes cast into the Jumna River. Exactly 40 years ago today General Jan Smuts ordered Ghandi's release from a South African prison following a sentence for civil disobedience.

Suicide pact at Mayerling may be murder

1889 Tragedy visited the royal Austrian hunting lodge of Mayerling today when Archduke Rudolf, the Crown Prince, and his 17-year-old mistress Baroness Marie Vetsara, were found dead. Rudolf was unhappy in his arranged marriage to Stephanie, daughter of the Belgian king. Officially the tragedy has been pronounced a double suicide. Rumour, however, maintains that Rudolf was murdered because of his sympathies with Hungarian nationalism, and to prevent his accession to the throne.

Hitler becomes Chancellor

1933 Adolf Hitler today became Chancellor of Germany, turning the tables on Paul von Hindenburg, the 85-year-old President who months ago rejected the charismatic leader out of hand. Last year Hitler narrowly lost the presidential election to Hindenburg. Virtual street warfare between Communists and Hitler's supporters, as well as the intrigues of army officers and bankers, has forced Hindenberg to send for the 43-year-old Hitler, a former painter. The cabinet is chiefly composed of right-wing Nationalists who are confident they will be able to control the man who has roused the people after the humiliations imposed as a result of the Great War.

"TRAITOR" CHARLES BEHEADED

1649 King Charles 1 of England, Scotland and Ireland today stepped on to the scaffold in front of the Banqueting House in Whitehall to deliver his final words. Liberty and freedom, said the monarch who had levied taxes without parliamentary consent, ruled for 11 years without any parliament, and had refused to recognize the court that condemned him, consisted of having a monarch like a loving father to run the government, not in having any share of that government. A subject and sovereign were "clear different things", he said. Then he placed his head on the block and the axe came down. Since his army's defeat at Naseby by Oliver Cromwell's Roundheads three years ago, Charles had manoeuvred desperately to escape this fatal day, offering Ireland, Rome, and even Scotland incentives to aid him. But the courts deemed him a "tyrant, traitor, murderer and enemy of the people".

How pleasant to know Mr Lear!
Who has written such volumes of
*   stuff!*
Some think him ill-tempered and
*   queer,*
But a few think him pleasant
*   enough.*
Edward Lear, on himself
– the "laureate of nonsense"
died today, 1888.

New genius of Paris fashion has first show

1958 The young genius of Paris fashion, Yves Saint Laurent, held his first major show in Paris today – at the age of 22. He was apprenticed to Christian Dior at 18, and on the latter's death last year became the head designer of the Dior fashion house. Dior's romantic New Look, which he introduced after the war, revitalized Paris fashion with its long, full skirts and narrow waists. His young successor is looking to the future; Saint Laurent sees the end coming for the one-off individual creation and a new wider market for couture fashion emerging, particularly in the United States. He plans to open boutiques offering high fashion at reasonable prices.

MORE THAN A MILLION DIE IN BLOODY STALINGRAD

1943 The Red Army has captured Stalingrad in the greatest – and bloodiest – land battle of this war. The German army is believed to have lost 850,000 troops and the Soviets almost as many in the seven-month struggle that has destroyed most of this strategic city on the Volga. The capture of German commander Von Paulus – who twice rejected Russian General Zhukov's surrender terms – came as he was promoted to Field Marshal by Hitler in a desperate attempt to stop him capitulating. But Hitler failed to live up to a promise to relieve the city with air drops and thousands of German soldiers starved to death in the bitter cold.

A desperate disease requires a dangerous remedy.
Guy Fawkes, justifying his Gunpowder Plot. He was executed today, 1605.

2000 Family GP Dr Harold Shipman has been sentenced to life for murdering 15 of his female patients, making him Britain's worst convicted serial killer. He is also suspected of killing more than 100 other patients. The judge, Mr Justice Thayne Forbes, said: "You brought them death, disguised by the attentiveness of a good doctor."

Viet Tet offensive may turn war

1968 Strategic buildings in Saigon, including the US embassy, came under surprise attack during a religious holiday today as Viet Cong troops broke a truce and launched a major offensive. The so-called Tet Offensive shows the determination and audacity of North Vietnam's generals, and is sowing doubts among US congressmen about the wisdom of prosecuting this ever more unpopular war. Although the Communists are losing large numbers of men, they have proved their ability to strike even at supposedly secure cities. With American casualties now exceeding 1000 per day, domestic American hostility to the war is burgeoning. Tet could prove the turning-point in the war.

Assassin's guns jam: President's life saved

1835 US President Andrew Jackson was saved by the lucky double misfire of a would-be assassin's pistols as he was attacked at close range on Capitol Hill today. His assailant, a house painter called Richard Lawrence who claims to be the rightful heir to the English throne, was quickly disarmed. He appears to represent no political faction. This is the first attempt on the life of a president of the United States, but President Jackson, a man of strong convictions, an iron will and fiery temperament, is no stranger to violence. Earlier gunfights over gambling debts have left two bullets lodged in his body.

1950 US President Truman today gave the go-ahead for the development of a hydrogen bomb, which scientists say could prove to be 1000 times more powerful than the bombs that destroyed Hiroshima and Nagasaki at the end of World War II. The hydrogen bomb is based on the atom bomb, which is then surrounded by a layer of hydrogenous material. Tests are likely to take place within two years.

JANUARY 31

1747 The first clinic for the treatment of venereal diseases is opened at the London Lock Hospital.

1788 Bonnie Prince Charlie, the Jacobite pretender to the English throne, dies in exile in Rome.

1858 Brunel's steamship *The Great Eastern* is finally launched at Millwall after a three-month delay.

1876 All American Indians are ordered to move on to reservations.

1910 Dr Crippen poisons his wife then chops her into bits and buries her in the cellar.

1917 The US enters World War I after Germany torpedoes American ships.

1955 RCA introducs the first musical synthesizer.

1956 The creator of *Winnie-the-Pooh*, A. A. Milne, dies.

1958 The first satellite to orbit the earth, *Explorer I*, is launched from Cape Canaveral.

1974 American film producer Sam Goldwyn dies.

BIRTHDAYS

Franz Schubert 1797, Austrian composer who wrote a prodigious amount including his famous *Unfinished Symphony*.

Zane Grey 1872, American writer of western novels, including *Riders of the Purple Sage*.

Anna Pavlova 1885, Russian ballerina who came to London and formed her own company which travelled worldwide.

Mario Lanza 1921, American tenor singer who ruined a promising career with drugs and alcohol.

Jean Simmons 1929, English stage and screen actress who starred in *Black Narcissus* and *The Big Country*.

Norman Mailer 1923, American writer and novelist whose career spans 40 years with books like *The Naked and the Dead*.

Phil Collins 1951, English rock musician who has a successful solo career after drumming for the group Genesis.

FEBRUARY

"I cannot and will not give any undertaking at a time when I, and you, the people, are not free. Your freedom and mine cannot be separated."

Message from **Nelson Mandela**
read by his daughter to a rally in Soweto
in 1985, five years and one day before his release
from prison on February 11, 1990.

DE KLERK TAKES APARTHEID APART

1990 South African President F.W. de Klerk today knocked out the main props of the racist apartheid system that has held the white minority in power for the last 42 years. In an epoch-making speech to parliament in Cape Town today he said it was now time to get rid of the cornerstones on which the apartheid system is based. He also announced the end of the 30-year ban on the African National Congress, the South African Communist Party and other anti-apartheid organizations, and promised that Nelson Mandela, a political prisoner for 27 years, would be free within a fortnight. In the Johannesburg townships blacks demonstrated joyfully at the news, but white conservative groups are accusing De Klerk of betraying his people.

1650 Death of René Descartes, the "father of French philosophy".

1790 The US Supreme Court meets for the first time.

1893 In New Jersey, Thomas Edison opens the first film studio.

1896 Puccini's opera *La Bohème* is premiered in Turin.

1908 Portuguese King Carlos I and Prince Luiz are killed by soldiers after a failed revolution.

1924 Britain's first Labour government recognizes the Soviet government.

1942 Vidkun Quisling is made Norwegian Premier under German occupation.

1944 Dutch abstract painter Piet Mondrian, most famous for his use of geometric design in painting, dies in New York.

1958 The first US satellite, *Vanguard*, is launched.

1966 The great silent screen actor Buster Keaton dies.

1977 The Pompidou Centre, designed by English architect Richard Rogers and Italian Renzo Piano, opens in Paris.

1981 Norway elects its first woman prime minister, Gro Harlem Bruntland.

1985 Twenty-six alleged killers of Filippino opposition leader Benigno Aquino, gunned down as he stepped from the plane on his return from exile, go on trial in Manila.

1989 Millions of Kenyan Luo tribesmen mourn the death of Omiuri, a 16 ft (7.6 m) python believed to have magical powers.

BIRTHDAYS

John Ford 1895, American film director, best known for western classics including *Stage Coach* and *How the West Was Won*.

Clark Gable 1901, American film actor who became an international heart throb. He played Rhett Butler in *Gone With the Wind*.

Sidney Joseph Perlman 1904, American humorist and writer who wrote scripts for several Marx Brothers' films including *Monkey Business*.

Caruso goes mass-market

1903 Those unable to afford a seat at New York's Metropolitan Opera to see Enrico Caruso in person can still hear the great Italian tenor sing. His new 10-inch phonograph recording of "La Donna e Mobile" was released today, a sequel to his hugely popular English recording of "Vesti la Giubba" from *I Pagliacci*. The 30-year-old Caruso, currently starring in *L'Elisir d'Amore* made his debut only nine years ago, but his beautiful voice soon took the public by storm. After first hearing him sing, the famous conductor Arturo Toscanini said, "This Neapolitan will make the whole world talk about him." His prophecy has certainly been fulfilled.

Democracy means government by the uneducated, while aristocracy means government by the badly educated.
G. K. Chesterton, iconoclastic English writer, 1931.

Space shuttle disintegrates

2003 The US space shuttle Columbia broke up as it re-entered the earth's atmosphere, killing all seven astronauts on board. This marks a major setback for the US space program and has left the nation stunned. This is the first time an accident has occurred on landing in the 42 years of space flight. The shuttle disintegrated 16 minutes before it was due to land at Cape Canaveral in Florida. Nasa spokesman Sean O'Keefe, said: "This is indeed a tragic day for the Nasa family, for the families of the astronauts and likewise, tragic for the nation."

Ayatollah back in triumph

1979 Iran's religious leader Ayatollah Khomeini ended 16 years of exile today, returning to a frenzied welcome at Tehran airport. A huge crowd of supporters hailed the old man who has forced the Shah of Iran to flee. Much of Khomeini's success was due to his command of the media – when international radio stations denied him airtime, his supporters flooded Iran with audio cassette tapes of his speeches. Today the 79-year-old Ayatollah promised to intensify the struggle against the enemies of his radical Shi'ite Islamic sect. He announced, "I will strike with my fists at the mouths of this government. From now on it is I who will name the government." Prime Minister Shahpur Bakhtiar's authority is dwindling hourly.

LONG DID SHE REIGN OVER US

1901 As guns fired in salute from a phalanx of British and foreign battleships, a naval escort this afternoon led the royal yacht *Alberta* and its precious cargo of the body of Queen Victoria into Portsmouth harbour en route to her funeral in London tomorrow. In the sunset scene the cortège was hardly visible through the pall cast by the smoke from the guns, which kept booming out on the minute until the *Alberta* reached harbour. The Queen died at Osborne on the Isle of Wight on January 22, surrounded by her children and grandchildren. She was 82, and had lived and reigned longer than any other British monarch; her descendants have occupied seven thrones. Queen Victoria was only 18 when she ascended the throne 63 years ago. She has left it immeasurably strengthened, her empire circling the globe.

1801 Ireland is represented for the first time in the British parliament.

1852 The first public convenience for men opens in Fleet Street, London.

1870 Press agencies Reuters, Havas and Wolff sign an agreement which enables them to cover the whole world.

1878 Greece declares war on Turkey.

1914 The first pack of Cub Scouts is formed in Sussex, England.

1915 Germany begins U-boat blockades of British waters, while the US warns Germany against attacking American ships.

1943 The German Army offers its surrender to the Soviet Army at Stalingrad.

1970 English philosopher, writer and Nobel Prize-winner Bertrand Russell dies.

1986 Lichtenstein allows women to vote for the first time.

BIRTHDAYS

Nell Gwynne 1650, English actress who started her career as an orange seller at the Drury Lane Theatre and went on to become the mistress of Charles II.

Charles Maurice de Talleyrand-Périgord 1754, French foreign minister to Napoleon Bonaparte and King Louis XVIII and ambassador to Britain.

Havelock Ellis 1859, English psychologist noted for his studies of human sexual behaviour.

James Joyce 1882, Irish novelist whose most famous work, *Ulysses*, was originally banned in Britain and the US.

Jascha Heifitz 1901, Russian-born violinist who became an American citizen in 1925.

Jussi Björling 1911, Swedish operatic tenor.

Stan Getz 1927, American jazz tenor saxophonist who played with all the big name bands from the age of 16.

Elaine Stritch 1927, American star of stage and screen.

Soviet army finally quits Afghanistan

1989 The Soviet Union's nine-year military occupation of Afghanistan ended today as the final armoured column of Red Army forces set off home from the capital, Kabul. The USSR agreed two years ago as part of the Geneva accords that the last of its forces would be gone by February 15 this year. These last 120,000 troops are now making their way up the Salang Highway, watchful for ambush by US-backed mujahideen guerrillas.

The Russians have left large amounts of arms behind for the government forces. Afghan President Najibullah, who continues to rule under emergency powers, said today that a life-or-death struggle with the guerrillas would now begin.

1972 Protesters in Dublin burned down the British embassy in an act of revenge for the "Bloody Sunday" shootings in Londonderry last weekend, in which British troops killed 13 Catholic youths and wounded another 17. Angry crowds today would not let firemen approach the blazing embassy until the roof had fallen in.

I'll wager you that in 10 years it will be fashionable again to be a virgin.
Barbara Cartland, British romantic novelist, 1976.

I said 10 years ago that in 10 years' time it would be smart to be a virgin. Now everyone is back to virgins again.
Barbara Cartland, 1987.

CASTAWAY SAILOR RESCUED AFTER 4 YEARS ON DESERT ISLAND

1709 A castaway sailor has been rescued after spending more than four years alone on a desert island. Alexander Selkirk could hardly speak English when Capt. Woodes Rogers found him on one of the uninhabited Juan Fernandez islands off the coast of Chile in South America. He had survived with the aid of a musket, a hatchet, a knife and a flint to strike a flame, improvising all his other needs. Selkirk had been left on the island after an argument with the master of his buccaneer ship, the *Cinque-Ports*. As Captain Rogers described it in his ship's log today, the longboat brought on board "a man cloth'd in goat-skins, who look'd wilder than the first owners of them. For the first eight months he had much ado to bear up against melancholy, and the terror of being left alone in such a desolate place". Rogers has appointed him ship's mate. He plans to help Selkirk publish a report of his solitary sojourn. The story could interest the London writer Daniel Defoe, who has been exploring the use of real events as the basis for his tales of fiction.

Vicious death

1979 Sid Vicious, punk bassist with the defunct Sex Pistols, died of a heroin overdose at a party in New York tonight. He was 21. Vicious (born John Ritchie) was arrested last October for murdering his American girlfriend Nancy Spungen in their New York hotel room. He was charged and sent to a prison drugs detoxification unit, where he tried to kill himself. Another member of the group eventually stood bail for him. Vicious had been trying to stay off heroin, and the shock of tonight's dose was too much for him. He died in the flat of his current girlfriend, Michelle Robinson.

New Amsterdam gets yorked

1665 A British fleet today captured New Amsterdam, the centre of the Dutch colony in North America. The British force outnumbered and outgunned the Dutch garrison, and Dutch governor Peter Stuyvesant, under pressure from anxious civilians not to open fire, finally surrendered without a fight. The flourishing trading settlement on the island of Manhattan is to be called New York in honour of the Duke of York, its new governor and the younger brother of England's King Charles II. The Dutch bought the island from the Manhattan Indians in 1626 for a few dollars' worth of trinkets, and made it a base for Dutch settlement. The colony thrived under Peter Stuyvesant's iron rule, but the settlers are relieved to see the last of their evil-tempered governor. Stuyvesant had lost a leg to a Portuguese cannonball, and replaced it with a wooden peg bound with silver. He was a puritanical tyrant, given to punishing offenders for such moral crimes as playing tennis while religious services were being held. The English style is rather different – last year the continent's first race course opened at Newmarket in British-held Long Island.

Father of printing dies in poverty

1468 Johann Gutenberg, a blind, impoverished German goldsmith from Mainz, has died in obscurity. It was he who developed the letterpress printing method and oil-based inks that are now making a fortune for Johann Fust and his son-in-law, Peter Schoffer. They have used Gutenberg's techniques to mass-produce copies of the Bible. Gutenberg had also transformed a wine press into a press capable of printing pages of his Gothic type. In 1450 he borrowed a large amount of money from Fust to develop his system of movable type cast in lead. Five years later Fust foreclosed on the mortgage and took possession of the type and presses, setting himself up as a printer. Despite Gutenberg's personal failure, his cheap method of mass-producing printed pages has freed the written word from the jealous monopoly of the monasteries.

HOLLY LEGEND LIVES ON

1963 Rave reviews greeted Buddy Holly's long-awaited new LP released today – four years after the great rock singer and guitarist was killed in a plane crash. Holly had chartered a light plane to take him on the next leg of a tour of the Mid-West. The plane crashed in a snowstorm minutes after take-off. Holly was 22 and had been married for five months. The bespectacled guitar ace started playing at 13, and at 19 his group opened for Elvis Presley. Then, with the Crickets, came a cluster of rock'n'roll hits. The new LP, *Reminiscing,* consists of unissued tapes which have been remixed. The title track was in the UK charts three months ago. There is no sign of his popularity waning.

Nazi supporter Stroessner ousted

1989 Eight successive presidential terms and 35 years of rule for Generalissimo Alfredo Stroessner ended suddenly today in Paraguay as a military coup toppled the old dictator. General Andres Rodrigues, Stroessner's former aide, took over the capital, Asuncion, after heavy fighting. He has announced that he has locked Stroessner in a military barracks. Meanwhile, Brazil is negotiating political asylum for the ousted dictator. Stroessner, the son of a German immigrant, was notorious for harbouring fugitive Nazis after World War II. Rodrigues has promised to bring democracy to Paraguay, but diplomats here do not expect the changeover to have much real effect on daily life.

Macmillan predicts "wind of change"

1960 A "wind of change" is blowing through Africa, bringing a new national consciousness, Britain's prime minister warned South Africa's whites-only parliament today. Harold Macmillan told the astonished white politicians in the Cape Town parliament they should accept racial equality. Britain is trying to establish racial equality throughout the Commonwealth, but Macmillan's speech has raised a storm of criticism from white South Africans resentful of British meddling. Macmillan forecast that the coming challenge was whether the emergent nations of Africa and Asia would align themselves with the ex-colonial powers of the West or with the communist Eastern bloc.

1989 BT, the British telecommunications company, banned "chatlines" today because of the chatline junkie problem – people get hooked on the faceless chatter and run up huge telephone bills which they cannot pay. The company has been criticized following the widely reported case of a woman whose 12-year-old son landed her a chatline bill of £6,000.

"Pom" Queen still welcome

1954 Australia gave away a close-kept national secret today. Despite what Australians tend to say about the derisory shortcomings of the "Poms", what looked like the whole of Sydney turned out today to welcome Queen Elizabeth II. Elizabeth, who is on a three-month Commonwealth tour, is the first reigning British monarch to visit Australia. Huge crowds cheered as she and Prince Philip stepped ashore: the "aussies" love their English queen.

There will certainly be no one to blame if I should kill myself, even if the immediate cause should for instance appear to be F.'s behaviour. I can find no other solution. I can't live without her and must jump, yet – and this F. suspects – I couldn't live with her either.

Franz Kafka, novelist, writes in his diary, 1914.

1399 Death of John of Gaunt, father of King Henry IV of England.

1488 Portuguese explorer Bartholomeu Diaz becomes the first European to land on African soil, putting ashore at Mossel Bay on the eastern side of the Cape.

1730 The London *Daily Advertiser* publishes the first stock exchange quotations.

1762 English dandy and gambler Richard "Beau" Nash dies.

1877 "Chopsticks", a piece of music composed by Arthur de Lull (in reality 16-year-old Euphemia Alten), is registered at the British Museum.

1919 The League of Nations holds its first meeting in Paris, chaired by US president Woodrow Wilson.

1931 New Zealand is struck by an earthquake which kills 216.

1966 A Soviet unmanned spacecraft, *Luna IX*, achieves the first landing on the moon.

1969 Yasser Arafat becomes the leader of the Palestine Liberation Organization.

1969 English actor Boris Karloff, who made a speciality of horror parts, dies aged 82.

1970 British police seize Andy Warhol's film *Flesh* on the grounds that it is obscene.

1989 P. W. Botha quits as South Africa's ruling party chief.

BIRTHDAYS

Felix Mendelssohn-Bartholdy 1809, German composer of *Fingal's Cave* and *The Midsummer Night's Dream.*

Gertrude Stein 1874, American writer and critic who lived in Paris and was friend to many famous painters and writers.

Clarence Mulford 1883, American writer who created Hopalong Cassidy.

James Michener 1907, American novelist who has written a number of blockbuster novels, including *Hawaii.*

Simone Weil 1909, French writer whose work was published posthumously.

FEBRUARY 4

BIRTHDAYS

Fernand Léger 1881, French Cubist painter who also designed ballet sets, tapestries, stained glass and ceramics.

Charles Lindbergh 1902, American aviator who made the first solo flight over the Atlantic.

Dietrich Bonhoeffer 1906, German theologian who was one of the group that plotted the assassination of Adolf Hitler and who was subsequently executed in a concentration camp.

Byron Nelson 1912, American golf champion who won the first two US Masters titles.

Alice Cooper 1948, American pop singer who loved to shock his audiences with hits like "Welcome to my Nightmare".

LINCOLN'S UNION LOSES SOUTHERN STATES

1861 In an atmosphere of looming conflict with American President Abraham Lincoln and his Northern Republicans, delegates from seven Southern states met today in Montgomery, Alabama, to draft a separate constitution for what they are now calling the Confederate States of America. Led by South Carolina, which seceded from the Union last year, Mississippi, Florida, Alabama, Georgia, Louisiana and Texas have all formally broken ties with Washington in the last three weeks. Lincoln's convincing election victory in the rapidly industrializing North and his implacable opposition to slavery in the rural South tipped the scales towards secession. The South says it cannot survive without its slaves. The Confederates face the choice of abandoning their almost feudal way of life or fighting to defend it. Jefferson Davis is to be their first president.

CHARLESTON MERCURY

EXTRA:

Passed unanimously at 1.15 o'clock, P. M., December 20th, 1860.

AN ORDINANCE

To dissolve the Union between the State of South Carolina and other States united with her under the compact entitled "The Constitution of the United States of America."

THE UNION IS DISSOLVED!

If a woman like Eva Peron with no ideals can get that far, think how far I can go with all the ideals that I have.
Margaret Thatcher
in a *Sunday Times* interview – she became head of Britain's Conservative Party today, 1975.

"Hot jazz" Baker outrages Nazis

1928 The black American "hot jazz" dancer Josephine Baker has raised a storm of protest in Vienna. Members of Adolf Hitler's fast-growing Nazi party are outraged by her stage act. Broadway star Miss Baker made a string of bananas the most provocative dress of the 20s in her Paris revue, but in Vienna she drew angry complaints from Austria's Nazis, who accused her of public indecency. But what they really find offensive is not the amount of Miss Baker's skin on view but its colour.

President for post-Shah Iran

1980 Revolutionary Iran today installed its first elected president. However, President Abolhassan Bani-Sadr will follow the line of the country's de facto ruler, religious leader Ayatollah Khomeini. Bani-Sadr is a moderate economist who, like Khomeini, spent a long exile in Paris. Though he was elected president last month with as much as 75 per cent of the popular vote, Bani-Sadr does not command a majority in the Iranian parliament, where fundamentalist Shi'ite Muslim clerics are firmly in control. However, Khomeini is now planning to strengthen Bani-Sadr's powers in order to deal with the crisis of the US hostages held captive in the Tehran embassy by Revolutionary Guards. Meanwhile, in New York, the United Nations is preparing to mount a commission of inquiry into the exiled Shah of Iran's affairs.

Philippines take on USA

1899 Fighting broke out today in America's newest colony, the Philippines, which declared itself a republic last month. The US had supported the Filipino nationalist revolutionary General Emilio Aguinaldo against the islands' Spanish colonial masters during the Spanish-American war. Aguinaldo had thought the US would back Filipino independence after the war, and last month he declared the Philippines a republic, with himself its first president. But the rebels had won their freedom only to lose it again – the US annexed the islands as a prize of war. Aguinaldo and his army have risen up against their new colonial masters, so now Aguinaldo is fighting his former allies.

America gets its Cup back

1987 After an embarrassing four-year sojourn in Australia, the America's Cup is finally back in America – in the trophy room of the San Diego Yacht club. The US catamaran *Stars & Stripes*, skippered by Dennis Connor, has beaten the *New Zealand*, a 133-ft (40.5-m) monohull, in races off Perth. But what the New Zealanders lost in the water, they plan to win back in court – they are claiming that the rules require competing yachts to be of similar design, and the catamaran's twin hull therefore disqualifies it. The cup was first presented to the New York Yacht Club by the owners of the schooner *The America* in 1851. It quickly became the world's premier yachting challenge trophy. It stayed in American hands for the next 132 years, until Australia's triumph in 1983.

Stones gagged

1967 The Rolling Stones appeared on British ITV's *Eamonn Andrews Show* tonight and showed why the group is falling foul of the establishment – and delighting the younger generation. The group's current hit "Let's Spend the Night Together" is soaring to No 1, but they weren't allowed to play it tonight because of a Musician's Union ban. They had a similar problem on the *Ed Sullivan Show* in the US last month, and had to change the lyrics to "Let's Spend Some Time Together". Since they first hit the big time in 1963 the Stones have created chaos in the sanitized world of pop, where teenage love is "Sealed with a Kiss". It's not just their loutish behaviour and their lyrics: singer Mick Jagger's uninhibited stage act is outrageously sexy. The howling mobs that storm the stage have had to be subdued with teargas. Parents are appalled,

but to a generation clamouring for under-age access to the Pill it's a breath of fresh air. Meanwhile, Jagger announced on the show that he will sue a Sunday newspaper for an article connecting him with drug-taking pop stars.

Meters hit town

1958 London's exclusive Mayfair is no place for squatters – or their cars. From today motorists had to pay for the privilege of parking in a Mayfair street. In a trial scheme to ease the city's endemic traffic congestion, each kerbside space now has a parking meter. Feeding coins into the slot buys parking time, registered on a dial. When the dial runs out, the car is illegally parked, and its owner liable to a fine. Drivers greeted the new arrangement with suspicion today and many metered spaces stayed empty while cars jostled for parking in unmetered streets nearby. The meters were first used in America in 1935. The fines are nothing new, however – Mr William Marshall earned the first parking summons in 1896 after leaving his car awkwardly parked in a street in London's City.

Germany refuses to pay war debts

1920 Just a month after signing an agreement to pay its former enemies £10 billion over the next 40 years as reparations for the Great War, Germany says it cannot afford to make the payments. Government spokesmen have captured German popular feelings of "indignation" over the conditions imposed as part of the Peace of Versailles, and are trying to avoid coming up with the cash. Today's debate in the Reichstag heard that the agreement would lead to "economic and political pauperization" and could drive Germans to extreme nationalism. Meanwhile, in Britain, post-war economic gloom has put a million people out of work.

> *Give me a laundry list and I'll set it to music.*
> **Gioacchino Rossini**, whose Barber of Seville was premiered today, 1816.

Wit and wisdom in bite-sized chunks

1922 A new monthly magazine was launched in New York today with an appealing formula – the *Reader's Digest* offers 31 condensed articles from the leading magazines, each one "of enduring value and interest". It is the brainchild of DeWitt Wallace, a former book salesman. Unable to find backers for his idea in his native Minnesota, Wallace finally published the magazine himself, on a shoestring budget. He already has 1500 subscribers and promises the magazine will entertain and inspire them. Wallace, the son of a Presbyterian minister, has struck just the right note with the readership: the first issue reflects the puritan, conservative tone still prevalent in America, while recognizing that few today have enough time for reading and reflection.

> *He's stoned on himself. He's always in complete control and the whole thing is manipulation. It really bothers me that a twerp like that can parade around and convince everybody that he's Satan.*
> Ace guitarist **Ry Cooder** on Mick Jagger, 1967.

1679 The Third Treaty of Nijmegen ends seven years of war in Europe.

1782 Spain captures Minorca from British troops.

1881 Death of Thomas Carlyle, Scottish historian and essayist.

1935 Boxing authorities in New York rule that no fight can exceed 15 rounds.

1945 General MacArthur and US troops enter Manila.

1953 Walt Disney's Peter Pan goes on general release.

1957 Rock group Bill Haley and the Comets arrive to a riotous reception in London.

1974 Nineteen-year-old heiress Patti Hearst, granddaughter of multi-millionaire William Randolph Hearst, is kidnapped.

1983 Nazi war criminal Klaus Barbie is flown to France to face a war crimes trial.

1983 An unknown Mozart symphony is discovered in Odense, Denmark.

1989 Media mogul Rupert Murdoch launches satellite Sky TV.

1994 A mortar bomb explodes in the main market square in Sarajevo, killing 70 people.

BIRTHDAYS

Sir Robert Peel 1788, British prime minister and founder of the Metropolitan Police.

Adlai Stevenson 1900, American statesman and ambassador whose liberal views caused him trouble during the McCarthy witchhunts.

John Carradine 1906, American character actor who gave notable performances in *The Invisible Man* and *The Last Tycoon*.

William Burroughs 1914, American novelist who wrote *The Naked Lunch*.

Bob Marley 1945, Jamaican reggae composer and performer who introduced reggae to an international audience.

Charlotte Rampling 1947, British actress whose films include *The Night Porter* and *Stardust Memories*.

FEBRUARY 6

1493 Maximilian I of Germany takes the title Holy Roman Emperor.

1515 Death of Manutius Aldus, the first publisher of paperbacks and the inventor of italics.

1783 The great English landscape gardener Capability Brown dies.

1788 Massachusetts becomes the sixth state in the Union of American States.

1804 The first locomotive converted from a steam-hammer power source runs on a line near Merthyr Tydfil, Wales.

1804 The discoverer of oxygen, English clergyman Joseph Priestley, dies.

1838 Boer leader Piet Retief is executed by Zulu chief Dingaan.

1865 Robert E. Lee becomes commander of the Confederate Armies.

1917 British women over 30 get the vote.

1926 Child prodigy Yehudi Menuhin makes his violin-playing debut in Paris

1943 Errol Flynn is cleared of three rape charges by a Los Angeles court.

2000 The city of Grozny, Chechnya, falls to Russian troops.

BIRTHDAYS

Queen Anne 1665, last Stuart ruler of Britain.

Christopher Marlowe 1664, English poet and playwright who wrote *Tamburlaine the Great* and many other plays and poems.

George Herman (Babe Ruth) 1895, American baseball player with a tremendous batting record.

Zsa Zsa Gabor 1920, Hungarian actress who has made a career of frequent marriage.

François Truffaut 1932, French director of many fine films including *Day for Night* and *Jules et Jim*.

Rick Astley 1966, British pop singer best-known for "Never Gonna Give You Up".

1952 Britain's King George VI died peacefully at Sandringham tonight. Princess Elizabeth, the elder of his two daughters, will succeed him. The sad news is being rushed to the new Queen in Kenya, where she and her husband, the Duke of Edinburgh, are on an official tour.

Maoris under British rule

1840 Rather reluctantly, Britain today annexed New Zealand. Fifty Maori chiefs accepted British sovereignty in a treaty signed by Captain William Hobson, the governor, at Waitangi. The British move is for the protection of all concerned, but nobody is happy about it. Two factors forced Britain's hand: the need to forestall French settlement in South Island, and to protect the fierce but unsophisticated Maori tribes from unscrupulous Western land sharks, gun runners and liquor pedlars, many of them escaped English convicts from Australia. The Waitangi treaty gives the Maoris full rights and protects their land ownership: to prevent their being cheated, Maoris wanting to sell their land must now offer it to the British government first. But settlers, prevented from buying land, are refusing to accept the treaty, while Maoris are expressing doubt that the British government itself can be trusted.

"Butcher" Barbie brought to trial

1983 Nazi fugitive Klaus Barbie was charged in Lyon, France, today with crimes against humanity. Barbie was known as "the Butcher of Lyon" during World War II, when he headed the local Gestapo. He is alleged to have deported hundreds of French resistance fighters and Jews to the Nazi death camps; he is also alleged to have tortured and murdered resistance leader Jean Moulin. Barbie was tracked down in Bolivia by the French Nazi hunters Serge and Beate Klarsfeld in 1971, but was not extradited to France until this week. His lawyer claims that US intelligence agents protected Barbie after the war. He is also threatening to expose during Barbie's trial the hitherto concealed extent of wartime French collaboration with Nazi rule.

IS THE TSAR'S DAUGHTER STILL ALIVE?

1928 Reporters and curious onlookers crowded round the gangplank of a disembarking liner at New York to catch sight of a 25-year-old woman who may be the murdered Russian Tsar's youngest daughter. Anastasia Chaikovsky claims to be the only member of Russia's imperial Romanov family to survive the revolution. In 1918 the Tsar and his whole family were shot in a cellar at Ekaterinburg by Bolshevik soldiers. Mrs Chaikovsky says she hid under their bodies after being struck in the face with a bayonet, which broke her jaw. A sympathetic Russian soldier later took her to the frontier. There is no real evidence that her story is not a hoax, but the son of the Tsar's former physician said today that she really is the Grand Duchess he played with when they were children. There is some speculation that Anastasia may know the whereabouts of the substantial Romanov fortune which has not been traced since the Tsar's death.

Busby's Babes die in tragic crash

1958 British sports fans are in mourning tonight for the Manchester United football team, which has been virtually wiped out in an air crash at Munich. The team had just qualified for the European Cup semi-finals in a match at Belgrade, and was returning home via Munich when their plane crashed on its second attempt to take off from the snowbound runway. Seven players were killed, including four full British internationals. Other players and officials are gravely injured, among them Matt Busby, the Scottish manager who forged his "Babes" into one of the best teams in Europe.

Vienna: a raddled old city where one is surfeited with the music of Brahms and Puccini, with officers with women's bosoms and women with officers' chests.

Composer **Claude Debussy** writes in his diary today, 1911.

1845 A drunken visitor to the British Museum has smashed one of its greatest treasures. William Lloyd blundered into the Portland Vase, which fell to the floor, shattering into more than 200 pieces. The famous cameo-glass vase, dated 25 BC, belonged to the Roman Emperor Augustus. The museum's experts are painstakingly examining the pieces and are confident the vase can be rebuilt. Though no substitute, excellent copies of the Portland Vase have been produced in the factory of English master potter Josiah Wedgwood.

IRA strikes at No. 10

1991 In its most daring daylight raid yet, the IRA today fired three mortar bombs at the British Prime Minister's residence at No. 10 Downing Street. One bomb landed in the garden and a second shattered the windows of the room where John Major and his war cabinet were discussing the Gulf crisis, but nobody was seriously hurt. The mortars were hidden inside a commercial van parked nearby and fired through its roof by remote control. Prime Minister John Major said such terror tactics would not change Britain's Northern Ireland policy "one iota".

1301 AD The son of King Edward I of England becomes the first English Prince of Wales.

1792 Austria and Prussia sign a military pact against France.

1816 Italian missionary Giovanni Lantrua of Triora is executed by the Chinese.

1863 One hundred and eighty-five people die as HMS *Orpheus* is wrecked on the coast of New Zealand.

1959 Death of Daniel F. Malan, prime minister of South Africa 1948–54 and architect of apartheid.

1960 Israeli archaeologists unearth a number of Dead Sea Scrolls.

1964 Twenty-five thousand fans mass at Kennedy airport as the Beatles arrive for their first-ever visit to the US.

1971 Switzerland finally allows women to vote.

1974 Grenada gains its independence and Eric Gairy becomes its first prime minister.

1989 A violent storm causing updraughts results in a rain of sardines over Ipswich, Australia.

1990 The Central Committee of the Soviet Communist Party votes for a package of reforms that will end its monopoly of power.

1999 Death of King Hussein of Jordan, a symbol of stability in the Middle East, aged 64.

2001 Ariel Sharon is elected Prime Minister of Israel.

Vietnam heads for war

1950 East and West have backed rival factions in the French colony of Vietnam in Indochina, fanning the flames of civil war. Last week the Soviet Union granted formal recognition to the provisional government of Marxist guerrilla leader Ho Chi Minh. Today the United States and Britain endorsed the French-backed government of Emperor Bao Dai. This is no surprise: the US has been discreetly funding Paris in its battle against Ho's Viet Minh communists since fighting broke out in 1947. Ho declared Vietnam's independence from France at the end of World War II. He is a founder member of both the French Communist Party and the Comintern.

"Baby Doc" takes money and runs

1986 Haiti is celebrating the end of the bloodthirsty 28-year rule of the Duvalier dynasty. In the face of a national uprising, the self-styled "president for life", Jean Claude "Baby-Doc" Duvalier, fled the island late last night, bound for exile in France. With the celebrations came vengeance as angry crowds in Port-au-Prince, the capital, lynched members of the Tontons Macoute secret police force. Both Duvalier and his father, known as Papa Doc, used the Tontons Macoutes to maintain a reign of terror. Though Haiti is one of the world's poorest countries, Duvalier has reportedly accumulated a huge fortune of over £100 million – at his people's expense. It will be no surprise for Haitians that "Baby Doc" has taken the money with him to France.

Gold struck in South Africa's Transvaal

1886 An English carpenter, George Walker, struck gold today in the Transvaal in South Africa while building a cottage for a prospector. Walker's shovel uncovered a clear gold streak when he started digging the foundations. His discovery has geologists looking at the Boer republic's Witwatersrand ridge with growing excitement. Specks of the coveted metal have been found in nearby rivers for the last 30 years, but it is now thought that the whole ridge may be one massive field of gold. The Boers fear the strike will bring hordes of troublesome, money-seeking foreigners to the area.

> *He said once to myself that he was no atheist but he could not think God would make a man miserable only for taking a little pleasure out of the way.*
> **Gilbert Burnett**, Bishop, on Charles II's death, 1685.

MERRY MONARCH'S MYSTERY DEATH

1685 England is in mourning today for the "merry monarch" King Charles II – though nobody quite knows how he died. Some say he was poisoned, others that he died of apoplexy following days and nights of revelry with his mistresses and concubines. Charles loved women, horses, gambling and good times. He was much loved by his people in return, following the dreary years of Puritan rule under Oliver Cromwell. He was less popular with the politicians – he took bribes and had no compunction about lying and cheating to get his way. He even secretly took money from France to restore the Catholic religion to England. Following the execution of his father, Charles I, he spent 16 years in exile in France, constantly plotting – and failing – to win back the throne. Restored to the monarchy in 1660 after Cromwell's death, he was always at odds with parliament, and finally dissolved it in 1681. At least two duchesses were his mistresses, but his favourite was the popular comic actress Nell Gwynne, who bore him two sons. His last words to his brother James were, "Don't let poor Nelly starve." James, a Catholic, is now king.

BIRTHDAYS

Sir Thomas More 1478, English Lord Chancellor who was executed by Henry VIII for refusing to deny the authority of the Pope.

Charles Dickens 1812, great English novelist who wrote a number of well-loved classics like *Oliver Twist* and *David Copperfield*.

Alfred Adler 1870, Austrian psychoanalyst who introduced the concept of the inferiority complex.

Sinclair Lewis 1885, American novelist and Nobel prize-winner who wrote *Main Street*.

1725 Peter the Great of Russia dies and is succeeded by his wife Catherine.

1740 London sees the end of the Great Frost which started on Christmas Eve 1739.

1872 Indian viceroy Lord Mayo is assassinated by nationalists.

1884 Cetewayo, nephew of Shaka, the last king of independent Zululand who routed the British at the Battle of Isandhlwana in 1879, dies a fugitive.

1886 Unemployed people demonstrate in Trafalgar Square and looting and rioting break out along Oxford Street and Pall Mall.

1906 A typhoon hits Tahiti, killing 10,000 people.

1924 The gas chamber as a method of execution is used for the first time in Carson City, Nevada on Chinese gang-member Gee Jon.

1965 British health minister Kenneth Robinson announces that cigarette ads are to be banned from British television.

1972 Fans demonstrate outside the Albert Hall after Frank Zappa and the Mothers of Invention have their concert there cancelled due to the obscenity of one of their songs.

1974 Skylab space station astronauts return safely to earth after 85 days in space.

1990 American pop singer Del Shannon shoots himself.

BIRTHDAYS

John Ruskin 1819, English writer and art critic who wrote *Modern Painters*.

William Sherman 1820, American Union general during the Civil War who was eventually appointed head of the army when Ulysses Grant became President.

Jack Lemmon 1925, American film actor noted for comedy roles like those in *Mister Roberts* and *Save the Tiger*.

James Dean 1931, American film actor and cult hero who died young in a road accident.

MARY QUEEN OF SCOTS BEHEADED

1587 Mary Queen of Scots was beheaded today on the orders of her cousin, England's Queen Elizabeth I. She had been found guilty of plotting to assassinate the queen and restore England to Catholicism, believing that Henry VIII's marriage to Elizabeth's mother Anne Boleyn was illegal. Mary inherited the throne of Scotland at the age of six. In her teens she married the French Dauphin, and was Queen of France for a year until he died. Later she married Lord Darnley. After Darnley's murder – in which Mary may have been implicated – the Earl of Bothwell became her third husband. In 1568, defeated in battle in Scotland, Mary fled to England, but the jealous Elizabeth had her jailed for nearly 19 years. Witnesses at her execution told of Mary's fortitude in the face of death. It took the axeman two blows, and Mary's lips continued to move for 15 minutes afterwards. Her pet dog was found hiding in her skirts.

1983 Irish bandits have kidnapped a top race horse from a stable in County Kildare and are demanding a £2 million ($3.7 million) ransom. The horse is Shergar, winner of the 1981 Derby by a record 10 lengths, the biggest margin ever. Shergar, owned by the Aga Khan, is probably the world's finest horse. In the rarefied world of thoroughbred breeding, he is priceless. Whether the Aga Khan pays the ransom or not, rumour is that Shergar is destined to be catfood.

Irish leader kept quiet by jail

1929 Irish Free State leader Eamon de Valera has been sentenced to a month's imprisonment in a Belfast jail for entering Northern Ireland illegally. De Valera is the leading Irish nationalist and the head of Fianna Fail, the largest party in Dublin's Dail parliament. He narrowly escaped execution for his part in the Easter Uprising of 1916, and, as leader of the revolutionary Sinn Fein, he repudiated the treaty that established the Irish Free State in 1922. He is also a devout Roman Catholic. The British authorities do not want him spreading his message in the largely Protestant North. De Valera is a fiery mixture: he was born in New York, his mother Irish and his father Spanish.

> *A dead woman bites not.*
> **Lord Gray**,
> calling for the execution of
> Mary Queen of Scots, 1587.

Japanese catch Russians offguard

1904 The Russian imperial fleet anchored at Port Arthur in Manchuria has been crippled by a surprise night attack by Japanese warships, plunging the two countries into war. The Japanese sank two Russian battleships and a cruiser in the port, trapping the rest of the fleet. Tokyo now claims it has captured seven warships. Only after the battle did the Japanese emperor inform the Russians they were at war. Hostilities were sparked by mounting Russian ambitions in Korea and Manchuria – areas that rapidly-industrializing Japan sees as its spheres of interest.

Scout's honour for young Americans

1910 The Boy Scouts of America organization was inaugurated today, a cousin to the movement founded by Sir Robert Baden-Powell in Britain two years ago. Open to boys of eight and upward, it aims to develop good character and fitness of body and mind. It will be run on military lines, with uniforms and ranks, patrols and troops, countryside camps and community service. Baden-Powell is a British soldier who won fame during the Boer War in South Africa, holding the besieged town of Mafeking against Boer forces for seven months. After the war he wrote a manual on field reconnaissance for officers, but so many young people bought the book that he rewrote it as *Scouting for Boys* and founded his youth movement. Baden-Powell's wife, Lady Agnes, is planning a similar movement for girls.

Blasphemy ban on Beckett

1958 A play by the Irish author Samuel Beckett has been banned from the London stage – because of a blasphemy. The Lord Chamberlain has invoked ancient religious laws against *Endgame*, an extremely modern play. It is an existential drama of despair in an end-of-the-world setting during which almost nothing happens. It features a slave, his tyrannical master, and the tyrant's old parents (who live in dustbins). They talk, to little avail. It is even more bleak than Beckett's *Waiting for Godot*, which brought him worldwide acclaim. Yet, far from being a gloomy non-event, *Endgame* is brilliant, a potent image of bewilderment in the face of an indifferent universe. London's critics have not been much kinder to Beckett than has the Lord Chamberlain – the London premiere of *Waiting for Godot* saw a mass walkout. But in Paris he is a leading light in the pitiless "theatre of the absurd", along with Jean Genet and Eugene Ionesco. French critics see him as a strong candidate for a Nobel Prize for Literature.

1981 Poland's defence minister, General Wojciech Jaruzelski, has taken over today as prime minister and chief of the Communist Party. His promotion threatens a crackdown on the rapidly-growing Solidarity labour movement. General Jaruzelski has close links with the Soviet Union, where years ago he was trained as an army officer. He favours a strong hand in government – not surprisingly his relationship with Solidarity leader Lech Walesa is somewhat tense.

Fab Four sweep America

1964 The US crime rate plunged dramatically tonight as 73 million Americans cancelled everything to watch four lads from Liverpool appear on the *Ed Sullivan Show*. Six weeks ago nobody in America had ever heard of The Beatles. One week ago their single "I Wanna Hold Your Hand" hit the top of the US hit parade, and yesterday the British pop group arrived in New York for a 10-day US tour to meet scenes of mass hysteria and near-riot, with police out in force to keep the peace. Radio stations broadcast the progress of their trans-Atlantic jet as thousands of teenagers – mostly female – packed the airport to greet the "fab four" and follow them through the city. The Beatles swept to the top of the charts in Britain six months ago with a string of best-ever sellers, riding an unprecedented tide of mass adulation.

Massachusetts on verge of armed rising

1775 Hostilities are imminent between Britain and the American colony of Massachusetts. In London today parliament announced that there is rebellion, and approved new laws to control the situation. Dissatisfaction over British rule has been mounting for the last 10 years, and now it threatens to spill into war. The situation has deteriorated rapidly in the 14 months since American rebels disguised as Indians destroyed cargoes of British tea in Boston Harbour in protest against British taxes. The hated Tea Tax was imposed to save the British East India Company, which had built up a crippling surplus of tea in London. Settlers swore to pay no further taxes to Britain, and there has been sullen opposition to the laws Britain imposed to restore order – oppressive measures the colonists are calling the Intolerable Acts. Since late last year an illegal assembly known as the First Continental Congress has urged Americans to boycott British goods and to arm themselves.

Chinese rebels blame hardship on Christians

1899 A new tide of rebellion is sweeping through China. The Boxer rebellion is aimed at Westerners, especially Christians. The movement has gained a grip on China's peasants, whose crops were wrecked last year. "If the rain does not fall and the land dries up, it is because the churches stand in the way of Heaven, and the gods are angry," says a Boxer pamphlet. "To be converted to Christianity is to disobey Heaven, to abandon our gods, and to forget our ancestors . . .To be convinced of this, one only has to look at the barbarians' eyes, which are completely blue. The railways must be destroyed, the electric wires cut, and the ships demolished. This will frighten France and demoralize Britain and Russia." All three countries, as well as Germany, have forced China to relinquish land.

> *It's easy, you turn left at Greenland.*
> **John Lennon**, when asked how he found America, 1964.

1799 The US Navy draws first blood in a war with France.

1801 The signing of the Peace of Luneville between France and Austria dissolves the Holy Roman Empire.

1825 John Quincy Adams is elected US president, defeating Andrew Jackson, and ending a two-month impasse.

1830 Explorer Charles Sturt discovers the source of Australia's longest river, the Murray.

1881 Fyodor Dostoevsky, the great Russian novelist who wrote *Crime and Punishment*, dies at the age of 60.

1949 Actor Robert Mitchum is jailed for two months for smoking marijuana.

1966 The last of the "Red hot mamas", Sophie Tucker, dies.

1971 The first British soldier is killed in Ulster as the current troubles mount.

1972 The third month of the miners' strike causes Britain's prime minister Edward Heath to declare a state of emergency.

1981 Musician Bill Haley, whose "Rock Around the Clock" was one of the first ever rock 'n' roll records, dies.

1996 The IRA admits planting a bomb in the Docklands area of London, ending a 17-month ceasefire. British Prime Minister John Major said there is now "a dark shadow of doubt" where optimism had been.

BIRTHDAYS

Mrs Patrick Campbell 1865, English actress who had a close relationship with Bernard Shaw, playing Eliza Doolittle in his play *Pygmalion*.

Carole King 1941, American songwriter and singer who wrote many hits for other people before recording any of her own.

Mia Farrow 1945, American actress who first made her name in the television series *Peyton Place* and went on to make many films, notably comedies with Woody Allen.

1354 Students in Oxford cause death and mayhem in a running street battle with locals.

1482 The Florentine king of terracotta sculpture, Luca della Robbia, dies.

1837 Aleksandr Pushkin, Russian author of *Eugene Onegin* and *Boris Godunov*, is killed in a duel.

1840 Britain's Queen Victoria marries her first cousin, Prince Albert.

1840 French-speaking Lower Canada and English-speaking Upper Canada are reunited again, 50 years after their division into separate British provinces.

1889 The use of the revised Bible is authorized by the Church of England.

1923 Death of William Röntgen, German physicist who invented the X-ray.

1932 Death of Edgar Wallace, British novelist who wrote highly successful detective stories and film scripts.

1988 Octogenarian English actor Sir John Gielgud plays the longest role for a man of his years: Sydney Cockerell in *The Best of Friends* by Hugh Whitmore.

BIRTHDAYS

William Congreve 1670, English Restoration playwright best known for his plays *Love for Love* and *The Way of the World*.

Boris Pasternak 1890, Russian author famed for his prize-winning novel *Doctor Zhivago*.

Jimmy Durante 1893, American comedian and vaudeville star whose large nose became part of his very successful act.

Berthold Brecht 1898, German Marxist poet, playwright (*Mother Courage* and *The Caucasian Chalk Circle*) and librettist of composer Kurt Weill's best-known works, including *The Threepenny Opera*.

Robert Wagner 1930, American film and television actor, twice married to actress Natalie Wood.

Greg Norman 1958, Australian champion golfer dubbed "The White Shark".

Powers freed in Berlin bridge swop

1962 In an exchange worthy of a thriller, captured US spy-plane pilot Gary Powers tonight started walking from the Communist side of a Berlin bridge, while the highest-ranking Russian spy ever caught, KGB Colonel Rudolf Abel, set off from the American side. The two men passed in silence in the middle of the bridge, and walked on to freedom. Powers thus escaped the 10-year prison sentence imposed on him two years ago by a Soviet court following his high-altitude spying mission on Soviet military installations. His U-2 spy-plane could fly higher than the Russian jet fighters, but a Soviet surface-to-air missile brought it down near Sverdlovsk. The incident soured relations between the two superpowers and wrecked the "Big Four" summit meeting in Paris a few days later between Eisenhower, Khrushchev, Macmillan and De Gaulle. The US was finally forced to admit it had been spying. Colonel Abel was captured in New York five years ago and sentenced to 30 years for spying.

1763 The Treaty of Paris, signed today, has ended seven years of worldwide war. Britain emerges as the leading world power, gaining both Canada and Florida and establishing its dominance in the East. France has lost all its North American possessions except two colonies along the St Lawrence, while Spain regains Louisiana, Cuba and the Philippines. Meanwhile Russia has withdrawn from the war in Europe, leaving Austria no choice but to seek peace terms with the victorious Frederick the Great of Prussia.

Johannesburg police drive 60,000 blacks out of homes

1955 Thousands of armed South African police have begun evicting 60,000 blacks from their homes in Sophiatown near Johannesburg, with bulldozers flattening the township in their wake. They are forcing the angry Africans to move to a new settlement called Meadowlands, where there are no land rights – most of the residents owned their land. The African National Congress is staging a series of protests against the all-white government's latest imposition of its racist apartheid policies.

1942 American bandleader Glenn Miller was today presented with a special pressing of his hugely popular record "Chattanooga Choo Choo" – the pressing was made of solid gold. The swing hit has officially sold a million copies, the first record ever to do so.

Scott died just 11 miles from safety

1913 Thirteen months after British polar explorer Captain Robert Scott and his men disappeared on their expedition to the South Pole, a relief party has found a snow-covered tent containing the bodies of Scott and two of his companions. Photographic plates and diaries tell the harrowing story of how Scott, Wilson, Bowers, Evans and Oates died on the journey homeward, having lost the race against Norwegian Roald Amundsen's team to be first at the Pole. Evans fell from a glacier and was killed; Oates, crippled by frostbite, stumbled out into the blizzard to give the others a better chance of reaching their ship, the *Discovery*. The last three died of starvation and cold, trapped by the storm 11 miles from a food cache and survival.

So where to?
Johannesburg blacks' name for the new South Western Townships – "Soweto" – at the height of South Africa's urban removals of blacks in 1955.

Riccio's killer meets own untimely end

1567 Lord Darnley, the second husband of Mary Queen of Scots, has been murdered. His house at Kirk o' Field was blown up with gunpowder and he was found in the grounds, strangled. He was 22. He and Mary, his first cousin, were married only 18 months ago. Mary, who inherited the throne when she was six days old, wed the French Dauphin in her teens, but he died when she was 18. The marriage to her young cousin came after negotiations failed for a political match with Don Carlos, son of the King of Spain. But the new marriage quickly soured and Mary sought comfort with her Italian secretary, David Riccio. Last year the jealous Darnley had Riccio murdered in front of the distraught Mary, who was six months pregnant with her son James, born last June. Mary then turned to the unpopular Earl of Bothwell. Scottish nobles have now accused Bothwell of Darnley's murder, and some say the beautiful young queen knew of the plan to kill her husband and may now be planning to marry the Earl.

Mandela free – at last

1990 Nelson Mandela was freed today after 26 years in jail for his opposition to South Africa's white racist regime. President F.W. de Klerk unconditionally revoked the 72-year-old black leader's life sentence for treason and sabotage. Met at the prison by his wife Winnie and a crowd of supporters, Mandela set off to address a jubilant crowd in front of Cape Town's city hall. His message was one of "peace, democracy and freedom" – but he also endorsed the African National Congress's "armed struggle". In jail, he had refused offers of freedom in exchange for renouncing violence. Mandela, a lawyer, became an ANC leader in 1949, working under Nobel Peace Prize-winner Albert Luthuli. The ANC, founded in 1912, was committed to peaceful resistance for 48 years, in spite of the brutal official response to black protest. But when white police massacred black protestors at Sharpeville in 1960, Mandela started a sabotage campaign. In jail he became the symbol of freedom in the black struggle that has now forced de Klerk's government to renounce apartheid.

I have cherished the idea of a democratic and free society in which all persons live together in harmony and with equal opportunities . . . if needs be, it is an ideal for which I am prepared to die.
Nelson Mandela
echoes the words he spoke at his trial in 1964 on his release from jail 26 years later, 1990.

1991 Soviet President Mikhail Gorbachev today sent a letter to government leaders of the Warsaw Pact nations proposing that the military structure disbands by April 1. The Warsaw Pact military alliance was formed one week after a rearmed West Germany joined NATO in 1955. The Western NATO allies are celebrating the end of the Cold War.

ALLIED VICTORS CARVE UP POST-WAR EUROPE

1945 With victory in the war with Germany virtually assured, the three allied leaders, Winston Churchill, Franklin D. Roosevelt and Joseph Stalin, have mapped out Europe's future at a secret meeting in the Black Sea resort of Yalta. The three leaders agreed that Adolf Hitler's Nazi forces must accept an unconditional surrender. Post-war Germany will be split into four occupied zones, with Russia in control of the whole of eastern Germany. A deadlock over Berlin – which will be in the Russian zone – is still to be resolved. They also planned the invasion of Japan, and Stalin agreed to declare war on Japan once Germany surrenders. After the war the old League of Nations will be replaced by a new organization to be called the United Nations. The "Big Three" leaders will meet again later this year to complete their plans for the new world body.

14 year old claims Virgin appeared

1858 A 14-year-old girl claims to have had visions of the Virgin Mary near Lourdes in south-west France. Bernadette Soubirous says she has seen the Mother of Christ 18 times in a grotto in the foothills of the Pyrenees. The Pope is reported to be interested in the authenticity of the visions and emissaries from the Vatican are travelling to Lourdes to investigate. Large numbers of believers are also hastening to the site. A spring of water at the grotto is reputed to have healing powers.

Thatcher lifts torch of Tory crusade

1975 For the first time in its 300-year history, Britain's Conservative Party has a woman leader. Margaret Thatcher defeated four rivals to succeed ex-leader Edward Heath, who lost the last election to the Labour Party. Satirists had dubbed Heath "the Grocer"; Margaret Thatcher is the daughter of a grocer, and the wife of a wealthy businessman. Mrs Thatcher, 49, has two children. She has been in parliament since 1959, and was secretary for education in the last Conservative government. A woman of strong convictions, Mrs Thatcher is deeply committed to her vision of England's future. Cutting back the socialist welfare state is a personal crusade.

1810 French emperor Napoleon I marries Marie Louise, daughter of the first emperor of Austria, Francis I.

1858 Benito Juarez is declared constitutional President of Mexico by an assembly at Vera Cruz.

1929 Pope Pius XI and the Italian government of Benito Mussolini sign the Lateran Treaty which gives the Vatican City the status of an independent sovereign state.

1949 Swedish physician Axel Munthe, famed for his best-selling autobiography *The Story of San Michele*, dies.

1976 Ice skater John Curry wins Britain's first-ever gold medal for figure skating.

1983 Dennis Nilsen is accused of murdering 14 to 16 young men at his flat in a leafy suburb of north London.

1990 James "Buster" Douglas knocks out world heavyweight boxing champion Mike Tyson in Tokyo after a controversial late count in round eight when Douglas was floored.

2001 British yachtswoman Ellen MacArthur crosses the finishing line in second place in the Vendées Globe round-the-world race after 94 days alone at sea.

BIRTHDAYS

Henry Fox Talbot 1800, British botanist and physicist best known for his pioneering techniques in photography.

Thomas Edison 1847, prolific American inventor whose "firsts" include the electric light bulb, the gramophone and motion pictures.

Joseph Mankiewicz 1909, American film director who on two separate occasions won Oscars for best screenplay and best director for the same film: *Letter to Three Wives* (1949) and *All About Eve* (1950).

Mary Quant 1934, English designer and major fashion innovator of the 1960s.

Burt Reynolds 1936, American film actor noted for his tongue-in-cheek style.

1688 A "Glorious Revolution" brings the Protestant champion William of Orange and his wife Mary to the throne of England after the Catholic king James II flees to France.

1804 German philosopher Immanuel Kant, author of the doctrine of transcendental idealism, dies.

1831 J.W. Goodrich of Boston invents the rubber galosh.

1861 British teams Sheffield and Hallam play the first inter-club football match.

1894 Death of Hans von Bulow, outstanding conductor and one-time champion of Richard Wagner.

1898 A Brighton resident becomes the first British motorist to die in a car crash.

1929 Lillie Langtry, "The Jersey Lily", British actress, socialite and one-time mistress of King Edward VII while he was Prince of Wales, dies aged 76.

1935 The airship Macon crashes in America.

1948 The ashes of Mahatma Gandhi are placed in the holy waters of the Ganges at Allahabad.

1990 Dr Carmen Lawrence becomes Premier of Western Australia, the first woman premier of an Australian state.

2002 An Iranian airliner crashes, killing 117 of the passengers on board.

BIRTHDAYS

Charles Darwin 1809, British naturalist and author of the influential book *The Origin of Species*.

Abraham Lincoln 1809, US president who was assassinated a few days after the end of the American Civil War.

George Meredith 1828, British novelist and poet, best known for his novels *The Egoist* and *The Tragic Comedians*.

Marie Lloyd 1870, British music-hall star who sang risqué songs and scandalized society with her eventful private life.

Mary Tudor executes cousin

1554 The "nine days queen", Lady Jane Grey, lost her head today at the Tower of London. She was 16. The execution was ordered by her cousin Mary Tudor, the present queen. The protestant King Edward VI had proclaimed his cousin Jane, fifth in line to the throne, as his successor above his half-sister Mary, a Catholic, since Jane would keep England beyond the reach of Catholic Spain. Jane ascended the throne in July last year with her husband Lord Guildford Dudley. Mary deposed them nine days later and condemned them to death for treason. The new queen delayed the execution, but changed her mind when Jane's father was involved in an attempted rebellion. Dudley was beheaded first, and Jane was led past his body on her way to the block. Lady Jane was beautiful and intelligent, and had ambitious plans to restore the English economy and return land to farmers dispossessed by Henry VIII.

1999 American president Bill Clinton has been cleared of all charges in his impeachment trial. Prosecutors failed to secure either vote against him in the Senate trial for perjury and obstruction of justice, despite very close voting.

No man is an island, entire of itself . . . Any man's death diminishes me, because I am involved in mankind. And therefore never send to know for whom the bell tolls; it tolls for thee.

John Donne, writing about a distant funeral bell in 1624.

Donne defies death to preach

1631 Poet and preacher Dr John Donne, the dean of St Paul's Cathedral in London, rose from his sickbed today to deliver the last of his famous sermons. A packed congregation listened enthralled as he read "Death's Duel", a brilliant discourse on death and resurrection. Later today Donne posed for a portrait at his home, wearing a funeral shroud. Donne, who is mortally ill, has long been prepared for death. "Death be not proud, though some have called thee mighty and dreadful, for thou art not so," he once wrote. His sermons and poetry rank him as an expert on the subject of death – and on that of life, and of love both sacred and profane.

Australia tastes gold fever

1851 Fortune-hunters are rushing to the town of Bathurst in the Blue Mountains in New South Wales, Australia in search of gold. Veteran prospector Edward Hargraves started it when he panned some earth on a piece of land at Summerhill Creek that looked similar to what he'd seen in California – and found gold. The greedy and the gullible are swarming in like moths to a flame, lured by the myth that you can dig up a lifetime's wealth in a day. It is true that some are earning good money. The news has reached the world and boatloads of would-be prospectors are leaving from Britain and the United States. It's every man for himself when it comes to staking a claim, and the government is to impose a licensing system to prevent conflict and disorder.

Child emperor gives up dynasty

1912 China's five-year-old boy-emperor Pu Yi listened in his court in Peking today as his weeping aunt read out a letter. He could not have understood that it was his abdication, marking the end of the 267-year rule of the Qing dynasty and 3000 years of monarchy. The Manchurian Qing tribe conquered China during the chaos following the fall of the Ming Dynasty. Their rule has declined through 70 years of foreign wars and insurrection, with 16 rebellions in the last decade. The current uprising began on October 10 when an army revolt in the south became a full-scale nationalist rebellion. The revolutionary leader Dr Sun Yat-sen was made president of the new republic last month but, to avoid civil war, he has given up the presidency to General Yuan Shih-k'ai – suspected of planning to usurp the throne.

LINDBERGH BABY KILLER GOES TO CHAIR

1935 A New Jersey jury today found Bruno Hauptmann guilty of kidnapping and murdering flying ace Charles Lindbergh's infant son three years ago. The judge sentenced him to die on the electric chair. Hauptmann is an illegal immigrant who fled from a life of crime in Germany. Lindbergh, who made the first solo flight across the Atlantic in 1927, paid a $50,000 ransom after his son was snatched, but the baby's body was found two months later. Hauptmann was caught late last year spending ransom money, and more of it was found in his cellar. There was scientific evidence that he had made the ladder used in the kidnapping, and the ransom note contained spelling mistakes Hauptmann commonly made.

Campbells kill sleeping hosts at Glencoe

1692 The chief of the Macdonald clan and 36 of his warriors were murdered in a treacherous pre-dawn attack at their Glencoe stronghold today – by their guests. Robert Campbell of Glenlyon and his 128 men were acting under English orders. They sought shelter at Glencoe two weeks ago and, following the strict code of hospitality in the Scottish Highlands, were accepted. Last night Campbell received his orders from England's Secretary of State for Scotland, Sir Robert Dalrymple of Stair: "Fall upon the Rebells the McDonalds of Glenco and put all to the sword under 70." At 5 am the Campbells turned on their sleeping hosts. Clan chief MacIain was slain in his bed; 36 of his men and a number of women and children were killed. The rest of the clan escaped into the hills. The Macdonald chief's supposed crime was that he had not signed allegiance to the new king, William of Orange. In fact he had signed, though late, having been delayed by blizzards. Dalrymple deliberately suppressed the fact, wanting to make an example of a Jacobite clan for supporting the exiled King James II. It is suspected that King William knew about the unjust and murderous plot.

Milosevic trial begins in The Hague

2002 The trial of Slobodan Milosevic, the former Yugoslav president accused of genocide and war crimes over a period of 10 years in the Balkans, has begun in The Hague. Milosevic is the first former president to be charged with genocide, crimes against humanity and war crimes in the fighting which followed the dissolution of Yugoslavia. The trial at the International Criminal Tribunal for the former Yugoslavia is seen as the most important since Nazi leaders went on trial after World War II. Mr Milosevic is charged with presiding over the killings of nearly 250,000 non-Serbs in Croatia, Bosnia-Hercegovina and Kosovo. "Today as never before we see international justice in action," said the chief prosecutor, Carla Del Ponte, at the opening of the case. Milosevic refuses to recognise the legitimacy of the UN tribunal or the charges against him, and has not appointed any lawyers to defend him. However, one of his legal advisors, who met him for three hours, said he thought Mr Milosevic would make a statement.

1969 Human eggs removed from women volunteers have been fertilized in a test-tube at Cambridge University in England. Scientists R. G. Edwards and B. D. Bavister, working with specialist obstetrician P. Steptoe, found that when the eggs were mixed with male sperm in a nutrient solution, almost a third of them were fertilized. There is still a long way to go before such fertilized eggs could be reimplanted in a woman's womb for a normal birth. The scientists warn that the technique could produce deformities but the discovery will doubtless bring hope to many childless couples.

What's the Saudi national anthem?
"Onward Christian Soldier".
Joke circulating amongst US troops in Saudi Arabia during the Gulf War with Iraq, 1991.

Tyson loses crown in shock ko

1990 Boxer James "Buster" Douglas was today recognized as the new world heavyweight champion after knocking out Mike Tyson in Tokyo two nights ago in one of boxing's biggest-ever upsets. Douglas floored Tyson for the count in the 10th round, but Tyson had knocked Douglas down two rounds earlier – for a count of eight, Douglas said; but others claimed it was 12, and the title was frozen. Today both the world authorities ruled that Douglas had been down for only eight, and he gets the crown. Tyson was only 20 when he won the title in 1986, the youngest world heavyweight champion ever.

1542 The faithless wife of English king Henry VIII, Catherine Howard, is beheaded for treason.

1826 A rise in liquor sales is forecast as the American Society for the Promotion of Temperance is formed.

1866 The James Younger gang robs a Missouri bank of $60,000.

1883 Death of Richard Wagner, German composer whose masterpiece is *Der Ring des Nibelungen*.

1917 Dutch spy and *femme fatale* Mata Hari is arrested by the French.

1941 The wonder drug penicillin is used on a human for the first time – a policeman from Oxford, England.

1943 British motor manufacturer and philanthropist William Nuffield establishes a charitable institution called the Nuffield Foundation.

1958 British suffragette Dame Christabel Pankhurst dies.

1960 The French test their first atomic bomb in the Sahara.

1971 South Vietnamese troops aided by US aircraft and artillery enter Laos.

1971 US President Spiro Agnew hits three spectators with his golf ball during the Bob Hope Desert Classic tournament.

1991 Germany's Red Army Faction carry out a gun attack on the US Embassy in Bonn, claiming a link with the Gulf War.

BIRTHDAYS

Feodor Chaliapin 1873, Russian opera singer famed for his rendering of the bass part of Boris in Mussorgsky's opera *Boris Godunov*.

Georges Simenon 1903, Belgian crime novelist and creator of Maigret.

George Segal 1934, American film actor and star of many comedies, including *A Touch of Class* with Glenda Jackson.

Peter Gabriel 1950, British pop musician and former singer with the group Genesis, influential in the popularizing of "World Music".

FEBRUARY 14

1400 Mystery surrounds the death of English monarch Richard II at Pontefract Castle.

1797 British naval forces under Admiral John Jervis and Captain Horatio Nelson defeat the Spanish fleet off Cape St Vincent.

1852 Great Ormond Street Children's Hospital opens in London.

1876 American inventor Elisha Gray files a caveat with the US patent office announcing his intention to file a patent for a telephone – just a few hours after Alexander Graham Bell files just such a patent.

1906 Fifty-four people are arrested as suffragettes fight a pitched battle with police outside the British Parliament.

1933 Oxford students declare that they would not fight for "King and Country".

1973 An Israeli fighter shoots down a Libyan passenger plane over the Sinai Desert, killing 74 passengers and crew.

1975 Death of P. G. Wodehouse, creator of the incompetent Bertie Wooster and his exceedingly knowing butler, Jeeves.

1979 The US ambassador to Afghanistan is kidnapped in Kabul.

1984 British ice dance partners Torvill and Dean win the gold at the Winter Olympics in Sarajevo.

BIRTHDAYS

Thomas Malthus 1766, British clergyman and economist, famous for his theories of population.

Christopher Scholes 1819, American inventor of the typewriter.

Carl Bernstein 1944, American journalist who, with Bob Woodward, exposed the Watergate scandal.

Alan Parker 1944, British film director whose films include *Bugsy Malone* and *Midnight Express*.

Kevin Keegan 1951, British footballer, for many seasons a leading Liverpool and England international player.

ELEGANT DRESDEN DESTROYED BY BOMBS

1944 Dresden, one of Germany's most graceful cities, has been destroyed in a firestorm by the most destructive bombing raid of the war. Nearly 2000 RAF and US bombers laden with high explosives and incendiaries pounded the city mercilessly in three waves over 14 hours. Dresden was considered safe since it was not a war target, and was crammed with refugees. At least 130,000 civilians died in the raid, and many more were injured. Most of Dresden's public buildings were themselves art treasures, including superb examples of 17th- and 18th-century baroque and rococo architecture, while the city's famous galleries housed major collections of the Italian, Flemish and Dutch masters. Today Dresden is a pile of smoking rubble. Air Chief Marshall Arthur "Bomber" Harris, head of RAF Bomber Command, is facing a storm of criticism over the raid, both on humane grounds and strategically – senior Allied planners wanted to attack military targets. But Harris claims his "terror bombing" tactics will destroy the German will to fight.

HAWAIIAN SPEAR KILLS CAPTAIN COOK

1779 The explorer Captain James Cook is dead, killed by a native spear in Hawaii. Cook was a peaceful man, not given to brutalizing the native peoples he encountered on his epic voyages – but some of his men had started trouble with a local chief. The villagers retaliated by stealing the ship's cutter. Cook took 12 armed marines ashore to take a hostage to swap for the cutter. But the villagers had never seen guns and were not afraid of Cook's men. They attacked, felling the Captain.

Valentine's Day – but no love lost

1929 "Bugs" Moran's men were setting up an illicit beerhall on North Side this morning – the police in Moran's pay had not warned them of any plans for a raid. Five men, three in police uniform, burst into the garage, lined the seven gangsters up against the wall and opened fire. The five "police" were rival mobsters, probably from "Scarface" Al Capone's gang. Hundreds of mobsters have died in Chicago's gangland wars as Capone bids for control of the bootlegging trade, prostitution and protection rackets said to earn him $100 million a year. Almost half Chicago's police force is now under investigation for corruption.

1989 Iran's religious leader Ayatollah Khomeini has condemned the Anglo-Indian writer Salman Rushdie to death for blasphemy in his book *The Satanic Verses*. All those involved in its publication who were aware of its contents are sentenced to death also. The book has provoked uproar in the Islamic world. In London, Rushdie today cancelled an American tour and went into hiding under police guard, while publishers Viking Penguin have stepped up security. Ironically more people will now want to read the book.

Love notes pose postal problem

1822 Britain's postal services have had to employ extra mail sorters to make sure that the thousands of St Valentine's Day messages lovers have sent to each other arrive on time today. The quaint fashion is growing more popular by the year: today is the day to affirm your love, perhaps with an anonymous note, or written in the secret language lovers share. Nobody knows how the custom arose. It may have started in 1477, when a Norfolk woman sent a note to her lover saying: "To my right wellbeloved Voluntyne." There seem to have been two St Valentines, both third-century Italian priests, both martyred; before that came a pagan fertility festival the Romans celebrated in mid-February. Or it could simply be that love is in the air today – it's an old English belief that this is the day birds choose their mates.

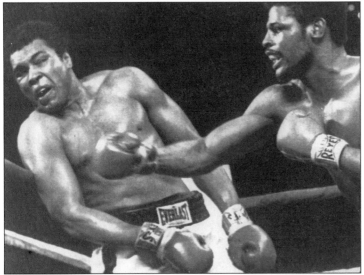

AGEING ALI LOSES TITLE

1978 Muhammad Ali lost his world heavyweight title to Leon Spinks in a 15-round decision at Las Vegas tonight. Ali first won the title in 1964, but was stripped of it for refusing to fight in Vietnam. He started fighting again in 1970 and won the title a second time when he beat the fearsome George Foreman in a sensational upset in 1974. Ali is 36, and after tonight's defeat punters are saying he is past it – but he is a superb athlete with enormous staying power. Spinks is only the third fighter ever to beat Ali. Joe Frazier did it in 1971, but Ali later beat him twice. Ken Norton defeated Ali in 1973, but Ali won the return bout. Now Ali wants a return match against Spinks. If Ali wins, he'll be the only man to hold the title three times.

Remember the Maine, *to hell with Spain!*
The warmongering slogan in William Randolph Hearst's *New York Journal* on the sinking of the USS *Maine* in Havana today, 1898.

He floats like an anchor, stings like a moth.
Sports writer **Ray Gandolf** updates Muhammad Ali's line "Float like a butterfly, sting like a bee" after Ali lost his title tonight, 1978.

FAREWELL TO BOBS AND TANNERS

1971 Britain has gone decimal, leaving millions of older citizens brought up with pennies, tanners, bobs, florins and half-crowns to fumble with unfamiliar coins inelegantly known as "p", short for "new pence" – as in "five p", which equals 12 old pennies (or one old shilling). If this all sounds confusing, that's because it is. New pence are more than twice the value of old pennies, and critics say the awkward conversion scale will mean higher prices and hidden inflation. But the government claims the changeover is going very smoothly.

Britain remembers wartime courage of George VI

1952 England's King George VI was buried today at Windsor after a state funeral. More than 300,000 silently paid their respects as his coffin lay in state at Westminster Hall in London. His brother Edward VIII's abdication in 1936 forced him to take the throne he had never wanted. Wartime leadership was thrust upon him, but he won wide affection and tremendous respect for his dedication, often risking his life on morale-building visits to troops in the war zones. The eldest of his two daughters is the new queen of England, Elizabeth II.

Police and pickets clash at Wapping

1986 London police in riot gear fought violently tonight with 5000 angry union pickets trying to stop distribution of the *Sunday Times* and *News of the World* newspapers. Australian press baron Rupert Murdoch moved the papers to the new computerized plant at Wapping in London's docklands to outflank the 2000 print union strikers who had brought production to a halt. The papers are now being produced by managers and journalists, and Wapping is virtually under siege.

Battleship blast edges US and Cuba close to war

1898 The US battleship *Maine* exploded and sank in Havana harbour today with the loss of 260 lives. She had been sent to Havana to protect American citizens during the current Cuban rebellion against Spanish rule. The US says today's tragic explosion was caused by a floating mine, but Spanish authorities say the ship's bunkers caught fire. The incident has brought the two countries to the brink of war. The American press is holding Spain responsible and demanding revenge. William Randolph Hearst's *New York Journal* is deliberately whipping up pro-war feelings: Hearst has agitated for US intervention in the brutal Spanish suppression of Cuba's peasant rebellion, and last week published a stolen letter in which Spain's envoy criticized President McKinley. In a now-famous cable to a cameraman sent to Havana, he promised to provide the war himself. Spain, meanwhile, is hastily trying to withdraw from Cuba without loss of face.

FEBRUARY 15

1882 New Zealand cargo ship *Dunedin* sails with the first consignment of frozen meat for the British market.

1922 The Permanent Court of International Justice holds its first session in the Hague.

1933 US president Franklin D. Roosevelt escapes an assassination attempt by Italian-born anarchist Giuseppe Zangara.

1942 Singapore falls to Japanese forces who capture thousands of British troops.

1944 The Allies begin to bomb the German-held strategic position of Monte Cassino in Italy.

1945 British forces reach the River Rhine in their advance to Berlin.

1970 Death of Lord Dowding, the architect of British Fighter Command's victory over the German Luftwaffe during the Second World War.

1974 A battle rages on the Golan Heights between Israeli and Syrian forces.

1982 Eighty-four die as a storm wrecks an oil rig off the coast of Newfoundland.

BIRTHDAYS

Galileo Galilei 1564, Italian mathematician, astronomer and physicist.

Louis XV 1710, French king whose weak rule and tendency to vacillation did much to foster the conditions for the French Revolution after his death.

Jeremy Bentham 1748, English philosopher and pioneer of utilitarianism, an ethical doctrine which held that the best action is one that will result in the greatest happiness and least pain for the greatest number of people.

Charles Tiffany 1812, American jeweller and founder of the famous New York store.

Ernest Shackleton 1874, British explorer who nearly reached the South Pole in 1909 and died on his fourth expedition to Antarctica.

Claire Bloom 1931, British film and stage actress.

Coco kills the corset

1923 Let women rejoice – the corset is dead. That is the clear message of the new haute couture collection shown in Paris today by the High Priestess of Style, Coco Chanel. Coco's New Woman of the Twenties is young and free, and will have no truck with the fussy fashions still lingering from the last century. Gone forever are the corsets, ruffles and cloying drapes, giving way to bobbed hair, low heels, shorter skirts and sweaters – and freedom. Coco Chanel opened a milliner's shop in Paris in 1909, and five years later she added clothes to her line. She sees fashion as architecture: "It's a matter of proportions," she says. Her new clothes are classics – simple and chaste, with an austere, youthful look.

1834 Lionel Lukin, the British inventor of the lifeboat, dies.

1887 The jubilee of British queen Victoria is celebrated in India with the freeing of 25,000 prisoners.

1932 Eamon de Valera's Fianna Fail party sweeps to power in the Irish general election.

1940 Hundreds of British merchant seamen are freed as the German auxiliary cruiser *Altmark* runs aground in a Norwegian fjord after being stalked by HMS *Cossack*.

1945 US forces capture Bataan in the Philippines.

1960 USS *Triton* begins her epic underwater voyage around the world, the first nuclear submarine to undertake such a journey.

1972 A miners' strike plunges Britain into darkness as electricity supplies are cut.

1983 Arson is suspected as fire devastates South Australia, leaving 8500 homeless.

1989 Harley Street specialist Dr Raymond Crockett resigns after allegations of his involvement in a "kidneys-for-sale" racket in which organs were transplanted from needy Turks to wealthy patients.

1989 The police announce that the Pan Am plane crash at Lockerbie in Scotland is the result of a bomb.

1991 During the Gulf War, two Scud missiles hit Israel.

BIRTHDAYS

Robert Flaherty 1884, US documentary film maker and former explorer whose classic *Nanook of the North* is regarded as the first significant documentary ever made.

Sir Geraint Evans 1922, Welsh operatic baritone.

John Schlesinger 1926, British film director whose films include *Midnight Cowboy* and *Sunday, Bloody Sunday*.

John McEnroe 1959, American tennis player who is famed as much for his fiery temper as his fine stroke play.

Americans go nylon crazy

1939 "Hurry while stocks last!" say the shops – and hordes of American women are doing just that. The new kind of women's stockings that went on sale today are causing a shopping frenzy. These stockings are just too good to be true: sheerer than pure silk, and stronger, easy to wash and dry – and, unlike silk, they're so cheap anyone can afford them. The stockings are made of nylon, the miracle material patented by the Du Pont Company two years ago. Nylon is entirely artificial, a polymer made from chemicals. It is extremely tough, can be made into sheets, moulded to any shape or spun into the finest yarn. The man who discovered it, chemist W. H. Carothers, died soon after it was patented and never saw it made into a useful product. The Nylon toothbrush went on sale the next year.

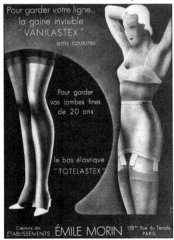

Pour garder votre ligne...
la gaine invisible
"VANILASTEX"
sans coutures

Pour garder
vos jambes fines
de 20 ans

le bas élastique
"TOTELASTEX"

Créations des ÉTABLISSEMENTS ÉMILE MORIN 158ᵗᵉ, Rue du Temple PARIS

Amin secret police murder Archbishop

1977 Ugandan dictator Idi Amin has murdered the country's Archbishop, the Most Reverend Janani Luwum. The Archbishop and two cabinet ministers were arrested at an opposition rally in Kampala by troops. Amin announced today that they had died in a car crash, but there is no doubt that he was murdered by Amin's notorious State Research Bureau secret police. Tens of thousands of people are known to have been murdered and many terribly tortured since Amin's coup in 1971.

SHOULD GULF WAR GO NUCLEAR?

1991 One in three people in a poll of seven of Europe's largest cities, published today, wants the allies to use nuclear weapons if Saddam Hussein uses chemical weapons in the Gulf War over Iraq's invasion of Kuwait. It is well known that Iraq has chemical weapons, and Saddam says he will use them in the ground war that now seems imminent. Iraq is also thought to have nuclear capabilities, but nuclear installations were an early target for the allied bombers. However, two more Iraqi Scud missiles hit Israel today, despite continuing allied raids on the Scud launching sites. One fell in the Negev desert near Israel's Dimona nuclear reactor. A broadcast from Baghdad announced that Scuds are targeted on the reactor.

"Ivan the Terrible" finally faces Israeli court

1987 John Demanjanuk, or "Ivan the Terrible", a former car worker who lived for 40 years in the US, has gone on trial in Jerusalem accused of the murder of hundreds of Jews at the Nazi death camp of Treblinka. Demanjanuk insists he is not guilty. "I'm not a human monster," he told the jury. Prosecution witnesses told how he strangled their relatives with his bare hands. He was extradited from the US, and is the second Nazi to be tried in Israel after Adolph Eichmann.

1659 A new way of paying money without using either coinage or a letter of credit was used in England today when Mr Nicholas Vanacker signed a "cheque" to a creditor, noting the sum owed. Creditors can present such notes at a goldsmith's or bank for payment. British bankers hope this will help England to catch up with the more sophisticated techniques used in Italy.

1959 Fidel Castro, 32, has been sworn in as the youngest-ever leader of Cuba just weeks after his rebel guerilla army drove the hated dictator Fulgencio Batista into exile. Cuba's constitution was amended to allow such a young leader to take office. Castro's administration has been well received internationally.

Chinese attack former allies in Vietnam

1979 Months of border skirmishes erupted into war today as Chinese forces poured into Vietnam. China had backed North Vietnam during the Vietnam War, but since Hanoi's victory in 1975 Vietnam has turned to the Soviet Union, causing tensions with China. Last month Vietnam invaded Cambodia and drove out Pol Pot's murderous Khmer Rouge regime – which China supports. There is rising panic among Vietnam's ethnic Chinese population as rumours of anti-Chinese purges spread, and thousands of refugees are fleeing to China or taking to small, crowded boats for a perilous voyage to freedom.

CND AIMS TO BAN THE BOMB

1958 Spurred by the threat of American nuclear weapons on British soil, a new pressure group was formed in London today to demand that Britain "Ban the Bomb". The Campaign for Nuclear Disarmament chose veteran peace campaigner Bertrand Russell as its president. CND is demanding that Britain take the initiative in stopping the arms race and abandon nuclear weapons – unilaterally if need be.

> *It is a great shock at the age of five or six to find that in a world of Gary Coopers you are the Indian.*
> **James Baldwin**, black US writer, in a speech at the Cambridge Union, 1965.

Mongol leader was ruthless but loved art

1405 Timur the Lame, the Mongol conqueror who built pyramids of skulls all over Central Asia, is dead – laid low by disease during an expedition to conquer China. He was 68. Timur (called Tamerlane in Europe) carved out a vast empire by the sword, stretching from Mongolia to India, from Baghdad to Egypt – although he was crippled in his youth and often had to be carried into battle on a litter. Claiming direct descent from Genghis Khan, he conquered his native Transoxiana (Uzbekistan) 35 years ago, and made Samarkand his capital. Then he attacked all his neighbours in turn. His terms were simple: surrender or death – and hesitation meant mass beheadings. A brilliant tactician, Timur routed the Golden Horde, conquered the Turks, Anatolians, Mamelukes, Arabs and Persians, and sacked Delhi, Damascus and Baghdad. He filled Samarkand with looted art treasures – for Timur loved art, and was a philosopher who impressed the great minds of his time, even though he was illiterate. His four sons now inherit the empire.

Geronimo dies with honour

1909 Geronimo, the legendary Apache warrior chief, died today at his ranch on an Oklahoma reservation, far from the homeland he fought to defend. He was 80. He cleverly and fiercely resisted white settler incursions in the Chiricahua Apache lands in Arizona and New Mexico. After the Chiricahua were forced on to a bleak desert reservation in 1876, Geronimo repeatedly broke out on hit-and-run guerrilla raids, and in 1881 led the last Apache uprising after US troops slew an Apache holy man. He finally surrendered in 1886 and took to ranching. The great warrior was selling Apache souvenirs at the Louisiana Purchase Exposition five years ago, and a year later he rode in President Roosevelt's inaugural procession.

1968 The great French Alpine skier Jean-Claude Killy has won all three men's gold medals at the Winter Olympics in Grenoble, France. He is only the second man to do so, following Austrian skier Toni Sailer's triple gold win in Italy in 1956. Jean-Claude Killy won the World Championship combined titles in 1965 and 1966 and the World Championship last year, proving him to be one of the greatest downhill skiers of all time.

1855 The imperial Chinese army finally ousts the Small Sword Triad gang from Shanghai with the help of French forces.

1856 Death of Heinrich Heine, German poet, writer and revolutionary sympathizer, author of *Buch der Lieder* and *Romanzero*.

1880 Tsar Alexander II narrowly escapes an assassination attempt by Russian Nihilists as a bomb explodes in the Winter Palace in St Petersburg.

1883 The Vacant/Engaged toilet door sign is patented by Mr Ashwell of Herne Hill, London.

1962 After the longest murder trial in British legal history, James Hanratty is found guilty of the murder of Michael Gregston in a layby on the A6 and is sentenced to hang.

1972 The German Volkswagen Beetle outsells the US Ford Model-T with over 15 million cars sold.

1982 Crackdown in Poland as General Jaruzelski imposes martial law and thousands are arrested.

1982 Death of Lee Strasburg, founder of the New York Actors' Studio where he developed Stanislavsky's theory of acting as the "method" approach.

1982 Death of Jazz pianist and composer Thelonius Monk, who was influential in the development of "bop".

BIRTHDAYS

Andrew "Banjo" Paterson 1864, Australian poet and journalist and author of the popular anthem "Waltzing Matilda".

Marian Anderson 1902, American contralto and the first black singer to perform on stage at the Metropolitan Opera House in New York.

Barry Humphries 1934, Australian entertainer and creator of Dame Edna Everidge and Les Patterson.

Alan Bates 1934, British stage and film actor whose notable successes on celluloid include *Butley*, *Far from the Madding Crowd* and *The Go-Between*.

1455 Death of Fra Angelico (Giovanni da Fiesole), Florentine painter and Dominican friar.

1478 George, Duke of Clarence, is drowned in a butt of wine in the Tower of London.

1855 Russian autocrat and precipitator of the Crimean War, Tsar Nicholas I, dies.

1876 A direct telegraph link is established between Britain and New Zealand.

1933 Death of James "Gentleman Jim" Corbett, US prizefighter and world champion from 1892 and 1897.

1948 The Fianna Fail party under Eamon de Valera is defeated in the Irish election.

1967 The father of the A-bomb, American physicist Robert Oppenheimer, dies.

1990 Demonstrators storm the headquarters of Romania's provisional government and demand the resignation of President Ion Iliescu and Prime Minister Petre Roman.

1991 The US assault ship *Tripoli* and the guided missile cruiser *Princeton* are damaged by mines in the Persian Gulf during the Gulf War.

BIRTHDAYS

Mary Tudor 1517, English queen known as "Bloody Mary" because of her relentless persecution of the Protestants.

Niccolò Paganini 1784, Italian virtuoso violin player and composer whose superlative skills inspired both Franz Liszt and Robert Schumann.

Milos Forman 1932, Czech-born American film director perhaps best known for his Oscar-winning film *One Flew Over the Cuckoo's Nest*, starring Jack Nicholson.

John Travolta 1954, American film actor who made his name in the hit film musicals *Saturday Night Fever* and *Grease*.

Yoko Ono 1933, Japanese-American artist, writer and performer, and second wife of John Lennon.

A LIFE OF GENIUS

1564 Michelangelo Buonarotti, the artistic paragon of the Renaissance Age and Italy's finest creative genius, has died in Rome at the advanced age of 89. He was still working at the end. Michelangelo was equally at ease with sculpture, painting, architecture, even poetry, but his first love was for marble and the chisel. The *Pietà* and the colossal *David*, both carved when he was in his twenties, are masterpieces, although the extraordinary frescoes of the Book of Genesis that adorn the ceiling of the Sistine Chapel are arguably his greatest work. They were commissioned by Pope Julius II, and took four years to complete. Twenty years later he returned to the Sistine Chapel to paint the famous *Last Judgement* on the wall behind the altar for Pope Clement VII. The sack of Rome and the destruction of the Florentine Republic left Michelangelo disillusioned, and his later works show a deep spiritual sorrow. His last sculpture, a second *Pietà*, was intended for his own tomb. He mutilated it in a fit of dejection, and never finished it. The figures are as powerful as ever, but filled with suffering – and with a passionate faith. It is an inspired portrait of the dead Christ, yet to rise again.

Too much work kills Luther

1546 Martin Luther, the father of the reformation, has died at his birthplace in Eisleben, Germany, at the age of 63, worn out by overwork. When he was 22 Luther was almost killed by lightning, and joined an Augustinian monastery. In 1511 he was appointed professor of scripture at Wittenberg. Luther's dedication to the common man brought his teachings into increasing conflict with the Roman Catholic church, and in 1521 he was excommunicated. He refused to recant, and sought refuge at Wittenberg. The elector Frederick III of Saxony refused to send him to Rome for execution. Luther set about reforming the church in the German states, abolishing confession and private mass, abandoning monasteries and allowing priests to marry. He married a former nun, and they raised six children. He also brought the Bible within reach of ordinary people, translating it into everyday German. He lived to see most of northern Europe abandon Rome for the new Protestant churches.

1930 An American astronomer, Clyde Tombaugh, today discovered a new planet, to be named Pluto after the Lord of Hades in Greek myth. Pluto is the Sun's ninth planet, and the smallest of them – it is so faint it can hardly be seen even with the most powerful telescopes. It is 3.7 billion miles from the Sun, 40 times as far as the Earth – a cold, dark, lifeless place.

South Africa tries to curb TV crews

1986 In a bid to muzzle international outrage over the brutal tactics it is using to suppress black rebellion, South Africa's white government has barred foreign television crews from filming "disturbances" in the black townships. The police say last weekend's bout of violence in Alexandra township near Johannesburg left 19 blacks killed in battles against the security forces. However protesters say four times as many were killed, and hundreds were wounded. The new press curbs do not yet affect foreign newspapermen, but correspondents fear they may soon have to face military censorship.

Unknown preacher writes masterpiece

1678 An itinerant English tinker and preacher with hardly any formal education has written a book that is being hailed as a masterpiece of English prose and human insight. John Bunyan, a 50-year-old Baptist, published the first part of his *Pilgrim's Progress* today. It is both an allegory of the inner journey from sin to salvation and a satire on life. Bunyan writes with a strength and direct simplicity that tells of experience more than mere theory; he is a field preacher who knows little of pulpits, charming simple folk face-to-face with his message of salvation for Everyman. Bunyan has spent 12 years in jail for preaching without a licence and for nonconformism, and has written 10 books in his cell.

General FRONTISPIECE to BUNYAN's Whole WORKS, with Notes, &c.

An Allegorical Representation of Mr JOHN BUNYAN, Late Minister of the Gospel and Pastor of a Congregation at Bedford

SPINNING ROTORS LIFT NEW CRAFT

1921 Etienne Oehmichen, a French engineer, has built a helicopter with two huge rotors powered by a mere 25-horsepower motor – and today it made a successful test flight in Paris. Oehmichen's secret is the craft's lightweight construction – it weighs only 220 pounds (100 kg). Helicopters built by other pioneers have been much too heavy. Though Oehmichen's helicopter takes off successfully, he admits he does not yet know how to keep it stable, nor can he control its direction.

Cod war: chips are down

1976 Iceland broke off diplomatic relations with Britain today in a further episode of the "cod war" that soured relations between the two countries four years ago. Conflict with Britain broke out in 1958 when Iceland extended its territorial waters from 3 to 12 nautical miles (4.8 to 19.2 nautical km) to protect its cod-fishing grounds. Britain finally recognized the 12-mile limit in 1961. In 1972 Iceland extended the limit to 50 miles (80 km). British fishermen took no notice until an Icelandic gunboat sank two British trawlers, starting a sporadic "war" which lasted a year. Last month an Icelandic gunboat rammed the Royal Navy frigate *Andromeda*, which was protecting British trawlers within the 50-mile limit. Following today's breakdown in relations, Britain is sending a fourth warship to the area.

1991 The USSR's two most powerful men are locked in a head to head power struggle. Boris Yeltsin, the president of the Russian Federation, today called on Soviet president Mikhail Gorbachev to resign. Speaking on television, Yeltsin said Gorbachev "has brought the country to dictatorship" in his hunger for "absolute personal power". As was to be expected Yeltsin's speech has provoked a furious backlash from his rival.

1861 Tsar Alexander II today signed a proclamation setting free 20 million serfs – almost a third of Russia's population. But the emancipation has strings attached: to become owners of the land they till, serfs must pay a redemption tax to the government and a fee to their former landlords. Very few have the means to do so.

Vital Dardanelles under attack

1915 A Franco-British fleet today began shelling Turkish fortifications along the strategic Dardanelles waterway in a bid to defeat Turkey and reopen the critical Black Sea supply route to Russia. The Russians desperately need war supplies from Britain and France, who in turn need the Ukraine's grain. Sixteen allied battleships are bombarding the Turkish forts at long range, for fear of mines. The big guns are being directed by spotter aircraft from the new aircraft carrier HMS *Ark Royal*.

Corn "flakes" for breakfast

1906 A new kind of "instant" breakfast went on sale in the US today, backed by an expensive advertising campaign. The Battle Creek Toasted Cornflake Company of Michigan is selling boxes of twice-baked wheat flakes – just add milk and sugar, and they're ready to eat. The company's founder, Will K. Kellogg, helped to develop the "new" flakes 30 years ago with his elder brother, Dr John H. Kellogg, at Dr Kellogg's sanitarium at Battle Creek. Dr Kellogg, a Seventh Day Adventist, used the flaked cereals as a vegetarian health food for patients with mental illnesses. He also claimed the flakes would help to curb the sex drive – but the advertisements his brother Will launched today failed to mention that.

1800 Napoleon Bonaparte proclaims himself First Consul of the newly established French dictatorship.

1855 Bread riots break out in the British city of Liverpool.

1897 Charles Blondin, the Frenchman who tightrope-walked his way across the Niagara Falls, dies.

1897 Mrs Hoodless of Ontario, Canada, founds the Women's Institute.

1909 Keen big-game hunter US president Theodore Roosevelt calls for a world conference on conservation.

1914 British explorer Campbell Besley announces in New York his discovery of lost Inca cities.

1937 Italian forces begin the pillage of Addis Ababa, capital of Ethiopia.

1942 The Japanese air force bombs the Australian city of Darwin.

1951 Nobel prize-winning French writer André Gide, author of *The Immoralist* and *The Vatican Cellars*, dies.

1959 Britain, Greece and Turkey guarantee the independence of the island of Cyprus.

BIRTHDAYS

Nicolas Copernicus 1473, Polish astronomer who propounded the theory of the earth and other planets revolving round the sun.

Adelina Patti 1843, Italian coloratura soprano with a reputation for high Cs and high fees.

Merle Oberon 1911, British film actress whose many films include *The Scarlet Pimpernel*, *Wuthering Heights* and *A Song to Remember*.

Carson McCullers 1917, American writer whose works include *The Heart is a Lonely Hunter* and *The Ballad of the Sad Café*.

Lee Marvin 1924, American film actor with a gravelly voice who specialized in tough guy roles.

Holly Johnson 1960, lead singer of the pop group Frankie Goes to Hollywood.

1513 Pope Julius II, patron of Michelangelo and Raphael, dies.

1653 Martin van Tromp's Dutch fleet is defeated off the coast at Portsmouth by the English fleet of Admiral Robert Blake.

1677 Death of Benedict Spinoza, Dutch philosopher of Jewish parentage, whose equation of God and nature was furiously attacked by Christian scholars.

1790 Holy Roman Emperor Josef II, whose sweeping reforms provoked rebellion in Belgium, Hungary and elsewhere, dies.

1811 Austria declares itself bankrupt.

1938 British Foreign Secretary Anthony Eden resigns over Prime Minister Neville Chamberlain's decision to hold talks with the Italian Fascist dictator Benito Mussolini.

1972 Influential US journalist Walter Winchell, who wrote for *The New York Mirror* between 1929 and 1969, dies.

1985 Contraceptives go on sale in the Irish Republic for the first time.

1997 Death of Deng Xiaoping, China's reformist and paramount leader, aged 92, three years after his retirement.

2001 Foot and mouth disease hits the UK for the first time in 20 years.

BIRTHDAYS

Voltaire 1694, French man of letters, philosopher, scientist and moralist who waged a lifelong campaign against intolerance and injustice.

Dame Marie Rambert 1888, British ballerina and founder of her own company, the Ballet Rambert.

Robert Altman 1925, American film director who sprang to prominence with the film *M*A*S*H*.

Sidney Poitier 1927, American film actor and the first black actor to win an Oscar, for *Lilies of the Field*.

Jimmy Greaves 1940, British footballer and later successful television commentator.

Glenn spins round the world

1962 Astronaut John Glenn circled the Earth three times in under five hours today to become the first American to orbit the planet. After 10 postponements because of bad weather and technical problems, the US Marine Corps pilot's flight aboard the tiny Friendship-7 capsule went without a hitch from blast-off at Cape Canaveral to splashdown in the Atlantic near Puerto Rico. During the flight a warning light at mission control indicated the capsule's vital heat-shield was loose, but re-entry to the earth's atmosphere went smoothly. This is the third manned flight in the Mercury

programme, but the US still lags behind the USSR in the space race – Yuri Gagarin was the first man in space in April last year. Glenn, who was a pilot in both World War II and the Korean War, said he felt "excellent" after the flight.

Mountbatten final viceroy for India

1947 Britain's Labour government has given Lord Louis Mountbatten the task of supervising a peaceful transition to independence for India after centuries of British rule. The government also announced that Britain will leave India by June next year. As the last viceroy, Mountbatten will try to negotiate agreement between the divided Hindus and Muslims, whose leaders are said to be considering partitioning the country. Mountbatten, a great-grandson of Queen Victoria, was Supreme Allied Commander for Southeast Asia during the War and recaptured Burma from Japan. His appointment is controversial: his predecessor, Field Marshall Lord Wavell, was dismissed from his post and opposition leader Winston Churchill (who had refused to free India) has demanded an explanation.

Last of the Moguls

1707 Aurangzeb, the sixth and perhaps the last of the great Mogul emperors of India, died today at 88, his empire crumbling about him. Aurangzeb seized the throne at Agra from his father, Shah Jahan, 49 years ago, killing two of his brothers and jailing the third to secure the succession. He moved his capital to Delhi, and his rule was stable until his third son backed a revolt by the Rajputs – the Hindu warriors of Rajasthan. Aurangzeb was at continuous war with the Hindu kingdoms ever after. His military excesses have brought the empire close to bankruptcy, his subjects taxed to starvation. He destroyed hundreds of Hindu temples, and his religious persecutions will leave a long and bitter legacy.

King of Scotland murdered in sleep

1437 Scotland's King James I has been assassinated by a group of nobles seeking to place a rival on the throne. He was 42. James was staying at the Dominican friary at Perth. His assassins, led by Sir Robert Graham, have failed in their plans since James's son is to succeed him. As a boy the late King sought safety in France, but was captured by the English en route and imprisoned for 18 years. While a prisoner he married Joan, a cousin of England's King Henry V. After assuming Scotland's throne in 1424 James executed many of the powerful nobility to establish control.

1915 Disregarding the Great War that is tearing Europe apart, San Francisco is staging a world fair at which several of the warring states are exhibiting. The Panama-Pacific Exhibition celebrates the opening of the Panama Canal between the Atlantic and Pacific Oceans, saving a 7000-mile (11,300 km) journey round Cape Horn. The canal was completed 15 months ago when President Wilson pressed a button, detonating the last area of land away.

Outer Space is no place for a person of good breeding.
Violet Bonham Carter, English writer and politician.

Nixon in China

1972 US President Richard Nixon landed in Peking today, extending the hand of friendship to Communist China. Speaking at a state banquet in the Great Hall of the People, Nixon invited Prime Minister Chou En-lai to join him in a new "long march" to world peace. Nixon and national security adviser Dr Henry Kissinger, who arranged the visit, were met by Chou En-lai at the airport. They then visited Chairman Mao Tse-tung in the Forbidden City. Nixon's visit reverses the hardline US policy on communist China – it is the first exploratory step towards full diplomatic recognition of the regime which is backing the other side in the Vietnam War. A major stumbling-block is US support for the Nationalist regime in Taiwan: Peking insists that the US must choose between the two Chinas before relations can be normalized between Peking and Washington.

GLORIOUS FONTEYN DIES IN PANAMA

1991 Dame Margot Fonteyn has died in Panama, aged 73. To millions the world over she was the epitome of the prima ballerina. Fonteyn made her debut in 1934 at London's Sadler's Wells. Her talent soon emerged and she became the company's lead ballerina. Under the direction of Sir Frederick Ashton, Fonteyn's interpretation of the classic ballet roles established her as one of the century's foremost dancers. She began her legendary stage partnership with Rudolf Nureyev in 1962, at the advanced age of 43. In 1955 she married Panama's ambassador in London, Roberto Arias. Four years later they were both arrested after a failed coup in Panama City. In 1965 Arias

was paralysed in an assassination attempt and Fonteyn devoted herself to caring for him. On her 60th birthday the Imperial Russian Ballet named her prima ballerina assolutta – an award given only twice before.

Secret burial for outspoken Molière

1673 In the dead of night and with no priest to bless his bones, the greatest showman of the age was buried in secret in a Paris cemetery tonight. Molière, playwright, actor, and provider of theatrical extravaganzas for the Sun King, Louis XIV, was acting the part of Argan the hypochondriac in his new play *Le Malade Imaginaire* four days ago when he collapsed and died. He was 51. Molière's scathing wit caused offence, and though he was mourned by the King and by the people, his enemies in the church and at court denied him a decent burial.

MALCOLM X GUNNED DOWN IN NEW YORK

1965 The American Black Muslim leader Malcolm X was shot dead today while addressing a meeting in New York. A rival sect is suspected of the killing. Malcolm X once preached black violence, but he converted to orthodox Islam after a pilgrimage to Mecca last year and abandoned his extreme, separatist stance for a more optimistic socialism. Born Malcolm Little, Malcolm X led a violent youth; his father was killed for backing black revolutionary Marcus Garvey. Malcolm drifted to New York in his teens, fell into a life of crime in Harlem and served six years for burglary. In jail he read the works of Black Muslim leader Elijah Muhammad, and once freed he joined the sect and changed his name to Malcolm X. Intelligent and articulate, he was soon the chief Black Muslim spokesman. But he proved too radical for the Muslims, and split with them two years ago.

> *President Nixon's motto was, if two wrongs don't make a right, try three.*
> **Norman Cousins** of the *Daily Telegraph*, on President Richard Nixon, 1979.

German guns batter Verdun

1916 Massed German artillery started a furious bombardment of a crucial 8-mile (13 km) sector of the French line at Verdun in the middle of the Western Front this morning. The deadly barrage has kept up all day, demolishing the French defences – which were weakened because, ignoring intelligence reports, French commander General Joseph Joffre was convinced the attack would come at Champagne and failed to reinforce Verdun in time. Joffre has now pulled back his troops to minimize losses and German infantry advancing behind the barrage are meeting only scattered machine-gun fire. The German lines are reinforced by half a million men withdrawn from the eastern front following German successes there. The battle for Verdun could be a long and bloody one.

1849 Following the end of the Second Sikh War, the Punjab is annexed by Britain.

1858 The first electric burglar alarm is installed by Edwin Holmes of Boston.

1952 Film actress Elizabeth Taylor weds hotel tycoon Conrad Hilton, Jnr.

1957 Israel defies a UN deadline and holds on to the Gaza Strip.

1960 Castro nationalizes all private businesses in Cuba.

1969 The US Patents Office grants a patent to King Hassan of Morocco for his device to monitor the function of the human heart.

1986 Shigechiyo Izumi, the world's oldest man, dies in Japan at the age of 120.

1989 Two members of Winnie Mandela's bodyguard are charged with the murder of 14-year-old Stompie Mocketsi.

1989 Czech writer Vaclav Havel goes to jail for initiating demonstrations.

BIRTHDAYS

Antonio Lopez de Santa Anna 1794, Mexican revolutionary who freed his people from Spanish rule only to institute his own dictatorship between 1839 and 1845.

John Henry Newman 1801, British cardinal noted for his theological and philosophical writings. His poem *The Dream of Gerontius* was set to music by Edward Elgar.

Leo Délibes 1836, French composer noted for the music for the ballets *Coppélia* and *Sylvia* and the opera *Lakmé*.

August von Wasserman 1866, German bacteriologist who invented a test for detecting syphilis.

W. H. Auden 1907, Anglo-American poet and, in collaboration with Christopher Isherwood, author of verse dramas.

Nina Simone 1934, American jazz singer and pianist who first scored a popular hit with her recording of *I Put a Spell on You*.

BIRTHDAYS

The five and dime money machine

1879 American storekeeper Frank W. Woolworth was convinced he had a winning idea, and when at first it failed he simply tried again. His first venture was a retail store in Utica, New York, where everything on sale cost the same cheap price – five cents. But the F. W. Woolworth Co. 5 Cent Store was not a success, and today he opened the new F. W. Woolworth Co. 5 and 10 Cent Store in Lancaster, Pennsylvania. The area's conservative Amish and Mennonite communities apparently approve of this aid to thrifty living and have given Woolworth's new venture a warm welcome. If the store succeeds, Woolworth's plan is to open a growing chain of 5 and 10 cent stores – he reckons centralized purchasing will help him keep prices down, and profits up.

1819 Spain has ceded Florida and all her colonies east of the Mississippi to the United States in a treaty signed today by Secretary of State John Quincy Adams. This follows General Andrew Jackson's invasion of Florida last year. Jackson grossly exceeded his orders to pacify Indian tribes on the Florida border, taking his army deep into Spanish territory to occupy Pensacola in a coup. Jackson faces an inquiry, but it is likely to be a mere formality.

5 year old is new Dalai Lama

1940 A five-year-old boy was enthroned in Lhasa today as the 14th Dalai Lama, spiritual and temporal ruler of Tibet, with a regent and council of ministers to guide him. Tenzin Gyatso was born in north-eastern Tibet on June 6, 1935, the very day that his predecessor died. According to Tibetan belief this was no mere coincidence – the Dalai Lamas are held to be the reincarnation of their predecessors, in an unbroken line stretching back 544 years. Lhasa's wise men located young Tenzin in 1938 and administered the time-honoured tests: the three-year-old little boy had to choose various objects that had belonged to his predecessor from a group of similar objects. Tenzin picked them all out, without any hesitation.

> *The latest definition of an optimist is one who fills up his crossword puzzle in ink.*
> **Clement King Shorter,** in the *Observer*, 1925.

Somoza executes rival Sandino

1934 General Augusto Sandino, the charismatic Nicaraguan guerrilla leader, has been executed by his rival, General Anastasio Somoza, commander of the feared US-trained National Guard. Sandino and three aides were seized by National Guards after a meeting with President Juan Sacasa, and shot. Somoza is now poised for a coup. Sandino's guerrilla army fought US forces which occupied the country from 1912. They were withdrawn last year when Sandino agreed to a ceasefire.

Farm revolutionary dies

1741 The great agricultural innovator Jethro Tull died today at his farm near Hungerford in England. He was 67. Ten years ago Tull published a book that is already a classic: *The New Horse-Houghing Husbandry, or an Essay on the Principles of Tillage and Vegetation.* The book is central to the ongoing revolution in agricultural technology. Tull had invented a steerable, multi-tined, horse-drawn hoe – not just a better hoe but a new type of tool for a new kind of farming. Tull's hoe is ideal for both grain and turnips, the new root crop. Turnips mean more winter stockfeed, which means more manure and therefore a more fertile soil – which no longer needs a whole year's rest to recover. Turnips fit in perfectly with two grain crops and one of grass and clover for hay and pasture – the highly productive four-course system now spreading through England. Tull's hoe was only half the answer: it requires crops planted in straight, evenly-spaced rows. So Tull invented a mechanical seed-drill – inspired by the pipes of the organ he played in church on Sundays.

> *I must rewrite the burial service; for there are things in it that are deader than anyone it has ever been read over; but I had it read because with all its drawbacks it is the most beautiful thing that can be read as yet.*
> **George Bernard Shaw,** writing on his mother's funeral, on this day, 1914.

US FLAG FINALLY FLIES OVER IWO JIMA

1945 The Stars and Stripes is flying today over Iwo Jima, a strategic island only 750 miles (1200 km) from Tokyo. After 74 days of bombardment and four days of bitter fighting on the ground, the invading force of 30,000 US Marines still has a tough fight on its hands. The crack Japanese garrison, believed to number 23,000, is fighting without quarter and almost no Japanese prisoners have been taken. They are still defending a network of deep underground bunkers. Losses on both sides have been heavy in some of the bloodiest fighting so far. Once conquered, the island-fortress will serve as an Allied air base for the final assault on Japan.

Juan Carlos confronts Fascists

1981 Fascist officers loyal to the memory of Spanish dictator Francisco Franco today stormed the Cortes, Spain's parliament, and held hundreds of parliamentarians hostage. The rebel leader, Colonel Tejero de Molina, pistol in hand, took the podium to announce the coup after his Guardia Civil unit raked the ceiling with machine-gun fire. Meanwhile the Francoist General Jaime del Bosch, the man behind the coup, declared a state of emergency in the east and sent his troops into Valencia. This evening King Juan Carlos responded with a resolute four-minute television address to the nation, saying he had ordered the army to "take measures" to suppress the revolt. The king was counting on popular support – the country's return to the monarchy after Franco's death in 1975 had brought the first free elections in 40 years of Fascism. And the Fascist general wavered: the troops returned to barracks, and Spain's fragile democracy has survived.

I shall soon be laid in the quiet grave – thank God for the quiet grave – O! I can feel the cold earth upon me – the daisies growing over me – O for this quiet – it will be my first.
John Keats, English poet who died on this day, 1821.

1732 Handel's *Oratorio* is performed for the first time in Britain.

1792 Death of Sir Joshua Reynolds, British painter and first president of the Royal Academy.

1836 The Mexican army lays siege to the Alamo in San Antonio, Texas.

1863 British explorers John Speke and J. A. Grant announce that they have discovered Lake Victoria to be the source of the Nile.

1898 Emile Zola is imprisoned for the publication of his letter *J'accuse*, which accused the French government of anti-Semitism and of wrongly imprisoning Captain Dreyfus.

1906 Johann Hoch is imprisoned in Chicago for murdering six of his 13 wives.

1917 French actress Sarah Bernhardt has her right leg amputated.

1924 Death of Thomas Woodrow Wilson, 28th president of the USA who proposed a plan for a League of Nations.

1931 Death of Dame Nellie Melba, Australian opera star who had a dessert named after her – Peach Melba.

1968 Theatre censorship ends in Britain.

1991 Thai premier Prem Tinsulanonda is overthrown in a bloodless coup.

BIRTHDAYS

Samuel Pepys 1633, English civil servant who wrote the famous Diary.

Meyer Rothschild 1743, German banker who founded a dynasty.

Sir George Watts 1817, English painter and sculptor who found popular fame and was one of the original holders of the Order of Merit.

Victor Fleming 1883, American film director best-known for *The Wizard of Oz*.

Erich Kästner 1899, German author who wrote the children's book *Emil and the Detectives*.

Cabinet bomb plot foiled by police

1820 Only a few days after the Prince Regent acceded to the throne as King George IV, London police have foiled a plot to murder his Cabinet. The plot was uncovered when a revolutionary group led by London estate agent Arthur Thistlewood was infiltrated by a police informer. Thistlewood had stored a cache of arms in the hay-loft at a house in Cato Street, West London. The plan was to plant a bomb at a house in Grosvenor Square where the Cabinet was to meet tonight for dinner. With the ministers despatched, the prisons were to be thrown open and London set afire. Police raided the house today and arrested Thistlewood and his followers. One policeman was killed in the scuffle.

WARHOL'S 15 MINUTES UP

1987 The man who found art in a Campbell's soup can has died on the operating table in New York. Warhol was the pope of Pop Art. In the early 1960s he started reproducing blown-up comic strip scenes for New York shop window displays, using a new technique of silk-screening outsized photographic enlargements. His "factory" churned out sequential mass-media images, each slightly different: the soup can or Marilyn Monroe's face. Warhol often hinted that he was taking both the public and the critics for a ride. "If you want to know anything about me, just look at the surface of my paintings. It's all there, there's nothing more," he once said, causing speculation about whether he implied profundity or shallowness about himself and his paintings.

1582 Pope Gregory XIII introduces the Gregorian calendar as a replacement for the Julian calendar.

1815 Death of Robert Fulton, American engineer who invented the steam boat.

1815 In New Zealand land is sold to whites for the first time, for a mission church.

1848 France becomes a republic for the second time as King Louis Philippe abdicates and flees to exile in England while rioters invade the Chamber of Deputies and declare a republic.

1887 Paris and Brussels establish a telephone line, the first cities to do so.

1920 The National Socialist German Workers Party announces its programme for establishing the Third Reich.

1932 Speed king Malcolm Campbell beats his own land speed record, reaching 253.96 mph at Daytona Beach.

1946 Juan Perón is elected President of Argentina.

1966 An army coup deposes Dr Kwame Nkrumah, first president of Ghana.

1977 US president Jimmy Carter cuts off aid to Argentina, Uruguay and Ethiopia for human rights violations.

1987 Memphis Slim, American blues singer, dies in Paris.

1989 Fifty-one die over the Pacific when a cargo door drops off a Boeing 747.

1999 Thirty-eight people are killed in twin avalanches which hit the small town of Galtuer in the western Austrian Alps.

BIRTHDAYS

Wilhelm Grimm 1786, German philologist and folklorist who, with his brother Jakob, compiled *Grimm's Fairytales*.

Michele Legrand 1932, French composer noted for his film scores, which included the Oscar-winning *The Summer of '42*.

Alain Prost 1955, French motor-racing champion.

AMERICAN ASTOR FIRST WOMAN MP

1920 American-born Nancy Astor was today the first woman to speak in Britain's House of Commons. Her husband, Conservative MP Waldorf Astor, succeeded his father as Viscount Astor last year and moved to the House of Lords. Lady Astor won his seat in the Commons in a by-election two months ago. Today she took her place in the Mother of Parliaments, and rose to speak in opposition to a proposal to abolish the Liquor Control Board. Lady Astor has strong opinions on temperance, and on women's rights and child welfare.

1825 Thomas Bowdler, the English editor who was more of a censor, died today aged 71. Bowdler was a prude – in 1802 he formed the Society for the Suppression of Vice. He doctored Shakespeare to produce his Family Edition, and excised parts of the Old Testament and Gibbon's *Decline and Fall of the Roman Empire*, removing "words and expressions which cannot with propriety be read aloud in a family". He gave a new word to the English language: "bowdlerizing" means literary emasculation.

Wars come because not enough people are sufficiently afraid.
Hugh Schonfield, British writer, on this day, 1948.

Missing Link forged

1961 British anthropologists Louis and Mary Leakey have found a second "Missing Link" in the ancient evolutionary chain between apes and men. Two years ago, after a painstaking 28-year search in East Africa's Olduvai Gorge, Mary Leakey uncovered the 1¾ million-year-old fossilized skull of the most ancient pre-human creature yet found, Australopithecus. Today the Leakeys uncovered another skull, that of a child, along with a collarbone and parts of a hand. This pre-human's brain was twice the size of the first skull and half the human size, with smaller teeth, and opposable thumbs. Stone tools were found near the skull. The Leakeys are calling it *Homo habilis* – "handy man". They say it is the earliest toolmaker, and a direct human ancestor.

Tet riposte captures Hue

1968 After a fierce battle, South Vietnamese and US Army troops today recaptured the old Vietnamese imperial citadel of Hue, which had been in Viet Cong hands for a month. Today's victory was a counter-attack to the recent three-week Tet Offensive, which cost communist North Vietnam 40,000 men. But the North may be winning the propaganda war – American television pictures have shown scenes of increasing brutality, including the summary execution of prisoners, and opposition to the war is swelling fast.

Telegram tips US towards war

1917 German foreign minister Arthur Zimmermann has sent a telegram to his ambassador in Mexico which could turn the tide of the war in Europe. The message found its way instead to the desk of US President Woodrow Wilson, who read it today to an outraged nation. British naval intelligence intercepted the telegram and managed to decode it. Zimmermann had offered Mexico an alliance against the US in return for restoring Texas, Arizona and New Mexico to Mexican control. Though Wilson won re-election last year with his slogan "He kept us out of the war," it now looks as if he will go down in history as the president who took the US into war.

1923 The 400-mile (640 km) journey from London to Edinburgh shrank to a mere day trip today as the "Flying Scotsman" set off to inaugurate the London and North Eastern Railway's new scheduled train service between the two cities. The powerful new steam engine is said to be capable of pulling its line of carriages at 100 mph (160 kph).

1964 As he'd promised, Cassius Clay floated like a butterfly and stung like a bee – and hammered Sonny Liston into the canvas at Miami Beach, Florida tonight in one of boxing's biggest-ever surprises. After six rounds an injured and humbled Liston, the 7-1 favourite, refused to come out of his corner and world champion loudmouth Clay is now also the world heavyweight boxing champion.

TV evangelist suffers severe "moral failure"

1988 American television evangelist Jimmy Swaggart has been banned from preaching for a year by the Protestant church elders of the Assemblies of God after being photographed with a prostitute. Swaggart confessed to "moral failure" on Sunday from the pulpit at his Family Worship Centre in Baton Rouge, Louisiana. He has been visiting the woman in question for the past three years at a house with a sign in the window saying: "Positively no refunds after 15 minutes."

1997 An adult sheep called Dolly, which was successfully cloned by scientists from a single cell at the Roslin Institute in Edinburgh, has been presented to the public. Many see Dolly the sheep as the first step towards human cloning and have expressed moral outrage. Others feel the new biotechnical advances will have a profound impact on medicine, offering lifesaving procedures.

GUERILLA WARFARE LANDS SUFFRAGETTE IN COURT

1913 Emmeline Pankhurst, the founder of Britain's suffragette movement, went on trial near London today accused of bombing Chancellor of the Exchequer David Lloyd George's villa in Surrey a week ago. Nobody was hurt in the explosion. Mrs Pankhurst described it today as "guerrilla warfare" and accepted responsibility for this and various other violent acts. She and her daughters Christabel and Sylvia have been jailed several times for inciting riots. Mrs Pankhurst founded the Women's Social and Political Union (WSPU) in 1903 to press for voting rights for British women – rights already established in the British colonies of New Zealand and Australia. Women of all classes joined in massive demonstrations, civil disobedience and hunger strikes – and have been harassed, jailed, and thrown bodily out of Parliament. It is the WSPU's militant tactics that have brought the suffragettes growing public hostility in this divisive issue.

Lincoln backs "greenbacks"

1862 With America locked in civil war, President Abraham Lincoln today introduced a new version of the dollar bill to finance the Union's mounting Civil War costs. Congress has authorized millions of the new notes, known as "greenbacks", all the same colour and all the same size, whatever the denomination ($1 to $1,000). The greenback is not redeemable in gold or silver – America's first true paper money, its buying power is a matter of confidence and faith. If the industrial North is suffering under the war burden, the South is worse off: the Confederate dollar started on a par with the Union's, but its value has slumped. The Confederacy is also printing money it doesn't have, despite a $15 million loan from a French bank.

He who begins by loving Christianity better than Truth will proceed by loving his own sect or church better than Christianity, and end by loving himself better than all.
Samuel Taylor Coleridge, romantic poet, son of an English clergyman.

1308 King Edward II of England is crowned.

1570 Queen Elizabeth I of England is excommunicated by Pope Pius V.

1841 China offers rewards for British heads as the Opium War rages.

1913 Federal income tax comes into force in the USA.

1914 Death of Sir John Tenniel, English artist who was best known for his illustrations for *Alice in Wonderland*.

1922 In France, Henri Landru is guillotined for the murder of at least 10 women, whose bodies have never been discovered.

1932 Austrian-born Adolf Hitler becomes a German citizen.

1939 The first Anderson bomb shelter is built in Britain.

1983 Death of Tennessee Williams, American dramatist whose plays included *Sweet Bird of Youth*, *A Streetcar Named Desire* and *Cat on a Hot Tin Roof*.

1989 American heavyweight boxer Mike Tyson defeats British champion Frank Bruno.

2001 Death of Sir Donald Bradman, the Australian cricketer who shot to fame in 1930 for scoring 334 runs against England at Headingley.

BIRTHDAYS

Pierre-Auguste Renoir 1841, French Impressionist painter who once said "I never think I have finished a nude until I think I could pinch it."

Enrico Caruso 1873, Italian operatic tenor, the greatest lyric tenor of his time.

John Foster Dulles 1888, American Republican politician and diplomat, secretary of state to Eisenhower.

Dame Myra Hess 1890, British pianist much loved for her lunchtime concerts in the National Gallery during World War II.

David Puttnam 1941, British film producer.

George Harrison 1943, British pop musician and former Beatle.

Cory wins as Marcos flees

1986 Power abruptly changed hands in the Philippines today. Right-wing dictator Ferdinand Marcos and opposition leader Mrs Corazon Aquino both claimed to have won the elections held two weeks ago, and today both held ceremonies to install them as president. Mrs Aquino, whose husband was shot by Marcos' troops in 1983, announced that "the long agony" of the 20-year Marcos tyranny was over. Marcos, whose supporters had rigged the polls, delivered a television address confirming his re-election – but the broadcast was blacked out. Within hours thousands of Aquino supporters mobbed Marcos's palace. He and his family escaped to the rooftop, to be whisked away by US Air Force helicopters.

1791 The Bank of England issues the first ever pound note.

1815 Napoleon Bonaparte escapes from his exile on the island of Elba.

1839 The first Grand National steeplechase is run at Aintree, Liverpool.

1848 The Second French Republic is proclaimed, following the overthrow of the Bourbon king Louis Philippe.

1885 A 15-nation meeting in Berlin under Bismarck divides up Central and East Africa among the European nations.

1935 Radar is demonstrated for the first time at Daventry in England by Robert Watson-Watt.

1951 The 22nd Amendment is passed, limiting US presidents to two four-year terms in office.

1980 Diplomatic relations are established between Israel and Egypt, to the outrage of other Arab nations.

1986 In the Philippines, President Marcos is deposed and Mrs Corazon Aquino is elected.

1991 Saddam Hussein orders Iraqi troops to retreat from Kuwait, declaring a great victory.

1993 A car bomb planted by Muslim fundamentalists explodes under the World Trade Center in New York, killing six people.

1995 Barings Bank in London goes into receivership after the Nick Leeson scandal.

BIRTHDAYS

Victor Hugo 1802, French novelist, dramatist and poet whose books include *Les Miserables*.

Honoré Daumier 1808, French caricaturist, sculptor and painter best-known in his lifetime as a social satirist.

Richard Gatling 1903, American gunsmith who gave his name to the Gatling gun.

Fats Domino 1928, American jazz singer and pianist.

Johnny Cash 1932, American country and western singer, musician and actor.

WREN'S OWN MONUMENT IS LONDON'S SKYLINE

1723 Sir Christopher Wren, builder of St Paul's Cathedral, died today. He was 90. By the age of 30, Wren was a professor of astronomy at Oxford, a renowned polymath and a founder member of the Royal Society. At 31 he turned to architecture, designing a college chapel at Cambridge and a theatre and college buildings at Oxford. Then the Great Fire of London destroyed 400 acres (161 hectares) of the city in four days. Reconstruction brought a building boom, and Wren replanned the whole city. His street plan was rejected, but he was asked to rebuild the skyline – 51 churches, and a replacement for the medieval cathedral of St Paul's, destroyed in the fire. It took him the rest of his life. St Paul's took 40 years to build – a work of splendour, its vast dome second only to St Peter's Basilica in the Vatican (on which he modelled it). With St Paul's and his many other commissions, such as Kensington Palace and the superb Royal Hospital for Seamen at Greenwich, Sir Christopher Wren left an indelible stamp on London.

Boxer leaders beheaded

1901 Two leaders of China's Boxer Rebellion were publicly beheaded by a court executioner in Peking today, ending the two-year uprising against the presence of foreigners in China. Japanese soldiers led the condemned rebels to their deaths while a combined foreign force guarded the route. Last August 10,000 allied troops captured Peking and ended a 56-day Boxer siege of the European legations. The Empress Dowager Tz'u-hsi, who shared the "Righteous Harmony Fist" resentment of foreigners and refused to act against the Boxer rebels, had fled the capital. She has not yet dared to return. Western diplomats say the Chinese government will be forced to pay indemnity for the death of 1500 foreigners in the rebellion and that Western troops will be permanently stationed in Peking.

Britain builds its bomb

1952 Britain has developed an atomic bomb and will test it in the Australian desert later this year. Prime Minister Winston Churchill's announcement in the House of Commons today comes three years after confirmation that the Soviet Union had the bomb. Churchill said the previous Labour government had developed the bomb in secret – while publicly opposing nuclear weapons. In the US, the Senate committee on atomic energy said that it would help to keep world peace.

1990 Playwright Vaclav Havel, Czechoslovakia's new president, announced in Moscow today that all Soviet troops will leave Czechoslovakia by July, ending 21 years of armed occupation. Most of the troops are expected to be gone by June, when elections are to be held.

If people behaved the way nations do they would all be put in strait jackets.
Tennessee Williams, American playwright, who died today, 1983.

Hitler launches people's car

1936 A new family car intended to rival Henry Ford's famous Model T has been unveiled in Germany. Chancellor Adolf Hitler today opened a factory in Saxony that will mass-produce a small, cheap saloon. This Volkswagen – the "people's car" – has been designed by Ferdinand Porsche of Auto Union, known for more luxurious models. The new Volkswagen is streamlined, and has a revolutionary four-cylinder air-cooled engine mounted over the rear axle. Hitler hopes the new car will transform the German economy.

Communists take power in Prague

1948 The Czechoslovakian Communist Party today seized power in Prague, and Western leaders fear the country will now become a Soviet satellite. Last week the liberal President Eduard Benes told his people a totalitarian Communist regime would never rule in Czechoslovakia. Today he was silent as the Communist Party leader, Prime Minister Klement Gottwald, announced that Benes had accepted a new Cabinet with Communists in all the top jobs. Czechoslovakia was the only one of the new countries in Central Europe to maintain a democratic government – until Nazi occupation in 1939. Benes, in exile during the war, afterwards resumed his post as president – under the shadow of the USSR. Concessions he was forced to make to the Czech Communists led directly to today's takeover.

Reichstag blaze suits Nazis

1933 A mysterious fire tonight gutted Berlin's Reichstag parliament. A Dutchman has been charged with arson, but with less than a week to the German elections, observers agree the blaze could not have been more convenient for the ruling Nazi party had they planned it themselves. Nazi leaders immediately blamed the Communist Party. At the scene, Chancellor Adolf Hitler called the fire a "God-given signal" that the Communists should be crushed. In less than two months in office, Hitler has virtually stamped out Communist and Socialist papers. Last week Police Minister Hermann Goering raided the Communist Party headquarters, claiming evidence of a revolutionary plot.

> *Matthew reminds us that the meek shall inherit the earth.*
> **George Bush**, US president, before the Gulf War, 1991.
>
> *The meek shall inherit nothing.*
> **Frank Zappa**, US rock musician, 1983.

Freed slaves get the vote – in theory

1869 Four years after the Civil War, the last of three amendments to the US Constitution enshrining the rights of freed slaves as full US citizens was passed by the US Congress today: the new 15th Amendment prevents state governments denying the vote to anyone "on account of race, colour, or previous condition of servitude". The defeated rebel states of the South must ratify it before they can be readmitted to the Union – but they can still use poll tax and literacy rules to stop blacks voting, and the current surge of terrorism by white racist secret societies like the murderous Ku Klux Klan is enough to stop most blacks insisting on their rights. For many blacks, very little has changed; the 15th Amendment is only a piece of paper.

> *God grant that this is the work of the Communists. You are witnessing the beginning of a great new epoch in German history. This fire is the beginning.*
> **Adolf Hitler**, German Chancellor, speaking to a foreign correspondent as the Reichstag burns, 1933.

GULF WAR OVER

1991 The Gulf War ended today. Saudi forces entered Kuwait City at first light as the Iraqi army fled northward, only to be cut off by allied forces which had moved behind them in a lightning strike. Later in the day the Iraqi government announced its unconditional acceptance of the UN resolutions on Kuwait, and US president George Bush announced tonight that the war is over. All allied military action will cease from tomorrow morning. No chemical weapons were used during the four-day ground battle which has ended the war, and allied casualties were light. The US lost 184 men in the war. The allies have taken 80,000 Iraqi prisoners, and allied leaders calculate that 85,000 to 100,000 Iraqis have been killed. Initial estimates are that Iraq's destroyed infrastructure will take $200 billion and a generation to repair, and that Kuwait's reconstruction will cost $50 billion.

1881 A British force that set out to teach Boers of the Transvaal a lesson was wiped out at Majuba today. General Sir George Colley was shot through the forehead – a chilling tribute to deadly Boer marksmanship. The Boers fled British rule in the Cape 50 years ago and declared the Transvaal a republic last year.

1784
John Wesley, founder of the Wesleyan faith, signs its deed of declaration.

1874
Claimant to the Tichborne fortune Arthur Orton is found guilty of perjury after 260 days, the longest trial in England, and sentenced to 14 years' hard labour.

1912
In Missouri, the first parachute jump is made by one Albert Berry.

1922
In a grand ceremony Princess Mary, daughter of King George V and Queen Mary, marries Viscount Lascelles in London.

1966
The Cavern Club, the venue where the Beatles and many other groups first made their mark, goes into liquidation.

1972
In Marseilles, French police seize 937 lb (425 kg) of pure heroin.

1975
Thirty-five people are killed in London when an Underground train accelerates into a dead-end tunnel at Moorgate station, crushing three of the six crowded coaches.

1989
In Venezuela, President Peres faces riots as food prices rise.

1991
Khaleda Zia, widow of President Rahman of Bangladesh, wins the freest national election in the country's history.

BIRTHDAYS

Sir John Tenniel 1820, British artist and cartoonist who supplied the original illustrations for *Alice in Wonderland*.

Charles Blondin 1824, French tightrope walker who crossed the Niagara Falls on stilts.

Professor Linus Pauling 1909, American chemist and physicist who won the Nobel Prizes for Chemistry (1934) and Peace (1962).

Sir Stephen Spender 1909, British poet and critic.

Zero Mostel 1915, American comedy actor who starred in Mel Brooks's cult film *The Producers*.

Brian Jones 1942, founder member of the Rolling Stones.

BOERS RETREAT AFTER RELIEF OF LADYSMITH

1900 The four-month siege of the British garrison at Ladysmith in Natal ended today as a relief column finally rode into the battered town and the Boer forces retreated. General Sir Redvers Buller's relief force had lost more than 1000 men in an encounter with the Boers at Spion Kop, only a few miles from Ladysmith. This followed three major British defeats in a week in December – all under Buller's command. Amongst the 2000 British dead during "Black Week" was the only son of Field Marshall Lord Roberts, who arrived in Cape Town three weeks later to replace Buller as overall commander. The fast-moving Boer commandos ran rings round the Redcoats after

they invaded British Natal at the start of the war in October. But they tied up their forces in sieges at Kimberley, Ladysmith and Mafeking, giving the British time to bring in reinforcements. The sheer weight of numbers is now tipping the scales against the Boers. Two weeks ago Lord Roberts relieved Kimberley, and today Buller stands vindicated – with a telegram of congratulation from Queen Victoria.

Palme, man of peace, gunned down

1986 Sweden's prime minister Olaf Palme was shot dead by an unknown assassin as he walked home from a cinema in Stockholm tonight. His wife was wounded in the attack. The lone gunman escaped, and nobody has claimed responsibility for the killing. There seems no obvious motive. Palme was a man of peace and, as such, an outspoken critic of the US war in Vietnam; he set up a panel to ban nuclear weapons in Europe and was a UN mediator in the Iran-Iraq war. He is the first European head of government to be killed in office in 47 years.

"Kill us again" dare Indian activists

1973 Militant American Indian activists seized the Sioux village of Wounded Knee in South Dakota today, and challenged the government to repeat the Indian massacre that happened there more than 80 years ago. The militants are holding 10 hostages. They are demanding free elections of tribal leaders, a review of all Indian treaties and full investigation of the Bureau of Indian Affairs – whose Washington headquarters were occupied for a week last November by protesting Indians. The militants are members of the American Indian Movement (AIM), formed five years ago. In December 1890, in the last clash between US troops and Indians, the US Seventh Cavalry opened fire on Sioux Chief Big Foot and his followers at Wounded Knee, killing 300 men, women and children.

1906
Tommy Burns beat Marvin Hart in 20 rounds at Los Angeles tonight to take the world heavyweight boxing title. The fans were more interested in the referee, one James J. Jeffries, who retired unbeaten as world champion last year. He was unbeaten in 22 fights – and only retired because he could not find a sufficiently worthy opponent.

Arms alone are not enough to keep the peace – it must be kept by men.
J. F. Kennedy,
US president, 1962.

Inquisition burns English sailors

1574 Two Englishmen and an Irishman were burned at the stake in Mexico City today – the Spanish Inquisition's first European victims in the New World. Since they arrived in New Spain three years ago the priests of torture have used their dreaded powers only to purify the hosts of Indian converts of any lingering traces of Aztec paganism. Today's three unfortunates stood guilty of "Lutheran heresy". Another 68 Englishmen were given public lashings and began long terms as galley-slaves. These men were themselves slave traders, the remnants of a fleet that sailed under Sir John Hawkins and Sir Francis Drake from Plymouth seven years ago, fetching slaves from Africa to sell in the Caribbean – in defiance of a Spanish ban. The Spanish navy ambushed the fleet off the Mexican coast, and though Hawkins and Drake escaped, they had to leave two ships and their crews behind. Today's Inquisition victims are the survivors.

BUNNY GIRLS LET LOOSE

1960 February 29 is the day chivalry is reversed and the girls ask the boys. Maybe that's why Hugh Hefner chose tonight to open his new Playboy Club in Chicago – but the only thing Hefner's "Bunny Girls" will ask is if you want a drink. These shapely young women in scanty black swimsuits, plus formal collar and tie, mesh stockings, high heels and big Bugs Bunny ears, with a fluffy white tail stitched on to their behinds, are strictly for looking at – the only things on offer are drink, entertainment and a flutter at the tables. Hefner, who was brought up in a strict Methodist home, started his magazine *Playboy* seven years ago with only $10,000 (£55,000), and is now a very wealthy man. He said tonight that the new club is just the first of a worldwide network of Playboy Clubs.

Nobel-winner Tutu arrested

1988 South Africa's Anglican Archbishop Desmond Tutu was arrested today for demonstrating outside the parliament building in Cape Town in defiance of a ban on political activity by the white minority government. He was leading a protest against the death sentence imposed on the "Sharpeville Six" for killing a black townships councillor. Archbishop Tutu is a focus for resistance to the apartheid system and a well-known figure worldwide. He won the Nobel Peace Prize in 1984, the second South African to do so (Albert Luthuli, president of the African National Congress, was the first). In a nation riven by strife, Tutu preaches non-violence. He has condemned the state of emergency in force since June 1986 and defies the emergency laws in calling for economic sanctions against South Africa and for foreign disinvestment. Archibishop Tutu is not likely to be held for long – jailing him would cause the government even more trouble than freeing him.

DANCER COST KING HIS THRONE

1868 King Louis I of Bavaria took his patronage of the arts further than most – and it cost him his throne. Louis's capital, Munich, was the cultural centre of Europe, a magnet for the great names in art, music and literature – and also for lesser names, like Marie Gilbert, a young Irish dancer whose stage name was Lola Montez. King Louis duly patronized Lola too. In return for her favours he made her a countess, and gave her increasing sway over the affairs of state. Her other affairs included notorious liaisons with the composer Franz Liszt and with romantic novelist Alexandre Dumas *père*. In 1848 Lola's scheming helped to provoke a revolution; Louis was forced to abdicate and Lola was banished. Lola died penniless in the US seven years ago. She was only 43. Ex-King Louis died today in Munich, aged 81.

Racial turmoil splits Alabama

1956 White segregationist groups are planning demonstrations against a US federal court ruling today that the first-ever black student at the University of Alabama be readmitted. Autherine Lucy had been suspended – to ensure her safety, the white college authorities insisted. She had been attacked by an angry mob when she first arrived. Today the court ordered that she be given proper protection on campus. Meanwhile turmoil continues over Alabama's segregated buses. It began when Rosa Parks (below), a black woman, insisted on sitting in a "whites-only" seat on a bus in Montgomery. She refused to pay her fine and was jailed, leading to a mass boycott of the buses – and 115 black activists were then jailed for staging the boycott. Among them is the leader of the burgeoning civil rights movement, the Rev. Martin Luther King Jnr.

642 St Oswald, bringer of Christianity to north-east England, is killed in battle.

1880 The St Gotthard tunnel, providing a rail link between Switzerland and Italy, is completed.

1908 Onnes, a scientist from Leyden, the Netherlands, announces he has succeeded in liquefying helium.

1960 An earthquake in Morocco destroys much of Agadir and kills about 12,000 people.

1984 Canadian prime minister Pierre Trudeau resigns.

1984 Death of Roland Culver, British stage and film actor who appeared in *Bonjour Tristesse* and *The Yellow Rolls-Royce*.

2004 The third film in the *The Lord of the Rings* trilogy wins 11 Oscars.

BIRTHDAYS

Anne Lee 1736, British blacksmith's daughter who emigrated to the USA and founded the religious group the American Society of Shakers.

Gioacchino Rossini 1792, Italian composer who wrote 36 operas, including *The Italian Girl in Algiers*, *William Tell*, *The Barber of Seville* and *The Thieving Magpie* – and invented a number of recipes, notably Tournedos Rossini.

John Holland 1840, Irish-American inventor of the submarine.

Ranchhodji Morarji Desai 1896, Indian prime minister who was imprisoned with Mahatma Gandhi.

His Majesty's Government view with favour the establishment in Palestine of a national home for the Jewish people, and will use their best endeavours to facilitate the achievement of this object, it being clearly understood that nothing shall be done which may prejudice the civil and religious rights of existing non-Jewish communities in Palestine.

Arthur Balfour,
British foreign secretary, in a letter to Lord Rothschild, 1917.

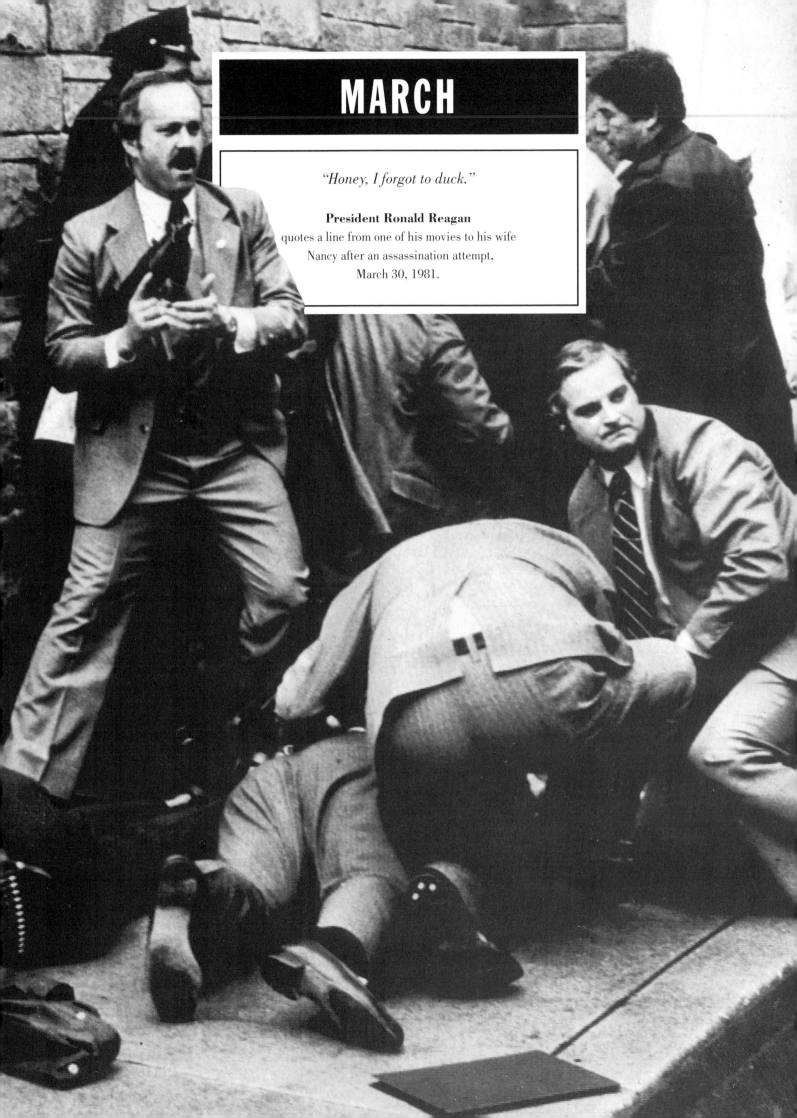

MARCH

"Honey, I forgot to duck."

President Ronald Reagan
quotes a line from one of his movies to his wife
Nancy after an assassination attempt,
March 30, 1981.

Aviator Lindbergh's baby snatched

1932 New Jersey police are searching for clues that might lead them to the kidnapper of the 20-month-old son of the aviator Charles Lindbergh. The baby vanished as Mr and Mrs Lindbergh were having dinner, and a $50,000 ransom note was found near the cot. Police have launched a massive manhunt to locate the boy. Lindbergh achieved fame with his solo Atlantic flight in 1927, and there is nationwide interest in the kidnapping: reporters are flocking to the Lindbergh home in New Jersey and President Hoover is being kept informed. The only clues so far are footprints in the Lindbergh's garden and a home-made ladder used to reach the nursery. The ransom note is crudely lettered and misspelt but promises "the child is in gut care".

Riddle of Nostradamus's future imperfect

1555 A "Book of Centuries" consisting of cryptic four-lined rhymed verses has been published in France by Michael Nostradamus, a provincial doctor. The book's 900 "Centuries" contain a series of prophecies about future events. Predictions include a massive fire in London in the year 1666, global war erupting twice in the far-distant 20th century, the coming of an anti-Christ from the deserts of Persia later in the same century and, most absurd of all, a revolution that will overthrow the mighty French monarchy before the 18th century is over. Snatches of Hebrew, Latin and Portuguese, and the use of anagrams, make the book very difficult to understand fully – yet it is impossible to dismiss.

NEW DISCOVERY LEIGH PICKS UP TOP OSCAR

1940 English actress Vivien Leigh has won an Oscar for her role as Scarlett O'Hara in the film *Gone with the Wind*, now breaking all box-office records in America. The film won five Oscars in all. Miss Leigh was a young unknown when Hollywood producer David Selznick chose her for the part coveted by every female star in Hollywood. She had only one obscure British film to her credit – though she won a record £50,000 movie contract five years ago following a successful stage debut in London. Miss Leigh plays a proud southern belle fighting to regain what her family has lost in the Civil War, using and discarding men along the way. She meets her match in the unscrupulous Rhett Butler, played by Hollywood King Clark Gable – but it is Miss Leigh who has won the Oscar. The film, a marathon four hours long, cost more than $2 million to make. It is based on the Pulitzer Prize-winning novel by Margaret Mitchell.

New hydrogen bomb wipes out island

1954 The US today exploded the most powerful bomb ever made – and tiny Bikini Atoll in the South Pacific died. The explosion was the equivalent of 15 million tons of TNT – hundreds of times more powerful than the weapons that destroyed Hiroshima and Nagasaki in 1945. The "Bravo" test of the world's first full-scale hydrogen bomb was a complete success. Cameras were there to record the awesome flash and the immense mushroom cloud – the symbol of our post-war era. But the bomb was apparently even more powerful than expected: the shock went right off the dials of the recording instruments. Though the atoll was cleared of islanders and the seas were patrolled, there are reports that Japanese fishermen on boats more than 70 miles from the blast have been seriously burnt by white ash that fell from the sky. In a smaller test blast two years ago, a complete island vanished. This puts the US well ahead in the arms race, but it is only a matter of time before the Soviets test their own H-bomb.

1815 Napoleon Bonaparte has landed at Cannes with 1500 soldiers and is returning to Paris with a rapidly growing army. The Austrian, British and Russian allies are appalled: having banished him to Elba, they believed they had freed Europe of the extraordinary military hero.

The number's up for baseball star

1969 When ace baseball slugger Mickey Charles Mantle retired today, he took his number with him, and the New York Yankees no longer have a No. 7. Mantle shares this honour only with Babe Ruth, Lou Gehrig and Joe DiMaggio. Mantle has played major league since 1951. When DiMaggio retired, Mantle replaced him in centrefield. In 1956, Mantle won the Hickock Belt for the professional athlete of the year. He broke Babe Ruth's record of 16 home runs in World Series play in 1964, and his 18 remains a record. Mantle hit a grand total of 536 home runs. He is one of the all-time greats in major league baseball – which is 100 years old this year.

St David's Day

1875 The US Congress passes the Civil Rights Act.

1880 Pennsylvania becomes the first US state to abolish slavery.

1896 Ethiopia routs 100,000 Italian troops after their attempt at invasion.

1912 Captain Albert Berry makes the first parachute jump in St Louis, Missouri.

1934 Peking's "Last Emperor" is crowned by Japan.

1946 The Bank of England passes into public ownership.

1949 Boxer Joe Louis retires at the age of 35 after beating 25 contenders for his title.

1950 British physicist Klaus Fuchs is found guilty of having passed classified information to the Soviet Union since 1943.

1959 Archbishop Makarios returns to Cyprus after almost exactly three years of exile.

1961 President Kennedy forms the Peace Corps of volunteers to work in Third World Countries.

1972 London boy Timothy Davey (14) is found guilty of conspiring to sell cannabis in Turkey.

1978 Charlie Chaplin's coffin is stolen from a Swiss cemetery.

2001 The Taliban demolish Buddhist statues in Afghanistan.

BIRTHDAYS

Frédéric Chopin 1810, Polish composer and pianist.

Lytton Strachey 1880, English author who wrote *Eminent Victorians* and was a member of the Bloomsbury Group.

Oskar Kokoschka 1886, Austrian-born Expressionist painter who became a British citizen in 1947.

Glenn Miller 1904, American band leader and composer.

David Niven 1910, British actor whose films included *The Guns of Navarone* and *The Pink Panther*.

Roger Daltrey 1945, British rock musician and actor, member of the group The Who and star of the film *McVicar*.

MARCH 2

BIRTHDAYS

Lone Star defiance starts Tex-Mex dust-up

1836 American settlers in Texas have declared their independence from Mexico and set up a new state with a new flag – the Lone Star. But the Mexican dictator General Antonio Lopez de Santa Anna has invaded Texas to reassert control. A small force of Texan rebels under Colonels William Travis and Jim Bowie rode out to meet the army but has now retreated. The rebel army leader, General Sam Houston, is retreating in the direction of San Jacinto Prairie. American settlers have been pouring into Texas for the last 20 years – a split with Mexico was inevitable. The Texans saw their chance last year when discontent with Santa Anna's policies stirred the Mexicans to revolt against his repressive government.

Doors singer busted for "lewd behaviour"

1969 To the young he is a hero, but to the American establishment pop singer Jim Morrison of The Doors is a drunken, disorderly, drug-taking, obscene rabble-rouser. Record companies have fired the group for Morrison's "objectionable" lyrics. Morrison, twice arrested and leader of a riot at a concert in Chicago six months ago, was yesterday arrested again after a concert in Miami. Today he was charged with "lewd and lascivious behaviour in public by exposing his private parts and by simulating masturbation and oral copulation", plus profanity, drunkenness and various minor charges – and this is the star all the kids love.

Dickens defeats the deadlines

1840 The novelist Charles Dickens has started a weekly periodical, *Master Humphrey's Clock*, in which he is publishing his two latest books, *The Old Curiosity Shop* and *Barnaby Rudge*, by instalments. The phenomenal success of Dickens's two previous works, *Oliver Twist* and *The Posthumous Papers of Mr Pickwick*, both of which were serialized, has shown that the British reading public likes fiction in regular, tantalizing doses. Dickens's extraordinary industriousness has kept him ahead of the close deadlines – when he began *The Pickwick Papers* by instalment in 1836 to illustrate a series of sketches he was writing on only two days' notice. Dickens is also editing a biography of a famous clown, and writing two books. *Oliver Twist* is only part-fiction. Dickens's father was imprisoned for debt, and for several months 12-year-old Charles worked in a factory, living alone amid London's poverty. His books are full of life, have depth, humour, and compassion.

> *The whole commerce between master and slave is a perpetual exercise of the most boisterous passions, the most unremitting despotism on the one part, and degrading submissions on the other.*
>
> **Thomas Jefferson**; today Congress banned the import of slaves to America, 1807.

SUPERSONIC BEAUTY TAKES TO THE SKY

1969 Concorde, the supersonic Anglo-French airliner, roared off the runway, straightened its pointed nose and took to the skies today, carrying with it the promise of space-age air travel for the common man. Today's successful maiden flight at Toulouse of the French prototype 001 brought to fruition the £360 million agreement between France and Britain to build a jetliner that will travel at twice the speed of sound. The five-year venture has produced an elegant aircraft: it has delta wings with subtly curved leading edges and a streamlined nose-cone that slopes down in a distinctive droop to give the pilot better visibility on takeoff and landing. The plane will seat 125 passengers. Initially, commercial service will be limited to first-class only, for businessmen in a hurry. Concorde will halve the flying time between London and New York.

Australia finally goes it alone

1986 Queen Elizabeth II today signed the Australia Bill, severing Britain's formal ties with its former colony almost two centuries after British convicts were shipped to Botany Bay in 1788. Australia has been virtually self-governing since the 1901 constitution was introduced; but in 1975 Sir John Kerr, Governor General, decided his powers included the right to sack the Prime Minister. He caused a furore by dismissing Labour leader Gough Whitlam. Outraged Australians decided that in future the Queen should have less to do with their government.

Scargill's army reluctantly admits defeat

1985 Britain's coal miners finally bowed to the inevitable today, voting to return to work after a year-long strike that was as much a political challenge to Prime Minister Margaret Thatcher as an industrial dispute. Mrs Thatcher is claiming a "famous victory" over the National Union of Mineworkers' leader Arthur Scargill, who has been a thorn in the side of the Conservative Party leadership since he

contributed to the downfall of a Tory government in early 1974. The strike was sparked by Mrs Thatcher's government insisting on closing loss-making pits. The miners' delegates today voted 98-91 to return to work, despite insistence by the National Coal Board management that they would have to accept financial penalties for their actions, and that those dismissed will not be reinstated. The bitter dispute leaves the state-owned National Coal Board facing a record £2.2 billion loss this year. It has accelerated the move away from coal, once the energy source of Britain's industrial strength.

Europe up in arms

1848 Revolution is sweeping across Europe, spurred by hunger, economic depression and the political demands of the growing middle classes. During a public outbreak of fury in Paris last month, King Louis Phillippe fled while a mob wrecked his palace then formed a government and "national workshops" for the jobless. Now the flames have spread to the Austrian empire, with demonstrations raging in both Vienna and Hungary. In Vienna, conservative statesman Klemens von Metternich has been driven from office. Hungary has declared its autonomy, while Croatia is in turn demanding its freedom from Hungary. Venice has renounced Austria's authority and proclaimed a republic. Serfdom in the Austrian empire is crumbling; there is no proper constitution. In Germany, unrest may cause the Prussian king to call a constitutional assembly.

Wayne claims Westerns are "art"

1939 "Westerns are closer to art than anything else in the motion picture business," said John Wayne at the premiere of *Stagecoach* in New York tonight. A tale of heroes, heroines and villains set in a stirring drama and coupled with the breadth of vision of the movie camera creates a formula that could never be achieved in theatre or opera. Art or no, John Ford's *Stagecoach* is a classic Western, and has all the ingredients of a spectacular Hollywood hit. This is the first major screen role of its star, John Wayne, but cowboy Wayne, whose real name is Marion Michael Morrison, has already carved out a niche for himself with his granite features and understated heroism. Ford began directing Westerns in 1917.

TIME DISTILS THE NEWS

1923 Americans with no time to read a daily newspaper can now buy *Time* magazine, which puts the week's news between two covers. Edited by Henry R. Luce, *Time* separates out the week's events, with an emphasis on photographs and analysis; there is social commentary and even some gossip. Mr Luce has a firm editorial policy: the reporters' individual styles are submerged by extensive rewriting, conservative in tone, favouring the Republicans. In a country with no truly national newspaper, there is room for a weekly news magazine distributed by rail – an idea others will no doubt copy.

Communists go international

1919 Plans to set Europe ablaze with Communist revolution were announced today by Russia's Bolshevik leader Vladimir Ilich Lenin. A new organization, the Communist International or "Comintern", has been set up to dictate policies to Communists in other countries. Its job will be to set up trade unions and Communist propaganda organizations. It is a more radical offshoot of the three Internationals that have existed since the Socialist movement started 35 years ago. Lenin believes he has a greater chance of establishing control if the Socialist creed spreads to neighbouring countries.

MARCH 3

1802 Beethoven's "Moonlight Sonata" is published.

1804 Giandomenico Tiepolo, close collaborator with his father Giambattista Tiepolo and famous in his own right for his etchings and engravings, dies aged 77.

1857 Britain and France declare war on China, using the killing of a missionary as the pretext.

1875 Bizet's opera *Carmen* is premiered at the Opéra Comique in Paris.

1924 President Kemal Ataturk abolishes the Caliphate and disestablishes the Islamic religion in Turkey.

1931 "The Star Spangled Banner" is adopted as America's national anthem.

1942 The West Coast of America is declared a military zone and 100,000 are evacuated.

1950 The US Congress votes to admit Alaska as the 49th state.

1959 Death of Lou Costello, comedy partner of Bud Abbott.

1974 A Turkish Airlines DC10 crashes into a wood near Paris, killing all 344 people on board.

1983 Arthur Koestler, Hungarian-born writer and active member of the Voluntary Euthanasia Society, commits suicide with his wife Cynthia as his health declines.

1990 Venezuela suspends foreign debt payments after widespread rioting.

1991 Queen Elizabeth II incurs a wound to her finger requiring three stitches while trying to break up a fight between corgi dogs in the grounds of Windsor Castle.

BIRTHDAYS

George Pullman 1831, American industrialist and inventor of the luxury railway carriage.

Alexander Graham Bell 1847, Scottish inventor who emigrated to the USA and invented the telephone.

Jean Harlow 1911, American actress and platinum blonde sex symbol.

Fatima Whitbread 1961, Olympic gold medallist.

1193 Saladin, legendary Muslim commander during the Crusades, dies in Damascus.

1634 Samuel Cole opens the first tavern in Boston.

1789 The first US Congress is held in New York with 59 members, each representing a district of approximately 30,000 people.

1824 The Royal National Lifeboat Institution is founded in Britain.

1873 The *New York Daily Graphic* becomes the first illustrated daily newspaper.

1882 The first electric trams in Britain run from Leytonstone in East London.

1941 British forces and Norwegian resistance fighters raid the German-occupied Lofoten Islands and destroy 11 German boats.

1971 Pierre Trudeau, 52-year-old Prime Minister of Canada, marries 22-year-old Margaret Sinclair in secret.

1975 Charlie Chaplin is knighted at Buckingham Palace.

1980 Robert Mugabe becomes the leader of newly independent Zimbabwe, which had been governed as Rhodesia by the British since 1889.

1989 Pope John Paul II brands Salman Rushdie novel *The Satanic Verses* blasphemous on account of its suggestion that part of the Koran was inspired by the devil.

BIRTHDAYS

Prince Henry the Navigator 1394, Portugese patron of explorers under whose auspices Madeira, and Azores and the Cape Verde Islands were colonized.

Antonio Vivaldi 1678, Italian composer best known for *The Four Seasons.*

Alan Sillitoe 1928, British author and playwright whose books *Saturday Night and Sunday Morning* and *The Loneliness of the Long Distance Runner* were both turned into films.

Kenny Dalgleish 1951, Scottish footballer and manager.

CHARLES II GIVES QUAKER NEW START IN AMERICA

1681 King Charles II has given his authorization for what promises to be a bold social experiment in his American colonies. Today, by Royal Charter, he granted William Penn, a Quaker, the right to set up a new colony at West Jersey. The King also paid off £16,000 of Penn's family debts. The Charter gives the 38-year-old Penn near-dictatorial powers over the new colony, its Indian population and its surroundings, which he proposes to name Pennsylvania.

Lincoln inherits country in turmoil

1861 Abraham Lincoln was sworn in today as the 16th president of a Federation of States united only in name: the country is divided and on the threshold of civil war. Lincoln's inaugural address did little to alter matters in the southern states where his hostility to slavery – the backbone of their way of life – is well-known. Lincoln, a prosperous lawyer and congressman, was about to give up politics when the issue of extending slavery into Kansas and Nebraska fired him to carry on. In 1856 he joined the Republicans but failed to

> *Let me assert my firm belief that the only thing we have to fear is fear itself.*
>
> **Franklin D. Roosevelt,** on his inauguration as US president during a period of chaos; American banks closed down as he took the oath in 1933.

get into the senate: last year he only narrowly secured his party's presidential nomination. His first challenge comes from Fort Sumter in South Carolina, which is being deprived of supplies by forces loyal to Jefferson Davis, the Confederate President.

Outrage as Lennon says "We're more popular than Jesus,"

1966 Fast-quipping Beatle John Lennon's quick Merseyside tongue may at last have taken him a quip too far. He has said the Beatles are more popular than Jesus Christ – and he said it to a newspaper reporter. Lennon was talking to Maureen Cleave, of London's *Evening Standard*, about rock 'n' roll. "I don't know which will go first, rock 'n' roll or Christianity," he said, rather carelessly. "We're more popular than Jesus Christ right now." He was just stating a fact: in England, the Beatles are more popular – the English churches are painfully aware of flagging attendances. And he didn't imply that religion is merely a matter of popularity polls. Even so, many people will be outraged and Lennon looks to lose a lot of fans.

AMATEUR BASTION GOES PRO

1968 The guardians of Wimbledon's hallowed turf have at last agreed to the unthinkable – allowing professional tennis players to compete in the world's oldest amateur tennis tournament. The British Lawn Tennis Association and the International Tennis Federation today voted to open the game to the highly-paid professionals who are drawing huge crowds at other international tournaments. This year about a dozen tournaments will be open to all comers, and a big boost in crowds is expected as amateurs slog it out with the tough new breed of tennis professionals in pursuit of ever-larger prizes.

MacArthur's thriller in Manila

1945 As promised, US General Douglas MacArthur has returned to the Philippines, where his troops have now taken the capital Manila after months of heavy fighting against the Japanese occupation forces. "I shall return," MacArthur promised the Filipinos in 1942, when he had to flee aboard a torpedo-boat as the Japanese advanced. Now he has fought his way up through the islands from New Guinea and, with the help of Admiral Nimitz's Pacific fleet, has virtually cut off Tokyo's lines of supply. The Japanese navy suffered its worst defeat so far in the Leyte Gulf last October. While US columns converged on Manila, US Army parachutists landed at the fortress of Corregidor to clear the last resistance. The Japanese are estimated to have

MAN OF STEEL DIES

1953 Joseph Stalin, who forged the Soviet Union into a global superpower at the cost of oppression by which millions were killed, has died of a brain haemorrhage. His body is lying in state in Moscow. No clear successor has yet emerged. Stalin, the son of a Georgian shoemaker, started his career robbing banks to raise Bolshevik funds. He seized power after Lenin's death in 1929. During World War II he broke Hitler's military power at Stalingrad – earning him the title of the country's saviour. He treated with Churchill and Roosevelt on equal terms – and demanded their acquiescence in the Soviet domination of Eastern Europe after the war. Stalin was a brutal leader obsessed with opposition. In his final weeks he suspected a plot by Kremlin doctors.

Seagulls inspire speedy Spitfire

1936 Britain's aircraft industry has produced a fighter plane the government believes has the speed and power to counter the startling build-up of military aircraft in Hitler's Germany. The new fighter, called the Spitfire, is built by Vickers and powered by a liquid-cooled Rolls-Royce Merlin engine. The plane made its maiden flight today. It was designed by Reginald Mitchell, who drew up his plans after spending many hours watching how seagulls fly. The single-seat, low-wing monoplane will enter service with the Royal Air Force in the next two years to counter the German Messerschmitt 109, which is said to be the world's best fighter. Britain's air defences, which opposition MPs led by Winston Churchill have criticized as incapable of meeting a threat, will be dramatically strengthened by the Spitfire and its companion the Hawker Hurricane.

I found myself at a ball with two queens. The Queen of Naples looks like a grocer's wife overcome with age. Her husband is handsome and stupid, but entirely hidden behind a wide blue ribbon. The Queen of Spain looks good-natured and friendly, but horribly common. The Queen of Naples has the irritated air of a benevolent curmudgeon, and seems to be fundamentally kindly.
Stendhal, French author, reporting on social life in Rome, 1841.

1966 The criminal overlords of London's East End, 35-year-old twins Ronald and Reginald Kray, were today jailed for 30 years for murder. Four of their underworld gang were also convicted. As they were led away, one of the Krays told the judge menacingly: "I'll see you later!" It was the longest murder trial ever held at London's famous Old Bailey, lasting 39 days.

Birdseye puts freeze on peas

1930 An American food scientist from New York has perfected a method of storing food that will revolutionize the American kitchen – and help farmers solve their overproduction problems. Clarence Birdseye's frozen fish has been on the market since 1925. His new method of quick-freezing peas is said hardly to change their taste and texture.

BRITISH TROOPS FIRE ON AMERICAN DEMONSTRATORS

1770 British troops opened fire on an unruly crowd in Boston today, killing five Americans. The incident has been dubbed the "Boston Massacre". It follows 18 months of simmering tension since they arrived in Massachusetts in a show of force to quell American resentment over the Stamp Act, which taxes all legal or printed documents. Massachusetts was said to be "on the brink of anarchy". The Americans saw the troops as oppressors, and there have been fights between soldiers and citizens ever since. Today a crowd gathered at the Customs House became unruly, and a squad led by Captain Thomas Preston opened fire, killing three men and mortally wounding two others. All troops were immediately withdrawn from the town and Preston and six soldiers are under arrest. But the damage has been done: the incident has given the Boston radicals opposing Britain a powerful propaganda weapon.

1461 Henry VI of England is deposed by the Duke of York in the course of the Wars of the Roses.

1534 Death of Antonio Corregio, Italian Renaissance painter of sensuous mythological scenes.

1778 Death of Thomas Arne, British composer of more than 50 operas and stage works and, most famously, "Rule Britannia".

1790 Death of Flora Macdonald, Scottish heroine who helped Bonnie Prince Charlie escape to safety after the Battle of Culloden.

1856 The Covent Garden Opera House in London is destroyed by fire.

1926 The Shakespeare Memorial Theatre in Stratford-on-Avon is engulfed by flames.

1933 In Germany, the Nazis win almost half the seats in the elections.

1946 Winston Churchill, on tour in the US, says "An iron curtain has descended across Europe" in a speech about the Russian threat.

1984 Tito Gobbi, Italian baritone, dies aged 69.

1991 Baghdad Radio announces that the Iraqi government has annulled the annexation of Kuwait and promised that Kuwaiti assets will be restored.

1991 The last Cruise missile leaves Greenham Common airbase in Berkshire to be dismantled in Arizona as part of the INF disarmament treaty.

BIRTHDAYS

King Henry II 1133, first Plantagenet king of England.

Lady Augusta Gregory 1852, Irish playwright and co-founder (with W. B. Yeats) of the Abbey Theatre in Dublin.

Rosa Luxemburg 1871, German socialist leader and founder of the left-wing Spartacus movement.

Rex Harrison 1905, debonair British star of stage and screen.

Elaine Page 1952, British musical star who shot to fame in the Lloyd Webber musicals *Evita* and *Cats*.

1853 Verdi's opera *La Traviata* receives its premiere in Venice.

1900 Death of Gottlieb Daimler, motor engineer and inventor of the motor cycle.

1901 An anarchist fails in his attempt to assassinate Kaiser Wilhelm of Germany.

1932 John Philip Sousa, American composer of military marches, dies aged 78.

1944 Daylight bombing raids on Berlin from US air bases in Britain begin.

1971 In London, 4000 women's libbers march from Hyde Park to 10 Downing Street.

1971 Pearl Buck, American author and Nobel Prize winner who wrote *The Good Earth*, dies at 81.

1983 Australian Christopher Massey sets a water skiing record of 143.08 mph (228.9 kph).

1988 Dr Kurt Waldheim, Austrian president and former director-general of the UN, admits he knew Allied commandos held by his unit in World War II would be executed contrary to the Geneva Convention.

1992 American boxer Mike Tyson is found guilty of rape.

BIRTHDAYS

Savinien Cyrano de Bergerac 1619, French novelist and playwright who is said to have fought over 1000 duels to avenge unkind remarks about the size of his nose.

Elizabeth Barrett Browning 1806, British poet who fought free of a repressive father to marry poet Robert Browning.

Oscar Straus 1870, Viennese-born composer (later a French citizen) who wrote *The Chocolate Soldier*.

Ring Lardner 1885, American humorist, sports reporter and writer of short stories.

Ronald Reagan 1911, former American Republican president.

Andrzej Wajda 1926, Polish film director whose films include *A Generation* and *Ashes and Diamonds*.

Dame Kiri Te Kanawa 1944, New Zealand soprano.

Mexican massacre of Alamo resistance

1836 The heroic stand by a small band of Texan rebels at the old Alamo mission was today crushed. The 187 besieged Texans have been slaughtered. After a continuous 12-day artillery bombardment, 6000 Mexican troops under General Antonio Lopez de Santa Anna stormed the crumbling mission and massacred the defenders. Santa Anna had the bodies burned as a warning to Texas never again to challenge Mexican rule. One of the few survivors, Susanna Dickinson, a blacksmith's wife, was set free with a message from Santa Anna to Texan General Sam Houston that further fighting would end the same way. Among the dead was the famous frontiersman Davy Crockett, who had only just returned to Texas after two terms in Washington as a US congressman. The Alamo rebels' commander, Colonel Travis, had refused to obey Houston's orders to withdraw to a less vulnerable position.

1888 The grief surrounding her father's funeral was too great for Louisa M. Alcott, the American writer, feminist, abolitionist and teetotal campaigner who died today, hours after he was buried. Famous for the largely autobiographical story *Little Women*, Alcott drew much of her material from a poor childhood in which she and three sisters slipped ever-deeper into poverty.

IRA activists shot by SAS in Gibraltar

1988 In a pre-emptive strike against IRA terrorism, British commandos have shot dead an "active service unit" of Irish Republican activists on the island of Gibraltar. The security forces claim the three – Sean Savage, Mairead Farrell and Daniel McCann – were planning to attack a military parade and had a car packed with explosives. But no evidence to support this has yet been produced and eye-witnesses say the three were walking unarmed when they were gunned down at close range without any warning. The search for the car and the supposed weapons cache has widened to Spain and there are suggestions that members of Britain's elite SAS commando squad may well have been precipitate.

Wonder drug kills headache pain

1899 A new pain relief drug was patented today, and pharmacists are claiming it has almost magical properties. The drug, called aspirin, is said to relieve even severe pain, particularly headaches, muscle aches and joint pains. It acts within minutes. The patent for aspirin, or acetylsalicylic acid, is held by the chemist Felix Hoffmann, who synthesized the drug in his laboratory. Aspirin's active ingredient occurs in nature in the willow and other plants, and has been known for its medicinal properties since ancient times – but this will be the first time a cheap, reliable pain-killer is made universally available. Aspirin has shown itself to be relatively safe in tests so far. Plans are going ahead for its large-scale manufacture and distribution.

It takes people a long time to learn the difference between talent and genius, especially ambitious young men and women.
Louisa May Alcott, author of *Little Women*, died today, 1888.

Zeebrugge ferry rolls into nightmare

1987 A British-owned cross-channel ferry overturned in shallow water today outside the Belgian port of Zeebrugge. More than 200 people are feared drowned in Europe's worst maritime disaster in recent years. Most of the passengers were British. The *Herald of Free Enterprise* had just set sail after taking scores of cars aboard through the open bow section, but rescuers could not yet say if the bow doors had been left open in error. Ships and helicopters from Belgian and Dutch ports arrived quickly to save passengers who had escaped death. Survivors are telling horrific tales of being hurled across the lounges as the ship suddenly turned turtle. In London, the government has promised an inquiry into safety measures.

Chinese shoot Tibetan rebels

1989 Chinese security forces opened fire on Tibetan monks and civilians in Lhasa today. Officially, 12 "agitators" were killed, but Tibetan sources claim there are many more dead and wounded. A Western businessman in the city reports seeing "piles of bodies", and some estimates put the number of deaths in the hundreds. Hundreds more Tibetans have been arrested. The shootings started two days ago during a demonstration to mark the first Tibetan uprising against China 30 years ago. The strife continues as Chinese forces search for demonstrators, while rioting Tibetans have wrecked Chinese-owned shops and offices. China invaded Tibet in 1950, claiming it as a Chinese province, but Tibetans have been pressing for independence since 1985, thwarted by Peking. Today's show of force is by far Peking's most brutal response yet. It does not bode well for the Chinese pro-democracy movement in Peking.

1989 A convicted murderer in South Carolina who successfully appealed against being sent to the electric chair was today electrocuted accidentally while sitting on the toilet mending a pair of earphones.

First jazz record — but it's all white

1917 From today, America has a new sound to swing to. It's called jazz, the music of the black community, or more precisely Dixieland jazz from New Orleans. The Victor Company has issued a new phonograph recording it says is the first-ever jazz recording, spelling an altogether new direction in American popular music. Recorded in New York by Nick La Rocca and his Original Dixieland Jazz Band, the disc is entitled "The Dixieland Jazz Band One-Step". The musicians are all from New Orleans, but they are all white, playing in a style learned from the city's blacks. It may be some time before black musicians record their music, for to do so they must be able to travel to studios in New York or Chicago.

1838 Jenny Lind, the "Swedish Nightingale", makes a triumphant debut at the Stockholm Opera in Weber's *Der Freischutz*.

1912 Frenchman Henri Seimet flies from Paris to London in three hours, the first aviator ever to make the journey non-stop.

1971 Swiss men finally vote to give women the right to vote and to hold federal office.

1971 English poet Stevie Smith commits suicide.

1975 The body of British heiress Lesley Whittle is found in a 60-foot drain shaft, 52 days after she was kidnapped by a man the press call "The Black Panther".

1984 Donald Maclean, British Foreign Office official and Russian secret agent who fled to the Soviet Union in 1951, dies aged 70.

1988 Death of American transvestite actor Divine (Harris Glen Milstead), who starred in cult films *Pink Flamingoes* and *Polyester*.

BIRTHDAYS

Joseph Niepce 1765, French doctor who produced the first photograph from nature using a camera obscura, pewter plates and an eight-hour exposure.

Edwin Henry Landseer 1802, English painter and sculptor of the lions in London's Trafalgar Square.

Piet Mondrian 1872, Dutch abstract painter famed for his geometric compositions and primary colours.

Maurice Ravel 1875, French composer whose works include *Bolero* and the ballet *Daphnis and Chloe*.

Lord Snowdon (Anthony Armstrong Jones) 1930, British photographer and former husband of Princess Margaret.

Viv Richards 1952, Antiguan cricketer and former captain of the West Indies cricket team.

Ivan Lendl 1960, Czechoslovakian tennis player.

Rik Mayall 1958, British comedian who found fame with the TV series *The Young Ones*.

BELL RINGS FOR TELEPHONE

1876 A revolutionary new device was patented today – the electric voice telegraph or telephone. Its Scottish-born inventor, Alexander Graham Bell, teaches vocal physiology at Boston University and is an expert on communication with the deaf. He discovered the principle behind his machine last year. The telephone converts sound waves into electrical oscillations, which can then be transmitted long distances via a cable. It is possible it could be used on a commercial scale – in which case Alexander Graham Bell's invention could make him a very wealthy man.

Hitler throws gauntlet down to Britain

1936 In contempt of the Versailles Treaty imposed after World War I, Germany's chancellor Adolf Hitler has marched his troops into the demilitarized zone east of the Rhine. First reports say the troops, who began arriving through the night by truck, are being met with rejoicing by the local population. In addition to violating the treaty that ended the Great War, Hitler's actions could force signatories of the 1925 Locarno Pact into action to maintain Europe's stability. France wants action but Britain appears unconcerned by the development. In its anxiety not to upset Hitler, the British government has made a naval pact that removes controls on Germany imposed after the Great War and allows it to build a powerful navy. Now Mr Baldwin's government wishes to prevent France from issuing a formal challenge to Hitler.

> *Jazz will endure just as long as people hear it through their feet instead of their brains.*
> **John Philip Sousa**, American composer.

Allies cross the Rhine into Germany

1945 Nine years to the day after Hitler's troops occupied the Rhineland, making war inevitable, American troops have seized a strategic bridge over the Rhine and have begun crossing into Germany. Tonight troops poured across the bridge at Remagen and are now securing other crossings for heavy armour. While Soviet troops are advancing on Berlin, the US is concentrating on southern Germany.

1702 Queen Anne accedes to the British throne after the death of William III in a riding accident.

1790 The French Assembly votes to continue slavery in the colonies.

1910 The first pilot's licences are granted to a British man and a French woman – J. T. C. Moore Brabazon and Mlle Elise Deroche.

1952 An artificial heart is used for the first time on a 41-year-old male patient, keeping him alive for 80 minutes.

1917 Count Ferdinand von Zeppelin, inventor of the Zeppelin airship, dies aged 79.

1966 In London, Ronnie Kray of the notorious Kray twins walks into the *Blind Beggar* pub in Whitechapel Road and shoots a rival gangster, George Cornell, through the head.

1983 Sir William Walton, British composer who wrote the film scores for the films *Hamlet*, *Henry V* and *Richard III*, dies on the Isle of Ischia, Italy.

1988 The writers of American soap operas go on strike for improved terms and there are fears that *Dynasty* and *Dallas* are threatened.

1988 Police in a south Indian village keep 3000 residents indoors to enforce a government ban on the nude worshipping of a Hindu god.

BIRTHDAYS

Kenneth Grahame 1859, Scottish author of the children's book *Wind in the Willows*.

Otto Hahn 1879, German physicist and chemist who won the Nobel Prize for chemistry in 1944 and discovered nuclear fission.

Cyd Charisse 1921, American dancer and actress whose many films included *Singin' in the Rain*.

James Dean 1931, American film actor and cult hero who starred in *Giant*, *East of Eden* and *Rebel Without A Cause*.

Lynn Seymour 1939, ballerina.

David Wilkie 1955, British swimmer, Olympic gold medallist at the 1976 Olympics.

1989 The Chinese authorities today declared martial law in Tibet following the massacre of pro-Dalai Lama demonstrators by Chinese police in Lhasa this week. All foreigners have been hustled out of the country, and the Chinese are reportedly making arrangements to deport thousands of Tibetans from the strife-torn capital.

Vatican dismisses loss-making banker

1989 The long-running Vatican bank scandal has finally claimed a victim in Holy Orders. Rumours of massive mismanagement of the church's financial affairs first became public seven years ago when an Italian banker hanged himself in London. Today the Vatican stripped Archbishop Paul Marcinkus of command of Ambrosiana, its loss-making bank which last year had a US $88 million deficit. It is expected to go further into the red as a result of dealings with Italian financiers Roberto Calvi and Michele Sindona. Calvi was found dead under London's Blackfriars Bridge in 1982.

Round the world Empire style

1906 A book published today by the British government tells how in theory it is now possible to travel round the world without ever leaving the dominions of Great Britain. The British are compulsive measurers, and the latest *Blue Book* contains the results of a statistical survey and census of the Empire, which now has a population of 400 million people and covers 12 million square miles, circling the globe in pink.

TSAR'S TIME SHORT AS REVOLT GROWS

1917 There have been widespread street demonstrations in Petrograd, provoked by food shortages. This is nothing new for the turbulent Russia of today, but for the first time the Tsar's soldiers have refused to fire on the crowds or suppress the uprising. The army, which has suffered terrible casualties at the German front, now seems more an ally of the people than the increasingly isolated Tsar Nicholas II, who left Petrograd's garrison commander General Khabalov with the hard task of maintaining order. The moderate parliament, or Duma, which began its new session last week, senses matters are moving to a head as revolutionaries and defecting soldiers roam the streets. The Tsar's days of absolute power are clearly numbered.

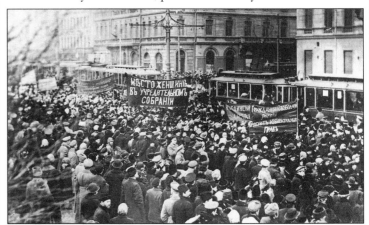

Satellite clash of titans

1971 Joe Frazier beat Muhammad Ali over 15 rounds tonight in a historic world heavyweight title fight. The fight grossed an estimated $20 million, which has to make it the most lucrative sporting contest ever. Most of that comes from closed circuit television receipts. Frazier was defending the world title he took from Ali four years ago without a fight. Ali was disqualified for refusing military service in the Vietnam War on religious grounds. He is a Black Muslim and a hero of black communities worldwide. His world-champion flamboyance makes him good news – the TV satellites have beamed him on to every small screen in the world. Both men were Olympic champions. Ali "dances like a butterfly, stings like a bee" – fast, deadly accurate. Frazier was unbeaten when he took the title. Last year the ban on Ali was lifted. Tonight they met in the ring for the first time – but not for the last.

Iran-Contra trial kicks off

1990 In a damning White House scandal, a former National Security Adviser has gone on trial on charges of conspiracy, obstructing Congress and lying to the nation. Admiral John Poindexter, President Ronald Reagan's top security adviser in 1985, became embroiled in the Iran-Contra affair as a consequence of secret agreements made by the Reagan administration to secure the release of US hostages in Iran in 1981. A covert arms sales fund of $30 million was diverted to finance right-wing guerrillas fighting Nicaragua's Sandinista government. In 1986 Poindexter resigned, and later told Congress he was to blame and that President Reagan had known nothing of the dealings.

Riots as poll tax protest sweeps England

1990 Six hundred years after England was last convulsed by popular unrest over government attempts to impose an unpopular poll tax, prime minister Margaret Thatcher is facing nationwide protest against her own version of the tax. The situation is scarcely as grave as the Peasants' Revolt of 1381 that almost toppled King Richard II, but the broad base of discontent with local councils' attempts to enforce the tax is widening rapidly. This week there have been a number of violent demonstrations as left-wing protesters sought to disrupt meetings in provincial cities where the tax was being set. Today dozens were arrested in south London as riot police broke up demonstrations. Mrs Thatcher claims the new tax, charged on all adults regardless of circumstance, is fairer than the old system of property rates. She also believes it will help ensure that local government gives tax-payers better value for local services. Her opponents say she has abused civil liberties and in the ruling Conservative Party there is mounting unease that the tax may prove to be her Waterloo.

"Terrorist" Makarios deported by British

1956 In a bid to stem the growing power and violence of the EOKA independence movement in Cyprus, British police have deported the leader of the Greek faction, the Orthodox Archbishop Michael Makarios. The Governor of Cyprus, Sir John Harding, claims that despite his clerical robes the bearded Makarios has been actively encouraging terrorist activity on the island. He was sent to exile in the Seychelles along with a key aide, Bishop Kyprianos. Since it took over the island in 1914 and built strategic military bases, Britain has been trying to keep the peace between the island's Greek and Turkish populations. Makarios is insisting on union with Greece. This is also the aim of EOKA (National Organization for the Cyprus Struggle), which has carried out bomb attacks against the British. Makarios's deportation has raised a storm of protest in Nicosia.

> *Now they're calling drugs an epidemic – that's 'cos white folks are doing it.*
> **Richard Pryor**, US comedian – ex-Beatle Paul McCartney has been charged with growing marijuana at his Scottish farm, 1973.

Cholesterol Kid bursts back

1987 Ex-world heavyweight champion George Foreman is making a comeback. He knocked out Steve Zouski in the fourth round tonight. Since nobody's ever heard of Steve Zouski, so what? This is what – it is 16 years since Foreman lost the crown to Muhammad Ali in Zaire. He's now 42 and bigger than ever before: he weighed in at an immense 263lb or 18st 3lb (down from 320) – a flabby, unpenitent, non-dieting heavy-eater. "I'm comfortable at 255," he says. The fans have dubbed him the Cholesterol Kid. But he won, in a style that commands notice – in fact he looked unstoppable. The man himself is determined to get a shot at the title. In 1977 Foreman had a religious experience in his dressing room after losing a fight to Jimmy Young. He retired from the ring and took to the pulpit for 10 years. Now he's back – with conviction.

Wild boy Tower unfit for defence

1989 The reputation of American Republicanism, already shaken by the Iran-Contra scandal, took another battering today when the US Senate decided that the man chosen to be in control of the world's most powerful armed forces was unfit for the post. They rejected Senator John Tower by a slender 53-47 margin. Senate hearings had focused on allegations of Tower's heavy drinking while in charge of sensitive arms control negotiations, lewd behaviour with secretaries, and using restricted government information for personal profit. Tower had been in charge of the Iran-Contra hearings.

Boney's Mme

1796 Napoleon Bonaparte, the brilliant young French officer who has just been made commander of the Army of the Interior, today married Josephine, a Creole divorcée and famous society beauty. A widow since her first husband the Vicomte de Beauharnais was guillotined in 1794, Josephine, 33, sought the marriage with Napoleon to protect her reputation after the two commenced a passionate affair which soon became very public.

1562 In Naples, kissing in public is made punishable by death.

1831 The French Foreign Legion is founded to serve in France's African colonies.

1864 General Ulysses Grant is made General-in-Chief of the Union Forces in the American Civil War.

1888 Death of Kaiser Wilhelm I of Prussia, who took the title in 1871, the first German ruler to do so since 1806.

1918 Frank Wedekind, German dramatist, actor, poet, singer and essayist, dies aged 54.

1923 Vladimir Ilich Lenin suffers a massive stroke and retires from the Soviet leadership.

1932 Eamonn de Valera is elected president of Ireland.

1937 *The Road to Wigan Pier*, George Orwell's powerful book on the effects of the Depression in northern England, is published.

1946 Thirty-three English football fans are killed when steel barriers collapse at Bolton Wanderers' football ground.

1967 Svetlana Alliluyeva, daughter of Joseph Stalin, defects to the West.

BIRTHDAYS

Amerigo Vespucci 1454, Italian navigator who discovered the mouth of the Amazon and gave his name to America.

William Cobbett 1763, British journalist who championed the cause of the underprivileged and wrote the book *Rural Rides*.

André Courrèges 1913, French couturier and inventor of the mini skirt in 1964.

Yuri Gagarin 1934, Soviet astronaut and the first man in space.

Bobby Fischer 1943, American chess champion who won the world title from Boris Spassky in 1972.

Micky Dolenz 1945, American actor and pop musician, founder member of the Monkees.

Bill Beaumont 1952, British Lions and England international rugby champion.

1661 Death of Cardinal Jules Mazarin, French statesman and chief adviser to the regent Anne of Austria, mother of King Louis XIV.

1914 In London's National Gallery, Mary Richardson, journalist and militant suffragette, attacks Velasquez' *Rokeby Venus* with a meat cleaver.

1968 In Wellington Harbour, New Zealand, a car ferry capsizes in a severe storm, drowning 200.

1969 James Earl Ray pleads guilty to the murder of civil rights leader Martin Luther King and is sentenced to 99 years in jail.

1980 Jean Harris, an American headmistress, murders her lover Dr Herman Tarnower, inventor of the Scarsdale Diet.

1981 Death of Sir Maurice Oldfield, the British intelligence chief thought to be the model for "M" in Ian Fleming's James Bond novels.

1985 Death of Konstantin Chernenko, General Secretary of the Soviet Communist Party since only 1984.

1986 Ray Milland, Welsh-born actor who starred in many films including *Beau Geste* and *Dial M for Murder*, dies aged 79.

1988 The Chinese army occupies Lhasa, capital of Tibet, after major demonstrations by Tibetans against continued Chinese rule.

1988 Andy Gibb of the Bee Gees dies of a drug overdose, aged 30.

BIRTHDAYS

Tamara Karsavina 1885, Russian ballerina who was one of Nijinsky's partners and co-founded the Royal Academy of Dancing in London.

Arthur Honegger 1892, French composer who was one of Les Six, a group of composers who united against Romanticism and Impressionism in French music.

Bix Beiderbecke 1903, American cornet player and composer who drew his inspiration from black jazz musicians.

Prince Edward 1964, youngest son of Queen Elizabeth II of England.

HOLLYWOOD? NEVER HEARD OF IT

1910 American film director D.W. Griffith thought he had found just the place to make his film *In Old California*, but he had to battle to get the producer's reluctant agreement to rent the old barn in the village where some of the action was shot. There was no reason why Griffith's bosses on the East Coast should have heard of Hollywood, but his discovery of a spot with the near-perfect natural light the cameras crave could start a studio stampede to the Los Angeles area. Griffith has transformed this young industry with the hundreds of short films he has made for Biograph: he pioneered the use of close-ups, travelling shots and modern editing techniques.

We don't want apartheid liberalized. We want it dismantled. You can't improve something that is intrinsically evil.
Bishop Desmond Tutu, South African clergyman, 1985.

It is strange how an old man of letters still feels stupid satisfaction at seeing his work printed in a newspaper. This morning, before seven o'clock, I went downstairs three times in my nightshirt to see if the Gil Blas *was in my letterbox and if it contained the first instalment of* Cherie. *Then I roamed around Paris, looking for my posters on the walls.*
Edmond de Goncourt, French diarist, writing in his journal

You expect your party to stay with you when the going gets tough. They got scared – so be it, so be it.
Margaret Thatcher, 1991.

Charles just avoids killer avalanche

1988 Prince Charles narrowly avoided disaster today on a skiing holiday in the Swiss Alps when a freak avalanche swept off two members of his royal party, killing one of them. The dead man was named as Major Hugh Lindsay, a member of the royal household. Mrs Palmer-Tomkinson, a close friend of the heir to the British throne, was injured. The Prince had been enjoying skiing off-piste in an area where rescue teams would have had difficulty in rescuing him had disaster struck. He is badly shaken by the incident.

US wins ex-Mex states

1848 The United States is today a million square miles larger thanks to the addition of California, New Mexico and parts of Texas – the spoils of victory in the war with Mexico. By today's congressional vote, reluctantly approving the terms of the Treaty of Guadalupe Hidalgo, Washington gains control of these lands but must pay their Spanish-speaking settlers $15 million compensation. The treaty ends a period of political hostility almost as bitter as the fighting: one group wanted to annex the whole of Mexico and throw it open to slavery. The abolitionists succeeded in banning slavery in new territories. The war has hardly been glorious – though casualties were light, almost a third of the 100,000-strong American volunteer army has succumbed to disease.

Iraqis sentence *Observer* reporter

1990 A journalist working for a British newspaper has been sentenced to death by a military court in Iraq. Farzad Bazoft, a 31-year-old Iranian-born reporter working for the *Observer*, confessed to spying charges after months in detention. Last year he tried to enter an Iraqi military base where it had been reported that a huge explosion, caused possibly by a ballistic missile, had caused as many as 700 deaths. A British nurse, Daphne Parish, who was driving with Bazoft, has received a 15-year sentence. There have been immediate pleas for clemency: British prime minister Margaret Thatcher has made a personal appeal to Iraqi strongman Saddam Hussein and journalists have begun a vigil outside the Iraqi embassy in London. But there is no sign that Saddam Hussein, who has reacted with fury to all attempts to expose the full range of his military might, will put off the hanging, ordered for next week.

1974 A Japanese soldier was today found in hiding on Lubang Island in the Philippines. He believed World War II was still being fought, and was waiting to be relieved by his own forces. Told the good news, he is now awaiting a potentially massive payoff from his war pension.

Chile awakens from Pinochet nightmare

1990 Chile today turned the page on 17 violent and bitter years of repression under General Augusto Pinochet, welcoming in the democratic era of Patricio Aylwin. Standing for a broad coalition, the 71-year-old lawyer soundly beat Pinochet's nominee Hernan Buchi in last November's polls. He was sworn in today, and stressed the need for reconciliation in a country where political passions have caused untold harm. Though moderate socialists and church and human rights leaders are celebrating the victory, Pinochet continues as army commander and has threatened to overturn the rule of law again if a single soldier is charged with human rights abuses. Chile's troubles began in 1970 when Salvador Allende became the world's first democratically elected Marxist leader. His confrontation with US capital interests and the local elite provoked the coup by his trusted aide Pinochet. Human rights organizations say thousands died as Pinochet set about eradicating what he called "the cancer of Marxism".

GORBACHEV IS LEADER OF THE USSR

1985 The youngest leader in the history of Soviet Communism has taken office in Moscow following the death yesterday of Konstantin Chernenko after a 13-month rule. The new general secretary is 54-year-old Mikhail Sergeyevich Gorbachev, who started his working life as a driver of tractors and harvesters. Western diplomats see Gorbachev as a potential reformer; his first official speech is being combed for favourable references to arms control and the prospects for detente with the west. Gorbachev first tried to implement political reforms in 1982 as an adviser to Yuri Andropov. After a period in which the Soviet Union has buried three elderly and ineffective leaders in as many years, Gorbachev could be just the kind of new blood the country needs.

The Americans cannot build aeroplanes. They are very good at refrigerators and razor blades.
Herman Goering
establishes the Luftwaffe, 1935.

Madrid shaken by bomb blasts

2004 Ten bombs ripped apart trains at three stations in Madrid during the morning rush hour, killing 190 and wounding 1,200. Spain's prime minister Jose Maria Aznar said the bombers would be brought to justice. Mr Aznar said he thought the Basque separatist group ETA was behind the blasts, but Interior Minister Angel Acebes later revealed that an Islamic tape had been found with detonators in a stolen van found near Madrid. Many observers say the bombings bear the hallmarks of the Islamic militant group al-Qaeda, which has threatened revenge on Spain for backing the American-led invasion and occupation of Iraq.

Britain puts down Indian Mutiny

1858 The Indian Mutiny has finally been put down after 10 months of strife that has forever changed the relationship between the British masters and their subjects. Henceforth, areas under British rule will be treated as vassal states and the Indian army will be more tightly overseen. The old intimacy is gone; stories of outrages by the mutineers have stoked British demands for revenge on India. The revolt was sparked off by British insensitivity to Indian customs: sepoys in the army mutinied after refusing to touch new rifle cartridges they believed were lubricated with animal fat that was either holy to Hindus or unclean to Muslims. It was the first clash against colonial rule.

US lifeline for warring allies

1941 America has handed a financial lifeline to friendly nations fighting Hitler and his allies by allowing President Franklin D. Roosevelt to apply US economic muscle without declaring war. Congress today approved the Lend-Lease Act, which will allow Britain, China, the USSR and other friendly powers to receive munitions, tanks, ships and other weapons on preferential credit terms. The Allies cannot otherwise afford to keep fighting the war.

1682 The Royal Hospital in Chelsea is founded to care for soldiers.

1702 The first daily paper in England, the *Daily Courant*, is published.

1844 In New Zealand, Maoris rise up against the British and burn a settlement.

1864 A reservoir near Sheffield in the north of England bursts its banks, killing 250 people.

1926 Eamonn de Valera resigns as leader of Sinn Fein in Ireland.

1945 The vast Krupps factory in Germany is destroyed when 1000 Allied bombers make the biggest-ever daylight bombing raid.

1955 Death of Sir Alexander Fleming, Scottish bacteriologist and discoverer of penicillin at St Mary's Hospital, London.

1957 Death of Erle Stanley Gardner, American lawyer and novelist who created Perry Mason.

1985 Harrods, the "top people's store" in Knightsbridge, is bought by the Fayed brothers, wealthy cotton brokers from Cairo.

1988 Death of Arthur d'Arcy Locke, South African golf champion.

1988 The Bank of England pound note ceases to be legal at midnight, replaced by the pound coin.

BIRTHDAYS

Sir Henry Tate 1819, British sugar magnate who endowed the Tate Gallery in London.

Sir Malcolm Campbell 1885, British holder of the world speed records on land and sea.

Harold Wilson 1916, British Labour Prime Minister 1964-70 and 1974-6.

David Gentleman 1930, British painter and designer, best-known for his scenes of London.

Douglas Adams 1952, British author of the cult radio serial *The Hitch-Hiker's Guide to the Galaxy* which became a book and a television series.

Rupert Murdoch 1931, Australian media tycoon.

604 AD Death of St Gregory, the Pope who initiated the Anglo-Saxons' conversion to Christianity.

1507 Cesare Borgia, once regarded as the saviour of Italy, dies at the siege of Viana in Navarre.

1789 The US Post Office is established.

1881 Tunisia is made a protectorate of France because of its strategic importance.

1912 Juliette Gordon Low founds the Girl Guides (later called Scouts) in the US.

1913 Canberra is made capital of Australia.

1940 The Russo-Finnish War is brought to an end with victory for the Soviet Union, the aggressor.

1945 Young Jewish diarist Anne Frank dies in a German concentration camp.

1955 Charlie ("The Bird") Parker, regarded as one of the greatest jazz musicians of all time, dies at the age of 35.

1969 The song *Mrs Robinson* is voted Record of the Year and wins a Grammy for US duo Paul Simon and Art Garfunkel.

1969 Beatle Paul McCartney marries Linda Eastman.

1999 Death of Yehudi Menuhin, violinist and conductor.

BIRTHDAYS

John Aubrey 1626, English antiquary whose novel *Brief Lives* was published 201 years after his death.

Kemal Ataturk 1881, Turkish statesman and soldier.

Gabriele d'Annunzio 1863, Italian poet, novelist, playwright and soldier.

Sir Henry Perkin 1838, English chemist who synthesized the first artificial dye, aniline purple.

Vaslav Nijinsky 1890, Russian dancer and choreographer whose tragically short career was brought to an end by mental illness.

Jack Kerouac 1922, American author of *On the Road*.

Liza Minnelli 1946, US singer, dancer and actress.

1991 Saddam Hussein's troops have crushed a rebellion in southern Iraq, where breakaway Shi'ites are demanding a separate Muslim state. Large numbers of civilians are said to have died. There are now reports that Shia Muslims in Baghdad have rebelled, and Kurdish rebels are resisting government forces in the north of Iraq.

I don't know what effect these men will have on the enemy, but, by God, they frighten me.
The Duke of Wellington, as his forces occupy Bordeaux, France 1813.

Gandhi starts Salt March to defy British

1930 Mahatma Gandhi, the spiritual leader of India's nationalist movement, today began a mass protest against British rule. Gandhi – who has been in and out of prison since he began his non-violent protests in South Africa – has chosen salt as his latest weapon. The Raj is insisting on its right to maintain a tax on its monopoly of the salt trade. Gandhi is walking from his house in Ahmedabad to the sea at Jalalpur to make salt with his own hands. About 100 followers have started out with him on the 300-mile journey, but many more are expected to join. He said he was "prepared for the worst, even for death, in defiance of the salt tax". Determined to stop this challenge to their authority, British administrators have ordered the destruction of salt pans on the coast and promised Gandhi will not reach the sea.

NAZIS ANNEXE AUSTRIA

1938 Adolf Hitler's troops marched into Austria today and made the country a German province. But Austrians, who have watched Hitler's plans for integrating the land of his birth into his Third Reich ever since the murder of Chancellor Engelbert Dollfuss in 1934 in an abortive Nazi putsch, are ecstatic over the Anschluss (annexation). Cheering crowds greeted the jack-booted troops as they poured in, and a massive welcome is being prepared for Hitler himself – he is expected in Vienna within 48 hours. The pretext for the Anschluss was the resignation of Austrian premier Kurt von Schuschnigg, who had been forced to include Nazis in his cabinet. Hitler is already turning his eye on Czechoslovakia, where oppressed native Germans in the Sudetenland seek integration with Germany.

Cubists baffle critics

1909 The current exhibition of avant-garde paintings by Pablo Picasso and Georges Braque at the Salon des Independants in Paris has revealed an extraordinary new style that the critics are treating with as much scorn as they did Impressionism in its early years. One writer, Louis Vauxcelles, says the new paintings "reduce everything to little cubes" – so the painters are proudly calling their new movement "Cubism". Picasso has abandoned his Rose Period harlequins, acrobats and dancers for increasingly abstract and simplified forms, while Braque favours fragments of still-recognizable objects like guitars, faces or wine glasses. The two invented the new abstract style last year, drawing on primitive art from Africa, Egyptian motifs and the geometric landscapes of modern painters like Paul Cézanne.

Truman launches Cold War by warning US of Communist threat

1947 Americans are coming to terms with a new piece of political jargon – "the Cold War". Financier Bernard Baruch borrowed the term from columnist Herbert Bayard Swope to describe the power struggle between Washington and Moscow. Now President Truman has put the Cold War at the top of the political agenda with a speech to the US Congress in which he urged the country to mobilize in a global crusade against expanding communism – a policy he is calling the Truman Doctrine. The US would give economic and military aid to countries deemed to be under Soviet threat, such as Greece and Turkey, he said. Washington would also "support free peoples who are resisting attempted subjugation by armed minorities or by outside pressures". The administration is preparing another foreign policy initiative, the Marshall Plan, which will pour billions of dollars into war-ravaged western Europe.

> *"Come unto me, all ye that are weary and heavy-laden."* Perhaps never, in all the history of suffering humanity, have these words been spoken to so great an assembly of the homeless, the penniless and the bereft. And when the address ended, as the Pope paused a moment before the Benediction, from thousands of throats came a cry of supplication, unforgettable to anyone who heard it – a cry which sounded like an echo of all the suffering that is torturing the world: *"Give us peace; oh, give us peace."*
>
> **Iris Origo**, in Nazi-occupied Tuscany, hears the Pope, 1944.

AMATEUR STARGAZER SPOTS NEW PLANET

1781 A new planet unknown to the ancient astronomers has been discovered by a German stargazer. William Herschel, an organist by profession, has a passion for grinding lenses and building telescopes with which to survey the heavens. He noticed that one of the stars in the constellation of Gemini had the characteristics of a planet. Today it was confirmed that a seventh planet in addition to Earth does indeed exist. The new planet, which is even further from the sun than Saturn, has yet to be named, but a possibility is Uranus, after the Greek god of the sky. Herschel is at work compiling a star catalogue.

1894 The first professional striptease takes place at the Davan Fayoneau Music Hall in Paris.

1900 British forces under the command of Field Marshal Roberts take Bloemfontein in the second Boer War.

1906 The American feminist Susan B. Anthony dies.

1926 The first commercial air route is established across Africa with the completion of a 16,000-mile London–Cape Town–London flight by Alan Cobham.

1928 Four hundred and fifty people are drowned when a dam near Los Angeles bursts.

1930 Pluto, the planet farthest from the sun, is discovered by Tombaugh as a result of calculations made by the astronomer Percival Lowell 14 years earlier.

1961 Artist Pablo Picasso, aged 79, marries his 37-year-old model, Jacqueline Rocque.

1972 Clifford Irving admits in a New York court that he has fabricated the "autobiography" of Howard Hughes.

1977 Czech secret police torture to death the leader of the Charter 77 movement, Jan Potocka.

1974 The Charles de Gaulle airport in Paris is opened.

1978 Moluccan terrorists hold 72 people hostage in government buildings in Assen, Holland.

DUTCH IN CAPE CATTLE BATTLE

1701 A marauding band of Griqua tribesmen rustled more than 40 cattle from Dutch settlers at the Cape of Good Hope today. Last month a hostile band of more than 300 raided outlying farms and took more than 200 cattle – though settlers shot three of the raiders. Such incidents are a feature of life here in a guerrilla war that has been festering almost since the colony was founded nearly 50 years ago. Trouble started when the local Khoisan natives became alarmed at foreign encroachments on their soil. In 1659, the Khoisan clans declared war on the colony, sweeping down in swift cattle raids.

The Dutch retaliated by taking Khoisan prisoners. The pattern was established – land encroachment on one side and cattle-stealing on the other – and intermittent warfare has continued ever since. It will grow worse as the white farmers expand into the South African hinterland.

1996 Sixteen pupils and their teacher were shot down by a lone gunman at their school in Dunblane. The man burst into the class of five- and six-year-olds in a random killing spree before turning the gun on himself. Twelve other children were taken to hospital, where one died of his injuries. The gunman has been named as Thomas Hamilton, 43, a local man and former scout master.

Grenada Marxists take over while PM away

1974 Sir Eric Gairy, the avuncular prime minister of the Caribbean island Grenada who has a passion for communication with other worlds, has been ousted in a very down-to-earth power struggle. With Gairy away in New York, political control of the island has been seized by 33-year-old Marxist Maurice Bishop and his New Jewel Movement. Bishop's ragged army of revolutionaries have taken over the radio station and announced they are setting up a government and army. A policeman was killed in the takeover. The former British colony only recently achieved its independence within the Commonwealth.

Tsar murdered by extremist bomb

1881 Tsar Alexander II has been murdered by extremists on the very day he had finally agreed to implement democratic reforms. Two bombs were thrown at the Tsar in St Petersburg. The first exploded harmlessly, but as the Tsar stood in the street asking questions about the attack a member of the *narodniki* extremist organization threw a second bomb that killed him. Alexander survived a string of assassination attempts after his proclamation ordering the emancipation of the serfs in 1861, but the *narodniki* were determined to eliminate him. This group of populist intellectuals condemned Alexander to death two years ago for refusing to summon a popular assembly. Ironically, Alexander signed a manifesto that would have created a national consultative assembly just before his death. The assassination itself will now postpone such a step.

Dr Joseph Priestley 1733, English chemist who discovered oxygen in 1774.

Sir Hugh Walpole 1884, English novelist perhaps best-known for his four-volume family saga, *The Herries Chronicle* (1930-33).

Tessie O'Shea 1918, English entertainer known as "Two-Ton Tessie" because of her size.

Neil Sedaka 1939, American singer-songwriter.

Joe Bugner 1950, Hungarian-born British heavyweight boxing champion who subsequently emigrated to Australia.

MARCH 14

1869 The third Maori rebellion in 15 years ends with the defeat of the guerrilla leader Titokowaru.

1891 The first underwater telephone cable is laid on the bed of the English Channel by the submarine *Monarch*.

1900 President McKinley puts America on the Gold Standard, a monetary system in which paper money is convertible into gold.

1915 The German cruiser *Dresden* is sunk.

1932 George Eastman, inventor of the Kodak camera, commits suicide.

1953 Nikita Krushchev becomes First Secretary of the Communist Party of the Soviet Union, replacing Georgi Malenkov.

1961 The *New English Bible* is published.

1966 Britain's first coloured policeman, Muhammad Yusuf Daar, is sworn in as a member of the Coventry force.

1975 The American film actress Susan Hayward dies.

1980 Twenty-two members of a US amateur boxing team die when a Polish airline crashes.

1991 Death of Howard Ashman, American lyricist, playwright and director – his best-known work was *Little Shop of Horrors*, Broadway's highest grossing and longest running musical.

BIRTHDAYS

Victor Emmanuel II 1820, the first king of a united Italy.

Albert Einstein 1879, German-born Swiss physicist and mathematician.

Quincy Jones 1933, American composer (*In the Heat of the Night*) and producer (Michael Jackson's huge-selling album *Thriller*).

Michael Caine 1933, English actor whose many films include *The Man Who Would Be King* and *The Ipcress File*.

Tessa Sanderson 1957, English athlete who won a gold medal at the 1984 Los Angeles Olympics for the javelin.

SPAIN EXPELS 150,000 JEWS

1492 Queen Isabella of Castile has ordered the 150,000 Jews in Spain to accept Christian baptism or face immediate expulsion. Most of the Jews are planning to leave rather than betray their faith, although they have nowhere to go. To Isabella and her husband Ferdinand, both devout Catholics, the offence of the Jews is twofold – in the past they were an important part of the Arab cultural renaissance in Iberia, contributing to the body of Spanish-Arab work on science, philosophy and other subjects that is proving a vital influence in today's Europe. Now the royals, who have forced the Arabs from Granada, are eager to sweep away the Jews, too. Encouraged by the monarchs, the Inquisition is enforcing absolute religious conformity.

> *Hegel says somewhere that all great events and personalities in world history reappear in one fashion or another. He forgot to add: the first time as tragedy, the second as farce.*
>
> **Karl Marx**.

Ruby guilty of Oswald TV murder

1964 Dallas night-club owner Jack Ruby has been found guilty of killing Lee Harvey Oswald, the presumed murderer of President John F. Kennedy. Two days after Kennedy's death last year, as Oswald was being taken from Dallas police headquarters to prison, Ruby shot him at close range. Now Ruby, 52, has been sentenced to death for silencing the only man who might have proved whether or not a wider conspiracy to kill Kennedy existed. The Warren Commission is investigating Oswald's motives, whether he had links with Ruby, and whether other assassins were implicated in Kennedy's death. Ruby simply said: "I did it for Jackie Kennedy."

The kaleidoscope choreographer

1976 Busby Berkeley, high priest of the Hollywood musical extravaganza, died today. His influence was greatest in the 1930s, when kaleidoscopic patterns of intertwining lines of massed dancers kicking their legs up – often filmed from above – became his trademark of thinly-repressed eroticism. On both stage and screen Berkeley went for grandiose choreography even when the intimate would have sufficed. At the time, films like the "Gold Diggers" series and *Footlight Parade* were big hits, but fashions – and society's perceptions of women – changed. Berkeley's overblown chorus-lines stepped back out of the limelight, and he had no choice but to follow them.

KARL MARX DIES

1883 Karl Marx died today in London – "the best-hated and most-calumniated man of his time", according to his colleague Friedrich Engels. As a revolutionary philosopher, his materialistic conception of history has established a method of social analysis that goes far beyond the movements of political exiles that took him as their guide. Even if the revolution of the proletariat that he preached never actually happens, socialism now has a prophet and a bible – Marx's *Das Kapital*. Marx settled in London after being expelled from Prussia and France for his ever-increasing radicalism. In 1848 Marx and Engels, both followers of Hegel, published *The Communist Manifesto*, which developed the theory of class struggle. In 1864 Marx, who lived in extreme poverty and spent most of his time reading and writing in the British Museum, helped create the International Working Men's Association, later known as the First International. In 1868 he published the first volume of *Das Kapital*, his masterwork, which used dialectical materialism to show that capitalist society would eventually be overwhelmed.

Tsar Nicholas abdicates

1917 Russia is today without a Tsar – the 300-year-old Romanov dynasty ended as Nicholas II abdicated. This follows food riots in Petrograd, where soldiers refused to act against the crowds. Today a special Duma committee and the Petrograd Soviet demanded that Nicholas relinquish power and appointed Prince Georgi Lvov as president. The Tsar tried to give the crown to his brother Michael, but Michael refused it. The Romanovs' undoing was sown in two disastrous wars. Nicholas preferred the advice of his headstrong wife Alexandra, and her sinister adviser the monk Rasputin. After Russia's defeat by Japan in 1905 the Tsar promised reforms and a democratic assembly, but later reneged. In the Great War he took command of his armies but failed to gauge the terrible suffering imposed on the Russian people. Tsar Nicholas has now gone to Pskov to bid farewell to his army.

CAESAR SLAIN

44 BC Julius Caesar should have listened to his fortune-teller. "Beware the Ides of March", he was told, but he insisted on attending a meeting of the Senate in Pompey's theatre. Caesar has recently compared himself to Alexander the Great, and was planning the conquest of Parthia. Many Romans were convinced he had to be stopped. Stabbed by Marcus Brutus, he fell with the words, "You too, Brutus?"

STALIN PURGES ON

1938 The Soviet dictator Joseph Stalin's infamous purges of the Communist Party reached their peak today with the execution of 18 senior figures, several of them Lenin's favourites. Among those shot at Lubyanka prison, after "confessing" extraordinary crimes against the state, was Nikolai Bukharin. Bukharin's revolutionary credentials appeared even more respectable than Stalin's – which perhaps contributed to his fate. The trials have also seen a former premier and an ex-head of the secret police confessing to the most improbable plots to overthrow the Soviet state – but Stalin considers the trials "healthy".

Baseball goes pro

1869 The Cincinnati Red Stockings are professionals, and out of their first 92 baseball games this season they have won 91. Their success as the first truly professional team is encouraging others to follow suit in the organized league, the National Association of Baseball Players. Baseball has come of age. It first appeared in the Eastern United States in the 1820s as a development of rounders. In 1845 the rules were laid out, and in 1857 they were amended by a convention of baseball clubs. Now the whole game is going professional.

Before us stands the last problem which must be solved and will be solved. It is the last territorial claim which I have to make in Europe, but it is the claim from which I shall not recede.
Hitler storms Prague, 1939.

Taylor and Burton tie the knot

1964 Britain today produced its answer to the Hollywood screen romance when two of its best-known actors tied the knot in Montreal. Richard Burton, the handsome Welshman whose work on Broadway and on the London stage is well-known even to those who have only seen him in films, married the violet-eyed beauty Elizabeth Taylor. The glamorous couple are said to be "very, very happy".

Brazil's Indiana Jones shoots the "tiger of inflation"

1990 Fernando Collor de Mello took office today as Brazil's first elected president in almost 30 years – and immediately announced dramatic measures to quell the country's runaway 250 per cent annual inflation. Collor, 33, narrowly won last year's elections on a populist ticket. He has confiscated $80 billion worth of private savings in a make-or-break economic plan that must now be approved by the congress. Many small savers have been left with less than $150 (£80) in the bank, with the promise of seeing their money back only in 18 months. Collor also plans to dismiss thousands of civil servants and sell off loss-making state companies. Collor compared himself to a hunter slaying the tiger of inflation with a single shot, while US President George Bush has compared him to the screen hero Indiana Jones. With film-star looks and a karate black belt, the new president comes from a wealthy family with media interests in Northern Brazil, where he briefly worked as a TV presenter. Collor's command of the small screen during the campaign swept him to power.

MARCH 15

1584 The reforming Russian tsar, Ivan the Terrible, dies.

1820 Maine becomes the 23rd state of the Union.

1900 British prime minister Lord Salisbury rejects US President McKinley's offer to mediate in the Boer War.

1909 The American entrepreneur G. S. Selfridge opens London's first American-style department store on a six-acre site in Oxford Street.

1915 American soldiers under the command of General Pershing enter Mexico to hunt down the revolutionary Pancho Villa.

1933 Adolf Hitler proclaims the Third Reich in Germany, prompting an exodus of Jews from the country – kosher food and left-wing newspapers are banned.

1937 Bernard Faustus sets up America's first blood bank.

1966 British singer Tom Jones wins a Grammy for Best New Artist.

1975 The death is announced of the Greek shipping tycoon Aristotle Onassis.

1989 The centre of the Hungarian city of Budapest fills with rival demonstrators who voice their opposition to or support for the Communist government.

1990 Farzad Bazoft, a journalist working for the British newspaper the *Observer*, is hanged as a spy in Iraq.

1991 Albania and the United States restore full diplomatic relations after a gap of 52 years.

BIRTHDAYS

Andrew Jackson 1767, who became seventh president of the United States in 1828, served two terms and finally retired in 1837.

Mike Love 1941, American singer and founder member of the Beach Boys.

David Wall 1946, British dancer, formerly with the Royal Ballet company, latterly director of the Royal Academy of Dancing.

Terence Trent d'Arby 1961, US pop singer and ex-boxer.

1802 The US military academy at West Point is established.

1815 William of Orange is made King of the United Netherlands and crowned William I.

1872 The Wanderers beat the Royal Engineers 1-0 in the first English Football Association final.

1888 In Paris, France, Émile Roger makes the first recorded purchase of a motor car, a Benz.

1914 Madame Caillaux, wife of the French finance minister, shoots dead the editor of the newspaper *Le Figaro* to protect her husband against libel.

1915 Britain's Jockey Club decides that war is no reason to stop horse racing.

1930 The death of the Spanish leader Miguel Primo de Rivera y Orbaneja is announced.

1935 Adolf Hitler renounces the terms of the Treaty of Versailles and introduces conscription.

1937 British statesman Sir Joseph Austen Chamberlain dies.

1971 In Britain, the Campaign for Real Ale (CAMRA) is set up.

1973 British monarch Queen Elizabeth II opens the new London Bridge.

BIRTHDAYS

James Madison 1751, fourth US President, who was first elected in 1809 and retired at the end of his second term, in 1817.

Georg Simon Ohm 1787, German physicist who in 1827 discovered the basic law of electric current, later known as Ohm's law.

Matthew Flinders 1774, English explorer after whom the Flinders River and Flinders mountain range in Australia are named.

Leo McKern 1920, Australian-born actor of stage, film and television, noted for character roles.

Jerry Lewis 1926, American film star famous for his zany roles and partnership with singer-actor Dean Martin.

Bernardo Bertolucci 1940, Italian film director whose films include *The Last Emperor* and *Last Tango in Paris*.

BEARDSLEY DIES AT 25

1899 The brilliant, shocking young London illustrator Aubrey Beardsley has died at the age of 25, at the height of his career. Beardsley's art nouveau, much of it published in the avant-garde *Yellow Book* to which Oscar Wilde has been a frequent contributor, is almost all explicitly erotic. Until he quar-

relled with Wilde, Beardsley was one of the entourage that gave the decadent London of the 1890s its sexually ambivalent flavour. Line drawings such as those in illustrated volumes of *Volpone*, *The Rape of the Lock* and *Lysistrata* were a slap in the face for staid Victorian values. His personal life was no less shocking – rumours abound about his overly-close relationship with his sister Mabel.

US troops massacre 300 villagers in ditch

1968 Reports are reaching Saigon of a massacre of 300 unarmed villagers by American troops in the South Vietnamese village of My Lai. Soldiers under the command of Lt William L. Calley were flown in to break a rebel stronghold. More than 300 women, children and elderly men were herded into ditches and riddled with automatic fire. Calley and his men were apparently not shamed by this mass murder, since it was carefully photographed. There are also reports of another horrifying mass killing of civilians by US troops at My Khe.

> *I am just going outside and may be some time.*
> **Lawrence Oates** leaves his tent and disappears into the Antarctic blizzard, 1912.

Space dream gets boost

1926 Man's dream of journeying to the stars took a leap forward today when the American physicist Robert Goddard successfully launched a liquid-propelled rocket. Goddard's latest rocket did not travel as far as many of the solid-fuelled versions he has been testing, but the new fuel means much greater payloads. The device uses a simple pressure-fed rocket that burns petrol and liquid oxygen. Goddard developed it in his spare time without any funding. He has published detailed papers about his rocketry experiments, but the United States government does not seem very interested.

EVANS FINDS ANCIENT HOARD AT KNOSSOS

1900 Just days after he started digging at what he suspected was the site of a Cretan Bronze Age palace, the British archaeologist Sir Arthur Evans today struck an incredible hoard of antiquities dating from 16 centuries BC. Sir Arthur has named the civilization whose ruins he is excavating at Knossos, on the Greek island of Crete, the Minoan culture – a reference to the mythical Cretan Minotaur. Sir Arthur says there are signs the Minoans worshipped bulls; he believes the sprawling palace may contain the labyrinth built by Daedalus described in the ancient tale. He has also uncovered the earliest known writing. The new find is the most exciting since German archaeologist Heinrich Schliemann excavated Mycaenae in 1874.

> *To the rooftop, where half the press were waiting for Ralph Richardson to inaugurate his rocket. Called Ralph's Rocket, this will be fired every night when the curtain goes up. "I love fireworks," he said, "they are so unnecessary."*
> **Peter Hall,** theatre director, writing on the opening of Britain's National Theatre, 1976.

India's most powerful sultan surrenders

1792 Tippoo Sahib, the most powerful Indian sultan still resisting the advance of British imperialism, has finally been beaten in battle. His defeat ends the third war fought over Mysore and means he will be forced to give up half his immense lands to the administration of the British East India Company. Tippoo's secret was that he studied western military operations and was able until now successfully to second-guess British moves. But against General Charles Cornwallis he did not fare as well as the American colonists, who soundly beat the British commander at Yorktown. After this defeat Cornwallis was sent to India as governor-general with the mission of crushing Tippoo Sahib. While the sultan has been beaten, he is still far from crushed.

GRANDMOTHER TAKES OVER IN ISRAEL

1969 A 70-year-old grandmother today took office as Israel's first woman prime minister. Golda Meir outflanked ultra-orthodox Jews opposed to seeing women in power when she took over the leadership of the Labour Party, following the death last month of Levi Eshkol. Born in the Ukraine, as a young woman she spent many years as a school teacher in the United States before moving to what was then Palestine in 1921. She held important posts in the Jewish Agency and the World Zionist Organization. After independence in 1948 she was Israel's ambassador to Moscow and held two ministerial posts. Defending Israel's borders against surprise Arab attack will be a major concern of the new prime minister. Meir has chosen General Moshe Dayan, the hero of the Six-Day War, as her defence minister.

Birth control clinic opens for London's poor

1921 Five years after police in the United States forced a birth control centre to close down for outraging public morals, a British campaigner today opened a clinic to advise mothers on how to avoid having more children. The Mothers' Clinic in North London has been set up by Dr Marie Stopes, the author of the widely publicized *Married Love* – one of the first books to discuss sexual relations in a straightforward manner. Dr Stopes, a well-known womens' rights campaigner, is facing stiff resistance to her new clinic from church leaders and doctors who insist that by making contraceptives freely available to poor women, immorality will increase. Margaret Sanger, whose American clinic was closed down for similar reasons, plans to reopen the clinic as soon as possible.

Britain repeals tax to save American colonies

1766 Parliament in London is tonight voting on the repeal of the controversial Stamp Act, which has been mainly responsible for the climate of rebellion in the American colonies. The Act, passed last year as a means of paying for the increasing cost of maintaining troops in the colonies, required Americans to pay a tax on all legal or printed documents and newspapers or pamphlets. Instead of helping to keep order, it gave the colonists – who have no voice in parliament – a rallying-cry: "Taxation without representation is tyranny." A boycott of British goods and refusal to buy the hated stamps has mushroomed into an organization called the Stamp Act Congress, which recently issued a bill of American rights. A simple repeal of the Act may come too late to stifle the rebellion.

VAN GOGH MOVES TO PARIS

1886 Vincent van Gogh, the young Dutch painter who has been studying at the art academy in Antwerp, has come to Paris to further his training under the supervision of his brother, Theo. The truth is that his family are exasperated by this 33-year-old who has been unable to support himself and shows signs of mental instability. He was sacked from his job at a gallery and abandoned another at a bookshop, failed to make headway with theological studies and was no success as a lay missionary working under the direction of his father, a clergyman. But Van Gogh's early paintings of peasant subjects, such as *The Potato Eaters*, show great promise.

USSR votes on unity

1991 Soviet voters have gone to the polls to decide whether or not their vast country will remain a single unit. President Mikhail Gorbachev has been passionately campaigning for a "yes" vote in the nationwide referendum, while his rival Boris Yeltsin has been urging a "no". Six breakaway republics have refused to participate because they are convinced the draft of the new Union Treaty being proposed by Gorbachev would undermine their freedom. Three have announced they will run their own referendum. A strong turnout is expected and analysts believe the "yes" lobby will win by a considerable margin.

1337 Edward, the Black Prince, is made first Duke of Cornwall by his father, King Edward III of England, giving him a 130,000-acre estate and a source of income.

1782 Swiss physicist Daniel Bernoulli dies.

1845 Briton Stephen Perry patents the rubber band.

1848 Violence breaks out in Berlin against the conservatism of Prussian ruler Frederick William IV.

1853 Death of Austrian physicist Christian Doppler, who coined the term Doppler effect to explain the apparent change in the frequency of a wave when the source is moving relative to the observer.

1899 A merchant ship run aground off the English coast sends the first radio distress call.

1958 Australian-born polar explorer Sir George Wilkins dies.

1959 The US submarine *Skate* surfaces at the North Pole after completing an historic under-ice voyage to reach its destination.

1968 Violent demonstrations against American involvement in the Vietnam War take place outside the US embassy in London.

1978 A tanker, the *Amoco Cadiz*, runs aground off the Brittany coast, splits in two and begins to release its massive cargo of crude oil.

1983 British premier Margaret Thatcher is the target of a letterbomb campaign by the IRA.

1992 South Africa's white population votes in favour of constitutional change.

BIRTHDAYS

Edmund Kean 1787, British actor.

Gottlieb Daimler 1834, pioneer German car maker and engineer.

Bobby Jones 1902, American golfer and first amateur to win the British Open championship held at Lytham St Annes (1926).

Nat "King" Cole 1917, American popular singer and pianist.

Rudolf Nureyev 1938, Russian ballet dancer, considered one of the greatest of dancers.

MARCH 18

BIRTHDAYS

Pakistan court condemns Bhutto to death

1978 An army judge in Lahore today condemned Pakistan's former prime minister, Zulfikar Ali Bhutto, to death after finding him guilty of ordering the murder of a political opponent in 1974. Despite the military court's ostensible respect for the forms of law, the decision is part of a brutal power struggle. Last July Bhutto's government was overthrown by the army chief of staff, General Muhammad Zia Ul-Haq. Zia stepped in after an allegedly rigged election victory for Bhutto was followed by rioting, with martial law imposed in some cities. In place of Bhutto's free-wheeling and often questionable political methods at the head of his Pakistan Peoples' Party (PPP), the anti-communist Zia has imposed Islamic rule and a political clampdown. Bhutto's lawyers have promised to appeal, but as the final decision rests with General Zia himself clemency is not expected.

> *It is very unreasonable for people to be depressed by unfavourable reviews: they should say to themselves "Do I write better than Wordsworth and Shelley and Keats? Am I worse treated than they were?"*
> **A. E. Housman**, British poet writing to a friend today, 1924.

KAISER SACKS BISMARCK

1890 Otto von Bismarck, the mighty German chancellor who has governed Prussia and later Germany with a policy of "blood and iron" since 1862, was today summarily dismissed from his post by Kaiser Wilhelm II. Despite his ability to build a huge empire, the strong-willed Kaiser wanted none of the old politician's advice. Even Bismarck's pioneering social welfare legislation, which in 1889 provided Germans with insurance against illness, accident, and old age, could not deflect the enmity of the socialists whom the 31-year-old Kaiser is trying to befriend. Bismarck seemed to court dismissal: he has often failed to turn up in Berlin, spending his time in the country nursing grievances or giving warnings of anarchist plots.

Tristram Shandy author dies

1768 Laurence Sterne, the creator of Tristram Shandy and his uncle Toby – two of the most amiable and comical eccentrics in English letters – has died of pleurisy. Sterne became famous overnight with *The Life and Opinions of Tristram Shandy, Gentleman* – a massive satirical digression into the nature of the novel and just about every other aspect of 18th-century life. The work also reflects Sterne's upbringing in Ireland and his career in the church. Sterne's book has had a strong influence on other writers: his Walter Shandy, Uncle Toby and Parson Yorick are characters of extraordinary realism. Toward the end of his life Sterne travelled to Europe, primarily for health reasons, and subsequently produced the delightful *A Sentimental Journey through France and Italy*.

Red Brigade kidnaps Italy's ex-prime minister

1978 Red Brigade terrorists today confirmed they are the kidnappers of former prime minister Aldo Moro, releasing a photograph of the Christian Democrat politician in captivity. Police have been unable to trace the hide-out where Moro is being held by at least six armed men who pulled him from his car in the centre of Rome. The far-left terrorists issued a communiqué accusing Moro of a number of "crimes against the people", for which they said he would be put on trial for his life. The Christian Democrat party, for which Moro headed five coalition governments, is refusing to make any deals with the kidnappers.

RUSSIAN SPACEMAN TAKES A WALK OUTSIDE

1965 Soviet cosmonaut Aleksei Leonov today became the first man to walk in space as he danced and somersaulted in orbit hundreds of miles above the earth, secured only by a slender lifeline. As co-pilot of the Soviet Union's Voskhod II craft, 31-year-old Colonel Leonov left the craft to take the first hand-held film images of the earth during his 15-minute adventure, spinning gracefully above the earth in a bright orange space suit.

University basketball star gets $1.2m deal

1969 Led by centre Lew Alcindor, UCLA won the NCAA basketball championship today for the fourth time in six years, beating Purdue 97 to 92. Alcindor won the Most Valuable Player award for the third year in a row, the first player to do so. Just how valuable he is was revealed by the Milwaukee Bucks, who have paid $1,200,000 for Alcindor's services for the next five years. Two years ago Alcindor, playing in his first varsity year, achieved an all-time high season field goal percentage of .667.

> *It is better to be violent, if there is violence in our hearts, than to put on the cloak of non-violence to cover impotence.*
> **Mahatma Gandhi** goes to jail for sedition, 1922.

END OF YARN FOR TARZAN'S CREATOR

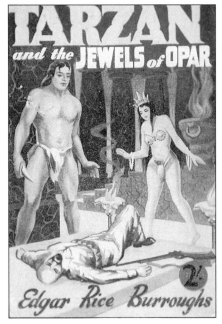

1950 American novelist Edgar Rice Burroughs, who created Tarzan of the Apes and sold more than 100 million copies of his 70 novels in 56 languages, has died aged 75. Educated at a military academy, followed by a short spell in the cavalry, his literary career began inauspiciously in 1911 with pulp magazine fiction. High art it wasn't, but it sold. After Tarzan first appeared in *All-Story Magazine* in 1912, Burroughs wrote 24 novels about the English aristocrat hero raised by wild apes in the African jungle, and now made famous through the cinema. From Burroughs' pen poured crime stories and westerns, adventure fantasies of lost cities, faraway civilizations and even distant planets, such as the popular "Warlord of Mars" series. Burroughs spun a rattling good yarn and is probably the century's most widely-read novelist.

There seems to be in the end of his voyage negligence, treason, hunger, sickness and death. He shall find many enemies in his return and have great loss of goods and honour: much villainy and treason shall be wrought.
Dr Simon Forman, astrologer, today warned the Earl of Essex against a military expedition in Ulster – 1589.

1913 *Boris Godunov*, the majestic Russian opera of 17th-century intrigue in the Kremlin, was tonight premiered in its full-length form at New York's Metropolitan Opera with Arturo Toscanini conducting. Modest-Mussorgsky's 1869 opera tells of Gudunov's ambition for the Tsar's crown and his pangs of guilt once he has gained it.

Tolpuddle martyrs transported

1834 As punishment for trying to set up a rural trade union, six southern England farmworkers have been sentenced to seven years' transportation to Australia. The punishment – effectively a death sentence because of the harsh conditions in the colony – has brought a huge public outcry. The convicts are being called the Tolpuddle Martyrs, after the name of their Dorset village. The men wanted to set up a branch of the Friendly Society of Agricultural Labourers. At the same time the Whigs are proposing the abolition of wage subsidies to help low-paid farmworkers like the Tolpuddle Martyrs stay out of the workhouses. Britain's harsh treatment of its poor is in stark contrast with its international campaign against slavery.

English cricket rebels banned for three years

1982 England's cricket authorities have banned 15 English players currently on a "rebel" tour in South Africa, breaking the international sports boycott of the land of apartheid. Test cricketers Graham Gooch, John Emburey and 13 other members of the so-called "Invitation XI" have been banned for three years. The cricket board's crackdown follows the threat that the Indian and Pakistani tours of England scheduled for this summer would be cancelled in the row over the English players' rebellion.

TV preacher resigns in sex and corruption scandal

1987 TV evangelist Jim Bakker has been forced to resign from his very lucrative Praise the Lord religious network in the southern United States after confessing a string of sexual adventures unfitting for a man of the cloth. Bakker and his wife Tammy LaValley were well-known on hundreds of religious networks in dozens of countries, exhorting viewers of the "Jim and Tammy Show" to follow their spiritual example. An extramarital group sex scandal dating from 1980 could now also force his unfrocking as a minister of the Assembly of God. In addition, Bakker is under investigation for having pocketed church funds donated by supporters.

1932 Sydney Harbour Bridge in New South Wales, Australia, was opened today, the world's longest single-span arch bridge. It has a 1650 ft (503 m) span, carries four railway tracks, a 56 ft (17 m) wide road and two footpaths.

MARCH 19

721 BC The Babylonians make the first-ever record of an eclipse of the sun.

1791 Equal rights are granted to French and English-speaking settlers in Canada.

1853 Chinese peasants led by the rebel Hong Xiu Quan capture Nanjing.

1861 An uneasy truce is established between Maoris and the colonial government of New Zealand in the two-year war over the enforced sale of Maori lands.

1920 The US Senate votes against joining the League of Nations.

1930 Former British prime minister Arthur Balfour (1902–6) dies.

1931 Indigestion aid Alka-Seltzer goes on sale in the US.

1958 Britain's first planetarium opens in London, at the famous waxworks museum, Madame Tussaud's.

1976 Princess Margaret, sister of the Queen of England, separates from her husband, photographer Lord Snowdon, after 15 years of marriage.

1992 The Duke and Duchess of York announce their separation.

BIRTHDAYS

Georges de la Tour 1593, French painter best-known for his nocturnal candle-lit scenes.

Tobias Smollett 1721, British writer of satirical novels.

Dr David Livingstone 1813, Scottish missionary and explorer and the first white man to discover the Victoria Falls.

Wyatt Earp 1848, American lawman famed for bringing order to Tombstone, Arizona.

Adolf Eichmann 1906, German SS colonel and war criminal.

Ursula Andress 1936, Swiss actress.

Courtney Pine 1964, British jazz saxophonist.

Philip Roth 1933, American author best known for *Portnoy's Complaint*, published in 1967.

1413 Death of the English king, Henry IV.

1653 Oliver Cromwell, Lord Protector of England, dissolves the Long Parliament.

1739 Persian ruler Nadir Shah sacks the Indian city of Delhi.

1792 The French Legislative Assembly approves the use of the guillotine for capital punishment.

1793 An army of peasant-royalists defeats the forces of the Republican government in the Vendée region of France.

1819 Burlington Arcade, the exclusive shopping mall, opens in London.

1934 Radar is first demonstrated in Kiel harbour, Germany.

1945 Lord Alfred Douglas, the one-time love of Oscar Wilde, dies.

1969 Beatle John Lennon marries Japanese-American artist Yoko Ono.

1980 British radio pirate ship Radio Caroline sinks.

1990 Namibia gains independence as South Africa pulls out to end more than a century of foreign domination.

1995 More than 5,500 people are rushed to hospital and 12 die when sarin nerve gas is released on the Tokyo subway by the Am Shinrikyo cult.

BIRTHDAYS

Ovid 43 BC, Roman poet best-known for the *Metamorphoses*.

Sir Isaac Newton 1727, English scientist who discovered the law of gravitation.

Henrik Ibsen 1823, Norwegian dramatist and poet whose early plays made strong criticism of the social mores in nineteenth-century Norway.

Beniamino Gigli 1890, Italian tenor who made his debut in 1920 at La Scala, Milan in Boito's *Mefistofele*.

Sir Michael Redgrave 1908, British stage and screen actor.

Dame Vera Lynn 1917, British singer dubbed the "Forces sweetheart" because of her popularity with Second World War servicemen.

First detective novel: Poe dunnit

1841 The poet and literary journalist Edgar Allan Poe has today published a horrifying yet fascinating work of fiction that critics are citing as the first example of a new style – the detective story. *The Murders in the Rue Morgue* is a challenging piece of work for the reader, who must exercise the deductive powers of a detective to keep pace with Poe's writing and discover who is really the villain before the final page. An orphan, Poe gave up a military career to write. Until recently he was editor of the *Southern Literary Messenger*, which has published much of his influential criticism, poetry and prose fiction.

US LAUNCHES MISSILES AT SADDAM

2004 American missiles have been launched at Baghdad, signalling the start of the US campaign to remove Saddam Hussein from power. President George Bush made a statement shortly after the bombings began, vowing to "disarm Iraq and to free its people". He said: "This will not be a campaign of half measures and we will accept no outcome but victory." The attack came shortly after the 48-hour deadline expired for Saddam Hussein to leave Iraq. American sources say the Iraqi leader himself was targeted in the first attacks. The Iraqis say some non-military targets have been hit and a number of civilians have been wounded. The air strikes began at 05.34 local time. A short time later, Iraqi TV broadcast what it said was a live speech by Saddam. In it he said: "I don't need to remind you what you should do to defend our country. Let the unbelievers go to hell, you will be victorious, Iraqi people."

> *I did not write it. God wrote it. I merely did his dictation.*
> **Harriet Beecher Stowe**
> on *Uncle Tom's Cabin*,
> published today, 1852.

Napoleon returns to Paris in triumph

1815 Napoleon Bonaparte today re-entered Paris as the returning hero after putting behind him a dreary year of exile on the Mediterranean island of Elba. His protestation of peaceful intentions has not been believed: King Louis XVIII fled to Belgium and the alliance of countries that beat Napoleon's armies last year – Russia, Britain, Prussia and Austria – are again preparing for war. The allies, who are in Vienna negotiating a complex peace agreement to cover the whole of Europe, have branded Napoleon "the enemy and disturber of the peace of the world". Later this week they will sign a specific pact to defeat the former emperor.

Princess Anne shot at in kidnap attempt

1974 Princess Anne, the daughter of Britain's Queen Elizabeth II, escaped unhurt today after an armed man tried to kidnap her in London. The attempt was part of a bizarre bid to draw attention to declining public health services for mental patients in Britain. The gunman, Ian Ball, ambushed the princess's car close to Buckingham Palace and fired six shots into it. After blocking the royal car with his own, Ball tried to drag out the princess but was beaten off by bodyguards and a passerby. He escaped into nearby St James Park but was soon hunted down and caught. Police are enquiring into Ball's psychiatric history.

Dutch form East India Company

1602 The Dutch East India Company has received a charter granting it the monopoly of all trade between Holland and the lands lying between the Cape of Good Hope and the Straits of Magellan. The initiative follows the establishment two years ago of the British East India Company. The company's purpose is to displace Portuguese traders from Asia and to deny the English a foothold in the lucrative trade in pepper, nutmeg and cloves from the Indies. The States-General's licence is for trade, but the company will occupy territories and act as a sovereign state to maintain itself. It is to be based at Batavia on the island of Java.

Lewis and Clark chart the wild west

1806 The Lewis and Clark expedition that is charting the vast unexplored territory between the Mississippi River and the Pacific Ocean has turned homeward after extraordinary adventures in the American wilderness. The expedition has proved there is no easy water route across the American continent. Army captains Meriwether Lewis and William Clark started out from St Louis almost two years ago. They travelled up the Missouri as far as the Rocky Mountains, crossed over to the Columbia River and thence to the Pacific coast. The original plan was to explore the newly acquired territories of Louisiana in a single year, but difficult navigation, hostile Indians and other hardships caused delays. After a second winter in the wilderness by the Pacific

shore, the party has split into two groups; one is exploring the Yellowstone River before they rendezvous at the Missouri River for the home leg of their 8,000-mile journey.

A judge is not supposed to know anything about the facts of life until they have been presented in evidence and explained to him at least three times.

Hubert Lister Parker, Lord Chief Justice of England, 1961.

Drugs bust as Bowie starts world tour

1976 Pop stars David Bowie and Iggy Pop were arrested in a hotel room in Rochester, Massachusetts, tonight on marijuana charges. They were later released on bail of $2,000 each. Sexually ambiguous mega-star Bowie has just started the US leg of a world tour. He has long been an admirer of Iggy Pop (Iggy is short for iguana). Nine months ago Pop suddenly vanished from view, into a psychiatric ward for drug rehabilitation. Bowie was his only visitor – perhaps not the ideal choice of company for a drug addict trying to come down to earth, since Bowie reckons he comes from the stars.

1978 Three black ministers were today sworn into the illegal government of prime minister Ian Smith in war-torn Rhodesia. The three, including the Bishop Abel Muzorewa, are underwriting an interim settlement providing the white minority with constitutional safeguards once elections are held. It excludes two black parties led by Robert Mugabe and Joshua Nkomo – observers are sceptical about peace chances.

Blacks massacred at Sharpeville

1960 South African police today perpetrated the worst civilian massacre in the country's history when they shot dead 56 black people and wounded another 162 at Sharpeville, a black township near Johannesburg. About 15,000 blacks had joined a peaceful protest against the hated pass laws that force blacks to carry travel documents at all times. The crowd was met at the township police station by a line of armed police. Rocks were thrown and the heavily-outnumbered police opened fire on the crowd. Meanwhile, seven people were shot dead in similar disturbances in Langa township near Cape Town. The government has reacted quickly to the protests, banning all black organizations such as the African National Congress and the Pan-Africanist Congress. Black leaders have gone underground, calling for a civil disobedience campaign and nationwide strikes.

Massive German attack at the Somme

1918 Germany's field commander General Erich Ludendorff today launched a massive offensive on the Somme in a bid to break the Allied line before fresh American reinforcements arrive. Crack German troops are advancing rapidly along a 60-mile front and the Allies have already been forced back several miles. British troops are bearing the brunt of the attack, which is the Germans' first major breakthrough since the early days of the war. Delays in reinforcing the British line are being caused by disagreements between French generals over whether it is more important to strengthen the line or defend Paris. Casualties on both sides are very high.

1556 England's first Protestant Archbishop of Canterbury, Thomas Cranmer, is burnt at the stake as a heretic under the Catholic queen Mary I, known as "Bloody Mary".

1788 Fire ravages the American city of New Orleans.

1804 A new civil code, the Code Napoléon, comes into force in France.

1829 The 60-year-old English prime minister, the Duke of Wellington, fights a bloodless duel with the Earl of Winchelsea over Catholic emancipation, of which the Duke is a convinced supporter.

1843 English Poet Laureate Robert Southey dies.

1871 A commune is declared in the French city of Lyons.

1871 Chancellor Otto von Bismarck opens the first parliament of the newly declared German Reich.

1896 Britain's first cinema opens in London's Piccadilly Circus.

1908 French aviator Henri Farman flies over Paris with the first air passenger.

1933 The first parliament of Nazi Germany, with Hitler as Chancellor, is proclaimed in the garrison church at Potsdam.

1946 British minister Aneurin Bevan announces his Labour Government's plans for a National Health Service.

1963 The notorious Alcatraz prison in the bay of San Francisco closes.

1989 Australian Prime Minister Bob Hawke breaks down on television as he confesses his adultery.

BIRTHDAYS

Johann Sebastian Bach 1685, German composer and organist.

Benito Pablo Juarez 1801, Mexican president who was deposed by colonial powers Britain and France before being re-elected as head of state.

Paul Tortelier 1914, French cellist and conductor.

Peter Brook 1925, British stage and film director.

1622 Three hundred and fifty American settlers at James River are killed by Indians, the first Indian attack for many years.

1687 French composer Jean Baptiste Lully dies of a gangrenous abscess on his foot.

1824 The British parliament agrees to the expenditure of £57,000 to purchase 38 paintings to establish a national collection.

1829 In London, a conference agrees the boundaries of independent Greece, free of Ottoman rule after nearly 400 years.

1888 The English Football League is formed in a hotel in Fleet Street, London.

1896 Thomas Hughes, British author of *Tom Brown's Schooldays* and Liberal MP, dies aged 74.

1903 The Niagara Falls run out of water due to a drought.

1904 In the USA, the *Daily Illustrated Mirror* runs the first colour newspaper pictures.

1906 In Paris, England beats France 35–0 in the first rugby international.

1907 The first taxis with fare meters take to the streets in London.

1942 The BBC begins morse code broadcasts to the French Resistance.

1988 For the first time in Australia, doctors turn off the life support machine of a terminally ill patient.

BIRTHDAYS

Sir Anthony van Dyck 1599, Flemish artist who became portrait painter to the English court and was knighted by Charles I.

Nicholas Monsarrat 1910, British author of *The Cruel Sea* and *The Tribe That Lost Its Head*.

Karl Malden 1913, American film and television actor.

Marcel Marceau 1923, French mime artist.

Stephen Sondheim 1930, American composer of musicals such as *A Little Night Music* and *Sweeney Todd*.

ALDRICH BOWS OUT WITH PANACHE

1981 "Rudy, if you ever need a friend, buy a dog," says fast-talking women's wrestling promoter Harry Sears (perfectly played by Peter Falk) in Robert Aldrich's final movie, *California Dolls*, released today. The movie is violent, indecent, sexist and disreputable – and it's also terrific, red-blooded fun, with a right rousing climax when the good guys (or rather girls) finally triumph, having had the daylights thumped out of them by a pair of wicked nasties – who are black. It's no surprise that the film is anathema to the critics. Aldrich is perhaps the most forceful American film director to emerge in the 1950s, with a string of hits such as *Whatever Happened to Baby Jane?* His later films brought increasing hostility as he trampled on society's corns, but none can deny their sheer power. With this last film Aldrich has retired, at the age of 63. "Eddie, don't move – I want to forget you just as you are," Sears says in *California Dolls*. But Aldrich's films aren't that forgettable.

Gandhi's disobedience stirs South Africa

1907 Asians living in South Africa today began a campaign of civil disobedience to protest against new laws that require the entire community to carry pass-books and register their fingerprints. The campaign is led by Mohandas Gandhi, a young London-trained lawyer born in India. The new laws, requiring all Indians to submit to the registration process, carry the threat of expulsion for those who refuse to comply. Gandhi's campaign applies the principle of non-violent protest he calls "satyagraha" or "steadfastness in truth".

Final words of Goethe the great thinker

1832 Johann Wolfgang von Goethe, one of the greatest thinkers of his age, has died at the age of 82. Characteristically, his last words were "More light!" Goethe certainly left more light behind him and his influence will be felt for generations to come. He was a literary giant, philosopher, pioneering scientist and political councillor. To Goethe, these roles were all one, parts of a luminous whole. Many of his works are seen as high points of literature, models for others to follow. At his death he was finishing the second part of his celebrated dramatic poem "Faust: A Tragedy". It is a modern version of the European myth of Dr Johann Faustus, the 16th-century scholar said to have sold his soul to the devil for unlimited knowledge. In 1788 Goethe dedicated himself fully to writing and to the many society love affairs that marked his life. He married a village girl who had already borne him several children.

Nazis open concentration camp at Dachau

1933 German Chancellor Adolf Hitler's ruling National Socialists today opened a concentration camp at Dachau near Munich to detain communists and other "political undesirables". Under emergency legislation approved last month following the Reichstag fire, the government and its Nazi storm troopers can detain anyone. Those being rounded up are almost all Jews, whom Hitler blames for all Germany's ills; in a recent speech he banned kosher food and encouraged a ban on all Jewish commerce. Jews now face random violence by street gangs of Nazi sympathizers. Some have had their property destroyed and many are making arrangements to flee the country. Hitler's power is rapidly growing into dictatorship: he is currently forcing passage of a new bill that will allow him, rather than the ageing president, to rule by decree without the control of the demoralized parliament.

1945 The Arab League has been set up by seven Middle Eastern countries to coordinate political action and safeguard their sovereignty. The members are Egypt, Saudi Arabia, Syria, Lebanon, Iraq, Jordan, and Yemen.

Moscow orders Lithuania back into line

1990 Moscow today warned the rebel Baltic republic of Lithuania it would strike back at its declaration of independence – announced just 10 days ago – if the new country does not disarm and disband the militia forces now coalescing into a small army. Soviet President Mikhail Gorbachev gave Lithuania 48 hours to remove the roadblocks and military posts on its border. Federal Soviet interior ministry troops and KGB forces are being seen in increasing numbers on the streets of Vilnius, the capital. Moscow's special concern is the state-owned publishing house generating the new republic's propaganda, which it is thought may be a target for the troops. The new government, however, insists that it will obey the restored 1938 Lithuanian constitution, not the Kremlin.

MUSSOLINI FOUNDS FASCIST PARTY IN MILAN

1919 In Milan, a group of disillusioned former socialists and Italian war veterans has formed a political party inspired by the most authoritarian period of the Roman empire. Led by Benito Mussolini, the editor of *Il popolo d'Italia*, the group is called the Fasci di Combattimento, after the fasces, the axe that was the symbol of ancient Roman authority. The "Fascists" are both revolutionary and nationalistic. Mussolini, the son of a blacksmith, was editor of the Milan Socialist party newspaper *Avanti!* before he was expelled for his stance in the war. He then founded his own paper. Now, in the current post-war economic and social turmoil, Mussolini and his new party are attacking both communism and liberal business. Their answer for Italy's problems is a strong state.

1925 Charles Darwin's theory of evolution was today outlawed in the southern US state of Tennessee. Governor Austin Peay signed a statute forbidding Darwin's work to be taught in state schools on religious grounds.

1953 His favourite subjects were garden parties, regattas and horse racing, flowers and nudes; his long career embraced styles from Impressionism through Fauvism to fashionable textile and book designs. French painter Raoul Dufy was a core member of the Fauvist group led by Henri Matisse – the "wild beasts" whose use of searing colour shocked the critics in 1905. Dufy died today and the world of painting, printmaking, and industrial design will miss him.

Drunken officers strangle mad Tsar

1801 In a brutal Kremlin coup tonight, the mentally unbalanced Tsar Paul I was strangled in his bed by a group of drunken Russian army officers. They then proclaimed his son Alexander the new emperor. The Tsar's harsh rule, as well as his alliance with Austria against Napoleon (although he later changed sides), alienated the military. He also alienated his people by repealing a law confining corporal punishment to serfs. Paul I's life was fraught with argument and instability. Catherine the Great conceived him in an adulterous love affair. Paul fought bitterly with Catherine and her policies; she isolated him from his sons and tried to disinherit him. After her death five years ago, he decreed that no woman could ever rule again.

Patient dies – artificial heart still "a success"

1983 Retired American dentist Barney Clark has died after gaining a three-month lease of life when an artificial heart was implanted in his chest. Clark's worn-out heart was replaced by a polyurethane and aluminum "Jarvik-7" artificial heart last December at the University of Utah Medical Center in the first operation of its kind. He died of circulatory collapse and other problems associated with the new heart – which his doctors are nevertheless describing as a success. Some medical experts believe, however, that artifical heart research should be banned on the grounds that it is too expensive and largely useless. The heart, designed by Dr Robert Jarvik, has two chambers replacing the natural heart venticles and was driven by an air compressor that stood by Clark's bedside.

New cathedral rises from war ruins

1956 England's Queen Elizabeth II today laid the foundation stone of the new cathedral being built in Coventry, a symbol of Britain's resurgence after the wartime horrors of the Blitz. The old 14th-century cathedral and most of Coventry's medieval city centre was destroyed in a single 11-hour air raid by the German Luftwaffe on 14 November 1940, with over 1000 people killed. Plans were made to rebuild the cathedral in the Gothic style, but Sir Basil Spence's bold modernist project won the design competition. Decorative works by Sir Jacob Epstein and Graham Sutherland have been commissioned.

Mill's short rap was heard at the door: but he stood there unresponsive, pale, the very picture of despair. My poor manuscript, all except some four tattered leaves, was annihilated! It had been taken for waste paper and so five months of as tough labour as I could remember of, were as good as vanished, gone like a whiff of smoke.

Thomas Carlyle, Scottish essayist, writes how John Stuart Mill had lost the manuscript of Carlyle's book on the French revolution – 1835.

1369 Pedro the Cruel, King of Castile and Leon, is murdered by his brother Henry.

1752 Canada's first newspaper, the *Halifax Gazette*, hits the streets.

1765 The Stamp Act comes into force, requiring the taxing of all publications and legal documents in British colonies.

1815 The British Corn Law halts the import of grain.

1842 French novelist Stendhal, author of *Le rouge et le noir*, dies aged 59.

1861 London's first tramcars go on the streets in Bayswater.

1918 Big Bertha, a giant German gun, begins shelling Paris from 75 miles away.

1933 A bill is passed in the German parliament allowing Adolf Hitler to rule by decree, so establishing a dictatorship.

1966 In Rome, the first official meeting for 400 years between the heads of the Catholic and Anglican churches takes place.

1983 In the USA, President Reagan dubs the Soviet Union "an evil empire" and proposes a "Star Wars" defence system.

1984 British civil servant Sarah Tisdall is sent to jail for six months for leaking the news to the *Guardian* that Cruise missiles were on their way to Britain.

BIRTHDAYS

Juan Gris 1887, Spanish Cubist painter, sculptor and book illustrator as well as stage and costume designer.

Joan Crawford 1908, American film actress whose many films include *A Woman's Face*, *Mildred Pierce* and *Whatever Happened to Baby Jane?*

Akira Kurosawa 1910, Japanese film director whose *Seven Samurai* inspired Hollywood's *The Magnificent Seven*.

Donald Campbell 1921, British world speed record-breaker.

Roger Bannister 1929, British sportsman who in ran the world's first sub-four-minute mile in 1954.

1877 The Oxford and Cambridge boat race ends in a dead heat for the first time.

1905 Jules Verne, French author of *Around the World in Eighty Days* and *Twenty Thousand Leagues Under the Sea*, dies aged 77.

1905 Death of J.M. Synge, Irish playwright whose *Playboy of the Western World* caused riots when it was premiered at the Abbey Theatre in Dublin.

1911 Denmark abolishes capital punishment.

1922 Only three out of 32 horses finish at the Grand National at Aintree.

1938 British prime minister Neville Chamberlain admits that he will not oppose Adolf Hitler's annexation of Czechoslovakia in the interests of avoiding war between Britain and Germany.

1953 Death of Queen Mary, widow of King George V of England.

1976 Argentinian president Isabel Perón, third wife of former president Juan Perón, is deposed by the army in a bloodless coup.

1976 Death of Viscount Montgomery of Alamein, British Field Marshall and Commander of the Eighth Army in World War II.

1988 Mordecai Vanunu is found guilty of revealing Israel's nuclear secrets to the *Sunday Times*.

1990 Indian peacekeeping troops pull out of Sri Lanka.

2002 Halle Berry becomes the first black female actor ever to receive an Oscar.

BIRTHDAYS

William Morris 1834, British designer, artist and poet who was associated with the Pre-Raphaelite Brotherhood.

Roscoe "Fatty" Arbuckle 1887, American silent film comedian whose career was ruined in 1921 after a sex scandal in which a young actress was found dead in sordid circumstances at a party.

Steve McQueen 1930, American film actor whose first major film was *The Magnificent Seven*.

China cracks down on opium trade

1839 Chinese troops blockaded the foreign traders' warehouses in Canton today as the Peking court's struggle to suppress the opium trade moves toward outright war. Commissioner Lin Ze-xu, the Emperor's special envoy, has surrounded the warehouses and has ordered the foreign merchants to give up more than 20,000 chests of the illegal drug, worth about $12 million. The merchants have little choice but to comply and the opium will be destroyed. The drug – first imported from India in the 17th century – is ruining China morally and financially, says Peking. But it is filling the coffers of the Scottish, English and American trading houses with entrepot facilities at Canton. It is a balance of addiction: the London exchequer was being drained of silver for the hard-currency payments China demanded for selling its tea to the thirsty British – until merchants forced them to start accepting payment in opium which the merchants could buy very cheaply in India. The matter will not end with Lin's tough action: for the Western powers, access to China's markets is at stake.

US resumes aid to Contras

1989 The US Congress today agreed to renew a $40 million aid programme for the right-wing Contra rebels fighting Nicaragua's Sandinista government. The condition is more Congressional oversight of the administration's affairs. The funding was stopped during the Iran-Contra scandal, in which it was revealed that CIA and National Security Council chiefs were secretly funding the Contras. The aid money will only be used for non-lethal equipment, but its resumption is an important coup for the Republican right wing.

ELIZABETH'S GLORIOUS REIGN ENDS

1603 Elizabeth I, England's virgin queen for 45 years, died today. So ends a reign that made England the leading Protestant and maritime power of Europe – and one in which the arts have flourished as never before. Without an heir, she is succeeded by the son of Mary Queen of Scots, uniting the thrones of England and Scotland; he will be James I of England and James VI of Scotland. Her final years were clouded with frustrations at the continuing Irish rebellions and the death of her handsome young favourite, the Earl of Essex. The Queen's last words were "All my possessions for a moment of time".

Madonna's mantelpiece full to bursting

1991 Madonna sang her hit "Sooner or Later" from the movie in which she starred, *Dick Tracy*, at the Academy Awards ceremony in Los Angeles tonight – and won an Oscar for it. But she'll hardly be able to find room for it on her mantelpiece. Earlier this month she won *Rolling Stone*'s Best Single, Best Video, Best Tour, Best Dressed Female Artist, Sexiest Female Singer, Best Video and Hype of the Year awards – no mean feat, considering that last year the magazine gave her the Worst Female Singer and Worst Video awards. Three days earlier her single "Vogue" won the International Single of the Year award, and the day before "Rescue Me" was the highest-debuting single by a female artist in history. Madonna has sold more than 80 million albums worldwide; at one time she had a No. 1 hit in 28 countries simultaneously. Only Elvis Presley and the Beatles beat her chart success.

NATO planes strike Kosovo

1999 Nato has launched air strikes against military targets in the Federal Republic of Yugoslavia. Key facilities, including a radar facility near the Pristina airfield and an ammunitions base, have been hit. Operation Allied Force, which is under the command of General Wesley Clark, comes after escalating violence between Serbian forces loyal to the Yogoslav president Slobodan Milosevic and the ethnic Albanians in the province. Milosevic has been accused of a campaign of ethnic cleansing, driving thousands of Albanians from their homes. UK Defence Secretary George Robertson has said air strikes will continue until Milosevic ends the violence in Kosovo. "Milosevic should think again, withdraw his troops and sign the peace accord," Mr Robertson told the MoD news conference.

A hurry of hoofs in a village street,
A shape in the moonlight, a bulk in the dark,
And beneath from the pebbles, in passing, a spark,
Struck out from a steed flying fearless and fleet:
That was all! And yet, through the gloom and the light
The fate of the nation was riding that night.
From *Paul Revere's Ride*, by **Henry Wadsworth Longfellow**, who died today, 1882.

> *Shakespeare – the nearest thing in incarnation to the eye of God.*
> **Laurence Olivier**, 1949.

Saudi prince kills King Faisal

1975 Saudi Arabia's King Faisal was murdered by his nephew today during a ceremony at the palace in Riyadh to celebrate the birthday of the Prophet Mahommed. The killer, 31-year-old Prince Faisal ibn Museid, is reported to be mentally deranged. If condemned under Saudi law he faces a public beheading. Faisal's death is a diplomatic blow for the United States, which had relied on the king as a moderating influence in the political powder-keg of the Middle East.

Alaskan oil disaster as grounded tanker splits

1989 The worst oil spill in US history was today threatening to decimate marine life over a wide area as 11 million gallons of crude oil poured uncontrolled into the open sea. The 987-ft super tanker *Exxon Valdez* ran aground and split open on a reef in Prince William Sound, Alaska, yesterday, releasing an oil slick into an area rich in marine wildlife and fishing stock. The cause of the accident has not been revealed but the US Coastguard has subpoenaed the tanker's captain and two crew to face federal investigators. There are rumours that the crew had been drinking. The ship's owners, Exxon Shipping, have promised to pay for the gigantic, months-long clean-up that will be necessary.

Robert the Bruce crowned King of Scots

1306 The eighth Earl of Carrick, Robert the Bruce, was today crowned King of Scotland at Scone, becoming Robert I. Bruce's grandfather lost his claim to the throne in 1292; Bruce won back the crown after murdering his rival John Comyn last year. Comyn was backed by the English under King Edward I. After a decade when his allegiance to the cause of Scottish nationalism was wavering, the murder and his accession to the throne have now committed Bruce to the fight to restore national independence to Scotland.

Olivier's Hamlet sweeps Oscars

1949 British actor and director Laurence Olivier was today the toast of Hollywood after his film version of *Hamlet* swept five Oscars. The production is the first British film to win the Academy Award for Best Picture; Olivier himself won the Best Actor award. Olivier, 41, also directed the film, which had a mixed reception at its premiere last year. Critics then said he was too old to play Shakespeare's hero opposite 18-year-old Jean Simmons as Ophelia. He was also attacked for hacking the classic down to a mere two and a half hours, but today's ceremony gives him the last laugh. Olivier's triumph confirms him as one of today's leading actors and directors. His screen credits include *Rebecca*, *Wuthering Heights* and *Pride and Prejudice*, while his work with London's Old Vic has endeared him to thousands of theatregoers.

Sugar Ray takes world title – again

1958 The great American boxer Sugar Ray Robinson won the world middleweight title for an unprecedented fifth time tonight when he outpointed Carmen Bastillo over 15 rounds in Chicago. Bastillo took the title last year when he outpointed Robinson in a savage fight. Many think Robinson is the greatest fighter of modern times. He is fast and poised, and his combination punches are devastating. Born Walker Smith in 1921, he took his name from a friend's birth certificate he borrowed so he could fight while still under-age. He won the welterweight title in 1946, and the middleweight title for the first time in 1951. In 1952 he retired, but returned three years later to take the middleweight title from Carl Olson. He lost the title twice last year, and has now regained it – twice.

Birth of a Euro-vision

1957 Six European countries took a historic step towards guaranteeing a future of peace and prosperity for their continent today when they signed the Treaty of Rome and formed the European Economic Community. The new EEC aims to create free movement of people, goods and money to generate an economic boom. The leaders of the founding member-states – France, West Germany, Italy, the Netherlands, Belgium and Luxembourg – signed the agreement in front of a transcontinental TV link-up broadcast. Tariffs between member states will disappear, common policies will be developed and the first steps towards a European political union will be taken.

1609 Commissioned by the Dutch East India Company, English navigator Henry Hudson sets off on his third attempt to find the North-West Passage.

1807 Influenced by the philanthropic MP William Wilberforce, the British parliament abolishes the slave trade.

1815 Britain, Austria, Prussia and Russia form a new alliance against Napoleon Bonaparte.

1876 The Scots win 4–0 in the first football match between Scotland and Wales.

1914 Frédéric Mistral, French poet, winner of the Nobel Prize for Literature and co-founder of the movement to preserve the culture of Provence, dies aged 84.

1929 Benito Mussolini, leader of the Fasci di Combattimento organization, claims to have won 90 per cent of the vote in the Italian elections.

1918 Claude Debussy, French composer of *Pellèas et Mélisande* and *La Mer*, dies aged 55 after a nine-year battle against cancer.

1999 A fire in the Mont Blanc tunnel between France and Italy kills 40 people.

2002 A powerful earthquake hits Afghanistan causing 1,800 deaths.

BIRTHDAYS

Arturo Toscanini 1867, Italian conductor who refused to conduct in Italy or Germany when they were ruled by the Fascists and the Nazis respectively.

Béla Bartok 1881, Hungarian composer and virtuoso pianist whose music blends East European folk music with dissonant harmonies.

A. J. P. Taylor 1906, British historian and broadcaster.

David Lean 1908, British film director who made *Lawrence of Arabia*, *Dr Zhivago* and *Bridge over the River Kwai*.

Aretha Franklin 1942, American singer dubbed the "Queen of Soul".

Elton John 1947, British songwriter, pianist and singer.

MARCH 26

BIRTHDAYS

Egypt and Israel sign peace accord

1979 Hopes of a lasting peace in the strife-torn Middle East were given a major boost today when the leaders of Israel and Egypt signed a historic peace treaty in the presence of US President Jimmy Carter. The agreement between Israeli Prime Minister Menachem Begin and Egyptian President Anwar Sadat to restore diplomatic relations opens a new era: 30 years of conflict between the two nations may now be solved. The treaty crowns two years of patient diplomacy following Sadat's surprise journey to Jerusalem to open peace negotiations. Both leaders face domestic problems getting today's bold step accepted. For Carter, the treaty will restore much of the prestige he lost during the Iranian revolution.

England monarchy certain to return

1660 The return of the monarchy to England is now all but certain after the longest Parliament in the country's history dissolved itself today. The so-called Long Parliament survived for 20 years through the Civil War. A new Parliament will be elected to prepare the way for the restoration of King Charles II, who has promised to rule as a constitutional monarch. The country is now looking forward to peace.

Jolly boating at Henley debut

1839 Watched by crowds sipping champagne and eating sumptuous picnics, the first rowing regatta at the English riverside town of Henley-on-Thames took place today. This unusual sport is growing in popularity across the country. Originally the means of carrying armies across the Mediterranean, it is now one of the favourite pastimes of the British upper classes. Organizers of today's regatta hope it will become an annual event.

> *The thing we secretly dread most often happens. When I was a little boy I used to tremble to think what it would be like to love someone and see her married to another. I exercised my mind with that thought. And you see!*
>
> **Cesare Pavese**, Italian poet, writing on this day, 1938.

"Fourth" man dead

1983 "The Fourth Man" of Britain's upper-class spy ring died of a heart attack today. Anthony Blunt was the Cambridge spymaster who in the 1930s recruited Donald Maclean, Kim Philby and Guy Burgess to the communist cause. They went on to penetrate the British security services, while Blunt climbed to the top as an art historian and was appointed by Queen Elizabeth to look after the royal art collection. The spy ring undermined security during the Cold War. Blunt's role was uncovered four years ago in the House of Commons, when it was revealed that he had confessed as far back as 1964 in exchange for immunity.

King of diamonds dies of broken heart

1902 British imperialist Cecil John Rhodes has died in Cape Town aged 48. Rhodes amassed huge wealth in South Africa's mining boom in the 1870s and '80s, finally controlling 90 per cent of the world's diamond production. In 1890 he became prime minister of the Cape Colony. His chartered British South Africa Company conquered black kings to establish the British crown in Northern and Southern Rhodesia. He was implicated in the piratical Jameson Raid on the Transvaal Boers in 1896, and forced from office. He sacrificed his chances of vindication in the scandal for the sake of England's honour. Friends say it broke his heart, and has brought him to an early death.

Final curtain for Bernhardt

1923 The great French actress Sarah Bernhardt died today after a long and extraordinarily successful career, loved by millions around the globe. She was 78. She took Paris, London and then New York by storm in the 1870s, making several world tours. On tour in South America, she injured her right knee jumping off a parapet in Tosca, and in 1915 her leg had to be amputated. Nine months later she was back on stage, performing with a wooden leg. Audiences were spellbound by her flashing eyes and lovely voice and she used her eccentricities, such as sleeping in a coffin, to promote her fascinating public image.

FATAL JUMBO COLLISION

1977 The worst accident in flying history shocked the world today when two Jumbo jets collided, claiming 574 lives. The two Boeing 747s, belonging to KLM and Pan Am, crashed on the runway at Tenerife on the Canary Islands, sending huge jets of flame and smoke into the air. The accident happened when the American plane turned on to the runway where the Dutch Jumbo was about to take off. Both had been diverted from nearby Las Palmas because of a bomb threat. All 248 KLM passengers perished in the ensuing fire, while some 70 Pan Am passengers were tonight being treated in hospital for horrific burns.

Strike brings Poland to a halt

1981 Millions of Polish workers today staged a general strike in protest at police harassment of activists belonging to the trade union Solidarity. They were urged to do so by union leader Lech Walesa. The strike is a show of strength against hard-line communists trying to reclaim concessions made last year when mass strikes won Solidarity recognition as the Warsaw Pact's first independent trade union. The union wants the hard-liners forced out of power. Walesa would be willing to make deals with the communist rulers to secure the union's position, but union militants are pressing for a more political line. Meanwhile Poland's new party leader, General Jaruzelski, is under pressure to declare martial law and ban

1794 The US Navy is established.

1802 Britain and France sign the Peace of Amiens.

1813 Prussia declares war on France and Russian forces occupy Dresden.

1835 Texan rebels are massacred by the Mexican army at Gohad.

1871 Scotland beats England in the first international rugby match between the two nations.

1914 Medical history is made in a Brussels hospital where the first successful blood transfusion is performed.

1958 Soviet prime minister Marshal Nikolai Bulganin is ousted by Nikita Kruschev in a Kremlin power struggle.

1964 Britain's Great Train Robbers are sentenced to a total of 307 years imprisonment after being found guilty of stealing more than £2.6 million from mail bags.

1968 Soviet astronaut Yuri Gagarin, the first man to orbit the earth, dies in a plane crash near Moscow.

1975 British composer and Master of the Queen's Musick Sir Arthur Bliss dies.

2002 Death of much-loved actor, comedian and musician Dudley Moore at 66 after a long illness.

2002 Death of Billy Wilder, director of films such as *Some Like it Hot* and *Sunset Boulevard*.

US TROOPS ROUT CREEK INDIANS

1814 Troops under General Andrew Jackson today inflicted an overwhelming defeat on the Creek Indians at the Battle of Horseshoe Bend in eastern Alabama. More than 800 Indians lost their lives in the battle, which marks the end of a year-long war. Much of the Creek territory in Alabama and Georgia will now be brought into the United States.

1980 A North Sea oil platform overturned during a storm late this afternoon and over 100 men are feared drowned. Phillips Petroleum's *Alexander Kielland* platform was used for recreation. About 200 workers were relaxing aboard when one of the five legs buckled and the platform turned turtle, trapping many inside. Rescue teams are rushing to the scene, 250 miles (400 km) from the Scottish coast.

End of Tiepolo's prolific talent

1770 The last great Italian painter of the Renaissance, Giambattista Tiepolo of Venice, died today after a lifetime of creativity which made him one of Europe's most sought-after artists. His huge output and extraordinary technical virtuosity gained him patrons in Italy, Germany and Spain, and he died in the latter country, working to the end. With flawless draughtsmanship and brilliant light and colour, Tiepolo's work sums up the magnificence of Italian decorative painting. A master of perspective, he painted large ceiling frescos which are spectacular illusions of space and light, the actual structure of the building vanishing in the scene. His Banquet of Cleopatra and Transport of the Holy House of Loreto, both in Venice, are perhaps his masterpieces. Tiepolo's two talented sons, trained by their father, will carry on painting in his style.

Britain strong-arms America

1774 The American colonists call them the Intolerable Acts. The British parliament prefers the label "coercive acts" and says they are needed to restore order after the episode of the Boston Tea Party. Whatever the name, London's latest package of legislation for its unruly colony is causing a furore. The Boston Port Act closes the harbour entirely until the colonists have paid compensation for the spilled tea. The Massachusetts Government Act has put the legislature under control of the crown, and banned all public meetings. In London, parliament is urgently considering further provocative legislation – one such is

a bill to try Americans in English courts, while another would give power to British soldiers to requisition any house they want for military quarters. The notion that enforced idleness will encourage Boston's traders to see the error of their ways is a curious one – their resolve to confront Britain is hardening daily.

> *The hungry hare has no frontiers and doesn't follow ideologies. The hungry hare goes where it finds the food. And the other hares don't block its path with the tanks.*
> **Lech Walesa**, 1981.

BIRTHDAYS

Baron Georges Haussmann 1809, French town planner and the man responsible for transforming Paris into a city noted for its long, wide boulevards and splendid vistas.

Sir Henry Royce 1863, British engineer and co-founder, with C. S. Rolls, of the Rolls-Royce motor company.

Gloria Swanson 1898, American star of silent films remembered for *Sunset Boulevard*, in which she played a faded movie star.

Sarah Vaughan 1924, American jazz singer popular for her rendering of middle-of-the-road songs.

1868 The Earl of Cardigan, who led the ill-fated "Charge of the Light Brigade" at the battle of Balaclava during the Crimean War, dies.

1881 Russian composer Modest Mussorgsky dies, aged only 42.

1910 The first seaplane takes off near Marseilles in France.

1912 Oxford and Cambridge boat crews take to the water in the annual Varsity race as both boats sink.

1941 The British Navy sinks seven Italian warships for no loss at the battle of Matapan, off the Greek island of Crete.

1941 The British writer and member of the Bloomsbury Group Virginia Woolf commits suicide.

1943 Russian emigré composer and pianist Sergei Rachmaninov dies in California.

1945 Germany mounts its last V2 rocket attack against Britain.

1969 Former US Republican President Dwight D. Eisenhower dies.

1979 The government of British premier James Callaghan falls over the Home Rule for Ireland question.

1985 Russian-born painter Marc Chagall, latterly famous for his ballet sets and costume designs, dies.

BIRTHDAYS

Raphael (Raffaello Sanzio) 1483, great Italian painter of the Renaissance.

St Teresa of Avila 1515, Spanish noblewoman who joined the Order of Carmelite nuns in 1533 and after several mystical experiences dedicated her life to reforming the movement.

Aristide Briand 1862, French socialist statesman and, with the German statesman Gustav Stresemann, joint winner of the Nobel Peace prize in 1926.

Dirk Bogarde 1921, British film actor and writer who starred in films such as Joseph Losey's *The Servant* and Luchino Visconti's *The Damned*.

King and Queen of Hollywood wed

1920 Douglas Fairbanks and Mary Pickford – known to millions as the King and Queen of Hollywood – married today surrounded by friends. Their marriage comes just one year after they broke away from the big Hollywood companies and formed United Artists with Charlie Chaplin. Fairbanks, 35, has had a meteoric rise to fame with productions such as *The Mask of Zorro*. Pickford, 26, became one of the movie industry's first true stars under the direction of D. W. Griffith in *Pollyanna* and *Rebecca of Sunnybrook Farm*. This is her second marriage.

> *I'm not interested in making an assessment of myself and stripping myself for the general public to view.*
> **Marlon Brando**, who refused an Oscar today, 1973, because of Hollywood's abuses of the American Indians.

Meltdown in US nuclear reactor

1979 A meltdown in the nuclear reactor core of the Three Mile Island power station at Harrisburg in Pennsylvania caused panic in the eastern United States today. Experts are warning that the reactor core may release radioactive clouds through the region but there are no facilities for a general evacuation of the immediate area. The accident appears to have been caused by the failure of valves controlling cooling water, followed by operator mistakes. Staff at the plant are trying to limit the inevitable release of radioactivity. Local residents are already demanding stricter controls.

British customs seize Iraqi nuclear triggers

1990 Forty switches which could be used to trigger a nuclear weapon were seized at London's Heathrow airport today by US and British officials in a "sting" operation. They were being exported by a Californian firm to Baghdad where they were destined for Iraqi president Saddam Hussein's nuclear programme – revealing his plans to build a nuclear bomb. British officials arrested the carrier as he boarded a plane.

Mine lift cage plunges a mile

1980 A mine lift cage at the Vaal Reef gold mine in South Africa plunged more than a mile today, killing all 23 aboard. It is thought to be the longest lift fall ever. Some South African mines reach down to 11,500 ft (3700 m) below the surface. Supplying air to the huge networks of deep tunnels is a major engineering problem; the tunnels seep water which must constantly be pumped out. The stuffy heat, noisy drills, dynamite and danger of rockfalls add up to an industrial hell, worked by many thousands of tribal blacks under white supervision. This is the latest of many disasters in pursuit of South Africa's gold.

Franco the victor as Spanish War ends

1939 After three years of destruction, the Spanish Civil War ended today when General Francisco Franco's nationalist forces took Madrid peacefully and the Republican government fled to Valencia. Tens of thousands have died, families have been split and the scars of battle will take generations to heal. It has also been a struggle between the forces of fascism and communism: Hitler and Mussolini have supplied Franco with troops, air support and provisions while the Soviet Union has given the Republicans valuable assistance. Idealists flocked from all over the world to fight on the Republican side. Many observers see the Civil War as a bloody dress rehearsal for a wider European war.

RADICALS PROCLAIM PARIS A COMMUNE

1871 Patriotic French radicals filled with the fervour of the Revolution of 1789 today proclaimed Paris a "commune of the people". They are seeking to turn France's lost war against the Prussians into a triumph for Jacobin-style socialism by installing proletarian rule. Led by intellectuals and workers and backed by a reformed National Guard, the "communards" aim to set up a municipal government independent of the national government, which has fled to Versailles. The communards are incensed that the government has accepted the humiliating peace terms imposed by the Prussians, including the loss of Alsace and Lorraine. But no one is predicting with confidence how long the Commune will last.

10,000 mourners at Beethoven's funeral

1827 Ludwig van Beethoven was buried today in Vienna, mourned by a crowd of more than 10,000 that came to bid farewell to this titan of modern music. Beethoven's work is surely guaranteed a place of honour in the musical repertoire for generations to come. His vast creative outpouring is all the more extraordinary given that in his last 20 years he was plagued by deafness that eventually prevented him performing publicly. He will doubtless always be best known for the mighty symphonies of his middle period.

COCA-COLA — A TONIC FOR THE BRAIN

1886 A new fizzy drink went on sale at a pharmacy today in Atlanta, Georgia. Coca-Cola, an "Esteemed Brain Tonic and Intellectual Beverage", will cure anything from hysteria to the common cold, claims its inventor, Dr John Pemberton. The non-alcoholic but nonetheless stimulating drink is made from a secret recipe including syrup, caffeine from the cola nut and a tincture of coca leaves. Dr Pemberton's brew faces stiff competition from other elixirs, such as Imperial Inca Cola.

1461 Henry VI's Lancastrian forces are crushed by the Yorkists at the bloody battle of Towton, Yorkshire, and the position of the newly proclaimed King of England, Edward IV, is secured.

1792 Enlightened Swedish king Gustavus III is gunned down at a masked ball.

1871 British monarch Queen Victoria opens the Royal Albert Hall in London.

1891 George-Pierre Seurat, developer of the style of painting known as pointillism, dies.

1891 British explorer Robert Falcon Scott dies in Antarctica after reaching the Pole.

1927 Malcolm Campbell's world land-speed record is smashed by Sir Henry Segrave driving his *Mystery* car on the hard white sands of Daytona.

1957 Irish-born writer Joyce Carey dies.

1970 Peace campaigner and writer Vera Brittain dies.

1973 US troops pull out of South Vietnam.

1988 Lloyd Honeyghan knocks out Jorgé Vaca to become the first British boxer to regain a world title since Ted "Kid" Lewis some 71 years previously.

1989 Space Services Inc of Texas becomes the first private company to make a commercial space launch, sending aloft an instrument package.

PARIS HATES MITTERRAND'S PYRAMID

1989 France's president François Mitterrand today inaugurated the vast glass pyramid at the entrance to the Louvre in Paris – the largest of the monuments his administration has built to celebrate the bicentennial of the French Revolution. The pyramid, which will form the main entrance to the art museum and former palace of French kings, is the work of Chinese-born American architect I. M. Pei. It includes a large underground addition to the Louvre. It has been criticized almost as fiercely as the Eiffel Tower was a century ago, but Mitterrand has stood firm over his latest project. However, Parisians have liked to throw stones in their many revolutions, and it is questionable whether a pyramid of glass will survive.

Idi Amin flees Ugandan capital

1979 Uganda's bloody dictator Idi Amin Dada has been driven from the capital, Kampala, and is hiding in the interior. His army is rapidly being worn down by Tanzanian forces sent by President Julius Nyerere to aid Ugandan rebels. Amin's invasion of Northern Tanzania late last year has been his undoing. International quiescence to the excesses of his rule, during which an estimated 300,000 Ugandans have been killed, finally ended when Nyerere struck back. Kampala has been besieged by Tanzanian forces and the Uganda Liberation Front, and even last-minute support for Amin from the Libyan leader Colonel Gaddafi has not helped his retreating army. Amin overthrew Milton Obote to become president in 1972. A flamboyant and unpredictable personality, he and his government have been notorious for their brutality. His departure will not be mourned by the Ugandans.

1929 Britain's suffragettes have won their battle at last, for tonight the House of Commons voted in favour of the Equal Franchise Bill that gives the vote to all women over the age of 21, amending earlier legislation that had enfranchised only women over 30.

Soviet's first real election since 1917

1989 Soviet citizens have turned their thumbs down to the ruling Communist Party in the first real choice they have had since the 1917 revolution. Communist candidates have been humiliatingly defeated in yesterday's elections for a new congress – the first contested multiparty election in Soviet history.

Soviet general secretary Mikhail Gorbachev has unleashed a whirlwind with his perestroika policy of openness – in Moscow Gorbachev's rival, Russian president Boris Yeltsin, won 90 per cent of the votes, and there were solid opposition gains in the Ukraine and in Leningrad. The Communists have not, of course, lost power – a proportion of the seats in the new assembly were reserved for Party members.

When the white man came, we had the land and they had the Bibles; now they have the land and we have the Bibles.
Dan George,
Canadian Indian chief, 1952.

Elihu Thomson 1853, English-born American inventor and co-founder, with Thomas Edison, of the General Electric Company.

Edwin Lutyens 1869, British architect known as the last English designer of country houses and for his work on the vice-regal palace of New Delhi.

William Walton 1902, British composer who first came to the public's attention with his composition *Façade*.

Pearl Bailey 1918, American jazz singer noted for her role in the all-black version of *Hello Dolly*.

1842 Ether is used as an anaesthetic for the first time, by American surgeon Dr Crawford Long.

1855 Afghan leader Dost Mohammed ends 12 years of hostilities by signing a peace treaty with the British.

1950 Léon Blum, French statesman responsible for introducing radical social reforms to France in the 1930s, dies.

1978 Leading ad agency Saatchi and Saatchi are hired by British Conservatives in a new political propaganda offensive.

1980 Twenty are killed as the funeral of the murdered Salvadorean rebel archbishop Oscar Romero turns into a bloodbath.

1986 James Cagney, American film actor who started his career in Vaudeville, dies aged 87.

1989 American actor Kurt Russell wipes the smile from Goldie Hawn's face by proposing marriage in front of a television audience of 1.5 billion people who are watching the couple present Oscars.

BIRTHDAYS

Francesco Goya 1746, Spanish court painter whose works grew increasingly gloomy, especially those inspired by the French invasion of Spain.

Vincent van Gogh 1853, Dutch Post-Impressionist painter driven by insanity to suicide who sold only one of his paintings during his lifetime and whose work now fetches record prices.

Melanie Klein 1882, Austrian psychiatrist noted for her studies of children.

Sean O'Casey 1884, Irish playwright whose best known works, such as *Juno and the Paycock*, were written for the famous Abbey Theatre in Dublin.

Warren Beatty 1937, American film actor and director, brother of Shirley MacLaine.

Eric Clapton 1945, British rock guitarist.

Glory of war dies in Crimea

1856 The Crimean War is over. The bloody three-year conflict between Europe and Russia ended with today's signing of the Treaty of Paris. The devastating power of the modern weapons used in the war has shattered any illusions of the glory of arms. Russia has been forced to agree to the demilitarization of the Black Sea and will demolish four of its naval bases there. Russia loses access to the Danube River and must give up claims to Rumanian territory. The European powers – Britain, France, Austria, Prussia and Piedmont – are guaranteeing the Ottoman empire against future Russian expansionism or any claims to the loyalty of Orthodox Christians living in Turkish lands. Britain rules the East Mediterrranean again.

McCarthyism is Americanism with its sleeves rolled.
Joseph R. McCarthy,
of whom President Harry S. Truman expressed his distaste today, 1950.

Death of mystic educator

1925 Rudolf Steiner, the Austrian mystic, scientist and educator who created the Anthroposophical Society, has died aged 64. Steiner tried to change the educational system – his schools reject aggressive games and competitive methods in favour of artistic activity and pure thought. He developed a highly productive method of "bio-dynamic" farming which rejects the new artificial fertilizers and poisons. His anthroposophy is a Christianized version of the mystical doctrine of theosophy.

1840 Beau Brummell, the Regency dandy and saviour of British sartorial elegance, died today in a lunatic asylum for the poor after a long exile in France, where he had fled to escape gambling debts. In happier days the dashing cut of Brummell's coats turned the head of Britain's Prince Regent. "Who's your fat friend?" the dandy asked when he first saw the prince. The two formed a friendship and Brummell became the arbiter of English fashion.

QUEEN MOTHER DIES

2002 Buckingham Palace has announced that the Queen Mother has died peacefully in her sleep, aged 101. The Queen was at her bedside when she passed away this afternoon at the Royal Lodge, Windsor. The news was announced two and a half hours later. Hundreds of people have begun paying their respects at royal palaces, describing her as a "fairy-tale grandmother", and tributes have been flooding in from all over the world. Prince Charles, who was believed to have been very close to his grandmother, is returning home early from Switzerland where he has been skiing with his two sons. He is said to be devastated. She will have a ceremonial funeral at Westminster Abbey on Tuesday 9th April.

America buys Alaska from Russia

1867 "An awful lot of ice for an awful lot of dollars," is how senators in Washington are describing the American proposal to pay $7.2 million to Russia for the frozen wastes of Alaska. An impassioned debate about the merits of buying Alaska is reaching its peak as the Senate votes on the issue. Today the two governments signed a treaty of cession, but the US Senate must now authorize payment. Secretary of State William Seward is adamant that the price is a bargain that will handsomely repay investment when the potential for gold and other minerals in exploited.

Reagan survives assassin's bullet

1981 President Ronald Reagan was seriously wounded today in an assassination attempt as he walked out of a Washington hotel. He was rushed to George Washington Hospital, where a bullet, which passed inches from his heart, has been removed from his lung. The 70-year-old president is reported to have survived the operation well. He told his wife Nancy: "Honey, I forgot to duck" – a line from one of his movies. His assailant, John Hinckley, Jr., fired six shots with a small .22 calibre pistol. Three other men were wounded: presidential press secretary Jim Brady received a head wound. Hinckley, 25, is the son of an oil executive. He dropped out of Yale University to work as a disc-jockey. In 1980 he was arrested with a gun at Tennessee airport when former president Jimmy Carter was arriving. He is reported to be obsessed with actress Jodie Foster and her role in the film *Taxi Driver*.

Charlotte Brontë dies

1855 Charlotte Brontë, the reclusive Yorkshire novelist and author of *Jane Eyre*, has died. The life of the Brontë sisters – Charlotte, Emily, and Anne – followed the quintessentially English pattern of mighty passions smothered by the grinding tedium of provincial life in Victorian England. But Charlotte's passion spilled out – the horrors of her schooling were transformed into *Jane Eyre*. The book, published under a pseudonym, was an immediate success, arousing great public curiosity in its secretive author. Her next book, *Villette*, was the result of a spell in Brussels as a governess, when she fell in love with a married man. Charlotte was held in great critical acclaim.

1980 Black American athlete Jesse Owens has died, aged 67. He was the star of the 1936 "Aryan" Olympics in Hitler's Germany, winning four Gold Medals – but Hitler refused to shake his hand at the Olympics because he was black.

Heyerdahl publishes Kon-Tiki saga

1950 The Norwegian explorer Thor Heyerdahl today published an English translation of his epic 1948 voyage across the Pacific Ocean aboard a raft. He and a crew of five made the 5000-mile (8050 km) journey aboard *Kon-Tiki* to test his theories about the diffusion of early civilizations. He believes Polynesia was settled by voyagers from Peru, and that there may have been contacts between Egypt and South America centuries before Columbus crossed the Atlantic. Sailing from Peru, the expedition proved that aboriginal South Americans could have voyaged to the Pacific islands.

1905 Britain's canniest criminals can no longer sleep easy in their beds, lulled by the sticky end of Sherlock Holmes, the world's most brilliant detective. Writer Arthur Conan Doyle tried to destroy his most successful creation, killed as he fell over the Reichenbach falls in 1893. But public demand for his hero was so overwhelming that he gave way and resurrected him.

Eiffel changes Paris skyline

1889 Paris, the graceful capital of measured stone architecture and mellowed historic buildings, received its tallest and brashest tourist attraction yet when the new Eiffel Tower was opened today by French premier Tirard. The soaring skeleton of exposed wrought-iron latticework is by far the tallest man-made structure in the world, standing at almost a fifth of a mile. Only the revolutionary engineering in Alexandre Eiffel's design makes the tower possible: its pylons are curved so precisely that the high wind pressures the top of the tower is subjected to compress the structure on to its base rather than weakening it.

Eiffel also built the steel structure that holds up the Statue of Liberty in New York. It has taken two years to complete the tower in time for this year's Paris Exposition celebrating the centenary of the French Revolution. A monument to the achievements of modern engineering, the 984 ft (300 m) tower dominates the whole city. Many Parisians, including the writer Guy de Maupassant, are far from happy that science should so dominate in this world capital of art. Visitors and Parisians both, however, will certainly enjoy ascending effortlessly in the Eiffel Tower' power-driven glass lift cages for the truly wonderful view.

DALAI LAMA FLEES TIBET

1959 The ruler and spiritual leader of Tibet, the Dalai Lama, has fled to safety in India after Chinese military occupation of his country has made his position in Lhasa impossible. He slipped quietly away on horseback, narrowly escaping capture by the Chinese. On his arrival in West Bengal the young priest-king was welcomed by thousands of Tibetans now also in exile. He was careful to avoid overt criticism of Chinese troops who are reported to be using force in their efforts to eradicate the country's ancient Buddhist faith. Tibet was an independent nation until 1951, when China's People's Liberation Army invaded, crushing all resistance, imposing Chinese law, language and customs. Resentment at the communist suppression of religious customs boiled up into violent protests earlier this year, which were harshly put down. According to Tibetan sources an estimated 65,000 Tibetans lost their lives, while an equivalent number fled to safety in India. The Chinese have installed Panchen Lama in the Dalai Lama's place.

1820 American missionaries arrive in Honolulu to spread the Word.

1854 Japan finally opens its doors to American traders.

1858 China capitulates to British and French demands for trade concessions.

1866 Chile sides with Peru in war against Spain.

1901 German inventor Gottlieb Daimler names his latest 53 mph, four-cyclinder creation after his daughter, Mercedes.

1913 New York's Ellis Island receives a record 6745 immigrants in one day.

1934 American bank robber John Dillinger escapes from police custody.

1939 The British government pledges to defend Poland under the terms of a new tripartite UK/French/Polish treaty.

1985 The British National Coal Board announces a record annual loss of £2225 million.

1989 The master of the *Exxon Valdez* tanker responsible for polluting a vast stretch of Alaskan waters is sacked for drunkenness by the Exxon company.

BIRTHDAYS

René Descartes 1596, French philosopher and inventor of the technique of methodical doubt.

Franz Joseph Haydn 1732, Austrian composer of symphonies, oratorios, operas and chamber works.

Nikolai Gogol 1809, Russian writer whose novel *Dead Souls* is considered one of the finest ever.

Robert Bunsen 1811, German physicist and chemist and inventor of the bunsen burner.

John Fowles 1926, British novelist whose books include *The French Lieutenant's Woman* which was made into a film starring Meryl Streep.

Richard Chamberlain 1935, American television and film actor who first came to prominence as Dr Kildare in the TV series of the same name.

APRIL

"Madam, even God himself could not sink this ship."

Crewman
to a passenger as the Titanic sets sail
on her maiden voyage from Southampton,
April 10, 1912.

LATEST PARIS FASHIONS

1867 Twelve years after staging her first great exhibition – in emulation of the London Exhibition of 1851 – France is again showing off her achievements to the rest of Europe. This year's star attraction at the Paris World Fair is the capital itself, which has been transformed by the rebuilding programmes of Baron Georges Haussmann. The remodelled capital has 85 miles (137 km) of new streets with wide roadways and pavements fringed with trees. The height and façade of all houses and shops along these boulevards have been subject to approval by M. Haussmann and his inspectors. The city also boasts a new drainage and water system and a landscaped park, the Bois de Boulogne. The finest gem in Paris's refurbished crown will be the luxurious new opera house, which is currently under construction.

Enquiring minds get royal approval

1662 The latest fashion at the court of British king Charles II is the pursuit of learning. Today His Majesty granted royal patronage to a group of scientists and academics who have since 1645 been holding informal meetings in the interest of furthering knowledge. The group's name is the Royal Society of London for the Improvement of Natural Knowledge. The King's interest should guarantee its support among courtiers.

April Fool's Day: This is the day upon which we are reminded of what we are on the other three hundred and sixty-four.
Mark Twain, in *Pudd'nhead Wilson's Calendar*, 1894.

Mercy, mercy me

1984 Marvin Gaye has died in Los Angeles, one day short of his 45th birthday, after being shot during a violent argument with his father, Church minister Marvin Gaye, Snr. The cocaine-addicted soul singer was living with his parents at the time of his death. Friends had been concerned about the singer's mental state for some time. Gaye had threatened to take his own life and had become increasingly unpredictable, largely due to his drug addiction. His most recent hit, "Sexual Healing", came out last year on CBS after Gaye had terminated his 20-year association with the Tamla Motown label of Berry Gordy.

Peace chain at Greenham

1983 Actress Julie Christie and nonagenarian CND supporter Lord Brockway were among the estimated 30,000 campaigners who today linked hands in the cause of world peace. The 14-mile (22 km) long protest chain enveloped the US Air Force base at Greenham, where a women's peace camp was set up last year, and also the centres of Aldermaston and Burghfield. This latest civil protest at the presence of nuclear missiles on English soil went off peacefully, thanks largely to a "softly, softly" approach by Thames Valley and military police. No arrests were made, despite several attempts by protesters to breach the perimeter fence of the base.

Berlin blockade segregates Soviets

1948 Relations between former wartime allies have been put under severe strain by the Soviets' sudden imposition of tough checks on all Western transport entering Berlin. The western Allies fear that this may signal an attempt to force the entire city into the communist sphere of influence. The city, which is divided into four occupation zones - administered by France, Britain, the United States and the Soviet Union – is already isolated within the Soviet-controlled eastern part of Germany. The Allies suspect the Soviets of planning a complete blockade of the former German capital. The Soviets say they are only responding to the Allies' decision to unify their three separately administered zones into one West German zone.

APRIL 2

1810 Napoleon Bonaparte marries Marie Louise, daughter of the Austrian emperor.

1860 The first Italian parliament meets in Turin.

1873 British trains are fitted with toilets – but only in the sleeping cars.

1921 The IRA first obtain Tommy guns from two gunsmiths in Hartford, Connecticut.

1938 The Spanish Civil War ends with General Franco's Fascists as the victors.

1969 The Los Angeles underground newspaper *Open City* ceases publication.

1974 Death of Georges Pompidou, President of France.

1979 Prime Minister Menachem Begin becomes the first Israeli leader to make an official visit to Egypt.

1991 Soviet coal miners go on strike across the USSR.

1991 British businessman Roger Cooper is released from an Iranian prison after serving five years of a ten-year sentence for alleged spying.

1991 Diego Maradona, star of Napoli football team, flies home to Argentina hours before being banned from every sporting activity in Italy after failing a dope test.

BIRTHDAYS

Hans Christian Andersen 1805, Danish writer of fairy tales.

William Holman Hunt 1827, English painter and member of the Pre-Raphaelite Brotherhood.

Émile Zola 1840, French realist novelist whose books included *Nana*, *Germinal* and *La Terre*.

Sir Alec Guinness 1914, British actor who won an Oscar for *The Bridge on the River Kwai*.

Sir Jack Brabham 1926, Australian world champion motor racing driver.

Marvin Gaye 1939, American soul singer and one of the foremost Tamla Motown artists.

Emmylou Harris 1948, American country and pop singer.

Argentina's junta snatches Falklands

1982 The British South Atlantic dependency of the Falklands Islands is now in the hands of Argentinian military forces. Falklands governor Rex Hunt ordered the company of British Marines stationed in the island's capital, Port Stanley, to surrender when it became clear that they were massively outnumbered by the invasion force. Fears were raised last week when a party of Argentinian "scrap metallers" landed on the sparsely populated British island of South Georgia, 150 miles (240 km) away. Observers believe that the military junta in Buenos Aires, led by President Leopoldo Galtieri, may have read the British Foreign Office's silence on this as a sign that Britain is prepared to give up her costly commitment to the 2000 islanders, the vast majority of whom reject Argentina's claim to their homeland. The British government is now discussing the possibility of sending a task force to eject the invaders.

NELSON BLAMES HIS BLIND EYE

1801 Never has a naval commander won so much popularity for disobeying orders. In a defiant gesture, British admiral Horatio Nelson, aboard HMS *Elephant*, sank the pro-French Danish fleet off its home port of Copenhagen. Nelson's squadron had come under fire from Danish shore batteries when the incident occurred. The British commander-in-chief, Sir Hyde Parker, signalled Nelson to withdraw his forces. On reading the C-in-C's signals, Nelson reportedly said "Damn me if I do!", placed his telescope pointedly to his blind eye and continued attacking the Danish ships. Nelson's action has opened up the Baltic to British shipping and increased chances of stemming the Napoleonic threat.

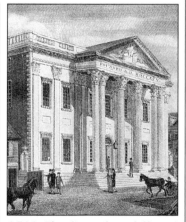

1792 The first silver dollar of America's new currency was struck today in Philadelphia by the Bank of the United States. Each coin contains 371 grains of silver metal. The American eagle on each dollar is a reminder of the fledgling country's determination to establish an identity that owes nothing to Britain.

Red Rum pulls off hat trick

1977 Red Rum, Britain's favourite racehorse, today crowned a magnificent career by becoming the first horse ever to win three Grand Nationals. The 12-year-old gelding galloped past the winning post to notch up another impressive victory at Liverpool's Aintree race course and add to his unprecedented record in Britain's premier steeplechase: wins in 1973 and 1974 and second places in 1975 and 1976. Red Rum made light of his 11st 8lb handicap, sailing over the 30 fences and finishing the 4 mile 856-yard (7.2 km) race 25 lengths ahead. His performance has surpassed the wildest dreams of his 89-year-old owner, retired businessman Noel Le Mare. Before "Rummy" was bought for him in 1972 by part-time trainer "Ginger" McCain for 6,000 guineas, Mr Le Mare had spent over £100,000 trying to realize his ambition of owning a National winner.

Khmer Rouge genocide exposed

1979 Vietnamese soldiers now occupying Cambodia are showing the world the unspeakable brutality of Khmer Rouge leader Pol Pot's ousted communist regime. Mass graves containing piles of skulls and bones of at least 2000 people have been found near the town of Stung Treng in north-eastern Cambodia. The new Vietnamese-backed administration in the Cambodian capital Phnom Penh estimates that one million people may have perished during Pol Pot's three-year experiment to take his people back to "Year Zero". A member of Ho Chi Minh's Indochinese Communist Party in the 1940s, Pol Pot committed his Khmer regime to a programme of enforced collectivization, involving the mass evacuation of city-dwellers to the Cambodian countryside. Many of the victims of this radical policy were either worked to death or murdered for resisting the Khmer Rouge's chilling brand of ideological purism.

WINDSOR JEWELS FETCH £31 MILLION

1987 Jewellery worn by the woman who once charmed a British king off his throne was today snapped up by latterday queens of Hollywood. The auction in Geneva included rings, necklaces, brooches and other personal possessions belonging to the Duchess of Windsor, who died 12 months ago. The £31 million raised from the sale will go to medical research. Observers believe that buyers, including Elizabeth Taylor and Joan Collins, were more interested in the "Edward and Mrs Simpson" connections than the real worth of the items. Wallis Simpson had few occasions to show off her baubles in Britain, for the Windsors lived in exile after the constitutional upset caused by Edward VIII's abdication in 1936. While their Paris home was elegant, it was hardly a royal court.

1682 Death of Bartolomé Murillo, Spanish painter of sentimental religious and genre scenes.

1862 Death of Sir James Clark Ross, English explorer who gave his name to Ross Barrier, Ross Island and Ross Sea, Antarctica.

1897 Death of Johannes Brahms, German composer of symphonies, piano and violin concertos, chamber music and choral works.

1922 In Russia, Joseph Stalin is appointed General Secretary of the Communist Party.

1969 Jim Morrison of pop group The Doors is arrested by the FBI in Los Angeles and charged with interstate flight to avoid prosecution for "lewd and lascivious behaviour in public" at a concert in Miami, Florida on March 1 that year.

1982 Buenos Aires celebrates the invasion of the Falkland Islands while the UN says Argentina must withdraw.

1991 Graham Greene, author of international repute, dies aged 86.

1991 Death of Martha Graham, dancer, choreographer and pioneer of contemporary dance in the USA.

Jesse James bites the dust

1882 The notorious outlaw Jesse James, head of the James Gang and mastermind of countless bank and train robberies, was gunned down today at his home in St Joseph, Missouri. Neighbours were shocked to learn that the man they knew as Thomas Howard had a $10,000 price tag on his head. James met his end at the hands of a new recruit to the gang, Bob Ford, who was staying with James, his wife and two children. Ford allegedly shot James in the back of the head as he stood on a chair to straighten a picture. James's 20-year life of crime began at the end of the Civil War after an apprenticeship with the pro-Confederate band of guerrilla fighters led by William Quantrill. After the war, James and his brother Frank founded their own gang. But in 1876 an attempted bank raid in Northfield, Minnesota went wrong and the gang was decimated. James re-formed the gang, but it never achieved the same success.

> *Any cook should be able to run the country*
> **Vladimir Ilich Lenin**, returning to Moscow from exile today, 1917.

Parliament curbs East India Company

1784 The India Act has at last been steered through the British Houses of Parliament to bring some measure of order to the affairs of the East India Company, Britain's agents in India. The struggle to modify the Company's powers and make it more accountable to the government in London cost Whig politician Charles Fox his job last year. William Pitt has now succeeded, but not without disturbing the interests of the directors of the Company. The imperial power wielded by the governor general in British India, Warren Hastings, has attracted adverse comment from liberal commentators who point to the taxpayers' money that is used to benefit the organization's employees and no one else.

Lonely Brahms ends a musical era

1897 Germany's foremost classic-romantic composer, Johannes Brahms has died at his home in Vienna at the age of 64. Supported by his father and by fellow musicians, notably the composer Robert Schumann, Brahms's big breakthrough came in 1868 with the first performance in Bremen of his German Requiem. Lauded across Europe, and with compositions for piano, chamber orchestra, and chorus, Brahms began work on his first symphony. He would deliberate over this for some 20 years, and then follow it almost immediately with a second. Work on all four symphonies was punctuated by piano and chamber pieces and songs. As a personality Brahms was a complex mixture: both gruff and tender, a bachelor who longed for love and yet shied away from committment.

1936 German-born carpenter Bruno Hauptmann today went to the electric chair for the kidnap and murder of the 20-month-old baby son of aviation hero Charles Lindbergh and his wife Anne. The execution had been delayed pending an appeal, which was turned down. Hauptmann proclaimed his innocence throughout the trial last year and denied receiving a $50,000 ransom and bludgeoning the child to death.

BIRTHDAYS

Washington Irving 1783, American historian and author of short stories, including "Rip Van Winkle".

Daisy Ashford 1881, English author who wrote *The Young Visiters* at the age of only nine.

Henry Luce 1898, American publisher who founded *Time*, *Life* and *Fortune* magazines.

Marlon Brando 1924, American Method actor who won Oscars for *On the Waterfront* and *The Godfather*.

Doris Day 1924, American actress and singer who delighted audiences with musicals such as *The Pajama Game* and *Calamity Jane*.

Helmut Kohl 1930, German statesman twice elected chancellor.

Eddie Murphy 1961, American comedian and film star.

APRIL 4

BIRTHDAYS

Pierre-Paul Prud'hon 1758, French historical and portrait painter who was a favourite of both Napoleon Bonaparte's empresses.

Muddy Waters 1915, American blues singer and guitarist whose hits include "I've Got My Mojo Working" and "Mannish Boy".

Maya Angelou 1928, American poet, playwright and novelist whose four volumes of autobiography are best-sellers.

Brixton is Britain's latest battle-zone

1981 Brixton, a predominantly black district of south London, tonight became a battle zone for the second night running. Police with protective shields faced an army of rioting youths – black and white – armed with petrol bombs and anything else they could lay their hands on. Whole streets were engulfed in the violence which ended in 200 police injured and some 213 arrests. Cars were overturned and wrecked and shops looted for valuables. What sparked the violence is disputed. Community leaders are citing years of heavy-handed policing and racial harassment as a potential powder keg waiting to erupt. Senior police deny that their methods provoked a confrontation or that the riots have a racial origin, pointing to the fact that blacks and whites were seen fighting shoulder-to-shoulder. A police presence is necessary, they argue, because of the high incidence of drug dealing and other crime in the area.

Murdoch tries to end ugly war in Wapping

1986 Media mogul Rupert Murdoch is ready to make peace with the workers who have been trying to disrupt operations at his new multi-million pound, super-tech factory at Wapping in London's docklands. The plant's new technology has been installed at the expense of compositors who now find themselves out of work. Murdoch is hoping that the apparently generous offer of giving the old Gray's Inn Road plant, in west central London, to the printers' union will bring the acrimonious dispute to an end. The strike, involving some 2000 print workers, has led to ugly scenes on the picket line at Wapping as police have attempted to ensure the safe passage of delivery lorries. Production of a number of Murdoch's papers, including the *Times*, *Sun* and *Sunday Times*, has been affected. The papers are being produced by management while journalists – traditionally allies of the printers – have been told they will be fired if they fail to cooperate.

> *If a man hasn't discovered something he would die for, he isn't fit to live.*
> **Martin Luther King,** who died today, 1968.

Shots just miss heir to British throne

1900 Prince Edward, heir to the throne of England, narrowly escaped death today when a teenage anarchist fired two shots at him. The Prince and his wife Princess Alexandra were on a train in Brussels railway station when the incident occurred. The would-be assassin, 16-year-old Jean-Baptiste Sipido, is said to have targeted the Prince because he holds him personally responsible for the many deaths suffered in the Boer War, especially under Lord Kitchener.

Drake's world tour a triumph

1581 England's latest hero, the navigator Francis Drake, was today knighted at Deptford by Queen Elizabeth after entertaining Her Majesty to a banquet aboard the *Golden Hind*, the ship in which he repeated Ferdinand Magellan's feat of circumnavigating the world. Drake's flotilla of five small ships carrying 160 men and boys left Plymouth on December 13, 1577. The three-year voyage was dogged with problems and passengers had to "haul and draw" with the mariners. Drake attacked Spanish ships off the coasts of Chile and Peru and annexed a "fair and good" bay which he named New Albion. The ship ran aground on a shoal in the East Indian Archipelago, but slid off it after 20 hours and headed for home.

Dream-maker King shot dead

1968 Civil rights leader Dr Martin Luther King, the man who inspired black and white Americans with his eloquence, vision and compassion, was today shot dead by an unidentified white assassin at a motel in Memphis, Tennessee. The son of a preacher, Dr King became world famous in 1963 for his "I have a Dream" speech in which he spelt out his vision for America's poor, both black and white. Dr King first played a major role in the civil rights movement in 1955 when he led a year-long bus boycott in protest against segregation on public transport in Montgomery, Alabama. Afterwards he established the South Christian Leadership Conference, which used non-violent marches and protests as a way of drawing attention to the issues of black rights and poverty. At the time of his death, King was planning a multi-racial Poor People's March. His award of the Nobel Peace Prize, in 1964, came at a time when he was coming under fire from more militant black activists increasingly frustrated by his pacifist approach. King's murder may help these elements within the civil rights movement win the argument against moderation in the continuing fight for equality.

WILDE ABOUT THE BOY

1895 A trial has opened at the Old Bailey which promises to become the talk of London society. Playwright Oscar Wilde, the author of the highly successful plays *The Importance of Being Earnest* and *Lady Windemere's Fan*, is sueing the Marquess of Queensberry for libel. The Marquess is alleged to have left a note at Mr Wilde's club accusing him of sodomy. Now the Marquess is threatening to produce an impressive list of witnesses to testify in support of his allegation. Insiders claim that the temper of the boxing-mad Marquess has been sorely tried by his son, Alfred, who has made no secret of the intimate nature of his relationship with Mr Wilde.

Churchill resigns

1955 An era in British politics came to an end today as Prime Minister Sir Winston Churchill announced his resignation. He will be succeeded by Foreign Secretary Sir Anthony Eden. Churchill's decision to pass the Conservative torch to a younger man is not unexpected. Two years ago he suffered a crippling stroke which has taken its toll of his 80 years. With characteristic candour, Churchill said he was too old to hold the reins of government, although he hopes to continue as MP for Woodford.

Washington's capital idea

1793 George Washington has approved plans for new public buildings and roads in America's capital city. Work will begin soon on the meeting place of the US Congress, the design for which has been awarded to William Thornton, who has no previous architectural experience. The runner-up in the design competition, Stephen Hallet, is to supervise the project. The president chose the site for the new capital as well as the site for this building – to be called the Capitol, after the centre of government in ancient Rome.

French architect Major Pierre L'Enfant is to be responsible for the overall design of the new city, which is to be laid out on classical lines.

Solidarity turns the corner

1989 The end of communist rule in Poland is now in sight after today's historic political pact between the independent trade union federation Solidarity and the government of Wojciech Jaruzelski. After weeks of seemingly hopeless negotiations, Solidarity has finally won the right to contest partially free elections and to publish its own newspaper. The pact also provides for a democratically elected senate and president. Opinion polls will be held in June. Solidarity has been banned by the Polish authorities since 1982. Its relegalization is well overdue, since martial law was finally lifted in the middle of 1983. However, throughout the ban, the organization continued to receive widespread support among a Polish population that is desperate for saviours. Many hopes are now riding on Solidarity and its charismatic leader, Lech Walesa. The current regime's apparent willingness to allow Solidarity to take part in the political process is widely acknowledged to be an indication of its own inability to provide answers to Poland's mounting economic problems in the absence of popular support.

> *Power tends to corrupt, and absolute power corrupts absolutely. Great men are almost always bad men . . . there is no worse heresy than that the office sanctifies the holder of it.*
> **Lord Acton,**
> British historian, 1887.

Guillotine turns on the revolutionaries

1794 Nine months after losing his place on the Committee of Public Safety which rules France, Georges Jacques Danton has also lost his head. Today the revolution's most dazzling speaker, a force for moderation, was guillotined for corruption. Executed with him were 14 members of his group, called the "The Indulgents". A lawyer by profession, Danton was one of the fathers of the Revolution. His call for a relaxation of the "Terror" and the policy of flushing out counter-revolutionaries received such heartfelt support from the public that Robespierre, fearing for his position in the regime, moved against him. Robespierre's action may have an unsettling effect on other National Convention members.

1199 Richard I of England dies from an infected wound while besieging Chaluz Castle during the Crusades.

1520 Raphael, Italian Renaissance painter and architect, dies on his 37th birthday.

1580 An earthquake in London damages St Paul's Cathedral.

1830 The Church of the Latterday Saints is founded at Fayette, New York by Joseph Smith.

1843 English poet William Wordsworth is appointed Poet Laureate.

1939 A Polish defence pact is signed in London by Britain, France and Poland.

1944 Pay As You Earn Income Tax is introduced in Britain.

1965 The US launches the first commercial communications satellite, *Early Bird*.

1968 Pierre Trudeau becomes Prime Minister of Canada.

1972 Russian-born composer Igor Stravinsky dies in New York.

1976 Millionaire recluse Howard Hughes dies in a plane while being flown to hospital, leaving a fortune of $2,000 million (£1081 million).

1982 Forty-four-year-old American Jim Princeton returns $37.1 million (£20 million) in negotiable bearer certificates which he finds outside 110 Wall Street.

1984 Seventeen-year-old South African runner Zola Budd is granted British citizenship only 13 days after signing her application so that she can run for Britain in the Los Angeles Olympic Games.

BIRTHDAYS

Harry Houdini 1874, American magician and escapologist.

Anthony Fokker 1890, Dutch aircraft designer.

Sir John Betjeman 1906, British Poet Laureate loved for his gentle social satire.

André Previn 1929, American composer, pianist and conductor.

Pete Tosh 1945, Jamaican reggae artist and founder member of the Wailers.

Boney gets the Elba

1814 French emperor Napoleon Bonaparte was today forced to abdicate unconditionally. The beginning of the end for the ambitious Corsican was his defeat last October at the so-called "Battle of the Nations" near Leipzig, where he lost a third of his half-million troops. With his once mighty army now reduced to a pathetic rump of fighting men, many of them conscripts, Bonaparte nevertheless refused to negotiate and in an audacious manoeuvre inflicted reverses on the advancing allied armies. However, it soon became apparent that the allies could outwit him by quickly reaching Paris and setting up a new government. Last week British, Russian, Prussian and Swedish troops poured into Paris. From his headquarters at Fontainebleau, Napoleon received news of the French people's enthusiasm for the return of the Bourbons and his own Marshals' reluctance to continue the struggle. He therefore had to step down. In return for relinquishing his empire, the allies have given him sovereignty over Elba, the island to which they are exiling him.

THE DOUGHBOYS ENTER WWI

1917 President Woodrow Wilson today signed the resolution which takes the United States into war on the side of Britain and France. America's participation had been made inevitable by Germany's intensification of its submarine campaign against the merchant shipping routes to Britain. American ships have been suffering increasingly heavy losses, despite Germany's earlier promise to abandon the campaign. The decision to enter the war represents a political about-face for Wilson, but the President nonetheless won ecstatic applause from Congress for his rousing call "to save democracy" and unanimous support for the war resolution.

Olympics anew

1896 A modern version of the ancient Olympic Games was opened today in Athens, initiated by French aristocrat Baron Pierre de Coubertin, who hopes to stimulate interest in physical fitness and promote understanding between nations. The first record of the Games dates from 776 BC, although it is thought that they were already 500 years old by then. The venue was Olympia, home of the Greek god Zeus in whose honour they were held every four years – until Greece lost its independence and the Christian Roman emperor, Theodosius, abolished them to discourage paganism, in AD 394.

> *Nothing easier. One step beyond the pole, you see, and the north wind becomes a south one.*
> **Robert Peary** on how he reached the North Pole, 1909.

1528 Albrecht Dürer, the German painter, engraver, designer of wood cuts and art theorist, has died in his home town of Nuremburg, aged 57. Dürer will be remembered for achieving a synthesis between his own northern European artistic heritage and the revolutionary ideas propounded by the Italian Renaissance artists of southern Europe. His work was enriched by his studies of the latter in his travels to Italy.

African presidents shot down

1994 The presidents of the African states of Rwanda and Burundi were killed when their plane crashed near Kigali, Rwanda. Some observers say the aircraft was brought down by rocket fire. Juvenal Habyarimana and Cyprian Ntayamira were returning from a meeting of African leaders in Tanzania, set up to discuss ways of ending the ethnic violence in their countries. Violent clashes between the Hutu tribe and the minority Tutsis has plagued both states for hundreds of years. The deaths of the presidents could make the situation worse. Heavy fighting has already been reported around the presidential palace in Rwanda and explosions have been rocking the city in Kigali.

Vesuvius kills hundreds

1906 Hundreds of Italians living in the vicinity of Mount Vesuvius have been killed in a cataclysmic volcanic eruption. Lava from the volcano has devastated the nearby town of Ottaiano and in Naples, some nine miles away, buildings have collapsed under the weight of the debris from the eruption. The volcano has been active since AD 79 when, after years of lying dormant, it erupted with spectacular, and tragic, effect. The thriving towns of Pompeii and Stabiae were buried under ash and the city of Herculaneum under a mud flow. The smoking giant has frequent outbursts, usually harmless. This latest is one of the most destructive in its fractious history and many are wondering how long they can go on living in its unpredictable shadow.

Anti-nuclear force on the march

1958 This Easter weekend has seen an extraordinary protest against Britain's nuclear bomb programme. Supporters of the recently established Campaign for Nuclear Disarmament (CND) walked from London all the way to Aldermaston, the Berkshire site of Britain's Atomic Weapons Research Establishment, where nuclear warheads are made. About 3000 men, women and children are estimated to have taken part in the ban the bomb march, and a further 9000 turned up for the rally outside the main gate of the high security defence plant.

> *You have a row of dominoes set up; you knock over the first one, and what will happen to the last one is that it will go over very quickly.*
>
> **President Dwight D. Eisenhower** on the "domino effect", during the Battle of Dien Ben Phu, 1954.

Turpin hangs

1739 Travellers in northern England may once more sleep easily in their beds after the hanging today of notorious highwayman Dick Turpin. The innkeeper's son from Essex had been operating in the area for about two years, after working on the fringes of London with his then partner-in-crime Tom King. The duo, whose haunts included Epping Forest and Hampstead Heath, built on the myth of highwaymen started by the dashing French rascal Claude Duval, who once stopped a coach in which a lady was travelling, took only £100 of the £400 she was carrying and ransomed the rest by dancing with her on Hampstead Heath. The 26-year-old one-time valet, and some say model for charming rogue Macheath in John Gay's musical hit *The Beggar's Opera*, was eventually caught in 1669 and hanged at Tyburn. A train of weeping women was said to have attended his magnificent funeral. The romance of these "kings of the road" is still alive, although the increase in their numbers is causing alarm with the authorities. A mob took away Turpin's body for burial after it was cut down from the Mount, outside the walls of York city.

Fire rips through ferry: 150 dead

1990 Fire-fighters are still trying to dampen down the inferno that may have claimed the lives of 150 people aboard the Danish ferry *Scandinavian Star*. The Bahamas-registered vessel was en route to the Danish port of Frederikshavn from the Norwegian capital of Oslo when the fire broke out in the early hours of this morning. Disturbing reports of serious breaches of safety regulations have been received from survivors, many of whom were rescued by a Swedish ferry. They are telling tales of fire alarms that did not work and a panicky crew, many of them Filipinos and Portuguese, more interested in helping themselves than the passengers. Some people had been allowed to sleep in their vehicles, in flagrant violation of maritime safety rules. The captain is allegedly convinced that the killer blaze was the work of an arsonist.

Motor ace killed

1968 British world racing champion Jim Clark was killed today when his Lotus hurtled out of control at an estimated 120 mph (192 kph) during the first race of the Formula Two championship in Hockenheim, Germany. Clark, 32, had a record 25 Grand Prix wins.

APRIL 7

1614 El Greco, Cretan-born painter, sculptor and architect, dies in Spain, his adopted country.

1827 John Waller, a chemist in northern England, sells the first matches, which he invented himself.

1862 General Ulysses Grant's troops vanquish the Confederate army at the Battle of Shiloh.

1943 Chemist Albert Hoffman synthesizes the drug lysergic acid diethylamide (LSD) at his laboratory in Switzerland.

1943 British economist John Maynard Keynes launches a plan for post-war reconstruction.

1947 Death of Henry Ford, American car manufacturer.

1948 The World Health Organization is founded in Geneva.

1949 Rodgers and Hammerstein's musical *South Pacific* opens on Broadway.

1953 Swedish civil servant Dag Hammarsköld succeeds Trygve Lie as secretary-general of the United Nations.

1971 Nixon promises to withdraw 100,000 troops from Vietnam by Christmas.

1978 President Carter backpedals on building the neutron bomb.

BIRTHDAYS

Ole Kirk Christiansen 1891, Danish toymaker who invented Lego.

Walter Winchell 1897, American journalist and broadcaster.

Billie Holiday 1915, American jazz singer par excellence.

Ravi Shankar 1920, Indian sitar player whose music was brought to Western attention by the Beatles.

James Garner 1928, American actor who starred in the television series *The Rockford Files*.

David Frost 1939, British television presenter and producer.

Francis Ford Coppola 1939, American film producer best known for *The Godfather* and *Apocalypse Now*.

APRIL 8

217 AD Roman emperor Caracalla is assassinated after a bloody reign.

1513 Spanish explorer Juan Ponce de Leon discovers Florida.

1904 Britain and France sign the Entente Cordiale, a mutual recognition of each other's colonial interests with particular regard to France's in Morocco and Britain's in Egypt.

1925 The Australian government and the British Colonial Office offer low-interest loans to encourage 500,000 Britons to emigrate to Australia.

1950 Russian ballet dancer Vaslav Nijinsky, who retired at only 29 suffering from schizophrenia, dies at the age of 60.

1962 Cuban leader Fidel Castro offers to ransom prisoners held since the invasion of the Bay of Pigs on April 19, 1961.

1977 The Damned play New York, becoming the first punk band to go on stage in the US.

1989 It is revealed that more than 40 Soviet submariners died after a nuclear-powered "Mike" class submarine refused assistance from nearby Western merchant ships when it caught fire.

1990 British golfer Nick Faldo wins his second successive US Masters.

BIRTHDAYS

Mary Pickford 1893, Canadian-born actress who became known as "America's Sweetheart".

Sir Adrian Boult 1889, British conductor particularly associated with the music of Elgar, Vaughan Williams and Holst.

Ian Smith 1919, Rhodesian prime minister who unilaterally declared independence from Britain in 1965 in the interests of retaining white supremacy.

Dorothy Tutin 1930, British stage and screen actress whose films include *The Importance of Being Earnest* and *Savage Messiah*.

Julian Lennon 1963, British pop musician, son of John Lennon.

Picasso draws last breath

1973 Spanish painter Pablo Picasso died today at his chateau at Mougins after suffering a heart attack. He was 91. His genius began to flower after he moved from his native Barcelona to Paris in 1904. Stimulated by the unique intellectual and artistic climate of the French capital, he threw off his "blue period" of limited colour variation and gloomy subject matter to concentrate on a lighter style, known as his "rose period". Picasso's early spirit of artistic adventure led him to originate the abstract style that became synonymous with his name - Cubism. His legacy consists of 140,000 paintings and drawings, 100,000 engravings, 300 sculptures and thousands of other documents, such as the menu cards he illustrated to pay for his dinners in the early days in Paris. Nevertheless, he still found the time for enjoying the good life, beautiful women and bullfighting.

Carmel makes Clint's day

1986 Clint Eastwood, the screen tough guy famed for his portrayal of "Dirty Harry", is to get the chance of playing the real-life role of mayor of the up-market Californian resort of Carmel. Eastwood, 55, gained a landslide victory today on a pledge to "clean up" the town where he has lived for 14 years. The townspeople hope that Clint will "make their day" by smoothing out relations between commerce-minded shopkeepers and residents who would like a respite from the hordes of visitors attracted to the bijou town. The Hollywood star intends to supplement his $200-a-month salary with film work, which he is sure will leave him sufficient time to carry out his mayoral duties.

1513 A new province in the Americas has been claimed for the Spanish throne by the man who completed the conquest of Puerto Rico. Juan Ponce de Leon set sail and found what seems like an island paradise – although it may not be an island at all. He has called his latest discovery Florida, the Spanish for Easter Day, Pascua Florida, when the island was first sighted.

Kenya jails Kenyatta

1953 British colonial administrators in Kenya today sentenced Jomo Kenyatta and five others to seven years' hard labour. Kenyatta is alleged to be the leader of the secret terror organization known as the Mau Mau, which has waged a gruesome campaign against white settlers in an attempt to drive the British out of East Africa. Jomo Kenyatta denied the charge against him and made a few allegations of his own, describing the trial as an attempt to trample the legitimate rights of the native African people. The white settlers in Kenya, however, hope that Kenyatta's imprisonment will bring an end to the bloody campaign which the Mau Mau launched last year.

BON VOYAGE!

1838 The massive new steamship *Great Western* left Bristol today on her maiden voyage across the Atlantic to Boston. Her designer, Isambard Kingdom Brunel, chief engineer of the Great Western Railway, estimates that the 236-ft (71 m) long wooden ship should reach her destination in 15 days. The *Great Western* is considerably longer than other vessels plying the Atlantic and has a huge capacity for coal, which drives her four boilers and provides steam for her paddle wheels. She also has a full complement of sails and rigging. The voyage has aroused interest among businessmen, who may be interested in using steamships as passenger liners.

1963 The British film *Lawrence of Arabia*, starring Peter O'Toole, won seven Oscars in Los Angeles tonight, including Best Picture, Best Director, for David Lean, and Best Score, for composer Maurice Jarre.

End to bloodshed in civil war

1865 General Robert E. Lee, leading the Confederate army of North Virginia, today surrendered to his opposite number in the Union army, General Ulysses S. Grant, at the Appomattox Court House in Virginia. The charismatic Lee had no choice but to surrender. His army had been reduced to almost a rag-bag because of mass desertions. At the finish he had only 9,000 fighting troops he could call on. An orderly retreat was out of the question: Sheridan's forces had cut off the most likely exit point. There was nowhere for his exhausted, starving men to go but into the arms of the enemy. Although Grant insisted on unconditional surrender, Lee's men have been allowed to keep their guns. Mopping-up operations are expected to continue for several weeks, especially as the army of North Carolina under General Johnson has still to surrender.

SADDAM STATUE TOPPLES WITH BAGHDAD

2003 Scenes of joy greeted US tanks as they rolled into the Iraqi capital Baghdad, confirming that Saddam Hussein is no longer in power. In the main square, a group of Iraqis tried to pull down a statue of Saddam Hussein in a show of contempt for their former leader. They climbed the statue to secure a noose around its neck but were unable to topple it. US troops joined in, using an armoured vehicle to gradually drag down the statue.

Just before the statue was down, a US soldier covered the face with a US flag. This was not well received so it was quickly removed and replaced by the old Iraqi flag, to roars of approval. As the statue fell, the crowd jumped on it, chanting as they danced on the fallen effigy, in a symbolic gesture of contempt as it was torn to pieces. They then cut off the head, tied chains around it, and dragged it through the streets. The US military campaign in Iraq is set to continue, although a US Army spokesman has made a very upbeat assessment of the gains made so far in Iraq.

> *The physician can bury his mistakes, but the architect can only advise his client to plant vines.*
> **Frank Lloyd Wright,** American architect, died today, 1959.

Namibia close to independence

1989 Namibia's fight for independence moved a step nearer success today with the announcement of a cessation of hostilities between South Africa's armed forces and guerrilla fighters of the left-wing nationalist movement South-West Africa People's Organization. Under the UN-sponsored agreement, guerrillas who have crossed into Namibia from their bases in Angola will withdraw to UN-run camps. In return, South Africa will continue preparations for free elections, which SWAPO is hot favourite to win. If all goes well, Namibia could be just months away from finally throwing off the shackles of colonial rule. Proclaimed a German protectorate in 1884, it has been occupied by a stubborn South Africa since World War I, after which the government in Pretoria was expected to order its forces to withdraw.

> *If a man will begin with certainties, he shall end in doubts, but if he will be content to begin with doubts, he will end in certainties.*
> **Sir Francis Bacon,** who died today, 1973.

Apple starts to rot

1970 One of the most exciting chapters in the history of pop ended today as singer-songwriter Paul McCartney issued a High Court writ winding up the business partnership of the Beatles. The move was not unexpected. McCartney was known to be losing patience with Apple, the quirky record company-cum-ideas bank set up to manage the group's financial affairs. Months of squabbling over money, power and the influence of Yoko Ono, wife of John Lennon who was, with McCartney, the creative driving force behind the Fab Four, have solved nothing. McCartney's action is a sad comment on the state of relationships within the band, especially between McCartney and Lennon, who first catapulted to fame in the early 60s under Brian Epstein's guidance. Perhaps now is the right time for the Beatles to "Let It Be", as the title track of their latest album advises, and go their separate ways.

1553 Death of François Rabelais, the French satirical writer who, though once a monk, was noted for the bawdiness of his work.

1869 The Hudson Bay Company cedes its territory to Canada.

1882 Death of Dante Gabriel Rossetti, English painter and poet who co-founded the Pre-Raphaelite Brotherhood.

1940 The Germans invade Norway and Denmark.

1945 Dietrich Bonhoeffer, German theologian who involved himself with anti-Hitler conspirators, dies in Buchenwald concentration camp.

1960 David Pratt, a 52-year-old white man, fires two shots at South African president Dr Hendrik Verwoerd and succeeds in wounding him.

1966 Film producer Carlo Ponti marries Sophia Loren in Paris, even though according to Italian law he is still married to his previous wife.

1981 *Nature* magazine publishes a paper containing the longest-ever scientific word, which boasts 207,000 letters.

BIRTHDAYS

Isambard Kingdom Brunel 1806, English engineer whose achievements included the Clifton suspension bridge in Bristol, the *Great Western* steamship and the Great Western railway track.

Charles Baudelaire 1821, French poet whose only volume, *Les fleurs du mal*, led to him being prosecuted for obscenity.

Paul Robeson 1898, American actor and singer whose left-wing views and civil rights activities brought him into conflict with the American administration during the McCarthy era.

Hugh Hefner 1926, American publisher of *Playboy* fame.

Carl Perkins 1932, American pioneering rock 'n' roller who wrote "Blue Suede Shoes".

Jean Paul Belmondo 1933, French actor who made his name in the *nouvelle vague* films of the 1960s.

1633 Bananas appear in British shops for the first time.

1809 Austria declares war on France and invades Bavaria.

1810 Pirate chieftainess "Dragon Lady" Zheng Yi Sao surrenders herself and the 1800 junks under her command to the Chinese authorities.

1820 The first British settlers arrive at Algoa Bay, South Africa.

1841 The *New York Tribune* is published for the first time.

1849 The safety pin is patented in the USA by Walter Hunt of New York.

1858 Chinese governor-general Ye Mingchen of Canton dies in Calcutta, a prisoner of the British.

1864 Archduke Maximilian of Austria becomes Emperor of Mexico.

1921 Sun Yat-Sen is elected president of China.

1932 In the German elections Paul von Hindenburg is elected president with 19 million votes to Adolf Hitler's 13 million.

1960 The US Senate passes the Civil Rights Bill.

1974 Golda Meir resigns as Israeli prime minister.

1989 Police and rioters clash in Tiblisi, capital of Georgia, USSR.

1989 Nick Faldo becomes the first Briton to win the US Masters.

BIRTHDAYS

William Hazlitt 1778, English critic and essayist whose best-known publication is *The Spirit of the Age*.

Joseph Pulitzer 1847, American newspaper proprietor who founded the Pulitzer Prize for achievements in journalism and literature.

Clare Boothe Luce 1903, American playwright, politician and US ambassador to Italy in 1952.

Max von Sydow 1929, Swedish actor who found success at home in Ingmar Bergman films and abroad in Hollywood.

Omar Sharif 1932, Egyptian actor whose many films include *Lawrence of Arabia* and *Doctor Zhivago*.

Zapata zapped

1919 People's champion Emiliano Zapata was today cut down in a hail of bullets after being ambushed by soldiers of the Carranza regime. Zapata took his first step along the revolutionary path in 1910 when the policies of dictator Porfirio Diaz ensured that land appropriated from the peasants remained in the possession of the wealthy. Power changed hands several times in quick succession, as first Diaz, then Francisco Madera, then Victoriano Huerta were unseated. Throughout this time Zapata fought for acceptance of his plan to return to a communal system of land ownership, under the slogan "Land and Liberty". An alliance with the unpredictable Pancho Villa brought some military successes but eventually ended when Villa's army was defeated. Zapata, now isolated, continued the fight. Essentially a man of principle, he died untainted by the desire for power and money evident in some of his lieutenants.

De Gaulle's brave gauntlet

1944 The announcement in Algiers yesterday that Brigadier General Charles de Gaulle is to be the commander-in-chief of all Free French forces has prompted an angry response from his rival for the post, First World War veteran, General Henri Giraud. Giraud has called his ousting "illegal". De Gaulle, who is number one on the hit list of the collaborationist Vichy government of Marshal Petain, fled to London from Paris after the fall of France in 1940. He persuaded the British government to let him use BBC radio to reach fellow Frenchmen willing to fight for the freedom of their country. As sole leader of the French government in exile, de Gaulle is now poised to unveil his ambitious plans for arming the Resistance to a dubious British government.

Abuse for King Cole

1956 Popular jazz musician Nat King Cole has been subjected to a violent assault by racists during a live appearance before a segregated audience in Montgomery, Alabama, his home town. Cole's reaction was to play down the incident, a stance which is attracting considerable criticism from blacks who feel that Cole is in danger of becoming a latter-day "Uncle Tom". Ten years ago Cole was the object of a racially-motivated campaign to drive him from his newly acquired home in a prestigious suburb of Los Angeles. Among the insults he endured was the desecration of his front lawn, into which was burnt the word "nigger".

NORTHERN IRELAND PEACE DEAL

1998 Peace talks between British Prime Minister Tony Blair and the Republic of Ireland's leader Bertie Ahern have ended in an historic agreement on the future of Northern Ireland. Dubbed The Good Friday Agreement, the plan is the result of nearly two years of negotiations. Tony Blair said the accord marked a new beginning: "Today I hope the burden of history can at long last start to be lifted from our shoulders." The agreement includes plans for a Northern Ireland Assembly and cross-border institutions involving the Irish Republic. The proposals will be presented to the people of Ireland and put to a referendum in May. Bertie Ahern said he hoped now a line could be drawn under Ireland's "bloody past".

End near for Hoxha

1985 The man who has safeguarded Stalinist-Leninist ideals in Albania for the last 40 years, Enver Hoxha, is on the point of death. The 76-year-old leader suffered a stroke a year ago and affairs of state have increasingly been dealt with by Ramiz Alia. Hoxha came to power in 1946 after murdering potential rivals. As many as 100,000 Albanians are estimated to have died trying to escape the drab, doctrinaire society he has created. Beards, private cars and religion are forbidden.

Mankind is not a tribe of animals to which we owe compassion. Mankind is a club to which we owe our subscription.

G. K. Chesterton, English writer, in the *Daily News*, 1906.

1841 News-hungry New Yorkers have an extra source of fodder from this morning – the *New York Tribune*. Launched by Horace Greeley, the former editor of Thurlow Weed's political campaign weeklies, the *Tribune* promises a lofty diet of Whig reformism and forward thinking in its pages. Greeley has the knack of wrapping his sound moral principles in a prose style that should guarantee the reader satisfaction as he swallows the *Tribune*'s edifying morsels.

MacArthur loses his stripes

1951 World War II hero General Douglas MacArthur, the man who accepted the Japanese surrender in Tokyo Bay in 1945 and went on to reform the Japanese constitution, has been stripped of all his commands by an irate President Harry Truman. He will be replaced by General Matthew B. Ridgway. Trouble between the commander-in-chief of the 16-nation UN force in Korea and the US president had been brewing since March 31, when the counter-offensive launched by the UN forces succeeded in bringing them to the 38th Parallel, the invisible line that divides pro-Western South Korea from Soviet-backed North Korea. MacArthur and his men reached this point last year and were on the brink of defeating the North Koreans when China stepped in. MacArthur unofficially publicly declared that UN forces should pursue the war into China if needs be. Truman read it as a direct challenge to his authority to determine the conduct of US foreign policy.

1514 Italian architect Donato Bramante dies while still engaged in the building of St Peter's in Rome, which he had begun in 1506.

1713 France cedes Newfoundland and Gibraltar to Britain.

1913 French aviator Gustave Hamel sets a record by flying the Channel from Dunkirk to Dover and back in 90 minutes.

1919 The International Labour Organisation is founded in affiliation with the League of Nations to improve living standards and working conditions.

1929 The cartoon character Popeye appears for the first time, in a William Hearst newspaper.

1960 Death of Sir Archibald McIndoe, New Zealand-born plastic surgeon who pioneered new techniques while treating RAF pilots burned in World War II.

1961 A young folk singer called Bob Dylan makes his first live appearance when he opens for John Lee Hooker at Gerde's Folk City in Greenwich Village.

1977 Death of Josephine Baker, black American singer and dancer who found recognition in France.

1988 Sir Kenneth Macmillan's ballet *Elite Syncopations* is performed at the Bavarian State Opera accompanied by only two pianos – it is based on music by Scott Joplin and the orchestra has claimed the right, under a 1937 Nazi law, not to play music written by a black person.

1989 English soccer clubs are readmitted to the European Cup after a ban imposed because of the behaviour of soccer hooligans.

Supergun for Saddam?

1990 The usual calm which pervades the British Foreign Office has been disturbed by the seizure at Teesport, Middlesbrough, of an Iraq-bound shipment of heavy "oil pipes" that look suspiciously like sections of a large gun. British Customs officials were certain that the contents of the eight crates offloaded from the Bahamas-registered merchantman *Gur Mariner* could be classified as munitions. An embargo on arms exports to Iraq introduced during the Iran-Iraq war is still in force. A spokesman for one of the companies involved in the manufacture of the "pipes", Sheffield Forgemasters, has described the allegations as "something out of a sci-fi fantasy". Despite the scepticism of some military experts about the feasibility of a 130-ft (39 m) long gun made of 140 tons of tubing, Ministry of Defence scientists are backing the theory.

GREEN LIGHT FOR ORANGE

1689 The joint coronation of William III, Prince of Orange and champion of Protestantism, and his wife Mary, Protestant daughter of the deposed Stuart king James II, sets the seal on a remarkable transition of power within British government. Since arriving in Britain last November, William has been involved in lengthy negotiations with the Lords and Commons over the future rule of the country. A Bill of Rights which excludes Roman Catholics from the throne, gives political and civil rights to the people and supremacy to parliament, is expected to reach the statute books later in the year. Meanwhile, the nation is breathing a collective sigh of relief at seeing the back of James II, whose obsession with promoting the Catholic cause brought about his downfall.

Nazi Eichmann finally faces trial

1961 Alleged Nazi war criminal Adolf Eichmann today entered a Jerusalem court to hear the 15 charges against him, 12 of which carry the death penalty. As head of the Gestapo's Jewish section, Adolf Eichmann is said to have been responsible for sending millions of Jewish men, women and children to their deaths during the Second World War. Eichmann fled to Argentina after the war in an attempt to evade capture but was eventually tracked down by the Vienna-based Nazi-hunter Simon Wiesenthal. Wiesenthal then tipped off the Israeli secret service. A team of secret service agents kidnapped Eichmann last year and brought him back to their own country to face a long overdue trial.

More pain for the Dust Bowl

1935 Disaster has already struck the hard-pressed folk of America in the shape of the Depression. Now, just as they were pinning their hopes on a brighter future with President Roosevelt's New Deal programmes, dust storms are threatening half the country. The worst-hit areas are the so-called "Dust Bowl" states of Kansas, Colorado, Wyoming, Oklahoma, Texas and New Mexico. In the 20s much of the vast prairie was planted with wheat which degraded the topsoil, leaving the land dusty and arid, ideal for the turbulent prairie winds to whip up into a huge black destructive mass that can devastate homes and crops. The government is being urged to declare the affected area a disaster zone.

1204 The Fourth Crusade, which started from Venice, is diverted by the Venetians to sack Constantinople and establish a Latin empire there.

1606 The Union Jack becomes England's official flag.

1817 Death of Charles Messier, French astronomer who made a list of nebulae known as the Messier catalogue.

1838 English settlers in South Africa vanquish the Zulus in the Battle of Tugela.

1877 Britain annexes the Transvaal, causing deep resentment amongst the Boers.

1914 George Bernard Shaw's play *Pygmalion* opens in London with Mrs Patrick Campbell and Sir Herbert Tree in the leading roles.

1954 Bill Haley and the Comets record "Rock Around the Clock".

1960 Ray Charles wins the Best Male Vocalist Grammy Award for "Georgia On My Mind" and Ella Fitzgerald wins Best Female Vocalist for "Mack the Knife".

1981 Death of Joe Louis, the US and world heavyweight boxing champion.

1989 Death of Sugar Ray Robinson, welterweight and middleweight boxing champion.

2004 Cricketer Brian Lara achieves 400 runs, the highest ever score in test cricket.

BIRTHDAYS

Henry Clay 1877, American statesman and founder member of the Republican Party.

Lionel Hampton 1913, American jazz bandleader and vibraphone player.

Maria Callas 1923, Greek operatic soprano.

Bobby Moore 1941, British footballer who played for England 108 times.

Alan Ayckbourn 1949, British dramatist whose plays combine farce with minute observation of British class structure.

David Cassidy 1950, American teenybopper idol.

Confederates challenge Lincoln

1861 Confederate forces today threw down the gauntlet to Republican president Abraham Lincoln by firing on Fort Sumter in Charleston Harbor. The fort, which is still under construction, and its garrison of around 85 Federal troops have been under threat since the new president first took office some five weeks ago. Lincoln's opposition to the second Crittenden amendment, which would have allowed states to be either pro-slavery or pro-freedom, resulted in six more states seceding from the Union and joining South Carolina to form the Confederate States of America. The Federal troops garrisoned in Fort Sumter and at other military installations within the confederacy were called on to surrender or face starvation. Lincoln responded by announcing that reinforcements would be sent to relieve the beleaguered fort, indicating his determination to bring the rebels to heel. It can only be a matter of time before President Lincoln, a firm believer in centralized government, mobilizes the vast resources available to his generals. Theoretically outnumbered by a ratio of 2:1 in manpower, and 30:1 in availability of arms, the Confederates can only be hoping that their cause will attract aid from overseas.

A politician is a man who understands government, and it takes a politician to run a government. A statesman is a politician who's been dead ten or fifteen years.
Harry S. Truman, 1958.

Russians win the human space race

1961 A new phase in the competition for top dog status between the Soviet Union and the United States opened today when Russian cosmonaut Major Yuri Gagarin became the first man in space. The single orbit of the Earth completed by Gagarin in the four-and-a-half ton Vostok 1 space vehicle took 108 minutes. Gagarin is said to feel fine and shows no immediate signs of the adverse effects that weightlessness and re-entry into the Earth's atmosphere can have on the body.

Four-term Roosevelt dies

1945 America is mourning the sudden loss of one of its greatest political figures, Franklin D. Roosevelt. He died today aged 63 after suffering a stroke. Roosevelt was no stranger to adversity, despite every material advantage and impeccable Ivy League credentials which suited him to a career in politics. In 1921, after 11 years in the Senate, he was crippled by poliomyelitis at the age of 39 and forced into temporary retirement. During his first presidential term of office (1932-36), Roosevelt developed his New Deal programme of spending America out of the Great Depression. In his fourth, and last, term Roosevelt's ideals for a safe and secure world inspired the foundation of the United Nations Organization, whose charter is to be unveiled in San Francisco at the end of the month. He will be a hard act to follow, and his successor, Vice-President Harry S. Truman, will no doubt be grateful for a honeymoon period with Congress, no matter how brief.

Falklands invader pays the price

1983 General Leopoldo Galtieri, the man who ordered the invasion of the Falklands Islands, has been sentenced to 60 days' imprisonment while the authorities decide what to do with him. Galtieri has criticized his fellow generals' part in the recent military defeat at the hands of the British. The feathers of General Mario Menendez, the former military governor of the Falklands capital Port Stanley and a member of Argentina's most powerful military family, were well and truly ruffled by Galtieri's accusation of cowardice, which appeared in the newspaper *Clarin*. Galtieri's attempt to spread the blame for the Falklands' débacle may be seen as an attempt to forestall his own downfall, which now seems inevitable.

1981 The Americans have marked the twentieth anniversary of the first manned space flight by Soviet cosmonaut Yuri Gagarin with the launch of the revolutionary Columbia space vehicle – which is reusable. The vehicle is launched in the usual way from a pad at Kennedy Space Center, but after re-entering the Earth's atmosphere lands on a runway like a conventional aircraft. The "space shuttle" will be tested at the end of the year.

Men have never been good, they are not good, they never will be good.
Karl Barth, Swiss Protestant theologian, and World War I pastor, 1954.

Soviets admit to Katyn massacre

1990 One of the Kremlin's best-kept lies was admitted today after decades of deception: the systematic murder of over 15,000 Polish army officers by the Soviet secret police, the NKVD, forerunners of the KGB. This crime, known as the Katyn massacre after the pine forest in western Russia where the executions were carried out in the spring of 1940, has always been officially blamed on the Germans. The evidence, though, has always pointed to the Soviet Union as the culprit. The announcement by the Soviet news agency Tass coincides with the visit to Moscow of the Polish leader, General Jaruzelski. The conspiracy of silence over Katyn began as a diplomatic necessity in World War II, when to tarnish the image of "Uncle Joe" Stalin would have spoiled the Allies' propaganda campaign. After the war, western governments preferred to continue the lie rather than admit that they had been party to the deception.

> *A hungry stomach has no ears.*
> **Jean de la Fontaine**, French fabulist who died today, 1695.

1997 American golfer Tiger Woods has stunned the sporting world and rewritten golf history. He has become both the youngest player (at 21) and the first black player ever to win the US Masters tournament. He also thrilled crowds of supporters by beating the previous record with his 72-hole score of under-18-par 270, having the widest ever winning margin of 12 strokes, and breaking records with his totals for the last 54 holes, as well as the second and third rounds. His brilliant career is just starting.

Poitier's Oscar boost

1964 Sidney Poitier, described as "the world's most handsome black man", won an Oscar tonight for his performance in Ralph Nelson's *The Lilies of the Field*. He is the first black actor to receive the award. At a time when the civil rights movement and its white liberal allies seem to be under threat from reactionary forces, Poitier's Oscar is a much-needed morale booster for the black community. However, whether Poitier's portrayal of a nice black man with nice wholesome views really deserved the film industry's most prestigious accolade is debatable.

Handel's *Messiah* triumphs

1742 The new choral work by the German-born composer George Frederick Handel, *Messiah*, has been received enthusiastically by audience and critics alike at its premiere performance in Dublin. Mr Handel, who has lived in England for the last 30 years, conducted the performance himself. Perhaps best known for his *Water Music*, composed for His Majesty King George I, Mr Handel has found his fortunes at a low ebb in recent years due to a decline in the popularity of the Italian-style operas in which he used to excel. He is now turning his attention to the writing of oratorios.

SPECIAL DELIVERY

1860 The banners were out today in Sacramento, California, to greet the arrival of the first delivery of mail by Pony Express. The name of the rider who brought the three newspapers and 49 letters the last leg of the 1800-mile (2900 km) journey between St Joseph, Missouri and Sacramento is Tom Hamilton. About 50 riders are needed to operate the relay system which involves each horseman riding between 10 and 15 miles on each of his three mounts. There are more than 150 staging posts along the route. The maiden run that was completed today took a total of 10 days, half the time taken by the Overland Mail Company by stage coach. It is possible to cross from east to west even faster: President Lincoln's inaugural address was taken across the continent in 7 days 17 hours. The operators of the service, Russell, Majors, and Waddell, are pinning their hopes for the financial success of the business on a lucrative government contract.

1598 Henry IV of France issues the Edict of Nantes to promote peace between Roman Catholics and Huguenots.

1605 Death of Boris Fedorovich Godunov, Russian statesman who became tsar on the death of Fyodor I, for whom he was regent and whose heir, Dimitri, he may have murdered.

1668 John Dryden, British poet and critic, is appointed Poet Laureate.

1829 The House of Commons passes the Catholic Emancipation Act.

1868 After his defeat by the British at Arogo, Ethiopian emperor Theodore II hills himself.

1882 The Anti-Semitic League is founded in Prussia.

1904 In the Russo-Japanese War a mine sinks the flagship of the Russian fleet, killing 600.

1912 The Royal Flying Corps, an armed service of the air, is formed in Britain.

1919 British troops under the command of Brigadier General Dyer open fire on an unlawful demonstration by Sikhs in the Holy City of Amritsar.

1935 Imperial Airways and Qantas inaugurate a London to Australia air service.

1939 Italian dictator Mussolini invades Albania.

2003 Paula Radcliffe breaks the world record in the London Marathon.

BIRTHDAYS

Frederick North, Earl of Guildford 1732, English prime minister who introduced the Tea Act that led to the Boston Tea Party.

Thomas Jefferson 1743, American president responsible for drafting the Declaration of Independence and founding the Democratic Party.

Frank Winfield Woolworth 1852, American chain store magnate.

Samuel Beckett 1906, Irish dramatist, winner of the Nobel Prize for Literature in 1969.

1471 In the English Wars of the Roses, the Yorkists defeat the Lancastrians at the Battle of Barnet.

1759 George Frederick Handel dies in London, leaving works such as the *Messiah* and the *Water Music* as his memorial.

1814 The US repeals its trade embargo with Britain.

1860 Fort Sumter falls to the Confederate Army.

1903 In New York, the typhus vaccine is discovered by Dr Harry Plotz.

1915 Russian composer and pianist Alexander Scriabin dies.

1931 Britain gets its first Highway Code.

1951 Death of Ernest Bevin, British Labour politician and minister of labour in the coalition government during World War II.

1954 Soviet diplomat Vladimir Patrov asks for political asylum in Australia.

1956 The first videotape is demonstrated in Chicago.

1983 The first cordless telephone is introduced in Britain.

BIRTHDAYS

Philip II 1527, Spanish king who sent his armada to conquer England in 1588 and met with total defeat and the loss of his fleet.

Arnold Toynbee 1889, British historian and author of a 12-volume work entitled *A Study of History*.

Sir John Gielgud 1904, British actor revered for his Shakespearean and other classical roles.

Francis Duvalier 1907, Haitian president and dictator nicknamed "Papa Doc", legendary for his corruption and brutality.

Rod Steiger 1925, American actor who won an Oscar for *In the Heat of the Night*.

Julie Christie 1940, British actress whose films include *Don't Look Now, Shampoo* and *McCabe and Mrs Miller*.

DRAMA OFF STAGE AS LINCOLN SHOT

1865 President Abraham Lincoln is failing fast after being shot in the back of the head at point-blank range. The president and Mrs Lincoln were attending a performance of *Our American Cousin* at Ford's Theatre in Washington when the attack occurred. His assailant, John Wilkes Booth, a member of one of America's most distinguished acting families and a Confederate fanatic, then jumped from the box on to the stage, shouting "Sic semper tyrannis! ['Thus always to tyrants'] - The South is avenged". He then ran out of the theatre, limping heavily, mounted a horse and galloped off into the night. Lincoln will go down in history as the man who saved the Union and in the process brought about the emancipation of America's black slaves. In his own words: "If I could save the Union without freeing any slave I would do it; and if I could save it by freeing all the slaves I would do it; and if I could save it by freeing some and leaving others alone, I would also do that." A manhunt is underway to bring the assailant to justice.

Spanish king deposed at the ballot box

1931 Spain's King Alfonso XIII has fled his native country for Rome after the landslide win for Republican parties in last week's municipal elections. The king's position has been precarious since the fall of the dictator Primo de Rivera last year. Alfonso had supported Rivera's overthrow of the parliamentary system eight years ago, and with Rivera gone and the army against him, a bloody end to his long run of luck looked in sight. Clearly he will not be missed.

1987 Soviet President Mikhail Gorbachev has wrong-footed the White House by proposing a round of arms cuts. The Soviet leader's offer to remove the Soviet Union's entire stock of short-range missiles in Eastern Europe would form part of an agreement on medium-range missiles. The initiative could lead to an early disarmament treaty with the United States, although President Reagan has never suggested going this far in arms cuts and may hold back for political reasons.

Hot air adventure

1872 After their miserable defeat in the Franco-Prussian War last year Parisians are lapping up escapist literature. The latest diversion is an amusing tale that is being serialized in the morning newspaper *Le Temps*. Called *Le Tour du Monde en Quatre-Vingt Jours* – which translates as "Around the World in Eighty Days" - it is about an upper-class Englishman, Phileas Fogg, who lays a bet of £20,000 ($37,000) with several friends in his London club that he and his long-suffering French manservant will circumnavigate the world in a hot-air balloon in 80 days. The author of this delightful nonsense is Jules Verne, master of fanciful adventure stories.

> *Die when I may, I want it said of me by those who know me best, that I have always plucked a thistle and planted a flower where I thought a flower would grow.*
> **Abraham Lincoln**, who was assassinated today, 1865.

De Beauvoir's feminist legacy

1986 Simone de Beauvoir, feminist writer and philosopher, died today in a Paris hospital. She was 78 and had been suffering from blood circulation problems. She and her lover Jean-Paul Sartre, who died six years ago, were for some 40 years the uncrowned heads of France's avant-garde philosophy fraternity. Best known for her book *The Second Sex* (1949), in which she explored sexism from a woman's standpoint, de Beauvoir is also credited, with Sartre, of developing "existentialism". Sartre was true to this philosophy, choosing his character and goals during his 50-year "open" relationship with de Beauvoir. De Beauvoir drew great intellectual rewards from their association but few emotional ones, and not even a Sorbonne training could help her argue away the jealousy prompted by his infidelities with attractive younger women. "I have grown accustomed to living in this world where men are what they are – oppressors," she said. A passionate campaigner for left-wing causes, an atheist, and painfully insecure of her own abilities, de Beauvoir would be amazed to learn that her influence in France is judged to far outweigh that of her once beloved oppressor.

LONDON VOTED TOPS

1966 *Time* magazine has declared London the city of the decade. In its eyes London is "a sparkling and slapdash comedy, switched on, a dazzling blur, buzzing, pulsing, spinning". Never before have young people in Britain had so much money and opportunity at their fingertips. There are jobs a-plenty, they have money in their pockets and new ideas of tolerance, free love and hedonism have replaced 50s caution and conservatism. The desire to be trendy in mini skirts, see-through blouses and knee boots bought from boutiques in the King's Road or Carnaby Street is shared by girls from all walks of life. And for the boys, a Beatles haircut and a Mini Cooper are the ultimate in style. The people the young look up to are from their own generation - designers Mary Quant and Barbara Hulanicki, models Twiggy and Patti Boyd, and pop singers like the Beatles and Rolling Stones. None of them want to grow into their parents' shoes – and who can blame them.

SHE ALWAYS WANTED TO BE ALONE

1990 Greta Garbo has died in New York after almost half a century of self-imposed isolation. At the height of her fame in Hollywood during the 1930s she avoided publicity, believing that "the creative artist should be a rare and solitary spirit". The daughter of an unskilled Swedish labourer, she was taken to Hollywood in 1925 by Russian director Mauritz Stiller and soon established herself in silent films then "talkies".

US go after Gaddafi

1986 The whereabouts of President Reagan's bogey-man, "mad dog" Colonel Gaddafi, were not known this evening after the US bombing of his presidential palace in the Libyan capital, Tripoli. Among the 100 people killed in the raid was Gaddafi's 15-month-old adopted daughter, Hanna. President Reagan ordered the attack in reprisal for Libya's firing of two missiles at the American manned radar base on the Italian island of Lampedusa. Neither missile hit its target. The US fighters that carried out the attack came from bases in the UK. There are fears that Gaddafi will not turn the other cheek over this incident.

1797 Revolutionary fever has spread across the Channel and infected the Royal Navy's fighting men at Spithead and Nore. The mutinies in the Channel fleet are caused by arrears in pay, bad food, ill treatment, lack of leave and arduous blockade duty. The unrest could not have come at a worse time, with Britain at war with Revolutionary France. Admirals Jervis and Howe are threatening draconian measures if order is not quickly restored.

Soccer fans crushed to death

1989 Ninety-five people were crushed to death and 200 injured this afternoon in Britain's worst sports disaster, at Hillsborough stadium, Sheffield. The day promised to be memorable for the quality of football played by FA Cup semi-finalists Liverpool and Nottingham Forest. Instead it turned into a nightmare. The tragedy occurred when a gate was opened to ease a crush of around 4000 Liverpool supporters who arrived shortly before the kick-off and were trying to get into the ground. Most of the fans then thronged into a packed stand, crushing those at the front who were prevented from escaping by a high wire mesh fence erected to stop pitch invasions. This is the second tragedy that has attended a Liverpool FC game: in 1985, 41 supporters of the Italian team Juventus were killed when Liverpool fans went on the rampage at Heysel stadium in Belgium.

1753 Dr Samuel Johnson publishes his Dictionary, the product of nine years' work.

1764 Death of Madame de Pompadour, powerful mistress of King Louis XVI of France.

1793 The Bank of England issues the first £5 notes.

1797 British naval personnel mutiny at Spithead, near Portsmouth, over poor conditions and low pay.

1865 President Andrew Jackson is sworn in as American president following the assassination of Abraham Lincoln.

1925 Sir James Barrie donates the copyright of *Peter Pan* to the Great Ormond Street Hospital for Sick Children in London.

1925 John Singer Sargent, American painter specializing in society portraits, dies in London where he has lived since 1884.

1945 Looted Nazi art treasures, including paintings by Rubens, Goya, Raphael and Leonardo da Vinci, are found in an Austrian mineshaft.

1955 The first McDonald's hamburger store opens, in San Bernardino, California.

1988 North Korean president Kim Il Sung receives 43,000 gifts as he celebrates his 76th birthday in style.

1998 Death of Pol Pot, aged 70, cruel dictator of Kampuchea (now Cambodia) and murderer of thousands of people.

BIRTHDAYS

Sir James Clark Ross 1800, English explorer of the Antarctic.

Henry James 1843, American novelist who spent much of his life in England.

Bessie Smith 1894, American singer considered by many to be the finest female blues singer ever.

Claudia Cardinale 1939, Italian actress who appeared in *The Leopard*, *The Pink Panther* and *Once Upon a Time in the West* among other movies.

APRIL 16

1446 Death of Filippo Brunelleschi, Florentine architect and sculptor who built the dome for the city's cathedral.

1515 Roman Catholic mass is banned in Zurich as the Lutheran reformation sweeps Europe.

1689 Death of Aphra Behn, British novelist and dramatist and early feminist.

1828 Death of Francisco de Goya, the Spanish painter whose deafness changed the nature of his work, making it frequently macabre and menacing.

1883 Paul Kruger becomes president of the South African republic.

1902 More than 20,000 people rally in Dublin Park to protest against British government legislation.

1917 Vladimir Ilyich Lenin returns to Russia after three years of exile in Zurich.

1953 The royal yacht *Britannia* is launched.

1969 Desmond Dekker becomes the first Jamaican artist to reach the top of the UK singles chart, with "The Israelites".

1975 The communist Khmer Rouge seize Phnom Penh, capital of Cambodia.

BIRTHDAYS

Jules Hardouin-Mansart 1646, French court architect to Louis XIV who designed the Gallery of Mirrors and the orangery at Versailles.

Giovanni Batista Tiepolo 1696, Venetian rococo painter, the greatest Italian artist of the 18th century.

Wilbur Wright 1867, American aviator who, with his brother Orville, invented the first powered aircraft.

Sir Charles Chaplin 1889, English-born comedian much loved for his portrayal of a tramp in baggy trousers and bowler hat.

Henry Mancini 1924, American composer responsible for many film scores.

PRINCE CHARLES NOT SO BONNY

1746 The hopes of the grandson of the deposed Catholic king of England, James II, regaining the throne of England for his family were dealt a severe blow today at Culloden Moor in Scotland. It was here that the so-called "Young Pretender", Charles Edward Stuart, decided to take on the might of the British Army under the command of William, Duke of Cumberland, the second son of George II. "Bonnie Prince Charlie" Stuart's 5000 Highlanders were no match for Cumberland's 9000 soldiers, many of them regulars equipped with the latest weaponry. Many are questioning the wisdom of Stuart's decision to make a stand on flat ground which offered every advantage to Cumberland's artillery. Stuart managed to escape the carnage and is thought to be in hiding somewhere in the area.

Tussaud waxes lyrical

1850 The founder of the famous museum of waxworks in London, Madame Marie Tussaud, died today aged 89. Madame Tussaud learnt the art of wax modelling from her uncle, Philippe Curtuis. When the French Revolution broke out she was art tutor at Versailles to Louis XVI's sister Elizabeth and, after a period of imprisonment, she was given the unpleasant task of making death masks from heads freshly severed by the guillotine. It is said that she recognized many of them as people she had known in happier times. She left Paris in 1802, accompanied by her collection of waxwork models and two sons from her unsuccessful marriage to a French engineer, François Tussaud. She spent the next 33 years touring Britain before opening a permanent display in London.

1988 The Palestine Liberation Organization's military commander, Khalil al-Wazir, was today mown down by bullets at home in Tunis, the Tunisian capital. The PLO say the killing is the work of an Israeli hit squad. Mr al-Wazir – or Abu Jihad – had been a thorn in the Israelis' sides for years and masterminded many attacks into Israel from Lebanon. He was also thought to have orchestrated the recent Palestinian unrest in the occupied territories.

Dear comrades, soldiers, sailors and workers! I am happy to greet in you the victorious Russian Revolution!

Vladimir Ilich Lenin, in a speech made at Finland Station in Petrograd, 1917.

Mandela plays Wembley

1990 Freed African National Congress leader Nelson Mandela tonight publicly thanked the world for its support during his 26-year imprisonment by the South African government. His platform was Wembley stadium, where about 72,000 people gathered to hear 50 top British, American and African stars pay him tribute. The globally transmitted concert attracted names like Simple Minds, Lou Reed, Tracy Chapman, Neil Young and Terence Trent D'Arby and cost an estimated £2 million. It is hoped that some of the revenues will go to charity. Some Conservative MPs have accused the BBC of left-wing bias: the concert broadcast ends with public criticism of the government's opposition to sanctions against South Africa.

The unsinkable does the unthinkable

1912 The British luxury liner the *Titanic* has sunk after hitting an iceberg during her maiden voyage to New York. Over 1500 people are feared drowned in the icy waters of the North Atlantic. The vessel collided with the "skyscraper" sized iceberg shortly before midnight on April 14, causing a 300-foot (91 m) gash in the vessel's right side. Five of the ship's watertight compartments were punctured, causing the ship to sink at around 2.20 am. The ship's double-bottomed hull, divided into 16 watertight compartments, was said to make her unsinkable. Reports from some of the 691 survivors suggest that there were not enough spaces on the lifeboats for the 2224 people on board. More lives would have been lost if the liner *Carpathia* had not reached the *Titanic* within 80 minutes.

LIBYAN EMBASSY SNIPERS KILL WOMAN PC

1984 A peaceful demonstration in London's St James's Square turned into a battlefield today when a gunman inside the Libyan embassy opened fire on the protesters. A tragic victim of the outrage was 25-year-old woman police constable Yvonne Fletcher, one of several police officers on duty in the square, who later died of her injuries in hospital. Ten other people were injured, none seriously. The embassy has been sealed off by police while the British government plans its response. Politicians are calling for diplomatic bags to be searched in future to prevent the importation of arms. The government-controlled Libyan media are portraying the incident as an attack on their embassy by British police and "other foreign agents".

1421 Over 100,000 people are drowned at Dort in Holland when the sea breaks through the dikes.

1790 Death of Benjamin Franklin, American diplomat, scientist and author.

1860 The first match between an American and English boxer takes place in Hampshire, England.

1924 Benito Mussolini's Fascist party wins the Italian elections.

1960 American rock star Eddie Cochran is killed in a car crash in England.

1963 In Moscow, British businessman Greville Wynne is charged with spying.

1964 The Rolling Stones release their first LP entitled simply "The Rolling Stones".

1970 Country singer Johnny Cash performs for President Nixon in the East Room of the White House.

1980 Rhodesia becomes independent Zimbabwe.

1982 The Polish Solidarity organization becomes legal after a 10-year ban.

1990 Moscow imposes a blockade upon Lithuania in an attempt to stem demands for independence.

2003 Death of John Paul Getty, aged 84, American oil magnate who founded the J. Paul Getty Museum in California and was one of the richest men in the world.

Artists unite for success

1919 Leading film-makers Charlie Chaplin, Mary Pickford, Douglas Fairbanks and D. W. Griffith have joined forces to launch their own company, called United Artists Corporation. The talented quartet want control of their own artistic destinies and feel that this can only be achieved if they control the production and distribution of their films. Fairbanks, the moving spirit behind the formation of the company, plans to produce a series of adventure epics which promise to make full use of his handsome physique and natural grace.

1961 A small force of about 1300 Cuban exiles has been thwarted in its aim of toppling the Communist regime of Fidel Castro. The invasion force ran into the Cuban army soon after landing in the Bahia de Cochinos (Bay of Pigs) and its members were either captured or shot.

> *In this world nothing is certain but death and taxes.*
> **Benjamin Franklin,**
> who died today, 1790.

Luther's Diet of Worms

1521 The congress of church and state heads meeting at Worms to decide the case of the nonconformist German priest Martin Luther has granted him an extra day's grace. At this afternoon's meeting Luther requested time to reflect on the assembly's demand that he acknowledge or deny the vast body of heretical works attributed to him. The 38-year-old firebrand is not without friends in high places, despite the open hostility of the Holy Roman Emperor Charles V. His refusal to accept the authority of the Church of Rome over individual conscience and the Bible has struck a sympathetic chord in many quarters of German society. Luther's supporters fear that any moral truimph will be at the price of a ban on his writings.

Chaplin will never go back to USA

1953 Charlie Chaplin, the world's most famous comic actor, today announced from his home in Corsier-sur-Vevey, Switzerland, that he will never return to the United States. London-born Chaplin left the States last year for Europe where he has been promoting his latest film, *Limelight*. He seems to be the latest victim of Senator McCarthy's campaign against "undesirables" – politicians and newspaper reporters have repeatedly accused him of being a communist sympathizer and of having links with subversive organizations, charges which he has strongly denied. The US government is also after Chaplin for non-payment of back taxes. After leaving the country Chaplin was informed that his re-entry rights would be questioned by the US Department of Justice if he attempted to return. He subsequently took the decision to surrender his re-entry permit in Geneva.

BIRTHDAYS

Sir Leonard Woolley 1880, British archaeologist most famous for his excavations at Ur in southern Iraq.

Nikita Khruschev 1894, Russian politician, prime minister of the USSR 1958-64.

Thornton Wilder 1897, American dramatist and novelist whose *The Matchmaker* was adapted to become the musical *Hallo Dolly*.

Lindsay Anderson 1923, British film director whose films include *If...* and *O Lucky Man*.

James Last 1929, Dutch bandleader, composer and arranger of international easy-listening renown.

APRIL 18

1775 Paul Revere rides from Charleston to Lexington to warn US militiamen of the British advance.

1791 William Wilberforce's parliamentary campaign to abolish the slave trade meets defeat in the House of Commons.

1934 The first laundrette is opened, in Fort Worth, Texas.

1942 Bombers from a US aircraft carrier bomb Tokyo.

1949 The Republic of Ireland Act comes into operation.

1954 President Neguib of Egypt resigns, leaving the government of the country to be carried on by a council of ministers.

1968 An American tycoon buys London Bridge for £1 million, confusing it with Tower Bridge.

1979 Jeremy Thorpe, former leader of the British Liberal Party, goes on trial accused of conspiring to murder his male lover.

1989 At the Royal Opera House, Covent Garden, Spanish tenor José Carreras gives his first concert for three years following his illness from leukaemia.

1991 Publisher Robert Maxwell launches his Mirror Group Newspapers towards public flotation on May 21, meanwhile complaining that the British press have never acknowledged his achievements.

BIRTHDAYS

Lucrezia Borgia 1480, Italian illegitimate daughter of Pope Alexander VI who was married three times by the age of 18 to further her father's political ambitions.

Leopold Stokowski 1882, English-born conductor and composer who became a US citizen in 1915 and conducted many of America's leading orchestras.

Hayley Mills 1946, British actress who first appeared in a film (*Tiger Bay*) at the age of 13.

Malcom Marshall 1958, Barbadian fast bowler who regularly pulverized the English cricket teams.

Hanging judge cheats gallows

1689 George Jeffreys, one of the cruellest of the deposed King James II's judges, died in the Tower of London today, aged 44. Charged by the King with the task of setting up a court to deal with the rebellion of 1685, led by the illegitimate Protestant son of Charles II, the Duke of Monmouth, Jeffreys set about his task with bloodthirsty zeal. Over 300 of Monmouth's peasant followers were hanged at Jeffreys' "Bloody Assizes" and 800 sent to forced labour in Barbados. Jeffreys, a Protestant, was then made lord chancellor by his grateful monarch, a position he held until the Glorious Revolution last year swept James from power. Jeffreys attempted to escape the country disguised as a sailor but was caught and imprisoned in the Tower. He was awaiting trial at the time of his death.

Pound circulates

1958 After being detained in a mental asylum for almost 13 years the American poet Ezra Pound is to be freed by the US authorities. Pound, 73, was arrested in Italy at the end of the war and charged with treason for making anti-US broadcasts to American troops on Rome Radio. Doctors considered Pound unfit to stand trial on his return to the States, whereupon he was incarcerated in St Elizabeth's hospital for the criminally insane in Washington D.C. Pound continued to write and completed several more of his Cantos, among other works, during the long years of his imprisonment.

EINSTEIN DIES

1955 Albert Einstein died in his sleep today at Princeton Hospital, aged 75. Regarded as one of the most creative intellects in human history, Einstein made his greatest contributions to scientific theory before the age of 50. He was awarded the Nobel Prize for Physics in 1921, for his photoelectric law and his work in the field of theoretical physics. His theory of relativity, which had its beginnings in an essay he wrote when he was only 16, was verified by the Royal Society of London in 1919. Einstein's commitment to world peace and Zionism brought him into conflict with right-wing opinion in his native Germany. When Hitler became Chancellor of Germany in 1933, Einstein renounced his German citizenship and went to America. In 1939, after Lise Meitner split the atom, he urged on President Roosevelt the importance of US scientists developing an A-bomb ahead of the Nazis, and his recommendation marked the beginning of the Manhattan Project at Los Alamos. The horror of Hiroshima in 1945 shocked Einstein into issuing letters calling for the establishment of a world government to prevent future use of the bomb, aware that without his theory of relativity the nuclear age would not have dawned.

San Francisco tumbles in massive earthquake

1906 At precisely 5.13 this morning San Francisco was hit by the most violent earthquake ever recorded in its history. Worst hit by the earthquake and subsequent fire is the central business district, where an estimated 512 blocks in the four square-mile (10 sq km) area are thought to have been either destroyed or to be currently under threat. Survivors who have been made homeless by the disaster are making for the relative safety of the 1000-acre (405 hectare) Golden Gate Park to the west of the town, where temporary accommodation is being erected by the emergency services. First estimates suggest that as many as 700 people may be dead and a further 250,000 made homeless. Earthquakes have hit San Francisco before – in 1864, 1898 and 1900 – but none has wrought such widespread devastation.

American rebels ready to fight

1775 The British government's impatience with its rebellious colonists in America has finally led to bloodshed. Yesterday a force of 700 Redcoats was dispatched by the recently appointed royal governor of Massachusetts, General Thomas Gage, to destroy the military stores at Concord. Local militiamen were ready and waiting for the British column, alerted to the danger by a member of the Sons of Liberty, Paul Revere, who had ridden through the night to warn them of the impending raid. Outnumbered by 10 to 1, the militiamen were soon put to flight at Lexington Green. The Redcoats went on to Concord only to find that the munitions had been hidden or destroyed and a force of about 400 armed rebels was ready to fight. The British were forced to withdraw and are now reported to be making their way back to Boston.

Sex shocks prudes

1927 The police raid on the Broadway show *Sex*, starring Miss Mae West, has been welcomed by moralists, who have been up in arms since the play opened last year. Even more satisfaction has been gained by the sentencing of Miss West to 10 days' imprisonment. The play, which was co-authored by its star, is an unedifying tale of prostitution, sailors and blackmail. The critics have described it as "vulgar" and "amateurish", but New York audiences love it and have flocked to each of the 375 performances. Another of Miss West's shows – *The Drag*, described as a "homosexual comedy" – is raising a few eyebrows at another New York venue at present. Miss West is reported to be pleased by the free publicity and has plans for even more scandalous shows in future. Just how much more, and different, dirt she can dig up to keep audiences interested is a moot point.

> *No, she will only ask me to take a message to Albert.*
> **Benjamin Disraeli**, British politician, on his deathbed today, declines a visit by Queen Victoria, 1881.

HUGE EXPLOSION SHAKES OKLAHOMA CITY

1995 A lorry packed with 4,000 pounds of explosives has blown up a government building in Oklahoma City, killing 168 people, some of them children attending a nursery there. The blast happened just after 09.00 local time when most workers were in their offices. Chaos ensued as paramedics treated survivors on the pavement and rescue workers dug others from the rubble. The ten-storey Alfred Murrah building housed the Federal Bureau of Alcohol, Tobacco and Firearms, as well as social security offices and a nursery. President Bill Clinton vowed "swift, certain and severe punishment" for those behind the attack. "The United States will not tolerate and I will not allow the people of this country to be intimidated by evil cowards," he said. The attack comes exactly two years after the seige at Waco, Texas and some commentators are linking the two. However, there are also suspicions that right-wing groups, or Middle Eastern terrorists are involved.

Waco cult seige ends in inferno

1993 At least 70 cult members are feared dead as fire swept through the beseiged headquarters of the Branch Davidian sect near Waco, Texas. Cult leader David Koresh is not believed to be among the survivors. White house officials say the fire was started deliberately by cult members when the FBI began a dawn raid. The cult's buildings have been surrounded since February when four agents with the Bureau of Alcohol, Tobacco and Firearms were killed as they tried to arrest Mr Koresh on firearms charges. Tear gas canisters and stun grenades were fired into the fortified compound and an armoured vehicle started to demolish the walls. By the time fire crews arrived the fire had taken hold on the wooden buildings. The fire worsened when the cult's store of munitions exploded. Eight cult members escaped from the blaze.

Darwin dies

1882 Charles Darwin, the most controversial scientist of the age, has died at his home in Kent, England, after 50 years of ill health. He was 73. Darwin rejected both medicine and the church before he took an unpaid job as naturalist on HMS *Beagle*'s five-year Pacific voyage in 1831. The unique Galapagos Islands fauna were the main inspiration for Darwin's theory of evolution, which has revolutionized biology with the idea that man's ancestry is bestial. Last year Darwin published *On the Formation of Vegetable Moulds*, about earthworms. He concluded that they show intelligence rather than mere instinct – like a man.

THE PRINCE AND THE SHOWGIRL

1956 The wedding today of Prince Rainier of Monaco and American screen actress Grace Kelly has set the seal on a story that is ripe for turning into a Hollywood movie. The couple met and fell in love last year at the international film festival in Cannes, which is only a few hours' drive from Rainier's home, a pink palace perched on a rock overlooking the Mediterranean. Over 1200 guests attended the televised Catholic wedding ceremony in Monte Carlo. Grace Kelly the film star was widely admired for her cool charm and classy good looks, but it was under the direction of the master of suspense, Alfred Hitchcock, that those attributes were tapped to best effect. Kelly's performance in *To Catch a Thief*, in which she played love scenes opposite Cary Grant, is said to have struck a raw nerve in husband-to-be Rainier, who tried to delay the film's release.

1588 Death of Paolo Veronese, Italian painter who specialized in enormous scenes of the splendour of Venice in its Golden Age.

1689 Death of Queen Christina of Sweden who abdicated in 1654.

1824 British poet Lord Byron dies of a fever at Missolonghi while fighting against the Turks alongside Greek nationalists.

1933 Britain bans all trade with the USSR.

1948 The US tests a plutonium bomb at Eniwatok atoll in the Marshall Islands.

1959 The Dalai Lama, Tibetan leader fleeing the Chinese invasion of his country, finds sanctuary in India.

1966 Australian troops leave Sydney to join the American forces in Vietnam.

1983 A car bomb destroys the US embassy in Beirut.

1989 Death of Daphne du Maurier, author of romantic thrillers such as *Rebecca* and *Jamaica Inn*.

1999 The German parliament returns to the newly-renovated Reichstag building in Berlin.

2004 Two fuel trains collide in North Korea, causing a massive explosion and 3,000 casualties.

BIRTHDAYS

Richard Hughes 1900, British novelist, author of *High Wind in Jamaica*.

James Mollison 1905, Scottish aviator and husband of Amy Johnson, with whom he made the first east-west air crossing of the Atlantic.

Sir Thomas Hopkinson 1905, British journalist, author, editor of *Picture Post* (1940-50) and *Drum International* (1958-61).

Jayne Mansfield 1933, American actress known as much for her chest measurement as her acting ability.

Dudley Moore 1935, British musician and comedian who became a Hollywood sex symbol following his appearance in *10* with Bo Derek.

Murray Perahia 1947, Chilean pianist noted for his Mozart interpretations.

1653 Oliver Cromwell dissolves the Long Parliament which governed England in the Civil War.

1768 Death of Canaletto, Venetian artist who specialized in painting views.

1857 West African Muslim leader Ai Hajj Uman lays siege to the French fort of Medine in Senegal.

1887 The first motor race occurs in Paris, with only one entrant.

1913 The two children of dancer Isadora Duncan are drowned when the car in which they are travelling rolls downhill and into the Seine.

1883 Edouard Manet, one of the first Impressionist painters, dies in terrible pain a week after having a gangrenous leg amputated.

1929 King Victor III of Italy opens a parliament composed entirely of Fascists under the leadership of Benito Mussolini.

1944 The RAF drops a record 4,500 tons of bombs on Germany in a single raid.

1969 Violence breaks out at a free pop festival in Venice, Los Angeles – 117 are arrested and many are injured.

1992 Death of British comedian Benny Hill.

1999 Two disaffected students at Columbine High School, Colorado, shoot 13 fellow pupils.

BIRTHDAYS

Napoleon III 1808, French emperor, nephew of Napoleon Bonaparte, who precipitated the Franco-Prussian War, thus losing his empire and causing his exile.

Adolf Hitler 1889, Austrian-born housepainter and subsequently German dictator, architect of World War II.

Joan Miró 1889, Spanish Surrealist painter, graphic artist and designer.

Sir Donald Wolfit 1902, English actor-manager and fine Shakespearean.

Ryan O'Neal 1941, American film actor who starred in *Love Story*, *Paper Moon* and *What's Up Doc?* among other movies.

ART NOUVEAU ATTRACTS OLD MONEY

1896 Fashionable Paris is being drawn like a magnet to the gallery opened recently by the well-known connoisseur, dealer and writer on Japanese art Samuel Bing. His "Maison de l'Art Nouveau" is devoted to showing both fine and applied works of art – but with a difference. All the works are examples of the so-called "new art" and owe their inspiration to the present. When M. Bing threw open his doors in the Rue de Provence last December he unveiled a vast and bewildering array of paintings and decorative objects, each of them executed as unique items and designed from scratch. This aesthetic ideal is currently in vogue all over Europe, and can be seen in poster and book illustration, glasswork, jewellery, textiles, furniture and architecture. The practitioners of the new art prefer naturalism to the formalized type of decoration seen in the past. The effects can be startling – writhing plant forms as patterns, heart-shaped holes in furniture, cast-iron lilies and copper tendrils. The one drawback to "art nouveau" is expense. However, a lowering of costs through standardization would kill the ethic behind the work and the interest of a fashionable clientele who love the new art for its exclusivity.

1912 The Dublin-born writer Bram (Abraham) Stoker has died at his home in London. He was 65. His one great success as a writer was *Count Dracula*. Stoker was also a journalist, a student of mathematics and philosophy, an accomplished athlete, a civil servant and the touring manager and secretary of actor Henry Irving.

Cook discovers Terra Australis

1770 The Royal Society of London has received an update on the progress of its scientific expedition to the Pacific which set sail two years ago. The 98-foot long coal-hauling bark *Endeavour*, commanded by 40-year-old Yorkshireman Lieutenant James Cook, has safely delivered a party of the Society's scientists to Tahiti. After observing the transit of the planet Venus from Tahiti, Cook struck out south and south-west in an attempt to find the southern continent, the so-called Terra Australis. Instead he reports finding a group of islands called New Zealand which he has charted over six months. He is currently running north along the south-east coast of Australia, surveying as he goes.

Battleship explosion kills 47

1989 A 16-inch gun turret of one of the oldest ships in the US Navy, the 45-year-old battleship *Iowa*, exploded during firing practice today, killing 47 sailors. The accident is thought to have been caused by a spark igniting one of the hundred-weight bags of cordite used to fire the one-ton shells. The ship is equipped to carry Cruise missiles, but her gun technology is of World War II vintage. *Iowa* was one of four warships taken out of mothballs recently to beef up the US Navy to the 600-ship target set by President Reagan. Today's accident questions the wisdom of re-commissioning nautical dinosaurs just to make the US Navy look good on paper.

Gorbachev plays hardball

1990 Nice guy Mikhail Gorbachev showed the iron fist concealed within the velvet-smooth glove yesterday by cutting off 85 per cent of gas supplies to the rebellious republic of Lithuania. Shortly before this move,

Gorbachev had ordered that the Baltic state's oil pipelines be shut down. A Soviet foreign ministry spokesman has warned that if Lithuania does not tow the Kremlin line and back down from its declared aim of independence "we may have to take other measures". The Lithuanian president Vytautas Landsbergis remains defiant, however: "We can hold out for 100 years without gas and oil". Despite pleas from the Lithuanians, the European Community has resolutely stayed outside the quarrel between Moscow and her Baltic satellites, urging restraint on both sides. Western governments are unwilling to pile yet more pressure on the beleaguered Soviet president, fearing that it may unseat him.

Heath given double-edged sword

1968 Conservative Party leader Edward Heath was today handed a political hot potato by fellow Tory and former Cabinet minister Enoch Powell, who has called for an end to non-white immigration from the Commonwealth. In a highly charged and emotive speech given in Birmingham, Powell likened the Labour government's policy of allowing 50,000 dependents of immigrants into the country each year to that of a people "busily engaged in heaping up its own funeral pyre". The liberal-minded Mr Heath, who has denounced the speech as racist and inflammatory, is expected to take a strong line with Powell, possibly ejecting him from the Shadow cabinet. Ironically, by supporting Powell he could revive his popularity with the British electorate, many of whom are worried by the number of immigrants entering the country.

1828 From this day on, no American will be able to plead ignorance of his or her own language. A new dictionary compiled by lexicographer and philologist Noah Webster promises to put some cultural distance between US citizens and their British cousins. The two-volume work, entitled *The American Dictionary of the English Language*, is the first attempt to standardize the American language and distinguish it from the English of the British.

Franklin sent off in style

1790 One of independent America's founding fathers, Benjamin Franklin, was buried today in one of the most splendid funerals ever seen in Philadelphia. Tributes to the man regarded as epitomizing New World sensibility have been flooding in – especially from France, where Franklin achieved hero status. One of the most sought-after men on the Parisian social scene, Franklin could be seen everywhere – literally, for his portrait could be found on all manner of objects, from snuff boxes to chamber pots. Fellow Americans will remember his many witticisms with affection and his role in the drafting of the US constitution will be remembered with deep gratitude.

Rio miffed by Brasilia

1960 Brasilia, the brain-child of President Juscelino Kubitschek, was today dedicated as the official capital of Brazil. Building work in the new capital is still underway and several of the more ambitious projects planned by architect Lucio Costa and his adviser Oscar Niemayer will take several more years to complete. The new city stands on a plateau some 580 miles (930 km) north-west of previous capital Rio de Janeiro. Miffed at their city's loss of status, and the pouring of huge amounts of money into developing the interior of the country, the citizens of Rio de Janeiro are denouncing the plan. President Kubitscek intends that Brasilia and the region in which it stands should be seen as a symbol of Brazil's future greatness. However, there are also fears that the ambitious programme may bankrupt the country, which has high inflation and has doubled its foreign debt since work began on planning Brasilia in 1957.

All you need in this life is ignorance and confidence; then success is sure.
Mark Twain, who died today, 1910.

RED BARON RUNS OUT OF LUCK

1918 The most feared fighter pilot of World War I, Germany's Baron Manfred von Richthofen, was killed today, shot by a single bullet. Competing claims for the deed have been received from a Canadian pilot of 209 Squadron, Roy Brown, as well as from British and Australian ground artillery. A report has also been received from the observer of a British reconnaissance plane who allegedly fired on a German in a scarlet plane as he passed him. By the time of his death, the "Red Baron" had notched up 80 "kills", most of them British. Von Richthofen's passion for shooting down enemy airmen was said to have been assuaged for 15 minutes by each "kill". It is doubtful that his victims would draw any consolation from the fact that the Baron would order a silver trophy for each plane he shot down.

1509 Henry VIII accedes to the English throne on the death of Henry VII.

1699 Death of Jean Racine, French dramatist and outstanding tragedian of the French classical period.

1831 The Texans vanquish the Mexicans at the Battle of San Jacinto.

1898 The US declares war on Spain.

1901 Sculptor Auguste Rodin shocks Paris when his semi-nude statue of Victor Hugo is exhibited at the Grand Palais.

1901 Mark Twain, American journalist and author of *The Adventures of Tom Sawyer* and *The Adventures of Huckleberry Finn*, dies aged 74.

1914 American troops occupy the Mexican city of Vera Cruz in order to stop German weapons reaching the Mexican command.

1916 Former British consular official Roger Casement arrives in Ireland from a German submarine to lead the Sinn Fein rebellion but is arrested by the British.

1946 Death of John Maynard Keynes, British economist who argued that unemployment can only be eased by increased public spending.

1989 More than 10,000 mass in Beijing's Tienanmen Square.

1992 Eurodisney opens its doors in Paris.

2003 Death of Nina Simone, singer and songwriter of jazz and blues music, aged 70.

BIRTHDAYS

Jan van Riebeeck 1634, Dutch naval surgeon and founder of Cape Town, South Africa.

Charlotte Brontë 1816, British novelist, eldest of the three Brontë sisters and author of *Jane Eyre*, *Villette* and *Shirley*.

Anthony Quinn 1915, Mexican-born actor who won an Oscar for *Viva Zapata*.

Norman Parkinson 1913, British photographer specializing in fashion and celebrities.

1500 On his way to India with 13 ships, Portuguese navigator Pedro Alvarez Cabral discovers Brazil and claims it for Portugal.

1838 The British packet steamer *Sirius* becomes the first steamer to cross from New York to Britain.

1915 The Germans use poison gas for the first time on the Western Front.

1933 Death of Frederick Henry Royce, motor car manufacturer.

1964 British businessman Greville Wynne, imprisoned in the Soviet Union a year earlier for spying, is exchanged for the Soviet agent Gordon Lonsdale.

1969 British yachtsman Robin Knox-Johnston completes his solo non-stop round-world trip in his ketch *Suhaili* in 312 days.

1972 John Fairfax and Sylvia Cook arrive in Australia, the first people to row across the Pacific.

1979 Keith Richard of the Rolling Stones escapes jail on a drug conviction in return for performing a benefit concert for the Canadian National Institute for the Blind.

1983 £1 coins are introduced in Britain to replace the paper £1 note.

BIRTHDAYS

Henry Fielding 1707, English novelist, author of *Tom Jones.*

Immanuel Kant 1724, German philosopher who maintained that there was an absolute moral law which can never be modified by expediency.

Vladimir Ilich Lenin 1870, Russian leader of the Bolshevik Revolution and first leader of communist Russia.

Vladimir Nabokov 1889, Russian-born novelist and poet, author of *Lolita.*

Robert Oppenheimer 1904, American nuclear scientist who developed the atom bomb.

Yehudi Menuhin 1916, American-born violinist who gave his first public recital at the age of six.

Charles Mingus 1927, American jazz musician.

End of hated Haitian

1971 Haiti's hated leader François Duvalier, known as "Papa Doc", has against all the odds died peacefully in bed, aged 63. By Haitian standards "Papa Doc" lived to a ripe old age – the life span of the average Haitian male is 47 – despite a string of ailments, including diabetes, heart problems and suspected cancer. Duvalier's 14-year regime was remarkable for all the wrong reasons: violent suppression of all opposition, a private army of thugs called the Tonton Macoute to terrorize the population, and sinister dabblings in witchcraft. He survived six assassination attempts. During the last two years of his life he felt secure enough to venture out of his huge white palace with its four obsolete armoured cars and 40 mm AA guns on the front lawn. He had a predilection for reading the future in chickens' entrails and keeping the heads of decapitated rivals.

USA cleans up baseball

1876 The reputation of the fast-growing game of baseball looks set to be saved by the formation of the National League of Professional Baseball Clubs. Most of the teams that made up the now discredited National Association of Professional Baseball Players, formed five years ago, are to join the new league. In five seasons the Association gained an unenviable reputation as a breeding ground for drunkenness, violence and corruption. The league has drawn up a constitution to which each of the eight founder-member clubs must subscribe. Alcohol is banned from sale at all League grounds and no play is allowed on Sundays. Any club which breaches these and other undertakings will be disqualified from the League.

1959 Angler Alf Dean could not believe his eyes yesterday when he landed a mammoth man-eating great white shark at Denial Bay, near Ceduna, South Australia. Dean's catch, which weighs 2664 lb (1208 kg) and is 16 ft 10 in (5.13 m) long, is the largest to be caught on a rod.

Nixon dies

1994 Richard Milhous Nixon, president of the United States 1969—74 has died age 81. During his two terms in office, the Republican president negotiated the withdrawal of American troops from Vietnam and began the process of reconciliation with China and Russia. But at home the Watergate conspiracies brought disgrace and his resignation.

1997 The siege of the Japanese embassy in Lima, Peru, has ended after four months as government troops stormed the building. All 14 Tupac Amaru guerrillas were killed. One Japanese citizen also died but the remaining 71 hostages were rescued. The rebels were demanding the release of 440 of their comrades.

AIDS breakthrough

1984 Medical researchers working in the United States and France have identified a type of human cancer virus that may be the causative agent in the killer disease AIDS, or Acquired Immune Deficiency Syndrome. The virus identified by the team of Robert Gallo, working at the US National Cancer Institute, has been identified as human T-cell lymphotropic virus, Type III, or HTLV-III. A very similar virus has been identified by the French team of Jean-Claude Chermann, Françoise Barre Simoussi and Luc Montagnier of the Pasteur Institute, Paris, and designated lymphadenopathy-associated virus, or LAV. The discovery has raised hopes of finding an anti-AIDS vaccine and the possibility of eventually developing antibodies that could be used to treat patients with full-blown AIDS. The disease, which was first described in 1981, suppresses the body's immune system, leaving it open to attack from life-threatening diseases such as cancer.

On your marks, get set, stake that claim

1889 An estimated 200,000 people were on the starting line at noon today for the start of a land run in Oklahoma territory. At the crack of the starting pistol the rush was on to stake claims to the two million acres which Congress has agreed should be released for new settlers. Each successful claimant will receive 160 acres of prairie. The race is intended to ensure a fair distribution of the land, but there are reports that some settlers are already in the new territory, making themselves at home. The pressure on the US government from the railroads and land-hungry whites to allow them into Indian territory has been immense. Organized groups of people called Boomers, have been settling here illegally since at least 1879. The Indians cannot be sure that today's land race will be the last State-endorsed appropriation of their territory.

Curtain down on Shakespeare

1616 Mr William Shakespeare, a gentleman of substance well-known in theatrical circles, has died at New Place, his home in Stratford-upon-Avon. He was 52. He entered the theatre as an actor and was soon engaged as a player by one of the foremost troupes of the day, the Lord Chamberlain's Men. The troupe was renamed the King's Men on acquiring the patronage of His Majesty King James I, a keen theatregoer, and went on to hold the pre-eminent position among the theatrical companies of the day. Mr Shakespeare's contribution to

their success was not inconsiderable, as he had by this time become a masterly playwright whose tales of life, love and the ever-changing nature of man's condition drew a devoted audience to the company's Globe and Blackfriars theatres. As a shareholder in the company, Mr Shakespeare reaped the rewards of his endeavours and shrewdly invested the proceeds in property in London and Stratford. None of Mr Shakespeare's large body of work, which includes poems as well as plays, is available in authorized editions, although plans are afoot to correct this state of affairs. Mr Shakespeare leaves a wife, Anne, and two daughters, Judith and Susanna.

> *I came, I saw, God conquered.*
> **Charles V**, Holy Roman Emperor, after the battle of Muhlberg, 1547.

De Sade's hot shocker

1791 That inflicting pain can give intense sexual pleasure is hardly a novelty: what is new is *Justine, or The Misfortunes of Virtue*, the scandalous new novel by aristocrat Count Donatien Alphonse François de Sade. The book's heroine, Justine, is branded with a hot iron, flogged, sodomized and repeatedly tortured. She is eventually rescued from this dire lifestyle by her sister, Juliette, the proverbial happy hooker. With happiness almost within her grasp, Justine is struck by lightning and dies. The idea for the novel came to de Sade while he was in jail for numerous sexual offences. He and his manservant had travelled around France abusing young prostitutes in an orgy of sexual encounters. In 1777 his mother-in-law, Madame de Montreuil, had him incarcerated. The last straw for her was the revelation that de Sade had succeeded in debauching her daughter. De Sade has spent the two years since his release revising and polishing his novel. Now living with the actress Marie-Constance Renelle, he is enjoying his notoriety. How long he will remain in favour with the authorities is uncertain, such is his ability to scandalize. According to his publisher, another blockbuster is already in the pipeline.

1983

1983 The German weekly magazine *Stern* announced yesterday that it has in its possession 60 volumes of hitherto unknown diaries kept by Nazi leader Adolf Hitler. The distinguished British historian Lord Dacre (Hugh Trevor-Roper) is convinced that the diaries are genuine. German historians, on the other hand, are expressing extreme scepticism. One, Herr Werner Maser, said that the whole business "smacks of pure sensationalism". Serialization in both *Stern* and the London *Sunday Times* is expected.

Kennedy killer sent to Death Row

1969 A Los Angeles jury decided today that Sirhan B. Sirhan should be sent to the gas chamber for the murder of Senator Robert Kennedy in June last year. Last week the jury rejected psychiatric evidence that portrayed Sirhan as a psychotic mentally incapable of premeditated murder. Sirhan claims to have shot Kennedy to bring attention to the plight of the Palestinian Arabs. He will now join the 80 men already on Death Row in San Quentin prison. State law allows him to appeal.

US hostage freed

1990 The release of the American professor Robert Polhill in Beirut last night after 39 months in captivity has raised hopes that more hostages held by Islamic fundamentalist groups may soon be freed. The call by Libya's Colonel Gaddafi for the release of all hostages has been taken as a sign of willingness on the part of the Lebanese kidnap groups to negotiate in earnest. Gaddafi specifically mentioned two Red Cross workers, Emmanuel Christen and Elio Erriquez, who are being held by Abu Nidal's Revolutionary Council, a group which has close ties with the Libyan leader. Polhill, 55, is the first Beirut captive to be freed since David Jacobsen was released in 1986.

St George's Day

1616 Death of Miguel de Cervantes, Spanish novelist and dramatist, author of *Don Quixote*.

1661 Charles II is crowned King of England.

1850 British poet William Wordsworth dies aged 80.

1860 Explorer John Stuart reaches the centre of Australia.

1879 The Shakespeare Memorial Theatre opens in Stratford-upon-Avon.

1915 British poet Rupert Brooke dies of blood poisoning on his way to active service in the Dardanelles.

1935 Joseph Stalin officially opens the Moscow Underground railway system.

1962 In the biggest-ever Ban the Bomb demonstration, 150,000 people rally in London's Hyde Park.

1968 The first decimal coins appear in Britain, easing the way to decimalization in 1971.

1986 Film director Otto Preminger dies aged 79.

1990 Death of Paulette Goddard, American actress who starred in Charlie Chaplin's *Modern Times*.

BIRTHDAYS

Joseph Mallard William Turner 1775, English painter and engraver controversial for his innovatory approach to landscape.

Sergei Prokofiev 1891, Russian composer and pianist best-known for *Peter and the Wolf*.

Lester Pearson 1897, Canadian statesman, diplomat and prime minister who won the Nobel Peace Prize in 1957 for his part in settling the Suez crisis.

Dame Ngaio Marsh 1899, New Zealand writer of detective novels.

Shirley Temple Black 1928, American child star who went on to become US ambassador to Ghana.

Roy Orbison 1936, American singer and songwriter who had massive hits with "Pretty Woman" and "Only the Lonely".

1731 Death of Daniel Defoe, British journalist, novelist and economist, author of *Robinson Crusoe* and *Moll Flanders*.

1895 Captain Joshua Slocum sets forth from Bristol in his sloop *Spray* to sail round the world single-handed.

1939 Robert Menzies becomes prime minister of Australia as leader of the United Australia Party.

1949 The remaining rationing of foodstuffs in post-war Britain comes to an end as British children gain unlimited access to sweets.

1967 The Russian spacecraft *Soyuz 1* crashes, killing astronaut Vladimir Komarov.

1986 Wallis, Duchess of Windsor, for whom a British king gave up his throne, dies in Paris aged 89.

1993 The IRA bombs the City of London for the second year in a row.

BIRTHDAYS

William III 1533, king of England known as William of Orange.

Anthony Trollope 1815, British novelist who wrote a series of novels set in an imaginary county of Barsetshire.

Philippe Pétain 1856, French general and statesman who signed an armistice with Hitler and led the collaborationist Vichy government, thus earning himself life imprisonment after the end of World War II.

Sir Stafford Cripps 1889, British Labour Party politician who, as chancellor of the exchequer, imposed an austerity programme upon Britain after World War II.

William Joyce 1916, American-born British traitor who made propaganda broadcasts for Germany during World War II.

Shirley MacLaine 1934, American actress, dancer and writer, Oscar-nominated for *Some Came Running*, *Irma La Douce* and *The Apartment*.

Barbra Streisand 1942, American actress and singer, Oscar-winning star of *Funny Girl*.

1989 Herbert von Karajan resigned today as chief conductor of the Berlin Philharmonic. Karajan has cited failing health as his reason for ending the 34-year relationship with the orchestra. Earlier this year West Berlin's Culture Senator, Volker Hassemer, agreed to the 80-year-old conductor's proposal that the annual number of his concerts in Berlin be halved to six. The recent election of a Social Democrat-Green Party coalition brought the less sympathetic Frau Anke Martiny to the post held previously by Herr Hassemer. Frau Martiny, who shares the Left's general dislike of the maestro for his alleged Nazi past, made it clear that Karajan should retire.

> *Any institution which does not suppose the people good, and the magistrate corruptible, is evil.*
> **Maximilien Robespierre**, in the declaration of Human Rights, on this day, 1793.

DISASTER IN THE DESERT

1980 An attempt by crack forces to rescue the 53 American hostages held captive in the US embassy in the Iranian capital Teheran since last November has ended in humiliating failure. Eight helicopters took off from US aircraft carriers in the Gulf of Oman early this morning to rendezvous with a 97-man "Delta" rescue team at a remote area in the desert, codenamed Desert One. Dust storms forced down two of the helicopters short of the target area and another aircraft developed hydraulic problems, forcing the abandonment of the rescue bid. As the helicopters and six giant C-130 Galaxy transports attempted to retreat, one of the five remaining helicopters flew into one of the Galaxies, engulfing the two in flames. The deaths of eight US servicemen and the loss of five pieces of expensive military hardware are a bitter blow to president Jimmy Carter.

Ben is back

1858 The best and biggest bell in the world, Big Ben, is at last ready to be hung in the clock tower of Westminster Palace, at the second attempt. Last year Messrs Warner of Cripplegate transported to London a giant bell cast at their Stockton works, only to have it cracked after being pounded by a 13-hundred-weight clapper fitted on the orders of Edward Denison, the man in charge of the project. The Whitechapel Bell Foundry are hoping that their recasting of metal from the cracked bell will fare better – it should have a four hundredweight hammer only. Londoners will hold their breath when the bell is sounded next month.

White supremists form the Klan

1866 President Andrew Johnson's programme of reconstruction in the wake of the Civil War is attracting much criticism. In the South a secret society called the Ku Klux Klan has been formed by ex-Confederates dedicated to the principle of "white supremacy". The Klan hopes to stem the libertarian tide towards blacks by waging a war of terror against them. Meanwhile, radical Republicans say that Johnson is allowing provisional governments in the South to undermine blacks' rights.

Bloody struggle for Irish freedom

1916 A bloody uprising against British rule has thrown Dublin into chaos. The day after Easter Sunday, a force of around 2000 Irish para-militaries has succeeded in seizing the General Post Office. Street fighting is continuing as the rebels battle to establish positions in other areas of the city. The leaders of the rebellion, named as Patrick Pearse, Joseph Plunkett and James Connolly, have proclaimed a provisional Republican government. Given the military weight against them, however, it can only be a matter of time before they are forced to surrender. The uprising comes two years after the decision by the British Liberal PM Herbert Asquith to suspend implementation of the Home Rule for Ireland bill until hostilities with Germany cease. In this time there has been an increase in support for para-military groups committed to the aim of immediate independence for Ireland.

Scientists crack the genetic code

1953 The world of science moved several steps closer to understanding man's genetic make-up today with the publication of a paper which establishes the structure and function of DNA. DNA stands for deoxyribonucleic acid, the molecules which store an individual's genetic code. British scientist Francis Crick and American biologist James Watson, both of whom work at Cavendish Laboratories in Cambridge, have built a model which shows how the strands of DNA are coiled in a double-helix and connected by hydrogen bonds between the bases. DNA has thus been identified as the most important substance in the transmission of hereditary characteristics. The implications for medical science cannot be over-estimated. The finding will undoubtedly help research into the prevention and detection of hereditary diseases. The breakthrough was made possible by the work of the Irish biophysicist Maurice Wilkins, whose X-ray diffraction studies enabled Crick and Watson to build their model.

1660 The English parliament votes for the restoration of the monarchy.

1719 Daniel Defoe's *Robinson Crusoe* is published in London.

1774 Death of Anders Celsius, the Swedish astronomer who devised the centigrade temperature scale.

1859 The building of the Suez Canal begins under the supervision of engineer and designer Ferdinand de Lesseps.

1926 Puccini's opera *Turandot*, is premiered with Arturo Toscanini as conductor.

1956 American heavyweight boxer Rocky Marciano retires unbeaten.

1964 The Little Mermaid statue in Copenhagen loses her head to thieves.

1982 Death of British actress Celia Johnson, perhaps best-known for *Brief Encounter*.

1988 Death of Clifford Simak, American journalist and science-fiction author.

1990 The Hubble space telescope is launched from the space shuttle *Discovery*.

US race riots

1960 Ten blacks were shot dead in Mississippi today after the latest in a succession of racially inspired incidents. Relations between white and black Mississippians have deteriorated since the Supreme Court's decision in 1954 to declare racially segregated schools unconstitutional. Whites have felt increasingly threatened by the demands for wholesale and immediate change that resulted from the court's decision. More extreme elements within Mississippi white society have resorted to bombing black churches and murdering civil rights workers to prevent the overturn of long-established practices. The black community has retaliated through sit-ins, boycotts and acts of violence.

French get upbeat anthem

1792 Patriotic fervour is still burning brightly in France almost three years after the storming of the Bastille. Captain Claude-Joseph Rouget de Lisle, an army officer stationed in Strasbourg, spent all last night composing an anthem dedicated to the ideals of the new republic – which include beating the Austrians whom de Lisle is fighting on the French border. The rousing tune and stirring words, also by de Lisle, should ensure the song's success with army units. The only let-down is the title – an uninspiring "Chant de guerre de l'armée du Rhin". However, that will surely change once the song reaches a wider audience.

Hit man kills train robber

1990 One of Britain's most notorious criminals, Charles Wilson, was murdered yesterday as he sat beside the swimming pool of his villa in Marbella, Spain. His killer coolly pumped three bullets into him before shooting his alsatian guard dog, then escaping on a yellow mountain bike. The killing is thought to be the work of a British "hit man" sent by a rival drug baron. Wilson, 57, was known to have been involved in drug smuggling and had ambitions to become the Mr Big of the trade on the Costa del Sol. The "treasurer" of the £2.6 million ($4.8 million) haul from the Great Train Robbery in 1963, Wilson moved to Spain with his wife Pat two years ago. He was released from prison in 1978 after serving 11 years 4 months of a 30-year sentence for his part in the robbery.

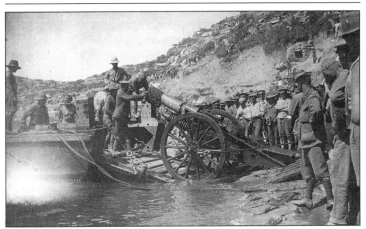

Troops storm ashore at Gallipoli

1915 Over 90,000 allied troops, most of them British and Australian, met stiff resistance from Turkish forces as they stormed ashore on the Gallipoli peninsula early this morning. The aim of the landings is to seize the Turkish forts guarding the approaches to Constantinople and open up a route to assist Russian forces. The landings have been described by observers as a triumph of naval improvisation, for no purpose-built landing craft were provided and the troops received no special training for the task. Luckily for the Allies, they landed at the extreme end of the peninsula and some way from the main Turkish forces, which are commanded by Mustapha Kemal under the direction of the German general Liman von Sanders. Since the failure of the Anglo-French fleet last month to penetrate the main Turkish defences, Kemal's two divisions have been reinforced to six, one more than the five at the disposal of the British commander, Sir Ian Hamilton.

BIRTHDAYS

King Edward II 1284, English monarch and first heir-apparent to take the title Prince of Wales.

Oliver Cromwell 1559, English soldier and statesman, Lord Protector of England 1653-8.

Guglielmo Marconi 1874, Italian electrical engineer who won the Nobel Prize for physics in 1909 for his work on the transmission and reception of radio waves.

Edward Murrow 1906, American broadcaster and journalist whose broadcasts to the US from London during World War II won much US sympathy for the embattled Britons.

Ella Fitzgerald 1918, American jazz singer.

Al Pacino 1939, American actor who found stardom in *The Godfather*.

1865 As the American Civil War draws to its close, General Johnston surrenders at Durham station.

1900 In Canada, a raging fire envelops Hull and Ottawa, rendering 12,000 homeless.

1915 Allied troops land at Cape Helles, in the Dardanelles.

1921 London sees its first motor cycle patrols.

1923 The Duke of York marries Lady Elizabeth Bowes-Lyon at Westminster Abbey.

1944 Russian and American forces meet near Torgau in east Germany.

1975 In Portugal's first free elections for 50 years, former exile Mario Soares emerges the victor as leader of the Portuguese Socialist Party.

1984 William "Count" Basie, American jazz pianist and bandleader, dies aged 79.

BIRTHDAYS

Marcus Aurelius 121 AD, Roman emperor who was known as the philosopher emperor on account of his work *Meditations*, which consisted of 12 volumes of aphorisms in the Stoic tradition.

Leonardo da Vinci 1452, Italian painter, sculptor, architect, scientist, engineer and inventor.

Eugène Delacroix 1798, French painter who left more than 9,000 paintings, pastels, and drawings in his studio upon his death.

Michel Fokine 1880, Russian choreographer who worked with Diaghilev's Ballet Russes in Paris, for whom he choreographed *The Firebird* and *Petrushka*.

Anita Loos 1893, American novelist, poet and screenwriter, best-known for the book and film *Gentleman Prefer Blondes*.

Rudolf Hess 1894, German Nazi leader who was Hitler's deputy in the early part of World War II but was imprisoned by the British when he flew to Scotland on a peace mission.

Duane Eddy 1938, American pop guitarist.

BURLESQUE LOSES A TROOPER

1970 The death was announced today of Gypsy Rose Lee, dubbed "the queen of burlesque". She was 56. Her career began when she was only six years old and encompassed striptease, the theatre, movies, writing and, latterly, hosting a TV chat show. The events of her colourful early life were the ingredients that went into a famous Broadway musical and, later, a movie. The chief character of *Gypsy* was the star's indomitable mother, Rose, the driving force behind Miss Lee's success. Lee, however, was quite a character in her own right, as two quotes of hers reveal: "Royalties are all very well but shaking the beads brings in the money quicker"; and, "God is love, but get it in writing".

Was he Lincoln killer?

1865 Doubts are being cast on the claim that the man shot in Virginia in the early hours of this morning was indeed the killer of President Lincoln. Federal troops arrived at the farm of Richard Garrett, near Port Royal, after a tip-off that John Wilkes Booth, the president's alleged killer, and an accomplice were hiding in Garrett's tobacco barn. At about 3 am the barn was set alight and "Booth" was shot, although whether by his own hand or a soldier's is unclear. The man lingered, conscious but saying very little, for some four hours before expiring. The body was then brought back to Washington. Unequivocal identification was not possible because the body was so badly disfigured. The authorities' wish to close the case as speedily as possible may be hampered by the allegation that Booth, an ex-Confederate secret agent, did not in fact mastermind the president's assassination.

1994 After three and a half centuries of white domination, South Africa has gone to the polls in its first ever multi-racial elections. Millions of black South Africans have voted for the first time after years of negotiations between F.W. de Klerk's National Party and the African National Congress. Nelson Mandela of the ANC is tipped to become president.

There's no such thing as a bad Picasso, but some are less good than others.
Pablo Picasso on Picasso – one of his paintings sold for a record $532,000 today, 1967.

Impressions of Impressionism

1874 French art critic Louis Leroy yesterday lampooned a group of artists, whom he terms "impressionists", whose works are currently on show at a studio in the Boulevard des Capucines in Paris. His satirical article appears in the periodical *Charivari* and centres on the lack of precision and concern for symmetry and detail in the pictures. It seems that the paintings have to be looked at from a distance if the viewer is to perceive the unifying elements in them, namely light and the interplay of coloured reflections. According to Leroy, art-lovers who appreciate classical art of the type practised by members of the French Royal Academy of Painting and Sculpture would be well advised to retreat as far away as possible – or avoid looking at them at all. The exhibition has not so far created much of a stir among Parisian art-lovers, but perhaps it will now as a result of M. Leroy's bit of mischief. Among the 28 painters exhibiting are Paul Cézanne, Edgar Degas and Claude Monet.

Fascists unleash terror on Guernica

1937 The civil war in Spain took a sinister and devastating turn today with the sudden and horrific bombing by German planes of the medieval Basque town of Guernica. The town was crowded with people who had come in from the surrounding area for market day. Much of the damage was caused by incendiary bombs which exploded into flames on landing. Survivors say that the aircraft also strafed the town with machine-gun fire, causing additional casualties. The attack will inflame Republican sympathizers who allege that the support given by the German and Italian governments to the rebel Nationalist forces of Fascist leader General Franco are in direct contravention of the non-intervention agreement reached by the League of Nations last year. The Soviet Union is the only country to extend a helping hand to the Republican government, although an International Brigade recruited from among opponents of fascism in several European countries has rallied to the Republican

War preparations

1939 The British government has announced its intention of setting up a ministry of supply and introducing conscription for the first time since World War I. The move comes in the wake of Prime Minister Neville Chamberlain's military guarantees to Poland, Romania and Greece. Six months' military service will be compulsory for men as they reach the age of 20. Both Liberal and Labour politicians are opposed to the plan, denouncing it as a surrender to militarism. The conscripts are to receive an unexpected perk - pyjamas, which have never before been provided for rank-and-file British servicemen.

1521 Portuguese navigator Ferdinand Magellan is killed by the inhabitants of the island of Mactan in the Philippines.

1882 American essayist and poet Ralph Waldo Emerson dies aged 78.

1932 Imperial Airways begin an air service from London to Cape Town in South Africa.

1950 The British government officially recognizes the state of Israel.

1968 In Britain, a new Abortion Act liberalizing the law on abortion comes into force.

1970 American actor Tony Curtis is fined £50 in London for possession of cannabis.

1972 Kwame Nkrumah, Ghanaian president who was deposed in 1966 by a military coup while he was in China, dies in Bucharest, Hungary.

1976 Pop star David Bowie's special train is halted for several hours on the Polish-Russian border while customs officers search baggage, confiscating Nazi books and mementoes.

1984 The Philadelphia radio station W-WSH has a "No Michael Jackson" weekend in reaction to the pop star's over-exposure during the past year.

Nuclear meltdown fears come true at Chernobyl

1986 The nightmare of meltdown in a nuclear reactor has finally come true. The first sign of trouble was picked up by US spy satellites which detected a fire at the Chernobyl nuclear power station, north of Kiev, Ukraine. Scientists at the Swedish Forsmark nuclear power station next reported a huge rise in radiation levels as fall-out spread to Scandinavia. No word of warning was issued by the Soviet authorities to neighbouring countries. Experts believe the accident may have been caused by catastrophic failure of one of the reactor's welded pressure vessels, allowing melt-down of fuel in the core. The reactor is of a water-cooled type not used in Britain or the US. The accident will undoubtedly refuel the ongoing debate between the pro- and anti-nuclear lobbies, while the lack of information from the Soviets will also lend weight to calls for more stringent checks on nuclear fuel facilities world-wide.

Slovo comes home

1990 The leader of the South African Communist Party, Joe Slovo, will arrive in Pretoria tomorrow to take part in peace talks with the administration of President de Klerk. The return of the 64-year-old Lithuanian ends a 27-year exile made possible because the South African government's has ceased to ban the SACP and ANC. Many white South Africans are very suspicious of the former Johannesburg lawyer, who is one of the most senior commanders of the ANC's military wing, Umkhonto we Siswe ("Spear of the Nation").

> *Your country needs you.*
> British conscription
> poster, 1939.

London welcomes its own zoo

1828 The Zoological Society of London has opened a zoological gardens in Regent's Park almost two years to the day after its founding in 1826. Although today's inauguration was restricted to Fellows of the Society it will not be long before the zoo is welcoming the general public. The Society's aim in opening the zoo is to advance our knowledge of the animal kingdom and introduce "new and curious subjects" to an even more curious human audience. The zoo already has monkeys, bears, emus, kangaroos, llamas, lizards and turtles. The royal menagerie at Windsor may be transferred to the gardens, as may the selection of animals kept in the Tower. The Zoological Society takes the well-being of its animals seriously – gentlemen visitors are not allowed to carry whips in the gardens and ladies are politely but firmly requested to refrain from poking the beasts through the bars of the cages.

Triumphant opening of Golden Gate bridge

1937 The new Golden Gate suspension bridge linking the city of San Francisco with Marin County reached completion today after four years. Among its remarkable features are 746-ft (227 m) high bridge towers, the tallest in the world, and 4200-ft (1280 m) span, the longest in the world. Fast-rising tides, frequent storms and fogs and the difficulty of blasting through bedrock 100 ft (30m) below the surface of the water to plant earthquake-proof foundations were among the many problems overcome. Users of the bridge are guaranteed a spectacular view from the six-lane roadway perched 250 ft (76 m) above the surface of the Golden Gate strait.

BIRTHDAYS

Edward Gibbon 1737, English historian who wrote the six-volume *The Decline and Fall of the Roman Empire*.

Mary Wollstonecraft 1759, English writer, political radical and feminist whose *A Vindication of the Rights of Women* demanded equal rights in education.

Samuel Morse 1791, American inventor of the magnetic telegraph and the Morse code.

Ulysses S. Grant 1822, American general of the Union army and 18th president of the USA.

Cecil Day-Lewis 1904, Irish-born novelist and Poet Laureate.

Anouk Aimée 1932, French actress, star of *A Man and a Woman* and *La Dolce Vita*.

1770 Captain Cook lands at Botany Bay in his ship the *Endeavour*.

1780 The first advertisement for an abortion clinic appears in London's *Morning Post*.

1788 Maryland becomes the seventh state of the Union.

1936 King Fu'ad of Egypt, who became monarch when Britain granted limited independence to Egypt in 1922, dies aged 68.

1953 Japan is finally allowed the self-government of which it had been stripped after World War II.

1977 In Germany, Baader-Meinhof group terrorists Andreas Baader, Gudrun Ensslin and Jan Raspe, dedicated to the violent overthrow of capitalist society, are jailed for life.

1988 Twenty-eight-year-old Sian Edwards becomes the first woman to conduct at the Royal Opera House, Covent Garden.

1996 A madman shoots dead 35 people and badly wounds 17 at Port Arthur in Tasmania.

BIRTHDAYS

King Edward IV 1442, English monarch, Yorkist leader during the Wars of the Roses who was crowned after defeating the Lancastrians at Mortimer's Cross and Towton in 1461.

James Monroe 1758, American statesman and fifth president whose Monroe Doctrine declared that no European power would colonize any part of America.

Charles Sturt 1795, English explorer who made his name for his Australian expeditions.

Lionel Barrymore 1878, American actor who appeared in 144 films between 1909 and 1953.

Ann-Margret 1941, Swedish-born actress, singer and dancer whose films include *Carnal Knowledge*, *The Cincinnati Kid* and *Tommy*.

Kenneth Kaunda 1924, Zambian president who was imprisoned in 1958 for founding the Zambian African National Congress when the country was still Northern Rhodesia.

Germany must pay for WWI

1919 After negotiations lasting three months the five Great Powers - Britain, France, Italy, Japan and the United States – have agreed the terms of the post-war settlement. Despite the moderating influences of British Prime Minister David Lloyd George and, especially, US President Woodrow Wilson, France insisted on her pound of flesh. French premier Georges Clemenceau, known as "the tiger", was hell-bent on recouping France's losses to Germany after the last conflict between the two countries in the 1870s. The major clauses of the Versailles Treaty agreed in Paris provide for war reparations to France, a limit on the size of Germany's armed forces and the creation of a League of Nations to safeguard world peace. Alsace and Lorraine have been restored to France and the Saar placed under French administration. The treaty may, though, sink without trace so far as America is concerned, for Congress has still to ratify it and rumour has it that many in the House are strongly opposed to the idea of a League of Nations.

Whoops! Wrong bridge

1987 American real estate agents have arrived in London with the intention of selling back to the Brits a famous purchase that they made 18 years ago. Yes, London Bridge is back on the market. The difference, apart from the price tag - £30 million as opposed to $1 million – is that the purchaser will not be allowed to transport the mammoth artifact back to Britain. Offered with the bridge is virtually the whole of downtown Lake Havasu City, the desert new town where oil mogul Robert McCulloch, now deceased, rebuilt his purchase, brick by brick. The story goes that McCulloch bought London Bridge in mistake for the more picturesque Tower Bridge. Only after spending $3.7 million (£2 million) erecting the bridge did he realize his error.

1945 Italian dictator Benito Mussolini was today shot and strung up head down by his own countrymen. The man once called "Il Duce", the leader, is now seen as little better than a common criminal. The same treatment was meted out to his mistress, Claretta Petacci.

"Non" to De Gaulle

1969 After emerging intact from the political debris resulting from last year's riots, President de Gaulle has fallen from power over the comparatively uncontroversial issue of regional electoral reform. His decision to resign after his failure to win the referendum of two days ago was inevitable because he had staked his presidency on this pet issue. De Gaulle will be suc-

ceeded by his former wartime aide and prime minister since 1962, Georges Pompidou. "It's like being cuckolded by your chauffeur," was de Gaulle's characteristically blunt comment on this reversal in his fortunes. By saying "Non" to the 79-year-old de Gaulle, the French people may be signalling their readiness to move to more liberal government.

MUTINY ON THE BOUNTY

1789 A mutiny is reported to have broken out on a British armed transport ship in the South Seas. The captain of the 94-ft (29 m) *Bounty*, Captain William Bligh, and 18 loyal crew members have been put in an open boat and are now drifting in the direction of Timor, near Java. The mutineers, led by master's mate Fletcher Christian, are thought to be returning to Tahiti, where the *Bounty* recently took on board a consignment of 1000 young breadfruit trees which Bligh intended taking to the West Indies as a food source for the African slaves there. The cause of the mutiny is unclear, but Bligh's harshness has been offered as a possible explanation. It has also been suggested that the sailors have been beguiled by the charms of the native Tahitian women. One mutineer, John Adams, talked of the possibility of starting a new life on one of the many remote South Sea islands.

Master of suspense dies

1980 The screen's master of suspense, Alfred Hitchcock, died in Los Angeles yesterday aged 80. The ghastly thrills which Hitchcock injected into his films were worked out in minute detail before he began filming. His unique brand of visual storytelling invariably centred upon his chief preoccupations of sin and confession, a reflection perhaps of his Jesuit upbringing. Some of Hitchcock's early work in Hollywood was marred by studio intervention. Potentially interesting subjects evident in *Spellbound* and *Notorious*, for example, tended to be submerged beneath a superficial Hollywood gloss. His most famous film, *Psycho*, starring Antony Perkins, was rejected by all the major studios, forcing Hitchcock to finance it himself. The film's success made him a millionaire. The film industry's ultimate accolade, an Oscar, eluded Hitchcock to the end, despite the fact that at least a dozen of his works are considered masterpieces.

1376 Sir Peter de la Mare takes office as first Speaker of the House of Commons.

1842 In Britain, a Corn Act is passed introducing a new sliding scale to the price of domestic corn at which foreign importation is allowed.

1930 A telephone link is established between Britain and Australia.

1937 American chemist Wallace Hume Carothers commits suicide just two months after he has patented nylon.

1945 German plenipotentaries in Italy sign terms of surrender.

1967 In London, 41 groups play at an all-night rave in Alexandra Palace.

1977 Trade unions are declared legal in Spain for the first time since 1936.

1987 The musical *Cabaret* is performed in London without music when the orchestra goes on strike.

BIRTHDAYS

Arthur Wellesley, Duke of Wellington 1769, English soldier and prime minister known ans the Iron Duke, who defeated Napoleon at Waterloo.

William Randolph Hearst 1863, American newspaper proprietor.

Sir Thomas Beecham 1879, English conductor famed for his acerbic tongue as well as his music-making.

Sir Malcolm Sargent 1895, English conductor who was the chief conductor of the Sir Henry Wood Promenade concerts from 1948 until his death in 1957.

Duke Ellington 1889, American jazz pianist, composer and bandleader.

Rudolf Schwarz 1905, Viennese conductor who survived Belsen concentration camp and went on to become conductor of the BBC Symphony Orchestra.

Zubin Mehta 1936, Indian conductor and violinist chiefly known for his association with the Israel Philharmonic Orchestra.

1985 The six-year wrangle between the family of the late Sir Charles Clore and the British Inland Revenue has been settled. A total of £67 million is to be paid to the Revenue on Clore's world-wide assets, estimated at £123 million. The Revenue originally claimed £84 million because, it alleged, he was living in England. His son claimed his father had lived in Monaco.

Blue stockings make strides

1885 The decision to allow women to sit the examinations of Oxford University is further evidence that the door of academe is widening – slowly. This advance is due almost entirely to the efforts of Emily Davies, guiding force behind a committee dedicated to securing higher education for women. Cambridge agreed to open its local examinations to women in 1865 after the success of a pilot project in 1863 when 91 women sat the exams. Four years ago women were allowed to sit the Tripos examination also. However, women are not to be awarded degrees.

> *Any reasonable system of taxation should be based on the slogan of "Soak the Rich".*
>
> **Heywood Broun**, US journalist, 1922.

What horrors herein?

1945 As the Allies continue their advance into territory previously held by German forces they are gradually uncovering evidence of unspeakable crimes against humanity perpetrated by the Nazis. The latest abomination has been uncovered on the outskirts of the small Bavarian market town of Dachau, just north-west of Munich. In this ironically picturesque setting Hitler's SS set up a death camp, possibly as early as 1933. More than 200,000 people, mainly of Jewish faith, are estimated to have been exterminated here or held before being transferred to another concentration camp.

Hair raises hackles on Broadway

1968 The new musical *Hair* has provoked a mixed reaction from its first-night audience at the Biltmore Theatre, New York. Comments included "vulgar", "dirty" and "juvenile backyard fence graffiti"

from the antis and "fresh", "frank" and "the most significant musical of the decade" from the pros. Sex, drugs, military service and religion are among the wide range of topics served up for the public's consumption in a number of new songs added since the original production, staged off Broadway last year. A nude scene has added fuel to the charge that *Hair*'s producers are more interested in cheap sensationalism than theatrical values. The show does have some influential friends among the critics, including *New York Times* columnist Clive Barnes, whose "yea" or "nay" can spell success or disaster for a Broadway show.

1772 The first dial weighing machine is patented by John Clais of London.

1803 The US purchases Louisiana and New Orleans from the French.

1900 The republic of Hawaii cedes itself to the US.

1904 St Louis Exhibition opens.

1912 A second reading of the Irish Home Rule Bill is moved in the House of Commons by Winston Churchill.

1936 Death of A. E. Housman, the English poet who wrote two volumes of lyrics, *A Shropshire Lad* and *Last Poems*, on the themes of human vanity and transience.

1948 The first Land Rover is exhibited at the Amsterdam Motor Show.

1957 Egypt reopens the Suez Canal to traffic.

1965 Bob Dylan opens his first UK tour in Sheffield.

1968 Frankie Lymon, the American pop star who had a hit at the age of only 14 with "Why Do Fools Fall in Love?" dies of a heroin overdose.

1983 Death of George Balanchine, Russian-born choreographer who was first artistic director to the New York City Ballet.

BIRTHDAYS

Daniel Thompson 1770, English-born Canadian who explored large parts of western Canada.

Joachim von Ribbentrop 1893, German politician who was Hitler's foreign minister.

Franz Lehár 1870, Hungarian composer best-known for *The Merry Widow*.

Jaroslav Hasek 1883, Czechoslovakian novelist who wrote the satirical novel *The Good Soldier Schweik*.

Jill Clayburgh 1944, American actress Oscar-nominated for *An Unmarried Woman*.

Saigon falls

1975 Communist North Vietnamese forces entered the capital of South Vietnam today, signalling an end to the 15-year Second Indochina War. Despite signing the Paris ceasefire two years ago, the Saigon government had continued its efforts to eliminate Communist power in its territory. It was a forlorn hope that this could be achieved with American help, let alone without it. The complete withdrawal of US troops in 1973 and Washington's decision to accord the Communist-backed Provisional Revolutionary Government equal status with Saigon signalled to the northern leadership in Hanoi that further American intervention would not be forthcoming. Communist forces in Vietnam have been trying to unite their country under a national government since World War II.

Washington takes the oath

1789 President George Washington was inaugurated in a ceremony at Federal Hall in New York today. The 67-year-old Virginian landowner is widely recognized within his own country, and indeed beyond, as the only man capable of giving the new federation the wise and sure leadership it will need in its infancy. Washington was the architect of the idea of a federal convention as the best way of organizing a union of states. His leading role in establishing this framework of government is said to have made him reluctant to accept the presidency when it was initially offered earlier in the year. The loud cheers which were heard as Washington took the oath have hopefully reassured him of the American people's faith in his integrity and ability, qualities which he demonstrated time and again during the War of Independence which only recently ended.

> *I wouldn't believe Hitler was dead, even if he told me so himself.*
>
> **Hjalmar Schacht**, German banker, 1945.

Ali stripped of his title

1967 In a dramatic and unprecedented move, Muhammad Ali has been stripped of his world heavyweight boxing crown for refusing to be conscripted into the US armed forces. Ali's claim that he is exempted from serving in Vietnam on religious grounds has been rejected. The boxing authorities have promptly taken away his title and revoked his licence. Ali, 25, first won the title as Cassius Clay in 1964. He changed his name to Muhammad Ali after converting to the Muslim faith and becoming a minister. He is expected to appeal, but until the case is resolved fans will be deprived of watching a man popularly regarded as the greatest boxer this century.

Adolf Hitler ends it all

1945 In a scene straight out of Wagner's epic music-drama *The Ring of the Nibelungen*, Adolf Hitler has ended his evil reign. After bidding farewell to the few aides remaining with him in his Berlin bunker hideaway, the megalomaniac who has reduced his country and much of Europe to ashes then retired to his suite and shot himself. His wife of just 48 hours and former mistress, Eva Braun, took a cyanide potassium capsule. In accordance with Hitler's instructions, both bodies were then burnt. During the last three months of his life Hitler is said to have been close to insanity as he bowed to the inevitability of defeat for his once all-powerful, super Reich.

1900 An Illinois Central railroad engineer, John Luther ("Casey") Jones, was the only fatality in a potentially horrific smash involving the famed *Cannonball Express* which runs between Chicago and New Orleans. Jones, 36, had been attempting to deliver the eight-hour-late mail on time when his locomotive, engine No 382, hit the caboose of a freight train which was protruding out of a siding. The management of the railroad have praised the dead engineer's conscientiousness.

PROGRAMME OFFICIEL
DES
BALLETS RUSSES

BAKST
1911

Costume de "NARCISSE"

1983 A poster advertising Sergei Diaghilev's Ballets Russes in 1911 for whom George Balanchine choreographed a number of ballets including *Apollo* and *The Prodigal Son*. Balanchine died this day aged 79.

MAY

"We made seats for ourselves in the snow,
and sitting there in reasonable comfort
we ate with relish a bar of mintcake."

Edmund Hillary
on reaching the summit of Everest,
May 29, 1953.

> *For, Heaven be thanked, we live in such an age,*
> *When no man dies for love, but on the stage.*
> **John Dryden**, English writer, who died today, 1700.

EMPIRE STATE SCRAPES THE SKIES OF NEW YORK

Explorer meets death in Africa

1873 The Scottish missionary and explorer David Livingstone has died of malaria in the middle of Africa. He was 60 years old. More than any other man, Livingstone helped to open Africa to the church – and to Western commerce. The London Missionary Society sent him to South Africa in 1841. He made the first-ever crossing of the Kalahari Desert, and, fired by a vision of peoples the church had not reached, began a dramatic journey further afield. It took him to Luanda on the west coast of Africa and to the Indian Ocean on the east coast, and he discovered the stupendous Victoria Falls on the way. Back in London his reports on central and east Africa aroused great interest. Livingstone then spent years searching for the source of the Nile, and was already feared to have died until the journalist Henry Morton Stanley found him two years ago, already a sick man, but determined to continue his search.

1994 Leading Formula One driver Ayrton Senna has been killed on the same stretch of track as fellow driver Roland Ratzenberger was two days earlier at San Marino Grand Prix.

Nijinsky dances into notoriety

1912 The brilliant young Russian dancer Vaslav Nijinsky scandalized Paris tonight with a performance so sensual some critics described it as "bestial". Nijinsky is a faun amongst nymphs in Claude Debussy's *L'Apres-midi d'un Faune*, premiered tonight – yet it was the final sequence, when Nijinsky danced alone with a long scarf, that was so outrageous. Nijinsky, 24, upsets and delights all at once – his performance, as ever, was stunning as is the whole ballet. Nijinsky's first effort at choreography, it brings alive the familiar friezes of ancient Greece. Like Debussy's score, it is pure impressionism. Nijinsky first came to Paris three years ago with Serge Diaghilev's Ballets Russes and was an instant sensation.

1931 US President Herbert Hoover opened the tallest building in the world in New York today – the 102-storey Empire State Building on Fifth Avenue, which stands an incredible 1250 ft (380 m) high. It is the city's third new "skyscraper" in just one year. It went up with lightning speed, the steel framework being finished in less than six months. It met its deadline for completion – today – with no time to spare – the day many New York office leases expire. The Empire State Building has more than 2 million sq ft (609,800 sq m) of office space, much more than the city can absorb with the Depression in full swing. The owners are hoping sightseers to the lofty observation decks will help to pay the taxes.

1960 Days before US President Eisenhower and Soviet Chairman Kruschev meet at a Paris summit, an American spy plane has been shot down over the Soviet Union today by a Soviet surface-to-air missile. The pilot, Francis Gary Powers, was captured. The US has denied Russian accusations that it was spying.

THE KING FINDS A QUEEN

1967 Elvis Presley, the King of Rock 'n' Roll and still the world's No 1 heart-throb, caused widespread female dismay this morning when he married his sweetheart of seven years, Priscilla Beaulieu. The couple wed at the Aladdin Hotel in Las Vegas at a civil ceremony with 100 guests. Priscilla wore a traditional flowing white dress and veil, and Presley a formal suit and black tie. The wedding cake was six tiers high. After the reception they flew to Palm Springs for a two-day honeymoon. Presley is due in Hollywood on Thursday for final work on his new movie, *Clambake*, and then they'll complete the honeymoon at Graceland, Presley's Memphis mansion.

May Day

1700 Death of John Dryden, English Poet Laureate.

1707 The Union between England and Scotland is proclaimed.

1808 Charles IV of Spain abdicates in favour of Joseph Bonaparte.

1840 The first Penny Black stamps bearing Queen Victoria's head go on sale five days before the official date of issue.

1851 Queen Victoria opens the Great Exhibition in the Crystal Palace in Hyde Park, London.

1862 The Union army occupies New Orleans.

1898 During the Spanish-American War, an American fleet squadron slips into Manila harbour and destroys the obsolete Spanish fleet.

1904 Death of Antonin Dvořák, Czechoslovakian composer best-known for his New World Symphony.

1936 Emperor Haile Selassie of Ethiopia flees the country.

1941 Orson Welles' film *Citizen Kane* is premiered in New York.

1945 In Germany, Hitler's propaganda minister Joseph Goebbels kills his wife, his six children and finally himself, the day after his leader's suicide.

1989 Anti-government protests in Prague demand the release of jailed playwright Vaclav Havel.

1997 Labour leader Tony Blair is elected UK Prime Minister.

BIRTHDAYS

Joseph Addison 1672, English essayist, poet and Whig statesman who co-founded the *Spectator* in 1711.

Glenn Ford 1916, Canadian-born American actor who appeared most notably in *Gilda*, *Blackboard Jungle* and *The Fastest Gun Alive*.

Joseph Heller 1929, American novelist best-known for his novel *Catch-22*.

Rita Coolidge 1945, American country rock singer and pianist.

1797 The British naval mutiny spreads to the North Sea fleet.

1857 French playwright and poet Alfred de Musset dies of a heart attack.

1923 Lieutenants Kelly and Macready make the first non-stop flight across America in 27 hours, travelling from Long Island to San Diego in a Fokker T-2.

1957 Death of Senator Joe McCarthy, who chaired the Permanent Subcommittee of Investigations that carried out the communist witch-hunts in 1950s America.

1965 The first satellite television programme links nine countries and more than 300 million viewers.

1972 Death of J. Edgar Hoover, head of the FBI.

1989 China imposes martial law as pro-democracy demonstrators camp in Tienanmen Square.

BIRTHDAYS

Catherine II 1729, Empress of Russia who gained the throne in 1762 in a coup in which her husband, Peter III, was murdered.

Theodor Herzl 1860, Austrian journalist who propounded the idea of a Jewish state and became first president of the World Zionist Organization in 1897.

Baron Manfred von Richthofen 1892, German air force officer who was nicknamed the "Red Baron" by the British because he flew a red Fokker in World War I.

Lorenz Hart 1895, American lyricist who collaborated with Richard Rodgers to produce musicals such as *Pal Joey*.

Bing Crosby 1904, American singer and actor whose "White Christmas" is the biggest-selling single ever recorded.

Dr Benjamin Spock 1903, American paediatrician whose books influenced generations of mothers.

Satyajit Ray 1921, Indian film director best-known for his "Apu" trilogy about a child growing up in modern-day India.

Renaissance man moves on

1519 The Florentine painter Leonardo da Vinci has died at Cloux in France at the age of 67. In an era of artistic genius he shared with the universally talented Michelangelo, the dazzling painters Titian and Raphael, and Bramante, giant of architecture, Leonardo was perhaps the greatest of them all. Born in Vinci, the illegitimate son of a notary, he trained in Florence under Verrocchio. His most famous works are indubitably the mural *The Last Supper* and the portrait *Mona Lisa*. Leonardo was court artist to the Duke of Milan for 18 years – as well as a civil and military engineer, and an expert mathematician and biologist, a grinder of lenses, a designer of clock mechanisms, of devices for transmitting energy, even of flying machines. In his quest for understanding of the natural world, he studied birds in flight, swirling streams and rock strata, his amazingly acute eye freezing motion in sketches and diagrams. After the French invasion of Milan in 1499 he returned to Florence, becoming military engineer and architect to Cesare Borgia. Leonardo was as great a scientist as he was an artist. To him art and science were one, part of the search for knowledge. Seldom has a search been so rewarded: Leonardo leaves an immensely rich body of work.

Furore over sinking of the *General Belgrano*

1982 The Argentinian cruiser *General Belgrano* was torpedoed and sunk today by the British submarine *Conqueror* – 30 miles (48 km) outside the 200-mile (320 km) "exclusion zone" Britain has declared around the Falkland Islands. Some 360 crewman perished. The Argentinian government has denounced the attack as "a treacherous act of armed aggression", but British prime minister Margaret Thatcher insists that the cruiser posed a threat. A Royal Navy task force set sail last month for the Falklands to dislodge Argentinian forces that occupied the British islands on April 4. Last week a British advance force recaptured the island of South Georgia. Argentina has for many years laid claim to the Falklands.

1952 Jet-age travel was born today as a de Havilland Comet jet airliner with 36 passengers aboard took off from London for Johannesburg on the first scheduled jet flight. The British Overseas Airways Corporation flight is scheduled to take 18 hours, flying via Rome, Beirut, Khartoum, Entebbe and Livingstone. It made its maiden flight in July 1949.

Pink Floyd's hit is black anthem

1980 British rock group Pink Floyd's hit single "Another Brick in the Wall" was banned by the South African government today. Rebellious black schoolchildren have adopted the song as an anthem. The brutally suppressed nationwide riots of 1976 were started by black schoolchildren rejecting the racist government's education system, which spends six times as much educating a white child as a black child. Now the young protesters chant Pink Floyd's lines: "We don't want no education, we don't want no thought control." Banning the song is not likely to stop them singing it – nor meaning it.

Jakie, is it my birthday or am I dying?
　　Nancy, Viscountess Astor, US-born British politician – her last words, said today to her son, who replied: "A bit of both, Mum." 1964.

League dithers as Ethiopia tumbles

1936 With Italian troops closing on the capital Addis Ababa, Ethiopian Emperor Haile Selassie and his family fled into exile today. The Italians have caused international outrage by bombing Ethiopian villages with mustard gas. Rejecting negotiations, Italy's Fascist dictator Benito Mussolini invaded Ethiopia last October with 100,000 men, plus bombers. Bent on vengeance, the Italians overwhelmed the border city of Adowa, where Ethiopian forces humiliated the Italians in 1896. Following Selassie's impassioned plea for help, the League of Nations called for sanctions against Italy, but both France and Britain vacillated on the crucial oil embargo. As Ethiopia succumbs to its fate the League loses all credibility as a peacekeeping force.

Best-selling romance for Hollywood?

1937 American writer Margaret Mitchell has won a Pulitzer Prize for her first novel, *Gone With The Wind*. The 1000-page romance, published last year, sold a million copies in the first six months. Set in Georgia, the novel portrays the destruction of the old South during the Civil War as wilful heroine Scarlett O'Hara struggles to regain her family's lost possessions. Her lovers, one a gentle aristocrat, the other as unscrupulous as Scarlett herself, are a symbol of the harsh new order's triumph over the old. There are rumours of discussion over film rights.

Czech officials made to blush over pink tank

1991 Czech president Vaclav Havel's foreign ministry apologized to the Soviet ambassador in Prague today over the "vandalism" that had "desecrated" a Soviet war memorial in the city. Two days ago an art student painted a Russian tank pink. He said it was "out of place in the current climate of disarmament". The incident is a symbol of continuing Czech confusion over the Soviet role; Prague remembers both the Russian tanks that crushed the "Prague Spring" of 1968 and those that liberated the city from the Nazis in 1945. Today the tank was painted green, ready for Independence Day.

> *In Flanders fields the poppies blow,*
> *Between the crosses, row on row,*
> *That mark our place.*
> **John McCrae**, Canadian poet, written on this day, 1915.

COLUMBUS CHINA TRIP FINDS JAMAICA INSTEAD

1494 On his second voyage across the Atlantic in search of a westward route to the East, the Italian navigator Christopher Columbus today discovered Jamaica, a tropical paradise of forests and mountains. But it is not the fabled Orient, and the fleet is turning back to Isábella, the colony Columbus founded on Hispaniola last month. Columbus returned to Spain last year after his first voyage west, carrying gold and some of the native people, and claiming to have reached islands off the coast of Asia. Encouraged, Queen Isabella funded the second voyage much more generously than the first, providing 17 ships and 1500 men. But Columbus has found no trace of the court of China and its gold – only a succession of beautiful islands peopled by primitive Indians. The 39 sailors Columbus left on Hispaniola on the first voyage had been killed by the Indians, he has found very little gold, and the new colony is proving troublesome. Columbus can expect a cool reception at court when he returns to Spain this time.

Bourbons take the biscuit

1814 France has a Bourbon king again after 22 years of revolution and conquest under Napoleon Bonaparte. Louis XVIII entered Paris today and took the throne following Napoleon's defeat by the allies and his forced abdication and exile to Elba last month. When Louis wrote to Napoleon from exile 12 years ago, asking him to restore the monarchy, Napoleon replied: "You must not expect to return to France. It would mean marching over a hundred thousand corpses." But it is Napoleon that has left Europe strewn with corpses, and Louis returned without a fight. He had fled France early in the Revolution and proclaimed himself King in exile when his nephew, Louis XVII, was guillotined. Talleyrand is to be the King's foreign minister.

1654 The first toll bridge in America comes into operation in Massachusetts.

1788 The first daily evening newspaper, the *Star and Evening Advertiser*, is published in London.

1790 Port Louis in Tobago is razed by fire.

1808 Above Paris, one of the contestants is shot dead in the first duel to be fought from hot air balloons.

1810 English poet Lord Byron takes one hour and 20 minutes to swim the Dardanelles strait in Turkey.

1917 The first US destroyers arrive in Britain to join the naval forces ranged against the Germans in World War I.

1958 Death of Henry Cornelius, South African-born British film director whose most notable films are the comedies *Passport to Pimlico* and *Genevieve*.

1969 Pop star Jimi Hendrix is arrested at Toronto airport for illegally possessing narcotics.

1988 *Time* magazine publishes advance extracts of the memoirs of Donald Regan, former chief of staff to President Reagan, which tell how astrologer Joan Quigley influenced White House decisions.

BIRTHDAYS

Niccolò Macchiavelli 1469, Italian political theorist who wrote *The Prince* in 1532, in which he argued that all means are permissible to achieve a stable state.

Golda Meir 1898, Israeli politician who became prime minister at the age of 70.

Mary Astor 1906, American film actress most notable in *The Maltese Falcon* and *The Great Lie*.

Pete Seeger 1919, American folk singer.

Sugar Ray Robinson 19290, American world middleweight and welterweight boxing champion.

Peter Oosterhuis 1948, British golfer.

James Brown 1933, American soul singer.

Britain fetes the new Elizabethan age

1951 The South Bank of the River Thames in London lit up this evening as King George VI and Queen Elizabeth opened the Festival of Britain. The five-month festival is designed to disperse the grey post-war cloud with a bright vision of Britain's future. Clusters of illuminations and the revolutionary architecture of the Dome of Discovery and the Festival Hall have drastically changed the South Bank, which was destroyed in the London Blitz. Festival entertainments include a large fun-fair, sculptures, a railway and the Festival Pleasure Gardens.

1799 Tipu Sahib, the formidable warrior Sultan of Mysore in southern India, fights to the death when the British overwhelm his capital at Seringapatam.

1839 The Cunard shipping line is founded by Sir Samuel Cunard.

1904 Charles Rolls and Henry Royce sign a provisional agreement to collaborate in the production of Rolls-Royce cars.

1970 Journalist Seymour Hirsch wins the Pulitzer Prize for his reporting of the My Lai massacre in Vietnam, when American troops killed the inhabitants of My Lai village, women and children included.

1980 Yugoslavian president Tito (Josip Broz) dies aged 87, having ruled his country since 1953.

1983 President Reagan announces his backing for the Nicaraguan Contras in their conflict with the Sandinistas.

1989 Christine Jorgensen, former US Army private who caused a storm when she had the first-ever sex change operation in 1952, dies of cancer.

2000 The Love Bug virus wreaks havoc with computers all over the world.

BIRTHDAYS

Bartolommeo Cristofori 1655, Italian harpsichord-maker and inventor of the piano.

John Hanning Speke 1827, English explorer who was the first European to see Lake Victoria and who, on a later expedition, identified it as the source of the Nile.

Alice Liddell 1852, English inspiration for Alice in Lewis Carroll's *Alice in Wonderland* and *Alice Through the Looking Glass*.

Audrey Hepburn 1929, Belgian-born actress whose most notable films were *Roman Holiday*, *War and Peace*, *Funny Face* and *Wait Until Dark*.

Tammy Wynette 1942, American country and western singer best-known for her song "Stand By Your Man".

Britain comes to a standstill

1926 Britain's workers downed tools today en masse and the country ground to a halt. The first-ever General Strike began at midnight after the general council of the Trades Union Congress voted in favour of supporting the miners' strike which began four days ago in protest at a wage reduction. Talks between the government and the TUC broke down late last night after printers at the *Daily Mail* refused to print an article by the editor which denounced the TUC as revolutionary. There have been reports of strikers in Glasgow trying to force public vehicles off the road, and the army has been put on full alert in Scotland, Yorkshire and South Wales. It is rumoured that volunteers and troops will be used to keep essential services running.

Vietnam protesters killed at Kent State

1970 US National Guardsmen shot and killed four students at Kent State University in Ohio today. The dead students, two men and two women, were taking part in a massed anti-war protest when the soldiers fired into the unarmed crowd. Nine students were wounded. Two more students were shot dead at Jackson State University, Mississippi. The killings follow three days of student rioting in which the National Guard used bayonets, teargas and finally bullets. Thousands of students came out today in defiance of a state ban on all public meetings. The Nationwide campus demonstrations erupted after President Richard Nixon sent US troops into Cambodia last week.

1982 A British destroyer, HMS *Sheffield*, has been sunk in the Falklands War, with 22 crewmen killed and many burned. *Sheffield* was hit without warning by an Exocet missile launched from 20 miles (32 km) away by an Argentinian Air Force fighter-bomber the ship's radar never saw. The Royal Navy has no defence against Exocets. Both missile and fighter are French-made.

Maggie jubilant

1979 Britain's first woman prime minister, Margaret Thatcher, moved into No. 10 Downing Street today after a resounding election win that gives her Conservative government a majority of 43 seats in parliament. A jubilant Thatcher said she felt an "aura of calm". Married to a businessman and the mother of two, she is a grocer's daughter. She espouses a monetarist economic policy. She took the reins of the Conservative Party in 1975 after ousting Edward Heath. Today she promised a complete transformation of Britain's economic and industrial climate. Thatcher is planning a war on inflation, privatization of the nationalized industries and a curb on trade union power. "Hands off," the Trades Union Council warned her tonight. But Thatcher-watchers say it is unwise to underestimate her.

Maoris strike back

1863 A 23-year running conflict in New Zealand erupted today in a pitched battle between Maoris and British settlers at Taranaki. A Maori leader, Rewi Maniapoto, has been urging his people to rise up and kill Westerners, and three weeks ago a war party attacked and killed eight British soldiers. There are growing signs of a widespread rebellion. The Maoris accuse the settlers of cheating them out of their land. Settlement has spread rapidly despite the Treaty of Waitangi, which enshrined Maori rights in 1840, and conflict has spread with it.

When dissent turns to violence it invites tragedy.
Richard M. Nixon, US president, commenting on the shooting of rioting students at Kent State University today, 1970.

Crusaders flee fallen stronghold

1291 Egypt's Mamelukes overwhelmed the last Christian stronghold in the Holy Land today. Sultan Qalawun's army battered the Crusader fortress-port of Acre into submission. Giant catapults lobbed bombs over the walls while engineers burrowed under them, and then blew them up with gunpowder. As the Egyptian troops poured in, crusaders fled to the port, fighting for places in the few remaining boats to escape to Christian Cyprus. Most were captured. The sultan attacked Acre because the Crusaders had broken a truce and slaughtered every Muslim in the town. He has sent his captives – 1000 Christian knights, their foot soldiers, women and children – to the slave market at Damascus.

1961 Alan B. Shepard today became the first American in space. His tiny Mercury spacecraft, Freedom 7, blasted off from Cape Canaveral atop a Redstone rocket for a 15-minute suborbital flight, reaching an altitude of 116 miles (186 km) before a splashdown 303 miles (488 km) downrange. The US is still well behind the Soviets: on April 12 Russian Yuri Gagarin blasted into orbit for 108 minutes and circled the Earth before landing safely.

NAPOLEON IS DEAD

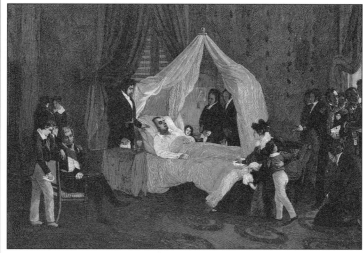

1821 Napoleon Bonaparte died today in exile on the remote British island of St Helena. He was 51. The military genius known as "the Little Corporal", Emperor of France and conqueror of Europe, could not survive more than six years in such a restricted prison. "There is no more oil in the lamp," he told Montholon, his secretary, late last year. Ill since then, he fell into a coma today and died a few hours later. In France he is widely revered, the legend underpinned by the memoirs he wrote in exile. His British captors had no hand in his death – though they did everything to make his life a misery, plaguing him with petty restrictions even during his illness. Napoleon had lost the three great loves of his life: France, power – and his empress. He rejected her in 1810 because she had not given him a male heir. She died seven years ago, but today, the last word Napoleon spoke was "Josephine".

PARIS RIOTS SWELL

1968 Paris was torn by violence today as 30,000 students ripped up the streets to make barricades and student "commando squads" clashed with riot police, answering the police teargas grenades with a hail of bricks and Molotov cocktails. Six hundred and fifty students were injured, and 350 police. The first demonstrations, six weeks ago, were anti-American, but student arrests prompted student leader "Danny the Red" Cohn-Bendit to stage a mass sit-in at the university. Two days ago the riot police broke it up, bringing accusations of police brutality – and today's riots. Tonight the city awaits the mass demonstration planned at the Arc de Triomphe for tomorrow morning. It is unlikely to remain peaceful. Meanwhile, millions of dissatisfied workers are said to be moving towards support for the left-wing students.

I used to say of him that his presence on the field made the difference of 40,000 men.
Arthur Wellesley, Duke of Wellington, on Napoleon, who died in exile on St Helena today, 1821.

SAS DARES TO STORM EMBASSY

1980 As millions watched live on television, commandos of Britain's secret Special Air Services stormed the Iranian Embassy in London's fashionable Knightsbridge to break a six-day terrorist siege. The gang was demanding the release of political prisoners in Iran. The commandos attacked without hesitation after the terrorists started to shoot hostages. The commandos killed four of the five gunmen and freed 19 surviving hostages. The Embassy building was gutted.

1760 The first hanging takes place at Tyburn, at the north-east edge of Hyde Park, London, when Earl Ferrers pays the penalty for murdering his valet.

1865 The first train robbery is carried out, near North Bend, Ohio.

1920 Bartolomeo Vanzetti and Nicola Sacco are arrested in New York City for possession of anarchist literature.

1949 Death of Count Maurice Maeterlink, Belgian poet and leading dramatist of the Symbolist movement who wrote *The Blue Bird*.

1955 The post-war occupation of Germany officially ends as the Allied High Commissioners meet for the last time in Berlin and Germany regains sovereignty, with the country split into two parts, East and West.

1955 The World Bank warns that poverty is a greater threat to world peace than the Cold War.

1963 Britain's first satellite is launched from Vandenburg air base, California.

1967 Scott Mackenzie's flower-power anthem "San Francisco" enters the US singles charts.

1972 Death of the Rev Gary Davis, legendary blind blues guitarist.

1988 Japanese television broadcasts the first transmission from the summit of Mount Everest.

BIRTHDAYS

Søren Kierkegaard 1813, Danish philosopher and prolific writer whose influence was seen in 20th-century existentialism.

Karl Marx 1818, German philosopher, economist and revolutionary, author of *Das Kapital*.

Tyrone Power 1913, American actor whose many films include *The Mark of Zorro*, *Alexander's Ragtime Band* and *The Sun Also Rises*.

Michael Palin 1943, British comedian, actor and writer who first became known as a member of Monty Python's Flying Circus.

MAY 6

1527 Rome is sacked by German mercenaries who daub Raphael cartoons with graffiti as they loot the city during battles between the Holy League and Charles V, Holy Roman emperor.

1851 American inventor Linus Yale patents the Yale lock.

1877 The Sioux chief Crazy Horse surrenders and gives up all claim to Nebraska.

1910 King Edward VII of England dies and George V accedes to the throne.

1959 The Cod War between Britain and Iceland over territorial fishing rights hots up when Icelandic gunboats fire live ammunition at British trawlers.

1983 Experts in Bonn announce that the Hitler diaries discovered by a Stern reporter are fake.

1990 P. W. Botha resigns from the ruling National Party in South Africa in protest at talks with the ANC.

1992 Death of Marlene Dietrich, German actress and entertainer who appeared in Hollywood films such as *Destry Rides Again*, *The Blue Angel* and *Shanghai Express*.

1994 The Channel Tunnel, linking Britain with mainland Europe, is officially opened by the Queen and president Mitterand.

BIRTHDAYS

Maximilien Robespierre 1758, French revolutionary who instituted the Reign of Terror but eventually fell victim to the guillotine to which he had condemned so many others.

Sigmund Freud 1856, Austrian psychiatrist and pioneer of psychoanalysis.

Rudolph Valentino 1895, Italian actor who became a star of Hollywood silent movies and caused female hearts to flutter with his performances in films such as *The Sheik*.

Orson Welles 1915, American actor, writer and film director, who starred in *Citizen Kane* and panicked Americans with a radio broadcast of *The War of the Worlds*.

Four-minute mile barrier just broken by Bannister

1954 Roger Bannister, a 25-year-old British medical student, broke an invisible barrier today when he ran a mile in three-fifths of a second less than four minutes. He was running at the Iffley Road track in Oxford, representing the university against the Amateur Athletics Association, with two fellow students setting the pace. Experts long held that it was impossible for man to run a mile in less than four minutes. Today Bannister took two seconds off the previous record, set by Swede Gunder Hagg in 1945. What will be next – a three-and-three-quarter-minute mile?

Under a government which imprisons any unjustly, the true place for a just man is in prison.
Henry David Thoreau, American writer and naturalist, who spent time in prison and laid the foundations for passive resistance in his book *Civil Disobedience*. He died today, 1862.

1840 For just a penny, you can now send a letter anywhere in the British Isles. The penny buys you a printed token – a "stamp" bearing the queen's portrait, with gum on the back so it can be pasted on to an envelope. The scheme is the controversial brainchild of Rowland Hill.

HINDENBURG EXPLODES

1937 The giant German transatlantic airship *Hindenburg* exploded while landing in New Jersey tonight and plunged to the ground in flames, killing 35 of the 97 aboard and injuring many others. Herb Morrison, a radio commentator for WLS in Chicago, described the scene to listeners. "Oh, the humanity, all the passengers, I don't believe it," he said before breaking down in tears. Sailors from the nearby naval base fought to rescue passengers from the burning wreck. The 1000 ft (304 m) airship was delayed by a thunderstorm at the end of her three-day crossing from Frankfurt, and it is thought lightning ignited her 7 million cubic ft of hydrogen gas as her wet mooring ropes touched the ground. This is the fifth airship to crash and today's tragedy must spell the end of the line for them.

Moors Murderers put away for life

1966 "Moors Murderer" Ian Brady was sentenced today to three concurrent life sentences and his accomplice, Myra Hindley, to two. Their crimes came to light when Hindley's brother-in-law, David Smith, saw them kill 17-year-old Edward Evans with an axe. A left-luggage ticket then led to tapes and photographs of missing Lesley Ann Downey, aged 10. The couple had recorded her ordeal before killing her, burying the body on the Pennine Moors in the north of England. They also killed 12-year-old John Kilbride, and police are still searching the moors for the bodies of two other children.

Dutch buy Manhattan for a song

1626 A Dutch official named Peter Minuit today bought the 22 sq mile (57 sq km) island of Manhattan from local Indians. He certainly got a good deal. The Indians refused his gold and silver – they wanted knives, beads, trinkets, and accepted an offer of them to the value of only 60 guilders (£13/$24). In fact Manhattan has belonged to Holland since 1609 when Henry Hudson, at the commission of the Dutch, explored the Hudson River while seeking a route to the Orient. The first settlers arrived two years ago, when the new Dutch West India Company's first governor, Cornelis Mey, arrived with 30 families and founded the colony of New Netherland, stretching from Manhattan up the Hudson River. Minuit today named the settlement New Amsterdam and is building a fort there. Manhattan was first discovered 100 years ago by the Italian explorer Giovanni da Verrazano, who thought Delaware Bay was the opening to the Pacific.

1974 West German Chancellor Willy Brandt resigned from office today after an East German spy was found on his staff. Gunter Guillaume had worked for Brandt for four years, despite warnings that he was a security risk. Brandt became foreign minister in 1966 and West Germany's first Social Democratic chancellor in 1969. In 1971 he won the Nobel Peace Prize for his policies of establishing detente with the Communist bloc.

Scientists can clone Abe Lincoln's genes

1991 A team of geneticists at Johns Hopkins University was given permission today to clone genes from the remains of US president Abraham Lincoln, assassinated in 1865. They will work with blood stains, bone chips and samples of his hair still preserved. Lincoln is thought to have inherited Marfan's syndrome, characterized by tallness, long arms and a weak heart. The scientists want to test whether Lincoln really had it.

> *I let down my friends, I let down my country, I let down our system of government.*
> **Richard Nixon**, speaking today, 1977.

Watergate Pulitzer for Woodstein

1973 With US President Richard M. Nixon under increasing pressure to admit a White House cover-up, the *Washington Post* today won the Pulitzer Prize for the work of investigative reporters Bob Woodward and Carl Bernstein in exposing the Watergate scandal. Woodward and Bernstein – now widely known as "Woodstein" – have been relentless in unravelling the tangle of deceit behind the illegal break-in and wiretapping at the Democratic Party headquarters in the Watergate complex in Washington last June by Nixon re-election campaign members. A White House investigation concluded that administration officials were not involved, and six months after the break-in Nixon was re-elected in a historic landslide. But his credibility has been damaged as new revelations pushed the suspicion of complicity ever higher, right to the desk in the Oval Office where it was once said: "The buck stops here." A week ago, with his most senior aides resigning and facing indictment, Nixon again denied involvement. In 10 days the Senate starts its hearings on the affair.

NAZIS SURRENDER

1945 Nazi Germany surrendered to the Allies early this morning and the war in Europe ended. German chief of staff General Alfred Jodl signed the instrument of unconditional surrender at 2.40 am and delivered his nation "into the victors' hands, for better or worse," as he remarked. Jodl was met by Britain's General Montgomery, US chief of staff General Bedell Smith and Soviet General Suslapatov at General Eisenhower's headquarters, a small schoolhouse in Rheims, northern France. The Nazis have collapsed in the last two weeks as the Allies advanced on all sides. Adolf Hitler killed himself a week ago as his once-mighty war machine was swept away. Mussolini was shot two days earlier and a million German troops in Italy and Austria surrendered the next day, followed by the German armies in Holland, Denmark, north Germany and Norway. Europe lies shattered, but the Nazi horror is over, and victory in the East is only a matter of time.

> *I was the seventh of nine children. When you come from that far down you have to struggle to survive.*
> **Robert Kennedy**.

1888 An ex-bank clerk named George Eastman, 34, put a new kind of camera on the American market today with the sales pitch: "You press the button, we do the rest." Eastman's Kodak camera is a simple black box with a viewer, a lens, a lever for the film – and the button. It comes preloaded with enough of Eastman's new fast, flexible film for 100 pictures.

French Indo-China hopes dashed

1954 "We will not surrender," French General de Castries told army headquarters in Hanoi as Viet Minh insurgents overran the besieged fortress of Dien Bien Phu today. But almost the entire garrison of 16,000 men has been killed. The victory of the communist forces today marks the end of France's hopes of retaining her colonies in Indochina after eight years of war. The next step is the negotiating table. Meanwhile President Eisenhower has announced that the US would join in "united action" to prevent a communist takeover in Southeast Asia.

1663 The Theatre Royal in Drury Lane opens with a performance of *The Humorous Lieutenant* by Francis Beaumont and John Fletcher.

1763 American Indian Chief Pontiac attacks the English garrison at Detroit.

1823 In spite of his deafness, Beethoven conducts the first performance of his Ninth Symphony.

1832 Greece is declared an independent kingdom under British, French and Russian protection.

1847 The American Medical Association is founded.

1918 A peace treaty between Rumania and the Central Powers is ratified.

1926 The voting age for British women is lowered from 30 to 21.

1942 Japanese and American naval forces engage in the Coral Sea.

1943 Allied forces capture Tunis from the Germans.

1977 Ninety thousand tickets for Bob Dylan's concerts at Earl's Court in London sell out within only eight hours.

1988 Boston sees the first gathering of people who claim to have been abducted by aliens.

BIRTHDAYS

Robert Browning 1812, English poet who found popular success with works such as "The Last Duchess".

Johannes Brahms 1833, German composer who wrote piano and violin concertos, four symphonies, choral works and chamber music.

Peter Ilich Tchaikovsky 1840, Russian composer chiefly known for his ballets *Swan Lake* and *The Nutcracker*.

Gary Cooper 1901, American actor and heart throb who won Oscars for *Sergeant York* and *High Noon*.

Jimmy Ruffin 1939, American soul singer whose greatest hit was "What Becomes of the Broken-hearted".

1819 Death of King Kamehameha, who united Hawaii.

1819 Death of King Kamehameha, who united Hawaii.

1873 Death of the English economist, philosopher and reformer John Stuart Mill.

1849 In the first international yacht race, Bermudan boat *Pearl* beats the American *Brenda*.

1876 Death of Tuganini, the last Tasmanian aborigine.

1880 Death of French novelist Gustave Flaubert, author of *Madame Bovary*, *Salammbô* and *La Tentation de Saint Antoine*.

1921 Sweden abolishes the death penalty.

1924 Afrikaans becomes the official language of South Africa.

1945 Street parties are held all over Britain as VE Day is celebrated, marking the end of World War II in Europe.

1947 Department store magnate Harry Gordon Selfridge dies, leaving only £1544.

1955 Hiroshima victims arrive in the USA for plastic surgery.

1961 Former British diplomat George Blake is jailed for 42 years for spying for the Soviets.

1977 Dutch art dealer Peter Menten goes on trial in Amsterdam, charged with murdering Polish Jews in 1941 for financial gain.

1990 Estonia adopts its 1938 constitution and affirms independence.

BIRTHDAYS

Henri Dunant 1828, Swiss philosopher who was the inspiration behind the founding of the Red Cross.

Harry S. Truman 1884, American president who ordered the atomic bombing of Hiroshima and Nagasaki.

Sonny Liston 1932, American heavyweight boxing champion.

Peter Benchley 1940, American novelist best-known for *Jaws*.

Candice Bergen 1946, American actress who appeared in *The Group*, *Carnal Knowledge* and *Rich and Famous*, among other movies.

Peasant girl recaptures Orléans

1429 France's warrior maiden, Joan of Arc, today led the Dauphin's troops to victory over the English laying siege to Orléans. Clad in full armour, the inspired and inspirational peasant girl drove the Earl of Salisbury and his 5000 men back over the Loire. The English knights' goal is yet more French land, while Joan's army fought with the religious fervour of crusaders – which is what they are. Since she was 13, Joan has heard holy "voices" giving her the mission to rid France of the English. Today, still in her armour, Joan gave thanks to God for her victory, which turns the tide against the enemies from across the Channel.

Affair of the Hart ends Gary's bid

1987 Democratic front-runner Gary Hart withdrew his bid for the presidency today following allegations of marital infidelity. The *Miami Herald* reported Hart's alleged affair with Donna Rice, a 30-year-old model, with whom he was seen in Washington and on board a yacht named *Monkey Business*. Hart said today the press shouldn't pry into people's private lives – but public figures such as American presidential candidates who expect to have private lives are surely naive.

1902 The town of St Pierre on the Caribbean island of Martinique was obliterated within minutes today as the nearby Mt Pelee volcano erupted unexpectedly. Only two of the 30,000 inhabitants have survived. The volcano had shown increased signs of activity.

Any woman who understands the problems of running a home will be nearer to understanding the problems of running a country.
Margaret Thatcher, 1979.

Nazi criminals go unchallenged in UK

1991 A British government investigation shortly after World War II identified dozens of Nazi war criminals living in Britain – but no action was taken and the report was kept secret for 40 years. It detailed SS men, members of death squads and notoriously cruel and perverse death camp doctors among the 200,000 post-war East European immigrants to Britain. But the investigation, run by MI5 intelligence men, was not looking for Nazis but for Communist sympathizers – and potential Communist agents. The report came to light in the wake of the new War Criminals Act which became law this week. Home Secretary Kenneth Baker is expected to give the MI5 report to a police team at London's Scotland Yard which has already started investigating war criminals in Britain.

I have got an infamous army, very weak and ill-equipped, and a very inexperienced staff.
The Duke of Wellington, in a letter to Lord Stewart at the beginning of the Waterloo campaign today, 1815.

1200 LOST AS U-BOAT SINKS LUSITANIA

1915 The Cunard transatlantic liner *Lusitania* was sunk today off Ireland by German torpedoes when a U-boat struck without warning. Of the 1924 people aboard, 1200 are feared drowned, including at least 50 infants. The U-boat fired two torpedoes, and the huge ship, queen of the Cunard fleet, sank in 20 minutes. There is widespread outrage at the attack, particularly in neutral America – 120 of those missing are Americans, and they include associates of President Woodrow Wilson. When war broke out in Europe last August Americans, almost to a man, wanted nothing to do with it, and the President vowed to keep the US neutral. But US shipping has been harassed and in February the Germans threw a U-boat blockade around Britain, declaring all vessels fair game to torpedoes. Today the Germans said the *Lusitania* was carrying munitions, and that they had advertised in New York newspapers warning Americans not to sail on her. But public sympathy is strongly against them, and President Wilson has sent a furious protest to Germany, demanding reparations and an instant halt to unrestricted submarine attacks.

OSBORNE'S ANGRY REALITY

1956 *Look Back in Anger*, a first play about an angry young man by John Osborne, opened tonight in London to reviews that ranged from indignant through puzzled to dazzled. The critics had lots of nasty things to say about Jimmy Porter, the play's "hero", but he's not supposed to be likeable; Jimmy is an educated working-class youth with a middle-class wife,

and his bitter railings at the mindless manners, smug values and entrenched class system bring them both to grief. Heroes are obsolete in Jimmy's grey welfare-state Britain. Critic Kenneth Tynan said Jimmy represents post-war youth "as it really is", and called it "the best young play of the decade".

1978 All 90,000 tickets for Bob Dylan's forthcoming performances at Earls Court in London were sold out in just eight hours today. Dylan started a world tour in Japan in March, and the London show opens the European leg of the tour. For this tour Dylan has refashioned his 60s classics to make them suitable for an electric rock group and female chorus. He has included tracks from an attractive new album, Street Legal, which is currently edging its way towards the UK charts.

Australia opens showcase Parliament

1988 Australia's new Parliament House in Canberra was inaugurated today in a glittering ceremony attended by Australian prime minister Bob Hawke and Queen Elizabeth II of England. The House, which took over 10 years to build, has been planned as a showcase for Australian art, with many specially commissioned works from Australia's leading sculptors, painters and craftspeople incorporated into the fabric of the building. Most notable among these is a vast tapestry which dominates the Great Hall, covering the whole of the main wall. The tapestry, reproduced from a painting by Australia's premier artist, Arthur Boyd, was four years in the making by the Victorian Tapestry Workshop, which followed with minute precision every nuance of colour and change of line of Boyd's work. The inauguration comes 87 years to the day since Australia's first federal parliament met in Melbourne.

Yeah, some of them are about 10 minutes long, others five or six.
Bob Dylan, asked to comment on his songs in an interview, 1965.

"God" stands for election

1991 Despite temperatures of 113°F (45°C), ageing politician N. T. Rama Rao is drawing huge crowds at his campaign meetings in South India. The adoring crowds don't care about the weather, for in the minds of a great many voters Rao is an incarnation of God. This is because Rao, a famous film star, often plays a god – usually Rama, an incarnation of Vishnu, one of the two main Hindu gods. Riding the Rama ticket, Rao swept to power in the opposition Congress Party stronghold of Andhra Pradesh state eight years ago, becoming chief minister. Poor performance lost him the job, but, a string of hit movies later, his popularity is now vast. Rao claims he isn't seeking re-election only to oust the Congress Party from the state.

There aren't any good, brave causes left. If the big bang does come . . . it'll be about as pointless and inglorious as stepping in front of a bus.
John Osborne, from *Look Back in Anger*.

Daring theft of crown jewels

1671 An Irish adventurer, Colonel Thomas Blood, talked his way into the Tower of London tonight disguised as a priest. He smuggled in several armed accomplices and they made off with the crown jewels. They escaped from the Tower but were arrested soon afterwards and are now in jail, awaiting the pleasure of the jewels' rightful owner, His Royal Highness King Charles I.

Florence mourns brilliant tyrant

1492 Lorenzo the Magnificent, Medici ruler of Florence, has died aged 43 after a 23-year reign of unequalled cultural brilliance. Lorenzo, a poet himself, was patron of a circle of influential philosophers and poets such as Pulci and Politian and artists such as Domenico Ghirlandaio, Fra Filippo Lippi, Andrea del Verrochio, Leonardo da Vinci and Michelangelo; plus musicians and architects – all the great figures of the time. Lorenzo was a tyrant, but a most refined one, and his city mourns him.

1657 Death of Pilgrim Father William Bradford, Governor of Plymouth Colony in Massachusetts.

1805 Death of German poet and playwright Friedrich Schiller.

1887 Buffalo Bill's Wild West Show opens in London.

1903 French Post-Impressionist painter Paul Gauguin dies at his home on the Polynesian island of Hiva Oa.

1904 Death of Sir Henry Morton Stanley, British explorer and journalist who was sent to Africa to find Dr Livingstone.

1911 The British parliament agrees to Home Rule for Ireland.

1918 British troops block the German army's attack on Ostend, Belgium.

1926 American explorer Richard Byrd becomes the first person to fly over the North Pole.

1946 Victor Emmanuel III of Italy abdicates in favour of Prince Umberto.

1962 The Beatles sign a recording contract with EMI's Parlophone label.

1972 Israeli troops storm a hijacked jet at Jerusalem, freeing 92 passengers held hostage by Palestinian Black September terrorists.

1978 The body of kidnapped Italian statesman Aldo Moro is found in a car in central Rome. He had been shot 11 times.

1991 William Kennedy Smith, nephew of Senator Edward Kennedy, is charged with sexual battery.

BIRTHDAYS

John Brown 1800, American abolitionist.

J. M. Barrie 1860, Scottish dramatist best-known for *Peter Pan*.

Pancho Gonzalez 1928, American tennis player who won the US men's singles title eight times.

Glenda Jackson 1936, British actress whose films include the Oscar-winning *Women in Love* and *A Touch of Class*.

1811 Britain announces that paper money is to be legal tender to stave off an economic crisis.

1818 Death of Paul Revere, who made the famous ride from Charlestown to Lexington to warn militiamen of the approach of English troops.

1849 Katsushika Hokusai, the great printmaker legendary for his pictures of "the floating world" dies at 89, asking for "yet another decade".

1866 The American Equal Rights Association is formed.

1933 The Nazis begin burning books by "unGerman" writers.

1941 Hitler's deputy, Rudolph Hess, flies to Scotland to attempt peace talks but is imprisoned by the British.

1971 Pop group Jethro Tull play a gig in Denver in a cloud of tear gas after police fire canisters of the gas into the audience.

1973 American Indian activists end their 10-week takeover of Wounded Knee.

1977 Death of American film star Joan Crawford.

1981 François Mitterand becomes president of France on his third attempt.

1990 Robert Maxwell launches the first European newspaper – called *The European*.

BIRTHDAYS

John Wilkes Booth 1838, American assassin who ended the life of Abraham Lincoln.

Dimitri Tiomkin 1894, Russian composer who emigrated to the USA and wrote numerous film scores, notably *High Noon*, *The High and the Mighty* and *Gunfight at the OK Corral*.

Fred Astaire 1899, American actor, dancer and singer much loved for movies such as *Flying Down to Rio*, *Top Hat* and *Follow the Fleet*.

David O. Selznick 1902, American film producer whose most notable success was the classic *Gone with the Wind*.

1967 Mick Jagger and Keith Richard of The Rolling Stones appeared in court in Chichester today to face drugs charges. They were released on bail of £1000 each and will stand trial by jury at a later date. Meanwhile a third Rolling Stone, guitarist Brian Jones, was arrested today when his London apartment was raided by police. Jones will also face drugs charges.

Mandela sworn in

1994 Leader of the African National Congress party, Nelson Mandela, has been sworn in as the first president of a multi-racial South Africa. The ceremony took place in Pretoria after an overwhelming victory in last month's elections.

22 KILLED IN WAR OF WORDS

1849 Troops fired into a rioting crowd in New York City today, killing 22 and injuring 56. The crowd had gathered outside the Astor Place Opera House to revile British actor Charles Macready, who has openly scorned the vulgarity of Americans and American life. The mob was armed with clubs, paving stones and bricks.

Let he who is without sin jail the first Stone.
Protest poster as Rolling Stones members appear in court on drugs charges, 1967.

Churchill will fight

1940 Following furious argument in Parliament over military bungling in Norway, Winston Churchill has replaced Neville Chamberlain as British prime minister and is forming an all-party war government. Meanwhile news came that Adolf Hitler's troops had stormed Holland and Belgium. If Belgium falls, the Maginot Line, the main British defence, will be broken. In Westminster today rebel Tory MPs refused to back Chamberlain unless the opposition Labour and Liberal Parties were brought into an emergency government, but Labour refused to serve under Chamberlain, pre-war champion of appeasement with Hitler. Chamberlain then resigned in favour of Lord Halifax, the foreign secretary. But Labour MPs rejected Halifax in favour of Churchill. With Britain in dire peril, he promised his people nothing but "blood, toil, tears and sweat."

STONEWALL SHOT BY HIS OWN TROOPS

1863 The brilliant commander in the Confederate army General T. J. "Stonewall" Jackson is dead. Shot accidentally by his own troops eight days ago after inflicting a crushing defeat upon the Union army at Chancellorsville in northern Virginia, he developed pneumonia as a result of his wounds and died today. He was 39. Stonewall Jackson graduated from West Point, distinguished himself in the Mexican War and taught for 10 years at the Virginia Military Institute. He joined the Confederates in 1861. As their outnumbered forces fell back at the battle of Bull Run that July, Jackson stood firm – "like a stone wall", said General Barnard Bee – winning the day for the South, and his nickname. Consistently successful in battle, Jackson's death is a great loss to the South.

US railroad links east and west

1869 The east and west coasts of the US were linked today by a transcontinental railroad. Bands played and crowds of railwaymen cheered as the Central Pacific Railroad from the west, and the Union Pacific Railroad from the east, met in Utah. Telegraph messages flashed news of the link-up across the nation as the Governor of California brought a sledgehammer down on the final railway spike, made of gold – and missed. The 1776-mile (2858 km) track has taken three years of digging, bridge-building and tunnelling to complete.

REGGAE KING

1981 Bob Marley died today of cancer. He was 36. Marley grew up as a "rudeboy" in the Jamaican slums where reggae music and the Rastafarian cult have their roots. He and his group the Wailers dedicated their concerts to Ras Tafari, the late Ethiopian emperor Haile Selassie, held to be the one true God. Marley brought reggae and his religion to world attention. It is hard to believe that the man who made such irrepressible music has died.

Indians defy British rule

1857 Britain's Indian sepoy troops have mutinied in Meerut, killing their officers and every European they could find. Thousands are marching to seize Delhi. The uprising started after troops of the 3rd Bengal Cavalry were jailed for refusing to handle new supplies of cartridges because they are greased with cow fat – cows are sacred to Hindus. Muslim soldiers, meanwhile, say the bullets are greased with pig fat, which no Muslim would touch. There is widespread resentment over British rule, which has run roughshod over Indian sensibilities. British reforms such as banning child marriages and suttee (widow suicides) have raised an outcry, and a new measure last year requiring sepoys to serve overseas, thus losing caste, brought further discontent. The British commander at Meerut was warned of today's rebellion but did not believe it could happen and took no precautions.

Cyclone death toll mounts

1991 The death toll from the cyclone which has devastated Bangladesh is climbing towards 250,000. The entire coastal plain, millions of acres of fertile rice land, is underwater following fierce floods that swept away whole communities. Now, with millions of people marooned in the midst of the flood, there is no water to drink, no food, no shelter, no medical care, and little help on the way. Supplies are needed instantly – foreign aid has been promised, but not much has yet arrived, and getting it to those who need it is a massive problem.

Blitz batters London

1941 A pall of smoke hid the ruins as a badly shaken London emerged this morning from the worst bombing raids yet. At least 1400 people died as 550 German planes unloaded hundreds of bombs and more than 100,000 incendiaries over the city last night. Only 33 bombers were shot down. Many people are still trapped beneath the rubble as rescue teams fight to free them. The damage is immense: the House of Commons, Westminster Hall, Westminster Abbey, the British Museum and all the big railway stations are badly damaged. St Paul's Cathedral was hit, but still stands. German radio announced the raid was a reprisal for the bombing of German cities. London has now lost a total of 20,000 killed in the Blitz and a further 25,000 have been injured.

CATS PURRING

1981 A new musical opened in London today – another immediate hit for composer Andrew Lloyd Webber. This show is different, even for the eclectic Lloyd Webber. *Cats* is a ballet-musical, setting T. S. Eliot's playful poems in *Old Possum's Book of Practical Cats* to Lloyd Webber's music, sung by a sinuously agile cast in vivid feline make-up. The score includes some good songs that could be hits, like "Memory", sung by Grizabella the Glamour Cat. Other characters are suave feline felon Macavity, Rumpleteazer, and the Jellicle Cats, who "are black and white and come out at night". As in *Jesus Christ Superstar* and *Evita*, Lloyd Webber hits all the right notes in *Cats*. It's a lot of fun – and that's what musicals are for.

> *Dangers by being despised grow great.*
> **Edmund Burke**, British politician, in a House of Commons speech today, 1792.

1778 Death of William Pitt (the Elder), first Earl of Chatham, British statesman known as the Great Commoner.

1812 British prime minister Spencer Perceval is shot dead in the House of Commons by bankrupt John Bellingham.

1824 The British capture Rangoon, using a steamship in war for the first time.

1858 Minnesota becomes the 32nd US state.

1900 US world heavyweight champion Jim Jeffries knocks out former champion James J. Corbett in New York after 23 rounds.

1904 Australian diva Nellie Melba signs a recording contract with the Gramophone Company.

1927 Spanish Cubist painter Juan Gris dies in Paris, where he has lived since 1906.

1956 Elvis Presley first enters the UK charts with "Heartbreak Hotel".

1960 The world's longest liner, SS *France*, is launched at St Nazaire by General de Gaulle.

1985 The main stand at Bradford City football ground in northern England catches fire, killing 40 and injuring more than 170.

1988 Kim Philby, former British intelligence officer who spied for the Soviets, dies in Moscow aged 76.

BIRTHDAYS

Irving Berlin 1888, Russian-born American composer of musical comedies and film scores.

Martha Graham 1893, American ballet dancer and choreographer, one of the most influential teachers of modern dance.

Salvador Dali 1904, Spanish Surrealist painter known as much for his megalomaniac exhibitionism as for the quality of his work.

Phil Silvers 1912, American comedian known for his role as Sergeant Bilko.

Eric Burdon 1941, British rock singer who had hits with the group The Animals before going solo.

1870 Canada purchases the Red River Colony (Manitoba) from the Hudson Bay Company.

1884 Bohemian composer Bedrich Smetana dies in an asylum for the insane.

1932 The kidnapped baby son of aviator Charles Lindbergh is found dead.

1935 Alcoholics Anonymous is founded in Akron, Ohio by William Wilson.

1937 The coronation in London of King George VI and Queen Elizabeth is broadcast live worldwide by the BBC.

1943 The Axis powers in North Africa surrender.

1957 Death of Erich von Stroheim, German-born actor and director.

1963 Bob Dylan refuses to appear on the *Ed Sullivan Show* on the grounds that the show is too square.

1969 The minimum voting age in Britain is lowered from 21 to 18.

1991 The first multi-party general election since 1959 is held in Nepal.

2003 A triple suicide bomb attack in Riyadh, Saudi Arabia, kills 34 people.

BIRTHDAYS

Edward Lear 1812, English artist and poet who wrote the *Book of Nonsense* for the grandchildren of his patron, the Earl of Derby.

Florence Nightingale 1820, English nurse whose experiences in the Crimean War led her to become a hospital reformer.

Dante Gabriel Rossetti 1828, English poet, painter and co-founder of the Pre-Raphaelite Brotherhood.

Gabriel Fauré 1845, French composer and organist best-known for his songs and his *Requiem*.

Burt Bacharach 1929, American composer whose collaboration with Hal David produced hits such as "Walk on By" and "What's New, Pussycat?"

USSR unblocks Berlin

1949 The Soviet Union has called off its blockade of Berlin after more than a year. Today cheering crowds in the four-power city met the first food convoy to arrive by road from the West. The former capital is entirely surrounded by Russian-occupied Germany. The Russians had closed the roads, stopped the trains and banned food imports from the Soviet sector in protest at the Western Allies' plans to create an independent republic in West Germany. Britain and America beat the blockade with a round-the-clock airlift, with up to 200 flights a day ferrying food and supplies to the city. Moscow agreed to lift the siege following negotiations at the United Nations.

IRISH REBEL LEADERS SHOT

1916 The leaders of the Easter Rising in Ireland have all been executed. General Sir John Maxwell announced that James Connolly, last of the seven Republican Brotherhood leaders who proclaimed an Irish Republic on Easter Monday, was shot today. He had been wounded, and was taken on a stretcher to face the firing squad. General Maxwell has refused to give up the body of writer Patrick Pearse, the rebel leader, for a Catholic burial, saying he did not want to create a martyr. Trouble has been mounting since the new Home Rule Bill was passed four years ago. However, the rebellion was swiftly suppressed.

1971 Rolling Stones singer Mick Jagger married a beauty from Nicaragua, Bianca Perez Morena de Macias, in a Roman Catholic ceremony at St Tropez in the south of France today. Paul McCartney, Ringo Starr and Eric Clapton were among the guests. Jagger met Bianca after a Rolling Stones concert in Paris six months ago. The Stones moved to France recently as tax exiles.

India's population hits one billion

2000 News that India's one-billionth citizen had been born was officially announced in Delhi today. In a ceremony at the Safdarjung hospital, the baby girl was presented to the media, one Astha Arora. India's government is using the occasion to highlight the problems of an expanding population. With ever increasing poverty, diminishing natural resources, illiteracy and unemployment, the government is trying to encourage smaller families. The United Nations has warned that India may face problems with food and water shortages in the near future if the population rise does not slow. The increasing population hampers all India's attempts at progress. One civil servant summed up the occasion by saying that while the event was a matter of joy for the family, it provided a moment of reflection for the government.

If you feel in a plight, to his journal you write
And get reparation in full.
So you'll all say with me, Good luck to H.B.
And continued success to John Bull.

Pantomime song, on Horatio Bottomley's magazine *John Bull*, which started publication today, 1906.

General Strike fails

1926 Britain's Trades Union Council has called off the General Strike that has brought the nation to a virtual halt for the last nine days. A bare skeleton of essential services kept the country going after public transport, rail, ports, post, supplies and industry as a whole simply stopped on May 4. Police barricaded vital centres and there were armoured cars on city streets as the army escorted convoys of emergency supplies. The middle classes, from students to City men (and their wives), volunteered at the official Organisation for the Maintenance of Supplies to drive lorries or sort mail. Meanwhile the miners' strike continues with the sympathy of the TUC.

Hard times ahead for new settlers

1607 Captain Christopher Newport sailed his three ships into Chesapeake Bay today to found a British colony. The newly chartered London Company's first colonists named the settlement Jamestown after King James I. However, some of the 104 settlers foresee problems ahead. Most of the settlers are gentlemen, unused to the hard manual labour required if the colony is to be secure. Most of the provisions were used up on the voyage and it is now too late to plant crops. The Company instructed the colonists to search for gold and find a route to the Pacific – but they may have to wait.

> *I used to say that politics was the second lowest profession and I have come to know that it bears a great similarity to the first.*
> **Ronald Reagan**, on the run-up to the presidential campaign trail, on this day, 1979.

Pope in Vatican shooting

1981 A crowd of 20,000 people in St Peter's Square in Rome today saw Pope John Paul II shot four times by a Turkish gunman. The Pope, in his white open-top jeep, was blessing the crowds during his weekly audience when the gunman opened fire, hitting the Pope and wounding two other people. The gunman was arrested as the jeep sped to safety. After a five-hour operation the Pope was declared out of danger and is expected to recover fully. The gunman, Mehmet Ali Agca, 23, had escaped from Turkey where he was apparently being held for murder. He shot the Pope in protest at "American and Russian imperialism".

US and Mexico at war

1846 The US declared war on Mexico today. Congress has authorized $10 million in war funds and the recruitment of 50,000 troops, blaming Mexico for the hostilities. The two countries have been doing battle around the Rio Grande for the past 10 days, and yesterday Mexican troops crossed the river. This was the excuse President James Knox Polk was waiting for – Mexico's aggression had shed American blood on American soil, he said. However, Washington has provoked this war. Mexico refuses to sell its Californian territory to the US at any price, and Polk now intends to take the area by force. In a deliberately provocative move, he sent General Zachary Taylor into Mexican territory at the Rio Grande in March, and today's declaration is the inevitable result.

1891 London drama critic Jacob Grein's new "free" theatre had its opening performance tonight – but audience and critics alike hated the play he chose. Norwegian playwright Henrik Ibsen's *Ghosts* might well be the brilliant theatre Grein says it is, but revelations of infidelity, incest and syphilis are just not what people go to the theatre to see.

Rivera mural drives New York up the wall

1933 The massive mural commissioned for the RCA Building, centrepoint of New York's huge new Rockefeller Center, has been destroyed. The painting, by the renowned Mexican artist Diego Rivera, so outraged New York society that Nelson Rockefeller, who commissioned Rivera for the job, asked him to remove it. He refused, so Rockefeller fired him and had the mural scraped off. The painting, *Man at the Crossroads*, showed man's progress through technology to a proletarian utopia, and included a large portrait of Lenin, father of the Russian Revolution. New Yorkers say a bastion of capitalism such as the Rockefeller Center is hardly the place for a portrait of Lenin.

1830 The republic of Ecuador is created on the break-up of the original state of Gran Colombia.

1835 Death of John Nash, English architect who was commissioned by King George IV to redevelop parts of London including Regent Street and Trafalgar Square.

1844 Spain establishes a military peacekeeping force known as the Guardia Civil.

1930 Death of Fridtjof Nansen, Norwegian explorer, zoologist and statesman who was the League of Nations' high commissioner for refugees, in which capacity he introduced the Nansen passport for displaced persons and won the Nobel Peace Prize in 1923.

1958 Right-wing French settlers, backed by the military, seize government buildings in Algiers as 40,000 demonstrators take to the streets to demand independence.

1971 On his 21st birthday, American musician Stevie Wonder receives $1 million as his childhood earnings - although he actually earned more than $30 million.

1989 British ex-pilot Jackie Mann is kidnapped in Beirut.

1990 A car bomb in Bogotá, Colombia, kills 26.

BIRTHDAYS

Josephine Butler 1828, English social reformer who campaigned for women's rights.

Sir Arthur Sullivan 1842, English composer who wrote 16 operettas with librettist W. S. Gilbert.

Georges Braque 1882, French painter who was, with Picasso, the joint creator of Cubism and was the first living painter to have his work exhibited in the Louvre.

Dame Daphne du Maurier 1907, English writer whose novels include *Rebecca*, *Frenchman's Creek* and *Jamaica Inn*.

Joe Louis 1914, American world heavyweight boxing champion known as the "Brown Bomber".

Jack Bruce 1943, British pop musician best-known as a member of the group Cream.

1796 British physician Edward Jenner carries out the first successful vaccination against smallpox.

1801 Pasha Yusuf Karamanli of Tripoli declares war on the US.

1804 Meriwether Lewis and William Clark set out from St Louis to find an overland route to the Pacific.

1847 HMS *Driver* arrives at Spithead on the south coast of England, completing the first round-world voyage by a steamship.

1900 The second modern Olympic Games open in Paris – and this time women are allowed to compete.

1948 Atlantic Records is founded in the USA by Ahmet Ertegun, son of the Turkish ambassador to the USA.

1955 The Eastern bloc signs the Warsaw Pact.

1956 A British frogman disappears while bugging the underside of President Khruschev's warship in Portsmouth.

1959 American jazz saxophonist Sydney Bechet dies on his 65th birthday.

1968 French workers go on a one-day strike to support demonstrating students.

1987 A coup takes place in Fiji, aimed at curbing the influence of Indian migrants in government.

1990 Anti-Semitism resurfaces in France with the desecration of a Jewish grave at Carpentras cemetery.

BIRTHDAYS

Thomas Gainsborough 1727, English painter of portraits, landscapes and sentimental rural genre scenes.

Otto Klemperer 1885, German conductor particularly renowned for his interpretations of Beethoven symphonies.

Bobby Darin 1936, American pop singer who reached the charts with "Splish Splash" and "Mack the Knife".

Fanatical monk stabs king

1610 France's Good King Henry IV was murdered today as he rode in his carriage in Paris. A fanatical Catholic monk, François Ravaillac, jumped on to the carriage wheel when the coach stopped in the traffic and plunged a dagger into the King's chest. Ravaillac's aim was to stop the King's planned war against Catholic Spain and Austria. Henry ended 50 years of religious war in France and won wide popularity through his reconstruction of the devastated country. He is succeeded by his son, Louis XIII, who is eight.

Goldwyn back in the big time

1939 Hollywood film producer Sam Goldwyn took control of United Artists today after buying out Charlie Chaplin, Mary Pickford and Douglas Fairbanks, who founded the movie corporation in 1919 with director D. W. Griffiths. Goldwyn sold his interest in Metro-Goldwyn-Mayer (MGM) in 1924, and has since been an independent producer. He is currently producing *Wuthering Heights* with director William Wyler. A Polish immigrant, Goldwyn is famous for his unusual turn of phrase.

1973 Space exploration entered a new era today as the US space station *Skylab 1* blasted off for orbit. Successive three-man crews will live on the space station for weeks on end. *Skylab* is the converted third stage of a Saturn 5 rocket.

Israel born in fire

1948 With eight hours still to run before the British mandate in Palestine runs out, the torn nation's 400,000 Jews today proclaimed the Zionist state of Israel and threw open the doors to Jewish immigrants, banned since 1944. US president Harry Truman immediately recognized the Jewish state. Meanwhile battle raged on between Jews and Arabs in a civil war that has claimed thousands of lives this year, and the Arab armies ranged around the new state prepared for invasion. With Britain's troops withdrawing, the 30,000-strong Jewish defence, Haganah, is on a full-scale war footing. After centuries as a scattered, persecuted nation, the Jews' determination is fearsome.

> *Every director bites the hand that lays the golden egg.*
> **Sam Goldwyn**, film producer, 1939.

Mighty Nile succumbs to progress

1964 Egypt's president Gamal Abdel Nasser and the Soviet premier Nikita Khrushchev today pressed a button, a huge sand barrier exploded and the River Nile changed its course. The river had to be diverted to build the next stage of the Aswan High Dam which is being funded by the USSR. It will cost $1 billion, but the dam will turn nearly a million acres of desert into irrigated farmland and will double Egypt's electricity output. Work started four years ago and the huge wall – 17 times the size of the Great Pyramid – will be finished in 1970. The dam will create a lake 6 miles (9.5 km) wide and 350 miles (503 km) long, displacing about 100,000 people – and inundating many of the ancient sites of the Pharoahs. Egypt has put the needs of the people before its historic remains. However, an international appeal is raising funds to have the temples and tombs moved to safety.

Goodbye to ol' blue eyes

1998 Veteran singer Frank Sinatra died today after a sparkling career spanning 60 years of show business. He first shot to fame in the 1930s singing in various popular bands but it was his 1954 album *Songs for Young Lovers* with which he established a major following. He will be perhaps best remembered for his hits *New York New York* and *My Way*. Sinatra was also a successful film star, winning an Oscar for his performance in *From Here to Eternity*. He starred in many other movies, including *High Society* with Grace Kelly.

1718 London lawyer James Puckle patents the machine gun.

1800 One James Hatfield attempts to assassinate King George III at Drury Lane Theatre, London.

1829 The US Congress designates the slave trade as piracy.

1833 Death of English actor Edmund Kean, who had his first big success as Shylock in *The Merchant of Venice*.

1895 Death of Joseph Whitaker, English publisher of *Whitaker's Almanac*.

1918 The world's first regular air mail service begins between Washington and New York.

1930 The first-ever air hostess, registered nurse Ellen Church, takes care of 11 passengers on a flight from Oakland, California to Cheyenne, Wyoming.

1936 Aviator Amy Johnson arrives in England after a record-breaking flight from London to Cape Town and back.

1957 Britain's first H-bomb is dropped on Christmas Island in the Indian Ocean.

1987 American actress and dancer Rita Hayworth dies after suffering from Alzheimer's disease.

1988 The USSR begins evacuating troops from Afghanistan.

Medics take to the skies of Oz

1928 Medical care went airborne in Australia today with the launching of a Flying Doctor Service. Dr K. St Vincent Welch of the Australian Inland Mission launched the service, to cover the vast area of Central Australia and Queensland. A DH50 aircraft and a pilot have been provided by QANTAS – the Queensland and Northern Territory Aerial Service. Dr Welch will be called to emergency cases by means of a radio transmitter-receiver with a 300-mile (482 km) range. He is based in Cloncurry and will serve 250,000 square miles (647,500 sq km) of the Australian outback – previously covered by only 10 doctors.

1990 Lindi St Clare, retired brothel keeper – previously known by her professional name of Miss Whiplash – today lost a 15-year legal battle against Britain's Inland Revenue, who had sued her for back taxes. She had refused to pay, supposedly for the Inland Revenue's own protection, claiming it would mean the government department would be breaking the law by living off immoral earnings. Today the judge ruled against her.

Brooklyn opens baseball grounds

1862 A new kind of sports field opened today in Brooklyn. The Union Grounds are exclusively for baseball. The game has become immensely popular in the US since the Knickerbocker Baseball Club was organized in New York 20 years ago and formal rules were drafted. Up to now, baseball has been played at recreation grounds, race courses, or anywhere available. With the Union Grounds the game comes of age.

Soviets and Chinese thaw icy relations

1989 Soviet leader Mikhail Gorbachev shook hands with China's leader Deng Xiaoping in Peking's Great Hall of the People today, breaking the ice in the long-standing quarrel between the two nations that has split the Communist world. But the historic occasion was upstaged by the extraordinary events that deliberately occurred just outside the Great Hall as half a million Chinese gathered in Tienanmen Square demanding democratic reform. The demonstrations, which started last month, are led by student protesters, some 3000 of whom are on hunger-strike. So far the demonstrations have been peaceful. China's leaders have been severely embarrassed in front of the Soviet leader by today's massive demonstrations. To the chinese leader they constitute a great loss of face.

Governor George gunned down by White assassin

1972 George Wallace, Governor of Alabama, is fighting for his life in a Washington hospital after an assassination attempt earlier today. Wallace, known for his racist and segregationist policies, was campaigning for the Democratic Party's presidential nomination in Maryland when a young white man shouted "Hey George" – and fired five shots at him at close range. Wallace was hit in the stomach, leg and in the spine. Doctors are confident Wallace will survive the shooting, but fear his spinal cord may have been damaged and he could be paralysed. The gunman, Arthur Bremer, 21, was arrested at the scene.

Frank Baum 1856, American children's author best-known for *The Wonderful Wizard of Oz*.

Katherine Anne Porter 1890, American writer mainly of short stories, whose only novel, *Ship of Fools*, won a Pulitzer Prize in 1962.

Joseph Cotton 1905, American actor whose films included *Citizen Kane* and *The Third Man*.

James Mason 1909, English actor who appeared in more than 80 films.

Mike Oldfield 1953, British composer and instrumentalist who had a big hit with *Tubular Bells*.

MAY 16

BIRTHDAYS

Edith for PM

1991 France has its first woman prime minister. Socialist president François Mitterand announced today that Edith Cresson will replace the unpopular Michel Rocard, who has been dismissed. Mrs Cresson's appointment gives Mitterand's government a new élan and, yes, glamour which were distinctly lacking. "Life is hellish for a woman in politics unless she is elderly and ugly," she told an interviewer today. Cresson is neither of those – she's an elegant redhead of 57 and doesn't look at all like a grandmother, though she is one. She is also a tough customer. Mitterand dubbed her his "little soldier" because of her record for taking on the worst tasks and winning. Cresson was Minister for European Affairs, and previously for Trade. She has pushed an aggressive trade policy to put France's exports on the map. Now she faces a recession and rising unemployment – and the task of rallying a sagging socialist vote before the next elections. But Cresson appears to relish the prospect.

1929 Paramount's *Wings* won the award for best film of the year today in a glittering ceremony as Hollywood presented its new Academy Awards for achievement in the movie industry. Janet Gaynor was Best Actress for her role in *Seventh Heaven*, and German Emil Jannings won Best Actor for *The Way of All Flesh*. Douglas Fairbanks presented the 12-inch (30 cm) gold-plated statuettes of a naked man plunging a sword into a film reel. The Academy was founded two years ago by Louis B. Mayer and other producers to enhance the prestige of the American film industry.

Derby crosses Atlantic

1875 A large crowd watched jockey Oliver Lewis ride Aristides to victory today in the maiden event of a prestigious new annual race, the Kentucky Derby, held at Churchill Downs in Louisville. The organizers intend the Derby to be one of the premiere Thoroughbred races of the American season, along with the Preakness Stakes at Pimlico in Maryland, now in its third year, and the Belmont Stakes at Jerome Park, New York, running since 1867. Horse-racing, the ancient sport of kings, is now the most popular spectator sport in America, with big prizes in the Thoroughbred stakes.

Bouncing bombs skip like stones

1943 The Ruhr Valley, the industrial heart of Nazi Germany's war machine, was crippled tonight by two RAF bombs. The raid breached two huge dams, the Mohne and the Eder, sending walls of water down the valley, sweeping away everything in their path. Dortmund and Mulheim ground to a halt, their steel plants swamped and the coal mines flooded. The Eder dam, the biggest in Europe, is still emptying. The low-flying Lancaster bombers dropped special bombs that bounced like skipping stones over the surface of the dams and sank behind the walls before exploding. Bombing the walls the conventional way was useless – they were simply too strong. The British aircraft designer Dr Barnes Wallis had the idea of bombing the inside of the walls, since explosions under water have much more force. With this in mind he designed his special bouncing bombs. The cost of tonight's raid to the RAF's 617 Squadron was heavy – sadly less than half the bombers returned. But the pilots' lives were not lost in vain – the cost of the raid to Germany is incalculable.

> *Men are not in any sense irreplaceable, except in one's private life.*
>
> **Edith Cresson**, who became France's first woman prime minister today, 1991.

Van Gogh knocked down for highest ever price

1990 A Japanese businessman paid $82.5 million for a Van Gogh in New York today, the highest price ever paid for a painting at auction. Paper manufacturer Ryoei Saito was the successful bidder for *Portrait of Dr Gachet* at Christie's (whose commission was included in the price). It was one of Van Gogh's last paintings before he shot himself. Mr Saito has not yet finished his buying spree – he is planning to attend Sotheby's New York sale tomorrow, and is said to have his eye on the superb *Au Moulin de la Galette*, Renoir's famous painting of models and artists at a Montmartre dance hall, which critics say could fetch almost as much as the Van Gogh did today.

Botticelli dies unsung

1510 The great Florentine painter Sandro Botticelli has died in his native Florence aged 65. Botticelli had hardly painted in recent years, and lived in poverty. He was at the height of his career when the downfall of his Medici patrons in 1494 brought disaster, in the shape of the Black Friar, Girolamo Savonarola. The Black Friar preached that art was immoral, and also accused Botticelli and Leonardo da Vinci of sodomy. After they were acquitted Leonardo left Florence, but Botticelli stayed, and suffered. Botticelli was the foremost of a new wave of Italian artists. He was only 25 when he was noticed by Lorenzo de' Medici, under whose patronage he did some of his finest work, including *The Birth of Venus*. He was taught by master of perspective Fra Filippo Lippi and sculptor Andrea del Verrocchio.

> *Writing free verse is like playing tennis with the net down.*
> **Robert Frost**, American poet, in a speech at the Milton Academy today, 1935.

Watergate secrets go public

1973 America watched in fascination as televised Senate hearings on the Watergate affair opened today. Senator Sam J. Irvin, Democrat of North Carolina, virtually accused the Watergate burglars of trying to steal America's "right to vote in a free election" when he opened public sessions of the Senate Select Committee on Presidential Campaign Activities. White House denials that President Richard M. Nixon's administration knew about the break-in at Democratic Party headquarters last June have worn thin as the scandal unfolded. A week ago senior Nixon aides John Mitchell and Maurice Stans were indicted for perjury. Today's first witness testified that Nixon's re-election campaign leader, Jeb Magruder, had hidden vital papers within hours of the burglary. Tomorrow one of the burglars, James McCord, takes the stand.

1861 The first colour photograph is exhibited at the Royal Institution in London.

1890 *Comic Cuts*, the first weekly comic paper, is published in London by Arthur Harmsworth.

1935 Death of Paul Dukas, French composer, teacher and critic, best-known for his orchestral scherzo *The Sorcerer's Apprentice*.

1962 Hong Kong puts up its own "Berlin wall" to keep out migrants.

1964 Bob Dylan makes his first major London appearance at the Albert Hall.

1969 Dubliner Tom McClean rows from Newfoundland to Ireland, becoming the first person to cross the Atlantic in a rowing boat.

1978 Charlie Chaplin's coffin is found 10 miles (16 km) from the Swiss cemetery from which it was stolen on March 2.

1989 The communist government of Czechoslovakia frees playwright Vaclav Havel after only three months of a nine-month jail term.

1993 Rebecca Stephens is the first woman to climb Everest.

2003 Casablanca, Morocco, is ravaged by terrorist bombs.

Churchill's ghost voice

1990 US speech researchers say they have proof that three of Winston Churchill's most famous wartime speeches were recorded by an actor. They are the promise to the nation of nothing but "blood, toil, tears and sweat", the Dunkirk rallying call "We shall fight on the beaches, in the fields, in the streets and in the hills", and the "finest hour" speech predicting the Battle of Britain. Churchill made the speeches himself in parliament, but the famous words broadcast to the public and sent to the US to rally war support were recorded in the BBC studios. Actor Norman Shelley long ago claimed he had done the job because "Churchill was too busy". This was recently confirmed by a BBC archivist. Researchers at Sensimetrics in Cambridge, Massachusetts, tested Churchill's speeches with a computerized system they developed for verifying tapes used as court evidence – and said the speeches in question were "quite different" to Churchill's.

Mafeking relieved - euphoria in Britain

1900 Extraordinary scenes of rejoicing have swept across Britain as a cable from South Africa brought news that the 217-day siege of the British garrison at Mafeking has been broken. London's streets filled with huge crowds of revellers as the tide turned in the Boer War following a humiliating string of defeats for the British forces. Reinforcements under Lord Roberts attacked the Boers from two sides, overwhelming the besieging army. Hero of the day is cavalry officer Colonel Robert Baden-Powell, the British commander in Mafeking. His unwielding defence tied down thousands of Boer troops and he has captured the British imagination.

1861 A party of British workers and their families set off from London for Paris today on a new kind of holiday. Overland travel, the Channel crossing, hotel accommodation and meals all come in one convenient "package", arranged by Thomas Cook of London. Packaged holidays, offered to groups, are cheaper – Cook buys the tickets and hotel coupons in bulk and passes on the discounts to clients.

BIRTHDAYS

Erik Satie 1866 French composer famed for his eccentricities and for the nonsensical titles he gave to his compositions.

Maureen O'Sullivan 1911, Irish actress who played Jane in six Tarzan movies.

Birgit Nilsson 1918, Swedish operatic soprano best-known for her roles as Brunnhilde, Turandot, Salome and Elektra.

Dennis Hopper 1936, American actor and director who first came to prominence with Peter Fonda in *Easy Rider*.

Grace Jones 1955, Jamaican-born model turned pop singer with a menacingly decadent and androgynous image.

Sugar Ray Leonard 1956, American boxer who has won world champion welterweight, light middleweight and middleweight titles.

1652 Slavery is banned in Rhode Island.

1803 Britain abandons the Treaty of Amiens, signed only the year before, and declares war on France.

1832 In Paris, French novelist George Sand publishes her first novel, *Indiana*, in which she makes a plea for women's right to independence.

1909 Death of British poet and novelist George Meredith.

1909 Death of Isaac Albéniz, Spanish composer and pianist best-known for *Iberia*, a collection of 12 piano pieces.

1954 The European Convention on Human Rights comes into effect.

1981 Death of American poet, playwright and novelist William Saroyan.

1987 Iraqi Exocet missiles hit the US naval frigate *Stark*, killing 26 – Baghdad says it is an accident.

1991 Muriel Box, British writer, feminist publisher and director of many films including *Rattle of a Simple Man* and *The Happy Family*, dies aged 85.

BIRTHDAYS

Nicholas II 1868, Russian tsar who was forced to abdicate at the beginning of the Revolution and was subsequently executed.

Bertrand Russell, 3rd Earl Russell 1872, British philosopher, mathematician and pacifist, winner of the Nobel Prize for Literature in 1950, who claimed that "longing for love, the search for knowledge and unbearable pity for mankind" were the ruling passions of his life.

Frank Capra 1897, Italian-American director whose films include the Oscar-winning *It Happened One Night* and *You Can't Take It With You*.

Dame Margot Fonteyn 1919, British ballerina whose most famous performances were in partnership with Rudolph Nureyev.

Rick Wakeman 1949, British pop musician.

MAHLER DIES

1911 Gustav Mahler, the inspired Austrian conductor and composer, has died of a heart disease. He was 51. Mahler had been expecting to die since he learned of his condition four years ago, yet he kept up a busy touring schedule in Europe and in New York, where he is a favourite. His Ninth Symphony is so charged with emotion that many find it over-powering. Mahler always tended towards the magnificent: his symphonies are long works requiring huge orchestras, music on a monumental scale not heard before. They are awe-inspiring, but only the Second Symphony has yet gained any popularity. Mahler was born a Jew, but converted to the Catholic faith to qualify as conductor of the Vienna Court Opera. His 10 years in the post are already seen as a high point of the art and his early death is an immense loss to German music.

This island is almost made of coal and surrounded by fish. Only an organizing genius could produce a shortage of coal and fish in Great Britain at the same time.
  Anuerin Bevan, opposition Labour politician, in a speech at Blackpool, 1945.

1990 In the face of strong Soviet disapproval, West and East Germany took the first step towards unity today when their two finance ministers met in Bonn to sign a formal accord on monetary union. From July 1 the two countries will have one currency – West Germany's deutschmark.

1975 Unstoppable Japanese climber Junko Tabei was today the first woman to reach the summit of the world's highest peak, the treacherous 29,078 ft (8863 m) Mount Everest in Nepal.

It is neither fitting nor safe that all the keys should hang from the belt of one woman.
  Thomas Brinton, Bishop of Rochester, on the influence of the unscrupulous Alice Perrers over her ageing lover, King Edward III, 1376.

Casey hits 100

1988 Said to be the world's most often recited poem, the epic baseball classic "Casey at the Bat" had its 100th anniversary today. It was first recited in a New York theatre on May 18, 1888 by William Hopper, a popular musical comedy actor. He repeated the recital more than 10,000 times, up to his death in 1935. The poem tells the story of a mighty baseball hero's downfall. It was written by a 25-year-old Harvard man, Ernest L. Thayer, who sold it to the *San Francisco Examiner* for $5.

India goes nuclear

1974 India exploded a nuclear device in the Rajasthan desert today. Prime Minister Indira Gandhi issued a statement saying the underground blast was for peaceful purposes, but experts on nuclear proliferation say India could be close to developing a military bomb – and it has the jets and missiles to deliver it. Today's test blast will create nervousness across the border in Muslim Pakistan, which was severely beaten four years ago in the third war between the two nations.

Napoleon claims crown

1804 Napoleon Bonaparte is to be crowned Emperor of France, 11 years after the Revolution guillotined King Louis XVI, ending the monarchy. Napoleon was asked to take the throne in a petition by his senate following the outcry in February over a royalist attempt to assassinate him. He has ruled as a virtual king since he was made consul for life two years ago, when a referendum brought him more than three million votes with only a few thousand against him. Napoleon has built a new order in France which has revolutionized law, education, industry and government, balanced the budget, restored the economy and established France as the major world power, and the French love him for it.

Anne Boleyn goes to the block

1536 Anne Boleyn, English King Henry VIII's second wife, was beheaded in London today. She was 29. She had been charged with incest with her brother and four counts of adultery, but her real crimes were to let the king tire of her, and to fail to bear him a male heir. She gave birth to a daughter, Elizabeth, soon after they were married three years ago. Earlier this year Henry had her arrested after the stillbirth of a boy. He had meanwhile become infatuated with Anne's lady-in-waiting, Jane Seymour, and with Anne out of the way, an immediate marriage is planned. Henry's first wife, Catherine of Aragon, died in January. When she failed to bear him a son he tried to have the marriage annulled, and when Pope Clement VII refused Henry broke with the Roman church so that he could marry Anne. In fact they had already married in secret.

The ballot is stronger than the bullet.
Abraham Lincoln, in a speech on this day, 1856.

1982 The Italian actress Sophia Loren was jailed today for tax evasion. She will spend a month in a women's prison near Naples. Loren, 47, had not paid £2500 ($4600) in tax in 1970 – "through a little error", she said. She must also pay a large fine.

MT ST HELENS EXPLODES

1980 At least 15 people were killed today when a long-dormant volcano in the US exploded. About 400 people were evacuated earlier when Mt St Helens in south-western Washington State started smoking a few weeks ago, but geologists did not expect the sudden violence of today's eruption, which started fires, mudslides and floods in areas thought to be safe. About 120 square miles (310 sq km) are devastated. The volcano is sending up a huge column of smoke and ash, darkening the sky 100 miles (160 km) away. It last erupted in 1857.

Jackie Kennedy to be reunited with John

1994 Jacqueline Kennedy Onassis has died today and will be buried next to her former husband President John F. Kennedy in Arlington National Cemetery. During her time as First Lady, Jackie became known for her fashion sense and her decoration of the White House. She was honoured for her dignity after the assassination of her husband in 1963. She went on to marry wealthy Greek shipping magnate Aristotle Onassis in 1968, then became a publishing editor after his death seven years later.

Lawrence of Arabia dies

1935 Retired hero T. E. Lawrence died today, five days after sustaining a fractured skull in a road accident. He was racing his motorcycle down a Dorset lane when he swerved to avoid two boys on bicycles and crashed. He never regained consciousness. During World War I Lawrence of Arabia won popular fame as the dashing young intelligence officer who led the Arabs in a guerrilla war against the Turks and finally captured Damascus. In 1922 he dropped from sight, changing his name to Shaw and joining the Tank Corps and then the RAF. Lawrence unsuccessfully championed the Arab cause at the Paris Peace Conference in 1919. Though his friend Sharif Hussein of Mecca had fought for Arab independence and was backed by Britain, the Arab lands emerged as British and French colonies. Maybe this was what Lawrence meant when he told Irish writer W. B. Yeats: "I was an Irish nobody. I did something. It was a failure. And I became an Irish nobody again." Lawrence refused to publish his book on Arabia, *Seven Pillars of Wisdom*, in his lifetime. It will now be published posthumously.

1312 After a fortnight's siege at Scarborough Castle in Yorkshire, Piers Gaveston, favourite of King Edward II, is taken prisoner.

1649 England is declared a Commonwealth by the Rump Parliament.

1795 James Boswell, biographer of Dr Samuel Johnson, dies at the age of 54.

1802 Napoleon institutes the title Légion d'honneur, which will be the highest honour awarded for civil and military distinction.

1864 Death of Nathaniel Hawthorne, American novelist and short story writer.

1898 British statesman William Gladstone, elected Liberal prime minister four times, dies aged 88.

1900 The 169 islands collectively known as the Kingdom of Tonga, or the Friendly Islands, become a British protectorate.

1906 The 12-mile (19 km) Simplon Tunnel linking Italy and Switzerland through the Alps is officially opened.

1954 Death of American experimental composer Charles Ives.

1971 Death of American humorist Ogden Nash.

1984 Poet Laureate Sir John Betjeman, gentle social satirist, dies aged 78.

1991 Helen Sharman, the first Briton in space, blasts off with two Soviet cosmonauts for a rendezvous with the Soviet Mir space station.

BIRTHDAYS

Dame Nellie Melba 1848, Australian operatic singer of world renown

William Waldorf Astor, 2nd Viscount 1879, English politician and proprietor of the *Observer*.

Ho Chi Minh 1890, North Vietnamese revolutionary leader.

Malcolm X 1926, American Black Muslim leader.

Edward de Bono 1933, British doctor who developed the concept of lateral thinking.

Pete Townshend 1945, British guitarist with pop group The Who.

1347 Popular Roman leader Cola di Rienzo, having gained the support of the people against the nobles, attempts to restore Rome as a republic.

1588 The Spanish Armada sets sail from Lisbon on its mission to conquer the English.

1609 The sonnets of dramatist William Shakespeare are published.

1802 France restores slavery and the slave trade in her colonies.

1867 Queen Victoria lays the foundation stone of the Albert Hall in London.

1895 In the USA, income tax is declared unconstitutional.

1939 In London, approximately 200,000 people attend the first Chelsea Flower Show, held in the grounds of the Royal Hospital.

1939 Pan-American Airways begins its first commercial flights between the USA and Europe.

1956 Death of British caricaturist and writer Sir Max Beerbohm, author of *Zuleika Dobson*.

1970 The Beatles' film *Let It Be* is premiered in London.

1975 British sculptor Dame Barbara Hepworth is killed by a fire in her St Ives studio.

2002 East Timor celebrates as it gains independence from Indonesia and becomes a new nation.

BIRTHDAYS

William Thornton 1759, American architect who created the Capitol in Washington.

Honoré de Balzac 1799, French novelist whose life's work was the cycle *La comédie humaine*.

John Stuart Mill 1806, English philosopher, economist and social reformer.

William Fargo 1818, American co-founder of the freight-carrying company Wells Fargo.

James Stewart 1908, American actor whose many films include the Oscar-winning *The Philadelphia Story*.

Cher 1945, American singer and actress.

Jet travel murders Orient Express

1961 The "king of trains and the train of kings", the once-luxurious Orient Express, set off from Paris today on its final journey to Istanbul. From its inauguration in 1883 until World War II stopped the service, the Orient Express was renowned as the epitome of luxury travel. It was used as the background to Graham Greene's *Stamboul Train* in 1932, and two years later was the setting for one of Agatha Christie's famous murders. Sadly, since the route reopened after the war, the standard of service has not been that preferred by kings – and these days, they fly.

China crisis

1989 Martial law was declared in Peking today as huge demonstrations calling for reform continue to shake China. Peking seemed to be in the control of the people as more than a million demonstrators gathered in support of pro-democracy student campaigners on hunger strike in Tienanmen Square. The campaign of mass defiance has spread to other major cities. The demonstrations started last month following the death of former party chairman Hu Yaobang, who was seen to be in favour of reform. Two days ago talks between the students and government leaders failed. But so far the protests have been peaceful.

1823 An estimated 100,000 people jammed the Union Course on Long Island today to see a horse race with a difference – and a purse of no less than $20,000. Sir Henry, a top Southern horse, was the challenger against American Eclipse, champion horse in the North, over three heats. Sir Henry lost the first heat, won the second – and lost the third. The result has caused widespread gloom in the Southern states.

World fails to end as comet passes

1910 Thousands of people prepared for the world's end today as the Earth passed through the fiery tail of Halley's Comet. In America, "comet pills" have been on sale, claiming to offer protection against the comet's effects, and miners refused to work, not wanting to die underground. Many people stayed at home to meet the end with their families. The comet lit up the night sky, passing its closest to the Earth today – 13 million miles away. The comet was first observed in 1682 by the English astronomer Edmond Halley, who predicted it would return every 76 years.

1979 A 23-year-old British nurse, Helen Smith, was found dead in Jeddah today, having apparently fallen six floors from the balcony of a flat. A drinks party was being held there by surgeon Richard Arnot, in breach of Saudi law. There are rumours that the death may not have been accidental.

COLUMBUS STILL BELIEVED IN ASIA

1506 Christopher Columbus died today at Valladolid in Spain, virtually penniless, and still believing he had reached Asia. He was 55. The Spanish court, 14 years later, still had not paid him the royalties owed him from his discoveries in the New World. Columbus spent seven years persuading Spain's Queen Isabella I to finance an expedition to search for a westward route to the Orient. Three months after leaving Europe his three ships reached the Bahamas. Columbus sailed back and forth across the Atlantic on three further voyages, none successful. On the third voyage he was returned to Spain in chains for having seven rebellious settlers hanged, and on his last voyage he was marooned on Jamaica for a year. But he was a master mariner: his discovery of favourable winds in both directions opened up the New World to European exploitation.

Solitary spirit of Lindbergh

1927 Charles Lindbergh landed his plane in Paris this evening to win the $25,000 prize for the first solo flight across the Atlantic. A crowd of 100,000 turned out to welcome the 25-year-old American pilot in his specially-built plane, the *Spirit of St Louis*, as it landed at Le Bourget airport. Lindbergh took off from Roosevelt Field in Long Island early yesterday and was in the air for 33 hours and 40 minutes. He learned to fly five years ago and was flying a mail run between Chicago and St Louis when he heard about the prize money on offer. Now he is an international hero. US president Calvin Coolidge is sending a Navy cruiser to take him back to the US.

1966 Cassius Clay is still The Greatest – British contender Henry Cooper failed to deprive him of the world heavyweight boxing title tonight. Clay knocked down Cooper in the sixth round in a bout in London.

Liberty is so much latitude as the powerful choose to accord to the weak.
Billings Learned Hand, US federal judge, in a speech at the University of Pennsylvania Law School today, 1944.

1924 Two Chicago teenagers kidnapped and murdered 14-year-old Bobby Franks – for "thrills". Richard Loeb and Nathan Leopold, both 19 and sons of millionaires, were arrested and have now confessed all.

1471 King Henry VI of England dies in the Tower of London, probably the victim of murder instigated by King Edward IV.

1542 Spanish explorer Hernando de Soto, the first European to cross the Mississippi, dies on the return journey.

1553 Lady Jane Grey, great-granddaughter of Henry VII, is forced to marry Lord Guildford Dudley, son of the Duke of Northumberland, who has ambitions for the throne of England.

1618 Death of Italian physician Hieronymous Fabricius ab Aquapendente, who discovered one-way valves in veins.

1804 Pere Lachaise cemetery is opened in Paris.

1840 New Zealand is proclaimed a British colony.

1894 Queen Victoria opens the Manchester Ship Canal.

1975 The Baader-Meinhof terrorist gang goes on trial in Stuttgart.

1990 Ion Ilescu wins the first free elections in Romania.

2000 Death of Sir John Gielgud, aged 96, an actor and director for almost 80 years. He was admired for his melodic speaking voice; his most famous role was Hamlet.

2003 More than 2,000 people die as a massive earthquake hits Algeria.

RAJIV GANDHI ASSASSINATED

1991 Rajiv Gandhi is dead. The former prime minister of India was blown up by a woman terrorist suicide bomber at an election rally in South India this morning. He was 46. Gandhi's party, campaigning in the general election, had just arrived in the small town of Sriperumbudur, where party officials and well-wishers rushed forward to greet him with garlands. A young woman knelt to kiss his feet, and as Gandhi stooped to help her up a powerful bomb strapped to her body exploded, killing both of them and many others. Sri Lanka's Tamil Tigers militants are suspected, since Gandhi's Congress Party plans to close down the Tigers' camps in India, but they have denied the charge. Rajiv Gandhi became India's prime minister when his mother, Indira Gandhi, was assassinated by her bodyguards in 1984. He had been an airline pilot and entered politics when his brother Sanjay, groomed for power, died in an air crash in 1980. The leaderless Congress Party is now in disarray.

Suharto resigns

1998 Indonesia is preparing for a new political era as President Suharto resigns after 32 years in power. His Vice-President, BJ Habibie, has been sworn in as the new president. The news was greeted by cheering from protesting students. Suharto had been under escalating pressure both at home and from abroad to step down amid the country's worst political and economic crisis since he came to power. During the televised announcement he asked "for forgiveness if there were any shortcomings."

Agincourt victor to rule France

1420 King Henry V of England is now ruler of France too, in terms of the Treaty of Troyes signed today. The agreement comes four years after Henry's spectacular victory at Agincourt and he hopes it will ensure "perpetual" peace between the two countries. The treaty means that Henry can now marry the French princess Catherine de Valois, and that he will become king on Charles de Valois' death. The English and French cultures are not expected to merge. One problem remains: who will succeed Henry? The Salic Law in France does not allow a woman to rule France. Unless Henry and Catherine produce a male heir, the French throne will again be occupied by a Frenchman.

The House of Lords is a model of how to care for the elderly.
Frank Field, British politician, 1981.

---

337 AD Constantine the Great, who in 313 AD issued the Edict of Milan which established toleration of Christians, is baptized on his deathbed, becoming the first Roman emperor to convert to Christianity.

1455 In the first battle of the English Wars of the Roses, the Yorkists are defeated by the Lancastrians at St Albans.

1795 Scottish explorer Mungo Park sets forth on his first voyage to Africa.

1885 French novelist, dramatist, poet and national literary hero Victor Hugo dies in Paris aged 83.

1915 A troop train collides with a passenger train at Gretna Green in Scotland, killing 227 people.

1932 Death of Irish dramatist Lady Augusta Gregory who, with W. B. Yeats, founded the Irish Dramatic Movement, a theatre company that moved into the Abbey Theatre in Dublin in 1904.

1972 Richard Nixon becomes the first US president to visit the USSR.

1974 After seeing Bruce Springsteen and the E. Street Band at Charley's Club in Cambridge, Massachusetts, rock critic Jon Landau writes "I saw rock and roll future – and its name is Bruce Springsteen".

1981 Peter Sutcliffe, nicknamed the "Yorkshire Ripper" is found guilty at London's Old Bailey of the murder of 13 women and the attempted murder of seven others.

1990 New Zealand boats take the first three places in the Whitbread Round the World yacht race.

BIRTHDAYS

Richard Wagner 1813, German composer famed for the operatic cycle *Der Ring des Nibelungen*.

Sir Arthur Conan Doyle 1859, Scottish novelist who created the great detective Sherlock Holmes.

Laurence Olivier 1907, British actor, producer and director of such stature he was made a peer of the realm, the only actor ever to be honoured in this manner.

WRIGHTS PATENT FLYING MACHINE

1908 Wilbur and Orville Wright patented their flying machine today, four years after their historic first powered flight at Kitty Hawk in North Carolina. That day the "Flyer I" made four flights, the longest lasting a minute and covering 852 ft (259 m). Today they still use the same machine, very much improved, to make flights of 40 minutes, travelling up to 25 miles (40 km) at altitudes of 150 ft (46 m) or more. Strangely the brothers are hardly known in America, except to a few hundred enthusiasts. But now their pioneering work is starting to bear fruit: last year the US Army Signal Corps contracted the Wrights to build a two-man aircraft capable of flying 125 miles (201 km), and later this year the brothers are to take their aircraft on tour in France – hence today's patent.

Rebels drive out Ethiopian president

1991 Ethiopian president Mengistu Haile Mariam fled to Zimbabwe today as rebel forces closed in on the capital, Addis Ababa. Mengistu's long civil war is largely held to blame for the environmental ruin which brought the famines of the 1980s. When Mengistu's Marxist regime came to power 40 per cent of Ethiopia was forested, but today only a tiny fraction of the trees are left and huge areas are uninhabitable. Mengistu spent $9 billion on Soviet arms to put down rebellions in Eritrea, Tigray and Oromo in the north, while only 3 per cent of the budget went to Ethiopia's farmers. The Ethiopian People's Revolutionary Democratic Front rebels now on the verge of victory, however, have worked with western agencies to help peasants and protect the environment in the areas they controlled.

British apologize over slur on Saudis

1980 British foreign secretary Lord Carrington publicly apologized to ultra-conservative Saudi Arabia today for a film shown on Britain's Independent Television last month. The film, *Death of a Princess*, investigated the public execution of a Saudi princess convicted of adultery. The Saudis are incensed by the film's allegations of loose living behind the strictly orthodox face of the Sunni Muslim state. In spite of a formal British apology, the Saudi Arabian Council of Ministers threatened to expel the British ambassador, break off diplomatic relations and use the immense Saudi oil wealth to apply economic measures.

1921 The Flying Finn, Paavo Nurmi, who won two gold medals at last year's Olympics in Antwerp, broke the world 10,000 metres record in a race in Stockholm today – knocking 18 seconds off the old record set 10 years ago.

US rebel chief tracked down

1865 In the aftermath of the US civil war, Jefferson Davis, the fugitive president of the defeated Confederate states, was caught today by Union cavalry colonel Benjamin Pritchard in Irwinville, Georgia. He was disguised as a woman. There is the handsome reward of $100,000 for his capture to collect: President Andrew Johnson has publicly accused Davis of complicity in President Lincoln's assassination. Davis fled from Virginia last month as the confederacy collapsed, with the intention of organizing a government in exile. He is now awaiting indictment in prison at Fort Monroe.

USA to USSR

1972 In a historic moment, Richard M. Nixon arrived in Moscow today, the first US president ever to visit the USSR. He was met by Soviet leader Leonid Brezhnev. The two world leaders will hold talks on arms limitation and the avoidance of military confrontation. Nixon's policy of detente with the communist world is beginning to bear fruit – the Strategic Arms Limitation Talks (SALT) that he started with the Soviets in 1969 have resulted in agreements that the two leaders will sign during Nixon's week in Moscow. He is also expected to address the Soviet people on television.

> *One is short of all-male preserves in present-day England.*
> **Roger Hearn**, member of the Marylebone Cricket Club, London, on this day, 1991.

PIRATE HANGS

1701 Captain William Kidd was hanged for piracy and murder in London today. His trial and sentence were widely publicized in an attempt to deter other seamen from hoisting the Jolly Roger and preying on merchant ships. Kidd, 56, was commissioned as a British privateer to wage war on Spanish and French ships, and became a wealthy man. Five years ago he turned to piracy, taking rich prizes off the coasts of Africa. Thinking his commission would protect him, Kidd returned to Long Island with his fleet, but he was arrested in Boston shortly afterwards and brought to London for trial. Mystery surrounds the proceeds of Kidd's buccaneering – most of his booty has simply vanished.

Sun loses libel case to 6-year-old

1991 A disabled English boy, six-year-old Jonathan Hunt, today won "substantial" libel damages from the *Sun* newspaper – which had dubbed him "the worst brat in Britain". He is the first British child to sue for libel. In an article in July 1989, the *Sun* said that Jonathan had set the furniture alight, cut his ear off, killed the cat in the washing machine, painted the dog blue and swallowed insecticide, amongst various other crimes. The newspaper failed to mention that the child is registered as disabled by behavioural problems caused by acute neo-natal meningitis. A letter of complaint from his mother, Josephine, yielded a visit by another *Sun* feature writer – which was followed by an even worse article, this time headlined "Living with Britain's naughtiest boy". In the High Court today the *Sun* apologized to Josephine and her son profusely – and paid compensation. How much was not disclosed.

Violent end for criminal couple

1934 Bank robbers and murderers Bonnie Parker and Clyde Barrow died in a hail of bullets today when they drove their car into a police ambush in Louisiana. More than 50 bullets hit the pair, police said. Parker and Barrow have terrorized the southwestern US during the last four years, killing 12 people in a series of armed raids on small-town banks and gas stations. Barrow was 25, and Parker 23.

1977 Armed South Moluccan terrorists took the 161 occupants of a Dutch passenger train at Assen and teachers and children at a school at nearby Bovensmilde hostage today. They are demanding independence for their homeland, now part of Indonesia.

Sea success for Da Gama

1498 The Portuguese navigator Vasco da Gama arrived at Calicut on India's Malabar coast today after almost a year, the first European to reach the Indies by sea. Da Gama sailed his four ships south from Lisbon to the Cape of Good Hope at the tip of Africa, and then up Africa's east coast. The sultan of Mozambique thought the voyagers were Muslims and gave them pilots for the journey north, but hostile Arabs attacked them at Mombasa. Da Gama's reception in Calicut could have been warmer: the gifts he took ashore today were more suited to Africa, and Calicut's ruler rejected them. Arab traders have tried to turn the Indians against their Portuguese rivals.

Nazi Eichmann caught in Israel

1960 Israeli prime minister David Ben-Gurion announced today that Nazi war criminal Adolf Eichmann has been captured and will stand trial in Israel. Eichmann, the "technician of death", was in command of the Gestapo section charged with exterminating the Jews and supervised the network of death camps where six million Jews died. He escaped at the end of the war. Reports in Israel claim that Nazi hunter Simon Wiesenthal tracked Eichmann down in Argentina, where he was living under the name Ricardo Klement. Israeli agents then kidnapped him and brought him back to Tel Aviv in an official plane. Wiesenthal, who lost 89 relatives in the Holocaust, has helped bring hundreds of Nazis to trial.

1498 Italian religious reformer Girolamo Savonarola is hanged and burnt at the stake for heresy by his political rivals.

1795 In Paris, troops put down an uprising caused by bread shortages.

1863 Death of American frontiersman Kit Carson.

1873 The North West Mounted Police are formed in Canada.

1887 The French crown jewels go on sale, raising six million francs.

1925 British publishing magnate Sir Edward Hulton dies after falling off his penny farthing bicycle.

1945 Heinrich Himmler, Adolf Hitler's minister of the interior, commits suicide.

1948 The *Empire Windrush* sets sail from Jamaica with the first boatload of West Indian immigrants invited to Britain to help with post-war reconstruction.

1988 Two Danish divers marry on an underwater reef in Mauritius, using divers' language to sign their vows to a Mauritian civil servant in a glass-bottomed boat.

1990 Death of Rocky Graziano, American boxer who was world middleweight champion in the 1940s.

1991 Chinese authorities mark the fortieth anniversary of their "liberation" of Tibet with low-key celebrations.

BIRTHDAYS

Carl Linnaeus 1707, Swedish botanist who established the principles for classifying and naming plants and animals.

Sir Charles Barry 1795, English architect who designed the Houses of Parliament.

Douglas Fairbanks 1883, American actor who specialized in swashbuckling roles.

Joan Collins 1933, British actress who had her biggest success in the television series *Dynasty*.

Richard Moog 1934, American inventor of the Moog synthesizer.

Anatoly Karpov 1951, Russian chess champion.

MAY 24

1689 The English parliament passes the Act of Toleration for the relief of Dissenters.

1809 Dartmoor Prison is opened in England to house French prisoners of war.

1814 Pope Pius VII, exiled by Napoleon Bonaparte, returns to Rome.

1833 Brooklyn Bridge is opened.

1856 American anti-slavery campaigner John Brown leads the Free-Staters in a massacre of the pro-slavers at Pottawatamie Creek.

1862 London's Westminster Bridge is opened.

1959 Death of John Foster Dulles, US secretary of state under Eisenhower.

1973 In Britain, Lord Lambton and Earl Jellicoe resign from the government in a call girl/security scandal.

1988 Snow falls on the Syrian desert and on Damascus for the first time in 50 years.

BIRTHDAYS

Gabriel Fahrenheit 1686, German physicist who invented the mercury thermometer.

Jean Paul Marat 1743, French politican, radical journalist and physician.

Queen Victoria 1819, English monarch whose ideas of duty and discipline influenced the nation for nearly a century.

Sir Arthur Wing Pinero 1855, British dramatist who wrote highly successful farces and, later, more serious plays about contemporary social problems.

Jan Smuts 1870, South African statesman and general, twice prime minister.

Suzanne Lenglen 1899, French tennis player who won the women's singles title at Wimbledon eight times.

William Trevor 1928, Irish novelist and and playwright.

Bob Dylan 1941, American rock musician.

COPERNICUS TURNS HEAVENS UPSIDE DOWN

1543 As he lay dying today, the canon of Frauenberg cathedral in Poland was brought the first copy of a treatise he has written that overturns church doctrine on man's place in the universe. According to Nicolaus Copernicus, our world is not the centre about which all else in the heavens turns, as Aristotle and Ptolemy claimed. His book, *On the Revolutions of the Heavenly Spheres*, claims that the Earth and the other planets revolve round the sun – which itself doesn't stay in one place. The universe, he says, is much bigger than was thought – and man's place in it is far from central. In fact Copernicus's scheme of things sounds very plausible. The book is bound to cause immense controversy. Copernicus is aware of this – he first wrote about his theories in 1514, but was very discreet about them.

Hard man Robespierre cheats death twice

1794 French revolutionary leader Maximilien Robespierre survived the second attempt on his life in two days when 25-year-old Cécile Renault tried to assassinate him today. Robespierre, a slight man with a reedy voice, wields the power of life and death in France. He demanded the execution of King Louis XVI and of the moderate Girondists, and his election to the Committee of Public Safety last year has brought bloody repression as he eliminated rival factions.

Private Eye's Ed. may be a banana

1989 A British jury today awarded libel damages of £600,000 ($1,110,000) to Sonia Sutcliffe, wife of sex killer Peter Sutcliffe, the "Yorkshire Ripper", against the satirical magazine *Private Eye*. *Private Eye* had said Mrs Sutcliffe had sold a newspaper the story of her marriage for £250,000 ($462,500). The magazine will appeal against the award – the highest in British legal history. Editor Ian Hislop commented, "If this is justice, I'm a banana."

1941 The Royal Navy's pride, the 42,000-ton battleship HMS *Hood*, has been sunk in a duel with the German battleship *Bismarck* in the North Atlantic. Nearly all the crew of 1400 have drowned.

> *The Catholic Church has always refused and continues today to refuse to make the market the supreme regulator and almost the model or synthesis of social life.*
> **Pope John Paul II**, on this day, 1991.

Duke leaves legacy of pure genius

1974 Duke Ellington, one of the greatest of all jazz musicians, has died of lung cancer. He was 75. Perhaps more than any other musician, Ellington helped bring jazz out of the black ghettoes of America and put it on the world map – it was through Ellington, Fletcher Henderson and Count Basie and their syncopated big-band arrangements that most white Americans first heard jazz. Ellington won popularity in New York when his 11-piece band took up residence at the famous Cotton Club in Harlem in 1927, and live broadcasts from the club soon made the unique Ellington sound famous. Virtually all the jazz greats have played with Ellington, who usually wrote special pieces to show off their skills. With some 3000 works to his credit, he is now acknowledged as America's greatest composer. Three years ago he toured Europe, Russia and Latin America, and his *New Orleans Suite* was awarded the title of record of the year.

Marx lunacy goes celluloid

1929 After six years on Broadway, the anarchic lunacy of the Marx Brothers now has movie audiences roaring. "Your eyes shine like the pants of my blue serge suit," leers Groucho Marx round his cigar in *The Coconuts*, premiered in New York tonight. Fast-talking Groucho (born Julius) with his bushy eyebrows and thick black moustache, Chico (Leonard), who mostly plays an Italian, Harpo (Adolph), who plays the harp but doesn't say a word, and fourth brother Zeppo (Herbert) who provides romantic relief, get full Marx for zaniness. The brothers are now making a film version of *Animal Crackers*, which opened on Broadway last year. The big money is in the movies – more than 80 million Americans go to the country's 23,000 cinemas every week. As Groucho says in *The Coconuts*, "What's a thousand dollars? Mere chicken-feed – a poultry matter."

1951 Two British diplomats have gone absent without leave in London. Both Donald MacLean and Guy Burgess had held senior Foreign Office positions in Washington. It is understood that police in Europe have been alerted, with checks in countries bordering the Soviet bloc. The Foreign Office has refused to comment.

Hot air as temperatures rise

1990 British prime minister Margaret Thatcher today warned of the dangers of global warming and pledged Britain to a 30 per cent reduction in carbon dioxide emissions, which are thought to be the main cause of global warming. The pledge breaks stride with the Bush administration, which has refused to commit itself, calling first for further research on the problem. But environmental groups are saying Mrs Thatcher's 30 per cent cut is not nearly enough. A United Nations report published today concludes that worldwide emissions of carbon dioxide, methane and chlorofluorocarbons will have to be cut by 60 per cent to stabilize atmospheric concentrations at current levels – which are already too high and continuing to esacalate. The report warns of global temperature increases of 2° F in 35 years, and 6° F by the end of the next century, with potentially disastrous consequences. The report was approved by scientists representing 39 countries.

Owens' record busting day

1935 Jesse Owens, a 21-year-old black student athlete from Alabama, set five new world records and equalled a sixth this afternoon – a world record in itself for a single day's achievement. In fact, Owens did it all in a single hour. He equalled the 100 yards record, then set new records for the long jump, 220 yards and 220-yard hurdles, relentlessly breaking the 200 m records on the way.

Monkey business

1925 Press men and religious sects both converged on the courthouse in the small Tennessee town of Dayton today to see the local schoolteacher, John T. Scopes, stand trial for teaching Darwin's theory of evolution. Tennessee passed a law two months ago outlawing Darwin and anyone else who contradicted the Bible's version of creation, but Scopes defied the new law. High drama is assured in the "Monkey Trial", as it is being called.

THOR'S REED ADVENTURE

1969 Intrepid Norwegian diffusionist Thor Heyerdahl and a seven-man crew from all over the world set sail today to cross the Atlantic in a reed boat named *Ra* after the Sun God of the Pharaohs. Heyerdahl, famed for his *Kon-Tiki* expedition across the Pacific in a balsa-wood raft the experts said would sink, now aims to prove that the ancient Egyptians sailed to America, which would account for the New World's pre-Columbian pyramids. His new craft was built by traditional boat-builders from Chad, using 12 tons of papyrus reeds. *Ra* sailed today from the old Moroccan port of Safi. Once again, the experts are predicting that the reed boat will sink.

History is more or less bunk. It's tradition. We don't want tradition. We want to live in the present and the only history that is worth a tinker's damn is the history that we make today.
Henry Ford, on this day, 1916.

Americans start to draft constitution

1787 A rather special group of Americans met in the State House in Philadelphia today to set about writing a new constitution for the United States. Among them are George Washington, hero of the Revolution; the Philadelphia lawyer John Dickinson, who helped draft the first constitution; the indomitable Benjamin Franklin, Pennsylvania's president, now 81; Alexander Hamilton of New York, at 32 a distinguished soldier and famous lawyer; Virginia leader James Madison, master of republican theory; and several dozen other brilliant men. The meeting was called because Congress faces bankruptcy and the states are alarmed by Shays's Rebellion earlier this year. The uprising by bankrupt farmers showed the need for a stronger central government, but under the Articles of Confederation the government has no control over commerce and cannot raise taxes or enforce its own laws.

1768 Captain Cook sets forth from England in his ship the *Endeavour* on a voyage to explore the Antipodes.

1850 The first hippopotamus ever seen in Britain arrives as an exhibit for London zoo.

1934 Death of Gustav Holst, British composer best-known for the orchestral suite *The Planets*.

1938 Alicante is bombed by General Franco's aircraft as his Falangists fight a bitter civil war against the Republicans.

1950 French troops clash with Viet Cong guerrillas in Vietnam.

1959 The US supreme court rules that Alabama's ban on boxing matches between black and white is unconstitutional.

1961 The Ku Klux Klan clash with civil rights "Freedom Riders" in Montgomery, Alabama.

1965 Heavyweight boxer Cassius Clay knocks out Sonny Liston in the first round of their fight at Lewiston, Maine.

1986 Worldwide, 30 million people run a "Race Against Time" for Sport Aid to raise money for the starving in Africa.

1986 South African troops drive 25,000 blacks out of Crossroads squatter camp.

BIRTHDAYS

Ralph Waldo Emerson 1803, American poet and essayist.

Bill "Bojangles" Robinson 1878, American tap dancer who appeared in several films including *Stormy Weather*.

Gene Tunney 1898, American heavyweight boxing champion.

Miles Davis 1926, American trumpeter and composer who had a huge influence on jazz music.

Beverley Sills 1929, American operatic soprano who became director of the New York City Opera when she retired from singing.

Sir Ian McKellen 1938, British stage and screen actor.

Paul Weller 1958, British pop singer with groups Jam and the Style Council.

735 AD The Venerable Bede, English scholar, monk, historian and writer, dies shortly after completing his translation of St John into Anglo-Saxon.

1660 King Charles II of England lands at Dover after a nine-year exile.

1791 The French Assembly forces Louis XVI to hand over the crown and state assets.

1805 Napoleon Bonaparte is crowned King of Italy in Milan Cathedral.

1908 A major oil strike is made in Persia, the first in the Middle East.

1942 British prime minister Winston Churchill signs a military pact with Russian leader Joseph Stalin, who promises him "close collaboration after the war".

1969 John Lennon and Yoko Ono begin a "bed-in" for world peace and invite the media to film them in Room 1742 of the Hotel de la Reine, Montreal, Canada.

1975 American stuntman Evel Knievel suffers severe spinal injuries in Britain when he crashes while attempting to leap 13 buses in his car.

1988 Andrew Lloyd Webber's musical *Cats* opens in Moscow with a British and American cast.

BIRTHDAYS

John Churchill, Duke of Marlborough 1650, English statesman and general.

Al Jolson 1886, American singer and entertainer who starred in the first movie with sound, *The Jazz Singer*.

John Wayne 1907, American actor who appeared in more than 250 flms, winning an Oscar for *True Grit*.

Peter Cushing 1913, British actor best-known for his roles in horror films such as *The Curse of Frankenstein* and *Dracula*.

Peggy Lee 1920, American singer, songwriter and actress with a distinctive smoky voice.

James Arness 1923, American actor noted most for his role in the television series *Gunsmoke*.

US Civil War over: half a million dead

1865 The last organized resistance in the US civil war ended today when General Kirby Smith surrendered Confederate forces west of the Mississippi. Resistance east of the Mississippi ended on May 4, following General Robert E. Lee's surrender to Ulysses S. Grant at Appomattox on April 9. The Confederate navy still holds the port of Galveston in Texas. The war has torn America: half a million are dead and the South is crippled. President Lincoln's death is a severe loss to the post-war healing process; he called for generous reconciliation in his last speech, three days after Appomattox. President Andrew Johnson is instigating plans for amnesty and to bring the rebel states back into Congress.

Pepys leaves coded diaries

1703 Samuel Pepys, a distinguished public servant in King Charles II's government, has died at the age of 70. He was twice secretary of the admiralty, and was elected to Parliament in 1679. He was interested in science, and became president of the Royal Society in 1684. He was forced into retirement when William III took the throne. Pepys leaves a diary which friends say ought to be published. It is a lively, very candid account of daily London life from 1660 to 1669, when Pepys stopped writing, fearing for his eyesight. But Pepys was nothing if not prudent – his diaries are written in code.

The history of the World is the World's court of justice.
Freidrich von Schiller, German dramatist, on this day, 1789.

I am not like a lady at the court of Versailles, who said: "What a dreadful pity that the bother at the tower of Babel should have got language all mixed up, but for that, everyone would always have spoken French."
Voltaire, French dramatist, in a letter to Catherine the Great, Empress of Russia, 1767.

Impeached president just survives defeat

1868 The US senate today found impeached US president Andrew Johnson not guilty – by only one vote. On February 21 Johnson defied last year's Tenure of Office Act, which Congress passed over his veto last year, by firing secretary of war Edwin M. Stanton – who refused to go, barricading himself in his office. Three days later Congress voted to impeach the president. The Senate trial began on March 13 – though the charges fell short of the "high crimes and misdemeanours" required for impeachment. Southern Democrat Johnson's main crime was reconstructing the defeated rebel states "according to his own will". Republican congressmen demanded much tougher measures. It is their "Radical Reconstruction" plans that are now going ahead.

French win new 24-hour race

1923 Watched by large crowds French drivers Lagache and Leonard won the new Le Mans 24-hour endurance race today, covering 1373 miles (2209 km) at an average speed of 57 mph (92 kph). The drivers were paired, taking turns at the wheel. Motor-racing has come far since the first race in 1894 between Paris and Rouen, when the winner averaged 14 mph (22.5 kph) over the 78-mile (125.5 km) course. Open-road racing was banned in Europe following an accident in 1903. The Le Mans track opened in 1906, and there are now circuits in most western countries.

MAKESHIFT NAVY EVACUATES BRITISH FROM DUNKIRK

1940 A strange armada of more than 700 boats set sail from Britain across the English Channel today as virtually everything that would float made for the beaches at Dunkirk in France to rescue 380,000 trapped Allied troops. The awesome Nazi war machine has taken just 10 days to sweep aside Allied defences in France and Belgium. In a lightning push through the Ardennes, German troops cut off the retreating British, French and Belgian armies now facing annihilation on the beaches. Helped by RAF air cover, the besieged troops are fighting a fierce rearguard battle to defend the beaches, but the makeshift flotilla of destroyers, ferries, fishing boats and pleasure craft are coming under heavy fire as they pick up the exhausted troops.

Whole lotta trouble goin' on for Jerry

1958 Southern rock star Jerry Lee Lewis has a whole lotta trouble goin' on. "The Killer" has been in the hot seat ever since his Bible school kicked him out because of the way he played the piano at prayer meetings, when he abandoned the preacher's daughter he'd married when he was 16 and took to playing in rough Southern bars. Then a bunch of good ol' boys insisted that he marry their sister Jane, never mind the preacher's daughter, and the following month he divorced the first wife while the second bore him a son. Meanwhile his electrifying brand of piano rock was getting somewhere. He recorded "Whole Lotta Shakin' Goin' On" – which sold six million copies – and "Great Balls of Fire", which sold a million in 10 days. Last week he arrived in London to start a tour, and reporters discovered the young girl with him was not only his cousin but his third wife, Myra, aged only 13. That's not too young for a Southern bride, but widespread public outrage forced the tour to close after only two concerts. "The Killer" is apparently baffled – okay, it was bigamy at first, but he then divorced Jane last month. The young couple flew back to the US today.

MAY 27

1564 Death of French Protestant reformer John Calvin.

1657 Lord Protector Oliver Cromwell refuses parliament's offer of the title of King of England.

1703 Russian tsar Peter the Great proclaims St Petersburg the new capital of Russia.

1851 Adolf Anderssen of Germany wins the first chess International Master tournament, held in London.

1900 Belgium becomes the first country to elect a government by proportional representation.

1957 Buddy Holly and the Crickets release their first record.

1963 Jomo Kenyatta becomes the first prime minister of Kenya.

1977 Punk band the Sex Pistols release the single "God Save the Queen" in the UK.

1988 In Canada, a man is acquitted of murdering his mother because he was sleepwalking. He drove to her home, hit her with an iron bar and then stabbed her.

1994 Novelist Alexander Solzhenitsyn returns to Russia after 20 years in exile.

Japan sinks Russian fleet

1905 Japan has won a great naval victory, annihilating the Russian Baltic fleet sent to relieve Port Arthur. Only three of the 38 Russian ships escaped from the straits of Tsushima in the Sea of Japan, while Japanese admiral Togo Heihachiro's fleet lost just three torpedo boats. Togo outmanoeuvred the Russians and sank all four Russian capital ships – including the *Admiral Nakhimov*, reputed to have been carrying $2000 million in gold and platinum. The Baltic fleet set sail 18 months ago for Vladivostok. It was too late to save Port Arthur, which surrendered to Japan on January 2 after a seven-month siege. On March 10 the Japanese routed the 200,000-man Russian army at Mukden. A humiliated Russia now has no choice but to concede defeat.

Communists take Shanghai

1949 After a month-long siege, the communist Chinese took Shanghai today with hardly a shot fired. The remnants of Chiang Kai-shek's routed Nationalist army are retreating towards Canton in the south and it is only a matter of time before communist leader Mao Tse-tung's victory is complete. Two years ago the Nationalists outnumbered the communist forces three to one and had vastly superior firepower, yet even with these advantages they were no match for Mao's guerrillas. Last year United States general David Barr reported to Washington that the Nationalists had "the world's worst leadership" and that there was "widespread corruption and dishonesty throughout the armed forces". Large numbers of Nationalists defected to the communist side, which conversely consists of motivated, disciplined and well-led men – and they have the additional support of China's peasants. Heavy US backing for the Nationalists could not counter this. Communist rule now stretches from Berlin to Shanghai.

There is no art which one government sooner learns of another than that of draining money from the pockets of the people.
Adam Smith, pioneering economist, 1776.

Virtuoso's final bow

1840 The illustrious Italian violinist Niccolo Paganini went to his Maker today – though opinion is divided on just which maker that might be. Many are convinced that the Devil himself played Paganini's violin for him. His skill was sheer wizardry – he could give stunning performances on only one string – and his music and dark good looks mesmerized audiences, not least people's wives and daughters. He died in Nice aged 58, and surely went to heaven.

Kremlin triggers shopping frenzy

1990 The Kremlin announced its new economic package today – and provoked an unprecedented shopping frenzy in the Soviet Union. Hordes of panic buyers emptied shops of everything, and many left empty-handed. The reforms mean the traditional food subsidies will be phased out to create what the Kremlin calls a "regulated market economy". Meat prices and sugar will double and bread will cost three times as much. But the new package is not law until parliament approves it, and there may be a referendum.

BIRTHDAYS

James "Wild Bill" Hickok 1837, American frontiersman and US marshal.

Amelia Bloomer 1818, American women's rights campaigner who invented the loose trousers gathered at the ankle and worn with a shorter skirt which gained the name "bloomers".

Isadora Duncan 1878, American dancer who pioneered a new style which greatly influenced modern dance.

Vincent Price 1911, American actor who starred in numerous horror movies.

Sam Snead 1912, American golfer who won 135 tournaments between 1936 and 1965.

Henry Kissinger 1923, German-born US secretary of state who shared the Nobel Peace Prize in 1973 with Le Duc Tho for his part in ending the Vietnam War.

1805 Death of Luigi Boccherini, Italian cellist and prolific composer.

1891 The first world weightlifting championships are held at the Café Monico in Piccadilly, London.

1937 Death of Alfred Adler, Austrian psychiatrist whose theories introduced the concept of the inferiority complex.

1940 The Belgian army surrenders to the Nazis.

1967 The 65-year-old British yachtsman Francis Chichester receives a hero's welcome when he arrives in Plymouth 119 days after setting out on a solo round-the-world trip.

1972 The Duke of Windsor, English king who abdicated to marry American divorcée Wallis Simpson, dies in Paris.

1982 Barcelona football club buys Argentinian footballer Diego Maradona from Argentinos Juniors for a record £5 million ($9 ¼ million).

1985 Thousands drown as a cyclone hits Bangladesh.

BIRTHDAYS

Joseph Guillotin 1738, French physician and revolutionary who developed the machine of execution which was so heavily used during the Reign of Terror.

William Pitt (the Younger) 1759, English statesman who became prime minister at the age of 24, the youngest British prime minister ever.

Thomas Moore 1779, Irish poet who found great success with *Irish Melodies* and the oriental romance *Lalla Rookh*; he was responsible, with the publisher John Murray, for burning Lord Byron's memoirs after his death.

Ian Fleming 1908, British novelist who created James Bond.

Patrick White 1912, Australian novelist who won the Nobel Prize for Literature in 1973.

Edward Seaga 1930, Jamaican politician and prime minister.

Kylie Minogue 1968, Australian actress and pop singer.

Teenager lands plane in Red Square

1987 A West German teenager's prank caused world-wide mirth today and seriously embarrassed the Soviet Union. Mathias Rust, 19, flew his light Cessna plane from Helsinki to Moscow, buzzed the Kremlin and landed in Red Square – evading the entire Soviet air defence system. He alighted to sign autographs for astonished Moscow passersby before being taken away by bemused policemen. Extremely unamused are the hard men in the Kremlin, who are unlikely simply to dock Mathias's pocket money. The young prankster is in deep trouble.

No, my dear, it is I who am surprised; you are merely astonished.
Noah Webster, American lexicographer, to his wife, who had found him embracing the maid. Webster died today, 1843.

1990 IRA gunmen shot dead two Australian tourists in Holland today – mistaking them for British soldiers. The IRA has admitted responsibility for the killings. Stephen Melrose and Nick Spanos, both lawyers, had stopped their British-registered car in Roermond, near the German border, planning to spend the night there, when a car pulled up and two men opened fire with machine-guns.

PARIS COMMUNE DROWNS IN BLOOD

1871 The Paris Commune collapsed today after a two-month siege, brutally suppressed by government troops in a week of bitter street-by-street fighting which has left 33,000 killed and part of the city in ruins. The communes at Lyons and Marseilles have already collapsed and the movement is dead. Backed by the National Guard, the communards set up a revolutionary municipal government in Paris in protest at the humiliating peace terms imposed by the victorious Prussian army, which had besieged the city for four months. The national government at Versailles then besieged the city in their turn. The Versailles troops stormed in when the communards abandoned a fort defending the west of the city.

Dutch hold back North Sea's tide

1932 Dutch engineers completed the world's biggest dam today – a major victory in their 800-year battle to push back the sea. The new dam wall, or dike, is 18 miles (29 km) long, and turns the Zuider Zee into a vast freshwater lake, called the Ijsselmeer. The dam cuts off Amsterdam from the sea, and ships must now use the 14-mile (22 km) deepwater North Sea Canal, completed in 1876. The dam will eventually provide cramped Holland with 500,000 acres (203,000 hectares) of reclaimed land. It is a slow process: flooded land is diked, pumped dry, then leached with fresh water to remove the salt and treated with gypsum before it can be used for agriculture. Most of the new land will be below sea level, needing continuous pumping. Holland's thousands of windmills maintain the complex system of water levels, though they are steadily being replaced with motor-driven pumps.

Maiden voyage steals headlines

1990 The yacht *Maiden*, skippered by Tracy Edwards, arrived in Southampton today to finish the Whitbread Round the World Race – the first yacht to do so with an all-woman crew. New Zealand yachts took the first three places. *Steinlager 2*, captained by Peter Blake, came in first with a time of 128 days and 9 hours, winning all six legs of the 32,000-nautical mile race, but it was *Maiden* that caused a sensation. The race is held every four years.

CHEERS FOR CHARLES

1660 Charles Stuart entered London today on his 30th birthday to become King Charles II, restoring England's monarchy following Oliver Cromwell's commonwealth. He was well received – the public actually asked him to come home. Apart from a short and disastrous visit in 1650 when he led a Scottish army to defeat at Worcester, Charles has been in exile since Cromwell had his father, Charles I, beheaded in 1649. Oliver Cromwell died two years ago and his son Richard's weak rule brought public demands for restoration of the monarchy. Charles issued a declaration at Breda in Holland agreeing to full cooperation with parliament, and an English fleet was sent to bring him home, arriving in Dover four days ago. When Charles arrived in London today, flowers littered the streets, bells were ringing and old Cavaliers wept for joy. The new King has brought considerable cheer following Cromwell's Puritan rule.

> *The Queen is most anxious to enlist everyone who can speak or write to join in checking this mad, wicked folly of "Women's Rights", with all its attendant horrors, on which her poor feeble sex is bent, forgetting every sense of womanly feeling and propriety.*
> **Victoria**, Queen of England, in a letter, 1870.

European Cup violence kills 41 at Heysel

1985 Britain's hated soccer hooligans went on the rampage at Heysel Stadium in Belgium tonight, causing a riot which left 41 fans crushed or trampled to death and about 350 injured. Most of the casualties were Italian football supporters. Chanting, flag-waving hooligans from Liverpool charged Italian fans in the stands during the European Cup Final between Liverpool and Juventus, causing immediate panic as a wall and safety fence collapsed under the surge of people. The fighting went on as police struggled to rescue those who were trapped, with the hooligans using lethal iron bars and bottles – whatever they could sieze – as weapons. Bodies were being laid out in the car park as mounted riot police rode in to stop the fighting. Europe has been plagued by marauding bands of British hooligans in recent years. Tonight's mindless violence will surely see them – and their teams – banned.

Diaghilev's Riot of Spring

1913 Serge Diaghilev's wonderful Russian ballet has delighted Paris for seven years, but tonight an outraged first-night crowd rioted and the first performance of *Le Sacre du printemps* (The Rite of Spring) ended when the police arrived. The ballet combines the violent, crashing music of Igor Stravinsky, the weird stage sets of Nikolai Roerich and the unbridled choreography of Vaslav Nijinsky. The story centres around a primitive fertility rite that ends with a human sacrifice. The controversial, modern performance of an unusual theme divided the audience into two camps – jeerers and hushers – who soon came to blows.

EVEREST CROWNED BY HILLARY AND TENZING

1953 A British team has "crowned" Mount Everest, the world's highest peak, reaching the summit just four days before Britain crowns its new queen, Elizabeth II. New Zealand-born climber Edmund Hillary and the Sherpa guide Tenzing Norgay reached the 29,001-ft (8839.5 m) summit at 11.30 this morning. They stayed for about 15 minutes to take photos and plant the Union Jack, the Nepalese flag and the UN flag side by side in the snow, with biscuits and cake as a Buddhist offering. Then they began the downward climb, tired but elated at their success. For 30 years men have tried and failed to scale Everest – or "Chomolungma" as it is called in Tibetan, "goddess mother of the world". Hillary and Tenzing used up-to-date mountaineering equipment, including special nylon clothing and oxygen equipment, and expedition leader Colonel John Hunt planned the assault meticulously, making a close study of previous climbs. An attempt earlier this month failed in high winds, but today the weather was perfect.

1453 Constantinople finally falls to the Turkish army after a siege lasting for a year.

1500 Portuguese navigator Bartholomeu Diaz drowns at sea during a storm.

1795 The Virginia Assembly opposes Britain's Stamp Act.

1911 British librettist and playwright W. S. Gilbert drowns in his own lake while trying to rescue two damsels in distress.

1914 Canadian Pacific liner the *Empress of Ireland* is wrecked in the St Lawrence River, drowning over 1000 people.

1958 French statesman Charles de Gaulle is summoned from retirement to deal with a crisis in Algeria, where French settlers are in revolt against prospective Algerian independence.

1972 Presidents Nixon and Brezhnev sign the first arms reduction pact.

1979 Bishop Abel Muzorewa, one-time president of the African National Congress, becomes the first black prime minister of Rhodesia.

1979 Mary Pickford, American actress known as "America's Sweetheart" in her heyday, dies at the age of 86.

1989 Russian politician Boris Yeltsin is elected to the Supreme Soviet after popular protests at his exclusion.

BIRTHDAYS

Isaac Albéniz 18860, Spanish composer and pianist.

G. K. Chesterton 1874, English novelist, essayist and poet.

Joseph von Sternberg 1894, Austrian film director and actor whose innovative films include *The Blue Angel* and *Shanghai Express*.

Bob Hope 1903, English-born American comedian who won five special Oscars for his services to the entertainment industry.

John F. Kennedy 1917, American politician who was the first Roman Catholic – and the youngest – president ever elected.

Goddess of Democracy outfaces Chairman Mao

1989 A defiant Goddess of Democracy and Freedom confronted the huge portrait of Chairman Mao in Peking's Tienanmen Square this morning. The 30 ft (9 m) figure, modelled on New York's Statue of Liberty, was sculpted overnight by Chinese art students out of fibreglass and plaster. A million people flooded the square again today to demand democratic reform, defying the martial law declaration of 10 days ago in an awesome confrontation with authority. The pro-democracy campaign is now nationwide. The divided party leadership will be forced to act soon – but how?

Japanese Red Army raids Tel Aviv

1972 Three Japanese Red Army terrorists opened fire on unsuspecting passengers at Lod international airport in Tel Aviv today, killing 26 people. The three men passed through security without any difficulty before taking automatic rifles from their bags and opening fire on the terrified crowds in the baggage hall. Two of the terrorists were shot by security guards and the third was arrested. They are reported to have been working for a Palestinian group in Lebanon.

2003 One of America's greatest entertainers, Bob Hope, celebrates his 100th birthday. Festivities include a fly-past by 1940's aeroplanes and the renaming of a Hollywood square in his honour. Today has been declared Bob Hope Day in 35 US states.

War should belong to the tragic past, to history: it should find no place on humanity's agenda for the future.
Pope John Paul II, in a speech in Coventry on this day, 1982.

Marlowe killed in pub brawl

1593 The English playwright Christopher Marlowe is dead, killed in a London tavern brawl after an argument over religion. He was 29, and had published only one of his plays, *Tamberlaine the Great* – already recognized as a classic. His *Doctor Faustus* remains unpublished. His work has greatly influenced his contemporaries Thomas Kyd and William Shakespeare. But last year Marlowe was arrested for counterfeiting, and earlier this month he was arrested again, accused of heresy.

Indianapolis 500 is fast but safe

1911 The new face of high-speed motor racing made its debut today when Ray Harroun won a 500-mile (804 km) race held on a special 2.5-mile (4 km) brick-paved circuit at Indianapolis. Harroun, who came out of retirement to drive his Marmon Wasp to victory, covered the 200 laps at an average speed of 74.59 mph (120 kph). The prestige Vanderbilt Cup race on Long Island has now been banned since today's racing cars are too fast for safety on the open streets. The Indianapolis Motor Raceway's three-million-brick track points the way forward – drivers may risk their necks but the spectators are safe. The Indianapolis 500 will be held every Memorial Day, the last Monday in May.

Joan left to burn

1431 Joan of Arc was burnt at the stake, accused of being a witch, in Rouen today. The last word she spoke before succumbing to the flames was "Jesus". She was 19. The peasant maid whose "voices" led her to drive the English from Orléans and put King Charles VII on the throne was wounded in battle a year ago and captured. Her Burgundian captors sold her to the English Duke of Bedford for 10,000 crowns. The duke, not daring to execute her, handed her over to a church court in Rouen for a secret Inquisition trial. The judges declared Joan's visions diabolical and charged her with heresy and witchcraft. Interrogated and tortured for months, she was finally tricked into admitting her guilt. She retracted the confession, and was then condemned as a relapsed heretic and sent to the stake. King Charles VII did not lift a finger to help her.

"UN-AMERICAN" MILLER WON'T TELL TALES

1957 The American playwright Arthur Miller was convicted today of contempt of Congress for refusing to finger other writers as communists. Miller was called before the House Un-American Activities Committee last June and grilled on his alleged communist leanings. Miller was candid about his own affairs but said his conscience prevented him naming others. Today a federal judge lauded his motives but found him guilty nonetheless. Miller could face a year in jail. He was released on bail and will appeal. Miller won the Pulitzer Prize in 1949 for his classic modern tragedy *Death of a Salesman*. In 1953 his Tony award-winning play *The Crucible* (right), about the Salem witch-hunts, was a thinly-veiled attack on Senator Joe McCarthy's crusade against subversion.

1989 The speaker at the US House of Representatives resigned today following investigations by the House Ethics Committee into financial impropriety. Jim Wright is the first speaker in US history forced to resign.

Perhaps it is God's will to lead the people of South Africa through defeat and humiliation to a better future and a brighter day.
Jan Smuts, Boer general, at the Boer War peace conference, 1902.

Venice's little dyer dies

1594 The great Venetian painter Tintoretto died today at the age of 76. The "little dyer", nicknamed after his father, a "tintero", or dyer, combined Titian's brilliant use of colour with Michelangelo's draughtsmanship in some of the world's biggest paintings. Among his master works is the cycle of paintings in the Scuola of the Confraternity of San Rocco in Venice which took him six years working at great speed with a phalanx of assistants, including his two sons and daughter. Tintoretto's *Paradise*, the largest canvas in the world, measures 84 ft by 34 ft (25.5 m by 10.3 m). He will be buried in the church containing the 50-ft (15.2 m) painting *Last Judgement*.

OUTGUNNED BOERS QUIT

1902 "With grief", South Africa's Boer generals formally surrendered to Britain tonight. The Boer War started with humiliation for the British – mere farmers overwhelmed the imperial forces in battle after battle. In the end 450,000 of Britain's elite troops were pitted against only 80,000 Boer fighters, who relied on mobility and expert guerrilla tactics. Britain's Lord Kitchener finally countered this by cordoning off the land and herding the Boer women and children into concentration camps, where more than 20,000 – one in three – died of disease and malnutrition. The camps have caused deep dissent in Britain and outrage in Europe, where Britain has been dubbed the "Dirty Dog". The peace treaty provides for eventual self-rule for the Boer republics, with the issue of votes for natives to be dealt with after that.

The last Model T

1927 The last Model T Ford, No. 15,007,003, rolled off the assembly line today. It is to be replaced by the Model A. Retooling the Ford production lines will take six months and cost at least $200 million. Henry Ford has held on to the Model T too long, and has now lost first place to General Motors. Ford introduced the moving assembly line technique of mass production in the US. One result has been a drop in price – the first Model Ts cost $850 in 1908, but they now sell for under $300. But the thriving second-hand market has hit sales. Other companies are countering this by making their cars slightly different every year. Nonetheless the automobile has become an essential part of American life.

1809 Death of Austrian composer Franz Joseph Haydn, who began his musical career at the age of eight as a cathedral chorister in Vienna and went on to become kappellmeister to the Esterhazy family.

1837 Joseph Grimaldi, English clown whose success was based on his skills as dancer, singer and acrobat as well as his gift for comedy, dies aged 57.

1939 Britain interns fascist leader Sir Oswald Mosley and thousands of other fascist sympathizers and aliens as the government consolidates emergency war powers.

1958 The Kremlin agrees to talks with the US on an atmospheric test ban treaty.

1961 South Africa declares itself a republic independent of the British Commonwealth.

1962 Nazi war criminal Adolf Eichmann is hanged in Israel.

1965 British racing driver Jim Clark becomes the first non-American driver to win the Indianapolis 500.

1983 Jack Dempsey, American boxer who was world heavyweight champion, dies aged 87.

1991 The 17-year civil war in Angola comes to an end.

BIRTHDAYS

Walt Whitman 1819, American poet who expressed his democratic idealism in *The Leaves of Grass*.

Walter Sickert 1860, British Impressionist painter and etcher who used a more sombre palette than the French Impressionists.

William Heath Robinson 1872, English illustrator and cartoonist .

Clint Eastwood 1930, American actor and director who hit the big time with spaghetti westerns such as *The Good, the Bad and the Ugly*.

Brooke Shields 1965, American actress and child model who leapt to public attention playing a child prostitute in Louis Malle's film *Pretty Baby*.

JUNE

*"... we shall fight on the beaches,
we shall fight on the landing grounds,
we shall fight in the fields and in the streets,
we shall fight in the hills;
we shall never surrender."*

Prime Minister Winston Churchill
in a speech to the House of Commons,
June 4, 1940, four years before D-day.

Glimmer of hope for *Mayflower* Pilgrims

1621 Settlers in the New England colony of New Plymouth have been wondering just how secure their settlement is, but a patent, issued today by the Council for New England, has put their minds at rest. When the Pilgrims, a group of religious dissenters, set sail in the *Mayflower* from Plymouth, England, on their 66-day voyage last year, they carried with them a patent from the Virginia Company granting them territory in Virginia and allowing the right to self-government. Their plans went wrong, however, when severe weather at sea put them off course, forcing them to land outside the limits of the grant. Although the new patent has given them the title to the land, the Pilgrims have had to sort out the government question for themselves. Fortunately, before disembarking, they had already entered into a solemn covenant with each other, which they call the Mayflower Compact. The terms bind them, as a body, to form a government, and to abide by any laws it may make.

Pepper assault

1967 The Beatles, indisputably the foremost British pop group of the decade, today released their new album, *Sergeant Pepper's Lonely Heart's Club Band*. The new release – a distinctive blend of pop, symphonic and Indian musical forms – is the greatest achievement in their creative output so far, and looks set to become a Beatles classic. Over the eight years since their beginnings in Liverpool, the group have continued to experiment, producing ever more inventive and sophisticated work, and their enormous contribution to the pop music industry cannot be overestimated.

How reconcile this world of fact with the bright world of my imagining? My darkness has been filled with the light of intelligence, and behold, the outer daylight world was stumbling and groping in social blindness.
The deaf and blind author **Helen Keller**, who died today, 1968.

1935 In the interests of road safety, the British government is introducing a test for would-be motorists. The test will put drivers through their paces, checking how well they can manoeuvre a vehicle, how good their eyesight is, and how well they know the rules of the road.

1880 The inhabitants of New Haven, Connecticut, are today trying out a new public facility – the world's first "public" telephone, located in the Connecticut Telephone Company office in the Yale Bank Building. Those wishing to use the telephone must pay a toll to an attendant.

THE QUEEN CELEBRATES HER GOLDEN JUBILEE

2002 Many Britons are taking part in wide-ranging celebrations to mark the Queen's Golden Jubilee. Today there is a classical prom in the grounds of Buckingham Palace, hosted by the Queen and the Duke of Edinburgh. The People's Party begins on Monday with garden and street parties and a three-hour concert at the palace. Irish band The Corrs will play at the Queen's Golden Jubilee concert with many other artists as varied as Ozzy Osbourne and Will Young. On Friday, a fleet of warships sailed into Chatham Historic Dockyard to take part in the three-day maritime and military celebration attended by the Princess Royal. On Tuesday, there will be a ceremonial procession in central London, the day the Jubilee weekend celebrations come to an end.

Royal family massacred in Nepal

2001 The Himalayan kingdom of Nepal has been thrown into deep crisis with the murders of 11 members of the Royal Family, including King Birendra and Queen Aiswary, during a banquet. Prince Dipendra, heir to the thrown, has been named as the killer. It is believed he shot dead his parents and relatives, then turned the gun on himself. There has been no official word about what triggered the violence, though reports suggest the incident followed an argument about the Prince's choice of bride. Although the Prince is gravely ill in hospital, royal tradition means he is the rightful successor to the throne. King Birendra's brother, Prince Gyanedra, has been appointed regent until the fate of the crown prince is known.

BIRTHDAYS

John Masefield 1878, English novelist and Poet Laureate who served in the merchant navy and wrote about the sea in his first publication, *Salt Water Ballads*.

Marilyn Monroe 1926, American actress who led a turbulent life and became an icon after her death.

Edward Woodward 1930, British actor best known for the television series *The Equalizer*.

Pat Boone 1934, American singer.

Jason Donovan 1968, Australian actor and pop singer who came to the public eye in the soap opera *Neighbours*.

1780 Lord George Gordon foments riots to protest against the ending of penalties against Roman Catholics in the Roman Catholic Relief Act of 1778.

1868 Britain crushes the Marathas in India and annexes their lands.

1882 Italian nationalist leader Giuseppe Garibaldi dies aged 74.

1909 Vaslav Nijinsky and Anna Pavlova lead in the Paris premiere of *Les Sylphides*.

1946 Italy's monarchy is abolished and the country becomes a republic.

1954 Eighteen-year-old jockey Lester Piggott wins his first Derby on Never Say Die, the first American horse to win the Derby since Iroquois in 1881.

1962 Death of Vita Sackville-West, British novelist and gardener who wrote *All Passion Spent* and created the garden at her home, Sissinghurst Castle, Kent.

1964 The PLO is formed in Jerusalem.

1966 American automatic spacecraft *Surveyor* lands in the south-west part of the moon's Oceanus Procellanum.

1985 English football clubs are banned indefinitely from playing in Europe on account of hooliganism by British fans abroad.

BIRTHDAYS

Marquis de Sade 1740, French writer who was imprisoned in the Bastille for his sexual perversions, where he wrote the novel *Justine*.

Thomas Hardy 1840, English novelist and poet whose books were set in imaginary Wessex.

Sir Edward Elgar 1857, English composer best-known for the *Enigma Variations* and the *Pomp and Circumstance* marches.

Lotte Reiniger 1899, German film animator who made the first full-length animated film in 1920 – *The Adventures of Prince Achmed*.

Sally Kellerman 1938, American actress best-known for her role as Hotlips Houlihan in the film version of M*A*S*H.

VIVAT REGINA!

1953 In a scene of ritual pomp and splendour at London's Westminster Abbey today, the Archbishop of Canterbury solemnly lowered the Crown of St Edward on to the head of Princess Elizabeth Alexandra Mary, to make her Queen Elizabeth II of Great Britain and Ireland. Outside, in the cold and wet, thousands of spectators waited for the new Queen to emerge and make her journey to Buckingham Palace in the ceremonial golden coach. Black-market tickets for the event were going for as much as £50 ($92), while a balcony with a good view commanded up to £3500 ($6500). Those who could not make it were glued to the screens of a record two and a half million televisions. Ironically, had it not been for the abdication of her uncle Edward VIII in favour of her father George VI, Elizabeth would not have had the starring role in today's ceremony. Married in 1947 to her distant cousin Prince Philip of Greece, now Duke of Edinburgh, Elizabeth has been representing her father on state occasions since 1951, due to the gradual decline in the King's state of health. It was while on a state visit with her husband in Kenya, en route to Australia and New Zealand, that the Queen heard of her father's death and her accession to the throne.

Poland's Pope comes home

1979 There was an emotional welcome waiting for Pope John Paul II as he set foot again on the soil of his native Poland. Born 59 years ago in Wadowice and christened Karol Wojtyla, John Paul was only elected to office on October 16 last year – the first non-Italian to be elected Pope in 456 years. Although Poland is under Communist rule, much of the population remains true to its Roman Catholic roots. The Pope's visit marks a major opening-up in the relationship between the Church and the countries of the Communist block.

'Iggins in 'Eaven

1990 Rex Carey Harrison, better known as the actor Sir Rex Harrison, died today at the age of 82. Sir Rex began his long career in theatre and films at the Liverpool Repertory Theatre in 1924, going into films five years later in 1929. Known for his suave manner, he excelled in playing the "English gentleman" type. He will be best remembered for his role as Professor Henry Higgins in the musical *My Fair Lady*, a part that he played both on Broadway and on the London stage from 1956 to 1958, and in the film version of 1964, winning not only a Tony but also an Academy Award.

Marconi invention: no wires attached

1896 Italian-born physicist Guglielmo Marconi, now living in London, has taken out the first patent for a wireless telegraphy apparatus, a device that transmits spoken messages over long distances without the aid of wires or cables. Using a transmitter and a receiver, Marconi's invention broadcasts sound by means of invisible electro-magnetic, or radio, waves – a phenomenon first demonstrated by the German physicist, Heinrich Hertz. Although at present transmission is limited to a distance of under 12 miles (19 km), Marconi aims to extend its range still further, perhaps even to France.

1987 In Australia, Lindy Chamberlain, the mother convicted of murdering her baby in the sensational "dingo murder" case, has finally received an official pardon. Lindy Chamberlain has consistently maintained her innocence, claiming that her baby was killed and carried off by a dingo, a wild Australian dog.

I doubt that art needed Ruskin any more than a moving train needs one of its passengers to shove it.

British playwright **Tom Stoppard**, 1977.

1780 A new horse race is being run today at Epsom Downs in the south of England. Named the Derby after Edward Stanley, 12th Earl of Derby, the race takes place over a 1 ½–mile (2.4 km) course, with a field limited to three-year-old colts and fillies.

NEW SHIP-BASED PLANES FOR US TO CRACK JAPANESE

1942 The Midway Islands, lying about 1150 miles (1850 km) west-northwest of Hawaii, are the scene of a new kind of warfare – airborne attack between American and Japanese carrier-based planes. After last month's humiliating surrender of United States troops under the command of General Jonathan Wainwright, the Americans hope that this bold, new-style offensive will help them to reclaim the Pacific islands from the Japanese, who have established a massive military presence there. If these hopes are fulfilled, the Battle of Midway – as it is being called – could prove a turning point for the Allies in the Pacific war.

Edward weds Wallis, his crown rejected

1937 Former King Edward VIII of Great Britain and Ireland married his American bride, Wallis Warfield Simpson, in a ceremony in Paris today. The marriage marks the end of a Royal scandal that rocked the nation. Edward and Mrs Simpson met in 1931. His relationship with her caused a major rift in the Royal family and outraged the Church of England hierarchy. Mrs Simpson divorced last October and in November Edward – realizing that he might have to choose between his crown and the woman he loved – told Prime Minister Baldwin that if he could not marry her and remain king, he was "prepared to go". A possible solution was suggested that would have been constitutionally acceptable: the couple could marry but Mrs Simpson would not be given Royal status.

Given time, the idea might have won popular support had the story not become headline news in the British press soon afterwards, forcing an instant decision. Only a week later, in December 1936 – less than a year after he was crowned – Edward signed the papers of abdication. The couple are now known as the Duke and Duchess of Windsor. Only the Duke, however, will bear the title.

1965 Joined to his Gemini 4 spacecraft by a Space Age "umbilical cord", astronaut Edward H. White today became the first American to take a walk in space. The walk lasted 20 minutes, and is part of a programme investigating the effects of prolonged space flight on man.

Lovelorn Abelard guilty of heresy

1140 The controversial views of leading French scholar Peter Abelard have landed him in serious trouble: in a dramatic verdict, a church court today has found him guilty of heresy. Abelard is no stranger to controversy and this is just one in a series of confrontations with the Church. Personal tragedy, too, has brought him fame of another kind, through his celebrated love affair with his beautiful pupil, Héloïse. The discovery of the couple's liaison so enraged Héloïse's uncle that he ordered Abelard's castration. After this brutal attack, the couple separated, Abelard to become a monk and Héloïse to enter a convent. They did manage to renew contact some years later, however, in a series of letters.

1924 German novelist and short story writer Franz Kafka died today in a sanatorium at Kierling, near Vienna after losing his seven-year battle with tuberculosis. With his pessimistic view of the world and of the despair and alienation of modern man, Kafka characteristically saw his illness as psychosomatic – a conspiracy between his head and his body to put an end to his internal anguish. Kafka was always reluctant to publish and before his death he exacted a promise from his friend Max Brod not to allow the publication of any more of his writings. If this promise is honoured, much of the work of a potential literary giant may be lost forever.

1665 British naval forces under the Duke of York defeat the Dutch fleet off the coast of Suffolk.

1864 In the American Civil War, more than 6,000 Unionists are killed or wounded in less than an hour at Cold Harbor.

1875 Death of French composer Georges Bizet, best known for his opera *Carmen*.

1899 Death of Johann Strauss the Younger, composer of *The Blue Danube*.

1946 The first bikini bathing suit goes on show in Paris.

1956 British Railways end third class travel.

1964 The Rolling Stones begin their first US tour.

1972 In Cincinnati, Sally Priesand is ordained as the first woman rabbi.

1981 Shergar, one of the Aga Khan's many horses, wins the Derby – by a record 10 lengths.

1984 The British government admits there is a higher level of leukaemia than average around Sellafield nuclear station.

1995 UN Rapid Intervention force is sent to Bosnia.

1998 High-speed train crash kills 98 in Germany.

BIRTHDAYS

Jefferson Davis 1808, American president of the Confederate states.

Raoul Dufy 1877, French painter and textile designer who developed a highly personal style.

Paulette Goddard 1911, American actress who starred in Charlie Chaplin's *Modern Times* and *The Great Dictator* and married the great comedian.

Tony Curtis 1925, American actor whose many films include *Some Like It Hot*, *The Boston Strangler* and *The Vikings*.

Allan Ginsberg 1926, American poet and leading light of the Beat movement.

Suzi Quatro 1950, American rock guitarist and singer.

1789 The Dauphin Louis, son of Louis XVI and heir to the French throne, dies at the age of seven.

1805 The first ceremony of the Trooping of the Colour is held in Horse Guards Parade, London.

1831 Prince Leopold, of the House of Saxe-Coburg-Gotha, becomes the first king of Belgium, although King William III of the Netherlands refuses to acknowledge Belgian independence.

1926 Death of Frederick Spofforth, the Australian cricketer known as the demon bowler.

1937 The first supermarket trolley bowls along the aisles of a supermarket in Oklahoma.

1941 Former German emperor Wilhelm II, forced to abdicate after Germany's defeat in World War I, dies in exile at Doorn in the Netherlands.

1944 Rome is liberated by the Allies.

1946 Juan Perón is elected president of Argentina.

1959 Charles de Gaulle stuns French colonists in Algeria by telling them they must integrate with the Muslim Algerians if they wish to stay.

1973 A Russian supersonic airline built on the lines of Concorde explodes at the Paris Air Show, killing six crew and 27 onlookers.

1988 Death of Sir Douglas Nicholls, governor of South Australia, the first aborigine to govern a state and to receive a knighthood.

BIRTHDAYS

George III 1730, English monarch of erratic mental health whose mishandling of the American colonies was responsible for the War of Independence.

Stephen Foster 1826, American composer of songs such as "Swanee River".

Rosalind Russell 1908, American actress who appeared in film and Broadway dramas and musicals such as *Night Must Fall*.

Italian seducer dies

1798 Today sees the death, in Bohemia, of one of this century's most flamboyant characters, Giovanni Giacomo Casanova, Chevalier de Seingalt. Casanova was born in 1725 in Venice, the son of an actor. His expulsion from the Seminary of St Cyprian for "scandalous conduct" launched him on a varied and infamous career, in which he was writer, traveller, adventurer, soldier, spy, diplomat and dedicated ladies' man. One of the more daring exploits of this man of many parts was his escape – under the nose of the Doge himself – from Venice's Piombi prison, where he was serving a five-year sentence after being denounced as a magician. Among his writings are *Icosameron*, a futuristic adventure fantasy, and his fascinating memoirs, *Histoire de Ma Vie*.

Massive train explosion

1989 Over 460 people are thought to have died in a massive gas explosion that wrecked two crowded passenger trains about 740 miles (1190 km) east of Moscow. The accident occurred as the two trains, travelling on the Trans-Siberian railway, passed each other. It seems to have been caused by sparks from the line that ignited gas leaking from the huge long-distance pipeline that runs alongside the track. All that remain of the trains are the wrecked and blackened shells of the carriages lying overturned by the side of the line. Soviet leader Mikhail Gorbachev has been to visit the scene of the accident.

Ragged armada rescues Allies

1940 As the might of the German army sweeps northwards through France, a massive Allied military operation has been taking place at the coastal town of Dunkirk in northern France. In the small hours of this morning, under fire from German guns, a flotilla of naval and civilian craft completed the safe evacuation of some 335,000 out of a total of 400,000 Allied troops. British prime minister Winston Churchill has hailed the operation as "a miracle of deliverance", but admits that in military terms it is a massive defeat for the Allies.

1844 Scientists are excited by the discovery today in Iceland of a great auk. This large flightless bird, also known as the garefowl, was thought to be totally extinct.

> *The war against hunger is truly mankind's war of liberation.*
> **John F. Kennedy**, in a speech at the World Food Congress, 1963.

Chinese army brutally halts democratic revolt

1989 Up to 2600 people are thought to have been killed and 10,000 injured as soldiers opened fire on student demonstrators in Tienanmen Square, Beijing, it was reported today. Since the removal of moderate party chairman Hu Yaobang in 1987, the conflict between moderates and old-style Maoist hardliners has escalated to crisis point. In a massive demonstration for greater democracy, huge crowds of student protesters had, by last night, barricaded themselves into Tienanmen Square. In a show of force, the government ordered the army into action. Reaching the square from the Avenue of Eternal Peace, the troops showered the students with a hail of bullets, and their armoured vehicles crashed through the barricades. The square and surrounding city became a scene of horror and chaos. Emergency services could not get through. At one o'clock this morning, the soldiers – only a day ago hailed as "brothers and comrades" – made a final onslaught on those who were left. Marching forward, they shot indiscriminately into the crowd. In their wake came the tanks, mercilessly flattening all in their path.

War chief Kitchener drowns at sea

1916 The long and distinguished military career of Herbert, Viscount Kitchener was abruptly brought to an end today when the SS *Hampshire*, carrying him on a mission to Russia, hit a German mine and sank off the Orkney Islands, north-east of the Scottish mainland. Born on June 24, 1850, near Listowel in County Kerry, Lord Kitchener held many prominent posts during his lifetime, among them commander-in-chief during the South African War, when – in one of the less savoury episodes of his career – he herded Boer women and children into concentration camps in his fight against guerrilla resistance. He will be best remembered for his lead in World War I, which he predicted would be a long, drawn-out war, to be decided by the "last million men" that Britain could put into battle. He organized "Kitchener armies" of volunteers trained to a professional standard and on a scale unseen in British history, since when the general public have come to see him as a symbol of national victory.

Scandal-scarred Profumo quits

1963 In a dramatic statement today, British Secretary of State for War John Profumo has admitted that he lied to the House of Commons about his association with model Christine Keeler. He has resigned from his parliamentary seat and from his Cabinet position. "The Profumo Affair", as it has come to be known, has rocked the nation and has almost led to the downfall of the government. At the time of John Profumo's liaison with Miss Keeler she was allegedly also involved with Russian diplomat Captain Ivanov, a former naval attaché at the Soviet Embassy, a link which has caused very serious security concerns.

Hot air powers balloon brothers to success

1783 Astonished local government officials in Annonay, France, today watched as a "hot air" balloon made by brothers Joseph-Michel and Jacques-Etienne Montgolfier slowly rose 6000 ft (2000 m) into the air, where it remained suspended for a full 10 minutes. The balloon, made of linen and paper, was "powered" by an ingenious method whereby heat from a fire on the ground warmed the air inside the balloon, thus causing it to rise. Today's demonstration is a culmination of earlier experiments by the brothers, working both together and independently. Joseph-Michel – head of the Rives branch of the family paper-making business since 1770 – devised an air pump for removing paper from moulds and, in November of last year, found a way of inflating a small silk container by suspending it over a fire. This was followed by a public demonstration with a larger, oblong-shaped silk balloon. The experiments continued, Joseph-Michel being joined by his younger brother, who runs the family's Vidalon factory. The Academy of Sciences in Paris are likely to be extremely interested in the work of the Montgolfiers.

The great nations have always acted like gangsters, and the small nations like prostitutes.
Stanley Kubrick, American film director, on this day 1963.

1991 Record compensation has been awarded in a British court to 14-year-old Heidi Everett, who was left brain-damaged by a motor accident 11 years ago.

Bobby Kennedy is shot

1968 Doctors are fighting to save the life of 42-year-old Senator Robert Kennedy, who was shot in the head and shoulder just after midnight this morning. The shooting took place at the Ambassador Hotel in Los Angeles, where the Senator had been making a speech after winning the California primary election in his campaign for the Democratic presidential nomination. He has not regained consciousness since being rushed to hospital, and hopes for his recovery are not high. The alleged gunman, a Jordanian Arab by the name of Sirhan Bishara Sirhan, has been arrested. The shooting comes five years after the assassination of Robert Kennedy's brother, President John Kennedy.

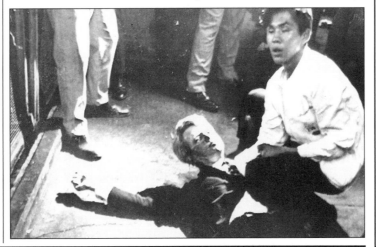

755 AD English missionary Boniface, known as the Apostle of Germany, is murdered with 53 companions in Germany by unbelievers.

1806 Louis Bonaparte is declared king of the Netherlands.

1826 German composer Carl Maria von Weber dies in London, where he has been conducting his opera *Oberon*.

1910 Death of American short-story writer O. Henry.

1915 French sculptor and draughtsman Henri Gaudier-Brzeska is killed in action in World War I, aged 23.

1967 War breaks out between Israel and the neighbouring countries of Egypt, Jordan and Syria.

1972 The Duke of Windsor, briefly King Edward VIII of England, is buried at Frogmore, Windsor.

1988 Kay Cottee sails into Sydney harbour, becoming the first woman to sail solo round the world non-stop.

1989 Solidarity beats the Communists in the first free Polish elections since World War I.

1990 Iran demands that British author Salman Rushdie is handed over to British Muslims.

1991 The Land Acts of 1913 and 1936 and the Group Areas Act of 1950 are nullified in South Africa, restoring land which had been

BIRTHDAYS

John Couch Adams 1819, English astronomer who in 1845 predicted to within 2° the position of the planet Neptune, which was certified in 1846.

Pancho Villa 1878, Mexican revolutionary who raided Texas and New Mexico with an irregular army and supported revolts against Mexican governments.

Federico Garcia Lorca 1898, Spanish poet and dramatist whose masterwork is the trilogy of plays *Blood Wedding*, *Yerma* and *The House of Bernardo Alba*.

Tony Richardson 1928, British film and theatre director.

1683 In Oxford, Elias Ashmole opens the first public museum, the Ashmolean.

1891 Death of Sir John Alexander Macdonald, first prime minister of Canada.

1933 The first drive-in movie opens at Camden, New Jersey.

1936 Gatwick Airport opens in Surrey, UK.

1941 Death of Louis Chevrolet, American car designer.

1956 Death of American archaeologist Hiram Bingham, who located the lost Inca city of Machu Picchu in Peru.

1976 American oil billionaire Jean Paul Getty, who made his first million by the time he was 22, dies in England aged 83.

1982 Stars such as Stevie Wonder, Jackson Browne, Bob Dylan and Linda Ronstadt appear at an anti-nuclear rally at the Rose Bowl in Pasadena, California.

1984 At the order of Prime Minister Indira Gandhi, Indian troops storm the Golden Temple in the Holy City of Amritsar to arrest Sikh militants who have taken refuge there – 712 Sikhs and 90 soldiers are killed.

1987 Pop star Michael Jackson ends his long-term support for the Jehovah's Witnesses.

BIRTHDAYS

Pierre Corneille 1606, French dramatist most famous for *Le Cid*.

Nathan Hale 1755, American revolutionary who was hanged for spying on the British.

Aleksandr Pushkin 1799, Russian poet, novelist and dramatist who wrote the epic verse novel *Eugene Onegin* and the historical drama *Boris Godunov*.

Captain Robert Falcon Scott 1868, English explorer of the Antarctic.

Thomas Mann 1875, German novelist who wrote *Death in Venice*.

Björn Borg 1956, Swedish tennis champion who won the men's singles at Wimbledon five times.

Orwell's bleak view

1949 In his novel, *Nineteen Eighty-Four*, published today, George Orwell has painted a grim picture of the dangers awaiting society if it allows politicians excessive power. In Orwell's view, this would lead to the establishment of a totalitarian state, in which citizens have little say and government has a stranglehold on the spread of information, systematically distorting truth to suit its own ends. The argument is one which the author has brooded on for some years and picks up the theme of his 1945 bestseller, *Animal Farm*, which centred on the corrupting effects of political power. Although suffering from tuberculosis, Orwell was determined to complete the book and wrote the last pages in a remote house in the Hebrides, in between periods of hospitalization.

Thinker's thinker dies

1961 Carl Gustav Jung, the founder of analytical psychology, died today in Switzerland at the age of eighty-five. Jung's contributions to the study of the psyche include his division of personality types into introverted and extroverted, his ideas on the four functions of the mind – thinking, feeling, sensation and intuition – and his belief in a "collective unconscious" linking all mankind. A highly original thinker who loved the simple life, Jung spent his last years with his wife Emma in the house they had built by the shores of Lake Zurich.

ALLIES SEND A MILLION MEN TO FREE EUROPE

1944 As morning dawned over France today, five desolate beaches on the northern French coast – code-named Utah, Omaha, Gold, Juno and Sword – became the scene of the largest military invasion in the world's history. Under the supreme command of US General Dwight D. Eisenhower, around 1 million men, in 4000 ships, disembarked to begin their assault on Rommel's "Atlantic Wall" and to battle their way into France. The combined Allied troops, including French, Canadians, British and Americans, were spearheaded by units of the US 82nd and 101st Airborne Divisions who landed near the town of Saint Mère–Eglise; British commandos were meanwhile taking key bridges and knocking out Nazi communications. Plans for the Normandy Invasion – also known as Operation Overlord – have been underway since January, but were threatened by the worst Channel weather in 25 years. Taking advantage of a break in the weather, Eisenhower ordered the fleet to set sail. Four of the beaches surrendered early, but Omaha proved more of a problem. This evening, however, sizeable sections of all five landing areas are under Allied control. The final campaign to defeat Germany has begun.

1988 In New York City today, David Stern became the world's biggest bubble blower. He blew a bubble measuring a record 50 ft (15.24 m) in length.

Show me a sane man and I will cure him for you.
Carl Gustav Jung, Austrian psychoanalyst who died today, 1961.

Mourners tear off Ayatollah's shroud

1989 There were scenes of hysteria at the funeral of Ayatollah Khomeini in Tehran, it was reported today. As the open coffin of the 87-year-old Iranian leader was born over the heads of the crowd on its way to its resting place on the outskirts of the city, grief-stricken mourners clutched frantically at the body, unwrapping it and tearing up the shroud. Today's funeral ends a decade which, under the Ayatollah, has seen the revival of militant Islamic fundamentalism, of terrorism and war, and of hostility to the West. This came to a head nine months after Khomeini's rise to power with the seizure in Teheran of 52 US embassy staff; the Americans were kept hostage for 444 days. Then the Iran-Iraq war intensified into a full-scale conflict in 1982. Despite repeated Iraqi bids for a cease-fire, fighting did not cease until August 1988.

Israeli first strike on Iraqi reactor

1981 Israeli jets have carried out a bombing raid on a nuclear reactor near Baghdad, Middle Eastern sources claimed today. The raid succeeded in destroying the plant. Prime Minister Begin justified the attack on the basis of the defensive "strike first" theory, saying that Iraq was planning to manufacture nuclear weapons to use against Israel. The event comes at a particularly difficult time in Arab-Israeli affairs. Negotiations, led by US envoy Philip Habib, are currently underway to prevent further confrontation between Israel and Syria over the Syrian establishment of Soviet surface-to-air missiles in Lebanon's Bekaa Valley in April.

1970 New York's Metropolitan Opera House, temple of classical music, is ringing to the strains of a very different tune today as British group The Who perform their rock opera, *Tommy*. The story centres around the experiences of the eponymous hero, a "deaf, dumb and blind kid", and is an ambitious undertaking for any group. This is expected to be the opera's last performance.

Spain and Portugal divide up world

1494 The ongoing dispute between Spain and Portugal over territorial rights was finally resolved today as ambassadors from both countries signed a treaty at Tordesillas in northern Spain. The dispute goes back to last year when Pope Alexander VI set a line of demarcation running from pole to pole 100 leagues west of the Cape Verde islands off the African coast, giving Spain exclusive rights to the region west of the line, and Portugal rights to the east. Both powers have sent expeditions to explore unknown territories, and the Pope's ruling was an attempt to settle any rival claims to land. While accepting the principle of demarcation, Spain has feared Portuguese incursions and there have been protests from Portugal that the division does not allow enough room at sea for her African voyages. Today's agreement has affirmed the papal division, but has moved the demarcation line a further 270 leagues west of its original position.

The King's palace open to his people

1982 The palatial mansion known as Graceland, in Memphis, Tennessee – home of rock superstar Elvis Presley, who died five years ago – today opens its doors to the public for the first time. Thousands of adoring fans will now have a chance to see how their idol lived. After his first hit of 1956, "Heartbreak Hotel", Elvis dominated the pop music charts, having at least one, if not two, releases in the Top Ten for the next 16 months. His gyrations during his performances drove teenage audiences wild and earned him the nickname "Elvis the Pelvis" – but critics saw them, and his music, as signs of moral decline. With his blend of white country and western and black rhythm and blues, Elvis was one of the key figures in the development of rock 'n' roll. Those who make the pilgrimage to Graceland will be coming to honour the memory of a legend – a man who has become one of the icons of the twentieth century.

Hero of Bannockburn dies

1329 All Scotland is in mourning today for the death of her king, Robert I, who finally succumbed to leprosy, from which he had been suffering for some time. Familiarly known as Robert de Bruce, the King seized the throne in 1306, at a time when his country was under English domination, and was immediately attacked and driven into hiding by English forces. Refusing to accept defeat, he returned to earn a place in Scottish history with his legendary victory at the Battle of Bannockburn in 1314, when he routed the armies of Edward II and drove the English off Scottish soil. Despite his victory, it would be another 14 years before the English finally agreed to accept Robert as the rightful king of Scotland.

> *That these United Colonies are, and of right ought to be, free and independent states.*
> **Richard Henry Lee**, American patriot and senator, Motion in Philadelphia, 1776.

1566 Sir Thomas Gresham lays the foundation stone of the first Royal Exchange in London.

1712 Philadelphia bans the import of slaves.

1905 Norway declares its independence from Sweden.

1933 The ballet *The Seven Deadly Sins* is premiered in Paris with choreography by Georges Balanchine and music and libretto by Kurt Weill and Bertolt Brecht.

1937 Hollywood star Jean Harlow, the original platinum blonde, dies at the age of only 26 of cerebral oedema.

1945 Benjamin Britten's opera *Peter Grimes* is premiered at Sadler's Wells Theatre in London.

1970 English novelist E. M. Forster, author of *A Room with a View*, *Howard's End* and *A Passage to India*, dies aged 91.

1971 India seals its border with newly independent Bangladesh to keep out cholera-stricken refugees.

1977 Street parties are held all over Britain to celebrate Queen Elizabeth's silver jubilee.

1980 American novelist Henry Miller, author of *Tropic of Cancer*, dies aged 88.

1983 Rock 'n' roller Jerry Lee Lewis marries his fifth wife, Shawn Michelle Stevens.

1990 President de Klerk lifts the state of emergency in South Africa.

BIRTHDAYS

Paul Gauguin 1848, French Post-Impressionist painter who went to live and work in the South Pacific.

Jessica Tandy 1909, English-born American actress who in 1990, at the age of 80, became the oldest person to receive an Oscar for her part in *Driving Miss Daisy*.

Pietro Annigoni 1910, Italian painter who is chiefly known for his portraits – and particularly that of Queen Elizabeth II.

Prince 1960, American singer and musician best-known for the film and album *Purple Rain*.

JUNE 8

BIRTHDAYS

Robert Schumann 1810, German composer.

Sir John Millais 1829, English painter who was one of the founders of the Pre-Raphaelite Brotherhood and was the most popular with the general public.

Frank Lloyd Wright 1869, American architect whose buildings include the Guggenheim Museum in New York.

Professor Sir Frances Crick 1916, British biologist who, with J. D. Watson, discovered the structure of DNA.

Nancy Sinatra 1940, American singer, daughter of Frank.

Prophet's blissful abode

632 Mohammed, prophet and founder of Islam, died today in Mecca. Mohammed took up his calling late in life: at 40, a revelation from Allah convinced him that he must spread the word of the one true god, and he began to forge the new religion. By the time of his death, and after several jihads (holy wars), most of the Arab peninsula had come to accept Islam, with Mohammed as its leader. Central to the Islamic message is a belief in the afterlife, in which the good will be rewarded by entry to Paradise: Mohammed will now pass into that "blissful abode – garden and vineyard" where there will be "girls with swelling breasts . . . and a brimming cup . . . a recompense from [the] Lord".

King's killer caught in London

1968 A man has been arrested in London for the killing of black civil rights leader Dr Martin Luther King last April. James Earl Ray, an escaped convict, is accused of firing the fatal shots that killed Dr King as he came out on to the balcony of his motel room in Memphis, Tennessee. Dr King was in the city to support a strike of local dustmen. Profoundly influenced by the teachings of Mahatma Gandhi, King insisted that protest should be non-violent, yet since he came to prominence in the civil rights movement in 1955 it was always on the cards that he himself would meet a violent end. He was awarded the Nobel Peace Prize in 1964. His funeral was held in his birthplace of Atlanta, Georgia, and was attended by 150,000 people.

"Angel of Death" is dead

1985 A skeleton dug up by Brazilian police today is said to be that of arch-Nazi Joseph Mengele, the man known as the sinister "Angel of Death". Camp doctor at Auschwitz from 1943 to 1945, Mengele was notorious for the medical experiments he performed on inmates. After escaping from capture by the British after the war, Mengele went to ground. He surfaced for a time in West Germany and then, in 1951, appeared in Buenos Aires, going by the name of "Gregorio Gregori". He later moved to Paraguay, where he was granted citizenship, but since that time his whereabouts, or his fate, remain unknown.

> *Government, even in its best state, is but a necessary evil; in its worst state, an intolerable one.*
> **Thomas Paine**, British writer and political philosopher, who died today, 1809.

1978 New Zealander Naomi James today became the first woman to sail solo round the world, having set out from Dartmouth in England on September 9, 1977 in *Express Crusader*.

Brains behind the American revolution

1809 Thomas Paine, guiding light of the American Revolution and one of the most influential thinkers of the age, died in New York City today. Through his writings, Paine inspired and revived the nation's morale during the dark days of America's fight for independence from Britain. His famous pamphlet *Common Sense*, published in 1776 and including the words, "The cause of America is in great measure the cause of all mankind" sold more than 100,000 copies in three months. *The American Crisis*, published later in the same year, is credited with contributing to American success at the Battle of Trenton. While in France, Paine wrote *The Rights of Man*, a defence of the French revolution that earned him the brand "traitor" in his native Britain. Although a supporter of the revolutionary cause, he was opposed to the execution of Louis XVI: this aroused radical suspicions and landed him in the Luxembourg Prison, where he worked on the statement of his religious beliefs, *The Age of Reason*, published after his release.

Deserted Nero stabs himself

AD 68 Reports from Rome today claim that the Emperor Nero has taken his own life. He is said to have stabbed himself in the throat with a dagger. The suicide occurred after Nero returned from Greece to find that he had been deserted by his Praetorian Guard. Resentment against the Emperor has been brewing throughout the Empire, and there have recently been revolts in Africa, Spain and Gaul. High levels of taxation to fund the Emperor's excesses has been one cause of the hostility, as has his total lack of interest in government. Leaving affairs of state to his advisers, Burrus and Seneca, Nero preferred to think of himself as a creative artist: "I have only to appear and sing to have peace once more in Gaul," he boasted.

CRICKET CAPTAIN RUN OUT OVER BAD BEHAVIOUR

1988 Two days of tabloid reports over sexual frolics during the first Test match in Nottingham have led to the sacking of England cricket captain Mike Gatting. Gatting has denied the stories and has threatened legal action. Although they have accepted his denials, the board of selectors feel that Gatting behaved "irresponsibly" when he invited a hotel barmaid to his room for a drink, and that the affair has tarnished the image of the game. Four other players from the team have also been called to account over the allegations. Gatting, who led the successful Australian tour last year, has asked not to be considered for the next Test. His most likely successor as captain is said to be team-mate Mike Emburey, although nothing has been announced.

1993 Crown Prince Naruhito of Japan has celebrated his marriage in a splendid shinto ceremony at the Imperial Palace in Tokyo. The bride was Masako Owada, a former diplomat. The couple have married amid mounting political tension.

1441 Death of Netherlandish painter Jan van Eyck, court painter and equerry to Philip the Good, Duke of Burgundy.

1198 Otto of Brunswick is crowned German king and Holy Roman Emperor Otto IV.

1898 China grants Britain a 99-year lease on Hong Kong.

1899 US heavyweight boxing champion James Jackson Jeffries knocks out Britain's Bob Fitzsimmons in the eleventh round, thus becoming world champion.

1908 King Edward VII of England visits Tsar Nicholas II on board the royal yacht in the Baltic Sea, the first meeting between a British monarch and a Russian tsar.

1959 America launches the *George Washington*, the first nuclear submarine with Polaris missiles.

1964 Death of newspaper baron Lord Beaverbrook.

1967 Israel seizes the Golan Heights on the fifth day of war with Syria, Egypt and Jordan.

1970 Bob Dylan is given an honorary degree at Princeton University.

1975 The BBC and LBC relay the first live transmission from the House of Commons.

1989 In China, show trials begin of the leaders of the demonstration in Tienanmen Square.

1934 Mickey Mouse, the first character created by American cartoon king Walt Disney, has at last got some competition. Making his debut in *The Wise Little Hen*, Donald Duck is Disney's latest creation. Like Mickey, Donald has the gift of speech – but his voice is contrastingly strange and "quacky". Audiences will have to keep a keen ear open if they want to understand just what he is saying.

Last Nuremberg Nazi hanged

1951 The judgement of the Nuremberg court will be fulfilled today as the noose slips over the head of the last Nazi condemned to hang for "crimes against humanity". The trials, which took place between November 1945 and October 1946, were conducted by four judges and four prosecutors from the United States, United Kingdom, USSR and France. In all, 24 of Hitler's top men were accused on a number of different counts, including conspiracy to wage wars of aggression, killing of hostages and crimes against peace. Twelve men, including leading Nazis Goering and Ribbentrop, were given the death penalty – a fate Goering only escaped by killing himself.

Comedy, like sodomy, is an unnatural act.
Marty Feldman, British comedian, 1969.

Dickens dies in mid-classic

1870 Britain is in mourning today after the death of the nation's best-loved author, Charles Dickens, who died of a stroke at home. He was engaged in his latest novel, *The Mystery of Edwin Drood*, which remains half-finished. The punishing schedule of Dickens' last few years affected his health badly, and is largely to blame for his sudden death. While continuing to write, he also made a series of tours of England and the United States in which he gave readings from his own works to enraptured audiences. Dickens' professional success was partly marred by personal unhappiness – he and his wife separated in 1859, and his sons failed to live up to his expectations. He died at Gad's Hill Place in Kent, the house he had loved from boyhood and finally owned.

BIRTHDAYS

Peter I 1672, Russian emperor known as Peter the Great on account of the modernization programmes and many reforms he undertook.

George Stephenson 1781, English engineer who developed greatly improved steam locomotives.

Elizabeth Garrett Anderson 1836, English physician who, having had to study privately, pioneered the admission of women to the medical profession.

Cole Porter 1893, American composer and lyricist whose musicals include *Anything Goes* and *Can-Can*.

JUNE 10

BIRTHDAYS

Witch hunt fever sweeps Salem

1692 In the climate of fear that possesses the Massachusetts town of Salem, an ominous trial has been taking place – and the first hangings were today. The women hanged have been found guilty of witchcraft, the first victims of a witch hunt of such a terrifying scale that no woman can consider herself safe. It all began when certain young girls from the area, after listening to the voodoo tales of a West Indian slave, Tituba, claimed that they were possessed by the Devil. The girls accused three women, including Tituba herself, of witchcraft, and the hunt was on. Accusations have been flying – there has even been talk implicating the wife of the Governor, William Phips. In the wake of the accusations, a special court, presided over by judges Samuel Sewell, John Hathorne and William Stoughton, was set up to investigate the affair; although the court is a civil one, it has the full backing of the clergy. The trials began in May and are set to continue.

1990 Czechoslovak democrats have won a huge victory in the country's first genuine elections for 40 years, with Vaclav Havel's Civic Forum and its Slovak allies winning more than 170 seats out of 300. The new parliament must steer the country through tough economic reforms.

> *There were times my pants were so thin I could sit on a dime and tell if it was heads or tails.*
> **Spencer Tracy**, American actor, who died today, 1967.

Bavarian King saves Wagner's Ring

1865 *Tristan und Isolde*, a work once regarded as too revolutionary to perform, receives its first airing at the Munich Opera House today. Composed by Richard Wagner between 1857 and 1859, the three-act opera is based on a traditional English tale of lost love (life blends with legend in much of Wagner's work). In Tristan's obsession there are strong echoes of the composer's own hopeless love for Mathilde Wesendonk, wife of his former patron, that led to the break-up of his marriage. And in the miraculous discovery of a new patron, the young King Ludwig II of Bavaria, Wagner has his own knight in shining armour. Aged 51, penniless and facing financial ruin, Wagner was rescued by the King, who set him up in a villa, invited him to complete the unfinished Ring series and enabled *Tristan* to be performed today.

1829 The rivalry between England's two most prestigious universities, Oxford and Cambridge, took to the water for the first time today. Two eight-men crews raced each other along the River Thames at Henley in south-east England, in a contest of rowing power nicknamed simply "The Boat Race".

Air base empties as volcano erupts

1991 A mass evacuation of 14,500 US personnel is taking place at Clark Air Base in the Philippines after Mount Pinatubo erupted, raining a shower of ash and volcanic debris over the surrounding area. The volcano was thought to be dormant. US spokesman Lt. Col. Ron Rand confirms that the evacuees are being driven to the US naval base at Subic Bay, 30 miles (48 km) to the southwest. There are a total of 40,000 US personnel in the Philippines, half of whom were stationed at the Clark Air Base.

After six days of war Israel doubles its size

1967 Six days of hostilities between Israel and its Arab neighbours ended today with a decisive victory for the Israelis, and a 200 per cent expansion in the territory they hold. The so-called Six-Day War has been a clear demonstration of Israeli air supremacy. The war began on June 5, after Syria had asked for Egypt's help in withstanding threatened Israeli retaliation against Syrian border raids. Egypt's President Nasser called for the removal of UN peacekeeping forces at Suez, closed the Gulf of Aquaba, mobilized the army and moved troops into Sinai. Israel's answer was a burst of simultaneous air attacks on Syrian, Egyptian and Jordanian air bases that decimated its enemies' air capability. In the week that followed, Israel went on to defeat all enemy resistance.

> *We were the first fascists... Mussolini copied fascism from me.*
> **Marcus Garvey**, Jamaican-born black nationalist, who died today, 1940.

80,000 celebrate Mandela's birthday

1988 A crowd of 80,000 packed London's Wembley Stadium today in what must be the biggest 70th birthday party ever. The only person unable to attend was the birthday guest himself – black South African leader Nelson Mandela, who has been in prison since 1964, serving a life sentence on a conviction of attempting to overthrow the state. In tribute to him, singers and musicians from all over the world, including South Africa itself, came to join in the day-long concert, which was televised and broadcast live to an estimated audience of 1 billion in 60 countries. Deputy leader of the banned African National Congress, Mandela has come to epitomize the struggle against apartheid. Attempts to keep politics out of the affair were thwarted, and many performers made references to South Africa's "terrorist state" and to the lack of strong British opposition to apartheid.

England and Spain: keep it in the family

1509 At a private ceremony today in the chapel of the Franciscan Observants at Greenwich, near London, King Henry VIII finally married his former sister-in-law, Catherine of Aragon. Catherine – who is aged 24 and six years Henry's senior – was previously married to Henry's elder brother, Arthur, who died seven years ago. The couple have been engaged since 1503, but there has been much controversy about the validity of the marriage which, some argued, went directly against the laws of the Church. According to Biblical teaching, "If a man shall take his brother's wife, it is impurity . . . they shall be childless". The issue has hinged on a technicality – if the former marriage was never consummated, Catherine was never Arthur's "wife" and would therefore be free to marry his brother. The real truth may never be revealed, and there has been more at stake here than marriage. Catherine's mother, Queen Isabella of Spain has been keen to continue the Anglo-Spanish alliance secured by Catherine's earlier union. In an attempt to silence any opposition, she persuaded the Pope to issue a dispensation allowing the marriage, conducted today by the Archbishop of Canterbury.

Exit "The Duke"

1979 John Wayne, veteran Hollywood star, died earlier today. Born Marion Michael Morrison in Winterset, Iowa in 1907, after a slow start he made his name as a genial tough guy and all-American hero in a series of Westerns and war films, and became one of the best known and most successful actors in Hollywood. His first major screen appearance was as Ringo Kid in director John Ford's 1939 film *Stagecoach*, a part that set the tone for the rest of his film career. Nicknamed "The Duke", Wayne maintained his on-screen persona off screen, being a staunch supporter of law, order, and traditional American values; an anti-Communist, he also supported the Vietnam War. Shortly before his death earlier this month, he was awarded a commemorative gold medal by the US Congress.

1989 At the tender age of 17 years and 109 days, Michael Chang of the United States today became the youngest-ever winner of the French Open tennis championships. He beat Stefan Edberg of Sweden.

> *The notes I handle no better than many pianists. But the pauses between the notes – ah, that is where the art resides.*
> **Artur Schnabel**, Austrian concert pianist, 1958.

Merc goes beserk

1955 Horrified spectators saw the famous Le Mans racetrack in France become a scene of carnage today. One of the cars competing in the 24-hour Grand Prix – a Mercedes Benz – ran out of control and plunged into the grandstand, killing an estimated 80 people and injuring more than 100 more. The news has shocked the motor racing world. Questions will undoubtedly be asked about the safety of the sport, and tighter restrictions may be imposed.

1573 In Britain, a Puritan pamphlet calling for the abolition of episcopacy is suppressed in the House of Commons.

1727 George II of England accedes to the throne following the death of his father, George I, the first Hanoverian king of England.

1905 British golfer Harry Vardon wins his fourth Open golf championship at Prestwick.

1940 Italian dictator Benito Mussolini declares war on the Allies.

1946 Italy is proclaimed a republic.

1955 Twenty-two years of Liberal rule end in Canada with Progressive Conservative John G. Diefenbaker's victory.

1970 Aleksandr Feodorovich Kerenski, prime minister of Russia in 1917 until the Bolshevik Revolution, dies in exile in New York.

1977 Dutch marines storm the train in which South Moluccan terrorists are holding hostages.

1990 Right-wing politician and novelist Mario Vargas Llosa is defeated in the second round of the Peruvian elections.

1990 Two die as the tanker *Mega Borg* catches fire in the Gulf of Mexico.

BIRTHDAYS

Ben Jonson 1572, English dramatist and poet whose satirical plays include *Volpone*, *The Alchemist* and *Bartholomew Fair*.

John Constable 1776, one of the greatest British landscape artists.

Richard Strauss 1864, German composer and conductor whose operas include *Salome*, *Der Rosenkavalier* and *Ariadne auf Naxos*.

Jacques Cousteau 1910, French underwater explorer who invented a means of using television underwater and made films such as *The Silent World* and *The Living Sea*.

Gene Wilder 1935, American actor best-known for comedy films such as *The Producers*.

JUNE 12

BIRTHDAYS

Charles Kingsley 1819, English clergyman who wrote *The Water Babies* and *Westward Ho!*

George Bush 1924, American Republican politician and president.

Vic Damone 1928, American singer who had his biggest hit with "The Street Where You Live" from *My Fair Lady*.

Anne Frank 1929, Dutch Jewish schoolgirl who, in hiding from the Nazis, wrote her famous diary before going to her death in a German concentration camp.

THE UNTOUCHABLES FINGER AL CAPONE

1931 The days of notorious gangland chief Al Capone may at last be numbered. Today, in their crackdown on the bootleggers, the Chicago police elite known as the "Untouchables" closed in, charging him with 5000 offences under America's Prohibition laws. Also known as "Scarface" because of a razor slash on his left cheek, Capone has dominated the gangland scene since the infamous St Valentine's Day Massacre in 1929, when his henchmen, dressed as policemen, gunned down seven rival gang members. Capone's underworld empire has profited from gambling and prostitution, but its main income has been from bootlegging. In 1927, the man that started life in Naples the son of a poor barber is said to have amassed a fortune close to $100 million (£54 million).

New sport with bases and ball could catch on in USA

1839 A new kind of ball game was played today at Cooperstown, NY. Known as "baseball" because of its four-base infield, it is said to be the invention of Abner Doubleday, who is teaching local military cadets how to play. The game uses a soft ball to avoid injury – one way of putting out a player running from base to base is for a fielder to hit him with the ball. Although Cooperstown would like to claim all the glory for giving America a totally new sport, some have their doubts. Baseball, it seems, bears a striking resemblance to the American children's game Old Cat and the English rounders, and may simply be an adaptation of these earlier forms.

> *Once in the racket you're always in it.*
> **Al Capone**, Chicago gangster, charged today with 5000 prohibition offences, 1931.

RUSSIANS GO TO VOTE IN FIRST DEMOCRATIC ELECTION

1991 The people of Russia are making history today as they go to the polls in the country's first-ever democratic elections. As they cast their votes, frontrunner Boris Yeltsin is sweating it out, waiting to hear whether he has gained the 51 per cent share of the vote that he needs to make it through the first round. Yeltsin is one of six candidates. Individually, none of the others is likely to get a big enough vote to defeat him, but their combined share could present problems. Yeltsin supporters say that the other candidates have a subversive purpose in mind, and are standing only to undermine his chances of becoming president.

1991 The people of Leningrad have shown that they believe in the importance of "What's in a name?" In a referendum today they voted by 55 per cent to 43 per cent to change the name of their city back to St Petersburg, a name by which it has not been known since pre–Revolution days. The move is indicative of the radical changes in outlook taking place in Russia. "Two years ago people would not have supported the idea," says mayor Anatoli Sobchak. Street signs will be amended, but it will take time for people to use the new name.

Indian PM Gandhi may have fixed victory

1975 A shock verdict in Allahabad, India today has caused a political scandal and a crisis of confidence in the country's leadership. A judge in Allahabad, home constituency of Prime Minister Indira Gandhi, has ruled that her landslide victory in 1971 was invalid because civil servants illegally aided her campaign. Mrs Gandhi, who came to power in 1966, is the daughter of Jawaharlal Nehru, India's first Prime Minister after the country gained independence from Britain in 1947. Today's verdict has brought angry calls for Mrs Gandhi's resignation, and she is now faced with the biggest political storm of her career.

> *So greatly did she care for freedom that she died for it. So dearly did she love women that she offered her life as their ransom. That is the verdict given at the great Inquest of the Nation on the death of Emily Wilding Davison.*
>
> **Christabel Pankhurst** on Emily Davison, who died protesting for her cause June 4, 1913.

Mad King Ludwig in suicide riddle

1886 King Ludwig II of Bavaria and his physician drowned today in Lake Starnberg, near Munich. The death is being treated as suicide. The King has had a history of mental disorders and was declared insane earlier this month. His struggle with homosexuality, as revealed in his diaries, must also have added to his psychological distress. Ludwig ascended the throne at 18, in 1864. A devoted patron of the composer Richard Wagner, the King spent much of his energy in building magnificent, fairytale castles and staging extravagant artistic performances.

1774 Rhode Island has become the first American colony to ban the importation of slaves, and to assure their freedom. The new act, passed today by the General Assembly in Newport, states, "No Negro nor mulatto slave shall be brought in to this colony, and in case any slave shall be brought in, he or she shall be . . . rendered immediately free . . . "

Workers march against poll tax

1381 Flemish merchants were killed and the Savoy Palace – home of John of Gaunt, the king's uncle – was burnt down as a crowd of angry peasants marched on London today. The marchers, agricultural workers from Kent and Essex in south-east England, were led by Walter "Wat" Tyler. Urban workers are also said to have joined the marchers, and similar protests are being launched in East Anglia. Although economic unrest has been brewing since the 1350s, it is the unpopular new tax – "poll tax" – that finally brought matters to a head today. The workers are also angry about the imposition of a maximum wage – labour is in short supply since the ravages of the Black Death, and the new wage restrictions limit workers' pay claims. Today's protest has taken the government by surprise, and the peasants are in no mood to be ignored. There seems little doubt, however, that this "Peasants' Revolt" will be crushed – putting little pressure on the king to make changes.

DOODLE BUGS BATTER LONDON

1944 London came under shock attack today as Hitler let loose a devastating new weapon on the city. The so-called V1 flying bomb, or "doodle bug", as it has been nicknamed, is a long-range device that can be launched safely from within enemy territory. Travelling at lightning speed, it moves too fast for anti-aircraft guns to target it accurately, and its super-power warhead is likely to bring down any fighter plane attempting to intercept it. Nazi scientists are said to have been working on the bomb for some time, but British intelligence has not known where it was being made or when it would be used. Ultimately the only way to deal with it may be to discover and destroy its launch sites.

Boxers fight for China's pride

1900 A group of volunteer soldiers known as the Boxers went on the rampage through Peking today in protest against the "foreign devils" who have such a hold on their country. Weakened by a century of conflict – both internal and external – China has, over the years, agreed to a series of treaties which have given away large slices of the national cake to foreign powers, notably the United States, Europe and Japan. Resentment against the terms of these treaties has, until now, only bubbled below the surface; events today, said to have been actively encouraged by the Chinese authorities, show just how deep Chinese anger really is.

323 BC Alexander the Great, King of Macedon, who came to the throne at the age of only 20 and conquered Persia, Egypt, Babylon, central Asia and part of India, dies aged 33 returning from India.

1842 Queen Victoria becomes the first British monarch to travel by train when she takes a trip from Slough to Paddington.

1893 The first women's golf championship is held at Royal Lytham in Britain and is won by Lady Margaret Scott.

1930 Sir Henry Segrave, who broke the British land and water speed records, is killed when his speedboat capsizes at 98 mph (158 kph) on Lake Windermere in northern England.

1951 Princess Elizabeth, heir to the British throne, lays the foundation stone of the National Theatre on the South Bank in London.

1956 Real Madrid win the first European Cup in Paris, beating Stade de Reims 4–3.

1988 The first beauty contest is held in the Soviet Union.

1989 Mikhail Gorbachev and Chancellor Kohl agree that East and West Germany should be reunited.

BIRTHDAYS

Fanny Burney 1752, British novelist and close friend of Dr Johnson.

William Butler Yeats 1865, Irish poet, dramatist and co-founder of the Abbey Theatre in Dublin.

Elizabeth Schumann 1888, German-born soprano who excelled in the music of Mozart and Richard Strauss.

Basil Rathbone 1892, South African-born English actor who played Sherlock Holmes in 14 films and villains in many others.

Dorothy L. Sayers 1893, English writer of detective stories and creator of the aristocratic sleuth Lord Peter Wimsey.

Don Budge 1915, American tennis champion who was the first amateur to win the Grand Slam.

1755 Dr Johnson's *Dictionary* goes on sale at £4 10s for the two volumes.

1800 Napoleon's forces vanquish the Austrians at the Battle of Marengo.

1814 The Netherlands and Belgium are united by the Treaty of London.

1839 A regatta is held for the first time at Henley-on-Thames, Oxfordshire.

1917 German planes bomb London for the first time.

1927 Death of Jerome K. Jerome, author of the comic novel *Three Men in a Boat*.

1936 Death of G. K. Chesterton, British novelist, essayist and poet who published more than 100 volumes.

1940 German troops march into Paris.

1946 Death of John Logie Baird, British electrical engineer who invented an early form of television as well as radar and fibre optics.

1964 Nelson Mandela is sentenced to life imprisonment.

1983 Protests erupt in Santiago against the regime of Chilean dictator General Pinochet.

1990 In Bucharest, Romania, street battles break out between students demanding democracy and miners providing support for the interim government of Iliescu.

BIRTHDAYS

Che Guevara 1928, Argentinian-born revolutionary who fought with Fidel Castro's forces and then moved on to guerrilla warfare in Bolivia.

Harriet Beecher Stowe 1811, American novelist who wrote *Uncle Tom's Cabin* to draw attention to the plight of the slaves.

Burl Ives 1909, American singer and actor who won an Oscar for *The Big Country*.

Sam Wanamaker 1919, American actor and director.

Steffi Graf 1969, German tennis star who won the Wimbledon women's single title at 19.

CROMWELL LEADS DECISIVE VICTORY

1645 Parliamentary troops under the leadership of Oliver Cromwell are reported to have inflicted a heavy defeat on Prince Rupert's Royalist forces at Naseby, 20 miles (32 km) south of Leicester in the English Midlands. After a pursuit by Cromwell, the opposing armies took up positions on the ridges flanking the valley of Broad Moor – 10,000 Royalists facing 14,000 of Cromwell's men. The Royalists successfully attacked Cromwell's left wing, but then made the fatal error of pursuing the fleeing Parliamentarians. Cromwell seized his chance to regroup the right flank of his cavalry to make a crushing assault on the Royalist centre, routing Prince Rupert's army and scoring a decisive Parliamentary victory in the Civil War.

Argentines surrender: Falklands back to Britain

1982 "Britain is great again," boasted Prime Minister Margaret Thatcher as Argentinian troops today surrendered to the British commander of land forces in the Falklands. The surrender marks the end of a six-week conflict that has cost 254 British and 750 Argentinian lives. The conflict began on April 2 when, in a continuing dispute with Britain over the sovereignty of the Islands, Argentina invaded the Falklands and, on the following day, South Georgia. A large British task force was immediately despatched on the three-week voyage to the South Atlantic. Despite diplomatic attempts by the United States and others to prevent hostilities, fighting began later that month. Notable losses were the sinking of the *General Belgrano*, Argentina's second-largest warship, 30 miles (48 km) south of the 200-mile (320 km) exclusion zone imposed by Britain around the Islands, and the British destroyer HMS *Sheffield*, which was struck by an Argentinian Exocet missile.

Queen knights Sir Ronnie

1989 Former governor of California and US president Ronald Reagan today received another honour when he was given a knighthood by Queen Elizabeth. As president of the United States, Reagan was one of the architects of the new cordiality between East and West, and has personally met Soviet leader Mikhail Gorbachev on several occasions to have talks on disarmament. During his 1988 visit to Britain, he called for "a newer world of freedom and individual rights for all". The new knight retired from presidential office in January of this year, being succeeded by George Bush. He had been US president since 1980. At 73, he was the oldest man to be elected to the office.

> *When was a war not a war? When it was carried on by methods of barbarism.*
> **Henry Campbell-Bannerman** refers to the Boer War, 1901.

1789 After drifting an incredible 3500 miles (5600 km) in an open boat, Captain Bligh and 18 loyal crew members put ashore at the island of Timor today. Bligh captained the 215-ton *Bounty* on its voyage from Tahiti to the West Indies with a cargo of breadfruit trees. Tensions on board erupted when the vessel reached the Friendly Islands and large numbers of the crew, led by Fletcher Christian, mutinied.

Suffragette sacrifice

1913 Bearing banners with the words "Fight on and God will give the victory", suffragettes today attended the funeral of Emily Davison, who was killed by King George V's horse at the Epsom Derby earlier this month. Davison grabbed the reins of the horse as it thundered towards the winning post, intending only to publicize the suffragette cause – votes for women – but her bid for publicity went horribly wrong. Today's funeral was not attended by Mrs Emmeline Pankhurst, founder of the British movement, who is in prison. In the face of the stubborn and patronizing attitude of Liberal prime minister Asquith and his government, the suffragettes have adopted an increasingly violent strategy – including pouring acid into letterboxes. Such tactics have not endeared them to the populace, but the force-feeding of suffragettes on hunger strike in prison has aroused great public sympathy.

Marilyn's blonde bombshell rocks Hollywood

1953 Curvaceous blonde Marilyn Monroe has caused quite a stir in Hollywood in her first major starring role in the film comedy *Gentlemen Prefer Blondes*, released today. The film is based on the bestseller of the same name by Anita Loos, and centres around the adventures of a "dumb blonde", played by Monroe, and a worldly showgirl, played by co-star Jane Russell, who go to Paris in search of rich husbands. Monroe, a former photographic model, made it into the movies after a nude shot of her was spotted on a calendar. A succession of bit parts followed, then minor roles in *The Asphalt Jungle* and *All About Eve*, both released in 1950. In *Gentlemen Prefer Blondes*, Monroe reveals quite a talent for comedy, bringing a deceptive wide-eyed naïveté to her character, the beauty without brains.

New school for Nightingale

1860 Nursing pioneer Florence Nightingale today opened the world's first school for nurses at St Thomas' Hospital in London. The heroine of the Crimean War, Nightingale has done more than anyone to raise the standards of nursing and to improve the way in which the job is viewed. During the war, she not only tended the sick and wounded in the most primitive conditions, but pressed the British government for better food supplies and hygiene facilities. The £45,000 used to open the new school comes from the Nightingale Fund, established through public subscription to commemorate Crimea. The school will provide nurses with their first formal training courses.

1752 In a brave – or perhaps foolhardy – act, American founding father, diplomat and scientist Benjamin Franklin today flew a kite in a thunderstorm to prove his theory that electricity and lightning are the same phenomenon. He also believes that electricity is "an Element diffused among, and attracted by, other matter, particularly Water and Metals". If it is, it should be possible to harness its power.

Alcock and Brown cross Atlantic in one swoop

1919 Aviation history was made today as Capt. John Alcock and Lt Arthur Whitten Brown touched down on the green turf at Clifden, Ireland, thus completing the world's first non-stop flight across the Atlantic. Taking off from St John's, Newfoundland, yesterday, the two former World War I airmen completed their record-breaking flight – 1960 miles (3150 km) across the empty expanse of the Atlantic Ocean – in only 16 hours 12 minutes. Their aircraft, a Vickers-Vimy bomber, was kept aloft by two 350-hp Rolls-Royce engines.

BARON KNIGHTS SIGN DEAL

1215 King John and his barons met on the banks of the River Thames at Runnymede, near London, today to hammer out a new deal. The document signed is called the Magna Carta. Its effect will be a decentralization of power, taking total authority from the hands of the King and granting the people of England – and particularly noblemen – certain basic rights and liberties. The barons have been pressing for the agreement in the wake of years of heavy taxation and increasing power of the monarchy. In a show of good faith, the King has agreed to a penalty clause – if he does not keep to the terms of the charter, a council of 25 barons are allowed the ultimate sanction of taking him to war.

1381 English poll tax protester Wat Tyler is executed at Smithfield.

1790 French Protestant militia massacre 300 Roman Catholics.

1813 Britain forms a new coalition with Prussia and Russia against Napoleon.

1825 The Duke of York lays the foundation stone of London Bridge.

1844 In the US, Charles Goodyear patents vulcanized rubber.

1846 The 49th parallel is proclaimed to be the border between the US and Canada.

1888 Emperor Frederick III of Germany dies.

1904 The paddle steamer *General Slocum* catches fire in New York Harbor, killing 693 people.

1933 China and Tibet end a two-year war with a treaty that agrees mutual respect for the pre-war border.

1934 In Venice, dictators Hitler and Mussolini meet for the first time.

1954 Atom bomb inventor Robert Oppenheimer is declared a security risk by Senator Joe McCarthy's committee because of his opposition to the development of the hydrogen bomb.

BIRTHDAYS

Edward the Black Prince 1330, eldest son of Edward III of England who was renowned for his valour and gained his name from the black armour he wore in battle.

Edvard Grieg 1843, Norwegian composer whose work was influenced by the folk music of his country.

Harry Langdon 1884, American silent film actor who was at one time rated as one of the four top American comedians.

Erroll Garner 1923, American jazz pianist and composer.

Simon Callow 1949, British stage and screen actor whose films include *Room with a View*.

1722 John Churchill, first Duke of Marlborough, dies aged 72.

1869 Charles Sturt, English explorer who discovered much of Australia, dies aged 74.

1880 Salvation Army ladies wear their bonnets for the first time as they march through Hackney in London.

1929 The first four places in the Le Mans 24-hour endurance test are won by Bentleys.

1948 The first air hijack occurs when Chinese bandits attempt to take over a Cathay Airways Catalina flying boat – the crew fight back and the aircraft crashes, killing all but the hijack gang leader.

1958 Former prime minister of Hungary Imre Nagy is hanged for the role he played in the unsuccessful revolution of 1956.

1958 Yellow lines marking no-parking zones appear on British roads.

1963 Valentina Tereshkova of the Soviet Union blasts off in *Vostok 6* to become the first woman in space.

1972 German police capture Ulrike Meinhof, the last member of the Baader-Meinhof group still at large.

1977 Death of Werner von Braun, German rocket pioneer who pursued his career under the Nazis and then worked on the US space programme after the war.

1990 Belgian police arrest IRA members suspected of killing Australian tourists in Holland.

BIRTHDAYS

Gustav V 1858, Swedish monarch who reigned for 43 years.

Stan Laurel 1890, English-born comedian who went to the USA and formed a successful partnership with Oliver Hardy to make films such as *A Chump at Oxford*, *Hog Wild*, *Way Out West* and *The Flying Deuces*.

Tom Graveney 1927, British cricketer who is considered to be in the top 10 best British cricketers ever.

Europe back in space business

1983 Everything went according to plan when the European rocket Ariane 1, blasted off from the French National Space Centre at Kouron, French Guiana today. Ariane launched the one-ton ESCI into an elliptical "transfer orbit". Early tomorrow the satellite's booster rocket will be fired to thrust it into "geostationary orbit" 22,000 miles (35,000 km) above the equator. Ariane's future has been uncertain since it crashed on its second and fifth missions. Today's performance, however, means Europe is back in competition with the American space industry for satellite contracts.

> *I believe this government cannot endure permanently, half slave and half free.*
> **Abraham Lincoln** in a speech at Springfield, Illinois, today, 1858.

Napoleon's troops crush Prussia's

1815 After a bitter and bloody battle the French scored a resounding victory against the Prussians at Ligny, in Belgium, today. Napoleon opened hostilities at about 2.30 pm and by 3.15 pm the battle was fiercely engaged. At about 7.45 pm a contingent of elite French troops broke the Prussian centre. The Prussian commander of the Lower Rhine, Field Marshal Blucher, responded by leading his cavalry reserve to stem the French advance. There was a tense moment for the Prussians when Blucher was knocked from his horse and only the prompt intervention of his *aide-de-camp*, Count Nostitz, saved him from being trampled to death. By 9 pm it was all over. The Prussians lost an estimated 12,000 men, the French 8500.

> **1835** In response to the widespread disappointment with the political results of the 1832 Reform Bill, social reformer Mr William Lovett officially founded the London Working Men's Association today. Despite the Bill's famous six points for reform, Mr Lovett claims that fundamental issues of social inequality are still not being addressed.

BALLET STAR NUREYEV LEAPS TO FREEDOM

1961 A star dancer of the Leningrad ballet, forbidden at the last minute to fly to London with the rest of the troupe, has asked for political asylum in France. Twenty-three-year-old Rudolf Nureyev was waiting to board the London flight at Le Bourget airport in Paris today when officials from the Russian Embassy ordered him to return to Moscow immediately. He refused and ran to a police officer crying, "Protect me!" Nureyev was immediately taken to the police commissioner's office at Le Bourget where he made a formal request for asylum. He was later driven to the Ministry of the Interior.

Roosevelt takes on Depression

1935 President Roosevelt's complicated "New Deal" legislative package which is aimed at tackling the severe economic problems of the American nation took another step forward today. The Social Security Bill – embodying old-age pensions, unemployment insurance and public health aid – has been passed by the House of Representatives. This important Bill with its far-reaching implications is now the unfinished business of the Senate. A successful passage is predicted for early this week.

> *We'll start shooting rubber bullets when they start throwing rubber rocks.*
> **Jimmy Kruger**, South African Minister of Police, as the death toll mounts in nationwide riots, 1976.

Sweden's Queen goes

1654 Queen Christina of Sweden abdicated today in favour of her cousin, Charles Gustavus. Although respected by some for her patronage of literature and the arts, the general feeling is one of relief at seeing her go. For many years there has been increasing discontent with her luxurious and wasteful lifestyle, open contempt of the Protestant religion, and refusal to marry and produce an heir. Her total lack of concern for public opinion and dismissal of the necessities of the state have also contributed to her widespread unpopularity.

Break in at Watergate HQ

1972 Five men have been caught snooping around the Washington complex of flats, offices and hotel known as The Watergate, currently being used by the Democratic Party as their headquarters during the election campaign. The men were all equipped with electronic eavesdropping equipment. It is rumoured that the men were in the pay of the Republican "Committee for the re-election of the President" (CREEP). A major political scandal is feared.

> *Washington is the only place where sound travels faster than light.*
> **C. V. R. Thompson** in the *Reader's Digest*, 1949.

Cosmonauts duet in space

1963 Valentina Tereshkova, 26, and Valery Bykovsky, 28, liaised today for the world's first ever date in space. Valery and Valentina made their link-up 30 minutes after Valya's launch at 10 am B.S.T. and are now circling the Earth just 12 seconds apart. Colonel Bykovsky's Vostok V had already been in orbit for two days and nights when Valya's Vostok V1 streaked up to meet him. In Moscow there was dancing and singing in the streets to celebrate the historic event.

WORLD IN AIDS FIGHT

1991 Eight thousand scientists and researchers gathered today at Fortezza da Basso, Florence, for an international conference on AIDS. The disease has now spread across 163 countries and is rife in Africa. The World Health Organization estimates the true number of cases worldwide at more than 1.5 million, with a total number of people with HIV at between 8 and 10 million. WHO predicts that by the year 2000, 40 million people worldwide may be affected by HIV. AIDS has attacked more than 170,000 Americans since 1981, and another 6000 develop the disease every month. Britain did not have a single sufferer in 1981, but has since documented more than 4500 cases of the disease.

Battle of Bunker Hill

1775 The second battle of the American revolution commenced just before dawn today at Bunker Hill and Breed's Hill, just north of Boston, Massachusetts. After an unsuccessful attack on the American left flank, British general William Howe ordered his men to storm the central redoubt defended by 1600 patriots under the command of Colonel William Prescott. The British were repulsed with blistering fire and only on their third attempt – reinforced with extra troops from Boston – did they succeed in capturing the position. Although the British gained the military victory, the moral victory belonged to the patriots for the courage and discipline they displayed under fire. The Americans lost around 400 men, the British 1000.

Italian banker's mystery death

1982 A man was found hanging under Blackfriars Bridge in London today. He was carrying £10,800 ($20,000) in foreign currencies, a fraudulent passport, and his pockets were weighted with 12 lb (5.4 kg) of bricks and stones. Police believe him to be Roberto Calvi, a central figure in the Banca Ambrosiano scandal currently rocking Italy. Calvi made a suicide attempt in July last year after being convicted of currency offences and three days ago his secretary killed herself jumping from a window. Archbishop Marcinkus, president of the Vatican Bank, is also implicated in the scandal.

> *Don't fire until you see the whites of their eyes.*
> **American revolutionary** soldier William Prescott at the Battle of Bunker Hill, 1775.

MALVINAS LOSER DUMPED

1982 Fourteen generals met at an Army base in Buenos Aires at dawn today and voted unanimously to sack Leopoldo Galtieri, the president who led Argentina into the Falklands war it could never win. Air force chief Basilio Lami Doza, the only junta member to emerge from the war with credit, is expected to replace him. It is understood that the new regime will declare all hostilities with Britain at an end, thus enabling the 10,600 prisoners on the Falklands to be repatriated.

JUNE 17

1579 Francis Drake drops the *Golden Hind*'s anchor off the south-west coast of America and names the area New Albion.

1719 Death of Joseph Addison, English essayist, poet and Whig statesman who co-founded the *Spectator*.

1823 Charles Macintosh patents a waterproof material.

1867 In Glasgow Royal Infirmary, Joseph Lister performs a mastectomy upon his sister using carbolic acid as an antiseptic – thereby becoming the first surgeon to attempt any form of antiseptic treatment.

1944 Iceland becomes an independent republic.

1950 The first kidney transplant is carried out in Chicago.

1963 Death of John Cowper Powys, British novelist and poet.

1970 Edwin Land patents the first Polaroid camera.

1988 In Kingston, Jamaica, reggae poet Dennis Loban is found guilty of the murder of reggae star and ex-Wailer Pete Tosh and is sentenced to hang.

BIRTHDAYS

Edward I 1239, English monarch who encouraged parliamentary institutions and subdued Wales.

John Wesley 1703, English religious leader and founder of Methodism.

Charles Gounod 1818, French composer whose most successful works were the operas *Faust* and *Romeo and Juliet*.

Igor Stravinsky 1882, Russian-born composer who first found fame with the ballet scores Diaghilev commissioned for his Ballets Russes, which included *The Firebird*, *The Rite of Spring* and *Petrushka*.

Ken Loach 1936, British film director whose television play *Cathy Come Home* brought the plight of the homeless to public attention.

Barry Manilow 1946, American singer and songwriter of vast popularity.

JUNE 18

1037 Persian philosopher and physician Avicenna dies, leaving an encyclopedia of philosophy, *Ash-Shifa* (*The Recovery*), and the *Canon of Medicine*, which has become a valued source of knowledge throughout the Middle East and Europe.

1155 A thousand die in riots as the English-born Pope Hadrian crowns Emperor Frederick Barbarossa in Rome.

1583 The first life insurance policy is issued in London.

1789 Austrian troops occupy Brussels.

1902 Death of Samuel Butler, British novelist who wrote *Erewhon* and the autobiographical *The Way of All Flesh*.

1928 Roald Amundsen, the Norwegian explorer who reached the South Pole ahead of Captain Scott, dies in a plane crash while trying to rescue another explorer.

1936 Death of Maxim Gorki, Russian novelist and dramatist who became the first president of the Soviet Writers Union.

1975 The first North Sea oil arrives on shore in Britain.

1977 Sex Pistol Johnny Rotten is attacked with razors in a North London pub.

2000 At Dover, 58 Chinese immigrants are found suffocated in the back of a lorry while trying to enter Britain illegally.

BIRTHDAYS

Viscount Castlereagh 1769, British statesman who, as foreign secretary, played an important role at the Congress of Vienna which reconstructed Europe after the fall of Napoleon.

Jeanette McDonald 1901, American actress and singer who made a series of film operettas with Nelson Eddy.

Ian Carmichael 1920, British actor who appears in light comedy roles on stage and in films such as *Private's Progress*, *Lucky Jim* and *I'm All Right Jack*.

Paul McCartney 1942, ex-Beatle and major British pop musician.

FIRST WOMAN TO FLY ATLANTIC

1928 Thirty-year-old Amelia Earhart became the first woman to fly the Atlantic when the trimotor *Friendship*, in which she was a passenger, landed at Burny Port today. Miss Earhart, the daughter of a railroad attorney and graduate of Columbia University, is employed as a settlement worker in Boston. Aviation is a passionate hobby with her and she is a very accomplished pilot. A plucky girl, Miss Earhart hopes to make a solo flight across the Atlantic herself one day.

1940 Charles de Gaulle, founder of the Free French in England, made a radio appeal from London today urging his fellow countrymen to continue to resist the Germans. It was in response to Marshall Petain's announcement yesterday that the French have approached the Germans with a request for an Armistice.

Elated Carter turns SALT to SWALK

1979 The climactic signing of the Strategic Arms Limitations Talks took place at last at the magnificent State Hall of the Imperial Hofburg Palace in Vienna today. President Jimmy Carter and President Leonid Ilyich Brezhnev shook hands, sat down, signed the documents, and rose again. Then suddenly an elated Jimmy Carter threw pomp and protocol to the winds. Taking a quick step towards the "Old Contemptible", he threw his arms around his granite shoulders and kissed him Russian-style on both cheeks. Brezhnev was totally taken aback, while the American Press Corps present responded with a gasp of stunned delight.

Napoleon beaten in the mire of Waterloo

1815 British and Prussian forces under the command of the Duke of Wellington and Field Marshall Blucher finally defeated Napoleon in a bloody battle at Waterloo, in Belgium, today. Fighting started at about 11.30 am, and raged ferociously all day. Initially Napoleon's 74,000 men and 246 guns were pitched against Wellington's army of 67,000 men and 156 guns, but at 1 pm Blucher's army arrived to join the fray. The water-logged state of the cornfields made combat conditions even more appalling. Soldiers fell dead and dying at every turn and soon mutilated bodies were thick on the ground. Napoleon's first decided advantage was gained at 6 pm, when Wellington's position fell into his hands. But the Iron Duke kept a cool head, quickly readjusting his lines and fortifying his torn centre. The desperate fighting was ultimately concluded by a British-Prussian victory. The total number of casualties on both sides is estimated to be around 62,000.

> *I shall earnestly and persistently continue to urge all women to the practical recognition of the old Revolutionary maxim, "resistance to tyranny is obedience to God".*
> **Susan B. Anthony**, American feminist, in court, 1873.

Mexican execute corrupt Emperor

1867 Despite universal appeals for mercy, Emperor Ferdinand Maximilian Joseph was executed by firing squad in Mexico today. Born in Vienna, the brother of the Emperor Francis Joseph and Archduke of Austria, he accepted the crown in 1864. The position was created by France following its invasion of Mexico in 1863. Financially and politically he was wholly dependent on France, and Mexico opposed him from the start. He further antagonized the country of Mexico by his outrageous extravagance and the inefficiency of his corrupt, intrigue-ridden administration. In October 1866, Maximilian fled the country with the intention of abdicating. Persuaded to return, he was soon arrested and court-martialled.

Sir Robert tells London police: keep 'em peeled

1829 Home Secretary Sir Robert Peel founded the London Metropolitan Police today. The newly restructured force has been modelled along the lines of the highly respected Irish constabulary. The measures Sir Robert is taking to reform and humanize the criminal law – particularly those parts of it that relate to offences against property and offences punishable by death – are earning him much praise. As one prominent liberal Whig has said, Peel can rightly claim that all his legislation has sought "some mitigation of the severity of the criminal law, some prevention of abuse in the exercise of it, or some security for its impartial administration."

NO CLEMENCY FOR ROSENBERGS

1953 Thirty-five-year-old Julius Rosenberg and his wife Ethel, 37, were sent to the electric chair at Sing Sing tonight accused of passing atom bomb secrets to the Russians. While thousands worldwide continued to protest, President Eisenhower turned down a final plea for clemency. "They have received the benefit of our justice . . . I cannot intervene," he said, adding that their crimes were "worse than murder." The Rosenbergs' guilt – which they have never admitted to – is seriously doubted throughout the world. Prison officials reported that they made no last requests, either for visitors or for a special last supper.

Solid Solidarity

1989 The second round of the elections to a new Polish bicameral National Assembly were held today. In the first round the Solidarity Citizens gained 92 of the new 100 seats in the Senate, as well as all its seats in the Sejm. Today it won all but one seat. In the first round the Government's National List of 35 candidates failed – with two exceptions – to win the necessary 50 per cent of the vote to retain their seats. Solidarity's spectacular success in these elections reflects the bitterness the Polish people feel towards the 40 years of Communist rule.

At Elysian Fields it's a whole new ball game

1846 The Elysian Fields in Hoboken, New Jersey, today provided the venue for the first ever official baseball match. The New Yorks and the Knickerbockers played according to rules set out by Mr Alexander J. Cartwright. The New Yorks defeated the Knickerbockers 23-1 in four innings. The field has 90 ft (27 m) base lines and the batsman stands at home plate. Cartwright's rules prohibit the retirement of a runner by "plugging" – hitting him with a thrown ball while off base. Balls caught on the first bounce constitute an out and runs are called "aces".

Peter Pan's creator dies

1937 J. M. Barrie, the man who created the "boy who never grew up", died today aged 77. Born in Kirriemuir, Scotland, he settled in London when he was 25. Sir James Matthew Barrie wrote many books and plays, among which are *Quality Street*, *What Every Woman Knows*, *Dear Brutus* and *Mary Rose*. His most famous and best-loved work, however, was the children's play *Peter Pan* which he wrote in 1904. Barrie was made a Bart in 1913 and received the Order of Merit in 1922.

1312 Piers Gaveston, Earl of Cornwall and favourite of King Edward II, is beheaded at Deddington at the instigation of the Earl of Warwick.

1790 The French Assembly abolishes hereditary nobility.

1820 Sir Joseph Banks, British botanist and explorer who made a round-world trip with Captain Cook, dies aged 77.

1924 British climber George Mallory, who wanted to climb Everest "because it's there", disappears 1,000 ft (305 m) from the summit.

1935 The British government overrides the Treaty of Versailles, signed at the Paris Peace Conference in 1919, by agreeing to allow Germany a massive increase in its naval strength.

1963 In Britain, the contraceptive pill is made available to women free under the National Health Service.

1967 The Monterey Pop Festival draws thousands of flower children to hear stars such as Jimi Hendrix, Janis Joplin, The Who, Otis Redding, The Mamas and the Papas, and the Grateful Dead.

1993 Death of Sir William Golding, author of *Lord of the Flies* and *The Spire*, and winner of the Nobel Prize for Literature.

BIRTHDAYS

James I 1556, English monarch, son of Mary Queen of Scots and Lord Darnley, the first Stuart king of England and Ireland and, as James VI, King of the Scots.

Blaise Pascal 1623, French mathematician, physician and theologian who invented the first calculating machine.

Charles Coburn 1877, American actor who won an Oscar for *The More the Merrier*.

Joshua Nkomo 1917, Zimbabwean politician.

Salman Rushdie 1947, British novelist whose book *The Satanic Verses* led to a death sentence from the Ayatollah Khomeini.

JUNE 20

1597 Dutch navigator Willem Barents, who led three expeditions to find the north-west passage and discovered Spitzbergen on his final trip, dies at sea on the return voyage.

1789 In France, the Third Estate of the States General forms a National Assembly to oppose the aristocracy's domination of the proceedings.

1837 Eighteen-year-old Victoria accedes to the English throne on the death of her uncle, William IV.

1863 West Virginia, the Panhandle State, becomes the 36th state of the Union.

1887 Queen Victoria's Golden Jubilee is celebrated all over Britain and the Empire.

1949 American tennis player "Gorgeous Gussie" Moran creates a sensation at Wimbledon by exposing lace-trimmed panties under her short skirt.

1960 American Floyd Patterson knocks out the Swede Ingmar Johansson to become the first boxer to regain the world heavyweight title.

1990 Nelson Mandela gets a ticker-tape welcome in New York.

BIRTHDAYS

Jacques Offenbach 1819, German-born composer who lived and worked in France, producing a series of popular operettas such as *Orpheus in the Underworld* and one grand opera, *The Tales of Hoffman*.

Kurt Schwitters 1887, German Dadaist artist and writer who moved to Britain in 1940 to escape from the Nazis and was best-known for his invention of Merz – art made from refuse.

Catherine Cookson 1906, British novelist, immensely prolific and immensely popular.

Errol Flynn 1909, Tasmanian actor who specialized in swashbuckling and war hero roles.

Lionel Richie 1949, American singer and songwriter best-known for "Say You, Say Me" and "All Night Long (All Night)".

Film murder angers US

1979 American TV reporter Bill Stewart was gunned down by Nicaraguan National Guardsmen today as he walked towards a road block with a white flag in one hand and his official yellow press card in the other. He had been ordered to get more action shots, so left his film crew accompanied by his Nicaraguan driver and interpreter. Suddenly one of the guardsmen ordered him first to kneel, then lie on the ground. As Stewart complied, he shot him in the head. The sequence was filmed and relayed on American TV, shocking the nation. It is expected that President Carter will review the question of American support to the regime.

Classic red bus terminates here

1990 The Routemaster, the world-famous London double-decker bus, is to be phased out because of old age, it was announced today. In its 30 years of faithful service the red "open platform" bus has become a tourist attraction in its own right and passengers in a hurry have come to rely on being able to hop on and off the bus. But despite cannibalizing even older buses for spare parts, London Regional Transport is finding it an increasing struggle to keep the fleet on the road. "The problem is that earlier models are developing fundamental faults that cannot easily be repaired," a spokesman said. The news has saddened a lot of people; the Routemaster is universally acknowledged to be the "best designed bus of all times".

BROADWAY HOT FOR SATCHMO AND FATS

1930 The vogue for black music continues and people can't seem to get enough of it. Fats Waller and Louis Armstrong took New York by storm tonight when their hit revue, *Hot Chocolates*, opened on Broadway. *Hot Chocolates* – which takes its title from the 12 gorgeous dancers who feature in the show – first opened at Connie's Inn in May 1929 and critics couldn't praise it enough. Armstrong is at his gravelly best singing "Ain't Misbehaving", and special praise must also go to Jazz Lips Richardson and his colleague Baby Cox. Pianist and vocalist Thomas "Fats" Waller takes credit for several of the excellent songs.

> *If I had not been born Perón, I would have liked to be Perón.*
> **Juan Perón**, returning to Argentina as president after 20 years in exile, 1973.

BLACK HOLE HORROR

1756 Of the 146 British men thrown into Calcutta's notorious Black Hole prison today, only 23 have survived into the night. The Nawab of Bengal, Suraj ud-Daulah, attacked the English settlement in Calcutta because he feared invasion. Reports had reached him that the English in Bengal had fortified their settlements without his permission and were abusing the trading privileges granted by the Imperial firman of 1717. The Black Hole measures only 18 ft by 14 ft (5.4 m by 4.2 m) in size.

Steamship cracks the Atlantic

1819 The first steamship to cross the Atlantic – or any ocean at all, for that matter – arrived to a tumultuous welcome in Liverpool, England today. The *Savannah* sailed from Savannah, Georgia, and took 25 days to make the momentous crossing. The *Savannah* is 98 ft (27 m) long and her 90 horsepower engine is fuelled by wood and coal. She is also equipped with sails. During the crossing the crew regularly unfurled the sails when the engine was shut down to clean the salt from her boilers. This magnificent and innovative vessel was built by an American, Moses Rogers, for the express purpose of discovering if steamships can be considered practicable for ocean-going voyages. The *Savannah*'s success has proved that they most certainly can!

Brazil wins soccer trophy for ever

1970 Brazil carried off the third world cup in a thrilling match in Mexico today. Pele opened scoring with a header, but it was Gerson's goal in the 65th minute – a left footer no goal keeper in the world would have saved – which triggered off a dazzling display of Brazil's real talents. Pele, Tostao, Jairzinho and Rivelino all played with sublime artistry. When Carlos Alberto scored the last goal three minutes from time, the crowd responded with an ovation as ecstatic as the players would have got in their home city of Rio. Brazil's third triumphant victory means the Jules Rimet Trophy has found a permanent home.

It's a boy!

1982 The Princess of Wales gave birth to a lusty, 7 lb (3.1 kg) blue-eyed prince in St Mary's Hospital, Paddington, today. Prince Charles, who emerged two hours later, described his son as having "sort of blondish hair, though it'll probably turn into something else later on". He said that both mother and baby were extremely well, but "the Princess is a little tired as it has been a long time". Diana, 21 next week, was in labour for just over 16 hours. The new prince is second in line to the throne after his father.

For painters, poets and builders have very high flights, but they must be kept down.
Sarah, Duchess of Marlborough, in a letter to the Duchess of Bedford, written in 1734.

French King foiled in vain escape plan

1791 The escape plan of Louis XVI of France and his family was foiled as members of the National Guard caught the fugitive king at Varennes and brought him back to Paris today. He had been attempting to get away to safety across the country's eastern border. This final act of foolishness has undermined the King's credibility as a consititutional monarch, and the National Assembly have suspended his powers. Clearly underestimating the strength of popular demands for economic and administrative reforms, the King has allowed himself to be dominated by reactionary forces within the aristocracy. His reluctance to sanction the achievements of the National Assembly – such as the Declaration of the Rights of Man and of the Citizen, and the dismantling of the feudal regime – reveals a serious lack of foresight. The King is now in an extremely precarious position.

EARTHQUAKE SMASHES IRAN

1990 More than 25,000 people are reported killed and tens of thousands injured in the earthquake that struck north-western Iran near the Caspian Sea today. Hundreds of towns and villages have been razed to the ground and huge areas are without water or electricity. The quake, 7.3 on the Richter scale, lasted more than a minute and struck an area estimated at 40,000 square miles (104,000 sq km). Rescue operations are being hampered by aftershocks, mud slides and flooding caused by damaged dams. President Rafsanjani declared three days of national mourning and appealed to citizens to help dig survivors from wreckage. Iran will accept aid from any source except Israel and South Africa.

We have to believe in free will. We've got no choice.
Polish-born US writer, **Isaac Bashevis Singer**, 1982.

Stonehenge solstice threat eclipsed

1989 Police mounted a £1 million ($1.8 million) operation at Stonehenge today to combat the expected invasion of thousands of hippies for the summer solstice. To avoid a repetition of last year's violent clashes – when 5000 hippies invaded Stonehenge for a festival – 800 police were laid on. But the dreaded invasion never materialized. Only about 400 travellers tried to reach the ancient stones, of which only six actually succeeded in touching them.

1652 Inigo Jones, the famous architect who founded the classic English tradition of architecture, died today. Son of a humble clothworker, he was patronized by Queen Anne and members of the aristocracy – including the Earl of Salisbury, for whom he designed the New Exchange at the Strand. He also designed masques and major buildings for Charles I. It is generally agreed that Jones's crowning achievement is the magnificent Banqueting House in Whitehall.

1377 Edward III of England dies after a reign studded with successful military ventures.

1527 Italian political theorist Niccolò Machiavelli dies aged 58.

1675 The construction of Sir Christopher Wren's St Paul's Cathedral in London begins.

1788 The US constitution comes into force.

1796 Scottish explorer Mungo Park reaches the River Niger.

1843 The Royal College of Surgeons is founded in Britain.

1852 Death of Friedrich Froebel, German educationist who founded the first kindergarten in 1837 at Blankenburg.

1868 Richard Wagner's opera *Die Meistersinger von Nürnberg* is premiered in Munich.

1876 Mexican soldier and statesman Antonio López de Santa Anna, best known for his defeat of the Texans at Alamo, dies in poverty-stricken exile.

1908 Death of Russian composer Nikolai Rimsky-Korsakov, best known for *Scheherazade*.

1908 A suffragette demonstration in London attracts 20,000 supporters.

1919 The 27 vessels of the German fleet interned at Scapa Flow in the Orkneys are scuttled by their crews.

1942 General Rommel's troops take 25,000 Allied prisoners at Tobruk, on the Libyan coast.

1970 Tony Jacklin becomes the first British golfer to win the US open in 50 years.

1988 The Burmese government imposes a curfew as the regime totters in the face of student protests.

BIRTHDAYS

Jean-Paul Sartre 1905, French philosopher, novelist, dramatist and critic who propounded the philosophy of existentialism.

Mary McCarthy 1912, American novelist, critic and journalist, whose work includes *Memories of a Catholic Girlhood*.

1377 Richard II accedes to the throne of England.

1814 The Marylebone Cricket Club and Hertfordshire play the first match at England's Lord's Cricket Ground.

1906 President Roosevelt sues John D. Rockefeller's Standard Oil company for operating a monopoly.

1940 France accepts the armistice terms of Germany and Italy.

1941 Germany invades the USSR.

1956 Death of British poet and novelist Walter de la Mare, best-known for the poem "The Listeners".

1979 In Britain, Liberal politician Jeremy Thorpe is cleared of conspiring to murder homosexual Norman Scott.

1989 The captain of the capsized cross-Channel ferry *Herald of Free Enterprise* is charged with manslaughter.

1989 In China, seven students involved in the Tienanmen Square protests are shot after televised show trials.

BIRTHDAYS

George Vancouver 1757, explorer after whom Vancouver Island and Vancouver are named.

Erich Maria Remarque 1898, German novelist who is best known for his anti-war novel *All Quiet on the Western Front*.

Billy Wilder 1906, Austrian-born film director and writer whose string of hits includes *The Apartment*, *Sunset Boulevard*, *The Lost Weekend* and *Some Like It Hot*.

Kris Kristofferson 1936, American singer, songwriter and actor best-known for the album *Me and Bobby McGee* and the film *A Star Is Born*.

Meryl Streep 1949, American actress whose films include *Kramer v. Kramer*, *Out of Africa*, *Sophie's Choice* and *The French Lieutenant's Woman*.

End of the rainbow

1969 American singer Judy Garland was found dead in the bathroom of her Belgravia mews home in London this morning. An empty box of sleeping pills was also discovered. Miss Garland's husband, who found the body, said they had spent a quiet evening at home watching the BBC programme *Royal Family*. Born Francis Gumm, 47-year-old Garland shot to instant stardom for her portrayal of Dorothy in *The Wizard of Oz* when she was 17 and the song from the film "Over the Rainbow" became her trademark. Despite her success, Miss Garland's life was rocked by illness, lawsuits and broken marriages. She leaves three children.

FRENCH SURRENDER

1939 Today, eight days after German troops entered Paris, the French formally surrendered to Germany. President Petain's request for an armistice was transmitted to Hitler on the night of June 16. Hitler's terms were delivered to the French envoys two days later. Talks between the two countries took place while German troops continued to advance through the Loire. On June 22, however, the French bowed their heads and accepted all of Hitler's terms. The bitter event took place in Marshall Foch's old railway carriage in the forest of Compiègne – the same used by the French to humiliate the Germans when they accepted their surrender in 1918.

Magic bullets target sex disease

1910 Paul Ehrlich, the German bacteriologist and immunologist, announced the definitive cure for syphilis today. The renowned scientist, winner with Elie Metchnikov of the 1908 Nobel Prize for physiology, has discovered that certain substances are capable of functioning as "magic bullets", attacking specific bacteria in the body while leaving the rest of the organism unharmed. The "magic bullet" against syphilis micro-organisms is an arsenical compound called Salvarsan. Mr Ehrlich was appointed director of the Royal Institute for Experimental Therapy at Frankfurt in 1906.

Louis KO echoes world tensions

1938 Joe Louis celebrated his first anniversary as heavyweight champion by knocking out German Max Schmeling in the first round of their New York fight today. It was the "Brown Bomber's" sweet revenge for the knock-out defeat Schmeling dealt him in the twelfth round of their 1936 contest – and a resounding smack in the eye for Hitler, who hailed Schmeling's victory as evidence of Aryan racial superiority! Louis, the 24-year-old son of a cotton picker, was born in Lafayette, Alabama. He turned professional after the 1934 national amateur championships. He is a powerful fighter, and there is speculation that he will be the greatest heavyweight ever.

1987 Fred Astaire, one of America's best loved entertainers, has died at the age of 88. He began his career as a music-hall dancer and went on to make films, notably the musicals of the 1930s in which he danced with Ginger Rogers. They include *Top Hat* and *Shall We Dance?* He later co-starred with Judy Garland, Lesley Caron and Audrey Hepburn.

When Barbarossa commences, the world will hold its breath and make no comment.
  Adolf Hitler referring to the planned invasion of Russia, codenamed Operation Barbarossa, 1941.

Explorer cast adrift to die

1611 Early this morning the explorer Henry Hudson was bundled into a shallop by his mutinous crew and set adrift without food or water to die in the open sea. This act was the barbaric conclusion of Hudson's fourth attempt to find the North-west Passage to the Orient. Hudson left England on April 17, 1610 in the sailing ship *Discovery*. His roughneck crew were troublesome and rebellious – particularly during the hardships of the bitter Arctic night when the ship went into winter quarters in James Bay, Canada. Hudson's eldest son was set adrift with him. There is very little hope of finding the craft in time.

EMPIRE CELEBRATES GVR

1911 Despite the rather glum weather thousands turned out to celebrate the coronation of King George V in London today. Twelve thousand members of the Metropolitan Police lined the route where cheering crowds waited for the great moment when the robed and crowned King and Queen would drive by. Seven thousand people attended the coronation ceremony itself, including representatives from all over the world. It has also been a day of rejoicing for the whole of the Empire, which has joined with the Mother Country in rendering homage to the new King. Even in India – where the great official celebrations will not take place until the time of the Delhi Durbar – unofficial festivities of the most varied sorts were being held everywhere.

Dail gets tough with IRA

1939 A series of IRA bombings in England has led the Dail, the Irish parliament, to take tough measures against the organization, including provision for internment without trial. The bombings are just one in a long line of terrorist activities going back to the IRA's beginnings in 1919, when they took over from the militant nationalist group, the Irish Volunteers. The present IRA refuses to accept the division of Ireland or the Irish Free State, established after the war of independence of 1919-21 and contemptuously referred to as "the Six Counties". Its goal is a united Ireland, and it believes that the only way to achieve this is through armed struggle. Despite being declared illegal in 1931 and again in 1936, the IRA has defiantly continued to bomb, raid, ambush and sabotage in the blind pursuit of its dream.

Quaker Penn seeks peace with Indians

1683 William Penn, the English Quaker and advocate of civil and religious liberty, signed a treaty with chiefs of the Lenni Lenape Tribe today in a bid to ensure the peace of his colony. Penn was granted a huge tract of land in the New World by King Charles II, which he subsequently named "Pennsylvania" after his father. Since arriving from England in September 1682 Penn, author of *No Cross, No Crown*, has gone all out to establish friendly relations with the Indian tribes in the area. Today's solemn ceremony took place under an elm tree at Shakamaxon, Philadelphia.

Nasser raises Egyptian profile

1956 Colonel Gamal Abdel Nasser, the man who stands as a symbol of Arab nationalism from the Atlantic to the Persian Gulf, became President of Egypt today. Son of a humble postal clerk, Nasser graduated from the Royal Military Academy in Cairo in 1938, aged 20. He was wounded in the 1948 Arab-Israeli war and was a central figure in the military uprising that overthrew the government of King Faruk in 1952. Appointed prime minister in 1954, Nasser has the full support and affection of the Egyptian people.

1985 An Air India Boeing 747 exploded off the Irish coast today, killing the 329 people on board. The jet was en route from Canada, where it left Montreal airport late, 1 hour and 33 minutes after its scheduled departure time. Although no group has as yet claimed responsibility for the murders, it is believed that Sikh extremists planted the bomb that caused today's devastating disaster.

JUNE 23

1757 British troops under Robert Clive defeat the Nawab of Bengal, Siraj-ud Dawlah, at the Battle of Plassey, thereby making possible the British annexation of Bengal.

1796 Pope Pius VI signs an armistice with Napoleon.

1839 Lady Hester Stanhope, English gentlewoman who spent much time living with Arab tribes in the Middle East, dies in poverty.

1848 Adolphe Sax is granted a patent for the saxophone.

1980 Sanjay Gandhi, son of Indira Gandhi and next in line for political power, is killed in an air crash.

1980 Death of Olivia Manning, British novelist best known for her Balkan Trilogy.

1991 The International Monetary Fund agrees to offer associate membership to the Soviet Union.

2002 A fire in a youth hostel kills 15 backpackers in the town of Childers, Australia.

BIRTHDAYS

Empress Josephine 1763, Martinique-born wife of Napoleon Bonaparte whose marriage was dissolved when she failed to produce an heir.

Edward VIII 1894, British monarch who abdicated in order to marry the divorcée Mrs Simpson and took the title Duke of Windsor.

Alfred Kinsey 1894, American zoologist and sociologist best-known for his studies of human sexuality and his books *Sexual Behaviour in the Human Male* and *Sexual Behaviour in the Human Female*.

Alan Mathison Turing 1912, British mathematician and computer expert who pioneered the Turing machine, which greatly advanced computer development.

Sir Leonard Hutton 1916, British cricketer who made 364 runs against the Australians in 1938, the highest ever scored by an English batsman.

Bob Fosse 1927, American dancer, actor, director and choreographer who won an Oscar for *Cabaret*.

1314 Led by Robert the Bruce, the Scots defeat the English army at the Battle of Bannockburn.

1509 Henry VIII of England is crowned.

1519 Death of Lucrezia Borgia, illegitimate daughter of Pope Alexander VI.

1717 The Grand Lodge of English Freemasons is formed in London.

1902 King Edward VII has an emergency appendix operation two days before his planned coronation.

1947 A pilot sees nine unidentifiable circular objects in the sky above Washington state.

1948 The Berlin airlift begins as the Allies fly food and essential supplies to Berliners after the Soviets blockade the city.

1953 Jacqueline Bouvier announces her engagement to US senator John F. Kennedy.

1968 British comedian Tony Hancock commits suicide in Australia.

1973 Eamon de Valera resigns as president of Ireland aged 90.

1978 Twelve white missionaries are massacred in Rhodesia's bush war.

1983 Sally Ride becomes the first American woman in space when she blasts off in *Challenger* with four male astronauts.

1985 Keith Hardcastle, Britain's longest surviving heart transplant patient, dies six years after he received his replacement heart.

BIRTHDAYS

Horatio Herbert, Earl Kitchener 1850, British secretary of state for war in 1914.

Jack Dempsey 1895, American heavyweight boxing champion.

Juan Fangio 1911, Argentinian racing driver.

Professor Fred Hoyle 1915, British astronomer and notable science-fiction writer.

Claude Chabrol 1930, French film director who is credited with beginning the *nouvelle vague*.

Custer's last stand

1876 General Custer and his men were defeated today in a bloody battle with the Indian chief Crazy Horse and his Sioux warriors. Custer had been ordered to take his regiment up the Rosebud Creek and into the valley of the Little Bighorn River to ferret out the hostile Indians believed to be camping there. Early this morning Custer spotted a large Indian village and, unaware that it was harbouring more than 1500 fighting men, decided to attack at once. With Custer's army totalling about 650 men, it was a lost battle from the start. The General divided his regiment into four detachments and led his own detachment in an attempted strike on the village's eastern flank. He was unable to penetrate with mounted troops, however, and his cavalry were forced to dismount and fight on foot. The 225 officers and men were overwhelmed and every last one was killed.

Cabot takes Maine chance

1497 John Cabot sailed into Maine with his sons today just 35 days after leaving Bristol in his ship *Matthew*. Armed with letters patent from King Henry VII authorizing him to discover and possess lands "unknown to all Christians", he immediately went ashore and finalized ownership. Cabot – real name Giovanni Caboto – is a Venetian explorer in the service of the English crown. Cabot's mission, and the purpose for which he came to England in the first place, is to find an alternative westward route to "the Indies".

Women ordained Anglican priests

1990 For the first time in the history of Europe two women deacons have been ordained priests of the Anglican Church. The historic ceremonies were conducted by the Bishop of Connor and took place in St Anne's Cathedral, Belfast, today. The women are Kathleen Young, a 50-year-old physiotherapist of Carrickfergus, co. Antrim, and Irene Templeton, 49, from Belfast. The ordinations follow a two thirds majority decision by the general synod of the Church of Ireland last month to give women equal opportunity with men. The Bishop said afterwards that the ordinations heralded a new era for the Church.

Home videos in zero G

1985 The shuttle Discovery returns to Earth today, having taken millions of French and Arabic viewers on a televised tour of the craft. Prince Sultan Salman Saud of Saudi Arabia and Colonel Patrick Baudry of Air France took it in turns to float around the cabin telling their respective audiences about the pleasures and peculiarities of the weightless life aloft. The Prince confessed that praying to Mecca up there made him dizzy. Colonel Boudry revealed that "in zero G, you can put your trousers on two legs at a time." The shuttle had a flawless rendezvous with the satellite Spartan released into orbit two days earlier. Spartan was videotaping observations of super-heated gases in the constellation Perseus and at the centre of the Milky Way.

1901 An exhibition of work by Pablo Picasso, a new young Spanish painter, opened at the Ambrose Vollard gallery in Paris today. Because of the restricted space the works have been hung from floor to ceiling. There is some interesting work on display, notably the *Old Harlot* and *Dwarf Dancer*.

I don't care for war, there's far too much luck in it for my liking.
Napoleon III, Emperor of France, following a narrow and bloody French victory at Solferino, 1859.

WAR IN KOREA

1950 Open hostilities began today between Communist North Korea and the Republic of Korea in the South. There has been constant tension in the country since the end of World War II, when the USSR established a puppet government in the Russian-controlled sector and militarized the line of the 38th parallel. A United Nations commission was established to oversee free national elections, but North Korea refused to allow the delegates in. On August 15, 1948 the Republic of Korea was proclaimed in the south and Syngman Rhee was elected President. This was followed on September 9 by the formal establishment of the Democratic People's Republic in the north. Unrest, subversion, and border incidents began almost immediately and today's clash seemed inevitable. The North Korean army and air force total some 127,000 men, while the South Korean army numbers approximately 98,000.

Bovary writer in moral bovver

1857 Gustave Flaubert went on trial in Paris today for offences against public morality in his novel *Madame Bovary*. In this scandalous work – serialized over the past year in the *Revue de Paris* – Flaubert tells the story of a provincial wife who seeks escape from boredom in extramarital affairs and daydreaming. Her fantasies and the debts she accumulates finally drive her to suicide. *Madame Bovary* is Gustave Flaubert's only published work.

1962 The Italian film actress Sophia Loren is to be tried for alleged complicity in bigamy. The act of indictment was filed today by the enquiring magistrate before a Rome tribunal. Miss Loren married her husband, film producer Carlo Ponti, at Ciudad Juarez, in Mexico, six years ago. The problem facing the couple is that Mr Ponti's previous marriage is considered still valid. There is no divorce in Italy and Italian law does not recognize divorce obtained abroad by Italian citizens. The couple were unavailable for comment.

Radium find gives Curies Nobel chance

1903 Today scientist Marie Curie announced the discovery of radium. Mrs Curie began a systematic search for the element when research she was doing with her husband, Pierre, pointed to the existence of something even more radioactive than either uranium or thorium. Radium is a radioactive metallic element found in pitchblende and other minerals and is remarkable for its spontaneous disintegration. Many are predicting that the Curies will carry off the Nobel Prize for physics for this breakthrough discovery.

After all, science is essentially international, and it is only through lack of historical sense that national qualities have been attributed to it.

Marie Curie.

1953 John Christie was sentenced to death today for the murder of four women, the bodies of whom he had kept in his home at 10 Rillington Place in west London.

Slovenia and Croatia declare independence

1991 Yugoslavia plunged deeper into political crisis as Slovenia and Croatia declared their independence today. Despite warnings from the EC and the US that they would not be recognized, the two key republics voted overwhelmingly to "disassociate" from Yugoslavia, annul federal laws and gradually sever ties with the other republics. Croatian officials said that although the republic would consider itself part of Yugoslavia for the time being, it wants to negotiate with other republics to form an alliance of sovereign states. Slovenia's Interior Minister, Igor Bavcar, announced that a formal ceremony proclaiming independence will be taking place tomorrow. Faced with the break-up of the country, Yugoslavia's federal parliament called an emergency session and asked for army intervention to prevent any border changes. EC foreign ministers have agreed not to recognize the declarations of independence by the two republics and to freeze contacts with their leaders.

1788 Virginia becomes the tenth US state.

1797 Admiral Nelson is wounded in the arm in battle and the limb is amputated.

1867 Lucien B. Smith of Kent, Ohio, patents barbed wire.

1870 Queen Isabella II of Spain abdicates.

1925 The first car telephone is exhibited in Germany.

1932 The Indian cricket team play their first Test against England at Lord's and lose by 158 runs.

1969 Pancho Gonzalez and Charlie Paserell play the longest ever singles match at Wimbledon which lasts 5 hours and 12 minutes.

1975 Mozambique gains its independence after four centuries of Portuguese rule.

1976 Death of Johnny Mercer, American composer, lyricist and singer who wrote Broadway and Hollywood musicals including *Seven Brides for Seven Brothers*.

1987 Joan Collins obtains a 45-second divorce from her Swedish husband Peter Holm.

1997 Death of Jacques Cousteau, French underwater explorer and aqualung diver.

BIRTHDAYS

Louis, 1st Earl Mountbatten of Burma 1900, British admiral and colonial administrator, supreme Allied commander in south-east Asia in World War II, last viceroy of India then commander in chief of the Mediterranean fleet.

George Orwell 1903, British novelist whose books include *Animal Farm* and *Nineteen Eighty-Four*.

Carly Simon 1945, American singer and songwriter best known for "You're So Vain" and "Nobody Does It Better", the theme song for the James Bond movie *The Spy Who Loved Me*.

George Michael 1963, British pop musician who was one half of Wham! before going on to a successful single career.

363 AD Roman emperor Julian the Apostate, the first non-Christian emperor since Constantine, dies of spear wounds inflicted during a battle with the Persians.

1794 The French defeat the Austrians at the Battle of Fleurus.

1830 King George IV of England dies and his brother William IV takes the throne.

1857 The new military honour the Victoria Cross is awarded by Queen Victoria to 62 servicemen at a ceremony in Hyde Park, London.

1906 The first Grand Prix is held at Le Mans.

1913 Emily Dawson becomes the first female magistrate in London.

1930 Joseph Stalin announces that his murderous purges are "purifying" the Soviet Union.

1959 Ingemar Johansson becomes the first Swedish heavyweight boxing champion when he knocks out Floyd Patterson in New York.

1984 Death of Carl Foreman, American writer, producer and director whose films include *The Bridge on the River Kwai*, *High Noon* and *The Guns of Navarone*.

1984 The Rev. Jesse Jackson prevails upon Fidel Castro to release 22 jailed Americans.

1990 The IRA bomb the Carlton Club in London, a popular haunt of Conservative MPs.

BIRTHDAYS

Pearl S. Buck 1892, American novelist best-known for *The Good Earth*.

Willy Messerschmitt 1898, German aircraft designer best-known for his World War II planes.

Peter Lorre 1904, Hungarian-born actor whose many films include *Crime and Punishment*, *The Maltese Falcon* and *Casablanca*.

Laurie Lee 1914, British poet and author of the autobiographies *Cider with Rosie* and *As I Walked Out One Midsummer Morning*.

Mick Jagger 1943, British singer of the Rolling Stones.

Human genome draft completed

2000 An historical landmark has been reached as scientists announce that they have completed a rough draft of the human genome. Researchers across the world have worked for over a decade to decipher the biochemical instructions required to build and maintain the human body. They have determined the exact sequence of the three billion individual chemical building blocks that make up DNA, the long, double-stranded molecule which is hidden in the nuclei of nearly all cells. Even though the DNA code will require decades of further study, it will allow doctors to diagnose diseases much earlier, and help pharmaceutical companies design drugs tailored to individual patients.

Conquistador dies

1541 The Spanish conqueror of Peru, Francisco Pizarro, was attacked and killed in his house in Lima today. His assassins were followers of fellow adventurer, Diego de Almagro, with whom Pizarro had quarrelled and whom he later had executed. Pizarro's conquest of Peru was funded by the Spanish emperor Charles V. He will be remembered as a ruthless, greedy and ambitious man who played a major part in crushing the fabled Inca Empire.

V&A opens its doors

1909 The Victoria and Albert Museum opened its doors in southwest London today. The history of this museum is interesting in itself. Originally called the Museum of Ornamental Art, it moved from Marlborough House to its present site in South Kensington in 1857 to become part of a collective museum of science and art. Today the science collection and the art collection have been formally separated and the new Victoria and Albert Museum now houses the art collection alone. There are pictures, drawings and objects of art of every description, with collections from all over the world including Japan, China and Persia. There is also a whole section devoted to Indian art.

1939 Prolific British novelist Ford Madox Ford has died. During his lifetime he wrote 80 or more novels, books of criticism and memoirs, including *The Good Soldier* and the tetralogy *Parade's End*. He founded the *English Review* and, in Paris, the *Transatlantic Review*, publishing the early works of Joyce and Pound.

Americans land to boost Allied hopes

1917 The first unit of American troops to land in France – an advance guard of 1 million – arrived in a French port today and were met by escorting destroyers. No time was lost in unloading the stores. Negro labourers ran up and down gangways carrying tents, tinned meats, biscuits, coffee, sugar, etc. For obvious reasons, details of the arrival of General Pershing's army in France are being kept secret. It is known, however, that there will be a period of preparation before the American troops go to the battlefront.

JFK CHARMS THE SOCKS OFF BERLIN

1963 A million and a quarter West Berliners turned out to give a tumultuous welcome to President Kennedy today. It was a triumphant eight-hour tour during which the whole city was gripped by a frenzy of jubilation, the likes of which hadn't been seen since the days of Hitler. Kennedy appeared confident and relaxed. Addressing the 120,000-strong crowd in Rathaus Square, he declared, "Two thousand years ago the proudest boast in the world was 'civis Romanus sumi'. Today, in the world of freedom, the proudest boast is 'Ich bin ein Berliner'." He concluded his speech by saying, "All free men, wherever they may live, are citizens of Berlin, and, therefore, as a free man, I take pride in the words 'Ich bin ein Berliner'."

Queen Mum's 90 glorious years

1990 London offered a custom-made birthday parade to the Queen Mother to celebrate her ninetieth birthday this evening. She arrived at Horseguards Parade in an open landau accompanied by Princess Margaret and the Prince of Wales. From there she watched an hour-long spectacular involving all the regiments of which she is colonel-in-chief, and contingents from about 300 organizations with which she is involved. The turnout included the Black Watch and the Toronto Scottish, Fellows of the Royal Society and members of the Mothers Union. A 500-strong choir sang "Underneath the Arches" and "The White Cliffs of Dover".

1957 Malcolm Lowry, the English novelist and poet, died in Sussex today aged 48. His best-known novel was *Under the Volcano*. A restless man who had alcohol problems, Lowry travelled widely and finally settled near Vancouver with his second wife.

Liberty Bell peals again for American freedom

1778 Today the Liberty Bell has been returned to Philadelphia after spending a year hidden under the floorboards of the Zion Reformed Church in Allentown, Pennsylvania. It was taken there as a precautionary measure when the city was threatened by the British one year ago. The 2080 lb (943 kg) bell has a circumference of 12 ft (3.6 m) and was originally commissioned for the state house of the British province of Pennsylvania. It was cast by Thomas Lester's London foundry and bears the biblical inscription "Proclaim Liberty throughout the land unto all the inhabitants thereof." It was rung on July 8, 1776 to proclaim the Declaration of Independence, and has been a symbol of American Independence ever since.

No man knows my history . . . If I had not experienced what I have, I could not have believed it myself.
Joseph Smith, Mormon founder, who was murdered today, 1844.

Hubble trouble

1990 The Hubble space telescope – launched in April to claims from NASA that it would revolutionize the understanding of the universe – is fatally flawed. It was designed to see light that has been travelling through space for 15 billion years – time close to the "Big Bang". But NASA officials admitted today that the Hubble's light-gathering system, said to be "the most precise ever built", has a wrongly shaped mirror which will prevent it from functioning any better than ground-based telescopes. Although scientists claim this fault can be rectified, nothing can be done before 1993. The Hubble cost $2 billion dollars and is calculated to cost at least $8 billion more during its decade-long lifetime in space.

1989 Another wave of refugee boats from Vietnam has hit Hong Kong, whose closed refugee camps are already bulging with 45,000 "boat-people". They are fleeing poverty, and even caged in one of Hong Kong's crowded and sordid camps they have hope, believing they are bound for California. But there is talk of sending them back to Vietnam. Hong Kong is complaining that the western nations' low refugee quotas mean that Hong Kong must do more than its fair share to help, with scant resources. In fact Hong Kong is wealthy, and has hundreds of square miles of rural land, but it doesn't want the refugees competing for its people's jobs, homes and school places. Yet still the Vietnamese keep coming, despite the fact that the overcrowded camps are ripe for disease and violence and there have been riots in the past.

1693 The first magazine for women, the *Ladies Mercury*, is published.

1816 Death of Samuel, 1st Viscount Hood, British admiral whose military successes included defeating the French off Dominica in 1782 and capturing Toulon in the French Revolutionary Wars.

1871 A new system of currency based on the yen is introduced in Japan.

1900 The Central Line comes into service between Shepherd's Bush and Bank as part of the London Underground.

1939 Pan-American Airlines operates the first scheduled transatlantic air service, a 19-seater flying boat.

1954 The first nuclear power station is opened at Obninsk in the Soviet Union.

1971 The Fillmore East in New York, the rock club every rock star wanted to play, closes its doors for ever.

1974 Death of bluesman Lightnin' Slim.

1976 Six Palestinians hijack an Air France Airbus from Athens and force it to fly to Entebbe in Uganda.

1988 Intrepid British mountain climbers Dave Hurst and Alan Matthews become the first blind climbers to reach the summit of Mont Blanc in Switzerland, Europe's highest mountain at 15,781 ft (4810 m).

BIRTHDAYS

Louis XII 1462, French monarch whose reign was dominated by the wars his father, Charles VIII, had initiated.

Charles IX 1550, French monarch who ordered the massacre of the Huguenots on St Bartholomew's Day in 1572.

Charles Parnell 1846, Irish politician who led the Home Rule party in the House of Commons.

Helen Keller 1880, American blind, deaf and mute teacher, social worker and writer.

1836 Death of James Madison, fourth president of the United States whose influence at the Constitutional Convention which met in Philadelphia in 1787 to draw up the constitution gained him the name of "father of the American constitution".

1841 The ballet *Giselle* is premiered in Paris.

1861 Robert O'Hara Burke, Irish explorer of Australia who with W. J. Wills crossed the continent from north to south, dies of starvation on his return from the exploration of the mouth of the Flinders River.

1902 The United States authorizes the construction of the Panama Canal.

1937 In the Soviet Union, Joseph Stalin has 36 "confessed" German spies shot.

1940 The Russians seize Bessarabia from Romania.

1950 The novice US football team beats Britain 1–0 in the first round of the world cup in Brazil.

1961 Death of William Wyler, American film director who won Oscars for *Mrs Miniver* and *The Best Years of Our Lives*.

1988 The longest trial ever held in Spain comes to an end after 15 months during which 1500 witnesses are cross-examined to try to establish guilt in the selling of toxic olive oil that killed 600 and left thousands more maimed.

BIRTHDAYS

Henry VIII 1491, English monarch famous for his six wives and his rebellion against the Roman Catholic church.

Jean-Jacques Rousseau 1712, French philosopher and writer.

Sir Peter Paul Rubens 1577, Flemish painter and designer who was the most influential force in Baroque art in northern Europe.

Luigi Pirandello 1867, Italian novelist and dramatist best known for his play *Six Characters in Search of an Author*.

Mel Brooks 1926, American producer, director and writer. His work includes *The Producers*.

PEACE TREATY SIGNED AT VERSAILLES

1919 The peace treaty officially ending four years of devastating war was finally signed by the humiliated Germans today. The treaty was first presented to the six chief German delegates at the historic conference in the Trianon Palace Hotel at Versailles on May 7, 1919. The Germans considered the terms excessively harsh – they include demands for massive reparations – and refused to sign, causing British prime minister Lloyd George to make a gloomy prediction of another war. The Germans, however, quickly changed their minds when threatened with an occupation by Allied troops.

Send her Victorious

1838 From as early as 4 am this morning crowds began gathering in the streets for Queen Victoria's coronation in Westminster Abbey today. By 10 am the entire route was jam-packed and the atmosphere was one of excited jubilation. Victoria entered the Abbey wearing her parliament robes of crimson velvet trimmed with ermine and gold lace. The ceremony was not without hitches, however. One mistake was particularly appropriate in view of a legend about the Coronation Ring which says: "The closer the fit, the longer the reign." The Archbishop of Canterbury attempted to force the ruby ring on to her fourth finger, but it had been made for her fifth.

1914 In Sarajevo a 19-year-old student has assassinated Archduke Franz Ferdinand, heir to the Austro-Hungarian throne, and his wife, as they travelled past him.

Mormon murder

1844 Joseph Smith, founder of the Mormon Church, and his brother Hyrum were shot dead today by a mob who burst into the prison where they were being held in Illinois. Both men had been in jail since the incident 21 days ago when Smith, incensed by a sharp attack on him in a local paper, ordered the destruction of its press and sacking of its editor. Smith founded the Church when a series of visions led him to claim that he had discovered golden tablets containing the sacred Book of Mormon. He is expected to be succeeded by Brigham Young.

1990 At this time of year the picturesque streets of Florence are hot, overcrowded and littered with horse manure. To prevent this fouling of public thoroughfares the authorities decreed today that all horses within municipal limits must wear underwear. The ordinance will affect the 19 horsedrawn carriages known as *fiacchiere*. "Just think how ugly the horses will look wearing nappies full of *merd*," one driver told an Italian newspaper.

British soldiers of fortune to die in Angola

1976 Three British mercenaries were sentenced to death by the People's Revolutionary Tribunal in Luanda today for their part in Angola's civil war. The men who now await their end are Andrew McKenzie, John Barker and Costas Georgiou (known as "Colonel Callan", originally from Cyprus). A 34-year-old American and father of four young children, Daniel Gearhert, was also sentenced to death with them. Judge da Silva described Gearhert as "a highly dangerous character", who advertised himself as a mercenary in the American magazine *Soldier of Fortune*. Judge Da Silva also accused Britain and the United States of complicity in recruiting private armies "to bring down black Africa's revolutionary governments".

All the world over, I will back the masses against the classes.
British statesman **William Ewart Gladstone**, in a speech at Liverpool, 1886.

Chukka fracture

1990 Prince Charles broke his arm in two places today when he fell from his pony during a polo match at Cirencester Park, Gloucestershire. He was taken to Cirencester Hospital and later underwent an operation for a bad fracture just above the right elbow. Earlier he received a visit from King Constantine of Greece, a close friend. The Princess of Wales cut short a visit to the opera and arrived at her husband's bedside just before midnight.

Floyd headline at Hyde Park festival

1970 Midsummer madness swept London's Hyde Park today as music fans flocked in their thousands to take part in a new phenomenon that has recently hit Britain – the open-air rock festival. Massive festivals of this kind have been a feature of American youth culture for some time, but the idea has only caught on in the UK in the last couple of years: the first British rock festival was staged at Woburn Abbey, home of the enterprising Duke of Bedford. A number of bands are playing in today's day-long concert, but the main attraction is the progressive pop group Pink Floyd. As fans lazed on the grass, the strange and haunting strains of the band's music floated over their heads and out into the city. With its experimental electronic sounds and loose musical structure, Pink Floyd's music has pushed beyond the boundaries of conventional pop, to become, some would claim, a new art form.

White House rocked by rent boy scandal

1989 It was revealed today that federal investigators have uncovered a homosexual prostitution and blackmail ring whose client list includes military officers and leading members of Washington's political elite – one of the ring's clients took two male prostitutes on a night tour of the White House. The call-boy network, Professional Services, was run under the guise of a funeral home and payments for sex were entered as "cremation urn" or "prayer cards". Officials in the Bush and Reagan administration have been implicated, as have former staff of Jimmy Carter.

Atlantic Conqueror

1986 Pop and airline millionaire Richard Branson, and the crew of Virgin Atlantic Challenger II, beat the Atlantic crossing record by slicing two hours and nine minutes off the time set in 1952. They arrived at Bishop's Rock lighthouse, off the Scilly Isles, at 7.30 this evening.

South Africa imposes new racist laws

1925 The South African government today adopted racial inequality as a political policy, passing an act which bars black South Africans from holding skilled or semi-skilled jobs. Job inequality between blacks and whites has its roots in the gold-mining industry of the last century when mining bosses had an almost limitless pool of cheap, unskilled labour in the native population. Skilled labour, however, had to be attracted from overseas by the lure of high wages. Although by the 1900s the blacks had acquired the necessary skills for promotion and would still have been cheaper to employ, white employees refused to be ousted from their positions. In 1922, a move by the Chamber of Mines to reduce inequality and cut white wages met with a storm of violent protest. The white lobby has proved too powerful for the government to ignore, and today's legislation may be the first of many new laws, marking the rise of a new, systematic oppression of the majority black population.

Tobacco treat for Virginia

1620 The UK government has today banned the growing of tobacco in Britain. A tobacco-growing monopoly has instead been granted to the colony of Virginia, at a tax of one shilling per pound. Colonists have for some time been using the leaf as their main exchange commodity in return for manufactured goods from Europe. *Nicotiana tabacum*, named after the French ambassador to Lisbon who is said to have sent seeds to Catherine de' Medici, is of American origin, smoked by the Indians. But King James I of England denounced it as a health hazard in 1604.

Maradona on a roll

1986 Argentina took the World Cup again today – thanks to Maradona, who was indirectly responsible for all the goals. The West Germans did their best to keep him in check with Matthaus marking Maradona, shoulder to shoulder, so closely attached that they might have been a honeymoon couple on the dance floor. It was a thrilling game and Maradona was the undisputed star of the show.

48 BC Julius Caesar defeats his brother-in-law and former ally Pompey at Pharsallus and thus becomes absolute ruler of Rome.

1603 The Globe Theatre in London burns down as a cannon is fired for the king's entrance in Shakespeare's *Henry V*.

1801 The first census is carried out in Britain.

1855 The *Daily Telegraph* is first published in Britain.

1864 Samuel Crowther, Bishop of Niger, becomes the first black Church of England bishop.

1905 The Automobile Association is founded in Britain.

1921 Death of Lady Randolph Churchill, American mother of Winston Churchill.

1940 Death of Swiss painter and graphic artist Paul Klee, individual 20th-century artist.

1941 Polish pianist, composer and statesman, Paderewski dies.

1956 American playwright Arthur Miller marries Marilyn Monroe.

1965 The first US military ground action begins in Vietnam.

1967 American actress Jayne Mansfield is killed in a car crash.

1974 Isabel Perón takes over the presidency of Argentina when her husband succumbs to illness.

1976 The Seychelles become an independent republic.

1990 Lithuania announces it will suspend its declaration of independence for 100 days.

BIRTHDAYS

Giacomo Leopardi 1798, Italian poet with a pessimistic philosophy largely engendered by an unhappy childhood, poor health and failed love affairs.

Antoine de Saint-Exupéry 1900, French novelist and aviator best known for *The Little Prince*, a children's fable.

Rafael Kubelik 1914, Czech conductor and composer.

Nelson Eddy 1901, American singer and actor who partnered Jeanette McDonald in film operettas.

1789 The revolutionary mob in Paris attacks Abbaye Prison.

1822 In Spain, rebels take King Ferdinand VII prisoner.

1837 The use of the pillory is banned in Britain.

1894 Tower Bridge in London is officially opened.

1919 Death of British physicist Lord Rayleigh, who was awarded the Nobel Prize in 1904 for his discovery of argon gas.

1934 Adolf Hitler eliminates all his political opponents in the Night of the Long Knives.

1936 Margaret Mitchell's romantic novel *Gone with the Wind* is published.

1971 Three Russian astronauts are found dead after a record-breaking 24 days in space which ended in oxygen failure.

1974 Russian ballet dancer Mikhail Baryshnikov defects to the West while on tour in Canada.

1984 Death of Lillian Hellman, American playwright best-known for *The Little Foxes*.

1997 The first novel by J.K. Rowling, *Harry Potter and the Philosopher's Stone*, is published.

BIRTHDAYS

John Gay 1685 English poet and playwright best-known for the ballad opera *The Beggar's Opera*.

Sir Stanley Spencer 1891, British artist whose most famous paintings are those of biblical scenes set in his home village of Cookham, Berkshire.

Lena Horne 1917, American singer and actress whose films include *A Cabin in the Sky* and *Stormy Weather*.

Susan Hayward 1918, American actress who won an Oscar for *I Want to Live*.

Mike Tyson 1966, American and world heavyweight boxing champion.

Tightrope thrills as Blondin walks over Falls

1859 Crowds held their breath in stunned admiration as a daring Frenchman crossed the 167 ft (51 m) high Niagara Falls balanced on a tightrope today. The whole extraordinary feat took just five minutes. Thirty-five-year-old Charles Blondin, whose real name is Jean François Gravelet, is an acrobat and tightrope walker of world renown. Born at St Omer and trained at Lyons, he is currently engaged in a tour throughout the United States.

NIGERIA GRABS CONTROL OF ALL RELIEF

1969 All relief operations on both sides of the front line of the Nigerian civil war are being taken over by the Nigerian military government, a spokesman announced today. This means that the International Red Cross (ICRC), individual churches and various other relief organizations – of which there are 20 – will now have to operate exclusively through the Nigerian National Commission for Rehabilitation. This move comes from the Nigerian government's determination to prevent food and other supplies getting into the hands of Biafran troops. The rest of the world, however, is concerned for the fate of the starving millions of the devasted region of Biafra. ICRC officials in Geneva say they will be striving to resume food airlifts to Biafra as soon as possible.

Norman Bates is here

1960 Screams of terror filled the cinema when Norman Bates went into a killing frenzy in the film *Psycho*, which opened today. Director Alfred Hitchcock – who refused to give too much of the plot away in advance – limited himself to saying that the original novel was based on the true story of a man who kept his dead mother in the basement. An orchestra composed entirely of strings was used for the musical score and the shrieking of violins contributes greatly to the atmosphere of chilling horror.

HONG KONG IS GIVEN BACK

1997 Against a backdrop of celebrations all over China, Hong Kong has been handed back to the Chinese after 99 years of British administration. Attending the ceremony are Prince Charles and Prime Minister Tony Blair, as well as Chinese President Jiang Zemin who has promised to govern Hong Kong by the principle of "one country, two systems".

1981 At the Trooping of the Colour in London today a youth stepped from the crowd and fired a pistol at the Queen. Police immediately arrested the youth who, it transpired, had been firing only blank cartridges.

Superman sighted

1938 Thanks to Action Comics, a new super crime fighter from the distant planet of Krypton has made his appearance among us today. He can leap taller than the highest building, run faster than a speeding train, is invulnerable and possesses the strength of 200 men. Most of the time his true identity is hidden behind the mild, unassuming persona of Clark Kent, a reporter on the *Metropolis Daily Globe*. But when action calls he quickly materializes in a blue catsuit and red cape, with a big "S" emblazoned on his enormous chest. And what's his name? Why, Superman, of course!

Aztec king slain by Spain

1520 The Aztec sovereign of Mexico, Montezuma II, was killed today by the Spanish conquerors of Hernando Cortez who had overthrown his empire and taken him prisoner. Misled by the ancient prophecies of his race, Montezuma II and his people received Cortez and his men as divinities when they first arrived at the Mexican capital, Tenochtitlan. His father, Montezuma I, was a mighty ruler whose power stretched from the Atlantic and to the Pacific. Montezuma II himself was a successful conqueror until overthrown by Hernando Cortez.

1894 Amidst much celebration the Tower Bridge was opened by H.R.H. The Prince of Wales. His cavalcade made a double crossing before the bascules were raised to allow an impressive procession of boats to sail down the Thames.

JULY

"*For years politicians have promised the moon,
I'm the first one to be able to deliver it.*"

President Richard Nixon
in a radio message to the astronauts on the moon,
July 20, 1969.

China leases New Territories to Britain

1898 Britain today acquired a 99-year lease to the New Territories on mainland China in a continuing drive for trade dominance in the region. Currently in possession of Hong Kong island and the Kowloon Peninsula as a consequence of the two Opium Wars, this latest acquisition will further enhance Britain's standing as a major trading partner in the region. The wars forced open Chinese ports to British trade, particularly trade in opium from British India, which is used to pay for porcelains, silks and teas purchased from China. After the first Opium War (1840-42), Britain acquired Hong Kong under the Treaty of Nanking and at the end of the second Opium War in 1860, acquired the Kowloon Peninsula under the Peking Convention. The new territories, however, must be returned to the Chinese government in 99 years time.

> *Peace is indivisible.*
> **Maxim Litvinov**, Russian statesman, in a speech to the League of Nations, 1936.

Charles invested as Prince of Wales

1969 Prince Charles, heir to the British throne, was today invested as Prince of Wales by his mother Queen Elizabeth II at Caernarvon Castle, Wales. In preparation for his investiture, Charles spent a term at University College of Wales learning Welsh. The title is usually granted by the reigning sovereign to the heir apparent, but not automatically. Charles became Prince of Wales when he was ten years old – only now it is official. Once he becomes king the title will cease, until he bestows it on his son.

1989 Amidst a groundswell of nationalist feelings among a number of the Soviet republics, President Gorbachev has today announced on television throughout the USSR that he would not tolerate separatism. Independence movements are well advanced in the Baltic states and it is feared that other republics might follow suit resulting in clashes with the Soviet army.

Darwin presents theory of evolution

1858 Amidst controversy, eminent British scientist Charles Darwin has presented his views on evolution and the principles of natural selection to the Linnean Society in London. Churchmen are concerned that Darwin's theory refutes the Book of Genesis, scientists are sceptical because his ideas seem to dismiss the work of Lamarck. Darwin has based much of his work on observations made while serving as a naturalist on HMS *Beagle* between 1831 and 1836. During this time his observations convinced him that species evolved gradually and that natural selection is responsible for changing the genetic constitution of a species in favour of particular genes carried by successful individuals. Almost pipped to the post by naturalist Alfred Russell Wallace, who holds similar views on evolution, Darwin has presented his findings in the nick of time. He will publish a book next year.

WAR ENDS IN ALGERIA

1962 After eight years of war between the Algerian nationalist population and the French army and settlers and 132 years of French rule, Algeria looks set to gain independence. A referendum held in Algeria today has almost unanimously backed de Gaulle's independence plan. A ceasefire called in March prompted by the intensification of terrorist activity in the country during the early months of this year, has allowed discussions between the French government and the National Liberation Front's (FLN) provisional government to take place. In spite of the talks, acts of terrorism continued and a mass exodus of Europeans began as the prospect of a Muslim state became more likely. France is likely to hand over the reins of power to the leader of the FLN provisional government, Ben Khedda.

JULY 1

1847 The first adhesive stamps go on sale in the USA.

1860 Death of American inventor Charles Goodyear, pioneer of rubber processing.

1896 Death of Harriet Beecher Stowe, the American author of the anti-slavery novel *Uncle Tom's Cabin*.

1916 Coca-Cola launches its distinctively shaped bottle.

1916 The Battle of the Somme begins with heavy casualties.

1925 Death of Erik Satie, the French composer notable for the eccentricity of the titles of his work.

1929 The cartoon character Popeye first appears in the USA.

1937 The 999 emergency telephone call comes into force in Britain, the first of its kind in the world.

1941 The first-ever television commercial is shown on channel WNBT in New York, advertising a Bulova clock.

1984 Naples football club pays £1 million ($1.85 million) for Argentinian footballer Diego Maradona.

1990 The *deutschmark* becomes the official currency of both East and West Germany.

BIRTHDAYS

George Sand 1804, French novelist best remembered for her romance with composer Frédéric Chopin.

Charles Laughton 1899, English actor whose most famous performances were in *Mutiny on the Bounty* and *The Hunchback of Notre Dame*.

Olivia de Havilland 1916, American actress who won Oscars for *The Heiress* and *To Each His Own*.

Hans Werner Henze 1926, West German composer and musical innovator.

Carl Lewis 1961, American athlete who won three gold medals in the Los Angeles Olympic Games in 1984.

1644 In the English Civil War, the Battle of Marston Moor turns the tide in Oliver Cromwell's favour.

1778 Swiss-born French philosopher and writer Jean-Jacques Rousseau dies insane.

1843 Samuel Hahnemann, the founder of homoeopathy, dies in Paris.

1881 US president James Garfield is injured by an assassin's bullets.

1937 American pilots Amelia Earhart and Fred Noonan take off from New Guinea on their round-world trip but fail to arrive at their destination, Howland Island in the central Pacific.

1951 The worst floods in US history leave 41 dead and 200,000 homeless in Kansas and Missouri.

1954 Czech tennis player Jaroslav Drobny beats Australian Ken Rosewall to take the men's singles title after the longest-ever Wimbledon final.

1964 President Johnson signs the US Civil Rights Bill, which prohibits racial discrimination.

1990 A hundred Muslim pilgrims die of suffocation in a tunnel in the Holy City of Mecca.

1997 Death of James Stewart, Hollywood screen idol who won an Oscar for his performance in *The Philadelphia Story*.

BIRTHDAYS

Thomas Cranmer 1489, English cleric who was consecrated Archbishop of Canterbury for his support of Henry VIII in the latter's divorce dispute with the Pope but was burnt at the stake as a heretic during the reign of Queen Mary.

Christoph Gluck 1714, German composer who wrote over 40 dramatic works and is best-known for *Alceste* and *Orfeo ed Euridice*.

Hermann Hesse 1877, German novelist and poet best-known for *Siddartha*, *Steppenwolf* and *The Glass Bead Game*.

Patrice Lumumba 1925, Congolese statesman and prime minister from 1960 to 1961.

William Booth establishes Christian "army"

1865 British evangelist and itinerant preacher William Booth today founded the Christian Mission in Whitechapel, one of London's worst slums. Thirty-six-year-old Booth from Nottingham has been a minister of the Methodist New Connection church for some years but the church has been reluctant to accept his poor converts. As a result, he has established his own mission along military lines, with military titles, hierarchy and uniforms. More than a Christian evangelical church, Booth's "Salvation Army" acts as a social service and reforming organization for the most destitute members of society. He works with his wife and public preacher Catherine.

FIRST ZEPPELIN FLIGHT

1900 Aviation history was made today in Germany as Count Ferdinand von Zeppelin flew his first airship (a dirigible balloon with a rigid frame named zeppelin after its inventor). A great pioneer of German aviation, Count von Zeppelin has devoted himself to the study of aeronautics since he left the army in 1891. He began construction of his zeppelin in 1897. Although the dirigible concept is not a new one – a number of airships have been built by other designers based on the idea of a power-driven aircraft buoyed up by lighter-than-air gas, Zeppelin's airship is the largest yet to be built. The 420 ft (136 m) LZ.1 flew for an hour and a quarter over Lake Constance driven by two 16 hp Daimler engines reaching speeds of up to 20 mph (32 kph) before its steering gear seized up. Zeppelin has been hailed as a great master of airship design and plans to set up a factory to make the airships at Friedrichshafen.

VIETNAM REUNIFIED

1976 North and South Vietnam were reunified today in the aftermath of the fall of Saigon and the tragedy of the Vietnam War. The division 22 years ago into separate states under the terms of the Geneva Convention (to ensure peace after the Indo China War) resulted in continuous fighting and massive loss of life: the Communist Vietcong within South Vietnam attempted to seize power from the government, aided by North Vietnam and China. The US provided military support to the South Vietnamese government for a number of years and during the early 1960s their involvement increased and the war escalated. The bloody war continued for many years at the cost of hundreds of thousands of military and civilian lives, devastating the countryside and laying waste to the economies of both countries with no definite winner or loser.

The US, unpopular with Americans for its part in the war, withdrew in 1973 in the most humiliating political defeat it has ever suffered. A peace treaty was signed between North and South Vietnam in the same year, but in March last year North Vietnam invaded South Vietnam and Saigon fell in April. The resulting Socialist Republic of Vietnam proclaimed today faces enormous economic and social problems.

> *People will not readily bear pain unless there is hope.*
> **Michael Edwards**, South African businessman, 1980.

Betty Grable dies

1973 Hollywood star and American GI pin-up Betty Grable died today. The bouncy blonde who was never at a loss for words reached the peak of her career in the 1940s with such films as *Tin Pan Alley* (1940), *Moon over Miami* (1941) and *Coney Island* (1943). Her legs were said to be her best feature, so like any sensible young woman taking care of her assets, Miss Grable insured them for a staggering figure of $200,000 (£108,700).

1989 Russia's longest-serving foreign minister, Andrei Gromyko, has died in Moscow today aged 79. Foreign minister for 30 years, he was also president of the Supreme Soviet for three years. He became notorious in western diplomatic circles for his austere and humourless manner, pursuing the Cold War relentlessly.

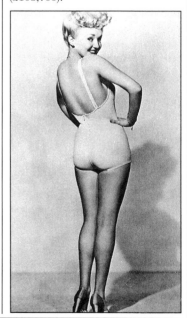

> *I am sick and tired of war. Its glory is all moonshine . . . War is hell.*
> **General William Sherman**, in his address to the Michigan Military Academy, 1879.

CHAMPLAIN FOUNDS CITY OF QUEBEC

1608 French explorer Samuel de Champlain today founded and named the city of Quebec, which lies on the St Lawrence river in Canada. In fact the city is an Iroquois village called Stadacona. Champlain has made two previous expeditions to Canada, a preliminary expedition in 1603, then an exploration of the coasts from 1604 to 1607. Champlain enjoys friendly and trusting relationships with the Algonquins and Hurons, and is not afraid to commit himself to long expeditions with his Indian guides. As a result he has been able to obtain information regarding the existence of three Great Lakes, a very large bay to the north as yet unexplored and another "South Sea" which is the Spanish name given to the Pacific Ocean. His understanding of the general shape of eastern North America is extraordinary.

Butcher of Lyons gets life

1987 Klaus Barbie, the Nazi SS commander in Lyons during World War Two, was convicted today, amidst cheering and clapping in court, of crimes against humanity. The 73-year-old listened to the verdict from his bullet-proof dock in silence. He had been living in Bolivia since 1951, enjoying the protection of various military regimes until he was turned over to the French authorities in 1983. Barbie was responsible for the deportation of Jews from the Netherlands in 1940. In 1942 he transferred to France as SS commander in Lyons where he tracked down resistance workers and Jews, including rounding up Jewish children from an orphanage at Iziev. He was also notorious for torturing resistance leader Jean Moulin, earning himself the name of "Butcher of Lyons". He escaped capture at the end of the war and was employed by US intelligence in Germany until moving to Bolivia in 1951.

Swede becomes youngest Wimbledon champion

1976 Twenty-year-old Swedish tennis player Bjorn Borg became the youngest ever men's singles winner at Wimbledon today defeating Ilie Nastase of Romania 6-4, 6-2, 9-7. A talented all-round sportsman, Borg showed early promise at tennis and at 11 won his first tournament. He has been in Sweden's Davis Cup team since he was 15. His superb athleticism and sportsmanlike temperament helped him win the Wimbledon Junior championship at 16 and the French championship at 18. Borg looks set to carry on for many seasons to come and will doubtless be much sought after for exhibition matches and by advertisers.

Hero of Chernobyl dies

1990 Anatoli Grishchenko, the Russian who braved radioactive fallout at the heart of Chernobyl to save the world from an even worse catastrophe, died of leukemia in an American hospital today. Grishchenko flew a helicopter over the damaged reactor and dropped the loads of sand and concrete needed to seal the plant and prevent meltdown. The disaster occured in April 1986 when fire broke out at the reactor causing the worst ever nuclear accident to date. There was widespread concern in Euope about the contamination of livestock and the long-term effects of widespread radiation (linked with cancer) on humans.

CONFEDERATES ROUTED AT GETTYSBURG

1863 With more than 51,000 dead and wounded, the Battle of Gettysburg is over and the Confederate Army has been routed. Superior numbers and strong defensive positions helped General George Meade's Union Army to defeat General Robert E. Lee just outside the market town of Gettysburg, Pennsylvania. It is estimated that General Lee has lost more than a third of his force of 70,000 men during the three days of conflict which began on July 1. This may prove to be a turning point in the grim and bloody struggle between the North and South.

323 AD Constantine I, Roman emperor in the West, defeats Licinius, the Eastern emperor, near Adrianople.

1898 Captain Joshua Slocum sails into Newport, Rhode Island in his boat *Spray*, becoming the first solo round-world sailor.

1905 In Odessa, Russian troops kill over 6000 to restore order during a strike.

1928 The first commercial television set goes on sale in the US at $75 (£40).

1940 Over 1000 French sailors die when the French fleet in Miersel-Kebr, Algeria, is destroyed at the order of Winston Churchill to prevent it falling into French hands.

1954 All goods finally come off ration in the UK as post-war shortages are ended.

1962 French property in Algeria is taken over as the country gains its independence.

1969 Rolling Stone Brian Jones is found drowned in a swimming pool.

1971 Jim Morrison, lead singer with the Doors, dies of a heart attack in Paris.

1988 The USS *Vincennes*, based in the Gulf during the Iran-Iraq war, shoots down an Iranian airliner with 286 people on board in the mistaken belief that it is a bomber.

BIRTHDAYS

Robert Adam 1728, Scottish architect and designer with an influential style.

Leos Janácek 1854, Czech composer whose operas include *Jenufa* and *The Makropulos Case*.

Franz Kafka 1883, Czech poet and playwright best-known for the stories *Metamorphosis* and *In the Penal Settlement* and the novels *The Trial* and *The Castle*.

Ken Russell 1927, British film director with an idiosyncratic and controversial style.

Tom Stoppard 1937, Czech-born playwright known for *Rosencrantz and Guildenstern are Dead*.

JULY 4

Independence Day

1712 Nine whites are killed in a slave uprising in New York.

1761 Death of Samuel Richardson, British writer whose novel *Clarissa* ran to seven volumes.

1829 The first horse-drawn buses go into action in London.

1848 The Communist Manifesto is published.

1892 In the British general election, James Keir Hardie wins the Holytoun constituency in Lanarkshire, Scotland, to become the first socialist MP in the House of Commons.

1934 Death of Marie Curie, the Polish-born scientist who discovered radium and won two Nobel Prizes, for Physics in 1903 and for Chemistry in 1911.

1934 French tennis star Suzanne Lenglen, winner of 15 Wimbledon titles, dies of leukaemia at the age of 39.

1979 Algerian leader Ben Bella is released after 14 years in jail.

1986 New York's Statue of Liberty gets a centenary facelift.

BIRTHDAYS

Nathaniel Hawthorne 1804, American novelist best-known for *The Scarlet Letter* and *The House of Seven Gables*.

Giuseppe Garibaldi 1807, Italian soldier who played a major role in the unification of Italy.

Stephen Foster 1826, American songwriter, composer of "Swanee River" and "Beautiful Dreamer".

Thomas Barnado 1845, Irish philanthropist who founded homes for destitute children.

Louis B. Mayer 1885, Russian-born Hollywood mogul and co-founder of MGM.

Louis "Satchmo" Armstrong 1900, American jazz trumpeter and bandleader, much loved for his appearances in films such as *High Society* and *Hello Dolly*.

Neil Simon 1927, American playwright of enormous popularity.

Billy the Kid shot dead

1881 Notorious outlaw William H. Bonney, better known as Billy the Kid, was shot dead today by lawman Pat Garrett as he tried to escape custody. Bonney, aged 22, was under sentence of death for the murder of a sheriff but escaped while in custody killing two guards in his bid for freedom. He was recaptured and shot while trying to escape again. A native of New York, Bonney is reputed to have killed his first man before he reached his teens, becoming a legend in his own time with his daring hold-ups and robberies in the south-western states.

Congress accepts Declaration of Independence

1776 In an historic session today the Continental Congress accepted, with minor amendments, the Declaration of Independence written by Thomas Jefferson under the instructions of a five-member committee. Although Congress voted on July 2 to declare independence, the declaration passed today formally severs American links with Britain. It has come about largely as a result of the War of Independence, which has raged for over a year. The document will be sent to King George III.

Dempsey is new heavyweight champ

1919 Boxing history was made today as Jack Dempsey beat Jess Willard in three rounds to win the World Heavyweight title. In front of a record crowd of 40,000 in Toledo, Ohio, Dempsey took control of the match, knocking Willard down seven times in the first round alone; after three rounds the fight was stopped.

We hold these truths to be self-evident, that all men are created equal, that they are endowed by their creator with certain unalienable rights, that among these are life, liberty and the pursuit of happiness.
American Declaration of Independence, 1776.

Hostage ordeal ends as Israeli commandos swoop

1976 While the rest of the world still debates the best course of action, a crack force of Israeli commandos has just made a daring midnight raid of Entebbe airport, ending this eight-day nightmare. In a dramatic swoop, 200 commandos have freed all but three of the 98 hostages who have been held there by Palestinian terrorists since June 27. The commandos arrived at the airfield in three Hercules C-130 transport planes and took just 53 minutes to complete their mission, overcoming airport guards and killing seven terrorists in the process. The hostage drama began when Palestinian terrorists hijacked an Air France A 300-B airbus shortly after take-off from Athens airport and demanded to be flown to Uganda. The passengers, a mix of Israeli and other nationalities, have been the pawns in an international drama which happily has ended in their favour. Overjoyed that their nightmare is over, they have been flown back to Israel.

1826 America has lost two of its founding fathers today as Thomas Jefferson and John Adams died on the anniversary of the acceptance by Congress of their historic Declaration of Independence. Both men were part of the five-member committee which drafted the original declaration.

Suffragette appears in trousers

1853 Controversial and outspoken suffragette Amelia Jenks Bloomer shocked her audience in Connecticut today by appearing in trousers while she delivered a speech denouncing the requirement that women should cover their legs. Mrs Bloomer has been appearing in this attire – a knee-length skirt combined with loose trousers bound in at the ankle and dubbed "bloomers" – since 1849 as a form of protest. The issues of women's rights in general and the issue of dress reform in particular are ones that Mrs Bloomer holds dear. She is the publisher of a reforming magazine titled *The Lily* and has shared a lecture platform in New York with Susan B. Anthony, the well-known campaigner for women's suffrage.

DIVA SAYS FAREWELL TO COVENT GARDEN

1965 In a stunning final performance, soprano Maria Callas tonight bade farewell to the operatic stage and her numerous fans at Covent Garden, some of whom had queued for 48 hours for tickets. In a voice noted for its fine range and gift of expression, Callas sang *Tosca* before a packed house. She has sung all of the most exacting soprano roles, excelling particularly in the *bel canto* style of the pre-Verdian Italian opera. She first came to international attention after a performance of *La Gioconda* at Verona in 1947 and since then has become an international star. Born in New York of Greek parents, Callas studied at Athens Conservatory and continues to spend time in Greece.

Ordination of women moves a step closer

1988 Amidst fears of a split, the Church of England voted today to move towards the ordination of women priests. The Archbishop of Canterbury, Robert Runcie, voted against the motion which passed with a majority of less than 60 per cent. It is understood that he is unhappy about the present proposition not because he is opposed to female ordination but because it allows bishops, priests and parishes the right to refuse women priests, which may provoke a split in the Church. This process toward the ordination of women priests will be taken a step further in 1992 when the Synod will vote on the matter.

Stones give free concert in Hyde Park

1969 Two days after the death of guitarist Brian Jones, the Rolling Stones gave a free concert in Hyde Park attended by a record 250,000 people. Policed by the London branch of Hell's Angels and recorded for television, the concert was a great success. During the evening Mick Jagger paid tribute to Jones by reciting Shelley while clouds of white butterflies were released over the stage. Jones' death has been attributed to alcohol and drug abuse.

Temperance turnout boosted by rail excursion

1841 The temperance movement got a boost today as Thomas Cook, entrepreneur and ardent temperance supporter, organized the first special rail excursion to transport the faithful to meetings. Today's excursion from Leicester to Loughborough and back again was pronounced a great success by Mr Cook. "All went off in the best style and in perfect safety we returned to Leicester," he said. When asked how he had come to organize such a venture he said, "I thought as I was walking one day, what a glorious thing it would be if the newly developed powers of railways and locomotion could be made subservient to the promotion of temperance." Thomas Cook has plans for more excursions using the railways.

> *I weep for Adonais – he is dead!*
> *O, weep for Adonais! though our tears*
> *Thaw not the frost which binds so dear a head!*
> A section from the poem *Adonais* by Shelley, quoted by Rolling Stone **Mick Jagger** on the death of the guitarist Brian Jones, 1969.

Raffles dies

1826 Colourful English colonial administrator Sir Thomas Stamford Raffles, best known for founding Singapore, died in London today after a brief illness. He was born in Jamaica but spent much of his career in the Far East. During 1811 he accompanied Lord Minto in an expedition against Java, taking it from the Dutch. While serving as Lieutenant Governor of Java, Raffles completely reformed the internal administration of that country; he wrote *The History of Java* in 1817 during enforced leave in England (due to illness). While in England he was knighted. Upon his return to the Far East as Lieutenant Governor of Benkoelen he formed Singapore and remained there until ill health again forced his return to England two years ago. On his way to England his ship caught fire, and he lost much of his natural history collection and his East Indian vocabularies. Undaunted by this loss and his illness, he established London Zoo and was its first president.

1791 George Hammond is appointed first British ambassador to the USA.

1811 Venezuela's revolutionary congress declares its independence from Spain.

1817 The first gold sovereigns are issued in Britain.

1830 The French capture Algiers and seize its ruler's fabulous jewellery collection.

1865 A 2 mph (3kph) speed limit is imposed in Britain, covering steam-driven and petrol vehicles.

1902 Edward VI foots the bill for 450,000 impoverished Britons to celebrate his coronation with a free dinner.

1919 French tennis player Suzanne Lenglen wins the Wimbledon women's singles title for the first time.

1975 Arthur Ashe beats Jimmy Connors to become the first black men's singles champion at Wimbledon.

1975 The Cape Verde Islands gain their independence from Portugal.

1977 Pakistani prime minister Zulfikar Ali Bhutto is ousted by a coup led by General Zia ul-Haq.

1989 Colonel Oliver North is fined $150,000 (£95,000) and given a suspended prison sentence for the role he played in the Iran-Contra affair.

BIRTHDAYS

Sarah Siddons 1755, English actress, the leading lady of her time.

Phineas Barnum 1810, American showman.

Cecil Rhodes 1853, English-born colonialist, financier and statesman in Southern Africa.

Dwight Davis 1879, American tennis player who founded the Davis Cup.

Jean Cocteau 1889, French poet and artist, best-known for *Orphée* and *Les Enfants terribles*.

Georges Pompidou 1911, French statesman and president from 1969 until his death in 1974.

1189 French-born Henry II of Anfland dies in Tours, France, to be succeeded by Richard I, known as "the Lionheart".

1801 The English and Spanish fleets are defeated by the French off Algeciras.

1809 Pope Pius VII is arrested for excommunicating Napoleon.

1892 American steelworkers are killed in a clash with armed Pinkerton men during a strike at the Carnegie plant in Homestead.

1892 Dadabhai Naoraji becomes Britain's first non-white MP.

1893 French author Guy de Maupassant dies in an asylum for the insane.

1928 *The Lights of New York*, the first all-sound feature film, is premiered.

1960 American author and Nobel Prize-winner William Faulkner dies aged 62.

1960 Death of Aneurin Bevan, British Labour politician who, as minister of health from 1945 to 1951, created the National Health Service.

1964 The Beatles' first film, *A Hard Day's Night*, is given a royal premiere in London.

1973 Otto Klemperer, German-born conductor particularly noted for his interpretations of Beethoven symphonies, dies at the age of 88.

BIRTHDAYS

Maximilian 1832, Austrian Archduke who was given the Mexican crown by the French.

Bill Haley 1925, American musician whose "Rock Around the Clock" was the first hit rock 'n' roll record.

Dalai Lama 1935, Tibetan spiritual leader in exile.

Vladimir Ashkenazy 1937, Russian pianist and conductor renowned for his interpretations of Mozart and Chopin.

Sylvester Stallone 1946, American actor best-known for his leading role in the popular series of "Rocky" movies.

North Sea rig explosion kills 166

1988 An explosion on the North Sea oil rig, *Piper Alpha*, has resulted in the loss of 166 lives. According to survivors of the disaster, a huge explosion wiped out the control room, and a further explosion propelled a fireball across the platform, destroying the superstructure. Amidst the twisted wreckage and flames 500 ft (162 m) high, men plunged 200 ft (65 m) into the sea to their deaths. The intense heat and the flames hampered rescue operations, and it is believed that many of the men could not swim. Braving the flames and cranes crashing into the sea, high speed dinghies picked up as many survivors as possible. Seven NATO warships, 21 smaller vessels and six helicopters are continuing the rescue operation. The fire continues to rage, fueled by oil pumping indiscriminately from beneath the sea bed. Occidental Petroleum, the firm operating the rig, is expected to call in famous firefighter and well capper Red Adair to try to bring the ferocious blaze under control.

1957 Sporting history was made today as American Althea Gibson became the first black Wimbledon champion beating fellow American Darlene Hurd 6-3, 6-2. An outstanding player, 30-year-old Gibson hasn't lost a single set throughout the entire fortnight's play.

Sir Thomas More executed

1535 Distinguished politician and author Sir Thomas More was executed today at the Tower of London after being found guilty of high treason. Formerly a favourite of King Henry VIII, More refused to take an oath of supremacy to the king as head of the Church in preference to the Pope, so was charged and found guilty of high treason. He has been held in the Tower for a year in hope that he would recant. Sir Thomas is greatly respected in the country and has had a most distinguished political and diplomatic career. London born, he studied at Oxford under Linacre and his religious beliefs were strongly influenced by Colet. More entered parliament in 1504 and from 1509, when he enjoyed the favour of the King, was employed on various foreign missions. He was appointed Speaker of the Privy Council in 1518 and became Speaker of the House of Commons in 1523, during which time he was knighted. Against his own strongest wishes he succeeded Wolsey as Lord Chancellor in 1529 and resigned in 1532 over King Henry VIII's ecclesiastical policy and his marriage to Anne Boleyn. As a devout Catholic, More refused last year to recognize the King as head of the Church and hence he lost his own head today.

Satchmo dies

1971 The musical world lost one of its best-loved stars today when jazz legend Louis Armstrong died of a heart attack at the age of 71. He had been battling with ill health for three years. Affectionately known as "Satchmo", Armstrong received international recognition for his virtuoso trumpet playing; he was also a bandleader, singer and star of film musicals, and became one of the foremost figures of 20th century popular music. He will be sadly missed by friends and fans, not only for his skill on the trumpet and inimitable gravelly voice, but also for his humour and warmth of personality.

Musicians don't retire; they stop when there's no more music in them.
Louis Armstrong, jazz trumpeter, who died today of a heart attack, aged 71.

NATO seeks a new role

1990 In the wake of the momentous events in Eastern Europe and the drive towards reunification by the two Germanies, NATO has declared that the Warsaw Pact is no longer a military threat to the West, and so must now seek a new role for itself in the 1990s. This declaration in London comes hard on the heels of the announcement in May by NATO defence ministers of major cuts to budgets. It is understood that NATO will become a primarily political organization.

US takes over occupation of Iceland

1941 President Franklin D. Roosevelt today ordered American troops to occupy Iceland, in a move to release British forces from Iceland and deter any attack from the Nazis. Although Iceland is an independent country, Britain occupied it earlier this year to prevent Germany from turning it into a base from which to further threaten British shipping. Although the United States is not at war with Germany at this point, the country is as committed to the Allied cause as is possible without actually declaring war on Germany. Roosevelt continues to stress that the US must remain an "arsenal of democracy".

1930 Sir Arthur Conan Doyle, creator of sleuth Sherlock Holmes and his sidekick Dr Watson, has died at 71. Edinburgh-born Doyle trained as a doctor and began writing while in practice at Southsea. His interest in science and history was reflected in many of his novels. In later life he became a spiritualist. He was knighted in 1902.

1985 Seventeen-year-old Boris Becker beat Kevin Curren today to become the youngest ever Wimbledon men's singles title holder. Becker is a powerful player, relying on enormous energy and physical strength to win.

1990 Martina Navratilova made Wimbledon history today by winning her ninth Wimbledon title, obtaining first place more times than anyone in the history of Wimbledon.

Japan open to trade after 250 years of isolation

1853 US Naval officer Commodore Matthew Perry today persuaded Japan to unlock its doors to trade with the rest of the world. Backed by armed ships in Edo Harbour, Perry convinced the current shogun that the Japanese should treat shipwrecked sailors with more consideration, that American vessels should be allowed to purchase coal and that American merchants should be allowed to trade in at least one port. Japan effectively closed its doors to the western world when it expelled the Spanish in 1624 and the Portuguese in 1639. Only the Dutch have been allowed extremely limited access to the country under very exacting restrictions and Japanese citizens are not permitted to travel outside the country. Although this surprise capitulation by the shogun will be greeted with delight in the West, it will cause some anxiety and unrest in Japanese society.

Great Italian architect dies

1573 Giacomo Barozzi da Vignola, the great Italian Renaissance architect, died today in Rome at the age of 66. He has had several important patrons and will be remembered for a number of great buildings. Two of the finest of these are Villa Giulia for Pope Julius III and the Villa Farnese at Caprarola. Perhaps he will best be remembered for the church of the Gesu, the mother church of the Jesuits, which has been used as a model for their places of worship throughout the world. The Gesu, with its cruciform plan and side chapels, has also had a significant influence on French and Italian church architecture.

Queen entertains intruder

1982 Early this morning Queen Elizabeth was awoken by a strange man sitting on her bed in the Royal suite at Buckingham Palace. Michael Fagin, 30, swigging wine from the Royal cellars, chatted amicably with the monarch who kept remarkably cool throughout what must have been an alarming experience. When Fagin asked for a cigarette, the Queen used the pretext of calling for some to summon help. She was unharmed by the incident and has been praised for her clearheaded response to a potentially extremely dangerous situation. Fagin has been remanded in custody and charged with the theft of the wine and with trespass. The incident further highlights concern about lax security at Buckingham Palace.

Where there is no imagination there is no horror.
Sir Arthur Conan Doyle.

1307 English king Edward I, conqueror of the Welsh, dies on his way to Scotland to fight Robert the Bruce.

1815 Following Napoleon's defeat at Waterloo on June 18, the victorious allies march into Paris.

1816 Irish playwright Richard Sheridan, best-known for *School for Scandal*, dies in poverty.

1937 The second Sino-Japanese war breaks out.

1950 The first airshow is held at Farnborough in Surrey, UK.

1970 Death of Sir Allen Lane, founder of Penguin and the first publisher to promote the paperback.

1984 Death of Dame Flora Robson, English stage and screen actress whose most notable films were *Black Narcissus*, *Fire Over England* and *Innocent Sinners*.

1988 An 11-year-old American boy pilot takes off from San Diego, bound for Le Bourget in Paris.

BIRTHDAYS

Joseph-Marie Jacquard 1752, French silk weaver and inventor of the Jacquard loom, which created figured patterns by means of punched cards.

Gustav Mahler 1860, Austrian composer and conductor who wrote ten symphonies and the song cycles *Kindertotenlieder* and *Das Lied von der Erde*.

Marc Chagall 1887, Russian painter and designer who spent most of his life in France and was the only other painter apart from Picasso to have his work exhibited in the Louvre in his lifetime.

George Cukor 1899, American film director whose most notable films include *Philadelphia Story*, *A Star Is Born* and the Oscar-winning *My Fair Lady*.

Vittorio de Sica 1901, Italian film director who won four Oscars for Best Foreign Film and is best-known for *Bicycle Thieves*, *Shoeshine* and *The Garden of the Finzi-Continis*.

Pierre Cardin 1922, French fashion designer.

1497 Portuguese navigator Vasco da Gama sets sail from Lisbon to attempt to find a sea passage to India.

1889 At a bareknuckle world heavyweight boxing match in Richburg, Mississippi, John L. Sullivan defeats Jake Kilrain in the 75th round.

1905 American tennis player May Sutton becomes the first foreigner to take a Wimbledon title.

1933 Death of British novelist Anthony Hope, author of *The Prisoner of Zenda*.

1939 Death of Henry Havelock Ellis, British psychologist and essayist best-known for his studies of human sexual behaviour.

1943 French Resistance leader Jean Moulin is executed by Nazi torturers who include Klaus Barbie.

1965 Starting gates for horse-racing are used for the first time at Newmarket in Britain.

1967 British actress Vivien Leigh, star of *Gone With the Wind*, dies of tuberculosis aged only 53.

1979 Death of Michael Wilding, British stage and screen actor and sometime husband of Elizabeth Taylor.

1990 One billion television viewers watch West Germany defeat Argentina to win the World Cup.

BIRTHDAYS

Joseph Chamberlain 1836, English politician who advocated free education and the creation of smallholdings.

Count Ferdinand von Zeppelin 1838, German aircraft manufacturer.

John D. Rockefeller 1839, American multimillionaire and founder of the Standard Oil Company.

Sir Arthur John Evans 1851, English archaeologist who excavated Knossos in Crete.

Percy Grainger 1882, Australian composer who derived much of his inspiration from folk songs.

SHELLEY DROWNED

1822 Leading figure in the Romantic movement Percy Bysshe Shelley drowned today in the Bay of Spezia, when his small boat foundered in a storm. He had just visited the poet Byron and Leigh Hunt at Leghorn and was returning home. A somewhat controversial figure, Shelley nevertheless has contributed enormously to English literary and intellectual life, leaving behind an impressive legacy of poetry, essays, pamphlets and letters. After the breakup of his marriage to Harriet Westbrook and her suicide, he left England for Italy with Mary Godwin with whom he had formed a liaison. He subsequently married her in spite of disapproving of marriage, royalty, meat-eating and religion. A great rebel and anarchist, his life and work reflect his intellectual courage, his keen sense of injustice and sharp sense of humour. Born in 1792 in Horsham, he was educated at Eton and University College, Oxford where he was expelled after only one year for writing a pamphlet titled *The Necessity of Atheism*.

SULLIVAN WINS LAST BARE-KNUCKLE FIGHT

1889 After a punishing 75 rounds, John L. Sullivan has won the the world heavyweight title against Jake Kilrain. Staged at Richburg, Mississippi, the bout, which is now the last bareknuckle defence of the world heavyweight crown under London Prize Ring rules, ended in a knock-out for the 31-year-old Bostonian in the 75th round. In future title fights combatants will have to wear large padded gloves. Professional boxing will now follow the Marquis of Queensberry rules, which amateur boxing has used for some years. Sullivan's great strength has been the hallmark of his success which began five years ago when he took the world heavyweight title from Paddy Ryan. His prowess has earned him a substantial amount of money although it is rumoured that heavy drinking outside the ring has used up much of it.

How wonderful is Death,
Death and his brother Sleep!
P. B. Shelley in *The Daemon of the World.*

The King bathes, and with great success; a machine follows the Royal one into the sea, filled with fiddlers who play "God Save the King" as his Majesty takes his plunge.
Fanny Burney, British novelist, referring to George III at Weymouth – a diary entry, 1789.

1978 Two German mountaineers, Reinhold Messner and Peter Habeler, today successfully scaled Mount Everest, without the use of oxygen, which has been crucial to the success of all previous expeditions to conquer the world's tallest mountain. Officially 29,028 ft (9416 m) high, Everest runs through Nepal between India and Tibet. Its name in Tibetan means "Goddess Mother of the World". It was first conquered in 1953.

Secret talks raise hopes of Mandela release

1989 News of a secret meeting three days ago between imprisoned ANC leader Nelson Mandela and outgoing president P. W. Botha has caused a stir of speculation in South Africa. The meeting at Cape Town's presidential offices, the Tuynhuys, was conducted without any press coverage and lasted a mere 45 minutes. Growing calls for the release of Mandela, who has been in jail for more than 26 years, and international pressure for the ending of apartheid has put the heat on the South African government. Liberals have taken today's news as a sign that the authorities may finally be prepared to come to the negotiating table, and that they accept Mandela as the man they will have to face. Others, however, are less pleased – Winnie Mandela suspects Botha's motives and right-wingers see any discussion with black leaders as a betrayal of the white minority.

ZIEGFELD GLORIFIES THE AMERICAN GIRL

1907 With the flashing of legs and the twitching of ostrich plumes, the Follies hit Broadway today. The theatre manager and producer Florenz Ziegfeld has brought an All-American version of the Folies Bergère of Paris to the New York stage, using that magic combination of beautiful girls, semi-nudity, great pageantry and comedy to ensure success; his theme - "Glorifying the American girl". Although less risqué than the original, Ziegfeld's Follies are bound to cause a stir. Ziegfeld is no stranger to the art of dramatic promotion and has in the past managed Sandow the famous strong man, as well as French actress Anna Held.

Sandinistas overthrow Somoza

1979 The civil war in Nicaragua is over – the Sandinista rebels have overthrown General Somoza, prompting his resignation and flight into exile. His family has ruled Nicaragua for 47 years. The bloody conflict between the Sandinista rebels and Somoza's army has cost the lives of thousands of Nicaraguans. Somoza's downfall was inevitable after he lost the support of conservatives, the business community and his biggest ally, the US. In fact the US has been instrumental in helping to work out a plan to replace Samoza. The man who will take Nicaragua through the transitional period is the new president Francisco Malianos.

> *Burke was a damned wrong-headed fellow, through his whole life jealous and obstinate.*
> **Charles James Fox**, on British political philosopher Edmund Burke, who died today, 1797.

1902 A German pharmaceutical company has today taken out a patent on a new compound which will alleviate insomnia. The company claims that barbaturic acid, a derivative compound of malic acid found in unripe apples and urea, can be used as a sleeping aid, as an anaesthetic for surgery and to help control epilepsy. Prolonged use may be addictive.

Lawn tennis championships inaugurated at Wimbledon

1877 Harrovian rackets player Spencer W. Gore today won the first ever men's singles tennis title at Wimbledon in matches played on the top quality croquet lawns of the All-England Croquet and Lawn Tennis Club. The club hopes that this championship will become an annual event open to the very best amateur players of lawn tennis. Lawn tennis was invented in its current form only a few years ago. Played on grass or on a composition court, today's game is derived from the 12th-century French game of real (or royal) tennis – the method of scoring, the rackets used and the rules of the two games are very similar.

Lightning causes York Minster fire

1984 York Minster Cathedral was struck by lightning today, causing a fire in the roof which destroyed the south transept of the 700-year-old building, which was fully protected against lightning. The fire was soon detected and the church clergy, working in relays, managed to save most of the treasures held in the building. The rescue operation continued until blazing beams and debris falling from the roof made it dangerous to continue. Some conservative critics within the Church of England have proclaimed the fire an act of retaliation by God over the consecration of Rt. Rev. David Jenkins, the Bishop of Durham, who has recently questioned some of the orthodox beliefs of the church. Archbishop of Canterbury Robert Runcie has retaliated by saying that God must certainly have intervened on behalf of the cathedral since only the south transept was destroyed and the famous Rose Window was left intact.

> *The greater the power, the more dangerous the abuse.*
> **Edmund Burke**, British political philosopher, who died today, 1797.

Crime writer jailed for contempt

1951 American crime writer Dashiell Hammett was jailed today for contempt of court when he refused to testify before the House Un-American Activities Committee. Senator Joe McCarthy's crusade against communism has led to the blacklisting of many in public life and the arts who are on the left of the political spectrum. Hammett, a former Pinkerton detective, has virtually given up the writing on which his reputation depends (his crime classics include *The Maltese Falcon* and *The Thin Man*). His partner, playwright and author Lillian Hellman, is also expected to be called before the Committee to testify.

1440 Flemish painter Jan van Eyck dies in Bruges, leaving the altarpiece of *The Adoration of the Lamb* at Ghent Cathedral and the double portrait *Giovanni Arnolfini and His Wife* as his main claims to fame.

1810 Argentina proclaims its independence from Spain at the Congress of Tucuman.

1850 Death of Zachary Taylor, American statesman and general, 12th president 1849-50.

1922 Eighteen-year-old American swimmer Johnny Weissmuller swims the 100 metres in 58.6 seconds.

1925 In Dublin, 22-year-old Oonagh Keogh becomes the first female member of a stock exchange.

1938 Thirty-five million gas masks go into the shops in Britain in anticipation of World War Two.

1943 British and US forces begin the invasion of Sicily.

1957 Nikita Krushchev, first secretary of the Soviet Communist Party, heads off a coup attempt and banishes ex-prime minister Georgi Malenkov to Kazakhstan.

1989 US president George Bush begins a tour of Europe, starting in Poland.

1990 Nairobi is closed down on the third day of rioting in Kenya.

1990 A 15-mile (24 km) stretch of the Cumbrian coast in north-west England is declared unsafe after items contaminated by the leaks from Sellafield nuclear plant in 1983 are washed up on the beach.

BIRTHDAYS

Elias Howe 1819, American inventor of the sewing machine.

Barbara Cartland 1901, British romantic novelist who has written over 500 books.

Edward Heath 1916, British Conservative politician, prime minister 1970-4.

David Hockney 1937, British artist of great repute probably best known for his paintings of Californian swimming pools.

AD 138 Death of Hadrian, Roman emperor who sponsored the building of a wall across northern Britain to keep the Scots out of England.

1778 King Louis XVI of France declares war on England in support of the American rebels.

1851 Death of Louis-Jacques-Mandé Daguerre, French pioneer of the photographic process.

1890 Wyoming becomes the 44th state of the Union.

1900 The Paris Metro opens.

1941 Jelly Roll Morton, American ragtime piano player and composer, dies in Los Angeles.

1964 The Bahamas gain their independence from Britain.

1984 The Nigerian junta tries to smuggle kidnapped foreign minister Umaru Dikko out of London in a diplomatic bag.

1978 Death of Giorgio de Chirico, Italian painter who was the originator of Metaphysical painting.

1992 Manuel Noriega is sentenced to 40 years in jail on drugs charges.

1995 Burmese Nobel Peace Prize winner Aung San Kyi is released.

2000 A giant landslide in Manila kills 200 people.

BIRTHDAYS

Camille Pissarro 1830, French painter who was a central figure of the Impressionist group, the only one of them to exhibit at all eight Impressionist exhibitions.

James McNeill Whistler 1834, American painter and graphic artist who spent most of his working life in England.

Marcel Proust 1871, French novelist whose masterpiece is the seven-volume *Remembrance of Things Past*.

Carl Orff 1895, German composer, teacher and conductor best-known for the oratorio *Carmina Burana*, based on 12-century German and Latin psalms found in a monastery in Bavaria.

Arlo Guthrie 1947, American singer whose biggest hit was the album *Alice's Restaurant*.

Benjamin Franklin calls for unification

1754 The representative for Pennsylvania, Benjamin Franklin, today presented the Albany Congress with a proposal for union between the British colonies. He and William Hutchinson have drafted a plan which would give this hypothetical union the power to build forts, raise armies, equip fleets, levy taxes, declare war, make peace and negotiate treaties with other nations. The so-called Albany Plan has not been ratified and it is unlikely that it will be for some time, because no consensus can be found. This situation, however, leaves the colonies divided in the face of a unified French presence in North America; some sort of union would allow for coordination of defence.

El Cid dies of grief

1099 The famed Spanish warrior Rodrigo Diaz de Bivar, or El Cid as he was more commonly known, has died today in Valencia, apparently of grief at the defeat of his forces against the Moors. His great achievement has been the capture of the Muslim city of Valencia, after a siege of nine months, which he has ruled absolutely for the past five years. It seems certain that with his death and the defeat of his forces, his wife Ximena will be unable to withstand the onslaught of the Moors and Valencia will be abandoned, once again becoming a Muslim city. Born at Burgos around 1043 of a noble Castilian family, El Cid rose to fame for his successes in the war between Sancho of Castile and Sancho of Navarre. El Cid became a combination of *condottiere* and compatriot at the tender age of 22 and has been fighting constantly since that time, sometimes for the Christians and sometimes for the Moors. He has served many rulers but none more faithfully than Alfonso VI of Castile, in spite of being exiled by the jealous king.

Poison cloud covers Seveso

1976 Leaked chemicals from a factory have created a cloud of poison over the northern Italian town of Meda near Seveso, causing panic among the residents. There is criticism that efforts to inform and evacuate have not already been made. A faulty pressure valve sprayed more than two tons of the toxic weedkiller TCDD, containing the cancer-causing agent dioxin, into the atmosphere. The dioxin has produced burning rashes, headaches, diarrhoea and vomiting in more than 250 people so far. Birds and animals have died and plant life and water supplies have also been contaminated.

1989 Sectarian feelings may be running a bit high in Glasgow tonight after Rangers Football Club announced that it had paid £1.5 million ($2.8 million) for a Catholic player. The signing of Scottish striker Maurice Johnston breaks Rangers 100-year-old tradition of fielding only Protestant players. Johnston, currently with the French club Nantes, had been expected to return to Celtic FC.

It has been discovered experimentally that you can draw laughter from an audience anywhere in the world, of any class or race, simply by walking onto the stage and uttering the words, "I am a married man".

Ted Kavanagh, British radio script writer, *News Review*, 1947.

Rainbow Warrior blown up in New Zealand

1985 The Greenpeace protest ship *Rainbow Warrior* sank today in Auckland harbour after two explosions tore the hull apart below the waterline. A Portuguese photographer Fernando Pereira was killed in the blast, but nine other people on board escaped uninjured. There are suspicions that French secret agents are behind the explosions – *Rainbow Warrior* was preparing to lead a flotilla of seven peace vessels into the French nuclear testing site of Muroroa Atoll in the Pacific to coincide with Bastille Day. The international implications of French Secret Service involvement in the *Rainbow Warrior* sabotage plan would be serious.

Chinese unearth a Terracotta Army

1975 Archaeologists in China today unearthed a vast army of 8000 terracotta figures, sculpted and fired in the shapes of warriors, chariots and horses all drawn up in battle formation. Found near the ancient Chinese capital of Xi'an, they were created more than 2000 years ago for Qin Shi Huangdi, the first emperor to unite China. He created the first totalitarian society and ruled it with efficiency and utter ruthlessness. He unified the Great Wall by building connecting walls in the gaps of existing walls, the construction of which cost the lives of more than 100,000 people. The figures are a mile (1.6 km) from the emperor's tomb and look as if they are guarding it. They range in height from 5 ft 8 inches (173 cm) to 6 ft 5 inches (195 cm), and are highly individual in their appearance. The horses, chariots and weaponry which were found reveal the enormous skill of the artisans who created this spectacular memorial. Their reward was to be walled up inside the emperor's tomb, so that the secret of the army would die with them.

1989 Tonight London's theatres dim their lights in honour of Sir Laurence Olivier who died early this morning at his Sussex home aged 82. Widely hailed as the greatest actor of his era, some of Olivier's Shakespearean roles are still considered the definitive interpretation. He was co-director of the Old Vic and director of the National Theatre company from 1962 to 1973, produced, directed and played in the films *Henry V*, *Hamlet* and *Richard II*. By way of contrast he shone as a broken-down comic in *The Entertainer*. Olivier was married three times, to English actresses Jill Esmond, the ravishing Vivien Leigh and to Joan Plowright with whom he made many films in later years. He was knighted in 1947, was the first actor to become a peer in 1970 and was awarded the Order of Merit in 1981.

BIRTHDAYS

Robert I 1274, Scottish monarch known as Robert the Bruce who seized the Scottish throne in 1306 and forced English recognition of Scottish independence in 1328.

Thomas Bowdler 1754, British doctor and editor whose expurgated *Family Shakespeare* and *History of the Decline and Fall of the Roman Empire* gave the word "bowdlerize" to the English language.

Yul Brynner 1915, American film star who grew up as a Russian refugee in Harbin, north-east China, and later became one of Hollywood's most magnetic stars.

Gough Whitlam 1916, Australian statesman and Labour prime minister 1972-75.

Leon Spinks 1953, American boxer who took the world heavyweight title from Muhammad Ali in February 1978.

William of Orange defeats James II

1690 Deposed Roman Catholic King of England James II met defeat today at the hands of the current king, William III or William of Orange, on the banks of the river Boyne in Ireland. James had recently raised a French/Irish army from his exile in France and landed in Britain intending to retake the crown. James was deposed in June 1688 shortly after the birth of his son when parliament became concerned about the possibility of a Catholic succession to the throne.

> *Acting is a masochistic form of exhibitionism. It is not quite the occupation of an adult.*
> **Laurence Olivier**, the British actor, who died today, 1989.

1960 One of the side benefits to today's Telstar communications satellite launch will be transatlantic television for Britain. The US Telstar, which forms part of the INTELSAT system that spans the globe, uses radio receivers, amplifiers and transmitters along with the electronic technique of multiplexing to relay many telephone and television signals simultaneously. Britain will now be able to receive American game shows.

CAPTAIN COOK SETS SAIL TO FIND THE NORTHWEST PASSAGE

1776 Explorer Captain James Cook set sail today from Plymouth harbour on his third important voyage of discovery, in search of a passage round the northern coast of America from the Pacific side. He is expected to retrace some of his earlier routes through New Zealand and the Pacific Islands. Cook joined the Royal Navy in 1755 and began his first major voyage of exploration in 1768, while in command of *Endeavour*. His success led to a promotion – as commander of *Resolution* and *Adventure* he set off in 1772 to determine how far northwards the lands of Antarctica stretched. Cook has proved an able commander – his last expedition only suffered one death throughout the whole three years. He returned last year having sailed 60,000 miles (96,000 km) in three years. This present expedition is expected to be equally long.

1705 Death of Anglican priest Titus Oates, anti-Catholic conspirator who alleged there was a plot to assassinate Charles II and place his Catholic brother James on the throne, thus causing the execution of 35 suspects and the exclusion of Catholics from parliament.

1789 Fire sweeps Paris after two days of rioting.

1799 Britain passes the Combination Act, which bars any combination of working men trying to improve working conditions in an attempt to prevent the spread of revolutionary ideas from France and the formation of trade unions.

1878 Turkey cedes Cyprus to Britain.

1944 The RAF becomes the first air force to use jet aircraft in operational service.

1952 Dwight D. Eisenhower resigns from the army in order to begin a presidential campaign.

1982 Hostilities between Britain and Argentina over the Falkland Islands are officially ended.

BIRTHDAYS

Julius Caesar 100 BC, Roman general and statesman who became a dictator and was assassinated on account of his monarchical aspirations.

Josiah Wedgwood 1730, English potter, industrialist and writer.

Henry Thoreau 1817, American naturalist and writer.

George Eastman 1854, American inventor of the Kodak camera.

Amedeo Modigliani 1884, Italian painter, sculptor and draughtsman known for his elongated, simplified forms.

Kirsten Flagstad 1895, Norwegian operatic soprano famous for her Wagnerian roles.

Oscar Hammerstein 1895, American lyricist and librettist who, in collaboration with Richard Rodgers, wrote *Oklahoma!*, *Carousel*, *South Pacific*, *The King and I* and *The Sound of Music*.

Bill Cosby 1937, American comedian and vastly popular actor.

Great scholar and humanist dies

1536 Desiderius Erasmus, the great classicist of the Renaissance, has died. He will be missed for his cultivated common sense and his ability to criticize kings and churchmen. His greatest work, *Colloquia*, opened new ground by exposing the abuses of the Church, paving the way for the likes of Martin Luther. Erasmus also published the first Greek text of the New Testament and a new Latin translation with the hope of reconciling faith and reason, so bringing Christianity and the culture of the Ancients closer together. An advocate of charity and moderation in all things, Erasmus was deeply critical of corruption in the church and fell out with Luther over methods of teaching; gentle reason and tolerance were his preferred tools. Erasmus spent much of his later life in Cambridge and in Basel. Though always surrounded by controversy, he became widely known and respected and advanced the revival of learning.

> *I have a Catholic soul, but a Lutheran stomach.*
> **Erasmus**, on why he failed to fast during Lent – he died today, 1536.

First British pilot is killed in crash

1910 British aviation claimed its first victim today when Charles Stewart Rolls, 33, crashed his French-built Wright biplane at a flying competition in Bournemouth. According to one spectator, the rudders of the biplane seemed to break during a tilt, causing the machine to crash nose-first to the ground. Rolls was still in his seat after the crash, but all attempts to revive him failed. An accomplished aviator, Rolls was the first person to fly non-stop both ways across the Channel. He was also a partner in the Rolls Royce car manufacturing company and won the 1000-mile (1600 km) motor-racing trial in 1900.

THE ROLLS-ROYCE IS AS SILENT AS ITS SHADOW

1920 The Panama canal, the world's largest engineering project, was opened officially today by President Woodrow Wilson. Construction began in 1881 but halted with the financial collapse of the French contractor de Lesseps. President Roosevelt took up the project, and construction was resumed in 1904. The first vessel sailed through on January 7, 1914.

Bradman's score breaks all records

1930 Australia's Don Bradman broke all Test cricket records today with a score of 334 runs against England at Leeds, breaking R. E. Foster's record at Sydney 27 years ago. He also set a record for the number of runs scored in a single day of play – 309 of his 334 runs were hit today.

Sunday Times in court over *Spycatcher*

1987 The *Sunday Times* newspaper found itself in the dock today over the controversial book *Spycatcher*, written by former MI5 agent Peter Wright. The government has stopped publication of the book in England and is attempting to prevent publication in Australia. The *Sunday Times* has gone against the government's injunction and has published excerpts of the book. The British government is insisting that the book is a breach of confidentiality. Wright has revealed the innermost workings of MI5 and highlights some of the illegal activities of the agency. It also suggests that Sir Roger Hollis, a former MI5 boss, was a Soviet spy, and that the agency attempted to undermine Harold Wilson's Labour government in 1974-76. The political implications are embarrassing for the present government and it has imposed an injunction on the *Guardian*, the *Observer* and the *Sunday Times*, forbidding even a mention of the book in the press.

Yeltsin resigns from Communist Party

1990 President of the Russian republic Boris Yeltsin resigned from the Communist Party today. He has been increasingly critical of President Gorbachev and of the slow pace of reform. This final severance with the Party concludes a process which has been going on since he was sacked by Gorbachev in 1987 for his impatience with economic reforms. Gorbachev, then as now, continues to walk a tightrope between hardliners and reformers. Yeltsin was a strong Gorbachev supporter for some time but has now emerged clearly in opposition to him, a position which was highlighted after demonstrations in Moscow by his supporters in March 1989. This support helped Yeltsin win a seat in the first election of a multi-candidate system later that month. In May of the same year he was elected to the Supreme Soviet. Continuing economic problems and trouble in the republics dog Gorbachev's administration, although his international stature is high. Gorbachev's ability to take the Soviet Union into a free market economy and his own political survival are, however, questionable.

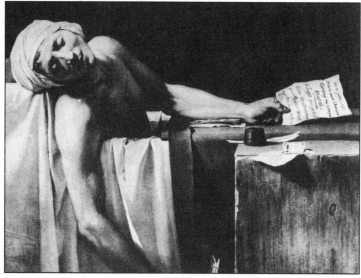

MARAT STABBED TO DEATH IN HIS BATH

1793 Leading figure in the French Revolution, Jean Paul Marat, has been stabbed in his bath by Charlotte Corday, a Girondist supporter. Although popular for his compassion for the poor and his concern for social justice, he may not be too sadly missed as he is largely responsible for denouncing deputies, ministers and kings, calling for innumerable executions. His paper *L'ami du peuple* provoked hatred but made him popular with the "scum" of Paris; it also gave him enormous power. Marat fled for his life on at least two occasions and it is rumoured that his flight into Paris' sewers caused him to contract a disease which was slowly killing him. He was elected a deputy of the Convention but was one of the most unpopular men in the House. Marat became involved in the Jacobin struggle with the Girondists and his death seems to be a further escalation of this violent struggle for supremacy. There are fears that the Jacobins will use his death as an excuse for a reign of terror.

1643 In the English Civil War, the Cavaliers take an early victory over Oliver Cromwell's Roundheads at Roundway Down.

1878 The Congress of Berlin ends with the European powers limiting Russian naval expansion, permitting Austria-Hungary to occupy Bosnia-Herzegovina and gaining Turkish recognition of the independence of Serbia, Romania and Montenegro and of Bulgarian autonomy under Turkish suzerainty.

1923 The British parliament passes a law banning the sale of alcohol to under-18s.

1930 The first World Cup soccer contest is held in Montevideo, Uruguay.

1947 Europe accepts the Marshall Plan, devised by US secretary of state George C. Marshall to aid European economic recovery after World War Two.

1951 Death of Arnold Schoenberg, Austrian-born composer best-known for his atonal works.

1957 Elvis Presley gets his first UK No. 1 with "All Shook Up".

1980 Death of Sir Seretse Khama, president of Botswana, who trained as a barrister in London and married Englishwoman Ruth Williams, as a result of which he had to renounce his chieftaincy of the Bamangwato tribe.

1990 The Italian port of Brindisi witnesses the arrival of 4500 Albanian refugees.

Blackouts hit New York City

1977 New York City is blacked out tonight after electrical storms knocked out power supplies for the city and for large parts of Westchester county. The police and emergency services have been under enormous pressure due to the blackout; there has been widespread looting and vandalism throughout the city which has largely gone unchecked. Security systems dependent on power have been put out of action, while traffic congestion is horrific. The underground system is not functioning and large numbers of office workers are trapped in skyscrapers dependent on elevators to get to the ground.

1955 Mother-of-two Ruth Ellis was hanged today at Holloway Prison for the death of her lover David Blakeley. At her trial the court heard how Ellis shot racing driver Blakeley, 25, outside a Hampstead pub in a fit of jealousy. The couple had lived together off and on for nearly two years.

General Tom Thumb dies

1883 Circus midget General Tom Thumb has died today aged 45. Part of P. T. Barnum's Greatest Show on Earth since the age of four, Charles Sherwood Stratton was 25 inches (62 cm) tall when Barnum found him, and over the course of his life reached a height of 40 inches (102 cm). As well as touring extensively with the circus, Tom Thumb performed at the American museum owned by Barnum. A master at massive public campaigning, Barnum made a fortune out of the likes of Tom Thumb and Swedish opera singer Jenny Lind.

Sir George Gilbert Scott 1811, English architect who was an advocate of the Gothic revival style and built the Albert Memorial and St Pancras Station in London.

Sidney Webb 1859, English economist and socialist who co-founded the Fabian Society and the London School of Economics.

Harrison Ford 1942, American actor whose films include *Star Wars*, *Raiders of the Lost Ark* and *Witness*.

Bastille Day

1823 King Kamehameha II of Hawaii and his queen die of measles during a visit to Britain.

1867 Swedish chemist Alfred Nobel demonstrates dynamite for the first time.

1900 The first governor-general of Australia is appointed.

1902 The campanile of St Mark's Cathedral in Venice collapses during a safety inspection.

1904 Death of Paul Kruger, head of the Boer Republic of the Transvaal during the Boer War.

1930 BBC television transmits its first play – *The Man with a Flower in His Mouth* by Italian dramatist and novelist Luigi Pirandello.

1959 The first nuclear warship, the 14,000-ton USS *Long Beach*, is launched.

1959 Death of the famous Swiss clown Grock.

1965 Democratic politician and co-founder of the UN Adlai Stevenson dies in London of a heart attack.

1967 The British parliament votes to legalize abortion.

1987 Martial law is formally lifted in Taiwan.

BIRTHDAYS

Emmeline Pankhurst 1858, English suffragette who suffered imprisonment and force-feeding in order to gain the vote for British women.

Irving Stone 1903, American novelist whose *Lust for Life* and *The Agony and the Ecstasy* were both made into films.

Woody Guthrie 1912, American folk singer, guitarist and composer.

Ingmar Bergman 1918, Swedish film and theatre director whose influential films include *The Seventh Seal*, *Wild Strawberries*, *Persona* and *Fanny and Alexander*.

Arthur Laurents 1918, American playwright and librettist who wrote *Home of the Brave*, *West Side Story* and *Gypsy*.

MOB STORMS THE BASTILLE

1789 Two days of rioting in Paris have culminated in the storming of the Bastille prison by a mob demanding munitions stored within its walls. Commander Marquis de Launay, who has been holding the prison with his men, refused to surrender the arms to the mob, fearing the volatile atmosphere throughout the city would be further heightened by weapons. The building has been stormed by the crowd, the munitions taken and the seven prisoners within have been released. The Bastille was built in 1370 as part of the defences of the city of Paris, but by the 17th century it had become a symbol of French absolutism, a prison which held political prisoners. The Bastille's hospitality has been savoured by some of France's most famous citizens, including the philosopher Voltaire and the notorious Marquis de Sade. There are fears that this civil unrest may be the beginning of a revolution, one which looks likely to be bloody, violent and long.

King Feisal is murdered

1958 King Feisal, his uncle the crown prince Abdul Illah and the Prime Minister Nuri el-Said were murdered in Iraq during a coup today. El-Said was reportedly kicked to death by a Baghdad mob as the monarch and his uncle were being murdered by a group of Iraqi army officers inspired by Nasser. The uprising of nationalist feeling and the coup have implications for the whole region. President Chamoun in nearby Lebanon has demanded aid from the West. The US is expected to respond by sending marines to Beirut – a move certain to be criticized as interventionist by the Soviet Union and its allies in the region.

> *Rien [nothing].*
> **Louis XVI**, King of France – the day the Bastille fell, diary entry, 1789.

Matterhorn conquered by British team

1865 The formidable Matterhorn has been conquered by an expedition led by British explorer Edward Whymper. Scaling the third highest peak of the Alps has not been without its price, though. During the descent four of the seven climbers in his team were killed. Situated in the Alps on the border between Switzerland and Italy, the Matterhorn is a comparatively low mountain at 14,700 ft (4480 m) high but is extremely difficult to climb due to its towering cliffs. More climbers have been killed here than on any other Alpine peak. Locals say that the mountain is protected by spirits and that climbers risk their lives attempting to scale the mighty peak. Edward Whymper is without doubt the most celebrated Alpine climber in Europe currently, having previously conquered a number of unscaled peaks in the mountain range.

Siberian miners go on strike

1989 More than 300,000 coal miners in seven Siberian cities have gone on strike for better pay and conditions, leaving the major Soviet coalfields idle. The strike is the most serious outbreak of industrial unrest since Gorbachev came to power four years ago. It looks likely that the strike will spread to other industries and other republics, causing great disruption and loss of revenue. The miners' union is a particularly strong and influential one in Soviet politics – the importance of coal to the struggling economy cannot be underestimated. Not surprisingly, the miners are also demanding greater political and economic independence for the mines along with a 40 per cent pay rise for night shifts and, more prosaically, soap to wash with and milk for their children.

> *It is far easier to make war than to make peace.*
> **Georges Clemenceau**, French statesman, 1919.

French sex-symbol marries

1966 French film star and sex-symbol Brigitte Bardot has married millionaire playboy Gunther Sachs in America. Her sex-kitten image has done much to popularize French films internationally and 34-year-old Bardot has received enormous media attention while in the US promoting her recent film *Viva Maria!*, with journalists comparing her to Marilyn Monroe. This is the third trip to the altar for "BB", as she is called in France, who has previously been married to film director Roger Vadim and to Jacques Charrier.

BRITAIN WINS RUGBY INTERNATIONAL IN AUSTRALIA

1989 The British Lions beat Australia by the narrowest margin – one point – in the third and final rugby international at Sydney today, winning the series by two matches to one. They lost the opening match to Australia but came back to win the series – the first time this century the Lions have won after losing an opening match. The victory, however, is not entirely down to great British skill: it was helped by an error on the part of Australia's David Campese. Instead of kicking into touch, he ran the ball out of defence and blew a pass, allowing Lions' player Ieuan Evans to intercept and score.

1685 James Scott, Duke of Monmouth and illegitimate son of Charles II, is beheaded in London for raising a rebellion against King James II.

1795 The Marseillaise, written by Claude Rouget de Lisle as "Le Chant du l'armée du Rhin" is officially adopted as the French national anthem.

1857 As the Indian Mutiny continues, 200 British men, women and children are chopped up and thrown down a well at Cawnpore.

1904 Death of Anton Chekhov, Russian dramatist and short-story writer whose major plays are *The Cherry Orchard*, *Uncle Vanya* and *The Three Sisters*.

1916 Edward Boeing sets up the Pacific Aero Products Company in Seattle.

1930 The British government orders 1000 Spitfire fighter planes.

1976 Death of American novelist Paul Gallico.

1989 Eleven people are killed and 127 injured in clashes between Georgians and Abkhazians in the Abkhazia enclave of Soviet Georgia.

1990 In Colombo, capital of Sri Lanka, Tamil Tigers massacre 168 Muslims.

We intend to remain alive. Our neighbours want to see us dead. This is not a question that leaves much room for compromise.
Golda Meir, Israeli stateswoman, 1971.

Crusaders take Jerusalem

1099 Jerusalem, long under Muslim rule, has been seized by Christian Crusaders led by Godfrey of Bouillon. The capture of this ancient city and the massacre of its Jewish and Muslim citizens is the culmination of the first armed pilgrimage organized by Pope Urban II to recapture places sacred to Christians. The army of French and Norman knights assembled in Constantinople, and proceeded to march through Anatolia, capturing Antioch on June 3 last year before moving on to Jerusalem. The massacre of the Muslim and Jewish inhabitants will further harden Muslim feeling against the Christians. Jerusalem is an important city to all three religious groups: for Jews, it is the focus of religious reverence and nationhood; for Christians, it is significant as the scene of Christ's final agony and triumph; and for Muslims, Jerusalem was the goal of their prophet's mystic night journey and is the site of the third most sacred shrine in Islam. The city has been under Muslim rule since the 7th century, with access to religious sites freely open to other groups until the recent takeover of Jerusalem by Seljuk Turks. The Seljuks have forbidden pilgrimages – hence Pope Urban's armed crusade.

Boeing 707 makes maiden flight

1954 Boeing today launched themselves into the world of jet air transportation with the maiden flight of their new Boeing 707. The new aircraft with its four engines hung on pods beneath the wings makes use of Boeing expertise in the world of jet bomber design. The British-built de Havilland Comet has shown the aviation world the advantages of jet travel. The Boeing 707, with a wing span of 130 ft (39 m) and length of 128 ft (39 m), has the capacity for 219 passengers at over 600 mph (960 kph). Boeing have also developed the Boeing 707 in tanker form to be used by the military for mid-air refueling. The US Air Force is now interested in the aircraft after early reluctance.

New record for round-the-world flight

1938 A new world record for round-the-world flight has been set by millionaire Howard Hughes and his crew of four. Flying a twin-engined Lockheed, Hughes and his men completed the journey around the world in just three days, 19 hours and 17 minutes after take off from Brooklyn airport. This cuts by half the previous record set by Wiley Post five years ago, with a time of 7 days, 18 hours. Hughes' 14,824-mile (23,718 km) flight via Paris, Moscow, Omsk, Yakutsk, Fairbanks and Minneapolis was made at an average speed of 208 mph (333 kph). He and his crew have been greeted in New York with a ticker tape parade.

Inigo Jones 1573, English architect whose best known buildings are the Queen's House in Greenwich and the Banqueting Hall at Whitehall.

Rembrandt van Rijn 1606, Dutch painter, etcher and draughtsman whose most famous picture is *The Night Watch*.

Iris Murdoch 1919, British novelist whose books include *A Severed Head*, *The Sea, the Sea* and *The Good Apprentice*.

Julian Bream 1933, British guitarist and lutenist.

Harrison Birtwistle 1934, British composer whose works include the opera *Punch and Judy* and the chamber ensemble *Medusa*.

1557 Death of Anne of Cleves, fourth wife of Henry VIII of England.

1791 Louis XVI of France is suspended from office until he agrees to ratify the French constitution.

1827 Death of English potter Josiah Spode I.

1945 The first atomic bomb is exploded on the White Sands Missile Range in New Mexico, USA.

1951 King Leopold III of Belgium abdicates.

1953 A new world air-speed record is set at 716 mph (1152 kph) by an F86 Sabre fighter.

1953 Death of Hilaire Belloc, British poet and essayist.

1967 The Biafran War begins as Nigerian troops march into the oil-rich secessionist region of Biafra.

1990 British explorer Ranulph Fiennes begins an expedition in Oman to find the lost city of Ubar, which has been buried for 2000 years.

1990 At least 100 people die in an earthquake in the Philippines.

BIRTHDAYS

Andrea del Sarto 1486, Florentine painter who excelled as a fresco decorator.

Sir Joshua Reynolds 1723, English painter who was the leading portraitist of his day and was the first president of the Royal Academy.

Mary Baker Eddy 1821, American founder of the Christian Science movement.

Roald Amundsen 1872, Norwegian explorer who was the first to reach the South Pole.

Barbara Stanwyck 1907, American actress whose long list of films includes *The Bitter Tea of General Yen*, *Stella Dallas*, *Double Indemnity* and *Executive Suite*.

Ginger Rogers 1911, American actress and dancer who partnered Fred Astaire in ten musicals.

Margaret Court 1942, Australian tennis player who won the Grand Slam in 1970.

Parisian patents idea for reinforcing concrete

1867 Joseph Monier, a Parisian commercial gardener, has received a patent for his idea of reinforcing concrete by embedding metal wires or rods in it. Monier, 44, has little technical training. Common sense told him, however, that his cement and concrete tubs and pots would be greatly strengthened by some form of iron-wire reinforcement. The concrete and the reinforcement act in tandem, with the former taking most of the compressive forces and the latter the tensile forces. Monier plans to show his invention at the Paris Exposition later in the year. Reinforced concrete, he believes, may prove useful in the engineering industry.

It is true that liberty is precious – so precious that it must be rationed.
V. I. Lenin flees to Finland after an unsuccessful revolt, 1917.

1970 The honeymoon period that new British governments traditionally enjoy has proved short-lived for Edward Heath's Conservative administration. Less than one month after being elected PM, Heath has declared a state of emergency in response to the national dock strike called by the dockers' union. Troops are on standby, ready to act should their labour be required to keep Britain's ports open. Industrialists have issued dire warnings about the consequences to Britain's overseas trade should the strike drag on.

RUSSIAN ROYALS SLAUGHTERED

1918 The Tsar of Russia, Nicholas II, and his family were murdered today in the cellar of the house in Ekaterinberg where they had been confined since May. Their bodies were then burned and thrown into a disused mine shaft. The local Bolshevik commander is thought to have ordered the killings when it became apparent that his men could not hold Ekaterinberg against the approaching White Russian forces and prevent the family's rescue. The Petrograd Soviet and the Revolutionary Workers' and Soldiers' Council insisted, against the wishes of the provisional government of Prince Lvov, that the family be sent to an area where Bolshevik sentiment is blood red rather than be allowed to leave the country.

Mont Blanc road tunnel opens

1965 The famous French engineer Lepiney suggested back in 1870 that it would be a good idea to link France and Italy by building a road tunnel through the Alps. His vision has at last been realized with the official opening today of a road tunnel running between Barats, four miles (6.5 km) from Chamonix, and the village of Entreves. It has taken a long 6½ years to complete the tunnel, which is 7¼ miles (11.6 km) long. The estimated average traffic flow will be about 600 vehicles per hour in both directions.

Cure for killer disease found

1885 French chemist and microbiologist Louis Pasteur, 63, has confounded his critics by proving beyond doubt that his ideas on the best way to tackle the killer disease rabies are correct. Nine-year-old rabies victim Joseph Meister is now making a rapid recovery thanks to receiving a weakened strain of the virus administered by Pasteur ten days ago. This latest success for Pasteur was only made possible by his previous research into disease-inducing micro-organisms such as anthrax and cholera. Sheep and chicken farmers – and indeed the animals themselves – have reason to be grateful to Pasteur for producing an effective vaccine against the diseases. The vaccine for rabies is obtained from the dried tissues of animals infected with the virus.

Invisible hand beckons Smith

1790 Adam Smith, author of the influential treatise on political economy, *The Wealth of Nations*, has died in Edinburgh after a painful illness. He was 67. Economics work best, Smith believed, by leaving them alone. The natural forces of competition and self-interest provide all the regulation necessary to ensure a healthy system that benefits all. The division of labour demanded by mechanization was regarded by Smith as the most efficient method of producing goods. Trade barriers, he thought, should be applied only in exceptional circumstances. Smith devoted a large part of the income he received as Commissioner of Customs and Salt Duties for Scotland to various secret acts of charity.

1954 The grounds of the Newport Casino on Rhode Island are the venue for a new jazz festival which was launched today. The festival has been organized by Louis and Elaine Lorillard as a non profit-making venture. George Wein, pianist and owner of Boston's Storyville Club, is the festival director.

US holds pirates at bay

1801 The United States is learning grimly that its former colonial status had at least one benefit – its shipping enjoyed immunity from attack by North African pirates. After making a series of humiliating financial concessions to the increasingly confident and voracious rulers of Algeria, Tunis and Tripoli, who control the pirates, two months ago the US dug in its heels and said "no" when the Pasha of Tripoli demanded that he be paid $225,000 (£122,000) now plus $25,000 (£13,500) annually. A US squadron under Commodore Richard Dale was dispatched to the Mediterranean and is currently blockading Tripoli. This show of force seems to have persuaded Algiers and Tunis that it would not be a good idea for them to join a war alliance with Tripoli. Morocco, however, is still willing to throw in its lot with the beleaguered pasha. Although Congress is taking pride in this display of US military muscle, some believe action is necessary.

"Lady Day" finds peace

1959 Billie Holiday, considered by many aficionados to be one of the greatest jazz singers of all time, died at Metropolitan Hospital, New York, today. She was 44. Born in Baltimore of unmarried teenage parents, "Lady Day", as she would become known, started her singing career in Harlem clubs aged 15 after several years as a prostitute. By the mid-30s she was an established artist, performing with the cream of musicians from the big bands. She formed a unique partnership with tenor saxophonist Lester Young, whom she nicknamed "the President". By the 1950s her health and vocal performance were beginning to show signs of the alcohol and narcotics to which she had become accustomed. She was admitted to hospital shortly after performing at the Phoenix Theatre in Manhattan. Holiday died as she had lived – the victim of a catalogue of personal disasters including rape, racism, imprisonment and unhappy love affairs. While she lay on her death bed, New York police served a warrant for her arrest – because narcotic addiction is an offence under US law.

> *If you have to ask what jazz is, you'll never know.*
> **Louis Armstrong**, jazz trumpeter – the first Newport Jazz Festival took place today, 1954.

PUBLISHED FOR THE PROPRIETORS, BY R. BRYANT, AT PUNCH'S OFFICE, WELLINGTON STREET, STRAND.

New weekly paper for London

1841 The first issue of a weekly newspaper called *Punch* was published in London today. The idea for the paper came from engraver Ebenezer Landells, who suggested to journalist Henry Mayhew that a publication along the lines of Philippon's audacious *Paris Charivari* would go down well in London. Mayhew and his fellow joint-editors Mark Lemon and Joseph Stirling Coyne hope to provide an entertaining mix of satiric humour, cartoons and caricatures.

1212 In Spain, the Christians win a military victory over the Muslims, defeating Caliph Mahommed al-Nasr near Toledo.

1453 The defeat of the English at Castillon ends the Hundred Years' War with France, leaving only Calais in British hands.

1790 Thomas Saint of London patents the first sewing machine.

1793 Charlotte Corday, a member of the Girondist right-wing republican party, is guillotined four days after she murdered French revolutionary leader Jean-Paul Marat by stabbing him through the heart with a breadknife as he sat in his bath.

1794 The Commune of Paris, set up in May 1791, is suppressed.

1815 Napoleon surrenders to the British at Rochefort.

1951 The Abbey Theatre in Dublin, founded in 1907 by poets Lady Augusta Gregory and W. B. Yeats, burns down.

1968 The Beatles' cartoon film *Yellow Submarine* is premiered at the London Pavilion.

1969 *Oh! Calcutta*, the show devised by influential critic Kenneth Tynan and condemned by many in Britain as obscene on account of its profanity and nudity, opens in New York.

1981 More than 100 people die when suspended walkways in the lobby of the new Hyatt Regency Hotel in Kansas collapse.

BIRTHDAYS

Maksim Litvinov 1876, Soviet statesman and diplomat who obtained US recognition of his country in 1934.

Erle Stanley Gardner 1889, American lawyer and prolific novelist who created the detective Perry Mason.

James Cagney 1899, American actor who began his career as a song-and-dance man but went on to specialize in tough guy roles in films such as *Mayor of Hell* and *Lady Killer*.

Wayne Sleep 1948, British ballet dancer and actor.

1721 French rococo painter Jean-Antoine Watteau, best-known for his *fêtes galantes*, dies of tuberculosis aged only 36.

1817 Death of English author Jane Austen, whose major novels include *Emma*, *Pride and Prejudice* and *Sense and Sensibility*.

1877 Thomas Edison records the human voice for the first time.

1913 Turkish forces recapture Adrianople from the Bulgarians who seized it four months ago.

1925 Adolf Hitler publishes *Mein Kampf* (My Struggle), which he wrote during a period of imprisonment for the Munich Putsch, the Nazi Party's abortive coup against the Bavarian government.

1936 Under the command of General Franco, the Spanish army rises up against the Republican government.

1990 Talks begin in Washington between the US and Vietnam over the future of Cambodia.

1996 TWA flight 800 explodes over Long Island, New York, killing all 228 passengers on board.

2003 Iraqi weapons expert, Dr David Kelly, is found dead.

BIRTHDAYS

Reverend Gilbert White 1720, English naturalist who wrote *The Natural History and Antiquities of Selbourne*.

William Makepeace Thackeray 1811, English novelist and poet best known for *Vanity Fair*.

Dr William Gilbert Grace 1848, English cricketer who scored 54,896 runs and took 2876 wickets in his illustrious career.

Vidkun Quisling 1887, Norwegian politician and Nazi collaborationist who led the occupation government in World War Two.

Nelson Mandela 1918, South African politician and oustanding black leader.

John Glenn 1921, American astronaut.

Richard Branson 1950, British entrepreneur, managing director of the Virgin Group.

Aggro artist dies

1610 The Italian artist Michelangelo Merisi da Caravaggio has died in exile in Porto Ercole at the age of 39. Caravaggio won fame and notoriety in Rome for his rejection of Renaissance ideals and insistence on painting directly onto the canvas. His use of low-life models, even in large religious works, caused much offence. Caravaggio fled Rome four years ago after killing a companion over a game of racquets. After a brief stay in Naples he moved on to Malta, but soon fell foul of the Order of St John by assaulting the highest grade of knight. Agents of the Order were sent after the fleeing Caravaggio and remained hard on his heels until the end. The violent temper of the peripatetic artist got him into trouble in Naples where he was wounded in a tavern brawl, forcing him to move on again. Alighting in Porto Ercole, a Spanish enclave on the Tuscan coast, he found himself the victim of wrongful arrest. On release, he made frantic efforts to catch up with a ship which he thought had all his belongings on board; these were, in fact, in Porto Ercole. This exertion brought on a fever to which he succumbed.

Arap Moi torches tusks

1989 Kenya's president Daniel arap Moi demonstrated his personal commitment to saving the elephant by putting the torch to 12 tons of stockpiled ivory worth approximately $3 million (£1.6 million). The elephant population of Kenya and Tanzania has been decimated by ivory poachers. The leaders of both countries are calling for an immediate permanent ban on the trade in ivory in hope of remedying the problem.

1955 A new entertainment experience opened near Anaheim, California, today. The creation of film producer Walt Disney, Disneyland aims to involve adults and children in a non-stop fantasy world. The 160-acre amusement park is divided into four sections: Fantasyland, Frontierland, Adventureland and Tomorrowland. Visitors may wander through a jungle filled with crocodiles and orchids, a picturesque small town street of the 1890s or take a ride on a Mississippi steam boat or blast off on a rocket voyage to the Moon.

750,000 war dead Commemorated

1920 A new national monument dedicated to the "Glorious Dead" of the Great War was unveiled in Whitehall today. Designed in Portland stone by the distinguished architect Sir Edwin Lutyens, it replaces the temporary plaster monument erected for the Allied Victory Parade last year. The only adornments on the new Cenotaph – from the Greek words *kenos* and *taphos*, meaning empty tomb – are the flags of the three armed services and the Merchant Navy. The new monument will be the focal point at the Armistice Day commemoration in November. Londoners are already treating it with suitable reverence, by doffing their hats on passing.

1984 In California today unsuspecting customers dining on burgers and chips in their local McDonalds hamburger restaurant were subjected to terror when a security guard began firing at random. Twenty people were massacred and 16 have been injured.

Tsar assassinated after abdicating

1762 The former Tsar of Russia, Peter III, has been assassinated at the village of Ropsha eight days after abdicating. He was being held in custody by Grigori Orlov, one of the ringleaders of the recent coup to oust the unpopular Tsar in favour of his wife, Catherine. Formerly Karl Ulrich, Duke of Holstein-Gottorp, Peter was an inept and insensitive ruler. He made no secret of his loathing for Russia, and for the Prussian ruler Frederick the Great. One of Peter's first moves on ascending the throne was to withdraw from the Seven Years' War, breaking the alliance with Austria and France, and form a pact with Prussia, their former enemy. There were also indications that he was about to divorce Catherine, his wife of 17 years. She struck first, however, by rallying the army to her side and, with the support of the senate and Church, having herself proclaimed empress. Although also German-born (Sophie Fredericke Auguste von Anhalt-Zerbst), the 33-year-old Catherine is perceived as being wholeheartedly dedicated to Russia.

Cloud over Kennedy's future

1969 In recent months Senator Edward Kennedy has given the appearance of a man destined to become the Democratic Party's presidential candidate in 1972. Today he looks like a man fighting for his political life. Last night the 37-year-old senator was involved in an automobile accident in which his passenger, 28-year-old Washington secretary Mary Jo Kopechne, died. The car is alleged to have swerved off a narrow bridge on Chappaquiddick Island, Massachusetts, and plunged into a pond. Serious questions are being raised about the senator's conduct, not least his decision to leave the scene of the accident and not contact the police until several hours later.

Nazi style rules

1937 Those wishing to discover what constitutes art in Hitler's Third Reich should make their way to the Bavarian capital, Munich, where two strikingly different exhibitions have been mounted for this purpose. What the Führer describes as "true German art" is of lofty subjects such as patriotism and family life and rendered in a stiff, academic style. "Degenerate, Bolshevik and Jewish art", on the other hand, is all modern art. Artists whose works are classifed as "degenerate" include Beckmann, Chagall, Dix, Grosz, Kandinsky, Klee, Kokoschka and Modersohn-Becker. In 1933 Goebbels ordered that "all artistic productions with cosmopolitan or bolshevist tendencies" should be removed from German museums and galleries. The examples of "degenerate" art currently on show have been taken from a stockpile of about 20,000 modern works seized at that time. According to one SS officer, the steel helmet is the most perfect object ever created.

> *The great masses of the people . . . will more easily fall victims to a great lie than to a small one.*
> **Adolf Hitler** in *Mein Kampf*, written from prison following an unsuccessful rising in 1923.

IRA ceasefire announced

1997 The IRA has announced a new ceasefire, its second in three years. It comes after republican political party Sinn Fein urged the IRA to call a truce, but the speed of the response has surprised many commentators. Northern Ireland Secretary Mo Mowlam will be monitoring IRA activity over the next few weeks to decide whether Sinn Fein will be admitted to the all-party peace talks scheduled for September. Sinn Fein President Gerry Adams said he supported the new ceasefire because of the "commitment by the two governments to inclusive peace talks".

Two-way reluctance in Poland

1989 General Wojciech Jaruzelski, the man who imposed martial law eight years ago, was voted in as Poland's first president today. The general won the required 50 per cent majority of valid votes cast by a mere one vote: 270 parliamentary deputies voted for him, 233 against and 34 abstained. Four Solidarity representatives declined to participate in the election, declaring it unlawful because Jaruzelski was the only candidate. The problems facing the new president are daunting: a bankrupt economy, no effective government and a resentful and cynical population. Jaruzelski was reluctant to offer himself for election, but to have turned his back would, in his words, "contradict the duties of a politician and soldier and also the logic of my public service in recent years".

Prince Albert launches world's largest ship, the *Great Britain*

1843 The Prince Consort of the United Kingdom, Albert, was at Wapping Dock today to launch the world's largest ship, the 3270-ton, 322-ft (98 m) long Atlantic liner *Great Britain*. The all-metal vessel was originally designed by Isambard Kingdom Brunel (right) as a paddle steamer. She has since been fitted with screw machinery, supplemented by sails on six masts.

1545 King Henry VIII's battleship the *Mary Rose* sinks in the Solent, off the south coast of England, with the loss of 700 lives.

1799 A stone slab inscribed with hieroglyphics is found at Rosetta, near Alexandria, Egypt.

1821 George IV is crowned King of England, but his estranged wife Caroline of Brunswick is barred from the ceremony.

1837 Isambard Kingdom Brunel's steamship *Great Western* is launched at Bristol.

1848 The first women's rights assembly begins at Seneca Falls, New York state.

1849 Sayid Ali Mohammed, founder of the Bathai religious sect, is executed in Persia by order of the Shah.

1870 Napoleon III declares war on Prussia.

1970 The first all-metal liner, Brunel's *Great Britain*, is brought back to Britain from the Falklands.

2001 Novelist and former Conservative deputy Chairman Lord Archer is sentenced to four years in prison for perjury and perverting the course of justice.

BIRTHDAYS

Samuel Colt 1814, American inventor responsible for the six-shot revolver and the first remote-control naval mine.

Edgar Degas 1834, French Impressionist painter and sculptor best known for his racecourse and ballet paintings.

Lizzie Borden 1860, American Sunday-school teacher who was falsely accused of murdering her father and stepmother with an axe.

Charles Horace Mayo 1865, American physician, member of a family of physicians who pioneered the idea of group practice and set up the Mayo Clinic in Rochester, Minnesota.

George Hamilton IV 1937, American country and western singer.

Ile Nastase 1946, Romanian tennis player noted for his erratic behaviour on court.

1588 The Spanish armada sets sail for England from Corunna, a day later than planned because of a storm.

1605 French cartographer Samuel de Champlain reaches Cape Cod in search of an ideal spot for French settlement in the New World.

1629 English adventurer Sir David Kirke seizes Quebec from the French.

1808 Joseph Bonaparte, brother of Napoleon, enters Madrid as Spanish patriots conquer the French army at Bailen.

1937 Italian physicist Guglielmo Marconi, inventor of radio telegraphy, dies aged 63.

1951 King Abdullah of Jordan is shot dead outside a mosque.

1954 The Geneva Agreement brings about a cessation of hostilities between North and South Vietnam.

1976 The American spacecraft *Viking* lands on Mars and starts sending back television pictures.

1979 The Sandinista National Liberation Front takes power in Nicaragua after ousting General Anastasio Somoza, whose family had ruled the country since 1933.

1982 An IRA bomb explodes outside the Horse Guards barracks in London's Knightsbridge, killing two guardsmen and seven horses.

1999 Death of King Hassan II of Morocco, prompting wide-spread mourning in the Arab world.

BIRTHDAYS

Sir John Reith 1889, Scottish engineer who became Director General of the BBC and laid down many of the tenets that still govern its standards.

Sir Edmund Hillary 1919, New Zealand mountaineer and explorer who, along with Sherpa Tenzing, was the first to reach the summit of Mount Everest.

Diana Rigg 1939, British actress who partnered Patrick MacNee in the Avengers television series but is better known for her classical roles on stage.

Jane Asher breaks off engagement

1968 Jane Asher stunned listeners to the BBC radio programme *Dee Time*, hosted by Simon Dee, today with the news that her engagement to Beatle Paul McCartney is off. The red-headed actress declined to give a reason for her decision. The couple announced their engagement last December. In February Asher joined the Beatles' controversial pilgrimage to the Rishikesh retreat centre of the Maharishi Mahesh Yogi in India. The only surprise about the break-up is that Asher should have chosen to announce it in this way – without telling McCartney first. According to insiders, the five-year-old relationship had been cooling rapidly in recent weeks.

1837 Euston Grove, an area of London once described as "a quiet scene of nursery gardens", is now home to a new terminus of the London and Birmingham Railway. The station, which replaces the old terminus at Chalk Farm, comprises two 420-ft (136 m) long platforms and a 200-ft (65 m) long double train shed designed by Charles Fox.

Bruce Lee found dead

1973 Kung fu film star Bruce Lee was found dead in the bathroom of actress Betty Ting Pei in Hong Kong yesterday. He was 32. Reputedly the fittest man on earth, San Francisco-born Lee (real name Lee Yuen Kam) is thought to have died of a swollen brain, possibly caused by an allergic reaction to aspirin. Lee's martial arts films – *Fists of Fury*, *Enter the Dragon*, *Way of the Dragon* and *Game of Death* – won him a large following. Many fans are refusing to believe that Bruce Lee is really dead, suggesting that cult status is not far off for the former king of kung fu.

NBC broadcasts war symphony

1942 A new composition by a living composer is a major musical event. Tonight's live broadcast by the NBC Symphony Orchestra of the Seventh Symphony by Dmitri Shostakovich was special on several counts. The work is, in the composer's own words, "an interpretation of war", dedicated to the city of Leningrad. The first three movements were written in that besieged city between July and December last year. Shostakovich finished the symphony in Kuibyshev after the Soviet authorities, fearful for his safety, insisted that he should move from Leningrad. The world premiere of the Seventh was given by the Bolshoi Theatre Orchestra in Kuibyshev last March. After the premiere a microfilm of the manuscript was smuggled through the German lines across Persia, Egypt and the Atlantic. As a musical representation of our times the 70-minute symphony is unique and will surely receive many performances.

Bomb plot fails

1944 Adolf Hitler narrowly escaped death today when a bomb exploded at his headquarters in Rastenburg. The bomb was left in a briefcase under the table of the conference room in which the Führer was meeting with his top military brass. The German leader was shielded from the full blast of the bomb partly by the heavy oak table top over which he was leaning and partly by the thick table leg against which the brief case had been leant. The bomb had been planted by a German officer with liberal sympathies, Colonel Klaus Schenk, Count von Stauffenberg. An attempt to capture Berlin has been foiled and several of the ringleaders have been rounded up and shot. A manhunt is now underway for the rest of the conspirators, who are thought to include several high-ranking officers. Hitler has taken his miraculous deliverance from what is estimated to be the seventh attempt on his life as a sign of God's favour.

Idleness is only the refuge of weak minds.
The Earl of Chesterfield, statesman, diplomat, writer and patron of many authors in a letter to his son, 1749.

THE EAGLE LANDS

1969 US astronauts Neil Armstrong and Edwin Aldrin completed the most breathtaking and perhaps the most hazardous part of the historic Apollo 11 space mission today. Michael Collins remained in the command-service part of the spacecraft, known as Columbia, while his two colleagues manoeuvred the lunar module, called Eagle, onto the surface of the Moon. Six-and-a-half hours after landing, Armstrong began what the hundreds of millions of television viewers round the world had been waiting for: the first Moon walk in human history. He stepped out onto the fine and powdery surface with the words, "That's one small step for a man, one giant step for mankind." During a two-hour moon walkabout the astronauts set up various scientific devices, and took rock samples and many photographs.

> *The United States has to move very fast to even stand still.*
> **John F. Kennedy**, quoted in the *Observer*, 1963.

> *Think of it, soldiers; from the summit of these pyramids, 40 centuries look down upon you.*
> **Napoleon I**, 1798.

MR BIG DIES

1809 Daniel Lambert, famed for his corpulence, died suddenly today at the Waggon and Horses inn, Stamford. He was 39. Lambert's weight did not begin to increase considerably until the early 1790s when he succeeded his father as keeper of Leicester prison. In 1793 he weighed 32 stone, despite an active and teetotal lifestyle. After resigning from the prison on an annuity of £50 ($92) a year, he began to turn his "mortal hugeness" to financial gain. He went to London and in April 1806 "received company" between the hours of 12 am and 5 pm at 53 Piccadilly. The following year he began touring the English shires. At the time of his death Lambert weighed 52 ¾ stone.

Khomeini ends war – reluctantly

1988 The eight-year Iran-Iraq war has been ended by Iran's spiritual leader, Ayatollah Ruhollah Khomeini. A statement read on Iran radio yesterday declared that Khomeini was prepared to accept UN Security Council Resolution 598, which called for a ceasefire. Khomeini had sworn to fight on until Iran had won total victory over Iraq and its leader Saddam Hussein, including his overthrow. In a statement Khomeini said the decision was "more deadly than taking poison". The cost of the war has been high for both sides: an estimated 1 million killed, 1.7 million wounded, 1.5 million made homeless and major cities reduced to rubble. A staggering $400 billion of the two nations' resources has also been expended in the struggle.

1985 A 20-year search for gold, silver and jewels in the wreck of a Spanish galleon has ended in triumph for chicken farmer-turned-treasure hunter Mel Fisher. His divers have found about half the original $400 million-worth (£217 million) of booty, in the wreck of *Nuestra Senhora de Atocha*, 40 miles (64 km) west of Key West, Florida. The galleon was one of nine Spanish ships sunk by a hurricane in 1622.

Robert Burns dies in hardship

1796 Scotland's unofficial Poet Laureate, Robert Burns, has died in Dumfries at the age of 37. His premature death from rheumatic heart disease is being attributed to the privations and hardship of his years as a struggling tenant farmer. Burns' success as a poet began on publication of his first volume, entitled *Poems, Chiefly in the Scottish Dialect*. Country people and Edinburgh sophisticates found much to admire in the book's blend of social satire, verse letters, nature poems and high-minded idealization of family life. Burns' low social status, however, prevented him from truly finding his niche, despite his undoubted intellectual abilities. He spent the last seven years of his life collecting and providing words for traditional Scottish tunes as well as working for the excise service.

JULY 21

1403 Sir Henry Percy, known as Harry Hotspur, is killed in battle near Shrewsbury while trying to overthrow King Henry IV.

1798 Napoleon defeats the Mamelukes at the Battle of the Pyramids.

1897 The Tate Gallery opens in London.

1904 The Trans-Siberian railway is completed after 13 years' work.

1906 Eleven years after his conviction on grounds of treason Captain Alfred Dreuyfus is pardoned and made a member of the Legion d'Honneur.

1954 Britain, the US and the World Bank turn down President Nasser's plea for aid to build the Aswan Dam on the river Nile.

1960 Sir Francis Chichester arrives in New York on his solo round-world journey, having crossed the Atlantic in a record-breaking 40 days.

1960 Mrs Sirimavo Bandaranaike, widow of the murdered prime minister of Sri Lanka Solomon Bandaranaike, replaces him and becomes the first woman prime minister in the world.

1990 At a huge open-air rock concert in Berlin, Roger Waters of the group Pink Floyd performs "The Wall" while a symbolic Berlin Wall is built and knocked down.

1994 Tony Blair is elected leader of the Labour party in Britain.

BIRTHDAYS

Baron Paul Julius von Reuter 1816, German-born founder of the Reuter's telegraph office, London, which supplied newspapers with international news.

Ernest Hemingway 1899, American novelist and short-story writer whose macho image was reflected in his books.

Karel Reisz 1926, Czech-born film director best-known for *Saturday Night and Sunday Morning* and *Morgan: A Suitable Case for Treatment*.

Jonathan Miller 1934, British doctor, opera and theatre director and documentary maker.

1789 A mob murder the Bailiff of Paris.

1790 The French clergy are removed from the control of Rome and property is nationalized.

1932 Death of American impresario Florence Ziegfeid, founder of the Ziegfeid Follies.

1950 Death of William Lyon Mackenzie King, Canadian statesman and Liberal prime minister three times, his chief political aim being national unity.

1957 BP and Shell decide to quit Israel under pressure from Arab oil producers.

1969 Spanish dictator General Franco names Juan Carlos, grandson of King Alfonso XIII, as his heir apparent.

1969 Apollo II leaves the Moon.

1976 Death of Sir Mortimer Wheeler, British archaeologist known for his skill in interpreting archaeological strata.

2003 Saddam Hussein's two sons Qusai and Udai are killed as American soldiers, backed by helicopters, storm a house in the northern city of Mosul following a tip-off from an Iraqi source.

BIRTHDAYS

Philip I 1478, Spanish monarch known as Philip the Handsome, son of Emperor Maximilian I and Mary of Burgundy and husband of Joan the Mad: she inherited the throne of Castile in 1504 but her insanity was such that Philip assumed sole control in 1506.

Gregor Mendel 1822, Austrian monk and botanist who discovered the fundamental principles governing the inheritance of characters in living things and summarized them in the Law of Independent Segregation and the Law of Independent Assortment.

Selman Abraham Waksman 1888, Russian-born microbiologist whose search for antibacterial substances in soil micro-organisms led to the discovery of actinomycin and streptomycin.

Terence Stamp 1940, British actor who won an Oscar for his first film, *Billy Budd*.

The last round-up

1934 The short but spectacular criminal career of bank robber John Dillinger came to a bloody end today. As Dillinger emerged from the Biograph Theater in Chicago he walked straight into an ambush sprung by a combined force of FBI agents and Indiana police. Since escaping from Indiana's Crown Point jail in March, Dillinger had led a charmed life, twice escaping FBI traps as well as shoot-outs with police in Wisconsin and Minnesota. A tip-off by a mysterious lady in red ensured that the law enforcement agencies got their man this time. Dillinger, 31, began his successful run as a bank robber last year, after finishing a nine-year sentence for a bungled hold-up in Mooresville, Indiana. His "tutors" in prison had been some of the best bank-busters in the business. Dillinger robbed seven banks in Indiana and Ohio before fleeing to Tucson, where he and his gang were arrested.

91 killed in Jerusalem bomb explosion

1946 A bomb planted in part of the King David Hotel in Jerusalem has left 91 people dead and 45 injured. The target of the terrorists – most likely the Jewish extremist organization Irgun Zvai Leumi – was the British military HQ and the civil secretariat. The extremist campaign against British administration in Palestine seems set to intensify, assisted, either actively or passively, by the the great majority of the Jewish population. The long-awaited report by the Analo-US committee of enquiry regarding the problems of European Jewry and Palestine recently concluded that any attempt to establish an independent state or states in the area would result in civil strife and that the mandate should be maintained.

Picnickers watch Confederates triumph in battle

1861 The first major set-to in the American civil war ended yesterday in a bloody nose for the Union army under General Irvin McDowell. Forced by his political masters into launching a premature attack against the Confederate forces holding Bull Run (or Manassas), McDowell found himself outnumbered by an enemy that had already received advance information of his battle plan. The Confederates were only marginally more competent in battle than their adversaries, however, and had it not been for the resolution of General Jackson's brigade all might have been lost for the southerners. Confusion and an air of unreality were intensified by the presence of Washington sightseers, picnicking while watching the action.

Don't let them eat bread

1946 Britons faced their first day of bread rationing today, more than a year after the end of World War Two. The extension of rationing to bread is due to a poor harvest, droughts and shortages in war transport and fertilizers. In the United States a voluntary system of restriction by customers is in operation. However, millers are required by law to produce not less than 80 lb (36 kg) of flour from each 100 lb (45 kg) of wheat, as opposed to the usual extraction rate of 72 lb (33 kg) or lower to each 100 lb.

Have strong suspicions that Crippen London cellar murderer and accomplice are amongst saloon passengers moustache taken off growing beard accomplice dressed as boy voice manner and build undoubtably a girl both travelling as Mr and Master Robinson.

Captain Kendall sends a telegram from his ship concerning the murderous Dr Crippen, 1910.

1933 One-eyed Texan Wiley Post today bettered his own record-breaking circumnavigation of the globe two years ago. This time flying solo in the veteran aircraft Winnie Mae, Post sliced some 21 hours off the time of 8 days 15 hours 51 minutes he set with navigator Harold Gatty. Post followed the same course plotted by Gatty, eastward from New York over the British Isles and Russia. Post, 34, has now bought Winnie Mae from his former boss, Oklahoma oilman F. C. Hall.

Who do you think you're kidding, Mr Churchill?

1940 The auxiliary force raised in Britain at the beginning of the French campaign last month has been given a new name. The Local Defence Volunteers are from now on to be known as the Home Guard. The one million-strong force, which has many World War One veterans in its ranks, is intended to protect Britain against the expected German invasion. The men who form Britain's last line of defence may have been bemused as much as encouraged by prime minister Churchill's proposed slogan "You can always take one with you" – wags may feel tempted to suggest the insertion of the word "home". Weapons are scarce and it is doubtful whether enthusiasm alone could offer effective resistance to Adolf Hitler's hordes of well trained Aryan supermen.

1986 Prince Andrew and commoner Sarah Ferguson married at Westminster Abbey today. The couple, both 26, met last year at Ascot and gave news of their engagement in March. Shortly before the ceremony the Queen announced that she had conferred on Andrew the title of Duke of York – traditionally reserved for the sovereign's second son.

I brought it all to life. I moved the whole world onto a 20-ft [6.5 m] screen. I was a greater discoverer than Columbus. I condensed history into three hours and made them live it.

D. W. Griffith, pioner US filmmaker who introduced the techniques of flash-back, crosscut, close-up and longshot, and who died today, 1948.

Tension mounts in Europe

1914 The Austro-Hungarian government has issued an ultimatum to Serbia in the aftermath of the murder of Archduke Franz Ferdinand, the heir to the throne of Austria-Hungary. It is demanding that all anti-Austrian activities on Serbian territory be forbidden, that one of the main Serbian nationalist parties, Narodna Odbrana, be outlawed and that Austrian officials be allowed to participate in the inquiry into the Archduke's assassination. If Serbia does not agree to the conditions, Austria-Hungary will mobilize her forces. Serbia is in a cleft stick: agreement would signify willingness to relinquish sovereignty; refusal would lead to a Europe-wide conflict.

Uprising ends on a downer

1803 The confused rebellion that was mounted in Dublin today does not augur well for the future of the cause of Irish nationalism. A combination of bad planning and misunderstanding prevented the various contingents of rebels from launching a coordinated attack. The architect of the uprising, 25-year-old Robert Emmet, and his small band found themselves marching on Dublin Castle alone. All they could achieve was the murder of Lord Kilwarden, the Lord Chief Justice, and his nephew. An operation is underway to round up the insurgents. Emmet, who spent from 1800 to 1802 with the exiled leaders of the United Irishmen in France, is believed to be hiding in the Wicklow mountains.

1637 King Charles I of England loses a court battle over the control of Massachusetts and power is handed over to Sir Ferdinand Gorges, a member of New England's governing council.

1757 Death of Domenico Scarlatti, Italian composer, organist and harpsichordist who wrote more than 400 innovative harpsichord sonatas.

1858 In Britain, the Oath of Allegiance is modified to allow Jews to sit in Parliament.

1916 Death of Sir William Ramsay, Scottish chemist who isolated neon, xenon and krypton and discovered helium.

1948 Death of D. W. Griffith, American film director most noted for *Birth of a Nation*.

1951 Philippe Pétain, French general and statesman who headed the collaborationist Vichy government in World War Two, dies in prison at 95, having been reprieved from a death sentence imposed in August 1945.

1967 British cyclist Bobby Simpson collapses and dies during the Tour de France.

BIRTHDAYS

Raymond Chandler 1888, American novelist with a distinctive and much-imitated style, author of *The Big Sleep* and *Farewell My Lovely*, both of which were filmed.

Haile Selassie I 1892, Ethiopian emperor who led the resistance to the Italian invasion in 1935 and was restored to the throne by the Allies in 1941.

Michael Wilding 1912, British stage and screen actor whose films include *The World of Suzie Wong* and *Lady Caroline Lamb*.

Coral Browne 1913, Australian actress who made her career on stage and screen in Britain, appearing in films such as *The Roman Spring of Mrs Stone* and *The Killing of Sister George*.

Richard Rogers 1933, British architect best-known for the Pompidou Centre in Paris and the Lloyd's building in London.

Freud dominates International Psychoanalytic Association

1914 The wrangle which brought about the resignation of the president of the International Psychoanalytic Association, Carl Gustav Jung, in April seems to have secured the future of the Freudian movement in a cast that is acceptable to its founder, Sigmund Freud. The 58-year-old Vienna-based doctor has circulated to all members of the Association his "History of the Psychoanalysis Movement" – his personal view of the dissent that has riven the movement in recent years. The paper makes plain that the ideas of Jung do not square with Freudian theory. Perhaps the most contentious issue between the two men has been the definition of the term "libido", which for Freud signifies sexual energy and for Jung also encompasses a general mental energy. The departures of Jung, Adler and Stekel leaves the Association in the hands of men dedicated to Freud's ideas.

JULY 24

BIRTHDAYS

Simón Bolívar 1783, South American soldier and statesman who liberated Colombia, Venezuela and Ecuador from Spanish rule and organized a federation of the newly independent states.

Alexandre Dumas *père* 1802, French novelist and dramatist best-known for *The Three Musketeers*, *The Count of Monte Cristo* and *The Black Tulip*.

Frank Wedekind 1864, German dramatist, actor, singer, poet and essayist whose *Erdgeist* and *Die Büchse der Pandora* formed the basis of Alban Berg's opera *Lulu*.

Amelia Earhart 1898, American aviator and the first woman to fly solo over the Atlantic.

Peter Yates 1928, British film director best-known for *The Dresser*.

Mormons find their place

1847 Mormon leader Brigham Young (above with his wives) and his party of 147 members of the Church of the Latter-Day Saints reached the safety of the Salt Lake valley today. The exodus from Nauvoo, Illinois, to a "land that nobody wanted" began early last year. The hazardous journey has claimed many lives, despite Young's excellent organization and preparation. Crops are already being planted on this day of their arrival. The Mormon appetite for hard work has not won them acceptance in any community, nor has their doctrinaire interpretation of God's word. They can make this new land their own, however, and all who enter it will have to conform to the Mormon way of life.

This is the greatest week in the history of the world since the creation.

Richard Nixon, US president, on the landing of men on the moon, three days before, 1969.

Archer awarded £½ million damages

1987 Multi-millionaire author Jeffrey Archer has won £500,000 ($920,000) in damages against the *Star* newspaper, the highest amount ever awarded in a British libel action. The jury at the Royal Courts of Justice in London took 4 hours 20 minutes to decide that Archer had not, as the paper alleged, paid prostitute Monica Coghlan £70 ($129) for sex. Archer was deputy chairman of the Conservative Party at the time of the alleged transaction. He resigned from the post last October when he admitted to paying Coghlan £2000 ($3680) to avoid possible scandal but denied paying her for sex.

The most important thing in the Olympic Games is not winning but taking part . . . The essential thing in life is not conquering but fighting well.

Pierre de Coubertin, French educator and sportsman, in a speech to Officials of Olympic Games, 1908.

Turkey and Greece end territorial dispute

1923 The Treaty of Lausanne signed by Greece and Turkey today concludes the peace settlement begun at the end of the Great War but aborted by Kemal Ataturk's nationalist overthrow of the Ottoman dynasty. Acceptance of the original Treaty of Sèvres would have reduced Turkey to a small area around Constantinople extending 25 miles (40 km) into Europe, and Anatolia (excluding Smyrna). Ataturk has surrendered all claim to territories of the Ottoman empire occupied by non-Turks and confirmed Greece in possession of all Adriatic islands (except Imbros and Tenedos, which are to be returned to Turkey). These concessions have been made so that the ancient commercial port and religious centre of Smyrna, and Eastern Thrace, may be restored to Turkey.

1989 Japan's Liberal Democratic Party has suffered its first defeat in 30 years, forcing the resignation of the prime minister, Sosuke Uno. The LDP had seemed to be on the road to political recovery under the premiership of Uno after the Recruit scandal claimed his predecessor. However, last month Uno's former mistress slung mud at his name, ruining his chances.

Peter Sellers dies from heart attack

1980 The British comic actor Peter Sellers died today in a London hospital after suffering a massive heart attack. He was 55. Sellers had stopped over in London for a reunion supper with fellow Goons Spike Milligan and Harry Secombe en route to Los Angeles where he was to undergo an important heart operation. Sellers began his 30-year career as a comic on radio, starring in *Ray's a Laugh* and, most famously, *The Goon Show*. International stardom beckoned when he made the transition to the big screen in the late 50s. The Inspector Clouseau films *The Pink Panther* and *A Shot in the Dark* brought him a steady stream of lucrative screen roles. It is arguable, however, whether his genius as a mimic and creator of illusion was best suited to this medium.

COUP ATTEMPT IN AUSTRIA

1934 A group of armed men broke into the office of the Austrian Chancellor Engelbert Dollfuss today and fatally wounded him. Meanwhile, a second group took over the radio station in Vienna and announced the appointment of the Nazi Rintelen as Chancellor. The recent upsurge in Nazi activity in Austria had given rise to speculation of a German-backed putsch. The reaction to the crisis by the Austrian authorities has been swift, as befits a government which has already succeeded in crushing opposition from the other end of the political spectrum, the Socialists. Mussolini, on whom the fascist government of the Catholic Dollfuss relied so much, has pledged his full support to help maintain Austria's independence.

Deathbed confession

1865 British Army surgeon Major-General James Barry could not take his most closely guarded secret with him when he died today in the London suburb of Kensal Green. Conclusive evidence that the slightly built five-ft (162 cm) tall septuagenarian officer was not what he seemed presented itself to the woman who laid out the body. James Barry had been Miranda Stuart. Barry, an orphan, went into the army after gaining an MD from Edinburgh College. In South Africa, the West Indies and the Crimea, Barry built up a reputation as a first-class surgeon and an able administrator, and ended a distinguished career in the office of Inspector General of all British hospitals in Canada. Described as a "perfect gentleman" with an eye for ladies, he had a long-standing affair with a Mrs Fenton. No one knows if he shared his secret with her.

Coal is transported by locomotion

1814 Killingworth is the latest colliery to experiment with locomotives for transporting coal out of mines. Their chief mechanic, George Stephenson, has built an engine that can draw eight loaded carriages bearing 30 tons of coal at four miles per hour (6.4 kph). Stephenson got the idea for "Blucher" after seeing the "steam boiler on wheels" built by Matthew Murray for John Blenkinsop in operation at a neighbouring mine. Blucher is an adhesion machine with vertical cylinders. A chain drive leads to the front tender wheels to increase grip. Stephenson is convinced that Blucher's power can be further increased, and is to continue experimenting with the engine.

Dance to death

1917 In peace time the French public might have raised a collective wry smile at the spectacle of a femme fatale dancer and courtesan called Mata Hari (Malay for "eye of the day") being charged with employing her sexual charms to weaken French Army officers into betraying their country. The exotic-sounding Mata Hari is a 41-year-old Dutch woman, Margaretha Geertruida MacLeod (née Zelle), who agreed to spy for the French in enemy-occupied Belgium despite already working for the German consul in The Hague. Apart from MacLeod's own admission that she had on one occasion passed out-of-date information to the Germans, the prosecution could produce no firm evidence of her spying activities

against France. The trial ended today with the military court at Vincennes finding her guilty as charged. She is to be shot by firing squad.

CONCORDE CRASH KILLS 113

2000 Concorde has crashed minutes after take-off, killing all 109 passengers on board and four people on the ground. The Air France plane, bound for New York, crashed into a hotel in Gonesse, 10 miles from Paris. It is understood the aircraft, which had taken off from Roissy Charles de Gaulle airport just two minutes earlier, fell out of the sky after one of the engines caught fire on take-off. A spokesperson for Air France said all the passengers were German tourists travelling to New York to join a cruise ship bound for Equador. Eye-witnesses reported a "huge fireball" followed by a cloud of black smoke after the jet hit the ground. Within minutes of the crash, emergency services were on the scene searching through the rubble for survivors. Flight AF4590 is the first Concorde in the aircraft's 31-year history to crash.

> *You cannot control a free society by force.*
> **Robert Mark**, British police commissioner, 1976.

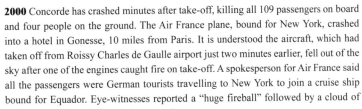

JULY 25

1554 The Catholic Queen Mary of England, known as "Bloody Mary" on account of her persecution of Protestants, marries Philip II of Spain.

1587 Christianity is banned in Japan and Jesuits accused of selling the Japanese as slaves are expelled from the country.

1835 Death of Samuel Taylor Coleridge, English poet and critic renowned for *Kubla Khan* and *The Rime of the Ancient Mariner* – and for his opium addiction.

1843 Death of Scottish chemist Charles Macintosh, inventor of waterproof clothing.

1909 French aviator Louis Blériot becomes the first man to fly the Channel, travelling from Calais to Dover in a Blériot XI.

1943 Italian dictator Benito Mussolini is forced by the Fascist Grand Council to resign following the Allied invasion of Sicily.

1956 Fifty lives are lost when an Italian ocean liner sinks off the Massachusetts coast after colliding in fog with a Swedish liner.

1959 The monarchy is abolished in Tunisia and the country becomes a republic with Habib Bourguiba as its first president.

1985 Film star Rock Hudson is admitted to hospital suffering from the killer disease AIDS.

BIRTHDAYS

Arthur James Balfour, 1st Earl 1848, British statesman and Conservative prime minister and foreign secretary from 1916 to 1919, during which time his Balfour Declaration promised to support the establishment of a Jewish homeland in Palestine.

Walter Brennan 1894, American character actor who won Oscars for *Come and Get It*, *Kentucky* and *The Westerner*.

Johnny "Rabbit" Hodges 1907, American jazz saxophonist.

Steve Goodman 1948, American songwriter whose "The City of New Orleans" gave Arlo Guthrie a hit.

1788 New York becomes the 11th state of the Union.

1830 King Charles X of France issues ordinances limiting political and civil rights.

1863 Death of Sam Houston, American soldier, president and Texan leader after whom the city of Houston is named.

1939 Death of Ford Madox Ford, British novelist who wrote more than 80 books and founded the *English Review* and the *Transatlantic Review*, in which he published the early works of Ezra Pound, James Joyce and Ernest Hemingway, among others.

1952 King Farouk I of Egypt abdicates after a military coup by General Neguib on July 22.

1953 Rebel leader Fidel Castro leads an unsuccessful attack on the Moncada barracks and is imprisoned by dictator Fulgencio Batista.

1956 President Nasser of Egypt nationalizes the Suez Canal just a month after coming to power.

1977 Israeli prime minister Menachem Begin defies a plea from US president Jimmy Carter and orders more settlements to be built on the occupied West Bank.

BIRTHDAYS

Jean-Baptiste-Camille Corot 1796, French painter who brought a new naturalism into the classical tradition of composed landscape.

George Bernard Shaw 1856, Irish dramatist, critic and man of letters, one of the founding members of of the Fabian Society.

Carl Jung 1875, Swiss psychiatrist and pioneer psychoanalyst who introduced the concept of introvert and extrovert personalities.

André Maurois 1885, French novelist and biographer.

Stanley Kubrick 1928, American film director whose works include *Dr Strangelove, 2001: A Space Odyssey* and *A Clockwork Orange*.

Mick Jagger 1943, British pop singer and founder member of the Rolling Stones.

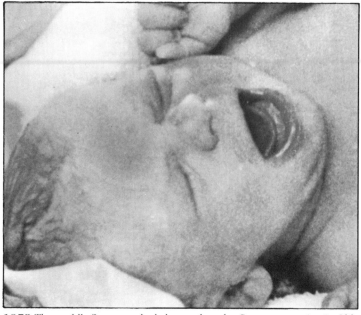

1978 The world's first test-tube baby was born by Caesarean section in Oldham General Hospital at 11.47 last night. For parents Lesley and John Brown of Bristol the birth is nothing short of a miracle after nine years of disappointment. The men whose expertise made the birth possible are Gynaecologist Patrick Steptoe and Cambridge physiologist Dr Robert Edwards. Together they succeeded in fertilizing an egg from Lesley's womb with her husband's sperm in the laboratory and then returning it to the mother for incubation.

It is uncertain whether the development and spread of electronic and computer technology will increase the spread of literacy or diminish the need for it and result in an oral culture overwhelming the present written one.
Eugene Radwin, US educationist, 1990.

Charles V sanctions new Pizarro expedition

1529 Francisco Pizarro's decision to go over the head of the governor of Panama and ask the Spanish Emperor Charles V to sanction another expedition to the wealthy kingdom south of Panama has paid off. The Council of the Indies has granted the 54-year-old soldier and explorer of South America the right of conquest, the governorship of the new lands and the title of Captain General for life. Last year Francisco Pizarro returned to Panama with gold, llamas and a few Indians as evidence of the riches that he believes are there for the taking. However, no funds appear to have been provided for the new expedition, nor have the contributions of Pizarro's partners, most notably Diego de Almagro, received recognition.

1908 The increase in the regulatory powers of the US government promoted by President Theodore Roosevelt was taken a stage further today with the establishment of a new investigative agency. This Federal Bureau of Investigation has been set up by Attorney General Charles J. Bonaparte within the existing Justice Department. The small group of FBI investigators will look into the nefarious dealings of land grabbers in the West and big business "trusts" in the East.

Argentina cries for "Evita"

1952 Eva Peròn, the wife of the President of the Argentine, Juan Peròn, died in Buenos Aires today after a long illness. She was 33. A former actress, Señora Peròn wielded enormous influence in public affairs. One of her main achievements was to win the vote for Argentinian women. "Evita", as she became known to Argentina's 18-million population, was recently proclaimed the "spiritual chief of the state" by Congress. That same body is expected to pass a bill ordaining that "for the rest of history" July 26 will be a day of national mourning for Argentina. Señora Peròn's body will lie in state until August 8 in the Ministry of Labour and Social Welfare.

Twenty-six die in railroad strike mayhem

1877 An America-wide railroad strike has brought in its wake violence and mayhem. Worst hit has been Pittsburgh, where three days of rioting have caused 26 deaths and an estimated $5 million (£2.7 million) worth of damage to property. Buffalo, St Louis and Chicago have also experienced rioting. The strike is in support of better pay and conditions for railroad workers, many of whom are immigrants. Some bosses regard the unrest as politically inspired by revolutionaries bent on the destruction of capitalism. Unionization is one of their chief bogeymen. Train crews are increasingly becoming unionized. Now other members of the railroad work force, which has grown rapidly since 1870, are similarly seeking to protect their interests.

ROBESPIERRE SLIPS IN HIS OWN BLOODBATH

1794 In an historic vote today the Convention in Paris decided to arrest the chief architect of the "reign of terror", Maximilien François Marie Isidore de Robespierre, and his supporters. They have become increasingly hostile to the 36-year-old lawyer and his aims, and yesterday were alarmed by his demand for a carte blanche regarding future use of the guillotine. Robespierre spoke in such menacing terms that few present could have doubted that their own necks might yet feel the kiss of that steely Madame. When Robespierre attempted to address the normally compliant Convention he was drowned out with cries of "Down with the tyrant". Support from the troops of the Commune, Robespierre's principal power base, was not forthcoming, and he was lost. Robespierre is now in custody awaiting execution.

Olympic athlete fails drugs test

1988 A life ban has been imposed by the British Amateur Athletic Board on Olympic pole vaulter Jeff Gutteridge. Two tests, one administered in Lanzarote in April and the other at a laboratory in London, revealed the clear presence of steroids. Gutteridge, 32, is the first British athlete to be banned for dope-taking. He denies the charge and intends appealing on the grounds that the testing procedure was not properly followed. Under the strict rules introduced by the BAAB to combat drug use, athletes who test positive have no right of appeal for reinstatement. Britain is the only country in the world to subject its athletes to spot checks.

Shah of Iran dies in Cairo

1980 The deposed Shah of Iran died in Cairo's Maadi Military Hospital today at the age of 60. The cause of death was internal bleeding and heart failure as a result of infection and lymphatic cancer. On his deathbed the Shah had requested to be buried ultimately in Tehran, named his eldest son, Prince Reza, as rightful heir to the Peacock Throne and prayed for the overthrow of Ayatollah Khomeini. The Shah lived in the Mexican mountain resort of Cuernavaca after leaving Iran in January 1979 but in recent months had been forced to seek medical treatment elsewhere for his deteriorating condition. Shortly before he died the Shah said that he was "fed up with living artificially". His wish for a very simple funeral is unlikely to be realized. President Sadat is expected to have his old ally buried with full military honours.

Spinoza challenges Scripture

1656 The Jewish religious authorities in Amsterdam have decided to excommunicate 24-year-old student Benedict Spinoza for failing to modify his unorthodox interpretations of Scripture. The civil authorities have also taken action by banishing him from Amsterdam for a short period. Neither bribes nor threats have persuaded Spinoza to change his contention that there is nothing in the Bible to support some orthodox views – for example, that God has no body, that angels exist or that the soul is immortal. The budding philosopher is said to be dismayed by the reaction to his ponderings. The Jewish fathers are in a difficult position, however, and fearful that Spinoza's "heresies" may reflect badly on the vulnerable Jewish community, whose members have still to win the right of citizenship in Holland.

> *Democracy passes into despotism.*
> **Plato**, Greek philosopher. Today military leaders in Greece handed power to civilian government, 1974.

1953 The Korean War formally ended today with the signing of a peace pact at Panmunjom. Lieutenant General William H. Harrison signed for the UN forces and General Nam II for the Chinese people's volunteers and North Korean forces. The armistice negotiations have taken just over two years, in which time the two sides have met 575 times. The three-year conflict has cost an estimated five million lives.

1789 Thomas Jefferson is made head of the new US department of Foreign Affairs.

1793 In France, Jacobin leader Maximilien Robespierre becomes a member of the Committee of Public Safety, established to guard against a coalition of European powers attacking France as a result of the execution of King Louis XVI.

1921 Sir Frederick Banting and Charles Best isolate insulin at the University of Toronto.

1941 Japan invades Indo-China.

1942 Death of Sir Fliders Petrie, British archaeologist who was the first professor of Egyptology at University College, London.

1946 American novelist and poet Gertrude Stein dies in Paris, where she was a leading figure in the American expatriate community.

1985 Ugandan president Milton Obote, who had regained power in 1980 after being deposed by General Idi Amin in 1971, is overthrown by a military coup.

1986 American cyclist Gregory James LeMond becomes the first non-European to win the Tour de France.

1996 A nail bomb explodes at the Olympics in Atlanta, killing two people and injuring over 100.

BIRTHDAYS

Alexandre Dumas *fils* 1824, French novelist and dramatist, illegitimate son of Alexandre Dumas *père* and author of the novel *La Dame aux Caméllias*, which he then adapted as the play *Camille* - later to be adapted again as Verdi's opera *La Traviata*.

Hilaire Belloc 1870, English poet, novelist and essayist best known for his light verse.

Anton Dolin 1904, British ballet dancer who with Alicia Markova founded London's Festival Ballet.

Bobbie Gentry 1942, American singer of "Ode to Billy Joe".

Christopher Dean 1958, British ice-skater who, with his partner Jayne Torvill, won an Olympic gold medal for ice dancing.

1655 Death of Cyrano de Bergerac, French soldier, writer and dramatist renowned for the size of his nose.

1741 Death of Antonio Vivaldi, Italian composer, violinist and priest who taught music at the Ospedale della Pietà in Venice.

1794 In Paris, Maximilien Robespierre goes to the guillotine himself, having presided over the Reign of Terror in which at least 25,000 were beheaded.

1835 Eighteen bystanders are killed as French king Louis Philippe escapes assassination.

1868 A treaty is signed allowing unrestricted Chinese immigration to the USA.

1914 Austria-Hungary declares war on Serbia.

1935 The Boeing B-17 Flying Fortress bomber makes its first flight at Seattle.

1945 A B-52 bomber crashes into the 78th floor of the Empire State building, killing the three crew and 11 passengers.

1960 UN secretary general Dag Hammarskjöld arrives in the Congo on a peace mission to end the civil war.

1965 President Lyndon Johnson sends another 50,000 US ground troops to Vietnam.

1989 In the Lebanon Israelis abduct leading Shia Muslim Sheikh Abduk Obeid.

BIRTHDAYS

Beatrix Potter 1866, English children's author and illustrator.

Marcel Duchamp 1887, French artist who became the leader of the New York Dada movement.

Malcolm Lowry 1909, British novelist best known for the semi-autobiographical *Under the Volcano.*

Sir Garfield Sobers 1936, Barbadian cricketer who scored a record 365 runs against Pakistan in the 1957-8 Test series.

Riccardo Muti 1941, Italian conductor and artistic director of La Scala in Milan.

New "potato" plant may provide animal fodder

1586 A new type of plant has been introduced into Ireland by some explorers associated with Sir Walter Raleigh. Called *Solanum tuberosum*, or the potato, it is a perennial herb thought to originate from the Andes region of South America. The tubers of the plant are eaten by the South American Indians. Sir Walter plans to plant some tubers on his estate at Youghall, near Cork, with a view to feeding the crop to his livestock.

WOMAN GETS LICENCE

1966 Lord Justice Denning has struck a decisive blow for equality between the sexes in the world of horseracing by ruling that 72-year-old Mrs Florence Nagle has to have a training licence "if she is to carry on her trade without stooping to subterfuge". After the hearing Mrs Nagle said that she had been trying for 20 years to get a licence from the Stewards of the Jockey Club. Undeterred by their refusal, she had circumvented the problem by taking out a licence in the name of her head lad. Mrs Nagles's most notable horse training success in recent years has been Elf Arrow, winner of the 1959 Liverpool St Leger and seven other races.

1868 The Fourteenth Amendment of the US Constitution was formally ratified today. The main purpose of this latest addition to the US statute book is to extend to the 4½ million or so black Americans the same personal and property rights enjoyed by other citizens of the United States. The Fourteenth Amendment builds on the provisions of the Thirteenth Amendment abolishing slavery by defining, for the first time, national citizenship and unequivocally including black Americans within that definition.

Henry VIII perhaps approached as nearly to the ideal standard of perfect wickedness as the infirmaties of human nature will allow.
Sir James Mackintosh, British historian, on King Henry VIII. Today, Henry beheaded Thomas Cromwell and then married Catherine Howard, 1540.

Great court composer and organist dies

1750 The court composer to the Elector of Saxony and director of Church music for Leipzig, Johann Sebastian Bach, has died in Leipzig at the age of 65. Herr Bach was one of the most accomplished heirs to a family tradition of music-making that stretches back 100 years or more. He spent the early part of his career as an organist and orchestral player. His interest in composing developed in an innovative direction when he became acquainted with the new styles and forms of music championed by the Italian masters, especially Vivaldi. Many of his cantatas, arias, concerto movements, fugues, chorales and large-scale vocal and keyboard works reflect this influence. Many more of Herr Bach's compositions are as yet unpublished. One of particular interest is "Das Wohltemperirte Klavier" – The Well-tempered [well-tuned] Clavier – in which Bach advocates adjusting tuning so that all keys of the instrument are pleasant to the ear.

Davies wins US Women's Open

1987 Laura Davies made golfing history today by becoming the first Englishwoman to win the US Women's Open. The number one player on the European circuit, Davies led throughout the 18-hole play-off at Plainfield Country Club, Edison, New Jersey. She finished the game with a one-under-par 71, ahead of the legendary Jo-Anne Carner (who at the age of 48 was bidding to become the oldest woman to win the title) and Japan's Ayako Okamoto. The most potent weapon in the golfing armoury of Davies, 23, is her long hitting. This, combined with the putting frailty of her opponents, brought the Surrey player victory and a cheque for $55,000 (£30,000), the largest amount she has won in her three-year professional career.

750 million watch royal wedding

1981 The heir to the British throne, Prince Charles, married Lady Diana Frances Spencer in front of 750 million people today. The ceremony in London's St Paul's Cathedral was televised live throughout the world. In Britain the official public holiday was celebrated in street parties by hundreds of thousands of people. Of the few people working, one – staunch trade unionist Harry Crapper of Sheffield – said he did not agree with "all this junketing". Another note of discord was sounded by the King and Queen of Spain who declined their invitation to the wedding because the royal couple's honeymoon plans include picking up the royal yacht *Britannia* in Gibraltar, a long-standing bone of contention between Britain and Spain.

1565 Mary Queen of Scots marries her cousin Henry Stewart, Lord Darnley.

1830 French liberals opposed to Charles X's restrictive new laws seize Paris.

1833 Death of William Wilberforce, British philanthropist who was a prime mover in the anti-slavery campaign.

1890 Dutch artist Vincent van Gogh dies two days after shooting himself in the chest.

1900 King Umberto I of Italy is shot dead by an anarchist.

1914 Following the murder of Archduke Ferdinand in Sarajevo, Tsar Nicholas II mobilizes 1.2 million troops.

1948 The first Olympic Games since World War Two opens at Wembley in London.

1966 Death of Gordon Craig, British actor, theatre designer and producer and son of actress Ellen Terry.

1968 The Pope condemns all birth control.

1974 Cass Elliott, singer with pop group the Mamas and the Papas, dies in London of a heart attack after choking on a sandwich.

1983 Actor David Niven, the quintessential English gentleman, dies of motor neurone disease.

BIRTHDAYS

Alexis de Tocqueville 1805, French political scientist, historian and politician who visited the USA and wrote *Démocratie en Amerique*, which also examined the constitutions of Europe.

Booth Tarkington 1869, American novelist who wrote *The Magnificent Ambersons*.

Benito Mussolini 1883, Italian founder of the Fascist Party and ally of Hitler in World War Two.

Sigmund Romberg 1887, Hungarian-born composer who wrote *The Student Prince* and *Desert Song*.

Dag Hammarskjöld 1905, Swedish politician and second secretary general of the United Nations.

German composer Robert Schumann dies

1856 The avant-garde German composer Robert Schumann, husband of the celebrated pianist Clara Schumann, has died in a private asylum at Endenich, near Bonn, at the age of 46. Schumann gave up studying law in order to devote himself to a career in music. He has left a large body of work ranging from piano pieces and songs to chamber music, choral works and symphonies. Schumann's music has not found wide acceptance among audiences and appreciation of it has been largely confined to a small clique of professional musicians and composers. Schumann's greatest contribution to contemporary musical life has been the journal *Die Neue Zeitschrift* (New Musical Journal) which since its inception in 1833 has brought young composers to the musical public's attention.

Japan grants US trade privileges

1858 US diplomat Townsend Harris has pulled off a spectacular trade coup for the US. He has persuaded the Japanese to agree to trade and diplomatic privileges with the United States. Harris has spent the past two years preparing the ground for this commercial treaty which opens five ports to US trade (in addition to those already opened under the terms of the Treaty of Kanagawa), exempts US citizens living in these areas from the jurisdiction of Japanese law, guarantees those same citizens religious freedom and arranges for diplomatic representation and a tariff agreement between the two countries. Japan's sudden willingness to negotiate may be explained by two factors: a change among the ruling élite; and the need to counter the mounting threat from Britain and France, whose joint naval force is currently on its way to Japan to obtain new treaties by force.

Spanish invasion receives calm British reception

1588 The armada of 130 ships sent by King Philip II of Spain to attempt an invasion of England was sighted today off Cornwall. The English fleet under Charles Howard, Baron Howard of Effingham, is confident of success, however. Howard has 197 ships with about 16,000 men, most of them seasoned sailors, at his disposal. His commanders seem equally nonchalant. Sir Francis Drake was playing a game of bowls on Plymouth Hoe when he received news of the armada's approach. He finished the game before making for the fleet assembly point at Portsmouth. Factors that may tell against the Spanish in battle include the lack of experience of their new commander, the Duke de Medina Sidonia, and the lack of pace and manoeuvrability of their ships.

1966 Singer Bob Dylan has been injured in a motorcycle accident near his home at Woodstock, New York. His injuries are thought to involve broken vertebrae in his neck. Precise details are scarce, however, although Dylan's manager has let it be known that the 25-year-old star has been completely incapacitated by the accident.

1718 Death of William Penn, Quaker founder of Pennsylvania.

1898 Death of Prince Otto von Bismarck, first chancellor of the German empire.

1930 In the first ever World Cup final, Uruguay beats Argentina 4-2.

1942 Canada approves conscription.

1958 A left-wing coup that overthrows the monarchy in Iraq arouses Western fears of a Middle Eastern domino effect.

1963 British double agent Kim Philby turns up in Moscow, seven months after his disappearance in Beirut.

1980 The New Hebrides, in the South-West Pacific, gain independence from Britain and France and take the name Vanuatu Republic.

1987 Saudi Arabian police open fire on Iranian zealots during the annual pilgrimage to Mecca.

BIRTHDAYS

Giorgio Vasari 1511, Italian painter, architect and writer who painted frescoes in the Palazzo Vecchio and built the Uffizi art gallery in Florence but is best known for his work on art history.

Emily Brontë 1818, English novelist, author of *Wuthering Heights*.

Henry Ford 1863, American car manufacturer.

Henry Moore 1898, English sculptor and graphic artist best known for his mother and child sculptures and reclining figures which show the influence of primitive African and Mexican art.

Northcote Parkinson 1909, British author, historian and journalist best known for the book *Parkinson's Law*, in which he stated that work expands to fill the time available for its completion.

Peter Bogdanovich 1939, American film and theatre director best-known for *The Last Picture Show* and *Paper Moon*.

Daley Thompson 1958, British athlete, winner of gold medals for the decathlon at two Olympics.

Speke names Lake Victoria

1858 British explorer John Hanning Speke, 31, has named the great lake he found in the heart of Africa today after Queen Victoria. He has until recently been exploring the region with Richard Burton, but after their joint discovery of Lake Tanganyika the younger man decided to make the homeward journey by striking out northwards. Speke's claim that in Lake Victoria he has found the source of the Nile is unlikely to be accepted by Burton, nor by many others in the scientific community. Speke developed an interest in exploration while serving with the British Army in India. His chance to join a pukka expedition came three years ago when he became a member of Burton's abortive attempt to explore Somaliland. Speke was badly wounded in the attack by Somali natives that put paid to the expedition.

IRA murder top UK politician

1990 Ian Gow, chairman of the Conservative backbench Northern Ireland committee and one of the most outspoken critics of IRA terrorism, was killed by a bomb concealed beneath the chassis of his car. The 5 lb (2.25 kg) bomb exploded at 8.39 am as Mr Gow prepared to drive out of the carport adjoining his East Sussex home. Mr Gow, 53, resigned from the Thatcher government over the Anglo-Irish agreement in 1985, remaining a stout defender of other Conservative policies. He knew his name was on an IRA hit list found last year.

England on top of the world

1966 England won the coveted Jules Rimet trophy, the World Cup of fooball, at Wembley Stadium this afternoon after an epic tussle with West Germany. It looked as though England were home and dry with a 2-1 victory, but then West Germany snatched a last-minute equalizer. Before the start of extra time, manager Alf Ramsey coolly told his exhausted players: "Well you've won it once. Now you'll just have to do it all over again, and you will. The Germans are all knackered". They did do it again, thanks to two goals by striker Geoff Hurst. At the final whistle the stadium erupted in celebration of England's 4-2 triumph.

Singing in the rain

1991 Not even the golden tones of Luciano Pavarotti could bring a smile to the heavens over London's Hyde Park last night and cajole the rain to stop. Fortunately the weather did not spoil the mammoth maestro's free open-air concert to celebrate his 30th anniversary in opera. More than 150,000 people turned up to hear Pavarotti's personal thank you to London and to cheer him hoarse. Among the dripping VIPs was the polythene-clad Princess Diana, to whom the 20-stone singer gallantly dedicated the aria "Donna Non Vidi Mai" ("I have never seen a lady like that"). The concert was televised live to an estimated 400 million people in 33 countries.

I have come to regard the law courts not as a cathedral but rather as a casino.
Richard Ingrams, British editor, 1977.

1973 The families of victims of the drug Thalidomide have been awarded £20 million ($11 million) in compensation after an 11-year legal battle fought on their behalf by the *Sunday Times* newspaper. The case began after it was discovered that the pill was associated with a high incidence of babies born with malformed limbs. The case has highlighted the need for greater stringency in the testing of new drugs.

First success for Ranger programme

1964 NASA scientists are on the brink of answering many questions about the composition of the moon. At the seventh attempt they have succeeded in landing a functioning camera-equipped spacecraft on the surface of the earth's only satellite. The 806-lb (365 kg) Ranger 7 probe reached its target area, the Mare Nubium, some 68 hours after blast off. The craft is fitted with six cameras, one covering a wide field of view, the other five taking close-ups of smaller areas. The pictures sent back so far reveal that part of the Moon is not covered with a deep layer of dust, as had been supposed. The surface material seems to have a spongy texture and is very different in composition from the rock found on Earth. Solar radiation and bombardment by meteors and other inter-planetary materials are only two of the phenomena that have gone into shaping the Moon's landscape.

Kidnapped US Marine hanged

1989 The Organization for the Oppressed of the Earth, a group of Shi'ite Muslim extremists closely linked with the pro-Iranian Hezbollah (Party of God), announced today that they had executed Lieutenant Colonel William Higgins, the US Marine abducted in Lebanon in February 1988. The group also released a video showing a bound and gagged man revolving slowly at the end of a rope. Close examination of the grisly low-quality tape has led the CIA to believe that William Higgins may have been killed at a much earlier date.

Tibetans rebel against China

1958 Kham tribesmen in eastern Tibet are reported to be increasing their guerrilla activity against Chinese troops. The armed resistance to the Chinese presence in Tibet is not as yet on the same scale witnessed last year in Kham province when tribesmen breached part of the main China-Tibet highway. But if the unrest spreads it may give the Chinese authorities an excuse to crack down on the rebels. Under the terms of the 1951 agreement Tibet supposedly enjoys full autonomy. In reality Peking makes all the decisions relating to domestic and foreign affairs.

Jim Reeves killed in plane crash

1964 Country singer Jim Reeves died today when his plane crashed into a hillside a few miles from Nashville, Tennessee. He was 40. "Gentleman Jim" Reeves shot to fame in the late 50s with his hit single "He'll Have to Go". He followed this up with "Welcome to my World", "I Love You Because" and "I Won't Forget You", all top ten records. Reeves set out to be a baseball star, but as a singer his distinctive voice and gentle style won him fans around the world. He made 375 records before his death and his widow Mary promises to ensure that they are released over the coming years.

1990 Four days ago cricketer Graham Gooch scored 333 runs, the third largest individual total by an England batsman. In 10½ hours he faced 485 balls. Back at the crease yesterday to open England's Second Innings against India, he scored 123 to become the first Englishman since Compton in 1947 to score centuries in successive innings.

All politicians have vanity. Some wear it more gently than others.
David Steele, British politician, 1985.

LISZT DIES

1886 The Abbe Liszt, Canon of Albano, died from pneumonia this evening aged 75. The great pianist was dogged with illness for the last two years of his life yet maintained a punishing schedule of teaching, composing and concert-giving. By the time he retired as a virtuoso pianist at 35, he had become a public idol. He died oppressed by much personal unhappiness that could not be relieved by his spiritual beliefs.

1556 Death of Ignatius Loyola, Spanish cleric who founded the Jesuit order to propagate the Roman Catholic faith.

1667 The Anglo-Dutch War ends with the Peace of Breda.

1875 Death of Andrew Johnson, Democratic president after the assassination of President Lincoln.

1910 Wife-murderer Dr Crippen and his mistress Ethel Le Neve are arrested on board the SS *Montrose*.

1914 Kaiser Wilhelm II of Germany rejects a British offer of mediation in the Austro-Serbian crisis as "insolence".

1919 The Weimar Republic is established in Germany, named after the town in which the new German constitution was formulated.

1932 The Nazi Party doubles its representation in the Reichstag.

1964 A Rolling Stones concert in Belfast is halted after only 12 minutes because of rioting fans.

1965 Cigarette commercials are banned on British television.

1975 Irish pop group the Miami Showband is ambushed and murdered by Protestant gunmen near Newry, Northern Ireland.

1979 Nigeria seizes British oil installations in a bid to persuade Margaret Thatcher to take a tough line on apartheid.

1990 In Trinidad, Muslim rebels release prime minister A. R. Robinson but continue to hold their other hostages in Port of Spain's television station.

BIRTHDAYS

Milton Friedman 1912, American economist and advocate of the free market economy, winner of the Nobel Prize in 1976.

Lynne Reid Banks 1929, British author best-known for *The L-Shaped Room*, which was made into a film starring Leslie Caron and Tom Bell.

Geraldine Chaplin 1944, American actress, the daughter of silent film comedian Charlie Chaplin.

AUGUST

"Forget the outside world. Life has different laws in here. This is Campland, an invisible country. It's not in the geography books, or the psychology books or the history books. This is the famous country where ninety-nine men weep while one man laughs."

Alexander Solzhenitsyn,
Soviet novelist - construction of the Berlin Wall started
August 17, 1961.

Poles urged to overthrow Nazis

1944 General Tadeusz Komorowski, commander of Poland's Home Army, has ordered his 40,000-strong Warsaw units to start fighting the German occupying forces in order to oust them from the city and, eventually, the country. Radio Moscow has been broadcasting to the population of Warsaw, urging them to rise up. The First Belorussian Army Group, under Marshal Konstantin Rokossovsky, has advanced to the Vistula River, outside Warsaw, so help for the Poles seems to be close at hand.

1873 Hallidie's Clay Street Hill Railroad Co promises to take the fatigue out of one of San Francisco's most daunting inclines. The new service, which opened today, has been made possible by the invention of the cable railroad. This was patented some six years ago by local cable manufacturer and mechanic Andrew S. Hallidie, who made his start by designing and building cableways for gold mines. Each of the new cable cars working the 2,800-ft (853 m) line is fitted with a device which grips a moving continuous cable embedded in the roadway.

Anne . . . when in good humour, was meekly stupid, and when in bad humour, was sulkily stupid.
T. B. Macaulay, English historian, on Queen Anne. She died today, 1714.

BRITONS NEVER NEVER SHALL HAVE SLAVES

1833 In a momentous move, Britain has finally ended its 400-year involvement in slavery. The act passed by parliament today frees all slaves in the nation's territories after a five- to seven-year apprenticeship. A sum of £20 million ($37 million) has been earmarked to compensate slave-owners. Today's news marks a victory for the Anti-Slavery Society (formed in 1823) and their parliamentary leader, Thomas Fowell Buxton, who have campaigned hard for this amendment. It also completes the work begun some 40 years ago by William Wilberforce. Wilberforce's bill abolishing the slave trade was eventually passed in 1807, after a series of setbacks to its progress since its inception in 1789. The new bill is expected to put fresh heart into the abolition campaign in the United States.

The thaw continues

1975 After three years of intensive negotiations the heads of government of the United States, Canada, the Soviet Union and all the states of East and West Europe – with the sole exception of Enver Hoxha's Albania – have signed the so-called Helsinki Agreement on security and cooperation. The accord is a landmark in the gradual process of detente in which East and West have been engaged since the 1960s. Soviet leader Leonid Brezhnev has been forced to agree to the future protection of a wide range of human rights in order to acquire the advantageous economic links his country so desperately needs. The performance of each state will be monitored by another co-signatory.

Lauda near death after inferno

1976 A 40-second inferno has left world motor racing champion Niki Lauda fighting for his life in the intensive care unit of a German hospital this afternoon. The accident happened on the second lap of the German Grand Prix at the 14-mile (22.5-km) long Nurburgring. According to eye witnesses Lauda's car spun out of control in the treacherous conditions, bounced off a safety barrier and then exploded. The struggling Lauda was released from the blazing cockpit by the combined efforts of several of his fellow drivers, whose selfless act has given the 27-year-old Austrian a slim chance of survival. In addition to severe burns to his face, Lauda has suffered near-fatal injury to his lungs as a result of inhaling raw, unvaporized petrol. The restarted race was won by James Hunt, Lauda's main rival for this season's drivers' championship.

1714 George Louis, Elector of Hanover, accedes to the British throne as George I on the death of Queen Anne.

1774 British chemist Sir Joseph Priestley announces that he has discovered oxygen.

1778 The first savings bank opens in Hamburg, Germany.

1798 Nelson attacks and annihilates the French fleet at Aboukir Bay, cutting off Napoleon's supply route to his army in Egypt.

1831 The new London Bridge is opened by William IV and Queen Adelaide.

1834 Death of Robert Morrison, the first English missionary to go to China and translator of the Bible into Chinese.

1914 Germany declares war on Russia.

1950 Australian prime minister Sir Robert Gordon Menzies promises to send troops to South Korea to join US forces in repelling the invasion by North Korea.

1969 The first pictures of the planet Mars are beamed back to earth by the US Mariner 6 unmanned spacecraft.

1985 America agrees to sanctions against South Africa in protest against apartheid and in response to violent race riots.

1989 John Ogdon, English concert pianist who suffered from schizophrenia, dies from pneumonia.

BIRTHDAYS

Claudius I 19 BC, Roman emperor who invaded Britain in AD 43 and made it a province.

Jean Baptiste de Lamarck 1774, French zoologist who coined the term vertebrate and invertebrate.

Francis Scott Key 1779, US poet, attorney and author who wrote the American national anthem "The Star Spangled Banner".

Jack Kramer 1921, American tennis champion and Wimbledon men's singles champion in 1947, who went on to promote tennis with great success.

AUGUST 2

1100 English King William Rufus is slain by an arrow while hunting in the New Forest – possibly assassinated by his younger brother, who became Henry I.

1589 Henry II, the last Valois king, is stabbed to death by a mad Dominican monk.

1718 The first quadruple alliance is formed between Britain, France, the Holy Roman Emperor and The Netherlands to maintain the Treaties of Utrecht, recently repudiated by Spain.

1788 Thomas Gainsborough, English landscape and portrait painter, dies.

1830 Charles X of France is overthrown and abdicates.

1834 The South Australian Association gains a charter to found a colony.

1918 British, French and US troops try to smash Lenin's communist revolution by supporting the White forces and seizing Archangel.

1945 The Potsdam Conference, the final allied summit of World War II, ends.

1948 "Reds under the Bed" in the US – American politician Alger Hiss testifies to the McCarthy hearings.

1964 US involvement in Vietnam escalates after a torpedo attack on the navy ship *Maddox* in the Tonkin Gulf: President Lyndon B. Johnson orders a retaliatory strike.

1980 A right-wing Italian terror group bombs Bologna railway station in Northern Italy, killing 84.

BIRTHDAYS

Sir Arthur Bliss 1891, English composer and Master of the Queen's Music from 1953: his work includes film scores and music for the ballet *Checkmate*.

James Baldwin 1924, American author well known for *Another Country* and *The Amen Corner* which explore black contemporary society.

Peter O'Toole 1932, Irish actor, most famous for his role in *Lawrence of Arabia*, for which he won an Oscar nomination.

Nelson catches French napping

1798 A 14-vessel naval squadron commanded by Rear Admiral Horatio Nelson has scored a brilliant tactical victory over a 17-strong French fleet in the Mediterranean. The wily Nelson caught the French with their ensigns down – at anchor in Aboukir Bay, north of the River Nile in Egypt. Most of the French ratings were ashore getting water, leaving their commander de Breuys with 120 guns but no one to fire them. As Nelson's fleet sailed into the attack on both sides of the anchored French men-of-war, de Breuys could not launch the classic response, a broadside. The battle, which started yesterday afternoon at around 4.30, did not end until early this morning. The French are reported to have lost 11 ships of the line and 2 frigates, 1700 of their men are dead, 1500 wounded and 3000 captured. The victorious British, whose losses amounted to only 1000 dead and wounded, aim to take home 6 of the captured vessels as prizes.

"Fastest gun" has no chance

1876 The man billed in his colourful shows as the "fastest gun in the West", "Wild Bill" Hickok fell victim to an assassin's bullet today. Hickok, 39, was playing poker in the saloon in Deadwood when killer Jack McCall struck, shooting the unsuspecting ex-lawman in the back from a vantage point behind the bar. As a federal marshal Hickok (real name James Butler Hickok) single-handedly tamed the notoriously rough frontier towns of Hays City and Abilene.

Ali out for the count

1849 The Egyptian ruler Muhammad 'Ali Pasha died in Alexandria today, aged 80, a year after retiring from office. The many economic and administrative reforms introduced during the former soldier's 44-year reign changed the face of Egyptian society. The traditional classes paid dearly for their ruler's primary objective of increasing his own wealth and power. His personal ambition eventually led him to challenge the dominance of the Ottoman sultan. The European powers stepped in to restore the status quo when the Sultan's fleet deserted to Muhammad 'Ali, in the wake of the decisive battle of Nezib (1839). However, Muhammad 'Ali did not entirely lose out; the right of hereditary succession to Egypt and Sudan was conferred on his family.

SADDAM SNATCHES OIL-RICH KUWAIT

1990 Saddam Hussein today made good Iraq's claim to the oil-rich state of Kuwait by invading it. Thousands of heavily armed Iraqi troops quickly cut through the paper-thin defences of their tiny Gulf neighbour and are now firmly in control of its capital, Kuwait City. The Al-Sabah family, which has ruled Kuwait for more than two centuries, has fled to Saudi Arabia. Tensions between the two countries have been high for several weeks since Saddam accused Kuwait of deliberately over-producing oil, thus depressing prices and damaging Iraq's fragile economy. Iraq's action has been condemned by world leaders, most forcibly by British PM Margaret Thatcher and US president George Bush who have not ruled out a military response to the crisis.

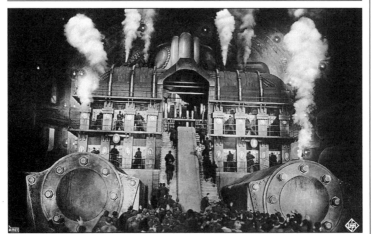

1976 German film director Fritz Lang has died. Lang won his reputation as a distinguished silent film maker with films like *Metropolis* (above), a nightmare vision of the future, and *M*, a study of a psychopathic murderer. He went to Hollywood in 1934 and tended thereafter to make commercial thrillers.

"Where shall I begin, please your Majesty?" he asked.
"Begin at the beginning" the King said, gravely, "and go on till you come to the end: then stop."
Charles Dodgson (Lewis Carroll) in *Alice's Adventures in Wonderland*, published today, 1865.

Golden voice finally stilled

1921 Enrico Caruso, the Neapolitan with the golden voice, has died at the Hotel Vesuvio in Naples aged 48. Signor Caruso was returning to Rome after a month's holiday in Sorrento when he suffered a recurrence of the illness that several operations and prolonged medical treatment had failed to cure: peritonitis and sepsis. The world has been robbed of one of the most individual operatic talents. Caruso invented his own vocal technique, developing a style that was just right for the verismo operas that came into vogue at the turn of the century and becoming a household name. The King of Italy has allowed the funeral to be held in the basilica of San Francesco di Paola in Naples – normally reserved for royalty.

Sumerland fun turns to terror

1973 At least 46 people, including children, have been killed and 80 injured in a fire that swept through the six-storey Summerland amusemement centre at Douglas, Isle of Man. Last night an estimated 7000 people were enjoying the amenities of the £2.5 million ($4.6 million) complex, reckoned to be the largest of its kind in the world. Just before 8 pm thick black smoke began to roll through the 3 1/2-acre (1.4-hectare) site and within minutes the whole building was ablaze. The pyramid-shaped acrylic sheeting covering the outside of the two-year-old centre melted, dripping on to people as they tried to escape. Police suspect arson or an electrical fault as the cause.

> *The lamps are going out all over Europe; we shall not see them lit again in our lifetime.*
> **Lord Grey**, British statesman, on the eve of the First World War, 1914.

Next stop - India

1492 Shortly before sunrise today a flotilla of three ships set sail from the Spanish port of Palos de la Frontera in search of a land called India. The leader of the expedition, Cristobal Colon (Christopher Columbus), thought to be a Genoese of Spanish-Jewish extraction, has spent the last eight years trying to get the project off the ground. The latest hitch came just seven months ago when his patrons, King Ferdinand and Queen Isabella of Spain, were told of Colon's price for undertaking the trip: a knighthood, the ranks of Grand Admiral and Viceroy (these to become hereditary) and 10 per cent of the receipts from his admiralty. The stunned monarchs dismissed Colon, but later recalled him and met all his demands. Colon claims to have received divine guidance in his career to date. He will need every iota to see him safely through the perilous adventure ahead.

216 In the Battle of Cannae a huge Roman army is defeated and its supply depot seized by a smaller army led by Carthaginian general Hannibal. Fifty thousand Roman soldiers are killed.

1460 Scottish king James II is killed by the English during the siege of Roxburgh Castle.

1792 Death of Sir Richard Arkwright, the Englishman who invented the the water-powered spinning frame.

1924 Death of Joseph Conrad, Polish-born British novelist whose books included *The Secret Agent* and *Lord Jim*.

1926 The first traffic lights in England are set up at London's Piccadilly Circus.

1966 American comedian Lenny Bruce is found dead after having taken an overdose of morphine – police place his body next to a syringe for the benefit of newspaper photographers.

1971 In London, three men are sentenced to between 9 and 15 months in jail for publishing the obscene "Schoolkids Issue" of the underground magazine *Oz*.

1989 A mysterious explosion in a London hotel blows a man to pieces and rips out two floors.

BIRTHDAYS

Stanley Baldwin 1867, British Conservative prime minister three times between 1923 and 1937.

Haakon VII 1872, Norwegian monarch who refused to surrender to the Germans in World War Two.

Rupert Brooke 1887, British war poet with a romantic image who was hailed as a hero for *1914 and Other Poems*.

Clifford D. Simak 1904, American author of *Way Station*.

P. D. James 1920, British crime writer of *A Taste of Death* and *Innocent Blood*.

Leon Uris 1924, American author famous for *Exodus* and the Cuban espionage novel *Topaz*.

Martin Sheen 1940, American actor, known for his roles in *Catch 22* and *Apocalypse Now*.

Fargo's final journey

1881 William George Fargo, the wealthy pioneer of the long-distance express service, has died at his home in Buffalo, New York, aged 65. Fargo was already established in the freight forwarding business when he hit upon the idea of offering a transcontinental express service between New York and San Francisco. The service went into operation in 1852 with hired stagecoaches. Their cargo was protected by armed guards on the long and perilous journey between the east and west coasts. In time Wells Fargo also offered a banking service to the many miners among its clientele, buying the miners' gold dust in exchange for cash.

Sir Roger hangs for treason

1916 One of Britain's most distinguished civil servants, Sir Roger Casement, was hanged in London today for his involvement in the Easter Uprising in Dublin. The former consul in Portuguese East Africa was an Ulster Protestant whose sympathy with the predominantly Catholic Irish nationalists led him to seek aid for their cause in Germany and the United States. His attempt to recruit Irish prisoners-of-war to a German brigade that would play a key role in the planned uprising was unsuccessful. Casement returned from the failed mission in a German submarine and was arrested by British forces soon after landing.

1778 Milanese society donned its finery tonight for the opening of the new opera house, the Teatro alla Scala, the magnificent replacement for the old Royal Ducal Theatre which burnt down two years ago. The theatre was designed by Milan's leading neo-classical architect, Giuseppe Piermarini. It opened with *Europa Recognized*, by Antonio Salieri.

BIRTHDAYS

Percy Bysshe Shelley 1792, English lyric poet whose poems include *Prometheus Unbound* and *Adonais*.

Sir Osbert Lancaster 1908, British writer, artist and cartoonist who had a daily cartoon published in the *Daily Express*.

David Russell Lange 1942, New Zealand Labour politician and prime minister 1984-9, controversial for his refusal to allow nuclear-armed ships to dock in New Zealand.

FAIRYTALE ENDING

1875 The death was announced in Copenhagen today of Hans Christian Andersen, famed the world over for his fairy tales and stories. He was 70. Andersen was born into poverty in Odense, the son of a cobbler and a woman who was both superstitious and illiterate. At the age of only 14 he left his job as a tailor's apprentice and went to Copenhagen to seek his fortune on the stage. The director of the Royal Theatre, Jonas Collin, took an interest in the boy, sending him to grammar school and eventually to university. His first book of fairy tales, published in 1835, soon became a bestseller throughout the world. His timeless tales do not pander to wish-fulfilment and leave the reader wiser rather than happier.

1955 The latest avant-garde play from Paris, Samuel Beckett's *Waiting for Godot*, provoked a mixed response from its first-night audience in London last night. About half of those present gave up on the nonsensical dialogue and absence of plot and walked out before the end. Those who stayed until curtain down cheered their support for the play's message – that the meaningless of life is reflected in our inability to communicate with others. The play, Beckett's first, was well received at its world premiere in Paris two years ago. London playgoers, however, are wondering what Beckett can possibly write next.

QUEEN MOTHER CELEBRATES CENTENARY

2000 Celebrations have been taking place all over the country to mark the 100th birthday of Queen Elizabeth, the Queen Mother. She is the first member of the Royal Family to reach her centenary and is said to be "very pleased indeed". Many presents and cards have been delivered to Clarence House, the Queen Mother's home in London. Accompanied by Prince Charles, the Queen Mother made her way to Buckingham Palace in a horse-drawn carriage adorned with flowers. More than 40,000 well-wishers gathered to watch the Queen Mother and her daughters step onto the balcony of the Palace. This evening, the Queen Mother will attend a performance by the Kirov Ballet at the Royal Opera House in Covent Garden. And it was not just in London that the occasion was marked. A 21-gun salute was fired from the ramparts of Edinburgh Castle in Scotland, from Hillsborough Castle in Northern Ireland, and from Cardiff City Hall. And at Glorious Goodwood, a race has been named in her honour.

We draw the sword with a clear conscience and with clean hands.
Kaiser Wilhem II, in a speech in Berlin, 1914.

All over by Christmas?

1914 The system of alliances by which the nations of Europe hoped to protect themselves looks set to bring about their destruction. The latest recruit to the European conflict is Great Britain. HM government has given Germany until 11 pm GMT this evening to signal its willingness to withdraw from Belgium. Confidence is high that the war, if it comes, will be a short one and will possibly be over by Christmas.

Human bull-board

1987 Luis Reina, a hard-up bullfighter from Extremadura in Spain, is having to fend off attacks from an unexpected quarter. By agreeing to advertise the name of the Japanese electronics giant, Akai, on his embroidered matador suit, Reina has brought a deluge of criticism from grizzled aficionados who regard the move as degrading to the art of bullfighting. For professional matadors, advertising spells financial survival in a game that offers handsome rewards only to the top 30 or so "artists". Reina received £10,000 ($18,500) today for promoting the Akai name. If other large companies follow Akai's lead, few matadors in Reina's league are likely to refuse the lucrative contracts.

Brilliant Owens blows Aryan myth

1936 The German Chancellor Adolf Hitler today turned his back on a living refutation of his theory of Aryan superiority. As 23-year-old black American athlete Jesse Owens was acknowledging the cheers of the vast crowd after his gold-medal triumph in the 200 metres final of the 11th Olympiad, the disgruntled Führer left the stadium. The multi-talented Owens has turned the Führer's rascist philosophy on its head by winning a gold in the 100 metres, 200 metres and the long jump. A fourth gold medal, in the 4 x 100 metres relay, is almost a certainty, too. After the long jump, in which Owens smashed the world record, Hitler privately congratulated silver medallist German Lutz Long, ignoring the American. The Führer's pique at having a "black mercenary" – the name given to Owens and his fellow black Americans by propaganda minister Josef Goebbels – threaten his party to glorify the Third Reich is not spoiling the genial American athlete's fun, however. He is revelling in the warmth of the Berlin crowd and his own hard-earned achievements.

1729 Death of Thomas Newcomen, the Englishman who invented the first automatic steam engine.

1792 Death of Lord North, British prime minister 1770-82, during which time his vacillation led to the loss of the American colonies.

1861 National income tax is introduced in the US, initially to fund the Civil War.

1895 Death of Friedrich Engels, German political theorist and co-author of *The Communist Manifesto.*

1914 The first electric traffic lights are installed in Cleveland, Ohio.

1979 British prime minister Margaret Thatcher says that rebel leaders in Rhodesia must hold talks.

1984 Welsh-born actor Richard Burton, twice husband of Elizabeth Taylor, dies of a stroke at his home in Switzerland.

1990 President Bush sends US marines into Liberia, capital of Monrovia, to evacuate American nationals and protect the US embassy.

1990 Iraq claims that its troops have begun withdrawing from Kuwait.

Oh brother!

1100 Henry I, the youngest son of William the Conqueror, was crowned in Westminster Abbey today, three days after the death of his brother, William Rufus, in a hunting accident in the New Forest. The 31-year-old monarch is not the rightful heir to the throne of England – that distinction belongs to Robert Curthose, Henry's elder brother, who is currently away on the First Crusade. He is not expected to return until some time next year. Observers believe that Henry will try to buy off his brother, probably by offering his own territories in Normandy – Robert already possesses much of Normandy in addition to the region of Maine – and a generous annuity. In an attempt to influence opinion in his favour, Henry has announced plans to issue a charter of liberties to end unfair taxation, the confiscation of Church revenues and other abuses perpetrated by his late brother.

> *Everybody has a right to pronounce foreign names as he chooses.*
> **Winston Churchill**, 1951.

1958 The nuclear-powered submarine *Nautilus*, under Commander William R. Anderson, has completed an historic 2000-mile (3200-km) underwater journey from Point Barrow in Alaska to the Greenland Sea. The 319-ft (97 m) craft passed directly under the North Pole during its five-day voyage. The achievement makes an appropriate finale to the 1957-8 International Geophysical Year.

US-UK LINK-UP

1858 The completion today of the world's first transatlantic telegraph cable is a dream come true for American financier Cyrus West Field, 39, who has sunk his considerable financial resources and mental energies into this monumental project. The cable, which runs between Ireland and Newfoundland, was laid jointly by the naval vessels USS *Niagara* and HMS *Agamemnon*. Later this month Queen Victoria and US President Buchanan will inaugurate the line by exchanging messages.

Sir Alec Guinness dies at 86

2000 One of Britain's most famous film actors, Sir Alec Guinness, has died at the age of 86. Sir Alec first made his name with classical roles in London theatre, but in a career which spanned nearly 70 years, he played comedy, tragedy and farce. His performances spanned a wide range of roles – from adaptations of the novels of Charles Dickens to blockbuster films such as *Star Wars*. He was always in demand during the 1950s, 60s and 70s, and built a close working relationship with British director, the late Sir David Lean, who directed him in *Lawrence of Arabia*. Sir Alec won an Oscar for his performance as the British colonel in another cinema classic, *The Bridge on the River Kwai*.

BIRTHDAYS

Edward John Eyre 1815, English explorer, colonial administrator, and Governor of Jamaica who discovered Lake Eyre

Guy de Maupassant 1850, French short story writer and novelist, who wrote *Boule de Suif* and *Bel Ami*.

John Huston 1906, American film director whose films include *The Maltese Falcon* and *The African Queen*.

Harold Holt 1908, Australian prime minister from 1966-7 who backed US intervention in Vietnam and sent Australian troops to fight there.

Jacquetta Hawkes 1910, English archaeologist, author of *A Land*.

Neil Armstrong 1930, American astronaut and the first man on the moon.

1497 Italian-born English explorer John Cabot returns to London after discovering what he thinks is Asia but what is in fact Cape Breton Island off the coast of Canada.

1623 Death of Anne Hathaway, William Shakespeare's wife.

1806 Holy Roman Emperor Francis II abdicates.

1890 The electric chair is used for the first time, to execute murderer William Kemmler in New York.

1962 Jamaica becomes independent after being ruled by the British for 300 years.

1962 Ugandan dictator Idi Amin throws 50,000 Asians out of Uganda.

1970 Members of the anarchist group of "Yippies" gather in Disneyland where, cheering for Ho Chi Minh and Charles Manson, they raise the Viet Cong flag on Tom Sawyer's Island.

1988 The Russian ballerina Natalia Makarova dances with the Kirov Ballet for the first time since she defected 18 years previously and gains a 35-minute standing ovation for her performance as Odette in *Swan Lake*.

2003 Gene Robinson becomes the first openly gay bishop in the Anglican communion.

BIRTHDAYS

Alfred, Lord Tennyson 1809, English poet famous for "The Lady of Shalott" and "The Charge of the Light Brigade".

Alexander Fleming 1881, Scottish scientist who discovered penicillin at St Mary's Hospital, London in 1928.

Charles Crichton 1910, English film director who directed *The Lavender Hill Mob* and other Ealing comedies and, 30 years later, *A Fish Called Wanda*.

Lucille Ball 1911, American comedienne who starred in the series *I Love Lucy*.

Robert Mitchum 1917, American actor who starred in *The Enemy Below*, *Cape Fear*, *The Longest Day* and many other films.

ATOM BOMB WIPES OUT HIROSHIMA

1945 At around 8.15 this morning an atomic bomb, dubbed "Little Boy", was released by a B-29 of the US Air Force, the Enola Gay, above the central Japanese city of Hiroshima. Two-thirds of the city has been destroyed and at least 140,000 people have been killed. Few people in the immediate vicinity of the epicentre are thought to have survived the blast. US President Harry Truman was made aware of the bomb's destructive capabilities three weeks ago. His decision to use it was made in the face of a terrible conundrum: how to end World War II. The Japanese military are committed to a fight-to-the-death policy and it would take a further half million American lives to force them into surrender by conventional means.

US woman smashes Channel record

1926 Sports star Gertrude Ederle put in a record swim today in a larger pool than she's used to – the English Channel. The 20-year-old New Yorker, the Olympic gold medallist (1924) and women's freestyle world record-holder for distances from 100 to 880 yards, completed the 35 miles (56 km) that separate Cap Gris-Nez and Dover in a lung-bursting 14 hours 31 minutes. The first woman to swim the Channel, she has dealt a blow to male pride by bettering the 51-year-old record, held by Englishman Matthew Webb, by 1 hour 59 minutes. Miss Ederle, a leading exponent of the eight-beat crawl (eight kicks for each full stroke with the arm), is now set to retire.

> *I am become death, the destroyer of worlds.*
> **Robert J. Oppenheimer**, nuclear physicist who developed the atom bomb, quoting Vishnu, 1945.

BLYTH SPIRIT OVERCOMES ALL

1971 A gauntlet of 200 yachts and an enthusiastic crowd greeted the return to the Hamble of round-the-world yachtsman Chay Blyth today. The 30,000 mile (48,000 km) voyage took Blyth just 292 days – beating the existing record by 21 days – although he was sailing east to west, against the prevailing winds instead of with them. The 31-year-old former paratrooper is no stranger to sea adventure - five years ago, he and fellow para John Ridgway rowed across the Atlantic. Looking tanned and fit after his voyage, Blyth said he would not do it again, even with a crew. Twice he had been almost swept overboard from the 59-ft (18 m) all-steel ketch *British Steel*, and for much of the voyage he sailed without the benefit of the self-steering gear, which had been broken in a storm. The physical hazards were accompanied by equally daunting mental struggles. Worst of these were flights of fantasy. Blyth puts his survival down to his sense of humour – "The worse the situation, the funnier I find it", he says.

BRITISH STEEL

Brush with death

1660 The death was announced in Madrid today of the Spanish court painter Diego Velazquez. He was 61. Señor Velazquez fell ill shortly after returning to the capital from a trip to France to arrange the decoration of the Spanish pavilion for the marriage of the Infanta Maria Teresa and the French king Louis XIV. Velazquez first came to the attention of Philip IV at the age of 24. The king was so pleased with the Sevillian's portrait of him that he vowed never to allow another to paint him. Philip had a key to Velazquez's workshop and is said to have dropped in almost every day to watch him at work. Velazquez was also responsible for buying paintings and antiques for the King and hiring artists to decorate the interiors of the royal apartments. The freshness and naturalness evident in his later paintings of the royal family set a new standard in portraiture.

1962 Film star Marilyn Monroe, 36, was found dead in the bedroom of her Hollywood home early yesterday morning. She had taken an overdose of Nembutal and chloral hydrate pills. Monroe had a history of sleeping problems and the overdose may have been accidental. Two months ago 20th Century Fox fired her for absenteeism from the set of *Something's Got to Give*.

Say bye bye to little sooty sweeps

1840 The British Parliament has passed a law forbidding the indenturing of child sweeps. Supporters of the bill have waged an emotive campaign against the practice, citing the appalling conditions in which climbing boys live and work. In addition to the risk of serious accident and misshapen limbs from climbing chimneys, the boys are also liable to suffer respiratory disease and cancer of the groin as a result of the fumes and soot. Some masters, it is claimed, deliberately starve their lads to keep them undersized, and reluctant climbing boys are driven up narrow flues by pricking or scorching the soles of their feet. Until an efficent sweeping machine is patented, however, there is every likelihood of the trade continuing unabated, especially if the new law is not strictly enforced.

1556 A UFO appears above Basle in Switzerland.

1830 Louis Philippe is proclaimed King of France on the abdication of Charles X.

1888 A killer, "Jack the Ripper" murders a London prostitute.

1913 American aviator Samuel Cody becomes Britain's first air fatality when his plane crashes at Farnborough.

1926 At the first British Grand Prix motor-race, held at Brooklands, the average speed of the winning car is 71.61 mph (115.24 kph).

1929 The Graf-Zeppelin airship takes off for a planned trip around the world.

1931 Legendary jazz pianist, trumpeter, cornet player and composer Bix Beiderbecke dies of pneumonia and alcoholism, aged only 28.

1938 Death of Konstantin Stanislavsky, the influential Russian theatre director, actor and teacher who founded the Moscow Art Theatre in 1898 and pioneered "method" acting.

Central cooling

1987 The leaders of Nicaragua, El Salvador, Guatemala, Honduras and Costa Rica signed a 14-page peace plan in Guatemala City today which aims to settle 10-year-old conflict in the region. The plan, the brainchild of Costa Rica's dynamic young president Oscar Arias, calls for a cease-fire in Nicaragua, El Salvador and Guatemala, an end to all foreign involvement in the region's affairs, including US sponsorship of the Nicaraguan Contra guerrillas, and an amnesty for political prisoners.

US embassies in Africa bombed

1998 At least 200 people have been killed and over 1,000 injured in explosions at the US embassies in Kenya and Tanzania, which took place within minutes of each other. No one has claimed responsibility for the blasts but US officials believe the attacks were the work of Osama bin Laden, an Islamic Muslim fundamentalist. The first blast occurred in the Tanzanian capital Dar es Salaam and caused widespread devastation, destroying the reception area of the embassy. The second, five minutes later, was in Nairobi, the capital of Kenya. The explosion demolished a five-storey office block, which crashed down onto the embassy next door. The US embassy was badly damaged and its bomb-proof doors ripped off. Two passing buses were also wrecked. Volunteers have worked hard to pull survivors from the rubble and cranes are freeing those who are trapped.

No more fine messes

1957 Oliver Hardy, the fat one in the Laurel and Hardy comic-duo, died of a stroke today, aged 65. Born in Harlem, Georgia, Ollie (real name Norvell) stumbled into films by chance after a series of career failures, including law and medicine. He made little headway in Hollywood until in 1927 producer Hal Roach teamed him with British-born ex-Vaudeville trooper Stan Laurel (Arthur Stanley Jefferson) in a comedy short, *Putting Pants on Philip*. From the start there was never any argument between the two men, despite Laurel's insistence on earning twice as much as his partner. While Laurel would spend hours rewriting scripts and involve himself in directing their films, the easygoing Hardy would head for the race track or golf course. The creativity that Laurel brought to the partnership was matched by Hardy's ineffable presence on screen, however. Laurel, now 67, is reportedly devastated by news of Hardy's death.

1987 In an unexpected move, Dr David Owen announced his resignation yesterday as leader of Britain's Social Democratic Party. The decision comes in the wake of his party's vote for merger with the Liberal Party. Dr Owen, one of the original "Gang of Four" who abandoned the Labour Party to set up the SDP in 1981, is vehemently opposed to such a union. A breakaway Social Democratic party with Dr Owen at the helm is on the cards, although the idea of a fourth political party is being ridiculed as pie in the sky.

BIRTHDAYS

Billy Burke 1885, American actress who is known for her role as Glinda the Good Fairy in the film *The Wizard of Oz*.

Louis Leakey 1903, Kenyan paleontologist who uncovered crucial evidence of man's early evolution, including a 1,750,000-year-old skull.

Ralph Johnson Bunche 1904, American diplomat who became the first Black American to hold an important position in the State Department, helped found the UN and won the Nobel Peace Prize for negotiating the 1949 Arab-Israeli truce.

Roland Kirk 1936, American saxophonist, flautist and composer who could produce a three-part harmony by playing three saxophones simultaneously.

Walter Swinburne 1961, Irish jockey who won the Derby in 1981 on Shergar.

117 Hadrian becomes emperor of Rome after the death of Trajan.

1576 Work begins in Denmark on the first purpose-built observatory.

1588 The Spanish Armada is finally defeated by the British.

1834 Britain introduces workhouses for the poor.

1900 The first Davis Cup tennis tournament begins at Brookline, Massachusetts.

1944 Hitler has four top men hung by piano wire for attempting to assassinate him.

1958 Seventeen-year old British singer Cliff Richard is signed to Columbia records.

1963 The US, Britain and the USSR sign the nuclear Test Ban Treaty in the Kremlin.

1964 At a Rolling Stones concert in The Hague in Holland riots break out and two girls get their clothes torn off.

1973 American vice-president Spiro Agnew goes under investigation for tax evasion.

1991 British journalist John McCarthy is freed by the Lebanese terrorist group who have been holding him hostage.

BIRTHDAYS

Marjorie Kinnan Rawlings 1896, American author who wrote *The Yearling*.

Ernest Lawrence 1901, American physicist who invented the first subatomic particle accelerator and the colour television picture tube and won the Nobel Prize for physics in 1939.

Jimmy Witherspoon 1911, American blues singer.

Dino De Laurentis 1919, American producer of *La Strada* and many other films.

Esther Williams 1923, American actress and former champion swimmer.

Dustin Hoffman 1937, American actor whose films include *Midnight Cowboy*, *The Graduate* and *Rain Man*.

Nigel Mansell 1954, British motor-racing champion.

Let us begin by committing ourselves to the truth, to see it like it is and to tell it like it is, to find the truth, to speak the truth and live with the truth. That's what we'll do.

Richard Milhous Nixon, nomination speech, 1968.

Train robbers net millions

1963 In one of the most audacious hold-ups of all time, thieves have got away with an estimated £2.5 million ($4.6 million) in unused, and therefore untraceable, bank notes from a night mail train travelling between Glasgow and London. The hijack was executed at about 3 am this morning. The robbers, masked and wearing combat fatigues, brought the high-security train to a halt at Sears Crossing in Buckinghamshire, by tampering with the signalling system. The engine and first two coaches were uncoupled and taken further down the track where the contents of the so-called High Value Package coach were offloaded into waiting vehicles. Driver Jack Mills offered resistance and was beaten over the head with a length of lead piping. The Post Office has offered a £10,000 ($18,500) reward for information leading to an arrest.

1844 The Mormon Church is slowly gathering itself in the aftermath of the death of founder Joseph Smith, at the hands of an Illinois mob on June 17. The man who has emerged to take Smith's place is Brigham Young, named third of the Quorum of the Twelve Apostles in 1835. The major task on Young's agenda is to find the sect a safe place to settle.

MONT BLANC CONQUERED

1786 Mont Blanc, at 15,771 ft (4807 m) the tallest peak in Europe outside the Caucasus, has been conquered at last. Twenty-five years ago a scientist from Geneva named Horace Benedict de Saussure offered prize money for the first ascent of this glory in the alpine chain. The prize has been claimed by a local man, Doctor Michel Gabriel Paccard of Chamonix, who completed the climb with his porter, Jacques Balmat.

The swizzles of Oz

1991 The scandal that led to the downfall of the National Party in the Queensland elections two years ago looks set to reach its denouement with the trial next month of 80-year-old ex-premier Sir Joh Bjelke-Petersen. Last week the state's former police chief, Sir Terence Lewis, was jailed after being found guilty on 15 charges of corruption. Sir Joh, a Bible-thumping free marketeer, is alleged to have received bribes and later perjured himself when giving evidence before the enquiry set up to allay public fears about corruption in the state. A four-year investigation has led to charges being brought against 213 people, including former National Party ministers as well as businessmen, policemen and judges.

Nixon quits

1974 Richard Nixon made history today as the first US president to resign his office. In an emotional television address to the nation, Mr Nixon admitted to errors of judgement which he said demanded that he stand down. Only four days ago the beleaguered president was forced to own up to his complicity in the break-in by members of his re-election committee to the Democratic Party Committee's HQ in the Watergate building, Washington, in June 1972. Evidence of political espionage and a dirty tricks campaign against his opponents had been mounting. The resignation will take effect as of noon tomorrow, when Nixon's deputy, Gerald Ford, will be sworn in as the 38th president of the United States.

> *If God wanted us to walk round naked, we would have been born that way.*
>
> **Anon** – Brighton's nudist beach opened today, 1979.

Creek tragedy

1814 A settlement of the dispute between the US government and the Creek Indians was formally concluded today with the signing of the Treaty of Fort Jackson. Under the terms of the treaty the Indians are to lose 23 million acres (9.3 million hectares) of land, comprising over half of Alabama and part of southern Georgia, to the US. The war flared up last August with the Creeks' fears about losing traditional hunting grounds to white settlers. Their first foray ended in the massacre of frontierspeople at Fort Mims, on the lower Alabama River. The response from the US authorities was swift. A 5000-strong militia under General Andrew Jackson wiped out two Indian villages and this spring, at the Battle of Horseshoe Bend, killed more than 800 warriors and took 500 women and children prisoner. The Indians' campaign was chaotic, for at no time were all 50 Creek towns united in aim, and some towns chose to fight with the US. Unfortunately, the punishment meted out to the Creeks is not selective and affects the many who supported Jackson.

1945 An atomic bomb identical to the one released by the US Air Force over the Japanese city of Hiroshima on August 6 has been exploded over Nagasaki. Fifty per cent of the city's area has been destroyed. The original target, Kokura, had to be abandoned when bad weather prevented the location of the aim point.

1974 Gerald R. Ford today became the first American president ever to take office without being chosen by the American people in a national election. The 38th president turned down offers to become a professional footballer to go to Michigan University then Yale Law School. He served in the navy in World War Two and was elected in 1949 as a Republican to the House of Representatives, and began his political career.

Real-life drama

1967 The bizarre life of playwright Joe Orton, 34, came to a bizarre end today. In a tiny Islington bedsit, police found Orton with his skull smashed in and his flatmate Kenneth Halliwell, 40, dead from an overdose. A note, written by Halliwell, was discovered nearby; it read, "If you read his diary all will be explained". Orton shot to fame in 1964 with the success of his first play, *Entertaining Mr Sloane*. This was followed in 1966 by *Loot*. Orton's unique brand of anarchic humour both shocked and entertained audiences. In his personal life, too, Orton cocked a snook at conventional morality and revelled in the danger of anonymous sexual encounters in public lavatories.

GRACE STUMPED BY HOBBS

1930 Surrey and England batsman Jack Hobbs notched up another milestone in his illustrious career today by scoring even more runs than cricketing giant W. G. Grace. In a perfectly judged 40 against Middlesex at the Kennington Oval, London, Hobbs overtook the great doctor's aggregate record of 54,896 runs. Five years ago Hobbs broke another of W. G. Grace's records, by exceeding 125 centuries. Hobbs is so thrilled that he intends inscribing his bat as a reminder of his historic achievement today.

BRIGHTON BEAUTIFUL

1979 Councillors in the Sussex seaside town of Brighton have caused a furore by agreeing to allow naturists to bare all on one of the less popular beaches in the borough. Opponents of the scheme fear that the designated area, Cliff Beach, which lies just below the Kemp Town area of Brighton, will attract all sorts of undesirables. Britain's 20,000 or so naturists, however, warmly welcome the move. Those of a nervous disposition need venture no further than the sign at the perimeter of the beach which gently points out that "Clothes Need Not Be Worn Beyond This Notice".

1653 Maarten Harpertzoon Tromp, the Dutch admiral who fought against Spain and England, is killed after a battle with the English fleet off the Dutch coast.

1794 General Napoleon Bonaparte is arrested in France on suspicion of Robespierrism.

1867 John Harrison Surratt is arrested as an alleged conspirator in the assassination of American president Abraham Lincoln.

1902 After a six-week delay due to an emergency appendectomy, 64-year-old Edward VII is crowned king of England.

1919 Death of Ruggiero Leoncavallo, Italian composer best known for the opera *I Pagliacci*.

1942 Mahatma Gandhi is arrested in Britain for his "Quit India" campaign, which demands that the British should immediately withdraw from India.

1965 Singapore is separated from Malaysia and becomes an independent state within the Commonwealth of Nations.

1975 Death of the Russian composer Dmitri Shostakovich, who wrote his first symphony at the age of 18.

BIRTHDAYS

Thomas Telford 1757, famous Scottish bridge engineer best known for his construction of the suspension bridge over the Menai Straits.

Leonide Massine 1896, Russian ballet dancer and choreographer who created more than 50 ballets for Diaghilev's Ballets Russes.

Solomon Cutner 1902, British pianist who performed at the proms when he was only eight years old.

Robert Aldrich 1918, American film director whose films include *Whatever Happened To Baby Jane?* and *The Dirty Dozen*.

Philip Larkin 1922, British poet who wrote *The Whitsun Weddings* and *High Windows*.

Rod Laver 1938, Australian tennis star who won the singles at Wimbledon four times.

843 A.D. The Treaty of Verdun divides the Frankish empire.

1675 The foundation stone of the Royal Observatory in Greenwich, London, is laid by King Charles II.

1846 The Smithsonian Institution for scientific research is established in Washington with a bequest from English scientist James Smithson.

1885 The first Promenade Concert, organized by Sir Henry Wood, is held at Queens Hall in London.

1896 Otto Lillenthal, the German aviation pioneer, dies after a glider crash which occurred yesterday.

1889 The screw bottle top is patented at the Hope Glass Works near Barnsley, Yorkshire, England.

1913 The Treaty of Bucharest is signed, ending the second Balkan War and partitioning Macedonia between Serbia, Greece, Romania and Bulgaria.

1961 Britain applies to join the EEC.

1964 Mick Jagger of the Rolling Stones is fined £32 ($59) for driving a car with no insurance in Liverpool.

1966 The first American moon satellite, Orbiter I, is launched.

BIRTHDAYS

Count (Camillo Benso) Cavour 1810, Italian statesman who played a large role in the unification of Italy and became prime minister in the new kingdom.

Aleksander Konstantinovich Glazunov 1865, Russian composer who was a pupil of Rimsky-Korsakov but whose symphonies, concertos and chamber and ballet music were influenced by Wagner and Liszt more than his Russian heritage.

Herbert Hoover 1874, American Republican president 1929-33 with a belief in individual freedom that led him to reject federal relief for unemployment during the Depression and lost him the 1932 election to Franklin D. Roosevelt.

HarmonIOUs

1788 August 10 seems a propitious day for Wolfgang Amadeus Mozart. Last year on this day the prolific Salzburg-born composer completed *Eine Kleine Nachtmusik*, a tuneful little piece, and today he finished his "Jupiter" symphony. Despite his almost constant composing, however – three complete symphonies since June 26 this year – and his appointment as Kammermusicus to write music for court balls, the 32-year-old Mozart is deeply in debt with no relief in sight.

Sharon Tate butchered

1969 Beautiful film actress Sharon Tate was found brutally murdered at her Hollywood home today. The bodies of four other people were also found at the rented house in Cielo Avenue, which Miss Tate shared with her husband, director Roman Polanski. He has cut short his trip to England, where he has been finishing a film. Miss Tate was eight-and-a-half months pregnant with the couple's first child.

1792 In a virtual re-run of the storming of the Bastille some three years ago, members of a new revolutionary Commune attacked the Tuileries this morning. In the forefront of the attack were the Bretons and Marseillais. The royal family has fled for protection to the Legislative Assembly, with no guarantee of safety.

US whitewash

1900 Torrential rain brought the first international tennis competition, the Davis Cup, to a premature close at Longwood, Boston, today. The United States held an unassailable 3-0 lead over the challengers, Great Britain, when the match was abandoned. The three-day competition is the brainchild of US doubles champion Dwight Davis, who has also donated the tournament trophy, a massive gold-lined solid silver punchbowl valued at $1,000 (£544). The winning team comprised Davis himself, M. D. Whitman and Holcombe Ward. With the three top British players unavailable, Arthur Gore, Ernest Black and H. Roper Barrett could only struggle manfully against seemingly overwhelming odds. These included a heat-wave on the first two days, grass twice as long as they are used to in England, a net that sagged 2-3 inches (5-7.5 cm) and tennis balls likened to "animated egg-plums".

Acid killer's ultimate price

1949 John George Haigh, 39, the infamous "acid bath" murderer, was executed in Wandsworth Prison today. Haigh confessed to nine murders after police found traces of a victim, Mrs Olive Durand-Deacon, 69, at his factory in Crawley, Sussex.

The self-styled engineer had shot Mrs Durand-Deacon for her valuables before putting her corpse in a 40-gallon (182-litre) drum which he then filled with sulphuric acid. By the time the police searched the factory, all that was left of the wealthy widow was an acrylic plastic denture. This was identified by Mrs Durand-Deacon's dentist, enabling the police to charge Haigh with her murder.

MARY'S ZOLA ECLIPSE

1984 Mary Decker, America's golden girl of athletics who was double-gold medallist at last year's world championships in Helsinki, crashed out of today's 3000 metre Olympics final in Los Angeles. The catastrophe came when she tripped over the leg of barefoot runner Zola Budd, the South African recently given UK citizenship in order to represent Britain in the Games. Budd was disqualified instantly by referee Andy Bakjian. His decision was later overturned by an eight-member jury who, after studying film of the race, ruled that 18-year-old Budd was not to blame – the accident had occurred because of Decker's "aggressive tactics".

Jackson Pollock killed

1956 Avant-garde artist Jackson Pollock was killed today when his car hit a tree near East Hampton, New York. He was 44. Pollock was recognized as a major talent, although recognition in some quarters was accompanied by derision in others. His search for a process by which he could transfer his personality into his art led him to develop "drip painting" – pouring paint on to a flat canvas in a seemingly haphazard manner. According to Pollock, this demanded a great deal of mental preparation first. Pollock the man was plagued by alcoholism and psychiatric problems for much of his adult life. Only through his art, it is said, did he achieve equilibrium.

1519 Johann Tetzel has died in Leipzig priory aged 54. Tetzel's forgiveness-for-cash career began when the Archbishop of Mainz hit on it as a way of raising money for the rebuilding of St Peter's in Rome. Tetzel saw nothing wrong in peddling indulgences, defending the practice in 50 theses.

HEATH TAKES THE HELM

1971 British PM Edward Heath proved his abilities as a team captain at sea today by leading the British contingent to victory in the 605-mile (973-km) Fastnet race for the Admiral's Cup. Heath, 55, will need all his skills at the political rudder if he is to steer his government's policy on Northern Ireland into calmer waters. So far the introduction of emergency powers enabling the army to round up 300 IRA suspects and intern them without trial has produced an escalation rather than a reduction in violence in the province.

1853 A French protectorate is established in Cambodia, following years of attacks by the Thais and Vietnamese.

1930 England goes broke – America and France each lend £25 million ($46 million), while US bankers extend another £60 million ($111 million).

1932 US president Herbert Hoover says it is time to scrap Prohibition.

1942 Russian composer Shostakovich's *Leningrad Symphony* is premiered in Leningrad by a half-starved orchestra, many of whose members had just returned from the Russian front-line.

1952 Crown Prince Hussein of Jordan is named successor to his schizophrenic father King Talal.

1962 Chad becomes independent from France.

1965 Violent race riots begin in the Watts area of Los Angeles.

1990 Forty Britons and five Irish people trapped in Kuwait by the Iraqi invasion celebrate their freedom after a dash across the desert in a convoy of four-wheel drive vehicles.

BIRTHDAYS

Richard Meade 1673, English physician to royalty and pioneer of preventative medicine.

Mary Roberts Rinehart 1876, American thriller writer whose books include *Haunted Lady* and *The Circular Staircase*.

Hugh MacDairmid 1892, Scottish dialect poet and founder of the Scottish National Party.

Enid Blyton 1897, British author of children's books and creator of "Noddy", the "Famous Five" and the "Secret Seven".

Alex Haley 1921, American author of *Roots*, which traced his ancestors from Africa to slavery and was made into a major television film.

Anna Massey 1935, English stage and screen actress who has made telling appearances in films such as *Bunny Lake Is Missing*.

The jockey knight dismounts

1954 Sir Gordon Richards, the king of flat race jockeys, announced his retirement yesterday. The decision was expected after the severe injuries he suffered at Sandown Park last month when his mount, the Queen's filly Abergeldie, threw him as they were leaving the parade ring. The fall left Sir Gordon with a broken pelvis and several cracked ribs. In his 38-year career, the diminutive Richards, 50, rode a staggering 4869 winners. He was champion jockey 26 times. The Derby, the world's most prestigious flat race, eluded him until his twenty-eighth and final attempt, when he romped home on Pinza. He was knighted in June 1953, the first jockey to be so honoured.

Abstract painting is abstract. It confronts you. There was a reviewer a while back who wrote that my pictures didn't have any beginning or any end. He didn't mean it as a compliment, but it was. It was a fine compliment.
Jackson Pollock, the innovative abstract artist who died today, 1956.

Diesel overheats

1893 The attempt by eminent German engineer Rudolf Diesel to devise a heat engine has once more almost cost him his life. In Augsburg yesterday, Diesel's latest model generated 80 atmospheres, the highest mechanically created pressure ever recorded, before the indicator plate exploded, narrowly missing the 35-year-old engineer's head. Despite this setback, Diesel plans to have a revised engine ready in six months. Diesel has spent 12 years developing his engine that can be adapted to suit all industrial requirements, including those of large-scale manufacturers. In 1888 Diesel was almost killed when the ammonia gas he was testing as a fuel for the engine exploded.

Steel man's gold heart

1919 Andrew Carnegie, the steel baron with a heart of gold, has died at his home in Lennox, Massachusetts. He was 84. The Carnegie family moved from Scotland to the US in 1848. Andrew joined the Penn Railway Co. and worked his way up to Superintendent. He first struck oil on his own land and in business invested in iron manufactures. By the turn of the century 25 per cent of steel output in the USA was produced by Carnegie-owned companies. In 1901 Carnegie retired. In his lifetime he set aside $350 million (£189 million) for philanthropic purposes. Foundations such as the Carnegie Corporation of New York will ensure he is not forgotten.

1791 African slaves in Santo Domingo, in the east of the island of Hispaniola, mount a violent revolt against plantation owners.

1848 Death of George Stephenson, who invented the steam locomotive "Rocket".

1883 The last of the quaggas dies in Amsterdam zoo.

1907 Prince Borghese of Italy wins the Paris-Peking motor race, having travelled 8,000 miles (12,874 km) in 62 days.

1955 Death of German novelist Thomas Mann, whose books include *Death in Venice* and *The Magic Mountain*.

1959 Parents and children in Arkansas riot over racial segregation in schools.

1960 Communications satellite Echo is launched at Cape Canaveral.

1964 Ian Fleming, the man who created secret agent James Bond 007, dies of heart failure.

1964 Great Train Robber Charlie Wilson escapes from jail.

1980 The first giant panda born in captivity is delivered safely at a zoo in Mexico.

1983 In Santiago, Chile, 17 people are killed in a demonstration against military dictator General Pinochet.

2000 Russian nuclear submarine *Kursk* sinks during training in the Barents Sea. After nine days of confusion and misinformation, an international rescue attempt to save the 118 crew proves too late.

BIRTHDAYS

George IV 1762, English king whose dissipation, extravagance and cruelty towards his wife Caroline of Brunswick undermined the popularity of the monarchy.

Robert Southey 1774, English poet and writer, close associate of Wordsworth and Coleridge.

Cecil B. De Mille 1881, American film director, legendary for large-scale Biblical epics such as *The Ten Commandments*.

Mark Knopfler 1949, British guitarist with Dire Straits.

FORD JUMPSTARTS MASS MOTORING

1908 The car which some are predicting will revolutionize motoring started rolling out of the factory today. The car in question is the Model T from the Ford Motor Company, a sturdy black four-cylinder number that comes in two versions, tourer and roadster. Both are retailing at incredibly low prices: the roadster at $825 (£445) and the tourer for just $25 (£13) more. The key to Ford's low pricing policy is volume production. The company intends concentrating its manufacturing muscle on the Model T, enabling it to utilize standardized parts and employ an assembly-line method of production. The new car represents a gamble for company president Henry Ford. Such is his faith in the Model T and the concept of motoring for all that he has parted company with Ford's erstwhile major backer, Detroit coal dealer Alexander Y. Malcolmson, who favoured an expensive car as the next project for investment.

Truth will out

1990 The Communist Chinese government's attempt to restore its tarnished image after the slaughter in Tienanmen Square has received a severe setback. The riots which broke out last March in the Tibetan capital Lhasa were brought under control relatively painlessly, according to Beijing. Official documentation of the disturbances now reveal that more than 450 were killed, the majority by bullets, 750 injured and 3000 detained. More embarrassing still for Beijing is the revelation that the riots were provoked by members of the People's Armed Police. Dressed as Tibetans, these *agents provocateurs* attacked and burned shops, offices and food stores, providing the authorities with the excuse they needed for cracking down on a native population whose resentment against Chinese rule was reaching boiling point.

> *Tiger! Tiger! burning bright*
> *In the forests of the night,*
> *What immortal hand or eye*
> *Could frame thy fearful symmetry?*
> **William Blake**, English poet
> and artist, dies, 1827.

At the cutting edge of hi-tech

1877 Thomas Edison, the 30-year-old wizard of new technology, is on the brink of developing his first wholly original invention. A small group of people at Edison's "invention factory" at Menlo Park, New Jersey, to witness a public demonstration of the new device – a phonograph – which records the human voice. They listened dumbfounded to a recording of Edison reciting "Mary had a little lamb". The phonograph has been ingeniously adapted from the telegraph repeater: a telephone diaphragm connects to an embossing needle which impresses on a suitable material the variations of the human voice.

1865 During an operation at Glasgow Royal Infirmary today British surgeon Joseph Lister, 38, demonstrated a method of preventing infection of an operation wound. It involves the use of carbolic acid as an antiseptic to protect the patient against microorganisms. Lister hopes that his method will lead to a drop in the current 50 per cent mortality rate among amputation cases.

Mystery of Cabinet suicide

1822 The British foreign secretary, Lord Castlereagh, slit his throat tonight with a penknife. He was 53. Despite holding the portfolio for foreign affairs, Castlereagh received much of the blame for the repressive policy in home affairs presided over by the prime minister, the Earl of Liverpool. He had a hard time of foreign policy matters, too, with few Cabinet colleagues understanding his aim of maintaining a balance of power between the leading European nations. Severe in manner and a poor public speaker, Castlereagh was always unpopular. It is unclear, however, whether political problems caused him to take his life. Some sources suggest that he may have committed suicide rather than face exposure for sexual misconduct.

Blake's heaven

1827 British artist and poet William Blake has died. He studied as a young man under Joshua Reynolds and became an illustrator, portraying Biblical scenes with prophetic vision. He did not receive recognition until his final years with works such as *Milton* and *Jerusalem*.

Soap artist dies

1896 Sir John Everett Millais, the President of the Royal Academy, died today. He was 67. An infant prodigy, Millais caused a scandal in 1850 with his painting *Christ in the House of His Parents*. The art-loving public was outraged by the artist's realistic depiction of the Holy Family and especially by the revelation that the initials "PRB" stood for Pre-Raphaelite Brotherhood, a group of artists who considered their work to be superior to that of Raphael and all who succeeded him. Millais soon turned his back on the Brotherhood. He eventually married Effie Ruskin, after the annulment of her six-year union with impotent art critic and Brotherhood member John Ruskin. Millais was reputedly the highest-paid painter in history. Ten years ago his painting *Bubbles* was used by the soap manufacturers A. & F. Pears to advertise their products. In 1885 Millais became the first artist to receive a baronetcy.

1978 A building which served as the Beirut HQ of the Palestine Liberation Front and contained the offices of their rivals, Al-Fatah, was ripped apart by a bomb today, leaving an estimated 150 people dead. Soon after the attack the pro-Iraqi PLF accused the pro-Syrian Popular Front of the Liberation of Palestine of attempting to annihilate its leadership. Later, however the PLF blamed "American and Israeli intelligence agents" instead.

Churchill's glory days

1704 The allied armies of the Grand Coalition won a resounding victory today over a numerically superior Franco-Bavarian force at Blenheim, north of the Danube. Led by John Churchill, Duke of Marlborough, and his "twin-captain", Eugene, Prince of Savoy, the allied army of 52,000 men mounted a surprise attack on the 56,000-strong enemy force. By the end of the afternoon the French and Bavarians had been routed, many drowning in the Danube as they attempted to escape. To add insult to the 21,000 French battle casualties, their commander, Marshall Tallard, was also captured. The Elector of Bavaria is reported to be heading for Hochstadt, leaving the encircled garrison of Blenheim to fend for itself. The victory has saved Vienna from imminent capture by the French and breathed new life into the flagging coalition. Recognition of Churchill as a soldier of genius also seems assured.

This strangely unequal painter – a painter whose imperfectly great powers always suggest to me the legend of the spiteful fairy at the christening feast. The name of Mr Millais's spiteful fairy is vulgarity.
Henry James on the painter Millais.

Ring leader released

1876 A glittering audience, including crowned heads and some of the world of music's most famous names, is expected to attend the performance in Bayreuth tonight of Richard Wagner's *Das Rheingold*. The opera, the prelude to Wagner's three-part opera cycle *Der Ring des Nibelungen*, inaugurates the new Festspielhaus, the theatre created by the 63-year-old composer to put into practice his unique concept of drama. *The Ring* took Wagner some 28 years to complete, beginning in 1848. Inspired by the composer's contempt for materialistic society, it is a realization of his belief that in opera, word, tone and drama should meld into one seamless entity. Rumour has it that the festival, which Wagner hopes will become an annual event, will be a financial, if not artistic, flop.

Bad dogs and Englishmen

1991 Britain's new Dangerous Dogs Act came into force yesterday. Under the act, fighting dogs such as the American pit bull terrier and Japanese tosa must be muzzled and leashed in public. Owners who fail to comply with the new law face a fine of £2000 ($3700) and six months' imprisonment. The British government were prompted into action by continuing public alarm at the level of dog attacks, which reached a crescendo in May when six-year-old Rucksana Khan almost died from injuries caused by a 65 lb (29 kg) pit bull terrier.

1814 The British take over the colony at the Cape of Good Hope from the Dutch.

1910 Death of nurse Florence Nightingale, the "Lady with the Lamp" during the Crimean War who transformed the appalling conditions in military hospitals and founded the nursing profession.

1915 George Joseph Smith, the "Brides in the Bath" murderer, who drowned his brides in a zinc bathtub after making sure that their finances were set up in his favour, is hanged.

1946 Death of the British novelist H. G. Wells, whose books include *The Time Machine* and *The Shape of Things to Come*.

1962 On the first anniversary of the erection of the Berlin Wall, an East-German, Peter Fechter, is shot and bleeds to death while trying to escape from the East.

1971 The American saxophonist King Curtis is stabbed to death in a fight outside his New York City apartment building.

1989 Twelve people are killed in Australia when two hot air balloons collide in the worst-ever hot air balloon disaster: one of them plunges 600 ft (182 m) to the ground.

BIRTHDAYS

Annie Oakley 1860, American markswoman who could hit the thin edge of a playing card at 30 paces.

John Logie Baird 1888, Scottish electrical engineer who invented television.

Jean Borotra 1898, the first Frenchman to win Wimbledon.

Alfred Hitchcock 1899, English film director who moved to Hollywood and directed such classics as *Psycho* and *The Birds*.

Archbishop Makarios III 1913, Cypriot churchman who became president of Cyprus 1960-77.

George Shearing 1919, British jazz pianist and composer.

Fidel Castro 1927, Cuban revolutionary who became socialist president in 1959.

1922 Death of Lord Northcliffe, founder of the *Daily Mail* and the *Daily Mirror* newspapers.

1932 Death of Rin Tin Tin, star dog from Hollywood.

1947 Pakistan becomes independent from India to satisfy the Muslim League's demand for a separate state for the Muslim minority.

1949 Konrad Adenauer becomes chancellor of West Germany.

1951 Death of Randolph Hearst, king of America's yellow press and inspiration for Orson Welles' film *Citizen Kane*.

1956 Death of Bertolt Brecht, Marxist German playwright and poet whose works include the play *Galileo* and the libretto for Kurt Weill's *The Threepenny Opera*.

1969 The first British troops enter Northern Ireland.

1980 Polish workers take over the shipyard at Gdansk in Poland.

1984 British novelist and dramatist J. B. Priestley, author of *The Good Companions*, dies at the age of 89.

1986 Benazir Bhutto, daughter of executed politician and former prime minister Zulfikar Ali Bhutto, is jailed by Pakistani dictator General Zia.

1994 Venezuelan terrorist "Carlos the Jackal" is arrested in Sudan.

2003 Blackouts cause chaos in north-east America and Canada as 50 million are without power.

BIRTHDAYS

Richard von Krafft-Ebing 1840, German psychiatrist who published his pioneering studies of sexual aberrations in *Psychopathia sexualis*.

John Galsworthy 1864, British novelist who wrote *The Forsyte Saga*.

Dave Crosby 1941, British guitarist with the Byrds and then founder member of the band Crosby, Stills and Nash.

Sarah Brightman 1961, British singer and ex-wife of Andrew Lloyd Webber, best-known for her role in his musical *Phantom of the Opera*.

All one's inventions are true, you can be sure of that. Poetry is as exact a science as geometry.
Gustave Flaubert, in a letter to Louise Colet, 1853.

BLOODSHED IN BROWNSVILLE

1906 Racial tension between soldiers and townsfolk are believed to have been responsible for the fatal shooting of a white bartender and the injuring of a white policeman in the town of Brownsville, Texas last night. Some 40 spent cartridges of a type used in the Army's Springfield rifles were found outside Fort Benson. As a result of this find, accusing fingers are being pointed at army personnel and, more specifically, at members of the three all-black companies of the 25th Infantry Regiment. The 25th Infantry Regiment arrived at Fort Benson two weeks ago. The arrival of the companies coincided with a series of minor incidents in the town, which were brought to an end by confining the soldiers to barracks. Army officials are centring their investigation into last night's violence on the men of "B" Company. The men have reportedly closed ranks and refused President Roosevelt's order that they name those responsible. The president is threatening to dismiss the entire Company unless someone breaks what he has termed "this conspiracy of silence".

"Black" Jack on a roll

1960 Jack Brabham today clinched the Formula One drivers' championship for the second year running with a sizzling win in the Portuguese Grand Prix at Oporto. "Black" Jack, as the greengrocer's son from Sydney is nicknamed, has already won five grand prix this season, at Zandvoort, Spa, Reims, Silverstone and now Oporto. His considerable driving and engineering skills have helped Cooper win their second consecutive constructors' championship. Their revolutionary lightweight rear-engined car is pointing the way ahead to other constructors. Next year will see the introduction of a limit (1.5 litres) on the size of engines in Formula One racing – and no doubt there will be more converts to the rear-engine concept, too.

Close encounters for the RAF

1956 Between 11 pm last night and 3 am this morning Royal Air Force personnel were involved in an extraordinary game of cat-and-mouse with several unidentified flying objects. One of these was tracked by ground radar and also seen with the naked eye by operators in the radar tower at RAF Lakenheath as a bright light passing overhead. An RAF pilot reported seeing the object streak beneath his aircraft. A second radar station was then alerted. After detecting a stationary target that suddenly raced northwards at 600 mph (965 kph), the second station called in an RAF fighter to investigate. The pilot made airborne radar contact with the object, only to have it move behind his fighter. Despite the pilot's best efforts, the object could not be shaken off. A second aircraft was called in, at which point the object moved off and all radar contacts were lost.

New colony goes legal

1619 The colony established in the New World in 1607 by the Virginia Company of London held its first legislative assembly in Jamestown today. The historic assembly was made possible by charters secured last year, which transferred the government of the colony from the Crown to the Company. The first of its kind in the New World, it may point the way forward to new colonies as and when they become established. Under the chairmanship of Governor Sir George Yeardley, the new assembly passed laws against drinking and gambling.

1979 The classic Fastnet Race ended in tragedy today when a Force 10 gale and mountainous seas claimed the lives of 15 sailors from competing yachts. Of the 306 yachts that lined up at the start of the race three days ago, only 177 completed the 605-mile (973 km) course; 23 sank or were abandoned and scores of others were disabled, a high number with broken rudders. Sailors had no advance warning of the severity of the storm, which changed dramatically from a bumpy but manageable Force 8 to a howling Force 10.

> *By yesterday morning British troops were patrolling the streets of Belfast. I fear that once Catholics and Protestants get used to our presence they will hate us more than they hate each other.*
> **Richard Crossman**, British politician, 1969.

Horse attitudes

1991 Tomorrow's famed Siena palio will go ahead, despite the enormous adverse publicity that the event has attracted. French film star Brigitte Bardot, a fervent animal rights campaigner, started the row when she denounced the 800-year-old horse race in Siena's medieval piazza as a cruel tradition. When the British-based World Society for the Protection of Animals echoed her criticisms, the Sienese, erroneously believing the Princess Royal to be a patron of the Society, lurched from indifference to all-out attack. The communist mayor of Siena, Pier Luigi Piccini, denounced Bardot and the Princess Royal as "publicity seekers". Film director Franco Zeffirelli joined the fray, defending the Princess and lambasting the Sienese for their "useless slaughter of the innocents". According to Buckingham Palace "the Princess has never voiced an opinion on the subject". The Sienese will fight to keep the palio and the tourism it attracts, despite allegations of routine doping and fatal injuries incurred as horses scramble to keep their footing on the cobbled stones. No one has spared a thought for the horsemen. Unlike their mounts, they are not comforted by a groom the night before the race, nor blessed in church.

1534 Former Spanish knight Ignatius Loyola today led his small band of followers to Montmartre in Paris, where they bound themselves by vows of poverty, chastity and obedience. Loyola has already appeared before the religious authorities in Spain and France to explain his unusual lifestyle. Between 1522 and his arrival in the French capital in 1528, this routinely included begging, scourging himself and spending several hours a day in prayer. The 43-year-old student now aims to study for the priesthood "to be able to help souls".

Woodstock 'n' roll

1969 An estimated 300,000 people are expected to attend the three-day Woodstock Music and Art Fair which opened at Bethel, in upstate New York, today. The outdoor rock concert has attracted many leading performers, including Jimi Hendrix, Joan Baez, Ravi Shankar, Janis Joplin, The Who and Jefferson Airplane. The thousands of young people fighting their way through the traffic jams to savour hippie culture may find the real thing a salutary experience. The hard facts of the peaceful communing are water and food shortages and large threatening clouds.

Jolly Rogers strike their flags

1967 The Marine Broadcasting Offences Bill introduced by the British Labour government looks set to sink the offshore pirate radio stations that have revolutionized broadcasting over the past few years. The bill, which comes into force today, is designed to starve the pirates of the revenue that keeps them afloat by making it illegal for British firms to advertise with them. Working for or supplying the vessels is also an offence. The government hopes that the new nationwide pop network to be launched by the BBC will compensate the public for the loss of the pirates. However, the station that started the pirate phenomenon, Radio Caroline, promises to continue broadcasting from international waters off the Essex coast.

> *Every country has the government it deserves.*
> **Joseph de Maistre**, 1811.

Tivoli's garden of delight

1843 The Tivoli Gardens in Copenhagen were opened today by George Carstensen. They provide a much-needed meeting place for the citizens of Copenhagen and are expected to attract visitors to the city from Denmark and all over the world. Laid out on part of the city's old defence works, the gardens offer a range of amenities, including eating places, amusement rides and amphitheatres for concert and stage performances. Thousands of gas lights illuminate the gardens at night, creating a magical atmosphere which is further enhanced by the backdrop of Chinese and Moorish buildings.

1057 The Scottish king Macbeth, who killed King Duncan I in 1040, is killed by Duncan's son Malcolm.

1914 The 52 mile (82 km) Panama Canal is opened, connecting the Atlantic and Pacific Oceans.

1947 India gains independence from Britain with Jawaharlal Nehru as her first prime minister.

1955 Twelve Indian protesters demanding the return of Goa are killed by Portuguese troops.

1965 Twenty thousand National Guards are called in to control the race riots which are being fought in the Watts area of Los Angeles, California.

1965 A Beatles concert draws 56,000 fans to Shea Stadium, New York, and creates a new outdoor audience record.

1987 Corporal punishment is banned in Britain except in independent schools.

1989 Giant mutant trees are found growing around the damaged Soviet nuclear reactor at Chernobyl.

1990 One hundred and fifty people are killed during violent clashes in the townships outside Johannesburg in South Africa.

BIRTHDAYS

Napoleon Bonaparte 1769, Corsican military man and Emperor of France 1804-15.

Sir Walter Scott 1771, British novelist whose works include the novels *Waverley*.

James Keir Hardie 1856, Scottish politican and founder of the British Labour Party.

Ethel Barrymore 1879, American actress who won an Oscar for *None but the Lonely Heart*.

T. E. Lawrence 1888, English soldier and writer known as Lawrence of Arabia who wrote *The Seven Pillars of Wisdom*.

Robert Bolt 1924, English playwright who wrote *A Man for all Seasons*.

Oscar Peterson 1925, Canadian jazz pianist and composer.

1886 Death of Ramakrishna, the Indian Hindu saint and religious educator who taught the essential unity and truth of all religions.

1886 Death of Ned Buntline, the American author who pioneered the dime novel.

1949 Margaret Mitchell, the author of *Gone with the Wind*, dies after being hit by a car two days previously.

1956 Bela Lugosi, the Hungarian actor who portrayed the vampire Count Dracula in such films as *Dracula*, *The Death Kiss* and *Mark of the Vampire*, dies in poverty after being released from a hospital in which he was being treated for drug addiction – he is to be buried, according to his wish, in a Dracula cloak.

1968 The first Poseidon missile is launched.

1975 Peter Gabriel leaves the band Genesis: his position as lead singer is taken over by drummer Phil Collins.

1979 Death of John G. Diefenbaker, Canadian statesman and Progressive Conservative prime minister who opposed nuclear weapons in Canada.

2001 Astronomers discover a new solar system.

BIRTHDAYS

Georgette Heyer 1902, English novelist much loved for her witty romantic novels in historical settings and her detective stories.

Charles Bukowski 1920, American poet, short-story writer and novelist.

Shimon Peres 1923, Polish-born Israeli statesman and prime minister of Israel 1984-86.

Menachem Begin 1913, Russian-born Israeli statesman who was prime minister of Israel 1977-83.

Ted Hughes 1930, British Poet Laureate best-known for his collections *Crow* and *Cave Birds*.

Madonna 1958, American pop singer and actress who has had a string of hits with records such as "Like a Virgin", "Material Girl" and "Justify My Love".

1991 The credibility of the English Football League was dealt a severe blow today when the 22 clubs that make up the First Division resigned en masse. Their intention is to form a breakaway super-league under the auspices of the Football Association. The clubs believe that this would enable them to generate more revenue from television contracts and sponsorship deals. The FA is in favour of the new league.

Elvis Presley, the Hillbilly Cat, Swivel Hips, the King of Rock and Roll, the King of Behop, the King of Country Music, simply, the King.

Michael Bane, American journalist, on Elvis, who died today, 1977.

Cyprus is a new republic

1960 The new republic of Cyprus came into being today. The road to independence has been a tortuous one for the eastern Mediterranean island, which lies between Turkey and the Levant. Led by Archbishop Makarios III, the Greek population (numbering some 80 per cent of the island's total) had been agitating for enosis, or union with Greece, for almost 100 years, since Britain took over administration of the island from the Ottomans. In return for independence the Cypriots have given undertakings not to participate in political or economic union with any other state. Future partition into separate Greek and Turkish enclaves has also been prohibited.

Idi Amin dies

2003 The notorious former Ugandan president Idi Amin died today. Amin gained control of Uganda in 1971 after overthrowing the government in a military coup and soon after announced plans to expel 50,000 Asians from Uganda. By 1977 he was coming under increasing pressure from around the world amid accusations of mass murder, including that of the Anglican Archbishop of Uganda. He headed a bloody incursion into Tanzania the following year but fled from his country a few months later when 45,000 Tanzanian troops invaded Uganda in revenge, ending his regime of terror.

BABE STRIKES OUT

1948 "Babe" Ruth, the most famous baseball player of all time, died in New York today aged 53. Baltimore-born Ruth (real name George Herman Ruth) will be chiefly remembered for his ability as a batsman. He broke the major league home-run record in three consecutive seasons (1919-21), and again in 1927 with a staggering score of 60.

The King is dead

1977 Elvis Presley, the king of rock 'n' roll, died today after collapsing at his mansion in Memphis, Tennessee. He was rushed to Baptist Memorial Hospital but failed to respond to treatment. Speculation is rife that the 42-year-old singer may have committed suicide. Presley took the world of popular music by storm in the mid-50s with a potent combination of blues-style singing and a sexually up-front stage act; the 60s revolution in pop music owed a great deal to him. Presley is estimated to have grossed $1000 million (£540 million) from records, films and other merchandise in his lifetime.

BLOOD SPILT FOR SUFFRAGE

1819 An orderly political reform meeting held in St Peter's Fields, Manchester, broke up in confusion and violence today, leaving 11 dead and some 400 injured. Magistrates, alarmed by the 60,000-strong crowd that had turned out for the event, ordered the Manchester yeomanry to seize the speakers, including fiery orator Henry Hunt. When the yeomanry also started setting about those carrying "revolutionary" banners, the chairman of the bench of magistrates ordered the 15th Hussars and the Cheshire Volunteers to clear the crowd. The incident is sure to aggravate the ill-feeling that exists between radicals and the Tory establishment. The rally itself was intended as a high point in the political campaign for universal suffrage.

Golden strike on the Klondike

1896 A massive influx of prospectors to the Yukon Territory of Canada is expected after the discovery yesterday of a major gold find at Bonanza Creek on the Klondike River. The three men who struck lucky, George W. Carmack and his two Indian brothers-in-law, made known their good fortune at the town of Forty Mile.

> *Baseball is very big with my people. It's the only time we can get to shake a bat at a white man without starting a riot.*
> **Dick Gregory**, US comedian, 1967.

Pakistan president blown out of the skies

1988 General Zia ul-Haq, Pakistan's iron-fisted ruler for the past 11 years, died today when the camouflaged C-130 Hercules plane in which he was travelling crashed shortly after take-off. Zia, 64, was on his way back to Islamabad after watching a demonstration of the capabilities of the US M1A1 Abrams tank at an army testing range near the airport of Bahawalpur. Among the 30 people on board were the US ambassador to Pakistan, Mr Arnold Raphael, and the US embassy's military liaison officer, Brigadier General Herbert Wassom. Pakistani and US intelligence officers suspect that the aircraft may have been downed by a bomb or ground-to-air missile. Zia is to be succeeded by former senate chairman Ghulam Ishaq Khan.

1998 President Bill Clinton was today giving evidence to the Grand Jury about his relationship with a young female intern. During the examination, President Clinton was questioned about the exact nature of his relationship with Monica Lewinsky, and whether he had previously lied under oath. An uncomfortable President Clinton was forced to defend previous statements about his affair with Miss Lewinsky by quibbling over the precise definition of his words. After facing the Grand Jury, the president now awaits the verdict of the American people.

Another brick in the wall of isolation

1961 There seems little doubt now that the East German authorities are intent on erecting a permanent barrier between the Eastern and Western sectors of the city. On August 13 the East German police began to string barbed wire and set up road blocks along the inner boundary of the eight districts of the Soviet sector of Berlin. This temporary barrier is now being replaced with a 9-ft (2.7 m) cement wall topped with barbed wire, complete with armed sentries in watchtowers. The decision to build the wall was taken by Communist leader Walter Ulbricht, with the backing of the Soviet Union, in the light of the continuing massive exodus of East Germans to the West, estimated to be running at around 2000 people a day.

Pugilist's Charter

1743 True to his word, champion bare-knuckle fighter Jack Broughton has published a set of rules to control boxing. He is said to have been determined on this course since Yorkshireman George Stevenson died of injuries sustained in a gruelling bout with him two years ago. Past practices now forbidden under the new rules include hitting an opponent when he is down, kicking, gouging, head butting and grasping an opponent below the waist. Broughton is also responsible for introducing 10-oz (300 g) gloves, called mufflers, to protect the hands and face from bruising during training. His gymnasium is among the many boxing establishments to benefit from the innovation, which has encouraged interest in the sport from young gentlemen previously put off by the prospect of disfigurement.

BABY SNATCHED BY DINGO

1980 A distraught 32-year-old mother, Lindy Chamberlain, has told Australian police of how she watched her nine-week-old baby daughter, Azaria, being carried off into the night by a dingo, a type of wild dog. The Chamberlain family, including Azaria's father, Michael, were camping at the legendary Ayers Rock, a sacred site used for centuries by Aborigines and now a major tourist attraction, when the snatch occurred. Police are to mount a search of the deserted bushland beyond the campsite for traces of the missing baby.

1590 John White, Governor of Roanoke Island, returns to find the British colony deserted and the first white child born in America vanished.

1896 The first pedestrian to be killed by a car is knocked down in Croydon, England – the car is travelling at just 4 mph (6.4 kph).

1945 After Japanese occupation during World War II, Indonesia declares itself a republic under the leadership of Dr Sukarno.

1973 Paul Williams, an original member of The Temptations, shoots himself dead in his car in Denver, Colorado.

1983 Death of Ira Gershwin, brother of George and composer of "Lady be Good".

1987 Donald Harvey, a former nurse's aide, is charged with the murder of 28 people in Ohio, having admitted to more than 50 murders.

1987 Death of Rudolf Hess, Hitler's close friend and deputy leader of the Nazi party.

1989 An Australian airliner becomes the first commercial plane to fly non-stop from London to Sydney.

1999 A massive earthquake hits north-western Turkey, killing more than 14,000 people and leaving hundreds of thousands without homes or essential services.

BIRTHDAYS

Davy Crockett 1786, American frontiersman and politician.

Mae West 1892, American comedy actress, scriptwriter and international sex symbol during the 1930s: she wrote most of her own stage-plays and film scripts.

Maureen O'Hara 1920, Irish-born actress who made her mark in Hollywood with films such as *The Hunchback of Notre Dame*, *The Black Swan* and *The Quiet Man*.

V. S. Naipaul 1932, Trinidadian writer and novelist.

Robert De Niro 1943, American actor, star of many films including *The Godfather*, *The Deerhunter*, *Raging Bull* and *Cape Fear*.

BIRTHDAYS

Virginia Dare 1587, American colonist, the first child of English parents to be born in the New World.

Meriwether Lewis 1774, American explorer who was joint leader with William Clark of the first overland expedition to the Pacific Northwest.

Franz-Joseph I 1830, Austro-Hungarian emperor who invaded Serbia and helped initiate World War I.

Marshall Field 1834, American department store magnate.

Caspar Weinberger 1917, American statesman and secretary of defence for Ronald Reagan.

Alain Robbe-Grillet 1922, French novelist and scriptwriter who provided the script for Alain Resnais' *Last Year at Marienbad*.

Shelley Winters 1922, American actress whose films include *The Poseidon Adventure* and *Lolita*.

Roman Polanski 1933, Polish film director who has worked in Europe and the USA, directing films such as *Repulsion*, *Rosemary's Baby* and *Tess*.

Robert Redford 1937, American actor whose films include *Butch Cassidy and the Sundance Kid*.

Legacy of brutality

1227 The Mongol ruler Genghis Khan, conqueror of a vast empire that extends from the Pacific to the Dnieper River, died today after falling from his horse. The son of Yesugei, a member of a royal Mongol clan, Genghis succeeded in uniting the Mongol tribes of nomadic horsemen and harnessing them into a terrifyingly effective war machine. The name Genghis Khan became synonymous with brutality as he pursued his goal of world conquest. Genghis was adaptable and willing to learn, however. Late in his career he came to recognize that power could be exercised without necessarily resorting to rape, murder and pillage. The future of the Mongols is now the responsibility of Ogodei Khan, Genghis' chosen successor.

Power-mad Pope damaged Papacy

1503 Pope Alexander VI, Spanish-born pontiff, has died in Rome after succumbing to a fever. He was 74. A member of the powerful Borgia family, he made rapid headway in the ecclesiastical hierachy, becoming a cardinal at the age of 25. His election as pope in 1492 brought about no change in his magnificent lifestyle. The murder of his favourite son, Juan, four years ago brought some curtailment of the decadence with which his court was associated, however. Pope Alexander's political and personal ambitions were never similarly held in check, and to his dying breath he used his energies in the pursuit of power. Critics believe that he has irreparably damaged the prestige of the papacy.

1984 British civil servant Clive Ponting, 37, has been charged under the Official Secrets Act after admitting to leaking two Ministry of Defence documents to opposition Labour MP Mr Tam Dalyell. Ponting's defence is that his duty is to Parliament and not just to the government. The documents related to the rules of engagement used in the controversial sinking of the Argentine cruiser *General Belgrano* in May 1982, during the Falklands War. The case is the latest in a series of breaches of confidence by senior officials out of sympathy with Thatcher's administration.

Span-tastic

1930 After seven years in the making the huge steel arch of the new Sydney Harbour Bridge has been completed. Some 38,390 tons of riveted, high-tensile silicon British steel has gone into the 1650 ft (503 m) arch, one of the largest in the world. Sydney Harbour is so deep that the bridge's British designers, Dorman Long of Middlesbrough, had to find a novel way of supporting the structure. The two halves were built out as cantilevers and supported by wire-rope anchorages situated on the north and south sides of the harbour. A target date of March 1932 has been set for its completion.

> *Protestant women may take the pill. Roman Catholic women must keep taking the* Tablet [a British Roman Catholic paper].
> **Irene Thomas**, British writer. The first oral contraceptive was marketed today, 1960.

Red Guards play Mao's game

1966 The systematic campaign by Chairman Mao to halt the trend towards right-wing thinking in every area of Chinese life is gathering pace. The first of eight huge demonstrations by semi-military groups called Red Guards took place in Peking today. These young radicals have poured into the capital from all over China to answer Mao's call for the denunciation and removal of senior officials held responsible by Mao for dampening down revolutionary ideals among his countrymen. The "great proletarian cultural revolution" launched by the 72-year-old Mao is committed to "purifying" the arts and education. In place of "the enemy within", he is proposing his own administration.

Last-ditch Soviet coup

1991 Mikhail Gorbachev, the Soviet leader who gave a nervous world two words of hope – *glasnost* (openness) and *perestroika* (restructuring) – has been toppled. Early this morning the Tass news agency issued a statement to the effect that the 60-year-old Gorbachev had fallen ill at his dacha on the Black Sea and was no longer able to run the country. An "emergency committee" has been formed to perform this task. The timing of the coup is significant – just one day short of the scheduled signing of the Union treaty, a document hated by hardliners because it signals the beginning of the end of the old Soviet empire they know and love.

1987 A lone gunman went on a six-hour rampage through the small British town of Hungerford, on the Wiltshire-Berkshire borders today, leaving 14 dead, including the gunman's mother, and a further 14 maimed from gunshot wounds. The man, ex-paratrooper Michael Ryan, 27, eventually turned his gun on himself. Ryan was said to have been deeply depressed by the death of his father two years ago. He had a passion for guns and had collected a vast personal arsenal.

PASCAL DIES

1662 Blaise Pascal, the French mathematician, physicist and religious philosopher, died in Paris today, aged 39. Pascal pursued his intellectual enquiries with an all-consuming passion. In November 1654 he experienced the "night of fire" that changed his life, and he temporarily abandoned the world of science – and inventions such as a calculating device, the syringe

and the hydraulic press – to go in search of religious truth among the austere moral precepts of Jansenism taught in the convent of Port-Royal. Thereafter, he wrote only at the convent's request and never again under his own name. *Les Provinciales*, his most popular work, is a beautifully written defence of Jansenist Antoine Arnaud, who believed that no amount of Communion could wash away sins not truly repented. At the time of his death Pascal was working on a treatise of spirituality.

Hitler gets the "Ja" vote

1934 The German people went to the polls today to give their verdict on Adolf Hitler's assumption of the titles Führer and Reich Chancellor. Of the 45.5 million eligible to vote, 38 million have voted "Yes", 4.25 million "No" and 870,000 spoilt their ballot papers. This is an impressive majority for the new German head of state, who announced on August 2, the day that President von Hindenburg died, his intention of merging the office of president with that of Chancellor.

> *If you want people to think well of you, do not speak well of yourself.*
> **Blaise Pascal**, French philosopher and mathematician, who died today.

14 AD Death of Augustus, the first Roman emperor.

1929 Death of Sergei Pavlovich Diaghilev, founder of the Russian ballet company Ballets Russes in Paris.

1936 Federico Garcia Lorca, the Spanish poet and playwright best-known for the trilogy *Blood Wedding*, *Yerma* and *The House of Bernarda Alba*, is shot by Nationalists during the Spanish Civil War.

1960 The Soviets sentence U-2 spy plane pilot Gary Powers to 10 years' detention.

1979 Pol Pot, ex-dictator of Cambodia, is sentenced to death for genocide in his absence by the Vietnamese-backed Cambodian government.

1989 Poland becomes the first country in Eastern Europe to end one-party rule as Solidarity's Tadeuz Mazowiecki takes office as prime minister.

1990 Iraqi leader Saddam Hussein offers to release all Western hostages in exchange for a US withdrawal from the Gulf region and an end to the blockade.

BIRTHDAYS

John Dryden 1631, British poet and critic, author of verse satires such as *Absalom and Architophel* and *MacFlecknoe*.

Antonio Salieri 1750, Italian composer and conductor who is suspected of poisoning Mozart.

Orville Wright 1871, American aviation pioneer, who, with his brother Wilbur, made the first powered and controlled flight.

Coco Chanel 1883, French fashion designer who revolutionized women's clothing.

Ogden Nash 1902, American humorist who immortalized such lines as "Candy is dandy/But liquor is quicker".

Willy Shoemaker 1931, American jockey who rode a record-breaking 7000 winners.

Johnny Nash 1940, American singer who had a hit with "I Can See Clearly Now".

Groucho leaves his Marx

1977 Groucho Marx, the wise-cracking comic who made his name by creating mayhem on stage and film, died of pneumonia in Hollywood today. He was 81 although, in true Marx brothers style, admitting to an age of 86! Groucho (real name Julius) and his real-life brothers – Leonard (Chico), Arthur (Harpo), Milton (Gummo) and Herbert (Zeppo) – owed their success to their indomitable mother, Minnie, who was convinced that her boys had talent, despite their own reservations. Their film career was launched in 1929, after success on Broadway. Groucho's trademarks of cigar, moustache and stooping walk and his way of orchestrating the antics of the equally zany Chico and Harpo won him massive popularity around the world in films like *A Day at the Races* and *A Night at the Opera*. After retiring from films at the end of the 40s, Groucho began a new career in radio and television, as host of the weekly show *You Bet Your Life*. Earlier this year the $2.9 million (£1.6 million) estate of the thrice-married Groucho was the subject of a bitter legal wrangle between his companion and secretary for 17 years, Erin Fleming, 37, and his only son, Arthur, 56. The court decided to place the ailing comic under the guardianship of neither, choosing his grandson, Andrew, instead.

AUGUST 20

1794 General Napoleon Bonaparte is freed from the jail where he was being held on suspicion of Robespierrism.

1912 Death of William Booth, the British founder of the Salvation Army.

1913 Adolphe Pégond bales out of an airplane at 700 ft (213 m) and parachutes safely to the ground, becoming the first person to parachute from a plane.

1913 Stainless steel is first cast in Sheffield by Harry Brearly.

1924 British sprinter Eric Liddel refuses to run in the 100 metres at the Paris Olympics on religious grounds because the event is held on a Sunday.

1940 Radar is used for the first time by the British during World War Two.

1956 The first nuclear power in Britain is generated at Calder Hall power station in Cumbria.

1969 Mick Jagger of the Rolling Stones is accidentally shot while filming *Ned Kelly* in Australia.

1970 Lieutenant Calley's sentence for the My Lai massacre in Vietnam is reduced by 20 years after public claims that he is a scapegoat.

1988 A ceasefire between Iran and Iraq takes effect.

BIRTHDAYS

Benjamin Harrison 1833, American Republican president whose administration passed the Sherman Anti-Trust Act in 1890.

H. P. Lovecraft American science-fiction author of macabre tales such as *The Case of Charles Dexter Ward* and *At the Mountains of Madness*.

Jack Teagarden 1905, American jazz trombonist, singer, composer and bandleader, best-known for his version of "The Ballad of Basin Street".

Bunny Austin 1906, British tennis player and four-times Davis Cup winner.

Jim Reeves 1924, American country and western singer.

1989 A birthday party held aboard a Thames pleasure boat ended in tragedy in the early hours of this morning when the 60-year-old vessel *Marchioness* was hit and run over by a 1475-ton sand dredger, the *Bow Belle*. The smaller craft sank in less than two minutes, leaving those below deck with little chance of escape. Police are questioning the crews of both vessels.

Axe falls for Trotsky

1940 Leon Trotsky, one of the leaders of the Russian Revolution in 1917, was stabbed to death with an alpine axe at his home in Coyoacan, near Mexico City today. He was 61. Ramon Mercader, a Spanish communist, has been charged with Trotsky's murder. Trotsky had lived abroad since January 1929, when Stalin finally lost patience with the steady stream of criticism issuing from the Ukrainian's place of exile at Alma-Ata in Central Asia and banished him from Soviet soil. His fall from grace in the Soviet hierarchy came swiftly after the death of Lenin in 1923. Outmanoeuvred by the wily Stalin, he found himself first ousted from the Politburo, then the Party, and finally the Soviet Union itself. Stalin then ordered the rewriting of the official history of the USSR to play down and denigrate Trotsky's place in Soviet history.

RAF invincible in battle for skies

1940 The offensive launched by Germany on August 13 in preparation for an invasion of the British Isles is being met with strong resistance and considerable victory by the RAF. Southeast England has borne the brunt of the attacks from fleets of bombers protected by fighter aircraft. So far 236 German aircraft have been downed for the loss of just 95 British, with the RAF's efforts concentrated on destroying the Luftwaffe's bombers. A switch of German tactics may well be on the cards as Luftwaffe supremo Hermann Goering searches for a way of cracking the British fighter command nut and winning air superiority.

Violent death for Born Free star

1989 British conservationist George Adamson, who with his wife Joy became world famous through the film about their tame lions, *Born Free*, was gunned down by bandits near his camp in the Kora National Reserve today. The men responsible for killing the 83-year-old Adamson and two of his assistants are thought to be the remnants of a gang of poachers recently driven out of Kenya's Meru and Tsavo national parks. Nairobi-born Adamson, the son of a coffee farmer, settled in the remote Kora Reserve 18 years ago, after his favourite lion, Boy (the mate of Elsa the lioness in *Born Free*), had mauled Mark Jenkins, the son of the Meru Park warden. Joy stayed behind at Meru and ten years ago was stabbed to death by a member of staff at the park.

> *From being a patriotic myth, the Russian people have become an awful reality.*
> **Leon Trotsky**, who died today, 1940.

Daguerre captures the real world

1839 A crowded joint meeting of the Académie des Sciences and the Institut de France in Paris heard yesterday of a revolutionary new photographic process sponsored by the French government. The process records an image by exposing to light a copper-coated silver plate sensitized by iodine which is then developed by bringing it into contact with heated mercury vapour. The government has agreed to pay L. J. M. Daguerre and Isidore Niepce, the son of Daguerre's now deceased partner in the project, Joseph Niepce, annual annuities of 6000 and 4000 francs respectively in return for the copyright. Although the image produced by the daguerreotype is of an exquisite tonal quality, it damages easily and cannot generate duplicates. The way ahead seems to be pointed by the negative-positive process of photography developed by Englishman Henry Fox Talbot, announced in February.

Think Cadillac

1902 Manufacturer Martin Leland has honoured Detroit's founding father, Antoine de la Motte Cadillac, by naming his new automobile after the French colonial administrator. The new Cadillac car is lightweight and has a single cylinder engine designed by A. P. Brush. Beautifully designed and finished, the Cadillac aims to carve a niche for itself as the Rolls-Royce of the American motor industry. Ironically, in order to start their venture in the luxury car market, Leland and his partner Faulconer bought the ailing Detroit Automobile Co. from that advocate of "Everyman" motoring, Henry Ford.

Benigno's Corazon takes heart

1984 A massive demonstration was held in Manila today to mark the first anniversary of the murder of Benigno Aquino, the leader of the anti-Marcos faction in the Philippines. Aquino was gunned down as he stepped on to the tarmac at Manila airport after returning from a three-year sojourn in the United States. The chant of "enough is enough" directed at the regime of Ferdinand Marcos is getting louder. The people of the Philippines are looking to Aquino's widow, Corazon ("Cory"), for a new champion who will challenge Marcos for the presidency he has held by force since 1972.

Now we are in a period which I can characterize as a period of cold peace.
Trygve Lie, first United Nations secretary general, 1940.

Anti-Gorby coup flops

1991 President Mikhail Gorbachev arrived back in Moscow today after the collapse of the attempt by hard-liners to depose him. All but one of the eight ringleaders of the plot has been rounded up. Gorbachev seems deeply saddened by the fact that several of his closest and most trusted colleagues, including the Kremlin chief of staff and the head of the KGB, were involved in the plot. Gorbachev's steadfast refusal to be coerced into resigning was echoed by mass demonstrations against the coup by the peoples of Moscow and Leningrad. There was also a disinclination on the part of many in authority – notably in the armed forces – to behave unconstitutionally. Russian Federation president Boris Yeltsin has identified the Communist Party as a stumbling block to further reform.

Volcanic gas wreaks havoc

1986 A cloud of toxic gas released from the volcanic Lake Nyos, near Wum in north-west Cameroon, has killed more than 1200 people. The 300 or so survivors are receiving treatment for gas poisoning in hospital. The eruption which released the killer gas – probably carbon dioxide – occurred during the night and is thought to have startled the villagers out of their homes and into a night air heavy with toxic fumes. The governor of the stricken province, Mr Walson Ntuba, said that "the few survivors were those who had the good sense to remain indoors".

1858 British Army officer Sam Browne of the 2nd Punjab Cavalry has come up with a novel new belt for sword or pistol. Browne, 34, lost an arm in action this year, so his design consists of a broad waist-belt supported at the left side by a narrow strap crossing the right shoulder. It is unlikely that the belt will become general issue in the foreseeable future.

1951 Death of Constant Lambert, English composer and conductor with Sadler's Wells Ballet, London.

1959 Hawaii becomes the 50th state of the USA.

1959 Death of Sir Jacob Epstein, American-born sculptor who became a British citizen and whose works include *St Michael and the Devil*.

1961 Britain releases nationalist Jomo Kenyatta, former president of the Kenya African Union who was imprisoned for his part in the Mau Mau rebellion: without him Kenyan politics cannot go forward.

1976 Twenty-five-year-old Mary Langdon joins the East Sussex fire brigade to become Britain's first female "fireman".

1988 British licensing laws are amended to allow pubs to stay open 12 hours a day, except on Sundays.

1989 The American fashion journalist Diana Vreeland dies.

BIRTHDAYS

William Murdoch 1754, Scottish engineer who pioneered the use of coal-gas for lighting in 1792 while working with James Watt and Matthew Boulton on their steam engines.

William IV 1765, English monarch known as "the sailor king" because he joined the Royal Navy at 13 and was a close friend of British admiral Nelson: William was renowned for his affairs and had 10 illegitimate children by actress Dorothea Jordan.

Aubrey Beardsley 1874, English illustrator who played a leading part in the Aesthetic movement. Despite ill health and an early death, his output was prodigious and includes illustrations for Pope's *Rape of the Lock*.

"Count" William Basie 1904, American jazz pianist and bandleader.

Chris Brasher 1928, English athlete and 1956 Olympic steeple chase gold medallist.

Princess Margaret 1930, English royal, sister of Queen Elizabeth II.

1815 Ultra-royalist reactionaries win the majority in the first parliamentary elections in France.

1849 Amaral, the Portuguese governer of Macao, is assassinated for anti-Chinese politics.

1862 Belgium signs a commercial treaty with Britain.

1868 Ten thousand Chinese plunder the China Inland Mission.

1940 Death of Sir Oliver Lodge, English physicist who pioneered wireless telegraphy.

1953 Iran's Shah returns to the Peacock Throne and Mossadegh is jailed after a military coup.

1963 Charlie Wilson is jailed for the Great Train Robbery.

1978 Death of Jomo Kenyatta, the first president of Kenya.

1989 British Telecom launch the world's first pocketphones which operate within 100 yards of a public base station.

BIRTHDAYS

Claude Debussy 1862, French composer best known for *Prélude à l'après-midi d'un faune* and *La Mer*.

Jacques Lipchitz 1891, Lithuanian-born US sculptor who began by exploring cubism but whose later work was of bold, bronze human beings and animals.

Dorothy Parker 1893, American writer, critic and humorist who was a founder member of the Algonquin Round Table, whose members were known for their sharp wit and intellectual liveliness.

Henri Cartier-Bresson 1908, French photographer, considered one of the greatest.

Ray Bradbury 1920, American poetic science-fiction writer of the *Martian Chronicles*.

Karlheinz Stockhausen 1928, German composer and conductor whose work includes *Kontakte*.

Steve Davis 1957, English snooker world champion, the first player to win more than £1 million ($1.8 million) from the game.

RED ROSE FLOWERS AGAIN

1485 The 30-year struggle between the houses of Lancaster and York for the throne of England ended today in victory for the Lancastrians. The decisive blow was dealt at Bosworth Field, 12 miles (19 km) west of Leicester, where key noblemen such as the Stanley brothers deserted Richard at his hour of greatest need to swing the battle Henry Tudor's way. Richard III fought on bravely before being unhorsed and killed. The 1000 or so mercenaries supplied by King Louis XI of France were a major factor in Tudor's success. Opposition to the 28-year-old usurper, who will be known as Henry VII, is likely to continue, however, until a way can be found of reconciling the white rose and the red, the well known emblems of the houses of York and Lancaster respectively.

Prague dragged back to Moscow

1968 Tanks belonging to a five-nation Warsaw Pact force have entered the Czech capital, Prague, to crush with military might the first flowering of Alexander Dubcek's reforms. Soviet leader Leonid Brezhnev had become increasingly alarmed by the consequences of Dubcek's championship of the "human face of socialism". Since January this year, first secretary Dubcek had introduced many economic, political and cultural reforms and promised further moves towards democratization. The Soviet Tass news agency is portraying the invasion as a timely intervention to save the Czech nation. The news film shot by Western sources, however, tells of a people in despair at the prospect of the political clock being turned back to Communist orthodoxy.

Charles challenges the Commons

1642 The divide separating King Charles I from the English Parliament seems to be hardening into a battle line. The King has raised his military standard in Nottingham town. It is almost certain that he will be able to count on the support of many peers and gentry who fear the consequences of a parliament infiltrated by the "common people". Three days ago both houses of parliament issued a joint statement denouncing as traitors any who join the King's cause. A parliamentary army of 10,000 has been mobilized.

Black year for airline travel

1985 Fifty-four people died today when a British Airtours Boeing 747 bound for Corfu caught fire at Manchester airport shortly after engine failure forced the pilot to abandon takeoff. The emergency services reached the aircraft within seconds of it coming to a standstill, but were unable to extinguish the inferno in time to save many passengers at the rear of the cabin. Today's disaster brings the 1985 death toll from aviation accidents to 1679, the worst annual figure on record. In addition to the Manchester disaster, on August 2 this month a Delta Airways Tristar crashed in a storm at Dallas-Fort Worth and on August 12 a Japan Airlines Boeing 747 came down near Tokyo, killing 520.

> *I have recently been all round the world and have formed a very poor opinion of it.*
> **Thomas Beecham**, British conductor, 1946.

Half-smile half-inched

1911 The world's most famous painting, Leonardo da Vinci's *Mona Lisa*, was stolen during the night from the Louvre in Paris. Museum officials are embarrassed by the loss of their most prized exhibit, which is one of the few works that the great Leonardo actually completed. Police have no clues as to the identity of the thief, or thieves, and seem to be banking on the *Mona Lisa* recovering herself. Just a glimpse of her smile should give away the whereabouts of the painting, said to represent the mystery of existence.

DEATH OF A DREAM LOVER

1926 Screen actor Rudolph Valentino, the idol of millions, died today of peritonitis in New York's Polyclinic Hospital. Valentino, 31, was in New York to publicize his latest film, *The Son of the Sheikh*. In five short years and a dozen films, including *The Sheikh* and *Blood and Sand*, Italian-born Valentino carved a unique image for himself as the epitome of virility. Recently, though, he had been the subject of unkind comments in the media. Last month the *Chicago Tribune* suggested that "pink powder puff" was a more apt label for the looks-conscious star than "the great lover". The revelation that both of his ex-wives, Jean Acker and Natacha Rambova, are lesbian also caused much speculation about Valentino's own sexual orientation. For many, though, he was the dream lover. News of his demise has reportedly provoked a rash of suicides worldwide.

My principal is: France before everything.
Napoleon I, French Emperor, in a letter to Eugène Beauharnais, 1810.

Love at first flight

1988 British Airways showed off its first husband and wife team of pilot recruits today. The couple, Anna and Danish-born Morten Riis, begin their intensive pilots' course with BA tomorrow. After training, they will be assigned to separate aircraft as co-pilots. The couple met on a commercial pilot's course at Perth in Scotland and married precisely two years and five days later.

Goths gatecrash Rome

410 The disintegration of the once-mighty Roman Empire is continuing apace with the fall of Rome to the Visigoths. Alaric, King of the Visigoths, ordered his men to storm the city after the refusal by the Roman emperor of the West, Honorius, to agree to his terms. The citizens of Rome are paying the price for their emperor's delusions of power. While he remains in the safety of his new and impregnable capital, Ravenna, they are being sacked. Two years ago, when Alaric first threatened the city, the Roman authorities contemplated offering sacrifices to the gods as a means of keeping the Visigoths at bay. On this occasion, the authorities needed only to offer land and subsidies. Fortunately for those who treasure Rome's beauty, first reports of the sack suggest that booty rather than wholesale destruction is the main aim of the invaders. The biggest loss from the fall of the capital is to Roman prestige.

1960 A new type of show is the talk of this year's Edinburgh fringe: *Beyond the Fringe*, the work of Alan Bennett, Peter Cook, Jonathan Miller and Dudley Moore, brings political satire to intimate revue. Critics are hailing it as the best thing to hit Edinburgh for many a year.

---

93 AD Julius Gnaeus Agricola, Roman general renowned for his conquests in Britain, dies in Rome.

1305 Sir William Wallace, Scottish patriot who demanded independence for his country, is hung, drawn and quartered in London.

1680 Death of Captain Blood, who tried to steal the Crown Jewels from the Tower of London in May 1671.

1818 The first steam ship service opens on the Great Lakes in North America.

1933 Gandhi is released from Poona jail after his hunger strike (against the government's attitude to untouchables) almost kills him.

1939 British driver John Cobb reaches 368.85 mph (590 kph) at Bonneville Flats, Utah.

1939 Germany and the USSR sign the Molotov-Ribbentropp nonaggression pact.

1940 German bombers begin night raids on London.

1944 The pro-Nazi dictator of Romania, General Ion Antonescu is overthrown.

1987 French racing driver Didier Peroni is killed in a power boat race off the Isle of Wight.

1990 The German states choose October 3 as the date for reunification.

BIRTHDAYS

Louis XVI 1754, French monarch responsible for the Revolution and the last king of France.

Edgar Lee Masters 1869, American author who wrote *Spoon River Anthology*.

Gene Kelly 1912, American dancer, choreographer, singer, actor and director who starred in Hollywood musicals, including *Anchors Aweigh*, *Singin' in the Rain* and his *Invitation to Dance*.

Peter Thomson 1929, Australian golfer who won numerous major victories at home and overseas.

Willy Russell 1947, English playwright from Liverpool whose plays include *Educating Rita*.

Prejudice threatens true justice

1927 In one of the most controversial cases in American legal history, Nicola Sacco and Bartolomeo Vanzetti went to the electric chair today. In July 1921 a jury found the men guilty of the murders of a factory paymaster and a guard during a robbery in South Braintree, Massachusetts. The guilty verdict was challenged on the grounds that the judge and jury had been prejudiced against the two political anarchists and immigrants. Calls for a retrial were denied, even when in 1925 condemned criminal Celestino Madeiros gave evidence that the murders had been committed by the Morelli Gang. Governor A. T. Fuller refused clemency for the two Italians, supported by an independent committee inspecting the case. Questions concerning the administration of justice remain to be answered.

79 AD In Italy Mount Vesuvius erupts and destroys Pompeii, Herculaneum, Stabiae and a number of smaller settlements.

1690 Job Charnock establishes a trading post on behalf of the English East India Company in Kalikata, West Bengal.

1906 Kidney transplants are carried out on dogs at a medical conference in Toronto, Canada.

1940 The *Lancet* reports the first purification of penicillin by professors Howard Florey and Ernest Chain.

1942 The Duke of Kent, youngest brother of George VI , dies in a flying boat accident while on active duty.

1951 The Mau Mau rebellion begins, led by Kenyan nationalists.

1954 Getulio Vargas, 71 year-old president of Brazil, shoots himself to avoid scandal and demands that he should relinquish power.

1975 Annabel Hunt gives the first official nude opera performance in Britain in *Ulysses* – it's also the first nude televized performance.

1990 The Irish hostage Brian Keenan is released from Beirut.

BIRTHDAYS

Robert Herrick 1591, English lyric poet and friend of Ben Jonson who wrote *Gather ye rosebuds while ye may.*

George Stubbs 1724, English animal painter and engraver, celebrated as the greatest of all horse painters. Virtually self-taught, he earnt his living as a portrait painter in his early career. In 1766 he published his famous book *The Anatomy of the Horse* which was an instant success. His paintings include *Mare and Foals in a River Landscape.*

William Wilberforce 1759, English philanthropist and anti-slave-trade campaigner.

Sir Max Beerbohm 1872, English caricaturist, writer and wit.

Jorge Luis Borges 1899, Argentinian author who dictated *The Book of Imaginary Beings* having gone blind.

Royal wedding toasted in blood

1572 Six days ago the exchange of marriage vows between the Catholic Marguerite de Valois, daughter of Henri II of France and Catherine de Medici, and Protestant Henri de Bourbon, king of Navarre, seemed to augur well for future relations between Roman Catholics and Protestant Huguenots in France. Today, the feast of St Bartholomew, the streets of Paris are running with the blood of the Huguenot nobles who attended the wedding. Only the bridegroom and the Prince de Conde have escaped the slaughter. The bridegroom's mother-in-law, Catherine, ordered the killing as part of her campaign against the Huguenot party and its influence over her son, Charles IX. The issuing of a royal order to stop the killing is expected shortly. The indications are, however, that the anti-Huguenot blood-lust is spreading to the provinces.

> *Latins are tenderly enthusiatic. In Brazil they throw flowers at you. In Argentina they throw themselves.*
> **Marlene Dietrich**, 1959.

1981 A Manhattan Supreme Court judge has jailed Mark David Chapman for 20 years to life for shooting dead John Lennon last December. Against his lawyers' wishes, Chapman had withdrawn his plea of not guilty by reason of insanity, saying God had ordered him to confess. Judge Edwards refused pleas of clemency and ordered that he should receive psychiatric treatment.

Pressure pushes poet to poison

1770 Poet Thomas Chatterton, 22, fatally poisoned himself with arsenic today at his lodgings in Brooke Street, in the city of London. He had become increasingly depressed by lack of recognition and persistent charges of "forgery". Born in Bristol, the son of an impoverished schoolmaster, Chatterton was first published before the age of 12. However, his enthusiasm for recreating the medieval world, in his Rowley Poems, came at the wrong time. Chatterton was denounced as a "forger" in the mould of the impudent James Macpherson, whose "rediscovery" of the works of the third-century Gaelic bard, Ossian, became the literary sensation of the 1760s.

Bitter British torch Washington

1814 The small but very bitter war currently being fought by Britain and America is continuing in the punitive vein struck towards the end of last year. Wanton destruction has been countered with wanton destruction. The latest target is Washington, which has been burnt by a 4000-strong British force of Peninsular War veterans under General Ross. The army, which was brought to the Washington approaches by ships of Admiral Cochrane's fleet, defeated local defence forces at Bladensburg before entering the capital and putting it to the torch. Among the casualties is the US president's official residence, the White House. The architect, James Hoban, will doubtless be asked to redesign it.

SPANIARDS FIND WOMEN WARRIORS

1542 The Spanish explorer Francisco de Orellana has reportedly discovered new lands east of Quito. Last April, Orellana and a group of around 50 men were sent ahead of the expedition, led by Gonzalo Pizarro to gather provisions. However, instead of returning, Orellana was persuaded to push on and explore the great river system that lay before them. The men's brigantine drifted with the current and eventually reached the mouth of the river. The explorers are said to be full of fantastic tales of treasure and, most curiously of all, tribes of women warriors resembling Amazons. Orellana is keen to return to his "Amazon River" region in order to exploit its enormous wealth. This may prove problematical, however, because Spain and Portugal are in dispute over ownership of the territory.

Vive la France!

1944 The four-year long ordeal that Paris and her citizens have suffered at the hands of the Nazis is almost over. With the forces of General Leclerc approaching the city and Resistance fighters continuing to attack from the centre, flushing out enemy nests, liberation is almost complete. Parisians owe thanks to the Commandant of Paris, General von Choltitz, who gave himself up today rather than carry out his Führer's order to blow up the capital's bridges and principal buildings to halt the advance. Tomorrow Free French leader General Charles de Gaulle will attend a liberation procession through the streets of Paris and a service of thanksgiving in Notre Dame cathedral.

1819 Death of James Watt, English engineer and inventor of the steam engine.

1804 Alicia Meynell completes a four-mile racecourse in York, Britain, to become the first known female jockey.

1830 A revolution begins in Belgium.

1837 Henry William Crawford of London patents a process for producing galvanized iron.

1841 Three women graduate from Oberlin Collegiate Institute, Ohio and are the first women to be granted degrees.

1867 Death of Michael Faraday, English chemist and physicist who invented the first electrical cell (battery).

1919 The first scheduled international air service begins between Paris and London.

1979 Death of Stan Kenton, American pianist, composer and jazz experimentalist.

Scorsese film crucified

1988 British film censors today risked damnation in this world and beyond by issuing the controversial film *The Last Temptation of Christ* with an 18 certificate. The film, by director Martin Scorsese, has raised a storm among Christian groups and Church leaders on both sides of the Atlantic. Many of those condemning it have yet to see it for themselves.

Reports of scenes in which Scorsese's Jesus fantasizes about having sex with Mary Magdalene are enough to upset people like veteran moral campaigner Mrs Mary Whitehouse, president of Britain's National Viewers' and Listeners' Association, however. Scorsese, a former altar boy who once entertained thoughts of entering the priesthood, denies that his film is an "intentional attack on Christianity", the view of its morality in the Media. It is, he says, his way of "getting closer to God".

> *Is Paris burning?*
> **Adolf Hitler**, before the liberation of Paris today, 1940.

Tsar punishes Potemkin rebels

1905 Eight of the mutineers from the Russian battleship *Potemkin* who recently returned to Russia after fleeing to Romania at the end of June have been sentenced to death. The remainder have been imprisoned. The mutiny, in which several officers were killed, was part of the nationwide campaign against the government of Tsar Nicholas II. Heavy taxation, the Tsar's refusal to introduce constitutional government and defeat in the Russo-Japanese War are the main issues fuelling the present wave of social unrest.

And now, live from Neptune

1989 To whoops of joy from scientists and journalists at Nasa's Jet Propulsion Laboratory in Pasadena, California, the spacecraft Voyager 2 beamed back to earth today pictures of Neptune. The pictures were taken as Voyager came within 30 miles (48 km) of the planet, which is revealed as pink and blue with a transparent atmosphere and a surface of glacial ice, ridges and cliffs. Especially stunning are the images of Triton, the largest of Neptune's eight moons, which show signs of recent volcanic activity. During its 4430 million-mile journey, *Voyager* has flown by Jupiter, Saturn, and Uranus. Once it passes Neptune, the craft will enter interstellar space, where it could go on travelling for billions of years.

WEBB CRACKS THE CHANNEL CHALLENGE

1875 Englishman Matthew Webb made history today by becoming the first person to swim the English Channel. The 27-year-old master mariner from Shropshire set off from Admiralty Pier, Dover, yesterday. Swimming breaststroke, he covered the 21-mile (34 km) stretch to Calais in 21 hours 45 minutes, emerging on the French side tired but triumphant. This feat would be sufficient to satisfy most people's yen for a challenge – but not Captain Webb's. His plans as a professional swimmer will, it seems, become progressively more ambitious.

BIRTHDAYS

Ivan the Terrible (Ivan IV) 1530, Russian tsar who executed more than 3000, including the royal heir.

Allan Pinkerton 1819, Scottish-born founder of the famous Pinkerton National Detective Agency in America, which specialized in railway theft.

Clara Bow 1905, American actress known as the "It" girl after her role in the film *It*.

Leonard Bernstein 1918, American composer and conductor best known for composing the music for *West Side Story*.

Sean Connery 1930, Scottish actor who played the leading role in seven James Bond movies and won an Oscar for best supporting actor in *The Untouchables*.

Wayne Shorter 1933, American saxophonist with Art Blakey's Jazz Messengers and then Miles Davis.

Elvis Costello 1954, British singer and songwriter well-known for songs such as "Oliver's Army".

1664 Jansenist nuns in a convent at Port-Royal in France refuse to renounce their views.

1748 The first Lutheran synod is founded in the American colonies.

1789 The French Assembly adopts the Declaration of the Rights of Man.

1850 Death of Louis Philippe, the "Citizen King" of France who abdicated rather than face a middle-class revolt.

1930 Death of Lon Chaney, American actor and "man of a thousand faces" whose appearances include *Phantom of the Opera*.

1952 The Soviets announce the first successful Intercontinental Ballistic Missile (ICBM) tests have taken place.

1958 Death of English composer Ralph Vaughan Williams whose works include *Sea Symphony*.

1970 A national women's strike causes chaos in New York.

1972 Death of Sir Francis Chichester, English yachtsman who was the first old-age pensioner to sail round the world singlehanded.

1987 A sex-crazed elephant "urgently in search of a mate" flattens a radio centre and kills two people in Bangkok.

1988 American swimmer Lynne Cox crosses the 11-mile (17.5 km) wide Lake Baikal in Siberia in 4 hours, 20 minutes – the first long swim in a cold water lake.

BIRTHDAYS

Joseph Michel Montgolfier 1740, French inventor and pioneer of the hot air balloon with his brother Jacques Étienne Montgolfier.

Prince Albert 1819, Bavarian-born consort to Queen Victoria, patron of the arts and organizer of the Great Exhibition of 1851.

Lee De Forest 1873, American radio and television pioneer and inventor of the Audion vacuum tube, which made broadcasting possible.

Malcolm Pyrah 1941, British showjumper.

Spandau loses last inmate

1987 A crowd of around 200 people, most of them young, attempted to force their way into the cemetery at Wunsiedel where Rudolf Hess, Adolf Hitler's one-time deputy, was due to be buried in the family grave today. Police successfully repulsed them with batons and dogs. A total of 90 people were arrested, 23 of them neo-Nazis. Hess, 93, who died on August 17 in Spandau Prison, Berlin after 46 years in captivity, is said to have been buried two days ago at an undisclosed location. The body will be reburied at Wunsiedel at a later date when there is less danger of neo-Nazi groups turning his internment into a political demonstration. The Hess family still disputes the Allies' assertion that Hess committed suicide by hanging himself. Spandau Prison will now be demolished.

Anyone who wants to carry on the war against the outsiders, come with me. I can't offer you either honours or wages; I offer you hunger, thirst, forced marches, battles and death. Anyone who loves his country, follow me.

Guiseppe Garibaldi – he was defeated by the Austrians at Morrazone today, 1848.

Mini marvel gets big cheer

1989 A very special car celebrated its 30th birthday today – the Mini. Few heads turned when the small wonder was first unveiled at the British Motor Corporation's Longbridge factory in Birmingham. Production was a modest 20,000 cars in the first year. In 1970 the figure leapt to 381,000. The Mini took off thanks largely to a series of major rally wins and its adoption by the rich and famous. The little car was seen roaring to victory in the Monte Carlo rallies of 1964, 1965 and 1967 and nipping about Swinging London piloted by the likes of John Lennon, Peter Sellers, Twiggy and Marianne Faithfull. Designer Sir Alec Issigonis, who died last year, would no doubt have joined the thousands of enthusiasts expected at Silverstone race circuit tomorrow to wish the 10-ft (3 m) marvel many happy returns.

US WOMEN VOTE

1920 The US legislature today ratified the Nineteenth Amendment giving American women the right to vote. The Amendment was bitterly opposed by some members of the Senate before eventually being submitted to the legislature in June last year. That American women now have equality with their sisters in Britain, Germany and Russia is largely due to the efforts of the 2 million-strong National American Woman Suffrage Association which, in different guises, has been campaigning for votes for women since 1869.

1936 The first high-definition television programmes seen in Britain were transmitted today from the BBC studios at Alexandra Palace, London, to the Radio Show at Olympia (Radiolympia). A regular service is due to open next November. Six weeks ago in New York the RCA station W2XBS started transmitting experimental high-definition television programmes.

French setback at Crécy

1346 An English army under Edward III has won an overwhelming, and unexpected, victory at Crécy today. This latest phase in hostilities between France and England – which the pessimists say looks set to last 100 years – opened when King Edward III, accompanied by his eldest son, Prince Edward, landed in Normandy last month. Their army sacked Caen and threatened Rouen before being pursued northwards by a large French force, estimated at around 50,000, under Philip VI. Battle was joined at Crécy-en-Ponthieu. Although numerically outnumbered by a ratio of 2:1, the English proved to have superior weaponry. Philip's 6000 Genoese crossbowmen were simply no match for Edward's 7000 well-trained longbowmen and the short-barrelled bombards aimed at the French ranks. For his battle performance, King Edward's 16-year-old son was awarded spurs and ostrich plumes and with them the mottoes *Homout* (Courage) and *Ich dene* (I serve).

1939 German aircraft manufacturer Ernst Heinkel's gamble to develop an aircraft propelled by a turbojet engine seems to be on the brink of paying off. It needs to, as Heinkel has sunk his own money into the project in the absence of interest by the German Air Ministry. Having completed a series of taxing trials, the He 178 aircraft powered by the revolutionary new engine, HeS 36, took off from the Marienehe airfield today. The designer of the engine is Hans-Joachim Pabst von Ohain, who Heinkel had to be persuaded to employ three years ago as a post-graduate student.

All right, then, I'll say it: Dante makes me sick.
Lope Félix de Vega Carpio, playwright of the Spanish Golden Age and the father of comedia, when told today that he was about to die, 1635.

Fab Four's guiding light

1967 Brian Epstein, the man who made the Beatles, died of a drugs overdose today at his elegant home in London's Belgravia. He was 33. Epstein "discovered" the Beatles in Liverpool's Cavern Club in the autumn of 1961 and determined to make them into stars. He succeeded beyond his, and their, wildest dreams. Lately Epstein had been chronically depressed and afflicted by insomnia and his business enterprises were not as sound as they had been. Despite two previous suicide attempts, friends are convinced he did not take his own life.

1576 Death of Venetian painter Titian (Tizano Vecelli).

1783 Jacques Alexandre César Charles launches the first hydrogen balloon to fly, helped by the Montgolfier brothers, Jacques-Étienne and Joseph-Michel.

1791 European monarchs back French King Louis XVI against the revolution.

1813 Napoleon defeats the allied army at Dresden.

1859 The world's first oil well is drilled by Edwin Drake at Titusville, Pennsylvania.

1910 Thomas Edison shows "talking pictures" for the first time at his New Jersey laboratory.

1919 Death of Louis Botha, first prime minister of South Africa.

1928 The Kellogg-Briand Pact, an international agreement to condemn all war as a means of settling disputes, is signed by representatives of 15 nations.

1951 US jets arrive in Britain to set up a US air base at Greenham Common.

1975 Death of Haile Selassie, deposed emperor of Ethiopia.

1987 A 13-year-old Chinese girl who was left to live with a family of pigs returns to normal life after three years special training.

1987 Honeymooners' amorous acts cause an American jet liner pilot to curtail their coast-to-coast inland flight and land in Houston.

BIRTHDAYS

Sam Goldwyn 1882, Polish-born co-founder of MGM, responsible for entertaining films like *Ben Hur* and *Porgy and Bess* reaching the screen.

Lyndon Baines Johnson 1908, American president who took over after Kennedy's assassination.

Mother Teresa of Calcutta 1910, Yugoslavian-born missionary dedicated to the poor and sick, particularly in India: she was awarded the Nobel Peace Prize in 1979.

Bernhard Langer 1957, German golfer.

Krakatoa blows its top

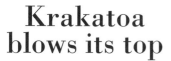

1883 The most catastrophic volcanic eruption witnessed by man reached its climax today on the Indonesian island of Rakata. In May the 6000 ft (1800 m) high Krakatoa volcano, which has its base 1000 ft (300 m) below sea level, began to show signs of rousing from its 200-year slumber. Activity died down only to resume again in June and become more terrifying in its effects. At 10 am this morning Krakatoa erupted with a fury that was heard in Australia, more than 2200 miles (3540 km) away. Debris has been tossed 50 miles (80 km) into the atmosphere, blotting out the sun and plunging the region into darkness. Gigantic tidal waves up to 120 ft (36 m) high have devastated the coastal towns of Java and Sumatra, leaving an estimated 36,000 people dead.

IRA MURDER MOUNTBATTEN

1979 Lord Louis Mountbatten was murdered today by an IRA bomb as he and members of his family enjoyed an outing on his 30-ft (9 m) fishing boat, *Shadow V*. The bomb exploded five minutes after the party had left the picturesque harbour of Mullaghmore in the Irish Republic. Killed with the 79-year-old former admiral and viceroy of India were his grandson, Nicholas Knatchbull, 14, local boy Paul Maxwell, 17, and Lady Brabourne, the mother-in-law of Lord Louis's daughter, Pamela. Later in the morning the IRA murdered 18 British soldiers at Warrenpoint in Northern Ireland.

Coke war in Colombia

1989 The proposed clampdown by the Colombian government on the Medellin drug-trafficking cartel has received a blunt response from that organization. "Total and bloody war" has been declared on the government of President Virgilio Barco. The cocaine-smugglers are particularly perturbed by the reinstatement of extradition to the United States, a process which bribery and threats of violence had forced the Colombian Supreme Court to abandon. Eduardo Martinez Romero, the cartel's leading money launderer, has already been arrested as part of the clampdown. The traffickers have repeatedly said that they would "prefer a grave in Colombia to a prison cell in the US" – not surprisingly, as the last drugs baron to head reluctantly northwards, Carlos Lehder, received a life sentence on arrival. The traffickers have offered to give up the trade in return for immunity from prosecution. The Colombian government is fighting for its credibility. This month alone the cartel was responsible for the murders of the front-runner in the presidential election, Senator Luis Galan Sarmiento, a police chief and a judge.

1850 Franz Liszt conducts the first performance of *Lohengrin* by his friend Richard Wagner, who has fled Germany to escape arrest for his role in the Dresden uprising.

1850 The Channel telegraph cable is finally laid between Dover and Cap Gris Nez.

1862 Garibaldi's army land at Calabria in their march to Rome.

1967 Death of Charles Darrow, American inventor of the board game Monopoly.

1988 Death of American film director John Huston whose films include *The Maltese Falcon*.

BIRTHDAYS

Johann Wolfgang von Goethe 1749, German poet, novelist, playwright and founder of modern German literature who led the Romantic *Sturm und Drang* movement.

Count Leo Tolstoy 1828, Russian author of novels such as *War and Peace* and *Anna Karenina*.

Peter Fraser 1884, Scottish-born New Zealand prime minister 1940-49.

Charles Boyer 1899, French actor who played romantic roles in international films and gained a reputation as the screen's "great lover".

Sir Godfrey Hounsfield 1919, British inventor of the EMI medical scanner and winner of the Nobel Prize for Psychology in 1979.

Lindsay Hasset 1913, Australian cricket captain.

Donald O'Connor 1925, American actor and dancer who co-starred in musicals such as *Singin' In The Rain* before concentrating on composing and on conducting the Los Angeles Philharmonic.

David Soul 1944, American actor and singer who co-starred with Paul Michael Glazer in the television series *Starsky and Hutch* and had a hit with "Don't Give Up On Us".

Emlyn Hughes 1947, Welsh-born England international soccer player.

Coe's Golden Age of the Mile

1981 Sebastian Coe proved last night that he is presiding over a golden age in middle-distance running. In the aptly named Golden Mile at the Heysel Stadium in Brussels, Coe regained the world record he had lost only two days ago to his great rival Steve Ovett. Seb slashed Ovett's time by 1.07 seconds, completing the four-lap race in an incredible 3 minutes 47.33 seconds. This has been a breathaking month for Coe, who has twice broken the world mile record within the last ten days. On August 19 in Zurich he pipped Ovett's year-old mile record by 27 one-hundredths of a second.

Dream sequence

1963 The eloquence for which civil rights leader Martin Luther King Jnr. has become renowned reached new heights today. The occasion was the interracial march on Washington, a peaceful demonstration by 200,000 people committed to the civil rights cause. Standing by the Lincoln Memorial, King gave his vision for America. "I still have a dream. It is a dream chiefly rooted in the American dream. I have a dream that one day this nation will rise up and live out the true meaning of its creed: We hold these truths to be self-evident, that all men are created equal".

CHARLES AND DIANA DIVORCE

1996 Today Britain's most infamous marriage came to end with the divorce of the Prince and Princess of Wales. The marriage lasted 15 years and bore the couple two sons, William and Harry, but finally broke down due to "irreconcilable differences". Both the Prince and the Princess have publicly admitted to adultery. The Princess is said to have received a settlement of around £17 million but she will no longer be able to use her HRH title. This is another blow to the Royal family and comes just four months after the divorce of Prince Charles' brother Andrew. The Duke and Duchess of York parted on good terms for the sake of their two young daughters, but the same cannot be said for the Prince and Princess of Wales.

1988 Three jet planes belonging to an Italian Air Force aerobatics display team collided today, killing 33 people. The aircraft were performing a complicated manoeuvre during their display to a crowd of 300,000 at the US Air Force base at Ramstein in Germany. The West German government is contemplating banning further air displays on its soil.

Thumbs down for the challenge of steam

1830 Inventor Peter Cooper's latest creation, a steam-driven locomotive called Tom Thumb, was today outstripped by the oldest kind of traction in the world – horse power. Since its inception three years ago the Baltimore and Ohio Railroad has relied on horse traction. Now it is looking to the future. On today's showing, though, the horse looks to be the more reliable of the two. After racing neck-and-neck for much of the race, the belt slipped from the loco's drum, the steam pressure dropped and the contraption slowed down. Cooper is sure that the technical hitch which handicapped Tom Thumb's performance today can be overcome. Race watchers agree that Tom Thumb completed the race looking fresher than the horse.

GANDHI COMES TO LONDON

1931 The Indian nationalist leader Mohandas Gandhi arrived in London today to attend the second Round Table Conference at St James's Palace. He is the sole representative of the Indian National Congress party. That Gandhi has agreed to call off the campaign of civil disobedience and attend the meeting is thanks largely to Lord Irwin, the former viceroy of India, who has publicly stated his commitment to India being accorded dominion status.

1929 The giant airship Graf Zeppelin returned to Lakehurst, New Jersey, today after completing a 21-day trip round the world. The hydrogen-filled craft, launched last September, made only three stops during its 21,500-mile (34,600 km) voyage. The flight has demonstrated the feasibility of using this type of craft as a commercial transatlantic airliner.

Beatles hit Klan-land

1966 The Beatles ended their controversial tour of the States with a concert for thousands of screaming fans in San Francisco's Candlestick Park tonight. John Lennon's widely reported comment about the group being more popular than Jesus Christ reached the States shortly before the group touched down to begin their tour. Lennon's apology at their first press conference in Chicago has done little to calm the wave of anti-Beatles sentiment sweeping the South. At Memphis the group was met by 8000 chanting Ku Klux Klan members. Manager Brian Epstein allegedly said tonight's performance will be the Beatles' last-ever live gig.

Candour that was tainted

1982 The Swedish actress Ingrid Bergman died on her 67th birthday at her London home tonight. Freshness and candour were the qualities that made Bergman a star of stage and screen – and it was these qualities that she seemed to betray in the minds of Middle America when she abandoned her husband and child for Italian film director Roberto Rossellini in 1950. The star of the Oscar-winning *Gaslight* was no longer welcome. Denounced in the US Senate for having Rossellini's illegitimate child, she left Hollywood for Europe. She returned 16 years later to collect an Oscar for *Anastasia*. After her third marriage ended in 1978, Bergman came to London. She wrote her memoirs and often appeared at the Chichester Festival.

> *I do not mind what language an opera is sung in so long as it is a language I don't understand.*
> **Edward Appleton**, British physicist, 1955.

One-way traffic at St Louis Olympics

1904 Christmas came early this year for the US Olympic team. Out of a total of 23 track and field events, US athletes collected an incredible tally of 21 gold medals. The major reason for the supremacy of the home team is that few European athletes came to St Louis – fewer than a twelfth of the competitors attending the Games were non-Americans. Apart from the cost and effort of attendance, overseas competitors were put off by the decision to make the Games part of the postponed Louisiana World Fair. Few people are sure about the precise status of the many events staged in St Louis.

Naval disaster at Spithead

1782 A first rate ship of the British fleet, *Royal George*, has sunk while undergoing repairs at Spithead. More than 900 people are feared lost, including most of the crew and many wives and children. Rear Admiral Richard Kempenfelt, 64, a distinguished veteran of the American War of Independence, was among those who perished. The survivors are to be tried for negligence at a court martial to be held at Portsmouth on September 9. The court will decide whether rotten timbers were responsible for the ship capsizing as she was being heeled or whether she was heeled so far that water entered the lower tier of gunports. Launched in 1756, *Royal George* was one of only three 100-gun ships in the British Navy.

1831 In London, Michael Faraday successfully demonstrates the first electrical transformer.

1835 John Batman and associates buy land from the Australian aborigines and officially establish Melbourne.

1842 The Treaty of Nanking is signed by the British and Chinese, ending the Opium War.

1877 Death of Brigham Young, Mormon leader and founder of Salt Lake City.

1885 The first motorcycle is patented by Gottlieb Daimler in Germany.

1918 More than 6000 British policemen go on strike, demanding better pay.

1975 Death of Eamon de Valera, three times Irish prime minister and president from 1959 to 1973.

1987 Lee Marvin, the American actor who won an Oscar for *Cat Ballou*, dies of a heart attack.

1989 Death of Sir Peter Scott, English former chairman of the World Wide Fund for Nature.

1990 The blockade of a bridge over the St Lawrence river in Canada by Mohawk Indians ends.

BIRTHDAYS

Maurice Maeterlink 1862, Belgian poet and playwright best known for *Pelléas et Mélisande* and the children's play *The Blue Bird*.

Elliot Gould 1938, American actor who starred in *M*A*S*H*, *The Long Goodbye* and *The Lady Vanishes*.

James Hunt 1947, British world champion racing driver.

Richard Gere 1949, American actor who first rose to fame with *Yanks* and *American Gigolo* and later starred in films such as *An Officer and a Gentleman* and *Pretty Woman*.

Lenny Henry 1958, British comedian and actor.

Michael Jackson 1958, American pop megastar whose hit albums such as *Thriller* and *Bad* are backed by equally successful videos.

1483 Death of Louis XI, responsible for the unification of France after the Hundred Years War.

1667 Charles II dismisses Lord Chancellor Edward Hyde over humiliating peace terms with Holland in the Treaty of Breda.

1860 The first trains in Britain begin running.

1862 "Stonewall" Jackson leads the Confederates to victory against the Union army at the second Battle of Bull Run in Virginia during the American Civil War.

1881 Clement Ader of Germany patents the first stereo system.

1901 The vacuum cleaner is patented by Scotsman Hubert Cecil Booth.

1937 Joe Louis flattens Britain's Tommy Farr to win the heavyweight boxing title at Madison Square Gardens in New York.

1939 Children start being evacuated from cities as war between Germany and Britain seems imminent.

1941 The Germans surround Leningrad.

BIRTHDAYS

Jacques Louis David 1748, French court painter to Napoleon who was actively opposed to Louis XVI during the revolution: his paintings include *The Rape of the Sabines*.

Raymond Massey 1896, Canadian actor of stage and screen who starred as Dr Gillespie in the television series *Dr Kildare*.

John Gunther 1901, American author and journalist who wrote *Inside USA* and *Inside Russia Today*.

Ernest Rutherford 1908, New Zealand physicist who led the way for modern atomic science at Cambridge.

Dennis Healey 1917, British Labour Party statesman and former Chancellor of the Exchequer.

Jean-Claude Killy 1943, French ski champion who won all three gold medals – the slalom, giant slalom and downhill – at the Winter Olympics in 1968.

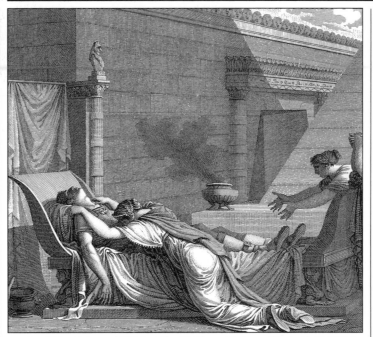

ALL FOR LOVE

30 BC The ruler of the eastern part of the Roman empire, Mark Antony, has committed suicide at the court of his Egyptian lover, Cleopatra. He was 52. Antony's political demise was signalled last year with his defeat by Roman emperor Caesar Augustus, the ruler of the western part of the empire, at the battle of Actium. The beautiful Queen Cleopatra was the cause of the break-up of the triumvirate Antony had formed with Augustus and Lepidus (the ruler of Africa) 10 years ago. Antony's loyalty to Rome was called into question after he made gifts of land to the Egyptian queen. Cleopatra is understood to be attempting face-to-face negotiations with the resolute Augustus. If she fails to mollify him, as seems likely, she will doubtless share a similar fate to Mark Antony.

Unions score victory strike

1980 A little over two weeks after seizing control of the Lenin Shipyard in Gdansk, Polish workers have succeeded in wringing significant concessions from their masters. Among the terms agreed by the Polish deputy prime minister, Mieczyslaw Jagielski, are the right to strike and the establishment of trade unions independent of the Communist Party. The government's initial refusal to negotiate gradually eroded as more Poles downed tools in support of the initiative taken by the Gdansk workers under Lech Walesa. He instigated a central committee to coordinate the country-wide strikes and draw up a list of demands. It remains to be seen whether the Polish government will honour the agreement.

> *During the last few weeks I have felt that the Suez Canal was flowing through my drawing room.*
> **Clarissa Eden**, wife of British prime minister Anthony Eden, as British and French troops sailed for Suez, 1956.

1963 A direct telephone line between the White House and the Kremlin became operational today. The agreement to have a "hot line" linking the US President with his opposite number in Moscow was struck in April. This may turn out to be a lifeline, preventing the delays in diplomatic communication which can lead to dangerous misunderstandings between the two super-powers – as occurred last year during the Cuban missiles crisis.

Ayatollah's regime shaken by bomb

1981 A wave of anti-government violence has culminated in the murder in Teheran today of the president of Iran, Muhammad Ali Rajai, and his prime minister, Muhammad Javad Bahonar. The two were victims of a bomb planted in the premier's office. Three other men were also killed in the blast. The government of Ayatollah Khomeini has been subjected to a series of violent attacks since the dismissal of president Bani Sadr two months ago. The president's dismissal was widely seen as a victory for religious forces over secular political forces in Iran. The speaker of the Iranian Parliament, Hojatoleslam Rafsanjani (below), said today that it was up to the Iranian people to ensure that the revolution continued on its course.

No one wants toxic waste

1988 A West German freighter, *Karin B* carrying 2000 tonnes of Italian hazardous waste is at anchor 18 miles (29 km) south-west of the British port of Plymouth awaiting news of its next destination. The ship has been denied entry to ports in Spain, West Germany, France, the Netherlands, Belgium and now Britain. The toxic cargo was first shipped from Italy to Nigeria where it was illegally dumped before being packed off. Britain's rapidly growing toxic waste industry would have obliged had it not been for the public outcry against it. Environmental groups say that the *Karin B* affair highlights the urgent need for an internationally agreed code of conduct for toxic waste shipments.

The great Grace declares at sixty

1908 W. G. Grace, who celebrated his sixtieth birthday last month, has decided to call it a day and retire from first-class cricket. In a first-class career spanning 43 years, Grace has scored a phenomenal 54,896 runs, notched up 126 centuries, knocked 2879 wickets and grabbed 871 catches. Such is his love of the game that Dr Grace intends to continue playing in minor cricket. His enormous success as a cricketer, and indeed his cricketing longevity, is put down to the solid technique instilled in him by his indomitable mother. A stickler for the straight bat, she coached him out of making loose shots during his formative years in county cricket.

1969 Rocky Marciano, former undefeated heavyweight champion of the world, died in an aircrash near Newton, Iowa, tonight, just hours before his forty-sixth birthday. Short by heavyweight standards (under 6 ft/1.8 m), stocky Marciano (born Rocco Marchegiano in Brockton, Massachusetts) had a remarkable record as a fighter, winning all 49 of his professional bouts, 43 of them inside the distance. A veritable brute in the ring, although unfailingly sporting, he was affable, modest and gentle outside it. He retired from the ring in April 1956 to devote himself to his business interests.

Spleen machine

1867 The French poet and critic Charles Baudelaire died in his mother's arms today in Paris. He was 46. Born into a well-off middle-class family, Baudelaire determined from an early age to live as an artist and embraced eccentricity, affectation and immorality. By his early twenties he was an opium addict and had acquired the venereal disease that would eventually kill him. He won plaudits for translating the works of Edgar Allan Poe, but few for his own work. *Les fleurs du mal* was a failure and labelled obscene. Most readers were either baffled by the poet's use of symbolism or deplored his themes. Declared bankrupt in 1862, Baudelaire died in poverty.

ANNE AND MARK SPLIT

1989 Buckingham Palace officially confirmed today that the marriage of Princess Anne and Captain Mark Phillips is on the rocks. Speculation heightened five months ago when it was revealed that the Princess' equerry, Commander Timothy Lawrence, had written affectionate letters to her. The statement issued today said that although the couple have agreed to separate, there are no plans for divorce proceedings.

1928 The taste of the critics and the Berlin public are poles apart if the reception given to Kurt Weil's Threepenny Opera is any guide. The audience loved its jazz rhythms but Berlin's most influential critics hated it, especially the libretto by Bertold Brecht. Any good words were reserved for the music.

Dylan blowin' again

1969 Bob Dylan, the "voice of a generation", appeared live on stage today for the first time since his serious motorcycle accident three years ago. With The Band he performed 17 of his compositions, including golden oldies like "Tambourine Man", for an appreciative 150,000-strong audience at the three-day Isle of Wight music festival.

DIANA DIES IN PARIS CAR CRASH

1997 Diana, Princess of Wales, has been killed in a car crash in Paris. She was taken to hospital in the early hours of Sunday morning where surgeons tried to save her life. In a statement, Buckingham Palace said the Queen and the Prince of Wales were both "deeply shocked and distressed" by the news. The accident happened after the princess left the Ritz Hotel in Paris with her companion Dodi Al Fayed, son of Harrods owner, Mohammed Al Fayed. Dodi Al Fayed and the car's chauffeur were also killed in the crash which happened in a tunnel under the Place de l'Alma in the centre of the city. The princess' Mercedes was apparently being pursued at high speed by photographers on motorbikes when it hit a pillar and smashed into a wall. Tributes to the princess have been pouring in from around the world.

1422 Henry V, King of England, dies of dysentery while in France: Henry VI accedes to the throne, aged nine months.

1688 Death of John Bunyan, English author famed for *Pilgrim's Progress*.

1900 Coca-Cola goes on sale in Britain.

1957 Malaya achieves independence from Britain.

1962 The former British possessions of Trinidad and Tobago become independent.

1962 Chris Bonington and Ian Clough become the first Britons to conquer the north face of the Eiger.

1963 Death of Georges Braque, French Cubist painter.

1965 India and Pakistan threaten war over Kashmir.

1972 American swimmer Mark Spitz wins five gold medals in the Munich Olympics.

1986 Death of Henry Moore, major English sculptor.

1994 IRA announces a "complete cessation of military activities".

BIRTHDAYS

Caligula 12 AD, Roman emperor remembered for his murderous reign.

Maria Montessori 1870, Italian educationist who developed the Montessori teaching system which encourages children to take the initiative.

Dubose Heyward 1885, American author of *Porgy*.

Sir Bernard Lovell 1913, English astronomer.

James Coburn 1928, American actor probably best known for his role in James Bond spoofs such as *Our Man Flint*.

Van Morrison 1945, Irish-born international singer whose songs such as *Moondance* and *Gloria* have stood the test of time.

Edwin Moses 1955, American athlete who made a world record when he ran in the 400 metre hurdles in 1976 – his first Olympics.

SEPTEMBER

" *We saw the fire as only one entire arch of fire
from this to the other side of the bridge, and in a bow up
the hill, for an arch of above a mile long. It made me
weep to see it. The churches, houses, and all on fire
and flaming at once, and a horrid noise the flames made,
and the cracking of houses at their ruine.*"

Samuel Pepys
London diarist on the Fire of London
which raged September 5, 1666.

SUN KING ECLIPSED

1715 France's Sun King, Louis XIV, died today at 77. Louis succeeded to the throne at the age of four and ruled France for 73 years, longer than any other monarch. His reign was absolute, brilliant and bloody. He was only 23 when he seized full control. A cultural extravaganza blossomed for 20 years at Louis' magnificent palace at Versailles, accompanied by an economic boom and French domination of the world stage. However, Louis' brutal suppression of the Protestant Huguenots was a disaster, and a long succession of wars subsequently sapped France's strength. In his final years his health was failing, and the last of his celebrated mistresses, Madame de Maintenon, had persuaded him that his sufferings were God's punishment for the blood he had spilled all over Europe. On his deathbed he counselled his five-year-old heir Louis XV to avoid wars and extravagance.

1557 Death of Jacques Cartier, French explorer of North America.

1666 Death of Franz Hals, Dutch portrait painter.

1830 The poem "Mary Had a Little Lamb" is published by Sarah J. Hales in Boston.

1920 The French create the state of Lebanon, naming Beirut as the capital.

1923 A massive earthquake in Japan kills more than 300,000, devastating Tokyo and Yokohama.

1948 Chairman Mao sets up a provisional government in China.

1951 The Anzus Treaty, a mutual defence treaty between Australia, New Zealand and the United States, is signed.

1951 Britain's first supermarket, the Premier, opens in London.

1967 Death of English poet Siegfried Sassoon, famous for his brutally realistic war poems.

1969 Libyan Colonel Muammar al-Gaddafi seizes power after the monarchy is overthrown.

1996 Footballer David Beckham earns his first senior cap in a game against Maldova.

1833 A 23-year-old printer published the first edition of a new kind of newspaper in New York today. The *New York Sun* is a daily, half the size of the big news-sheets (much easier to read on a crowded streetcar), and is a fraction of the price of all other New York papers. Written and typeset by proprietor Benjamin Day himself – the *Sun's* four pages are packed with articles calculated for popular appeal rather than merely to inform. Day has hit on an innovative way of selling the newspaper, employing boys to hawk it on the streets.

Fischer reels in title

1972 Bobby Fischer became the first American world chess champion today. The temperamental 29-year-old boy wonder from Brooklyn finally triumphed over defending champion Boris Spassky of the USSR after a marathon two-month struggle, which also established Fischer as the one of the world's unreasonable people. Fischer, who was US champion at 14 and an international grandmaster at 15, sailed undefeated through the qualifying matches to face Spassky, and then argued with the champion over petty details for months before agreeing to play. The showdown in Reykjavik in Iceland drew avid media attention – Fischer's constant tantrums made riveting viewing. The two men played in an atmosphere boiling with resentment, yet the chess was brilliant.

It is impossible to win gracefully at chess. No man has yet said "Mate!" in a voice which failed to sound to his opponent bitter, boastful and malicious.
A.A. Milne, English author, 1919.

Blind, deaf, and dumb but brilliant

1904 A young woman who has been both blind and deaf since the age of two graduated from college today, with honours. Helen Keller, 24, now holds a doctor's degree from Radcliffe College in Cambridge, Massachusetts. When she was an infant a brain fever left her in a silent, dark world. She was confined to hysterics, screams and tantrums until an inspired teacher, Anne Mansfield Macy, helped her to read braille and write using a special typewriter. Two years ago Helen published her autobiography, *The Story of My Life* – but her story is far from over.

GERMANY INVADES POLAND

1939 Adolf Hitler hurled more than a million German troops into Poland today, smashing the Polish defences in a move which has committed the Allies to war. The Poles met the massive armoured onslaught with gallantry but with little else – they even mounted a cavalry charge against the intimidating barrage of Nazi tanks. France and Britain – both treaty-bound to defend Poland – are fully mobilized. Hitler had tried to make a deal with Britain over Poland, but his offers were rejected.

Amilcare Ponchielli 1834, Italian composer of the opera *La Gioconda*.

Sir Roger Casement 1864, Irish nationalist and British diplomat, sentenced to death by the British after he attempted to arrange for Irish World War One prisoners in Germany to take part with him in a Republican rebellion.

Edgar Rice Burroughs 1875, American novelist who created the fictional character Tarzan in *Tarzan of the Apes* and many sequels, but who never visited Tarzan's native Africa.

Marilyn Miller 1898, American actress, dancer and singer who rose to fame with the Ziegfeld Follies in the 1920s.

Rocky Marciano 1923, American heavyweight boxer who became world champion in 1952 and remained undefeated in 49 professional fights.

1834 Death of Thomas Telford, Scottish engineer and canal and bridge builder.

1858 The anonymous song "The Yellow Rose of Texas" is copyrighted in New York.

1865 Boundary disputes end between the British settlers and the Maori Kingitanga in New Zealand.

1870 Louis Napoleon hands his sword to Kaiser William of Prussia, defeated after 40 days of war that confirm Germany as the most powerful nation in Europe.

1910 Death of "Le Douanier" Henri Rousseau, French primitive painter and customs officer, best known for his jungle scenes.

1937 Death of Baron Pierre de Coubertin, founder of the modern Olympic Games.

1942 The German SS destroys the Warsaw Ghetto, killing 50,000 Jews.

1945 Ho Chi Minh becomes president of the newly declared North Vietnam Republic.

1958 South Africa's new premier Hendrik Verwoerd promises to strengthen apartheid.

1976 The European Court of Human Rights says that the British torture Ulster detainees.

1979 Death of Felix Aylmer, British stage and screen actor.

1980 Canadian Terry Fox, with an artificial leg, completes a 3000 mile (4800 km) run and raises $24 million (£13 million).

1987 Philips launch the CD-video.

1988 Chilean exiles led by Salvador Allende's daughter return to Santiago.

2001 Death of heart transplant pioneer Dr Christiaan Barnard.

BIRTHDAYS

John Howard 1726, English prison reformer who campaigned for sanitary improvements and wages for gaolers rather than fees from prisoners.

Lord George Brown 1914, British Labour foreign secretary, 1966-68.

Jimmy Connors 1952, American tennis player.

Viet Minh boss goes for broke

1945 Nationalist leader Ho Chi Minh proclaimed the independent Democratic Republic of Vietnam in Hanoi today, with himself as its first president. Ho's Viet Minh guerrilla army marched into the capital last week when the Japanese withdrew from Vietnam after four years of occupation. Ho and other nationalists formed the Communist Viet Minh – the League for the Independence of Vietnam – in 1941, and have fought alone against the Japanese. Ho was trained in Moscow, was a founding member of the French Communist Party and founded the Indochinese Communist Party in 1930. The British arrested him in Shanghai, and he was a thorn in the side of the French colonial government in Vietnam before the war. Ho Chi Minh has wide public support, but France has no intention of giving up Indochina and is not likely to recognize the new republic.

WORLD'S WORST WAR ENDS

1945 Japan formally surrendered today to Supreme Allied Commander General Douglas MacArthur aboard the aircraft carrier *USS Missouri* in Tokyo Bay, and World War Two ended. Flanked by military leaders, the frock-coated Japanese foreign minister signed the unconditional surrender announced by Emperor Hirohito last month after US atomic bombs obliterated the cities of Hiroshima and Nagasaki. The capitulation is almost as humiliating for Japan as her defeat – according to the martial code of *bushido*, only cowards surrender; warriors choose death. US forces are now occupying Japan while final mopping-up operations continue in Southeast Asia. In a radio broadcast after today's ceremony, MacArthur expressed the hope that a better world would emerge from the carnage – and warned: "We have had our last chance. If we do not devise some greater and more equitable system, Armageddon will be at our door."

Though Tolkien lived in the 20th century he can scarcely be called a modern writer. His roots were buried deep in early literature, and the major names in 20th-century writing meant little or nothing to him.
Humphrey Carpenter, English writer, 1979.

Prussian blues

1792 More than a thousand people died in Paris today as fear of the advancing Prussian army degenerated into a drunken orgy of killing. The mob set out to execute alleged traitors and royalists still held in prison but ended up killing anyone in their way. Prisons were sacked and the inmates hacked to death. Some were subjected to mock trials with only one verdict: death. Most of the victims have been ordinary criminals. The rioting continues tonight.

Warring dervishes mown down at will

1898 General Sir Herbert Kitchener's 25,000-man Anglo-Egyptian army slaughtered a huge Mahdist dervish army at Omdurman in Sudan today. At least 10,000 dervish warriors were killed. They fought bravely but were simply mown down by Kitchener's Maxim machine guns. Kitchener lost 500 men. Thus ends 14 years of dervish rule after the Mahdi, Muhammad Ahmad, massacred General Charles Gordon and his entire garrison at Khartoum in 1885.

TOLKIEN DEPARTS MIDDLE EARTH

1973 J. R. R. Tolkien, Oxford scholar of mediaeval English, died today aged 81. He will be remembered for the story he wrote for his children about the adventures of Bilbo Baggins, a furry-footed hobbit who lived in a burrow in the Shire, a bucolic idyll of Anglo-Saxon Britain. The tale grew into a saga of warriors and wizards, elves, demons, trolls and goblins locked in an awesome struggle of good and evil, with the fate of Middle Earth hanging on a lost ring – the ring of the chillingly evil dark lord Sauron. Tolkien published his *Lord of the Rings* in 1955, but it was not until the 1960s that anybody really noticed the book. The otherworldly Tolkien suddenly found himself the revered guru of a whole generation of flower children, their psychedelic idyll threatened by the evil lord Nixon and his military industrial complex. Tolkien cared little – he was scarcely aware of the modern world outside of his imagination. Other books include the *Hobbit*, and the rings saga continues in the *Silmarillion*, to be published posthumously.

Lionheart grabs English throne

1189 Richard the Lionheart received his father's crown at Westminster today and became King Richard I of England. Richard's first royal act was to free his mother, Eleanor of Aquitaine, from the tower where King Henry II imprisoned her 16 years ago for supporting their warring sons in a rebellion against their father. Richard, Duke of Aquitaine in France, rebelled again, forcing the ailing Henry to conclude a humiliating peace earlier this year. Henry's favourite son, John, was amongst the rebels, and in July Henry died, brokenhearted. The King's last words to Richard were a prayer for revenge on his son and heir, who subsequently wept tears of remorse over his father's coffin. Richard, a petty and quarrelsome man who loves a fight, is looking to his new kingdom to finance a third Christian crusade to the Holy Land.

1650 The Scots are defeated by the English at Dunbar.

1651 The army of Charles II of England is beaten by Oliver Cromwell's army in a battle at Worcester.

1883 Death of Russian novelist and playwright Ivan Sergeyevich Turgenev, who wrote *A Month in the Country*.

1930 The first non-stop flight from Paris to New York is made by Diedonne Caste and Maurice Bellonte.

1939 New Zealand, Australia, Britain and France declare war on Germany after Germany's invasion of Poland on September 1.

1950 The first world driving championship is won by Nino Farina of Italy at the Monza Grand Prix.

1966 Captain John Ridgway and Chay Blyth complete their journey across the Atlantic in a rowing boat in 91 days, landing on the Isle of Aran in Ireland.

1969 Ho Chi Minh, president of North Vietnam during the Vietnam war, dies after a heart attack.

1976 The American spacecraft *Viking II* lands on Mars and sends photographs back to Earth.

1980 The opening night of the tragedy *Macbeth* at London's Old Vic, starring Peter O'Toole, has the audience roaring with laughter.

BIRTHDAYS

Matthew Boulton 1728, English engineer who invented and manufactured the steam engine with James Watt.

Sir Frank MacFarlane Burnet 1899, Australian virologist who was awarded the Order of Merit in recognition of his work on diseases such as influenza, polio and cholera.

Alan Ladd 1913, American leading film actor whose films include *This Gun For Hire* and *Shane*.

Pauline Collins 1940, British stage and screen actress who was nominated for an Oscar for her part in the film *Shirley Valentine*.

1916 England was raided tonight by 13 German Zeppelin airships, and a British fighter pilot, Captain Leefe Robinson, shot one of them down near London – the first of the giant bombers destroyed by the Flying Corps. The airship crashed in flames in Hertfordshire. Two people were killed and 13 hurt in the raids.

America united in state of freedom

1783 Britain finally recognized the independence of the United States of America today. The Treaty of Paris marks the end of the American Revolution following two years of secret negotiations between a beleaguered Britain and the colonial rebels. In an unprecedented war, Britain sent an army of 60,000 to fight a populous and well-armed people on their own ground. However France, Spain and Holland all sided with the rebels. The decisive blow came when rebel commander-in-chief George Washington trapped Lord Cornwallis's army in Yorktown, forcing him to surrender with 7000 men. The war lingered on, but the colonies were already severed from the empire. The new nation has emerged from its revolution with a burgeoning sense of freedom and purpose.

> *It is better to die on your feet than to live on your knees.*
> **Dolores Ibarruri**, Spanish politician, 1936.

CIVIL WAR VICTOR DIES

1658 Oliver Cromwell, Puritan Lord Protector of the English Commonwealth, died today of ague at the age of 60. His son, Richard, succeeds him. Following his civil war victories, Cromwell was made Lord Protector five years ago with army support. His austere military rule made him unpopular in his own country, though he rebuilt the national prestige: he defeated Holland and Spain and made England a great power with overseas possessions, reformed the law, established religious freedom and allowed Jews to settle while protecting Protestants abroad. Cromwell dismissed his second parliament in February, and has ruled alone since then. These last months have been filled with plots and rumours of plots. Colonel Titus even published a book entitled *Killing No Murder*, openly advising Cromwell's assassination. The strain told on his failing health, and the sudden death of his daughter was an added blow, from which he never recovered.

Colony rejects convict cargo

1849 Citizens of the Cape colony at Cape Town today took an oath to boycott the British colonial government and all civil servants with immediate effect. They are protesting against the arrival of the British ship *Neptune*, carrying a cargo of convicts. This follows a London decision to form a penal settlement at the Cape like that started in Australia 60 years ago. The citizens' strike appears to be total. The government will soon start to run out of supplies, and there is very little Governor Sir Harry Smith can do about it. He has given orders for the convicts to be kept on board the ship until he hears from London. The Cape Town journalists and lawyers who fought Lord Charles Somerset to establish press freedom organized today's strike and now want a new liberal constitution.

SEPTEMBER 4

1791 During the French Revolution King Louis XVI is forced to approve France's first constitution, which makes him a mere civil servant.

1797 A French army coup disposes of British-backed royalists in Paris.

1821 Tsar Alexander closes Alaska to shipping.

1870 Napoleon Bonaparte's nephew, Emperor Napoleon III, is deposed and the Third Republic is declared in France.

1871 The New York municipal government at Tammany Hall is accused of widespread corruption.

1907 Death of Edvard Grieg, Norwegian composer famous for composing the incidental music for Ibsen's play *Peer Gynt*

1923 *Shenandoah*, the first rigid airship to be built in the United States, is launched.

1929 The BBC invites Baird Co. to carry out experimental TV transmissions.

1948 Queen Wilhelmina of The Netherlands abdicates in favour of her daughter Juliana.

1965 Albert Schweitzer, French medical missionary, organist and Nobel Prize winner, dies in the Gabon.

1989 Death of Georges Simenon, Belgian novelist of world-wide acclaim who created the fictional detective Maigret.

BIRTHDAYS

Darius Milhaud 1892, French composer and one of the famous Les Six group of influential French composers, best known for his *La Création du Monde*.

Edward Dmytryk 1908, Canadian film director best known for *Crossfire* and *The Human Factor*.

Dawn Fraser 1937, Australian swimmer and one of the greatest ever – she broke the 100 metres freestyle record nine successive times.

Tom Watson 1949, American golfer and five-times winner of the British Open, also winning the US Masters in 1982.

KIROV STAR SEEKS ARTISTIC FREEDOM

1970 Leningrad's famous Kirov Ballet, currently in London on a European tour, lost its brightest star today when Natalia Makarova defected. The spectacular Makarova is widely considered the perfect ballerina. She told reporters today that Russian ballet is stifled by politics and she is seeking artistic freedom in the west. Makarova danced her first Giselle with the Kirov in London on the company's first European tour in 1961 – when her partner Rudolf Nureyev defected. The Kirov's artistic director, Konstantin Sergeyev, is reported to be furious at losing Makarova and is threatening to resign. Makarova's friends say there is more than artistic freedom at stake: she has fallen in love with a westerner.

Seeds sown in opium war

1839 British ships fired the first shots today as the illegal opium trade in China propels the two countries towards war. A British frigate hopelessly outmanoeuvred a fleet of lumbering Chinese junks and delivered two broadsides. The spectacular quantities of opium shipped to China from British Bengal earn vital revenues for Britain – and are ruining China. Earlier this year the Emperor's commissioner, Lin Ze-xu, blockaded the British and American merchants' warehouses in Canton, forcing them under siege to surrender 20,000 chests of the dream drug, which he then destroyed in quicklime pits, to great public acclaim. Lin has now blockaded Canton. In London, the belligerent foreign secretary Lord Palmerston is pushing parliament to send an expedition to force China to open its ports – in the name of free trade.

Monza glory for self-made man

1966 Australian Jack Brabham won the Italian Grand Prix at Monza today, winning the world championship and setting a new record at the age of 40 – and he is the first world champion to win in a car he built himself. With speeds varying between 25 and 160 mph (40 and 257 kph) on the twisting circuits, Grand Prix racing is one of the most exacting businesses there is, and Monza is one of the fastest Grand Prix courses.

Make light work

1881 The best-lit factory in America opened in New York today. The Edison Electric Light Company's new "central power station" in Pearl Street generates enough electricity to light up 7000 of Thomas A. Edison's new incandescent lamps. The company is now offering electricity for sale – power cables lead from the new plant's 900-horsepower steam-driven generators to the premises of 85 paying clients, and there is plenty of spare capacity. Edison, 34, invented the stockbroker's indispensable aid, the ticker-tape machine, when he was only 21, and made a small fortune. His laboratories in New Jersey have churned out valuable inventions ever since – the quadruplex telegraph, which doubled the capacity of the lines, and two years ago the first commercially practical electric light. Edison's carbon-filament lamp burns for more than 40 hours and is cheaply replaced.

How can you bear to go further, selling products injurious to others in order to fulfil your insatiable desire?
    Lin Ze-xu, Chinese imperial commissioner, in a letter to Queen Victoria complaining about the opium trade, 1839.

Double death trap

1978 Rebel guerrillas shot down a Rhodesian airliner with a Russian SAM-7 missile today, then massacred survivors. The missile blew the starboard wing off, killing 38 of the 56 people aboard when the plane crashed in the bush. The survivors were nursing their wounds when the guerrillas appeared and opened fire, killing a further 10 people. The rebels – fighting Prime Minister Ian Smith's illegal white regime – said the airliner was a "military target".

1987 Mathias Rust, the West German teenager who flew his light plane from Poland straight through the Russian air defence system and landed in Moscow's Red Square on May 28, will have plenty of time to think about his extraordinary prank. Today a Soviet court sentenced him to four years in a labour camp.

DEATH FIRE HOT ON HEELS OF PLAGUE

1666 The massive, city wide fire that has raged in London for a number of days started at Pudding Street bakery in London's East End. The flames quickly spread next door to a tar store, which exploded, igniting the neighbourhood. London's Lord Mayor refused to be disturbed by such a paltry matter as a fire and the next morning, as fire gripped the city, thousands of families fled their homes to seek safety in small boats on the River Thames and in the fields outside the city. Today the blaze was at last halted by Navy teams who blew up a swathe of buildings in the path of the flames. More than 13,000 homes and 90 churches have been destroyed, and 400 acres (162 hectares) of the city, from the Tower to the Temple, is reduced to smouldering rubble – yet only nine lives were lost. London was still reeling from last year's great plague, which cost 75,000 lives. The fire has cauterized the old wooden buildings that were still rife with disease. Now the homeless must be fed and sheltered – and a better city built.

USSR kills itself off

1991 The Soviet state is no more. In the past two weeks Russian president Boris Yeltsin and his supporters have foiled a coup, watched the demise of the Communist Party, seen independence in the Baltic and defeated the Soviet centrists. Today, under pressure from Soviet president Mikhail Gorbachev, the Congress of People's Deputies of the Soviet Union reluctantly wound up the Union and handed power to the Soviet republics. The new arrangement leaves Gorbachev a national figurehead – but without wealth.

FATTY FATED

1920 Scandal erupted in Hollywood today when the world's favourite fat man, movie comedian Roscoe "Fatty" Arbuckle, was accused of rape and manslaughter. Last night actress Virginia Rappe, seeking a movie part, went to a drinking party Arbuckle held in a San Francisco hotel room. She was raped, and later died in hospital of internal injuries. "Roscoe did it," she said before she died. Arbuckle weighs 23 stone. Arbuckle started his film career in the Keystone comedy studio – today the public is finding little to laugh at.

Mother Teresa dies at 87

1997 Mother Teresa of Calcutta, the Albanian nun who spent her life caring for the poor and dispossessed, has died at the age of 87. The Nobel Peace prize winner is best known for her work in India, especially Calcutta, where she founded her order, the Missionaries of Charity, in 1948. She was also active in East Pakistan, caring for refugees. Her worldwide profile was raised in 1971 when she visited the United States and set up a mission in the Bronx area of New York.

> *I have not ruled out the possibility of one day coming to power.*
> **Grand Duke Vladimir Kirillovitch**, head of the Romanov dynasty and pretender to the Russian throne, on this day, 1991.

Blackest September at Munich Olympics

1972 Eleven Israeli athletes died when Palestinian terrorists struck at the Munich Olympics early today. Eight hooded Black September terrorists broke into the Olympic Village and attacked the sleeping Israelis in their dormitories. Two athletes died in a hail of bullets while 18 escaped, and the remaining nine were taken hostage. The Games were stopped and 12,000 police surrounded the village. The terrorists demanded the release of 200 Palestinians held in Israel and safe passage out of Germany. The German leaders agreed and the gang and their hostages were taken to Munich airport. In a tragic blunder police sharpshooters opened fire, and all nine athletes were killed in the ensuing battle, as well as four terrorists and one policeman. Three of the gang were captured and one escaped. The Games will continue, albeit under a cloud.

1569 Death of Peter Breughel the Elder, Netherlandish painter of peasants, landscapes and religious scenes.

1800 French troops occupying Malta surrender to the British.

1922 American aviator James Doolittle makes the first American coast-to-coast flight, which takes 21 hours 19 minutes.

1963 Christine Keeler, call-girl at the centre of the Profumo scandal that has rocked the British Conservative government, is charged with perjury.

1969 Death of American blues singer and guitarist Josh White.

1980 The world's longest road tunnel is opened in Switzerland, stretching 10 miles (16 km) between Goshenen and Airolo.

1982 Death of Group Captain Sir Douglas Bader, British fighter pilot who lost both his legs in a flying accident but talked his way back into the RAF to serve in World War Two and became a national hero.

1987 The longest running comedy in the world, *No Sex Please – We're British*, closes at a London theatre after 6671 performances over 16 years.

BIRTHDAYS

Giacomo Meyerbeer 1791, German composer, notably of operas such as *Les Huguenots, L'Africaine* and *Robert le Diable*.

Victorien Sardou 1831, French dramatist who wrote *Fedora* (which starred Sarah Bernhardt) and *La Tosca* (used by Puccini for his opera).

Jesse James 1847, American outlaw who, with his elder brother Frank, led a gang which carried out daylight bank robberies.

Darryl F. Zanuck 1902, American film producer who began his career writing stories for Rin Tin Tin, Hollywood star dog.

Arthur Koestler 1905, Hungarian-born-writer, best known for the novel *Darkness at Noon*.

Frank Yerby 1916, American novelist who wrote *The Foxes of Harrow*.

SEPTEMBER 6

1666 The Great Fire of London is finally extinguished.

1879 The first British telephone exchange opens in Lombard Street, London.

1914 The Battle of the Marne begins.

1936 British aviator Beryl Markham flies solo across the Atlantic.

1940 King Carol II of Romania is forced to abdicate by pro-German Ion Antonescu.

1941 Yellow Star of David badges are compulsory for all Jewish citizens in Nazi Germany.

1968 The kingdom of Swaziland in Southern Africa gains its independence.

1985 All employees of ATV Publishing throughout the world are made redundant following a takeover by Michael Jackson and CBS Songs.

1987 The historic Venice regatta is held without the city's gondoliers, who are on strike to protest against the damage caused to the fabric of the city by powerboats.

1988 Eleven-year-old Thomas Gregory from London is the youngest person to swim the English Channel, completing the trip in 12 hours.

1989 A computer error in Paris results in 41,000 residents, who should have received traffic fines, receiving letters charging them with murder, extortion and organized prostitution.

BIRTHDAYS

Marquis de Lafayette 1757, French statesman and soldier who fought with the American colonists for independence, and was a major figure in the French Revolution.

Joseph Kennedy 1888, American founder of the dynasty that gave rise to the first Catholic American president.

Britt Ekland 1942, Swedish actress and former model who appeared in *The Man with the Golden Gun* and other films.

Sail round world takes its toll

1522 A battered Spanish ship with only 15 crewmen left alive reached Seville today after sailing round the world. The *Vittorio*, commanded by Sebastian del Cano, is the only survivor of the fleet of five ships that set sail three years ago seeking a westward passage to the Indies. Commander Ferdinand Magellan, a Portuguese navigator working for Spain, put down a mutiny and lost two ships in the narrow passage to the Pacific discovered at the tip of South America. In the Philippines Magellan was killed by natives, and a third ship was lost. The survivors sailed west, losing another ship in a skirmish with the Portuguese before rounding the Cape of Good Hope and heading north for home.

Clippers race home for a nice cup of tea

1866 Three British tea clippers reached London today within two hours of each other after a 16,000-mile (25,750 km) race all the way from China. Crowds of Londoners lined the Thames to see the great ships arrive. There are big bonuses for the first ships home with the new season's tea. *Serica, Taiping* and *Ariel* left Foochow at the end of May and raced neck-and-neck all the way. *Taitsing* and *Fiery Cross* are less than two days behind. The sleek 200-ft (61 m) clippers carry more than 1 acre (0.4 hectare) of sail and are the fastest ships ever built – they can sail at speeds of more than 20 mph (32 kph).

Magnificence or megalomania?

1566 Suleiman the Magnificent, the Ottoman sultan for 46 years, caliph of the Arabs and ruler of Islam, has died in Constantinople. Suleiman brought the Turkish Ottoman empire to the height of its power and grandeur, conquering the Arab world, Hungary and Mesopotamia, dominating the Mediterranean and the eastern seas, and bringing prosperity, justice and culture to his empire. Suleiman's father, Selim the Grim, took the throne by killing his brothers, and secured Suleiman's succession by killing all his other sons and grandsons. Suleiman, at the bidding of his scheming wife Roxelana, had his favourite son murdered. Roxelana died, and Suleiman withdrew from active rule, leaving his remaining two sons to fight over the succession. Selim, a drunken weakling, won, and murdered his brother Bayezid with all his sons. Selim took the throne today.

SOLIMANVS II.

Architect of apartheid

1966 Coloureds danced in the streets of Cape Town today after South African prime minister Dr Hendrik Verwoerd was assassinated in parliament. The grand architect of the white racist apartheid system was stabbed four times in the chest by a white parliamentary messenger wielding a stiletto – because the government "didn't do enough for whites". Since 1950, Verwoerd, 65, a socio-psychologist, has sub-divided the country's 73 per cent black majority into ethnolinguistic minorities, each with its pseudo-independent "homeland" (totalling only 13 per cent of the country), effectively exporting them from South Africa and leaving the whites as the majority. Millions of blacks have been forcibly relocated to the poverty-stricken homelands, which serve as cheap labour pools. Untold numbers now live illegally in what used to be their own country, at the mercy of the police. The hard-line minister of justice and police, B. J. Vorster, will succeed Dr Verwoerd.

> *Drugs have taught an entire generation of American kids the metric system.*
> **P. J. O'Rourke**, US journalist: today President Bush announced he would halve the US drug problem, 1989.

Soviets admit their jets downed KAL 007

1983 Soviet military chiefs called a highly unusual press conference in Moscow today to explain why a Soviet jet fighter shot down a South Korean airliner last week, with the loss of 269 lives. The Soviets maintain that flight KAL 007 was on a spying mission for the US. The night flight was far off course – it was shot down near secret Soviet military installations on the island of Sakhalin off Siberia, north of Japan. The Soviets say it refused to answer signals and was flying without navigation lights. Tonight the Soviet leaders expressed sympathy for the bereaved.

CHRISTIAN NAVIES PUMMEL OTTOMANS

1571 The Turkish Ottoman fleet was routed today by the combined Christian navies at Lepanto off the coast of Greece, and Ottoman dominance of the Mediterranean is weakening. The Muslim Turks lost 230 galleys, the Christians 17. Turkish commander Ali Pasha was killed and his head presented to Don John of Austria, commander of the navies of Spain, Venice and Rome. This is the first real Christian victory over the mighty Ottoman empire. The Christian princes combined forces when Sultan Selim II invaded Christian Cyprus, taking Famagusta. Today the opposing lines of galleys confronted one another. Fighting across the decks followed, and after two hours the mauled Turks withdrew. But they have not withdrawn from Cyprus.

> *This is the historic hour when our air force delivers its blows right into the enemy's heart.*
> **Hermann Goering**, Nazi field marshal, unleashing the Luftwaffe bombers on British cities, 1940.

1892 The Boston Strong Boy, world heavyweight bare-knuckle boxing champion John L. Sullivan, lost the title tonight in his first bout wearing the padded gloves required under the new Marquess of Queensberry rules. "Gentleman Jim" Corbett knocked Sullivan out in the 21st round in New Orleans. James Corbett, who invented the deadly left hook, is seven years younger than 33-year-old Sullivan and easily dodged the older man's punches.

The bombs rain down on London

1940 Hundreds of German bombers raided London today in waves that continued well into the night. Parts of the Docks and the East End are ablaze. However, the Air Ministry reported tonight that the Luftwaffe lost nearly 100 planes in the raid and the RAF only 22, and the city weathered the blitz with commendable courage. Every day that the battle for Britain's skies rages on means another day to strengthen the ill-equipped troops defending the coast against the expected Nazi invasion.

Tutu is Archbishop

1986 Bishop Desmond Tutu, the black general secretary of the South African Council of Churches, was today enthroned as Archbishop of Cape Town, the leader of two million South African Anglicans. He is the church's first black leader. Tutu was awarded the Nobel Peace Prize in 1984 for his opposition to South Africa's racist apartheid regime. He has condemned the state of emergency imposed in June to suppress the uprising in the black townships, and defies the emergency laws in calling for economic sanctions against South Africa and for foreign investors to leave. Last month the US senate voted for sanctions; British PM Margaret Thatcher wants voluntary sanctions by Commonwealth states.

> *The chances of peaceful change in South Africa are virtually nil.*
> **Bishop Desmond Tutu**, Nobel Peace Prize-winner, 1985.

Moon finally goes to the dark side

1978 Keith Moon, rock drummer with The Who, died today in his London flat of an overdose of drugs prescribed to combat his alcohol problem. The stick-twirling virtuoso has been described as one of the most talented of contemporary rock drummers. The Who's vocalist, Roger Daltrey, said today Moon was irreplaceable. In fact he has been replaced before. Moon has collapsed several times before from drinking. Moon and the band's guitarist Pete Townshend are famed for their on-stage violence – most performances end with guitars and drums smashed in a fury of destruction.

1812 Marching to Moscow, Napoleon's forces defeat the Russians at the Battle of Borodino, 70 miles (112 km) west of the city.

1838 During a storm at sea, Grace Darling, a lighthouse-keeper's daughter, rows a mile in a small boat to rescue four men and a woman from the small steamship *Forfarshire* which had struck rocks near the Longstone Lighthouse, Northumberland.

1848 The Vienna assembly abolishes serfdom.

1901 The Boxer Rising in China ends with the signing of the Peace of Peking.

1910 Death of William Holman Hunt, English Pre-Raphaelite painter.

1910 Polish chemist Marie Curie announces she has isolated pure radium.

1940 Romania returns southern Dobruja to Bulgaria.

1981 Death of Christy Brown, severely handicapped Irish author of the autobiographical *Down All our Days*.

BIRTHDAYS

Elizabeth I, 1533, English monarch, daughter of Anne Boleyn and Henry VIII.

"Grandma" Moses (Anna Mary Robertson) 1860, American primitive artist who began painting professionally at the age of 78.

Elia Kazan 1909, Turkish-born stage and film director and writer who emigrated with his Greek parents to the US and became a leading Broadway director with *A Streetcar Named Desire* and *Death of a Salesman*, and also co-founded the Actors Studio, which trained stars.

Anthony Quayle 1913, English actor of stage and screen who won an Oscar for his role in *Anne of the Thousand Days*.

Buddy Holly 1936, American rock singer and guitarist who was killed in an aircrash aged only 23; his hits include "That'll be the Day" and "Peggy Sue".

BIRTHDAYS

Richard I 1157, King of England known as "the Lion Heart" who began a crusade in 1190 which ended in the signing of a three-year peace treaty with Muslim leader Saladin.

Antonin Dvorak 1841, Czech composer best remembered for his *From the New World* symphony.

Siegfried Sassoon 1886, English war poet, novelist and biographer of George Meredith.

Hendrik Frensch Verwoerd 1901, South African prime minister who instituted the country's policy of apartheid and was stabbed to death two days before his 65th birthday.

Peter Sellers 1925, English actor best known for his comic roles, particularly as Inspector Clouseau in the Pink Panther series of films.

MONTREAL GIVES IN

1760 The French forces at Montreal surrendered the city to British General Jeffrey Amherst today, completing the British conquest of Canada. The British victory ends 70 years of repeated conflict during which the American colonies were caught up in Europe's wars. Britain declared war on France in 1756 as part of the Seven Years' War in Europe, and suffered a series of defeats in America until General Amherst's forces overwhelmed the French fortress at Louisbourg in 1758. General Amherst went on to conquer Ticonderoga and Crown Point, opening the way to Montreal. General James Wolfe then defeated the French garrison at Quebec, with both General Wolfe and the French commander-in-chief the Marquis de Montcalm dying in the battle. Today General Amherst attacked Montreal from three directions, quickly forcing the French to surrender.

Penguin charged for *Lady Chatterley*

1960 A bid by Penguin Books to publish D. H. Lawrence's notorious novel *Lady Chatterley's Lover* has brought the publishers a charge of public obscenity. Penguin will stand trial at London's Old Bailey next month. The book was first published privately in Italy in 1928. Lord Chatterley, an industrialist paralysed below the waist in the war, symbolizes the impotence of the upper classes; his wife Constance seeks solace in the arms of Mellors, His Lordship's gamekeeper. The prosecution says it contains 13 sexually explicit episodes with heavy use of certain Anglo-Saxon terms. Penguin, however, argue differently, saying the book is great art.

Michelangelo's David faces modern Goliaths

1504 Florence unveiled a magnificent symbol of its independence from its powerful neighbours today. The 29-year-old Florentine sculptor Michelangelo Buonarotti allowed nobody to see his enormous 13-ft (4 m) marble statue, which has taken him three years to carve, until it was unveiled. It is a wonderful figure of David, standing relaxed, his sling over his shoulder, about to face Goliath in battle. The statue was to have adorned the facade of the Cathedral of Florence, which commissioned it, but Michelangelo and the grand council of the new Florentine republic have placed it instead at the main entrance to the Palazzo Vecchio, the seat of the city's government, where its message is clear.

V-2 hurls terror at London

1944 A new German terror weapon struck at London today, adding to the havoc caused by the swarms of V-1 flying bombs thrown at the city since June. The 400-mph (644 kph) V-1 falls after the engine stops – "If you can still hear it, you're safe," the saying goes. But the new V-2 weapon, a long-range rocket carrying a ton of high-explosive, travels faster than sound and plunges out of the sky without warning. The first of them hit Chiswick today with a blast heard for miles, and killed three people. The rockets can be fired from anywhere. Up to 150 V-1s a day have hit London and thousands have been killed. For the second time in the war, London's children have been evacuated. The Germans are thought to have fewer V-2s, but their sudden devastation vastly increases the unnerving effect of the terror campaign.

This pictorial account of the day-to-day life of an English gamekeeper is full of considerable interest to outdoor minded readers. Unfortunately, one is obliged to wade through many pages of extraneous material. In this reviewer's opinion the book cannot take the place of J. R. Miller's Practical Gamekeeping.

Field and Stream, journal of British country life, reviewing D. H. Lawrence's *Lady Chatterley's Lover*, 1961.

ITALY'S WHITE FLAG

1943 Italy has surrendered to the Allies, according to an announcement today by US commander General Dwight D. Eisenhower. Marshall Pietro Badoglio, Italian prime minister since the Fascist dictator Mussolini's fall in July, signed the surrender at a secret meeting four days ago. Mussolini's power faltered when the Allies invaded Sicily, and King Victor Emmanuel deposed him. The Allies landed in Italy opposite Messina last week and further landings are underway. Eisenhower today appealed to Italians to oppose the German forces. Meanwhile Mussolini is believed to be in prison somewhere in Italy.

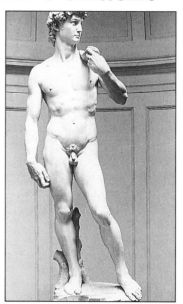

Race stirs riots in London

1958 Notting Hill in north London has been torn by three nights of race riots, with serious injuries and more than 150 arrests. The fighting was provoked by whites – police say extreme right-wing activists were at work. It started when white youths beat up five blacks, leading to petrol bombings and street battles between gangs of up to 2000. Meanwhile in Nottingham a television director was accused of starting a race riot by reconstructing a previous clash between black and white youths. The mock fight exploded into battle. A magistrate today jailed five rioters – and condemned the media.

Chairman unseated

1976 Mao Tse-tung has died after a series of strokes. He was 82. Chairman Mao was revered by 800 million Chinese whose lives he changed forever. In 1949 Mao's Communist guerrilla army overthrew Chiang Kaishek's US-backed Nationalists and established the People's Republic of China. Mao, the "Great Helmsman", charted the way forward, and today China's "starving millions" are history: the Chinese are universally fed, housed, educated, employed and kept healthy, there is little crime, and not nearly as much oppression as westerners believe. Political ferment continues, but then Mao saw revolution as an ongoing process.

THE VIOLENT SIDE OF NORMAN WISDOM

1087 William the Conqueror has died. As Duke of Normandy William conquered England in 1066 and took the throne as William I. The Norman king brought stability in a time of turmoil, but at great cost to the English: all land became Norman property and the English serfs were reduced to slavery. Early rebellions were harshly dealt with – William devastated Yorkshire. By law, poachers had their eyes gouged out; the Norfolk rebels of 1075 had their right feet cut off. Earlier this year the French king sneered at the ageing William because he'd grown so fat.

William declared war and besieged Mantes. Riding out to view the burning town, his horse trod on an ember and threw him off. Today, six weeks later, the Conqueror died of his injuries near Rouen. He was buried by a French knight in Caen and will be succeeded by his greedy, obnoxious second son, William Rufus.

> *Mao always wanted to tour America.*
> **Edgar Snow**, US journalist and chronicler of communist China, 1979.

Israeli whizkid hacked Pentagon secrets

1991 While Israelis sheltered from attacks by Iraqi Scud missiles during the Gulf War, a teenage computer wizard hacked into the Pentagon computers to find out how the top-secret Patriot anti-missiles protecting Israel worked. When he tired of browsing military secrets he turned to the Visa credit card computer, finding his way into the customer files. He provided details to an international network of teenage hackers, who promptly went on a spending spree at Visa's expense. Six of them were arrested in the US and Canada, and named 18-year-old Deri Schriebman of Israel as the source. Today he showed awed detectives how he did it, as well as how to make free long-distance telephone calls. "He's the most talented hacker we've ever seen," the police experts said.

Stunted artist felled by low life he painted

1901 Henri de Toulouse-Lautrec, Post-Impressionist artist and chronicler of Paris low-life, died today following a paralytic stroke brought on by syphilis and alcoholism. He was 36. Toulouse-Lautrec was a master draftsman and observer. Born

an aristocrat, he smashed both thighs in a fall from a horse when he was 14, and bone disease left him horribly stunted. The young Toulouse-Lautrec haunted the Montmartre red-light district in Paris and produced stylish Art Nouveau posters for nightclubs and performers, and charming, if cynical, paintings of his friends the Montmartre prostitutes.

1513 King James IV, King of Scotland, dies at the Battle of Flodden Field, defeated by English troops.

1583 English explorer Sir Humphrey Gilbert drowns on his return to England together with the entire crew of the frigate *Squirrel*, which sank off the Azores.

1835 The British Municipal Corporations Act reforms urban government, bringing about a system of local government.

1911 The first airmail service in Britain begins, operating between Hendon and Windsor.

1948 North Korea proclaims its independence.

1963 Twenty-seven-year-old Jim Clark from Scotland is the world's youngest motor racing champion, driving Colin Campbell's Lotus.

1971 British reporter Geoffrey Jackson is released after eight months by the Tupamaros, his kidnappers in Uruguay.

1978 Eighteen-year-old Czech tennis player Martina Navratilova defects to the West and asks the US for political asylum.

BIRTHDAYS

Cardinal de Richelieu 1585, French statesman and chief minister to Louis XIII from 1624, who crushed all opposition to the monarchy.

Max Reinhardt Goldman 1873, Austrian theatre and film director of great influence.

Cesare Pavese 1908, Italian poet and novelist who was imprisoned for his anti-fascist views in 1935.

Chaim Topol 1935, Israeli actor of stage and screen who won an Oscar for the film version of *Fiddler on the Roof*.

Otis Redding 1941, American singer and songwriter known for "Try a Little Tenderness" and "(Sittin' on) the Dock of the Bay".

John Curry 1949, British world-class ice-skating star who won the European men's single title, the winter Olympics gold medal and the World Championships in Stockholm in 1976.

1894 London taxi driver George Smith is the first person to be convicted for drunken driving while in charge of an electric cab. He is fined 20s (£1/$1.80).

1919 The allies sign the Treaty of Saint Germain with Austria at the Paris Peace conference.

1945 Nazi collaborator Vidkun Quisling, premier of Norway during World War Two, is sentenced to death.

1952 West Germany offers Israel £293 million ($540 million) in compensation for Nazi atrocities.

1956 Record shops are inundated with requests for "Love Me Tender" following Elvis Presley's first appearance on the *Ed Sullivan Show* on American television on September 9.

1962 Australian Rod Laver completes the Grand Slam after winning the US Tennis Championships.

1965 Yale University publishes a map showing that the Vikings discovered America in the 11th century.

1979 The Lancaster House conference on the future of Rhodesia opens.

1983 Death of Balthazar Johannes Vorster, former prime minister of South Africa who was interned during World War Two as a pro-Nazi leader.

BIRTHDAYS

Giovanni Domenico Tiepolo 1727, Italian rococo painter and engraver best known for his church frescoes.

Sir John Soane 1753, English neo-classical architect who is noted for the Bank of England in London and many country homes.

Mungo Park 1771, Scottish surgeon who explored the true course of the River Niger in Africa.

Robert Wise 1914, American film director whose productions include *West Side Story*.

Arnold Palmer 1929, American golfer, champion of four US Masters, two British Opens and the US and Spanish Opens.

Picasso's picture of pain comes home to Spain

1981 *Guernica*, Pablo Picasso's picture of pain, returned to Spain today after four decades in exile in New York. *Guernica* is Picasso's vision of the appalling destruction of the Basque capital by German bombers in 1937 during the Spanish civil war. The Spanish artist painted it at once, and later that year it was defiantly exhibited in Paris to counter a Nazi exhibition in Germany of Expressionist painters, titled "Degenerate Art". In 1940 Picasso sent the painting to New York for safekeeping during the war, and later refused to allow it to be shown in Spain until General Franco's Fascist rule ended and democracy was restored. Picasso died before that happened, in 1973. Today his masterpiece took its rightful place in the Prado Museum in Madrid, a memorial to both artist and subject for free Spain to treasure. *Guernica*'s wailing mother with the dead child, the crawling woman, the screaming horse, all are shorn of all abilities but one, the ability to suffer pain. The most famous painting of the century, for millions *Guernica* condemns all war.

East Germans stream west

1989 East German refugees flooded through Austria to West Germany today as Hungary lifted restrictions on its border with the West. The Hungarians started to dismantle the barbed wire "Iron Curtain" on their Austrian border in May, and East Germans saw it as an avenue to freedom, sidestepping the hated Berlin Wall. Allowed to travel within the communist bloc, more than 50,000 went "on holiday" through Czechoslovakia to Hungary, where many have been waiting in refugee camps. Abandoning the deadlocked negotiations with East and West Germany, Hungary today opened its borders to all East German citizens. The East German government has condemned Hungary's "treachery".

CONGRESS BACKS MAHATMA GANDHI

1920 The Indian National Congress voted today to adopt Mahatma Gandhi's campaign of non-cooperation with the British colonial government. "Non-cooperation is our only weapon," he said, and promised the campaign would lead to victory within a year. He has managed to unite the rival Hindu and Muslim parties in protest.

Wham Slam Danke Mam

1988 Steffi Graf, the 19-year-old West German tennis star, was today the third woman in history to win the Grand Slam – the Australian, French, Wimbledon and US open singles titles in the same year. Graf beat Gabriela Sabatini 6-3, 3-6, 6-1 to win the US Open. Last year she won 11 of her 13 tournaments, 75 of 77 matches and the French Open. This year she lost only one set in the entire Grand Slam – the second set against Sabatini today.

> *It would have been better if the experiment had been conducted in some small country to make it clear that it was a utopian idea, although a beautiful idea.*
> **Boris Yeltsin**, Russian president, on communism, *Newsweek*, 1991.

Bungle warfare at Sevastopol

1855 The Russian Black Sea naval base of Sevastopol finally fell to the British and French armies today after an 11-month siege. The campaign was fraught with bungles on both sides. The Allies could not even decide where to fight the war. When their armies eventually arrived at Sevastapol the Russians had not built proper defences and the Allies could have captured the fortress without a siege. But the British and French commanders argued over tactics and the opportunity was lost. The long siege took a high toll. British troops suffered the winter without proper cover, and more soldiers died of disease than bullets.

> *I want to be the white man's brother, not his brother-in-law.*
> **Martin Luther King Jr.**, black US civil rights leader, 1962.

Chile's Allende killed in army coup

1973 Chile's democratically elected Marxist government was overthrown today in a US-backed military coup, and president Salvador Allende is dead. Right-wing coup leader General Augusto Pinochet says Allende committed suicide, but surviving leftists say he was shot, fighting to the last, the presidential palace in Santiago burning around him. Thousands of Chilean leftists were slain. Elected in 1970, Allende's left-wing alliance instituted land reform and nationalized major industries – including the copper mines, 80 per cent US-owned. US big business acted with the CIA to destabilize the country. Chile's international credit suddenly dried up; the US forced down the world copper price, Chile's chief foreign exchange earner, and poured resources into Pinochet's army, while the CIA fomented strikes and plotted today's coup – in which Pinochet was little more than a US puppet.

Cromwell soaks Ireland in blood

1649 Oliver Cromwell today had 1500 Irish rebels put to the sword to prevent further bloodshed. When the city of Drogheda rejected his offer to surrender, Cromwell's Roundhead troops sacked the city. The Puritan English Commonwealth's military chief is leaving a welter of blood and destruction in his wake. Ireland has been in turmoil since the insurrection of 1641. The English Civil War left Parliament on a weak footing there, with the Royalist Marquis of Ormond controlling most Irish fortresses. He rebelled, claiming the exiled Charles II as king. Cromwell landed near Dublin with 16,000 troops, and his terror tactics have turned the tables. Today's massacre has left the remaining Royalist strongholds anxious to surrender.

Nazis flee as US enters Germany

1944 With the Nazis in retreat throughout Europe, the first Allied forces entered Germany today when the US First Army under General Omar Bradley crossed the German border at Eupen. Bradley's forces were with the Free French soldiers who liberated Paris on August 25. Last week British and US troops freed Brussels and Liege in Belgium and advanced on the Siegfried Line, Germany's main defence. The Line is under heavy US assault in the south near Nancy, the lynchpin in Adolf Hitler's southern defences. German soldiers are fleeing en masse, with large numbers surrendering and reports of widespread desertions.

Saudi front man takes BCCI rap

1991 The US Federal Reserve has seized the US assets of a Saudi Arabian financier and fined him $37 million (£20 million). Ghaith Pharaon was the US front man for the Bank of Credit and Commerce International, which was seized by international regulators in July amid allegations of widespread fraud. Forty BCCI officials were arrested in Abu Dhabi at the weekend. The bank was 70 per cent owned by the Gulf state. Last week a US grand jury issued indictments against six BCCI officials following investigations into drugs money laundering. A congressional report said the US government had information on BCCI corruption in the mid-1980s, and in London a judicial inquiry has been told that both the Bank of England and the Chancellor were warned about BCCI as early as 1986, but failed to act.

> *People of the same trade seldom meet together but the conversation ends in a conspiracy against the public, or in some diversion to raise prices.*
>
> **Adam Smith**, Scottish economist, in *An Inquiry into the Nature and Causes of the Wealth of Nations*, 1776.

AMERICA UNDER SIEGE

2001 The United States has become the victim of the worst terrorist attack ever launched. A hijacked American Airlines Boeing 767 has crashed into the North Tower of the World Trade Center, killing all passengers on board, and causing an enormous explosion. Fifteen minutes later, a second hijacked plane crashed into the South Tower. A third plane was flown at the Pentagon in Washington and a fourth crashed in Pennsylvania after the hijackers were overpowered. Both towers of the World Trade Center later collapsed and the number of dead has been estimated at 3,000. No one has claimed responsibility, but many believe it is the work of Al Qaeda.

1777 English forces under General Howe defeat George Washington's troops at The Battle of Brandywine Creek in the American War of Independence.

1841 The Brighton-London commuter express train begins a regular service, taking just 105 minutes.

1915 The first British Women's Institute is opened in Wales.

1948 Death of Mahammed Ali Jinnah, first governor of Pakistan.

1950 Death of Jan Smuts, the Boer guerrilla leader who became a British field marshal and a world statesman.

1971 Former Soviet premier Nikita Khrushchev dies in obscurity.

1987 Four men are arrested and charged with intending to steal a £25,000 ($46,000) dolphin from the Marineland Oceanarium in Morecambe, Lancashire.

1987 Pete Tosh, Jamaican reggae star and former member of the Wailers, is shot dead by three robbers who burst into his home.

2003 Swedish foreign minister Anna Lindh is murdered.

BIRTHDAYS

James Thompson 1700, Scottish poet who wrote "Rule Brittania".

O. Henry 1862, American short-story writer who established himself as a writer of merit with his first book, *Cabbages and Kings*.

D. H. Lawrence 1885, British novelist who examined human sexuality and social conditions in industrial society in *Sons and Lovers* and *Women in Love* and whose *Lady Chatterley's Lover* was banned when it first appeared.

Herbert Lom 1917, Czech-born actor who trained in London at the Old Vic and whose films include *War and Peace* and the Pink Panther films.

Ferdinand Marcos 1917, Filipino president whose conspicuously corrupt rule came to an end when he was deposed by Cory Aquino.

Barry Sheene 1950, British motor cycling champion.

1733 Death of French musician François Couperin, who taught and composed for the harpsichord.

1878 Cleopatra's Needle, the obelisk of Thothimes III, is erected on London's Thames Embankment.

1910 The world's first policewoman is appointed by the Los Angeles Police Department: Mrs Alice Stebbin Wells was a social worker in her previous career.

1935 American millionaire Howard Hughes achieves an aviation record, flying an aeroplane of his own design at 352.46 mph (564 kph).

1936 British tennis champion Fred Perry beats Donald Budge in the final of the US Tennis championships to become the first non-American winner.

1953 Nikita Khrushchev is elected first secretary of the Soviet Communist Party.

1972 Death of American actor William Boyd, internationally famous from 1934 as cowboy hero Hopalong Cassidy.

1974 Haile Selassie of Ethiopia is deposed by a military coup.

1987 American jockey Steve Cauthen wins the St Leger on Reference Point, setting a new record for trainer Henry Cecil of 147 wins in a season.

BIRTHDAYS

Herbert Henry Asquith 1852, British Liberal Prime Minister who introduced the old age pension.

H. L. Mencken 1880, American essayist, critic and author of *The American Language*.

Maurice Chevalier 1888, French acrobat, entertainer and actor.

Louis MacNeice 1907, Irish poet, playwright and broadcaster who belonged to the group of poets known as the Oxford Group together with Auden, Day Lewis and Spender.

Jesse Owens 1913, American track and field athlete who won four gold medals at the Berlin Olympics in 1936.

Police brutalize Biko

1977 The South African Black Consciousness activist Steve Biko has died after six days in police detention. There is little doubt that he was beaten to death and the news has sparked international outrage. Biko, 30, is the latest in a long line of deaths in custody. He was detained under Emergency powers in Port Elizabeth and interrogated for five days. Guards found him unconscious in his cell yesterday, foaming at the mouth, and he was then driven 750 miles (1207 km) to Pretoria, naked and handcuffed, to die in a prison hospital.

FORTUNE RUNS OUT FOR AMERICAN CHANCER

1860 William Walker, American filibuster and ex-president of Nicaragua, was shot today by a firing squad in the Honduras. Walker, 36, a failed lawyer turned soldier of fortune, landed in the Honduras last month on yet another military escapade, but he was captured by government forces, court-martialled and sentenced to death. Three years ago, backed by Cornelius Vanderbilt and other US businessmen, Walker took advantage of a civil war in Nicaragua to seize control with a force of only 250 men. He set himself up as dictator and won US recognition, but he argued with his business backers, who had him overthrown and expelled after only a year in power. Today Walker's dreams of heading a united Central America ended.

Relief waltzes in to save Vienna

1683 The two-month siege of Vienna ended today when the Turkish Ottoman army surrounding the city was routed by a European relief force. Grand vizier Kara Mustafa had led his army on a feint into Hungary and then turned towards Vienna, long the main Christian bastion against Muslim Ottoman expansion. Vienna's cannon kept the Turks at bay, but the city was weakening when Poland's King John III and Charles, Duke of Normandy's relief expedition arrived. Poor tactics cost Mustafa the battle, opening the way for a Christian attack on the Ottoman empire. The Sultan has ordered Kara Mustafa to commit suicide.

> *The most potent weapon in the hands of the aggressor is the mind of the oppressed.*
> **Steve Biko**, founder of South Africa's Black Consciousness Movement, 1971.

Hijackers blow up three jets

1970 Palestinian hijackers holding three Western airliners and more than 300 passengers hostage at a desert airfield in Jordan blew up the three aircraft today. The terrorists freed 250 hostages before destroying the jets but are still holding another 56 passengers and reiterating their demands for the release of Palestinian prisoners. The drama began on Monday when the terrorists seized a PanAmerican Jumbo, a Swissair DC8 and a TWA Boeing 707 in Europe, forcing the Jumbo to fly to Cairo and the other two to Jordan. The negotiations continue.

Kennedy - Bouvier the dream ticket

1953 America's most eligible couple were wed in Newport, Rhode Island, today. Senator John Fitzgerald Kennedy married the *Washington Times-Herald* photo-journalist Jacqueline Lee Bouvier, and you had to be somebody to be there — thousands were turned away from the wedding party. Rising star Kennedy, a Democrat and a Roman Catholic, defeated Henry Cabot Lodge to take the Massachusetts seat in the major upset of last year's elections. His father is the financier Joe Kennedy, former US ambassador to Britain. John shone at Harvard, was a Navy hero in the Pacific war and a Boston congressman for six years. Younger brother Robert, a Washington lawyer, ran his brilliant election campaign last year. A third brother, Edward, is in the armed forces, hoping to redeem himself after being caught cheating at Harvard. Tragedy has dogged the family: the eldest son, Joseph, was killed in the war, and the eldest daughter, Kathleen, died in an air crash five years ago.

Mystery crash leaves Chinese puzzle unsolved

1971 Peking is buzzing with speculation today following an official announcement that the man Chairman Mao Tse-tung named as his successor, People's Liberation Army chief Lin Piao, has been killed in a plane crash – while fleeing to the Soviet Union. The announcement said Lin had been plotting to assassinate Mao and take power. Lin was the master tactician whose victory over Chiang Kai-shek's US-backed Nationalists in 1949 made way for communism in China. He was Mao's closest ally, and it was only through Lin's support that Mao was able to quell the turmoil of the Cultural Revolution which had removed Mao's chief rivals: all except Lin Piao, perhaps. The truth may never be known.

1989 South Africa's biggest anti-apartheid demonstration in 30 years took place today in Cape Town. Twenty thousand people of all races marched to the City Hall in protest against the police killings of 23 protesters during the whites-only election last week.

PHILIP'S GOLDEN REIGN TARNISHED

1598 The world's most powerful ruler, the Habsburg king Philip II of Spain, died today at 71. His 40-year reign was a golden age for Spain, funded by the conquistadors' plunder of Latin America – and squandered in a succession of wars in Europe. Following the crushing defeat of Spain's "invincible Armada" by the English 10 years ago, beset by the Dutch revolt and the struggle with the Turks in the east, Philip's vast empire is close to economic ruin. Philip was a devout Roman Catholic and an austere but just ruler, well loved by his people. His fourth wife's fourth son, Philip III, is now Spain's new king.

1993 In an historic ceremony on the lawn of the White House, Israeli premier Yitzhak Rabin and PLO leader Yassir Arafat have signed a peace accord after months of secret negotiations. President Clinton was there to host the ceremony, which was attended by 3,000 dignitaries. The agreement makes provision for a transition to complete Palestinian autonomy in the Gaza Strip and West Bank. The accord, however, has many dissenters.

AIDS is global

1985 The World Health Organization announced in Geneva today that AIDS is now a worldwide epidemic. While virtually every major drugs company has joined the race to find an effective treatment, the WHO is coordinating a global AIDS prevention and education effort. But many traditional societies that are now affected have strong taboos against the open discussion needed, and even Western societies resist the implications.

Wolfe scales new heights

1759 A British expedition today defeated the French forces at Quebec. James Wolfe, the young general who led the attack, was killed in the battle – but he lived long enough to hear that he had won. The French commander, the Marquis de Montcalm, was fatally wounded. Wolfe led 5000 men up the St Lawrence River, intending to meet up with General Amherst's land forces, but Amherst did not arrive and Wolfe continued alone. He laid siege to Quebec in May, but was unable to break the French resistance until today, when he and his men scaled the cliffs behind Quebec and surprised the French on the Plains of Abraham. Wolfe has died a hero – Quebec is the key prize in the French and Indian war, now in its third year.

1592 Death of Michel de Montaigne, French essayist and diarist.

1788 New York becomes the federal capital of the United States.

1806 English statesman Charles James Fox is taken ill and dies at home in London, just as he was about to introduce a bill abolishing slavery.

1907 The British liner *Lusitania* arrives in New York at the end of her maiden voyage, having made the journey in a record five days, averaging 23 knots.

1955 Little Richard records a sanitized version of "Tutti Frutti" in Los Angeles.

1957 The 1998th performance of *The Mousetrap* makes it Britain's longest-running play.

1970 In Mexico for the World Cup, England football captain Bobby Moore is accused of stealing a diamond bracelet from a shop.

1989 A British banking computer error gives customers £2 billion ($3.7 billion) in just half an hour.

BIRTHDAYS

Clara Schumann 1819, German pianist remembered for her interpretation of the work of her husband, Robert, and Chopin.

Milton Snaveley Hershey 1857, American chocolate manufacturer who built the world's largest chocolate factory to make his Hershey Bars and established the Hershey Foundation, in which his wealth was used for educational purposes.

John Pershing 1860, American general who commanded the US Expeditionary force in Europe in World War I.

Claudette Colbert 1905, French-born film star who was one of Hollywood's most versatile light actresses.

Roald Dahl 1916, British author who wrote children's books, macabre tales for adults and the screenplay for the film *Chitty Chitty Bang Bang*.

BIRTHDAYS

Baron von Humboldt 1769, German scientist who explored Central and South America and published data which forms the foundation of the study of ecology, which he initiated.

Charles Dana Gibson 1867, American artist who created the *The Gibson Girl*, an idealized picture of woman which set a new style of American femininity.

Jack Hawkins 1910, British actor whose films include *The Cruel Sea* and *The Bridge on the River Kwai*.

Tragic Buffalo slaying

1901 US president William McKinley died early this morning in Buffalo, New York, eight days after being shot by an anarchist. He was 58. Vice-President Theodore Roosevelt took the oath this evening. McKinley was greeting visitors at the Pan-American Exposition in Buffalo when Leon Czolgosz, a young Pole, shot him twice in the stomach at point-blank range. President for five years, McKinley followed a foreign policy that turned the US into a world imperial power. He annexed Hawaii, conquered Spain in a two-year war, winning Puerto Rico, Guam and the Philippines, and sent troops to China to quell the Boxer Rebellion. At 43, Roosevelt is the youngest president yet. He returned a hero from the war in Cuba as a leader of the Rough Riders and was elected Governor of New York. He believes in a strong foreign stance.

US do Mexican wave

1847 General Winfield Scott's American forces have captured Mexico City and the Mexican War is over. Scott's artillery battered the hill fortress of Chapultepec on the outskirts of the city yesterday and today his infantry overwhelmed the defenders and entered the city. Mexican commander Antonio Lopez de Santa Anna has fled with his troops and Scott has hoisted the union flag over the National Palace. Scott has fought a brilliant campaign, defeating Mexico with only 14,000 men in five months. Meanwhile US forces have conquered in Texas, New Mexico and California. The war started two years ago over the US annexation of Texas, but President James Polk's real aim was California. Mexico has now lost a third of her land. The cost to the US forces is high – war casualties have been light, but nearly 12,000 have died of disease.

ISADORA'S WILD LIFE TAKES A FATAL TWIST

1927 "Goodbye, my friends, I go to glory," the American dancer Isadora Duncan called out as she set off for a drive near Nice in France. Seconds later she was dead. The end of her shawl had caught in the rear wheel of her Bugatti sports car, breaking her neck as the car pulled off. She was 49. Isadora Duncan revolutionized the world of ballet, winning worldwide acclaim for her free, barefoot interpretations of classics. She largely inspired Serge Diaghilev's spectacular Paris Ballets Russes. Her life was as tempestuous as some of her dances – her love affairs made headlines. Tragically, her two children (by different fathers) were drowned when the car they were in rolled into the Seine 14 years ago. She married the young Russian poet Sergei Yesenin, 18 years her junior, but he left her and hanged himself two years ago, having written his last poem in his blood.

1959 Man reached out and made contact with the moon today. Lunik II, a Soviet spacecraft, crash-landed on the moon after a two-day journey. It sent back a stream of scientific data during the trip. The Soviets are preparing a further space shot, Lunik III, set to fly round the moon and photograph the "dark side" which no man has yet seen.

CAR CRASH ROBS MONACO OF HER GRACE

1982 Princess Grace of Monaco was killed in a car crash today. Formerly the American film actress Grace Kelly, she was driving with her daughter Stephanie on a mountain road between Monaco and Nice when the brakes failed. The car went off the road and plunged 120 ft (36 m). Stephanie survived the fall, but Princess Grace died of head injuries. She was 52. Grace Kelly married Prince Rainier of Monaco in 1956, ending her acting career. She won fame as the cool beauty in films such as *The Country Girl*, for which she won an Oscar, and Alfred Hitchcock's *To Catch a Thief* – in which ironically she drives a sports car at breakneck speed along a mountain road near Nice.

Watergate burglars are Nixon aides

1972 Seven men were indicted in Washington today in connection with the break-in at the Democratic National Committee headquarters at the Watergate office building in Washington on June 17. They were charged with burglary, conspiracy, and wiretapping. Five of the seven were arrested at the scene, attempting to instal secret bugging devices. They were all members of the Republican committee to re-elect president Richard Nixon. The other two men were former White House aides Howard Hunt and Gordon Liddy, members of the same committee. A party spokesman said there was nothing to indicate any others were involved in the plot to bug the Democrat office.

Rocket tragedy

1830 William Huskisson, British MP and former cabinet minister, today became the first person to be killed by a train. Huskisson, head of the Board of Trade, fell under the wheels of George Stevenson's "Rocket" steam engine as it departed on the inaugural run of the Liverpool and Manchester Railway. He was crossing the track to greet the prime minister, the Duke of Wellington, who opened the new passenger line.

Hitler declares Jews "sub-human"

1935 Germany's persecuted Jews have now lost virtually all their rights. At a huge Nazi rally in Nuremberg today, the German Führer, Adolf Hitler, announced new decrees which relegate Jews to *untermensch* (sub-human) status. The Jews lose their German citizenship, they may not marry Aryans, are excluded from employment in the civil service, the media, entertainment and education and lose their pension rights. "Jews Not Wanted" signs are appearing in public places all over Germany. Jewish children are excluded from schools, Jewish businesses are boycotted and Jews are constantly in danger of abuse and open violence, with no recourse to justice.

1588 Final humiliation of the Spanish Armada, whose remnants return to Spanish harbours after defeat by the English.

1821 San Salvador declares its independence.

1859 Death of Isambard Kingdom Brunel, probably the greatest British engineer.

1871 The Army and Navy Cooperative begins the first mail order service to meet the needs of its members in Britain and abroad.

1917 Russian Socialist Revolutionary Party prime minister Aleksandr Kerenski proclaims Russia a republic.

1928 The first robot to be made in Britain is demonstrated at the Model Engineering Exhibition in London by inventors Captain Rickards and A. H. Renfell.

1966 Britain's first nuclear submarine, HMS *Resolution*, was launched by the Queen Mother.

1975 Civil war begins in Beirut between the Christians and Muslims.

BIRTHDAYS

Titus Oates 1649, English Anglican priest who successfully created anti-Catholic feeling by inventing a "Popish plot".

James Fenimore Cooper 1789, American author of 50 novels who is best remembered for *The Last of the Mohicans* and *The Deerslayer*.

Agatha Christie 1890, English crime writer and one of the most successful novelists of all time, creator of Belgian detective Hercule Poirot and spinster sleuth Miss Jane Marple.

Jean Renoir 1894, French film director and son of the famous painter. His productions include *Le Regle du Jeu* and *The River*.

Margaret Lockwood 1916, British stage actress and star of many popular post-war British films, including *The Man in Grey* and *The Wicked Lady*.

Jessye Norman 1945, American mezzo-turned-soprano concert and opera singer.

Warships with wheels launched into war

1916 Thirty-two massive steel "landships" lumbered into action on the Somme today, rolling over the German trenches and apparently impervious to the German machine-gun-fire. Two hours later the British and Canadian infantry had advanced 7 miles (11 km) and taken thousands of prisoners. The fearsome new weapon, codenamed the Tank, is the brainchild of Winston Churchill, Britain's First Lord of the Admiralty. Bristling with guns, the armour-plated monsters weigh nearly 30 tons and run at 4 mph (6.5 kph) on rolling steel tracks. It takes four men to steer them. Hundreds of tanks are being built in Britain.

1988 The Museum of the Moving Image, devoted entirely to the history of cinema and television, opened today on London's South Bank. The world's largest film museum, it is packed with exhibits such as cameras, costumes, props and relics from film sets, plus various gadgets including a self-recording video for visitors to use. It forms part of the South Bank complex of theatres and galleries.

1978 A Bulgarian defector has died in hospital in London four days after being stabbed with a poisoned umbrella tip. Georgi Markov was a broadcaster on the BBC's foreign service. He was standing at a bus stop on Tuesday evening when he was jabbed in the leg from behind. He never saw his assailant. Later he collapsed in a coma and did not recover consciousness.

Dante joins his Beatrice

1321 The Italian poet Dante Alighieri has died in Ravenna after 20 years exiled by papists from his native Florence. He was 56. Dante had only just finished his masterpiece, *La Divina Commedia* (The Divine Comedy), after 14 years' work. It is a 14,000-line fable of a journey through hell, purgatory, and finally paradise where, led by his beloved Beatrice, the poet glimpses God's heaven. A subtle allegory of religion, politics and life, the *Commedia* is being hailed as the greatest contemporary poem. In a sense it is dedicated to Beatrice Polinari, a Florentine Dante met twice and loved all his life.

He may be a little bad now and then – but what man isn't?
Victoria Gotti on her husband, Mafia chief John Gotti, 1991.

1498 Death of Tomas de Torquemada, principal architect of the Spanish Inquisition.

1824 Death of King Louis XVIII of France, whose attempts to be a moderate constitutional monarch were thwarted by the ultra-royalists.

1908 In the USA, Buick and Oldsmobile merge under the name General Motors.

1953 The wife of former British Foreign Office official and Soviet spy Donald Maclean disappears, two years after her husband fled to Russia with Guy Burgess.

1959 Charles de Gaulle, French President of the new Fifth Republic and former head of the committee of National Liberation in Algiers, offers Algeria a referendum on independence.

1963 Malaysia becomes independent and a mob of more than 100,000 burns down the British Embassy in celebration.

1977 Lead singer of T-Rex, Marc Bolan, dies in a car crash.

1988 Thousands of Americans queue up to apply for a new credit card, the Elvis Presley credit card which features the star and allows customers credit of up to $3500 (£1902).

BIRTHDAYS

Henry V 1387, English king who defeated the French at Agincourt.

John Gay 1685, English poet and playwright famed for *The Beggar's Opera*.

Sir Alexander Korda 1893, Hungarian-born film producer and dominant figure in the British film industry.

Lauren Bacall 1924, American actress who made her debut in *To Have and Have Not* opposite her future husband Humphrey Bogart.

Charlie Byrd 1925, American jazz guitarist, perhaps best known for the bossa nova album he recorded with Stan Getz.

B. B. King 1925, American blues guitarist and inspiration of a whole generation of rock musicians, including Eric Clapton.

Pilgrims seek freedom in New World

1620 A group of Puritan separatists set sail from Plymouth today in the *Mayflower*, bound for the New World and religious freedom. The group, most of them uneducated farmers, fled to Holland in 1608 to escape King Charles I's religious oppression. They settled in Leyden, free to follow their beliefs, but they were poor, and could not adapt to Dutch society. Church elder William Brewster went to London and found a sponsor for the voyage to America in Sir Edwin Sandys, treasurer of the Virginia Company. Sandys arranged a plantation grant and financing through London merchants hoping to profit from the venture. Another elder, John Carver, chartered the 180-ton *Mayflower* at Southampton. Brewster and William Bradford sailed from Leyden for Southampton with 35 other "Pilgrims" in the *Speedwell*, and the two ships set off twice before they abandoned the leaking *Speedwell* the third time and crowded onto the *Mayflower*, which sailed today with 102 passengers.

DUTCH TAKE CAPE WAR INLAND

1795 After a three-month standoff, an English fleet carrying a 4000-man army took the Cape Colony from the Dutch today with hardly a shot fired. Dutch Governor Sluysken's troops simply fled when the British landed at Muizenberg. A disgusted Sluysken managed to negotiate a truce, but soon afterwards he received a declaration of war from rebel colonists in the interior who had thrown out the Dutch officials and set up a republic. In despair he capitulated to the British. The English fleet arrived in June to protect the colony against France, but Sluysken held off the invaders with prolonged negotiations and sheer bluff – until today.

Priest uses pulpit to preach revolution

1810 A rural Mexican priest ended his Sunday sermon today with the fiery war-cry: "Death to the Spaniards!" and set a revolution in motion. Father Miguel Hidalgo y Costilla, the pastor of Dolores, is now leading a ragged army of more than 10,000 Indians and peasants against the Spanish colonial government. Hidalgo's academic career ended when his liberal attitudes enraged both the government and the Inquisition. He was sent to the provinces, where he continued to champion the oppressed. His plans to overthrow the Spaniards were discovered, forcing him to act today.

1992 Today Britain withdrew from the Exchange Rate Mechanism (ERM), despite vigorous assertions by the Conservative government of the importance of membership to its anti-inflation strategy. The market's doubts about the credibility of the ERM have at last overwhelmed the Treasury.

Treaty to save the ozone layer

1987 Seventy countries signed an agreement in Montreal today to curb the threat from industrial gases to the ozone layer. The upper atmosphere's layer of ozone, a form of oxygen, absorbs ultraviolet radiation from the sun that would harm all life if it reached the Earth's surface. Three years ago a seasonal "hole" in the layer was discovered over Antarctica, thought to be caused by chlorofluorocarbons (CFCs), gases used in aerosols and as refrigerants. CFC use will be frozen at current levels and reduced by half within 12 years.

1991 A man attacked Michelangelo's David with a hammer today, breaking off the second toe of the marble statue's left foot. The 13-ft (4 m) sculpture is one of the great masterpieces of Renaissance art. The attacker later told the Florence police he was merely following instructions from "Nani", a Venetian model who sat for Veronese in the 16th century. The museum director said the pieces had all been saved and the toe would be repaired.

1959 Soviet premier Nikita Krushchev, on a US tour, exploded in rage tonight during a banquet given in his honour by the City of Los Angeles. He took exception to Mayor Norris Poulson's speech and threatened to fly home.

Berlioz ups the decibel level

1837 The French composer Hector Berlioz has produced a *tour-de-force* at a premiere performance in Paris. Most orchestras have about 60 players, but Berlioz's mighty *Requiem*, commissioned by the government, used a 200-voice chorus, 110 violins, a swollen brass section and 16 timpani. With any other composer this would have been sheer excess, but Berlioz used

the huge ensemble to the full. Once the audience had recovered from the overwhelming scale, they were captivated. Berlioz's manipulation of each instrument's capabilities is masterful, yet he cannot play a single instrument properly. He has been a central figure in French music since his innovative *Symphonie Fantastique* won acclaim in 1830.

First air death as Orville Wright crashes

1908 A US army officer was killed today when Orville Wright's flying machine broke a propeller in mid-air and plunged 150 ft (46 m) to the ground. Wright was badly injured, but his passenger, Lieutenant Thomas W. Selfridge, was killed – the first passenger to die in an aircraft accident. Orville Wright made the first-ever powered flight in 1903. The Signal Corps has asked him and his brother Wilbur to build a two-seater aircraft for the army, and Selfridge was on a test flight today.

1977 Prima donna Maria Callas has died of a heart attack, alone in her Paris flat. She was 53. Callas, born to Greek parents in New York, dominated opera in the '50s and '60s. She retired in 1965, her range and power – and her rages and dramatic lovelife – had earned her great fame.

1701 Death of King James II of England.

1792 The Crown Jewels are stolen in Paris.

1796 George Washington gives his farewell address as president of the USA.

1877 William Henry Fox Talbot, British botanist and physicist who pioneered photographic techniques, dies aged 77.

1894 The first British musical on Broadway, *A Gaiety Girl*, opens at Daly's Theatre, New York.

1931 Long-playing records are demonstrated in New York by RCA-Victor.

1941 Reza Pahlavi sacks his unpopular father and becomes Shah of Iran.

1944 "Operation Market Garden" begins as British airborne forces land at Arnhem, Holland, aiming to secure a bridge over the Rhine to facilitate an invasion of Germany.

BIRTHDAYS

William Carlos Williams 1883, American poet and physician who wrote "Journey to Love".

Sir Francis Chichester 1901, English yachtsman and aviator who was knighted for sailing round the world solo in *Gypsy Moth IV* and flew his plane *Gypsy Moth* solo east to west across the Tasman Sea.

Sir Frederick Ashton 1906, British dancer, choreographer and director who worked with the Ballet Rambert and then the Royal Ballet, creating more than 30 ballets including *Façade* with music by William Walton.

Anne Bancroft 1931, American actress who made her name on Broadway in *The Miracle Worker* and won an Oscar for the film version. Other films include *The Graduate*.

Maureen Connolly 1934, American tennis player known as "Little Mo" whose career was brought to a premature end by a horse-riding accident, the year after she completed an historic Grand Slam.

Hong Kong sees swing to liberals

1991 With six years left before China takes over Hong Kong, the British colony today held its first direct elections – and liberals swept the board. Seventeen of the 18 seats contested went to candidates who are strongly opposed to both the Hong Kong and Chinese governments. The outspoken United Democrats won 12 seats. Conservative business-backed candidates, who are pro-China, were left out in the cold. Less than a third of the seats in the legislature were elected: 21 seats were chosen by a small elite and the governor appointed the rest. But the liberal legislators are determined to have an impact.

1961 London's biggest "Ban the Bomb" demonstration yet ended today with police battles and 830 demonstrators arrested – including actress Vanessa Redgrave, playwright John Osborne and the chairman of the Campaign for Nuclear Disarmament, Canon Collins. The trouble started when police tried to move thousands of demonstrators staging sit-down protests. Last week the philosopher Bertrand Russell, now 89, was jailed for incitement during a CND demonstration.

United States compose brand new Constitution

1787 George Washington, leader of the Philadelphia Convention, was today presented with a new Constitution for the United States of America. Thirty-nine delegates representing 12 of the 13 states (all but Rhode Island) signed the document after months of debate. The difficulty was to balance a strong central government with both democratic principles and adequate representation of the states. The result is mixed government: representatives in the lower house will be elected by popular vote, the states will have equal representation in the upper house and each state will decide how to choose its presidential electors. The public has its say in the ratification of the new Constitution by the states as the supreme law of the land. The constitution's lack of a bill of rights is already being criticized. The Convention's Federalists say no such bill is needed, but the Anti-Federalist faction strongly disagrees.

They don't just want to be sawn in half by males, they want to do the sawing as well.
Greville Janner, British MP, on the admittance of women to the Magic Circle, 1991.

96 AD Roman Emperor Domitian is murdered by assassins in the pay of his wife, Domitilla.

1759 French forces at Quebec surrender to the British.

1851 The first edition of the *New York Times* is published.

1914 The Irish Home Rule Bill is given Royal Assent.

1934 Britain hears Lord Haw-Haw (Irishman William Joyce) make a Nazi propaganda broadcast.

1955 Four years after they fled to Russia, the British government admits Donald Maclean and Guy Burgess really were Soviet spies.

1961 UN chief Dag Hammarskjöld dies when a DC-6 plane carrying 130 other passengers crashes in the jungle in Northern Rhodesia – sabotage is suspected.

1967 Death of Sir John Cockroft, English nuclear physicist who first split the atom.

1981 Under President Mitterand, France abolishes the guillotine.

1988 The military seize power in Burma.

BIRTHDAYS

Samuel Johnson 1709, English lexicographer and celebrated conversationalist whose *Dictionary* was used as the authoritative reference book for more than a century.

Greta Garbo 1905, Swedish-born Hollywood film legend who remained in the public consciousness decades after she stopped making films in 1941.

Kwarne Nkrumah 1909, Ghanaian prime minister and then president from independence in 1957 until a military coup in 1966 sent him to exile in Guinea.

Bob Dylan 1933, American singer, songwriter and poet who became a cult figure writing folk songs such as "The Times They are A-Changin'" and went on to use electronic instruments in the album *Highway 61 Revisited*.

Frankie Avalon 1939, American singer and actor who began as a child trumpeter and later had hits as a singer with *Venus* and *Why?*

No help for desperate Hendrix

1970 Early this morning rock superstar Jimi Hendrix called his ex-manager Chas Chandler from his girlfriend's flat in London's Ladbroke Grove, but Chandler wasn't home. Hendrix left a message on Chandler's answering machine: "I need help bad." But no help came, and Hendrix was pronounced dead on arrival at St Mary's Hospital at 11.45 am, killed by an accidental overdose of sleeping pills. He was only 27. Jimi Hendrix is probably the most powerful thing that ever happened to the guitar – a rock 'n' roll genius with a solid background in the blues, and an outrageously sexy stage act. He was the highest-paid act at Woodstock Festival last year and the star of the Isle of Wight Festival last month. But he has been beleaguered by law suits over royalties and contracts, squabbling managers and bands that broke up around him. He ended a troubled tour in Denmark four days ago, leaving the stage in mid-performance with the fateful words: "I've been dead for a long time."

> *What dreadful hot weather we have! It keeps me in a continual state of inelegance.*
> **Jane Austen**, British novelist, in a letter, 1796.

Hearst: jail not bail

1975 A San Francisco court today refused 21-year-old newspaper heiress Patty Hearst bail on bank robbery charges. Hearst, the granddaughter of "yellow press" millionaire William Randolph Hearst, was kidnapped last February by a radical terrorist group, the Symbionese Liberation Army. Ten weeks later she was filmed on closed circuit television with other Symbionese Liberation Army members robbing a San Francisco bank, gun in hand. She was captured by the FBI this week after a 20-month hunt.

Nile explorer shoots himself

1864 English explorer John Hanning Speke shot himself in a tragic accident this morning, and died soon afterwards. He was 37. Speke discovered the source of the River Nile six years ago at the huge African lake he named after Queen Victoria. Last year he tracked the Nile even further south to the Kagera River, which he said was the true source of the Nile. But his claim has been disputed by Sir Richard Burton, with whom he explored East Africa. Burton led their expedition from the coast to Lake Tanganyika but fell ill with malaria, and Speke travelled on without him to discover Lake Victoria. Today the two adventurers were to meet in public debate to settle their argument over the Nile.

SADAT PEACE AGREEMENT WITH ISRAEL AROUSES ARAB WRATH

1978 President Anwar Sadat of Egypt and Israel's prime minister Menachem Begin reached a peace agreement today. Meeting at Camp David in the US under president Jimmy Carter's sponsorship, they agreed that Israel will withdraw from the Sinai (but not yet from the other occupied territories of Gaza and the West Bank), and Egypt will establish normal relations with Israel. The agreement is the culmination of Sadat's peace mission to Jerusalem last year. But it has appalled Israeli hard-liners, and Sadat's Arab allies regard him as a traitor.

Tsar's PM gunned down

1911 Russian premier Pyotr Stolypin died today after being shot down at the opera in Kiev last week by a police double agent. Emperor Nicholas II and his daughters saw the shooting from the royal box. It took a true statesman to hold down Stolypin's job in the turmoil of today's Russia, and he held it for six years. His predecessor only lasted a year. Stolypin even achieved something with his reforms, but his tactics were ruthless – he crushed dissent and simply ignored the constitution. Faced with a reluctant Tsar Nicholas, reactionary civil servants and the socialists in the Duma legislative assembly, nothing short of ruthlessness would have worked; but it won him few friends. Recently he fell out with the Tsar, his council of ministers and the Duma simultaneously. Now he has been removed.

DISNEY SPEAKS MICKEY SQUEAKS

1928 Hollywood artist Walt Disney today released the first sound cartoon film, *Steamboat Willie*. The film features Mickey Mouse and Disney himself provides his squeaky voice on the soundtrack. Mickey – originally Mortimer Mouse when he was conceived in Disney's animation studio last year – is a clever caricature of an impish child. Disney and his chief collaborator Ub Iwerks are working on more cartoon characters.

Ocean ahoy for Spanish

1513 A Spanish conquistador, Vasco Nunez de Balboa, today reached the west coast of the Americas and became the first European to cast his eyes on the western ocean. He has called it the South Sea. Balboa came to the New World in 1500 and took up farming on the island of Hispaniola, but after 10 years his farm failed and he fled to the mainland to escape his creditors. He founded a Spanish colony in Panama, which he named Darien. Four weeks ago he led an expedition to the west, hacking a way through thick jungle and fighting off hostile Indians. Today the expedition reached a mountain, which Balboa climbed alone to see the new ocean spread out below him.

Try stubbing out cigarettes with both feet while rubbing your back with a towel.
Chubby Checker's advice on how to do the Twist – his hit song entered the US charts today, 1960.

Earthquake wrecks Mexico City

1985 A massive earthquake devastated large parts of Mexico City and the surrounding area this morning and many thousands of people are feared killed. Thousands of buildings and homes have been destroyed. The earthquake, measuring 8.1 on the Richter scale, is the worst to hit Mexico this century. Amid fears of a second quake, a huge rescue operation is seeking out those trapped in the wreckage and providing relief for survivors.

Louis XVI watches sheep fly

1783 Two French papermakers, Joseph and Jacques Montgolfier, thrilled King Louis XVI and his court at Versailles today when they sent a giant balloon filled with smoke into the sky, carrying a sheep, a rooster and a duck. The balloon ascended 1500 ft (457 m) and landed 1 mile (1.6 km) away. The rooster was killed in the landing, but the sheep and the duck were unharmed. Three months ago the brothers sent their first balloon aloft at Annonay. Today they wanted to test the effect of altitude on living creatures.

1356 Led by the Black Prince, Edward, the English defeat the French at the Battle of Poitiers.

1876 American inventor Melville Bissell patents the carpet sweeper.

1881 Death of James Abram Garfield, 20th US president, who was shot on July 2 having been in office just four months.

1888 The world's first beauty contest takes place in Belgium and is won by 18-year-old Bertha Soucaret from Guadeloupe, who collects the 5000-franc prize.

1905 Death of Thomas Barnardo, British doctor, philanthropist and founder of homes for destitute children.

1945 Lord Haw-Haw is sentenced to hang for treason.

1952 Charlie Chaplin is dubbed "subversive" by rightwingers in the US.

1955 Juan Perón is ousted by a military junta in Argentina.

1968 Death of Chester Carlson, American inventor of the Xerox photocopying system.

1981 Simon and Garfunkel get back together after 11 years to play to an audience of 400,000 in New York's Central Park.

1994 US troops are sent to Haiti after months of negotiations and a mounting tide of refugees floods out of the Republic; the aim is to return the ousted President Aristide to power.

BIRTHDAYS

Sir William Golding 1911, British author best known for *The Lord of the Flies*.

Zandra Rhodes 1940, British fashion designer.

"Mama Cass" Elliot 1943, large American who began as singer of the Mamas and the Papas then went solo and had hits like "Dream a Little Dream".

Jeremy Irons 1948, British leading actor of stage and screen.

Twiggy (Lesley Hornby) 1949, British actress and singer who first found fame as a model in the 60s.

The Who-oomph

1967 The British rock group The Who ended their two-month US tour with an even wilder performance than usual. The group are famous for ending their shows by smashing their instruments in a savage fury, but they didn't plan to wreck the studio when they made a live appearance on *The Smothers Brothers* TV show tonight. Drummer Keith Moon had put a flash powder charge in one of his drums, but used far too much powder. The explosion demolished the drum kit and enveloped wildman guitarist Pete Townshend in flames, leaving him singed and deafened.

SEPTEMBER 20

1519 Ferdinand Magellan sets sail from Seville in Spain with a fleet of five small ships in an attempt to circumnavigate the world.

1792 France's untried army defeats the Duke of Brunswick's, attacking Prussian troops at Walmy.

1928 In Rome the supreme legislative body, the Chamber of Deputies, is taken over by the Fascists.

1946 The first Cannes Film Festival opens.

1959 America's Disneyland turns down a visit by Soviet prime minister Nikita Khruschchev for security reasons.

1961 Argentinian Antonio Albertondo begins the first non-stop swim across the Channel.

1961 Rhodesian premier Ian Smith bans the black opposition party.

1984 Forty die as a suicide bomber attacks the US Embassy in Beirut; the bomber drove into the compound with a lorry load of explosives.

BIRTHDAYS

Sir George Robey 1869, English comedian and star of the music hall, billed as "The Prime Minister of Mirth".

Upton Sinclair 1878, American prolific author whose books include *The Jungle* and *Oil!*

Jelly Roll Morton 1885, American pianist, singer and composer and one of the first jazz musicians, who made his first recording in 1923.

Kenneth Moore 1914, English actor who was usually typecast in likeable, if chauvinistic, roles on stage and screen, such as that of World War II fighter pilot hero Douglas Bader in *Reach for the Sky*.

Sophia Loren 1934, Italian actress who married the man who groomed her for stardom, Carlo Ponti, won an Oscar for *Two Women* and proved her abilities as a comedienne in *The Millionairess*.

Drake bowls round world

1580 Francis Drake made landfall in Plymouth, England today, his ship laden with treasure and spices. Drake, the first captain to sail round the world, has captured tons of silver, gold, coins and jewels from Spanish galleons in the Americas. Spain has complained bitterly and wants Drake hanged for piracy, and Queen Elizabeth I has launched an inquiry. But Drake is a public hero – and Elizabeth herself backed his expedition. Drake set off three years ago with five small ships, but only his *Golden Hind* survived the treacherous Straits of Magellan to reach the Pacific. His first prize was a Spanish treasure galleon and others followed. Drake landed at San Francisco Bay and claimed it for England, then crossed the Pacific to trade in the Spice Islands before setting course for home, via the Indian Ocean and the Cape of Good Hope.

1947 English cricketer Denis Compton ended the season in dashing style today with three all-time records. He has scored the highest number of runs and the most centuries ever in a single season of first-class cricket – and he is the first man to hold both titles at once. He scored 18 centuries and a total of 3816 runs – 298 more than the previous record, set 41 years ago.

VIOLENCE THREATENS SOUTH AFRICA'S PEACE ACCORD

1991 South Africa's hard-won peace accord has failed to stop the political violence that has caused hundreds of deaths this month. President F. W. de Klerk, ANC leader Nelson Mandela and the ANC's arch-rival, Chief Mangosuthu Buthelezi, head of the Zulu Inkatha movement, signed the "national peace accord" last Saturday after a week of violence that claimed 120 lives nationwide. It is hoped the agreement will be the basis of further negotiations on a new constitution. But the two most extreme black parties refused to sign, and the heavily armed far right-wing white groups refused even to attend. They have accused De Klerk of treachery and are threatening a new "Boer War". The fighting in the black townships continues unabated.

Cricket is a game which the British, not being a spiritual people, had to invent in order to have some concept of eternity.
Lord Mancroft, 1967.

Crisis-ridden Britain tries to stem gold rush

1931 Britain has abandoned the gold standard, devaluing the pound by almost a third. The government said the move was essential to halt foreign speculation in sterling and to prevent further gold withdrawals. Foreign banks lost confidence in the pound on Tuesday when 12,000 Royal Navy sailors went on strike over a pay cut. The cut was part of an austere emergency package rushed through as Britain's worst-ever economic crisis deepened. The Labour government collapsed last month, and was replaced by a national coalition. The crisis is causing great hardship, and both the government and a worried press are trying to soothe public discontent. Two weeks ago King George V took a voluntary pay cut – of £50,000 ($92,500) a year.

Dako KOs Bokassa

1979 Africa's most bizarre dictator, self-styled Emperor Jean Bedel Bokassa of the Central African Empire, was overthrown today in a coup by his cousin, David Dacko. Dacko was president until Bokassa, then an army colonel, overthrew him in 1965. Bokassa's brutal excesses rival those of the genocidal Idi Amin, who was forced to flee Uganda six months ago. Bokassa has terrorized his people, tortured and murdered, and sacked the poverty-stricken country's coffers to support his grotesque pretensions. He crowned himself emperor two years ago, donning a $2 million (£1.1 million) crown and ascending a massive golden throne. France paid the $30 million (£16.2 million) bill. Now Bokassa has fled to France – amid horrifying accusations of child cannibalism in the palace.

HURRICANE HUGO IN A HUFF

1989 Hurricane Hugo, the worst storm this decade, hit the US coast last night and left widespread destruction in South Carolina and Georgia. Charleston is badly damaged. Hugo's 140 mph (225 kph) winds swept through the Caribbean, leaving death and chaos in Puerto Rico, the Dominican Republic and the Virgin Islands – where riots and looting followed the storm. Whole towns are wrecked and many have been killed and injured.

Scott burns out as debts pile up

1832 Sir Walter Scott, the most popular writer in the world, has died in Edinburgh, his health ruined by overwork as he struggled to pay off his debts. He was 61. His novels had made Scott a wealthy man with a large home in the country, but six years ago a printing firm he had an interest in went bankrupt and Scott took on the debt. He worked ceaselessly, producing a large number of novels, and managed to clear his name. Last year, exhausted, he went on a Mediterranean cruise, but it tired him even more. He never recovered. Scott, a barrister and a poet, wrote his first novel in 1814, a historical romance called *Waverley*. Published anonymously, it was immensely popular. The Waverley series followed – ever popular with today's fast-growing reading public.

My God! This is a wonderful land and a faithless one; for she has exiled, slain, destroyed and ruined so many Kings, so many rulers, so many great men, and she is always diseased and suffering from differences, quarrels and hatred between her people.
Richard II, King of England, imprisoned in the Tower of London, 1399.

TEMPERATURE RISES AS NATIONS BICKER

1991 The latest round in the negotiations to hammer out an international treaty on climate change and greenhouse gases ended in deadlock in Nairobi today, blocked by the US refusal to set targets for reducing carbon dioxide output. Europe pushed for targets, having agreed last December to stabilize its CO_2 output at 1990 levels by the year 2000 – but in Brussels that agreement is breaking down into further argument about output levels. Japan wants promises without targets. Meanwhile a billion tons of carbon dioxide poured into the atmosphere during the two weeks of talks, mostly from the industrial countries. CO_2 levels are higher than ever before and are reliably predicted to force up global temperatures at unprecedented rates, with catastrophic effect.

1915 Stonehenge was sold today for £6600 ($12,210), bought with the surrounding fields by a local farmer. The finest and most elaborate of Europe's prehistoric megaliths, the concentric circles of standing stones are a powerful mystery. The antiquarian William Stukeley said 150 years ago Stonehenge was a Druid temple, but it is now known that it was already ancient when the Druids arrived in England and dates back to before Christ. In 1136 Geoffrey of Monmouth wrote that the stones had magical healing powers. How they were transported also remains a mystery.

QUEEN BEATS KING IN POKER GAME

1327 England's King Edward II has been murdered in prison. Fearful shrieks from the dungeons broke the silence in Berkeley Castle in the early hours today, and this morning the citizens of Bristol were called to look on the horribly distorted face of the dead king. It is believed he was killed with a red-hot poker. Many think Edward's queen, Isabella of France, and her lover Roger de Mortimer plotted the murder to ensure the succession of the King's son, 15-year-old Edward – under Isabella's regency. Edward II was a weak and foolish king whose lavish treatment of his favourites constantly raised the ire of England's nobles. Two years ago Isabella met Mortimer in France and fell in love with him. The couple raised a mercenary army and invaded England. The disaffected English barons sided with Isabella, and eight months ago Edward was deposed.

1745 The Battle of Prestonpans in Scotland is won by Bonnie Prince Charlie and his Jacobite army, defeating the English.

1792 France abolishes the monarchy.

1857 British forces retake Delhi from Indian mutineers.

1903 The first recorded Western film opens in the US, titled *Kit Carson* – it is 21 minutes long.

1944 US general Douglas MacArthur returns to the Philippines, attacking the Japanese near Manila.

1981 Belize is granted independence.

1989 Divorcee Mary Sue Davis is awarded by a Tennessee judge temporary custody of seven frozen embryos which had been fertilized by her former husband, who had complained that he did not want to become a father against his will.

1993 Russian President Boris Yeltsin dissolves the Russian Parliament pending elections to a new legislative body.

BIRTHDAYS

John London MacAdam 1756, Scottish engineer and inventor of the macadam road surface.

H. G. Wells 1866, English author who pioneered science fiction when he wrote *The Time Machine*, his first work.

Gustav Holst 1874, British composer and teacher whose best-known work, *The Planets*, is also one of the most popular orchestral suites with audiences.

Sir Allen Lane 1902, English publisher who founded Penguin Books and brought about the paperback revolution.

Larry Hagman 1931, American actor and director best known for his role as mean oil tycoon JR Ewing in the TV serial *Dallas*.

Leonard Cohen 1934, Canadian poet and singer whose gloomy songs, which include "Suzanne" and "That's No Way to Say Goodbye", and growling delivery won him a cult following in the 1960s and 70s.

1735 Sir Robert Walpole occupies the new prime minister's residence at No.10 Downing Street, just five minutes' walk from the Houses of Parliament.

1792 The French Republic is proclaimed.

1860 China's Emperor flees Peking as Anglo-French forces advance.

1862 President Abraham Lincoln issues his Preliminary Emancipation Proclamation freeing slaves in the South.

1972 Idi Amin gives the 80,000 Asians in Uganda 48 hours to leave the country.

1980 The war between Iraq and Iran begins in the Gulf.

1986 The youngest heart and lung transplant patient, a two-and-a-half-month-old baby, is given new organs at the Harefield Hospital, Middlesex.

1988 Two women crawl out of their grave in a village in South Sumatra, having been buried by robbers in the belief they were dead.

BIRTHDAYS

Michael Faraday 1791, English physicist who invented the dynamo and formed many of the principles of electricity.

Dame Christabel Pankhurst 1880, English suffragette and daughter of Emmeline, who led the suffragette movement.

Erick von Stroheim 1885, Austrian-born Hollywood film director and actor whose eccentric leather-clad image and autocratic ways won him the title "The Man You Love to Hate", and whose desire for perfection frequently led him to go wildly over budget.

John Houseman 1902, Romanian-born producer, actor, writer, stage director and founder, with Orson Welles, of the famous Mercury Theatre in New York.He became a star actor in his seventies.

Fay Weldon 1931, English author brought up in New Zealand whose novels include *The Life and Loves of a She-Devil*.

Outrage in NZ as France admits to *Rainbow* bombs

1985 French prime minister Laurent Fabius today admitted that the *Rainbow Warrior* was sunk by French agents. A crew member was killed when the Greenpeace ship was rocked by two explosions in Auckland Harbour, New Zealand, on July 10. She had been due to lead a flotilla of peace ships into the French nuclear test zone at Muroroa Atoll in French Polynesia in a protest action. The incident brought international condemnation. The French defence minister has resigned amid a storm of protest and demands for the head of the secret service to be sacked. In New Zealand, Labour PM David Lange's anti-nuclear stance has gained wide support from the public indignation at the French action.

I only regret that I have but one life to lose for my country.
Nathan Hale, hero of the American Revolution, in a speech before being hanged by the British as a spy, 1776.

THE ZULU NAPOLEON

1828 Shaka, King of the Zulus, was murdered today at Dukuza, his capital in Natal, by his half-brothers Dingaan and Mhlangana. Dingaan has taken the throne. Shaka was a great and terrible king, a military genius who has been compared with Napoleon. The Zulu were a small clan when Shaka became their chief, but through bloody conquest he welded them into the mightiest nation in Southern Africa. Shaka abandoned the traditional light throwing spear and adopted a short, broad-bladed stabbing spear for his regiments, along with a tall shield of tough hide. Ardent disciplined warriors, his troops ran barefoot into battle, the flanks separating to attack from three sides. None could stand against them. Shaka's revered mother, Nandi, died last year, and the grief-stricken king lost his mind. Thousands of Zulus have been executed for showing insufficient grief – Shaka ordered an entire regiment to march off a cliff to their deaths, and they did so to a man. Now the bloodbath has ended.

Poland's workers found Solidarity union

1980 Polish workers today exercised the new freedom they have wrested from the Communist government and formed an independent labour union. The new Solidarity union's leader, electrician Lech Walesa, led the Gdansk inter-factory committee which coordinated the massive shipyard strikes this summer. The wave of work stoppages forced the government to concede, allowing independent unions, freeing jailed dissidents and lifting press censorship. Party leader Edward Gierek has now been replaced by security chief Stanislaw Kania.

1989 A powerful IRA bomb blasted the Royal Marines School of Music at Deal in Kent, England, this morning, killing 10 bandsmen and injuring 22. Twelve marines are in hospital. The IRA admitted responsibility. Britain is shocked by the attack: the men were musicians, not combatants.

TUNNEY SURVIVES "LONG COUNT" TO BEAT DEMPSEY

1927 World heavyweight champion Gene Tunney won his return bout with ex-champion Jack Dempsey in a sensational fight tonight. In a furious attack, Dempsey, the "Manassa Mauler", knocked down Tunney in the seventh round. Tunney fell – but the referee refused to start the count because Dempsey hadn't retired to a neutral corner. Five seconds elapsed before the count began, giving Tunney time to stagger to his feet. Ringside experts said he'd been down for 13 seconds. Tunney went on to win. Dempsey said he'd been robbed of the title and promised to appeal against the decision. The Chicago fight was the richest ever, with a purse of $2.6 million (£1.4 million).

British caught out by *Spycatcher*

1987 *Spycatcher*, the memoirs of former British intelligence officer Peter Wright, will be published in Australia in spite of top-level British efforts to have the book suppressed. MI5 man Wright retired to Australia 10 years ago. Last year a High Court judge banned British newspapers from publishing extracts from the book and the British government brought a court case against Wright in Australia – unsuccessfully. Britain appealed, and lost the appeal today. London's *Sunday Times* is in court for contempt after publishing extracts from the book, many copies of which have been smuggled into Britain, and which is openly on sale in the US. Wright insists there is nothing new in his book.

Astronomers row over new planet

1846 Two German astronomers have discovered another planet, the eighth in distance from the Sun, about a billion miles beyond Uranus. Johann Galle and Heinrich d'Arrest of the Berlin Observatory were told just where to look by the young French astronomer Urbain Leverrier. He had concluded that the irregular orbit of Uranus could only be explained by the gravitational pull of another planet, and calculated its position to within one degree. The announcement has brought a protest from 24-year-old English astronomer John Adams, who claims he made the same prediction nine months ago, and the credit should be his. British scientists scoffed at his findings at the time. Further controversy surrounds a name for the new planet. Leverrier wants to call it "Leverrier", but others favour Neptune.

1780 During the War of Independence, British agent John André, carrying information that Benedict Arnold is about to betray the revolution by surrendering West Point, is captured by the Americans.

1870 The siege of Paris begins during the Franco-Prussian War.

1940 The George Cross is instituted for civilian acts of courage.

1942 Australian troops under US general Douglas MacArthur start an offensive in New Guinea to drive back the Japanese.

1974 The world's first Ceefax teletext service begins on BBC television in Britain.

1987 Death of Bob Fosse, American dancer who became a director, and produced the autobiographical film *All that Jazz*, which he also choreographed.

2000 Rower Steve Redgrave wins his fifth Olympic Gold medal in the coxless 4's during the Sydney Olympics.

BIRTHDAYS

Gaius Octavius Caesar 63 BC, first Roman emperor, the adopted son and heir of Julius Caesar, a powerful genius who brought stability to the Roman empire and defeated Julius Caesar's assassins at the Battle of Philippi in 42 BC.

Armand Hyppolyte 1819, French physicist who first measured the speed of light.

Mickey Rooney 1920, American actor who was particularly popular in the late 30s, when he starred in a series of films as Andy Hardy.

John Coltrane 1926, American tenor saxophonist.

Ray Charles 1932, American singer of classics like "Georgia on My Mind" and "I Can't Stop Loving You".

Julio Iglesias 1943, Spanish popular romantic singer.

Bruce Springsteen 1949, American singer-songwriter who achieved great success in 1975 with his album *Born to Run*.

Third World pays to stay in debt

1991 The World Bank took more money from Third World countries than it gave them last year, according to the bank's annual report, released today. Interest and capital repayments were $1.56 billion more than the bank paid in new loans and assistance. The African countries were net recipients, but the Caribbean and Latin America paid out $2 billion more than they received. The figures have brought bitter criticism from the poorer countries, which are anxious not to lose out as the bank shifts its focus to the needs of the Soviet Union and Eastern Europe.

1912 King of comedy Mack Sennet's new slapstick short *Cohen Collects a Debt* was released today and was an instant success. The film features policemen known as the Keystone Cops, whose antics had the audience in stitches.

Silent U-boats are new lethal weapon

1914 The German submarine U-9 has sunk three British cruisers off the Dutch coast, with 1500 lives lost. The war at sea started in earnest on August 28, when a British fleet raided the Heligoland Bight and sank four German ships. Today's battle off Holland shows the new shape of sea warfare: powerful warships were helpless against the silent attack of one small submarine. The German fleet is outnumbered and blockaded in the North Sea, but the U-boats are not so easily stopped. German mines have claimed several British ships.

NUCLEAR TESTING DENIED BY SOUTH AFRICANS

1979 A special US satellite used for monitoring nuclear explosions today reported a brilliant double flash over the south Atlantic between South Africa and Antarctica. A South African Navy ship was seen in the area. US analysts said South Africa had exploded a clandestine nuclear bomb, but South Africa has denied the charge. The US Vela high-altitude satellites were built to detect nuclear detonations in the Earth's atmosphere and in deep space: they can spot a nuclear blast 100 million miles away. Previously a US military satellite photographed installations hidden in the Kalahari desert which the US associated with a nuclear test, and South Africa was forced to remove the structures. South Africa has operated a reactor near Pretoria since the mid-60s, and a nuclear power station is planned near Cape Town even though the country has huge coal reserves.

> *At bottom God is nothing more than an exalted father.*
> **Sigmund Freud**, father of psychoanalysis, who died today, 1939.

1200 refugees slaughtered on train

1947 A trainload of Muslim refugees fleeing to Pakistan has been massacred by Sikhs at Amritsar in the Punjab, with at least 1200 defenceless people shot and hacked to death. This is the worst single incident so far in the communal violence that has swept the sub-continent since the partitioning of India on August 15. Millions of refugees caught on the wrong side of the Hindu-Muslim divide are fleeing to safety – some estimates put the number as high as 15 million. Nobody knows how many have died as sectarian hatred spilled over, creating a vicious cycle of retaliation. Sikhs in the western Punjab, now in Pakistan, have been slaughtered by rioting Muslims, and more than two million are fleeing east to India. Hindus caught in Pakistan are in the same desperate position, with killings in most towns.

Black Friday as golden bubble bursts

1869 Panic hit Wall Street today as the bottom fell out of the gold market – and the entire stock market followed it down. Thousands of gold speculators led the plunge towards bankruptcy. The blow fell when President Ulysses S. Grant told the US Treasury to release its gold. The sudden glut knocked the price down, killing a bid by financiers Jay Gould and James Fisk to corner the gold market. They had said they'd succeeded in stopping the president selling government gold, and many believed them. But Grant had simply been slow to react. Fisk and Gould are not noted for integrity. Today they fled in a storm of acrimony.

1842 The brother of the Brontë sisters dies of drugs and drink: Bramwell Brontë was the model for the drunkard Hindley Earnshaw in Emily Brontë's *Wuthering Heights*.

1852 A hydrogen-filled airship, the first of its kind, makes its maiden flight at Versailles, powered by a 3 hp steam engine built by Henri Giffard.

1941 The Siege of Leningrad begins: the British RAF support the Red Army.

1960 The first nuclear-powered aircraft carrier, the USS *Enterprise*, is launched at Newport, Virginia.

1960 Death of Melanie Klein, Austrian-born child psychoanalyst who spent the last 34 years of her life living in London and who wrote *The Psychoanalysis of Children*.

1975 The first all-British team reaches the summit of Mount Everest, having also made the first ascent of the steep south-west face of the mountain.

1983 Italy jails chemicals executives responsible for the Seveso dioxin disaster, when a poisonous gas cloud escaped from a factory in Seveso contaminating a wide radius of land.

BIRTHDAYS

F. Scott Fitzgerald 1896, American novelist and short story writer whose first success was with his autobiographical novel *This Side of Paradise*.

Anthony Newley 1931, British actor, co-author and lyricist who made his name as a child in the film *Oliver Twist*, in which he played the Artful Dodger, and who also wrote musicals with Leslie Bricusse, such as *Stop the World, I Want to Get Off*.

Svetlana Beriosova 1932, Russian prima ballerina with the Grands Ballets de Monte Carlo and the Sadler's Wells Ballet, creating the leads in *Le Baiser de la Fée* and *Persephone*.

Linda McCartney 1942, American photographer married to ex-Beatle Paul McCartney and campaigner for animal rights.

Old-style Samurai meet brutal reality

1877 Japan's modern army today crushed a rebellion by 40,000 feudal samurai warriors fighting for their old way of life and their honour. The Meiji Restoration of 1868 broke the closed military rule of the Shoguns as Japan moved to transform itself into a modern world power. Thus ended 700 years of unchanging feudalism and warfare. The samurai armies and their *bushido* code of honour were an anachronism. The new Meiji government cut their pay, stopped them carrying swords – and six months ago refused to invade Korea. At this the incensed samurai rebelled. Today their leader committed ritual suicide amidst the fallen; many of the survivors followed suit.

1980 Iraq invaded Iran in force today and destroyed the huge oil refinery at Abadan as months of border incident flared into full-scale war. Iraq, taking advantage of the domestic chaos in fundamentalist Iran, is hoping for a quick victory over its bigger neighbour. The prize is dominance in the Persian Gulf.

1930 Noel Coward and Gertrude Lawrence star in Coward's new stage comedy *Private Lives*, about two lovers who abandon their spouses.

India is a geographical term. It is no more a united nation than the Equator.
Winston Churchill, 1931.

Perón and on

1973 Former dictator Juan Perón was re-elected president of Argentina today after nearly 20 years' exile. Perón's second wife, Eva, an actress, was the mainstay of his first rule. "Evita", idolized by the people, was virtually co-president, and Perón's regime never recovered after she died in 1951. Perón returned from exile in Spain following a recent Perónist election victory. His third wife, Isabel, is his vice-president.

BISMARCK'S CREED OF IRON AND BLOOD

1862 The Prussian statesman Otto von Bismarck has rescued his beleaguered king from a losing battle with the Liberal government. Vetoed because of his militarist budget proposals, King William appointed Bismarck chancellor. Bismarck defied the Chamber of Deputies, took control of taxes, completely ignored the budget, and forced through King William's military reforms. It was Prussia's power that won respect, he said, not Prussia's Liberals. "The great questions of the age are not settled by speeches and majority votes, but by iron and blood," he told the deflated Democrats in the Chamber today.

Big guns make Little Rock respect black student rights

1957 Protected by a thousand army paratroopers with fixed bayonets, nine black children took their places in the all-white Central High School in Little Rock, Arkansas, today. Meanwhile angry whites demonstrated outside the school, and eight were arrested. The Federal district court in Little Rock ruled that the nine students be admitted to the Central High following a Supreme Court ruling that segregated schools contravene the Fourteenth Amendment. But Arkansas Governor Orville Faubus flouted the order, and when the black children arrived at the school they were barred by armed National Guardsmen while whites jeered "Niggers go home!" President Eisenhower intervened, and the troopers were withdrawn – only to be replaced by a white mob. In an unprecedented move, Eisenhower removed the National Guard from Faubus's control and sent in the 101st Airborne Division. Furious southern governors have demanded their withdrawal.

> *Women and small people are the most difficult to deal with.*
> **Confucius** (551-479 BC), Chinese sage and founder of Confucianism.

Bandaranaike cut short by Buddhist monk

1959 Sri Lankan prime minister Solomon Bandaranaike has been assassinated. Bandaranaike led the People's United Front leftist alliance which won the 1956 election. His Sinhalese nationalism has angered the large Tamil Hindu minority – Sinhalese is now the sole national language. Yet he was shot by a Sinhalese Buddhist monk. He is to be succeeded by his wife, Sirimavo Bandaranaike, a radical socialist.

Turin unveils "Shroud of Christ"

1933 More than 25,000 believers gazed in awe at a miraculous image of Jesus Christ today. Church custodians at the cathedral of Turin in Italy showed the famous Turin Shroud to the public for the first time in 400 years. The stained, 14-ft (4.2 m) long cloth is believed to have been the burial shroud of Jesus Christ. At the cathedral today it was impossible not to be moved by the cloth's imprint of a body, front and back, and the clear picture of a man's face, eyes closed. Scientific opinion is that the image is the actual imprint of the body of a man. Today's crowd had no doubt about whose face it showed.

West says Hung is a Taiping error

1851 More than 20,000 Taiping rebels chose the Christian prophet Hung Hsiu Chuan as king at their mountain stronghold in China today. Invasions, droughts, floods, famines and lawlessness have left China ripe for rebellion. Some years ago Hung, 39, read a Christian pamphlet entitled *Good Advice to the World*. Later he fell into a 40-day coma and awakened to claim he had met God and Jesus and that he was "Jesus's younger brother". God had ordered him to "kill the demon Manchus", he said. He plans to abolish property ownership, redistribute the land to everyone (including women, who are to have equal status), educate everybody, share everything, and end poverty, famine and injustice. Western missionaries, however, condemn Hung as a heretic.

FLOYD FLOORED BY PATTERSON'S PISTON

1962 World heavyweight champion Floyd Patterson lost his title tonight in a first-round knockout. Two minutes into the first round, giant Sonny Liston hit Patterson with four fearsome punches, and the champion fell, staying down for the count and longer. After the fight Patterson said he will retire. He took the crown from Archie Moore in 1956 to become the youngest-ever champ at 21. In 1959 he lost the title to Swede Ingemar Johansson, but regained it a year later. It was thought Liston's shady underworld past might disqualify him as a contender.

CIAO GIACOMO

1977 Italian ace motorcycle racer Giacomo Agostini today announced that he is set to retire. He was a record fifteen times world champion between 1966 and 1976, racing both 350cc and 500cc bikes.

1818 The first blood transfusion using human blood (as opposed to animal blood), takes place in London at Guy's Hospital.

1897 Britain's first motor bus service starts in Bradford.

1932 Catalonia in Spain becomes autonomous: it has its own parliament, language and flag.

1954 "Papa" Doc (Dr Francois Duvalier) wins the presidential elections in Haiti.

1960 Death of Emily Post, American columnist and writer on etiquette.

1970 Death of Erich Maria Remarque, German author of *All Quiet on the Western Front*.

1986 In Wales a British police constable is jailed for biting off part of a colleague's ear during a rugby match.

2000 Sportswoman Cathy Freeman races to victory in the 400-metre race in front of her home crowd.

BIRTHDAYS

Jeanne Philippe Rameau 1683, French composer best known for his opera *Castor et Pollux*.

William Faulkner 1897, American novelist and 1949 Nobel Prize-winner for literature.

Mark Rothko 1903, Russian-born American painter who was one of the pioneers of Abstract Expressionism.

Dmitri Shostakovich 1906, Russian 20th century composer who began his first opera, *The Gypsies*, at the age of nine and whose other famous works include his seventh symphony, *The Leningrad*.

Sir Robert Muldoon 1921, New Zealand prime minister from 1975 to 1984.

Michael Douglas 1944, American actor and producer who, like his father Kirk, has established himself as a major star. He starred in, produced and co-scripted *The China Syndrome*.

Christopher Reeve 1952, American actor best known for his role as Superman.

1815
The Holy Alliance is signed by Tsar Alexander I of Russia, Francis I of Austria (formerly Holy Roman Emperor Francis II), and Frederick William III, King of Prussia.

1820
Death of US frontiersman Daniel Boone.

1903
Women get the vote in the Connecticut state elections.

1907
New Zealand becomes a Dominion.

1945
Hungarian composer Béla Bartok dies in poverty in the USA; his stage works include the opera *Duke Bluebeard's Castle*, and his most popular work is *Concerto for Orchestra*.

1957
The first performance of the Bernstein-Sondheim musical *West Side Story* is given in New York.

1984
Britain and China agree that Hong Kong will revert to Chinese rule when lease expires in 1997.

1989
The last Vietnamese troops pull out of Cambodia.

BIRTHDAYS

T. S. Eliot 1888, American-born poet, playwright and highly influential critic whose poem *The Waste Land* established him as one of the most important 20th century poets and who went on to develop a more lyrical style, as in *The Four Quartets*, in which to treat the experience of the discovery of faith.

George Raft 1895, American actor who specialized in gangster and tough-guy roles which were not far from his real-life experience with the Mafia, with whom he had close associations; his films include *Scarface* and *Some Like It Hot*.

George Gershwin 1898, American composer who worked chiefly with his brother, lyricist Ira Gershwin, to produce songs and musicals such as *Funny Face* and *Porgy and Bess*.

Bryan Ferry 1945, British pop singer, pianist and composer who was lead singer of Roxy Music.

Olivia Newton-John 1948, British singer who starred with John Travolta in the film *Grease*.

BESSIE DIES SINGING MISSISSIPPI BLUES

1937 The Empress of the Blues is dead. And Bessie Smith's friends are saying she would still be alive if she'd been white: Miss Smith was hurt in a car smash today in racist Mississippi, and bled to death waiting for an ambulance that simply didn't bother to hurry. She was 43. Bessie Smith learnt to sing in a gospel church in Tennessee, and started her singing career in honky tonk bars. She got her big chance in 1923 when she went to New York to make a "race record" for sale in the black communities. She was an instant sensation, and her success quickly spilled across the race barrier. Bessie Smith is a household name, her records are landmarks of blues and jazz singing. And now she has died, a victim of prejudice and stupidity. That's how the blues were born, and that's why people like Bessie Smith sing them.

Johnson runs into drug shame

1988 Canadian sprinter Ben Johnson flew home in disgrace from the Seoul Olympics today, stripped of his gold medal after failing a drugs test. Two days ago Johnson was a hero after winning the 100 metres with a new world record. But tests proved that he'd taken anabolic steroids to boost his strength. The scandal hit the world's front pages today, but Johnson isn't the only one to have failed the drugs tests – so have nine other athletes. Following the US-led boycott of the Moscow Olympics in 1980 and the inevitable Eastern-bloc boycott of the 1984 Games in Los Angeles, this is the first Olympics since 1976 where east and west have met, and the west has not shone. Russia has swept up the most medals, and the heroes are the East German swimmers and African long-distance runners.

Australians win America's Cup

1983 An Australian yacht has won the America's Cup, at last wrenching the famous trophy from the New York Yacht Club, its home for 132 years. *Australia II*, owned by Australian millionaire Alan Bond and skippered by John Bertrand, beat the US yacht *Liberty*, skippered by Dennis Conner, in the last of seven races off Newport, Rhode Island, today. The victory was greeted with a national celebration in Australia. Newport has been the scene of the America's Cup for 53 years. Next time the race will be held in Australian waters.

Temple of war takes direct hit

1687 The masterpiece of ancient Greek architecture, the Parthenon, has become a casualty of war. Turkish forces that have besieged the Acropolis were using the old temple as a powder magazine, and today the attacking Venetian army scored a direct hit on it with a mortar bomb. The powder exploded, blowing off the roof, ruining the frieze-covered walls and damaging much of the marble sculpture. But still the battle continues. The Parthenon is the temple of Athena, Goddess of War. It was designed by Ictinus and Callicrates under the direction of the great sculptor Phidias and completed in 432 BC. Phidias's huge image of Athena was destroyed by the Crusaders. Over the years the Parthenon has been used as a Catholic church, a mosque and a harem.

This was no actress, no imitator of women's woes; there was no pretence. It was the real thing.
Carl van Vechten in *Show Business Illustrated*, writing on blues singer Bessie Smith, who died today, 1937.

1977 270 people paid only £59 ($109) to fly from London to New York today on the first flight in Freddie Laker's Skytrain. They had queued for 24 hours at London's Gatwick airport to save £131 ($241). Single fares cost £190 ($350) on other airlines. This is no-frills travel, with few comforts and meals extra. The big airlines had tried to stop the new service. Laker called it the beginning of a new air travel era.

Top model can't marry as she was born a he

1990 Glamorous British model Caroline Cossey has failed to overturn a law that won't let her get married – because her birth certificate says she's male. And so she was, until a sex-change operation 15 years ago transformed her into the beautiful and successful model "Tula". She appealed against the ruling in terms of the European Convention on Human Rights, but the European court today upheld the British law.

SLAVES BY THE SHIPLOAD

1672 A new British company chartered today has been given a monopoly of the African slave trade. The Royal African Company is now arranging shipments of slaves from the African coast to the markets in the Americas, offering special terms for entire shiploads. A healthy slave costs less than £20 ($37) on delivery in America. The new company's chief competition is the Dutch West India Company, which has had a monopoly of the West African slave trade for 50 years. Britain and France are at war with Holland, and last month a Dutch fleet attacked New York. Regardless of European hostilities, the number of slave ships plying the Atlantic is bound to grow. The New World plantations cannot operate without slaves and enormous profits are to be made from the trade in "black gold".

"No plot" behind Kennedy killing

1964 The Warren Commission has officially rejected conspiracy as a factor in the killing of US President John F. Kennedy last November. Neither has it found a motive. The Commission, appointed by President Lyndon B. Johnson to investigate the assassination, published its report in Washington today. Killer Lee Harvey Oswald acted alone, the report said, and neither Oswald nor Jack Ruby, Oswald's killer, was involved in a wider conspiracy. The report criticized the FBI, the secret service, which it said must be overhauled, and the Dallas police for poor security. The FBI knew Oswald had lived in Russia and had a job in a store overlooking Kennedy's route – but the secret service didn't know, yet its role is to protect the president.

1975 Jamaica's big reggae stars, Bob Marley and the Wailers, have a first European hit as "No Woman No Cry" enters the UK Charts.

Mr Stephenson having taken me on the bench of the engine with him, we started at about 10 miles [16 kph] an hour. You cannot imagine how strange it seemed to be journeying on thus, without any visible cause of progressing other than that magical engine, with its flying white breath, and rhythmical unwearying pace.
Fanny Kemble, British actress (1809-93), in *Record of a Girlhood*.

Tokyo joins Berlin-Rome Axis

1940 Imperial Japan signed a 10-year economic and military alliance with Nazi Germany and Fascist Italy in Berlin today. The Tripartite Pact formalizes the Berlin-Rome-Tokyo Axis which began in 1936 when Japan signed the Anti-Comintern Pact with Germany; Italy signed a year later. Today's pact is a coup for Nazi leader Adolph Hitler, whose *Blitzkrieg* in Europe has gained him conquests, but no allies other than Italy and an increasingly reluctant Spain. Japan is also a useful buffer against the United States. Japan and Russia, however, have been bitter enemies since their war over Manchuria in 1905, and the peace treaty that was signed by Russia and Germany a year ago is looking ever more shaky.

1968 Just one day after the end of theatre censorship in Britain, 13 naked actors faced a London audience tonight as the rock musical *Hair* opened in the West End to a packed house. The nude bit only lasted one short scene and impressionistic stage lighting left most of the crucial details discreetly shadowed, but the show was nonetheless a big hit with the audience.

Commuters do the Locomotion

1825 A new era of travel began today when George Stephenson's steam engine Locomotion pulled a full load of passengers from Shildon to Stockton via Darlington, inaugurating the world's first passenger railway service. Stephenson operated the engine himself, and the 27-mile (43 km) journey took less than three hours. The passengers travelled in a long line of 32 carriages fitted with special wheels which glide smoothly along the steel rail track. Stephenson built the Locomotion for the Stockton and Darlington Railway and also surveyed the route, avoiding steep gradients wherever possible. He and his talented engineer son Robert are designing a more powerful engine which they say could have a top speed of as much as 30 mph (48 kph). It is understood that Stephenson has been approached by the Liverpool and Manchester Railway.

1791 Jews are granted French citizenship.

1888 The Central News Agency in London receives a letter, signed "Jack the Ripper" about the current spate of horrific prostitute murders.

1917 Death of Edgar Degas, French painter and sculptor who initially painted portraits in the style of the old masters, but in the mid-1860s began painting contemporary scenes, particularly of ballet and racecourses.

1921 Death of Engelbert Humperdinck, German composer who wrote the well-loved opera *Hansel and Gretel*.

1922 Constantine I, King of Greece, abdicates following the Greek defeat in Turkey.

1930 American golfer Bobby Jones completes the first-ever golfing Grand Slam when he wins the US National Amateur Championships.

1960 Europe's first "moving pavement", the travelator, is opened at Bank Underground Station in London.

1979 Death of Dame Gracie Fields, singer and entertainer whose songs include "The Biggest Aspidistra in the World" and "Sally" (her theme song).

2002 A Senegalese ferry sinks with 1,000 fatalities.

BIRTHDAYS

Samuel Adams 1722, American revolutionary who was involved in planning the Boston Tea Party, an anti-taxation raid on British ships.

George Cruikshank 1792, British political cartoonist who also illustrated more than 850 books, including Charles Dickens' *Oliver Twist*.

Louis Botha 1862, South African prime minister, the first of the Union of South Africa, who encouraged reconciliation between the British and the Boers.

Vincent Youmans 1898, American composer of popular music whose hits included "I Want to Be Happy" and "Tea for Two".

1066 Norman invaders land in England.

1868 Rebel generals oust Queen Isabella in Spain.

1891 Death of Herman Melville, American author of *Moby Dick*.

1895 Death of Louis Pasteur, French chemist and micro-biologist who developed vaccines for anthrax and rabies.

1964 Death of the mute harp-playing member of the comic team of Marx Brothers, Harpo Marx.

1975 Dictator General Franco executes five Basque terrorists.

1978 John Paul I is found dead after only 33 days as Pope.

1986 British welterweight boxer Lloyd Honeyghan becomes world champion in just six rounds with American boxer Donald Curry, who was forced to retire with a badly cut eye.

1989 Ferdinand Marcos, ex-President of the Philippines, dies in exile.

BIRTHDAYS

Caravaggio 1573, Italian baroque painter noted for his dramatic canvasses of light and shade.

"Gentleman John" Jackson 1769, English pugilist who managed to get boxing accepted as a legitimate sport and after his retirement as English boxing champion set up a self-defence school in Bond Street, where his pupils included Lord Byron.

Georges Clemenceau 1841, French prime minister from 1917 to 1920.

Al Capp 1909, American cartoonist who drew the "Li'l Abner" strip which first appeared in 1934.

Peter Finch 1916, Australian actor of stage and screen whose appearances in the films *Sunday, Bloody Sunday* and *Network*, for which he was awarded a posthumous Oscar, won him a new audience.

Brigitte Bardot 1934, French actress and international sex symbol who first caused a stir in *And God Created Woman*.

Marines enter Beirut after Lebanese massacre

1982 US president Ronald Reagan has sent marines into Beirut on a peace-keeping mission. They will be joined by Italian and French contingents, and Reagan said both Syrian and Israeli forces would leave the Lebanon. This follows the massacre of hundreds of Palestinian civilians 10 days ago by Israeli-backed Lebanese Christians in the Sabra and Chatila refugee camps in West Beirut. The massacre was the Christians' revenge for the assassination four days earlier of Lebanese Christian president-elect Bashir Gemayel, now replaced by his brother, Amin. On Saturday 300,000 Israelis demonstrated against Israeli involvement in the massacres.

Ptolemy kills Pompey Caesar not impressed

48 BC The Roman general Pompey the Great has been assassinated, stabbed to death as he landed in Egypt on the orders of Egyptian king Ptolemy XIII. Pompey had sided with the Roman senate against Julius Caesar, who was campaigning in Gaul, but Caesar marched on Rome, forcing Pompey to retreat to Greece with his army. Caesar followed him, and defeated Pompey at Pharsalus last month. Pompey fled to Egypt and Ptolemy granted him refuge – and then had him killed, seeking to curry favour with Caesar. Caesar, however, is furious at the ignoble end of his adversary and to Ptolemy's dismay is leading an expedition to Egypt. The young King Ptolemy, who is only 15, is in the middle of a civil war with his 21-year-old sister, Cleopatra.

AXIS LEADERS PROMISE PEACE

1937 A million people gathered at a floodlit rally in Berlin tonight to hear Nazi leader Adolf Hitler and Italy's Fascist dictator Benito Mussolini deliver a message of peace. The *Führer* and the *Duce* were speaking at the Field of May, scene of last year's Berlin Olympics. They announced that the Berlin-Rome Axis was not a threat to other peoples. Mussolini went on to denounce the League of Nations' current sanctions against Italy as "criminal". The sanctions follow Italy's invasion and conquest of Abyssinia last year. Tonight's message of peace is incompatible with Hitler's prime objective of *lebensraum* - more living space for Nazi Germany.

1994 The passenger ferry *Estonia* has sunk in the Baltics, with the loss of 910 of the crew and passengers on board.

2000 In the worst violence since the 1993 peace agreements, riots broke out in the Israeli-occupied territories today, sparked by a visit to Haram-al-Sharif by Ariel Sharon.

International debut for Marx

1864 A group of socialist radicals in London has formed an International Workingmen's Association to help unite the world's workers in revolution. They are known as the First International, led by German emigré Karl Marx, an economist and (with Friedrich Engels) the philosopher of modern revolution. Marx has branded religion a social evil – "the opium of the people" – and wants private property abolished. In 1848 he and Engels wrote their *Communist Manifesto* for a London workers' organization, stating that all history was the history of class conflict. The modern capitalist system of production would inevitably drive the proletariat to communist revolution, they said. Karl Marx has charted a path for today's "alienated" society to cast off its yoke and achieve unity and abundance through the elimination of greed.

The workers have nothing to lose in this revolution but their chains. They have a world to gain. Workers of the world unite!
Karl Marx and Friedrich Engels, the closing words in *The Communist Manifesto*, 1848.

Dirty tricks sully pristine White Sox

1920 Eight members of the Chicago White Sox were indicted today on charges of taking massive bribes to lose last year's World Series to the Cincinatti Reds. Baseball fans are appalled – the national game is revered as something quite beyond corruption, and the World Series, first played in 1903, is the game's main celebration, and the biggest event in American sport. Sports writers are calling the eight players the "Black Sox".

ATHENS WREAKS REVENGE ON PERSIA

480 BC Though outnumbered two to one, the Greeks today routed a huge Persian war fleet in the straits of Salamis. Themistocles of Athens led the Greek fleet and won as much by trickery as valour, with a strategy of feints and about-turns that left the Persian fleet divided and exposed. The lines of ram-prowed Greek ships, each propelled by 200 oarsmen, ploughed into King Xerxes' Persians with devastating effect, sinking scores of galleys outright. After fierce fighting, the remnants of the invading Persian fleet fled, leaving more than 200 wrecked galleys and thousands of casualties. The Greeks lost 40 ships. Earlier this year Xerxes invaded and burnt the city of Athens. Today Athens had her revenge. Three years ago, with today's battle in mind, Themistocles persuaded the city to use the profits of a new silver mine to build 200 war triremes, the biggest fleet in Greece. Without naval support, the Persian army's chances of conquering the Greeks are slim.

UK goes cap in hand to IMF

1976 A broke Britain asked the International Monetary Fund for a $3.9 billion (£2.1 billion) loan today – the limit of its entitlement. Britain needs the money to prop up the ailing pound, which collapsed this week following market jitters caused by loud left-wing noises at the ruling Labour Party's annual conference. Meanwhile inflation is soaring, fuelled by poor productivity, high government spending and an energy crisis, while rising prices bring embarrassing wage demands by unions which support the Labour Party. Prime minister James Callaghan has ruled out left-wing demands for lower taxes and a bigger welfare budget.

1986 The Soviet Union today freed American journalist Nicholas Daniloff, jailed a month ago on improbable spying charges. His release follows US agreement to drop charges against Russian diplomat Gennadi Zakharov, previously arrested for spying in New York.

Ulster Protestants vow to fight home rule

1913 Ireland edged one step closer to civil war today as the Protestant majority in Ulster province vowed to fight rather than be ruled by Catholic Dublin. At a meeting in Belfast, the Ulster Unionist Council agreed to set up a provisional government if the British parliament approves Irish home rule, and council chairman Sir Edward Carson promised to make Ulster ungovernable by Dublin. Meanwhile the Protestant Ulster Volunteer Force held a military parade near the city. Britain's Liberal prime minister Herbert Asquith needs the Irish nationalist votes to stay in power. Under pressure from nationalist leader John Redmond, he introduced the Irish Home Rule Bill in parliament last year. But Ulster's Protestants are committed to British rule to avoid becoming a small minority in an Irish state.

> *Long Island represents the American's idea of what God would have done with Nature if he'd had the money.*
> **Peter Fleming**, British writer, 1929.

> *No one owes Britain a living.*
> **James Callaghan**, British Labour prime minister, 1976.

Day of death as Nazis shoot 30,000 Jews

1941 A special Nazi death squad has murdered thousands of Russian Jews in Kiev, machine-gunning them systematically in Babi Yar ravine. The shooting continued all day, and more than 30,000 men, women and children are feared dead. Nazi Gestapo secret police chief Heinrich Himmler sent four *Einsatzgruppen* (strike squads) into Russia behind the advancing German war machine with the express mission of exterminating Soviet Jewish civilians and other "undesirables". Kiev fell to the Nazis 10 days ago, and Leningrad is under siege. Meanwhile some 700,000 Jews have died in the Polish ghettoes since the Nazi occupation two years ago. Himmler and his henchmen, Reinhard Heydrich and Adolph Eichmann, are reported to be planning a "final solution" to the Jewish "problem".

1650 A border pact is signed which recognizes the English claims to parts of the Long Island coastline.

1902 French writer Emile Zola dies, accidentally gassed by charcoal fumes.

1911 Alleging mistreatment of Italians in Libya, Italy declares war on the Ottoman (Turkish) Empire.

1930 George Bernard Shaw turns down a peerage.

1938 The Munich Conference begins, attended by Neville Chamberlain, Edouard Daladier, Adolf Hitler and Benito Mussolini.

1950 The first automatic telephone answering machine is tested by the US Bell Telephone Company.

1952 John Cobb, British and world waterspeed record holder, is killed on Loss Ness in Scotland when his vessel *Crusader* disintegrates after hitting waves at a speed of 240 mph (384 kph).

1987 John M. Poindexter officially resigns from the Navy over the Iran-Contra scandal.

BIRTHDAYS

Tintoretto 1518, Italian painter, one of the most important of the Venetian school, whose works include *The Ascension* and the ceilings at the Prado, Madrid.

Miguel de Cervantes 1547, Spanish playwright best known for his novel *Don Quixote*.

Viscount Horatio Nelson 1758, British naval commander who became a national hero despite the scandal of his love affair with Emma, Lady Hamilton.

Gene Autry 1907, American singing cowboy and actor who wrote and recorded more than 200 songs.

Stanley Kramer 1914, American film producer and director whose films include *Guess Who's Coming to Dinner*.

Jerry Lee Lewis 1935, American rock 'n' roll star who first appeared on stage at the age of just 14. His first big hit was "Great Balls of Fire".

1630 John Billington is executed in New Plymouth for murder – the first capital crime in America.

1791 Mozart's opera *Die Zaubefflote* receives its premiere in Vienna.

1792 French troops take Speyer in the Rhineland.

1882 Water power is first used to produce electricity at a plant on the Fox River near Appleton, Wisconsin, USA.

1931 Pay cuts in the British Navy prompt mutinous protest by 12,000.

1933 Franklin D. Roosevelt announces $700 million New Deal aid to the American poor.

1949 Mao Tse-Tung formally becomes chairman of the Peoples' Republic of China.

1970 Britain swaps hijack hostages for Palestinian terrorist Leila Khaled.

1989 Death of Virgil Thomson, American composer, music critic and conductor.

1993 An earthquake claims the lives of 10,000 villagers in western and southern India.

BIRTHDAYS

Lewis Milestone 1895, Russian-born American film director who won an Oscar for *All Quiet on the Western Front*.

David Oistrakh 1908, Russian violinist most renowned for his interpretations of the Brahms, Tchaikovsky and Prokofiev concertos.

Truman Capote 1924, American novelist and short story writer whose books include *Breakfast at Tiffany's* and the "non-fiction novel" *In Cold Blood*.

Angie Dickinson 1931, American actress and star of the TV series *Police Woman*. Her films include *Dressed to Kill* and *Charlie Chan and the Curse of the Dragon Queen*.

Johnny Mathis 1935, American ballad singer who had a hit with "Wonderful! Wonderful!" in 1957 and continued to record best-sellers over the next 20 years.

Dean just too fast to live

1955 Screen rebel James Dean has been killed in a car crash. The 24-year-old star died like he lived – too fast. He crashed his high-powered Porsche sports car while on his way to compete in a motor race. Dean starred in only three movies: the first, *East of Eden*, was based on John Steinbeck's novel. His second role was as the misunderstood teenager in *Rebel Without a Cause*, released this year. It instantly made him the object of mass teenage adulation and his death has caused widespread heartbreak. Dean's third film, *Giant*, in which he played opposite Rock Hudson, will be released next year, a rags-to-riches tale of an oil millionaire.

Babe Ruth home and dry

1927 Babe Ruth slugged his way to immortality today when he hit his 60th home run of the season, an all-time record. The New York Yankees star smashed the record on a Tom Zachary pitch playing the Washington Senators. The "Sultan of Swat" broke his own previous record of 59 home runs set in 1921 – which in turn broke the record 54 he hit the previous year, his first with the Yankees. Before he joined the Yankees, George Herman Ruth broke records as a pitcher for the Boston Red Sox. Ruth has breathed fresh life into the game. When he first took the bat for the Yankees, baseball was at a low ebb, deep in the "Black Sox" bribery scandal. It was a pitcher's game without much running: Ruth must take most of the credit for the exciting slugger's game it has become today.

> *Freedom of the press is for he who owns one.*
>
> **H. L. Mencken**, iconoclastic American journalist – Canadian press baron Lord Thomson bought the *Times* of London today, 1966.

1949 Victorious communist Chinese leader Mao Tse-tung was elected Chairman of the new People's Republic of China in Peking today. Chou En-lai was elected foreign minister. After three years of civil war, Mao's guerrillas have roundly defeated Generalissimo Chiang Kai-shek's US-backed Nationalist army and the communists are now in control of the huge country. Chiang is a spent force, the remnants of his regime bottled up in the south.

RIPPER STRIKES WITH CLINICAL PRECISION

1888 Jack the Ripper murdered two more prostitutes in the streets of London's East End early this morning. His first victim was Liz Stride, in her late 30s. Her body was found at 1 am. The mad killer had left her with a cut throat. An hour later he struck again a mile away, killing Cathy Eddows, also in her 30s. The Ripper slit her throat expertly and then performed his dreadful ritual on the corpse, disembowelling her with all the skill of a surgeon. This morning's victims were his third and fourth. London is aghast at the latest killings, and the city's prostitutes are terrified. There seems no doubt that unless he is caught the maniac will strike again. The police have made little headway in the case: they are not even certain that the man who wrote the taunting letter signed "Jack the Ripper" is indeed the killer. The murderer's surgical skills suggest an upper class background, and dark rumours are circulating of conspiracy in high places.

Chamberlain "peace with honour"

1938 British prime minister Neville Chamberlain returned from the crisis conference in Munich tonight and told cheering crowds at the airport "I believe it is peace for our time." Chamberlain and French premier Edouard Daladier flew to Munich to meet Germany's Adolf Hitler and Italian premier Benito Mussolini to find a solution to the Czechoslovakian crisis. Hitler had demanded immediate German occupation of German-speaking Sudetenland in western Czechoslovakia following a series of staged riots. France is treaty-bound to defend Czechoslovakia, but Daladier, under pressure from Chamberlain, agreed to the German occupation, and Chamberlain agreed to withdraw British support for the Czechs in return for Hitler's promise that this would be his last bid for more territory. Tonight Chamberlain called the agreement "peace with honour". The Czechs are calling it treachery.

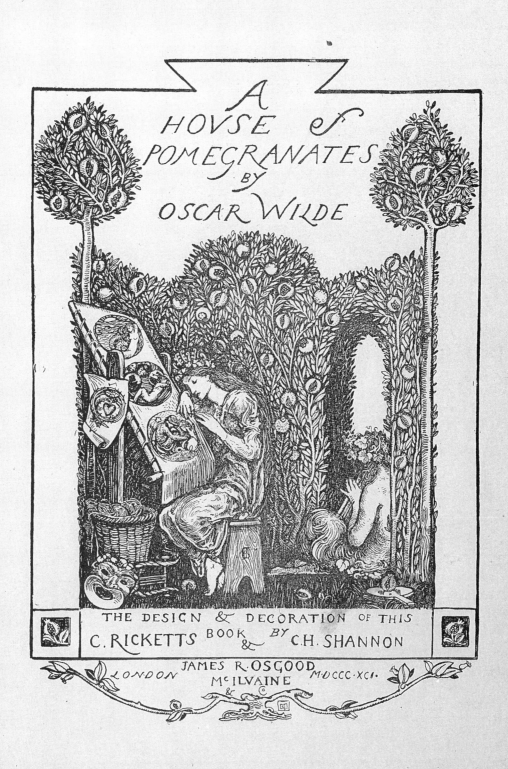

A HOVSE of POMEGRANATES BY OSCAR WILDE

THE DESIGN & DECORATION OF THIS BOOK C. RICKETTS & BY C.H. SHANNON

LONDON JAMES R. OSGOOD McILVAINE & MDCCC·XCI·

1900 Writer and wit Oscar Wilde has died today in Paris where he has been living in exile. One of several collections of fairy stories, *A House of Pomegranates* was published in 1891.

OCTOBER

*"England expects
that every man will do his duty."*

Signal hoisted on **Lord Nelson's** ship
prior to the Battle of Trafalgar, October 21, 1805.

Siamese catharsis

1868 Mongkut, king of Siam, has died in Bangkok, aged 64. In only 17 years as ruler he implemented sweeping political, economic and social changes with western help. Mongkut's decision to reverse centuries of isolation was formulated during the 27 years he spent as a Buddhist priest. During this time he travelled widely and saw that radical steps were needed to solve the country's problems. Siam had one large and venerable commodity to offer the US in return for all their advice – elephants. These, Mongkut thought, could be used in the development of the USA. Siam's experience of imperialism was soured last year when France forced him to relinquish his vassal state, Cambodia, and make it a French protectorate.

It is my Royal and Imperial command that you . . . exterminate first the treacherous English, and . . . walk over General French's contemptible little Army.
Wilhelm II, King of Prussia and Emperor of Germany, referring to the British Expeditionary Force, 1914.

1936 General Francisco Franco Bahamonde, 44, was today proclaimed "Chief of the Spanish State" by the nationalist military junta that is trying to seize power in Spain. His elevation comes a month after the death in a plane crash of the former leader, General Sanjurjo. The nationalists are looking for a speedy end to the chaos gripping the country – unlikely because the capital, Madrid, and the east of the country are firmly in control of government forces.

City of the Angels shaken and stirred

1987 An earthquake rocked Los Angeles for 20 seconds this morning, killing seven people and injuring at least 100, 12 seriously. The quake struck at 7.40, the height of the morning rush hour. Traffic snarled up as freeways were closed due to structural damage. Frightened office workers poured out of their skyscrapers and on to even more hazardous streets. The area of the city worst hit was downtown Whittier, where some 50 businesses and 100 homes suffered extensive damage. The earthquake registered 6.1 on the Richter scale and was felt 200 miles (321 km) away in Las Vegas. It was the strongest tremor to hit the area since February 1971, when a quake in the Sylmar community in the San Fernando Valley resulted in 64 deaths.

Controversial Leakey dies

1972 The controversial archaeologist and anthropologist Louis Leakey died in London today, aged 69. Leakey will be remembered for the discoveries of the 1,750,000-year-old Zinjanthropus fossil at Olduvai Gorge and the contemporaneous *Homo habilis* at Lake Natron in Tanzania between 1959 and 1964. Leakey believed that *Homo habilis* was a human ancestor of man but Zinjanthropus was not. This brought him into conflict with those scholars who classifed Zinjanthropus as an Australopithecine, the fossil widely thought to be most closely related to man, and disputed the existence of a *Homo habilis* lineage. Leakey's wife, Mary, and their son, Richard, will continue his work piecing together the jigsaw of human evolution.

China to be Mao's Republic

1949 China has been proclaimed a People's Republic under the leadership of Mao Tse-tung, as Chairman, and Chou-En-Lai, as Prime Minister. The defeat of the Nationalist forces of Chiang-Kai-shek leaves the Communists with a clear path for the implementation of their radical social and economic policies. A few months ago the new leaders warned that the struggle ahead would be as difficult as the revolutionary armed struggle that is just coming to an end. One of the primary objectives of Chairman Mao is the industrialization of his Republic, which he hopes will raise China to the status of a great power. His ultimate goal of seeing the rise of Communism throughout the world will begin with the creation of a socialist society in China.

1880 The Edison Lamp Works begin operations in New Jersey to manufacture the first electric light bulbs.

1903 European railways link with Russia.

1918 British officer T. E. Lawrence (Lawrence of Arabia) and the Arab forces of Emir Faisal capture Damascus from the Turks.

1936 The BBC begins regular television broadcasts from Alexandra Palace in London.

1938 German forces enter Sudetenland, once part of Czechoslavakia which, ironically, Hitler claimed he had liberated.

1969 The sound barrier is broken by Concorde 001 for the first time, during a test flight in France.

1974 The Watergate trial begins.

1987 Forty-eight-year-old surrogate grandmother Mrs Pat Anthony gives birth to triplets for her daughter Karen Ferriera-Jorge in Johannesburg, South Africa.

BIRTHDAYS

Annie Besant 1847, English social reformer and theosophist who together with radical atheist Charles Bradlaugh promoted birth control, for which they were prosecuted.

Stanley Holloway 1890, English actor and entertainer who was Oscar-nominated for his Alfred Doolittle in the film *My Fair Lady*, a role he created for the original New York stage production.

Vladimir Horovitz 1904, Russian concert pianist with an enormous repertoire who once gave a series of 25 recitals which included more than 200 works.

Walter Matthau 1920, American actor who won an Oscar for his part in *The Fortune Cookie* and was the leading man in the Broadway and, later, film productions of *The Odd Couple*.

Jimmy Carter 1924, American president and peanut farmer, who was instrumental in getting Israel and Egypt to sign the Camp David agreement, ending hostilities between the two countries.

322 BC
The great Greek philosopher Aristotle dies of a stomach illness.

1780 British officer John André, who negotiated with the treacherous American revolutionary General Benedict Arnold for the surrender of West Point, is executed as a spy.

1803 Death of Samuel Adams, American statesman and one of the signatories of the Declaration of Independence.

1871 Mormon leader Brigham Young is arrested for bigamy.

1925 London's first almost entirely enclosed red double-decker buses begin service.

1935 Italian forces invade Abyssinia – Mussolini's bombers have already pounded border towns.

1940 Child evacuees sailing to Canada in the *Empress of Britain* come under attack from a German submarine – most of the 634 crew and passengers are rescued.

1950 A new cartoon strip by Charles M. Schulz called *Peanuts* appears, featuring Charlie Brown.

1987 Death of Sir Peter Medawar, biologist and Nobel prize-winner.

2003 J. M. Coetzee wins the Nobel Prize for Literature.

BIRTHDAYS

Mohandas Karamchand Gandhi 1869, Indian leader who used civil disobedience in his campaign for Indian independence.

Cordell Hull 1871, American statesman, diplomat and secretary to Franklin D. Roosevelt who was awarded the Nobel Peace Prize in 1945.

Roy Campbell 1901, South African poet whose vigorous and often aggressively satirical work includes *The Flaming Terrapin* and his autobiography *Light on a Dark Horse*.

Graham Greene 1904, British novelist, playwright, short story writer and *Times* journalist whose novels include *Our Man in Havana* and *Brighton Rock*, which was made into a film.

FRENCH STRENGTHEN HAND AT SPANISH COURT

1700 The death was announced today of the Spanish king, Charles II. He was 39. Alarm bells will have rung in England, Austria and Holland with the announcement that before his death, Charles, who leaves no heir, named Philip, Duke of Anjou, as his successor. Two years ago the nations with an interest in the succession agreed that Joseph Ferdinand, the electoral prince of Bavaria, should get the crown. Spanish territory would be ceded to pay off the rival French and Austrian claimants – Philip, the second grandson of Louis XIV, and the Archduke Charles, the second son of the Hapsburg emperor Leopold I. This ingenious plan went awry when Joseph Ferdinand inconveniently predeceased Charles, leaving the physically and mentally handicapped Spanish monarch susceptible to the blandishments of the French party at his court. War looks inevitable.

Texans up in arms against Mexico

1835 Texan-Americans today struck the first blow for an independent Texas by staging an armed uprising against the centralist government of Antonio de Santa Anna in the town of Gonzales, 67 miles (108 km) east of San Antonio. American immigrants, with their slaves, first settled here in 1825 when Texas was largely undeveloped and there was little interference from the Mexican government. Santa Anna's bid to change Mexico from a federation of states into a centralized system with himself as undisputed head is popular with the army but has little support among the general population, especially the Texan-Americans who have a great deal to lose from Santa Anna's policy. The situation may prove to be a heaven-sent opportunity for America to expand westwards.

AIDS hits screen hunk

1985 Screen star Rock Hudson died at his Beverly Hills mansion early today. Ten months ago the 59-year-old star had told the world that he was dying of AIDS (Acquired Immune Deficiency Syndrome). Pushed as the all-American boy in the 50s, Hudson quickly established himself as a Hollywood heartthrob. However, the public image of Rock Hudson bore no resemblance to reality. The Hollywood publicity machine helped him to hide his homosexuality. Hudson spent the last two years of his life denying his illness and refusing to believe that it would prove fatal. News of Rock Hudson's death hit the media barely 40 minutes after it occurred. A horde of photographers was at the scene before the mortuary van had departed with the body which was to be immediately cremated – Rock had not wanted a funeral.

> *There are many reasons why novelists write, but they all have one thing in common – a need to create an alternative world.*
> **John Fowles**, British novelist, 1977.

Tatters of papal power

1870 The meeting of the Vatican Council in Rome, the first general assembly of the Church of Rome for 300 years, is drawing to a close amid mounting criticism at home and abroad. Of the decrees issued by the Council during its 10-month sitting, the one relating to papal infallibility on matters of faith and morals has raised most hackles. Secular governments fear that this will lead to clerical interference in politics. The papacy has lost all territorial power since Italian forces invaded Rome. The Papal States no longer exist and Rome is set to become the capital of a united Italy. The pope, Pius IX, regards himself as a virtual prisoner in his own palace, but will continue to wield what little power he has left.

1931 Tea tycoon and yachtsman Sir Thomas Lipton has died in London at 81. Glasgow-born Sir Thomas was a grocer, expanded and sought a cost-effective way of supplying his shops: he bought tea, coffee and cocoa plantations in Ceylon and farms, bakeries and bacon-curing establishments in England. The one success which eluded him was victory in the America's Cup yacht race.

OJ SIMPSON ACQUITTED OF MURDER

1995 OJ Simpson has been found not guilty of the murders of his ex-wife Nicole and her companion Ronald Goldman. The jury took just a few hours to reach a unanimous decision in the trial that has gripped America. Nicole Brown Simpson and Ronald Goldman were stabbed to death outside her Brentwood house on June 12. Former American football star Simpson was arrested soon after the killings but insisted from the start he was innocent. Orenthal James Simpson's fate has become essential television viewing ever since 95 million Americans watched police give chase to his car on the day of his arrest.

DPP's career sadly curbed

1991 Sir Allan Green, QC, the British Director of Public Prosecutions, resigned today after being stopped by police for alleged kerb crawling. He had been seen talking to prostitutes in the red light district around King's Cross station on more than one occasion, it was claimed.

Sir Allan, 56, was an able and popular DPP and his fall from grace has been greeted with disbelief tinged with sadness by those who worked with him. During his four years as DPP head, Sir Allan reorganized the service with the aim of making it "fair, competent and nationwide". Prostitute Lindi St Clair, the leader of the Corrective Party, has urged Sir Allan to back her calls for the legalization of prostitution.

NO MORE MORRIS

1896 William Morris, the author and designer, has died at his Hammersmith home, Kelmscott House, aged 62. He had recently returned from a sea voyage to Norway intended to revive his failing health. In 1861 Morris founded the firm of Morris & Co to produce wallpapers, furniture, tapestries, carpets, furnishing materials and stained glass windows (many of them by Burne-Jones). This association of "fine art workmen" held to the principle that the artist-designer should "honour" his material. Morris put much of his considerable energy into promoting Socialist ideals through his writings and, latterly, the formation of the Socialist League.

Berlin backs Willy Brandt

1957 The Berlin city assembly made history today by voting in its youngest ever *Oberburgermeister*, or Mayor. The man entrusted with this difficult office is 44-year-old Willy Brandt. He was elected unopposed by 86 out of the 118 members who voted. Herr Brandt's Social Democratic Party (SPD) was the only party to put up a candidate. Speculation that he would face a challenge by fellow SPD politician Willi Kressmann proved groundless. The composition of the Berlin senate remains unchanged, with the SPD maintaining its one-seat advantage over the Christian Democratic Union party.

British nuke own warship

1952 The first British atomic weapon was exploded today off the Monte Bello Islands, west of Australia. The test was designed to assess the effect of an atomic bomb exploding in a harbour. The ship in which the weapon was exploded, the 1370-ton frigate HMS *Plym*, vapourized except for a few fragments which landed on the nearby islands and started fires in the vegetation. Watching newsmen felt the force from 65 miles (104 km) or so away about four minutes after the flash.

> *I don't want art for a few, any more than education for a few, or freedom for a few.*
> **William Morris**, British designer, who died today, 1896.

1226 Death of St Francis of Assisi, founder of the Franciscan order who received the wounds of Christ (the stigmata) and endured great pain during the first two years of his life.

1867 Death of Elias Howe, who patented the sewing machine and made $2 million (£1.1 million) from it.

1906 SOS is established as the international distress call, replacing the call sign CDQ (sometimes interpreted as "Come Damn Quick!").

1959 Post codes are introduced in Britain.

1967 Death of Sir Malcolm Sargent, hugely popular British conductor perhaps best-loved for his Promenade concerts.

1967 Woody Guthrie, American singer and songwriter of "This Land is Your Land" dies from Huntington's Chorea.

1987 Death of French dramatist Jean Anouilh, whose works include *Antigone* and *L'Alouette*.

BIRTHDAYS

Eleanora Duse 1859, Italian actress for whom the play *La Gioconda* was specially written by her lover, D'Annunzio.

Pierre Bonnard 1867, French painter mainly of Paris scenes who, with Vuillard, also developed the type of intimate domestic interior scene to which the term Intimiste is applied.

Gore Vidal 1925, American satirical author and critic who wrote *Myra Breckinridge* and the screenplay of *Suddenly Last Summer*.

Eddie Cochran 1938, American singer whose hits include "Summertime Blues" and "C'mon Everybody"; he died in England in a car crash, and became a rock 'n' roll legend.

Chubby Checker 1941, American singer whose "The Twist" became an international dance hit and was followed by more hits such as "Let's Twist Again" and "Slow Twistin'".

1535 Miles Coverdale's English translation of the Bible is published.

1824 Mexico becomes a republic.

1859 Death of German publisher Karl Baedeker, whose series of travel guides became internationally famous.

1883 In Glasgow, Sir William Alexander Smith founds the Boys' Brigade.

1895 The first European edition of the *New York Herald* is published in Paris.

1895 American Horace Rawlins wins the first US Open Gold tournament, played at Newport, Rhode Island.

1904 Death of French sculptor Frederic Auguste Bartholdi, creator of the Statue of Liberty.

1905 Orville Wright is the first person to fly an aircraft for more than 33 minutes.

1910 Portugal is proclaimed a republic – King Manuel II flees to Britain.

1952 An external device called a pacemaker developed by Dr Paul Zoll of the Harvard Medical School is fitted to David Schwartz to control his heartbeat.

1961 Death of the painter Max Weber.

BIRTHDAYS

Giovanni Battista Piranesi 1720, Italian architect and engraver.

Jean-François Millet 1814, French painter, chiefly of romanticized scenes of peasant life.

Rutherford B. Hayes 1822, American statesman and Republican president from 1877 to 1881, during which time he supported the welfare of minority groups and reformed the civil service.

Buster Keaton 1895, American actor, director and screenwriter who began his career at the age of three as a human mop in the family comedy act and went on to make some masterful Hollywood comedies such as *The Navigator* and *The General*.

RUSSIAN REBELS SURRENDER IN WHITE HOUSE SIEGE

1993 Troops and tanks loyal to President Yeltsin have opened fire on the White House in Moscow and finally put an end to the pro-Communist rebellion. The rebels were occupying the building together with Moscow's mayoral offices, and had attempted a partial take-over of the national television centre. The siege followed escalating running battles between the pro-Communists and the security forces loyal to President Boris Yeltsin in Moscow. Riot squads had been moved in to clear the streets after protesters erected barriers and set car tyres alight across the Garden Ring Road, Moscow's main thoroughfare. The riot police drafted in reinforcements and used water cannons to disperse the crowds but were driven back with home-made missiles. The protests have been sparked by President Yeltsin dissolving parliament and calling for fresh elections on 21 September. The rebels have demanded Yeltsin reverse his earlier decision to dissolve the conservative parliament. Vice President Alexander Rutskoi, a key player among the hard-line communists and nationalist parliament rebels, was claiming the presidency. He called on people to take to the streets and urged police officers to switch their allegiance. Several people were injured in the clashes between riot police and the 600 demonstrators who were armed with steel bars, petrol bombs and rocks. Police fired warning shots in the air, but they were beaten back by a powerful and determined crowd of rioters. An estimated 146 people have died in the struggle. President Yeltsin has pardoned the ringleaders.

RUSSIA WINS FIRST HEAT OF SPACE RACE

1957 Two years ago both Russia and America announced that satellite programmes would form part of their respective contributions to International Geophysical Year 1957-58. Artificial satellites are believed to have potential as monitors of scientific and meteorological phenomena and also as communications relay stations. The Russians have taken a step closer to discovering the possible uses of satellites by successfully launching the world's first artificial satellite, Sputnik I. The 22-inch (53 cm), 185-lb (84 kg) disc of Sputnik I is at this moment circling the earth at an estimated 18,000 mph (29,000 kph). On each 96-minute orbit, Sputnik comes to within 143 miles (231 km) of the Earth at one extreme of its trajectory and to within 584 miles (942 km) at the other. It is expected to continue sending signals from its two radio transmitters until early next year.

1669 The Dutch painter Rembrandt van Rijn has died in Amsterdam at 63. In his 30s Rembrandt earned large sums from painting portraits of Amsterdam's upper crust. After his wealthy wife died in 1642 he gradually went bankrupt. However, he continued to paint and to receive commissions and he leaves a vast legacy of about 600 paintings, 1500 drawings and 350 etchings.

IRA calls off death strike

1981 The IRA has called off the seven-month old hunger strike that has cost the lives of ten republicans held in H-block of the Maze prison in Belfast. The Maze became the focus of interest for the world's media after the first batch of hunger strikers died, including the MP for Fermanagh and South Tyrone, Bobby Sands. The men in the Maze wanted the British government to give them the status of political prisoners.

Quantum sleep

1947 The German physicist Max Planck has died at his home in Gottingen, aged 89. He was awarded the Nobel Prize in 1918 in recognition of his contribution to the advancement of physics through the discovery of energy quanta. This quantum theory had been established by Planck at the end of 1900 to explain how energy is distributed according to wavelength in the so-called black-body radiation of a cavity. Ironically, the theory went against the tenets of classical physics to which Planck himself adhered. It only became accepted by the majority of physicists after the Dane Niels Bohr demonstrated beyond all doubt that it was not an ad hoc hypothesis invented purely to prove the correct radiation formula for Planck's experiment.

> *They called me everything from a rambling honky-tonk hitter to a waterlogged harmonica player. One paper down in Kentucky said what us Okies needed next to three good square meals a day was some good music lessons.*
> **Woody Guthrie**, legendary US folksinger and songwriter, who died today, 1967.

Janis ODs

1970 Rock singer Janis Joplin was found dead today in a Hollywood hotel room. She had taken an overdose of heroin. Joplin, 27, was known for her uninhibited singing style. She would routinely drink a bottle of Southern Comfort on stage to improve her performance. Recently, though, she had eschewed this method of getting "high", relying instead on the music, and had fought her heroin addiction. Nine years ago Joplin ran away from home in Port Arthur, Texas, to become a singer. She hit the big time following the Monterey Pop Festival in 1967.Her hits include "Piece of My Heart".

Jarrow's unemployed march without food

1936 A British workers' movement has hit on the idea of hunger marches as a way of bringing public attention to the plight of the unemployed in depressed areas of the country. In the formerly prosperous Tyneside ship-building town of Jarrow, which now has a permanent jobless rate of two-thirds of its population, 200 unemployed were given a rousing send-off. They are taking with them on a long march to London a petition with more than 11,000 signatures. The government's attempt to revive the four areas of the country officially recognized in November 1934 as depressed – including Tyneside – has failed. The marchers believe the capitalist system has broken down.

FLYING CIRCUS READY FOR TAKE-OFF

1969 A new 13-episode comedy show to be launched by the BBC on late-night television seems set to raise a few eyebrows: *Monty Python's Flying Circus* is the brainchild of a team of five Oxbridge graduates – John Cleese, Graham Chapman, Eric Idle, Terry Jones and Michael Palin – and an American cartoonist, Terry Gilliam. The style of the new "satire show" has its origins in the successful Thames Television children's comedy programme *Do Not Adjust Your Sets*. Few at the BBC seem to realize that Monty Python will not be like the old late-night satire shows. The audience for the first two shows has been recruited from an old people's home.

2000 Slobodan Milosevic has finally been swept from power as President of the Federal Republic of Yugoslavia amid gathering protest nearly two weeks after he failed to acknowledge defeat in the general elections of September 24. Crowds stormed the parliament building and state-owned television station in Belgrade in protest. Finally Vojislav Kostunica has been able to claim the presidency.

Tea-time

1952 Her majesty's government has taken a significant step towards reviving the nation's addiction to tea by removing it from the list of rationed commodities. The British people's burden remains great, however – meat, bacon (excluding cooked gammon), sugar, butter, margarine, cooking fats, cheese, eggs, sweets and chocolates are all still subject to strict rationing.

1998 The US Congressional committee is debating whether to begin impeachment proceedings against President Clinton over his affair with Monica Lewinsky. It follows a report by Kenneth Starr which said there was evidence the President was guilty of abuse of power and witness-tampering.

Spain tries French dressing

1796 Spain signed the Treaty of San Ildefonso today, thus throwing in her lot with Revolutionary France. Many Spaniards are hostile to the alliance. The man most in favour of it is Manuel de Godoy, Spain's Prime Minister and the lover of Charles IV's lascivious wife, Maria Luisa. He is convinced that Britain is an enemy of Spain. By backing France, however, he is further weakening Spain's dwindling imperial clout. Spain will now be on the opposite side of the fence from her natural allies, the anti-Revolutionary coalitions engineered by Britain. She will also lose her markets in America.

My opinion is, that power should always be distrusted, in whatever hands it is placed.
Sir William Jones, British jurist, in a letter, 1782.

1880 Death of Jacques Offenbach, French composer who wrote *The Tales of Hoffman*.

1908 Bulgaria declares its independence from Turkey.

1917 Sir Arthur Lee donates the country residence Chequers to the nation as a retreat for British prime ministers.

1930 The R-101 rigid airship crashes on the edge of a wood near Beauvais, France, killing 48 passengers including Air Minister Lord Thompson, who may well have contributed to the disaster by bringing luggage on board equivalent to the weight of about 24 people.

1968 Police use water cannons and batons to break up a civil rights march in Londonderry.

1989 The Moulin Rouge in Paris celebrates its centenary.

1994 Fifty members of the Solar Temple cult are found dead in Switzerland.

1999 A train crash near London's Paddington station kills 31 people.

BIRTHDAYS

Chevalier d'Éon 1728, French spy who conducted missions for his country disguised as a woman; a brilliant fencer, he gave exhibitions in London and was fatally wounded in 1810, when an autopsy revealed his masculinity.

Donald Pleasance 1919, British character actor best known for his threatening roles in films such as *Hallowe'en*.

Vaclav Havel 1936, Czech playwright and human rights spokesman who was jailed four times before the collapse of the Communist regime in December 1989, when he became the nation's president.

Bob Geldof 1954, Irish pop musician who was lead singer with the Boomtown Rats and the instigator of Live Aid, an international pop concert to raise funds for famine relief; he received an honorary knighthood and was nominated for the Nobel Peace Prize for his efforts.

OCTOBER 6

1536 English reformer and Bible translator William Tyndale is strangled and burnt at the stake at Vivarde near Brussels on the orders of Henry VIII.

1807 Sir Humphrey Davy discovers a new metal, and names it potassium.

1860 The Franco-British force captures Peking.

1891 Death of Irish nationalist politician Charles Stewart Parnell, described as the "uncrowned king" of Ireland.

1892 Death of Alfred, Lord Tennyson, great English poet who won the Chancellor's medal for English as a young man with the poem "Timbuctoo", and later wrote the famous "The Charge of the Light Brigade".

1895 Promenade concerts, initiated by Sir Henry Wood, begin at the Queen's Hall in London.

1902 A 2000-mile (3200 km) railway line running from Cape Town in South Africa to Beira, Mozambique, is completed.

1928 Chang Kai-shek is China's new president.

1941 Two men with the unfortunate names of Willburn and Frizzel go to the electric chair in Florida.

1968 British drivers Jackie Stewart, Graham Hill and John Surtees come first, second and third in the US Grand Prix.

BIRTHDAYS

Jenny Lind 1820, Swedish operatic soprano dubbed the "Swedish Nightingale".

Le Corbusier 1887, French architect born in Switzerland who promoted the idea of the house as "a habitable machine" and was commissioned at home and abroad to devise town-planning schemes.

Thor Heyerdahl 1914, Norwegian explorer and anthropologist who led a 5000-mile (8000-km) expedition on the raft *Kon-Tiki* from the western coast of South America to the islands east of Tahiti.

You ain't heard nothin' yet

1927 New York is abuzz with the latest entertainment phenomenon – a film with sound, called a "talkie". Warner Brothers premiered their revolutionary film, *The Jazz Singer*, at the Warner Theatre tonight. The omens are good for the company, which has taken a considerable risk in pioneering talkies and in particular the Vitaphone sound process. The star of *The Jazz Singer* is the hugely popular stage entertainer, Al Jolson. People are expected to come in droves to hear him sing on film and speak a couple of lines of dialogue. Warner Brothers hope to release their first all-talking film next year. The film industry is hoping that talkies will revive its flagging fortunes.

VIP victim of rubber war

1951 The British High Commissioner in Malaya, Sir Henry Gurney, was killed today in an ambush by Communist terrorists in the Pahang Hills. The assassination is the most serious incident so far in a year that has seen a marked increase in casualties among the security forces. The Chinese Communists are fighting on two fronts in the fledgeling Malay Federation. Attacks on the security forces are supplemented by an economic war in which rubber trees are slashed and plantation workers intimidated. These tactics are already bearing fruit in that rubber output has decreased. According to the British authorities only a small number of terrorists is involved in the unrest, but the terrorists are very well organized. A long campaign to flush them out is envisaged.

Camp David avenged

1981 The president of Egypt, Anwar Sadat, was assassinated today while attending the military parade marking the anniversary of Egyptian successes in the 1973 Yom Kippur War. Sadat, 62, was rushed to the Maadi Armed Forces Hospital, south of Cairo, but died soon after arrival. Sadat and other ministers were watching a fly-past when men dressed as soldiers opened fire with grenades and automatic weapons from a truck that had stalled in front of the reviewing stand. Seven other senior Egyptian officials and guests were also killed. Sadat's signing of the Camp David treaty with Israel in 1979 won him a host of enemies in the Arab world. Chief among these was the exiled opposition leader Lieutenant General Saad El-Shazli, who is thought to have masterminded the killing.

1014 The Byzantine emperor Basil II has brought his country's 28-year-war with Bulgaria to an end with an act of unprecedented savagery. Tsar Samuel's defeated army of 15,000 men has been blinded. One eye has been left to each 100th man to ensure that the army finds its way back to the Tsar. Meanwhile, the whisker-twirling Basil will be looking for further lands to incorporate into his already vast empire. Sicily, now in the hands of the Arabs, is next on his list of military conquests.

> *You ain't heard nothin' yet, folks.* A line from the film *The Jazz Singer*, the first picture with sound, which hit the screen today, 1927.

Arabs attack as Israel prays

1973 One of the holiest days in the Jewish calendar, Yom Kippur ("Day of Atonement"), has turned into one of the bloodiest. As Israelis were beginning Yom Kippur (when past sins are atoned for through fasting and prayer), a joint Egyptian-Syrian invasion force was attacking their country on two fronts. After initial confusion, the Israeli defence force has been mobilized. The Arabs are unlikely to win this latest round of hostilities on the battlefield, such is Israel's military superiority. The wily Egyptian leader Anwar Sadat believes that a bloody nose might persuade Israel to negotiate seriously over the Arab territory lost during the 1967 Six-Day War.

ARNIE ELECTED GOVERNOR

2003 Hollywood film star Arnold Schwarzenegger has won the race for governor of California, ousting the Democrat incumbent Gray Davis. It is the first time that Californians have voted to sack their governor mid-term. With almost all the votes counted, Schwarzenegger – running as a Republican – has secured almost 48%. In a victory speech, Mr Schwarzenegger thanked the people of California for giving him their trust: "I know that together we can make this the greatest state in the greatest country in the world."

US to root out terrorists in Afghanistan

2001 Today President George Bush announced the start of Operation Enduring Freedom whose aim is to root out al-Qaeda members, particularly Osama bin Laden, from Afghanistan. US and UK troops will join with those of the Northern Alliance, a federation of groups opposed to the Taliban regime in Afghanistan. The terrorists, who were behind the September 11 attacks, are thought to be hiding out in caves in the Afghan White Mountains.

1858 A non-stop mail coach reaches Los Angeles 20 days after leaving St Louis – having travelled 2600 miles (4160 km).

1908 Crete revolts against Turkish domination, seeking unity with Greece.

1919 The first airline, KLM of Holland, is established – scheduled flights are forecast to take place in 1920.

1922 The Prince of Wales makes the first royal broadcast on British radio.

1959 Pictures of the far side of the moon are relayed back to Earth for the first time by the Russian spacecraft *Lunik III*.

1985 Italian cruise liner the *Achille Lauro* is seized by Palestinian terrorists, endangering the lives of more than 400 passengers on board.

1986 A new national newspaper, the *Independent*, is published in Britain.

1988 After an Alaskan hunter spots grey whales trapped in the ice an international rescue operation is planned.

Matisse & Co. get the bird

1905 The paintings of a group of radical artists exhibiting at this year's Salon d'Automne have provoked an unusually hostile response from Parisian art lovers. "A paint pot has been flung in the face of the public," said one critic. Another, Louis Vauxcelles of Gil Blas, has described the room where a sculpture in the classical style by Albert Marque is displayed with the offending paintings by Henri Matisse, André Derain and others, as "Donatello parmi les fauves" ("Donatello among the beasts"). Matisse's *Woman with the Hat* epitomizes the "fauves" approach to art – deliberate disharmonies of intense colour and seemingly little attention to draughtsmanship. Parisians have taken to gathering in front of the painting and jeering at it. However, the American modern art collector, Leo Stein is reported to be interested in buying the painting.

POE POURRI

1849 The poet, short-story writer and critic Edgar Allan Poe has died in Baltimore after a heavy drinking bout. He was 40. In 1845 Poe won fame throughout the United States for his poem "The Raven". His gift for writing in many different styles found expression in, at one extreme, horror and detective stories and, at the other, pseudo-learned discourses. Controversial though he could be – with a libel suit brought by the subject of one of his gossipy sketches on the "Literati of New York" – Poe could also be humorous, kind and gentle as well as ascerbic and self-centred.

Journey's end for Bishop

1904 Isabella Bird Bishop, the first woman to be made a Fellow of the Royal Geographical Society of London, died today. She was 73. She was a sickly child so the family doctor advised her to travel, and in 1854 she made the first of many journeys overseas, to the western United States. Thereafter she travelled all over the world. After each journey she would write a detailed account of her adventures. Her first book, *The Englishwoman in America*, became widely known. She went on her last journey, to Morocco, aged 70. Towards the end of her life she became increasingly involved in the missionary cause and established several small hospitals in China and India.

> *Decades of pain and humiliation – that is precisely what differentiates Central European countries from their Western counterparts.*
> **Czeslaw Milosz**, Polish novelist and 1980 Nobel Prize for Literature winner, 1991.

Turks invincibility blown at Lepanto

1571 A Holy League of naval forces from Spain, Venice and the Vatican has exploded the myth of Turkish military invincibility by annhilating their fleet at the battle of Lepanto in the eastern Mediterranean. The Turkish commander, Ali Pasha, was killed in the bloody fray along with 25,000 of his men. The fleets were evenly matched with about 200 galleys and 80,000 men on either side. Christian galley slaves accounted for half of the Turkish fleet's manpower; 12,000 of them were freed at the end of the battle. Turkish galley losses are estimated at about 150 to the allies' 15. The architect of the Holy League's victory is the dashing Don John of Austria, 24, who has managed to weld disparate fleets into an effective force. It remains to be seen whether the same high degree of cooperation can be maintained.

BIRTHDAYS

Heinrich Himmler 1900, German head of the Gestapo and, from 1929, Hitler's second-in-command.

June Allyson 1923, American actress of stage and screen who could play a tomboy or a tease and appeared in the film *Best Foot Forward* and in numerous musicals such as *Two Girls and a Sailor* and *The Glenn Miller Story*.

Reverend Desmond Tutu 1931, South African archbishop of Cape Town and general secretary of the South African Council of Churches who was awarded the Nobel Peace Prize in 1984.

Thomas Keneally 1936, Australian author whose novel *Schindler's Ark*, based on a true story, won him the Booker Prize.

Jayne Torville 1957, British ice-skating champion who dominated the sport in the mid-'80s with her partner Christopher Dean.

OCTOBER 8

BIRTHDAYS

Sir Alfred Munnings 1878, English artist, critic and president of the Royal Academy whose speciality was horses and sporting pictures.

Juan Perón 1895, Argentinian general and president who was deposed in 1955 and returned to office in 1973.

Cesar Milstein 1927, British molecular biologist who in 1984 shared the Nobel Prize for Medicine for his work on techniques to produce antibodies in order to immunize against specific diseases.

Ray Reardon 1932, Welsh-born World Professional Snooker Champion in 1970, and from 1973 to 1976

Reverend Jesse Jackson 1941, American politician and black civil rights campaigner.

Ferrier loses fight

1953 British contralto Kathleen Ferrier has died at a nursing home in London after a long fight against cancer. She was 41. A late starter, Ferrier reached the summit as a singer in a remarkably short time, thanks to a beautiful voice that was rich in tone and character. She established herself in the first rank of concert singers during the war years. Her stage debut came in 1946, in the world premiere of Britten's *The Rape of Lucretia* at Glyndebourne. The title part in Gluck's *Orfeo* became closely identified with her and, together with appearances at the Edinburgh and Salzburg festivals, won her international acclaim.

Haitian despot takes own life

1820 Henri Christophe, the Haitian leader who believed that despotism was the only form of government for his people, has shot himself. He was 53. A former slave, Christophe rose to prominence as a military commander during the war against the French in 1791. After 1806, when his efforts to become overlord of the entire country had been thwarted, Christophe established his own fiefdom in northern Haiti. He built a fortress, Citadelle Laferrière, south of his capital, Cap-Haitien. His people have been in revolt for the past two months – since hearing that their despotic ruler, now calling himself King Henri I, had suffered a stroke. Christophe could expect no mercy.

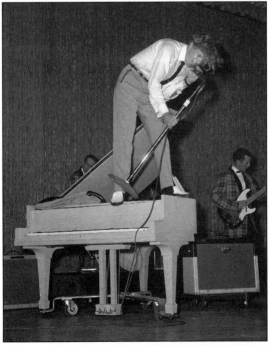

DOW JONES TRACES UPS AND DOWNS

1897 A New York news agency has come up with the novel idea of charting the general trends in the trading of stocks and bonds on Wall Street. The company, Dow Jones & Co, Inc, computes a daily industrials average by using a list of 12 stocks and dividing their total price by 12. The creator of this unique statistical measure is the highly respected financial journalist Charles Henry Dow, 46, the founder and editor of the *Wall Street Journal*.

Multi-million bullion rescued

1981 Treasure worth £45 million ($83 million) which has lain in the Barents Sea for almost 40 years was retrieved last night. For the past three weeks a team of 10 divers has been working round the clock to recover 431 gold bars, weighing 23 lb (10.5 kg) apiece, from the hull of the British cruiser, *Edinburgh*. In May 1942 the ship was transporting the bullion from Russia to Britain when she became involved in a running battle with German destroyers and a U-boat and was eventually sunk. The companies involved in the salvage operation, Wharton Williams and Jessop Marine Recoveries, will receive 45 per cent of the value of the gold. The British and Soviet governments will receive the rest.

Another scandal for Jerry Lee

1984 The death of the fifth wife of singer Jerry Lee Lewis, 49, is the topic of a major article in this month's *Rolling Stone* magazine. Shawn Lewis, 25, died last August, apparently of a methadone overdose. *Rolling Stone* now reveals that bloodstained clothes were found in the room where she died and that blood and bruising were found on her body. Shawn's mother is reported to have said that her daughter had called her the day before her death and said she was going to leave the violent Lewis – nicknamed "The Killer". Lewis has many problems on his plate at present, not least the Internal Revenue Service, after him for back taxes.

Killer fire sweeps through Chicago

1871 Fire has devastated the mecca of the MidWest, Chicago. The inferno began yesterday in the south-western part of the city and quickly spread northwards. The flames were so immense that they licked across the Chicago River and only died out when they reached Lake Michigan. The recent long spell of dry weather rendered the city's many wooden buildings into ideal tinder. About 300 people are estimated to have lost their lives, and a further 90,000 their homes, to the fire. In all, four square miles of the city have been destroyed, including the business sector, at a cost of $200 million (£108 million). Improved safety standards are expected to be the priority of any reconstruction programme for the city.

1192 King Richard the Lion Heart abandons the Holy Land after an unsuccessful Crusade, leaving Jerusalem in Muslim hands.

1651 The Navigation Act is passed, allowing only English ships to import goods from Africa, America and Asia to England.

1760 Russians and Austrians pillage Berlin.

1897 Henry Sturmey sets off in his 4.5 hp Daimler from Land's End in Cornwall, aiming to be the first person to drive from Land's End to John O' Groats in Scotland – a distance of 929 miles (1486 km).

1962 Uganda receives formal independence.

1963 Three thousand lives are lost when the Vaiont Dam in the Italian Alps is wrecked by a rock slide.

1967 Death of André Maurois, French author and biographer.

1973 Elvis Presley divorces Priscilla.

1987 Death of multi-talented Clare Boothe Luce, former US congresswoman, ambassador, novelist, editor and playwright who wrote *The Women*.

THE KINGMAKER TRIES AGAIN

1470 In the ongoing struggle for the English throne the sands of fortune have shifted in favour of the House of Lancaster. Richard Neville, Earl of Warwick, who abandoned the Yorkist cause after his protegé Edward secretly married the beautiful young widow Elizabeth Woodville, has restored the pious and mentally unstable Henry VI to the throne. The strong-willed Edward wanted the woman of his choice and not an arranged marriage to a French princess. Henry VI is used to abdicating responsibility in political matters so the alliance between himself and the power-hungry Warwick should suit them both. However, observers point to Henry's inability to govern as the major cause of the war that has riven the country for the past 15 years and for the loss of English-held lands in France. The days of the Lancastrian dynasty as represented by Henry seem to be numbered.

> *If Botticelli were alive today he'd be working for* Vogue.
> **Peter Ustinov**, British actor, 1962.

CHE SHOT DOWN ON THE JOB

1967 Ernesto "Che" Guevara, the Argentine-born revolutionary who helped Fidel Castro win power in Cuba, has been shot dead after being captured by Bolivian Army troops. He was 39. Che Guevara was in Bolivia as part of a Cuban-sponsored expedition to topple the military government of President Barrientos and export Fidel Castro's brand of Communism to other countries in Latin America. The revolutionary struggle in Bolivia is expected to be carried on under the leadership of Inti Peredo, although without the charismatic Che Guevara the long-term prospects of the movement do not look very good.

Nobel problems for Solzhenitsyn

1970 The winner of this year's Nobel Prize for Literature, dissident Soviet writer Aleksandr Solzhenitsyn, has excused himself from attending the award ceremony in Stockholm in December, for "personal reasons". It is unclear whether the Soviet authorities refused to permit him to leave the USSR or whether Solzhenitsyn declined to go for fear that he would not be re-admitted. The championing of Solzhenitsyn in the West – where he is now a best-selling author – has made life difficult for him with the Soviet authorities, who view the award as provocation. Last year he was expelled from the Soviet Writers' Union.

Jordan hands olive branch to Egypt

1984 A five-year severance of relations between Amman and Cairo was formally ended today with the visit by President Hosni Mubarak of Egypt to Jordan. Egypt has been in the Arab dog-house since 1979 when the late Anwar Sadat signed a peace treaty with Israel. King Hussein's decision to resume diplomatic relations with Egypt and bring her back into the Arab fold has met with hostility, especially among radical Arab states such as Libya and Syria. One reason for King Hussein's decision to extend the hand of friendship to Egypt is Jordan's economy, which is badly in need of a large export market to offset the general downturn in trade caused by the Iran-Iraq war.

BIRTHDAYS

Camille Saint-Saens 1835, French composer and pianist who is perhaps best known for his opera *Samson and Delilah* and his symphonic poem *Dance Macabre*.

Aimee Semple McPherson 1890, American theatrical "evangelist" who was one of the first to use radio as a means of reaching a large religious audience.

Jacques Tati 1908, French actor, film director and screenwriter remembered for *Monsieur Hulot's Holiday* and *Mon Oncle*.

John Lennon 1940, English pop singer, musician and songwriter who rose to fame with the Beatles and later formed the Plastic Ono Band with his wife Yoko Ono.

Steve Ovett 1955, British middle-distance runner who won the gold medal at the Moscow Olympics in 1980.

1794 The Russians crush the rebel Polish army, taking its leader prisoner.

1881 Charles Darwin publishes what he considers his major work, the result of a 45-year ecological study – *The Formation of Vegetable Mould through the Action of Worms with Notes on their Habits.*

1903 British suffragette Mrs Emmeline Pankhurst forms the Women's Social and Political Union in Manchester to fight for female emancipation.

1911 The Chinese revolution breaks out at Wuchang in Central China.

1935 George Gershwin's *Porgy and Bess* opens in New York, the "first American opera".

1940 A German bomb destroys the high altar of St Paul's Cathedral in London.

1954 Ho Chi Minh returns to Hanoi as the French evacuate.

1957 A major radiation leak is detected at the Windscale atomic power station in Cumbria following a nuclear accident on October 7.

1975 After a tumultuous past during which time they have already married and divorced, Richard Burton and Elizabeth Taylor remarry in a remote village in Botswana.

1985 Death of Yul Brynner, bald-headed American actor whose most famous films include *The King and I* and *The Magnificent Seven.*

BIRTHDAYS

Antoine Watteau 1684, French rococo painter of the famous in rural backgrounds (*fêtes galantes*).

Benjamin West 1738, American-born history and portrait painter who spent most of his career in England, becoming President of the Royal Academy.

Giuseppe Verdi 1813, Italian romantic opera composer whose works include *Rigoletto* and *Aida.*

Thelonius Monk 1920, American jazz pianist and composer who led the way in bebop.

CITIZEN WELLES

1985 Orson Welles died at his Los Angeles home today, aged 70. Wisconsin-born Welles (real name George Orson) knew success early in his career. In 1938, when he was only 23, he came to the attention of Hollywood with his radio production of H. G. Wells' *The War of the Worlds*, which had several million Americans believing that Martians had landed in New Jersey. His first film, *Citizen Kane*, which he directed, produced, wrote and starred in, was highly praised. But there was no way but down from this pinnacle of perfection. Disillusioned, he left Hollywood after the war to act in Europe. Eventually he drifted into television, providing voice-overs for commercials.

Yale break at New Haven

1718 Puritan leader Cotton Mather definitely seems to have the Lord on his side. He has received a generous response to his request for further assistance for the Saybrook School from its principal benefactor, wealthy British trader Elihu Yale. Mr Yale responded with gifts worth £800 ($1470). The money from the sale of these items – which included a portrait of George I – will be used to construct a building, to be called Yale College, at the university's new home in New Haven. The university's curriculum emphasizes classical studies and rigid adherence to orthodox Puritanism. Mather and his fellow Congregationalists determined from the outset that their college would not be based on the Harvard model – that bastion of learning is also a hotbed of religious dissent.

Agnew damned by lies

1973 The man twice chosen by US President Richard Nixon to be his deputy resigned this afternoon before appearing in a federal district court in Baltimore to face charges of income tax evasion. Spiro Agnew, 54, pleaded "no contest" ("guilty") and was fined $10,000 (£5400) and placed on probation for three years. Until today, Agnew had described the charges against him as "lies, damned lies". His last-minute reversal means that the Federal prosecutors will not bring more serious charges against him. These relate to the source of the income which Agnew concealed from the Revenue. From the time of his election as Governor of Maryland in 1967, Agnew had accepted cash bribes from engineering firms in return for lucrative state contracts. Agnew's fall from grace is the heaviest of the many miscreants who have so far inhabited the corridors of power in the Nixon administration.

Diamonds aren't his best friend

1979 The political fall-out generated by the overthrow of the self-proclaimed Emperor of the Central African Empire, Marshal Jean Bedel Bokassa, last month has now alighted on the shoulders of French president Valéry Giscard d'Estaing. If he wished for relief from France's domestic problems – which include rising unemployment and inflation – he would not have found it in the satirical newspaper *Le Canard Enchaîné*, which claims he accepted gifts of diamonds from Bokassa. The opposition Socialist party are playing the Bokassa affair for all its worth, demanding an enquiry into relations between the deposed emperor's corrupt and nasty regime and France.

Blast from afar

1913 The last obstacle to the completion of the Panama Canal was overcome in spectacular fashion today by President Woodrow Wilson. From the safety and comfort of the Oval Office, he pressed a red button to detonate the explosives laid over 4000 miles (6400 km) away to clear the final stretch of the Canal. American military engineers, headed by Colonel Goethals, have spent the past nine years on the US-financed waterway. This link between the Atlantic and Pacific oceans is 51 miles (82 km) long, has six locks and traverses two natural lakes, one of which – Lake Gatun – is the largest in the world. The Canal is due to open to shipping next August.

EDITH AND JEAN – THE COCTEAU TWINS

1963 France is today mourning the loss of Jean Cocteau and Edith Piaf. Cocteau died in Paris, aged 74, Piaf in the south where she was convalescing after treatment for drug and alcohol abuse. The two had been firm friends since 1940 when Piaf's newly acquired star status gave her the entrée to move in the same artistic circles as Cocteau. By this time he was almost a French institution, lionized for his artistic experiments in poetry, drama, fiction, drawing, design and film. Such was his admiration for Edith that he wrote a play for her, *Le Bel Indifférent*. He described her as "a star who burns in the nocturnal solitude of the sky over Paris".

1727 George II is crowned in London.

1809 Death of Meriwether Lewis, American explorer who with William Clark found the overland route to the Pacific.

1871 The Great Fire of Chicago is finally extinguished.

1919 The first in-flight meals are served on board a Handley-Page flight from London to Paris at a cost of 3 shillings (15p/28 cents) each.

1961 Death of Leonard "Chico" Marx, piano-playing member of the Marx Brothers comedy team.

1968 *Apollo 7* is launched, carrying US astronauts Walter Schirra, Don Eiselle and Walter Cunningham.

1976 The third wife and widow of Mao Tse-tung, Qiang Qing, is arrested in Berlin with three associates: the "Gang of Four" had attempted to seize power on Mao's death.

1980 Soviet cosmonauts return to earth after a record 185 days in space in the craft *Salyut 6*.

BIRTHDAYS

Sir George Williams 1821, English social reformer who founded the YMCA.

Eleanor Roosevelt 1884, American writer and civil rights campaigner who was married to US president Franklin D. Roosevelt.

Friedrich Bergius 1884, German industrial chemist who invented a process to extract coal from oil.

François Mauriac 1885, French novelist, dramatist and critic who won the Nobel Prize in 1952.

Art Blakey 1919, American jazz drummer and leader of the Jazz Messengers.

Ennio Morricone 1928, Italian composer whose film scores such as *A Fistful of Dollars* have won him international acclaim.

Maria Bueno 1939, Brazilian tennis player who first won Wimbledon at the age of 17, and subsequently won many other major championships.

Algeria stricken

1980 The Algerian city of El Asnam was hit by an earthquake of catastrophic proportions yesterday. Algerian radio said that 80 per cent of the city was destroyed. Twenty thousand are feared dead. The first shock wave registered 7.5 on the Richter scale, and its ferocity broke monitoring equipment at the Swedish Seismological Institute in Uppsala. The effects of the quake were felt in Valencia, Spain, causing cracks to open in a number of houses. El Asnam (formerly Orleansville) had to be almost totally rebuilt after the last earthquake, in 1954, which damaged an area of 30 square miles (78 sq km). The city stands on a section of an unstable fault zone stretching from Gabes, Tunisia to Agadir, Morocco. President Bendjedid Chadli has proclaimed a week's national mourning.

Politicians can forgive almost anything in the way of abuse; they can forgive subversion, revolution, being contradicted, exposed as liars, even ridiculed, but they can never forgive being ignored.
Auberon Waugh, British novelist and critic, 1981.

Rough trade

1834 Sir William Napier, Britain's Chief Superintendent of Trade in China, has died in Macao at the age of 48. He had recently returned from Canton after a disastrous attempt to persuade the imperial government of China to trade directly with Britain rather than through the Hong merchants. Angered Chinese viceroy Loo had no wish to alter established custom. He ordered Napier to return to Macao, and when he refused kept him in confinement. He also called a halt to trade with Britain. Within weeks Napier was dangerously ill, weakened by the heat, and by sheer anxiety, anger and frustration.

JODRELL REACHES FOR THE STARS

1957 The world's largest steerable radio-telescope went into operation at the Jodrell Observatory of the University of Manchester today. The instrument, which has a 250-ft (81-m) diameter parabolic bowl, is mounted on a trunnion 180 ft (58 m) above ground level. The telescope's designer, Bernard Lovell, has completed his project in time for tracking the first Sputnik, which was launched a week ago. Indeed, had it not been for the Russian "first", Lovell's project might have been halted because of spiralling costs.

Tact consists in knowing how far we may go too far.
Jean Cocteau, who died today, 1963.

1987 The latest in sonic wizardry has been brought in to settle the long dispute over the existence of the Loch Ness monster. Known affectionately as Nessie, it was first sighted by an unimpeachable source – St Columba – back in 565. Since then there have been numerous claims of sightings, including photographic evidence. Today's trawl of the loch by some 24 boats fitted with sophisticated sonic detectors revealed a large moving object at a depth of around 180 ft (58 m). A positive identification of the object has yet to be made, and the world's press is eagerly awaiting the outcome.

OCTOBER 12

BIRTHDAYS

Cavell pays high price for humanity

1915 The German authorities in Belgium have executed British nurse Edith Cavell, 50, for her role in an underground operation to help Allied soldiers escape from Belgium to the Netherlands, a neutral country. Cavell had confessed to providing shelter for escapees at the Berkendael Institute in Brussels, a Red Cross hospital of which she was matron. There the men received money and guides from Philippe Baucq, who was arrested and subsequently shot with Nurse Cavell. Reports suggest that responsibility for her death lies solely with the occupation administration in Belgium, which committed the deed before telling the Berlin authorities.

2002 Terrorists have stuck again, this time in the Indonesian tourist resort of Bali. Nearly 200 people were killed and 300 injured, many of them Australian holidaymakers, when a bomb exploded outside a nightclub. The blast is thought to be the work of Muslim groups linked to al-Qaeda.

Boers get first strike

1899 The Boer states have responded to Britain's dispatch of troops to South Africa by issuing a declaration of war, and they have drawn first blood. The British military garrison at Mafeking, under Colonel Robert Baden-Powell, is under siege by Boer forces. If the siege drags on, as seems likely, it may become a symbol of the wider struggle between a colonial power intent on defending its commercial rights and Dutch Boers who resent British inroads in South Africa.

Terra firma is not a mirage

1492 After a month of experiencing mirages of land, explorer Christopher Columbus and his three ships sighted terra firma at dawn today. Columbus went ashore and took possession of the island in the name of his patrons, Isabella and Ferdinand, but is already keen to set sail to find the Island of Cipango.

IRA strikes at the very heart of British Cabinet

1984 The IRA has launched its most daring attack yet on the British government. At 3 am this morning a 20 lb (9 kg) bomb exploded at the Grand Hotel, Brighton, where most of the Cabinet are staying during this year's Conservative Party Conference. Several floors of the hotel collapsed, killing four people and leaving 30 injured. Among the dead are former deputy whip Sir Anthony Berry and the wife of the Tory government's chief whip John Wakeham. The bomb is thought to have been planted on the sixth floor, above the suite occupied by Prime Minister Margaret Thatcher, whose bathroom was devastated by the blast. Despite the turmoil, the party conference started punctually at 9.30 am. Mrs Thatcher told a nonetheless packed assembly that "all attempts to destroy democracy by terrorism will fail".

Rebel with many a cause

1870 Robert E. Lee, the man who by example encouraged the people of the defeated Confederate states of America to believe in a new and better tomorrow, has died in Lexington at the age of 63. The years of hardship endured by Lee as commander of the Army of Northern Virginia during the Civil War took their toll, and he never regained his health. He fought a defensive war, believing that the Confederates could not win against the superior Union army. After the war, Lee accepted the post of president of Washington College in Lexington, Virginia. He proved to be a progressive educator, inspiring in his students the desire to rebuild their state and become good citizens of a united republic.

> *Patriotism is not enough. I must have no hatred or bitterness towards anyone.*
> **Nurse Edith Cavell**, English nurse in World War One, before her execution, 1915.

TURIN SHROUD A FORGERY

1988 The Turin Shroud, for centuries regarded as the burial cloth of Jesus Christ, is believed to be a fake. The results of exhaustive carbon dating tests, carried out on the shroud at laboratories in Oxford, Zurich and Arizona, were revealed today. Speaking at a press conference in London, Professor Edward Hall, the head of the Oxford team, said that the data showed with 95 per cent certainty that the 14-ft (4.5 m) linen cloth dated from between 1260 and 1390, a period when forgery was rife. The Catholic Church, which has consistently expressed caution over the shroud's origins, accepts the findings, but one regular visitor to the Turin Cathedral chapel, Signora Angela Bosso, 72, remarked: "I don't believe in those scientists."

Twelve good men unite Jewry

1843 Twelve men met in a café on New York's Lower East Side today to establish a new fraternal order of Jews in the USA. Their aim is to bring a sense of community to the 15,000 Jewish people living in the United States.

They plan to concentrate initially on arranging private rituals and providing assistance to the elderly, widows and orphans and victims of tragedy and persecution. The name of the new organization is B'nai B'rith, meaning "Sons of the Covenant".

> *My definition of a free society is a society where it is safe to be unpopular.*
> **Adlai Stevenson**, US politician, 1952.

Princesses take to the airwaves

1940 Fourteen-year-old Princess Elizabeth, daughter of King George VI, today made her first public contribution to Britain's war effort by broadcasting to the children of Britain and the Commonwealth. The Princess's father has been much admired for his morale-boosting efforts in these dark days. Princess Elizabeth followed his example in her address to the BBC radio *Children's Hour* audience. She told them: "We know, every one of us, that in the end all will be well." At the end of the programme the Princess encouraged her 10-year-old sister, Margaret, to utter her first public sentence: "Goodnight, and good luck to you all".

1982 The Detroit marathon is certainly not as famous as its counterparts in Boston and New York, but it seems to attract a special strain of competitor. Anthony "Scott" Weiland is one such unusual competitor. He completed this year's Detroit super run in the world record time of 4 hours 7 minutes and 54 seconds – backwards.

DIE CLAUDIUS

AD 54 The Roman emperor and historian Claudius I (Tiberius Claudius Drusus Nero Germanicus) has died, allegedly after consuming poisoned mushrooms dished up by his fourth wife, his niece Agrippina. He was 64. Shortly before his death, Claudius had agreed to acknowledge Nero, Agrippina's son by a former marriage, as his heir instead of his natural son, Britannicus. Claudius was made emperor 13 years ago by the Praetorian Guards, the imperial household army, after the murder of his nephew, Caligula. Until then, Claudius had been encouraged by the imperial family to keep a low profile and concentrate on studying. Ill health, ugliness and an absence of social grace did not recommend him to the public eye. But as emperor he invited popularity and glory – shown in his decision to extend the Roman empire in Africa and Britain – but won neither. He was, however, an able and enlightened administrator.

1399 Coronation of Henry IV, the first King of the House of Lancaster.

1792 US President George Washington lays the foundation stone of the White House.

1857 Prioress wins at Newmarket, becoming the first American horse to win a major British race.

1884 Greenwich is adopted as the universal meridian.

1904 *The Interpretation of Dreams* by Austrian psychoanalyst Sigmund Freud is published.

1930 Hitler's 107 Nazi deputies turn up in uniform to take their new seats at the Reichstag.

1939 Hitler tries without success to persuade US president Roosevelt to intermediate a peace between Germany, France and Britain.

1988 The Law Lords lift an injunction and allow British newspapers to print extracts from Peter Wright's book *Spycatcher*.

BIRTHDAYS

Lillie Langtry 1853, English society beauty known as the "Jersey Lily" who was intimate with Edward VII when he was Prince of Wales.

Yves Montand 1921, Italian-born French actor-singer whose films include *The Wages of Fear* and *Let's Make Love.*

Lenny Bruce 1924, American social satirist who was arrested and charged with obscenity on several occasions, deported from Britain in 1963 and banned from Australia after a single performance in Sydney.

Margaret Thatcher 1925, British Conservative politician and prime minister from 1979 to 1990.

Paul Simon 1941, American pop singer, songwriter and musician who, as part of the duo Simon and Garfunkel, produced big hits such as "Bridge Over Troubled Water" and "Mrs Robinson" and whose solo hits include "Fifty ways to Leave Your Lover" and the album *Graceland.*

1791
The Society of United Irishmen is set up in Belfast to demand rights for Catholics.

1893
The first musical comedy, *The Gaiety Girl*, is performed in London.

1912
President Theodore Roosevelt is shot in an attempted assassination.

1913
An explosion at Universal Colliery in South Wales kills 439 miners – Britain's worst mining disaster.

1939
Eight hundred and ten die as The Royal Navy battleship *Royal Oak* is torpedoed and sinks in Scapa Flow.

1969
The British ten shilling note is replaced with a 50 pence coin.

1973
Egypt and Syria invade Israel as the nation celebrates the holy Day of Atonement, Yom Kippur.

1976
Death of Dame Edith Evans, leading British stage actress who made occasional films and is perhaps best known for her performances in *The Queen of Spades* and *The Importance of Being Earnest*.

BIRTHDAYS

William Penn 1644, English Quaker leader who founded the American Quaker colony of Pennsylvania.

Eamon de Valera 1882, American-born Irish politician who was president of the newly declared Irish Republic from 1919 to 1922, three times Irish prime minister and subsequently president from 1959 to 1973.

Dwight D. Eisenhower 1890, American military commander in charge of the Allied invasion of Europe in World War Two, and twice president of the USA after the war.

Lillian Gish 1896, American heroine in many silent film classics, including *Birth of a Nation*.

Cliff Richard 1940, British pop singer who rose to fame in the '50s and has had chart-topping hits ever since.

William conquers as Harold falls at Hastings

1066 The dispute over who should succeed the late Edward the Confessor as king of England was settled in a hard-fought battle near Hastings today. On his deathbed Edward is thought to have named the warlike Earl Godwin's son, Harold, his successor in order to prevent bloodshed between two other claimants, William, Duke of Normandy and Harald Hardrada, king of Norway. But he had already made William his heir in the 1050s when the Godwin family was in exile. When they heard that Harold had been crowned, William and Hardrada joined forces and set sail for England. Harold threw back the challenge from the north, killing his Norwegian namesake. But today English slings and spears were no match for Norman cavalry. The English peasant army lost heart soon after their leader fell, mortally wounded. The Normans are now heading for London, to secure the capital and William's position.

I do not dislike the French from the vulgar antipathy between neighbouring nations, but for their insolent and unfounded airs of superiority.
Horace Walpole, British writer, in a letter, 1787.

Nobel Prize gives hope to Burma

1991 This year's Nobel Peace Prize has been awarded to the Burmese opposition leader Aung San Suu Kyi. The daughter of the martyred General Aung San, father of Burmese independence, she returned to Burma in 1988, after an absence of 28 years. The formation of a military government in Burma motivated her to found an opposition party, the NLD (National League for Democracy). She denounced the government and in July 1989 was put under house arrest and barred from participating in the May 1990 elections. Despite winning only 10 out of 485 seats, the military refused to hand over power to the NLD, which won 81 per cent of the seats they contested. The Peace Prize may be seen as part of an international effort to win her release.

TRAGIC END FOR BRAVE "DESERT FOX"

1944 Mystery surrounds the death today of one of Germany's finest military leaders, Field Marshall Erwin Rommel, who commanded the Afrika Korps with distinction during the North African campaign (1941-43). He was 53. Three months ago the Field Marshall suffered serious head injuries when his car somersaulted off the road after being strafed by British fighter-bombers. He was thought to be recovering well from these injuries, however. Today heart failure has been given as the cause of death, but other sources say that Rommel poisoned himself because Hitler had made it known that he was aware of the Field Marshall's involvement in the recent July plot to assassinate him. Rommel was left to choose between trial before the People's Court, under the notorious Nazi judge, Roland Freisler (who has already had the other plotters put to death by slow hanging from a noose of piano wire suspended from a meat-hook), or suicide.

Crooner Bing's last swing

1977 The much-loved entertainer Bing Crosby collapsed and died today after completing a round of golf near Madrid. He was 73. Hollywood was quick to exploit Crosby's vocal talent, and in 1940 he began an association that would last 20 years with Bob Hope and Dorothy Lamour in the Road films. One of his most successful films was *High Society*, with Grace Kelly and Frank Sinatra. His records have sold more than 400 million copies.

Yeager smashes sound barrier

1947 Another chapter in the history of aviation was written today when the Bell X-1 became the first aircraft to fly faster than sound. The rocket-powered craft, piloted by Major Charles Yeager, USAF, was taken to a height of 30,000 ft (9700 m) under a B-29 Superfortress mother-plane. The test began at 70,000 ft (22,700 m). The maximum speed achieved was Mach 1.05, held for several seconds. Once the test was completed, the X-1 glided to land at Edwards Air Force Base in California. There was severe buffeting at around Mach 0.94, but comparatively little as the sound barrier was broken.

Judge just scrapes in

1991 The US senate today elected Clarence Thomas to the Supreme Court by 52 votes to 48, the highest ever number of "no" votes ever cast against a nominee. Ten days ago it seemed likely that the Democrat-dominated Senate would back Thomas by a handsome margin. Then it was revealed that a 35-year-old law professor, Anita Hill, had accused Thomas of sexual harassment while he was chairman of the Equal Employment Opportunity Commission in the early 1980s. The Administration had been aware of her allegations but dismissed them out of hand. The Senate hearings to determine Thomas' suitability for the Supreme Court were broadcast live, but became a trial of character rather than his stance on legal matters.

1993 ANC leader Nelson Mandela and President F. W. de Klerk of South Africa have today been awarded the Nobel Peace prize, an acknowledgement of their commitment to build a peaceful, multi-racial South Africa. The prize comes after years of negotiations between the two.

Genius gets away with murder

1534 The artist and goldsmith Benvenuto Cellini looks set to get away with cold-blooded murder on account of his arch-rival and fellow artist Pompeo outside a chemist's shop on the corner of the Chiavica in Rome. Fortunately for Cellini the new Pope, Paul III (formerly Alessandro Farnese), is a great admirer of his work. So keen is Pope Paul said to be for Cellini to make his coinage that he is prepared to award him a safe conduct until the next Feast of the Assumption (August), when he will grant the goldsmith a full pardon.

THE MELODIES LINGER ON

1964 The American composer and lyricist Cole Porter died today in Santa Monica, California, at the age of 71. The grandson of a millionaire speculator, Porter inhabited the glittering society world that so often provided the backdrop to his musicals and songs. The richest creative period of his life was between 1928 and 1948, culminating with his greatest musical, *Kiss Me Kate*. In 1958, 21 years after a horseriding accident left him crippled, Porter underwent the amputation of one leg.

Millions march to end Vietnam War

1969 The biggest anti-war demonstration in America's history was staged today. Millions of Americans took part in organized rallies and marches to register disapproval of their country's continuing involvement in the Vietnam War. The protesters want a moratorium, an end to the war that has, after eight years of US involvement, cost the lives of 40,000 US servicemen.

He put the gym in Germany

1852 Friedrich Ludwig Jahn, the founder of the Turnverein (gymnastic club) movement in Germany, has died at Freyburg an der Unstrut aged 74. Jahn, a nationalist, sought to improve the moral and physical powers of his fellow Germans through gymnastics. At Jahn's first gymnasium in Berlin his pupils dressed in a kind of medieval costume. Jahn suffered in the reaction of 1819 along with other German democrats and individualists. His gymnasium was closed down and he was imprisoned for six years. In 1840 he was awarded the Iron Cross, and eight years later was elected to the German parliament.

> *I'm not interested in the bloody system! Why has he no food? Why is he starving to death?*
> **Bob Geldof**, Irish rock musician, in Ethiopia during the famine, 1985.

1582 Pope Gregory XIII has decreed that 10 days be dropped from the calendar. The Julian calendar calculated a year as 365 ¼ days, overestimating it by 11 minutes 14 seconds. The equinox this year fell on March 11, 14 days earlier than in Caesar's time. By losing 10 days this month and counting years ending in hundreds as leap years only if they are divisible by 400, the new calendar should now work.

1522 Spanish emperor Charles V promotes Hernán Cortés to the status of governor general in the new Mexican colony founded by the expedition leader in 1521.

1821 The Central American Federation wins independence from Spain.

1880 Victorio, military genius and leader of the Warm Springs Apache, is finally trapped by Mexican troops and fights until his ammunition gives out, then kills himself.

1927 Britain's Public Morals Committee attacks the use of contraceptives, which allegedly cause "poor hereditary stock".

1928 The airship *Graf Zeppelin* lands in New Jersey after making its first transatlantic crossing from Germany.

1945 French politician Pierre Laval, who led the Vichy government which collaborated with the Germans in World War Two, is executed.

1964 Harold Wilson wins the British elections for the Labour Party with a majority of just four to become the youngest British prime minister of the 20th century.

1997 *Thrust* sets the first supersonic land speed record, breaking the sound barrier at 766 mph (1226 kph).

BIRTHDAYS

Virgil 70 BC, Roman epic, didactic and pastoral poet.

Evangelista Torricelli 1608, Italian mathematician who invented the barometer in 1643.

Friedrich Wilhelm Nietzsche 1844, German philosopher who developed the idea of the *Ubermensch*, or superman, in his book *Thus Spake Zarathustra*.

P. G. Woodhouse 1881, English author of more than 90 books who created the famous butler Jeeves.

C. P. Snow 1905, British author and parliamentary secretary to the Ministry of Science and Technology who wrote the Strangers and Brothers series of novels, which include *The Corridors of Power*.

OCTOBER 16

BIRTHDAYS

White House invite lands Booker T. in trouble

1901 President Roosevelt's invitation to black American educator Booker T. Washington to visit the White House has unleashed a fury of opposition. The consensus among the protesters is that the invitation constitutes a "breach of etiquette". Mr Washington spends most of his time encouraging his fellow blacks to absorb American values. Last year he formed the National Negro Business League, which emphasizes vocational skills, thrift and enterprise. One suspects that the protesters are really objecting to a breach of the colour bar, for there is no hint of radicalism in his aims. The controversy will not have helped Washington's cause among his own people.

1946 Ten leading Nazis found guilty of crimes against humanity by the International War Crimes Tribunal a fortnight ago were hanged in the gymnasium of Nuremberg prison today. Hermann Goering chose to exit via a different door, taking poison less than two hours before he was due to be executed.

Marie-Antoinette loses her head

1793 The execution today of Marie-Antoinette, queen-consort of the late King Louis XVI, and the prospect of further deaths by guillotine of both counter-revolutionaries and revolutionaries suggest that France is slipping even deeper into anarchy. The Queen, who was 38, had been held in prison for more than a year, since August in solitary confinement. Two days ago she was brought before the Revolutionary Tribunal to face a catalogue of her sins. Ironically, high on the list of public prosecutor Fouquier-Tinville was immorality, the charge – almost certainly spurious – which her enemies at the old court used so effectively to discredit the monarchy. Those who glimpsed the Queen on her journey to the scaffold say that her good looks had quite disappeared.

> *The greatest disorder of the mind is to let will direct belief.*
> **Louis Pasteur**, French biologist, 1890.

Worst storm, but no warning

1987 The London Weather Centre is battening down its hatches to meet a deluge of criticism after failing to alert southern England to the imminent arrival of the worst storm to hit Britain in 300 years. The violence of the Force-11 storm brought down roofs, chimneys, trees and power lines, claimed the lives of 18 people and caused an estimated £100 million ($184 million) of damage. Life was brought to a halt on land and sea as police advised people to stay at home rather than add to the chaos. Sevenoaks in Kent has lost six of the giant oak trees which gave the town its name, while experts at Kew Gardens said that it would take about 200 years to replace some of the trees lost from their arboretum. The Met Office is blaming a computer error for its miscalculation.

Pinochet arrested

1998 The former Chilean military dictator Augusto Pinochet has been arrested in London in the first step of extradition proceedings. Spain has applied to have Pinochet brought to justice on human rights charges relating to the war which followed his overthrow of President Allende in 1973. His arrest has caused much controversy around the world, with some believing the former dictator should have sovereign immunity from prosecution.

CHOPIN SPREE COMES TO AN END

1849 Frederic Chopin, the composer and virtuoso pianist, has died of tuberculosis in Paris. He was 39. The half-French, half-Polish Chopin was an infant prodigy, at seven writing a march that the Grand Duke Constantine had scored for his military band to play on parade, and a year later making his first public appearance as a soloist. In 1831 he moved to Paris where he quickly established himself as a fashionable recitalist and teacher able to command high fees. The nervous strain of performing, however, did not help his already weak constitution. Chopin was calm at the end, and asked only that his unfinished manuscripts be destroyed and that Mozart's *Requiem* be sung at his funeral. This will be held at the Church of the Madeleine on October 30.

1651 Defeated by Oliver Cromwell at Worcester, Charles II of England flees to France.

1806 The tyrannical Emperor Jacques I, first ruler of independent Haiti, is assassinated.

1914 German U-boats raid Scapa Flow, the main base of the British Grand Fleet, off the north coast of Scotland in the Orkney islands.

1956 Britain's first nuclear power station, Calder Hall, is opened by the Queen.

1985 The House of Lords votes to allow doctors to prescribe contraceptives to girls under the age of 16 without parental consent, ending a campaign by Catholic mother Mrs Victoria Gillick against such action.

1988 Beethoven's tenth symphony is performed for the first time in London – researcher Barry Cooper has pieced together fragments of the manuscript and sketches discovered in Berlin.

BIRTHDAYS

John Wilkes 1727, English journalist and political agitator who campaigned for press freedom and was elected to Parliament four times but not allowed to take his seat until 1774.

Baroness Karen Blixen 1885, Danish author of *Out of Africa* under the pseudonym of Isak Dinesen.

Nathaniel West 1903, American novelist whose *Lonelyhearts* was made into a film and who drew a scathing picture of Hollywood in *The Day of the Locust*.

Rita Hayworth 1918, American actress and dancer who partnered Fred Astaire in *You Were Never Lovelier* and caused a sensation in *Gilda*.

Montgomery Clift 1920, American actor usually given introspective roles, whose films include *From Here to Eternity* and *The Misfits*.

Evel Knievel 1939, American stuntman who specialized in leaping over rows of cars or buses on a motorcycle or in a car.

Oil countries blackmail West

1973 The ten Arab members of Opec announced an enormous 70 per cent hike in oil prices and a cutback in production in response to America's support for Israel in the Yom Kippur War. President Nixon had proposed a $2200 million aid package to the beleaguered nation. Western Europe will be particularly hard hit by the decision because it relies on the Arab producers for 80 per cent of its oil. Inflation and petrol rationing are expected. The Arabs' policy is likely to drive a wedge between the US, on whom an oil embargo has also been imposed, and Europe, which is fearful of further retaliatory measures for America's support for Israel.

Perón woos Argentina

1945 Tonight Argentina found the saviour it has been searching for. Juan Domingo Perón addressed a 300,000-strong crowd from the balcony of the presidential palace in Buenos Aires, and told them of his desire for a just and strong nation. In his speech, which was also transmitted to millions more listening on the radio, ex-military man Perón promised that he would lead the people to victory in the forthcoming presidential election. Two weeks ago Perón's ambition to become undisputed leader of the Argentinian people received a severe setback when he was ousted from his positions of vice-president and minister of war. His re-emergence is due largely to his forceful and politically astute mistress, Eva Duarte, who helped rally support. With her by his side and with the backing of the labour unions, 55-year-old Perón looks set to put into practice his plans for reshaping the nation.

1967 French skiier Sylvain Saudan made the steepest descent in alpine history today, from the north-east side of Mont Blanc down the Couloir Gervasutti to gradients of about 60 degrees.

Politicians are the same everywhere. They promise to build bridges even when there are no rivers.
Nikita Krushchev, Soviet statesman, 1960.

Italy's Achille's heel

1985 The Italian government under Socialist Bettino Craxi fell from power today as a consequence of its inept handling of the *Achille Lauro* affair. The cruise ship *Achille Lauro*, carrying 454 passengers, was hijacked by Palestinian terrorists ten days ago. They threatened to blow it up if 50 Arab prisoners held in Israeli prisons were not released. After tortuous negotiations the release of the ship and its passengers, minus one elderly man, Leon Klinghoffer, whom the terrorists had murdered, was secured and the Palestinians promised its safe passage to Tunis. On the orders of President Reagan, US jet fighters intercepted the terrorists' plane, forcing it to land in Sicily. The US were keen to apprehend Mohammed Abbas, the mastermind of this hijack, suspected of many other terrorist attacks. US forces and Italian *carabinieri* then clashed over who had the right to arrest the hijackers. The US bowed to Italian sensitivities. Abbas was arrested and then allowed into neighbouring Yugoslavia by the Italian authorities.

OCTOBER 18

BIRTHDAYS

Canaletto 1697, Italian painter best remembered for his dramatic and picturesque views of Venice.

Pierre de Laclos 1741, French author of *Les Liaisons Dangereuses*, his single masterpiece.

Chuck Berry 1926, American rock and roll pioneer whose hits included "Maybelline" and "Sweet Little Sixteen".

George C. Scott 1927, American actor who was awarded an Oscar for his leading part in *Patton*.

Martina Navratilova 1956, Czech-born American tennis champion who won the Wimbledon women's singles title nine times and numerous other Grand Slam events.

Bay devastation as quake rocks Cisco

1989 An earthquake measuring 7.1 on the Richter scale yesterday claimed 67 lives and caused billions of dollars in damage in the Bay area of San Francisco. A section of the two-tier Interstate 880 in Oakland collapsed, crushing motorists driving on the lower deck. The 15-second quake also caused damage in the Marina and to the San Francisco-Oakland Bay Bridge.

French suffer braindrain

1685 The French king Louis XIV has turned the screw still further on the Protestants among his people by revoking the Edict of Nantes. In 1598 Henri IV issued this edict to safeguard the civic and religious rights of French Protestants – Huguenots – and to usher in a new age of toleration. Thousands of Protestants are expected to respond to today's action by fleeing the country. Some commentators are warning of dire consequences to the French economy as a result of such a skills drain.

Quebec freedom fighters kill again

1970 The Canadian separatist group, Quebec Liberation Front (FLQ), has responded to Canadian premier Pierre Trudeau's get-tough policy by murdering Pierre Laporte, the Quebec minister of Labour and Immigration who was kidnapped with British diplomat James Cross eight days ago. Laporte's body was found in a car boot. Negotiations had opened with the kidnappers, but two days ago Trudeau declared a state of "insurrection" in Quebec, introducing emergency powers to deal with the crisis. The FLQ were outlawed and 250 of its members arrested.

Ordeal over as hostages freed

1977 The five-day ordeal of passengers aboard a German Lufthansa jet hijacked by Palestinian terrorists ended today when a squad of crack troops stormed the aircraft at Mogadishu airport when it became likely that passengers would be killed. Three of the four Palestinians were killed in the shoot-out. The terrorists had already killed the pilot, Jurgen Schumann. The hijack was in support of the left-wing Baader-Meinhof urban terrorist group.

Hardliner sidelined

1989 Erich Honecker, East Germany's hardline ruler, has been ousted from the job he has held for the past 18 years. His economic chief, Gunter Mittag, and minister for propaganda and agitation, Joachim Herrmann, have also been forced to quit. The unsmiling, bureaucratic Honecker, 77, had failed to respond to the desire among East Germans for change. The new ruler the 21-man Politburo are pinning their hopes on is the youthful Egon Krenz, 52. Reform groups are not convinced that Egon Krenz, formerly head of internal and external security, will set the wheels of reform moving. In their eyes he is closely associated with the policies that have created the discontent.

1922 Marconi and the General Electric Company are among the major wireless manufacturers who have formed a new company to be responsible for the broadcasting of radio programmes throughout Great Britain. Pressure has been mounting for a central service of this kind. The new British Broadcasting Company will operate from Marconi House in London, under the management of John Reith, and will begin a daily service of programmes from November 14.

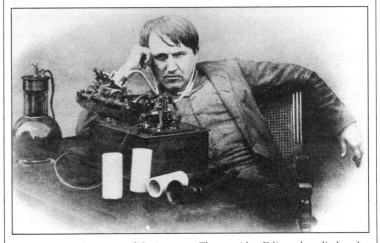

1931 America's most prolific inventor, Thomas Alva Edison, has died at the age of 84. Edison's lack of formal education proved no handicap: his inventions include the phonograph, microphone and the kinetoscope, and he designed a complete electrical distribution system for lighting and power.

No way out for British

1781 British commander General Charles Cornwallis, 46, delivered his 8000 troops into the hands of the besieging American forces at Yorktown today. Two days ago Cornwallis had signalled his willingness to come to terms. He had been hemmed in by superior forces on land and at sea for the past three weeks with no relief in sight. He could only surrender, allowing General Washington to win the War of Independence for the colonists.

Nightmare on Wall Street

1987 Wall Street has experienced the worst day in its history, with the Dow Jones Industrial Average plummeting a record 508.32 points, wiping $500 billion (£270 billion) off the value of shares. The percentage decline was 22.6, almost 10 per cent higher than the big crash of 1929. Last Friday a record 338.5 million shares changed hands as wave after wave of sell orders hit traders. The dramatic sell-off has hit stock markets around the world. In London the FT index fell 250 points, responding to the overnight collapse in Tokyo and other Far Eastern markets and slashing more than £50 billion ($92 billion) off share values. There was no sign, however, of the panic selling that has turned Wall Street from a bull to a bear market almost overnight. The change in mood has been caused by fears about America's persistent trade deficit, now $15.7 billion (£8.4 billion), a 40 per cent depreciation in the value of the dollar over the past year and the spectre of further increases in interest rates.

> *You cannot shake hands with a clenched fist*
> **Indira Gandhi,** on this day 1971, at a press conference in New Delhi.

French start long, cold walk home

1812 Napoleon's 12-week campaign in Russia seems to have reaped a meagre reward. The Russians abandoned Moscow after the indecisive battle of Borodino six weeks ago. The French entered the city to find it in flames, three-quarters destroyed. Tsar Alexander's refusal to negotiate and renewed Russian military activity to the south of Moscow left Napoleon with no alternative but to withdraw to winter quarters. The retreat began today, the 50-mile (80-km) column heading in the direction of Smolensk. The road ahead is fraught with danger for the Grand Army – danger from the enemy force and the weather, which is fine at present but could turn very quickly.

1897 George Mortimer Pullman, the US industrialist and inventor of the Pullman sleeping car, has died in Chicago. He was 66. The first and most famous of the sleeping cars that would become synonymous with his name was Pioneer, built in 1863 with the help of his friend Ben Field. In 1867 Pullman set up the Pullman Palace Car Company to lease his cars to the railroad companies; he built the town of Pullman to house his employees.

De Lorean shutdown hits Belfast hard

1982 The announcement by the Northern Ireland Office that the De Lorean sports car plant at Dunmurry is to close has brought further despondency to Belfast, which has the highest unemployment rate in the UK (21 per cent). Some £70 million ($129.5 million) of taxpayers' money was injected into the project, the brainchild of American entrepreneur John de Lorean. The car built at the factory was a revolutionary stainless steel gull-winged design for the American market. The receivers were called in eight months ago. The company's demise has been blamed on under-capitalization and a deep recession in the US market. The high salaries paid to De Lorean executives and the cost of running a suite of offices in New York were also contributory factors. Some 1500 jobs will be lost as a result of the closure.

1741 The actor David Garrick gives his debut performance as Richard III at London's Goodman's Fields Theatre, and receives an ovation.

1860 The first company to manufacture internal combustion engines, designed by Barsanti and Matteuci, is formed in Florence.

1864 The American Civil War battle of Cedar Creek ends with the victory of General Sheridan over the Confederates.

1901 Brazilian aviator Alberto Santos Dumont circumnavigates the Eiffel Tower in his airship to win the first aviation prize.

1950 The North Korean capital of Pyongyang falls during the Korean War.

1963 Sir Alec Douglas-Home succeeds Harold Macmillan as British prime minister.

1987 One of Britain's finest cellists, Jacqueline du Pré, dies from multiple sclerosis, aged 42.

2000 The oldest ever cave painting is discovered near Verona.

2003 Mother Teresa of Calcutta is beatified.

BIRTHDAYS

Adam Lindsay Gordon 1833, Australian horsebreaker, steeplechase rider and poet, the first to write in an Australian idiom.

Alfred Dreyfus 1859, French army officer who was falsely accused of treason and sent to Devil's Island, which caused a national scandal.

Auguste Lumière 1862, French moving picture pioneer who, with his brother Louis, developed and manufactured the cinématographe - a motion-picture camera and projector.

John Le Carré 1931, British novelist whose job in the British Foreign Service influenced his writing, which includes *The Spy Who Came in From the Cold* and *The Looking Glass War*.

Peter Tosh 1944, Jamaican reggae musician who was with Bob Marley's Wailers before going solo in 1975 with hits like "Don't Look Back".

1818 Britain and the US establish a border across the 49th Parallel.

1822 The first edition of the *Sunday Times* is published in Britain.

1827 In Greece the Battle of Navarino comes to an end as British, French and Russian fleets annihilate the Turkish and Egyptian fleets.

1911 Roald Amundsen of Norway and four companions leave the Bay of Whales on the east side of Antartica's Ross Ice Shelf for the South Pole; they are on skis and have dog sleds carrying necessities.

1943 The UN War Crimes commission is formed.

1944 General MacArthur returns to the Philippines with 250,000 troops to fulfil the promise he made when his forces retreated from the Japanese.

1949 Britain recognizes the People's Republic of China under Chairman Mao.

1973 Attorney General Elliot L. Richardson resigns in connection with the Watergate Scandal.

1994 Death of Burt Lancaster, Hollywood actor whose long film career included *Elmer Gantry*.

2001 A fishing boat sinks off the coast of Australia, drowning 350 refugees.

BIRTHDAYS

Sir Christopher Wren 1632, English architect famous for many major English buildings including St Paul's Cathedral in London.

Thomas Hughes 1822, English author of *Tom Brown's Schooldays*.

Charles Ives 1874, American composer who set an American style and was to influence 20th century music.

Bela Lugosi 1884, Hungarian actor who settled in the US and became the master of the horror film, first appearing in the title role of *Dracula*.

Dame Anna Neagle 1904, British actress and former chorus dancer who starred in many films, including *Victoria the Great* and *Nurse Edith Cavell*.

THE PERFUMED GARDENER

1890 Sir Richard Burton, the explorer, soldier, diplomat and scholar, has died of a heart attack in Trieste. He was 69. England was the only country where Burton never felt at home and he spent much of his life abroad. He discovered Lake Tanganyika and was one of the first non-Muslims to enter the secret cities of Mecca and Medina. A gifted linguist, Burton was a writer-translator of the first rank. A posting to Trieste as British Consul in 1872 bore unexpected intellectual fruits, including the 16-volume *Arabian Nights*, an unexpurgated translation of the sexual wisdom of the East. This frank work ruffled many feathers in England. The abuse heaped on Burton's head caused great pain to his devoutly Catholic wife, Isabel, and it is feared that she may prevent publication of the new edition of *The Perfumed Garden*, which Burton was working on at the time of his death.

Mao's march of destiny

1935 Three hundred and sixty-four days ago military pressure by the Nationalist army of Chiang Kai-Shek forced the evacuation of Kiangsi Province, where the Communists, under Mao Tse-tung had established their Chinese Soviet Republic. An estimated 90,000 people began the migration to the relative safety of Shensi Province on the Yellow river. Today the survivors of that long and arduous march through difficult mountain terrain reached their destination. More than half the marchers perished during the 6000-mile (9600 km) journey. The first task for Communist leader Mao Tse-tung will be to organize a strong defensive position. Shensi has the potential to provide a more secure power base for the Communists, but only if its defences can thwart future Nationalist attacks.

1944 The US First Army, commanded by General Hodges, has announced that the German city of Aachen is now firmly in its control after a battle lasting over a week. More than 10,000 prisoners have been taken. The city is the first major German centre to fall to the Allies in its attempted push through the Siegfried Line. Much of the ancient city has been destroyed.

Lawrence's "Lover" gets Britain buzzing

1960 Writer D. H. Lawrence's last novel, *Lady Chatterley's Lover*, the unexpurgated version of which has been banned in England for the past 30 years, is the subject of a court case which opened in London today. Penguin Books have been prosecuted for publishing Lawrence's original full text, deemed by the Crown to be obscene. To equip them for the case, the jury has been told to read the book. The nation awaits their verdict.

A chance to serve

1915 Less than three months after 30,000 women marched down Whitehall shouting the slogan "We demand the right to serve", Prime Minister David Lloyd George has granted them their wish. The war now raging in Europe has left Britain with a labour shortfall and given women the opportunity to step into the breach. Most areas of employment will now receive a large influx of women. Government departments have vacancies for 200,000, private offices for about half a million, and agriculture and engineering a million between them. Trams and buses up and down the country are to team a male driver with a female conductor. Trade unionists are concerned lest the move depresses wages.

> *One starts to get young at the age of sixty and then it's too late.*
> **Pablo Picasso**, 1963.

Grenada explodes

1983 Maurice Bishop, prime minister of the tiny Caribbean island of Grenada since 1979, was shot dead yesterday in St George's, the capital. He was 39. Last week the conflict between Bishop and his even more hard-line Marxist colleague, Bernard Coard, the deputy prime minister, came to a head. When an attempt to remove Bishop from head office failed, he was put under house arrest. Bishop was released by supporters and then gunned down by the army in a bloody confrontation on the streets. The education minister, Jacqueline Creft, the mother of Bishop's five-year-old son, Vladimir, was also killed. The United States had no love for the Bishop regime. The more ideologically-inclined Bernard Coard will be even less to their liking.

OPERA HOUSE'S VERY OWN DRAMA

1973 After almost 20 years of wrangling and dispute the Sydney Opera House was officially opened today by Her Majesty the Queen. The unique design of the building caused costs to soar, from an estimated A$7 million (£3 million) to an astronomical A$100 million (£43 million) plus. The most striking features of the house are its three sets of roof shells. These contain about 2000 panes of glass in more than 700 different sizes. The functions of the two main halls in the building remain in doubt – concerts are to be given in the larger hall, operas in the smaller. Concern has been expressed about the small size of the orchestra pit in the hall designated for opera. There has even been talk of the need for a "proper" opera house.

Nelson triumphs

1805 Since January the British and Allied fleets have been engaged in a game of cat and mouse as Admiral Sir Horatio Nelson has pursued the French admiral Villeneuve backwards and forwards across the Atlantic. Threatened with losing his command, Villeneuve was forced earlier this month to break out of Cadiz with his combined Franco-Spanish fleet. Nelson was again in hot pursuit and this time Villeneuve had no alternative but to fight. After four hours of fierce exchanges and superlative manoeuvring by the British commanders, the Allied Fleet was beaten, losing 18 ships – more than half its strength. The worst blow of all, however, was the loss of Admiral Nelson, who was mortally wounded by a French sniper as he stood on the deck of his flagship *Victory*. The Battle of Trafalgar will be remembered as his finest victory.

1979 Grete Waitz, the first lady of distance running, has won the New York marathon for the second consecutive year. In last year's event – her first ever marathon – she finished the race in the world record time of 2 hours 32 minutes 30 seconds, slicing more than two minutes off the previous best time. This year, the 26-year-old Norwegian schoolteacher reduced the record by nearly five minutes, finishing in 2 hours 27 minutes 33 seconds.

Now, gentlemen, let us do something today which the world may talk of hereafter.

Lord Collingwood, British admiral, before the Battle of Trafalgar, 1805.

End of the Road for Beat guru

1969 The most famous spokesman for the Beat generation of writers, Jack Kerouac, has died in Florida at the age of 47. Kerouac inhabited the same sub-culture as his characters in *On the Road*, his best-known work – about writers, poets, mystics and eccentrics who thrived on a footloose existence enlivened by sex, drugs and jazz. He has now paid the price for his philosophy of fast living. He despised the mundane and discarded a conventional writing technique after publication of his first novel in 1950. His new method of writing prized energy and spontaneity above structure and polish – *On the Road* was written in just three weeks.

Huge river of coal crushes Aberfan

1966 The tiny Welsh coalmining community of Aberfan was hit by disaster today when a 500-ft (162-m) coal tip slipped, crushing Pantglas Junior School, a row of cottages and a farmhouse. The death toll of 144 includes 116 children aged between seven and 11 years. One eyewitness described the river of coal sludge that buried the village as "a black flood with a noise like thunder". The cause of the disaster is to be established by a special tribunal. The safety procedures operated by the National Coal Board, who run the Merthyr Vale colliery, are expected to come under close scrutiny.

1652 The exiled boy-king, Louis XIV, returns to Paris.

1789 Martial law is imposed in France.

1858 The first performance of French composer Jacques Offenbach's *Orpheus in the Underworld* is given in Paris.

1923 The world's first planetarium opens in Munich.

1931 Death of Arthur Schnitzler, Austrian-Jewish dramatist, novelist and physician, whose works include the dramatic cycles *Anatol and Reigan* and his prose masterpiece *Leutnant Gustt*.

1952 President of the Kenya African movement Jomo Kenyatta is arrested as Britain crushes the Mau Mau rebels.

1967 Norman Mailer is arrested in an anti-Vietnam peace demo.

1969 Willy Brandt is elected Chancellor of West Germany.

1979 In Britain unions agree to suspend the *Times* newspaper strike.

BIRTHDAYS

Katsushka Hokusai 1760, Japanese painter, engraver and printmaker whose Japanese colour prints continue to be sold worldwide.

Samuel Taylor Coleridge 1772, English poet who maintained that the true end of poetry is to give pleasure "through medium of beauty".

Alfred Nobel 1833, Swedish industrialist and chemist who invented dynamite and founded the Nobel Prize to award the world's leading scientists, artists and peacemakers.

Dizzie Gillespie 1917, American trumpet player and band leader responsible for the jazz classic "Night in Tunisia", and one of the originators of bebop.

Carrie Fisher 1956, American screen actress and novelist, whose roles include that of Princess Leia in *Star Wars* and who wrote the books *Postcards from the Edge* and *Surrender the Pink*.

OCTOBER 22

1835 Sam Houston is sworn in as president of the Texas republic.

1909 Elise Deroche becomes the first woman to fly solo.

1906 Death of the great French Post-Impressionist painter Paul Cézanne.

1910 Dr Hawley Harvey Crippen is found guilty of murdering his wife.

1917 The Trans-Australian Railway is opened, running from Kalgoorlie to Port Augusta.

1934 The American gangster Charles Arthur "Pretty Boy" Floyd is killed by FBI agents.

1962 ANC leader Nelson Mandela goes on trial for treason in South Africa, pleading not guilty.

1975 Death of Arnold Toynbee, historian and philosopher whose Study of History explores patterns of growth and decay of civilizations.

1987 The first volume of the Gutenburg Bible fetches $5.39 million (£3.26 million) in New York auction rooms.

1987 A deer hunter discovers an unmanned aircraft in the branches of a tree in Star Lake, New York – its pilot had crank-started its propeller 65 miles (104 km) away and it had taken off without him, eventually running out of fuel.

BIRTHDAYS

Franz Liszt 1811, Hungarian composer of Romantic music and creator of the symphonic poem, most popularly known for the Hungarian Rhapsodies.

Sarah Bernhardt 1844, French stage actress who was hugely successful and continued to perform after a stage accident caused the loss of a leg.

Joan Fontaine 1917, British actress who was initially typecast as a shy English rose but later made efforts to play sophisticated roles, winning an Oscar nomination for Rebecca and an Oscar for her role in The Constant Nymph.

Catherine Deneuve 1943, French actress whose films include Belle de Jour.

Eiffel high fall

1797 Parisians were treated to a demonstration of parachute-jumping today by 28-year-old Frenchman, André-Jacques Garnerin, a former Army officer. Garnerin jumped from a height of about 3200 ft (1000 m) after ascending in a hot-air balloon. He was assisted in the demonstration by his brother, Jean-Baptiste-Olivier. Although he is not its inventor, Garnerin has perfected the device to enable him to jump from greater heights than had been possible before. His parachute is of white canvas and is approximately 23 ft (7 m) in diameter.

I dedicate this prize to all those who suffer in public and in private and who never give up dreaming.
Ben Okri, Nigerian author of *The Famished Road*, on winning the Booker Prize, 1991.

The Windsors drop in on Hitler

1937 The Duke of Windsor, former heir to the British throne, and his wife, Wallis, rounded off their tour of Germany today with a visit to Adolf Hitler's mountain eyrie at Berchtesgaden in Bavaria. The Führer and all the top Nazi officials were there to meet the Windsors, who are said to be enthusiastic supporters of the Nazi regime. The Nazi achievements which have particularly impressed the Duke are full employment and workers' housing. The unofficial tour has caused some consternation in British government circles. The Duke had been advised to avoid such visits because of the adverse criticism they would attract. He seems keen, however, to show that, his abdication notwithstanding, he is still a man of consequence.

1881 An experiment in concert-giving was launched tonight in Boston's Music Hall in the form of the Boston Symphony Orchestra, founded by banker Henry Lee Higginson. He is determined to bring some élan to music-making in Boston, a city which ironically is said to be "dull as a symphony concert" in this sphere of the arts. Higginson wants the orchestra "to play the best music in the best way and give concerts to all who could pay a small price".

1983 The announcement by Washington that Pershing II and Cruise missiles are to be deployed in Europe has met with the largest anti-nuclear demonstrations ever seen, with rallies in Germany, Britain and Italy so far.

KENNEDY EYEBALLS KRUSHCHEV OVER CUBA

1962 US president John F. Kennedy has made his first major move in the showdown with the USSR over the building of ballistic missile sites in Cuba. In a speech broadcast live to the American people the president said that he would take whatever steps were necessary to force the removal of offensive weapons and installations from Cuban soil. Cuba will be placed under a naval "quarantine" – a blockade – until the Soviets remove them. Kennedy also said that the launch of one of the missiles against any nation in the western hemisphere would be viewed by his administration as a declaration of war on America. Flights by U-2 spy planes recently confirmed the presence of a ballistic missile at a launch site in Cuba, one of many shipped from the USSR during the past three months as part of Krushchev's promise to defend the fledgling Communist state against further Bay of Pigs-type attacks by the US.

Superspy scrambles out of Scrubs to freedom

1966 KGB master spy George Blake has escaped from the maximum security wing of Wormwood Scrubs prison in West London. Blake, a former M16 officer, had spied for the Russians for 12 years, revealing Britain's spy ring in East Berlin to the KGB and also the location of the tunnel from where US and British intelligence agents tapped Warsaw Pact communications. The sentence meted out to him in 1962 was the longest ever: 42 years, one year for each of the lives that Blake's treachery is estimated to have cost. Blake used a home-made rope ladder to scale the Scrubs' high perimeter wall. The media are pointing the finger at the KGB as his likely rescuers, although they can put forward no sound reason for Russian involvement in such a high-risk enterprise since the man is of no further use to them.

Lester gets the ultimate handicap

1987 Former champion flat race jockey Lester Piggott was jailed for three years by Ipswich Crown Court today after pleading guilty to charges of tax evasion. Piggott, 51, had amassed a fortune of some £20 million ($37 million) during his 30-year career as a jockey while at the same time evading HM tax inspectors to the tune of £3.1 million ($5.7 million). His magic touch on the turf brought him more than 4000 winners and the jockeys' championship 11 times. He was one of the few jockeys to make a successful transition to race horse training. His wife will run the stables during his absence.

> *It's a funny kind of month, October. For the really keen cricket fan it's when you discover that your wife left you in May.*
> **Denis Norden**, British humorist, 1977.

NY opera lovers build own theatre

1883 A small group of wealthy New Yorkers realized their dream last night at the opening of the new Metropolitan Opera House at Broadway and 34th Street. Frustrated at not being able to get boxes for the opera season at the Academy of Music, they decided to finance their own opera house. Last night's musical offering was Gounod's *Faust*, with Christine Nilsson in the role of Marguerite. Architect Josiah Cleaveland Cady has provided luxurious furnishings for the 3600-seater auditorium. His inexperience as a theatre designer may soon begin to show at the sharp end, however. Doubts have already been raised about the adequacy of the stage equipment and the backstage facilities.

> *The man that hath not music in himself*
> *Nor is not moved with concord of sweet sounds*
> *Is fit for treasons, stratagems and spoils . . .*
> **William Shakespeare** in *The Merchant of Venice*.

TB pioneer wins Nobel Prize

1952 The Ukrainian-born microbiologist Selman A. Waksman has been awarded the Nobel Prize for Medicine or Physiology for discovering the antibiotic streptomycin, an agent effective in the treatment of tuberculosis. A naturalized US citizen, Waksman, 64, has spent most of his career at Rutgers University. He and his team succeeded in extracting streptomycin from soil cultures in 1944. Subsequent clinical trials confirmed their belief that it would be effective against the micro-organism that causes tuberculosis.

Sexual slavery no longer legal

1991 A husband's immunity from a charge of rape under British law was consigned to the dustbin of history today. Five Law Lords have ruled that the statement by 18th-century Chief Justice Sir Matthew Hale that "by their mutual matrimonial consent and contract the wife hath given herself in this kind unto her husband which she cannot retract", forms no part of English law. The decision upholds a Court of Appeal ruling in March that the marital exemption from prosecution was an "anachronistic and offensive fiction". Women Against Rape, the pressure group that has campaigned for reform since 1977, said the decision overturned "250 years of legal sexual slavery".

1906 The Brazilian aviator and inventor Alberto Santos-Dumont won the Deutsch-Archdeacon Prize today for making the first officially observed powered flight in Europe. Santos-Dumont performed the feat in an aircraft of his own design, a biplane called the 14-bis. The next project on his agenda is a design for a new monoplane. He first won the Deutsch Prize five years ago, flying his airship from St Cloud to the Eiffel Tower and back again in 30 minutes to collect a handsome prize and an award from the Brazilian government.

1942 The British Eighth Army today opened a massive offensive against Field Marshall Rommel's Afrika Korps at El Alamein. British field commander General Bernard Montgomery has targeted Rommel's gun emplacements, which have been pounded with air and artillery fire. Since the inconclusive first battle of Alamein in July, the British have been resupplied and brought up to strength (230,000). The Axis forces number just 80,000.

1642 Charles I's Cavaliers clash with Oliver Cromwell's Parliamentary Roundheads in fierce fighting at the Battle of Edgehill in the Cotswolds.

1812 An anti-Napoleonic faction in Paris tries to mount a coup d'état, believing Napoleon to be dead in Russia.

1915 Death of legendary English cricketer W. G. Grace.

1921 Death of John Boyd Dunlop, Scottish veterinary surgeon who invented the pneumatic bicycle tyre.

1926 Leon Trotsky is expelled from the Communist Party.

1950 Death of American singer and entertainer Al Jolson.

1954 Britain, the US, France and the USSR agree to end the occupation of Germany and allow West Germany to enter NATO.

1970 American dare-devil Gary Gavelich breaks the world land speed record in his rocket-propelled car "Blue Flame", driving at 631.367 mph (approximately 1010 kph) on Bonneville Salt Flats, Utah.

1989 Sixty-two members of the Lebanese parliament sign an agreement to distribute power equally between the Muslims and Christians.

BIRTHDAYS

Pierre Larousse 1817, French lexicographer and encyclopaedist.

Robert Bridges 1844, English poet, playwright and prose writer who was a physician in London for 13 years and eventually became Poet Laureate in 1913.

Johnny Carson 1925, American entertainer and leading chat show host.

Diana Dors 1931, British actress and post-war sex-symbol whose films include *Yield to the Night* and *There's a Girl in my Soup.*

Pele 1940, Brazilian football player who began playing internationally at the age of 16 and scored more than 1000 goals during his long professional career.

OCTOBER 24

1537 The third wife of Henry VIII, Lady Jane Seymour, dies shortly after giving birth to a son.

1648 The Treaty of Westphalia is signed, ending the Thirty Years' War.

1901 Mrs Ann Edison Taylor remains unhurt after going over Niagara Falls in a padded barrel to help pay the mortgage.

1925 On the eve of the British parliamentary elections, a letter urging socialists in all countries to revolt is leaked to the British press; it is thought to be from Soviet politician Grigori Zinoviev.

1937 New Zealand aviator Jean Batten breaks the record, flying from Australia to England in just five days, 18 hours and 18 minutes.

1957 Death of French fashion designer Christian Dior, who was responsible for the "New Look" after World War Two.

1987 Heavyweight boxing champion Frank Bruno knocks out Joe Bugner at White Hart Lane stadium in London and wins £750,000 ($1,380,000).

1989 Fake American television preacher Jim Bakker is sentenced to 45 years in jail and fined $500,000 (£272,000) for swindling his followers to the tune of millions.

BIRTHDAYS

Antonie van Leeuwenhoek 1632, Dutch microscopist who was the first man to see bacteria.

Dame Sybil Thorndyke 1882, English actress who gave her finest performance as George Bernard Shaw's Saint Joan.

Moss Hart 1904, American playwright and lyricist who wrote comedy hits, usually with George S. Kaufman, such as *The Man who Came to Dinner*.

Tito Gobbi 1915, Italian baritone whose most famous roles were as Mozart's Don Giovanni and as Scarpia in Puccini's *Tosca*.

Bill Wyman 1936, British bass guitarist and founder member of the Rolling Stones.

1861 The successful completion of the first transcontinental electric telegraph has forced the closure of the Pony Express service between St Joseph and Sacramento. The telegraph will be a boon to all citizens and business people east and west. The military are also said to be interested in its uses at a tactical level in the battlefield.

Quisling swings

1945 Vidkun Quisling, the former head of the "puppet" government established in Norway by the Germans in 1940, was executed at Akershus Fortress, Oslo, today. An ex-army officer, he joined the fascist Nasjonal Samlung (National Union) Party in 1933. He encouraged Hitler to invade Norway. Once a pro-German government had been installed, he embarked on a campaign of converting the Church, schools and youth to National Socialism, a move which made him deeply unpopular with his fellow Norwegians. Quisling was arrested after the liberation of Norway in May and charged with treason. He was also held responsible for sending nearly 1000 Jews to die in concentration camps.

Capone cornered on tax charge

1931 The American legal system proved today that there is more than one way of skinning a cat. The cat in question is notorious Chicago gangster Al Capone. The 32-year-old New Yorker has dominated organized crime for the past six years. The famous St Valentine's Day massacre two years ago was one of many inter-mob killings masterminded by Capone. The law has finally managed to make a charge against Capone stick. Today he received an 11-year sentence and an $80,000 (£43,000) fine for tax evasion.

Hungarian powder keg about to go off

1956 The new Hungarian hardline leader, Erno Gero, seems to have succeeded in igniting the political powder keg put in his hands for safekeeping by the Soviet Union. Yesterday thousands of Hungarians took to the streets to demonstrate against the reimposition of strict Communist control over their lives. Gero responded with a bruising speech that heightened tensions still further. Taking their cue from Gero, the police fired into the crowds. What was a peaceful demonstration has turned into a revolution, with the army supporting the revolutionaries. The return to power of the recently deposed Imre Nagy, whose relatively liberal regime awakened the Hungarian desire for greater freedom, looks like it is on the cards.

CONCORDE FLIES FOR THE LAST TIME

2003 Concorde is making its final flights today, after 27 years of supersonic travel. Celebrities will experience the last of three flights, as the plane completes the last leg of a return flight to New York carrying about 100 people, including actress Joan Collins and British broadcaster and frequent flyer Sir David Frost. Thousands of people are expected to gather at Heathrow airport to see the three planes touch down. British Airways chief executive officer Rod Eddington said the company was feeling a "mixture of sadness and celebration" about the retirement of Concorde. He said one of the reasons for retiring the plane was because economic conditions had meant the "vast majority" of Concorde's regular customers had not been flying on the plane over the last two years.

Washington sniper suspects arrested

2002 Police in Frederick County, Maryland, have arrested two men in connection with the sniper shootings in Washington over the past three weeks. They have been named as John Allen Muhammad, a 41-year-old Gulf War veteran, and his 17-year-old protégé John Lee Malvo. The men were in possession of a car which had apparently been adapted for shooting from the tailgate. Ten people have been killed and three injured in the shooting spree, each with a single bullet while they went about their daily business. There is still no obvious motive for the attacks.

> *A business that makes nothing but money is a poor kind of business.*
> **Henry Ford**. Today the New York stock exchange crashed, 1929.

1986 The British satirical fortnightly magazine *Private Eye* celebrates its 25th birthday today. Originally a magazine filled with jokes and parodies, it broadened its content two years after its launch in 1961. Editor Richard Ingrams decided to unearth and print the scandal and gossip that other papers would no doubt love to, but dare not. This decision has won the magazine mixed reactions from victims and critics.

France's finest fail

1415 The defeat of France's finest at the hands of an invading English army under King Henry V has brought to a violent end the lull in hostilities between the two countries. Henry landed in France two months ago with the intention of reclaiming lost English lands. The English magnates accompanying him on this new adventure are indulging to the full their love of fighting. The English were close to exhaustion when the French caught up with them at Agincourt, but had the advantage of being lightly armoured and more mobile than the opposition. Knee-deep in mud and weighed down by heavy armour the French were cut to ribbons. By the end of the day they had lost a dozen high-ranking noblemen, some 1500 knights and about 4500 men-at-arms. English losses were by comparison negligible.

Theirs not to make reply,
Theirs not to reason why,
Theirs but to do and die:
Into the valley of Death
Rode the six hundred.
Alfred, Lord Tennyson,
British poet, on the Charge of the Light Brigade, which took place today, 1854.

Glorious, but totally pointless

1854 A misunderstanding has resulted in heavy British losses for no strategic gain in the Crimea. The incident occurred at Balaclava where the Russians were attempting to disrupt the siege on Sebastopol by attacking the British lines of communication. After the British had repulsed the move, their commander, Lord Raglan, noted that the Russians were trying to evacuate some British-made Turkish guns. He sent instructions for the Light Brigade to capture them. Visibility was very poor and the only guns that Lucan, the divisional cavalry commander, could see were in the main Russian battery at the end of the North Valley. Believing this to be the objective, he ordered his brother-in-law, Lord Cardigan, to lead the Light Brigade in the charge against it. Despite suffering high casualties – 247 men killed or wounded and 475 horses lost – the Brigade succeeded in reaching the battery and scattering the Russian gunners. The cavalrymen's gallant but futile action was summed up neatly by General Bosquet: "C'est magnifique, mais ce n'est pas la guerre".

NY joins Lakes

1825 The future prosperity of the American upper MidWest region seems assured with the opening today of the Erie Canal, which connects the Great Lakes with New York City via the Hudson river. Under pressure from Governor DeWitt Clinton the New York state legislature agreed in 1817 to foot the $7 million (£3.7 million) construction bill. The decision is expected to pay handsome trade dividends to New York, which will now be regarded as the most important port on the Atlantic seaboard. The Canal is 363 miles (584 km) long, 40 ft (12 m) wide and 4 ft (1.2 m) deep and has 82 locks to cross the rise in elevation.

Chaucer tails off

1400 Geoffrey Chaucer, the courtier, diplomat, civil servant and poet, has died at his home in the gardens of Westminster Abbey. He found little time for writing until the 1380s when the pressures of the unsettled political situation in England seem to have encouraged him to seek relief in that direction. The much-praised love poem *Troylus and Cryseyde* dates from this period. At the time of his death Chaucer was working on a poem about a group of pilgrims journeying to the shrine of Thomas à Becket at Canterbury who pass the time by telling stories.

1556 Charles V, King of Spain and Holy Roman Emperor, retires to a Spanish monastery, dividing his possessions between his son and his brother.

1647 Death of the Italian inventor of the barometer, Evangelista Torricelli.

1760 Death of King George II of England.

1839 The world's first railway timetable is published in Manchester.

1900 The British annexe the mineral-rich territory of the Transvaal, especially renowned for its gold.

1906 American professor Lee de Forest patents the three-diode amplification valve.

1936 A radio station in Berlin broadcasts the first radio request programme called *You Ask – We Play*.

1952 The US blocks Communist China's entry to the UN for the third year running.

1971 Taiwan is expelled from the UN to allow the People's Republic of China to join.

1976 The Queen officially opens the National Theatre on London's South Bank.

BIRTHDAYS

Lord Macaulay 1800, English Liberal MP and a member of the supreme council of India from 1834 to 1838 who pressed for parliamentary reform and the abolition of slavery.

Johann Strauss the Younger 1825, Austrian composer best known for his waltzes such as the ever-popular "The Blue Danube", and for operettas such as *Die Fledermaus*.

Georges Bizet 1838, French composer of the internationally famous opera *Carmen*, which he completed shortly before dying from heart disease.

Pablo Picasso 1881, Spanish painter, sculptor, graphic artist, ceramicist and designer, one of the greatest and most versatile 20th-century artists.

1860 Guiseppe Garibaldi, Italian soldier and hero of the Italian movement for unification, proclaims Victor Emmanuel King of Italy.

1954 An assassination attempt on Egyptian prime minister Gamal Abdel Nasser fails.

1955 The underground American newspaper *Village Voice* is first published, backed by Norman Mailer.

1956 The Hungarian rebellion against Soviet rule is crushed.

1958 Pan American Boeing 707 jets and BOAC Comet airliners start flying regular jet services across the Atlantic.

1973 President Nixon prepares to launch World War III after hearing that the Russians are sending arms to the Middle East War.

1986 Jeffrey Archer resigns as deputy chairman of the British Conservative Party following allegations that he had paid a prostitute to make her leave the country in order to avoid a scandal.

1988 Soviet leader Mikhail Gorbachev promises to free all political prisoners by the end of the year.

BIRTHDAYS

Giuseppe Domenico Scarlatti 1685, Italian composer and harpsichordist who composed more than 600 sonatas.

Leon Trotsky 1879, Russian communist leader who, with Lenin, organized the October Revolution, was forced into exile by Stalin, sentenced to death in a Soviet court and murdered in Mexico, where he had found asylum.

Jackie Coogan 1914, American child actor whose case against his parents, who withheld his earnings from him as a child and would not allow him access after he came of age, led to a law known as the Coogan Act, which protects child stars in the US.

François Mitterand 1919, French president from 1981, founder of the French Socialist Party.

BEATLES AT BUCK HOUSE

1965 The four members of the Beatles pop group were formally presented with their MBEs by Queen Elizabeth at Buckingham Palace today. The Fab Four were probably relieved not to find a picket of irate war verterans and other pillars of the British establishment waiting for them outside the Palace gates. Some returned their Medals of the Most Excellent Order of the British Empire in response to the announcement in June that the Beatles were to receive the same honour. Prime minister Harold Wilson included the group in his Honours List. His decision is thought to reflect his desire for popularity rather than his taste in music.

Moscow theatre siege ends in tragedy

2002 The Moscow theatre siege has come to an end with the deaths of most of the rebels and more than 100 of the hostages. On the day the rebels were due to start executing hostages, Russian special forces pumped a paralysing gas into the auditorium. The authorities have declined to identify the gas which killed so many and hospitalised hundreds of others. Chechen separatist rebels stormed the building three days ago and have since held the 850-strong audience hostage, threatening to blow up the building unless the Russian authorities called an end to the war in Chechnya. Among the militants were a number of veiled women with explosive strapped to their bodies. President Putin has made a televised statement asking the nation for forgiveness for the civilian deaths.

Gunfight at OK Corral

1881 The gunmen's cemetery of Boot Hill in Tombstone, Arizona, received three more inmates today, courtesy of the Earp brothers, Wyatt (see right), Morgan and Virgil, and their sidekick, the tubercular gambler and gunslinger John H. ("Doc") Holliday. The streets were clear as the Earps and the "Deadly Dentist" began their walk to the OK Corral. Waiting, lined up against the adobe wall of the Assay Office backing on to the Corral, were Ike and Billy Clanton, the two McLowery brothers, Tom and Frank, and Billy Claiborne . . . The fight was short and bloody. Within a minute the McLowerys and Billy Clanton fell, fatally wounded, and Virgil and Morgan Earp were wounded. Ike Clanton and Billy Claiborne survived the carnage.

Norway goes her own way

1905 As of today Norway is a truly independent nation, its sovereignty underlined by the accession to the throne of a new king chosen, in Scandinavian style, by election. He is Prince Charles of Denmark, second son of Frederick VIII, who will be known as Haaken VII. The link between Norway, Denmark and Sweden dates to 1397 when Margaret I succeeded in uniting the three countries. That union lasted some 120 years, until its dissolution by Gustav I in 1523. Norway was then ruled by Danish governors until 1814 when the country was ceded to Sweden under the terms of the treaty of Kiel. Isolated voices calling for complete Norwegian independence grew into a chorus after the adoption of universal suffrage in 1898.

Doubt over serial killings

1440 After one of the most extraordinary trials in French history, nobleman and valiant soldier Gilles de Rais, 36, went to the gallows in Nantes today. He was charged with a catalogue of crimes by two courts: satanism and heresy were levelled against him by a Church court; abduction, torture and murder by a civic court. His 140 or so alleged victims were children. The courts were told that despite inheriting great wealth and extensive lands, Rais' extravagant lifestyle had landed him in financial difficulties. Rais turned to alchemy and satanism in the hope that these would help him secure more riches. The accused changed his plea to guilty under the threat of torture. Some observers believe that the case against Rais was only slim and was brought because of pressure from the powerful Duke of Burgundy, who had a financial stake in his ruin.

Reagan defends Grenada invasion

1983 US President Ronald Reagan has defended his decision to send a 2000-strong force of Marines and Army Rangers into the Caribbean island of Grenada. The invasion, he said, had saved the country from becoming a "Soviet-Cuban colony". The seven-nation expeditionary force is now in control. A spokesperson for the Organization of Eastern Caribbean States said that concern about the military build-up in Grenada prompted the member states to ask the US for help. The further destabilization caused by the overthrow of Grenada's PM Maurice Bishop earlier this month was the final straw. Beyond the Caribbean the invasion is seen as a violation of international law.

I want to take this occasion to say that the United States will never again seek one additional foot of territory by conquest.
Woodrow Wilson, US president, 1913.

Christ in this country would quite likely have been arrested under the Suppression of Communism Act.
Joost de Blank, South African churchman, 1963.

Hogarth's Hanover cure

1764 The engraver and caricaturist William Hogarth has died at his house in Leicester Fields, London, aged 67. A Londoner born and bred, Hogarth was from an early age a keen observer of city life and human behaviour. He placed little value on formal training in art and instead trained his visual memory. For fun he produced a series of engravings about contemporary life, moral yet amusing tales about the follies and nastiness of Hanoverian society. These were an instant hit with the public. Aware that his work would become a target for "art pirates", Hogarth pushed for legislation to protect artists' copyright – the so-called Hogarth Act, passed by Parliament in 1735. Hogarth also supported worthwhile causes, such as St Bartholomew's Hospital, of which he was a governor, and the Foundling Hospital.

Quakers can't shake off persecution

1659 If the Religious Society of Friends, or Quakers as they are more commonly called, hoped to find respite from persecution in the New World, they must have been deeply disappointed. The latest arrivals have been flogged from settlement to settlement and refused admittance wherever they have tried to establish homes. Four Quakers, including a woman, Mary Dyer, were hanged in Boston today. So deep is the antipathy towards the sect's non-conformist religious beliefs and social customs that the only answer would seem to be for them to live in their own separate part of the country.

1904 New York, usually a trend-setter, has fallen behind Boston in its attempts to develop a successful subway transport system. Things may change, though, with the inauguration today of a new subway line from City Hall to Broadway and 145th Street.

1810 President Madison has taken a direct hand in deciding at least one of the boundaries of the Louisiana Purchase, sold to the US by France. Unbeknown to Congress, which is in recess, he has decided that West Florida is also part of the Purchase and has ordered troops to annexe it forthwith. The Spanish will be keeping a weather eye open in Texas for similar moves there.

Commons votes for Euro-vision

1971 Ten years of campaigning to persuade his own Conservative Party and the country that Britain's future prosperity lies within the European Economic Community are beginning to bear fruit for Prime Minister Edward Heath. In an historic vote, the House of Commons backed the Heath Cabinet's decision to apply for membership of the Community by a margin of 132 votes. The EEC aims to promote the social and economic integration of Western Europe by working towards the gradual elimination of all trade and customs barriers and the establishment of common price levels and monetary union.

1505 Death of Ivan the Great (Ivan III), the first Tsar of Russia.

1662 Charles II of England sells Dunkirk to Louis XIV for 2½ million livres.

1792 French troops invade the Austrian Netherlands.

1871 Britain annexes the diamond region of Griqualand West in South Africa.

1936 Mrs Wallis Simpson is granted a divorce from her second husband.

1953 British gunboats foil a leftist coup in British Guiana.

1971 The Republic of the Congo changes its name to the Republic of Zaire.

1986 The deregulation of the money market brings about a "big bang" in the City of London.

BIRTHDAYS

Captain James Cook 1728, English navigator whose voyages of discovery in the ship *Endeavour* led to the European discovery of Australia, New Zealand and the Hawaiian Islands.

Niccolò Paganini 1782, Italian virtuoso violinist and composer.

Theodore Roosevelt 1858 American statesman and president who won the Nobel Peace prize for his efforts in ending the Russo-Japanese war.

Dylan Thomas 1914, British poet whose first work, *Under Milk Wood*, spoken in the Welsh idiom, began as a radio play and has since been staged and filmed as well.

Roy Lichtenstein 1923, American painter and pioneer of Pop Art with his magnified comic strip pictures.

Sylvia Plath 1932, American poet and novelist who wrote the autobiographical *The Bell Jar* and was married to British poet Ted Hughes, committing suicide a year after their separation.

John Cleese 1939, British comedian who established himself as a cult figure with the Monty Python team on British television, and gained wider fame in the film *A Fish Called Wanda*.

OCTOBER 28

1746 An earthquake completely destroys Lima and Callao in Peru.

1899 Death of Otto Morgenthaler, German inventor of the Linotype machine.

1914 George Eastman announces a colour photographic process, following his invention in 1888 of the Kodak camera, containing wind-on celluloid film replacing the paper-based film he patented in 1884.

1958 The state opening of British parliament is televised for the first time.

1975 Death of French boxer Georges Carpentier, world light heavyweight champion from 1920 to 1922.

1977 Yorkshire police announce that a multiple murderer is on the loose in Britain.

1982 Forty-year-old Felipe Gonzalez becomes Spain's first Socialist prime minister with a landslide victory.

BIRTHDAYS

Robert Liston 1794, Scottish doctor who performed the first operation in Britain on an anaesthetized patient.

Auguste Escoffier 1846, French *chef de cuisine* of the Carlton and Savoy hotels in London who was made a member of the Légion d'Honneur.

Evelyn Waugh 1903, British journalist and satirical novelist, author of *Decline and Fall*, *Brideshead Revisited* and *The Ordeal of Gilbert Pinfold*.

Francis Bacon 1909, British painter who began his career as an interior decorator in London and had no formal art training.

Sir Richard Doll 1912, British cancer researcher who proved the link between cigarette smoking and lung cancer.

Jonas Salk 1914, American microbiologist who developed an anti-polio vaccine.

Cleo Laine 1927, British singer and actress who became internationally famous following a series of US tours.

LIBERTY BELLE

1886 The largest present ever sent to the American people was inaugurated on Liberty Island in the Upper Bay of New York Harbour today by President Grover Cleveland. Weighing 225 tons and measuring over 151 ft (49 m) high without its pedestal, the gift – a statue called Liberty Enlightening the World – commemorates the friendship of the peoples of France and the US. French historian Edouard de Laboulaye suggested the idea at the end of the American Civil War. Funds were raised from public donations in France and work began under the sculptor Frederic-Auguste Bartholdi. The bright beacon will also make a useful navigation aid.

1831 Physicist and chemist Michael Faraday has succeeded in inventing a device that converts mechanical energy into electrical energy. After discovering that a current of electricity could be generated by plunging a magnet into a coil of wire, he set about trying to generate a steady current. He achieved this by spinning a copper disc between the poles of a magnet. The 40-year-old Englishman left school at 14 and was offered a job by Humphrey Davy, director of the Royal Institution's laboratory.

Wales wails

1988 The Prince of Wales renewed his attack on modern architectural thinking and planning in a BBC television programme broadcast today. The film took the form of a royal tour of Britain's architectural black and white spots. Two examples of the "terrible damage" that had been done to the inner-city landscape were Birmingham's Bullring and Convention Centre and London's Paternoster Square. A spokesman for Birmingham Council called the Prince's criticism of his city as a "stab in the back from someone in an ivory tower". Among the white spots were Kirkgate Old Market in Leeds and the Ministry of Health in Whitehall. The president elect of the Royal Institute of British Architects, Max Hutchinson, said that the Prince's thinking was "strangely nostalgic and . . . out of time with current architectural thought and criticism".

Krushchev forced to blink by JFK

1962 The world breathed a collective sigh of relief today when it was confirmed that the Soviet leader, Nikita Krushchev, had informed President Kennedy that work on the missile sites under construction in Cuba would be halted and that the missiles already delivered would be shipped back to the USSR. Krushchev has also offered to allow the UN to carry out on-the-spot inspections to check that the installations have been removed. The US will no doubt rely on its own U-2 spy planes for such confirmation. The US has been on a war footing for the past week, underlining Kennedy's determination not to allow alien missiles on America's doorstep.

Harvard grant to set up American Oxbridge

1638 The future of the college established in Cambridge, Massachusetts, by Puritan emigrants from England two years ago has been assured by a generous bequest. The college is to receive some 400 volumes and £779 17s 2d (approximately $1440) from the estate of Mr John Harvard, assistant pastor of the First Church of Charleston, who died of tuberculosis last month at the age of 31. The donation will certainly help the college fathers towards achieving their aim of providing an education that is the equal of Oxford or Cambridge in England. On October 28, 1636 the General Court of Massachusetts founded the college on the comparatively modest sum of £400 ($740). Harvard's generosity is worth a lasting gesture of thanks.

NEW YORK BANKS TRY TO STEM WALL STREET PANIC

1929 The crisis of confidence that has hit the New York stock market during the past few days reached epic proportions today. By the end of trading 16,410,030 sales had taken place, driving the Dow Jones index down rapidly a further 43 points and wiping out the unprecedented stock market gains of the past year. Investment trusts have suffered most. Financial leaders had hoped that by pooling resources they could arrest the decline. Yeaterday, however, four days after their collective effort, prices began to slide steeply again. Out-of-town banks are estimated to have withdrawn over $2 billion (£1 billion) from Wall Street. The nerves of the New York banks are strengthening – they have increased their lending by some $1 billion (£540 billion) to prevent a money panic.

Tide of fortune turns for Raleigh

1618 Sir Walter Raleigh, the English adventurer and writer, was executed for treason in the Tower of London today. He was 54. Raleigh came to prominence during the reign of Queen Elizabeth, whose favourite he became. Lucrative monopolies, properties and influential posts ebbed and flowed with the tide of her affection. When the possessive Elizabeth discovered that Raleigh had secretly married she cast him and his wife into the Tower. He succeeded in buying their release and returned to adventuring overseas. His aggressive policies towards Spain led the newly crowned James I to believe that Raleigh was plotting to overthrow him. The death sentence was lifted at the eleventh hour and he was released without a pardon. It was reinvoked two years later after his return, empty-handed, from a gold-finding expedition to Guiana. While Raleigh had lain ill with the fever a Spanish settlement had been burnt on the orders of his lieutenant. Nothing could save him this time.

It's not the bullet with my name on it that worries me. It's the one that says "to whom it may concern".
Resident in Belfast, Northern Ireland, 1991.

Dingo baby verdict

1982 Lindy Chamberlain, the mother who claimed that her baby daughter had been run off with by a dingo, was found guilty of murder by a court in Darwin today. Mrs Chamberlain, 34, who is expecting her fourth baby, was sentenced to life imprisonment with hard labour. Her husband, Michael, a Seventh Day Adventist pastor, was found guilty of being an accessory after the murder and helping her dispose of baby Azaria's body. A murder charge was brought after British forensic expert Professor James Cameron examined the torn and bloody jumpsuit recovered seven days after Azaria's disappearance in 1980. He concluded from this evidence that the baby's throat had been cut. At the trial itself scientific opinion on key parts of the evidence was divided. A consensus could not even be established regarding the likely behaviour of a dingo. No motive for the murder was established by the prosecution. No body was found. The "Dingo Baby Murder Mystery" looks set to run and run.

I will make you shorter by a head.
Queen Elizabeth I, from Chamberlin's *Sayings of Queen Elizabeth*.

BATTENBERG SLICED

1914 Prince Louis Alexander of Battenberg, Britain's first sea lord, announced his resignation today. The 60-year-old Admiral has been forced to resign because of his German birth. Although naturalized as a British subject in 1868 when he entered the Royal Navy, the Prince was born in Graz, Austria, of a German princely family. After giving more than 40 years of loyal service to his adoptive country the Prince could be forgiven for feeling aggrieved. One wonders whether the British royal family will be made to feel similarly uncomfortable about their origins.

1886 Champion English jockey Fred Archer rides the last of his races at Newmarket, retiring after 16 years and 2746 wins.

1927 The tomb of Genghis Khan is discovered by Russian archaeologist Peter Kozlov.

1956 Israeli forces cross into the Sinai Peninsula, pushing towards the Suez Canal.

1963 Swiss philanthropist Henri Dunant founds The Red Cross.

1964 Tanganyika and Zanzibar unite; from now on they will be known as Tanzania.

1985 Nine-times Derby winner Lester Piggot ends his horse-racing career at Nottingham.

1987 Multi-adaptable boxer Thomas "Hit Man" Hearns wins the world middle-heavyweight title – he has now won a world title at four different weights.

1998 The Truth and Reconciliation Commission, set up to investigate the causes and results of Apartheid, reports after two years of hearings.

1998 Death of Ted Hughes, Poet Laureate for 14 years, whose last collection, *Birthday Letters*, was written after he knew he was dying of cancer.

BIRTHDAYS

James Boswell 1780, Scottish writer and biographer of Samuel Johnson.

Jean Giradoux 1882, French author, diplomat and playwright whose work includes the play *Amphitryon* and a satire of 20th-century society, *The Madwoman of Chaillot*.

Fanny Brice 1891, American Broadway star whose life story was immortalized in the musical *Funny Girl*.

Joseph Goebbels 1897, German Nazi propaganda chief who poisoned himself when the Allies entered Berlin.

Richard Dreyfus 1949, American film star who won an Oscar for his part in *The Goodbye Girl* and whose other films include *American Graffiti* and *Jaws*.

BIRTHDAYS

Orson: the man who panicked America

1938 A 23-year-old actor-director succeeded in taking millions of Americans across the narrow line that divides fact from fiction tonight with his gripping radio dramatization of H. G. Wells' sci-fi thriller, *The War of the Worlds*. Despite several reminders that the CBS presentation by Orson Welles and the Mercury Players was pure fantasy and that New Jersey was not really being invaded by giant green men from Mars, thousands of New Yorkers panicked. Police switchboards were packed with anxious callers seeking information and advice, and roads and churches were jammed by people desperate to escape the clutches of the menacing Martians.

Communist critic killed

1984 The body of the kidnapped pro-Solidarity priest, Father Jerzy Popieluszko, was found by police frogmen in Wloclawek Reservoir in northern Poland today. Father Popieluszko, who was famed for his outspoken criticism of Communism, disappeared 12 days ago while driving between his parish in Warsaw and the city of Torun. Three secret police officers have already been charged with abducting the popular 37-year-old priest, but the Polish government has admitted that other, more important people must have ordered the killing. Hardline opponents of Prime Minister Wojciech Jaruzelski are thought to be the most likely culprits.

At last women can study

1838 Oberlin Collegiate Institute in Lorain County, Ohio, has become the first college in the United States to open its doors to women students. The Institute trains both ministers and teachers for work in the West. The town and college of Oberlin were founded five years ago by the Rev. John L. Shipherd, a Presbyterian minister, and Philo P. Steward, a former missionary to the Choctaw Indians. They chose the name Oberlin to honour the Lutheran pastor, educator and philanthropist Johann Friedrich Oberlin, who died 12 years ago after a life dedicated to improving the standards of living and education among his Alsatian parishioners.

1918 Lieutenant Colonel Thomas Lawrence ("Lawrence of Arabia") shocked King George V today by refusing to receive from him the Order of the Bath and the Distinguished Service Order. Lawrence, 28, is deeply disillusioned with the outcome of the recently ended hostilities in Palestine, where instead of realizing his dream of an Arab nation, he witnessed the Arabs' seemingly incurable factionalism and a carve-up of the region by the French and British.

Tragedy is if I cut my finger. Comedy is if I walk into an open sewer and die.
Mel Brooks, US film director, 1978.

Wed-in bells ring for 13,000 Moonies

1988 The head of the Unification Church, Rev. Sun Myung Moon, today presided over one of the biggest mass wedding ceremonies in history at Yongin in South Korea. In the appropriate setting of a production-line factory, the identically clothed brides and grooms paraded before their Moonie master. The 6516 couples had all been personally matched by the controversial cult leader. In some cases the two sides of Moon's ready-matched equation were meeting for the first time. The newly-weds will spend the next 40 days getting to know each other – and, in a few instances, each other's language – before being allowed to consummate their vows. The Moonies' last wed-in was held six years ago, when 5837 couples tied the knot.

SUEZ CANAL SPLITS ATLANTIC ALLIANCE

1956 A bitter row has erupted between Washington and London and Paris over the bombing of Egypt by Anglo-French aircraft. The attack follows an ultimatum by Britain and France that Israel and Egypt should withdraw their forces from the Canal zone. Two days ago Israeli forces moved into the Sinai Peninsula, ostensibly in retaliation for Egyptian attacks on Israel. The alacrity with which the British and French produced the 12-hour ultimatum and then brought their military forces into play suggest that the timing of the Israeli action came as no surprise. It came as a great surprise to President Eisenhower, who finds himself in the Soviet camp on this issue. Anglo-French thinking is that the Suez Canal – nationalized by Nasser in July – must be kept open to international traffic, thereby securing Europe's supply of oil. President Eisenhower regards the action as a threat to world peace and wants an immediate ceasefire.

Duty's sad call

1955 In a broadcast to the British people last night, Princess Margaret said that she had decided not to marry divorced Group Captain Peter Townsend. There has been intense speculation in the press about the possibility of the marriage since Townsend's (her late father's equerry) recent return from an enforced two-year posting to Brussels. Had the princess married him she would have lost her income from the Civil List and her place in line to the throne.

Bodyguards kill Gandhi

1984 The Indian prime minister Mrs Indira Gandhi was shot dead today as she walked in the garden of her home in New Delhi. She was 67. Ironically her killers were the men detailed to protect her, constable Satwant Singh and sub-inspector Beant Singh. The two men, both Sikhs, had riddled Mrs Gandhi with bullets before police loyal to the prime minister intervened, shooting dead Beant Singh. Mrs Gandhi had ignored repeated warnings about the potential danger of keeping Sikh bodyguards. Three months ago Mrs Gandhi outraged Sikh feelings by ordering the Army to storm the holy Golden Temple of Amritsar. Her assassination is almost certainly linked to that act. Rajiv Gandhi is expected to be sworn in as his mother's successor later today.

> *Gentlemen, it was necessary to abolish the fez, which sat on the heads of our nation as an emblem of ignorance, negligence, fanaticism and hatred of progress and civilization, to accept in its place the hat, the headgear worn by the whole civilized world.*
> **Kemal Ataturk**, Founder of the Turkish Republic, 1927.

Houdini can't escape death

1926 Escapologist and conjuror Harry Houdini died in a Detroit hospital today aged 52. The man who delighted in cheating death in his daring stage act succumbed to peritonitis after suffering a seemingly minor injury. The Hungarian-born master magician began his career as a trapeze artist. He changed his name from Erik Weiss to Houdini, after the famous French conjuror Jean-Eugene Robert Houdin. By the early 1900s his stage act had earned him an international reputation. Time and again he would enthrall audiences by escaping from all manner of straitjackets, handcuffs, prison cells and locked, weighted and submerged containers. He attributed his success to his immense strength and (tongue in cheek) to his bow legs.

RATE OF INFLATION

1888 A Scottish veterinary surgeon's efforts to reduce the vibration emanating from the solid rubber wheels of his son's tricycle has resulted in him being awarded a patent for a new type of tyre. John Boyd Dunlop's pneumatic tyre consists of an all-rubber inner tube covered by canvas with a rubber tread. The flaps of the canvas jacket are affixed to the wheel of the vehicle by means of rubber cement. The idea is not new – some 40 years ago Robert William Thomson was given a British patent for his pneumatic tyre. However, such is Dunlop's determination to find applications for his tyre that he intends to start commercial production in the near future.

OCTOBER 31

1517 Martin Luther nails his 95 theses against the corruption of the papacy in Rome to the church-door at Wittenberg.

1864 Nevada becomes the 36th state of the Union.

1940 The Battle of Britain ends: the Royal Air Force has lost 915 aircraft, the Luftwaffe 1733.

1958 Nobel prize-winning author Boris Pasternak is expelled from the Soviet Writers' Union and is likely to be exiled for his *Dr Zhivago*.

1958 The first internal heart pacemaker is implanted by Dr Åke Senning in Stockholm.

1961 Death of Welsh portrait painter and graphic artist Augustus John, renowned for his outstanding draughtsmanship.

1971 An IRA bomb explodes at the top of London's Post Office Tower.

1987 Two young people are said to have committed double suicide near Canberra, Australia, when they are found beheaded and strapped in the front seat of their car with their heads mysteriously placed in the back.

BIRTHDAYS

Jan Vermeer 1632, Dutch painter of exquisitely realistic scenes of serene and harmonious domestic life.

John Keats 1795, English Romantic poet best-known for his "Ode to a Grecian Urn" and "Ode to a Nightingale".

Benoit Fourneyron 1802, French inventor who further developed the water turbine, taking over where Claude Burdin left off.

Sir Joseph Swan 1828, English chemist credited with Edison for inventing the electric lamp.

Chiang Kai-shek 1887, Chinese leader of the Kuomintang (Nationalist People's Party), exiled in Taiwan after being ousted by the Communists.

Eddie Charlton 1929, Australian snooker champion 15 times and World Matchplay champion in 1976.

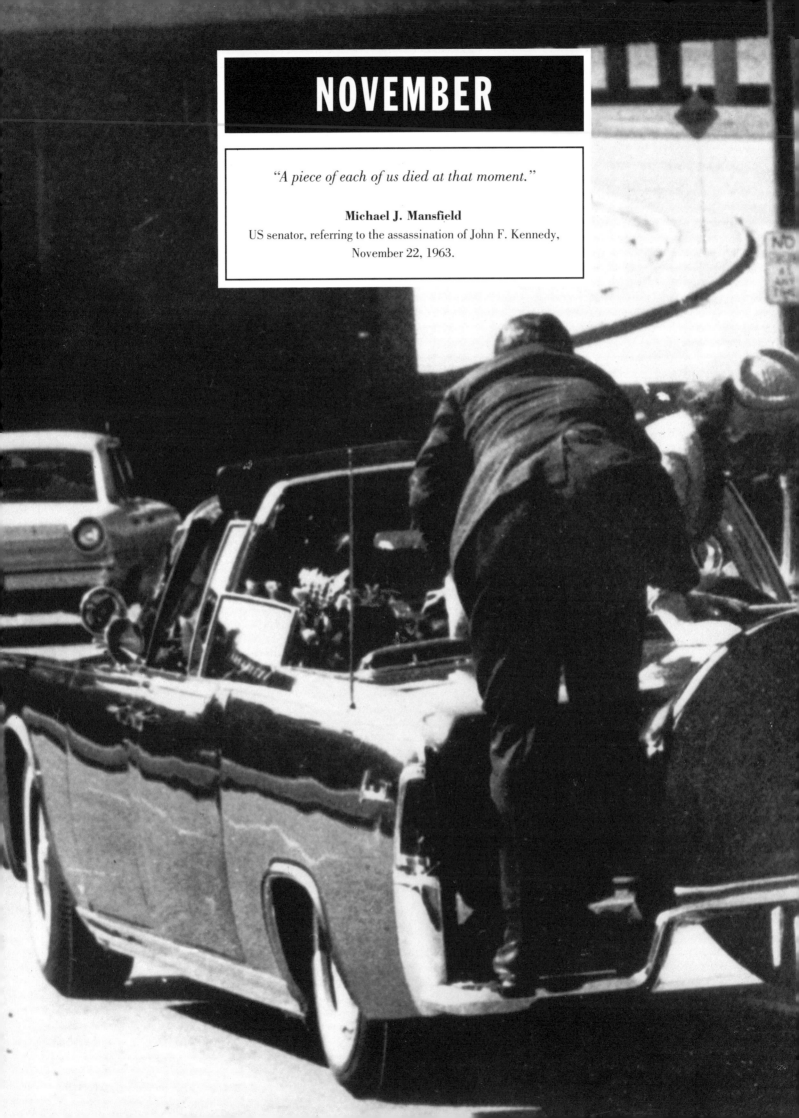

NOVEMBER

"A piece of each of us died at that moment."

Michael J. Mansfield
US senator, referring to the assassination of John F. Kennedy,
November 22, 1963.

Victoria proclaimed India's ruler

1858 The East India Company's long reign over India came to an end today when the administration of the country passed to Queen Victoria. Her Majesty announced a policy of non-interference with religious expression and the opening of higher administrative office to qualified Indians. Lord Canning, already Governor General, will be her Viceroy. The East India Company, formed in 1600 to exploit trade with the East, has acted as an agent of British imperialism since the early18th century, though abuses of power by shareholders were curbed by the Regulating Act (1773) and Pitt's India Act (1784). The Company's influence has finally been broken by the violent and bloody events of the Indian Mutiny, which developed from a revolt of Indian sepoys in Bengal into a widespread uprising against British rule in India. Although British reconquest was completed with the relief of Lucknow in March of this year, reform was inevitable.

1793 The British anti-Catholic Lord George Gordon dies in Newgate Prison convicted of libelling Marie Antoinette – he stirred up the so-called Gordon Riots in 1790.

1814 Following Napoleon's defeat, the European Congress opens in Vienna.

1895 The first motoring organization, the American Motor League, is founded.

1922 The first radio licences go on sale in Britain – they cost 10s (50p/90 cents).

1950 US President Truman survives an assassination attempt as two Puerto Rican nationalists shoot their way into his private residence, killing one of his guards.

1954 Algerian nationalists begin a war of independence against the French.

1967 Rolling Stone magazine makes its debut – it is the first national rock'n'roll periodical in the US.

1972 American poet Ezra Pound dies in Venice aged 87.

1984 Rajiv Gandhi is sworn in as India's premier.

1988 Batman's faithful sidekick Robin is no more, dynamited to death by the Joker in edition No. 428 of DC Comics' *Batman* following a readers' poll which voted that he should go.

Earthquake destroys Lisbon

1755 Severe earth tremors devastated the Portuguese city of Lisbon today, the Feast of All Saints. Within 15 minutes two-thirds of the city was in ruins. Those unfortunates who fled towards the sea to escape the falling buildings were drowned by a huge tsunami, or tidal wave. Because it was a Sunday the cathedrals and churches were packed with worshippers, and many thousands lost their lives when the buildings collapsed. As if this were not enough, towards evening the remains were engulfed by fire. The estimated death toll stands somewhere between 30,000 and 60,000, but the true figure will probably never be known.

A lie can be half-way round the world before the truth has got its boots on.
James Callaghan, British prime minister, 1976.

The European Union is born

1993 From today, the EC will now be known as the European Union (EU) and a tight timetable for economic and monetary union will bring member states closer together. The EU will take on new responsibilities for a common foreign and security policy on affairs such as asylum, immigration, terrorism and drugs. The new terms were laid down in the Maastricht Treaty which followed many years of negotiations between the foreign and finance ministers of the EC member states. Britain has opted out of the social chapter which concerns workers' rights, but citizens in all 12 countries are now Europeans with rights to live and work in any other EU state. Many countries have held a referendum to determine their entry into the EU. The Danes rejected the treaty and will not be joining. The French referendum gained only a marginal victory, and in Germany the treaties were referred to the constitutional courts, but were eventually voted in. The treaties scraped through the British Parliament and, despite the rough ride, will finally come into force today.

The nuclear power station needs electronic devices such as those used at airports, but there is not even a machine to make passes for the staff.
Yanko Yanev, Bulgarian Atomic Energy Committee chairman, 1991.

1961 The Soviet Communist Party Congress's "de-Stalinization" theme has had a dramatic result: during the night Stalin's body was removed from the mausoleum in Red Square where it has lain next to Lenin's since his death in 1953. Even Stalingrad, one of the most resonant names from Russia's struggle against the Nazis, has been renamed Volgagrad.

BILKO DEAD

1985 Comedian Phil Silvers died today aged 73. His showbiz career started on the vaudeville stage, and his many films include *Cover Girl*, *It's a Mad, Mad, Mad World*, *A Funny Thing Happened on the Way to the Forum* and *Buona Sera, Mrs Campbell*. He will be remembered worldwide for his role as Sergeant Bilko in the TV series *You'll Never Get Rich* (later retitled *The Phil Silvers Show*) between 1955 and 1958. The adventures of the crooked but lovable King of the Motor Pool and his sidekicks as they sought ever-more ingenious ways of subverting military authority (and making a buck) endeared him to millions, and are still popular today.

BIRTHDAYS

Spencer Perceval 1762, British prime minister from 1809 who was assassinated in the House of Commons.

Benvenuto Cellini 1500, Italian sculptor and goldsmith who killed a rival goldsmith and was absolved by Pope Paul III.

Stephen Crane 1871, American author of *The Red Badge of Courage*, a remarkably realistic account of the American Civil War.

L. S. Lowry 1887, English painter of distinctive matchstick figures.

Gary Player 1935, South African golfer who has won all four of the world's major golfing championships.

1810 The US establishes freedom of trade with France.

1889 Suffragettes Susan B. Anthony and Elizabeth Cady Stanton are stopped while trying to vote in the national election.

1899 The Siege of Ladysmith in Natal begins as Boers encircle the town.

1903 The *Daily Mirror* is published in Britain, marketed as a newspaper for women.

1917 The possibility of a permanent national homeland for the Jews in Palestine comes a step closer today with the issue by the British government of the so-called Balfour Declaration.

1920 KDKA in Pittsburgh becomes the world's first regular broadcasting station.

1953 It is announced that Pakistan is to adopt Islamic law.

1957 Elvis Presley sets an all-time record with eight simultaneous UK Top 30 entries.

1963 Death of Ngo Dinh Diem, first president of the Republic of South Vietnam.

1963 Archaeologists in America discover evidence of the Vikings dated 500 years before Columbus.

1984 Joseph Stalin's daughter Svetlana Alliluyeva goes home to Moscow 17 years after she went into exile and was stripped of her Soviet citizenship.

1990 Ivana Trump files for divorce from Donald Trump.

BIRTHDAYS

Daniel Boone 1734, American frontiersman and hunter who was captured and adopted as a son of the Indian Shawnee chief Blackfish before returning to settlement.

Burt Lancaster 1913, American Hollywood actor and former circus acrobat whose films include *The Sweet Smell of Success*, *The Birdman of Alcatraz* and *From Here to Eternity*.

Ken Rosewall 1954, Australian tennis player who first made history playing in the longest singles match and who reached the Wimbledon finals four times.

Haile Selassie I crowned emperor

1930 Ras ("Duke") Tafari, King of Ethiopia, was crowned Emperor Haile Selassie I in Addis Ababa today, amid immense pomp and splendour. Thousands of tribesmen in lionskin cloaks, waving spears and shields, lined the streets as the Emperor drove past in the ex-Kaiser's coronation coach. His accession follows the death of Empress Zauditu, with whom he has shared power since 1928. He has been regent and heir apparent since 1917; his liberal, westernizing influence acted as counterbalance to the conservatism of war minister Hapta Giorgis, and he secured Ethiopia's admission into the League of Nations in 1923. Haile Selassie (his name means "Might of the Trinity") intends to give Ethiopia her first written constitution. Ethiopia and Liberia are currently the only countries in Africa with black rulers.

TV AGE BEGINS

1936 The world's first regular high-definition (405-line) TV service was inaugurated by the British Broadcasting Corporation today. An estimated 100 TV owners, all living within a radius of 25 miles (40 km) from the studios at Alexandra Palace, north London, saw the Postmaster General perform the opening ceremony. The BBC is using the system developed by Mr John Logie Baird, which at present involves a 40-second delay between the event being shown and the actual transmission; during this 40 seconds a film is developed, printed and projected. It is believed that a simultaneous system will shortly be introduced. For the time being there will be two one-hour transmissions a day. Although television sets cost up to £100 ($184) it is thought that the number of owners will increase rapidly now that programmes can be transmitted regularly.

1947 In California the world's largest aircraft, the Hughes Hercules flying-boat, or "Spruce Goose", flew for the first time today. It has a wingspan of 319 ft 11 inches (97.51 m), is 218 ft 8 inches (66.64 m) long, has eight 3000 hp engines and seats 700 passengers. The brainchild of millionaire Howard Hughes, it has been under construction in Culver City since 1942 and cost $40 (£22) million to build.

Carter goes to Washington

1976 The Democratic outsider Jimmy Carter, former Governor of Georgia, defeated the incumbent Republican Gerald Ford to become the 39th President of the United States today. Carter and his running mate, Senator Walter Mondale of Minnesota, won by the narrow margin of 297 electoral votes to 241, capturing 51 per cent of the popular vote. The 52-year-old from Plains, Georgia, is a liberal and a populist, and a symbol of the "New South"; he has received support from prominent blacks such as Representative Andrew Young of Georgia. He intends to institute an energy conservation programme, to reduce the wastefulness of government bureaucracy, and to appoint women to his cabinet.

1960 A British jury has decided that the controversial novel *Lady Chatterley's Lover*, by D. H. Lawrence, is indeed a book that they would wish their wives or servants to read. Despite the prosecuting counsel's spirited, if puritanical, attempt to persuade them otherwise, the 12 jurors found that the book was not obscene, nor liable to deprave or corrupt those who read it.

North Sea oil starts to flow

1975 The Queen today officially opened the world's first underwater pipeline, which will bring 400,000 barrels of North Sea oil ashore each day at Grangemouth Refinery on the Firth of Forth in Scotland. Oil was first discovered in the North Sea in the mid-1960s, although the first major oilfield, Ekofisk, was not discovered until 1969. The task of extracting the oil and bringing it ashore has been extremely demanding, with unpredictable weather and currents, and depths of water up to 495 ft (160 m). The global oil crisis of 1974-5 has increased the urgency of the project, and the UK is aiming to be self-sufficient in oil by 1980.

> *Russians and Italians sing like birds, with enormous pleasure and excitement. The English are locked more inside. Every Englishman has in his heart a Chubb lock.*
> **Mstislav Rostropovich**, 1991.

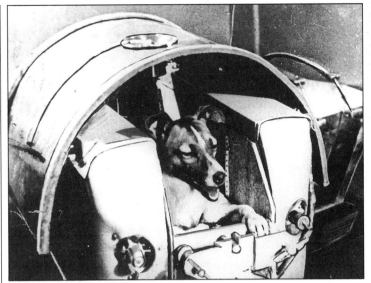

Russian dog in space

1957 The Soviet satellite *Sputnik 2* was fired into orbit today with a dog called Laika on board. The satellite, which is much more visible from Earth than its predecessor *Sputnik 1*, will carry out a variety of scientific tasks, including the study of ultraviolet radiation and cosmic rays. Laika is sealed in a cylindrical cabin containing a food store, air conditioner, and various devices for measuring her vital signs. Her cardiac and respiratory rates normalized satisfactorily after the stress of acceleration into space, although the process took three times as long as it would have done on Earth. Sadly, in spite of her importance to science, it will not be possible to bring Laika home.

Japanese will attack

1942 US ambassador to Tokyo Joseph Grew today cabled the State Department in Washington warning yet again that a Japanese attack on a United States position is imminent. He believes that the decision to go to war will be taken in the next few days. He says that the Japanese "might resort with dangerous and dramatic suddenness to measures which might make inevitable war with the United States." He continued, "It would be shortsighted for US policy to be based on the belief that Japanese preparations are no more than sabre-rattling."

1870 The photographing of every prisoner in England and Wales was made compulsory today. A photograph was first used on a wanted poster in 1861 with some success, and it is anticipated that this so-called "Rogues' Gallery" will help the police in the apprehension of criminals.

Grant is 18th US president

1868 General Ulysses Simpson Grant, Commander-in-Chief of the Union armies in the Civil War, was elected President of the United States today on the Republican ticket. He received 214 electoral college votes to the 80 of his Democratic opponent Horatio Seymour. Grant's aggressive tactics in the early battles of the Civil War earned him the nickname of "Unconditional Surrender" Grant. His inadequate preparations almost lost him the Battle of Shiloh, and he was criticized for his apparent indifference to heavy loss of life, but his victories at Chattanooga and Appomatox, and the subsequent Confederate surrender, proved the correctness of his strategic thinking. Before this year Grant had been unconcerned with politics (he has voted only once in his life – for a Democrat), but his unanimous nomination by the Republican convention persuaded him to stand. The impressive margin of his victory in the subsequent campaign came despite his refusal to make any speeches.

1706 Fifteen thousand people die as the town of Abruzzi in Italy is destroyed by an earthquake.

1839 An expeditionary force begins to be assembled after deteriorating relations between Britain and China over the opium trade have led to war.

1903 Panama proclaims its independence from Colombia.

1926 Death of Annie Oakley, the legendary American shooter with Buffalo Bill's Wild West Show.

1942 British field marshall Bernard Law Montgomery's troops break through commander of the Afrika Corps Erwin Rommel's front line in Africa and capture 9000 prisoners.

1954 Death of the French painter and sculptor Henri Matisse.

1984 The Indian prime minister Mrs Indira Gandhi is cremated.

1985 Two French agents in New Zealand plead guilty to sinking the Greenpeace ship *Rainbow Warrior* and to the manslaughter of the photographer on board.

1988 Koo Stark is awarded £300,000 ($550,000) libel damages following the publication of articles in the *Sunday People* which implied she had had an adulterous affair with Prince Andrew.

1992 Bill Clinton, the 46-year-old Governor of Arkansas, is elected President of the United States of America, winning a decisive victory in the presidential election and defeating the existing President George Bush.

BIRTHDAYS

Karl Baedeker 1801, German publisher famous for his guide books.

Vincenzo Bellini 1801, Italian opera composer whose work includes *Norma* and *La Sonnambula*.

Alfredo Stroessner 1912, Paraguayan dictator.

Charles Bronson 1921, American actor who appeared in films such as *The Magnificent Seven* and *Death Wish*.

1797 US Congress agrees to pay an annual "anti-piracy" tribute to Tripoli.

1847 German composer and pianist Felix Mendelssohn dies of a stroke aged only 38; his work includes the overture to *A Midsummer Night's Dream* and the oratorios *St Paul* and *Elijah*.

1852 The House of Commons Press Gallery is opened.

1890 The Prince of Wales travels on the Underground from King William Street to the Oval to mark the opening of the first electrified underground railway system.

1914 The first fashion show is held at the Ritz-Carlton Hotel in New York, organized by Edna Woodman Chase of *Vogue* magazine.

1921 Japanese prime minister Takashi Hara Kei is assassinated by a Korean.

1931 Indian campaigner Mahatma Gandhi, in London for the Round Table Conference on the question of dominion status for India, goes to Buckingham Palace for tea with King George V.

1946 A United Nations Educational, Scientific and Cultural Organization (UNESCO) is established.

1980 Ronald Reagan is elected 40th US president.

1987 Millionaire Peter de Savary buys Land's End, Cornwall, the southernmost tip of the British mainland.

BIRTHDAYS

William III 1650, Dutch-born King of England, Scotland and Ireland who landed at Torbay with an army of English and Dutch troops and, when Parliament declared the throne empty, was proclaimed king.

Walter Cronkite 1916, American award-winning journalist, television newsreader and commentator with CBS.

Art Carney 1918, American actor of stage and screen who starred in the Broadway play *The Odd Couple* and in films such as *Harry and Tonto*, for which he won an Oscar.

Militants seize US embassy

1979 A major international crisis blew up for President Carter today when up to 500 militant Iranians, mostly students, seized the US embassy in Tehran. Approximately 90 people have been taken hostage, blindfolded and handcuffed, including 65 diplomatic staff. The demonstrators burned two US flags and built a mock gallows intended for the Shah, chanting, "USA, we want the Shah soon." The Shah is in America at the invitation of President Carter for cancer treatment, having fled his country last January. The Iranians want him returned to face charges of alleged torture, murder and robbery. The Revolutionary Guards occupied the US embassy earlier this year, but were ordered out by the Ayatollah Khomeini; this time they claim they are acting on his authority.

1791 Miami Indian chief Little Turtle today defeated a mixed force of regulars and volunteers under the command of General Arthur St Clair. It is Little Turtle's second victory against the invaders of his territory; last year he disposed of General Josiah Harmer's forces at Fort Recovery on the Wabash River. Because his mother was a Mohican, Little Turtle cannot become a full chief of the Miami tribe. Nevertheless, his forceful leadership has made him revered among his people.

Roosevelt ends arms embargo

1939 President Roosevelt signed an amendment to the Neutrality Act into law today, repealing the US embargo on arms sales to foreign powers. Arms can now be shipped to belligerent powers provided they pay cash and use non-US ships for transport. Roosevelt urged the repeal in his annual message to Congress in January, but the proposal was blocked by the Senate Foreign Relations Committee. The Russo/German non-aggression pact announced on August 21, followed by the outbreak of the War itself, ended resistance. Although the amendment in theory applies to all nations, in practice the beneficiaries will be Britain and France, thus effectively ending US neutrality. It is hoped this will mean that the Allies will now be able to win the war without active US involvement.

We are not at war with Egypt. We are in an armed conflict.
Anthony Eden, British prime minsister, refers to the Suez crisis, 1956.

NELSON CLIMBS HIS COLUMN

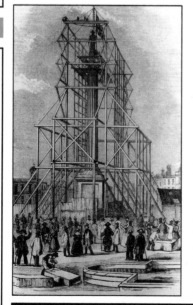

1843 In Trafalgar Square today the monument in honour of Lord Nelson, to commemorate his last and greatest victory at the Battle of Trafalgar, was finally completed after four years' work. The 17-ft (5.5 m), 16-ton statue, the work of E. H. Bailey, was hauled up the column in two pieces and placed on a capital cast in bronze from guns taken from the *Royal George*. The 184-ft (60 m) column cost £50,000 ($92,000), nearly half of which was contributed by Parliament, the balance by public subscription. Last weekend the statue was viewed by 100,000 people, not all of them admirers: one critic compared it to a ship's figurehead, and claimed that it displayed "a daring disregard of personal resemblance".

RABIN ASSASSINATED

1995 Israel is in shock after the assassination today of Prime Minister Yitzhak Rabin. Mr Rabin was addressing a peace rally in the Square of the Kings in Tel Aviv when a 27-year-old law student, a right-wing Jewish extremist, emerged from the crowd and killed him. The Prime Minister has been deeply unpopular with some Israelis since he shook hands with Yasser Arafat, the PLO leader, at the White House. His death brings grave doubts about the future of the Middle East peace process.

MAXWELL DEAD

1991 Colourful and controversial press baron Robert Maxwell drowned today after mysteriously falling from his luxury yacht off the Canary Islands. He was not missed for some hours, and it was only after an intensive air and sea search that his naked body was found floating in the sea. Maxwell was taking a short break amid rumours about his own health, the financial health of his businesses and his possible involvement with Mossad, the Israeli Secret Service. Born Ludwig Hoch in Czechoslovakia in 1923, Maxwell served with distinction in the British Army in World War Two, winning the Military Cross. After the war he parlayed his publishing company, Pergamon Press, into a huge media empire that includes the London Mirror Group and the New York *Daily News*. His ability to recover from apparently terminal setbacks (he was once stigmatized as an "unfit person to run a publicly quoted company") earned him the nickname of "the Bouncing Czech". Speculation about whether his death was accident, murder or suicide is intense.

> *I shall not be satisfied unless I produce something that shall for a few days supersede the last fashionable novel on the tables of young ladies.*
> **Lord Macaulay**, British historian, in a letter, 1841.

Plot to blow up Parliament foiled

1605 There was great rejoicing today at the narrow escape of His Majesty James I and Their Lordships, after a plot to blow up the Houses of Parliament was discovered late last night. Lord Monteagle, a Catholic peer, received a letter warning him to stay away from today's State Opening, and hinting at an explosion. On investigating the cellars beneath the House of Lords he and the Lord Chamberlain discovered a man piling wood who gave his name as Guy Fawkes, and claimed that the wood belonged to his master, Lord Percy. They let him go on his way, but on further investigating the pile of wood discovered 36 barrels of gunpowder at the bottom. Fawkes, a 35-year-old Yorkshireman, was arrested when he returned at midnight to make the final preparations. It appears that this was a plot hatched by Catholics, headed by Robert Catesby, in protest at increasingly oppressive treatment by the King and his ministers. The plotters had tunnelled into the cellars from a house adjoining the Parliament buildings, and had recruited Fawkes, who is noted for his coolness and bravery, in the Netherlands, where he was serving in the Spanish Army.

1586 Queen Elizabeth's favourite, Sir Philip Sidney, dies after a reckless cavalry charge during a campaign in the Netherlands.

1854 The combined British and French forces defeat the Russians at the Battle of Inkerman during the Crimean War.

1912 The British Board of Film Censors is appointed.

1912 Taking advantage of a split in the Republican opposition, Woodrow Wilson wins the US presidential elections to become the first Democrat in the White House for 20 years.

1914 Cyprus is annexed to Britain.

1919 The great American screen lover Rudolph Valentino marries actress Jean Acker and is locked out on his wedding night.

1956 Soviet tanks crush the Hungarian revolt.

1979 Death of American cartoonist Al Capp, who created Li'l Abner.

2003 *Voyager I* becomes the first man-made object to leave the solar system.

BIRTHDAYS

John Haldane 1892, English physiologist and geneticist who pioneered research in population genetics and evolution.

Roy Rogers 1912, American actor thought to be worth more than $100 million (£54 million), known as "King of the Cowboys" for his role as a singing cowboy in films and television.

Vivien Leigh 1913, British actress perhaps best known for her Oscar-winning role as Scarlett O'Hara in *Gone with the Wind*.

Elke Sommer 1940, German actress fluent in seven languages whose films include *A Shot in the Dark*, *The Prize* and *Deadlier Than the Male*.

Art Garfunkel 1942, American singer who rose to fame with Paul Simon with hits such as "The Sound of Silence", "Mrs Robinson" and "Bridge Over Troubled Water".

BOY EMPEROR EXPELLED FROM FORBIDDEN CITY

1924 The last Manchu emperor, 18-year-old Pu-yi, was forced to leave his palace in Peking today by Christian warlord Feng Yu-hsiang, who has taken control of the city. He was compelled to abdicate in 1912 by the revolutionary government in Nanking after the Wuchang uprising, ending 268 years of Manchu rule and over 2000 years of imperial tradition. The abdication agreement allowed him to live in the Forbidden City and retain all privileges. He was returned to the throne by General Hsun's coup in 1917, but was dethroned again after only 12 days. The Emperor has sought the protection of the Japanese in their concession at Tien-tsin. He now calls himself Henry Pu-yi.

Akbar victorious

1556 The 13-year-old Mogul leader Akbar defeated his only rival, Afghan general Hemu, at the second Battle of Panipat today. It was at the first Battle of Panipat in 1526 that Akbar's grandfather Babar defeated Sultan Ibrahim II to establish the Mogul dynasty. Akbar's army faced Hemu's 30,000-strong army, which very swiftly overcame the Mogul flanks. Hemu then attacked the centre with a force of 1500 elephants, and was on the point of victory when he was hit in the eye by an arrow and fell to the ground unconscious. Akbar mutilated the body and finally hacked off the head, whereupon Hemu's hordes fled. This victory gives Akbar unchallenged sovereignty over Delhi and Agra, and ensures the survival of the Mogul empire.

1429 Henry VI is crowned King of England.

1656 Death of King John V of Portugal.

1813 Mexico is proclaimed independent from Spain.

1924 Tory party leader Stanley Baldwin is elected prime minister of Britain.

1956 The construction of the Kariba High Dam on the Zambezi river begins.

1975 The Sex Pistols play their first-ever gig amid scenes of mayhem at London's St Martin's College of Art: after ten minutes the college's social secretary pulls the plug on them.

1984 A Dublin High Court judge freezes striking British mineworkers' money after a High Court decision that the strike, now in its 35th week, is illegal and that the union must pay a fine in 14 days or have its assets seized.

2003 Michael Howard becomes the new Conservative party leader.

BIRTHDAYS

James Gregory 1638, Scottish mathematician and astronomer who gave a description of the first practical reflecting telescope.

Adolphe Sax 1814, Belgian musical instrument maker and inventor of the saxophone.

John Philip Sousa 1854, American conductor and composer of marches known as the "March King" whose compositions include "The Stars and Stripes Forever".

James A. Naismith 1861, American physical education director of the International YMCA in Springfield, Massachusetts and inventor of basketball.

Sir John Alcock 1892, English aviator who in 1919 made the first non-stop flight across the Atlantic with Sir Arthur Whitten-Brown.

James Bowman 1941, English counter tenor known for singing many of the castrato roles in Handel's operas.

Mike Nichols 1931, German-born American director who won an Oscar for *The Graduate*.

German inflation soars

1923 The German mark reached the incredible figure of 4.2 trillion to the US dollar today, as against 4.2 to the dollar ten years ago. Workers can be seen taking their wages home in wheelbarrows and crates, worthless Monopoly money in a country where a loaf of bread costs 200 million marks.

1987 Rail passengers have often wished that TV screens on station platforms would show something more interesting than train times. Passengers on Patna station, India, today suddenly saw a pornographic movie on the screens. The official explanation was that a "mistake" had occurred.

Tchaikovsky dies

1893 Tchaikovsky, the most famous Russian composer of his age, has died at the age of 53. There are rumours that he died of cholera from drinking a glass of unboiled water, but it seems more likely that he committed suicide by poison, having been ordered to do so by a hastily convened Court of Honour of old classmates from the School of Jurisprudence, who were fearful of a scandal because of Tchaikovsky's homosexual relationship with a member of the Imperial family. His death came only six days after he conducted the first performance of his *Pathétique* symphony. "I am a *Russian, Russian, Russian* to the marrow of my bones," he wrote to his patroness Nadezhda von Meck, and this was apparent in every note he ever wrote: his symphonies, his concertos, his operas (most notably *Eugene Onegin* and *The Queen of Spades*, both after Pushkin), and of course his three great ballet suites, *Swan Lake*, *Sleeping Beauty* and *The Nutcracker*. Although he had more than fulfilled the promise of his brilliant early years at the St Petersburg Conservatory, he died as he had lived, a tortured and frustrated man.

RAF's new fighter

1935 The Hawker Hurricane, the RAF's first monoplane fighter, flew for the first time today and inaugurated a new era in military aviation. Heavily armed, with 4 machine-guns in each wing, it is claimed to be the fastest interceptor in the world, with a top speed of 325 mph (520 kph) at 20,000 ft (6500 m).

> *Every Communist must grasp the truth, "Political power grows out of the barrel of a gun".*
> **Mao Tse-tung**, Chinese Communist leader, 1938.

1991 Boris Yeltsin, President of the Russian Federation, today issued a decree banning the Communist Party of the Soviet Union (CPSU) and the Russian CP, and nationalizing their property. He said that the Party's role in the failed coup of last August proved that the CPSU was not a legitimate political party but a "special mechanism for exercising political power".

Abraham Lincoln triumphs in elections

1860 Abraham Lincoln and his Republican running-mate Hannibal Hamlin triumphed over a split Democrat vote in today's Presidential elections, with official Democrat candidate Stephen A. Douglas receiving only 12 electoral votes to Lincoln's 180. The remainder were split between John C. Breckinridge, Southern Democrat (72) and John Bell, Constitutional Union Party (39). The popular vote was another matter, however, Lincoln receiving nearly 200,000 votes less than the combined Democratic vote. The key issue of the campaign was slavery, and Lincoln's strong anti-slavery speech at the Cooper Union in New York in February made him front-runner for the Republican candidacy. Lincoln challenged Douglas to debate the issue publicly, and the seven great Lincoln-Douglas debates the candidates conducted as they crisscrossed the country during the campaign enthralled the electorate. Now that Lincoln is in the White House it is certain that the pro-slavery states will secede from the Union.

GUNMAN DRAWS A BEAD ON GORBACHEV

1990 In Red Square today a man fired two shots from a hunting rifle during the parade to mark the 73rd anniversary of the October Revolution. Police spotted the man taking aim at the reviewing stand on top of the Lenin Mausoleum, only 142 ft (46 m) away, where President Gorbachev was taking the salute, and wrestled him to the ground. The shots went wide and no one was injured. The gunman, Alexandr Shimonov from Leningrad, was charged with "attempting a terrorist act".

Lewis and Clark sight the Pacific

1805 The expedition of Captains Meriwether Lewis and William Clark reached the coast of Oregon today, 18 months after they set out from St Louis on their epic journey into the unknown, at the instigation of President Jefferson, to open up a trade route to the Pacific. Their party includes 26 soldiers and two French-Canadian interpreters. They have crossed thousands of miles of wilderness, including the Rocky Mountains, encountering many savage beasts and unfriendly men, with only one fatality – that of Sgt Charles Floyd, who died of a ruptured appendix near Sioux City, Iowa.

Mussolini is "Il Duce"

1921 Benito Mussolini, the 38-year-old blacksmith's son from the Romagna, today became official leader of the 35 parliamentary members of the National Fascist Party. Before World War One he was a socialist, editing the Milan Socialist Party newspaper *Avanti*, but moved to the right during and after the War, eventually involving himself in the foundation of the Fascists. He is a fanatical supporter of the nationalist poet Gabriele d'Annunzio in his struggle to annex the port of Fiume and pre-empt the Paris Peace Conference; his "squadristi", or black-shirts, have been active in anti-Bolshevik riots in Bologna, Florence and Milan, and are relentless in hunting down and breaking up Communist meetings. Mussolini's proud boast is that Fascism is both "aristocratic and democratic, reactionary and revolutionary".

Bolshevik revolution in Russia

1917 Vladimir Ilyich Ulyanov, known as Lenin, and his Bolsheviks successfully made a bid for power in Petrograd (St Petersburg) today. Since the abdication of the Tsar in March and Lenin's return from exile in Switzerland in April, political turmoil has presented Aleksandr Kerensky's provisional government with many problems, not least a German counter-attack which threatens Petrograd itself. Armed workers, soldiers and sailors began to take over various points throughout the city this morning. The cruiser *Aurora*, anchored in the River Neva, fired a single blank shell, and by evening the Red Guards had seized the Winter Palace, seat of the government. The Council of Commissars has confirmed Lenin as its head, with Leon Trotsky as Minister of Foreign Affairs. Kerensky has fled to Paris, vowing to return, though his failure to get to grips with the war or the country's economic crisis make this unlikely. The Bolsheviks' most immediate task is to make good their promise of "Peace, Land and Bread", and to this end it is their declared intention to conclude a peace treaty with Germany as soon as possible.

Canada's Golden Spike

1885 The coast-to-coast Canadian Pacific railway was completed today. The government of British Columbia had made it a condition of joining the Confederation, rather than be annexed to the US, that they be linked to the rest of the country by a railway by 1891. But the work has been completed five years early, thanks to the efforts of Cornelius van Horne and his team, and enthusiastic backers like Donald A. Smith. It was Mr Smith who drove in the final "golden" spike (actually iron) at 9.22 Pacific time near Craigellachie, in the Rockies. When trains start to run next year the journey time from Montreal to Port Moody, British Columbia, will be between five and six days.

1659 The Franco-Spanish war ends.

1862 The "Gatling" Gun, which is transported on wheels and has six barrels which fire in rotation mounted round a central axis, is patented by 44-year-old inventor Richard J. Gatling.

1865 The Repeating Light Company of Springfield, Massachusetts, manufactures the first pocket lighter.

1916 Jeanette Rankin of Montana becomes the first woman member of the US Congress.

1960 In Moscow missiles appear for the first time at the annual parade in Red Square.

1961 Konrad Adenauer is elected German chancellor for the fourth time.

1978 Death of American heavyweight boxing champion Gene Tunney.

1980 Death of American actor Steve McQueen, whose films include *The Great Escape*.

BIRTHDAYS

Marie Curie 1867, Polish-born physicist.

Sir Chandrasekhara Venkata Raman 1888, Indian physicist who won the Nobel prize for Physics in 1931 for his discovery of the changing wavelengths of light when diffused through transparent material.

Herman J. Mankiewicz 1897, American screenwriter who collaborated with Orson Welles in writing the screenplay of the Oscar-winning *Citizen Kane*.

Albert Camus 1913, French author associated with Existentialism who won the Nobel prize for Literature in 1957 and is perhaps best known for his novels *L'Étranger* and *La Peste*.

Helen Suzman 1917, South African anti-apartheid and civil rights campaigner.

Dame Joan Sutherland 1926, Australian operatic soprano for whom the role of Jenifer in Sir Michael Tippett's *The Midsummer Marriage* was created.

1793 In France the revolutionary government lets the public see the royal art collection in the Louvre for the first time.

1827 The *Canton Register*, the first English language newspaper in the Far East, starts publication in Guangzhou.

1939 Seven people are killed and more than 60 injured when a bomb explodes in Munich shortly after Hitler has left after his traditional speech on the anniversary of his abortive Beer Hall *putsch* – many suspect it was a propaganda ploy.

1974 London's Covent Garden ceases to be the location of the city's famous flower and vegetable market, leaving the site to be rejuvenated.

1987 A man serving 17 years for murder in a California prison decides to sue a juror for $24 million (£13 million) for sleeping through most of his trial and contributing towards what he claims was an incorrect conviction.

1988 Republican candidate George Bush wins the US presidential elections comfortably, carrying 40 states against only ten for his Democratic opponent, Michael Dukakis.

1989 In Virginia, Douglas Wilder becomes the first black state governor in the US.

BIRTHDAYS

Edmond Halley 1656, English astronomer and mathematician who was the first to realize that comets do not appear randomly, and who is best known for identifying the comet named after him.

Christiaan Barnard 1922, South African surgeon and heart transplant pioneer.

Margaret Mitchell 1900, American author of *Gone with the Wind*, her only book.

June Havoc 1916, American actress whose ambitious mother ensured she was a vaudeville star at five and who married her first husband at 13; her films include *My Sister Eileen*.

First black senator elected

1966 Former Massachusetts Attorney General Edward Brooke became the first black senator in US history today, elected to the Senate with a majority of more than 500,000. Born in Washington DC in 1919, Brooke took his BSc at Howard University in 1941, and his LlB at Boston in 1949, in between winning a Bronze Star with the Infantry in Italy in World War II. He served as Chairman of the Boston Finance Commission from 1960 to 1962. Elected as Attorney General in 1962, he was re-elected in 1964 by the largest majority in State history, and during his term of office indicted more than a hundred officials, private citizens and corporations on graft and bribery charges.

ROOSEVELT LANDSLIDE

1932 Franklin Delano Roosevelt was swept into the White House by a landslide today, carrying 42 out of 48 states against sitting Republican president Herbert Hoover. Although partially paralysed by polio, Roosevelt ran an energetic campaign, forcing Hoover to defend a record of bankruptcies, bank closures and unemployment. In his "New Deal", Roosevelt promised to boost public spending on railways, roads, utilities and farming; to regulate banks and stock markets; and to provide unemployment insurance for all. "No American will starve," is his claim.

Allies land in North Africa

1942 Early this morning four divisions of Allied troops, under the overall command of Lieutenant-General Eisenhower, landed on the coast of French North Africa in the largest combined operation of the War so far, codenamed Operation Torch. A convoy of more than 500 ships, protected by 350 ships of the Royal Navy and fighter squadrons of the Royal Air Force, made landfall at several points. Resistance from Vichy French defenders faded after General Eisenhower secured the cooperation of Marshal Pétain's deputy François Derlan, who was in Algiers. The First Army, under General Anderson, is now moving eastward to confront the Germans, and will join the Eighth Army under General Montgomery, now heading west after victory at El Alamein.

"Lucky" Lucan disappears after murder

1974 Scotland Yard have enlisted the aid of Interpol in their search for Lord Lucan, known to his friends in the gambling community as "Lucky" Lucan. They wish to interview him in connection with the murder of the family nanny, Sandra Rivett. At 9.45 yesterday evening his wife, the Countess of Lucan, staggered in her nightdress into the Plumber's Arms near the family home in Belgravia, bleeding from head wounds. She shouted, "Help me! Help me! I've just escaped from a murderer . . . He's murdered the nanny."

John Milton dies

1674 The poet John Milton died of gout at his home in London today. He was 66. Born in 1608 in Cheapside, he was educated at St Paul's School and Christ's College, Cambridge. A painful period of separation from his first wife prompted him to publish a pamphlet advocating the desirability of divorce on grounds of incompatibility of mind and spirit; he consequently spent the 1640s and '50s mired in controversy. By 1651 he was almost blind, and was aided by Andrew Marvell in his work as translator to the Council of State. The restoration of Charles II in 1660 saw him no longer in government employ, giving him time to write his greatest work: *Paradise Lost*, completed in 1667. Milton is to be buried beside his father in St Giles's, Cripplegate.

Remembrance Day blast kills 11

1987 A huge bomb went off today in Enniskillen, Co Fermanagh, as marchers were gathering for a Remembrance Day parade. The bomb, which had been placed in a disused school, claimed the lives of 11 people, including 3 married couples, and injured 63, some critically. The IRA admitted responsibility for placing the device, but blamed the British army for triggering the explosion with a high-frequency scanning device. Gordon Wilson, 60, was buried in the wreckage with his daughter Marie, a nurse, who died. The distraught father still had the generosity to say of her killers, "I shall pray for those people tonight and every night."

NIGHT OF TERROR IN GERMANY

1938 The Jewish community in Germany endured a night of terror when Nazi thugs went on the rampage, attacking Jewish businesses, synagogues and property. Thirty-six people were killed during the night, and 20,000 arrested; more than 7000 shops were looted and 267 synagogues burnt down. Dr Goebbels, Minister of Public Enlightenment and Propaganda, claimed that the violence was a "spontaneous reaction" to the assassination in Paris of Ernst von Rath, a German diplomat, by a young Polish Jew. There is no doubt, however, that the pogrom was carried out on the instructions of the Gestapo. A chilling development was the involvement of the "respectable" middle classes; fashionable women clapped as Jews were beaten by youths wielding lead piping. So that the insurance companies are not bankrupted by state hooliganism, the Nazis have declared their intention to confiscate insurance payouts and return them to the insurers. The huge amount of glass broken has led to the night being dubbed "Kristallnacht"; replacement glass will have to be imported and paid for in foreign currency. "They should have killed more Jews and broken less glass," grumbled Hermann Goering.

Bonaparte takes reins of power

1799 Thirty-year-old Corsican General Napoleon Bonaparte became France's new leader today. After a night of confusion – during which at one point he fainted in the crush – he emerged as First Consul and *de facto* head of government, supported by his brothers Joseph and Lucien and by Talleyrand. Bonaparte's rise to the top has been rapid, aided in part by luck and in part by his skill in negotiating the rocks and shoals of Revolutionary politics. He made his name by his daring defeat of the British fleet at the Revolt of Toulon in 1793; he was jailed as a terrorist after the fall of Robespierre but soon released; his defence of the Tuileries against the mob in 1795 – administering "the whiff of grapeshot", as he put it – made him the hero of Paris. His exploits in Italy and Egypt – despite the shattering of his fleet by Admiral Nelson at Aboukir Bay last year – made him world-famous and instinct told him that now was a good time to return to France from Egypt; with luck he got through the British blockade. Ironically, Corsica was only ceded to France by Genoa in 1768; had Bonaparte been born a year earlier he would not be French.

1988 The Pentagon took the wraps off the Air Force's new attack plane today. A sinister, all-black aircraft, the Lockheed F-117A employs the latest stealth technology – radar-absorbent materials and a "faceted" surface that deflects radar signals at odd angles. The aircraft's key feature is that it can supposedly arrive undetected over a target.

Israel admits Vanunu capture

1986 Israel admitted today that Atomic Energy Commission worker Mordechai Vanunu, 31, is in "lawful detention" in Haifa, but denies that he was kidnapped from the UK by Mossad. On October 5 the London *Sunday Times* printed his revelations about Israel's nuclear arsenal at the plant at Dimona, backed up with his photographs. The *Sunday Mirror* had printed a photograph of Vanunu on September 28, and by September 30 he had disappeared; he never collected the money due to him from the *Sunday Times*. One theory has it that he was lured from London by a "mystery blonde", presumably a Mossad agent; another that he was shipped to Israel as diplomatic baggage in a crate. In any event, there is no record of anyone holding a passport in his name leaving the UK.

> *Sire, you no longer have an army.*
> **Wilhelm Groener**, German general, to the Emperor Wilhelm II of Germany, 1918.

The light dies for Dylan Thomas

1953 "Do not go gentle into that good night./Rage, rage against the dying of the light," wrote Dylan Thomas to his father. Today at the Chelsea Hotel in New York, where he has been on a lecture tour, the flamboyant Welsh bard went raging into that good night at the age of 39, dying of pneumonia brought on by alcoholism. His heavy drinking and wild living are legendary. Thomas's *Collected Poems* were published last year. His verse drama for radio, *Under Milk Wood*, is to be broadcast by the BBC next year.

1794 The Russians enter Warsaw, ending Polish rebellion.

1813 Victorious allies offer Napoleon peace terms at Frankfurt.

1922 The SS is formed in Germany.

1937 Ramsay MacDonald, formerly Britain's first Labour prime minister but now despised by the party he nurtured and then betrayed, dies on a voyage to America.

1940 Death of former British prime minister Neville Chamberlain, who advocated a policy of appeasement towards the fascist powers in Germany but was forced to abandon this policy after Hitler's invasion of Czechoslovakia; Chamberlain had resigned as war prime minister in May this year.

1960 John F. Kennedy becomes US president.

1970 Death of the French president Charles de Gaulle.

BIRTHDAYS

Ivan Sergeyevich Turgenev 1818, Russian writer whose work includes the play *A Month in the Country* and the acclaimed novel *Fathers and Sons*.

Dr Herbert Thomas Kalmus 1881, American inventor of Technicolor.

Anthony Asquith 1902, British film director and producer whose films include *The Millionairess*.

Katherine Hepburn 1909, American actress who won eight Oscar nominations and four Oscars for films which include *Guess Who's Coming to Dinner*, *The Philadelphia Story* and *On Golden Pond*.

Hedy Lamarr 1913, Austrian-born American actress who was billed as the most beautiful woman in the world and whose films include *Samson and Delilah*.

Ronald Harwood 1934, South African-born playwright, novelist and television writer and presenter best known for his award-winning play *The Dresser* which was made into a film.

1775 By resolution of the Continental Congress, the raising of two battalions of men, to be known as the "Continental Marines", is authorized to create a seaborne military police.

1913 Battersea elects the first coloured mayor in Britain, John Archer.

1914 The Australian cruiser *Sydney* sinks the German cruiser *Emden* off Sumatra.

1918 The German emperor Kaiser Wilhelm II appears at the Dutch frontier having abdicated, leaving behind a country gripped by revolutionary fervour.

1928 Emperor Hirohito ascends the Japanese throne at the age of 27.

1952 The 77-year-old doctor-philosopher Albert Schweitzer, who decided that he would devote the first 30 years of his life to himself and the rest to mankind, is awarded the Nobel Peace Prize in recognition of his humanitarian work in Africa.

1987 The wreck of the US brig *Somers,* rumoured to be haunted after three of her crew were hanged and subsequently sunk in the US-Mexican war in 1846, is reported discovered off the coast of Veracruz, Mexico.

BIRTHDAYS

Martin Luther 1483, German religious reformer who began the Reformation.

François Couperin 1668, French composer and harpsichordist.

William Hogarth 1697, English painter and engraver famous for his series of cartoons *The Rake's Progress* and for *Marriage à la Mode*.

Sir Jacob Epstein 1880, American-born British sculptor whose masterpieces such as *Adam* were once the subject of controversy.

Richard Burton 1925, British stage and screen actor who was twice married to Elizabeth Taylor and whose films include *The Spy Who Came in from the Cold* and *Who's Afraid of Virginia Woolf?*

BREZHNEV IS DEAD

1982 Leonid Ilyich Brezhnev, hard-faced old-guard Soviet leader for 18 years, has died of a heart attack at the age of 75. His years of power saw Russia achieve superpower status, and strategic parity with the USA, but also saw her exerting an ever-stronger grip on her satellites, most notably Czechoslovakia in 1968. He was born in Dneprodzerzhinsk in the Ukraine, and studied as an engineer. His political career was advanced by his relationship with his compatriot Nikita Khrushchev, whom ironically Brezhnev toppled in 1964 to reach the top. His state funeral in Red Square will be attended by statesmen and political leaders from 70 countries. The new leader of the Soviet Union, only the fifth since 1917, is Yuri Andropov, former head of the KGB and a man adept at crushing dissent.

Stanley finds Livingstone

1871 "Doctor Livingstone, I presume?" were the first words spoken by Henry Morton Stanley to David Livingstone when Stanley tracked down the missing explorer and missionary to Ujiji on the shores of Lake Tanganyika. "Yes," said the Doctor, lifting his cap slightly. Livingstone, a 58-year-old Scot, is famous as the explorer of the Zambezi and discoverer of Victoria Falls, and as the first European to cross the continent from coast to coast. His search for the sources of the Nile and Congo rivers has occupied him to the point of obsession for several years. Stanley, also an explorer of some note, was commissioned to find Livingstone by James Gordon Bennett, proprietor of the New York *Herald*, although it is a moot point whether he was actually "missing" or merely out of reach. Since receiving his orders in 1869 Stanley has found time to attend the opening of the Suez Canal, sail up the Nile, visit Jerusalem, Constantinople, the Crimea and Caspian, and travel through Persia to India, before setting out on his quest. Whether it was a publicity stunt or not, Stanley's arrival was timely indeed. Doctor Livingstone had arrived at Ujiji a "living skeleton", to find that the supplies set aside for his arrival had been sold off by the *shereef* (headman) of the village.

Flanders carnage halted - for now

1917 British General Douglas Haig's grandiose plan of smashing through the German lines and on to the Channel was finally abandoned today, after 156 days and anything up to 250,000 casualties – nobody will ever be quite sure of the exact number. Canadian troops took control of Passchendaele Ridge and found themselves in possession of a few square miles of worthless swamp and a village which has almost ceased to exist. The battle – the third on the Ypres Salient – started in June with the mining of the Messines Ridge (the tremors could be felt in Downing Street), but the wettest August in living memory turned the ground to quagmire. Allied troops were faced with the choice of paths under a constant barrage of fire from the Germans, or death by drowning in the mud. The verdict of British prime minister Lloyd George is succinct: "The most grim, futile and bloody fight in the history of war", the result of "stubborn and narrow egotism, unsurpassed among the records of disaster".

> *This is not the end. It is not even the beginning of the end. But it is, perhaps, the end of the beginning.*
> **Winston Churchill** refers to the Battle for Egypt, 1942.

Berlin Wall breached

1989 A million East Germans poured into West Berlin early today, free at last to leave their country without special permission. Bulldozers made new holes in the 28-mile (45 km) Wall as the joyous crowd flooded the streets of West Berlin, drinking champagne and hooting car horns till dawn. East German leader Egon Krenz appealed to his fellow citizens to stay, promising multi-party elections, freedom of speech and a new criminal code, but since the borders with Hungary and Czechoslovakia were opened 167,000 have already left. On November 4, one million East Berliners marched for reform, gathering in Alexanderplatz, half a mile from the hated wall, shouting "Egon, here we come." Two days later, half a million marched in Leipzig. It was the biggest show of opposition in East Germany since Soviet tanks crushed a workers' revolt in 1953.

Great War ends

1918 After four years and 97 days the guns finally fell silent today. In a carriage of Marshal Foch's train in the Forest of Compiègne, Foch, General Weygand and British Admiral Sir Rosslyn Wemyss accepted the German surrender from a civilian, Reichstag Deputy Matthias Erzberger, and two junior generals. The German High Command had no intention of getting involved in surrender negotiations and stayed away. The Armistice document requires Germany to hand over 5000 heavy guns, 30,000 machine guns, 2000 aircraft, all U-boats, 5000 locomotives, 150,000 wagons and 5000 lorries; the surface fleet will be interned; the Allies will occupy the Rhineland and the blockade of German seaports will remain in force. The Kaiser abdicated and fled to Holland yesterday. The number of lives lost in the War is thought to be around 9 million, with another 27 million injured. The War has cost the Allies some $126 billion (£68.5 billion), the Central Powers $60 billion (£32.6 billion). It has been the most destructive war the world has ever seen.

Nat Turner hanged

1831 Nat Turner, the rebel slave, was hanged today in Jerusalem, Virginia. Turner, a 31-year-old of some education and a persuasive preacher, became convinced that he had been chosen by God to lead the slaves from bondage. With five others he rose up on August 21 and killed his master, Joseph Turner, and family. A growing band of rebels then marched on Jerusalem. By August 23, at least 57 white men, women and children had been slaughtered. A force of local men and militia hunted Turner's band down in the next 24 hours, and the revolt was crushed. Turner was caught six weeks later. Sixteen other men were hanged with him.

1940 The Willys-Overland Company launched its new general-purpose vehicle for the US Army today. The four-wheel drive vehicle, named "Jeep" for GP (general purpose), is in competition with a similar prototype from the Ford Motor Company. Trials will be carried out to decide which is to be selected.

> *My life's work has been accomplished. I did all that I could.*
> **Mikhail Gorbachev**, Soviet statesman, 1991.

Hitler arrested after beerhall *putsch*

1923 Adolf Hitler, leader of Bavaria's National Socialist Party, was arrested today in the village of Essing, outside Munich. Three nights ago the city's largest beerhall, the Burgerbraukeller, was the scene of a meeting to be addressed by the State Commissioner of Bavaria, Gustav von Kahr, on the subject of "the moral justification for political leadership". Hardly had he started when the hall was invaded by large numbers of Hitler's Brownshirts waving guns. Hitler stood on a chair, fired a shot in the air, and shouted, "The National Revolution has begun." He enlisted General von Lossow, local Army commander, and Colonel von Seisser of the State Police to his cause. His support evaporated over the next few days, however, and in a confrontation with police at the Royal Palace the man with whom he had linked arms was shot, whereupon he fled.

Smith declares UDI

1965 Ian Smith's Rhodesian Front government today declared Rhodesia, Britain's last African colony, an independent state, underlining Smith's party's opposition to sharing power with the black majority in the country. There are just 220,000 whites in Rhodesia, as opposed to 4 million blacks. Smith's Unilateral Declaration of Independence brought condemnation from Black African and Commonwealth leaders as well as from the United Nations. The British government under Harold Wilson immediately imposed trade sanctions and an oil embargo, although it is thought that the South Africans will probably aid the Rhodesians by sanctions-busting. The use of force has so far been ruled out, despite demands from neighbouring Black African countries. Joshua Nkomo and Robert Mugabe, leaders of Rhodesia's most prominent black nationalist organization, Zimbabwe African People's Union, are both in jail.

1807 Britain extends her naval blockade to Russia after the Anglo-Russian alliance against France is broken.

1855 Death of Søren Kierkegaard, Danish philosopher who greatly influenced 20th-century existentialism.

1880 Australian bank robber Ned Kelly goes to the gallows two years after becoming an outlaw.

1920 The bodies of unknown British and French soldiers are buried at Westminster Abbey and the Arc de Triomphe respectively.

1921 The British Legion holds its first Poppy Day to raise money for the wounded of World War I.

1975 Angola gains its independence from Portugal.

1987 Van Gogh's painting *Irises* is sold at Sotheby's in New York for $53.9 million (£29.3 million).

1987 An amateur pilot who has repeatedly buzzed the Champs Elysées in Paris is fined £5,000 ($9250) and banned from flying for three years.

1991 Martina Navratilova equals Chris Evert's record of 157 career titles when she beats Monika Seles to win the Virgina Slims of California tournament in Oakland.

1992 In the UK, the General Synod votes in favour of the ordination of women.

1995 Dissident writer Ken Saro-Wiwa and eight human rights activists are executed in Nigeria.

2000 A fire on a funicular railway in the Austrian resort of Kaprun results in the deaths of 155 holidaymakers.

BIRTHDAYS

Fyodor Mikhailovich Dostoyevsky 1821, Russian novelist whose major works include *The Brothers Karamazov* and *Crime and Punishment*.

Kurt Vonnegut 1922, American novelist best-known for *Slaughterhouse Five*.

Bibi Andersson 1935, Swedish actress chiefly known for her appearances in Ingmar Bergman films.

1035 Death of Canute II, Danish King of England.

1859 French trapeze artist Jules Leotard makes his debut at the Cirque d'Eté in Paris.

1865 Death of Mrs Elizabeth Gaskell, English writer whose works include the novel *Cranford* and a biography of her friend Charlotte Brontë.

1901 Gales sweep Britain, killing 200 and capsizing many ships.

1903 Death of French Impressionist painter Camille Pissarro.

1905 The Russian occupation imposes martial law on Poland.

1918 The House of Commons votes for a war loan of £700 million ($1295 million), bringing British war debts to £7100 million ($13,135 million).

1974 Karen Silkwood, who worked at the Kerr McGee nuclear fuel plant and was investigating irregularities there, dies in a mysterious car crash.

1988 In Sydney, West Indies cricket captain Viv Richards scores his 100th century.

1990 A demonstration in Paris by over 200,000 French schoolchildren demanding better education turns into a riot.

2001 Two hundred and sixty people die in a passenger plane crash in New York.

BIRTHDAYS

Alexander Porfirevich Borodin 1834, Russian composer and professor of chemistry and medicine, best-known for the opera *Prince Igor*.

Auguste Rodin 1840, French sculptor whose realism in works such as his figures of a nude Victor Hugo and a dressing-gowned Balzac initially caused hostility.

Grace Kelly 1929, American actress who was arguably the most beautiful of her day and who went on to marry Prince Rainier of Monaco.

Nadia Comaneci 1961, Romanian gymnast who won three Olympic gold medals at the age of 14.

Demonstration of new anaesthetic

1847 The eminent obstetrician Sir James Simpson, Professor of Midwifery at the University of Edinburgh, today gave the first public demonstration of a new anaesthetic. Its chemical name is trichloromethane, but it is more popularly known as chloroform; Sir James claims that it has three times the potency of ether and will quickly supersede it for long operations, and, in particular, for childbirth, where its practicality and ease of administration give it great advantages. The public trial immediately brought swift and vehement criticism from Scottish Calvinists, who oppose all use of anaesthetics in childbirth, but Sir James is not to be moved.

> *I confess I did my best to accommodate as many women as I could.*
> **"Magic" Johnson**, HIV positive US basketball star, 1991.

Tirpitz sinks

1944 *Tirpitz*, the last survivor of Hitler's formidable fleet of "unsinkable" pocket battleships, is lying upside-down on the bottom of Tromsø Fjord today. She had been lurking in Norwegian waters for several years, forcing the Allies to allocate warships that were badly needed elsewhere to convoy-protection duties. Lancaster bombers of 617 Squadron, the famous Dambusters, sank her at the third attempt with direct hits from three 12,000-lb (5500 kg) "Tallboy" bombs, dropped from 14,000 ft (4500 m) right on to the decks of the *Tirpitz*. Incredibly, a squadron of German fighters assigned to protect the ship did not even take off. Over 1000 of the ship's crew were entombed below decks as she turned turtle.

BROTHERS SET OFF FOR AUSTRALIA

1919 Two Australian brothers, Captain Ross and Lieutenant Keith Smith, set off from Hounslow, Middlesex, today, in an attempt to make the first flight from the UK to Australia. Their converted Vickers Vimy bomber, with its two Rolls-Royce Eagle engines (the same type as that in which Alcock and Brown flew the Atlantic in June), must carry the Smiths and their two mechanics the 11,130 miles (17,912 km) to Darwin in less than 30 days. Their planned route will take them through Cairo, Karachi, Calcutta, Bangkok and Singapore. If they make it they will win the prize of £10,000 ($18,400) put up by the Australian government. It is said that the registration of their aircraft, G-EAOU, stands for "God 'elp All of Us".

Lay preacher jailed

1660 John Bunyan of Elstow, Bedfordshire, was jailed today for preaching without a licence. The authorities have undertaken to release him on condition that he gives up preaching. Bunyan remains adamant on this score, however: "If you let me go today, I will preach again tomorrow," he has declared. The son of a tinker and goldsmith, 32-year-old Bunyan served in the Parliamentary army under Sir Samuel Luke. After the war he became deeply interested in religion, studying the Bible at every opportunity. He joined the new Baptist sect in 1653 after a period of inner religious struggle. Preaching to the poor in the isolated rural villages around Bedford brought him into conflict with the Quakers. Bunyan aired his doctrinal quarrel with them in two pamphlets, *Some Gospel Truths Opened* and *A Vindication*. He is now in conflict with a much more powerful adversary: the re-established Church of England.

YELTSIN FIRED

1987 Moscow Communist Party boss Boris Yeltsin has been fired by President Gorbachev after Yeltsin had the temerity to criticize him for the slow pace of perestroika (reconstruction). Yeltsin, an enthusiastic supporter of reform, also attacked Yegor Ligachev, number two in the Kremlin, for opposing Gorbachev's initiatives. He accepted criticism of what was termed his "political errors" and "personal ambition", and was replaced by Lev Zaikov.

Henry the Navigator dies

PRINCE HENRY OF PORTUGAL

CEUTA

1460 Prince Henry of Portugal, popularly known as Henry the Navigator, died today aged 66. The son of King John I of Portugal and Philippa of Lancaster (daughter of John of Gaunt), he gained an early taste for navigation when he joined his father's expedition to conquer Ceuta, in Morocco. His appointment by the Pope as General of the Order of Christ helped him to fund the well-prepared expeditions that he regularly dispatched from his home port of Segres. His captains discovered the Madeira and Canary Islands and the Azores, and in 1433 rounded Cape Bojador, previously a major navigational hazard and an object of superstitious terror to seamen. By the mid-1450s the Senegal and Gambia Rivers and Cape Verde had been opened up, and a lively trade was being conducted with West Africa. Meanwhile Henry surrounded himself with a brilliant circle of adventurers, astronomers and students of navigation. Although Henry never travelled further than North Africa, he earned himself a lasting reputation for his encouragement of exploration.

"Brassiere" patented

1914 A patent has been taken out today for an item of female underwear to be known as the "backless brassiere". In contrast to the all-embracing undergarments of the Victorian and Edwardian eras, the brassiere covers and supports the breasts only; its inventor, Mrs Mary Phelps Jacob (better known as Caresse Crosby), constructed her prototype out of two handkerchiefs and baby ribbon. Mrs Jacob has been making brassieres for her friends for some years, and has only now been persuaded to patent her idea.

The tree of liberty must be refreshed from time to time with the blood of patriots and tyrants. It is its natural manure.
Thomas Jefferson, American statesman, in a letter, 1787.

Vertical flight

1907 The rapid development of aviation took another step forward today. M. Paul Cornu, a French bicycle-maker and engineer from Lisieux, Normandy, rose 4 ft (1.5 m) vertically into the air in his "Direct Lifter", as he calls it, and hovered there for about 60 seconds. M. Cornu successfully tested his theories with a working scale model last year. The full-size machine, which was completed in August, uses a 24-hp water-cooled Antoinette engine to drive two 20-ft (6.5 m) rotors by means of belt and pulleys. In fact his achievement was even greater than he intended, for his brother, fearing the machine was getting out of control, jumped on to steady it and was also lifted into the air. M. Cornu anticipates that the machine will achieve a forward speed of about 7 mph (11 kph), making use of an ingenious system of movable vanes to deflect the downward wash of the rotors and thus provide propulsion.

De Gaulle Elected

1945 By the unanimous vote of all 555 deputies, General Charles de Gaulle was elected President of the French Provisional Government today. After the fall of France in 1940 de Gaulle carried a torch of hope for his countrymen, providing a rallying point for Free French forces. On many occasions, however, his pride and prickly temperament made him a difficult ally for Roosevelt and Churchill. The Pétain regime condemned him to death in his absence, but de Gaulle, who had served under Pétain in World War I, spared his old commander's life when he was in his turn sentenced to death for treason last year.

Thousands feared dead in Colombia

1985 Nevado del Ruiz, the 17,717-foot (5400 m) Colombian volcano dormant since 1845, erupted in a ferocious explosion today. Melted snow swept down the mountain in huge torrents, creating a mud avalanche which completely buried the town of Armero huddled below. There are very few survivors from the town's 25,000 population. A 28-inch (11 cm) layer of ash and rock has covered a 70-sq-mile (181 sq km) area around the volcano, 80 miles (128 km) west of Bogota. Expert warnings of an imminent eruption were largely ignored and there was no attempt to evacuate the area, which has now become a sea of mud in which thousands of people are entombed for ever.

1851 A telegraphic service between London and Paris comes into operation.

1909 Two bombs are thrown at the Viceroy of India, the Earl of Minto.

1914 General Botha's forces vanquish the rebel commandos of General Christiaan de Wet in the Orange Free State, leaving the way clear to march on the German colonists in South-West Africa.

1920 The first full session of the League of Nations begins in Geneva, with 5,000 representatives from 41 nations.

1923 In Italy, Benito Mussolini introduces a bill granting women the vote in national elections.

1925 The South African government calls for more segregation of blacks.

1926 In Italy, Mario de Bernardi sets a world seaplane speed record of 246 mph (396 kph).

1941 An Italian submarine sinks HMS *Ark Royal* near Gibraltar.

1973 Death of Italian fashion designer Elsa Schiaparelli, inventor of "shocking pink".

1974 Death of Vittorio de Sica, Italian neo-realist film director most famous for *Bicycle Thieves*.

2001 Kabul, the capital of Afghanistan, falls to the Northern Alliance, who are working alongside US and UK troops to rid the country of the Taliban regime and root out terrorists.

BIRTHDAYS

Edward III 1312, English monarch who was defeated at Bannockburn by Robert the Bruce.

Charles Frederick Worth 1825, Anglo-French fashion designer who found favour with the Empress Eugénie.

Robert Louis Stevenson 1850, Scottish author whose classic tales include *Treasure Island*, *Kidnapped* and *The Strange Case of Dr Jekyll and Mr Hyde*.

Adrienne Corri 1930, British actress who appeared in *Bunny Lake Is Missing* and *A Clockwork Orange* among other films.

1689 Death of Nell Gwynn, English actress and favourite mistress of King Charles II of England, by whom she had two children.

1896 A new Highway Act declares it is no longer necessary for a man with a red flag to walk ahead of motor vehicles and raises the speed limit from 4 mph to 14 mph.

1900 Dr Karl Landsteiner of the Pathological and Anatomical Institute in Vienna announces the discovery of three different blood groups.

1908 Foul play is suspected on the death of Tsu-Hsi, Dowager Empress of China.

1915 Death of black leader Booker T. Washington, first principal of the Tuskegee Institute (Alabama) for Blacks.

1918 Tomas Masaryk is elected first president of Czechoslovakia.

1938 Jews are expelled from colleges in Germany.

1988 In Algiers, the Palestine National Council declares a Palestinian state in Gaza and the West Bank.

1989 During his visit to Poland, West German chancellor Helmut Kohl visits Auschwitz.

1989 After five days of voting in Namibia's first elections, the South West African People's Organization (Swapo) is declared the largest party.

1990 In New Zealand, a gunmen kills 11 of the 50 inhabitants of Aramoana, near Dunedin.

BIRTHDAYS

Claude Monet 1840, French painter who was one of the pioneers of Impressionism.

Jawaharlal Nehru 1889, Indian statesman, first prime minister of independent India.

Aaron Copland 1900, American composer best-known for his works in popular style, such as the ballets *Rodeo* and *Billy the Kid*.

Joseph McCarthy 1908, American senator who led the Senate inquiry into alleged communists in the 1950s.

It's the Top Ten

1952 Britain's first pop chart was published in the *New Musical Express* today. It contains three discs by Vera Lynn, "Homing Waltz", "Auf Wiedersehen" and "Forget Me Not", while Jo Stafford's "You Belong to My Heart" is No. 2, and Nat "King" Cole's "Somewhere Along the Way" is at No. 3. And Britain's first Number One? "Here in My Heart", by Al Martino.

Iceland gets new island

1963 Iceland is constructed of volcanic rock, and there is volcanic activity around her shores, too. As a result an entirely new island appeared about 5 miles (8 km) off her southern coast today. The island, which has been named Surtsey, is currently 30 ft (10 m) high and growing, throwing ash thousands of feet into the air. Sightseers are queuing up in Reykjavik for flights over the spectacular new island, which is not hard to find – a plume of smoke 24,000 ft (7800 m) high marks the spot. Vulcanologists are warning of the dangers of getting too close, however, since the rapid cooling effect of seawater on red-hot lava creates a much greater explosive force than that of land-based volcanoes. A Japanese research vessel which was directly above an ocean-floor eruption in 1952 was blown to bits.

Coventry blitzed

1940 The Luftwaffe visited Coventry last night in one of the most destructive raids of the Blitz so far. Making use of a "bomber's moon", 449 bombers dropped 503 tons of bombs and 881 incendiaries, turning the centre of the city into a raging inferno. Out of the 250,000 population, 554 were killed and 865 seriously injured. The medieval cathedral, one of the city's glories, was almost completely destroyed.

A new royal prince

1948 A son, their first child, was born to Princess Elizabeth and the Duke of Edinburgh today. The boy, to be named Charles Philip Arthur George, will be first in line to the throne when Her Royal Highness eventually succeeds her father, George VI.

Around the world in less than 80 days

1889 Nellie Bly, intrepid reporter for *New York World*, set sail from New York today in an attempt to beat Phileas Fogg's round-the-world time of 80 days as described in Jules Verne's 1873 novel. Twenty-two-year-old Miss Bly is planning to travel by sea, sampan, horse and rail, and will hold a competition for readers to guess her final time. Miss Bly, whose real name is Elizabeth Cochran (her pen-name was taken from a Stephen Foster song) is no stranger to difficult situations. She made her name writing on divorce and the plight of women and children in factories for the *Pittsburgh Dispatch*; and she had herself committed to Blackwell's Island asylum for a story on conditions among the insane that made her famous overnight.

Surrealist exhibition in Paris

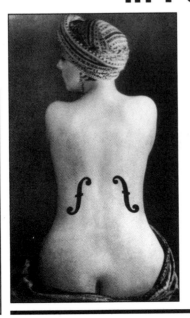

1925 A controversial exhibition of art by the Surrealists has opened at the Galerie Pierre in Paris. Those featured include Joan Miró, Georgio de Chirico, Paul Klee, Hans Arp, Man Ray, Pablo Picasso and Max Ernst. Although Surrealism is primarily a literary movement, developed out of Dadaism by André Breton (author of the *Surrealist Manifesto*) and Paul Eluard, the visual arts have not been far behind. Ernst's *Reunion of Friends*, André Masson's *Trees* and Miro's *Ploughed Land* and *Harlequin's Carnival*, all of which are in the exhibition, illustrate well the Surrealist theory that art should be "uncontrolled by reason and independent of all aesthetic and moral preoccupation".

1983 The world's largest airport, King Khalid International, opened today near Riyadh, Saudi Arabia. The £2100 million ($3864) airport covers 86 sq miles (221 sq km) of desert, a greater area than Manhattan. It also boasts the world's tallest control tower, at 243 ft (74 m) high.

The bells ring out

1918 Today was Victory Day in Britain as a war-weary nation celebrated the peace. At 11 am, to the accompaniment of church bells and fireworks, the all-clear was sounded for the last time with bugles and sirens. Factories closed, and there were scenes of unprecedented public revelry and rejoicing as what seemed to be the entire population took to the streets, waving flags and raising servicemen shoulder-high. Big Ben struck one for the first time in four years. Huge crowds gathered outside Buckingham Palace to sing "God Save the King" and "Rule Britannia", and later the King and Queen drove to Hyde Park. Hundreds thronged to Downing Street to hail the Prime Minister, Lloyd George. The police turned a blind eye to the licensing laws and pubs stayed open until they had been drunk dry.

1837 Published today by Samuel Bagster at 4d is a curious and interesting little book entitled *Stenographic Sound-Hand*, by one Isaac Pitman, a 24-year-old schoolmaster from Trowbridge in Wiltshire. The book expounds Pitman's theory of "stenographic phonography", or the practice of shorthand by the phonetic method. He believes that the present methods, notably Mr Taylor's, are inadequate.

I am MacWonder one moment and MacBlunder the next.
Harold Macmillan, British politician and prime minister, 1973.

Queen Elizabeth docks for the last time

1968 The largest passenger liner in the world, Cunard's flagship *Queen Elizabeth*, docked in Southampton today at the end of her last transatlantic voyage. She was launched in September 1938 as a sister ship to the *Queen Mary*, but the war broke out before she went into service. She spent the war as a troopship, based in Sydney, and did not leave Southampton for her first commercial voyage until October 1946. Since then she has crossed the Atlantic hundreds of times, carrying thousands of passengers, including royalty, movie stars and politicians, in unparalleled luxury. Sadly the jet age has made her into an anachronism, and she can no longer compete economically. Her future is uncertain, although a group of Florida businessmen have expressed interest in her as a tourist attraction. Cunard's new liner, *Queen Elizabeth II*, will carry twice as many passengers and will be used mainly for cruising.

Anglo-Irish agreement signed

1985 Mrs Thatcher and Irish leader Garrett Fitzgerald met at Hillsborough Castle in Belfast on what both parties claimed was a momentous day in Irish history. They signed into being the Anglo-Irish Agreement, which for the first time gives the Republic a consultative role in the running of Northern Ireland. Mrs Thatcher was quick to insist that the interests of both Ulster communities are being catered for. In Dublin, Charles Haughey, leader of the opposition *Fianna Fail* party, described it as "a sad day for Irish nationalism".

Sherman burns Atlanta

1864 General Sherman and his army set out for Savannah on their March to the Sea today, leaving Atlanta a smoking ruin behind them. Atlanta, an important strategic strongpoint for the Confederates, had been in Sherman's hands since General Hood had given up his brave resistance on September 1. Sherman, determined that the Confederates should have no further use out of Atlanta, gave orders that all public buildings, machine-shops, depots and arsenals should be burnt to the ground, all civilians having been evacuated. To the accompaniment of military bands playing martial airs and operatic selections, and the din of exploding ammunition, spectacular destruction was achieved. "Behind us lay Atlanta smouldering and in ruins, the black smoke rising high in the air and hanging like a pall over the ruined city," said General Sherman.

1802 Death of George Romney, English portrait painter who did numerous studies of Lady Emma Hamilton, mistress of Lord Nelson.

1901 An electrical hearing aid is patented by Miller Reese of New York.

1902 Anarchist Gennaro Rubin fails in his attempt to murder King Leopold II of Belgium.

1912 Viscount Astor turns 21 and gains a £15 million ($27.7 million) inheritance from his father.

1913 In Mexico, rebel leader Pancho Villa takes Ciudad Juarez.

1922 The first scheduled broadcast is made from Marconi House in London's Strand.

1923 In order to end rampant inflation – a loaf of bread now costs over 200,000,000 marks – the German government introduces a new unit of currency worth 1,000,000,000 marks.

1954 Death of Lionel Barrymore, American actor who made many films and continued to act after being confined to a wheelchair.

1956 Elvis Presley's first film, *Love Me Tender*, is premiered in New York.

1965 Craig Breedlove of the USA sets a world land speed record of over 613 mph (986 kph) in his jet engine car *Spirit of America* at Bonneville Salt Flats, Utah.

2003 Twenty-five people die in an explosion in a synagogue in Istanbul; Muslim fundamentalists claim responsibility.

BIRTHDAYS

William Pitt the Elder, 1st Earl of Chatham 1708, English statesman known as the Great Commoner.

Gerhart Hauptmann 1862, German dramatist and novelist whose plays include *Before Dawn*.

Erwin Rommel 1891, German general, commander of the Afrika Corps in North Africa during World War II.

Daniel Barenboim 1942, Israeli pianist and conductor, musical director of the Orchestre de Paris since 1975.

BIRTHDAYS

Tiberius 42BC, Roman emperor whose days ended in depravity on the Isle of Capri.

Paul Hindemith 1895, German composer and viola player whose work was banned by the Nazis.

George S. Kaufman 1889, American playwright and collaborator on musicals such as *Of Thee I Sing*.

Burgess Meredith 1908, American character actor who appeared in *Of Mice and Men* and *The Story of GI Joe* among other films.

Frank Bruno 1961, British boxer who put the British and European heavyweight titles under his belt.

King of Hollywood is dead

1960 Clark Gable, known the world over as "The King of Hollywood", died today aged 59. In a career that spanned nearly 30 years he made dozens of movies, from *The Painted Desert* in 1930 to his last, *The Misfits*, earlier this year. In the '30s he starred with Garbo in *Susan Lenox*, Jean Harlow in *Red Dust* and Claudette Colbert in *It Happened One Night*, for which he won an Oscar. But it is for his portrayal of the arrogant Rhett Butler in *Gone with the Wind*, playing opposite the young Vivien Leigh, that he will always be remembered. Gable served with distinction as a documentary film-maker in the US Army Airforce during World War Two. The fact that he was married five times did nothing to dent his popularity with his female fans, who were captivated to the end by his easy manner and impudent grin on screen.

Estonia calls for self-determination

1988 In an astonishing display of defiance the Estonian Supreme Soviet today rejected President Gorbachev's plans for reform of the Soviet constitution and adopted their own, although they stopped short of demanding outright independence from Moscow. Key provisions included the establishment of "the sovereignty of Estonia", a human rights guarantee, the right to own private property for all, and the bringing of all land and national resources under Estonian control. Gorbachev's reforms envisage retaining such matters under the central control of Moscow. Estonia's initiative makes it likely that the other Baltic states, Lithuania and Latvia, will follow suit. It remains to be seen whether Moscow will react with force.

Britain to build air-raid shelters

1937 The House of Commons voted in favour of a national programme of air-raid shelter construction today. The Labour Party, concerned at the possible cost to the taxpayer, voted against the motion, but Sir Winston Churchill described the move as "indispensable", and claimed that once the nation was thus protected an enemy would find it "not worthwhile" to mount air-raids.

> *It is beginning to be hinted that we are a nation of amateurs.*
> **The Earl of Rosebery**, British statesman, 1900.

Britain blockades Long Island Sound

1813 Britain's mastery of the sea in the so-called war of 1812 was further emphasized today when a mixed force of Royal Navy ships under the general command of Admiral Warren, including frigates, sloops and 74-gun ships of the line, took up positions in a blockade of Long Island Sound. All major American routes to the sea, including Chesapeake and Delaware Bays, the ports of New York, Charleston, Port Royal and Savannah, and the Mississippi, are now denied to US ships, and the blockade is beginning to cause severe economic losses to the young country, despite her successes in the land war.

Discovery of great Australian river

1824 The interior of Australia was further opened up today when the explorers Hamilton Hume and William H. Hovell became the first white men to see a great river, with many tributaries, which winds from high up in the Great Dividing Range to somewhere on the coast. The two men have been despatched from Sydney by Governor Sir Thomas Brisbane with authority to open up a route to the southern coast. After a hellish journey plagued by ticks, leeches and quarrels, Mr Hovell's first act on reaching the river, at a place called Albury, was to carve "W. H. Hovell, 1824" on a nearby tree. Nevertheless he insisted that the river be called the Hume in honour of his companion; it is thought, however, that the Murray River is a more likely name.

Blacks allowed on South Africa's beaches

1989 An important pillar of apartheid crumbled today when all restrictions on access to South Africa's beaches were removed. President F. W. de Klerk, announcing the move, said that "all members of the public" were henceforth allowed on all beaches, and promised that the Separate Amenities Act, the instrument which permits whites to monopolize public places, will be repealed next February.

> *Force is not a remedy.*
> **John Bright**, British politician, in a speech, 1880.

CATHERINE THE GREAT DIES

1796 Russia's great ruler died of a stroke today at the age of 67. Like Elizabeth I, she was a woman who will forever be identified with a decisive epoch in her country; during her long reign she made Russia a force to be reckoned with in European politics, and by her expansionist policies added more than 200,000 square miles (320,000 sq km) to her territory, bringing millions of Russian-speakers into the fold. Her brilliant court attracted the greatest minds of Europe, such as Voltaire and Diderot, who heavily influenced her thinking. But she could also be ruthless: in 1762 she overthrew her husband, Peter III,

with the help of her lover Orlov (one of a long string of lovers), and quite possibly connived at his subsequent assassination. The lot of the serfs deteriorated during her reign, particularly after the bloody suppression of Pugachev's rebellion in 1774, although some of her reforms increased the efficiency with which her vast country was run. She has been aptly described as "an enlightened despot".

Benazir Bhutto wins

1988 Benazir Bhutto became the first woman leader of an Islamic country today in the first democratic elections in Pakistan for 11 years. Her Pakistan People's Party, while falling short of an absolute majority, requires the backing of only 12 out of the 40 independent MPs to form a government. Benazir's father, Zulfiquar Ali Bhutto, was the country's leader from 1971 until he was deposed by a military coup headed by General Zia in 1977; two years later he was hanged. His daughter inherited the People's Party leadership, and was a thorn in the side of the military regime until Zia's death in an air crash last August. She has promised democratic reform.

I am not a crook.
Richard Milhous Nixon, 1973.

1917 The French sculptor Auguste Rodin has died at the age of 77. Rodin's artistic life was attended by controversy. The realistic – and increasingly erotic – nature of his work offended an aesthetic which revered the idealization of the human form as presented by classicism. Those with eyes to appreciate the radicalism of his art hailed Rodin as a master and by 1900 many were calling him the greatest sculptor of the age. Through his works, the most famous of which are perhaps *The Kiss* and *The Thinker*, Rodin has opened an innovative new chapter in the history of sculpture.

Suez Canal opens

1869 From the days of Haroun al-Raschid onwards it has been the dream of many men to cut a canal across the Isthmus of Suez. Thanks to a French diplomat and engineer, Ferdinand de Lesseps, that dream finally came true today, cutting the London-Bombay journey from 11,220 miles (17,950 km) to 6332 (10,130). Construction began on April 25, 1859, and the workforce initially consisted of 8213 men and 368 camels before they were replaced by steam shovels. The Canal concession was granted to de Lesseps by Said Pasha, after whom the city of Port Said has been named. The journey from Port Said to Suez takes about 16 hours, an hour for each million pounds the canal cost ($29 million). The canal will be managed by a French-Egyptian joint stock company, whose rights will expire in 1968.

The so-called new morality is too often the old immorality condoned.
Lord Shawcross, British Labour politician and lawyer, 1963.

Death of England's first queen

1558 Britain's first ruling queen, Mary Tudor, has died a broken and disappointed woman, hated by her subjects, after five years on the throne. Born in 1516 to Henry VIII and Catherine of Aragon, she was at first her father's favourite, but her loyalty to her mother and to the Catholic Church led to harsh treatment. On the death of her half-brother Edward VI she outmanoeuvred Lord Dudley's attempt to put Lady Jane Grey on the throne, and there was widespread rejoicing. However, her marriage to Philip II of Spain dragged England into the war between France and Spain, and in the struggle she lost Calais, which had been an English outpost since the time of Edward III. There was further resentment at the restoration of the Catholic Church in England, when many Protestants, notably Latimer, Cranmer and Ridley, were burned at the stake. Her final torment was the knowledge that her husband favoured as heir her Protestant half-sister Elizabeth over the Catholic Mary Queen of Scots.

1603 Sir Walter Raleigh goes on trial for treason.

1798 Irish nationalist leader Wolfe Tone commits suicide while in jail awaiting execution.

1880 The first three British female graduates receive their Bachelor of Arts degrees from London University.

1903 In London, Russia's Social Democrats officially split into two groups – Bolsheviks and Mensheviks.

1904 The first underwater submarine journey is undertaken, from Southampton across the Solent to the Isle of Wight.

1913 The steamship *Louise* becomes the first ship to travel through the Panama Canal.

1913 In Germany, Kaiser Wilhelm bans the armed forces from dancing the tango.

1922 Siberia votes for union with the USSR.

1970 The unmanned Soviet spaceship *Luna 17* lands on the Moon.

1990 A mass grave, believed to be that of of World War Two prisoners of war, is discovered by the infamous bridge over the River Kwai in Thailand.

1990 The Soviet government agrees to change the country's constitution.

Louis XVIII 1755, French monarch, the first to take the throne after the fall of Napoleon.

Bernard Law, 1st Viscount Montgomery of Alamein 1887, English field marshal whose many victories in battle included the defeat of Rommel in North Africa.

Sir Charles Mackerras 1925, Australian conductor.

Rock Hudson 1925, American film and television star whose successes included light romantic comedies with Doris Day and the television series *Macmillan and Wife*.

Martin Scorsese 1942, American film director whose films include *Taxi Driver* and *Raging Bull*.

1626 St Peter's in Rome is consecrated.

1852 A massive state funeral for the Duke of Wellington is held in London.

1901 Britain and the US agree terms for a canal to be built through Central America.

1904 In Rhodesia, a major source of gold is discovered 200 miles (322 km) to the south of Salisbury.

1910 Suffragettes attack the House of Commons; 119 people are arrested.

1922 Death of Marcel Proust, author of the seven-volume *Remembrance of Things Past*.

1938 Twenty people are trampled to death at the lying-in-state of Kemal Ataturk, founder and president of modern Turkey.

1977 President Sadat becomes the first Egyptian leader to visit Israel.

1988 A million Serbs demonstrate in Belgrade to demand independence.

1991 Gustav Husak, former president and Communist Party leader of Czechoslovakia who crushed the Prague Spring in 1968, dies in Prague aged 78.

2000 Young Welsh actress Catharine Zeta Jones marries Hollywood actor Michael Douglas.

BIRTHDAYS

Carl von Weber 1786, German composer best-known for his opera *Der Freischütz*.

Louis Daguerre 1789, French pioneer of the photographic process.

Ignacy Paderewski 1860, Polish pianist, composer and statesman who was the first prime minister of the newly independent Poland but resigned after only ten months to resume his concert career.

Sir Alec Issigonis 1906, Turkish-born British car designer who created the Morris Minor and the Mini Minor, both of which became classics.

Linda Evans 1944, American actress best known for her role as Krystle in the soap opera *Dynasty*.

KING'S CROSS UNDERGROUND INFERNO

1987 Up to 34 people died today as fire swept through King's Cross underground station, one of London's busiest interchanges. It is thought the fire started under the wooden treads of an escalator, used by an estimated 200,000 passengers a day, where an accumulation of rubbish and oily fluff was ignited by a cigarette. A combination of administrative confusion and understaffing meant that the station remained open; passengers arriving on the Piccadilly Line were trapped in an inferno of flame and smoke while a fireball roared up the escalator and incinerated those in the booking hall. There were no sprinklers, London Regional Transport having ignored recommendations made in 1984 that they should be installed.

1940 The prospect of alliance with the USA in the struggle against the Axis Powers inched closer to reality today when Winston Churchill confirmed a lend-lease deal to allow the US to establish military bases in St Lucia, Guyana, Trinidad, Antigua, the Bahamas, Jamaica and Bermuda. In return, Britain gets 50 destroyers.

Women's Christian Temperance Union is formed

1874 Cleveland, Ohio, today saw the foundation of the Women's Christian Temperance Union under the secretaryship of the charismatic Miss Frances Elizabeth Caroline Willard, president of the Evanston College for Ladies. The aims of the WCTU are to protect the home and develop Christian citizenship through individual commitment to abstinence and the abolition of the liquor trade. Its formation is a consequence of the Women's Temperance Crusade of 1873-4, in which militant women frequently invaded saloons to sing hymns and kneel in prayer; indeed there is a political element to the Union's aims, since insobriety and the ill-treatment of women so often go hand in hand.

Waite and Sutherland released

1991 The Briton Terry Waite and the American Thomas Sutherland were released today by the pro-Iranian Islamic Jihad for the Liberation of Palestine, as part of a UN-brokered three-way exchange of Western hostages, Arabs held by Israel and Israelis missing in Lebanon. Terry Waite, the Archbishop of Canterbury's special envoy, was kidnapped on January 21, 1987, while on a mission to secure the release of other hostages. His release immediately revived speculation about his links, involuntary or otherwise, with Colonel Oliver North and the Iran-Contra affair. It has been claimed that he had near!y 20 meetings with North between 1985 and 1987, and that three US hostages, in whose release he had been involved, had in fact been traded for arms. Thomas Sutherland, Dean of Agriculture at the American University in Beirut, was kidnapped on June 9, 1985.

Necessity is the plea for every infringement of human freedom. It is the argument of tyrants; it is the creed of slaves.
William Pitt the Younger, British Statesman, in a speech in the House of Commons, 1783.

Axis recognizes Franco

1936 Germany and Italy both issued proclamations today recognizing the Falangist administration of General Franco (who proclaimed himself Caudillo, equivalent to Führer, on October 1) as the legitimate government of Spain. The move follows the formation of the Rome-Berlin axis on November 1. The rightist revolt against the Republican Popular Front government has led to the Civil War which has been raging since July; the Germans are providing equipment and technical assistance, while the Italians have promised 75,000 troops. The Russians meanwhile are providing similar assistance to the Republicans. The British and French, fearing a Europe-wide war, are pressing for a non-intervention pact, to which all parties, even Germany, Italy and Russia, have committed themselves; at the same time thousands of private individuals of all political persuasions, fired by idealism, are flooding to Spain to join in the bitter struggle. To complete a worldwide alliance of Axis powers, Germany is due to sign the Anti-Comintern pact with Japan next week.

Lincoln makes masterful speech at Gettysburg dedication

1863 "Four score and seven years ago our fathers brought forth on this continent, a new nation, conceived in liberty and dedicated to the proposition that all men are created equal . . ." So began a two-minute speech by President Lincoln at the dedication of the cemetery where the dead of the Battle of Gettysburg are buried. His 15,000 listeners were exhausted by a two-hour oration full of learned detail from noted orator Edward Everett. The President was disappointed by their lack of enthusiasm, but Everett said admiringly, "I should be glad if I could flatter myself that I came as near to the central idea of the occasion in two hours as you did in two minutes."

Pilgrim Fathers land at Cape Cod

1620 The 180-ton wine ship *Mayflower* made landfall at Cape Cod today, just over two months after setting sail from Plymouth. The passengers, 87 members of a separatist Protestant sect founded in Northamptonshire by William Brewster, intend to start a new life in America. Having received from the Virginia Company a charter to found a trading post in that territory, to land outside the northern limits seemed at first sight disastrous, but after discussion the group have decided to settle without rights in Massachusetts Bay. Forty-one men, including Elder Brewster and William Bradford, are drawing up the "Mayflower Compact", a preliminary plan of government.

1984 A huge explosion rocked Mexico City today as ten tanks of liquid gas blew up at a chemical factory. Flames shot 300 ft (100 m) into the air, and surrounding slum areas were showered with burning debris and a cloud of poisonous gas. More than 500 people lost their lives and some 10,000 homes were destroyed in the teeming *barrio*: around a quarter of a million citizens had to be evacuated. Firemen fought for 18 hours to bring the fire under control.

Death of Franz Schubert

1828 One of the greatest musical geniuses the world has ever seen, Franz Schubert, died today aged 31. Worn out by overwork, delirious from the syphilis he contracted in 1822, he expired at 3pm in a damp room in the Neue Wieden suburb of Vienna, attended by his devoted brother Ferdinand and stepsister Josefa. In a furious burst of activity over the past few months he had completed three piano sonatas, a string quintet, and a number of songs. Schubert had been confined to his room for over a week, too ill to eat or drink, his only occupation the correction of the proofs of his recent song cyc!e, *Winterreise*.

1905 British steamer *Hilda* is wrecked off St Malo, France, drowning 128.

1908 A court in St Petersburg is adjourned when the prosecuting council refuses to deal with Russia's first female barrister.

1914 In Britain, Austrian and German internees riot at a detention camp on the Isle of Wight.

1917 A Revolutionary Diplomatic Committee is established in Petrograd with Leon Trotsky as its head.

1919 In Italy, Benito Mussolini and 37 Fascists are arrested after rioting over the election of the Socialists.

1920 One hundred thousand White Russian refugees from the Crimea arrive in Constantinople.

1925 The British parliament votes for a four-month prison sentence for drunken driving.

1988 Death of Christina Onassis, Greek shipowner and daughter of Aristotle Onassis.

BIRTHDAYS

Charles I 1600, English monarch who lost his head after the Civil War.

Viscomte Ferdinand de Lesseps 1805, French diplomat who supervised the building of the Suez Canal.

Hiram Bingham 1875, American senator and archaeologist who discovered the lost Inca city of Machu Picchu in Peru.

Clifton Webb 1891, American actor who appeared in *Laura*, *The Razor's Edge* and *Three Coins in a Fountain* among other films.

Anton Walbrook 1900, German actor whose best-known films are *Gaslight*, *The Red Shoes* and *La Ronde*.

Indira Gandhi 1917, Indian politician, prime minister 1966-77 and 1980-4.

Calvin Klein 1942, American fashion designer.

Jodie Foster 1962, American actress who won an Oscar for *The Silence of the Lambs*.

CORRUPT TAMMANY HALL CHIEF JAILED

1872 Corrupt New York City politico William M. "Boss" Tweed was sentenced to 12 years on Blackwell's Island today, having been found guilty of corruption and fraud on a massive scale. Tammany Hall, popular name for the Democrats (after the Society of St Tammany, formed in the 1780s as an anti-aristocratic pressure group), has become synonymous with evil and corruption in New York politics since the 1850s, when Democrat Mayor Fernando Wood made the city his own private fiefdom. The 49-year-old Tweed was elected to a board set up to stamp out electoral corruption in 1856, but he used this position to promote his friends to public offices. By 1868 Tweed all but controlled the entire State, milking municipal funds of millions of dollars. This was a second trial, the first having resulted in a hung jury.

BIRTHDAYS

POMP AND SPLENDOUR IN THE RAIN

1947 Princess Elizabeth, heir presumptive to the British throne, married Lieutenant Philip Mountbatten today amid scenes of pomp and splendour not seen since before the war. Undeterred by the rain, the crowds slept overnight in the streets to secure the best view, and were standing 50 deep in the Mall and Whitehall to cheer the King and his daughter on their way to Westminster Abbey. The Princess's ivory dress, covered with flowers of beads and pearls, and her tulle veil with a circlet of diamonds, were designed by Norman Hartnell. Her new husband, who is also her cousin, was created Prince Philip, Duke of Edinburgh, by the King at a private ceremony at Buckingham Palace this morning.

1992 Fire has swept through Windsor Castle, causing extensive damage to rooms and ruining furniture, paintings and other treasures belonging to the Royal Family. This disaster comes in a long line of set backs for the Royals this year, including the separation of the Duke and Duchess of York, the divorce of Princess Anne, and widespread press coverage over the marital difficulties of the Prince and Princess of Wales. The Queen is said to be devastated.

Nazis in the dock

1945 The trial of 24 senior Nazis accused of war crimes and crimes against humanity opened in Nuremberg today. The defendants are representative of 35,000 on whom the Allies have opened dossiers. The most notable are Hermann Goering, Luftwaffe leader and founder of the Gestapo; Julius Streicher, one of the earliest proponents of the Nazis' anti-semitic philosophy; Rudolf Hess, Hitler's deputy until his flight to Scotland in 1941; and foreign minister Joachim von Ribbentrop. Martin Bormann, Hitler's deputy since Hess's defection, has escaped and is being tried in his absence. Also conspicuous by their absence are Goebbels, Himmler and Hitler himself, all of whom committed suicide rather than face trial.

1926 At the Imperial Conference in London today the oldest colonies of the British Empire – Canada, Australia, New Zealand, South Africa and Newfoundland – were granted the status of self-governing dominions, masters of their own destiny and of equal status with Great Britain. The Irish Free State is also to become a dominion outside the United Kingdom, and the King is no longer its sovereign; the status of India is unchanged.

Something that everybody wants to have read and nobody wants to read.
Mark Twain defines a classic of literature, 1900.

Nuclear scientist joins peace campaign

1972 One of Soviet Russia's most prominent nuclear physicists, Andrei Sakharov, who was involved in the development of the Russian H-bomb, today put himself on a collision course with the authorities in Moscow. He joined 50 other civil rights campaigners and liberal intellectuals, including world-famous cellist Mstislav Rostropovich, in urging the Kremlin to abolish the death penalty and to free all political prisoners. Sakharov, 51, co-founded the Moscow Human Rights Committee in 1970, but as early as 1963 his concern about the threat of nuclear war led him to use his influence on Khrushchev to persuade him to negotiate a partial ban on nuclear testing.

Death of Spain's strong man

1975 Spain's Fascist era came to an end today with the death of Generalissimo Francisco Franco, victor of the Civil War and head of state since 1939. Having declared himself President for Life in 1947, Franco ensured the Royalist succession by nominating Don Juan Carlos Borbon y Borbon in 1969 as his "heir". Juan Carlos (left) will be the first occupant of the Spanish throne since his grandfather Alfonso XIII was exiled by the Republican government in 1931. Franco will be buried in the mountainside mausoleum built in the "Valley of the Fallen" to house the men who died under his command during the Civil War. Juan Carlos will be crowned in Madrid in two

Leo Tolstoy dies

1910 Count Leo Tolstoy, Russian author of *War and Peace* and *Anna Karenina*, died today in a railway carriage at Astopovo. He had been there since his flight from his estate at Yasnaya Polyana, after quarrelling with his wife, the Countess Sophie. He had previously made over his fortune to her and had been living as a peasant on the estate. "There are millions of people suffering in the world. Why are so many of you looking after me?" were his last words to his daughter Tatiana as doctors, priests and well-wishers milled around him. His wife had followed him, but was not admitted until he had slipped into his final coma.

Super powers reach agreement

1985 The so-called "Fireside Summit" between presidents Reagan and Gorbachev, their first, ended today with a broad measure of agreement to work for a 50 per cent cut in their respective strategic nuclear arsenals. A range of other issues was also discussed, such as the emigration of Soviet Jews and the need to avoid a repetition of the Korean Airlines tragedy. The two men spent six hours together, alone except for interpreters. Gorbachev was optimistic for the future, saying, "The world has become a safer place." President Reagan was more guarded in his enthusiasm, but did agree that he and his opposite number now "understand each other better".

1783 A balloon built by the Mongolfier brothers and piloted by François Pilatre de Rozier and the Marquis d'Arlandes made the first untethered flight in history today. Ascending from the gardens of the Château de la Muette, in the Bois de Boulogne, the balloon travelled some 5 miles (9 km) over Paris, reaching a height of 500 ft (162 m), before making a safe landing near the Luxembourg wood.

Junk bond king gets 10 years

1990 Michael Milken, the so-called "Junk Bond King" was sentenced to 10 years in jail today after pleading guilty to violating federal tax and securities laws. Charges against him included manipulating stock prices, bribery and insider trading. In a plea bargain with the federal authorities back in April Milken also agreed to pay $200 million (£109 million) in fines and $400 million (£217 million) in restitution. The severity of the sentence shocked some observers, but the judge firmly

rejected defence pleas that it be replaced by community service. She did, however, leave the door open for a sentence reduction in return for further cooperation. Milken's huge success as head of the "Junk Bond" department at Wall Street finance house Drexel Burnham Lambert – in 1987 he earned $500 million (£272 million) – made him the personification of the predatory financial ethics of the 1980s.

FRANCIS XAVIER RETURNS

1551 Papal legate Francis Xavier and his fellow Jesuits returned from their epoch-making two-year journey to Japan today, the first missionaries to attempt baptism in this eastern country. The trip has been a moderate success – Francis has left behind 2000 Christians who, it is hoped, will form a thriving community. The latest mission found favour with the Mikado who at first, unimpressed with Francis's humble dress and bearing, refused to see him; but when Francis returned suitably dressed and bearing gifts, he gave his support, even offering a disused Buddhist monastery for the mission's work. "Among all unbelievers no finer people will be found than the Japanese," said Francis on his return.

1695 Death of Henry Purcell, English composer and organist who wrote sonatas, songs, anthems, cantatas and music for the stage; his best-known work is the opera *Dido and Aeneas*.

1791 French navigator Etienne Marchand arrives in China after a record Pacific crossing of 60 days.

1818 The Congress of Aix-la-Chapelle, held to determine European affairs, reaches its close.

1904 A typhoon off Mindanao, the Philippines, renders 30,000 people destitute and homeless.

1906 In Glasgow, a man dies when 200,000 gallons of hot whisky bursts out of vats.

1913 Death of Tokugawa Keiki, last of the Japanese shoguns who controlled the country from 1603 to 1867.

1916 Death of Emperor Franz Josef, ruler of the Austro-Hungarian Empire since 1848.

1934 Cole Porter's musical *Anything Goes* opens in New York.

1964 The Verrazano-Narrows Bridge across New York harbour is opened – the longest single-span bridge in the world.

BIRTHDAYS

Voltaire 1694, French philosopher, scientist, moralist and man of letters who spent his life campaigning against injustice and intolerance.

Harpo Marx 1888, American comedian who, as one of the Marx Brothers, remained entirely mute, expressing himself by whistles, mime and playing the harp.

René Magritte 1898, Belgian Surrealist painter who made ordinary objects seem potentially menacing by their juxtaposition with each other.

Coleman Hawkins 1904, American jazz saxophonist of considerable influence.

Goldie Hawn 1945, American actress whose daffy blonde image belies a considerable facility as a businesswoman in the film industry.

1774 Baron Clive of Plassey, the English soldier and colonial administrator known as Clive of India, dies of an overdose of opium shortly after being vindicated of improper behaviour in the affairs of the East India Company.

1900 Death of Sir Arthur Sullivan, composer of the Savoy Operas with librettist W. S. Gilbert.

1901 Richard Strauss's opera *Feuersnot* receives its premiere in Dresden.

1902 Fire destroys the Williamsburg Bridge over the East River in New York.

1902 Death of Germany's wealthiest man, steel magnate Friedrich Krupp.

1907 The Cunard liner *Mauretania* arrives in New York, completing her maiden voyage.

1916 Death of American novelist Jack London, author of *Call of the Wild* and *White Fang*.

1918 One hundred women police officers go on patrol in the streets of London.

1980 Mae West, American film star who was the archetypal sex symbol of the 1930s, dies aged 88.

1989 A 550-pound (250 kg) remote-control bomb kills Lebanon's president René Moawad and 23 others.

1990 Twenty thousand protesters march in Bulgaria to demand the resignation of the communist government.

BIRTHDAYS

Thomas Cook 1808, English travel agent who pioneered the concept of the package tour.

Benjamin Britten 1913, British composer whose works include the operas *Peter Grimes* and *Billy Budd*.

Billie Jean King 1943, American tennis player who won 20 Wimbledon titles.

Boris Becker 1967, German tennis star who won the men's singles title at Wimbledon at the age of only 17.

KENNEDY ASSASSINATED

1963 The world is in mourning today at the news that President John F. Kennedy has been shot and killed in Dallas, Texas. The 46-year-old President and Mrs Kennedy were in Texas, on the latest leg of a tour of the southern states to gather support for the Democratic Party. The fatal shooting occurred this morning as the presidential motorcade swept through Dealey Plaza in downtown Dallas. The president died in his wife's arms during the dash to the nearest hospital. Accounts of the event are confused, with witnesses claiming to have heard one or more shots from several directions, but a high-powered rifle was found in an upstairs room of the Texas School Book Depository, the window of which overlooked Dealey Plaza. Later today Lee Harvey Oswald was arrested and charged with the murder. Vice-President Lyndon B. Johnson was sworn in as President on the flight back to Washington.

VICTORY FOR ENGLAND

2003 In a moment of sheer unadulterated glory, the England team have achieved victory by winning the Rugby World Cup 2003. Sports fans have described the win as England's greatest sporting triumph since 1966. England fly-half Johnny Wilkinson has achieved massive public popularity following his last-minute drop kick which won England the game. The team was led by England rugby captain Martin Johnson who was euphoric at the 20–17 win over Australia. Millions have celebrated the historic win and plans are under way to honour the squad with a victory parade in London and a Downing Street reception on their return to Britain. There are even rumours of knighthoods for the team.

1986 The awesome punching power of Mike Tyson made him the youngest-ever heavyweight boxing champion in Las Vegas today at the age of 20. He took the World Boxing Council heavyweight crown of Trevor Berbick in under two rounds.

New York greets Concorde

1977 The Anglo-French Concorde, the world's first supersonic airliner, finally entered service on the New York run today, eight years after her first flight, and more than a year after the inaugural Washington service. The British Airways Concorde, piloted by captains Walpole and Oudal, arrived in New York at the same time as the Air France Concorde flight from Paris. There has been an acrimonious campaign against the plane by anti-noise protesters, who had pressured the New York Port Authority into taking the issue all the way to the Supreme Court. Among the charges levelled at Concorde was that it had been responsible for the severe winter of 1976–77! Planned demonstrations turned out to be a non-event, with TV crews reduced to pressing a passing cab-driver into service as a protester.

Try a biro!

1946 A revolutionary new pen which will write 200,000 words without refilling, blotting or smudging goes on sale in Britain today at £2.75 ($5). It is the invention of Hungarian journalist Ladislaw Biro, inspired by the quick-drying printer's ink he saw in Budapest before the Second World War. The business end is a rotating ball point, connected to a capillary tube which holds the ink. In the last year of the war 30,000 biros were produced for RAF flyers, who found them invaluable in the air.

Blackbeard meets his match

1718 The notorious English pirate Edward "Blackbeard" Teach met his death today in hand-to-hand combat with Lieutenant Robert Maynard of HMS *Pearl*. For the past five years Teach has been the scourge of shipping in the Caribbean and off the coast of Virginia and the Carolinas. Recently North Carolina planters, despairing of help from their corrupt governor Charles Eden (who was in fact in league with "Blackbeard"), turned to Virginia governor Alexander Spotswood. He in turn sent two British frigates, the *Pearl* and the *Lyme*, to bring to an end Teach's long reign of terror.

CRIPPEN IS HANGED

1910 Dr Hawley Harvey Crippen was hanged at Pentonville Prison today, only a few hundred yards from the house in Hilldrop Crescent where he poisoned his wife Belle and dismembered her body. American-born Crippen was the manager of a London patent medicine company when he met and fell in love with a pretty typist named Ethel le Neve in 1907. By 1910 he had decided to murder his wife, a formidable ex-music-hall entertainer. He bought supplies of a narcotic called hyoscine, and on January 31 Belle vanished. Crippen told the police that she had died in the USA. Suspicions were aroused when le Neve moved into Hilldrop Crescent, but Scotland Yard's enquiries were frustrated by lack of evidence. The pair's sudden disappearance in July led to the discovery of Belle's remains in the coal cellar. Crippen and le Neve had set sail on the SS *Montrose* for Montreal, she disguised as his son, but the Captain was suspicious of their affectionate behaviour and radioed London. Chief Inspector Dew of Scotland Yard gave chase in a faster ship and arrested the pair in Canada on July 31. At the trial Ethel le Neve was acquitted of any involvement in Belle's death.

1499 Perkin Warbeck, a Flemish-born impostor who claimed to be the Duke of York, presumed killed with his brother Edward V in 1483, is hanged after two unsuccessful attempts to escape from the Tower of London.

1670 Molière's satirical play *Le Bourgeois Gentilhomme* is premiered in Paris.

1921 In the US, President Harding bans doctors from prescribing beer.

1956 Petrol is rationed in Britain and driving tests are suspended as a response to the Suez crisis which threatens oil supplies.

1979 Death of Merle Oberon, Anglo-Indian actress whose films included *The Scarlet Pimpernel*, *A Song to Remember* and *Wuthering Heights*.

1988 Sumo champion Chionofuji becomes the fifth sumo wrestler ever to win 50 consecutive matches.

2003 Eduard Shevardnadze resigns after a decade as president of Georgia amid allegations of corruption in his party.

Put another nickel in...

1889 The world's first jukebox was unveiled today in the Palais Royal Saloon, San Francisco, by Mr Louis Glass, General Manager of the Pacific Phonograph Company. It was Mr Glass's idea to fit coin slots on an electrically-operated Edison phonograph. For a nickel, four customers at once can listen to two minutes' worth of music through listening tubes, but it has to be the same music, since the wax cylinders must be changed manually.

It is not possible for a poet to be a professional. Poetry is essentially an amateur activity.
Lord Barrington, British barrister, 1978.

1852 Britain's first pillarboxes were introduced today at four points in St Helier, Jersey. The six-sided boxes are of cast iron, 4 foot (1.3 m) high and painted red. They are the brainchild of Anthony Trollope, a surveyor for the Post Office and part-time novelist, who noticed while on a trip to the Channel Islands to inspect the postal services that there were many places where the islanders could buy stamps but only one place to post letters.

1963 The BBC premiered a new sci-fi TV show today. Called *Doctor Who*, it tells of the adventures of the eponymous Doctor, one of the Time Lords, and his struggle against his implacable enemies, gravel-voiced robots called Daleks. The Doctor, played by William Hartnell, travels about the universe in a time-machine called the Tardis, which from the outside bears a remarkable resemblance to a police telephone box.

US cash squeeze forces UK out of Suez

1956 Under intense pressure from the US, the British government has agreed to begin a military withdrawal from the Suez war zone, following the ceasefire on November 8. Foreign Secretary Selwyn Lloyd said that troops will leave as "an act of faith" in UN undertakings to ensure the reopening of the Canal. The hostility of President Eisenhower and Secretary of State John Foster Dulles to the Anglo-French invasion has caused a run on the pound, and the US Treasury has made it clear to British Chancellor of the Exchequer Harold Macmillan that financial help in preventing a collapse of sterling depends on a UK withdrawal. Many senior Tories are critical of the government's handling of the crisis, while Prime Minister Sir Anthony Eden is to fly to Jamaica for three weeks, suffering from what is described as "overstrain". It is no secret that his relations with Dulles have almost completely broken down. Leader of the House R. A. Butler is acting Prime Minister in his absence.

William Bonney (Billy the Kid) 1859, American outlaw who finally met his death at the gun of Sheriff Pat Garrett.

Valdemar Poulson 1869, Danish inventor of the tape recorder.

Manuel de Falla 1876, Spanish composer best-known for *Nights in the Gardens of Spain* and the ballets *El Amor Brujo* and *The Three-Cornered Hat*.

Boris Karloff 1887, English actor who specialized in horror roles – most notably as Frankenstein – and starred in *The Mask of Fu Manchu*, *The Mummy* and *The Body Snatcher*.

Sir Peter Saunders 1911, British impresario who staged Agatha Christie's *The Mousetrap*, which broke the world record for the longest-running play.

Michael Gough 1917, British actor whose films include *The Boys from Brazil* and *The Go-Between*.

1572 Death of John Knox, Scottish Protestant reformer whose *Confession of Faith* was adopted by the Scottish church in 1560.

1642 Dutch navigator Abel Tasman discovers a new land and names it Van Diemen's Land after his captain.

1859 Charles Darwin publishes his book *Origin of the Species*.

1902 The world's first conference for professional photographers opens in Paris.

1924 Egyptian prime minister Zaghlol Pasha resigns after refusing to apologise to Britain for the assassination in Cairo of Major-General Lee Stack, Governor-General of the Sudan.

1934 Swedish tenor Jussi Björling makes his debut at the Metropolitan Opera House in New York singing the role of Rudolfo in *La Bohème*.

1979 Saudi Arabian troops storm the Great Mosque in Mecca to oust Iranian religious fanatics.

1990 White extremists attack 300 black children in a park in Louis Trichardt.

BIRTHDAYS

Laurence Sterne 1713, Irish novelist and clergyman best-known for *Tristram Shandy*.

Grace Darling 1815, English lighthouse-keeper's daughter who became a heroine when she rowed out to rescue survivors from the wreck *Forfarshire*.

Frances Hodgson Burnett 1849, English novelist famous for *Little Lord Fauntleroy*, *The Little Princess* and *The Secret Garden*.

Henri de Toulouse-Lautrec 1864, French artist who was stunted by a childhood accident and turned his back on his aristocratic background to live among the music halls and cafés of Montmartre and paint their inhabitants.

Scott Joplin 1868, American ragtime pianist and composer.

Billy Connolly 1942, Scottish comedian.

FREDDIE MERCURY DIES OF AIDS

1991 Freddie Mercury, one of rock's most flamboyant characters, has died of AIDS at the age of 45. Yesterday Mercury issued a statement confirming rumours that he had the disease. Mercury and his group, Queen, hit the music world in the 1970s with a teasing mixture of transvestism and original rock. In the early days the music press wondered at Mercury's outrageous persona with headlines like "Is This Man a Prat?" Meanwhile, the fans were flocking to buy the group's records. Throughout the '70s and '80s the effervescent Mercury kept them royally entertained with "Bohemian Rhapsody", "Crazy Little Thing Called Love", "We Are the Champions" and many more. The fans loved him, his songs and the way he sang them. He was a mesmerizing performer, uninhibited and totally involved. Unashamedly homosexual, Freddie Mercury the man was both kind and gentle.

Oswald shot

1963 Lee Harvey Oswald, the man arrested and charged with the assassination of President John F. Kennedy in Dallas two days ago, was himself shot and killed today. While being transferred under police custody to the County Jail he was approached in the underground car-park of the Dallas Police Headquarters by Jack Ruby, a Dallas strip-club owner, who produced a revolver and shot him from point-blank range. Ruby was immediately overpowered and arrested in his turn.

1989 The extraordinary events in Eastern Europe continue: today Alexander Dubcek, secretary of the Czechoslovak Communist Party during the short-lived "Prague Spring" of 1968, made his first public appearance in Prague for over 20 years. Appearing alongside dissident playwright Vaclav Havel in Wenceslas Square, he told a crowd of 200,000 cheering Czechs, "We have been too long in darkness. Once already we have been in the light, and we want it again."

US troops take Luzon

1899 The US Expeditionary Force made a major advance in its long-running struggle against insurrectionist leader Emilio Aguinaldo today when it gained control of the Philippines' largest island, Luzon. The roots of the struggle go back to the Spanish-American War, when Aguinaldo and his forces threw in their lot with the Americans against their hated Spanish oppressors. Bitterly disappointed by the transfer of control of the country to the US as part of Spain's war reparations, Aguinaldo declared the Malolos Republic last year and took to the mountains, from where he has been waging an effective guerrilla campaign. Though today's defeat is a considerable setback for him, he has vowed to continue the struggle.

"GOLDEN CITIES" REMAIN UNDISCOVERED

1642 Don Francisco Vazquez de Coronado, Governor of Nueva Galicia, arrived back in Mexico City a broken and disappointed man today. Two years ago he set off with a party of 336 Spaniards and hundreds of Indians in search of the legendary seven Golden Cities of Cibola. A certain Friar Marcos de Niza had earlier returned from an expedition to New Mexico talking of glittering cities. As a result, the Viceroy, Antonio de Mendoza, commissioned Coronado to lead an expedition. The glittering cities turned out to be simple adobe settlements, so the party struggled on to the north-east, looking for more fabled riches in "the land of Quivira". The exhausted Spaniards found nothing but squalid villages in the vast prairie of the Wichita Indians, and found small consolation in being the first white men to do so. The Viceroy was uninterested in their reports of "shaggy cows", or buffalo.

A piece of each of us died at that moment.
Michael J. Mansfield, US senator, on the assassination two days ago of John F. Kennedy, 1963.

My wife is French. That means she is both logical and badly organized, as we shall shortly discover in Europe.
Peter Ustinov, British actor, 1991.

Band Aid record for Ethiopia

1984 When Boomtown Rat Bob Geldof watched a BBC TV report on the famine in Ethiopia he was so appalled at what he saw that he resolved to do something about it. The results of that something were seen today when an extraordinary gathering of British rock stars gathered at Sarm Studios in London to record "Do They Know It's Christmas?" Those who turned up free of charge to sing the song, written by Geldof and Ultravox member Midge Ure, included Phil Collins, Sting, George Michael, Bono and Boy George. The single will be released on December 7, and all of the proceeds will go directly to Ethiopian famine relief.

1915 The white supremacist secret society the Ku Klux Klan was revived today at Stone Mountain, Georgia, by Colonel William Simmons. The original Klan (from the Greek "kuklos", circle) was formed in 1886 as a secret Confederate army. Its "night riders" in their hooded costumes were notorious for terrorizing blacks. The new Klan has spread its net wider, and opposes Catholics, Jews, immigration, birth control, the repeal of prohibition, pacifism and Darwinism as well as Negroes.

Mishima dies a Samurai death

1970 Japan's most widely read writer, Yukio Mishima, committed ritual suicide today. Increasingly angry at Japan's rejection of the austere, militaristic Samurai heritage, Mishima and four members of his paramilitary organization, the "Shield Group", seized control of a military barracks in Tokyo by taking its Commandant, General Mashita, hostage. Mishima then harangued a watching crowd of soldiers on the dangers of not allowing Japan to rearm. By this time the alarm had been sounded, and the noise of police helicopters made Mishima nearly inaudible. Returning to Mashita's office, Mishima disembowelled himself with some ceremony, being beheaded – at the third attempt – by his second-in-command Masakatsu Morita. Another of Mishima's acolytes beheaded Morita in his turn before the three survivors gave themselves up.

Ceasefire in former Yugoslavia

1995 A ceasefire has been declared in the former Yugoslav republics of Bosnia, Serbia and Croatia following a peace agreement signed by the republics' leaders in Dayton, Ohio. The Dayton Peace Agreement comes after a summer of military operations which have left the Bosnian Serbs politically and militarily weakened. The United States and NATO have been threatening direct military action if the fighting does not stop. The deal provides for Bosnia to become a single state comprising the Muslim-Croat Federation and the Serb Republic. Sarajevo will once again become a unified city, and the central Bosnian government will have jurisdiction over trade, monetary policy and foreign affairs. In addition, individuals charged with war crimes will be banned from holding public office.

> *The question is this: is man an ape or an angel? I, my lord, am on the side of the angels.*
> **Benjamin Disraeli**, British statesman, 1864.

"Hollywood Ten" blacklisted

1947 The so-called "Hollywood Ten" today refused to testify before the House UnAmerican Activities Committee enquiry into possible communists in the movie capital – on the grounds that the enquiry is unconstitutional. The ten screenwriters and directors – Alvah Bessie, Herbert Biberman, Lester Cole, Edward Dmytryk, Ring Lardner Jr, John Howard Lawson, Albert Maltz, Samuel Ornitz, Adrian Scott and Dalton Trumbo – face a professional ban and jail sentences for their lack of cooperation.

1688 King Louis XIV declares war on the Netherlands.

1901 Britain and Italy agree a frontier between Eritrea and the Sudan.

1902 New Zealand's Progressive Party wins the general election for the fifth consecutive time.

1922 Archaeologist Howard Carter and his sponsor the Earl of Caernavon make a hole in the door of Tutankhamun's tomb and are able to distinguish the contents by candlelight.

1928 The first twins to be born in Britain by Caesarean section are delivered in Manchester.

1942 Soviet troops encircle a quarter of a million German troops at Stalingrad, relieving the siege and routing General von Paulus's Sixth Army.

1956 American bandleader Tommy Dorsey chokes to death in his sleep at the age of 51.

1990 President Lee Kuan Yew of Singapore resigns after 26 years in office.

BIRTHDAYS

William Cowper 1731, English poet who, with evangelical curate John Newton, published *Olney Hymns*; in spite of mental instability and frequent suicide attempts he found great popularity with the comic ballad "John Gilpin's Ride".

Cyril Cusack 1910, Irish actor who made his film debut at the age of seven and went on to appear at the Abbey Theatre over 14 years and make many films.

Eugène Ionesco 1912, French dramatist who initiated the Theatre of the Absurd and, in his later plays, used surrealistic techniques to express his nihilistic view of society.

Charles Schultz 1922, American cartoonist who created the highly successful "Peanuts" strip.

Tina Turner 1939, American singer who had hits such as "River Deep, Mountain High" with her husband Ike before gaining massive success as a solo artist.

Roosevelt comes home

1906 President Theodore Roosevelt has returned to Washington from Central America, having made history by being the first US President to travel abroad while in office. His 17-day trip aboard the battleship *Louisiana* took him to Puerto Rico and then on to Panama to see for himself the building work on the canal he did so much to promote – or "to see how the ditch is get-

ting on", as he put it. The cab of a 95-ton steam shovel made an excellent vantage point for the President as he viewed the awe-inspiring work of engineering, which will reduce the voyage between the Atlantic and Pacific by around 7000 miles (11,200 km). It's a good time for Mr Roosevelt – next month he is to go to Stockholm to receive the Nobel Peace Prize, awarded for his mediation between Russia and Japan to end their armed conflict.

Cream say farewell

1968 Hippie heroes Cream, the world's loudest, fastest, most overpowering rock band, played their last concerts tonight and last night at London's Albert Hall in front of 10,000 fans torn between ecstasy and sorrow. The group – Eric Clapton on lead guitar, Jack Bruce on bass and Ginger Baker on drums – has spent the past two years blowing minds with their own compositions, such as "Strange Brew", "I Feel Free" and "Sunshine of Your Love", and original renditions of blues classics like "Crossroads" and "Spoonful". Clapton's playing has inspired "Clapton is God" graffiti on both sides of the Atlantic, and the group's *Wheels of Fire* double album topped the US charts for four weeks. Fans suffering withdrawal symptoms will be able to comfort themselves with Tony Palmer's film of the concert.

> *I think Prohibition a piece of low, provincial persecution of the dirtiest and most dismal sort. I defy anybody to say what the rights of a citizen are if they do not include the control of his own diet in relation to his health.*
> **G.K. Chesterton**, writing in the *Illustrated London News*, 1921.

NEW YORK GETS STREETCARS

1832 New York's public transport system was inaugurated today when Mr John Mason's horse-drawn streetcars, the city's first, went into operation between Spring and 14th streets.

1966 The world's first tidal power station was opened by General de Gaulle today on the Rance Estuary near St Malo in Brittany. Its developer, Albert Caquot, first drew up plans to harness the power of the tides in 1955, but his scheme was rejected as too ambitious. The present station cost FF420 million (£42 million/$77 million). The 2640 ft (850 m) barrage contains 24 turbo alternators which produce 544 million kW.

UK's biggest gold robbery

1983 A daring and efficient gang of thieves pulled off Britain's biggest-ever robbery today: £25 millions' ($46 million) worth of gold bullion. They coolly broke into the Brinks-Mat security warehouse at Heathrow Airport, neutralized the alarm system and tied up six guards. They then spent an hour loading the gold, which weighed 25 tons, into a truck before making their getaway.

> *Venice is like eating an entire box of chocolate liqueurs at one go.*
> **Truman Capote**, US novelist, 1961.

TAR McADAM

1836 John McAdam, Scottish inventor of the macadam road surface which has done so much to improve the comfort of travel on Britain's roads, has died at the age of 80. McAdam was prompted to find a way of improving the appalling standard of road surfaces in Britain after a trip to America opened his eyes as to how good these could be. He started work on the problem in 1783, and by the time he came up with his system had expended a considerable amount of his own fortune on experiments. The McAdam system makes use of crushed rock and gravel on a raised surface for good drainage. McAdam was appointed Surveyor General of Metropolitan Roads in 1827. He loved Scotland and in retirement would frequently revisit the scenes of his boyhood. It was while returning from one of these expeditions that he died.

Custer kills Chief Black Kettle

1868 Blood flowed on the Washita river in western Oklahoma today when Lieutenant Colonel George Custer and his 7th Cavalry attacked and burned the village of Cheyenne chief Black Kettle. The Cheyenne have been bitterly resisting the building of the railroad in their territory, but it seems that Black Kettle had been negotiating for peace at the time of his death. The 29-year-old Custer is a controversial figure – his daring, reckless style attracted attention at the Battle of Gettysburg and he has only recently been restored to active duty following a court-martial for unauthorized absence from his command and for mistreating deserters. Within an hour after the dawn attack, 103 warriors were dead, according to Custer's unverified estimate. The 23 US dead, among them Major Joel Elliott, were slaughtered while in hot pursuit of a group of fleeing Indians.

Bush in Iraq for Thanksgiving

2003 US President George Bush helped serve a Thanksgiving meal to American troops in Baghdad in a surprise visit to Iraq to mark America's Thanksgiving holiday. The event was kept secret until Mr Bush left the Iraqi capital because of security concerns. Mr Bush spent two hours having dinner with about 600 stunned US troops. Even they had not been told that Mr Bush was coming to Iraq, the first visit ever by a US president. "I was just looking for a warm meal somewhere," Mr Bush told the troops. "Thanks for inviting me to dinner. I can't think of a finer group of folks to have Thanksgiving dinner with than you all." The visit will have given the troops a much-needed morale boost, after a month of heavy American losses.

1893 New Zealand went to the polls today, and for the first time in a national election anywhere in the world women voted too, a female suffrage bill having been passed in parliament by just two votes. The women of New Zealand owe this advance to the flamboyant Liberal leader Richard John Seddon, known as "King Dick", whose unwillingness to alienate a powerful feminist-temperance alliance helped force the measure through parliament, albeit with so narrow a margin. The women returned the favour by electing Seddon and the Liberals to power.

Eugene O'Neill dead

1953 American playwright Eugene O'Neill, Nobel Prize-winner in 1936 and four-times Pulitzer Prize-winner, has died. He was 65. Although at times inconsistent, his best work, such as *Mourning Becomes Electra* and *The Iceman Cometh*, is equal to any other 20th-century playwright's. Born in a hotel room on Broadway and 43rd in New York City, he came from Irish theatrical stock. His discovery that his mother had been addicted to morphine while she carried him so shattered O'Neill that it led to an erratic life of drink and family feuding, which is reflected in his work. His last years were tragic: he was estranged from his children, his eldest son Eugene Jr committed suicide at 40 and a tremor in his hands prevented him from writing. He died in a Boston hotel with the words, "Born in a goddam hotel room and dying in a goddam hotel room!"

> *If, therefore, war should ever come between these two countries, which Heaven forbid! it will not, I think, be due to irresistible natural laws, it will be due to the want of human wisdom.*
> **Bonar Law,** British statesman, referring to Britain and Germany, 1911.

1811 Death of Andrew Meikle, Scottish inventor of the threshing machine.

1875 Britain buys shares worth £4 million ($7.4 million) in the Suez Canal Company.

1895 Death of Alexandre Dumas *fils*, French novelist and dramatist who wrote the novel *La Dame aux Caméllias* and adapted it for the stage as *Camille*.

1919 A massive meteor lands in Lake Michigan.

1942 The French fleet is scuttled by its crews six hours after German tanks arrive in the naval base of Toulon.

1944 The explosion is heard as far away as Geneva when 4000 tons of explosive stored in a cavern in Staffordshire, England, blow up, destroying a farm and killing 68.

1967 President de Gaulle turns down British entry into the Common Market.

1970 The Gay Liberation Front holds its first demonstration in London.

1970 In Manila, capital of the Philippines, a knife-wielding man is seized as he attempts to attack Pope John Paul.

1991 A 15th-century Bible is sold at Christie's in London to a New York antiquarian bookseller for £1.1 million ($2 million).

First women on the beat

1914 The first policewomen in Britain to complete their official training and assume active duty, Misses Mary Allen and E. F. Harburn, were patrolling the streets of Grantham, Lincolnshire, today. Reporting to the Provost Marshal of the county, the women are at present unpaid. They are in Grantham in response to a request from the military authorities – there is a military camp containing 18,000 soldiers just outside town (only 2,000 fewer than the population of Grantham), and it is felt that the women's presence on the streets could help to reduce tension. Wartime demands on manpower are expected to lead to the recruitment of more women to the force.

BIRTHDAYS

Anders Celsius 1701, Swedish astronomer who invented the Celsius temperature scale.

Alexander Dubcek 1921, Czechoslovakian politician who, as secretary of the Czechoslovak Communist Party in 1968, instigated the liberal reforms that led to the "Prague Spring" which was crushed by the Soviet Union in August of that year.

Jimi Hendrix 1942, American singer and ace guitarist who, with the group the Jimi Hendrix Experience, had massive hits with songs such as "Purple Haze" and Bob Dylan's "All Along the Watchtower".

1905
Austrians gain universal suffrage.

1907
King Leopold II of Belgium hands over control of the Congo to the Belgian government, ending 20 years of absolute rule by the monarch.

1909
In Paris, a law is passed to allow pregnant women eight weeks' maternity leave.

1919
Nancy Astor is elected member of parliament for Plymouth, becoming Britain's first woman MP.

1945
Death of Dwight F. Davis, founder of the Davis Cup tennis tournament.

1948
The first Polaroid cameras go on sale in Boston.

1967
All horse-racing is banned in Britain owing to an outbreak of foot and mouth disease.

1971
In Rome, 100,000 demonstrators march against fascism.

1978
The Iranian government bans religious marches.

2002
Suicide bombers drive a vehicle full of explosives into an Isaeli-owned hotel in Mombasa, Kenya, killing 13.

BIRTHDAYS

Jean Baptiste Lully 1632, French composer who worked as a scullion in an aristocratic French household and rose to be composer, violinist and dancer to King Louis XIV.

William Blake 1757, English visionary poet, painter and engraver.

Friedrich Engels 1820, German socialist whose books include *Condition of the Working Class in England in 1844* and *Anti-Dühring*.

Alberto Moravia 1907, Italian novelist whose books include *The Woman of Rome* and *Two Women*.

Claude Lévi-Strauss 1908, French anthropologist whose books include *Structural Anthropology* and *From Honey to Ashes*.

Randy Newman 1943, American singer and songwriter whose hits include "Short People" and "I Think It's Gonna Rain Today".

THATCHER RESIGNS

1990 Margaret Thatcher, Conservative prime minister since May 1979 (and the longest-serving this century) handed her resignation to the Queen early today. Later this morning John Major was formally appointed in her place. The leadership crisis was precipitated by the November 1 resignation of Sir Geoffrey Howe, deputy prime minister and the last serving member of Mrs Thatcher's original 1979 cabinet. Howe was openly critical of her hostile attitude to Europe, especially over monetary policy. Ex-minister Michael Heseltine, another Thatcher critic, challenged her for the leadership of the Conservative Party and in the ensuing ballot she failed by four votes to secure the 15 per cent margin needed to avoid a second ballot. Although she announced her intention to stand again, she finally stood down after protracted consultations with senior colleagues.

A new scientific truth does not triumph by convincing its opponents and making them see the light, but rather because its opponents eventually die out, and a new generation grows up that is familiar with it.

Max Planck, German physicist, 1934.

Chinese enter Korean conflict

1950 The Korean War took a devastating new turn today when an estimated 200,000 Chinese troops poured over the River Yalu. Chou En-Lai, the Chinese foreign minister, had repeatedly warned that his country would resist if US forces crossed the 38th Parallel into North Korea, but his warnings were ignored by the West. Now the US Eighth Army, along with large forces of Marines and South Koreans, is in humiliating retreat in appalling weather.

Spycatcher witness "economical with the truth"

1988 Cabinet Secretary Sir Robert Armstrong, the British government's chief witness in its attempt to prevent publication of retired MI5 agent Peter Wright's memoirs, admitted to the Sydney court today that he had unintentionally given "misleading evidence". In his book *Spycatcher*, Wright alleges that the late Sir Roger Hollis, former MI5 chief, was a Soviet double agent. Wright's attorney, Malcolm Turnbull, previously questioned Sir Robert about the government's apparent selectivity in going after Wright but not prosecuting two previous authors who had made similar accusations. Armstrong's contention was that Wright was a government employee, and therefore subject to different criteria, and that the decision not to prosecute was made by the Attorney General, Sir Michael Havers. Today he admitted that the decision had in fact been taken by "a group of advisors", not by Havers; inadvertently, he said, he had been "economical with the truth".

Rip Van Winkle's creator is dead

1859 Washington Irving, the first successful American-born writer, died at his Tarrytown, New York, home today, aged 76. In 1820 he published *The Sketch Book of Geoffrey Crayon, Gent*, a collection of amusing stories that included "Rip Van Winkle" and "The Legend of Sleepy Hollow". The book launched him as a writer, which was all he had ever wanted to be, although he never quite reproduced its success; latterly he concentrated on non-fiction, producing biographies of Christopher Columbus, Oliver Goldsmith and George Washington – after whom his father had named him and by whom he was blessed at his inauguration in 1789. A modest and kindly man of great charm, Irving never married, although there is a persistent legend that Mary Shelley was in love with him in the 1820s.

Massacre at Sand Creek

1864 At least 150 Indian warriors, women and children were killed today at Sand Creek, Colorado Territory by 750 US cavalry under the command of Colonel John M. Chivington. Some 200 Cheyenne and Arapho warriors along with 500 women and children had surrendered at Fort Lynn, 40 miles (64 km) away, after three years of war. Having been disarmed and sent to Sand Creek they were helpless in the face of the dawn massacre.

> *Ours is composed of the scum of the earth.*
> **The Duke of Wellington,**
> British general, on the British army, 1831.

Corpses from mass suicide discovered

1978 Horrified rescue workers came across a bizarre mass suicide at the site of the Reverend Jim Jones's People's Temple in Guyana today. Alerted by the disappearance of Congressman Leo Ryan and his five colleagues on a mission to investigate Jones's cult, they found more than 900 corpses scattered about the Temple grounds. Survivors found huddled in the bushes testified that the dead had drunk Kool-Aid laced with cyanide on the orders of their leader Jones; he apparently described it as "an act of revolutionary suicide" before shooting himself in the head. Jones was formerly a Methodist minister.

DEATH OF EMPRESS MARIA THERESA

1780 The death has been announced in Vienna of Maria Theresa, Archduchess of Austria, Queen of Hungary and Bohemia, widow of Holy Roman Emperor Francis I. She has been a key figure in the politics of 18th-century Europe, and has been described as "the most human of the Hapsburgs". Although deeply pious and intolerant to the point of bigotry, she has been an enlightened ruler, introducing compulsory primary education and a rudimentary penal code, and encouraging the eminence of Vienna as a centre for the arts. The most prominent of her 16 children are the emperors Joseph II and Leopold II, and Marie Antoinette of France, consort of Louis XVI. The death of her father, Charles VI, in 1740, precipitated the War of Austrian Succession, in which she lost Silesia to Frederick the Great of Prussia but secured the Imperial crown for her husband. Her rivalry with the latter for European power was a major cause of the Seven Years' War (from 1756 to 1763).

2001 The death has been announced of former Beatle George Harrison. Known as the "quiet one" of the Fab Four, Harrison continued with his musical success after the break up of the Beatles, having his own hits such as "My Sweet Lord", and playing with The Travelling Wilburys. He also had a film production company, Handmade Films. Harrison was 58 and had been suffering from cancer.

Allied leaders meet in Tehran

1943 The first summit conference between Russian prime minister Joseph Stalin, US president Franklin D. Roosevelt and British prime minister Winston Churchill opens today in Tehran. The intention is to discuss the progress of the war and to plan for the future – in particular the coordination of the Normandy landings planned for June 1944 with a simultaneous Russian attack on Germany from the east. Also on the agenda are the possibilities of Russia entering the war against Japan and the post-war foundation of a United Nations organization.

1990 Following intensive diplomacy from President Bush and Secretary of State James Baker, the UN Security Council today approved Resolution 678, authorizing member governments to use "all necessary force" to ensure Iraq's complete withdrawal from Kuwait by January 15 next year. This is the first authorization of force by the UN since the Korean War, and marks a significant stepping-up of the pressure on Iraq.

1641 The first English newspaper is published.

1902 Carl Nielsen's opera *Saul and David* is premiered in New York.

1909 Russian novelist Maxim Gorky is expelled from the Revolutionary Party for his bourgeois lifestyle.

1924 Death of Italian composer Giacomo Puccini, whose works include *Tosca* and *La Bohème*.

1965 In Britain, housewife Mary Whitehouse announces the formation of the National Viewers' and Listeners' Association, a watchdog body to halt sex, violence and bad taste in the BBC.

1971 The British government announces a fund of £3 million ($5.5 million) for thalidomide victims.

1974 German terrorist leader Ulrike Meinhof is jailed for eight years.

1986 Death of debonair British-born actor Cary Grant, star of many films including *The Philadelphia Story*, *Arsenic and Old Lace* and *To Catch a Thief*.

1989 Romanian gymnast and Olympic gold medal-winner Nadia Comaneci escapes to Hungary and asks for political asylum.

1994 Russian aircraft launch a bombing raid on the Chechen capital, Grozny.

1999 The Northern Ireland power-sharing executive is set up.

BIRTHDAYS

Gaetano Donizetti 1797, Italian composer of more than 75 operas, including *Lucia di Lammermoor* and *Daughter of the Regiment*.

Louisa M. Alcott 1832, American novelist best-remembered for *Little Women*.

C. S. Lewis 1898, Irish scholar and writer of science fiction, works on religious subjects, and popular children's books set in the land of Narnia.

Berry Gordy 1929, American songwriter and record producer who founded Tamla Motown, the first all-black record company.

1919
Women are allowed to vote for the first time in the French elections.

1924 The last French and Belgian troops withdraw from the Ruhr.

1925 The US sends warships to Hankow, China, to prevent Communist attacks on foreigners.

1956 American boxer Floyd Patterson becomes the youngest boxer to win the world heavyweight title when he knocks out Archie Moore in Chicago.

1957 Death of Beniamino Gigli, Italian tenor who was regarded as the successor to Caruso.

1967 Aden gains its independence from the British.

1979 Death of Zeppo Marx, one of the four Marx Brothers.

1983 Dutch brewery millionaire Alfred Heineken is kidnapped in Amsterdam.

1988 PLO leader Yasser Arafat is refused a visa to enter the US in order to address the UN General Assembly in New York.

1989 Germany's left-wing terrorist group the Red Army Faction blow up Alfred Herrhausen, the head of Deutsche Bank, in Frankfurt.

1989 In the Philippines, rebels attack Cory Aquino's presidential palace and seize parts of three military bases.

BIRTHDAYS

Andrea Palladio 1508, Italian architect whose neo-Classical style was much imitated throughout Western architecture.

Mark Twain 1835, American novelist, author of *The Adventures of Tom Sawyer* and *The Adventures of Huckleberry Finn*.

Sir Winston Churchill 1874, English statesman who, as prime minister, steered Britain through World War Two.

Virgina Mayo 1920, American actress who starred in films such as *Up In Arms* and *The Secret Life of Walter Mitty*.

Efrem Zimbalist Jr 1923, American actor whose films include *Wait Until Dark*, *The Chapman Report* and *Airport 74*.

Crystal Palace destroyed by fire

1936 One of London's best-loved landmarks, the Crystal Palace, burned down this evening. Designed by Joseph Paxton, the Duke of Devonshire's head gardener, the huge glass building, 1848 ft (600 m) long by 408 ft (132 m) wide, was originally constructed in Hyde Park to house the Great Exhibition of 1851. Six million people passed through the building during the Exhibition; Queen Victoria herself visited it 29 times. When the Exhibition closed the building was dismantled and rebuilt on a hill in Sydenham, South London, where it was still a great draw – one-and-a-quarter million Londoners visited it in 1854. The flames were first noticed at 8 pm, and by 8.30 the entire centre transept was ablaze, with flames shooting 300 ft (100 m) into the sky. Visible from all over the city and as far away as Brighton, the blaze attracted a huge crowd of sightseers and special trains were laid on from Central London. Five hundred firemen fought to save the building, but in vain.

Oscar Wilde is dead

1900 Oscar Wilde, the noted – and notorious – Irish wit and playwright, has died in a Paris rooming-house aged 46, in poverty and all but forgotten by his once large circle of admirers. He had lived in Paris since his release from imprisonment for sexual offences in 1897, broken by the scandal and the severity of his sentence. He was born in Dublin in 1854 and was educated at Trinity College, Dublin and Magdalen College, Oxford, where he first attracted attention by his flamboyance and his aestheticism. It is his four plays of the 1890s which will ensure his long-term reputation: *Lady Windermere's Fan*, *A Woman of No Importance*, *An Ideal Husband* and *The Importance of Being Earnest*. He is to be buried in Père Lachaise cemetery.

Reagan's men dismissed

1986 The rapidly developing Iran-Contra scandal has claimed two prominent heads: Admiral John Poindexter, President Reagan's National Security Advisor, and Lieutenant Colonel Oliver North (right) of the National Security Council staff, a much-decorated ex-Marine known as the President's "swashbuckler-in-chief". It has emerged that the $30 million (£16 million) profits from secret sales of embargoed arms to the Iranians were passed on to the US-backed Contras in Nicaragua to finance their struggle against the democratically elected Sandinista government. President Reagan has come under intense pressure over the extent of his involvement in the affair, but it is likely that the sacrifice of his two aides will defuse the crisis.

> *The legal profession is a kind of prostitution: lawyers are paid to find intellectual justifications for other people's actions.*
> **Lisa Forrell**, lawyer and dramatist, 1991.

House of Lords throws out people's budget

1909 After seven months of argument the House of Lords threw out Chancellor Lloyd George's controversial tax package "until it has been submitted to the judgment of the country". Prime Minister Herbert Asquith and the Liberals are bracing themselves for a constitutional crisis; a General Election is now inevitable, and a key issue will be whether their Lordships are too powerful. The Budget proposes taxing the 10,000 citizens with incomes of more than £5000 ($9200) a year an extra 6d (2½p/4½ cents) in the pound above the standard 1s (5p/9 cents) payable by all who earn over £2000 ($3700); unearned incomes are to be taxed 1s 2d (5½p/10 cents) in the pound. The money raised will finance rearmament and old-age pensions. The Tories describe the proposals as an attack on the propertied classes.

1954 Sir Winston Churchill was 80 today, and at a party in the House of Commons Mr Attlee, leader of the Opposition, presented him with a specially commissioned portrait by Graham Sutherland. Sir Winston received the gift with a marked lack of enthusiasm, and described it as "a remarkable example of modern art" that "certainly combines force with candour".

British actress Deborah Kerr today celebrates her birthday. Born in 1921 her films include *From Here to Eternity* and *The King and I*, in which her performances brought her two of her six Oscar nominations.

DECEMBER

"Yesterday, December 7, 1941 - a date which will live on in infamy - the United States of America was suddenly and deliberately attacked by naval and air forces of the Empire of Japan."

Franklin D. Roosevelt
on the attack on Pearl Harbor.

Boers outraged as slaves freed

1834 The slaves of the British Cape Colony were emancipated today. Their freedom has caused a deep split in Cape society, with Dutch-speaking Boer farmers in outlying districts threatening to rebel. The issue has become the focus of Boer resentment of the harsh British rule. Labour shortages caused by Britain's abolition of the slave trade in 1807 have driven the Boers ever further into the hinterland. Raising beef makes more profit and needs less labour than raising crops, and the Boers graze their cattle over large areas. Their expansion has brought them into constant conflict with the black tribes. To the Boers, blacks are savage heathens or slaves. British Governor Sir Benjamin D'urban is unsympathetic to their grievances. Some Boers are talking of leaving the Cape for the unexplored north.

1824 No clear winner has emerged in today's US presidential election. None of the four candidates received an electoral majority, though Andrew Jackson had the most votes, with John Quincy Adams second. The vote will now go to the House of Representatives.

Post-war Britain to abolish want

1942 The British government was today presented with a plan to turn post-war Britain into a "welfare state". The plan is the work of a government committee headed by Sir William Beveridge, charged with finding solutions to the problems of poverty after the war. It revolves around a compulsory national insurance scheme to provide all adults with free medical treatment, unemployment benefits, old age pensions and death cover. Both employers and employees will contribute. Britain introduced limited unemployment and old-age insurance in 1911, and the scheme was broadened in 1925. Beveridge's plan brings security for all "from cradle to grave".

RAMPARTS OF MT EREBUS

TREATY RESERVES ANTARCTICA FOR SCIENCE

1959 Twelve countries today agreed to preserve Antarctica for peaceful scientific research in the first international agreement of its kind. The Antarctic Treaty was signed by the US, the Soviet Union, Britain, France, Belgium, Norway, Australia, New Zealand, Chile, Argentina, South Africa and Japan. It freezes all territorial claims on the last unexploited continent, throws the continent open to all scientists, and bans military bases, nuclear explosions and the dumping of nuclear wastes. Antarctica is the coldest place on Earth. If it melted, the oceans would rise 200 ft (65 m).

Europe and Britain joined

1990 Today the two halves of the Channel Tunnel were joined under the sea. A joint British-French effort, excavations for the high-speed rail tunnel were started from both the French and British sides of the English Channel. This morning the two construction teams broke through to meet in the middle.

Fish feast kills King Henry

1135 England's King Henry I has died at St Denis in Normandy. He fell ill seven days ago after eating too many lampreys, and never recovered. He was 66, and had ruled for 35 years. Henry seized the throne after his eldest brother, King William Rufus, was killed. Henry defeated the rightful heir, his second brother Robert, Duke of Normandy, and seized Normandy as well. Robert died several months ago in Cardiff Castle, where Henry had imprisoned him 29 years ago. Henry's only son, William, drowned in 1120, (it is said that Henry never smiled again) and, left heirless, the king extracted an oath from his nobles to accept his stormy daughter Maud as his successor. But the barons see it as a disgrace for men to submit to a woman's rule – especially Maud's. They are backing the claim of Henry's nephew Stephen, Earl of Bois, first prince of the blood royal and a popular favourite, who is now hastening to London. Meanwhile Maud is preparing to invade England to get her father's throne.

BIRTHDAYS

BIRTHDAYS

Georges Seurat 1859, French painter who pioneered the technique of Pointillism, typified by his *Sunday Afternoon on the Island of La Grande Jatte*.

Sir John Barbirolli 1899, English conductor best-known for his association with the Hallé Orchestra.

Maria Callas 1923, Greek operatic soprano renowned for her dramatic interpretations.

General Alexander Haig 1924, American soldier and politician.

"HANDS OFF" MONROE TELLS EUROPE

1823 US President James Monroe today warned Europe to keep its hands off *both* American continents. In his annual message to the US Congress, Monroe defended the newly-won independence of the Spanish colonies in Latin America and said the American continents were no longer subjects for European colonization. The warning follows concerted moves by US secretary of state John Quincy Adams and British foreign secretary George Canning to head off reported French plans to send troops to help Spain regain her New World colonies. Canning persuaded France to renounce its New World ambitions in October, and Monroe knows Britain will enforce the agreement if necessary. However, Monroe sent a similar "hands off" message to Russia in July, following the Tsar's claims to part of the American Pacific coast.

Mercenary coup fails in Seychelles

1981 White mercenaries posing as golfers on holiday today failed in an attempt to overthrow the left-wing government of the Seychelles. They got no further than the airport, where a golf bag fell open to reveal a gun. Led by the notorious ex-Congo mercenary Colonel "Mad Mike" Hoare, the 44 men shot their way out of the airport building and hijacked an Air India jet to South Africa, which is believed to be the source of their backing. The men were arrested on arrival, but most of them have already been released.

John Brown hanged for treason

1859 The radical abolitionist John Brown was hanged today in Charleston for treason against Virginia. Three years ago Brown and his sons murdered five pro-slavery settlers in a raid in Kansas. His latest project was to found a republic in the Appalachians as a base for abolitionists and runaways to fight slavery. On October 16, Brown and an armed force of 21 men attacked Harpers Ferry in West Virginia, seized the federal arsenal and occupied the town. Federal troops commanded by Robert E. Lee recaptured the town the following morning, wounding Brown and killing 10 of his men. Brown was charged with treason. His trial was a sensation: Brown played on abolitionist sympathies in the North, where he is being hailed as a martyr, but his extremism has horrified the South, where he is seen as a murderous traitor. The whole affair has served to widen the rift over abolition.

1990 West German chancellor Helmut Kohl has won the first all-Germany election since 1933. Kohl's Christian Democratic Union and their allies have won more than half the vote, with a 20 per cent lead on the Social Democrats. East Germany's communist ex-rulers won a few seats in the new united German parliament.

1954 The end of four years of anti-communist hysteria in the US was in sight today when a special session of the US Senate voted to condemn the chief instigator of the witchhunt, Senator Joseph McCarthy, for conduct unbecoming to a senator.

Napoleon crowns himself emperor

1804 Monarchy returned to France today when Napoleon Bonaparte crowned himself Emperor Napoleon I at Notre Dame, 11 years after King Louis XVI was guillotined. Pope Pius VII presided over the ceremony, but Napoleon placed the crown on his own head, and then crowned his wife Josephine as empress. Ironically, the train of events that has put the "little corporal" from Corsica on the throne was sparked off by an attempt to kill him. In February, disgraced police minister Joseph Fouche won his job back when he uncovered a British-financed plot by renegade French royalists to assassinate Napoleon. The plot was thwarted, but a wave of anti-royalist feeling followed, encouraging the Senate to ask Napoleon to found an hereditary dynasty and take the throne.

As I write, they are leading old John Brown to execution . . . This is sowing the wind to reap the whirlwind, which will soon come.
Henry Wadsworth Longfellow, American poet, today, 1859.

Jackson is president

1828 John Quincy Adams lost the US presidential election to his arch-rival Andrew Jackson today. Adams's term as president was blocked at almost every turn by the Jacksonian faction. Frontier soldier Jackson, of Tennessee, is backed by the new Democratic Party, supported by southern farmers and northern workers. A noisy crowd of farmers and other supporters invaded the White House in Washington tonight to celebrate Jackson's victory, causing considerable upset and some damage.

It is no accident that the symbol of a bishop is a crook, and the sign of an arch-bishop is a double-cross.

Dom Gregory Dix, British monk, 1977.

3000 killed in Bhopal pesticide spill

1984 More than 3000 people are feared killed and hundreds of thousands injured in the world's worst-ever industrial accident following a chemical spill at a pesticide factory in India. A storage tank at the Union Carbide (India) plant in Bhopal, central India, began leaking just after midnight, sending a deadly gas spreading silently through the sleeping city. In three hours the tank leaked more than 30 tons of the chemical, methyl isocyanate (MIC). Most of those killed suffocated or choked to death. Many survivors have suffered severe lung damage, while others are blinded or have heart, kidney or liver damage. The plant was shut down as soon as the spill was discovered, and five Union Carbide officials have been arrested. The government has declared the city a disaster area and asked for assistance. Union Carbide has pledged to compensate victims as if the accident had happened in the US.

1918 Death-rates in the worldwide epidemic of killer influenza are beginning to fall. Almost every country has been hit since the deadly new strain of the disease first arose earlier this year. Called Spanish 'flu, where it really came from is a mystery. The Far East has been worst hit, with millions dead in China and India.

RENOIR DIES

1919 The most sensual of the French Impressionist painters, Auguste Renoir, has died at his villa near Cannes in France. He was 78. Though crippled by rheumatism, he was still painting hours before he died. Renoir and Claude Monet launched the Impressionist movement at a notorious exhibition in 1874. They worked outdoors, capturing nature's caprice in fleeting moments of light and colour. The critics sneered at the works' "half-finished" appearance, but a wiser world now sneers at the critics.

The Cold War is over

1989 The Cold War ended today after 52 years of superpower rivalry. With communist rule crumbling in Eastern Europe, Soviet leader Mikhail Gorbachev and US President George Bush ended their shipboard summit meeting off Malta and hailed the start of a new era of peace and cooperation. The leaders announced two arms treaties to be signed next year, reducing strategic nuclear forces by half and cutting conventional forces in Europe. Both sides have already dismantled their intermediate-range nuclear missiles.

Surgeons give man new heart

1967 A South African heart surgeon, Dr Christiaan Barnard, has successfully performed a human heart transplant operation. Leading a large team of surgeons at Groote Schuur Hospital in Cape Town, Barnard replaced the mortally diseased heart of Louis Washkansky, a 53-year-old grocer, with the healthy heart of a 25-year-old motor accident victim, Denise Darvall. Barnard said the main problem was not the operation itself but persuading the patient's immune system not to reject the new heart.

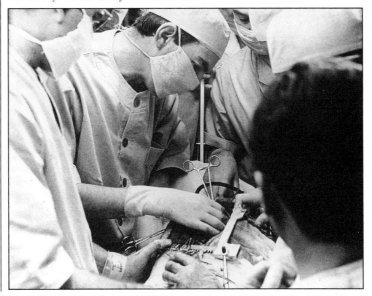

DECEMBER 3

1552 Death of Spanish Jesuit missionary Francis Xavier, who helped Ignatius Loyola found the Jesuit order and subsequently worked mainly in Japan, India and the Indies.

1894 Death of Scottish novelist Robert Louis Stevenson, author of *Treasure Island*.

1905 British troops put down a riot in Georgetown, British Guiana.

1909 King Edward VII dissolves the British parliament and taxes on alcohol, tobacco and cars are suspended as no Budget has been passed.

1910 France occupies the Moroccan port of Agadir.

1920 British writer Rudyard Kipling wins damages of £2 against a medical company that had used part of his poem "If" in an advertisement.

1925 In New York, police smash the biggest bootlegging ring since Prohibition began and arrest 20 people.

1926 British novelist Agatha Christie disappears from her home in Surrey.

1989 In India, 800 people are arrested during a demonstration to commemorate the fifth anniversary of the Bhopal chemical disaster.

1990 Argentinian president Carlos Menem foils an attempted coup.

BIRTHDAYS

Joseph Conrad 1857, Polish-born English author whose books include *Lord Jim* and *Heart of Darkness*.

Anton von Webern 1883, Austrian composer whose music influenced Boulez and Stravinsky, among others.

Walt Disney 1901, American film producer and film animator who created such immortals as Mickey Mouse and Donald Duck.

Andy Williams 1930, American ballad singer.

Jean-Luc Godard 1930, French film director, one of the pioneers of the *nouvelle vague* of French cinema in the 1960s.

1154 Nicholas Breakspeare becomes the first Englishman to be Pope.

1732 Death of John Gay, English poet and dramatist best-known for the ballad opera *The Beggar's Opera*.

1791 In Britain, the *Observer* Sunday newspaper is published for the first time.

1912 Turkey reaches an armistice with all the Balkan allies except Greece.

1913 Suffragette Emmeline Pankhurst is arrested in Plymouth on her return to the UK from the US.

1915 Georgia officially recognizes the Ku Klux Klan.

1937 In Britain, *The Dandy* comic is published for the first time.

1947 Tennessee Williams' play *A Streetcar Named Desire* is premiered on Broadway, with Marlon Brando and Jessica Tandy in the leading roles.

1974 Death of British composer Benjamin Britten, whose best-known works include the operas *Billy Budd*, *Peter Grimes* and *Death in Venice*.

1992 Twenty-eight thousand US troops land in Somalia to support the relief effort as hundreds of thousands face starvation due to civil unrest.

BIRTHDAYS

Thomas Carlyle 1795, Scottish historian and essayist whose works include *Sartor Resartus* and *The French Revolution*.

Samuel Butler 1835, English satirical novelist best known for *Erewhon* and the autobiographical *The Way of All Flesh*.

General Francisco Franco 1892, Spanish dictator from 1939 until his death in 1975.

Deanna Durbin 1922, Canadian actress who first found fame as a teenage star in films such as *Three Smart Girls* and *One Hundred Men and a Girl*.

Jeff Bridges 1949, American actor whose films include *The Last Picture Show* and *Thunderbolt and Lightfoot*.

Mystery of the *Marie Celeste*

1872 The American brigantine *Marie Celeste* has been found adrift in the Atlantic between the Azores and Portugal, her captain and crew mysteriously missing. The British brigantine *Dei Gratia* came upon the ship and boarded her when she failed to respond to their signals. The ship was deserted and the lifeboat was not on board. The rigging was slightly damaged, but the cargo of 1700 barrels of alcohol had not been touched. The captain's table was set for a meal which was never eaten. The *Marie Celeste* sailed from New York on November 7 bound for Genoa, commanded by Captain Benjamin S. Briggs and carrying a crew of eight and the captain's wife and daughter. They left no message aboard and there is no indication of what can have happened to them.

1973 The original Fuller Brush Man has died. Alfred Fuller started working as a brush salesman in Boston at the turn of the century. Later he started his own company, making the wire brushes and selling them himself door-to-door. The Fuller Brush Company was incorporated in 1913, with a nationwide direct sales organization. In 1960 Fuller published his autobiography, "A Foot in the Door".

Many, if not most, of our Indian wars have had their origin in broken promises and injustice on our part.

Rutherford B. Hayes, US President, in a message to Congress, 1877.

Fatty Arbuckle acquitted of fatal rape

1921 Roscoe "Fatty" Arbuckle, comic star of the silent screen, was today found not guilty of rape and manslaughter. The jury voted 10-2 in Arbuckle's favour. The charge arose from the death last year of Hollywood starlet Virginia Crabbe following a drinking party in Arbuckle's hotel room. She was raped at the party and accused Arbuckle before dying in hospital of internal injuries. The prosecution is pressing for a retrial following today's verdict.

KRENZ OUSTED AS COMMUNIST RULE CRUMBLES

1989 East Germany's head of state, Egon Krenz, was forced to resign today only six weeks after he replaced a beleaguered Erich Hoenecker. Strongman Hoenecker was toppled after huge public protests at government corruption and abuse of power, followed by a mass exodus to the West through Czechoslovakia. With communist rule crumbling about him, Krenz agreed to free elections and opened the Berlin Wall. New revelations, however, have linked him to large-scale corruption. Liberal Democrat leader Manfred Gerlach is acting head of state for the time being.

King's cardinal dies

1642 Armand du Plessis, Cardinal Richelieu, who has ruled France for his king for 18 years, died today, aged 57. Richelieu had survived constant conspiracies by jealous nobles, always one step ahead in the plot. Richelieu was foreign secretary when young King Louis XIII overthrew his mother to take the throne. He almost had Richelieu murdered, but fired him instead. Later Louis came to understand what he had in this pragmatic priest: a brilliant man, totally dedicated to France – and to the throne. In 1624 Louis made him chief of the royal council and gave him total authority. Richelieu has ruled ever since, with an iron hand and unerring skill. As a result, Louis has survived the Thirty Years' War, and France is at the forefront of European power – to the cost of her enemy, Spain. With Richelieu dead, King Louis has lost his right arm.

US celebrates end of Prohibition

1933 The US is celebrating the end of 14 long years of Prohibition today. Utah became the last state to ratify the 21st Amendment, which effectively nullifies the 18th Amendment of 1919 prohibiting the "manufacture, sale, or transportation of intoxicating liquors". The 18th Amendment, passed over President Woodrow Wilson's veto, was the result of long campaigning by the Temperance Movement and the Women's Christian Temperance Union – boosted unexpectedly by the World War One grain shortage. The "Noble Experiment" just did not work. Americans did not stop drinking – the law simply pushed the lucrative liquor trade into the hands of criminals like Al Capone and many others. Enforcement proved impossible, and unpopular even with the police. Anti-Prohibition "wets" have now won their campaign to restore individual freedom of choice.

1792 George Washington is re-elected president of the US.

1870 Death of Alexandre Dumas *père*, author of *The Count of Monte Cristo* and *The Three Musketeers*.

1904 The Japanese destroy the Russian fleet at Port Arthur.

1905 The roof of Charing Cross Station in London collapses, killing five.

1906 Russian admiral Niebogatov goes on trial accused of surrendering ships to the Japanese.

1910 A convoy of barges on the River Volga in Russia sinks, drowning 350 workmen.

1912 Italy, Germany and Austria renew the Triple Alliance for a further six years.

1920 In a referendum, the Greek people vote for the return of their monarch, ex-King Constantine, removed by the Allies in 1917.

1956 Rose Heilbron becomes Britain's first female judge.

1977 President Sadat of Egypt severs links with Syria, Libya, Algeria and South Yemen.

1978 The USSR signs a 20-year treaty of friendship with Afghanistan.

BIRTHDAYS

George Armstrong Custer 1839, American cavalry commander known for his "last stand" against the Cheyenne and Sioux Indians.

Fritz Lang 1890, Austrian film director whose many fine works include *Metropolis*, *M* and *The Big Heat*.

Otto Preminger 1906, Austrian film director whose best-known films include *The Man with the Golden Arm* and *Anatomy of a Murder*.

Little Richard 1935, American pioneer of rock 'n' roll whose hits include "Tutti Frutti" and "Good Golly, Miss Molly".

Jose Carreras 1946, Spanish operatic tenor who overcame leukaemia and resumed his successful career as one of the superstars of the heroic arias.

Death of man who drew the world

1594 The great Flemish cartographer Gerardus Mercator has died, aged 82. Mercator was a many-sided man, a philosopher, calligrapher, technician, instrument-maker and engraver, but it is his maps that won him renown – and helped the Netherlands grow into a sea-power. Mercator was at the centre of the great advances in mapmaking technique made this century. His method of depicting the world's curved surface on flat paper using straight lines of longitude and latitude soon became standard practice. Mercator designed a map of the world in 1538, and three years later a globe based on maps and descriptions by Ptolemy, Marco Polo and the Spanish and Portuguese navigators. In 1569 he published a series of world maps for use by navigators. Mercator worked on a world atlas and history of the world for 20 years, but never completed it. His son is now planning to publish it in its unfinished state.

Pauper's burial for Mozart

1791 Wolfgang Amadeus Mozart has died in Vienna of kidney failure. He was only 35, and at the height of his genius. Mozart wrote his first compositions when he was five, played before the Vienna court at the age of six, went on a concert tour of Europe when he was seven and composed his first symphony at the age of nine. He has written more than 600 works. Mozart's work was often too deep and complex for his audiences, though he has had a profound influence on other musicians, and he was dogged by money problems to the end. Only the gravedigger attended his burial in a Viennese suburb.

PLANES VANISH NEAR BERMUDA

1945 Six US navy aircraft carrying 27 airmen are missing without trace in the Atlantic near Bermuda. Five bombers took off this morning from Fort Lauderdale, Florida on a training flight. When radio contact was lost with the bombers, a sixth plane was sent to find them. It too lost radio contact. Subsequent searches have found nothing. It is thought the planes came down somewhere within a triangle of ocean between Bermuda, Puerto Rico and Florida.

1906 After a sensational nine-month trial by an ecclesiastical court, Episcopalian rector the Rev. Algernon S. Crapsey of Rochester, New York, was today convicted of heresy and expelled from ministry. The church had charged that Crapsey, influenced by the writings of Karl Marx and the French theologian Ernest Renan, had questioned the divinity of Christ. The case has created widespread controversy on both sides of the Atlantic.

Your parole officer has not yet been born.
   Edwin Torres, US judge, sentencing a murderer, 1991.

DECEMBER 6

1774 Austria becomes the first nation to establish a state education system.

1793 Madame du Barry, last mistress of King Louis XV of France, is sent to the guillotine by the Revolutionary Council.

1882 Death of English novelist Anthony Trollope, who made his name with a series of novels set in an imaginary county called Barsetshire.

1889 Death of Jefferson Davies, former president of the Confederate States of America.

1905 Norwegian explorer Roald Amundsen lands at Fort Egbert, Alaska, after a 2½ year voyage along America's Arctic coast in his 47 foot (14 m) cutter.

1911 Mongolia is declared a Russian protectorate.

1914 The Germans capture the Polish city of Lodz.

1988 American rock 'n' roll singer and songwriter Roy Orbison dies of a heart attack at the age of 52.

1989 In Colombia, more than 40 people are killed by a bomb at the headquarters of the security police.

1990 An Italian military aircraft crashes in flames into a secondary school near Bologna, killing 12 and injuring a further 65.

1990 Saddam Hussein announces that all 3400 foreign hostages held in Iraq since the invasion of Kuwait are now free to leave.

BIRTHDAYS

Warren Hastings 1732, English colonial administrator and first governor-general of India who was impeached for corruption on his return to England and acquitted after a trial before the House of Lords which cost him £70,000 ($129,000).

Ira Gershwin 1896, American lyricist who, with his brother George, wrote such hits as "Lady be Good" and "I Got Rhythm".

Dave Brubeck 1920, American jazz pianist and composer who had a big hit with "Take Five".

Cromwell purges Parliament

1648 Oliver Cromwell's troops surrounded Parliament at Westminster today and refused to admit 200 Presbyterian MPs, purging the whole of the majority that opposes Cromwell's Independents. The remaining 50 MPs, all Independents, voted hearty thanks to Cromwell for his great services, and moved on to discuss the fate of King Charles, who Cromwell is holding captive on the Isle of Wight. The Presbyterian faction tried to make a deal with the king. They hardly expected Cromwell's simple solution to the threat.

Monet dies at Giverny

1926 The French painter Claude Monet died yesterday at his home in Giverny in Normandy, France, aged 86. Monet founded the Impressionist movement with his friends Auguste Renoir, Camille Pissarro and Alfred Sisley. Impressionism was named after a Monet painting called *Impression: Sunrise*, a misty view of Le Havre. Monet painted scenes of rippling light and colour. The lovely garden he built at Giverny became his favourite subject, especially the lily pond: he painted its ever-shifting moods again and again.

Murder at Altamont

1969 An 18-year-old black youth was murdered in front of the stage while the Rolling Stones performed at a free concert at Altamont Speedway in California today. Meredith Hunter was stabbed to death by Hell's Angels bikers when he pulled out a gun during a confused scuffle at the stagefront. The whole incident was recorded by the crew filming the concert. Shocked and frightened, the Rolling Stones rushed through the rest of their numbers before escaping in a helicopter. This was the final performance of their US tour. The group had previously hired tamer English Hell's Angels as security guards, and they did the same in California, not realizing the difference.

> *The Soviet Union has disintegrated.*
> **Leonid Kravchuk**, president of the Ukraine, 1991.

> *Guy was happy, I was happy, the team was happy, the crowd was happy, everybody was happy. There is just one word to describe it all – happiness.*
> **Yannick Noah**, captain of the French Davis Cup tennis team, 1991.

1963 Christine Keeler sobbed in a London court today when she was jailed for nine months for perjury. The English "model", 21, admitted lying about two men hiding in her bedroom when an ex-boyfriend assaulted her. She was the protegé of Dr Stephen Ward who ran a high-society sex ring. Her lovers included John Profumo, Minister of War.

Ireland split as Free State is born

1921 Ireland's 26 southern states were granted independence from Britain today, becoming the Irish Free State. Six of the eight Protestant-majority counties of Ulster in the north will remain part of the UK, splitting the country in two. The agreement was signed in Downing Street early this morning following negotiations between Prime Minister David Lloyd George's team and the rebel Irish nationalist leaders. A special council will be set up to discuss eventual reunification. Both sides would prefer a single Irish parliament in Dublin, but Ulster's Protestant leaders refuse to bow to the Catholic South.

French pole-axe US to win Davis Cup

1991 French President François Mitterrand honoured the victorious French Davis Cup tennis team at a reception at the Elysée Palace in Paris tonight. The French players are national heroes. Against all odds they pole-axed the US team, winning back the trophy after 59 years. Star players were Guy Forget and Henri Leconte, but the real star was the non-playing captain, Yannick Noah, who has set an entirely new style for team captains. His high-powered encouragement from the courtside was the key to the trophy. Noah pleaded and ranted and genuinely inspired his players, while his opposite number, US captain Tom Gorman, sank into his chair in despondency. Today Noah can do no wrong in France.

JAPAN ATTACKS PEARL HARBOR

1941 A Japanese task force has launched a massive surprise attack on the US base at Pearl Harbor in Hawaii. Five US battleships and 14 other ships have been wrecked or sunk, 200 aircraft destroyed and 2400 men killed. Though intelligence reports had warned of Japanese fleet movements in the Hawaii area, the US base was completely unprepared. America is outraged at the news, announced by the White House within hours. Japan and the US are not even at war – the attack comes during negotiations between the two governments. Yesterday President Franklin D. Roosevelt made a personal appeal to Japan's Emperor Hirohito to avoid war. In spite of strong isolationist opposition, the US now has no choice but to declare war on Japan, and thus on her allies, Nazi Germany and Fascist Italy.

Serbs bombard besieged Dubrovnik

1991 Following a 67-day siege, Yugoslavian federal army and navy forces have wrecked Dubrovnik's historic Old Town in a savage two-day bombardment. Many people have been left dead or homeless. Some 50,000 civilian refugees were sheltering in the Old Town because the army had so far avoided shelling the historic area. The vicious civil war between Serbs and Croats continues unabated. European and United Nations peacemaking efforts have proved useless – the 14th ceasefire lies in tatters. The Croats held free elections last year in a bid for an independent Croatia, which is rejected by Yugoslavia's Serbian majority. The resulting war has been rife with atrocities, mostly against Croatian civilians by federal troops and Serbian irregulars.

PITT IS PRIME MINISTER AT 24

1783 William Pitt has been made British prime minister and chancellor of the exchequer, at the age of only 24. He replaces the Duke of Portland, dismissed after only eight months when King George III persuaded the House of Lords to reject his Indian government bill. Pitt is already acknowledged by all parties to be one of the finest orators and the ablest statesman of the day, but he has a formidable task before him. The king and public support him, but in parliament he faces a large and hostile majority led by experienced parliamentary tacticians, and he has no able speakers on his side.

Opera House opens in Covent Garden

1732 London's new Royal Italian Opera House in Covent Garden opened its doors to an élite crowd tonight for a sparkling performance of John Gay's *The Beggar's Opera*. It was a fine tribute to Gay, who died three days ago. The Opera House apes the Italian style, Covent Garden, Inigo Jones's square above the Strand, apes the style of an Italian piazza, while *The Beggar's Opera* is an outrageous burlesque of Italian opera. It is also a biting satire of prime minister Sir Robert Walpole and his Whig government, presented in the guise of low-life London villains and prostitutes. With music by John Pepusch, it is a most innovative work, using both songs and speech on stage to tell its story of high-society vice and corruption. It was immensely successful when Gay first staged it six years ago, and tonight's gala performance showed its popularity has not waned. However, it is not at all popular with certain government figures, who have called for stronger censorship laws.

EARTHQUAKE KILLS 100,000 IN ARMENIA

1988 More than 100,000 people are feared dead in an earthquake which devastated northern Armenia today. The cities of Spitak and Leninakan near the Turkish border have been virtually wiped out, with thousands buried alive in collapsed buildings. Survivors tried to reach trapped relatives, struggling to move the shattered concrete and rubble that are all that remain of most of the apartment blocks. The shocked country has appealed for international help as emergency teams start a massive rescue operation. On hearing the news, Soviet leader Mikhail Gorbachev cut short his US trip and returned to Moscow to co-ordinate relief efforts. The earthquake follows a year of ethnic violence between Armenia and Azerbaijan over the disputed region of Nagorno Karabakh.

> *Praise the Lord and pass the ammunition.*
> **Howell Forgy**, US naval lieutenant, when Japan attacked Pearl Harbor, 1941.

43 BC Roman orator and statesman Marcus Tullius Cicero is executed for the *Philippics*, a series of attacks on Mark Anthony.

1815 Marshal Ney, Napoleon's most illustrious general, is executed in Paris for treason for supporting Napoleon at Waterloo instead of arresting him as he had been instructed by the allies to do.

1817 Death of Rear-Admiral William Bligh, captain of the Bounty when its crew mutinied.

1909 A royal proclamation creating the self-governing Union of South Africa, comprising the Cape of Good Hope, Natal, Orange River and Transvaal, is read from the steps of the Royal Exchange in London.

1917 In Washington, President Woodrow Wilson declares war on Austria.

1982 Charles Brooks Jr, a Death Row prisoner at Fort Worth Prison in Texas, becomes the first American to die by lethal injection.

1988 President Gorbachev announces that Soviet military strength will be cut by ten per cent within the next two years.

1988 Nelson Mandela is moved to a luxury home in the grounds of Pollsmoor Prison.

1989 A revolt in the Philippines ends as 400 rebel troops abandon their siege of Manila's business centre.

1989 A feminist-hating gunman shoots 14 women in Montreal.

1995 A link is revealed between the cattle disease BSE and CJD, a brain disease in humans.

BIRTHDAYS

Gian Lorenzo Bernini 1598, Italian sculptor and architect whose major works include the piazza and colonade of St Peter's in Rome.

Pietro Mascagni 1863, Italian composer best-known for the one-act opera *Cavalleria Rusticana*.

Eli Wallach 1915, American actor specializing in tough-guy roles.

Ellen Burstyn 1932, American actress who won an Oscar for *Alice Doesn't Live Here Anymore*.

DECEMBER 8

BIRTHDAYS

Mary, Queen of Scots 1542, Scottish queen who was forced to abdicate in favour of her son, James VI (James I of England), and was later imprisoned and executed by her cousin, Queen Elizabeth I of England.

James Thurber 1894, American humorist, writer and cartoonist whose satires on intellectual fashions appeared in the *New Yorker* over many years.

Richard Fleischer 1916, American film director whose works include *Twenty Thousand Leagues under the Sea*, *The Vikings* and *The Boston Strangler*.

Sammy Davis Jr 1925, American actor, dancer, singer and comedian whose films include *Porgy and Bess*, *Ocean's Eleven* and *Sweet Charity*.

David Carradine 1940, American actor most associated with the television series *Kung Fu*.

Jim Morrison 1943, American singer with cult rock group the Doors.

Virgin Mary was without sin, Pope decrees

1854 Pope Pius IX has settled an ancient controversy in a papal bull issued in Rome today. It declares that the Virgin Mary, Jesus Christ's mother, was preserved from all sin from the moment she was born, by the grace of God. This doctrine is now binding on all Roman Catholics. The Gospels tell of Jesus' virgin birth, and of Mary's holiness. They also talk of Jesus' younger brothers, but 300 years later the church took the view that Mary had remained a virgin all her life. A subsequent argument, whether she was the mother of God or only the mother of Christ, was settled in 431, when she was proclaimed the mother of God. Other disputes raged through the centuries: did Mary ascend bodily to Heaven? And how had she escaped original sin, which stains all humans, to become the mother of God? Which led back to questions about Christ's immaculate conception. This is the issue the Pope has now ruled on – using arguments which the great theologian St Thomas Aquinas rejected 600 years ago.

1991 Wildlife investigators have uncovered an illegal scheme to sell 15,000 elephant tusks worth £6 million ($11 million) to ivory dealers in defiance of the international trade ban on ivory. The 83 tons of poached tusks, the world's largest ivory stockpile, have been bought from the government of Burundi by two South African businessmen. They plan to fly the ivory out of Burundi and sell it in secret in the Far East. Four-fifths of Africa's elephants have been slaughtered for their tusks in the past 10 years.

JOHN LENNON SHOT DEAD

1980 Forty-year-old ex-Beatle John Lennon was murdered in New York tonight. Lennon and his wife Yoko Ono were walking into their apartment building when a man approached and shot Lennon five times. Lennon was rushed to hospital, but did not recover. Police said the killer, Mark Chapman, 25, had shadowed Lennon since arriving from Hawaii three days ago. Earlier today he asked Lennon for his autograph, and Lennon obliged. Chapman was calm after the shooting, and offered no explanation.

Explorer of dreams dies

1859 Thomas de Quincey, opium addict, essayist and master of English prose, has died in Scotland after a difficult but fruitful life. He was 74. De Quincey ran away from his boarding school at 17 and was living as a beggar in London when his family rescued him. He was sent to Oxford, but left before graduating. Plagued by facial neuralgia, he began taking opium to sooth the pain, and became addicted to it for life. He had constant financial problems, and wrote essays for periodicals to pay his debts. He wrote biographies of his friends, the poets William Wordsworth and Samuel Coleridge, literary criticism, history, essays on economics and fiction. But it was his autobiography that won him acclaim: *Confessions of an English Opium-Eater* appeared in two parts in the *London Magazine* in 1821. He had planned it as a journal of his addiction, but it became a pioneering exploration of dreams and their nature. He never completed its sequel.

> *Not in vain is Ireland pouring itself all over the earth . . . The Irish, with their glowing hearts and reverent credulity, are needed in this cold age of intellect and scepticism.*
> **Lydia M. Child**, US anti-slavery campaigner, 1842.

Superpowers agree to destroy missiles

1987 The US and the USSR have agreed to dismantle all 2611 medium- and short-range nuclear missiles based in Europe – the first agreement to cut the nuclear arsenals. President Ronald Reagan and General Secretary Mikhail Gorbachev signed the Intermediate-Range Nuclear Forces (INF) treaty in Washington today at the end of what was clearly a cordial summit meeting. The treaty provides for full on-site verification. It must be ratified by the US Senate before it becomes effective.

Argentina's generals jailed

1985 Jorge Videla, former military president of Argentina, was jailed for life today in Buenos Aires for human rights abuses during the murderous seven-year rule of the right-wing military junta. Videla mounted a campaign to eradicate terrorism, and thousands of left-wingers and others simply disappeared. Some were shot outright, others imprisoned and tortured first. The fate of many of the victims may never be known. Videla was commander-in-chief when the generals overthrew Isabel Peròn's ailing government in 1976, and he became president. He was succeeded in 1981 by Roberto Viola. Viola was sentenced to 17 years' imprisonment today. Several other military leaders were also jailed. Viola's successor, General Leopoldo Galtieri, is being tried separately, for negligence in the Falklands War with Britain in 1982. Civilian rule returned in 1983 when Raul Alfonsin won the presidency.

We know what happens to people who stay in the middle of the road. They get run over.
Aneurin Bevan, British Labour politician, 1953.

Walesa is Poland's president

1990 The Solidarity trade union founder and leader Lech Walesa was elected president of Poland today in the country's first ever direct presidential elections. Ten years ago Walesa led Solidarity in a workers' confrontation with the communist regime. Initial concessions were followed by a severe crackdown, and Walesa was jailed for nine months. In 1983 he was awarded the Nobel Peace Prize. Again in 1988, Walesa led a wave of strikes which forced the regime to negotiate. Elections followed in June 1989, and Solidarity candidates won easily. August Mazowiecki became PM. Early this year the Communist Party was finally dissolved, and in May Solidarity candidates won majorities in the first local council elections. Walesa has played a major role throughout. But as president he will not have it all his own way: with the communists gone, divisions are appearing in the Solidarity movement as a democratic opposition begins to emerge.

Millions missing from Maxwell pensions

1991 At least £420 million ($773 million) is missing from pension funds controlled by billionaire Robert Maxwell. Maxwell died at sea a month ago, apparently after falling naked from the deck of his luxury yacht in the middle of the night. Sensational revelations have followed as the Maxwell empire collapsed amid massive debts and evidence of shady deals to

prop up share prices. Maxwell's younger son Kevin is tonight fighting a court order stopping him and his brother Ian leaving Britain. This follows evidence that money continued to flood out of the Mirror Newspaper Group pension fund even after Maxwell's death. The court order also freezes Kevin Maxwell's assets worldwide.

Dame Edith Sitwell dies

1964 The English poet Dame Edith Sitwell died today, aged 77. With her brothers Osbert and Sacheverell, also poets, Edith Sitwell led the 1920s avant-garde – though both she and her work was often derided. Her "Façade", written to music by William Walton, drew titters and mockery from the audience at its premiere – with Sitwell intoning the lines through a megaphone from behind a curtain. It was later parodied on stage by Noel Coward. Sitwell eventually fled to France. "I am like an unpopular electric eel in a pond full of flatfish," she said. Today her work is much appreciated.

1978 A better picture of the planet Venus emerged today after two US Pioneer spacecraft launched earlier this year reached it. Pioneer Venus 1 went into orbit round the planet four days ago, probing the atmosphere and the surface with radar. Pioneer Venus 2 had meanwhile launched four probes which descended into Venus's atmosphere today. One of the probes survived the landing and transmitted data from the surface for an hour. The orbiter has mapped mountains higher than Everest, and the solar system's biggest canyon.

VAN DYCK DIES AT 42

1641 The Flemish painter Sir Anthony van Dyck has died in London, where he settled nine years ago. He was only 42. Van Dyck opened his own studio in Antwerp at 16 and was a master of the artist's guild at 18. He worked with Peter Paul Rubens and was much influenced by him; he also studied in Italy. He won fame after England's King Charles I knighted him and appointed him chief court painter in 1632. Van Dyck painted perfect portraits of England's nobility. But there is more to his paintings than flattery: he has revolutionized English portraiture.

DECEMBER 9

1783 Newgate Prison in London sees its first executions.

1814 Death of Joseph Brahmah, English inventor of the beer pump.

1902 British and German warships seize the Venezuelan navy in an attempt to force the repayment of losses incurred during a coup in 1899.

1910 The Turks suppress an Arab uprising in Palestine.

1917 The British capture Jerusalem from the Turks.

1945 In Frankfurt, General Patton suffers chest injuries in a road accident and is paralysed from the neck down.

1955 Sugar Ray Robinson regains the world middleweight boxing crown by knocking out Carl Olson.

1967 Nicholae Ceausescu becomes president of Romania.

1971 Three hundred children die when Indian planes bomb an orphanage in Dacca, East Pakistan.

1992 Prime Minister John Major announces to a hushed House of Commons that the Prince and Princess of Wales will separate.

BIRTHDAYS

John Milton 1608, English poet whose greatest works were *Paradise Lost*, *Paradise Regained* and *Samson Agonistes*.

Clarence Birdseye 1886, American pioneer of deep-frozen food.

Elisabeth Schwarzkopf 1915, German operatic soprano particularly noted for her interpretations of Mozart and Richard Strauss.

Douglas Fairbanks Jr 1909, American actor whose films include *The Prisoner of Zenda*, *Catherine the Great* and *Sinbad the Sailor*.

Kirk Douglas 1918, American actor who specialized in tough, dramatic roles as typified by *Lust for Life*, *Paths of Glory* and *Spartacus*.

Bob Hawke 1929, Australian politician, Labour prime minister 1983-91.

1902 In Egypt, the 1¼ mile (2 km) long, 130 foot (39 m) high Aswan Dam on the Nile is completed after four years of work.

1910 Puccini's opera *La fanciulla del West* is premiered in New York with Toscanini conducting.

1963 A state of emergency is declared in the South Arabian Federation after a grenade is thrown at a group of government ministers and British diplomats at Aden airport.

1978 Millions of Iranians demonstrate in the streets to demand the abdication of the Shah and an end to the month-old military government.

1984 In Oslo, Desmond Tutu, Anglican Bishop of Johannesburg, has to wait an extra 20 minutes to receive his Nobel Peace Prize when the ceremony is interrupted by a bomb threat.

1989 In Czechoslovakia, president Gustav Husak swears in the first majority non-communist government since 1948 and immediately resigns his post.

1990 In the Serbian republic in Yugoslavia the Communist Party win a free election.

1990 Australia's oldest newspaper empire, the Fairfax Group, goes into the hands of the receivers with debts of A$1500 million (£660/$1222 million).

BIRTHDAYS

César Franck 1822, Belgian composer who developed a "cyclic form" – the use of the same theme in more than one movement of a work.

Emily Dickinson 1830, American poet who wrote over 1700 poems, only seven of which were published in her lifetime.

Olivier Messiaen 1908, French composer and organist whose works include the symphony *La Turangalîla* and the opera *St Francis d'Assise*.

Dorothy Lamour 1914, American actress best-known for the "Road" films she made with Bob Hope and Bing Crosby.

Peace prize for Mother Teresa

1979 Calcutta's Mother Teresa has been awarded this year's Nobel Peace Prize for her ceaseless work helping the destitute. Born in Albania in 1910, she joined a convent at 18 and taught in her order's school in Calcutta. In 1946 she heard "a call within a call" to help the desperately poor people around her, and was given permission to leave the convent. She found people dying in the streets and took them into a home to die in dignity, rescued orphans and cared for them. Other women joined her, and in 1950 she formed the Missionaries of Charity, dedicated to the destitute. Today they run 700 shelters and clinics. Calcutta is the world's most crowded place, with millions living in grinding poverty. The "living saint" and her sisters in Christ are often their only hope of survival.

England's young say "no" to marriage

1991 Weddings have never been less fashionable. The marriage rate in England is less than half that of 20 years ago, according to government figures released today. Nearly one in three couples in their twenties are living together. At least one in 10 marriages now ends in divorce within five years. The divorce rate is growing at record speed, and only a quarter as many divorcees remarry as 20 years ago. The rate of births outside marriage has almost tripled in 10 years, with more than 200,000 babies born to unmarried parents in England and Wales last year. The abortion rate is also soaring.

Master of the universe

1921 Albert Einstein today received the Nobel Physics Prize in Stockholm. The gentle Jewish genius of Berlin is world famous, though he has never sought fame. In the public eye he is a hero of science, the pure thinker whose piercing vision reaches beyond time and space to peel away the mysteries of the universe. Time and space are not absolutes, Einstein said, they are relative to each other. Nothing is fixed, and nothing is straight, since gravity bends space-time. The only constant is the speed of light, and even light bends: if a ray of starlight grazes the Sun's surface, the pull of the Sun's gravity will bend it by slightly less than one two-thousandths of a degree, Einstein predicted. Two years ago scientists put this theory to the test during the solar eclipse – and found bent starbeams. Einstein's theory of general relativity had triumphed.

WYOMING GIVES WOMEN THE VOTE

1869 With the campaign for women's suffrage gaining ground on both sides of the Atlantic, Wyoming today became first American territory to grant the vote to women. American feminists founded a women's rights movement 14 years ago, but earlier this year the movement split over endorsing the 15th Amendment, which gives the vote to blacks, but not to women. There are few women in Wyoming, which only became a territory last year. It is frontier country, just emerging from five years of Indian wars against the Sioux. However, the Wyoming stretch of the new Union Pacific Railroad has just been completed, and small towns are springing up along the line in the south.

> *We must use time as a tool, not as a couch.*
> **John F. Kennedy**, 1961.

First Nobel Prizes awarded

1901 The man who invented the most powerful explosives the world has ever seen hoped that they would put an end to war. "On the day two army corps can annihilate each other in one second all civilized nations will recoil from war in horror," the Swedish chemist Alfred Nobel wrote to the Peace Congress in 1892. It was dynamite that Nobel invented, and he made a fortune from his explosives factories. When he died in 1896, he left most of that fortune to a foundation to award annual prizes "to those who, in the preceding year, shall have conferred the greatest benefit upon mankind". The first Nobel Prizes, worth $30,000 (£16,300) each, were awarded in Oslo and Stockholm today, the fifth anniversary of Alfred Nobel's death, for literature, chemistry, physics, medicine and peace. The first-ever Peace Prize was shared by Jean Henri Dunant, founder of the Red Cross, and Frederic Passy, founder of the French Society of the Friends of Peace.

The riddle of the horse

1877 Englishman Eadweard Muybridge, photographer of the American West, has used his camera to solve an ancient riddle – and won a five-year-old bet for a millionaire. The Governor of California, rail magnate Leland Stanford, bet a friend that a running horse's feet are all off the ground simultaneously once every stride. Stanford commissioned Muybridge to settle the matter, and today Muybridge presented an astonishing series of "frozen-frame" photographs of a galloping racehorse – and proved Stanford right. Muybridge made the photographs by running wires across a racetrack, each connected to a camera. The horse tripped the camera shutters as it raced past. Muybridge's work was interrupted while he went on trial for murdering his wife's lover – hence it took him five years. Now acquitted, he is using the technique to study dancers and runners in motion.

1688 King James II of England flees the country.

1769 Venetian blinds are patented in London by Edward Beran.

1894 The first motor show opens in Paris with nine exhibitors.

1909 A 2147 mile (3455 km) section of the Cape-to-Cairo railway is linked up at the Sudan-Congo border.

1914 In the Battle of the Falklands, all British ships survive while four German cruisers are sunk.

1922 At London's Old Bailey, Edith Thompson is found jointly guilty with her lover, Frederick Bywaters, of murdering her husband and sentenced to death.

1963 In Los Angeles, Frank Sinatra Jr is set free after his father pays kidnappers $240,000 (£129,729).

1965 Death of American journalist and broadcaster Ed Roscoe Murrow.

1987 At Christie's auction house in London, Charlie Chaplin's cane and bowler sell for £82,500 ($152,625) and his boots for £38,500 ($71,225).

1990 The British government announces it will award £42 million ($77.7 million) to British haemophiliacs who became infected with the HIV virus after being treated with contaminated Factor VIII.

King renounces throne for love

1936 Britain's King Edward VIII has abdicated, less than a year after his accession to the throne. The king ended months of rumour and controversy tonight in a radio broadcast to the nation from Windsor Castle. "I have found it impossible to carry the heavy burden of responsibility and to discharge my duties as king as I would wish to do without the help and support of the woman I love," he said. After the broadcast he boarded a Royal Navy destroyer in Portsmouth, taking him to exile in France to join the twice-divorced Mrs Wallis Simpson. Edward's younger brother has now become King George VI. Edward and Mrs Simpson first met in 1931 but their love affair did not begin until 1934, since when they have been inseparable. His resolve to marry her could not be shaken even by the combined forces of the royal family, the cabinet and the church. Prime minister Stanley Baldwin finally told the king to choose between his throne and Mrs Simpson. He chose Mrs Simpson.

Things are being done in Ireland which would disgrace the blackest annals of the lowest despotism in Europe.
Herbert Asquith, former prime minister of Britain, 1920.

BIRTHDAYS

Elliott Carter 1908, American composer whose works include the *Double Concerto* and *Symphony for Three Orchestras*.

Alexander Solzhenitsyn 1928, Russian writer best-known for *The Gulag Archipelago*.

Jean-Louis Trintignant 1930, French actor whose films include *A Man and a Woman* and *My Night with Maud*.

Rita Moreno 1931, Puerto Rican actress whose career in films and television and on Broadway encompassed an Oscar-winning performance in *West Side Story*.

MARTIAL LAW IN IRELAND

1920 Britain today declared martial law in large parts of Ireland in a bid to contain the Irish Republican Army's rebellion. Britain has over 40,000 soldiers in Ireland, and 7000 of the hated Black and Tans (ex-soldiers serving as police), whose brutality has been much criticized in England. Their "retaliations" in search of IRA gunmen has left whole villages ablaze. The IRA's hit-and-run tactics have tied the British forces in knots. The British brought in mainland experts to improve army intelligence, and two Sundays ago, in a series of dawn raids, the IRA killed 14 of the experts in their beds. By nightfall 14 Irishmen were dead at the hands of the Black and Tans. Tonight, towns are ablaze in the wake of a massive army clampdown.

Rushdie calls for paperback of *Satanic Verses*

1991 Salman Rushdie, the British writer who is under an Islamic death sentence for blasphemy, invited renewed wrath tonight. Rushdie is in New York on his first trip abroad since he went into hiding in 1989. Tonight, under tight security, he addressed a dinner at Columbia University to mark the 200th anniversary of the First Amendment, which guarantees freedom of speech. He said his book *The Satanic Verses* must be "freely available and easily affordable", and called for its publication as a paperback. Angry Muslim spokesmen later said Rushdie had again put his life in serious danger. A year ago Rushdie recanted, proclaimed his belief in Islam and promised not to publish the book in paperback. Iran, however, responded by renewing the death sentence and doubling the reward for his murder to $2 million (£1 million).

1952 Two British teenagers were found guilty today of murdering a London policeman. Derek Bentley, 19, was sentenced to death – although it was his accomplice, Christopher Craig, who fired the fatal shots. The judge described Craig as a highly dangerous criminal, but at only 16 he is too young to hang. The policeman was killed on the roof of a warehouse after a bungled burglary.

DECEMBER 12

1889 Death of Robert Browning, English poet who wrote "The Last Duchess".

1900 In London, the War Office announces that more than 11,000 British troops have so far lost their lives in the Boer War, over two-thirds of that number falling prey to disease.

1906 In South Africa, the Transvaal is given autonomy with white male suffrage.

1907 Dinizulu, King of the Zulus, surrenders with several hundred of his followers to the commandant of the Natal forces, Colonel Sir Duncan Mackenzie.

1907 In New York, a rule is introduced forcing women to sign affidavits attesting to their age and good character before they marry.

1911 King George V is crowned Emperor of India and founds New Delhi as the new capital to replace Calcutta.

1988 In Britain, rock star Elton John is awarded damages of £1 million ($1.85 million) against the *Sun* newspaper for its libellous allegations about his private life.

1990 US president George Bush agrees to send a $1000 million (£540 million) food aid package to the Soviet Union.

BIRTHDAYS

Carl Maria von Weber 1786, German composer who wrote the first opera in the German Romantic tradition – *Der Freischütz*.

Gustave Flaubert 1821, French novelist whose first book, *Madame Bovary*, aroused accusations of immorality.

Edvard Munch 1863, Norwegian painter and printmaker whose symbolic paintings reflect his profound pessimism.

Edward G. Robinson 1893, American actor who was a menacing heavy in films such as *Little Caesar* and *Key Largo*.

Frank Sinatra 1915, American popular singer par excellence.

Emmerson Fittipaldi 1946, Brazilian motor-racing champion.

Marconi sends radio signal across Atlantic

1901 The Italian inventor Guglielmo Marconi has sent a wireless signal across the Atlantic Ocean with his radio wave apparatus. The signal was sent via a 160-ft (52 m) aerial in Cornwall, and Marconi received it almost instantly in St John's, Newfoundland, using an even higher aerial kept aloft by a kite. The feat is being applauded on both sides of the Atlantic: instant long-distance communication without the need for telegraph wires has huge potential.

Russia votes to scrap USSR

1991 The Russian parliament today voted overwhelmingly in favour of replacing the Soviet Union with a loose Commonwealth of Independent States. Russia immediately withdrew its MPs from the Kremlin in a boycott supported by Ukrainian and Byelorussian MPs. This left the Soviet parliament without a quorum, and it adjourned. Soviet general secretary Mikhail Gorbachev is left with his job, but no apparent function. Russia, the Ukraine and Byelorussia reached agreement on the Commonwealth plan last week, and Russian president Boris Yeltsin, architect of the plan, is due to meet the five Muslim Central Asian leaders this weekend. There are already rifts in the new Commonwealth before it has been born, with new demands from the Byelorussian opposition, and radical Ukrainian amendments to the text of the agreement. However, the Soviet Union has no option left but a transfer of power.

ANTI-CRUISE WOMEN LINK HANDS ROUND AIRBASE

1982 More than 20,000 British women today linked hands around Greenham Common airbase in Berkshire in an all-women protest against plans to site US nuclear cruise missiles there next year. The women started camping around the base four months ago and are proving a strong force. Moves to evict them have been unsuccessful, and although several have been jailed, it has not deterred them. The women's plan is to blockade the airbase tomorrow, confronting US airmen as they arrive for work.

1955 British electronic engineer Christopher Cockerell today patented a new kind of vehicle, half-ship and half-aircraft. His "hovercraft" floats on a cushion of air produced by fans, and is pushed forward by air propellers.

Billionairess fined $7 million

1989 New York billionairess Leona Helmsley was today fined $7 million (£3.8 million) and sentenced to four years in prison for tax evasion. Owner of the luxury Helmsley Palace hotel, she was convicted in August of evading tax of more than $1 million (£540,540). "Only little people pay taxes," she was quoted as saying. The "little people" are no doubt applauding the sentence.

1913 Leonardo da Vinci's famous *Mona Lisa*, stolen from the Louvre in Paris two years ago, has been recovered. It was found today hidden under a bed in a small hotel in Florence. Four men have been arrested. Police were tipped off by a Florentine art dealer who received a note from one of the thieves, an Italian house-painter named Vincenzo Peruggia. He stole the painting because he was incensed by French chauvinism.

Voyager circles Earth without refuelling

1986 The super-light experimental aircraft Voyager touched down today to complete its extraordinary non-stop flight round the world without refuelling. It took nine days, and pilots Richard Rutan and Jeana Yeager broke the endurance record as well as the distance record. Voyager's hollow plastic body holds four tons of fuel. She has a truly original design, with two engines, propellers fore and aft, very long wings and huge double fins, on a strange three-pod body quite unlike that of former spacecraft. Modern superstrong, ultralight materials have opened up new vistas in flying, including a host of do-it-yourself options with advanced designs developed with computer models on PCs.

I called the New World into existence to redress the balance of the Old.
George Canning, British foreign minister, on his defence of Latin American independence, 1826.

"We got him"

2003 Ousted Iraqi President Saddam Hussein is in custody following capture by US forces. "Ladies and gentlemen, we got him," US administrator Paul Bremer told journalists today. Saddam Hussein was found in a tiny cellar at a farmhouse about 15km (10 miles) south of his hometown Tikrit. British Prime Minister Tony Blair has welcomed the news, saying it "removes the shadow" hanging over Iraq. Saddam was the most wanted man on the list issued by US authorities but had not been seen since Baghdad fell to US forces in April.

GORE CONCEDES ELECTION TO BUSH

2000 Vice-President Al Gore has conceded the US Presidential election to Texas Governor George W. Bush, over a month after votes were cast. Al Gore won only a 0.3% majority over his opponent in the popular vote on November 8, and the electoral college vote rested on the contested results of Florida alone. Early indications suggested that Bush had won Florida. Al Gore phoned Bush to concede the election, but rang back an hour later to retract when it was clear the margin was extremely narrow. After a month of allegations of poll irregularities, manual recounts, inconclusive ballot papers and legal challenges, Gore has conceded, much to the relief of Americans. Out of the 102 million votes cast in the country, the election rested on a margin of just 537 votes cast in Florida.

Lee mauls Burnside's army at Fredericksburg

1862 Confederate general Robert E. Lee has inflicted a bloody defeat on the Union Army of the Potomac. Federal general Ambrose Burnside had just taken over the army from General George B. McClellan and today's futile assault on Lee's lines at Fredericksburg in Virginia was his major action in command. Burnside was planning to sweep Lee aside and push on to Richmond, but his plans went horribly wrong. Lee had taken up a heavily fortified position on the ridge at Marye's Heights. Again and again the Federal forces surged up the ridge, to be repulsed each time. Burnside has lost 12,500 men, and Richmond remains in Confederate hands.

Grandma Moses dies at 101

1961 Grandma Moses, the renowned American primitive painter, has died at the age of 101. Self-taught, Anna Robertson Moses only began painting in her 70s. Her bright pictures of American rural life were discovered by a New York art dealer, who exhibited them in his gallery in 1940. The following year one of her paintings, *The Old Oaken Bucket*, won her the New York State Prize, and in 1949 President Truman presented her with the Women's National Press Club award for her achievements in art.

> *If a man had time to study one word only, "wit" would perhaps be the best word he could choose.*
> **C. S. Lewis**, 1960.

Irish bomb kills 12 in London

1867 Irish bombers blew up the outer wall of Clerkenwell prison in London today in a bid to rescue a jailed comrade. The blast demolished the wall, as well as several nearby houses, killing 12 people and injuring more than 100. But the bombers failed to rescue the jailed Irishman. No arrests have yet been made. Police said the bombers are members of the Fenians, or Irish Republican Brotherhood, founded 10 years ago with the help of Irish Americans to overthrow British rule in Ireland. Last year the American wing of the Brotherhood mounted raids on Canada. The Fenians are in open rebellion in Ireland and have mounted a number of attacks upon British property. They have taken their name from Finn McCool, the third-century Irish folklore hero who led his Fianna warriors against the evil Fomor giants.

US ICE CREAM GOES CONICAL

1903 The ancient Chinese found that if you beat air into fresh cream while freezing it, you get ice cream. Explorer Marco Polo took the secret back to Italy in 1295, and within centuries Italian ice cream was a popular Mediterranean dessert. In America, Baltimore milk dealer Jacob Fussell built an ice cream factory in 1851, and Americans became avid ice-cream eaters. But something was still lacking – until today. New York ice-cream merchant Italo Marcione has patented his new ice-cream cone, the perfect container – easy to hold, no spoon required, and when you've finished the ice cream, you eat the cone. A work of genius.

1294 Pope Celestine V abdicates.

1784 Death of Samuel Johnson, English poet, critic and lexicographer.

1904 Government opponents wreck the interior of the Hungarian parliament building in Budapest.

1904 The first electric train comes into service on London's Metropolitan Railway.

1907 The liner *Mauretania* runs aground at Liverpool.

1909 British explorer Ernest Shackleton is knighted.

1911 The P & O liner *Delhi* founders with the Princess Royal on board but she and most of the other passengers are rescued.

1923 In London, Lord Alfred Douglas, former lover of Oscar Wilde, is sentenced to six months' imprisonment for libelling Winston Churchill.

1967 King Constantine of Greece flees his country after an unsuccessful attempt to topple the Greek military junta.

1988 In Brazzaville, South Africa signs an accord granting independence to Namibia.

1989 In South Africa, ANC leader Nelson Mandela meets President F. W. de Klerk for the first time.

1989 The first Vietnam refugees are repatriated from Hong Hong, escorted to a plane at dawn by police in riot gear.

BIRTHDAYS

Heinrich Heine 1797, German poet and writer.

Sir Laurens van der Post 1906, South African novelist, travel writer and conservationist whose books include *The Lost World of the Kalahari* and *The Hunter and the Whale*.

Dick Van Dyke 1925, American actor and comedian best-known for the television series *The Dick Van Dyke Show* and the film *Mary Poppins*.

Christopher Plummer 1929, British stage and screen actor whose films include *Waterloo*, *The Sound of Music* and *The Fall of the Roman Empire*.

1837 British troops crush rebellion in Canada.

1861 Prince Albert, consort of Queen Victoria, dies of typhoid.

1906 The first German submarine, the U1, enters service.

1907 In St Petersburg, 38 soldiers are sentenced to life imprisonment for surrendering to the Japanese at Port Arthur.

1927 In China, Chiang Kai-shek's Nationalist forces put down an attempted communist coup in Canton.

1959 Death of British artist Sir Stanley Spencer, notable for his paintings of religious subjects transposed to Cookham, the Berkshire village in which he lived.

1962 US *Mariner II* sends back the first close-up photographs of the planet Venus.

1973 Teenager John Paul Getty II is set free by his Italian kidnappers after his oil tycoon grandfather pays a ransom of $750,000 (£405,400) on receiving his ear through the post.

1988 PLO leader Yasser Arafat announces that he renounces all forms of terrorism and accepts Irael's right to exist within secure borders.

1988 Eight million workers in Spain go on strike against government economic policies.

1990 ANC president Oliver Tambo returns home to South Africa after 30 years of exile.

BIRTHDAYS

Nostradamus 1503, French astrologer and physician who, in *Centuries*, made a number of prophecies in rhyming quatrains.

George VI 1895, English monarch who succeeded to the throne when his brother, Edward VIII, abdicated to marry Mrs Simpson.

Lee Remick 1935, American stage and screen actress whose films include *Anatomy of a Murder, A Severed Head* and *The Days of Wine and Roses*.

Stan Smith 1946, American tennis player who won the men's singles title at Wimbledon in 1972.

PLANCK FINDS BUNDLES OF ENERGY

1900 The German physicist Max Planck today unveiled a completely new theory of energy. Up to now science has assumed that energy flows in a continuous stream. Planck's theory says energy is not continuous, it exists in tiny, indivisible bundles, or "quanta", almost like the atoms of matter. And it doesn't flow in a stream, nor in waves. What it does do is more like climbing a flight of steps. A "bundle" can only increase its energy level by absorbing exactly enough energy to "jump" to the next step, or quantum. In between the two steps, it simply does not exist. Planck's theory upsets Isaac Newton's orderly world – but it explains anomalies in physics which no other theory can account for.

Industry blocks Europe's CO_2 tax

1991 Industry opposition has indefinitely delayed a proposed tax aimed at cutting European carbon dioxide emissions. Energy and environment ministers were expecting to approve the tax at a meeting in Brussels this week, but officials say it could now be delayed for years. The proposal had already been watered down in the face of industry opposition. The Eurelectric energy lobby called for the tax to be scrapped in favour of voluntary restraints by industry. The tax was to be levied on both fuel use and carbon dioxide emissions, to encourage fuel economy and discourage the use of fossil fuels, which emit large volumes of carbon dioxide. Carbon dioxide is a "greenhouse gas", and rapidly increasing atmospheric levels of the gas are causing global climate change. Scientists are predicting potentially disastrous temperature increases in the not-so-distant future.

> *It becomes no longer a matter of choice, but the moral obligation and bounden duty of every responsible writer to bear witness to the times he lives in.*
> **Cecil Rajendra**, Malaysian poet, in an address to the Asian PEN writers' conference in Manila today, 1981.

Rail union president jailed

1894 American Railway Union president Eugene V. Debs was jailed for six months today for ignoring a court injunction to end the Pullman strike. The strike started on May 11 at the Pullman Palace Car Company plant in Pullman, near Chicago, when the company cut back wages but did not reduce rents for workers in company housing. ARU representatives protested, and when they were fired Debs called for a boycott of all Pullman cars. A violent strike followed, with riots and the burning of railroad cars. Attorney General Richard Olney obtained an injunction to halt the strike on the grounds that the strikers were obstructing the mails, and when this was ignored federal troops arrived in Chicago to enforce it. By July 10 the strike was broken.

America mourns George Washington

1799 George Washington has died at his Mount Vernon estate in Virginia. He was 67. Washington occupied a unique place in America's affections, and the nation is in deep mourning for the "father of his country". He retired two years ago, refusing to accept a third term as president. Washington first came to prominence as a young colonel in the last colonial wars of the 1750s. He strongly supported independence and in June 1775 Congress was unanimous in selecting him as commander-in-chief of the Continental forces. Washington led America to victory and independence. In May 1787 he led the Virginia delegation to the Constitutional Convention in Philadelphia. He was unanimously elected first president in 1789 when the constitution came into force, and was re-elected in 1792. The skill with which he guided the new republic through its first years laid a firm foundation that will long outlast him.

1911 The Norwegian explorer Roald Amundsen was today the first man to reach the South Pole, having left the British team led by Captain Robert Scott far behind in the race. Amundsen's five-man team used dog sleds, crossing the 2000 miles (3200 km) of treacherous ice without difficulty, while Scott's motorized team has been dogged with trouble. Amundsen planted a Norwegian flag at the Pole and left a sympathetic note for Scott before starting back.

1926 In a puzzle as mystifying as one of her plots, the missing British thriller writer Agatha Christie was found today staying under an assumed name at a hotel in Harrogate, Yorkshire. She disappeared from her home in Surrey on December 3. She told mystified detectives she had no recollection of how she came to be in Yorkshire. Mrs Christie, 36, specializes in murders rather than mere disappearances. She leapt to fame in 1920 with *The Mysterious Affair at Styles*. Her hero, an eccentric Belgian detective named Hercule Poirot, has been hailed as the best fictional sleuth since Sherlock Holmes.

US Bill of Rights ratified by states

1791 The Virginia state legislature today ratified the Bill of Rights, the 10th state to do so, and the Bill's 10 amendments became part of the United States Constitution. President Washington accepted the new Constitution in September 1787, but its lack of a bill of rights caused wide dissatisfaction. By popular demand, the state conventions called to ratify the Constitution proposed amendments to cover individual rights. James Madison led the movement in Congress to adopt the proposals and drafted 12 amendments to the Constitution. In 1789 Congress voted to submit Madison's amendments to the states. Two were defeated, and the remaining 10 are now enshrined in law. Unlike the Declaration of the Rights of Man and of the Citizen adopted in France in 1789, the US Bill of Rights provides specific protection for the basic rights of the individual to free expression and association, privacy and justice.

700,000 dead at Verdun

1916 The nine-month Battle of Verdun is finally over, at appalling cost and with little gain. The lines are more or less where they were in February – and more than 700,000 soldiers are dead. Meanwhile the Somme offensive has ended in a deadlock, again with little gained. It has cost the British 420,000 men, the French 195,000 and the Germans 600,000.

1961 Nazi mass murderer Adolf Eichmann showed no emotion when a Jerusalem court today sentenced him to be hanged. Eichmann was found guilty of murdering millions of Jews in the Nazi death camps. After the war he escaped to Argentina, where the Jewish Nazi hunter Simon Wiesenthal tracked him down. Last May the Israeli secret service kidnapped him and brought him to Israel to face trial.

South African army funded Inkatha

1991 South African president F. W. de Klerk's government was under renewed pressure today following further disclosures in the "Inkathagate" scandal over covert government support for Zulu chief Gatsha Buthelezi's Inkatha movement, the arch-enemy of Nelson Mandela's African National Congress. Police admitted funding a Buthelezi rally long after De Klerk had said the support had ended. Evidence also emerged that military intelligence poured millions into Inkatha – and sent Inkatha warriors to Israel for training.

1890 Chief Sitting Bull of the Sioux Indians has been shot dead. Sitting Bull fled to Canada after his victory over General Custer at Little Bighorn in 1876. He was jailed for two years on his return five years later. For several years he performed with Buffalo Bill's travelling Wild West Show, but his people's hunger and suffering drove him to join the new Ghost Dance cult, dedicated to destroying the whites and restoring the Indians' vanished world. The government sent troops to arrest the Sioux leaders and suppress the cult, and Sitting Bull was shot in the skirmish that followed. He was 69.

> *Our country is the world – our countrymen are all mankind.*
> **William Lloyd Garrison**, US abolitionist, 1837.

Walt Disney dies

1966 Walt Disney has died at the age of 65. Disney's Mickey Mouse is possibly the most famous character in the world, fictional or living. Mickey first appeared in 1928 in *Steamboat Willie*, the first sound cartoon film, and he was soon joined by Donald Duck and the rest of the Disney stable. In 1938 another world first, the feature-length *Snow White and the Seven Dwarfs*, was a phenomenal success. Disney also made live films such as *Treasure Island*, and beautifully photographed full-length nature films like *The Living Desert*, winning 30 Oscars for his film work. He expanded beyond his film studios with the giant amusement parks, Disneyland and Walt Disney World. Disney's brand of sentimental nostalgia has often been criticized – but the world loves him for it.

1683 Death of Izaak Walton, best known for his treatise on fishing, *The Compleat Angler*.

1840 Napoleon's body is interred at Les Invalides in Paris.

1904 In London, British statesman Joseph Chamberlain calls for curbs on immigrants from Europe, claiming they are responsible for crime and disease.

1913 The world's biggest battle-cruiser, HMS *Tiger*, is launched in Glasgow.

1918 Portuguese president Sidonio Paes is assassinated.

1920 Austria and China are admitted to the League of Nations.

1927 In China, the Nationalist government orders the closure of the Soviet consulate in Shanghai and begins rounding up communists following the attempted communist coup in Canton the day before.

1943 Death of Fats Waller, jazz pianist and composer.

1962 Death of Charles Laughton, British actor whose most notable films are *Mutiny on the Bounty* and *The Hunckback of Notre Dame*.

1989 In Colombia, police kill Gonzalo Gacha, one of the leaders of the Medellin cocaine cartel.

1989 In Bulgaria, 50,000 demonstrators lay siege to the parliament building in Sofia to demand the end of communist rule.

1991 A ferry sinks in the Red Sea, drowning 476 people, mainly Egyptians returning from pilgrimage or work in Saudi Arabia.

BIRTHDAYS

George Romney 1734, English portrait painter best-known for his studies of Lady Emma Hamilton.

Alexandre-Gustave Eiffel 1832, French engineer who built the Eiffel Tower in Paris.

Jean Paul Getty 1892, American oil billionaire and founder of the J. Paul Getty Art Museum in Malibu, California.

Alan Freed 1922, American disc jockey who first coined the phrase "rock 'n' roll".

1809 Napoleon divorces his beloved wife, Joséphine Beauharnais, because she is not able to provide him with an heir.

1850 The first immigrant ship, the *Charlotte Jane*, arrives in New Zealand.

1900 France and Italy agree to respect each other's rights in North Africa.

1902 An earthquake in Turkestan, Central Asia, kills 4000.

1909 US marines force the resignation of President Jose Zelaya of Nicaragua.

1921 French composer, pianist and organist Camille Saint-Saëns dies aged 86.

1922 Polish president Gabriel Narutowicz is assassinated after only two days in office.

1965 British novelist and playwright William Somerset Maugham dies in Nice at the age of 91.

1990 Forty-five-year-old pop singer Rod Stewart marries a 22-year-old model, Rachel Hunter.

1991 Cigarettes manufactured by the American multinational Philip Morris become illegal in Italy as the government attempts to crack down on a cigarette smuggling industry that nets the mafia and the Camorro about $2 billion (£1.1 billion) annually.

1991 In London, the new director-general of the security service MI5 is officially named for the first time – and the name is Stella Rimington, who becomes the first-ever female boss of the agency.

BIRTHDAYS

Jane Austen 1775, English novelist whose major works include *Emma*, *Pride and Prejudice* and *Sense and Sensibility*.

Sir Noël Coward 1889, English playwright, composer and actor whose best-known plays include *Hay Fever* and *Blithe Spirit*.

Liv Ullman 1939, Norwegian actress who has appeared most notably in Ingmar Bergman films such as *Cries and Whispers* and *Autumn Sonata*.

OPERATION DESERT FOX

1998 American and British forces have launched air-strikes against Iraqi military installations. The action, code-named Operation Desert Fox, comes after the Iraqi authorities suspended co-operation with UN weapons inspectors. Detractors are criticising the action as it has not been sanctioned by the UN. The air-strikes have provoked a storm of reaction in the Arabic-language and Middle East press, ranging from outright condemnation of the US and UK in many regional dailies to the analytical approach of the London-based Arabic press.

1944 American bandleader Glenn Miller is presumed dead after his flight went missing over the English Channel today. Miller was flying to join his band in France for a series of concerts for troops. His Christmas Day radio concert will be broadcast as scheduled.

Currie resigns with egg on her face

1988 Edwina Currie, Britain's outspoken Junior Health Minister, has been forced to resign in the wake of her statement two weeks ago that most British eggs are infected with Salmonella. The statement brought furious protests from farmers. Sales of eggs plummeted, and egg-producers are demanding compensation. However, eggs have played a leading role in an unprecedented series of food poisoning scares this year. Organic farming organisations say there is no way of keeping chickens healthy in the overcrowded conditions of a modern battery farm.

It was not the non-whites' freedom that drove us to such lengths, as their being placed on an equal footing with Christians, contrary to the laws of God.
Anna Steenkamp, Boer farmer's wife, writing about the Great Trek in her diary, 1836.

Tea party in Boston

1773 Whooping and brandishing axes, a band of intrepid colonists thinly disguised as Indians boarded three ships in Boston harbour tonight and emptied 342 chests of tea worth £9000 ($16,500) into the sea. This latest protest against the Tea Tax is a deliberate challenge to Crown authority, and a tough response is expected from London. In 1765 Britain's Stamp Act imposed new taxes on the colonies to help pay for the costs of the Seven Years' War. The taxes met with protests, boycotts and violent rejection, and the Act was repealed – to be replaced by the Townshend Acts' new taxes on tea, lead, glass, paper and paint. Protests swelled to a rejection of all forms of taxation, and angry colonists started to form defence associations. In 1770 the Townshend Acts were repealed, except for the Tea Tax, which was renewed this year to rescue the East India Company from bankruptcy.

Cromwell made Lord Protector

1653 Oliver Cromwell was today made Lord Protector of England, giving him the powers of an uncrowned king. The great Civil War general intends to rule in the old constitutional way, through the parliament – if he can find one that doesn't try to thwart him. Cromwell lost patience with the last parliament in April. "Get you gone," he roared at the members, "and give way to honester men!" He stamped on the floor, and hundreds of musketeers poured into the House. "Take away that bauble!" Cromwell told them, pointing to the mace. The soldiers did so, and cleared the hall. Cromwell locked the door as he left, and kept the key. An Assembly of 140 Cromwell supporters took Parliament's place, but four days ago it dissolved itself, resigning its power into the hands of Cromwell.

South Africa unveils national shrine

1949 A quarter of a million white Afrikaners attended the opening of an imposing memorial to South Africa's Boer pioneers in Pretoria today. The Voortrekker Monument is more than a memorial: it is a shrine. Today, December 16, is a religious holiday in South Africa. On December 9, 1838, Boer commander Andries Pretorius and his 460 men vowed to observe an annual day of thanksgiving if God granted them victory over the Zulus. Seven days later they met 10,000 Zulu warriors in battle. Afterwards, 3000 Zulus lay dead, with only two Boers injured. Pretorius thanked God, and kept his promise. In 1864 the Boer Transvaal Republic proclaimed December 16 a religious holiday. In 1877 Britain annexed the Transvaal, and on December 9, 1880, the anniversary of the vow, 9000 armed Boers vowed to fight for their freedom – and won it when 75 Boers routed 700 British soldiers at Majuba, with only one Boer killed. Again, they thanked God. Divine protection did not help them in the Boer War, but this did not dim their fervour. The foundation stone of the Voortrekker Monument was laid on December 16, 1938. Last year the right-wing Afrikaner National Party won the South African elections, and today the Boers thanked God for it.

WRIGHT BROTHERS MAKE FIRST POWERED FLIGHT

1903 In spite of an underwhelming audience of five people, the Wright brothers made aviation history today when their aircraft managed the first powered flight. Flyer I, or Kitty Hawk as it is more commonly called, made four flights in all, the longest lasting almost a minute, achieving 850 ft (276 m) of distance and an altitude of several feet. Orville and Wilbur Wright have been interested in aviation since 1896, when they learned of the European interest in sustained flight. While running a bicycle building shop, they have studied aviation and built kites and gliders to learn the essentials of aircraft control before attempting powered flight. They made 900 successful glider flights in 1902 in North Carolina while they solved the problems of getting an engine light enough and powerful enough to lift a plane off the ground. In the end, the brothers built their own 12-16 hp engine and propeller as well as the body of the aircraft. Kitty Hawk weighs only 605 lb (300 kg) and is launched off a trolley rolling along a greased 60 ft (19.5 m) launching track.

The airplane stays up because it doesn't have the time to fall.
Orville Wright explains, after making the world's first powered flight, 1903.

Brazil chooses new president in free elections

1989 In the first free elections for 29 years, Brazilians have chosen Ferdinand Collor de Mello as president defeating Jose Sarney. The new president will be faced with enormous problems, not least of which is the servicing of massive foreign debt. Interest payments on loans use up 40 per cent of the country's export income. Although Brazil has experienced rapid development, the repayments look set to destroy the economy. The International Monetary Fund has forced the government to impose austerity measures to try to guarantee that the loans will be repaid. Consequently prices have risen, wages have been cut and the annual inflation rate is around 700 per cent. It was the 80s economic decline that inc-reased demands for democracy.

Children . . . have no use for psychology. They detest sociology. They still believe in God, the family, angels, devils, witches, goblins, logic, clarity, punctuation, and other such obsolete stuff . . . When a book is boring, they yawn openly. They don't expect their writer to redeem humanity, but leave to adults such childish illusions.
Isaac Bashevis Singer, writer, on winning the Nobel Prize for Literature, 1978.

1830 Death of Simón Bolívar, South American revolutionary who gained the name "the Liberator" by expelling the Spanish from Colombia, Ecuador, Peru and Venezuela.

1907 Death of British physicist William Thomson, 1st Baron Kelvin, after whom the Kelvin scale of temperature is named.

1909 Death of King Leopold II of Belgium.

1939 The German battleship *Admiral Graf Spee* is scuttled in the River Plate off Montevideo, Uruguay by British warships.

1987 In Britain, Davina Durbin becomes the world's first triple heart, lungs and liver transplant patient.

1989 In Romania, as many as 2000 anti-government protesters are massacred in the city of Timisoara.

1990 Radical priest Jean-Bertrand Aristide is elected president of Haiti.

1991 Joseph Robert Smallwood, Canadian politician who led Newfoundland into the Canadian Confederation in 1949 and became its first premier, dies just short of his 91st birthday.

BIRTHDAYS

Sir Humphrey Davy 1778, English chemist who invented the safety lamp for miners and discovered sodium, calcium, barium, magnesium, potassium and strontium by passing electricity through molten metal compounds.

William Lyon Mackenzie King 1874, Canadian politician, Liberal prime minister three times.

Erskine Caldwell 1903, American novelist and journalist best-known for *God's Little Acre* and *Tobacco Road*.

Willard Frank Libby 1908, American chemist who developed radio-carbon dating.

Tommy Steele 1936, British entertainer who began his career as a pop singer before developing into a star of stage and screen musicals such as *Half a Sixpence*.

Britain faces a three-day week

1973 Prime Minister Edward Heath's confrontation with striking miners as part of his campaign to control inflation has provoked a crisis for the economy. Miners have continued their overtime ban and as a result coal supplies to power stations are down by 40 per cent. As of today, industry and commerce will only be allowed five days' electricity in 14 until December 30, then will be allowed three days' worth a week in the New Year. Television will shut down at 10.30 pm throughout the country. The government is cutting £1200 million ($2208 million) from public spending in response to the crisis. The chancellor has also imposed tighter credit controls and tax on developmental gains are up from 30 per cent to 50 per cent. This drive to fight inflation, combined with the tough stance against the strikers just when OPEC oil prices have increased by 70 per cent and production has been cut back, could well require Mr Heath to call a general election.

Australian PM disappears while swimming

1967 The Australian prime minister Harold Holt has disappeared and is presumed to have drowned near his holiday home at Portsea, Victoria, some 30 miles (48 km) from Melbourne. Although Holt, 59, is a strong swimmer and diver, it is understood that he almost drowned under similar circumstances just a few weeks ago. Military and civilian divers and search teams are hunting for him and the search will continue for some time. In the meantime, an interim prime minister will have to be appointed. The son of a teacher, Holt was Minister of Labour from 1940 to 1941, then again from 1949 to 1958 and Federal Treasurer from 1958 to 1966 when he succeeded Sir Robert Gordon Menzies as prime minister.

BIRTHDAYS

Joseph Grimaldi 1779, English clown who created the white-face clown make-up.

Paul Klee 1879, Swiss painter and etcher who was associated with Der Blaue Reiter group which aimed to unite the Expressionist style with symbolic and spiritual elements.

Jules Dassin 1911, American film director who went to Europe during the McCarthy witch-hunts and made films such as *Rififi* and *Never on Sunday*.

Willy Brandt 1913, German statesman, chancellor of West Germany 1969-74.

Betty Grable 1916, American actress, singer and dancer whose famous legs made her a forces' pin-up during World War Two.

Keith Richards 1943, British guitarist with the Rolling Stones.

Steven Spielberg 1947, American film director whose hugely successful films include *Jaws*, *Close Encounters of the Third Kind*, *ET* and *Hook*.

French naturalist and evolutionist dies

1829 Jean Baptiste Pierre Antoine de Monet Lamarck, one of France's best scientists, has died today at the age of 75. His most important work has been the study of evolution. Lamarck felt that acquired characteristics are inherited, that the use of an organ or limb strengthened it, and this strengthening could be passed down by reproduction. In 1774 he became a member of the French Academy and keeper of the royal garden, where he remained for 25 years. He published his *Philosophie zoologique* in 1809.

International project to save Brazilian rainforest

1991 The first international project to help save rainforests was launched today when the World Bank, the European Commission and the Group of Seven leading industrialized nations granted Brazil $250 million (£136 million) for conservation work in the Amazon basin. Of that sum, at least $100 million (£54.5 million) will go to scientific research. The money will also fund the establishment of national parks, tribal reserves, and the creation of new zones for non-destructive use of the rainforest's resources such as rubber tapping and collecting brazil nuts. All such projects must be approved by the World Bank and Brazil itself will have no control over how the money is spent.

Stradivari dies at Cremona

1737 Master violin maker Antonio Stradivari has died at his home in Cremona, after a life spent bringing violin making to perfection. Born in 1644, Stradivari apprenticed to the great Amati but by 1684 had diverged from his mentor and was producing larger violins with deeper coloured varnish, and was experimenting with small details. From 1690 his long models represented a complete innovation with regard to the proportions of the instrument. In the early 1700s Stradivari broadened and improved his model, and began making fine cellos and violas as well. Stradivari created the standards by which violins can be judged and devised the current form of the bridge, also setting the proportions for the today's violin with its shallower body that yields a more powerful and penetrating tone than earlier violins.

1865 More than two years after Lincoln's Emancipation Proclamation theoretically abolished slavery, the dream has become a reality with the 13th Amendment. The earlier proclamation in January of 1863 applied only to areas not under Union control.

I don't mind your being killed, but I object to your being taken prisoner.
Lord Kitchener, British field marshal, answers the Prince of Wales' request to go to the World War One frontline, 1914.

British railways and ports to be nationalized

1946 Clement Attlee's Labour government has won the vote on state ownership and it looks like railways and ports will be the first industries to be nationalized. Despite the prospect of severe economic handicaps, Attlee has committed himself to a vigorous programme of reform. The Bank of England has already been nationalized and coal mines, civil aviation, cable and wireless services, railways, road transport and steel will follow. The British National Health Act came into force in November, providing comprehensive medical care for every member of society. Attlee also has ideas of giving India and Burma their independence.

Hong Kong's fate sealed?

1984 Britain and China have signed an historic agreement today settling the fate of Hong Kong after the 99-year lease expires in 1997. Amid much protest it seems that Britain is to return all of its holdings in return for assurances that Hong Kong's social and economic freedom and capitalist lifestyle will be preserved for at least 50 years after China takes control. Hong Kong is to become a special administrative region within China, with its own laws, currency, budget and tax system. It will retain free port status and the authority to negotiate separate international trade agreements. Whether China will honour these commitments remains uncertain. The Hong Kong community feels that Britain has betrayed its responsibilities. Although the New Territories were secured by Britain on a 99-year lease in 1898, both Hong Kong Island and Kowloon Peninsula were already in Britain's possession, acquired in 1842 and 1860 respectively.

Scurvy claims Danish explorer

1741 Vitus Bering, the Danish explorer in the service of the Russian Tsar, has died of scurvy after being shipwrecked along the Commander Islands off the Alaskan coast. An excellent navigator and explorer, he is credited with having discovered Alaska and the strait between it and Russia. In his first journey of exploration he discovered the strait while exploring a route around Siberia to China. On a second expedition he managed to map much of the Siberian coast. His third and fateful trip this year, using two ships, reached and explored the south-west coast of Alaska and some of the Aleutian Islands before the two ships were separated. The crews of both ships were wracked with scurvy, and after Bering's ship was wrecked he died of the disease.

> *There is a holy, mistaken zeal in politics, as well as religion. By persuading others we convince ourselves.*
> **Junius** (unidentified English writer of letters), 1769.

Kasparov keeps world chess title

1987 Gary Kasparov, the reigning world chess champion from the USSR, retained his crown today in Seville against former champion and fellow countryman Anatoly Karpov. Although the series was tied at 12 games each, Kasparov as challenger wins the title under current international rules. He first took the title from Anatoly Karpov in 1985, becoming the youngest world chess champion ever. Karpov had held the title from 1975 to 1985.

> *For my name and memory, I leave it to men's charitable speeches, and to foreign nations, and the next ages.*
> **Francis Bacon**, English philosopher, in his will, on this day, 1625.

1932 The British Broadcasting Corporation today inaugurated its Empire shortwave broadcasting service to the farflung corners of the globe via its new Daventry transmitter. Now news from home can reach every corner of the British Empire. This new service is the brainchild of director general John Reith who has also developed radio broadcasting throughout the British Isles in the past year.

Gorbachev resigns

1991 Mikhail Gorbachev has resigned as president of the United Soviet Socialist Republics, a country which ceased to exist on December 12. Although he survived the hardline coup last summer, his position became weaker as independence for all the republics looked certain and leaders within the republics took more responsibility upon themselves. His former ally and rival Boris Yeltsin has effectively backed him into a corner, making resignation the only possibility. Whether Gorbachev will continue to have some role is unknown, but the West will view his departure with trepidation and sadness, since Gorbachev is largely the author of the momentous changes which have been taking place throughout the eastern bloc. Both perestroika and glasnost would have been impossible without his bravery and his vision.

1154 Henry II accedes to the throne of England.

1848 Emily Brontë, English author of *Wuthering Heights*, dies of tuberculosis at the age of 30.

1851 Illustrious English artist Joseph Mallord William Turner, renowned for his luminous and atmospheric landscapes in the Romantic tradition, dies at the age of 76.

1900 In France, the National Assembly passes a bill granting an amnesty to all those involved in the Dreyfus Affair.

1905 The first-ever motorized ambulance service for road accident victims is set up in London.

1927 In China, 600 communists are executed by the Nationalists.

1985 Senator Edward Kennedy announces that he will not run in the 1988 presidential campaign.

1988 Violence erupts during the presidential elections in Sri Lanka.

1991 The Australian Labour Party caucus deposes prime minister Bob Hawke after eight years in office and replaces him with his treasurer, Paul Keating.

BIRTHDAYS

Leonid Brezhnev 1906, Soviet statesman and president of the Soviet Union 1977-1982.

Sir Ralph Richardson 1902, British stage and screen actor who excelled equally in Shakespearean and other classic roles and in modern dramas.

Jean Genet 1910, French novelist and dramatist whose autobiographical *A Thief's Journal* recounts his life in prison and among the criminals and prostitutes of various European cities.

Edith Piaf 1915, French chanteuse whose life of lovers, drugs and alcohol was reflected in her haunting and powerful voice.

Gordon Jackson 1923, British actor who appeared in many films, notably *Whisky Galore* and *Tunes of Glory*, but is best-known for the TV series *Upstairs, Downstairs*.

DECEMBER 20

BIRTHDAYS

Sir Robert Menzies 1894, Australian statesman, prime minister as leader of the United Australia Party and then the Liberal Party.

Errol John 1924, Trinidadian dramatist and actor who wrote *Moon on a Rainbow Shawl*.

Jenny Agutter 1952, British actress whose films include *I Start Counting*, *The Railway Children* and *Walkabout*.

Biggest land deal in history settled

1803 The United States and France have concluded the biggest land deal in history today – some 831,321 square miles (2,153,121 sq km) have been bought from France for a mere $15 million (£8.2 million), doubling the size of the United States in the stroke of a pen. The Louisiana Purchase, as it is called, was offered for sale by French foreign Minister Talleyrand in a surprise move. There has been uncertainty regarding the whole region for some time. New Orleans, Louisiana, was transferred from Spain to France three years ago after some French bullying. The Americans, alarmed at the prospect of an ambitious Napoleon on their doorstep, began negotiations to buy New Orleans with very little success. Negotiations had been bogged down until Talleyrand's surprise offer to sell the whole territory to the US. It is understood that US president Thomas Jefferson was prepared to ally himself to his old enemy Great Britain in order to get the French out of the New World, but France's capitulation marks the end of Napoleon's plans for an empire and makes the US one of the largest countries.

A bill of rights is what the people are entitled to against every government on earth, general or particular, and what no just government should refuse to rest on inference.

Thomas Jefferson, US statesman, in a letter, 1787.

NEW DANCING STAR EMERGES

1933 The smash hit film *Flying Down to Rio* looks as though it will make stars of its leading man and lady, Fred Astaire and Ginger Rogers. A former vaudeville song and dance man who teamed up with his sister Adele on stage, Astaire didn't look to have the stuff stars are made of – the verdict of his Hollywood screen test was "can't act, slightly bald, can dance a bit". But Astaire managed to get a part opposite Joan Crawford in *Dancing Ladies*, then was paired with newcomer Ginger Rogers for *Rio* with undeniably fantastic results.

1989 At the end of a year noted for the resurgence of nationalist feeling throughout the Soviet Union, the Lithuanian Communist Party has voted to break away from the Soviet Communist Party. This move by the Lithuanian Communists must be seen as a survival tactic as popular fronts throughout the Baltic States have eclipsed official local communist parties as the driving force in internal affairs. Gorbachev will not tolerate separatism.

Arafat forced to retreat – again

1983 Yasser Arafat, leader of the split and beleaguered Palestinian Liberation Organization, has had to retreat from Lebanon today. Surrounded by the Syrian army and rebel Palestinian guerillas, Arafat and 4000 of his loyal followers have left their last Lebanese stronghold in Tripoli. This evacuation comes at the end of three weeks' fighting in the camps, leaving 700 dead. The UN Security Council arranged the safe passage out of the camps for Arafat and his men, in an attempt to bring the fighting to a finish. Bowed but not defeated, Arafat vows to march to Jerusalem.

Allies retreat from the Dardanelles

1915 The Allies are retreating from the Dardanelles after one of the most costly and ill-managed campaigns of the war. The Gallipoli campaign, under Sir Ian Hamilton, attempted and failed to force the narrows and link up with Russia, costing the lives of 25,000 men with 76,000 wounded, 13,000 missing and 96,000 sick. In the fateful April 25 landing at Gallipoli many thousands of Australian and New Zealand troops were lost. The Turkish strait connects the Sea of Marmara with the Aegean Sea, and its shores are formed by the Gallipoli peninsula to the north-west and the Turkish mainland in Asia to the south-east. From here the Turks with German backing have been able to seal off the Russians in their Dardanelle ports. Now it looks as if this situation will remain as the campaign is abandoned.

Pan American flight crashes at Lockerbie

1988 A Pan American jumbo jet blew up and crashed in the Scottish border town of Lockerbie this evening killing all 259 passengers on board and at least 11 people on the ground, making this the worst air disaster Britain has suffered. En route from London Heathrow to New York, the jumbo disappeared from radar screens at 7.19 pm as it exploded in the air, scattering wreckage over a large area. The wing of the plane came down in a residential part of Lockerbie, destroying six houses and creating a huge crater on impact. The nose of the plane with the dead crew still inside has been found about three miles (5 km) from the town. Dozens of fires have been burning in the town and the RAF has flown medical teams to Lockerbie to assist the emergency services with casualties. American embassies were warned that a Pan Am flight would be targetted. Flight 103 originated in Frankfurt, stopping at London Heathrow before departing for New York. Questions about the efficiency of airport security will again be on the agenda. No group has claimed responsibility for what was probably a bomb – Arab extremists are suspected.

Patton dies after car crash

1945 American general George "Blood and Guts" Patton, has died as a result of a car crash. The sixty-year-old general, famous for his drive and guts, had a glowing military record: during the current war he commanded the First Armoured Corps and in 1941 led the first US troops to fight in North Africa. Patton was given command of the 7th Army in 1943 which swept through Sicily. As head of the 3rd Army, Patton swept across France in 1944, reaching the Czech frontier by this year. He demanded rigorous standards of fitness among his men and exacted high standards of unit training. His death from a car crash seems ironic after surviving a dangerous and active military life.

1790 American industrialist Samuel Slater opened a cotton mill in his native country today, the first of its kind. The mill has 250 spindles which are powered by water and will be operated by a child labour force. Slater was previously apprenticed to a partner of British water frame inventor Richard Arkwright, during which time he learnt his trade.

Jane Fonda marries Ted Turner

1991 Actress Jane Fonda has married media tycoon Ted Turner at a ceremony held at Turner's Capp's Florida ranch. Both are thrice married. Thirty people attended a very private wedding, and Fonda's son Troy gave his mother away. Fifty-four-year-old Jane Fonda has won two Oscars for her roles in *Klute* and *Coming Home* and has made millions selling keep-fit videos and tapes. Ted Turner, who is 53, founded the Atlanta-based Cable News Network in 1980 and has five children.

Mosley presents proposals to cure Depression

1930 The former British Labour government minister, Oswald Mosley, has published a set of policy proposals which he is convinced provide an answer to the country's present economic ills. The wealthy Mosley is regarded with not a little suspicion in those quarters of the Labour Party that remain firmly wedded to the idea of free trade. He is advocating a firmer governmental hand on the economic tiller, to plan foreign trade, direct industry and use public finances to promote expansion. These proposals have already been rejected by Ramsay MacDonald and his Cabinet – whose response to the Depression has been to blame the capitalist system – and are supported by only 17 Labour MPs. Without support, Mosley could decide to found a new political party.

Like being savaged by a dead sheep.
Denis Healey, British Labour politician, refers to an attack by opposition MP Geoffrey Howe on his budget proposals, 1978.

1375 Death of Giovanni Boccaccio, Italian writer and poet who wrote the *Decameron*, a collection of a hundred stories told by people escaping the plague in Florence in 1348.

1846 Anaesthetic is used for the first time in a British hospital when Scottish physician Robert Liston amputates a leg at University College Hospital in London.

1909 American doctor and explorer Frederick Cook is publicly disgraced when his claim to be the first to reach the North Pole is rejected by experts in favour of that of Commander Robert Peary.

1935 Walt Disney's *Snow White and the Seven Dwarfs* is premiered in the USA.

1940 Death of F. Scott Fitzgerald, American author who chronicled the Jazz Age in books such as *Tender Is the Night* and *The Great Gatsby*.

1964 Britain bans the death penalty.

1983 Fifteen French soldiers die in Beirut when a lorry carrying bombs is driven into their post.

1988 Soviet cosmonauts Musa Manarov and Vladimir Titov return to Earth after a record 365 days in space.

1989 American troops invade Panama and oust dictator Manuel Noriega, installing a new government led by Guillermo Endara.

BIRTHDAYS

Anthony Powell 1905, British novelist best-known for the novel sequence "The Music of Time".

Heinrich Böll 1917, German Nobel Prize-winning novelist whose books include *The Train Was on Time* and *The Lost Honour of Katharina Blum*.

Jane Fonda 1937, American actress whose many fine films include *Coming Home*, *The China Syndrome* and *On Golden Pond*.

Frank Zappa 1940, American rock musician and singer.

Chris Evert 1954, American tennis player.

BIRTHDAYS

Peter Rabbit's creator dies

1943 Beatrix Potter, the creator of Peter Rabbit and many other well loved children's book characters, has died today. Born an only child of wealthy parents, Miss Potter was never sent to school and as a result led a lonely life as a child. To amuse herself, she taught herself to draw and paint small natural objects. Her first book, the *Tale of Peter Rabbit*, was written for the son of her former governess in 1893, in the form of letters. Beatrix Potter illustrated the book herself and went on to write many more books. She lived at Sawrey in the Lake District from 1905 and in 1913 married William Heelis, a solicitor in the area. The rest of her life was chiefly devoted to her farms and to the newly established National Trust which aims to preserve Britain's heritage.

Invisible light can see through flesh

1895 Willhelm Rontgen has today photographed his wife's hand to reveal the bones underneath the skin using his newly discovered X-rays. This discovery was made quite by accident while Rontgen was experimenting with electrical discharges in an evacuated glass tube. In the experiment electrons were accelerated to high velocities, then struck the walls of the tube, giving rise to penetrating radiation. It seems this invisible electromagnetic radiation is of much shorter wavelengths than visible light. X-rays can pass through objects or substances with a low density but are stopped by heavier or denser materials, so skin and muscles allow rays to pass through, while bone reflects them. The medical applications for this discovery have already sparked much interest.

> *You mustn't think I advocate perpetual sex. Far from it. Nothing nauseates me more than promiscuous sex in and out of season.*
>
> **D. H. Lawrence**, British novelist, refers to *Lady Chatterley's Lover*, 1928.

First US soldier dies in Vietnam

1961 US soldier James Davis today became the first American to die in Vietnam since America's involvement in the conflict. At the moment US involvement is limited to military advisers – some 200 Air Force members are joined by 700 Army training personnel in providing military advice, including bomber training. However, President Kennedy has just announced that the US will increase the number of advisers by as many as 16,000 over the next two years, giving rise to fears that American participation in the war will become entrenched and that direct military activity will soon follow.

1975 Palestinian terrorists have seized more than 70 hostages at the Austrian Opec summit held in Vienna. Led by Venezuelan killer Carlos, the terrorists have taken a number of oil ministers and have demanded a plane to fly them to an undisclosed destination. It seems that the authorities are willing to comply with the terrorists' wishes.

CEAUSESCU OVERTHROWN

1989 The civil war in Romania has ended tonight and with it the 24-year-long reign of terror by one of Europe's worst dictators, Nicolae Ceausescu. Tonight the dictator and his wife fled from the roof of their burning palace by helicopter to an unknown destination. Their flight follows the fighting which exploded after Laszlo Tokes, a priest, was threatened with arrest in Timisoara. Around 5000 were killed in Timisoara alone, but accurate numbers of fatalities on both sides will be difficult to determine. Securitate forces have been fighting the Romanian army, who support the protesters, leaving hundreds dead. Tanks have been deployed to try to quell the uprising but the protesting forces hold the TV and radio stations, and have set up a Committee for National Salvation. Last night Ceausescu spoke to the people from the balcony of his palace demanding the return of peace, but was met with jeers from the crowd.

ROYAL FAMILY RETURNS TO ITALY

2002 Victor Emmanuel, the son of Italy's last king, has returned to Italy after more than 50 years in exile. He and his family landed in a private plane on Monday morning for a private audience with Pope John Paul II. Victor Emmanuel spoke of "indescribable emotion" at his return. Hours later the family left for Switzerland, after a lightning visit which took commentators by surprise. But Emmanuel's decision to make his first visit to the Vatican has earned criticism from some who saw it as inappropriate. Sergio Romano, a former ambassador, described the decision as "a combination of arrogance, political insensitivity and bad upbringing." The visit was made possible by a series of votes in the Italian parliament earlier this year, reversing the post-war ban on the royals' return. The family swore their loyalty to the Italian republic as part of the terms of the lifting of the ban on them returning to Italy.

SAKHAROV RETURNS TO MOSCOW

1986 Soviet dissident and physicist Dr Andrei Sakharov and his wife Yelena Bonner, released on December 19 from the closed city of Gorky, returned to Moscow today. They have been in internal exile in Gorky since 1980. Their release comes following a telephone call from the Soviet president Mikhail Gorbachev, whose policies of Glasnost have made their freedom possible. Sakharov, considered to be the father of the Russian H-bomb, is also an outspoken civil rights campaigner. He has openly protested against Soviet nuclear testing, he founded the Soviet Human Rights Committee and won the Nobel Peace Prize in 1975 for his outspoken and dangerous stance on civil rights. He and his wife were exiled to Gorky after criticism of Soviet action in Afghanistan. It is understood that Dr Sakharov will resume his position at the Soviet Academy of Science.

> *It is the overtakers who keep the undertakers busy.*
> **William Pitts**, British Chief Constable, 1963.

General Tojo tries to cheat executioner

1948 A number of high ranking Japanese war criminals have been executed today after standing trial for crimes against humanity. One of the most infamous of the lot, General Tojo, attempted suicide – hari kiri – in the hope of cheating the executioner and regaining his self esteem: suicide is viewed as the only honourable course under the circumstances in Japanese culture. He was not successful. Tojo was Japanese PM from 1941 to 1944, during which time he became the chief instigator of the attack on Pearl Harbor, which brought the US into World War Two. After the war he was arrested, tried and sentenced.

1922 In Britain today the world's first regular radio broadcasts intended purely for entertainment are being transmitted by the British Broadcasting Corporation. The British Post Office has already begun instituting licences. The British wireless industry is responding to popular demand for receivers, which is being generated by the broadcasts.

1814 Andrew Jackson halts the British forces at New Orleans.

1834 English architect Joseph Aloysius Hansom patents a "safety cab".

1944 Death of American illustrator Charles Dana Gibson, creator of the "Gibson Girl".

1973 The Shah of Iran doubles oil prices.

1973 Charles Atlas, the original strongman, dies aged 79.

1985 In South Africa, six whites die in a bomb blast in Durban.

1989 The Romanian army announce the capture of President Ceausescu and his wife Elena.

1990 In a Yugoslavian referendum, the republic of Slovenia votes in favour of becoming an independent state.

1997 Venezuelan terrorist "Carlos the Jackal" is sentenced to life imprisonment after being arrested in Sudan three years earlier.

BIRTHDAYS

Sir Richard Arkwright 1732, English inventor and industrialist who invented mechanized spinning processes such as a spinning frame powered by water.

Alexander I 1777, Russian tsar who defeated Napoleon's invasion of Russia in 1812.

Joseph Smith 1805, American founder of the Mormons.

Samuel Smiles 1812, English writer who wrote biographies of Josiah Wedgwood and George Stephenson but is best known for self-improvement books such as *Self-Help* and *Thrift*.

Maurice Denham 1909, British stage and screen actor whose many films include *Sunday, Bloody Sunday*, *Our Man in Havana* and *Julia*.

Yousuf Karsh 1912, Turkish-Armenian photographer who emigrated to Canada, found fame as a portrait photographer and always signed his work "Karsh of Ottawa".

Helmut Schmidt 1922, German statesman, former chancellor of the Federal Republic of Germany.

Van Gogh cuts off his earlobe

1888 Dutch Post-Impressionist artist Vincent Van Gogh has cut off his earlobe in a fit of madness. He has been staying at Arles in the south of France for some time, painting with his friend and fellow artist Paul Gauguin. According to Gauguin they quarrelled, and the disagreement precipitated an attack of dementia for Van Gogh. During this attack of madness Van Gogh, in remorse for having threatened to wound Gauguin with a razor, cut off his own earlobe. He has been placed in the safety of a St Remy asylum.

Author William Thackeray dies

1886 Author of the best selling novel *Vanity Fair*, William Makepeace Thackeray, has died in England at the age of 52. Although *Vanity Fair* is his best known novel, he wrote many other novels and lighter works. *Vanity Fair* first appeared in monthly instalments illustrated by Thackeray himself. Born in Calcutta, his family sent him home to England to be educated at Charterhouse, then Trinity College, Cambridge. After university he studied law at Middle Temple, then art in Paris for a time. On his return to London, Thackeray began to work as a journalist, contributing to many publications, among them the magazine *Punch*.

1508 London houses receive piped water for the first time.

1828 William Burke goes on trial in Edinburgh, accused of robbing graves to sell corpses for medical research.

1851 Fire destroys part of the Capitol building in Washington and the whole of the Library of Congress.

1908 In Paris, French president Armand Fallières opens the first international aviation show.

1914 The first German bomb lands on British soil.

1924 Eight people die in Britain's worst air crash yet as an Imperial Airways plane dives into a housing estate at Croydon immediately after take-off.

1943 President Roosevelt appoints General Dwight D. Eisenhower commander-in-chief of the invasion of Europe.

1974 The Beatles' partnership is legally dissolved.

1980 Death of German commander Grand Admiral Karl Doenitz, who was briefly Führer in 1945.

1989 Deposed Panamanian leader Manuel Noriega gives himself up to the papal nuncio in Panama City, having dodged American troops determined to capture him.

1990 A cyclone sweeps the Queensland coast of Australia with wind speeds of 150 mph (241 kph).

BIRTHDAYS

John 1167, English monarch who was forced by his rebellious barons to sign the Magna Carta at Runnymede.

Ignatius Loyola 1491, Spanish founder of the Jesuit order.

Kit Carson 1809, American frontiersman and Indian agent at Taos.

Ava Gardner 1922, American actress who appeared in *The Barefoot Contessa*, *The Sun Also Rises* and *Night of the Iguana* among other films.

Verdi's *Aida* opens in Cairo

1871 After a year of delay the Italian Theatre in Cairo staged the first performance of Giuseppe Verdi's long-awaited opera *Aida* tonight. The first-night audience was unequivocal in its enthusiasm for this most personal of grand operas. The work was commissioned by the Khedive of Egypt, Ismail Pasha, last year. Verdi had turned down several requests for a new opera from the Khedive before his interest was aroused by a 23-page synopsis of *Aida* devised by Mariette Bey, the eminent Egyptologist. With the Khedive's generous terms (150,000 francs/£15,000/$27,600 for the Egyptian rights) safely committed to a contract, Verdi set to work with a will, finishing the opera in under five months. The delay in the production was caused by the outbreak of the Franco-Prussian War, which prevented the shipping of the French-made costumes and scenery to Egypt. The composer was not in Cairo to witness the triumph of his new opera. He will be present in Milan, however, for the opera's European debut in seven weeks' time.

Stonehouse bobs to the surface

1974 John Stonehouse, the former British Labour minister who was thought to have drowned off Miami Beach, Florida, last month, has turned up in Melbourne, Australia. Police, suspicious of the Englishman who made regular trips to the post office to collect mail, apprehended Stonehouse in the belief that he was the Earl of Lucan, wanted in Britain for the murder of his children's nanny. Stonehouse disappeared after telling associates he was going for a swim. Shortly afterwards it emerged in Britain that overdrafts had been raised in his name, funds of companies he headed had been plundered and life insurance policies had been taken out. In his fight against extradition, Stonehouse is expected to claim to be a victim of blackmail and persecution in Britain. Under Australian law British MPs are entitled to enter the country freely, so the fact that Stonehouse used a forged passport will not count against him.

> *I am very sorry to know and hear how unreverently that most precious jewel, the Word of God, is disputed, rhymed, sung and jangled in every ale-house and tavern, contrary to the true meaning and doctrine of the same.*
> **King Henry VIII** comments on the translation of the Bible into English, 1545.

Business as usual

1814 In Ghent today representatives of Britain and America signed a peace treaty ending the two-and-a-half-year conflict between the two countries. The nub of the agreement is that the two sides are to stop fighting. This stalemate treaty is appropriate to the position on the ground in North America, where neither side has made gains. The issue of maritime rights, the main cause of the war, has been a dead letter since the ending of the Napoleonic Wars in Europe, hence British willingness to settle the dispute with America.

> *I do not want people to be very agreeable, as it saves me the trouble of liking them a great deal.*
> **Jane Austen**, British novelist, in a letter, 1798.

Libya declares independence

1951 King Idris I formally declared the independence of Libya in a broadcast from the balcony of the Mahara palace in Benghazi today. It is just over two years since the United Nations set a time limit for Libya's independence at January 1, 1952. For the preceding six years, since the defeat of Axis forces in the area, the country had been administered by the French and the British: Fezzan by France and Cyrenaica and Tripolitania by the British. The new constitution of the federal democratic kingdom provides for two legislative chambers: one elected on a proportional representation basis, and the other nominated. Elections to the new parliament will be held early next year. King Idris, 61, was chosen as ruler of the new state by a Libyan National Assembly which met last year.

Christ's birth date is official

440 AD The leaders of the Christian Church have decided that the date of the birth of Jesus Christ should be fixed. At present some people observe it in May, some in January and some combine it with the feast of Epiphany. The date mooted is December 25, the day that the Romans celebrate the winter solstice. The Celtic and Germanic tribes as well as the Norsemen also hold this period dear. The Church authorities do not want their celebration to be tainted by an association with heathen customs, however, and are thought to be engaged in the task of creating rites that will underline the differences between their faith and any of an ungodly nature.

Christmas Day

800 AD In Rome, Charlemagne, King of the Franks, is crowned Emperor of the West by Pope Leo III.

1066 William the Conqueror is crowned King of England at Westminster Abbey.

1497 Florentine friar and charismatic preacher Giralomo Savonarola denounces the Pope for corruption and accuses Leonardo da Vinci of sodomy.

1800 Britain's first Christmas tree is put up at Windsor by Queen Charlotte.

1913 In New York, a couple are arrested for kissing in the street.

1914 British and German soldiers observe an impromptu truce on the Western Front.

1926 Hirohito accedes to the throne of Japan on the death of his father, Emperor Yoshihito.

1972 Managua, capital of Nicaragua, is destroyed by an earthquake.

1983 Death of Spanish Surrealist artist Joan Miró, whose painting was influenced by dreams and by poetry.

1987 Israeli forces crack down on Arab rioters.

1989 President Ceausescu and his wife are executed by the Romanian army.

1991 French actress Orane Demazis, known for her roles in Marcel Pagnol's Marseilles Trilogy, dies aged 87.

Dalai Lama flees Lhasa

1950 The 15-year-old Dalai Lama, the temporal and religious leader of Tibet, is thought to have fled the Tibetan capital, Lhasa, to enlist further help for his country's struggle to maintain its status as the only country in the world entirely under the control of priests. The crisis has deepened since October when China first invaded Tibet. The Indian government has tried putting pressure on the Chinese to reach agreement with Tibet, but to little effect. Last month the Tibetan government took the unusual step of investing the Dalai Lama with full powers of office three years before he was due to receive them. It remains to be seen whether this further legitimization of his rule will deter the Chinese from "liberating Tibet by force".

1950 The Coronation Stone was stolen from its resting place beneath the Coronation Chair in Westminster Abbey early this morning. Scotland Yard believe that the thieves may be Scottish nationalists. The 336 lb (152 kg) Stone of Scone, on which all Scottish kings were crowned, was brought to England as a trophy by King Edward I in 1296, a symbol of the English monarch's claim to Scottish rule. Many Scots would like to see the Stone returned permanently to Scotland.

William orders day of reckoning

1085 King William I has ordered a complete survey of England. Seven or eight groups of commissioners will gather detailed information of the accounts of the estates of the King and of those who hold land by direct services to him (his tenants-in-chief) in each county of the realm. The subjects of William's "description of England" are already referring to the impending investigation as "Domesday". From each manor information will be collected on the dimensions and the ploughing capacity of the land, the number of workers, and any extra amenities such as mills and fishponds. The King and his officers will then have an estimate of what every holder of land in the kingdom is worth.

> *I have spent a lot of time searching through the Bible, looking for loopholes.*
>
> **W. C. Fields**, misanthropic comic actor, on his deathbed – he died today, 1946.

CHARLIE CHAPLIN DIES

1977 Sir Charles Chaplin, KBE, died today at his home in Switzerland. He was 88. Chaplin's career in the cinema spanned 50 years but his reputation as a comic genius will rest most securely on a core of films made between 1916 and 1928, which include the Oscar-winning *The Circus*. The star's love-hate relationship with Hollywood was resolved in 1973 when, after a 20-year exile in Europe, he was awarded a special Oscar for his lifetime contribution to film and commemorated with a statue at the corner of Hollywood and Vine. In 1975 he was made KBE in the New Year's Honours list.

Maurice Utrillo 1883, French painter, illegitimate son of the artist Suzanne Valadon, known for his Parisian street scenes.

Humphrey Bogart 1889, American actor whose legendary films include *Casablanca*, *To Have and Have Not* and *The Maltese Falcon*.

Sissy Spacek 1949, American actress who appeared in *Coalminer's Daughter*, *Badlands* and *The Shining* among other films.

Annie Lennox 1954, British pop singer, one half of the Eurythmics.

DECEMBER 26

1900 Auguste Strindberg's play *Dance of Death* is premiered in Sweden.

1904 Following months of unrest and riots, Tsar Nicholas II of Russia decrees that the conditions of the people, and particularly the peasants, will be improved.

1907 The first session of the Indian National Congress is suspended after clashes between moderates and extremists.

1957 Death of French film pioneer Charles Pathé.

1972 Death of Harry S. Truman, American statesman and Democratic president 1945–53.

1974 Death of American comedian Jack Benny, whose act was based around his parsimony and his violin-playing.

1989 Nobel Prize-winning Irish dramatist Samuel Beckett dies in Paris at the age of 83.

1989 Death of Sir Lennox Berkeley, British composer whose works include *Serenade for Strings* and *Four Poems of St Teresa*.

2003 A massive earthquake destroys the historic city of Bam in Iran, killing 25,000 people.

BIRTHDAYS

Thomas Gray 1716, English poet best-known for "Elegy Written in a Country Churchyard".

Henry Miller 1891, American novelist who wrote *Tropic of Cancer* and *Tropic of Capricorn*, both originally banned as pornography.

Mao Tse-tung 1893, Chinese Communist statesman who, as chairman of the Chinese Communist Party, proclaimed the establishment of the People's Republic of China in 1949.

Richard Widmark 1914, American actor whose many films include *The Alamo* and *Madigan*.

Phil Spector 1940, American songwriter and record producer whose distinctive sound was to be heard on many records of the 1960s.

Great archaeologist dies in Naples

1890 The German archaeologist Heinrich Schliemann died yesterday in Naples, Italy, after collapsing while out walking. He was 58. He had been travelling Europe in search of a cure for the painful ear condition that afflicted him. The son of an impoverished pastor, Schliemann made a fortune at the time of the Crimean War, mainly as a military contractor. He retired from business at the age of 36 in order to devote himself to the study of archaeology. Since boyhood he had nurtured a fervent belief in the existence of Homeric Troy. After extensive study he theorized that the site of the great civilization was at Hisarlik, Turkey, and not at Bunarbashi, a short distance south of it. In 1873 he uncovered fortifications and remains of great antiquity. Further work revealed evidence of a Bronze Age city that had existed long before Troy. In 1876 he discovered a second civilization, at Mycenae in Greece.

Johnson wins boxing crown

1908 The Texan boxer Jack Johnson outclassed world heavyweight champion Tommy Burns at Rushcutter's Bay, Sydney, today with a dazzling display of fighting skills. He finally got the better of Burns in the 14th round when police stopped the contest. The 6-foot (1.8 m) negro challenger had followed the Canadian round the world in the hope of forcing a title match. Burns eventually agreed, but only after Snowy Baker had guaranteed him a purse of $30,000 (£16,300), the largest ever offered a fighter. The road to the top has been a long one for the flamboyant 30-year-old Johnson, who has been a victim of racial attitudes which discourage bouts between black and white boxers.

British sink mighty German battlecruiser

1943 The sea lanes of the North Sea have been made several degrees safer for Allied convoys by the sinking today of the mighty German battlecruiser *Scharnhorst*. The ship, commanded by Admiral Bey, left her lair in Altenfjord yesterday to attack convoy JW55B. Due to bad visibility *Scharnhorst* missed her prey and became separated from her escort of five destroyers. She continued the hunt alone, unaware that a Royal Navy long-range protection group comprising the battleship *Duke of York*, cruiser *Jamaica* and four destroyers was closing in fast. The convoy's cruiser and destroyer escort kept *Scharnhorst* at bay until the *Duke of York* could launch its attack.

Romanian king refused entry to his country

1990 The exiled King of Romania was back in Switzerland tonight after spending less than 12 hours in the homeland he left at the point of a gun in 1947. Ex-King Michael, 69, landed at Bucharest airport in a private plane yesterday with his wife, Princess Anne of Bourbon-Parma, and his daughter Sophia. Two hours later, en route to the Curtea de Afges monastery where family members are buried, Michael's car was stopped by police and escorted to Bucharest. After several hours of argument over the validity of their travel documents, the family were flown back to Geneva. The Romanian authorities, keen to damp down enthusiasm for a return of the monarchy, are insisting that Michael will be allowed "free access" after the elections.

> *Why must you write intensive here? Intense is the right word. You should read Fowler's* Modern English Usage *on the use of the two words.*
> **Winston Churchill**, British prime minister, in a note to the director of Military Intelligence on the Normandy invasion plans in 1944 – H. W. Fowler died today, 1933.

Frederic Remington dies

1909 The documentary artist and reporter Frederic Remington died today near Ridgefield, Connecticut. He was 40. The son of a wealthy newspaper publisher, Remington decided upon the precarious career of an artist after a trip to the West, his spiritual homeland. By his late 20s Remington had built up an enviable reputation as an illustrator of the Western scene. His work appeared in books and magazines, often as accompaniments to his own text. Remington broadened his artistic ambition in 1895 when he discovered his talent for sculpture and produced pieces such as *The Bronco Buster*.

Worldwide scientific expedition sets sail

1831 The Royal Navy vessel HMS *Beagle* under the command of Captain Robert Fitzroy set sail from Devonport today on a five-year scientific expedition round the world. The purpose of the trip is to survey the coasts of Patagonia, Tierra del Fuego, Chile and Peru, to visit some Pacific islands and to set

up a network of chronometrical stations. The official naturalist on board is recent BA graduate Charles Darwin, 22, whose task it will be to study the rocks and life of the places visited and to collect specimens. The post is unpaid but provides a unique opportunity for studying a wide range of phenomena.

Peter Pan's premiere

1904 Five days later than originally planned, J. M. Barrie's *Peter Pan* or *The Boy Who Wouldn't Grow Up* opened tonight at the Duke of York's theatre in London. Peter Pan is an ageless, motherless boy who comes into the nursery of three children called Darling, teaches them to fly and then takes them off into the night sky for fantastic adventures with exotic beings such as Indians, mermaids, wolves and pirates.

Showboat is a hit for Ziegfeld

1927 Impresario Florenz Ziegfeld has yet another hit on his hands in *Showboat*. The two-act musical, lyrics by Oscar Hammerstein II and music by Jerome Kern, captivated the audience at the Ziegfeld Theatre on Broadway tonight. The showboat of the title is *Cotton Blossom*, run by husband and wife team Cap'n Andy and Parthy Ann. The story, based on Edna Ferber's novel of the same title, centres on the lives and loves of the people who inhabit this floating playhouse. The unique aspect of *Showboat* is its unashamed American authenticity – the setting is 19th-century America and the songs use American musical idioms.

Britain signs Bretton Woods agreements

1945 The last obstacle to the signing of the historic Bretton Woods agreements was removed today when the British signified their willingness to take part in the 28-nation ratification ceremony at the State Department in Washington tomorrow. The Bretton Woods agreements provide for the establishment of an international monetary fund and a world bank. The purpose of the IMF is to bring about stability in the relative values of national currencies, thereby avoiding a repeat of the disastrous depreciations which followed World War I, and to free international trade from exchange control. The world bank is intended to help rebuild the economies of countries ravaged by war and supply the needs of industrially undeveloped nations.

1979 The Soviet Union has executed Afghan president Hafizullah Amin in a bid to restore order in the country. Babrak Karmal, a former deputy prime minister in exile in Czechoslovakia, has been installed in his place. Thousands of Soviet troops are now heading into the countryside to deal with the Muslim rebellion which the Kremlin fears may spread to the USSR if it is not put down quickly.

Every picture tells a story

1968 The pioneering news photographer "Weegee" died in New York yesterday at the age of 69. Born Usher H. Fellig in Zloczew, Poland, he emigrated to the US in 1910. The name Weegee was not adopted until about 1938, when his uncanny knack of arriving at the scene of an incident was so remarkable that it was thought he must have some direct line to a greater power, such as via the clairvoyant's ouija board. In fact, he had a radio that picked up the emergency signals of the Manhattan police and firemen.

I am going to build the kind of nation that President Roosevelt hoped for, President Truman worked for and President Kennedy died for.
Lyndon B. Johnson, US president, 1964.

1904 The Abbey Theatre in Dublin, the first state-subsidized theatre in the world, has its opening night.

1929 The All-India National Congress in Lahore threatens civil disobedience if independence is not granted.

1972 Death of Lester Pearson, Canadian statesman, Liberal prime minister 1963-8, chairman of Nato and winner of the Nobel Peace Prize in 1957 for the part he played in settling the Suez Crisis in 1956.

1965 The Sea Gem oil rig collapses in the North Sea, drowning 13.

1983 Mehmet Ali Agca begs the Pope's forgiveness when the latter visits his would-be assassin in jail.

1980 Egypt and Syria resume full diplomatic relations after a ten-year break.

1981 Death of American pianist and composer Hoagy Carmichael.

1984 In Poland, four policemen go on trial for the murder of Father Jerzy Popieluszko.

1992 French novelist and photographer Herve Guibert dies of AIDS at the age of 36.

BIRTHDAYS

Johannes Kepler 1571, German astronomer who discovered that planetary orbits were elliptical in shape.

Louis Pasteur 1822, French chemist and microbiologist whose many discoveries included the process of pasteurization and vaccines for anthrax and rabies.

Sydney Greenstreet 1879, British actor who made his main claim to fame playing heavies in films such as *The Maltese Falcon* and *Casablanca*.

Marlene Dietrich 1901, German actress and entertainer who made her mark in Hollywood with films such as *The Blue Angel*, *Shanghai Express* and *Destry Rides Again*.

Gerard Depardieu 1948, French actor who came to international fame in the film *Green Card*.

1694 Queen Mary II of England dies of smallpox.

1734 Death of Rob Roy (Robert Macgregor), Scottish outlaw whose exploits were romanticized by Sir Walter Scott in the novel *Rob Roy*.

1904 The first weather reports by wireless telegraphy are published in London.

1908 The most violent earthquake ever recorded in Europe destroys the city of Messina in Sicily, killing more than half the 150,000 inhabitants and causing a giant tidal wave.

1937 Death of Maurice Ravel, French composer of the Impressionist school whose works include the ballet *Daphnis and Chloe* and two piano concertos, one for the left hand only.

1984 Death of American film director Sam Peckinpah, maker of films such as *Ride the High Country* and *The Wild Bunch*.

1989 An earthquake in New South Wales, Australia, kills 11 and injures more than 100.

1989 Alexander Dubcek, secretary of the Czechoslovak Communist Party in 1968 and instigator of liberal reforms which were crushed by a Soviet invasion in August of that year, is elected chairman of the communist-dominated parliament after 20 years of political obscurity.

BIRTHDAYS

Thomas Woodrow Wilson 1856, American statesman and Democratic president 1913-21 whose Fourteen Points peace plan in 1918 contained a proposal for a League of Nations that was incorporated into the Versailles Treaty.

Earl "Fatha" Hines 1905, American jazz pianist, composer and bandleader.

Lew Ayres 1908, American actor whose films included *All Quiet on the Western Front* and *The Carpetbaggers*.

Maggie Smith 1934, British actress who won Oscars for *The Prime of Miss Jean Brodie* and *California Suite*.

TAY BRIDGE DISASTER

1879 Part of the Tay bridge collapsed this evening as the 7.15 Edinburgh to Dundee train was passing. All 300 passengers and crew are feared dead. Gale-force winds sweeping the area at the time are thought to have caused the collapse of 13 girders in the central part of the bridge. Early attempts to reach the train by steamboat have failed due to the severity of the weather. The bridge, at 10,612 ft (3442 m) the longest of its kind in the world, was hailed as a feat of engineering at its completion in May 1878. Construction was not problem-free, however, and on two occasions in 1877 accidents involving the collapse of girders during high winds occurred.

> *The next world war will be fought with stones.*
> **Albert Einstein**, 1949.

Sukarno moves into palace

1949 Ahmed Sukarno, the leader of the Indonesian Nationalist Party, has arrived in Batavia (Djakarta) to take up residence in the magnificent palace of the Dutch governors general. Since proclaiming Indonesia a republic after the Japanese surrender in 1945, Sukarno, 48, has defied all Dutch attempts to regain control of their former colony. Yesterday the Netherlands government formally bowed to the inevitable, their representative A. H. J. Lovink signing the protocol transferring sovereignty to an Indonesian delegation.

Coalition party wins election

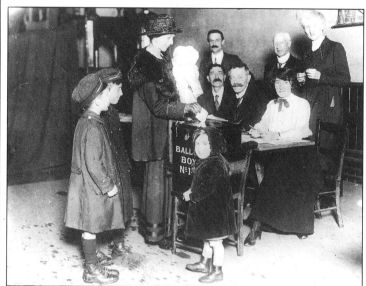

1918 The results of the General Election held in Britain on December 14 were announced today. They reveal that the Coalition Party under David Lloyd George has romped to victory, with a majority of 262 seats over all the other non-Coalition parties. It is the first election in which women have been allowed to vote, albeit not on an equal footing with men; only women of 30 years and older are eligible and those who have lived in the UK for six months. Of the 15 women candidates who stood for election only one, the notorious Sinn Fein leader Madame Markiewicz (Constance Gore-Booth), was elected. The Liberal Opposition under Herbert Asquith has been annihilated; only 26 Liberal followers of Asquith have been returned. The results are being read as a thumbs-up for the forces of stability and staunch nationalism.

TW3 is put firmly in the past

1963 The governors of the BBC have decided that tonight's edition of the satirical series *That Was the Week That Was*, affectionately known as TW3, will be the last. The premature demise of the hugely popular Saturday-night show, which attracts some 12 million viewers, is due to political sensitivity. Politicians were not relishing the prospect of front man David Frost and his team picking meaty morsels out of the week's news in election year. Politicians and the clergy have borne the brunt of the programme-makers' barbs since TW3's inception in November 1962 and the paranoia in establishment circles compelled the Postmaster General to ask to see the scripts in advance. For a short period the BBC was also ordered to expunge sensitive issues such as sex, religion, royalty and politics from the controversial show.

1931 A team of scientists led by Professor Harold Urey of Columbia University and including F. G. Brickwedde and G. M. Murphy has announced the discovery of a heavy form of hydrogen known as heavy water or deuterium. Professor Urey's research began in the 1920s. His team detected deuterium in the residue of a sample of liquid hydrogen.

ARCHBISHOP OF CANTERBURY MURDERED

1170 Four of King Henry II's knights murdered the Archbishop of Canterbury, Thomas à Becket, in Canterbury Cathedral this evening. The Archbishop had only recently returned from a six-year exile in France after incurring Henry's displeasure over the question of church vs crown rights in England. The tussle between the two had led to excommunication for the bishops Roger of York and Foliot of London and several royal servants hostile to Becket, and the fear that the Pope might slap an interdict on England. There is little doubt that Henry was the unwitting architect of the Archbishop's murder. It seems that Henry's exclamation "Will no one rid me of this troublesome cleric?" – uttered in a moment of extreme duress – was interpreted by the four knights who carried out the execution as a call to action.

1798 Britain, Austria, Russia, Naples and Portugal form a second military alliance against Napoleon.

1911 Chinese revolutionary leader Dr Sun Yat-sen becomes the first president of the Republic of China.

1924 John D. Rockefeller donates $1 million (£540,540) to the Metropolitan Museum of Art in New York.

1926 Death of Austrian poet Rainer Maria Rilke.

1952 Death of American jazz composer, pianist and bandleader James Fletcher Henderson.

1984 Rajiv Gandhi wins a landslide victory in the Indian general election.

1986 Harold Macmillan, 1st Earl of Stockton and prime minister who presided over the break-up of the British Empire, dies aged 92.

1989 Playwright Vaclav Havel is elected president of Czechoslovakia.

1989 In Hong Kong, thousands of Vietnamese boat people battle with riot police.

British Admiralty launches ship of iron

1860 The world's first true ironclad warship, *Warrior*, was launched at Blackwall on the river Thames today. The 9210-ton battleship is the first capital ship in the world to be built of iron throughout. The British Admiralty first showed interest in the idea of iron-built warships as a consequence of the calamitous showing of wooden-built vessels during the Crimean War. The decision to build such a vessel was not taken until last year, however, when the launch of the French ironclad *La Gloire* threatened British naval supremacy. *La Gloire* (displacement 5600 tons) is built of oak but with a belt of iron extending from the upper deck to 6 ft (1.8 m) below the waterline.

> In our country the lie has become not just a moral category but a pillar of the state.
> **Alexander Solzhenitsyn**, Soviet novelist, 1974.

Aircrash survivors resort to cannibalism

1972 Ten of the 16 survivors from a Uruguayan aircraft that crashed in the Andes mountains ten weeks ago admitted at a press conference in Montevideo today that they ate the raw flesh of their dead companions in order to stay alive. The Old Christians rugby team – pupils or old boys of the exclusive Catholic Stella Maris College in Montevideo – had chartered the aircraft for a tour of Chile. Fifteen of the 45 passengers died as a consequence of the crashlanding; eight died later in an avalanche. Starvation and cold killed another six. The survivors were rescued after two of them found their way down to an upland pasture where a farmer was checking his stock.

Sioux massacred at Pine Ridge

1890 An attempt to disarm Miniconjou Sioux Indians on the Pine Ridge Reservation, South Dakota, ended in bloodshed today. Trouble flared unexpectedly when a force of about 500 US cavalrymen, commanded by Colonel James W. Forsyth, rode into the Indian camp at Wounded Knee Creek, where the authorities had placed Big Foot and about 350 of his people. According to the Seventh Cavalry, a medicine man incited the young braves to resist disarmament. Big Foot was among more than a hundred Sioux that died in the action; 44 were wounded. About half of the Sioux casualties were women and children, lending weight to claims that the encounter was a massacre, not a battle. The violence will come as a further blow to General Nelson A. Miles, who had been hoping to settle the recent Indian unrest peacefully. News of the incident has prompted thousands of Indians to barricade themselves in a large camp north of Pine Ridge Agency.

Not child's play for Ibsen

1879 Norwegian dramatist Henrik Ibsen seems to have a knack for hitting the raw nerves of polite society. His play *The Doll's House*, which opened at the Royal Theatre in Copenhagen on December 21, has become a major talking point. The play ends with the main character, Nora, a pampered wife, leaving the family home. She literally slams the door on her successful lawyer/banker husband and, most controversially of all, her children. The play has been denounced by some as militant suffragist propaganda.

BIRTHDAYS

Jeanne Antoinette Poisson, Marquise de Pompadour 1721, French mistress of King Louis XV and as such the holder of political influence and a notable patron of artists and scholars.

William Ewart Gladstone 1809, English statesman and Liberal prime minister who dominated British politics in the latter half of the 19th century.

Pablo Casals 1876, Spanish cellist of great stature who refused to live or play in Spain while Franco ruled the country.

Mary Tyler Moore 1937, American actress who co-starred in the *Dick Van Dyke Show* and went on to have her own television series and appear in films such as *Ordinary People*.

Jon Voight 1938, American actor who first found fame in *Midnight Cowboy* and went on to win an Oscar for *Coming Home*.

BIRTHDAYS

Rudyard Kipling 1865, English novelist and poet, most of whose works are concerned with India, where he was born.

Stephen Leacock 1869, English-born Canadian humorist whose more than 30 books include *Literary Lapses* and *Nonsense Novels*.

Sir Carol Reed 1906, British film director best-known for *Odd Man Out*, *The Fallen Idol*, *The Third Man* and the Oscar-winning *Oliver!*

Bo Diddley 1928, American rhythm and blues singer who was a major influence on pop groups such as the Rolling Stones in the 1960s.

Tracy Ullman 1959, British comedienne who transplanted successfully to America, where she scored a hit with the *Tracy Ullman Show*.

RASPUTIN MURDERED

1916 The influential royal favourite Grigory Rasputin was murdered last night at the home of Prince Feliks Yusupov in St Petersburg. He was 44. The behaviour of the Siberian peasant turned mystic had scandalized Russian society and seriously undermined the standing of the Russian royal family which had persistently protected him against all allegations of wrongdoing. Rasputin's influence over the royal family came about after he succeeded in easing the suffering of the Tsar's haemophiliac son, Aleksey Nikolayevich. Once established as a royal favourite, Rasputin lived up to his acquired name, which means "debauched one". The monk met his end at the hands of a group of Conservatives, including Yusupov, Purishkevich (a member of parliament) and Pavlovich (the Tsar's nephew), committed to saving Russia from his malign influence. Yusupov first plied the visiting Rasputin with poisoned wine and tea cakes. When this ploy appeared to be having no success, the noblemen shot him, then tied him up and threw his body into the freezing river Neva, where he finally died by drowning.

1887 The British monarch, Queen Victoria, has received a unique celebration of her Jubilee year from the women of England. The Home Secretary accepted on her behalf this afternoon a memorial signed by 1,132,608 women in favour of the Sunday closing of English public houses and the banning of sales of intoxicating liquors on the Lord's day.

Richard Rodgers dies

1979 Richard Rodgers, one of this century's best-known composers of musicals, died in New York City today. He was 77. In a long and prolific career Rodgers formed long-standing working relationships with lyricists Lorenz Hart and Oscar Hammerstein II. His collaboration with Hart began in 1919 when the two were still at Columbia University. *The Boys from Syracuse* and *Pal Joey* are perhaps two of their most famous collaborations. Hammerstein became Rodgers' regular librettist after Hart's untimely death in 1943. Over the next 17 years, until Hammerstein's death in 1960, the two men had an outstanding run of success with one hit after another, including *Carousel*, *South Pacific*, *The King and I* and *The Sound of Music*.

Gilbert and Sullivan musical mayhem

1879 Arthur Sullivan and W. S. Gilbert are going to great lengths to secure the copyright of their latest operatic offering, *The Pirates of Penzance*, on both sides of the Atlantic. The first UK performance of the still-to-be-completed work was given today at the Royal Bijou Theatre, Paignton, Devon, despite only one rehearsal, no overture or proper costumes and a dearth of sheet music. *Pirates* should receive a more professional premiere at the Fifth Avenue Theatre in New York tomorrow night, with both Gilbert and Sullivan on hand to help out with the production. The two are in town for the staging of their official version of *HMS Pinafore*. Sullivan almost scuppered the duo's chances of mounting *The Pirates of Penzance* as well, however. He forgot to bring the draft of Act One to the States with him and has had to rewrite the act from memory. The overture is still not written, but Sullivan is confident that he can complete it by the opening.

I'm furious about the Women's Liberationists. They keep getting on soapboxes and proclaiming that women are brighter than men. That's true, but it should be kept very quiet or it ruins the whole racket.
Anita Loos, in the *Observer*, 1973.

US renegotiates for Noriega

1989 Negotiations between Washington and the Vatican have restarted to bring an end to the refuge of the Panamanian dictator General Manuel Noriega in the Vatican embassy in Panama City. Noriega fled to the embassy on Christmas Eve to escape the clutches of the US marines sent by President Bush to arrest him. Vatican officials tried unsuccessfully to persuade Noriega to leave of his own accord, but refused to hand over Noriega directly to the marines besieging the building. The US lost patience: Noriega and his reluctant hosts were treated to round-the-clock rock music played at full blast from loudspeakers erected by the US forces. Noriega faces prosecution in the US on drug trafficking charges.

US to open immigration depot

1891 The new year will see the opening of the US government's new depot for handling immigrant arrivals to New York. Last year the government assumed sole responsibility for the screening of arrivals, a task formerly performed in the New York area by the state of New York as the government's local agent. The new depot, on Ellis Island in the upper bay area, will be the nation's major immigration station. It is being trumpeted as a major improvement on the old reception facilities at the Battery on Manhattan Island and better able to cope with massive numbers of arrivals. The island is named after Samuel Ellis, who owned it in the 1770s.

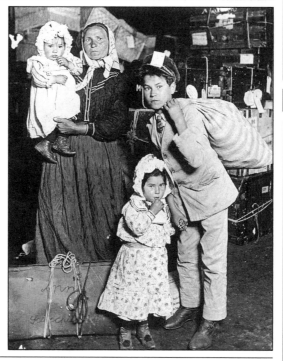

1687 The first Huguenot emigrants to South Africa set sail from France, taking vines with which to start a wine industry in their new colony.

1719 Death of John Flamsteed, the astronomer for whom King Charles II built the Greenwich Observatory.

1903 Five employees of the Iroquois Theatre in Chicago are arrested for manslaughter after the previous day's fire.

1922 The French government turns down a German offer of a non-aggression pact.

1985 American rock and country singer Rick Nelson is killed, along with his fiancée and four band members, when a chartered DC3 carrying them between concerts in Guntersville, Alabama and Dallas, Texas catches fire and crashes.

1986 The oil company Esso announces it is disinvesting in South Africa.

1988 In Islamabad, capital of Pakistan, prime ministers Rajiv Gandhi and Benazir Bhutto sign the first agreement between India and Pakistan in 16 years.

1990 The giant Christmas tree in London's Trafalgar Square was attacked by a man with a chainsaw early this morning. Police came upon Patrick Harward-Duffy, a 36-year-old Glaswegian, at 2.30 am as he was making his protest against the unfairness of the Norwegian legal system. Harward-Duffy had sliced one-third of the way through the trunk of the 70-ft (23 m) pine, a present from the people of Oslo who since 1947 have expressed their gratitude for British liberation from the Nazis by sending a tree each year.

Cambodia breaks off relations with Vietnam

1977 The Cambodian government announced today that it is breaking off diplomatic relations with neighbouring Vietnam and also suspending all air services between them. The two Communist countries are at loggerheads over which of them is to blame for the recent outbreaks of intense fighting along their borders. Full-scale battles at regimental level are reported to have taken place in the region known as Parrot's Beak which juts into South Vietnam. Much of the problem seems to have its roots in the movement of Cambodians across the frontier in the Mekong Delta soon after the fall of Saigon and before the North Vietnamese could establish full control in the area. The conflict is being exacerbated by ideological differences, with the Chinese-sponsored Cambodian regime laying claim to a more "revolutionary" outlook than that of Soviet-backed Vietnam.

Ghanaian government overthrown

1981 Former flight lieutenant Jerry Rawlings has overthrown the government of President Hilla Limann and seized power again in Ghana. In a radio broadcast to the nation, Rawlings described Limann and his associates as "a pack of criminals who bled Ghana to the bone" and said that they had ·brought about the country's "total economic ruin". Rawlings has given no indication of how long his Provisional Military Council will retain power, but he did remind his fellow citizens of the fact that he voluntarily returned the government to civilian rule three months after he toppled the military government of Lieutenant-General Fred Akuffo in June 1979.

1999 After eight and a half years in the Kremlin, Russian President Boris Yeltsin has resigned his presidency six months before the end of his official term. Mr Yeltsin said his ill health was the reason, and nominated Prime Minister Putin as acting President, a move which will strengthen Putin's hand in the Presidential elections which will take place in June 2000.

I'd not know what I may appear to the world; but to myself I seem to have been only a boy playing on the sea-shore and diverting myself in now and then finding a smoother pebble or a prettier shell than ordinary, whilst the great ocean of truth lay all undiscovered before me.

Isaac Newton, 1726.

BIRTHDAYS

Charles Edward Stuart 1720, Scottish royal known as Bonnie Prince Charlie or the Young Pretender whose attempt to regain the Scottish throne ended in failure.

Henri Matisse 1869, French painter and sculptor who initiated the vibrantly coloured style known as Fauvism.

George Marshall 1880, American general and statesman who, as secretary of state, devised the Marshall Plan for post-war economic recovery in Europe.

Anthony Hopkins 1937, British actor who won an Oscar for *The Silence of the Lambs*.

Ben Kingsley 1943, British actor best-known for his performance as Gandhi in Richard Attenborough's film of the same name.

INDEX

400

ACKNOWLEDGMENTS

The Publishers would like to thank all those who have supplied photographs for use in this book and apologize to any whose contribution may have been inadvertently omitted from these acknowledgments. We are particularly grateful to Peter Newark, Mike Hollingshead at Topham, Dawn Wyman at the Hulton Picture Company and Tony Oudot at Popperfoto.

(Abbreviations: A.P. = Associated Press. P.A. = Press Association. Bett = Bettman)

Aquarius Aug 15
Allsport Ltd Jul 30b (Pressens Bild); Aug 29b
American Heritage Publishing Co Mar 27b
Associated Press Jan 28t; Feb 1t; Feb 2t; Feb 4b; Feb 15t; Mar 8b; Mar 25t; Mar 27t; Mar 31b; Apr 20b; Apr 22b; May 18b; May 25b; May 27b; May 30t (Jeff Widener); Jun 7 (Mark Humphrey); Jun 12b; Jun 17b; Sep 21t; Sep 28t; Oct 14b; Oct 18t/rgt title page; Nov 18t; Nov 23b; Dec 1b; Dec 8b; Dec 17b
BBC Photo Library Jul 24b
Bettman Apr 11 (UPI); May 12t; Jul 15b; Dec 8t (UPI)
Boy Scouts of America, National Office Feb 8b
Bridgeman Art Library Feb 18t (Sistine Chapel); Mar 17t (Musée D'Orsay); Apr 8t (Tate Gallery); May 16b; May 17t (Galleria Degli Uffri); Aug 13t (Tate Gallery); Sep 8b (Accademia, Florence); Oct 3b (Victoria & Albert Museum); Nov 17b (Musee Rodin, Paris); Nov 18b
British Pathé News Apr 4b; Apr 16b; Apr 17b; Apr 19b; Apr 26; Apr 27t
Allan Cash Ltd Aug 8t
Camera Press Mar 18t; Jun 5cl
Colorsport Feb 13b
Culver Pictures Inc, N.Y. Nov 3b
Zoë Dominic Sep 4t
E.T. Archive/Documentation Photographique de la Réunion des Musées Nationaux Mar 1b
Mary Evans Picture Library Jan 6b/lft title parn Collection); Jan 20t; Jan 21b; Jan 29b; Jan 31t (Alexander Meledin Collection); Feb 1b; Feb 3t; Feb 4t; Feb 12t; Feb 16b; Feb 18b; Feb 19b; Mar 3b; Mar 4t; Mar 7c; Mar 13b; Mar 16t; Mar 16b; Mar 17b/lft title page; Mar 22b; Apr 20t; Apr End; May 11t; Jun 5; Jun 8b; Jun 10t; Jun 13t; Jun 17t; Jun 18b; Jun 20b; Jun 21t; Jun 22t; Jun 23b; Jun 24b; Jun 26t; Jun 28t; Jul 7b; Jul 8t; Jul 10t; Jul 14t; Jul 19b (Institute of Civil Engineers); Jul 23b (Sigmund Freud Copyrights/W.E. Freud); Jul 25c/lft title page; Jul 26b; Jul 27t; Jul 28t; Jul 28t; Aug 1t; Aug 3t; Aug 5b; Aug 10t; Aug 16b; Aug 18t; Aug 19t; Aug 22t; Aug 24b; Aug 24b; Aug 25b; Aug 26b; Aug 30t/Intro; Sep 3t; Sep 13t; Sep 20t; Sep 22t; Sep 29t; Oct Opener; Oct 14; Oct 19t; Oct 21b; Nov 19t; Nov 21b; Nov 29t; Dec 5b; Dec 10b; Dec 23b; Dec 27t; Dec 29t; Dec 29b
John Frost Newspapers Oct 9t
The Granger Collection, N.Y. Apr 2b; Nov 24b
Ronald Grant Archive Jan 24; Mar 14t; Apr 9; Apr 15b; May 24b; Jun 2b; Jul 2b; Jul 11b; Aug 2b; Aug 19b; Aug 31b
Giraudon/Louvre Aug 22b
Robert Harding Picture Library Mar 29b; July 11t
Hulton-Deutsch Collection Jan Opener; Jan 1t; Jan 2b (Bett); Jan 3t; Jan 3b; Jan 9b; Jan 10t (Bett); Jan 11t; Jan 12b; Jan 16t (Bett); Jan 22t; Jan 24t (Bett); Jan 25t; Jan 26t; Jan 27 b; Jan 30b; Jan 31b; Feb 5t; Feb 5b; Feb 10t (Bet); Feb 10b (Bett); Feb 12b; Feb 14t; Feb 15b (Bett); Feb 16t; Feb 17t; Feb 19t; Feb 21b; Feb 22 (Bett); Feb 26t; Feb 27t; Feb 28b; Mar 5t; Mar 9b; Mar 12t; Mar 15t (Bett); Mar 18b; Mar 19t (Bett); Mar 20t; Mar 24t; Mar 28b (Bett); Mar 29t (Bett); Mar 30t (Bett); Mar 31t; Apr 3t; Apr 3b (Bett); Apr 5b; Apr 10b (Bett); Apr 12t; Apr 15t; Apr 24b; Apr 25t (Bett); Apr 25b; Apr 28t; Apr 29t (UPI); May 9t; May 10b; May 15t; May 25t (Bett)/lft title page; May 31b; Jun 3b (Bett); Jun 20t (Bett); Jun 23t; Jun 25b; Jun 26b; Jul 1t; Jul 2t; Jul 8b; Jul 9t (Bett); Jul 12b; Jul 22t (Bett); Jul 24t; Jul 29t; Jul 29b; Jul 30t; Jul 31t; Aug 2t; Aug 5t; Aug 9; Aug 14t; Aug 16b (Bett); Aug 21b; Aug 23t; Aug 26t (Bett); Aug 27; Sep Opener; Sep 2b; Sep 6t; Sep 8t; Sep 22b (Bett); Sep 30t (Bett); Oct 6t; Oct 8t; Oct 8b (Bett); Oct 20t; Oct 30t; Nov 4b; Nov 7t; Nov 7b (Bett); Nov 10b; Nov 13t; Nov 15b (Bett); Nov 17t; Nov 25b (Bett); Nov 26b (Bett); Dec 5t (Bett); Dec 6b; Dec 18t; Dec 20t; Dec 24t; Dec 24b; Dec 31t
Kobal Collection Mar 10t; Mar 22t; July 20b; Aug 7b; Sept 23b; Sep Ending; Oct 2b; Oct 10; Nov 16t; Dec 15b; Dec 20b; Dec 25b/Intro; Dec 27b; Dec 30b
London Features International May 2b (Neal Preston); May 9b; Jun 11t; Sep 27b
Magnum Photos Ltd 29b (Philippe Halsman); Sep 16b; Nov 27t (Leonard Freed);

Mansell Collection Feb 2b; Apr Opener; May 31b; Jun 14t; Jun 19t; Jun End; Jul 21b; Aug 4t; Oct 2t; Nov 23t
Don Morley International Sports Photo Agency Sep 25b
National Baseball Library, Cooperstown, N.Y. Sep 28b
National Film Archive, London Mar 1
Peter Newark's Pictures Jan 1b; Jan 20; Jan 22b; Jan 26b; Jan 27t; Jan 28b; Jan 29t; Feb 3b; Feb 11b; Feb 17t; Feb 23t; Feb 24t; Feb 28t; Mar 2t; Mar 6t; Mar 7t; Mar 11b; Mar 12b; Mar 21t; Mar 21b; Mar 23; Apr 5t; Apr 6t; Apr 6b; Apr 6t/half title; Apr 8bl; Apr 10t; Apr 18b; Apr 22t; Apr 27b; May 1t; May 5t; May 8b; May 23t; May 30b; Jun 12t; Jun 13b; Jun 24t; Jul 4t; Jul 4b; Jul 13b; Jul 18t; Jul 23t; Aug 3b; Aug 4b; Aug 6t/lft title page; Aug 11b; Aug 12t; Aug 20t; Aug 28b; Aug 31t; Sep 1b/Intro; Sep 5t; Sep 10t; Sep 14t; Sep 16t; Sep 17b; Oct 10b; Oct 17t; Oct 18b; Oct 23b; Oct 24t; Oct 25t; Oct 25b; Oct 26b; Oct 28t; Nov 5t; Nov 6b; Nov 11b; Nov 19b; Nov 26t; Nov 28t; Dec Opener; Dec 2b; Dec 4t; Dec 7; Dec 16b; Dec 21b; Dec 25t/lft title page; Dec 26b
Robert Opie Collection Jan 18b
Pictorial Press Jun 1t; Jun 22t
Popperfoto Jan 2t; Jan 4t/Intro; Jan 5t; Jan 6t; Jan 13t; Jan 14t; Jan 14b (Reuter); Jan 17t; Feb 9t; Feb 11b; Feb 20t; Feb 21t; Feb 25b; Feb 26b; Feb 27b/rgt title page; Mar Opener; Mar 3t; Mar 8t; Mar 11t; Mar 14b; Mar 25b; Mar 30b; Apr 7b; Apr 7t; Apr 8bl; Apr 13b; Apr 17t; Apr 18t; Apr 19t; Apr 21t; Apr 23t; Apr 26t; May 1b; May 3b; May 4t; May 6b; May 7b; May 8c; May 10t; May 13b; May 19t/Intro; May 21t; May 22b; May 26t; May 27t; May 28t; May 28b; Jun 10b; Jul Opener; Jul 3t; Jul 5t; Jul 9t; Jul 13t; Jul 15t; Jul 16b; Jul 19t; Jul 20t; Jul 25b; Jul 26t; Aug Opener; Aug 7t; Aug 10b; Aug 11t; Aug 17t; Aug 18b; Aug 21b; Aug 22c; Aug 29t; Sep 4b; Sep 6b; Sep 10b; Sep 12t (A.P.); Sep 13b; Sep 17t; Sep 18t; Sep 19t; Sep 19b; Sep 21b; Sep 26b; Sep 29b; Sep 30b; Oct 1b; Oct 7t; Oct 9b; Oct 15b; Oct 20b; Oct 21t (Reuter); Oct 27t; Oct 29; Oct 31b; Nov 10t; Nov 15t; Nov 16b; Nov 20b; Nov 22b; Nov 27b; Nov 30t; Dec 3b; Dec 4b; Dec 11t; Dec 11b; Dec 12b; Dec 13b; Dec 14t; Dec 19b; Dec 22b; Dec 26t; Dec 28t; Dec 28b; Dec 30t; Dec 31b
Press Association Jun 29b; Aug 13b
Punch Magazine Jul 17b;
David Redfern Photography July 17t (Bob Willoughby); Nov 24t (Bob King)
Reed International Books Ltd May 20b; Sep 24; Nov 14b
"Ingres' Violin" 1924, Man Ray (C ADAGP, Paris and DACS, London 1992)
Retna Pictures Ltd Mar 24b (Fiona Simon); Oct 4b (Stevenson)
Rex Features Jan 19t; Mar 9t; Mar 20b; May 15b Jun 27b; Jun 29t; Jul 14b; Aug 14t; Nov 8b; Nov 13b; Dec 21
Roger-Viollet (Harlingue-Viollet) Jan 19b
Royal Geographical Society May Opener
Royal Photographic Society/Antoine Claudet Aug 20b
Roger Saunders Oct 5b
Science Museum Dec 17t
Phil Sheldon July 28b
Frank Spooner Pictures Jan 7b (Kaku Kurita/Gamma)
Syndication International Feb Opener; Oct 3t (Aldus Archive/Nat. Collection of Fine Arts, Smithsonian)
Theatre Museum/V&A Feb 9
Times Library/Sporting Pictures (UK) Ltd Aug 1b
Topham Picture Source Jan 4b; Jan 5b; Jan 8b; Jan 9b; Jan 12t Jan 12b; Jan 15t; Jan 15b; Jan 16b (A.P.); Jan 17b (A.P.); Jan 21t (A.P.); Jan 25b; Jan 30t; Feb 6; Feb 7t (P.A.); Feb 8t; Feb 13t (A.P.); Feb 14b; Feb 20b; Feb 23b (A.P./Copyright The Estate and Foundation of Andy Warhol, 1992 courtesy ARS, N.Y.) Feb 24b; Feb 25t; Feb 29t; Feb 29b (A.P.); Mar 2b (A.P.); Mar 4b; Mar 5b; Mar 6b (P.A.); Mar 7b (A.P.); Mar 10b; Mar 13t; Mar 15b (A.P.); Mar 19b; Mar 26t; Mar 26b; Mar 28t; Apr 1t; Apr 1b; Apr 2t (A.P.); Apr 4t (P.A.); Apr 16t; Apr 11b; Apr 12t; Apr 13t; Apr 14; Apr 21b; Apr 23b (A.P.); Apr 28b; Apr 29b; May 2t; May 3t; May 4 (A.P.); May 5b; May 6t; May 7t; May 8t; May 11b; May 12b; May 13t; May 14t; May 14b; May 16t; May 18t; May 19b; May 20t; May 21b (A.P.); May 23b; May 26b; May 29t; May 29b; Jun 1b; Jun 2t/rgt title page; Jun 3t; Jun 4t; Jun 4b (A.P.); Jun 5b (A.P.); Jun 6t; Jun 6b; Jun 9t; Jun 9b; Jun 11b; Oct 30b; Oct 31b; Nov Opener (A.P.); Nov 1t; Nov 1b (A.P.); Nov 2t; Nov 2b; Nov 3t; Nov 4t (A.P.); Nov 5b; Nov 8t; Nov 9t; Nov 9b; Nov 11t; Nov 12/rgt title page; Nov 14t (A.P.); Nov 20t (P.A.); Nov 21t (A.P.); Nov 22t; Nov 25t; Nov 28t (A.P.); Nov 29b; Nov 30b; Dec 2t; Dec 3t; Dec 6t; Dec 9t (A.P.); Dec 9b (P.A.); Dec 10t (A.P.) Dec 12t (A.P.); Dec 14b; Dec 15t; Dec 16t; Dec 18b; Dec 19t (A.P.); Dec 22t (P.A.); Dec 23t (A.P.)
U.S. Signal Corps Dec 13t
Victoria & Albert Museum Nov ending
Welcome Institute Library, London May 24t
Reg Wilson Photography Apr 24t; Jun 16
Whitworth Art Gallery Aug 12b